A CONTRACTS ANTHOLOGY

A Contracts Anthology

Edited with Comments by
Peter Linzer
Professor of Law
University of Houston Law Center

With the Assistance of
Patricia A. Tidwell

Anderson Publishing Co.

A CONTRACTS ANTHOLOGY

Library of Congress Cataloging in Publication Data

A Contracts anthology / edited, with comments, by Peter Linzer.
   p.   cm.
  Includes index.
  ISBN 0-87084-417-2
  1. Contracts—United States. 2. Contracts. I. Linzer, Peter.
KF801.A7C558 1989
346.73'02—dc20
[347.3062]

89-6677
CIP

Second Printing—August, 1989

To Kathryn and Alex

I know at times The Book became the enemy. I know that it took me away from you in spirit. You still gave me support and love. I love you both. More than I love this book.

THANK YOU

Joy Lowry. You typified the transition in the role of the secretary from typist to computer coordinator. You typed Part I, but when we switched to optical scanning for Parts II, III and IV, you handled the changes and coding between two sets of computers and frequently made sense out of chaos. As always, you put up with my tantrums and last minute emergencies while also tending to nine other faculty members.

The authors of the books and articles that make up this anthology. You are the book, and your cooperation and encouragement enabled me to get it done.

Dean Bob Knauss and Associate Dean Ira Shepard. You supported me intangibly and tangibly. I appreciate what you did.

The University of Houston Law Foundation and the Law Center alumni. You came up with the money that paid Pat Tidwell and Disc, Inc., of whom more below. Support of faculty writing projects is one of the most selfless ways that law alumni can help their schools, and you have been generous despite the depressed Texas economy.

Jan Cunningham and the Law Center secretarial staff. You were there when we needed you.

Disc, Inc. When I started this book I didn't know you (or optical scanning) existed. You took pasted-up copies of articles, sometimes seventy years old, and magically put them on computer disks, saving us hundreds of pages of typing when time was of the essence.

Anderson Publishing Co., particularly Dale Hartig and Bob Booth. You had faith in this project, even when I ran late and long.

My friends and colleagues, particularly Morley White, Laura Oren and David Dow. You gave me moral support and put up with my prattling on ad infinitum when you had things to think about that were just as important.

Janet Largen. You've done so much for all of us.

Finally, and most of all,

Pat Tidwell. It wouldn't have gotten done without you. You did so many different things, some interesting and challenging, some tedious but indispensable. And when the money ran out and the credit ran out and you had graduate school and law school *and* your family to worry about, you still came through.

Thanks y'all.

Contents

Indented italic headings are editor's comments.

Prologue

There is a very rich literature of contract, but one that is hard for lawyers and law students to get at, both because the books and articles have to be physically retrieved from the law library and because many of the articles are overwritten. Even well-written articles are often too detailed for readers who are not sure how much time they want to spend on a particular piece of writing. This collection is not a Condensed Book Club Edition; I have tried hard to keep the intellectual challenge of the writings and to let the readers know what has been removed so that they may decide whether to read a piece in full. But I have wanted to allow readers a chance to read important parts of significant writings right away, without compromise in quality but often with drastic editing and with a certain amount of background comment to help put the work in perspective.

Though I hope and believe that practicing lawyers (particularly those with sophisticated contracts practices) and upper-class law students will benefit from the collection, I especially want to give first-year law students an accessible way to read these pieces. However, this very aim creates problems. If the book assumes familiarity with cases, personalities and terms that we get to know in the first year of law school, beginning students will be at sea. If it explains everything, even first-year students will grow impatient before the year is out.

My attempt at a solution is a compromise in which topics and authors are discussed in comments preceding the articles and occasional editorial comments are made to explain or modify the quoted text. I did not want to dish out easy-to-digest pablum, but at the same time I understand that many law review articles are hard going for all but the most sophisticated law professors; even practitioners of ability are turned off by 100 pages of complex sentences studded with innumerable footnotes. I have cut out most of the footnotes and often summarized whole sections of articles so that I could give the reader discrete sections—not snippets—in readable form and at manageable length.

One of the most important questions was where to begin. Perhaps reflecting my interests, I chose to begin with a group of writings dealing with what contract is (or is it "what contracts are"?). This section debates just how important contract law is to our culture, why we enforce contracts, the history of contract law, and some viewpoints that are not based in our Anglo-American, secular and above all, masculine, mainstream. (On this last topic, see Part ID, "Other Voices.")

Entering law students may find this too abstract, although to my mind it is an obvious starting point. Those who disagree should feel free to browse through the table of contents to find something that looks interesting, and should start wherever they please. There is nothing magical about the order of the book. Even within the very first subtopic one can skip around to one's profit. Stewart Macaulay's *An Empirical View of Contract Law* is very easy to get into and is valuable reading. I considered beginning the book with it. Though I agree with much of Macaulay's ideas and have a lot of opinions of my own, this anthology is not my soapbox, and I preferred to begin with an essay by Fritz Kessler, one of the greats of twentieth-century contract law, followed by a debate of sorts between Kessler and his colleague and co-author Grant Gilmore. Kessler is pretty readable, but his essay does take a little more work than some of the pieces following it. (Gilmore himself told his students not to read the Kessler essay until later in the term, even though the essay appears on page one of their joint casebook.) I think Kessler is a good place to start, but if the reader finds it tough going, my advice is to skip to Gilmore or to Macaulay—or to go to a different part of the book altogether, for example, Eugene Moody's *Old Kontract Principles and Karl's New Kode* in Part IIC or the note on *Public Policy From Sunday Contracts to Baby M* in Part IIIB.

This anthology can serve many functions. It can be assigned as a direct supplement to a course. It can be a place to dip and browse. It can be a place to look for a little background on a particular topic. Or it can be all of the above. Readers of various backgrounds may, for example, find interest in the different treatments of the well-known case of *Wood v. Lucy, Lady Duff-Gordon* in Walter Pratt's *American Contract Law at the Turn of the Century* in Part IC ("Where Did Contract Law Come From?") and in Mary Joe Frug's *Re-reading Contracts: A Feminist Analysis of a Contracts Casebook* in Part ID ("Other Voices"). In the back of the book there is a Table of Classroom Favorites that allows similar comparison of various writers on a number of other famous cases.

Sections II, III and IV deal more directly with doctrinal topics that are studied in depth in the Contracts course, such as contract formation, the role of the Uniform Commercial Code, excuses, and remedies. Even there, however, I have avoided narrowly doctrinal articles; there are plenty of other places to find an article on whether the mailbox rule applies to electronic mail. Although it is essential (repeat: essential) for a lawyer to know the details of contract doctrine thoroughly, there are several excellent doctrinal texts already on the market. Looking at contracts as well from a bigger, more thoughtful perspective makes for better lawyers and is much more fun than mere technical mastery.

There was, of course, no way to include as many articles as I would have liked. Those who would like to read more of the classics of contract writing should try to find a copy of the Association of American Law Schools' *Selected Readings on the Law of Contracts* (1931), a wonderful collection that is out of print but available in most law libraries. An AALS committee made up a list of suggested readings in the mid-seventies and it was updated in 1981. It may still be available from the AALS headquarters in Washington. In addition, I have suggested additional books and articles in the notes accompanying the material in this anthology.

I hope that you find the enterprise worthwhile.

Part I
The Essence of Contract

A. What Is Contract, And How Important Is It?

This seems like a sensible question. To offer a partial answer, this section collects discussions by a fairly wide-ranging collection of writers. The word "contract" brings with it a lot of associations. We speak of social contracts, of freedom of contract, of marriage contracts, even of contracts coming out of psychotherapy or family counseling. In more overtly legal areas contract is bound up with notions of individualism and liberty. The more that we believe that legal duties come primarily from consent and agreement rather than society's dictates, the more we look to contract as a protector of liberty and free will, including the liberty to bind yourself voluntarily. The "classical" view of contract law—dominant from the post-Civil War period to the eve of the Second World War—required clear language and a symmetrical bargain to hold people into promises, and was reluctant ever to excuse them from performance if a contract was found. This mirrored a society that did not easily impose social duties through (non-consensual) tort, and that often denied government's power to "interfere" with the "right" to enter into contract.

The traditional approach was strongly criticized by many writers in the first third of this century, most notably Arthur Corbin, whose influence pervades contemporary contract law. In addition to Corbin, the Legal Realists, who encompased many of the progressive thinkers of the twenties and thirties, often wrote on contracts. Two important articles from that era, not included here for space reasons, are Karl N. Llewellyn's *What Price Contract?—An Essay in Perspective*, 40 Yale L.J. 704 (1931) and Morris R. Cohen's *The Basis of Contract*, 46 Harv. L. Rev. 553 (1933). Since the nineteen thirties we have taken a less rigid view of contract and of the need for focused consent to the imposition of duties. This approach is sometimes described as "neo-classical," in that it does not seek to undermine the whole contract system, but does seek to cleanse the classical system of its many inequities. The first article below, by Professor Kessler, discusses this progression.

A Dialogue Between Kessler and Gilmore

Friedrich Kessler and the late Grant Gilmore were both Sterling Professors of Law at Yale. Both also taught at the University of Chicago. They collaborated on the second edition of what is now Kessler, Gilmore and Kronman, *Contracts* (3d ed. 1986). Professor Kessler was raised and educated in Germany and emigrated to the United States during the Nazi rise to power. Throughout his long career, he has drawn on his continental Civil Law background to question dogmas of Anglo-American contract law. One of his most important articles is *Contracts of Adhesion—Some Thoughts About Freedom of Contract,* 43 Colum. L. Rev. 629 (1943). It is fair to say that his writings were iconoclastic when they appeared and have been seminal to many contemporary attacks on traditional contract theory and on an unbridled notion of freedom of contract. Nonetheless, Professor Kessler has continued to state a belief in the importance of contract and of the freedom to enter into it or to remain out, and it can be argued that his approach seeks to conserve the traditional Anglo-American contracts system while cleansing it of the excesses that robbed many parties of the freedom that they were supposed to have.

Professor Gilmore was, at least outwardly, the quintessential Ivy League professor, with a walrus mustache and a distinctive way of speaking. Before going to Yale Law School, he had earned a Ph. D. in French literature, also from Yale. An authority of secured transactions, he was a principal draftsman of Article 9 of the Uniform Commercial Code and author of the leading treatise on the subject.

Though he wrote at a high level of scholarship, Gilmore often showed irreverence. He too was an iconoclast, though different both in style and in substance from Kessler. In 1970 he gave a series of lectures that were published in 1974 as *The Death of Contract,* an elegant and funny little book that has been bitterly attacked as unhistorical, but which has proven very influential. The reader is urged to read *The Death* in full, but to remember that Gilmore frequently wrote with his tongue in cheek, and expected his readers to know when to discount his more outrageous remarks. (In fact, Gilmore's comment about Oliver Wendell Holmes's *The Common Law* is equally applicable to Gilmore, himself: "Holmes amused himself by dressing his lectures in a deceptive overlay of history.") The material excerpted below from the Kessler and Gilmore Teacher's Manual is illustrative both of the style and the substance of *The Death.*

While Professors Kessler and Gilmore were cordial friends and co-authors (see Kessler's memorial to Gilmore, below), they were often in friendly disagreement. Below we have four pieces that produce a serendipitous "debate" between these giants. We begin with Professor Kessler's introductory essay to the Kessler, Gilmore and Kronman casebook, originally written for its first edition in 1953 and updated for the later editions. That essay is followed by comments written in the early 1970's by Professor Gilmore for the Teacher's Manual to the second edition of the book. The comments refer in part to the Kessler essay, and have dissenting footnotes by Kessler ("F.K."). This in turn is followed by a short excerpt from Gilmore's *The Death of Contract,* in which he puts forth his notion of "contorts." Finally, there is a brief quotation from Professor Kessler's memorial to Gilmore in which he states his skepticism about Gilmore's "contorts" approach. In both of Gilmore's pieces he reacts strongly to what he dubbed "the Contract is Dead School." One of the leaders of this "school" is Professor Stewart Macaulay of the University of Wisconsin, whose own writings follow immediately after the Kessler-Gilmore exchange.

Friedrich Kessler, *Introduction: Contract As a Principle of Order*, from Friedrich Kessler, Grant Gilmore and Anthony T. Kronman, *Contracts* (3d ed. 1986)

. . .

Most of us take contract for granted. Together with family and property, contract is one of the basic institutions of our social fabric. Price bargains, wage bargains, and rent bargains . . . belong to our daily experience. Indeed, contract is a principle of order of such universal usefulness that even a socialist economy cannot dispense with it.

A profitable approach to the law of contract, and perhaps to law in general, is to view legal doctrine, rules, principles, and standards as reflecting the value system of the culture in which the legal system is embedded. In our modern society, a tension exists between those values favoring individual freedom and those favoring social control.[4] Whatever the merits of the claim that a society without tension is conceivable (and desirable), in our society we encounter every day the tension between individual freedom and social control in debates over government regulation of the economy, abortion, use of marijuana and laetrile, sexual practices between consenting adults, gun control, the rights of criminal defendants, busing, affirmative action, and the teaching of evolution. The list is virtually endless. Small wonder, then, that modern contract law reproduces this same tension within itself, drawing much of its drama and vitality from our divided commitment to individual freedom and social control.

The law of contracts comprises many different doctrinal elements and encompasses exchange relationships of limitless variety. If these relationships were arranged along a continuum, we would find at one end transactions based on free bargain and genuine agreement, or at least on promises voluntarily given. Here, the dominant theme is respect for the autonomy of the parties and noninterference in the arrangements they have made for themselves, provided all the ground rules laid down to insure the smooth working of the system have been observed. Social control is at a minimum. As we proceed along the continuum, the freedom of the parties increasingly is limited by a system of judicial and legislative control designed to protect the community interest. And finally, at the opposite end of the scale, we find the so-called compulsory and adhesive contracts, the first type entered into under an enforceable duty to serve the public and the second unilaterally dictated by the stronger to the weaker party in need of goods or services. In recent years, there has undoubtedly been a shift all along this vast continuum in the direction of greater social control, a phenomenon reflecting the socialization of modern law in general. But the idea of private autonomy remains influential in wide areas of contract law and even where it is no longer dominant, its appeal can still be heard, albeit often only as a distant echo.

To better understand the main tenets of modern contract law, and its distinctive tendencies, it will be helpful to recall the outlines of what has been called the "classical" theory of contractual obligation. Classical contract theory starts from the belief that the individual is the best judge of his own welfare and of the means of securing it, and is inspired by the hope that given a "suitable system of general rules and institutions there will arise spontaneous relationships also deserving the term 'order' but which are self-sustaining and within the limits prescribed by the rules need no detailed and specific regulation." To achieve such order, according to the proponents of the classical theory, all that is required besides a system of general rules is "a free market guaranteeing and guiding the division of labor through a system of incentives it provides to the interest of the individual producers." Within this framework, contract provides the legal machinery required by an economic system that relies on free exchange rather than tradition, custom, or command.

The triumph of capitalism during the eighteenth and nineteenth centuries, with its spectacular increase in the productivity of labor, was possible only because of a constant refinement of the division of terprisers could depend on a continuous flow of goods and services exchanged in a free market. And to be able to exploit the factors of production in the most efficient way, enterprisers had (and still have) to be able to bargain for goods and services to be delivered in the future and to rely on promises for future delivery. Thus, it became one of the main functions of our law of contracts to keep this flow running smoothly, making certain that bargains would be kept and that legitimate expectations created by contractual promises would be honored. "The foundation of contract," in the language of Adam Smith, "is the reasonable expectation, which the person who promises raises in the person to whom he binds himself; of which the satisfaction may be extorted by force." In this sense, contract liability is promissory liability. In an indus-

---

[4] This conflict is reflected in the two main theories of contractual liability. One, the will theory, emphasizes the autonomy of the individual. The other, the objective theory, bases contractual liability on the social consequences of promise-making, or, as Hume put it, on the fact that "[p]romises are human inventions founded on the necessity and interests of society." The former view has found powerful support in Kantian ethics, which in recent years has experienced renewed interest if not a philosophical revival, e.g., J. Rawls, A Theory of Justice (1971). . . .

Kennedy, Form and Substance in Private Law Adjudication, 89 Harv. L. Rev. 1685 (1976), has pointed out that the conflict between individual freedom and social control is played out even in the choice of forms of legal regulation, specifically in the choice between narrowly defined rules and broad-based standards.

trial and commercial society, whose wealth, as Pound said, is largely made up of promises, the interest of society as a whole demands protection of the interest of the individual promisee.

Contract, to be useful to the business enterpriser within the setting of a free-enterprise economy, must be a tool of almost unlimited pliability. To accomplish this end, the legal system has to reduce the ceremony necessary to vouch for the deliberate nature of a contractual transaction to the indispensable minimum; it has to give freedom of contract as to form. Furthermore, since the law must keep pace with the constant widening of the market without being able to anticipate the content of an infinite number of transactions into which members of the community may need to enter, parties must be given freedom as to the content of their contractual arrangements as well. Contract, then, in the sense of a system of free contract, enhances the mobility of factors of production in the interest of the enterpriser who wishes to utilize them in the most efficient way and to be able to experiment rationally with new methods of satisfying wants. For that matter, such a system is required by every member of the community who seeks to achieve rationality of conduct in the adaptation of means to ends, and who does not want to adhere passively to the compulsory uniformity of behavior imposed by tradition and custom. Thus, its emergence has greatly increased the area and the potentialities of rational conduct.

Within the framework of a free-enterprise system the essential prerequisite of contractual liability is volition, that is, consent freely given, and not coercion or status.[13] Contract, in this view, is the "meeting place of the ideas of agreement and obligation." As a matter of historical fact, the rise of free and informal contract within western civilization reflected the erosion of a status-organized society; contract became, at an ever-increasing rate, a tool of change and of growing self-determination and self-assertion. Self-determination during the nineteenth century was regarded as the goal towards which society progressed; the movement of progressive societies, in the words of Sir Henry Maine, is a movement from status to contract, Ancient Law [163-165 (1864)]. "It is through contract that man attains freedom. Although it appears to be the subordination of one man's will to another, the former gains more than he loses."[15] Con-

tract, in this view, is the principle of order par excellence and the only legitimate means of social integration in a free society. Translated into legal language this means that in a progressive society all law is ultimately based on contract. And since contract as a social phenomenon is the result of a "coincidence of free choices" on the part of the members of the community, merging their egoistical and altruistic tendencies, a contractual society safeguards its own stability. Contract is an instrument of peace in society. It reconciles freedom with order, particularly since, as we have been told, with increasing rationality man becomes less rather than more egoistic.

The high hopes with regard to the potentialities inherent in the contractual mechanism found admirable expression in Henry Sidgwick's Elements of Politics 82 (1879):

> In a summary view of the civil order of society, as constituted in accordance with the individualistic ideal, performance of contract presents itself as the chief *positive* element, protection of life and property being the chief *negative* element. Withdraw contract—suppose that no one can count upon the fulfillment of any engagement—and the members of a human community are atoms that cannot effectively combine; the complex cooperation and division of employments that are the essential characteristics of modern industry cannot be introduced among such beings. Suppose contracts freely made and effectively sanctioned, and the most elaborate social organisation becomes possible, at least in a society of such human beings as the individualistic theory contemplates—gifted with mature reason, and governed by enlightened self-interest. . . .

Thus, a system of free contract did not recommend itself solely for reasons of sheer expediency and utilitarianism; it was deeply rooted in the moral sentiments of the period in which it found strongest expression. The dominant current of belief inspiring nineteenth-century industrial society—an open society of "removable inequalities," to use Burke's phrase—was the deep-felt conviction that individual and cooperative action should be left unrestrained in family, church, and market, and that such a system of laissez-faire would protect the freedom and dignity of

---

[13] Freedom of contract thus means that, subject to narrow limits, the law, in the field of contracts, has delegated legislation to the contracting parties. As far as the parties are concerned, the law of contracts is of their own making;

society merely lends its machinery of enforcement to the party injured by the breach. . . .

[15] W. G. Miller, Lectures in the Philosophy of Law 216 (1884).

the individual and secure the greatest possible measure of social justice. The representatives of this school of thought were firmly convinced, to state it somewhat roughly, of the existence of a natural law according to which, at least in the long run, the individual serving his own interest was also serving the interest of the community.[18] Profits, under this system, could be earned only by supplying desired commodities, and freedom of competition would prevent profits from rising unduly. The play of the market, if left to itself, would therefore maximize net satisfactions and establish the ideal conditions for the distribution of wealth. Justice within this context has a very definite meaning. It means freedom of property and of contract, of profit making and of trade. A social system based on freedom of enterprise and competition sees to it that the private autonomy of contracting parties is kept within bounds and works for the benefit of society as a whole.

It is hardly surprising that contract played a significant role in the evolution of free enterprise capitalism in this country, in England, and for that matter, in western continental Europe. In America, the law of contract underwent an extraordinary process of expansion and refinement in the first three-quarters of the nineteenth century. During this formative period, when the country was still, for the most part, an elemental and unexplored vastness, the "hands-off" attitude of classical contract law facilitated what J. W. Hurst has called a "release of creative human energy."[23] With the constant widening of the market, exchange transactions became more numerous and complex, and the principle of freedom of contract established itself as a paramount postulate of public policy.[24] Though the expression itself did not acquire wide currency until later, its underlying philosophy was already implicit in the case law of the early nineteenth century (if not before), and its influence was felt in every branch of our developing law of contracts. The idea of freedom of contract found expression, for example, in the general opposition to compulsory contracts of every sort, in the rise and short-lived triumph of the will theory of obligation, in the rejection of older, equitable approaches to the

problems of consideration and contract damages, in the rule of caveat emptor and, finally, in the nearly universal acceptance of the axiom that courts do not make contracts for the parties.

Of course, it was often said that fraud, misrepresentation, and duress must be ruled out by the courts in the exercise of their function of making sure that the "rules of the game" are adhered to. But these categories were narrowly defined (at least by the nineteenth-century common law) due to the strong belief in the policing force of the market. It was taken for granted that oppressive bargains could be avoided by careful shopping around. Contracting parties were expected to look out for their own interest and their own protection. "Let the bargainer beware" was (and to some extent still is) the ordinary rule of contract. It is not the function of courts to strike down improvident bargains. Courts have only to interpret contracts made by the parties. They do not make them. Within this framework contract justice is commutative and not distributive justice.[28] This attitude is in keeping with liberal social and moral philosophy according to which it pertains to the dignity of man to lead his own life as a reasonable person and to accept responsibility for his own mistakes. If the diligent is not to be deprived of the fruits of his own superior skill and knowledge acquired by legitimate means, the law cannot afford to go to the "romantic length of giving indemnity against the consequences of indolence and folly, or a careless indifference to the ordinary and accessible means of information."[29] Sir George Jessel, one of the great defenders of freedom of contract remarked:

[I]f there is one thing more than another which public policy requires, it is that men of full age and competent understanding shall have the utmost liberty of contracting, and that their contracts entered into freely and voluntarily shall be held sacred and shall be enforced by Courts of Justice.[30]

These pronouncements, however, are representative only of the main current of thought that shaped our law of contracts in its formative period. Anglo-American law never became the perfect mirror image of free enterprise capitalism, but always retained a

---

[18] Adam Smith, Wealth of Nations 423 (Cannan ed. 1937): "By pursuing his own interest the individual member of society promotes that of the society more effectively than when he really intends to promote it."

[23] Law and the Conditions of Freedom in the Nineteenth Century United States 6 (1956). . . .

[24] 2 M. Weber, Economy and Society 889-892, 668-681 (G. Roth & C. Wittich eds. 1978). . . .

[28] F. A. Hayek, Constitution of Liberty 232, 464 (1960).

[29] 2 J. Kent, Commentaries *485 (O. W. Holmes 12th ed. 1873).

[30] Printing and Numerical Registering Co. v. Sampson, 19 L. R.-Eq. 462, 465 (1875). "Freely and voluntarily" should not be underemphasized.

measure of independence from the underlying market relations it was helping to rationalize, a characteristic that neo-Marxist writers describe as its "relative autonomy."[31] Interestingly, however, the independence or autonomy of contract law did not significantly impede the evolution of the free enterprise system, which seems, for the most part, to have developed in accordance with an inner law or logic of its own.

Pound [Roscoe Pound, 1870-1964, long-time dean of Harvard Law School, and a major writer on legal philosophy in the first half of the twentieth century — ed.] is entirely correct when he states that "there has never been in our law any such freedom [of contract] as they [i.e., the advocates of doctrinaire liberalism] postulate."[35] Thus, common law courts have never hesitated to deny enforcement, for reasons of public policy, to contracts contemplating a crime, a tort, or an immoral act. Nor have they hesitated, to take another example, to strike down contracts in restraint of trade. Furthermore, courts became increasingly aware of the presuppositions underlying the doctrine of caveat emptor, and began around the middle of the last century to enlarge the responsibility of the seller for the quality of his goods in favor of the buyer who does not trade face to face with his neighbor for merchandise there to be seen. So-called implied warranties were added to express warranties to make sure that goods bought were of fair merchantable quality, or fit for the buyer's purpose provided he had relied on the seller's judgment for the determination of quality.

Turning to equity, this branch of law has for centuries given relief against contractual penalties and forfeitures. For example, equity granted the mortgagor a right to redeem his property, even if he had failed to so stipulate, and did not permit him to bargain away in advance his "equity of redemption." Equity also interfered with contracts in order to protect the interests of weak, necessitous, and unfortunate persons. These doctrines were too firmly established to be dislodged by the spirit of laissez-faire.[40]

In the eighteenth century, there was a tendency, at least in this country, toward a more equitable conception of contractual obligation, a conception that emphasized, among other things, a substantive theory of consideration which allowed courts to scrutinize the fairness of a bargain by using an objective theory of commodity value. This view of the matter was, as we know, short-lived, and a subjective theory of value soon emerged to replace it [i.e., that a court could not judge value because everyone had individual preferences —ed.]. As a result, the consideration doctrine was forced to pay tribute to the great principle of freedom of contract and the adequacy of the quid pro quo was (in theory at least) left to free bargaining. But courts quickly came to realize the usefulness of the consideration requirement as an instrument of social control, and in the subsequent elaboration of this requirement many of the equitable ideas that had been so widely accepted in the previous century enjoyed a second (if somewhat disguised) existence. Throughout the nineteenth century, the doctrine of consideration was used to implement and enlarge notions of public policy that a judicial commitment to the philosophy of laissez-faire made impossible to promote more directly.

The tendency to control contractual freedom received support from growing movements of protest and reform which, toward the end of the nineteenth century, began everywhere to share political and social power and to influence the formation of social policy. These movements gained strength during the great depressions of the late nineteenth century, fueled by the vigorous public reaction against railroad amalgamations and the pioneer trusts, child labor, unregulated working conditions, social insecurity, and other evils of contemporary industrial society. Experience in dealing with these problems strengthened doubts as to the universal validity of the belief in the success of unregulated individualism. Society, in granting freedom of contract, does not guarantee that all members of the community will be able to utilize it to the same extent. The use that can actually be made of contract depends on the system governing the distribution of property: to the extent that the law sanctions an unequal distribution of property, freedom of contract inevitably becomes a one-sided privilege. Society, by guaranteeing that it will not interfere with the exercise of power by contract, enables the enterpriser to legislate by contract in a substantially authoritarian manner without using the appearance of authoritarian forms. According to a theory that has gained wide popular appeal, many an

---

31 See, e.g., Tushnet, A Marxist Interpretation of American Law, 1 Marxist Perspectives, Spring 1978. . . .

35 Pound, Liberty of Contract, 18 Yale L.J. 454, 482 (1909). Even Sir George Jessel's famous formula leaves a

wide berth for different, and perhaps restrictive, interpretations.

40 Williston, Freedom of Contract, 6 Cornell L.Q. 365, 373 (1921). . . .

industrial empire has strengthened its power by employing contract as a weapon of industrial warfare.

Only slowly did American courts recognize the dangers inherent in the inequality of bargaining power. Convinced of the justice of the system of property, upon which the justice of freedom of contract rests, they believed that the existence of large industrial empires served the interest of society as a whole. Only the fittest deserved to survive, and the failure of many enterprises to survive the competitive struggle simply indicated that their services did not sufficiently benefit society as a whole. Antitrust laws, designed to promote freedom of competition, were in some famous cases interpreted in ways favorable to the power of industrial combinations. State statutes attempting to protect the weaker contracting party against abuses of freedom of contract by fixing minimum wages and maximum hours in employment and by attempting to outlaw discrimination against union members by means of yellow dog contracts did not fare any better at the hands of American courts. The climate of opinion prevailing at the end of the last century and well into this one is strikingly illustrated by the celebrated cases of Lochner v. New York, 198 U.S. 45 (1904), Adair v. United States, 208 U.S. 161 (1907), and Coppage v. Kansas, 236 U.S. 1 (1914). Declaring such statutes unconstitutional under the due process clause of the fourteenth amendment, these decisions elevated liberty of contract to the status of a fundamental property right. Pitney, J., speaking for the majority of the court in Coppage v. Kansas, which declared an anti-yellow dog statute unconstitutional, formulated the then-prevailing philosophy of Social Darwinism.

. . . No doubt, wherever the right of private property exists, there must and will be inequalities of fortune; and thus it naturally happens that parties negotiating about a contract are not equally unhampered by circumstances. This applies to all contracts, and not merely to that between employer and employee. Indeed a little reflection will show that wherever the right of private property and the right of free contract co-exist, each party when contracting is inevitably more or less influenced by the question whether he has much property, or little, or none; for the contract is made to the very end that each may gain something that he needs or desires more urgently than that which he

proposes to give in exchange. And, since it is self-evident that, unless all things are held in common, some persons must have more property than others, it is from the nature of things impossible to uphold freedom of contract and the right of private property without at the same time recognizing as legitimate those inequalities of fortune that are the necessary result of the exercise of those rights. But the Fourteenth Amendment, in declaring that a State shall not "deprive any person of life, liberty or property without due process of law," gives to each of these an equal sanction; it recognizes "liberty" and "property" as co-existent human rights, and debars the States from any unwarranted interference with either.[44]

It is significant that the opposing viewpoint had already found expression ten years earlier in the dissenting opinion of Mr. Justice Holmes in Lochner v. New York. (The majority had declared unconstitutional a New York statute imposing maximum hours for work in bakeries.) In the words of Mr. Justice Holmes:

The case is decided upon an economic theory which a large part of the country does not entertain. If it were a question whether I agreed with that theory, I should desire to study it further and long before making up my mind. But I do not conceive that to be my duty, because I strongly believe that my agreement or disagreement has nothing to do with the right of a majority to embody their opinions in law. It is settled by various decisions of this court that state constitutions and state laws may regulate life in many ways which we as legislators might think as injudicious or if you like as tyrannical as this, and which equally with this interfere with the liberty to contract. Sunday laws and usury laws are ancient examples. A more modern one is the prohibition of lotteries. The liberty of the citizen to do as he likes so long as he does not interfere with the liberty of others to do the same, which has been a shibboleth for some well-known writers, is interfered with by school laws, by the Post Office, by every state or municipal institution which takes his money for purposes thought desirable, whether he likes it or not. The Fourteenth Amendment does not enact Mr. Herbert Spencer's Social Statics.[45]

---

[44] 236 U.S. 1, 17 (1914). As late as 1936 a New York act fixing a minimum wage for women was held invalid in Morehead v. New York ex rel. Tipaldo, 298 U.S. 587 (1936). The whole doctrine was abandoned a year later. West Coast Hotel v. Parrish, 300 U.S. 379 (1937). . . .

[45] 198 U.S. 45, 75 (1904). . . .

It was several decades before the spirit of Holmes' *Lochner* dissent, with its recognition that freedom must sometimes be limited in the interest of its own preservation, began to have an appreciable influence on the law of contracts. As Aaron Director observed:

There may once have been substantial merit in the notion that the free-market system would steadily gain in strength if only it were freed of wide-spread state interference. By 1934 it became evident that a combination of a hands-off policy, which permitted the proliferation of monopoly power, and promiscuous political interference, which strengthened such power, threatened "disintegration and collapse" of the economic organisation. And only the "wisest measures by the state" could restore and maintain a free-market system.[46]

Very gradually the conviction took hold that political democracy is not sufficient by itself to secure the meaningful liberty men rightly desire. To overcome the deep sense of frustration felt by many, and to establish the material conditions needed to give existing legal freedoms something more than paper worth, political democracy (many argued) had to be supplemented by economic and social democracy.[47] In the course of this debate, the rhetoric of freedom of contract was drowned out by the rhetoric of freedom from contract, and equality of opportunity.[48]

Social control of contractual association, which began as a counter-current in the early days of laissez-faire libertarianism, has finally swelled into a main current of thought. One consequence of this development has been the breakdown of the classical conception of contract law as a unitary body of legal doctrine and the emergence (typically through legislative enactment) of whole branches of specialized law, and even specialized tribunals, associated with particular contracts. Labor law now regulates a substantial number of contracts between employer and employee. Securities law regulates the purchase and sale of corporate securities. Public utilities must make contracts with persons in their service areas on terms set by a governmental body. Special consumer legislation abounds, many insurance contracts are standardized by statute in whole or in part, and government contracts, which play an increasingly important role in our economy, have peculiar characteristics of their own. It has been said that special law has increased to such an extent that the general law of contract now covers only a small portion of the actual contracts made.[53] And even within this restricted field, the law is said to have little practical effect, since businessmen are inclined to view contracts as flexible commitments and to avoid litigation whenever possible.[54]

Today, therefore, the individual member of the community continuously finds himself involved in contractual relations, the contents of which are predetermined for him by statute, public authority, or group action. The terms and conditions under which he obtains his supply of electricity and gas will in all likelihood be regulated by a public utility commission. So will his fare, should he use a public conveyance going to work. The rent he will have to pay may be fixed by governmental authority. The price of his food will depend partly on the government's farm support program and not solely on the interplay of supply and demand in a free market. Many of the goods he uses in daily consumption will have prices that reflect suggested list prices. The wages he earns, or must pay, may also have been fixed for him beforehand. And if he is a businessman, he must take care not to violate the antitrust laws which, during the last half century, have grown steadily in importance, transforming the business environment.

This picture of our world has led many to the conclusion that the idea of contract has undergone a dramatic change. Some view contract as an anachronistic concept, anticipating its merger with the general law of obligations,[57] or argue that Maine's famous

---

[46] Aaron Director's Prefatory Note to H. Simons, Economic Policy for a Free Society vi (1948). A school of thought, influenced by both Simons and Director, has emerged in recent years that advocates the testing of contract doctrines in terms of economic efficiency and wealth maximization. See R. Posner, Economic Analysis of Law (2d ed. 1977); A. Kronman & R. Posner, The Economics of Contract Law (1979). The views of Simons and the Chicago School are not identical.

[47] This is taken from Kessler, Natural Law, Justice and Democracy—Some Reflections about Law and Justice, 19 Tul. L. Rev. 32, 59-60 (1944). On the changing meaning of democracy, see C.B. Macpherson. The Life and Times of Liberal Democracy (1977). See also Kronman, Contract Law and Distributive Justice, 89 Yale L.J. 472 (1980).

[48] The phrase "freedom from contract" is taken from Patterson, An Apology for Consideration, 58 Colum. L. Rev. 929, 949 (1958). See also W. Friedmann, Law in a Changing Society 90 et seq. (1959).

[53] L. Friedman, Contract Law in America 20-24 (1965).

[54] Macaulay, Non-Contractual Relations in Business: A Preliminary Study, 28 Am. Soc. Rev. 55 (1963). [This article is discussed immediately following the Kessler-Gilmore "debate." —ed.]

[57] G. Gilmore, The Death of Contract (1974).

formula has to be qualified if not reversed. Closely connected with this criticism is the idea that more attention should be given to the difference between discrete (transactional) exchanges and continuing relations, since many of the terms of the latter type of transaction must be left open for further negotiation.[59] It has also been suggested that the modern law of contracts can be more meaningfully explained in terms of a tripartite distinction between benefit-based, detriment-based, and promise-based obligations. Most challenging is the controversial suggestion to merge law with economics.[61] No less challenging are the ideas developed by the Critical Legal Studies movement.

These observations doubtless have some validity. Today, few judges (and fewer legislatures) feel enthusiasm, or even respect, for the elegant simplicities of the classical law of contracts. On the contrary, the carefully delimited classical defenses of mistake, fraud, and duress—the only defenses allowable in a strict libertarian regime—seem continually on the verge of further expansion and have recently been supplemented by a revitalized, and potentially far-reaching concept of unconscionability. Social policy arguments are frequently advanced to strike down obnoxious clauses. Caveat emptor is a mere shadow of its former self. The rules of the contracting game have been softened, and bargainers are expected to act in good faith toward one another.[63] The old model of arm's length dealing is in retreat, along with the notion that a contractual relation is one of "limited commitment." In their place, the confidential relation—the relation of fiduciary trust—has emerged or is emerging as the new model for both bargaining and contract performance in a large number of cases.

Despite all this, however, the classical theory of contract reflects a set of values that continue to enjoy wide acceptance in our society. Most special legislation leaves considerable freedom to the parties to arrange their affairs as they wish. Labor law, for example, while imposing a duty to bargain in good faith, does not require that the parties come to terms. Disclosure statutes, such as those found in the consumer field, may require that the provisions of the contract be set out clearly, but mandate very few terms. The federal government in recent years has shown a marked reluctance to impose mandatory wage and price controls, even in times of high inflation. Faith in market forces, or perhaps a lack of faith in governmental controls, is widespread and growing. Despite paternalistic arguments for directly regulating the consuming habits of the poor, consumer legislation has not gone so far. Self-reliance, it would seen, is still a valued concept in late twentieth-century America, and even those who argue that we are turning back to status after a brief flirtation with contract recognize that the roles that define a person's rights and responsibilities are not ascribed to one at birth, but are assumed more or less freely, and just as freely given up. Finally, the planning element of contract, so important in the field of business, has in recent years become increasingly important in the domain of interpersonal relations, such as marriage and cohabitation, where traditionally the contractual freedom of the individual was restricted or nonexistent. As freedom of contract wanes in one area, it waxes in another, and the overall result is a world that may well be more free than its nineteenth-century counterpart (though it is certainly free in different ways).

Any society that sees value in individual autonomy must have a strong commitment to contract and to contract values. For those who think contract is dead, Selznick provides the following balanced view of the role of contract in contemporary society.

The idea of contract is not wholly suited to modern experience; it does not help the law to grasp the realities of an administered society. Voluntarism is eroded when standardized "contracts of adhesion" leave little or no room for negotiation and when "private governments" largely determine the conditions of participation in economic life. The contract model presumes a world of independent, roughly equal actors who enter relationships of limited duration and limited commitment. A world of large-scale organizations, with their clients and constituencies, is forced into that mold only at the cost of significant distortion.

Nevertheless, contract remains a pervasive and

---

[59] Macneil, The Many Futures of Contracts, 47 S. Cal. L. Rev. 691 (1974); Goetz & Scott, Principles of Relational Contracts, 67 Va. L. Rev. 1089 (1981). [Ian Macneil and the "relational" approach to contracts, are discussed in Part IB, below. —ed.]

[61] See Posner, Some Uses and Abuses of Economics in Law, 46 U. Chi. L. Rev. 281 (1979), and the Comment by Michelman, id. at 307; see further Leff, Economic Analysis of Law: Some Realism about Nominalism, 64 Va. L. Rev. 451 (1974).

[63] Kessler & Fine, Culpa in Contrahendo, Bargaining in Good Faith and Freedom of Contract: A Comparative Study, 77 Harv. L. Rev. 401 (1964). [This article by Prof. Kessler and Edith Fine has proven very influential. See Part IIIB, below. —ed.]

powerful instrument of facilitative law. Its premises have sometimes required reconstruction to account for stubborn realities, as when a new type of "collective" contract was evolved to make sense of labor relations. But the appeal of contract as a general idea has not yet waned significantly. In part this is so because contract, being firmly embedded in common-law experience, casts a benign

light of legitimacy over rules and relationships elaborated in its name and applied to new contexts. Furthermore, the law of contracts since the nineteenth century has embodied values of freedom, equality, self-government, and legal competence. Contract preserves the integrity of the parties and upholds the principle of authority founded in consent.[69]

---

[69] Selznick, The Ethos of American Law, included in The Americans 1976, at 221 (I. Kristol & P. Weaver eds. 1976). The persistence of contract values in our society is reinforced by the emergence of the school of thought that stresses the economic efficiency of classical contract doctrines and thereby the wisdom of laissez-faire economics.

Grant Gilmore, *Introduction* and *Teaching Notes* from Teacher's Manual (1972) to Friedrich Kessler and Grant Gilmore, *Contracts* (2d ed. 1970) (footnotes by Friedrich Kessler ("F.K."))

What might be called the classical theory of contract is, we have been told, dead. Being dead it is no longer relevant to what is going on in the real world or to what we may guess may be going on tomorrow. Being irrelevant, the classical theory is no longer worth studying. The first-year course in Contracts, if it survives in any form, should be cut loose from the burden of history. Analysis of the moribund consideration doctrine should be scrapped in favor of analysis of the economic and social forces which determine the decisions of businessmen and their lawyers and shape the transactions which, by accident or design, they enter into.

The editors of this book have no quarrel with the premises of the argument sketched in the preceding paragraph. It is clear beyond the possibility of argument that contract theory, as magisterially elaborated in Williston's treatise and in the first Restatement of Contracts, is dead or dying.[1] From that premise, however, we draw a conclusion which is at the opposite pole from the conclusion which we have attributed, perhaps unfairly, to the proponents of the Contract is Dead school. The most cursory glance at

the Table of Contents of our casebook will reveal that the bias of these materials is frankly, even aggressively, historical. It seems appropriate to preface these Notes with some explanation of why, for one example, our treatment of the concededly moribund doctrine of consideration runs on, through Chapters 4, 5 and 6, for several hundred pages.

The general or classical theory of Contract is hardly a hundred years old—symbolically we may take the 1871 publication of Langdell's Cases on Contracts as the birth date of the theory. However, neither Langdell's collection of cases nor the Summary of the Law of Contract which he added to the 1880 edition of the casebook contributed a great deal by way of theoretical insight.[2] Holmes, in the astonishing series of lectures which make up The Common Law (1881), became the great theoretician of our law of civil obligations. No one reads The Common Law any more; indeed it has become unreadable. The generalization will be ventured that the Holmesian formulation of contract theory and in particular of the consideration doctrine was, taken as of its own time, revolutionary. It represented a sharp break with the

---

---

[1] F.K. disagree with the last two sentences. His reaction to the second sentence is similar to that of Mark Twain on reading his own obituary.

---

[2] F. K. dissents: To be sure, Langdell was on occasion doctrinaire and inflexible. . . . Still his analytical structure was a remarkable achievement for his day.

past, not a continuation of it. Holmes amused himself by dressing his lectures in a deceptive overlay of history. From what we know of his sardonic turn of mind, we can be sure that he knew perfectly well that he was proposing novel doctrine for a new era. That, fifty years later, the revolutionary preaching of his youth should have become the orthodoxy of the First Restatement of Contracts must have been a source of quiet amusement to him in his old age. The theory, so brilliantly formulated by Holmes, was elaborated almost without change by Williston: Williston on Contracts (1920) does little more than restate in several volumes what Holmes had originally covered in fifty or sixty pages.

The received orthodoxy of our own century, was, viewed chronologically, a late nineteenth century construct. Its immediate and spectacular success is sufficient evidence that it responded, in Holmes's phrase, to "the felt necessities of the time." Jurisprudentially, the theory was formal in the highest degree—the apparent triumph of logic over experience. The "rules" were put forward as absolutes of universal and eternal validity. Purity of doctrine, on this side of the Atlantic, was achieved by paying as little attention as possible, in casebook or treatise, to the obvious diversity of American case law and by promoting English cases, mostly of then relatively recent vintage, to the rank of "leading cases" of unquestioned and unquestionable authority. The "rules" for which the English cases thus promoted were said to stand seem not infrequently to go well beyond anything decided or even suggested in the cases themselves . . . . Socially, as we suggest in the Introductory Note to Chapter 15 on Third Party Beneficiaries, "the most striking feature of nineteenth century contract theory [was] the narrow scope of social duty which it implicitly assumed." The function of the restated consideration doctrine often appeared to be to insulate actors from liability. Nor was any provision made for the recovery of benefits conferred under quasi-contractual or restitutionary theories or for the recovery of losses suffered through detrimental reliance on a promisor's assurances under what later came to be called the doctrine of promissory estoppel. Within the narrowly restricted confines of contractual liability, the theory purported to announce a doctrine of absolute liability—no discharge or excuse by reason of change of

circumstance, however catastrophic and unpredictable—but this aspect of the theory may well have been honored at least as often in the breach as in the observance. Along with the insistence on absolute liability went an insistence on minimizing the remedies available for breach of contract—damages in lieu of specific performance and damages cut back almost to the vanishing point.[3]

As the neat and tidy universe hypothesized by the nineteenth century theorists has dissolved into the war, social revolution and technological insanity of our own century, we should expect that one of the minor casualties of the dissolution would be the neat and tidy nineteenth century theory of civil obligations—our classical theory of contract. It is the underlying thesis of this book that the story of contract law in this century has been the story of the gradual breakdown of the "classical" theory. In the past fifty years we have come almost full circle. It is hardly an exaggeration to say that most, if not all, of the late nineteenth century rules have been replaced by their own opposites. As the narrow, rigid, formal theory has disintegrated, we have witnessed what might be described as an explosion of liability. The stages of the process of breakdown and disintegration are chronicled in the extraordinarily rich literature of the field. The two great treatises on Contracts are constantly at war, with Corbin systematically denying every proposition which Williston had affirmed. (Corbin's extraordinary discussion of the consideration doctrine is in essence a point by point refutation of the Holmesian theory as reformulated by Williston.)[4] The fascination of the first Restatement of Contracts [written in the 1920's and published in 1932 —ed.] lies in its essential ambiguity—poised uncertainly between past and future, pointing resolutely in both directions at the same time. The "contract" provisions of the Uniform Commercial Code, drafted in the 1940's, clearly reveal the great theory in an advanced stage of decay. And there are, finally, the valiant generalizations of the second generation of Restaters [writing in the 1960's and 1970's —ed.], bending the Restatement format to breaking point and beyond in fulfilling their appointed task of assembling chaos in a sort of order.

It is our thought that the decline and fall of the nineteenth century contract theory is a story which is fascinating in its own right as well as ideal material

---

[3] Here again F. K. dissents.
[4] See, however, Corbin's essay in 50 Harv. L. Rev. 449, 453-457 (1937). For a criticism of Corbin based on his own

treatment of the consideration doctrine see, 61 Yale L.J. 1092, 1101-1103 (1952) (F. K.).

for a first-year law school course. Most of us who end up teaching law agree that we are not, or should not be, principally engaged in peddling facts or pumping our students full of useful knowledge. Our aim is rather to communicate to our students some insight into the complex and obscure process by which the law, itself constantly in course of transformation into its own opposite, nevertheless maintains itself as a structure of rational discourse. Contract law in the twentieth century is an admirable habitat in which to observe that process.

Since decline and fall is a meaningless concept without some understanding of what it is that we are declining and falling from, we have devoted a considerable proportion of these materials to establishing the base line of nineteenth century theory. . . .

The breakdown of a formal system in any field of law is not an orderly process. The resulting pattern, as it evolves through time, is jagged, uneven, out of proportion. The prevalent disorder is particularly notable in an area which, like Contract, has so far resisted anything like a general codification (apart from the quasi-statutory formulations of the successive Restatements).[5] In selecting these materials we have tried to resist the temptation of making it appear that everything fits together in a well-designed and neatly carpentered structure. The case law of the past half century is notable for its chaotic richness and its unruly diversity. The new synthesis, if there is to be one, is not yet discernible. A variety of conflicting hypotheses about our future course can be rationally and plausibly deduced from the evidence so far available. All this adds up to a great deal of intellectual confusion. Students who like, or think they like, their ideas clearly articulated and neatly categorized will, at least initially, find themselves repelled by this sprawling diffuseness. This may seem like strong medicine for entering law students but, on the other hand, it is at least arguable that the great strength of the first year curriculum in American law schools lies in its startlingly close resemblance to a guided tour through hell.

. . .

The three chapters (17, 18, 19) in Part II deserve a special mention. Chapter 17 is designed for background reading as a brief introduction to the two following chapters. Chapter 18 on the Automobile Dealer Franchise and Chapter 19 on Status and Contract in Insurance might be described as case studies in commercial arrangements which have traditionally been analyzed in terms of contract theory, but which have in truth split off from general contract to follow an independent development. . . . [T]hey can be used to demonstrate the proposition that the conventional idea of a unitary theory of contract, which covers all A's and all B's in all conceivable relationships to each other, is sadly deficient and that we will be well advised to start thinking in narrower categories. . . .

Professor Arthur Corbin once remarked that he had always made it a rule never to put a question to a student unless he was reasonably well satisfied that he knew what the answer to the question should be. The editors of this casebook make no pretense to having lived up to Professor Corbin's high but stern ideal. The casebook is riddled with questions and hypotheticals to which, it may be, there is no answer or to which there may be contradictory answers on which reasonable and knowledgeable men may well differ. . . . Our purpose in setting out so many questions to which neither we nor, it may be, any one else knows the answers is not mere perversity of mind and spirit. It seems to us that it is vital for first year law students to be made to come to grips with the idea that the law is an imperfect tool or technique and that there are many more questions which can be asked than there are questions which can be answered (except by a majority of the judges on a court of last resort) and that it is usually folly to think that you can successfully predict how the next case is going to be decided. We deal in a range of possibilities, not in easy answers to hard questions.

[Turning to the Kessler essay, Gilmore continues:] This essay, by Professor Kessler, has been carried forward without substantial change from the 1953 edition of Kessler and Sharp. As a jurisprudential statement about the theory and function of contract, the essay thus represents a formulation set down at the mid-point of the century. Differences of emphasis and detail will no doubt be apparent between this essay and the Introduction to these Notes written by Professor Gilmore in 1971. On the other hand, it is believed that the fundamental coincidence of views represented by the two essays is more significant than the occasional minor discrepancies. Between the 1950's and the 1970's a great deal of water has passed over the dam, but the river is still demonstrably the same river.

It may be that statements on the level of jurispru-

---

[5] Codification of the law of Contracts in times of rapid transition like ours would be most undesirable. . . . (F. K.).

dential abstraction represented by Professor Kessler's essay on Contract as a Principle of Order will be of more help as well as of more interest to instructors than to entering law students. It is the practice of one of the editors to advise his students not to read the essay until toward the end of the course (when, it may be hoped, they will have acquired enough background to enable them to control the ideas advanced with at least some degree of critical independence).

The author of the "essay," by contrast, has experienced no difficulties with assigning and discussing it right at the outset. The reference to Macaulay's well-known and challenging study and the introductory pages of L. Friedman's Contract Law in America [see Kessler essay n. 53 —ed.], might tempt the user of the casebook, particularly the instructor, to explore the implications of the "Contract is Dead School." This school, to put it somewhat crudely, maintains that the role of contract in business activities is overrated and that contract, in the sense of free contract, is a residual category, a leftover, since typical transactions of today's business life are governed by special rules. The author of the essay does not share the iconoclasm this view entails. The proponents of this view, which unduly narrows the concept of contract, do not sufficiently take into account that many transactions they classify as non-contracts are taking place against the background of a highly developed, sophisticated and flexible legal framework. Its value consists in "being." To be sure, legal sanctions are quite frequently not invoked should a "breach of contract" occur. A valuable business contract may be more important than a successful damage suit. Many contractual relationships are of a continuing nature and resemble in this respect collective labor agreements as described by the late Dean Shulman [Harry Shulman of Yale Law School —ed.]. But the possibility of a legal sanction as the "ultima ratio" is always in the background. A canner, for instance, may use a law suit to force a recalcitrant supplier and other suppliers to toe the line. The Campbell Soup case referred to in UCC § 2-302, comment 1 is an illustration of such strategy—although it was unsuccessful. A distinction might be made between continuing relationships and "one shot deals," between dealings among members of the "ingroup" and dealings with outsiders. A study of the practices of some members of the New Haven wire industry, unfortunately never published, seems to confirm Patterson's observation that a contract is not regarded as a "steel chain" but only as "a tentative arrangement even after the legal requirements of contract have been satisfied." Suppliers, the researcher was told, permit the buyer of "stock goods" to cancel with impunity and buyers of goods in the process of being manufactured to cancel upon reimbursement of the expenditures. Of course, sellers may invoke the law of contracts to prevent what they regard as abuse of the cancellation privilege. The student may also find a reference to modern consumer legislation and the right to cancel in door-to-door selling of interest in this connection.

. . .

The beginning of wisdom in the study of law comes no doubt with the student's perception of the fact that the apparently separate subjects of Contracts and Torts (if they are not separate subjects, why are they taught in separate courses?) are in truth two different ways of talking about the same thing.* An unquestionable desirable reform in legal education would be to replace the separate courses in Contracts and Torts with a combined or comprehensive course in the theory of civil obligations (which we might christen Contorts). So long as the traditional distinction is maintained (as it is in this and all the other current case books), it seems desirable to draw the student's attention at an early point to the propositions that liability in "contract" (or even in "quasi-contract") is not the whole story, that liability in "tort" lies within the same universe of discourse, that there has always been an interplay between contract theory and tort theory and that the dividing line between contract and tort has never been clear and, indeed, can never be made clear. . . .

---

* For a possible explanation of the meaning of this statement see, [among other articles] Fuller and Perdue, The Reliance Interest in Contract Damages, 46 Yale L.J. 52, 57 (1936). The emancipation of contract from tort was of great importance. It shifted the emphasis to the phenomenon of private autonomy. The objective theory of contracts should not be allowed to obscure this fact. Today tort law is needed to serve as a corrective of rigid contract law. (F.K.)

Grant Gilmore, *The Death of Contract* 87-90 (1974)

Speaking descriptively, we might say that what is happening is that "contract" is being reabsorbed into the mainstream of "tort." Until the general theory of contract was hurriedly run up late in the nineteenth century, tort had always been our residual category of civil liability. As the contract rules dissolve, it is becoming so again. It should be pointed out that the theory of tort into which contract is being reabsorbed is itself a much more expansive theory of liability than was the theory of tort from which contract was artificially separated a hundred years ago.

We have had more than one occasion to notice the insistence of the classical theorists on the sharp differentiation between contract and tort—the refusal to admit any liability in "contract" until the formal requisites of offer, acceptance and consideration had been satisfied, the dogma that only "bargained-for" detriment or benefit could count as consideration, and notably, the limitations on damage recovery. Classical contract theory might well be described as an attempt to stake out an enclave within the general domain of tort. The dykes which were set up to protect the enclave have, it is clear enough, been crumbling at a progressively rapid rate. With the growth of the ideas of quasi-contract and unjust enrichment, classical consideration theory was breached on the benefit side. With the growth of the promissory estoppel idea, it was breached on the detriment side. We are fast approaching the point where, to prevent unjust enrichment, any benefit received by a defendant must be paid for unless it was clearly meant as a gift; where any detriment reasonably incurred by a plaintiff in reliance on a defendant's assurances must be recompensed. When that point is reached, there is really no longer any viable distinction between liability in contract and liability in tort. We may take the fact that damages in contract have become indistinguishable from damages in tort as obscurely reflecting an instinctive, almost unconscious realization that the two fields, which had been artificially set apart, are gradually merging and becoming one.

A number of the developments which we noted in the preceding Lecture in tracing the twentieth century decline and fall from nineteenth century theory illustrate this basic coming together of contract and tort, as well as the "instinctive, almost unconscious" level on which the process has been working itself out.

The idea which we have come to know as "quasi-contract" was not part of the nineteenth century theory. We think of quasi-contract as a sort of no-man's-land lying between contract and tort. In the early part of the century the concept served to blur the sharp edges both of contract theory and tort theory. It was, as the courts readily admitted, a legal fiction: the "quasi-contract" was no contract at all but the admitted legal fiction served, or so it was thought, the ends of justice.

The "promissory estoppel" cases, like the quasi-contract cases, began to appear in the reports shortly after the turn of the century. The two concepts were, indeed, twins. As a matter of usage it came to be felt that quasi-contract was a better way of talking about the situation where plaintiff was seeking reimbursement for some benefit he had conferred on the defendant, while promissory estoppel was better for the situation where plaintiff was seeking recovery for loss or damage suffered as the result of reliance on the defendant's promises or representations. It would seem, as a matter of jurisprudential economy, that both situations could have been dealt with under either slogan but the legal mind has always preferred multiplication to division. And it may be that we still feel that the "benefit conferred" idea is a little closer to contract than it is to tort, so that contract (or quasi-contract) language is appropriate, while the "detrimental reliance" idea is a little closer to tort than it is to contract, so that tort (or quasi-tort) language is appropriate.

. . .

We seem to be in the presence of the phenomenon which, in the history of comparative religion, is called syncretism—that is, according to Webster, "the reconciliation or union of conflicting beliefs." I have occasionally suggested to my students that a desirable reform in legal education would be to merge the first-year courses in Contracts and Torts into a single course which we could call Contorts. Perhaps the same suggestion would be a good one when the time comes for the third round of Restatements.

The most recent, and quite possibly the most important, development in the promissory estoppel or §90 cases has been the suggestion that such contract-based defenses as the Statute of Frauds are not applicable when the estoppel (or reliance) doctrine is invoked as the ground for decision. This line, if it continues to be followed, may ultimately provide the doctrinal justification for the fusing of contract and tort in a unified theory of civil obligation. A remarkable passage in the *Restatement (Second)* §90 Commentary explains how most "contract" cases, if not all of them, can be brought under §90 so that resort to §75 [now §71 —ed.] and consideration theory will rarely, if ever, be necessary. By passing through the magic gate of §90, it seems, we can rid ourselves of all the technical limitations of contract theory. And if we choose to follow the alternative route of recovery under theories of quasi-contract or unjust enrichment—§89 A [now §86 —ed.] in *Restatement (Second)*—the argument that the contract limitations no longer apply seems to be quite as strong as it is in the §90 cases. If we manage to get that far, the absurdity of attempting to preserve the nineteenth century contract-tort dichotomy will have become apparent even to the law professors who write law review articles and books—the academic mind is usually a generation or so behind the judicial mind in catching on to such things.

Friedrich Kessler, *Grant Gilmore As I Remember Him*, 92 Yale L.J. 4 (1982)

. . .Grant also prepared a teacher's manual. It is a pity that the manual is not available to the general public. It not only guides the reader through the labyrinth of contract law, but it also contains an introduction of its own that offers a gentle critique of my own introduction in the casebook.

Although we never talked about it, Grant and I were convinced that collaboration was possible despite differences in opinion. And we did have many differences in opinion. I have not radically changed my views as to the central position of freedom of contract nor do I believe in what Grant was fond of calling "contorts." By introducing the concept of contort, Grant meant to express his belief that contracts and torts would eventually be absorbed into a general law of obligation.[5] I would express the idea somewhat differently and more cautiously. In the language of Patterson, "Anglo-American law, with its consensual-relational duties, its feudal survivals and its original tort theory of contract, can stretch its conception of consensual obligation pretty far."[6] But consent will remain a vital ingredient of contractual obligations; though there are many bridges between contracts and torts, their distinctive features will endure. However deep our disagreement on this or other scores, Grant and I had a most successful collaboration.

Grant was an eminently private person. He was also a very kind and tolerant friend to whom I owe an immense debt of gratitude. What he said about me in a most generous essay in the *Yale Law Journal*[7] applies with equal force to him. The evenings in his house, the hospitality of the Gilmores on Edgehill Road, belong to my fondest memories. They made my return from Chicago to New Haven a most enriching experience.

[5] G. Gilmore, The Death of Contract 87-94 (1974).

[6] Patterson, Compulsory Contracts in the Crystal Ball, 43 Colum. L. Rev. 731, 743 (1943).
[7] See Gilmore, Friedrich Kessler, 84 Yale L.J. 672 (1975).

Stewart Macaulay and the "Wisconsin School"

Stewart Macaulay is Malcolm Pitman Sharp Professor of Law at the University of Wisconsin. In 1963 Macaulay published *Non-Contractual Relations in Business: A Preliminary Study*, 28 Am. Soc. Rev. 55 (1963), in which he published the results of interviews and questionnaires in which business people and business lawyers were asked about their actual practices in contract situations. Macaulay's data suggested that the actual rules of contract law had little impact on working businesses, and that business people rarely used contract remedies or insisted on all of their contract rights.

The article was very much in a Wisconsin tradition of empirical research testing law by looking at everyday business practices. It was received with less than enthusiasm, especially by lawyers and law professors. "For the first few years after publication of the article, the only response to it came at a social function from a sociologist. Although perhaps not suspecting, as law students have, Professor Macaulay's revolutionary tendencies, the sociologist nonetheless suggested to Professor Macaulay that his article had taken up space in the *Review* that could have been used for a real contribution by a sociologist or, at least, for an article by a young sociologist who needed the space to gain tenure." Mark H. Van Pelt, *Introduction* to *Symposium on Law, Private Governance and Continuing Relationships*, 1985 Wis. L. Rev. 461, 463.

By the 1970's, though, Macaulay's 1963 article gained influence both as an example of empirical research in law and as a challenge to those who put forth what Macaulay called elsewhere "elegant models" of legal theory. Ironically, Macaulay's attack on excessive theorizing has in fact played an important role in the development of the "relational" theory of contracts, which will be discussed in the next section. In addition, it was the writings of Macaulay and his colleagues at Wisconsin that gave the title to Grant Gilmore's *The Death of Contract*, where Gilmore dubbed them the "Contract is Dead School."

Macaulay's 1963 Article

We begin with a summary of Macaulay's 1963 article. While the article deserves to be read rather than paraphrased, space limitations prevent my including two articles here, and Macaulay has written a more recent article that is reprinted following this note.

The reason that the 1963 article appeared in a sociology journal was that Macaulay did not use conventional methods of legal research. Instead of relying on appellate opinions and law review articles, Macaulay interviewed in depth 68 businessmen and lawyers from 43 companies, corresponded with 125 more, and examined standard order forms from 850 firms. (He did, however, also look at all reported cases involving the 500 largest manufacturing corporations in the previous fifteen years.)

Many of Macaulay's findings flew in the face of conventional contract wisdom about the importance of contract law in the conduct of business. In short, Macaulay found that contract law was largely, though not entirely irrelevant to most business dealings. "Businessmen often prefer to rely on 'a man's word' in a brief letter, a handshake, or 'common honesty and decency'—even when the transaction involves exposure to serious risks." An examination of a large packaging manufacturer's records showed that its "battle of the forms" with customers (the exchange of order and acceptance forms with conflicting "boiler-plate" terms in small print on the back) had failed to produce an enforceable agreement sixty to seventy-five percent of the time.* Thus, frequently there would be no relief available from the courts if a dispute arose. But few of the businessmen and their house counsel thought that the lack of available legal remedies was of any importance. Despite the lack of legal planning, especially over

---

* Macaulay's discussion of the battle of the forms is reproduced or discussed in some detail in many contracts casebooks and texts.

sanctions and the effect of defective performance, the business people found that they were able to deal with the good faith disputes that were inevitable during the business relationship. Macaulay wrote that they were able to do so because the norm of business conduct was to adjust the deal as it went along. For example, Macaulay interviewed ten purchasing agents and seventeen sales people. All of them said that they expected to see an order cancelled if the buyer no longer could use the product, this despite clear contract law to the contrary. Macaulay quoted a paper seller: "You can't ask a man to eat paper . . . when he has no use for it." Also, a factor beyond business decency was involved. Most of the the business people made clear that lawyers were the last people they wanted involved when a contract dispute arose, and that a breach of contract lawsuit was an absolute last resort, since it would inevitably ruin any future business dealings with the other party.

Macaulay found further that business people were able to operate exchange relationships with relatively little attention to detailed planning or legal sanctions because both sides usually understood their primary obligations, even if they hadn't foreseen all foreseeable contingencies. Specifications are usually written by professionals for professionals "who will know the customs of their industry and those of the industries with which they deal. Consequently, these customs can fill gaps in the express agreement of the parties." Even more, contract and contract law were often deemed unnecessary because of two widely-accepted norms: "(1) Commitments are to be honored in almost all situations; one does not welsh on a deal. (2) One ought to produce a good product and stand behind it." Businesses exist to fulfill obligations and business people get to know each other. They want to satisfy their customers and suppliers, and they need to keep a good business reputation. As a result, the detailed planning that is envisaged by classical contract law may in fact hamstring flexible dealing and indicate a lack of trust.

Macaulay concluded that contract "often plays an important role in business, but that other factors are significant." He called for further examination of "the whole system of conducting exchanges" and of what he called "types of business communities." During the next two decades, he and others carried on that kind of research, and his findings led many writers to rethink the question of the centrality of contract and of contract law.

In 1985 the Wisconsin Law Review put together the symposium mentioned a few pages back. In it Macaulay discussed his earlier writing, and gave his opinion of the role of contract in the present day.

Stewart Macaulay, *An Empirical View of Contract*, 1985 Wis. L. Rev. 465

I. Introduction

When Grant Gilmore called his lectures "The Death of Contract," he gave a name to a body of work that includes some of mine. He called me the "Lord High Executioner" of the "Contract is Dead" movement. However, Gilmore was not very interested in my empirical description of contract. He said this kind of work lacked theoretical relevance. I must credit him with an attention catching title. Nevertheless, he failed to see that the very limited practical role of what professors call contract law poses signifi-

cant theoretical problems that we are only beginning to confront.

In a way, Gilmore's title is misleading. Contract as a living institution is very much with us. In the day-to-day flow of dealings, vast numbers of significant transactions take place to the reasonable satisfaction of all concerned. People and organizations bargain, they write documents, and they avoid, suppress, and resolve disputes little influenced by academic contract law. Some cases are taken to court and the formal process begun, although lawyers settle most of them before courts reach final decisions. There are even opinions by judges relying on traditional contract law, but they are relatively rare.

Furthermore, contract within the academy is still very much alive. Every morning in law schools all over the United States beginning law students struggle with offer, acceptance, and consideration. I never argued that contract law died. Rather, academic contract law is not now and never was a descriptively accurate reflection of the institution in operation Moreover, this inaccuracy matters in many ways.

At the end of September in 1984, there was a conference in Madison marking the 21st birthday of the publication in the *American Sociological Review* of my article on non-contractual relations in business. I am pleased that the article has had a long shelf-life and people still find something in it. After listening to others at the conference consider long-term continuing relationships, it is a good time for me to reflect on developments over the past two decades. We must remember that my article reports research done when Dwight Eisenhower was President of the United States, and I wrote it when John Kennedy was in office. Both the business executives and lawyers interviewed and the author were living in the United States before the decline and fall of the American empire. Indeed, any article that uses Studebaker taxis as an example was written in the pre-word processor age. A great deal has happened in 21 years. We also know much more about the American legal system in operation today than anyone did when I wrote the article.

To reconsider what I wrote, I will summarize the argument of my 1963 article, including some of my later research as well. Then I will note what I would add were I to write the article today. Finally, I will consider what difference all of this makes to those interested in contracts and law and society research.

. . .

II. The 1963 Article As Supplemented By Two Decades Of Work In Dispute Processing Research

The 1963 article challenges a model of contract law's functions, explicit or implicit in the work of contracts scholars and social theorists. This model makes contract law far more central than its actual role in society.[5] One version of the model suggests that in a state of nature we are all selfish. Law supports needed interdependence by coercing us to honor obli-

gations to others. The historical story is that we begin with trading within real communities. Capitalism breaks this up, and we become alienated strangers. Then the legal system supplies a kind of synthetic community based on rights and duties enforced by courts. A variant of the story is that market capitalism changes all personal relations into autonomous market trades—capitalism replaces a spirit of interdependence by "what's in it for me?" Contract law supplies the needed glue to hold individualists to their bargains.

More particularly, writers assume a number of things about the institution of contract. First, there is careful planning of relationships in light of legal requirements and the possibilities of nonperformance. We must spell out everything because parties will perform only to the letter of a contract, if they go that far. Second, contract law is a body of clear rules so that it can facilitate planning. It provides formal channels so that we know the right way to proceed to produce desired legal consequences. Finally, contract litigation is a primary means of deterring breach and directly and indirectly resolving disputes. Without contract law and the state's monopoly of the legitimate use of force, performance of contracts would be highly uncertain.

However, all of these assumptions about history and about human relationships are just wrong or so greatly overstated as to be seriously misleading. Contract planning and contract law, at best, stand at the margin of important long-term continuing business relations. Business people often do not plan, exhibit great care in drafting contracts, pay much attention to those that lawyers carefully draft, or honor a legal approach to business relationships. There are business cultures defining the risks assumed in bargains, and what should be done when things go wrong. People perform disadvantageous contracts today because often this gains credit that they can draw on in the future. People often renegotiate deals that have turned out badly for one or both sides. They recognize a range of excuses much broader than those accepted in most legal systems.

There are relatively few contracts litigated, and those that are have special characteristics. Few of those cases litigated produce anything like adequate compensation for the injuries caused. Frequently, limitations on liability in written contracts block remedies based on the reasonable expectations of the

---

[5] I am indebted to Professor Anthony Kronman of the Yale Law School and Professor Robert Gordon of the Stanford Law School for some of the ideas in this paragraph. I sketched the implicit academic model of contract in Macaulay, Elegant Models, Empirical Pictures, and the Complexities of Contract, 11 Law & Soc'y Rev. 507 (1977).

party who did not draft the instrument. At best, formal legal procedures usually are but a step in a larger process of negotiation. Filing a complaint and pretrial procedure can be tactics in settlement bargaining; appeals often prompt reversals and remands, leaving the parties to settle or face continuing what seems to be an endless process. When final judgments are won, often they cannot be executed because of insolvency.

How do we explain this gap between the academic model and an empirical description of the system of contract law in action? Academic writers often make individualistic assumptions. Their theories rest on worlds of discrete transactions where people respond to calculations of short-term advantage. However, people engaged in business often find that they do not need contract planning and contract law because of relational sanctions. There are effective private governments and social fields, affected but seldom controlled by the formal legal system. Even discrete transactions take place within a setting of continuing relationships and interdependence. The value of these relationships means that all involved must work to satisfy each other. Potential disputes are suppressed, ignored, or compromised in the service of keeping the relationship alive.

While we often read that increasing bureaucratic organization has made the world impersonal, this is not always the case. Social fields cutting across formal lines exist within bureaucracies, creating rich sanction systems. Individuals occupying formal roles ignore organizational boundaries as they seek to overcome formal rationality to achieve goals, gain rewards, and avoid sanctions. Social networks serve as communications systems. People gossip, and this creates reputational sanctions.

Power, exploitation, and dependence also are significant. Continuing relationships are not necessarily nice. The value of arrangements locks some people into dependent positions. They can only take orders. The actual lines of a bureaucratic structure may be much more extensive than formal ones. Seemingly independent actors may have little real freedom and discretion in light of the costs of offending dominant parties. Once they face sunk costs and comfortable patterns, the possibility of command rather than negotiation increases. In some situations parties may

see relational sanctions as inadequate in view of the risks involved. However, instead of contract law, they usually turn to other techniques to provide security, ranging from collateral to vertical integration.

Furthermore, contract law as delivered is a misrepresented product. American doctrine is not clear and easy to apply. Rather it is contradictory, uncertain, and offers arguments rather than answers.[17] This is particularly true of the Uniform Commercial Code's Article II, governing transactions in goods. I often tell my classes that if lawyers of equal ability represent clients with equal resources and willingness to invest them in a case falling under Article II, the case will end in a tie.[18] If one side wins and the other loses, it is not because of the power of legal doctrine. I can match any argument you make with one equally as good. Also, courts have interpreted the Code's rules concerning failure to perform so that settlements and compromises are promoted, and those who would vindicate their rights are punished.

American contract remedies are limited and reflect a fear of awarding too much. . . . Limiting remedies can benefit a weaker party, making breach of contract less burdensome. However, often it benefits stronger parties. They have less need for legal remedies to achieve their ends because they have other-than-legal leverage. Limited remedies allow stronger parties to walk away from burdensome obligations at low or no cost. Courts frequently find that a stronger has breached a contract, but so limit the remedy awarded the weaker that the victory is hollow.

Even when contract law might offer a remedy, the legal system in operation promotes giving up or settling rather than adjudicating to vindicate rights. One must pay for one's own lawyer, and one must win enough to offset all the costs of the endeavor. Thus, using the legal process always is a gamble. Furthermore, crafty lawyers use delay and procedural technicality for advantage. Galanter has discussed what he calls "megalaw." Those who can afford to play invest in the skills of large law firms. They play the litigation game by expanding procedural complexity to draw out the process. Others who cannot afford to invest as much must drop out. This kind of power is not distributed equally. In another famous article, Galanter tells us "why the 'haves' come out ahead."[26] The "haves" are repeat players who can spread the

[17] See, e.g., Macaulay, Private Legislation and the Duty to Read—Business by IBM Machine, the Law of Contracts and Credit Cards, 19 Vand. L.Rev. 1051 (1966).

[18] I have been accused of exaggerating every now and then to make a point.

[26] See Galanter, Why the "Haves" Come Out Ahead: Speculations on the Limits of Legal Change, 9 Law & Soc'y Rev. 95 (1974).

costs of litigation over many similar transactions. They can afford to play for rules and treat disputes as test cases which may help them in the future. They can run up the costs of a particular case in order to reinforce their reputation as difficult defendants to sue.

Technical complexity and delay gain greater impact in a legal system marked by overload. While America has more lawyers per person than any Western nation, the number of judges is relatively small. Many factors have contributed to the rise in recent years of judges who coerce parties to settle rather than try cases that will take time in court. Our judges have long done this, but recently they have brought the role out into the open. They are proud of their efforts, and they are teaching each other how best to force parties to settle rather than litigate. Of course, legal rights matter in settlement negotiations, but such considerations as the immediate need for money also play an important part.

III. In 1984, What Should Be Added To This Picture?

The original article does not rest on naive functionalist assumptions of harmony. Nevertheless, today I would stress that relational sanctions do not always produce cooperation or happy situations. Trust can be misplaced. There are always failures to perform and mistakes. Usually, business people take an insurance approach. They write off these incidents as long as there are not too many or one of them does not involve too much money. Business scandals always have been with us, and they prompt attempts to use care and countermeasures. By and large, the contracting system works well enough. However, even large famous business corporations can suffer major losses as the result of incomplete planning and trusting the wrong people.[32]

When long-term continuing relationships do collapse, those disadvantaged often turn to contract law and legal action. We have seen litigation prompted by major shocks to the world economic system. OPEC and the energy crises of the 1970s provoked many cases where contracts had rested on relational sanctions and assumptions about the costs of energy.[35] Relational considerations gave way to the large amounts of money that businesses would have lost had they performed their commitments. Westinghouse, for example, promised electric utilities buying its nuclear reactors that it would guarantee the price of fuel.[36] A world cartel sent the price soaring far beyond the price Westinghouse had guaranteed. Westinghouse found a plausible excuse in the Uniform Commercial Code[37] and announced that it would not perform. After elaborate rituals before the courts, the cases were settled. Westinghouse injured its reputation, but the alternative might have been the destruction of a major multinational corporation. Contract doctrine played a part in the resolution of this dispute, but it would be hard to call it the principal actor.

The decline of the American industrial economy produced other controversies about how to spread the costs throughout society. Employment security provides a good example. Unlike Europe, the United States does not have laws regulating job security of most workers. We did not see such laws as needed as long as we had a growing economy and a strong ideology of competition and rewarding merit. Events have shaken our assumptions. It is not easy for even the upper part of the working class or middle class white collar workers to move to comparable employment today. Many older middle managers have been fired to save their higher salaries, medical benefits, and pensions. The women's movement has made sexual harassment salient.

These developments plus the great reductions in the workforce have provoked atrocity stories that have come before the courts. The traditional American rule is that non-unionized employees of a private corporation could be fired for good reason, bad reason, or no reason unless they had enforceable employment contracts for a specified duration—and only a few highly valued employees had these.[42] Lawyers

---

32 See, e.g., J. Stewart, The Partners 152-200 (1983); Eagan, The Westinghouse Uranium Contracts: Commercial Impracticability and Related Matters, 18 Am. Bus. L.J. 281, 282-83 (1980); Joskow, Commercial Impossibility, the Uranium Market and the Westinghouse Case, 6 J. Legal Stud. 119 (1977); Parisi, Westinghouse Faces Hefty Financial Losses While the Case Puts Gulf Oil's Reputation in Peril, N.Y. Times, July 9, 1978, sec. 3, at 1, col. 1.

35 See, e.g., Aluminum Co. of America v. Essex Group, Inc., 499 F.Supp. 53 (W.D. Pa. 1980); Missouri Pub. Serv. Co. v. Peabody Coal Co., 583 S.W.2d 721 (Mo. Ct. App. 1979), cert. denied 444 U.S. 865 (1979).

36 See J. Stewart, The Partners 152-200 (1983); Macaulay, Elegant Models, supra note 5, at 515 for the story of the Westinghouse case.

37 Westinghouse relied on U.C.C. § 2-615(a) (1978) which provides an excuse "if performance as agreed has been made impracticable by the occurrence of a contingency the nonoccurrence of which was a basic assumption on which the contract was made . . ."

42 See, e.g., Comerford v. International Harvester Co., 235 Ala. 376, 178 So. 894 (1938) (court held that worker who alleged he was fired because of his wife's refusal of his supervisor's sexual advances, failed to state a cause of action).

brought cases to court involving outrageous terminations of employees at will, and some judges responded. At first, courts fashioned rather sweeping doctrines that would have offered a great deal of employment security. As American attitudes have shifted to the right, the courts have become concerned with going too far. Later cases have qualified what had seemed to be a growing trend. Many writers say we need a statute, but most arlgree that those who would benefit from such a statute lack the power to promote one.

Other cases have been provoked by the shift to new technologies that industry has mastered imperfectly. This has left a wide gap between expectations and what manufacturers have been able to deliver. Traditionally, American manufacturers of complex machines promised products that would produce certain results. They did their best while containing costs and keeping up production. Often the product sent was a first draft. Engineers from the seller and those from the buyer then would work something out by trial and error.

In the computer age, the expectations created by manufacturers' promises have been unrealistic, and the "working out" approach has often failed. This has led to litigation testing the contract drafting of elite lawyers. Even experienced business people are tricked by a sales person's assurances that are contradicted by a lawyer-drafted standard form contract. Courts often enforce these standardized documents to aid deception and fraud[50] or to help large bureaucracies control their street-level personnel. It is fascinating to watch the doublethink when they explain these decisions on the basis of the victim's consent and choice. Usually a major question is whether a court will honor the various warranty disclaimers, remedy limitations, and other evasions of responsibility hidden in fine print. Some courts have seen these clauses as just part of the business game; others have recognized that form contracts can be licenses for sales people to trick customers and evade responsibility when things go wrong.

Another body of reported litigation involves those in dependent relationships such as dealerships and franchises trying to fight to defend their assumptions

about continuing their business. All kinds of contract and tort doctrines have been mobilized, and these groups have organized to lobby statutes through the various state legislatures.[53] Dealers have won some notable victories. However, in recent years, bureaucratic rationality and flexibility in the face of changed marketing conditions have won out over the interests of the dependent.

While our court reports have registered a great deal of contracts litigation in recent years, all of these attempts to use contract law have revealed that the second part of my 1963 critique still has force. The legal system in operation simply fails to vindicate rights or offer much to those who seek redress from the courts. Often it offers only symbolic victories, probably producing great frustration. For example, as I have mentioned, we have enacted statutes granting rights to dealers who hold franchises to sell automobiles, gasoline, and the like. Members of the trade associations that worked to pass this legislation saw enactment as a great victory. Yet again and again the courts have read these statutes narrowly so that franchisers escape real harm. The statutes may have had indirect impact. Franchisers may have modified the behavior of their agents to avoid atrocity cases that might prompt courts to interpret the new rights broadly, but this is only supposition.[55]

Usually, contract litigation becomes an elaborate, drawn out morality play affecting only back stage negotiations. Gottlieb points out *"[i]n sustained and inextricable relations a principal use of contracts is to provide a basis for renegotiations* once a defective performance occurs." For example, many scholars have discussed *Aluminum Company of America v. Essex Group, Inc.*[57] In that case, increases in the price of fuel made a long-term contract very unprofitable for ALCOA, the supplier. The written contract contained a price escalator clause which failed to take into account great increases in energy costs. ALCOA stood to lose millions of dollars if a court enforced the contract as written. A federal trial judge rewrote the contract to produce a pricing arrangement that he thought fairly reflected the risks actually assumed by the parties. In light of all the declarations by American courts that they will not rewrite contracts to re-

---

[50] I think judges, just as most Americans, have conflicting views about deception. Fraud may be bad, but a sharp operator evokes a smile and admiration. Sometimes our judges confuse the loveable con man of fiction and film with a Fortune 500 company.

[53] I have told this story in some detail in S. Macaulay, Law and the Balance of Power: The Automobile Manufacturers and Their Dealers (1966); Macaulay, Law Schools and the

World Outside Their Doors II: Some Notes on Two Recent Studies of the Chicago Bar, 32 J. Legal Educ. 506, 536-40 (1982). See also Jordan, Unconscionability at the Gas Station, 62 Minn. L. Rev. 813 (1978).

[55] Franchisers have attacked franchise protection statutes, and this may indicate that the statutes have some effect. . . .

[57] 499 F. Supp. 53 (W.D. Pa. 1980).

flect the bargain the parties ought to have made, the opinion seems surprising. Perhaps, it symbolizes a very difficult role for courts.

However, the trial judge's decision never went into effect as the case was settled. The parties renegotiated their arrangement. During the oral argument on appeal, a federal appellate court managed to convey to the parties its doubts about the innovative decision that favored ALCOA. After a huge investment in lawyers, expert witnesses, court costs and the like, the reaction of the appellate court prompted ALCOA to offer a settlement to Essex Group that was too good to refuse.[58] What remains is an opinion by the district court for scholars to write about.[59] However, while most of these articles are excellent, most of the authors write as if they were unaware that the innovative, and perhaps offensive, judicial revision never was put into effect.[60] Many of these articles discuss judges imposing their views on the parties and rewriting contracts. That did not happen in the ALCOA case, and it probably would not happen in many cases even if *Aluminum Company of America v. Essex Group, Inc.* were recognized as the law everywhere. The District Judge's opinion and the uncertain result of the appeal changed the balance of bargaining power, but it did not impose a final result on the parties. The decision plus the appellate process worked as a form of coercive mediation. Faced with the situation, the parties worked out their own solution. The chance that a judge might rework a written contract after circumstances had changed also could affect bargaining situations. Perhaps this kind of coercion toward settlement is a good way to handle contracts that have gone on the rocks; perhaps it is a terrible way. Nevertheless, it is hard to evaluate a process without describing it accurately.

Other contracts disputes that provoke written opinions end in token settlements because almost always American contract law awards only money damages. However, a major reason that relational sanctions fail and contracts are breached is that the defaulting party is in or on the borders of bankruptcy. As some lawyers put it, a judgment against a bankrupt plus 65 cents will buy a bus ride in Madison, Wisconsin (of course, 65 cents alone will do the same

thing). The threat of bankruptcy often is a potent weapon in settlement negotiations; it is a form of strength through weakness.

IV. What Difference Does All This Make And To Whom?

What should we make of this gap between the academic model of contract law and the system as it works? At minimum, we need a complex model of contract law in operation if we wish to be descriptively accurate. Contract law operates at the margins of major systems of private government through institutionalized social structures and less formal social fields. We must establish rather than assume the actual influence of this doctrine. Contract law as discussed by scholars frequently is but a rhetorical ploy in a much larger struggle. Lawyers may use its vocabulary in the process of dealing with a dispute. Often, however, the real issue between the parties is transformed to fit a law school model far removed from the transaction. As such, classic doctrine may affect negotiations, but not in the way assumed by most scholars. Perhaps lawyers skilled in playing the contract game do better for their clients, but defenders of orthodoxy must prove this. Perhaps bargaining in the shadow of the law implements those values explicit or implicit in contract doctrine to some degree. This cannot be assumed but must be established by investigation.

The contract process in action seldom is a neutral application of abstract rationality. The party with the best argument as judged by a contracts professor will not necessarily win the case. An opponent with a plausible argument, little need to settle, and resources to play the lawyering game is unlikely to bow to arguments favored by law professors at elite schools. Indeed, all an attorney may need are arguments that seem more or less plausible to judges and other lawyers. Even those disliked by scholars such as "unilateral contract" and "the meeting of the minds" often will do in the actual dispute resolution process.

We cannot be sure what functions orthodox contract doctrine serves. However, what we know so far suggests that contract doctrine incorporates major conflicting strands of political philosophy. It does not

---

[58] The statement in the text is based on interviews with lawyers for the parties in the ALCOA case.

[59] See, e.g., Dawson, Judicial Revision of Frustrated Contracts: The United States, 64 B.U.L. Rev. 1 (1984); Speidel, The New Spirit of Contract, 2 J. Law & Com. 193 (1982); Speidel, Court-Imposed Price Adjustments Under

Long-Term Supply Contracts, 76 NW. U.L. Rev. 369 (1981). [Articles by Dawson and Speidel discussing ALCOA appear in Part IIIC of this anthology. —ed.]

[60] Both Dawson and Speidel are well aware of the settlement. Most of what I know about it comes from following up what Dick Speidel told me about the case.

stand apart from the cross currents of political debate over time. At a particular time, one conception is emphasized. Later, as times change, another view takes its turn. In areas such as the parol evidence rule, the Statute of Frauds and misrepresentation, we find decisions in a single state bouncing from one position to the other. This makes contract law contradictory.

At the most basic level, contract law promises to remedy breaches of contract and provide security of expectations. It does this only indirectly and imperfectly. It helps reassure us about the stability of an ever changing and frightening world. It deters breach by those unaware that counterrules neatly match most contract rules or that most contract rules are qualitative and open-ended. Much of law operates under the Wizard of Oz principle of jurisprudence—you will recall that the Great Oz was a magnificent and wonderful wizard until Dorothy's dog knocked over the screen so all could see that the Wizard was a charlatan.

Nonetheless, contract law curbs power to some degree. Those who can command may not want to appear arbitrary and all powerful. It is good public relations to channel their actions into the forms of contract to gain the symbolism of bargain and free choice. Even this modest effort offers a degree of leverage for limiting the exercise of power. Scholarly notions of free contract are a frail defense against those with power seeking to achieve illegitimate ends. Nonetheless, there are few other defenses short of revolution.

Perhaps classic contracts scholarship can safely ignore the way the contract system works. This scholarship may be irrelevant to most of practice, and so it does not matter how articles are written. However, this scholarship has influence in some instances, and this leaves us with a puzzle. In the face of many studies challenging its descriptive accuracy, many scholars and theorists continue to paint a simple instrumental picture. What purposes are being served by all this traditional scholarly effort? Perhaps it is a form of denial. The formal contract system claims to be neutral and autonomous and to rest on simple rationality. A descriptively accurate model of the process challenges these assumptions. We must remember that long-term continuing relations are not always nice situations for those short of power. Instead of free individuals making informed choices, many are dependent and must choose between unpleasant options. Courts seldom come close to putting aggrieved parties in the position they would have been had the contract been performed. Cases are often won by lawyer ploys and the strategic and tactical advantages flowing from greater wealth. Instead of vindicating rights, our legal system offers deals. As a result, often one party feels cheated while the other thinks he got away with something.

At least in the United States, we want to believe that a lawyer, armed only with reason, can champion the weak and overcome the powerful. This myth drew many of us to law school, and it is hard to give up. A descriptive model reduces many lawyers to little more than captive intellectuals serving those who control significant resources in society. In short, classical contracts scholarship allows us to maintain a comforting image of what it is that typical lawyers do. A system of individual rights prompts higher thought. Descriptive accuracy requires us to confront the dark side of the society and its legal system. Many find it easier to ignore reality than to cope with it. . . .

. . .

Perhaps many academics ignore the functioning legal system for a much simpler reason. Looking at it makes things messy. As Betty Mensch notes:

> Viewed in retrospect, Williston's majestic doctrinal structure may have been silly, but . . . appeals to reasonableness and justice appear sloppy and formless by comparison. Williston's structure was, at least, a real structure, however misguided. Perhaps much Willistonian dogma survives simply because it provides a challenging intellectual game to learn and teach in law school—more fun than the close attention to commercial detail required by thorough-going realism.[67]

V. A Not Totally Pessimistic Conclusion

Having said all this, I must note that I still teach contracts to beginning law students. (Of course, I am not sure that many American teachers would accept that what I teach is true contracts material.) I try to blend study of rhetoric and doctrine with a portrait of the system in operation. There are at least two reasons for doing this. One is to train lawyers better. Students must understand a game to learn to play it well. The other is that the approach raises major

---

[67] Mensch, Freedom of Contract as Ideology, 33 Stan. L. Rev. 753, 769 (1981).

questions about law and society. Put most simply, why does American society promise so much more than it delivers? Or, looking at the situation another way, what functions does the system as it actually operates serve and for whom?

However, I try to teach a not entirely negative lesson and guard against cynicism. There is enough truth in the image of law as rationality above politics and power so that a few lawyers representing a few clients can make their society a little less hostile place. I think visions of a better future are important, but in the here and now lawyers can make a contribution to smoothing rough edges from the society. I would rather teach my students some ideal of law than leave the impression that practice can be no more than just selling advocacy to the highest bidder.

My colleague, Marc Galanter, says that if we demystify the nature of dispute processing and paint an empirically accurate picture, we must face the challenge of:

> devising new ways of measuring the performance of legal institutions and new ways of redesigning those institutions to facilitate interchange with a more alert public. To get there from here, we need a new generation of research about what law means in people's lives; what gives it its hold, its influence, its attraction; why it repels or frightens; whether it is dependent upon illusions about its character. . . .[69]

This is an optimistic statement. Those who see law as but one of many cloaks for power and privilege may object. We can expect them to argue that an accurate view of law in operation would violate so many legitimating assumptions that a new normative justification would be impossible. Bargaining and negotiation are not examples of disinterested application of apolitical norms—they necessarily take into account all sources of power. The nice guys do not always win. Indeed, they may have to be content with token settlements. We can ask whether citizens in

modern welfare states can face the nature of their legal system? Do they need to believe in a rule of law? In absolute rights and wrongs? In a wholly autonomous legal system? Can they accept both the virtues and costs of bargaining in the shadow of the law?

Perhaps citizens need an idealized picture of their legal system. Perhaps it is what most of us want to believe. However, before we discard the possibility of working toward new rationalizations for modern legal systems as they operate, we must remember that the public is somewhat informed, often cynically aware of the true nature of law in action. Indeed, the citizens' recognition that the legal system's claims are belied by its day-to-day performance may produce that cynical awareness. Understanding the system as it is might reduce some of the cynicism. Perhaps, however, attempts to justify law as delivered might force us to consider a number of reforms which some would see as threatening to their position and privileges. If awareness provokes debate, it would be healthy.

Perhaps the only people fooled by classic images of law are law professors and social theorists misled by legal scholars. On the other hand, perhaps a few professors are playing a cynical game. Scholars can gain grants and support by fashioning their work to serve the interests of those who provide pleasant lives for academics. Most, however, are just more comfortable with a traditional structure that provides focus and coherence rather than an indeterminate empirical picture, whatever its accuracy.

The challenge is to find a way to avoid cynicism, recognize the values of classic views of law, and rationalize a dispute processing system that does not turn on litigation and doctrine. All of this must be done without becoming a pet intellectual for those who can pay. Perhaps it would be easier to square the circle or turn lead into gold than bring this off. Nonetheless, this is the challenge of an empirical perspective on law.

[69] Galanter, Knowledge Transcends Pessimism About the Law, Legal Times, Sept. 24, 1984, at 6, col. 1.

Critical Legal Studies

Contrast with the approaches of Kessler, Gilmore and Macaulay, the position of two leading members of the Critical Legal Studies movement, Peter Gabel and Jay M. Feinman. Gabel, who was formerly the President of New College in California, is presently teaching at New College of California School of Law and is Associate Publisher of Tikkun, a journal of Jewish progressive thought. Feinman is Professor of Law at Rutgers-Camden. The Critical Legal Studies movement is rather difficult to describe briefly. It is a wide-ranging amalgam of law teachers and others who are dissatisfied with the present state of law and of legal education. Many of its adherents apply Marxist analysis to law; some profess to be radical in politics as well, some do not. It is common for CLS articles to spend a fair amount of space on a revisionist history of their topic. Another common (if rather incomprehensible) device is "deconstruction" or "trashing" of legal rules and theories to show that they are indeterminate and infinitely manipulable. On this, see Kellman, *Trashing*, 36 Stan. L. Rev. 293 (1984).

If there is anything like a unifying thread (besides their fondness for poly-syllables), it is probably that most CLS people (sometimes called "crits," with varying degrees of fondness), believe that the legal system's ostensibly neutral rules favor hierarchy, wealth and the existing power structure. (Of course, many non-adherents, such as Macaulay, also believe this.) Many of their critics accuse the CLS'ers of being nihilists. Others, even when they reject much of the CLS corpus, believe that it has much of value and that we have much to learn from the "crits." For more on Critical Legal Studies, see *Symposium on Critical Legal Studies*, 36 Stan. L. Rev. 1 (1984); *Kennedy and Klare, A Bibliography of Critical Legal Studies*, 94 Yale L.J. 461 (1984); and *Unger, The Critical Legal Studies Movement*, 96 Harv. L. Rev. 561 (1983).

The Gabel and Feinman article is from *The Politics of Law* (Pantheon Press 1982), a collection of essays by Critical Legal Scholars specifically aimed at law students. A new edition of the book will appear in 1989.

Peter Gabel and Jay M. Feinman, *Contract Law As Ideology*, from The Politics of Law (David Kairys, ed. 1982)   [Pantheon Press]

The recent rise of right-wing forces in the United States has been brought about in large part through the shaping and manipulation of collective fantasies. Among the most powerful of these fantasies is a resurgence of what one might call the utopian imagery of freedom of contract. As Reagan "lifts the government off of our backs," we are told that we all will once again be able to stand as free and equal individuals, ready to take whatever action serves our respective self-interests. The image conveys a sudden release of personal power, as if it had only been "government" that had been obstructing the realization of our individual desires. At the same time, the image also conveys a new feeling of social solidarity, a feeling that once that obstruction is removed, we Americans will return to a time when a deal was a deal, when as plain-speaking people we could hammer out our collective destiny through firm handshakes enforceable in a court of law.

For this resurgent ideology to enjoy a temporary measure of success, it makes no difference that it is based upon a lie. The truth is that those of us living in the United States today cannot actually achieve our desire for increased personal power, for freedom, and for genuine social connection and equality so long as we are trapped within ubiquitous hierarchies that leave us feeling powerless, alienated from one another, and stupefied by the routines of everyday activities. And the truth also is that this reduction of our humanity will be overcome only by our own sustained efforts to abolish these hierarchies, to take control over the whole of our lives, and to shape them toward the satisfaction of our real human needs. This sort of concrete, practical movement would embody the *realization* of the utopian content of "freedom of contract," but no such movement is needed for the utopian imagery of the present period to have a profound catalytic effect; instead, the imagery can tap the suppressed needs that people feel as they are numbed into quasi-oblivion in front of industrial machines, word-processors, and television sets, and can jettison those needs into fantasies of fulfillment. The efficacy of the imagery, in other words, derives precisely from the fact that people experience little possibility of achieving personal power, freedom, or genuine social connection in the concrete context of their everyday lives.

A principal vehicle for the transmission of such ideological imagery has been and continues to be "the law." In order to understand the present and historical function of the legal system, and of contract law as a part of this system, one must grasp the relationship between the utopian images transmitted through legal ideas and the socioeconomic context that these ideas serve to justify. In this essay, we provide a brief introduction to a method for understanding this ideological power of law by tracing the relationship between the history of contract law and the development of capitalism over the last two hundred years.

. . .

[Building on the work of Morton Horwitz, the authors argue that contract law in the eighteenth century was based on a vision of traditional norms, primarily involving the transfer of title to things, and customary obligations based on status, occupation or social responsibilities. Horwitz's very important thesis has been challenged, particularly by Professor A. W. Brian Simpson of the University of Michigan Law School. The Horwitz-Simpson debate appears in Part IC, below.

[The authors then argue that in the nineteenth century, the importance of capital in the economy because of the Industrial Revolution was one factor that undermined the traditional status and property-based law of contracts. —ed.]

The second great change in society was the dissolution of many of the traditional bonds among people

that had characterized the social relations of earlier periods. The social meaning of work, property, and community were increasingly fragmented as socioeconomic processes based on competition and individual self-interest reorganized the social universe. Traditional social environments had hardly been idyllic and certainly embodied forms of alienation and class domination that ought not to be idealized. But the rise of capitalism—with its universal market in which people and things were everywhere made subject to the exigencies of money exchange—generated a dramatic and dislocating social upheaval. Within a short stretch of historical time, people experienced and were forced to adapt to the appearance of the factory and the slum, the rise of the industrial city, and a violent rupture of group life and feeling that crushed traditional forms of moral and community identity in favor of that blend of aggression, paranoia, and profound emotional isolation and anguish that is known romantically as the rugged individual.

How could people have been persuaded or forced to accept such massive disruptions in their lives? One vehicle of persuasion was the law of contracts, which generated a new ideological imagery that sought to give legitimacy to the new order. To speak of "ideological imagery" is to imply that there is a reality behind the image that is concealed and even denied by the image. The reality was the new system of oppressive and alienating economic and social relations. Contract law denied the nature of the system by creating an imagery that made the oppression and alienation appear to be the consequences of what the people themselves desired.

Denial and legitimation were accomplished by representing reality in ideal terms, as if things were the way they were because the people wished them to be so. This representation was not the product of conspiratorial manipulation by power-mad lawyers and judges. Instead, the legal elites tended to identify with the structure of the social and economic order because of what they perceived to be their privileged position within it, and they expressed the legitimacy of that structure when arguing and deciding cases in their professional roles. During this period important members of the bench and bar associated themselves emotionally and intellectually with the capitalist transformation and became imbued with the "logic" of the new system. In arguing and deciding cases, they fit the situation presented within that logic to resolve the conflict represented by the dispute at issue. Those resolutions tended to legitimate the basic social relations, no matter how unjust, oppressive, and alienating they actually were. In the process of resolving many cases, legal concepts were built up that embodied the new social relations. The result was a system of contract law that appeared to shape economic affairs according to normative principles but that was, in fact, only a recast form of the underlying socioeconomic relations.

The legitimating image of classical contract law in the nineteenth century was the ideal of free competition as the consequence of wholly voluntary interactions among many private persons, all of whom were in their nature free and equal to one another. From one point of view this was simple truth, for the practical meaning of the market system was that people conceived of as interchangeable productive units ("equality") had unfettered mobility ("freedom") in the market. From another point of view, however, this was denial and apology. It did not take account of the practical limitations on market freedom and equality arising from class position or unequal distribution of wealth. It also ignored other meanings of freedom and equality having to do with the realization of human spirit and potential through work and community. The legitimation of the free market was achieved by seizing upon a narrow economic notion of freedom and equality, and fusing it in the public mind with the genuine meaning.

The legal consequences of this legitimating mystification were the separation of contract law from the law of property and the law of nonconsensual relations, the representation of all social relations as deriving from the free and voluntary association of individuals without coercion by the state, and the allocation of responsibility for the coercion worked by operation of the market to personal merit or luck. In an economy founded upon the accumulation of capital through exchange transactions occurring in a competitive market, the proper role of the state was conceived to be that of the relatively passive enforcer of the "free will" of the parties themselves, of their "freedom of contract." As a result, the nineteenth-century law of contracts consisted of a series of forms ostensibly designed solely to realize the will of free and equal parties, as that will was objectively manifested in agreements.

Some leading contracts cases taught to first-year law students illustrate the power and effects of this mystification. The rules for contract formation and performance were extensions of the principle of objectively manifested free will. A son and his wife worked for his father on the father's farm for some twenty-five years without pay, in the expectation that the father would will the farm to him on his death. When the father died without a will, the farm was divided among all his heirs. Could the son, like the eighteenth-century physician, recover in contract, if not for the farm, at least for the value of his services? No, because there was no clear expression of an agreement between father and son, without which the court would be invading the freedom of the parties if it imposed liability. On the other hand, where the parties had made a definite agreement, it bound them absolutely. Thus, a builder contracted to build a schoolhouse; the partly finished building was blown down by a windstorm; and after being rebuilt, it collapsed again due to soil conditions that could not be remedied. Was the builder liable for failure to build a third time? Indeed he was, for "where a party, by his own *contract*, creates a duty or charge upon himself, he is bound to make it good if he may, notwithstanding any accident by inevitable necessity."

The most important and in some ways the most peculiar rules of classical contract law concerned the doctrine of "consideration," which grew out of the principles of freedom and equality. Since the market was the measure of all things, only those promises were enforceable that represented market transactions—those for which the person making the promise received something, a "consideration," in return. Thus, a promise to make a gift was not enforceable because it was gratuitous. Further, if a person offered to sell his house to another and agreed to give the other person until Friday to decide whether to buy or not, he could change his mind and revoke the promise because it was, like a gift, a gratuity. Conversely, when a bargain had been struck, it was firm, and the courts would not inquire into the "adequacy of consideration," i.e., the fairness of the bargain. If a person promised to pay a large sum of money in return for a worthless piece of paper, the nineteenth-century court, unlike the eighteenth-century jury, would "protect" the exercise of free will between supposedly equal parties and bind him without weighing the substantive fairness of the transaction.

The results in these cases may seem unfair or irrational today, but to the judges of the time they were neither. The courts could not easily have intervened to protect a party or to remedy unfairness without violating the ideological image that the source of social obligations rests only upon the bargain that the parties themselves have evinced, not upon the community's version of justice. This imagery, drawn as it was from the exigencies of competitive exchange, served to deny the oppressive character of the market and the lack of real personal liberty experienced by people in their private and work lives. Most important, it served to deny that there was a system at all that was coercively shaping and constricting the social world, because the imagery made it appear that this world was simply the perpetual realization of an infinite number of free choices made by an infinite number of voluntary actors.

Contract Law In The Twentieth Century

Today judges applying contemporary contract law would probably reach different results in these cases. The son might receive a recovery for the value of the services conferred on the father. Liberalized doctrines of excuse for nonperformance might relieve the builder. In many circumstances, a "firm offer," such as the offer to sell the house upon acceptance before Friday, is binding without consideration; in other cases, the court might not enforce the offer but would at least compensate the buyer for expenses incurred in reliance on the offer. And, purportedly, courts today will in extreme cases correct any gross unfairness in a bargain.

Contemporary contract law views these cases differently not because twentieth-century judges are wiser or smarter than their nineteenth-century counterparts, or because a new and more equitable style of legal reasoning has somehow sprung into being through a progressive maturation of the judicial mind. The old rules disintegrated for the same reason they were conceived: there has been a transformation of social and economic life that has brought about a parallel transformation in the ideological imagery required to justify it.

The transformation from the nineteenth-century to the twentieth-century forms of American capitalism was the consequence of a variety of factors that can only be summarized here: competition among businesses produced ever larger concentrations of capital within fewer and fewer companies; workers organized in response to their collective dependence on these emerging monopolies and challenged in a revolutionary way the myths of freedom and equality; exploitation of the Third World, advancing technology, and efficient organization of production facilitated the partial assimilation of the American labor movement, allowing for the payment of higher wages while deflecting more radical labor demands; this increase in the level of wages, the use of part of the

economic surplus for unemployment insurance, Social Security, and other types of welfare benefits, and the greater psychological control of consumer purchases through the mass media helped to alleviate the system's persistent tendency toward underconsumption. The basic requirement for understanding contemporary contract law is to look at the socioeconomic system thus produced and to observe its transposition, through the medium of law, into an imaginary construct that attempts to secure the system's appearance of legitimacy.

The essential characteristic of contemporary capitalism is the substitution of integration and coordination in the economy for the unbridled competition of the free market. Coordination is accomplished first by monopolistic corporations that are vertically and horizontally integrated (meaning there are but a few "horizontal" corporations at the top of the major industries that own the capital that controls "vertically" production and distribution in each industry); and second, by a massive involvement of the state in regulating and stabilizing the system. In place of the unrestricted mobility of productive units that characterized the operation of the market in the nineteenth century, we now have integration, coordination, and cooperation to above all maintain systemic stability through an ever more pervasive and efficient administration.

A brief look at the dominant American industry, the automobile industry, will illustrate. The industry is composed of three giant companies and one smaller firm, which account for three fourths of the vehicles sold annually. The firms are vertically integrated in fact; every step of the production and distribution process, from raw material production to retail sales, is accomplished either within the company itself, by basic industry firms such as the steel companies, which are closely allied in interest with the automakers, or through legally independent entities, such as parts suppliers and dealers, which are actually subject to the economic control of the manufacturers. Although General Motors, the largest of the "Big Three," may have the capital and market power to significantly increase its market share at the expense of some of its competitors, it has not usually done so, preferring a relatively predictable shared monopoly to cutthroat competition. State intervention occurs to support the industry through massive purchases of its products for civilian and military use, and the provision of highways as public goods for the use of cars; to coordinate the production of goods that market forces alone do not produce, such as safety devices;

and even to ensure the continued existence of the firms, as in the federal welfare scheme to bail out Chrysler.*

The rise of the coordinated economy has created a major problem for the law—how to transform the ideology of "freedom and equality" and its adjunct, "freedom of contract," into a new image that might retain the legitimating power of the older images while modifying them to conform more closely to the actual organization of daily life in the era of monopoly capitalism. The strategy for solving this problem has been to transform contract law into a relatively uniform code for business transactions that is predominantly defined not by the individualist principle of unregulated free competition but by the more collective principle of competition regulated by trade custom. Since most "trades" (whatever nostalgia for a bygone era that term may evoke) are actually integrated production networks subject to supervision by dominant firms, the modern law of contracts is able to retain the legitimating features of private agreement while effectuating the regulatory and stabilizing component that is a central principle of the contemporary economy.

The principle of regulated competition leads to different results in the kinds of cases mentioned earlier. The twentieth-century counterpart to the case of the son who could not recover from his father's estate because of the absence of an express promise is the 1965 Wisconsin case of *Hoffman v. Red Owl Stores* [26 Wis. 2d 683, 133 NW 2d 267 (1965) —ed.]. The Hoffmans were small-town bakers who were induced to sell their bakery and move to a new town in reliance on the promises of an agent of the Red Owl supermarket chain that they would be granted a franchise, which never came. Under classical contract law, the Hoffmans would be without a remedy because the formal franchise contract had never been executed; in the twentieth century, however, the Wisconsin court discarded that restricted notion of agreement and held that they could recover because their reliance on the agent's representation had been commercially reasonable.** The strict nineteenth-century requirement of bargain was rejected in favor of a broader standard of social obligation more expressive of the realities of the late-capitalist economy.

Hoffman v. Red Owl is a leading case for the principle that atomistic, concrete agreement is no longer the sole principle of contract law; people's tendency to act in reliance on less formal representations must be protected as well. It also illustrates the doctrine that private economic actors have a duty to act in "good faith." Both principles embody the ethic of cooperation and coordination reflective of the modern economy.

These principles apply in other cases also. The promise to keep open until Friday an offer to sell a house would now frequently be enforced because that is recognized as an appropriate and necessary way to do business today. In rare cases, courts can even be moved to inquire into the fairness of a bargain—into the adequacy of consideration—under the recently developed doctrine of unconscionability. While this doctrine has more theoretical significance than practical effect, sometimes consumers and other parties with little economic power can be protected from the more outrageous excesses of economic predators. In sum, people are conceived to be partners in a moral community where equity and the balancing of interests according to standards of fair dealing have supplanted the primitive era, when every moral tie was dissolved in "the icy waters of egotistical calculation." And the state as passive enforcer of private transactions has become the state as active enforcer of the newly conceived notion of the general welfare.

Conclusion

. . . [A]t each stage in our history the ideological imagery of contract law served to legitimate an oppressive socioeconomic reality by denying its oppressive character and representing it in imaginary terms.

This is a very different explanation of the role of contract law from liberal or leftist instrumental analyses, which suggest that particular rules of law or particular results "helped" capitalists by providing a framework for legal enforcement of market activity. Instrumental analyses of contract law confuse the role of direct force with the role of law in the development of sociohistorical processes. Social processes like "free-market capitalism" do not get "enforced" by "laws." Rather, these processes are accepted through social conditioning, through the collective in-

* [The authors seem to have used a rather outdated example, even for 1982, when this article was first published; in recent years foreign cars have created the most competition in the auto industry since the 1920's. The authors' point is not foolish, despite their unfortunate example. —ed.].

** [Note that the recovery was limited to the Hoffmans' loss (reliance damages) and did not include their promised gain from the abortive bargain (expectation damages) —ed.]

ternalization of practical norms that have their foundation in concrete socioeconomic reality. Since these norms are alienating and oppressive, the process of collective conditioning requires the constant threat of force and the occasional use of it. For example, if you fail to perform your part of a bargain, it *may* be the case that a sheriff with a gun will attach your bank account to pay the aggrieved party his or her damages. The occasional deployment of direct force serves to maintain the status quo as well as to get people to accept its legitimacy.

"The law" does not enforce anything, however, because the law is nothing but ideas and the images they signify. Its purpose is to justify practical norms (and in so doing to help constitute them by contributing to the collective conditioning process). One important way that this justification process occurs is through judicial opinions. Judicial opinions "work" as ideology by a rhetorical process in which oppressive practical norms are encoded as "general rules" with ideological content; these "rules" then serve as the basis for a logic ("legal reasoning") that supposedly determines the outcome of the lawsuit. The key social function of the opinion, however, is not to be found in the outcome and the use of state power which may follow from it, but in the rhetorical structure of the opinion itself, in the legitimation of the practical norm that occurs through the application of it in the form of a "legal rule." That enforcement of bargains was much more likely to occur under nineteenth-century contract law than under eighteenth-century law is, of course, true; but this does not mean that the function of nineteenth-century contract law was to "enforce bargains." The reverse expresses the truth more accurately—that the enforcement of bargains functioned to permit the elaboration of contract law as legitimating ideology.

The central point to understand from this is that contract law today constitutes an elaborate attempt to conceal what is going on in the world. Contemporary capitalism bears no more relation to the imagery of contemporary contract law than did nineteenth-century capitalism to the imagery of classical contract law. Contemporary capitalism is a coercive system of relationships that more or less corresponds to the brief description given here. The proof of this statement inheres in the situations we all face in our daily lives in the functional roles to which we are consigned: lawyer, secretary, student, tenant, welfare recipient, consumer of the products and services of Exxon, Citibank, and Sears. Despite the doctrines of reliance and good faith, large business corporations daily disappoint our expectations as to how they should behave. Despite the doctrine of unconscionability, unfairness is rampant in the marketplace. In this reality our narrow functional roles produce isolation, passivity, unconnectedness, and impotence. Contract law, like the other images constituted by capitalism, is a denial of these painful feelings and an apology for the system that produces them.

Most of the time the socioeconomic system operates without any need for law as such because people at every level have been imbued with its inevitability and necessity. When the system breaks down and conflicts arise, a legal case comes into being. This is the "moment" of legal ideology, the moment at which lawyers and judges in *their* narrow, functional roles seek to justify the normal functioning of the system by resolving the conflict through an idealized way of thinking about it.

But this also can be the moment for struggle against the narrow limits imposed in law on genuine values such as freedom, equality, moral community, and good faith. By questioning whether the legal system helps or hinders the actual realization of those values in a meaningful sense in everyday life, the critical approach permits us to expose the illegitimacy of the system and to explore the possibility of a different order of things.

B. The Basis Of Contract

Introduction

Part IA explored some of the discussions of the centrality of contract to law and society, and of law and society to contract. Now we explore the basis of contracts and ask why our legal system enforces them. There are many explanations, some of which were alluded to in the Kessler essay that began Part IA: free will and the liberty to bind yourself; promise as a morally binding act; reliance by the promisee; the economic needs of the society; the relationship between (or among) the parties; community; solidarity.

Throughout the topic runs the notion of consent to be bound. How important is consent? Is it consent that distinguishes contract from tort? How focused does consent have to be? May consent be inferred from acts? If so, how attenuated may the inference be, and does the act of stretching to find consent really move us back into tort? (This, of course, brings us back to Gilmore and Kessler's debate over "contorts.")

While it may seem arcane to argue over the basis of contract, if promise (or even the weaker concept of consent) is essential to contract, government intervention is circumscribed. Courts have less justification for the imposition of duties that were neither promised nor consented to, and legislation that does interfere with promises may be vulnerable constitutionally as an interference with "freedom of contract." (Freedom of contract is usually discussed under the rubric of substantive due process in the basic course in Constitutional Law; it has been in eclipse since 1937, but seems to be making a judicial and academic comeback in recent years. The controversies of earlier years are briefly discussed in the Kessler essay in Part IA, and in many law review articles, among them M. R. Cohen's *The Basis of Contract*, 46 Harv. L. Rev. 533 (1933).)

Promise or Consent as the Keys to Contract

Section 1 of the Restatement (Second) of Contracts defines a contract as "a promise or set of promises for the breach of which the law gives a remedy, or the performance of which the law in some way recognizes as a duty." Putting aside for the moment the question whether there can be a contract *without* a promise, we may consider why the law ever enforces promises, and whether a promise alone justifies judicial intervention to force compliance. Charles Fried discussed the issue at length in his important book, Contract As Promise (1981). Fried is Carter Professor of General Jurisprudence at Harvard Law School, and has written extensively on moral questions. Fried argues that a promise inspires trust; it invites reliance and permits future exchanges to be transformed into present exchanges by "a conventional device which we both invoke, which you know I am invoking when I invoke it, which I know that you know I am invoking, and so on." But on top of this "utilitarian counting of advantages" Fried adds a moral obligation: "[b]y virtue of the basic Kantian principles of trust and respect, it is wrong to invoke that convention in order to make a promise, and then to break it." In addition, the freedom to bind yourself involves "taking responsibility not only for one's present self but for one's future self."

Fried's promise approach to contract has provoked controversy. If, as has been suggested, emphasis on promise as a basis for duty limits governmental involvement, Fried's approach may explain his attractiveness to the Reagan Administration, in which he served as Solicitor General from 1985 to 1989. Many politically liberal academics were distrustful of Fried's role in the Reagan Justice Department, and one can readily see that his opening premise of the supremacy of human will and its implicit superiority to things that are "merely part of external nature" can be attacked as an example of collective megalomania. (Think of what we've done to the whales and to the ozone layer.) But Fried's favoring of "the basic Kantian principles of trust and respect" over "utilitarian counting [of] advantages" puts him more in the company of the politically liberal philosopher John Rawls than that of political conservatives like Robert Bork and the Chicago School economists. who frequently treat moral bases as nothing more than matters of subjective individual utilities. Thus, it is a mistake to make a simplistic political analysis of Fried. On the other hand, it is equally incorrect to ignore the political implications of his thesis.

If most private rights and duties come only from a voluntary undertaking (contract, promise, consent, etc.), substantive responsibility to others is greatly narrowed. Consider the ordinary example of leaving your car in a parking lot. In law this is a bailment for hire, an ancient concept—giving someone possession but not ownership of your personal property and paying him a fee. Bailments involve elements of tort, contract and property. While you may receive a ticket (and it may even have the word "contract" somewhere on it), parking your car is rather far removed from our usual notion of contract. No bargaining takes place; you may even leave the fee in a slot or receive your ticket from a machine. Is the lot owner responsible if your car is burglarized? If, as is typically the law, a bailee for hire has a duty to exercise ordinary care over the bailed property, we may assume that he is in fact liable. But does this duty come from "the law" or is it "implied" ("inferred?") from the "contract"? What if the ticket or a sign disclaims responsibility for thefts? If the duty is imposed by the law the courts will find it harder to allow the owner out of his "legal" duty than they would if the duty is merely inferred from his alleged consent in entering into a contract. After all, how can we infer consent from someone who expressly denies that he consents?

In tort, we spend rather less time worrying about consent. Is consent more important in contract? Is it the essence of contract? Does consent justify enforcement of contracts even if there is no formal promise?

Many of these questions are discussed in the writings of Randy Barnett. Barnett teaches at Illinois Institute of Technology, Chicago-Kent College of Law, and has written on both contracts and legal philosophy. His *A Consent Theory of Contract,* 86 Colum. L. Rev. 269 (1986), is an extensive argument that consent rather than promise or free will is "a potentially valuable approach to explaining contractual obligation." Most of this article is devoted to criticism of other theories, including Fried's, and to explanations of when it is proper to infer consent in the absence of express promise. (On this last point, see also Juliet P. Kostrisky's *A New Theory of Assent-Based Liability Emerging Under the Guise of Promissory Estoppel: An Explanation and Defense,* 33 Wayne L. Rev. 895 (1987).)

As was suggested two paragraphs ago, the more basic question is whether consent deserves the central position that Barnett and many other writers give it. Barnett gave his rationale for a consent-based view of contracts in a 1984 book review of E. Allan Farnsworth's *Contracts.* The relevant part of that book review follows. Immediately after it is an excerpt from Barnett's 1986 article *A Consent Theory of Contract.*

Not every writer would agree with the rather bright distinctions that Barnett makes among tort, contract and property in his 1986 article. We have previously seen challenges to the tort-contract distinction. Barnett's theory raises questions of the role of property concepts as well. To the extent that his theory is one of consent to the transfer of alienable rights, a key question will be who owns the right. Another problem is how we define alienable rights. For example, a woman may have a right to decide whether to allow her child to be adopted. But can she bind herself in advance to give up custody to her unborn child for a fee? If the right to decide can be sold, Barnett's approach would hold that she should be bound by her consent. But we are left with a heavy moral question of whether all rights are alienable. (The Declaration of Independence, after all, speaks of "certain inalienable rights.")

Barnett discusses some of these issues in his 1986 article *Contract Remedies and Inalienable Rights,* 4 Social Philosophy & Policy 179 (1986). Another important discussion is Margaret Jane Radin's *Market-Inalienability,* 100 Harv. L. Rev. 1849 (1987). Some of these ideas are discussed further in the note on *Public Policy From Sunday Contracts to Baby M* in Part IIIB of this anthology.

Randy E. Barnett, Book Review (of E.A. Farnsworth, *Contracts* (1982)) 97 Harv. L. Rev. 1223 (1984)

. . .

As good as it is, though, the book is not without its weaknesses. Farnsworth seeks primarily to promote an understanding of existing doctrines and their historical development. But where these doctrines reflect unresolved tensions and conflicts among underlying theories of contractual obligation and liability, the book does little to resolve the disputes. In particular, the book fails to mediate the apparent conflict between the bargain theory of consideration and the classic cases that seem to base contractual obligation on principles of reliance. This conflict cannot be resolved at the doctrinal level; any solution requires an analysis of the philosophy that underlies contractual obligation. It is here that the realms of jurisprudence and the treatise intersect.

The premise that contractual obligation derives from the act of promising, together with the theory that contractual freedom should be maximized, suggests the need for a formal theory of consideration. If contractual obligation is essentially promissory, courts need some means of distinguishing enforceable promises from unenforceable promises. The protection of contractual freedom seems to require as formal a criterion as possible, for the more formal the criterion, the less courts will be able surreptitiously to substitute the judge's terms for those of the parties.

. . .

[Barnett discusses bargain and reliance as bases for enforcement of promises, and continues: —ed.]

Farnsworth's justification for reliance-based recovery highlights its extracontractual nature:

> The possibility of an answer founded on principles of tort law is inescapable, particularly if recovery is limited to the reliance measure. One person has caused harm to another by making a promise that he should reasonably have expected would cause harm, and he is therefore held liable for the harm caused. (Pp. 97-98).

When Farnsworth alludes to this basis of recovery later in his discussion of *Hoffman v. Red Owl Stores*,[62] the tension created by such a justification becomes clearer: "[A]lthough the court spoke of promissory estoppel, its decision may fit better into that field of liability for blameworthy conduct that we know as tort, instead of that field of liability based on obligations voluntarily assumed that we call contract" (p. 192). In short, if a court finds a party's verbal conduct to be "blameworthy," it may impose liability even when it is aware that the promisor did not intend to bind himself.

It is a significant deficiency of the book that Farnsworth nowhere attempts to resolve this tension. Instead, he sidesteps the issue by pointing out that because such reliance cases involve the enforcement of a promise, they are contracts cases "within our definition of the term" (p. 98). Clearly, a definitional discussion of the tort-contract distinction is inadequate to account for, much less resolve, the apparent tension between freedom of contract and reliance-based liability. Without a substantial treatment of this problem, no comprehensive book on contract law can be considered entirely satisfactory.

It might be more productive and realistic to conceive of contractual obligation in the following way. Parties bring to transactions pre-existing rights to resources in the world; some of these rights are alienable, others are not. Verbal commitments should be enforceable as contracts when the parties effectuate the unilateral or bilateral transfer of alienable rights to resources in the world by manifesting their consent to a legally binding transfer. Thus, in an agreement to transfer a present or future right to property, the consensual transfer of alienable rights is itself the object of the agreement. In an agreement to perform or refrain from performing an act in the future, the object of the agreement is to obtain performance, but legal enforcement of the agreement should be available only if both parties have manifested a commitment to pay damages for breach. Such a commitment is a transfer of rights to the money, conditioned on nonperformance—a transfer that serves the purpose of providing a legal incentive for performance. The manifestation of consent to transfer alienable rights that characterizes both

---

[62] 26 Wis. 2d 683, 133 N.W.2d 267 (1965).

types of agreements may best capture what has traditionally been meant by the phrase "consent to be legally bound." Similarly, consent to alter ordinary tort duties of care and thereby to alter the presumptive legal distribution of risk of loss is also consent to transfer preexisting rights.

Laying the theoretical foundation for actual application of this approach would require a two-step analysis. The first step would be an inquiry into rights: what rights do we have, which of them are alienable, and by what means are they alienated? Such an analysis would have to establish that one way in which rights may be alienated is by a manifestation of consent on the part of the rightholder.[65] The second step would be an analysis of what constitutes a manifestation of consent sufficient to indicate the presence of a contract.[66] Thus, to decide a contracts dispute, a court would occasionally have to carry out the first-level inquiry to determine enforceability; in most cases, however, the court would simply apply the principles and doctrines discerned in the second step—the determination of what constitutes consent—to the facts of the dispute to see if consent was present.

Under such a consent theory of contract, the existence of a bargained-for exchange would be viewed as important *evidence* of consent to transfer rights. But this form of evidence would be neither a necessary nor even always a sufficient condition of recovery. In the absence of a bargain, a court could enforce commitments and still act consistently with the notion of contractual freedom if a party had manifested his consent to a transfer of rights in some other way. For example, the exchange of nominal consideration of one dollar for a promise would signify consent to the legal enforcement of a damage award for nonperformance. By "tak[ing] the trouble to cast their transaction in the form of an exchange,"[67] the parties would have manifested such consent. By contrast, under a traditional bargain theory, nominal consideration of this sort would be considered a "sham" without legal effect, because the promisor has not bargained for the dollar.[68]

In the same manner, acts undertaken by one party in reliance on the commitment of another might un-

der certain circumstances (usually present in the "hard" cases) provide valid evidence of a manifested consent to the transfer of rights. For example, a promisor's silence in the face of substantial reliance by the promisee might manifest to the promisee a legally binding intention. Under a consent theory, the enforcement of an obligation because of reliance or formalities would not be an *exception* to a regime of bargained-for exchange. Instead, some instances of reliance, like formalities, would demonstrate that the other party had in fact consented to transfer rights even absent the conclusion of a "bargain."

Stanley D. Henderson has noted that reliance has sometimes been viewed as evidence of a bargain rather than of consent. "Reliance, under this approach, functions not as a substantive ground for enforcement, but as a vehicle for identification of some other ground for enforcement." The problem with this approach is that, "[b]ecause the cases which most clearly warrant the application of Section 90 [of the Restatement of Contracts] seldom involve reliance which is beneficial to the promisor, a causal relation between putative bargain and factual reliance is likely to be difficult to find." Although reliance would serve a similar function under a consent theory, it is a much better indication of *consent* than of a bargain, because the promisor's consent can be, and in such cases usually is, manifested by silence in the face of the promisee's acts of reliance even when the promisor has received no demonstrable benefit.

The source of the problem for Farnsworth and others who are not unsympathetic to freedom of contract but are stymied by instances of "reasonable reliance" is their acceptance of a definition of contract that is limited to promises of future performance. This definition excludes from the category of contract all transactions that involve present exchanges of rights—transactions including such obviously bilateral transfers as cash sales. Farnsworth argues that "[b]ecause no promise is given in . . . [such] exchanges, there is no contract" (p. 4). The exclusive focus on future performance in the definition of contract blinds the theorist to the fact that promises to perform in the future are enforceable only when they

---

[65] Cf. P. Atiyah, The Rise and Fall of Freedom of Contract, 177 (1979) "[P]romising may be reducible to a species of consent, for consent is a broader and perhaps more basic source of obligation."). Of course, acts other than the consent of a rightholder—for example, torts—may transfer rights noncontractually, and a rights theory must specify the nature of these acts as well.

[66] "Now consent takes many forms, of which the explicit promise is only one; other types of consent may sometimes

be regarded as justifying the implication of a promise, but they are often more naturally described without reference to the concept of promises at all." Id. at 179-80.

[67] Fuller, Consideration and Form, 41 Colum. L. Rev. 799, 820 (1941).

[68] See Restatement (Second) of Contracts § 79 comment d (1979). Id. § 87(1), however, makes even recitals of purported consideration sufficient to render an offer enforceable as an option contract.

display the same moral component as do present exchanges of property: a present consent to transfer alienable rights manifested by one person to another.

Finally, a consent theory of contract might also provide a way to alleviate the other failing of the bargain theory: its apparent inconsistency with the courts' refusal to enforce certain formally valid contracts, such as slavery contracts or contracts to violate the rights of another. If contractual obligation is based on consent to transfer or alienate *rights*, the existence of a contract requires more than consent. Underlying any inquiry into the existence of a contract is an implicit or explicit inquiry into the nature of the rights at stake in a transaction. If a court identifies the rights involved in a particular transaction as inalienable ones, the question whether there has been consent to a transfer becomes simply irrelevant; regardless of consent, no transfer can occur. Under a consent theory, therefore, even a commitment manifested by a bargain or other evidence would not always be enforceable.

Questions regarding the nature of the rights subject to contractual alienation cannot be answered solely in terms of contract theory; their answers require the sort of moral inquiry we associate with political and legal philosophy. But resort to such concerns in a particular instance does not signal the failure of the consent theory. On the contrary, the theory specifies that such concerns should play an integral role in resolving the deeper moral problems that a finding of consent may sometimes raise. Indeed, the moral justification for consent-based enforceability can be provided only by underlying notions of rights. The two-step analysis under a consent theory—that is, the bifurcated inquiry into rights and consent—shows the proper relationship between contract theory and a more fundamental theory of justice based on rights. The analysis can thus explain the source of many of the extracontractual considerations that courts currently incorporate into contract law under the loose heading of "public policy" but that are completely unaccounted for by either a bargain or a reliance theory of contractual obligation.[74] The consent theory's capacity to encompass these extrinsic concerns points the way toward the integration of contract doctrine with more fundamental theories of justice based on rights.[75]

III.

In this otherwise excellent book, Professor Farnsworth makes no attempt to resolve some basic tensions created by contract theory. As a result, he can describe but cannot resolve the conflicting doctrines that have arisen in response. It would be premature to conclude from this deficiency, however, that contract law must be collapsed into torts. What is needed—and, I suggest, possible—is a theory of justice that explains when legal force, whether it is exercised in the realm of contract or of tort, is morally justified. Such a theory must articulate the rights people have and the ways in which these rights may be consensually or nonconsensually alienated. The fact that this is precisely the mission upon which the new moral and legal philosophers have embarked highlights the importance of legal philosophy and the direct role it can play in developing legal doctrines. The treatise writer is not only dependent on the philosopher to demonstrate the legitimacy of his enterprise. He or she is also in need of the philosopher's theory of justice, without which a completely coherent doctrinal analysis will remain elusive.

[74] Although I have not specified the defects of a reliance theory of contract, they are both numerous and serious. See, e.g., Cohen, The Basis of Contract, 46 Harv. L. Rev. 533, 579-80 (1933) (a reliance theory does not specify which types of reliance merit protection and which do not).

[75] Of course, I can only sketch the rough outlines of a consent theory here. Complete explication of the theory (including, for instance, an elaboration of the important differences between a consent theory and a will theory) is a much broader enterprise, in which I am currently engaged.

Randy E. Barnett *A Consent Theory of Contract*, 86 Colum. L. Rev. 269, (1986)

. . .

II. A Consent Theory Of Contract

A. *Entitlement Theory and Contract: The Central Importance of Consent*

1. *Entitlements as the Root of Contractual Obligation.*—The function of an entitlements theory based on individual rights is to define the boundaries within which individuals may live, act, and pursue happiness free of the forcible interference of others. A theory of entitlements specifies the rights that individuals possess or may possess; it tells us what may be owned and who owns it; it circumscribes the individual boundaries of human freedom. Any coherent theory of justice based on individual rights must therefore contain principles that describe how such rights are initially acquired, how they are transferred from person to person, what the substance and limits on properly obtained rights are, and how interferences with these entitlements are to be rectified.

These constituent parts of an entitlements theory comport substantially with the traditional categories of private law. The issue of initial acquisition of entitlements in real and chattel resources is dealt with primarily in property law; tort law concerns the protection of and proper limits of resource use; and contract law deals with transfers of rights between rights holders. Each category contains principles of rectification for the breach of legal obligations.

Viewing contract law as part of a more general theory of individual entitlements that specifies how resources may be rightly acquired (property law), used (tort law), and transferred (contract law) is not new. And, of course, the actual historical development of these legal categories has not perfectly conformed to the conceptual distinctions that an entitlements approach suggests. But this approach has long been neglected as a way of resolving some of the thorniest issues of contract theory and doctrine.

According to an entitlements approach, rights may be unconditionally granted to another (a gift), or their transfer may be conditioned upon some act or reciprocal transfer by the transferee (an exchange).

Contract law concerns ways in which rights are transferred or alienated. Accordingly, the enforceability of all agreements is limited by what rights are capable of being transferred from one person to another. Whether a purported right is genuine or can be legitimately transferred is not an issue of contract theory only, but is one that may also require reference to the underlying theory of entitlements—that is, the area of legal theory that specifies what rights individuals have and the manner by which they come to have them. In this respect, the explanation of the binding nature of contractual commitments is derived from more fundamental notions of entitlements and how they are acquired and transferred.

The subjects of most rights transfer agreements are entitlements that are indisputable alienable. In such cases the rules of contract law are entirely sufficient to explain and justify a judicial decision. However, in rare cases—such as agreements amounting to slavery arrangements or requiring the violation of another's rights—contract law's dependency on rights theory will be of crucial importance in identifying appropriate concerns about the substance of voluntary agreements. For example, agreements to transfer inalienable rights—rights that for some reason cannot be transferred—or to transfer rights that for some reason cannot be obtained, would not, without more, be valid and enforceable contracts.[100]

Although existing theories of contractual obligation have failed to recognize this dependent relationship explicitly, such a notion may sometimes be implicit. For example, it is difficult to understand how any theory based on the "will" of the individual or the rectification of "harm" to an individual caused by reliance makes sense without assuming a background of more basic individual rights. One would not care at all about an individual's expressed "will" or any reliance injury she might have sustained unless that person has a pre-contractual right to "bind herself" or a right to be protected from certain kinds of harm. Efficiency-based theories also depend on a (usually assumed) set of entitlements that form the basis of sub-

[100] Other bases of obligation are possible besides contractual obligation, however, such as those recognized under the law of tort and restitution.

sequent "efficient" exchanges. The many gaps in these articulate theories of contract are, in practice, most probably filled by our shared intuitions about fundamental individual rights. Making this conceptual relationship explicit helps to clarify what continues to be a hazy understanding of contractual obligation.

As Part I demonstrated, a proper understanding of contractual obligation and its limits requires an appeal to something more fundamental than the concepts of will, reliance, efficiency, fairness, or bargain. A framework or theory is needed to order these fundamental concerns, to show where each "principle" stands in relation to others. Recognizing the necessity of such an inquiry places the contract theorist in the realm of entitlements or rights theory. The legitimacy of principles of contract that determine which transfers of rights are valid depends upon the nature of individual entitlements and the extent to which rights have been or will be acquired by the parties to a transfer. The process of contractual transfer cannot be completely comprehended, therefore, without considering more fundamental issues, namely the nature and sources of individual entitlements and the means by which they come to be acquired.

2. *The Allocative and Distributional Function of Individual Rights.*—Any concept of individual rights must assume a social context. If the world were inhabited by one person, it might make sense to speak of that person's actions as "good" or "bad." Such a moral judgment might, for example, look to whether or not that person had chosen to live what might be called the "good life." It makes no sense, however, to speak about this person's rights. As one court noted: "Unless and until one is brought into relation with other men, or property, or rights, he has no obligation to act with reference to them; and this is true whether the obligation be called legal, moral, or reasonable."[103]

From the moment individuals live in close enough proximity to one another to compete for the use of scarce natural resources, some way of allocating those resources must be found. In short, some scheme of specifying how individuals may acquire, use, and transfer resources must be recognized. Certain facts of human existence make certain principles of allocation ineluctable. For example, it is a funda-

mental human requirement that individuals acquire and consume natural resources, even though such activity is often inconsistent with a similar use of the same resources by others.

"Property rights" is the term traditionally used to describe an individual's entitlements to use and consume resources—both the individual's person and her external possessions—free from the physical interference of others. That possession and use of resources is by "right" suggests that any attempt at physical interference with possession and use may be resisted by force if necessary. Additionally, if another interferes with a rightful distribution of resources, this violation may be rectified by *re*distributing resources. Some rights to property can be exclusive and other less so. The exact contours of a proper theory of rights need not be specified here. Only the recognition that *some* allocation of rights to resource possession and use is an unavoidable prerequisite of human survival and of human fulfillment is relevant to this discussion.

Although entitlements to resources can be acquired directly from nature by individual labor, in a complex society they will more likely be acquired from others. Contract law, according to an entitlements approach, is thus a body of general principles and more specific rules the function of which is to identify the rights of individuals engaged in transferring entitlements, and thereby indicate when physical or legal force may legitimately be used to preserve those rights and to rectify any unjust interference with the transfer process.

3. *Consent as the Moral Component of a Contractual Transaction.*—The areas of moral obligations and legal obligations are not coextensive. A moral obligation is something we ought to do or refrain from doing. A moral obligation that is not also a valid legal obligation can only be legitimately secured by voluntary means. That is, one may have a moral obligation to do something, but unless there is also a valid legal obligation, one cannot legitimately be forced by another to do it. A moral obligation is only a legal obligation if it can be enforced by the use or threat of legal force. This added dimension of force requires moral justification. The principal task of legal theory, then, is to identify circumstances when legal enforcement is morally justified.

---

[103] Garland v. Boston & M.R.R., 76 N.H. 556, 557, 86 A. 141, 142 (1913). As the court colorfully put the point in its discussion of duties of care: "The rule of reasonable care, under the circumstances, could not limit the conduct of Robinson Crusoe as he was at first situated; but as soon as he saw the tracks in the sand the rule began to have vitality." Id. at 563, 86 A. at 141; see also Demsetz, Toward a Theory of Property Rights, 57 Am. Econ. Rev. 347, 347 (1967) ("In the world of Robinson Crusoe property rights play no role.").

Entitlements theories seek to perform this task by using moral analysis to derive individual legal rights, that is, claims that may be justifiably enforced. A theory of contractual obligation is the part of an entitlements theory that focuses on liability arising from the wrongful interference with a valid rights transfer. Until such an interference is corrected—by force if necessary—the distribution of resources caused by the interference is unjust. Justice consists of correcting this situation to bring resource distribution into conformity with entitlements.

To identify the moral component that distinguished valid from invalid rights transfers, it is first necessary to separate moral principles governing the rightful acquisition and use of resources from those governing their transfer. Rights are the means by which freedom of action and interaction are facilitated and regulated in society, and thus the rights we have to acquire previously unowned resources and to use that which we acquire must not be subject to the expressed assent of others. Although societal acquiescence may be a practical necessity for rights to be legally respected, no individual or group need consent to our appropriation of previously unowned resources or their use for our right to *morally* vest.

Similarly, principles governing rights transfer should be distinguished from principles governing resource use. Tort law concerns obligations arising from interferences with others' rights. A tortfeasor who interferes with another's rights (rather than obtaining a valid transfer of those rights to herself) is liable because of that interference, not because she consented to be held liable for her actions that impair another's rights. A tortfeasor can be said to "forfeit" (as opposed to alienate or transfer) rights to resources in order to provide compensation to the victim of the tort.

In contrast, contract law concerns enforceable obligations arising from the valid *transfer* of entitlements that are *already vested* in someone, and this difference is what makes consent a moral prerequisite to contractual obligation. The rules governing alienation of property rights by transfer perform the same function as rules governing their acquisition and those specifying their proper content: facilitating freedom of human action and interaction. Freedom of action and interaction would be seriously impeded, and possibly destroyed, if legitimate rights holders who have not acted in a tortious manner could be deprived of their rights by force of law without their consent. Moreover, the moral requirement of consent mandates that others take the interests of the rights holder into account when seeking to obtain the rights she possesses. Wallace Matson succinctly describes the view of justice that makes consent the moral component of contractual transfer:

> [Justice is] . . . rendering every man is due. A man's due is what he has acquired by his own efforts and not taken from some other man *without consent*. A community in which this conception is realized will be one in which the members agree not to interfere in the legitimate endeavors of each other to achieve their individual goals, and to help each other to the extent that the conditions for doing so are mutually satisfactory . . . . Such a community will be one giving the freest possible rein to all its members to develop their particular capacities and use them to carry out their plans for their own betterment . . . . [T]his activity is The Good for Man . . . .

Consequently, the consent of the rights holder to be legally obligated is the moral component that distinguishes valid from invalid transfers of alienable rights in a system of entitlements. It is not altogether novel to suggest that consent is at the heart of contract law, although the claim that contractual obligation arises from a consent to a transfer of entitlements and is thereby dependent on a theory of entitlements is not widely acknowledged. Yet it is certainly a commonly held and plausible conception of ownership that owning resources gives one the right to possess, use, and dispose of them free from the use or threat of force by others.

In a modern society the chain between initial acquisition of resources and their ultimate consumption can be quite long and complicated. While controversies may exist, even among those who acknowledge the legitimacy of property rights in principle, about the proper mode of resource acquisition and the proper manner of resource use, a valid transfer of rights must be conditioned on some act of the rights holder. The allocative function that an entitlements theory is devised, in part, to fulfill suggests that the way rights are transferred is by consent.

In sum, legal enforcement is morally justified because the promisor voluntarily performed acts that conveyed her intention to create a legally enforceable obligation by transferring alienable rights. Within an entitlements approach, contractual obligation, as distinct from other types of legal obligation, is based on that consent.

. . .

Reliance, Expectation and Civil Obligation

Patrick Atiyah is Professor of English Law at Oxford and edits the *Oxford Journal of Legal Studies*. One of his important contributions to contract law is *The Rise and Fall of Freedom of Contract* (1979), a 791 page book in which Atiyah drew a very different picture of contract from the promise-based theory of Charles Fried discussed in the note preceeding the Barnett articles. (Fried wrote a critical book review of Atiyah's book at 93 Harv. L. Rev. 1858 (1980) as did Professor William M. McGovern of UCLA, whose review appears at 68 Minn. L. Rev. 550 (1982).) Atiyah's book has been influential, and has been followed by further work continuing his investigation of contract theory. These books are too massive to be included in this anthology. However, in 1978 Atiyah published in the Law Quarterly Review, a leading British law review, a short paper summarizing his conclusions; that paper follows.

Atiyah refers in his title to the "law of obligations." That is a term more commonly used in the civil law (i.e., continental European law) than in Anglo-American common law. In the civil law there is less of a distinction between tort and contract; while tort and contract are recognized as distinct jurisprudentially, "civil obligations" is taught as one subject. Indeed, Gilmore used the term in the discussions of "contorts" that were reprinted in Part IA of this book. Atiyah takes a very different view from Fried of the promise model and of the enforcement of "fully executory contacts" (exchanges of promises where neither party has performed or in any way relied on the other's promise). His claim that this is a nineteenth century anomaly has been criticized. The question of why we give full expectation damages (typically lost profits) to a disappointed promisee who has not relied on the broken promise flows through both Fried and Atiyah, and will reappear in the "Horwitz-Simpson" debate over contract history that appears in Part IC. But from our present point of view, of greater interest are Atiyah's arguments that detriment and reliance are more justifiable reasons to find liability, that receipt of a benefit is more important than intention to be bound, and that the lines between contract and tort have been drawn too sharply. These obviously diverge from the Fried and Barnett approaches.

Their relation to Kessler and Critical Legal Studies is rather subtler but worth pondering.

Patrick Atiyah, *Contracts, Promises and the Law of Obligations*, 94 L.Q. Rev. 193 (1978)

I.

For at least 100 years—and in many respects for more like twice that time—common lawyers have operated within a particular conceptual framework governing the law of obligations. Within this framework, the fundamental distinction has been that between obligations which are voluntarily assumed, and obligations which are imposed by law. The former constitutes the law of contract, the latter falls within the purview of the law of tort. There is, in addition, that somewhat anomalous body of law which came to be known as the law of quasi-contract, or in more modern times, as the law of restitution. This body of law was accommodated within the new conceptual framework by the academic lawyers and jurists from the 1860s onwards, and, after a considerable time lag, their ideas came to be part of the accepted orthodoxies. The law of quasi-contract, it came to be said, was part of the law of obligations which did not arise from voluntary acts of the will, but from positive rules of law. Quasi-contract thus took its place alongside tort law on one side of the great divide. Contract alone remained on the other side. Nobody ever paid much attention to the place of the law of trusts in this scheme of things. Equity, after all, was peculiarly English invention and theorizing about the law of obligations was very much a Roman and subsequently a

Continental fashion. It is true that much time and trouble was devoted to the problem of fitting equitable obligations into another typically Roman distinction, namely that dividing a *jus in rem* from a *jus in personam*. But nobody seems to have troubled overmuch about the place of equitable obligations in the great divide between voluntarily assumed and legally imposed obligations.

These broad distinctions reflected a set of values. and ways of thought which also exercised a most profound influence on the conceptual pattern which was imposed on Contract law itself. Contractual obligations came to be treated as being almost exclusively about promises, agreements, intentions, acts of will. The function of the law came to be seen as that of merely giving effect to the private autonomy of contracting parties to make their own legal arrangements. It is, of course, well known, indeed has become part of the modern orthodoxy, that the private autonomy, this extreme freedom of contract, came to be abused by parties with greater bargaining power, and has been curtailed in a variety of ways, both by legislative activity and by the judges themselves. That is a familiar story and I do not wish to pursue it here. What I do wish to discuss is the conceptual framework of Contract and its place in the law of obligations as a whole. I want to suggest that, despite the increasing attacks upon freedom of contract, and the great divide between Contract and Tort, the conceptual apparatus which still dominates legal thinking on these issues is the apparatus of the nineteenth century. It goes, indeed, far beyond the law itself. Our very processes of thought, our language in political, moral or philosophical debate, is still dominated by this nineteenth-century heritage to an extent which, I venture to suggest, is rarely appreciated. I want to suggest, further, that this conceptual apparatus is not based on any objective truths, it does not derive from any eternal verities. It is the result, quite specifically of a nineteenth-century heritage, an amalgam of classical economics, of Benthamite radicalism, of liberal political ideals and of the law, itself created and molded in the shadow of these movements. The result, I will argue, is that our basic conceptual apparatus, the fundamental characterizations and divisions which we impose on the phenomena with which we deal, do not reflect the value of our own times, but those of the last century. It is true that they reflect much that many will still think most admirable about the nineteenth century, the liberal tradition, the belief in the value and rights of the individual, adherence to an economic and social system which had the

confidence to reward enterprise, initiative and success. But to recognize that many of the values of our society today are opposed to much that was admirable in the last century is not to denigrate our predecessors. And to argue the case for revising our concepts so that they conform more closely to the value of today involves no judgment that those values are better than the values of yesterday. Indeed, the revision may prove useful to those who think otherwise, for it will bring into greater relief precisely what is involved in today's values.

II.

It is time to turn away from these generalities, and I propose to begin by spending a few moments on the paradigm of modern contract theory. If we were asked today to indulge in the fashionable exercise of constructing a model of a typical contract, I suspect most common lawyers would come up with something like this. A typical contract is, first, a bilateral executory agreement. It consists of an exchange of promises; the exchange is deliberately carried through, by the process of offer and acceptance, with the intention of creating a binding deal. When the offer is accepted, the agreement is consummated, and a contract comes into existence before anything is actually *done* by the parties. No performance is required, no benefit has to be rendered, no act of detrimental reliance is needed, to create the obligation. The contract is binding because the parties intend to be bound; it is their will, or intention, which creates the liability. It is true that the law has this technical requirement known as the doctrine of consideration, but except in rare and special cases, mutual promises are consideration for each other, and therefore the model, by definition, complies with the requirement of consideration. When the contract is made, it binds each party to performance, or, in default, to a liability to pay damages in lieu. Prima facie these damages will represent the value of the innocent party's disappointed expectations. The plaintiff may, therefore, bring suit on a wholly executory contract, for example, because the defendant has attempted to cancel his offer or acceptance, or withdraw from the contract, and may recover damages for his disappointed expectations even though he has not relied upon the contract in any way, and even though the defendant has received no benefit under it. The whole model is suffused with the idea that the fundamental purpose of contract law is to give effect—within limits of course—to the intentions of the parties. It is their decision, and their free choice, which makes the contract binding, and determines its interpretation, and its result in the event of breach. It is, of course, a commonplace today that all legal obligations are, in the last resort, obligations created or at least recognised by the law, but the classical model of contract is easily enough adjusted to take account of this truism. The law of contract, it is said, consists of power-conferring rules. The law provides facilities for private parties to make use of them if they so wish. Those who wish to create legal obligations have only to comply with a simple set of rules and the result will be recognized by the law.

There is no doubt that this model has been of astonishing power. For 100 years it has had no serious rival. Today many lawyers would probably want to qualify it, or modify it in a variety of respects. Many would admit, perhaps insist, that the model is primarily useful in connection with the business transaction, and it does not fit the consumer transaction, or the family arrangement, or other agreements which cannot be characterized as business deals. Even in transactions among business men, many lawyers will want to qualify this model. At the least many will recognize that the role of free choice on the part of contracting parties has declined, and that courts may, in the interests of justice as they perceive it, sometimes impose solutions in the teeth of contracting parties' intent. But making all allowances for the necessary qualifications, I do not think it would be seriously disputed that this is the paradigm model of contract which we have inherited from nineteenth-century lawyers. Indeed, a glance at the Contract textbooks will confirm that the model is still alive and well.

. . .

Before proceeding further to examine the reality of this model of contract, it is worth pausing to consider some of its underlying presuppositions which are rarely made explicit. The first of these is that the classical model assumes that contract law is fundamentally about what parties *intend*, and not about what they *do*. Here again, of course, qualifications, and important qualifications, have to be made. It is the manifestation of intention and not actual intention that matters most; and what the parties *do* is obviously crucial in measuring the extent to which performance falls short of promise. Nevertheless, classical contract theory assumes that contractual obligations are created by the intention of the parties and not by their actions. The classical model is thus

concerned with executory arrangements, with forward-looking planning. Contracts have a chronology, a time sequence, as can be seen by looking at the Table of Contents of any Contract textbook published in the last 100 years. They are *created* first, and performed (or not performed) thereafter. In this respect, of course, contractual obligations necessarily differ from those on the other side of the great divide. The law of torts, and the law of quasi-contract are concerned with what parties do. It is human action, or inaction, which creates liability in tort, or in restitution. Among other results, this means that Contract lawyers focus on a different time sequence. In tort, or in restitutionary claims, it is the causing of damage or injury on the one hand, or the rendering of benefits on the other, which is the immediate object of interest. In contract, likewise, damage or injury may be caused, or benefits rendered, but it is not these consequences, or the actions giving rise to them which are the focus of attention of the classical model. It is the intention of the parties which (it is assumed) must necessarily precede the causing of the damage or the rendering of the benefits, and which is therefore the source of the obligation. I will suggest later that this difference in the time which is the focus of attention has led, not merely to an exaggeration of the role of intentional conduct in the creation of contractual obligations, but also to a minimisation of the role of intentional conduct in the creation of other forms of obligation.

The second presupposition of the classical model of contract is that a contract is a *thing*, which has some kind of objective existence prior to any performance or any act of the parties.[1] Of all the examples of legal reification, none is surely more powerful than this. A contract is a thing which is "made," is "broken," is "discharged." So powerful is this reification that most lawyers see nothing odd about the notion of anticipatory repudiation, that is, about the idea that a promise can be treated as broken even before its performance is due. The tendency to reify legal concepts is, in the case of contract, given powerful impetus by the fact that so many contractual arrangements are in written form. Even today, lawyers constantly use the words "the contract" to signify both the legal relations created by the law, and the piece of paper in which those relations (or some of them) are expressed. Here again, there is a profound difference in the lawyer's way of looking at legal obli-

---

[1] See Arthur Leff, "Contract as Thing," 19 Am. U. Law Rev. 131 (1970).

gations on the other side of the great divide. A contract may be a "thing" but nobody would conceptualize a quasi-contract or a tort as a thing. One reason why the tendency to reify the concept of contract has had important results is that it has reinforced the respect for the private autonomy of the contractual relationship. If a contract is a thing created by the contracting parties, it is easier to see it as a relationship within defined and limited parameters. Within these parameters, concepts such as fairness, justice, reasonableness have far less room to operate than they do with diffuse concepts like tort or quasi-contract.

The third presupposition of the classical model of contract concerns the function of the court in the enforcement of contracts. I take it as axiomatic that, in principle, the judicial process is designed to serve either or both of two important social ends. The first is, by the threat of penalties or the promise of rewards, to encourage the citizenry to comply with socially desired standards of behavior. And the second is to provide machinery for the settlement of disputes by peaceful and fair means. Now the classical model of Contract with its emphasis on intentional conduct and future planning, presupposes that the first of these two goals is the primary function of the courts in dealing with contractual litigation. The purpose of contract law is to encourage people to pay their debts, keep their promises and generally be truthful in their dealings with each other. The enforcement of contracts, like the protection of property and the punishment of crime, is thus perceived as important primarily for its deterrent or hortatory purpose. It is no coincidence that these were historically linked together as the essential functions of the state even by Adam Smith and the classical economists. By contrast, other parts of the law of obligations are more likely to be dominated by the dispute-settlement functions of the courts, rather than by their deterrent or hortatory functions. In the law of quasi-contract, in particular, the court is almost invariably called upon to deal with a problem by resolving a conflict of equities. Some misfire has occurred, some untoward and unplanned benefit has been rendered. Is it right that the beneficiary should pay for it, or are there grounds on which it is more just that he should be permitted to retain an unpaid for benefit? It is not generally regarded as an important function of the court to discourage (for example) people from paying debts twice over, or rendering benefits to another without ensuring that there has been an agreement to pay for them. Similarly with the modern law of torts, the im-

portance of the deterrent function of the law has declined at the expense of the dispute-settlement function. Increasingly, the emphasis is on the function of the court in dealing with what are essentially perceived as accidents. . . .

The fourth presupposition of the classical model of Contract is that there is indeed *one* model, that it is possible and useful to think still in terms of general principles of Contract. The continued vitality of our textbooks and of our university law courses on Contract attest to the faith which lawyers still have in the generalizing effect of the concept of Contract. We know, of course, that most contracts fall into particular categories which have their own rules and qualifications derogating from the general law. There are, for example, special rules applicable to contracts of employment, consumer credit contracts, consumer sales, leases, mortgages, insurance contracts, house purchase, matrimonial agreements and many others. Indeed, there are few contracts today which are *not* governed by specific rules which in some measure derogate from the general law. But none of this has shaken the power of the classical model of Contract. This model is, without doubt, based on an economic model, that of the free market. Historically there is every reason to believe that this classical model grew up under the influence of the classical economists and of the philosophical radicals. There is no need to subscribe to the crude and exaggerated myth that these nineteenth century thinkers wanted to reduce all relationships to economic terms, or to encourage a purely materialist approach to all human motivation. But it is true that many of them saw much in the classical contract model which they felt was both admirable and applicable far beyond the commercial sphere. They thought it desirable that men should learn to order their lives according to some definite plan, that they should be encouraged to aim for particular goals, that they should co-operate with others in attempting to seek those goals, that those who let down their fellows should be made to pay the cost of doing so; they thought it desirable that men should be free to develop their skills and ambitions, and they accepted the natural corollary that some would rise and some would sink. It was partly for these reasons (though there were certainly others too) that the classical model of Contract was so unified, and no doubt, it was partly its unity which gave it so much power.

In the law itself, it was the nineteenth century which very largely saw the supersession of the importance of special kinds of contract by the general principles of contract. It was, of course, an Age of Principles—principles of morality, principles of political economy, principles of justice, and principles of law. When Addison published his *Treatise on Contracts* in 1847 he insisted that Contract law was not a mere collection of positive rules but was founded "upon the broad and general principles of universal law." Indeed, he went further: "The law of contracts," he wrote in his Preface, "may justly indeed be said to be a universal law adapted to all times and races, and all places and circumstances, being founded upon those great and fundamental principles of right and wrong deduced from natural reason which are immutable and eternal." Naturally, a concept of Contract which could dismiss all differences of time and place, of circumstances and people, had no need for trivial distinctions between sale and hire-purchase, mortgages and leases, commercial and consumer contracts.

III.

It is necessary now to cast a somewhat more critical eye at this conceptual structure. How far does it stand up to more detailed examination? Is it reconcilable with the value systems of the modern world, and in particular, of modern England? Is it even reconcilable with the developments in positive law which have taken place within this conceptual framework? Is it true that contractual obligations normally arise from agreements or exchanges of promises? How far is it true to suggest that contracts are intentionally made with a view to future performance? To what extent is it correct to regard contractual liability as depending on voluntarily assumed obligations? To what extent is it possible to adhere to the very concept of a single basic model of Contract?

Let me begin with this last question.

If we look at the law as it is stated in the books and the case law we shall see that the concept of contract is applied in a very wide range of situations and to a very large variety of relationships. Before it is possible to construct a model even of a typical or paradigm case of contract it is necessary to have some idea of what it is that we are trying to achieve. Typical of *what*? Paradigm of *what*? Quite apart from the circular nature of the definitional problem, it is hard to understand how one is to measure the typicality of a particular relationship. If we are concerned with the most *numerous* types of transaction then presumably the typical contract would be the bus ride, the train journey, or the supermarket purchase. But even this is somewhat speculative and only empirical research could actually tell us what are the most commonly made transactions. (Alternatively, we may be

concerned with the *value* of the transactions) we are examining. Commercial transactions are doubtless typically of greater individual value than consumer transactions; but it is unlikely that they are of greater aggregate value. And anyhow commercial transactions are so far removed from the ordinary experience of the average person that it is hard to believe a contractual model based on the commercial transaction would today have a wide and pervasive application outside the particular sphere of business. A third possibility is that the typical contract is that of which practicing lawyers have the most experience. But here again there are obvious difficulties. If we are concerned with the experience of solicitors, then there can be no doubt that house purchases and mortgages are the most typical of contracts. If we are concerned with the experience of a barrister in commercial chambers, then the typical contract might be an international sale, an insurance contract, a building contract, and it would almost certainly be a contract made by business parties.

The truth is, I would suggest, that there is no such thing as a typical contract at all. Moreover, modern society has plainly rejected the values of the market outside the increasingly narrow area in which the market is permitted to operate. The classical model of Contract thus continues to exist though with increasingly little content. The *principles* of Contract law sometimes govern new or marginal or residuary situations, but it is hard to see in what sense they can continue to be called *general* principles. They remain general only by default, only because they are being superceded by detailed ad hoc rules lacking any principle.

Let me turn now to a more challenging question. To what extent is it true to say that contractual liabilities arise from agreement or promises or depend on the voluntary assumption of obligation? I want to begin by suggesting that the power of the classical model here derives largely from its stress on the executory contract. If two parties do exchange promises to carry out some performance at a future date, and if, immediately on the exchange of promises, a binding legal obligation comes at once into existence, then it seems inexorably to follow that the obligation is created by the agreement, by the intention of the parties. If they have done nothing to implement the agreement, if no actions have followed the exchange of promises, then manifestly the legal obligation cannot arise from anything except the exchange of promises. Thus far the classical model appears to be impregnable. But closed examination suggests that the area of impregnability is really rather small.

The first point to note is that wholly executory contracts are rarer, more ephemeral in practice, and somewhat less binding than the classical model of Contract would suggest. In the classical model as I have suggested, the executory transaction lies at the very heart of Contract. It is precisely because the classical model largely defines Contract in terms of executory transactions that it necessarily locates the source of contractual liability in what the parties intend rather than in what they do. But large numbers of contracts are regularly made in which the making and the performance, or at least part performance, are simultaneous or practically simultaneous events. Consider such simple transactions as the boarding of a bus, or a purchase of goods in a supermarket, or a loan of money. Is it really sensible to characterize these transactions as agreements or exchanges of promises? Is it meaningful or useful to claim that a person who boards a bus is promising to pay his fare?* If so, would it not be just as meaningful to say that when he descends from the bus and crosses the road he promises to cross with all due care for the safety of other road users? I do not, of course, deny that all these transactions involve some element of voluntary conduct. People do not generally board buses, buy goods in a supermarket, or borrow money in their sleep. But they involve much else besides voluntary conduct. They usually involve the rendering of some benefit, or actions of detrimental reliance, or both. A person who is carried by a bus from point A to point B after voluntarily boarding the bus can normally be presumed to have derived some benefit from the arrangements. Does his liability to pay his fare have nothing to do with this element of benefit? A person who borrows money and actually receives the loan is, according to the classical model of Contract, liable to repay the money merely because he promised to repay it. The fact that he received the money appears to be largely irrelevant. . . .

If we look at a normative system not encumbered by the doctrine of consideration—say the moral basis of promissory liability—the position is even more starkly clear. An obligation to perform a promise to pay Ł100 is generally considered to be precisely the same whether the promise is to make a gift or to repay a loan. Since the basis of the obligation lies in

the promise in both cases it makes not a particle of difference that in the former case the promisor receives nothing for his money, while in the latter case he has already received full value. Is it not evident that there is some grotesque distortion here?

Consider next the possibility of detrimental reliance by the promisee. Is it not manifest that a person who has actually worsened his position by reliance on a promise has a more powerful case for redress than one who has not acted in reliance on the promise at all? A person who has not relied on a promise (nor paid for it) may suffer a disappointment of his expectations, but he does not actually suffer a pecuniary loss. The disappointment of an expectation may of course be treated as a species of loss by definition, as indeed, the law generally does treat it, if the expectation derives from Contract. But no definitional jugglery can actually equate the position of the party who suffers a diminution of his assets in reliance on a promise, and a person who suffers no such diminution.

But this is not all, for both in morality and in law the rendering of benefits and actions of detrimental reliance can give rise to obligations even where there was no promise at all. The law of quasi-contract is almost entirely concerned with situations in which one party is entitled to recompense for a benefit rendered to another even though the latter made no promise to pay for it. The rendering of a benefit is thus in some cases a sufficient ground for liability even without an agreement or promise to repay. Of course, the law of quasi-contract has "nothing at all" to do with the law of Contract, as classical contract theory tells us. But that is itself, as I shall suggest later, an idea which is quite unacceptable, both historically and analytically. And if the law of quasi-contracts concerns liability for the restitution of uncovenanted benefits, the law of torts and the law of trusts frequently provide redress for acts of reliance performed in the absence of an express promise. Moreover, the law of Contract itself, together with associated parts of the law sometimes characterized as distinct sets of rules, provide many examples of provisions plainly designed for the protection of acts of reasonable reliance, rather than for the imposition of promissory liability. The law of misrepresentations, of warranty, of estoppel and promissory estoppel, no

* [In many English buses a conductor goes through the bus collecting fares from passengers who previously entered the bus. —ed.]

matter how they are conceptualized, provide many illustrations of what can only be rationally regarded as reliance-based liability.

And so far I have said nothing about one of the most obvious bodies of legal doctrine which is not easy to reconcile with the theory that contractual and promissory obligations rest on voluntary obligation. I refer, of course, to the so-called "objective-test" theory of contractual liability. Every law student is taught from his earliest days that contractual intent is not really what it seems; actual subjective intent is normally irrelevant. It is the appearance, the manifestation of intent that matters. Whenever a person is held bound by a promise or a contract contrary to his actual intent or understanding, it is plain that the liability is based not on some notion of a voluntary assumption of obligation, but on something else. And most frequently it will be found that that something else is the element of reasonable reliance. One party relies on a reasonable construction of an offer, or he accepts an offer, reasonably thinking it is still open when the offeror has revoked it but failed to communicate his revocation. All this is standard stuff but I suggest that cases of this type have for too long been regarded as of marginal importance only, as not affecting the fundamental basis and theory of liability. In a simple world of simple promises and contracts this might have been an acceptable perspective. But the arrival of written contracts and above all the standard printed forms has surely rendered this approach much less defensible. A party who signs an elaborate printed document is almost invariably held bound by it not because of anything he intended; he is bound in the teeth of his intention and understandings except in some very exceptional cases of fraud or the like. The truth is he is bound not so much because of what he intends but because of what he does. Like the man who is bound to pay his fare because he boards a bus, the man who signs a written contract is liable because of what he does rather than what he intends. And he is liable because of what he does for the good reason that other parties are likely to rely upon what he does in ways which are reasonable and even necessary by the standards of our society.

What I suggest then, is that wherever benefits are rendered, wherever acts of reasonable reliance take place, obligations may arise, both morally and in law. These obligations are by no means confined to cases where explicit promises are given, for they may arise in cases where we would imply a promise, but they also arise in many cases where any attempt to imply a promise would be nothing but a bare fiction. The man who boards a bus without any intention of paying for his fare is bound to pay it though it is difficult to see what reality there can be in claiming that he impliedly promises to pay. The man who signs a document without reading it does not make an implied any more than an express promise in any genuine sense.

. . . Frequently, both in law and in moral discourse we appear to determine whether there should be an obligation first, and then decide how the language should be construed afterwards. And it follows that the existence or non-existence of the obligation is then being decided independently of the existence of any promise.

Much the same occurs where conduct rather than language is in question. Consider a recent example of the creation of what is, in essence, a new species of liability. The courts have recently decided that a local authority which is guilty of negligence in supervising the construction of a house in accordance with the Building Regulations may be liable to an ultimate purchaser of the house. The liability is, of course, a liability in tort. Now that the liability is established as a matter of law, it would not seem unreasonable or odd to say that a local authority impliedly undertakes or promises to exercise due care in supervising the construction of houses. But it would have been difficult to argue for the existence of such an implied undertaking or promise prior to the establishment of legal liability. Here it is clear that the liability is first created on independent grounds, and the implication of a promise can then be read into the conduct which leads to the liability.

. . . Now I must repeat that I am not arguing that consent, promise, intention, voluntary conduct, are irrelevant to the creation of obligations even where an element of reciprocal benefit is present, or some act of reasonable reliance has taken place. In the first place, where liability arises out of conduct rather than from the voluntary assumption of an obligation, the conduct itself is usually of a voluntary character. Even if liability on a part executed arrangement can properly be said to be benefit-based rather than promise-based, a man is normally entitled to choose what benefits he will accept—normally, though by no means invariably. Similarly, with reliance-based liability; it is normally open to a person to warn others that they are not to rely upon him, but must trust to their own judgment. Obviously this raises difficulty where a person wants to have his cake and eat it, where he wants to influence others to behave in a certain manner but wants also to disclaim responsibility for their doing so. There is little doubt that in such circumstances the trend is towards insisting on the imposition of responsibility. The striking down of exemption clauses and disclaimers of liability are evidence of the unacceptability of these attempts to have things both ways. This trend may reflect the increased emphasis on reliance and the declining stress on free choice.

But secondly, and much more important, I would argue that even where obligations can be said to be primarily benefit-based or reliance-based, explicit promises may have a valuable role to play. I referred earlier to the conventional wisdom of English common lawyers which some decades ago suggested that the only rational function of the doctrine of consideration was to serve as evidence of the seriousness of a promise. I now want to suggest that the truth lies more closely in the precise converse of this assertion. Where obligations arise out of the rendering of benefits or from acts of reasonable reliance, the presence of an explicit promise may, I suggest, serve valuable evidentiary purposes. Consider the simple example of a loan of money which I referred to earlier as an illustration of a liability which could not, without distortion, be viewed as purely promissory. The presence of an explicit promise may nevertheless serve valuable evidentiary purposes. First, it helps to avoid doubt about the nature of the transaction. The possibility of a gift is ruled out by the express promise to repay. Then it helps clarify who the parties to the transaction may be, for the handing of money by A to B may create a loan from X to Y where A and B are acting as agents or in a transaction of any complexity. An explicit promise may resolve any ambiguities about such matters. . . .

. . .

It may, of course, be said that these cases are no illustration of the general nature of contractual liability, but on the contrary serve to illustrate the difference between contractual and other forms of liability. For (it may be urged) the whole point of contractual liability is to permit parties to determine conclusively their own obligations. The promise creates the liability, and does not merely evidence it. In non-contractual cases, *per contra*, the duty is in the first instance created by the law; and the promise cannot be treated as creating the obligation. But I suggest that this analysis is the result of treating the executory con-

tract as the paradigm of contract, the heritage of the classical law which I have already criticized. In the part-executed transaction, as I have argued, it is in fact frequently the case that there would be a liability even apart from any express or implied promise. Promises are not a necessary condition of the existence of a liability or the creation of an obligation. The performance by one party of acts which are beneficial to the other, the rendering of services to another, for instance, would normally be thought of as creating some sort of obligation even in the absence of a promise. Similarly, acts of reasonable reliance would often create liability in tort, or by way of trust, or other equitable obligation, even where there is no express or implied promise. Indeed, did not the whole law of trusts arise because property was entrusted to other hands, usually no doubt because of some understanding that the trustee would behave in a certain fashion? In circumstances of this kind, therefore, where obligations would normally be thought of as arising from what has been done, rather than from what has been said, there seems to me no difficulty in regarding promises as having primarily an evidentiary role.

Treating explicit promises as prima facie evidence, and as strong prima facie evidence of the fairness of a transaction, of the appropriate price to be paid for goods and services, is an indispensable tool of efficient administration in a free market society. For any other rule would leave it open to a dissatisfied party to any and every transaction to appeal to a judge to upset an agreed price and fix a new one. But the *extent* of the indefeasibility of a promise, the *extent* to which it is to be treated as a conclusive admission of the fairness and reasonableness of the terms of an exchange, is a much less simple proposition. All promises and contracts are defeasible in *some* circumstances. A promise or agreement extorted by violence is no evidence of the fairness of a transaction, and is therefore naturally set aside by the courts. Promises given as a result of certain types of mistake may likewise be set aside. Alternatively, the courts may uphold the validity of the exchange but adjust the obligations of the parties (for example by implying appropriate terms) so as to ensure, so far as possible, that the exchange is a fair or reasonable one, despite the disparity between the literal obligations assumed by the parties.

The extent to which the courts and the law are prepared to go in treating promises as defeasible, or merely as prima facie rather than conclusive evidence of the fairness of an exchange, is obviously something determined by the degree of paternalism which commends itself to the society and the judiciary in question. A society which believes in allowing the skillful and knowledgeable to reap the rewards of their skill and knowledge is likely to have a higher regard for the sanctity of promises than a society which wishes to protect the weak and foolish from the skillful and knowledgeable. As we shall see, this point is a good deal more important in the case of executory transactions.

IV.

So far I have been trying to place the part-executed, or the wholly-executed transaction, more firmly back into the central role of Contract, and to suggest that the classical model, based on will theory and the executory transaction, does not fit a large part of law and life. But in the case of wholly executory arrangements, it may seem that things are different. If a person is liable, morally or legally, on a wholly executory arrangement, if he is liable on a promise prior to the receipt of any benefit, and prior to any act of reliance by the promisee, then it would seem that the liability must be promise-based and nothing else. Morally, few would doubt that, prima facie at least, a promise is *per se* binding; and lawyers, while insisting on the requirement of consideration, would largely agree with the moralists. Now the requirement of consideration or, at least, the satisfaction of that requirement, in the case of the wholly executory contract, is one of the puzzles of the common law. A, let us say, orders goods from B, to be specially made to his requirements. The next day, A discovers he can buy what he wants ready made elsewhere and cancels the order. B, let it be supposed, has so far done nothing whatever under the contract. There is no doubt in law that B can hold A liable and sue him for damages without having to lift a finger to perform his part of the contract. A receives no benefit, B suffers no detriment, no reliance, and yet he is entitled to damages. How can this be so, and how is it that common lawyers have continued to define the doctrine of consideration in terms of benefit and detriment when this definition does not fit the paradigm case of classical contract theory? The answer to this conundrum, which led to a vast quantity of ponderous legal literature, particularly in America, early in this century, lies I suggest, deep in our legal history. The story is long and complex and I have no time to explore it fully. But in essence I believe it is correct to say that until the end of the eighteenth and beginning

of the nineteenth century, the recognition and enforcement of executory contracts was a very different thing from what it is today.

. . .

[Atiyah argues that until the late eighteenth century a party recovering for breach of a purely executory contract remained liable to perform his own promise. Thus, while courts might then have treated contract as based on promise, there were two independently enforceable promises involved, since the failure of A to perform his promise did not excuse B from performing hers. (Atiyah's historical analysis is strongly disputed by Fried in his book review of Atiyah, 93 Harv. L. Rev. 1858 (1980). The argument parallels the debate between Morton Horwitz and A.W.B. Simpson reproduced in Part IC, below. —ed.)]

Now as we know, in modern law, all this is different. A plaintiff is unquestionably entitled to expectation damages for breach of an executory contract, without any actual consideration passing. There is no need to show any actual benefit, any detrimental reliance. The modern law is squared with the doctrine of consideration by saying that the mere promises constitute consideration for each other. That indeed was what judges had been saying since the time of Elizabeth I, but it has not generally been perceived what an enormous difference has come over the practical import of this formula. For in the reign of Elizabeth I, a promise was good consideration for a promise precisely because both promises had to be performed. In our modern law, a plaintiff's promise is good consideration for the defendant's promise even though the plaintiff is discharged from performing his promise by the defendant's breach. It is only since these rules grew up, therefore, that liability on the wholly executory contract has truly become promise-based, rather than benefit-or reliance-based.

But although this form of liability must be treated as promise-based, we are entitled to ask how extensive it is in relation to the rest of the law, and whether it deserves to occupy the central role in Contract and even in promissory theory that it occupies today. It is, I think, worth observing that wholly executory contracts are generally nothing like as binding in practice as legal theory might suggest. Consumers and even business men often expect to be able to cancel executory agreements with the minimum of penalty, paying perhaps only for actual expenses laid out in reliance on the promise. And such reliance expenditures would, by definition, not exist if the arrangement were still wholly executory. And even in strict law, it must be stressed that the expectations protected by executory contracts are limited. They are not generally expectations of performance but expectations of profit. Where there is no difference in the market price of the goods or services which are the subject of the contract, and the market price of comparable goods or services, the contract may in law be broken with impunity. In practice this must comprise a high proportion of cases in which executory arrangements are broken. Then again, the binding force of wholly executory contracts is normally of an ephemeral nature. Executory contracts do not normally remain executory for very long. Even if made well before the time for performance, the whole purpose of making them is frequently to enable the parties to make preliminary arrangements in confident reliance on reciprocal performance. Thus action in reliance is likely to follow hard on the heels of the making of most executory contracts, and it is only in the rare cases where cancellation is sought very soon after making the contract, or where, despite the lapse of some longer period of time no action in reliance has been commenced, that the source of the obligation has to be rested in the promise alone. Whatever the paradigm of actual Contract may be, there can be no doubt that the paradigm of a *breach of contract* is not the breach of a wholly executory contract. And this surely reflects the intentions of most parties who enter into executory contracts. The primary purpose of making such a contract is usually to agree upon the terms which are to regulate a contemplated exchange, when and if it is carried through; it is surely a subordinate and less obvious purpose that the contract binds both parties to see that the exchange is indeed carried through.

If this is correct, it is not difficult to see how, even in the case of wholly executory arrangements, the principal functions of the promise are evidentiary, as they are in the case of the executed or part-executed arrangement. For when the parties begin to carry through the exchange which they have contracted about, obligations would anyhow arise even in the absence of the contract. The transaction would then become part executed, and as before, there is no reason why obligations should not then arise even in the absence of promises. It is, therefore, only in relation to the bare, unperformed, unpaid for, and unrelied upon promise, or contract, that the evidentiary theory of promissory or contractual liability cannot be supported. Upon what, then, does liability rest in such circumstances? Wherein is the source of the obligation?

V.

To stress the limited nature of the issue I must again draw attention to the fact that promises, especially when given as part of some mutual arrangement, do not usually remain unrelied upon for very long. And there are, of course, obvious and complex issues involved in defining what is meant by action in reliance for these purposes. Does it include inaction? Does a sort of generalized action in reliance serve as sufficient to take the case out of the category of the wholly executory arrangement? These are important and difficult questions but I want to put them aside here and face squarely up to the case where there is no reliance of any kind at all; and equally as I have said, where there has been no payment, no benefit rendered. Perhaps an illustration is in order. Let me take an example discussed by Sir James Fitzjames Stephen in the first number of the *Law Quarterly Review* in 1885.

> "A wanted to take a furnished house, expecting to have to pass the summer in London. He made a verbal agreement to take the house of B, a friend and a man in his own position in life, who was going out of town. The day after the agreement was made, A was ordered to return to his appointment in India instantly. A, being thus prevented from occupying the house, asked B to release him from his agreement, which I think most men in B's position would have done, as nothing had been done under it, and B had been put to no expense or inconvenience. B, however, refused. A reminded B of the Statute of Frauds, but added, that having given his word, he would if required, fulfil his agreement, whatever he might think of B's conduct. In this case,"

Stephen concludes, "I think A did his duty as a man of honor."

To a lawyer, this case is clear. A contract was made, and if it was not for the Statute of Frauds, the contract would be binding. Moreover, the modern lawyer is likely to share the moral perspective of Stephen himself. A contract is morally binding as well as legally binding, even though it is purely executory and nothing has been paid, nothing been done under the arrangement. These conclusions do not appear to me to be as self-evident as they have seemed to most Englishmen at least since the days of the Natural Lawyers. . . .

. . .

. . . The modern, and perhaps, even, by now, the traditional legal view would probably be that promises and executory contracts give rise to reasonable expectations and that it is the function of the law to protect reasonable expectations. But this is itself a somewhat circular justification. We all have a large number of expectations, many of which are perfectly reasonable, but only a few of them are protected by the law. Besides, the reasonableness of an expectation is itself something which turns largely upon whether it is in fact protected. If the law did not protect expectations arising from a wholly executory arrangement, then it would be less reasonable to entertain such expectations, or at any rate to entertain them as entitlements.

Then again, the explanation appears to prove too much. For reasonable expectations may arise from assertions or representations of fact as much as from promises. Yet the law seldom or never protects such expectations unless and until they have been acted upon. If we can, as I think we should, conceptually equate the idea of action in reliance on representations with the notion of detrimental reliance as a consideration in the case of promises, then we must recognize that representations can only give rise to a contractual-type obligation in the case of a part-executed transaction. And this remains true even in the extreme case of fraud. No matter what expectations are thereby generated, a person who tells a downright and deliberate falsehood is not subject to legal obligations unless and until someone suffers loss through acting upon it. Indeed, even when it is acted upon, it is widely thought that the measure of any consequent liability is fixed by the extent of the reliance losses and not by the expectations generated.**
This, at least, is said to be the measure of damages in tort for fraud, although it is certainly not the measure in cases classified as warranty or estoppel. It is, perhaps, possible that the explanation for this otherwise puzzling distinction between the law's treatment of promises and assertions lies in the too ready acceptance of the idea that words or conduct are in practice easily classifiable as the one or the other. Perhaps the reality is that in more cases than lawyers are willing to admit, words or conduct are classified as promises or assertions precisely because in the particular circumstances the expectations aroused are, or are not, felt worthy of protection. But if this is the case, then it is clear that we cannot defend the protection of bare expectations by pointing to the fact that they derived from a promise.

Another puzzling feature of the law's willingness to protect bare expectations is that a disappointed expectation is a psychological rather than a pecuniary injury, and the law is generally sparing in its willingness to award compensation for injuries or losses which are neither physical nor pecuniary. And if it should be urged that, at least in the commercial sphere, expectation damages are more widely justifiable, a problem might then arise about the extent to which companies and other commercial bodies can be said to suffer from a disappointment of their expectations. If disappointment is a psychological phenomenon can a company suffer disappointment? Now I would not suggest that the disappointment of reasonable expectations is no ground at all for holding contracts or promises to be binding. To raise an expectation and then to decline to fulfil it is, in some measure to worsen the position of the promisee, certainly an individual promisee. Prima facie this is something that should be avoided, other things being equal. But I am bound to say that it does appear to me to be a very weak ground for the enforcement of executory contracts, and one that could very easily be counterbalanced by proof that other things are not equal. In the example discussed by Stephen, it might well be thought by most people that the inconvenience to the promisor of being held to his contract would be enough to outweigh the prima facie desirability of not disappointing the promisee.

The second possible argument for upholding executory contracts is the argument for principle. Executory contracts are made so that the parties can rely upon each other and take the necessary preliminary steps to performance. The whole point of such contracts is that they invite reliance. Therefore, it may be urged, *even if there has in facts been no reliance yet*, it is desirable that the principle of upholding the sanctity of contracts should be maintained. Supporters of this argument, however, must explain why a shift in the onus of proof would not meet the case. Certainly, it may be justifiable to throw upon the promisor the burden of showing that the promisee has not yet acted upon the promise; but if in fact he can show this, or if it is conceded, can the argument on principle be maintained? What principle is it that requires contracts to be held binding because they may be relied upon where in fact it is conclusively demonstrated that the particular contract has not been relied upon? Here again, I do not think the argu-

---

** [This is not always true in American Law. —ed.]

ment is as weak as it may look. Contracting parties will not always know whether the other party has relied upon the contract, and it may be undesirable to encourage the promisor to take the chance that the promisee has not yet acted in reliance. And even if, to take the strongest case, as in Stephen's example, the promisor knows that the promisee has not yet acted upon the contract, the argument on principle is not necessarily to be discounted. There *is* a case for saying that the sanctity of a general principle is likely to be better maintained if people are generally persuaded to observe it *as a matter of principle*, without pausing to examine, in every case, whether the reasons justifying the principle cover the case in hand. But it must be admitted that this is not an argument which seems to carry much weight with the public or our legislators in modern times. Given the temper of the times I doubt if it will much longer be possible to blur the line between holding a promise to be binding because it *may* be relied upon and holding it binding because it *has* been relied upon.

The third possible argument in support of the executory contract concerns the case where the contract is a deliberate exercise in risk allocation. Where the primary purpose of a contract is to shift a risk of some future possibility from one party to another, and where, in particular, the risk is thereby shifted to a party who in a commercial sense is better able to take the risk, or to take avoiding action against the risk eventuating, there appears to be a strong economic case for the executory contract. I believe that this argument lies at the heart of the historical development of the binding executory contract in English law, but it is imperative to note the limits upon its application. It is very far from being true that all contracts, even all executory contracts, are exercises in risk allocation. Frequently, it is the interpretation of the law which converts a simple postponed exchange into a risk-allocation exercise, rather than any deliberate intent of the parties. And it is also far from being always the case that the purpose of an executory contract is to shift a risk to a party whose business it is to handle such risks and who can, therefore, be assumed to be generally more efficient at handling them. Indeed, the clearest and most widespread example of a contract of a risk-allocation character is the simple bet. Even business contracts frequently partake of the nature of a bet in so far as they allocate future risks, though in these cases there is a greater likelihood of some social purpose being served inasmuch as the risk is likely to be shifted to a party better able to handle it. In the ordinary bet, of course, this is not so, and that is why there would appear to be no social purpose in investing bets with a binding contractual force.

I suggested earlier that the extent to which promises are treated as conclusive evidence of the fairness of transactions must reflect the degree of paternalism in any society. I must now observe that if the primary justification for the enforcement of executory contracts is that they are risk-allocation devices, then it follows that the enforcement of such contracts raised profoundly value-laden questions. The justification for the executory contract becomes, in effect, an economic justification, an argument for greater economic efficiency. The purpose of enforcing such contracts is that of facilitating the use of greater skill, intelligence, foresight, knowledge and perhaps even resources by those who possess these advantages. To the extent that the law refused to recognize the binding force of executory transactions in order to protect the weak, the foolish, the improvident or those who lack bargaining power, it must necessarily weaken the incentives and indeed the power of those not suffering these disadvantages. I must not be thought to be arguing for or against developments of this nature in the law. I have in the past had my share of arguing for a greater willingness to protect contracting parties from their own follies and weaknesses. But I have more recently come to appreciate the importance of the inevitable costs associated with such protection.

[When the law, for paternalistic reasons, makes it harder for parties to bind themselves, the] result naturally protects those who are less able and skillful at managing their affairs from making a commitment which turns out to be disadvantageous. But it inevitably does so by depriving those who are perfectly capable of managing their affairs, of the opportunity of using their skills. The dilemma is, I think, inescapable. The economic arguments for the binding executory contract, like those in favor of the institution of property itself, involve a tendency to a perpetuation of existing inequalities. To strike down, or limit the binding force of executory contracts in order to protect some people from their own folly or ignorance is, by contrast, a redistributive device, and like all such devices must impose costs as well as benefits.

The fourth argument, which I have left to the last, for the binding executory contract is the moral argument. It is simple and appealing to argue that promises are morally obligatory, and that this remains the case whether they have been paid for, or relied upon or not. But as the case for the morally binding nature of promises is examined more closely, it bears a curious resemblance to the case for the binding nature of legal contracts rather than offering an independent reason in support of the law. One of the most commonly adduced reasons for arguing that promises are morally binding is that they have a tendency to be relied upon. We then find it being argued that, if that is the only justification, it is a somewhat circular one. For if promises were not binding, they might not be relied upon. And again, it is argued that if the tendency to rely on promises is the source of their binding character, what of the case where reliance is distinctly disproved? The argument on principle, too, has generated a debate among philosophers which closely parallels the legal and social issues hinted at previously. Principles may be useful as rules of thumb but if it is shown that, in some particular case, adherence to the principle produces worse results than non-adherence, is it not merely rule-worship to insist on maintaining the sanctity of the principle? . . . And finally, the argument that executory contracts may be risk-allocation devices has its parallel in the writings of philosophers like John Rawls and H. L. A. Hart who argue that to promise is to deliberately take part in a social practice, accepting the benefits of that practice and therefore necessarily subordinating oneself to its burdens.

But when all is said, I do not find the moral contribution to the problem to be a very satisfying one. For moralists and philosophers, like the lawyers themselves, have not generally perceived the need to separate off the wholly executory arrangement for independent justification. Virtually all discussion of the source of contractual and promissory obligation, in law and in morality, has failed to draw the all important distinction between promises and contracts which rest purely in intention, and promises and contracts which depend partly on action. Surely, nobody can doubt that morally speaking promises are more strongly binding where payment has already been received, or where there is a clear and significant act in reliance which would worsen the position of the promisee if the promise were not performed. And just as I have suggested that, in the law of part executed contracts, explicit promises may play a useful evidentiary role, so it may be suggested that promises themselves are frequently of an evidentiary character. The purpose of a promise, far from being, as is so often assumed, to create some wholly independent source of an obligation, is frequently to bolster up an already existing duty. Promises help to clarify, to quantify, to give precision to moral obligations, many

of which already exist or would arise anyhow from the performance of acts which are contemplated or invited by the promise. The promise which is given without *any* independent reason for it is a peculiarity, just as the wholly executory contract is a legal peculiarity. Is it pure coincidence that the phrase, a "gratuitous promise" means both a promise without payment and a promise without reason? Could it then be that the refusal of English law to recognize the binding force of executory gratuitous promises is not the peculiarity, the idiosyncrasy it has so long been thought to be? Might it not be that the real oddity lies in the belief that a bare promise creates a moral obligation and should create a legal obligation, without any inquiry into the reason for which the promise was given, or the effect that the promise has had?

VI.

These arguments, of course, require much greater development than I can give them here; but enough has been said to show that, if they stand up to further examination, they should suffice to dethrone the executory contract from the central place which it occupies in Contract theory. The consequences of this would be to require some drastic redrawing of the lines of the conceptual structure of contractual and promissory obligation. In the first place, the distinction between contract and quasi-contract would surely come crashing to the ground. This distinction was not anyhow indigenous to English law. It is well known that until the middle of the nineteenth century at least, the common lawyers distinguished between express and implied contracts not between contracts and quasi-contracts. To the early common lawyers, the important point in common between express and implied contracts was that both usually involved a claim for payment or reimbursement for a benefit which had been conferred by the plaintiff on the defendant. Whether the defendant had promised to pay for that benefit was a secondary question. In the nineteenth century, when the executory contract became the pivotal key to the law of obligations, when will theory flourished and when, we may add, renewed study of the classics reminded common lawyers of the Roman law distinctions and terminology, the old common law distinction fell into disrepute. The process began with academics and writers like John Austin, Henry Maine and Martin Leake. Will theory, which emphasized the importance of free choice and the voluntary creation of obligations was plainly inconsistent with the indigenous common law. The newer ideas got into the books and—after the lapse of a couple of generations—into the Law Reports. They passed into orthodoxy. Everybody began to say that quasi-contracts had nothing to do with contracts. I am afraid that I said it myself. The Contract textbooks expelled the subject. Universities even began to run separate courses on the Law of Restitution.

Plainly, if the part-executed contract is to replace the executory contract as the centre piece of Contract theory, we shall have to turn our back on these exciting new ideas. We may then discover that, far from being new, they derive from the intellectual climate of the early nineteenth century. Free choice in all things, rational planning, calculated risk assessment, and the severest limitation of the active role of State and judge, these are the themes which underlie the distinction between contract and quasi-contract. It is scarcely necessary to add that they are the themes of the last century.

A similar fate may well await the distinction between Contract and Tort when once the executory contract is removed from the central place in the law of obligations. I have already suggested that our nineteenth century heritage has led us to place undue emphasis on the extent to which contractual obligations depend upon intentions and the voluntary assumption of liability. But is it not equally true that, perhaps by way of reaction, Tort theory was swung too far in the opposite direction? In their reaction away from Contract, lawyers and judges have tended to stress the positive nature of tortious liability. Tort duties are imposed by law, not assumed by the parties. They are the reflection of society's standards of fairness and reasonableness and not the result of deliberate submission to a mutual binding arrangement, and so on. I want to suggest that all this has tended to draw far too sharp a line between Contract and Tort. It is not true that consent, intention, voluntary conduct is irrelevant to tort liabilities. The modern law of negligence is, in many respects, an offshoot of nineteenth century Contract law. Historically, the tort of negligence which dominates modern Tort law, grew almost entirely out of contractual-type arrangements. Personal injury actions brought against occupiers of premises, against employers, against railway companies were the forerunners of the modern running down case. The road accident between strangers was not the typical tort action of the last century. And even today it remains true that nearly all tort liabilities arise in the course of the performance of voluntary actions. A person who negligently injures another while driving his car is voluntarily on the road, volun-

tarily driving his car, and may be said to submit himself to the requirements of the law with as much or as little truth as the seller of goods. The liability of the bus company to pedestrians or other road users does not, in this perspective, differ significantly from its liability to passengers inside the bus. In both cases, I suggest, liability arises primarily from what is voluntarily done, from the element of reciprocal benefit and from the fact of reliance. It is, of course true that the sharp distinctions drawn by the law between tortious and contractual liability have, over the years, led to various accretions of positive law. In particular, contractual liability is often stricter than tortious liability. The seller of defective goods is liable even without proof of negligence for any injury caused by the goods to someone who can claim that he has contracted to buy them. But this distinction is, in a way, an illustration of the theme I am attempting to state. For here too, lawyers and reformers are rejecting the traditional approach. Most lawyers would today prefer to decide what the obligations of a vendor of goods should be, and would then construe his behaviour to support those obligations. Thus if it is thought, as it widely is, that a vendor of defective goods should be strictly liable to anyone who uses the goods and not only to those who buy the goods, the vendor can be said to give an implied warranty that his goods will be safe. But this implied warranty does not necessarily mean that the vendor is thought to voluntarily accept that liability; he voluntarily sells the goods, and the liability is imposed upon him. If we ask, further, why the obligations should be imposed, we will find, in most cases, that the twin elements of benefit and detriment underlie the judgment. In this particular case, for instance, it would be widely agreed that the vendor gets the benefit of the sale, that the purchaser or user relies upon him to distribute goods which are not dangerous, and that these two factors, together with the fact that the sale is a voluntary transaction, suffice to justify the obligation.

. . .

I do not, of course, want to suggest that the whole law of obligations can be rewritten in terms of a few simple principles drawn from the notions of benefit and reliance. Society and social and economic relationships are too complex in the modern industrial world for oversimplifications of this nature. But what I do want to suggest is that the great divide between duties which are voluntarily assumed, and duties which are imposed by law is itself one of these oversimplifications. A more adequate and more unifying conceptual structure for the law of obligations can be built around the interrelationship between the concepts of reciprocal benefits, acts of reasonable reliance, and voluntary human conduct.

Economic Rationales of Contract

In the past twenty years the economic analysis of law has become one of the dominant approaches. While economics was never completely ignored by lawyers, the seminal modern work is universally thought to be Ronald Coase's *The Problem of Social Cost*, 3 J. Law & Econ. 1 (1960). Most of the early "law and economics" writing was limited to efficiency (or welfare) economics; many of the writers were associated with the University of Chicago Law School, particularly Richard Posner, author of *Economic Analysis of Law* (3d ed. 1986). A number of leading members of the "Chicago School," not all of whom taught at Chicago, were appointed to the federal courts by President Reagan: Posner himself, Robert Bork, Antonin Scalia and Frank Easterbrook, among others. Because of the combination of academic writing, increased economic sophistication among practicing lawyers and judges sympathetic to economic reasoning, it is becoming more common to see economic reasoning in judicial opinions.

The Chicago School has been much accused of masking political judgments as the ineluctable results of value-free "scientific" reasoning. See, e.g., Duncan Kennedy, *Cost-Benefit Analysis of Entitlement Problems: A Critique*, 33 Stan. L. Rev. 387 (1981); C. Edwin Baker, *The Ideology of the Economic Analysis of Law*, 5 Philosophy & Pub. Aff. 3 (1975). Regardless of the truth of that perception, it should be noted that not all economists use only efficiency analysis and that not all efficiency analysis reaches politically conservative conclusions. See, e.g., Guido Calabresi and Philip Bobbitt, *Tragic Choices* (1978); Jeffrey L. Harrison, *Egoism, Altruism, and Market Illusions: The Limits of Law and Economics*, 33 U.C.L.A. L. Rev. 1309 (1986); Barbara A. White, *Coase and the Courts: Economics for the Common Man*, 72 Iowa L. Rev. 577 (1987).

Besides Posner's *Economic Analysis of Law*, other important collections on the topic include a text-essay, A. Mitchell Polinsky, *An Introduction to Law and Economics* (1983); an anthology, Anthony T. Kronman and Richard A. Posner, *The Economics of Contract Law* (1979); and several symposia, among them *Symposium on Efficiency as a Legal Concern*, 8 Hofstra L. Rev. 485 (1980); *A Response to the Efficiency Symposium*, 8 Hofstra L. Rev. 811 (1980); and *Symposium: Risk as a Legal Concern*, 41 Md. L. Rev. 563 (1982). Several law reviews are primarily devoted to law and economics, among them the Journal of Law and Economics and the Journal of Legal Studies. The total number of economics-influenced legal articles is incalculable (except, perhaps, by an empirically oriented economist).

Contract has proven to be a popular topic for economic analysis, but the bulk of the writings has concerned remedies. (Some of these will be referred to later in this anthology.) For the present, we are interested in whether economic analysis can provide any insights into the basis of contract. What follows are excerpts from a sixty page article by Professors Charles J. Goetz, an economist, and Robert E. Scott, a lawyer. Both teach at the University of Virginia School of Law. As they note in the excerpt, they tried to minimize the technical terms and formal mathematics while applying economics to the question why we enforce some promises, but not others. Goetz and Scott are much less doctrinaire than some of the Chicago School. Nonetheless, their point of view can be contrasted with some of the other writers in this section. Consider their statement that

> The principal normative justification for permitting promises is the belief that, on balance, promissory benefits exceed harm. Legally enforcing promises can sometimes increase this net social gain by encouraging cost-reducing behavior by both promisors and promisees.

Charles J. Goetz and Robert E. Scott, *Enforcing Promises: An Examination of the Basis of Contract*, 89 Yale L. J. 1261 (1980)

The obligation to keep promises is a commonly acknowledged moral duty. Yet not all promises—however solemnly vowed—are enforceable at law. Why are some promises legally binding and others not? Orthodox doctrinal categories provide only modest assistance in answering this persistent question. Conventional analysis, for example, has distinguished promises made in exchange for a return promise or performance from nonreciprocal promises. Indeed, common law "bargain theory" is classically simple: bargained-for promises are presumptively enforceable; nonreciprocal promises are presumptively unenforceable. But this disarmingly simple theory has never mirrored reality.[4] Contract law has ventured far beyond such narrow limitations, embracing reliance and unjust enrichment as additional principles of promissory obligation.[5]

. . .

These often overlapping, yet seemingly unconnected, principles of bargain, detrimental reliance, and unjust enrichment characterize all legally enforceable promises. They, in turn, are linked with corresponding sanctions that determine the level of enforcement for a given set of promises. Contract damage rules embrace a variety of remedial choices. But the principles determining this choice of remedies are largely unarticulated. In most cases *A* can seek the value of what he expected from *B*'s promise. Such standard "compensatory" recovery puts *A* in the economic position he would have occupied had *B* fulfilled his obligation. There are alternatives to the compensation rule, however. Thus, *A* may seek restitution of any benefit conferred on *B* as a result of *B*'s promise. Alternatively, *A* may seek to recover identi-

fiable casts incurred in reliance on *B*'s promise. Recovering conferred benefits and reliance expenditures has the stated objective of returning the parties to the same economic position they occupied before the promise was made.

How can these interlocking doctrinal patterns be explained? Damage and liability rules have both redistributive and behavior-adaptive functions. In an earlier paper we commented on the apparently random—and arguably regressive—distributive effects of the basic contract remedial options. The adaptive effects of contract rules seem to offer greater explanatory possibilities. A liability or damage rule induces contracting parties to adapt their behavior in ways that will affect social welfare. The rules of promissory liability can, therefore, be examined usefully in terms of these welfare effects. It is important to emphasize that the proper focus here is on prospective effects, that future promising is the behavior to be influenced by the rules summarized above. If only promises already made were considered, ease of measurement is a primary factor that might commend the compensation rule over any more complex damage measure. With respect to past promises, choosing among reliance, compensatory, or punitive remedies involves primarily a distributional issue; the damage rule allocates the gains or losses from any particular broken promise between the promisor and promisee. But, considered prospectively, rules of promissory liability have efficiency consequences as well: they frequently alter the actual magnitude of the gains or losses to be divided between the parties. Whether a particular type of promise will be enforceable, and to what extent, are choices that may powerfully modify the nat-

[4] Professor Grant Gilmore has argued provocatively that a clearly defined "bargain theory" of contract never really existed in the first place. The "theory," he argues, was simply the creature of nineteenth-century formalism. See G. Gilmore, The Death of Contract (1974).

[5] The first breach in the armor of classical bargain theory is credited to Professor Corbin. See id. at 62-66. See generally 1 A. Corbin, Contracts 109, 110 (1963). Subsequently, the pioneering scholarship of Lon Fuller and Stanley Henderson has demonstrated that the environment of

promissory liability differs markedly from conventional assumptions. See, e.g., Fuller & Perdue, The Reliance Interest in Contract Damages (pt. 1), 46 Yale L.J. 52 (1936); Henderson, Promises Grounded in the Past: The Idea of Unjust Enrichment and the Law of Contracts, 57 Va. L. Rev. 1115 (1971) [hereinafter cited as Unjust Enrichment]; Henderson, Promissory Estoppel and Traditional Contract Doctrine, 78 Yale L.J. 343 (1969) [hereinafter cited as Promissory Estoppel].

In addition to Professor Gilmore's essay, the development of contract theory is thoughtfully explored by Lawrence Friedman, see L. Friedman, Contract Law in America (1965), and by Patrick Atiyah, see P. Atiyah, The Rise and Fall of Freedom of Contract (1979).

ure and amount of future promising. We will evaluate these choices by separating the enforcement question into two parts:

First, which system of promissory enforcement yields the maximum net social benefits from promise making?

Second, does such an optimal enforcement scheme explain current doctrinal patterns?

Part I of this Article considers the first of these questions by developing an analytical model that examines both the function of promises and the impact of liability on the making of promises. Clarifying the function of promising is a necessary first step in deriving an optimal enforcement model. It is critically important to realize that a promise is conceptually distinct from the actual transfer that it announces. As advance information signaling a future transfer, a typical promise prospectively carries *both* benefit if kept and harm if broken. This entanglement of benefits and harms substantially complicates the enforcement question. Thus, the enforcement of promises may have harmful consequences by deterring socially useful future promising. Alternatively, nonenforcement encourages more promises but also reduces the reliability of the announcement; the promisor's intent to perform is not tested against a potential penalty for its nonperformance. The value of social welfare is maximized by a system of legal rules that provides the optimal balance between the beneficial and the harmful effects of promising.

In Part II, we discuss the practical compromises necessary to implement efficient regulation of promises in a world of costly legal process and imperfect information. We examine common law rules of liability as proxies for theoretically optimal rules rendered impractical by the inherent difficulties of measuring the true social effects of promising. We conclude that a substantial congruence exists between traditional contract rules and optimal promissory enforcement. Indeed, this congruence offers a persuasive explanation for the peculiar patterns of promissory liability observed in actual practice.[17]

I. Optimal Enforcement of Promises

Attempts have been made to explain the overlapping patterns of promissory liability in terms of the economic implications of promise-making. Bargained for promises support value-enhancing exchanges. Such promises are thus seen as fully enforceable under the compensation rule in order to protect and encourage value-maximizing resource allocation. Measuring damages in terms of expectation rather than reliance is said to encourage more efficient breach decisions once the contract is made. A nonreciprocal promise, on the other hand, is frequently labeled as a "sterile transaction," which does not facilitate the movement of resources to more valued uses. On this basis, enforcement is justified only as a deterrent to the harm caused by any detrimental reliance on the promise. In sum, these lines of analysis suggest that full enforcement of bargains consolidates benefits while protection of reliance-based promissory interests minimizes harms.

But existing explanations of the legal enforcement of promises are incomplete and perhaps misleading. A principal limitation has been the failure to consider the effects of various levels of legal enforcement on the making of promises. Inquiry has generally focused instead on the effects of legal sanctions on decisions to breach or perform, assuming that the promise has already been made.[22] Yet, a decision to enforce promises, and the subsequent choice of remedy, does not merely mold the performance behavior of contracting parties; it also shapes both the nature and amount of promise-making activity. Appropriately calibrated enforcement rules can be used to

---

[17] A recent scholarly debate has centered on the hypothesis that the common law can be explained in terms of principles of economic efficiency. See, e.g., R. Posner, Economic Analysis of Law 404-05, 439-41 (2d ed. 1977); Rubin, Why is the Common Law Efficient? 6 J. Legal Stud. 51 (1977); Priest, The Common Law Process and the Selection of Efficient Rules, 6 J. Legal Stud. 65 (1977); Michelman, A Comment on Some Uses and Abuses of Economics in Law, 46 U. Chi. L. Rev. 307 (1979). We take no position on the extent to which economic efficiency is a dominant or merely subsidiary element in explaining the development of common law doctrine in general. Our intent is the more modest one of measuring a relatively narrow segment of legal doctrine against some underlying economic optimality considerations.

[22] . . .In order to increase its accessibility to a legal readership, this Article uses relatively nontechnical terms to present an underlying economic model that typically would be articulated by economists in highly formal mathematical terms. The formal model developed in the economic literature by Shavell and extended by Rogerson differs conceptually from ours in some important areas. For instance, we focus upon the influence of potential remedies on the quality and quantity of promises, rather than upon the optimal enforcement of a promise, the character of which is already determined. In addition, our definition of reliance damages differs because we incorporate the notion of "reasonableness." Hence, the implicit model underlying this Article is somewhat more complex conceptually than are those cited above.

achieve the optimal number and type of promises based on the degree and form of adaptation by promisor and promisee. Thus, the effects of legal enforcement on promise-making are critical factors in evaluating the seemingly disparate liability and damage rules of contract. In Part I we examine these effects by first describing the reactions of both the promisee and promisor to the risks inherent in promising. We then specify an enforcement model that encourages the socially optimal interaction between the promising parties.

. . .

C. *Optimizing Promisor-Promisee Interaction*

To what extent do legal sanctions optimize the interactions between promisor and promisee? In the present context, optimization is defined as maximizing the net social benefits of promissory activity—that is, the benefits of promises minus their costs. This approach is equivalent to the balancing of prospective costs and benefits under the widely accepted Learned Hand test for the required duty of care in potential tort-producing activities.[34] Indeed, there are strong theoretical parallels between the production of dangerous, but useful, products and the making of promises.

The role of damages or sanctions in generating socially optimal behavior can be focused more sharply by observing the distinction between internal and external effects.[36] Because self-interested maximizing behavior entails consideration of only internal costs and benefits, unfettered individual behavior is incompatible with social optimization in circumstances in which significant external costs or benefits are present. Individuals will oversupply activities with external costs and undersupply those with external benefits. By imposing costs and creating incentives, the law can cause individuals to consider external effects in their decisionmaking and thus "internalize" them.

Inducing optimal promise-making therefore requires that the promisor's costs of promising be adjusted to reflect any external effects on the promisee.

But this adjustment process is complex. Changes in the costs and benefits of promising are highly interactive in two senses. First, an individual's adjustment may substitute one category of his costs for another. Second, the actions of one party may produce reactions by the other and, in turn, feedback responses to the first party. The role of legal damages in optimizing this interaction depends upon whether a promise is reciprocal or nonreciprocal. Nonreciprocal or gratuitous promises, which are not conditioned upon performance of a return promise, do not typically enjoy the presumption of enforceability attached to reciprocal or bargained-for promises. As the analysis below reveals, the critical variable that distinguishes these categories of promises is whether the parties can interactively influence the nature and amount of promise-making through bargaining. It is the existence of effective impediments to interaction in the case of nonreciprocal promises that seems to explain why the law treats these two types of promises in such different fashions.[38]

1. Nonreciprocal Promises

Consider the case of a gratuitous promisor who has adjusted his promise-making to an arbitrarily assumed level of extra-legal sanction so that he cannot further improve his situation. In addition, assume that social considerations effectively prevent the promisee from influencing the promisor's calculations through bargaining. Under these conditions, when does the intervention of the law lead to optimal results? We shall first discuss the conditions under which nonenforcement of such a nonreciprocal promise will produce suboptimal reassurance and precautionary adjustments. We then derive an optimal damage formula for those cases in which some level of enforcement is suggested.

a. *Legal Enforcement and Reassurance*

Legal enforcement of a particular class of nonreciprocal promises increases the reliability of the promises. This added reassurance increases social benefits in three situations. First, legal enforcement

---

[34] Under the Hand definition, an actor is guilty of negligence if the loss caused by the accident multiplied by the probability of its occurrence exceeds the burden of taking adequate precautions. United States v. Carroll Towing Co., 159 F.2d 169, 173 (2d Cir. 1947).

[36] Internal effects are those costs and benefits felt by the individual actor. External effects are those consequences of an act that are felt only by individuals other than the actor. Only if a party makes decisions as if he were experiencing all of the consequences of his behavior, external as well as internal, will his behavior be socially optimal.

[38] Barriers to effective interaction between parties to promises may arise from many different sources. Ordinary transaction-costs impediments may exist as a result of the time and trouble involved in negotiating. Alternatively, there may be something inherent in the very relationship of the parties that renders interaction impractical, such as a social taboo, a status relationship, or an institutional environment that obstructs meaningful communication. See Leff, Injury, Ignorance and Spite—The Dynamics of Coercive Collection, 80 Yale L.J. 1, 41 (1970).

increases the net benefits of promissory reassurance if a legal sanction such as money damages displaces existing extra-legal penalties such as guilt or social pressure. If the total level of the sanction stays the same, the promisor's costs, benefits, and behavior all remain the same while the promisee's benefits are increased by the receipt of the damages. The promisee's self-protection costs also fall. Because the consequences of a regret contingency are reduced by a prospect of legal compensation, the promisee can spend less on mitigating the risk of uncompensated detrimental reliance. In the event of breach, damage payments reduce the cost of nonperformance to the promisee. Thus, his beneficial reliance on the promise will increase. In essence, the substitution of one type of sanction for the other provides the promisee with the benefits of more reassurance against the regret contingency at no additional cost to the promisor. Hence, the imposition of legal sanctions may increase net reassurance benefits, if extra-legal sanctions are replaced by legal enforcement.

Second, legal enforcement may increase net reassurance benefits regardless of the degree of substitutability of sanctions. Such an opportunity arises when a gratuitous promisor assesses the risk of a regret contingency at zero, because he is certain he will perform. In this case, if the law intervenes by raising the sanction for breach, the promisor's prospective regret and precautionary costs remain at zero. The prospect of sanctions is largely irrelevant to such a promisor. If the promisee knew that the risk of a regret contingency were in fact zero, he too would be unaffected by a stronger sanction. He would be perfectly assured already and, consequently, would incur no self-protection costs. Generally, however, a promisee's subjectively perceived risk of a regret contingency will be greater than the actual zero risk known to the promisor. Therefore, the increased sanction provides greater reassurance and permits a promisee who was originally engaging in excessive self-protection to decrease his self-protection costs.

Third, even the gratuitous promisor who is not totally certain of future performance may prefer more enforcement. This will occur, for instance, when the promisor cares about the welfare or the reaction of the promisee. Then, the net benefit of promising to the promisor may be enhanced by the provision of additional reliability to the promisee through legal enforcement. Although enforcement puts such promisors at additional risk, the greater reassurance to the promisee may generate increased benefits to the promisor that outweigh any increased costs.

Under what circumstances, then, will legally induced increases in the reliability of nonreciprocal promises be socially optimal? When the mutual interests of both parties are furthered by more assured promises, the promisor will voluntarily seek legal mechanisms for providing additional reassurance. However, often it will not be in the self-interest of the promisor to undertake voluntarily a more reliable promise. Even when some benefits to the promisor are produced by additional reassurance, the external benefits from performance may be inadequately communicated to the promisor by self-sanctions. As a general empirical premise, therefore, enforcement will be more likely to optimize promissory reassurance when extra-legal sanctions are relatively ineffective. The social desirability of enforcement, however, ultimately depends upon whether those gains are offset by corresponding costs. Before proposing a sanction for particular nonreciprocal cases, therefore, we must consider the societal effect of the promisors' precautionary adjustments triggered by legal liability.

b. *Legal Enforcement and Precautionary Action*

Although legal enforcement of nonreciprocal promises will initially increase the reliability of such promises, it may induce both qualitative and quantitative precautionary action by promisors. The net societal effect of legal enforcement of a class of promises depends on the relative social value of these interacting adjustments.

Qualitative precautionary adjustments by promisors to increased sanctions may be thought of as merely the converse of reassurance. These precautionary moves entail a lessening of the scope of the promise and a shifting of the risk of potential regret contingencies to the promisee, while reassurance enhances the value of the promise and constitutes an assumption of risk by the promisor. These qualitative dimensions of a promise encompass two conceptually distinct effects: first, risk minimization by providing the promisee with better information on which to determine his degree of reliance; and, second, risk allocation by dividing the costs of regret contingencies between promisor and promisee. Analysis of these two factors suggests that legal sanctions can be used to induce risk-minimizing precautionary adjustments by both parties, but are much less successful in directing risk-bearing choices.

By providing the promisee with information concerning regret contingencies, precautionary adjustments by the gratuitous promisor improve the accuracy of the promisee's degree of reliance. Without a legal sanction, the benefits generated by the information effect of precautionary adjustments may not be maximized. The promisor is motivated to make precautionary adjustments only to the extent that his increased precautionary costs are outweighed by decreases in his regret costs. For instance, when only minimal extra-legal sanctions are imposed on breach, the savings in regret costs are relatively trivial, and precautionary moves by the promisor are not likely to be cost-effective. Under these circumstances, the promisee will be insufficiently forewarned about the risks of breach and will consequently overrely, failing to protect himself adequately against the prospect of breach.

Thus, where the external costs of a nonreciprocal promise are unlikely to be conveyed to the promisor, legal enforcement can induce the promisor to make optimal precautionary adjustments. Alternatively, the promisee must optimize self-protection and reliance in the light of the information he now possesses about the reliability of the promise. Paradoxically, if promises are unenforceable, the promisee has the correct incentives to protect himself to the optimal level against risks. Because the promisee bears all risks of breach, in this environment, he will rely on a promise only to the extent that the prospective cost of reliance is outweighed by prospective benefits. In contrast, if a promise is legally enforceable, and the regret costs shift to the promisor, the promisee may engage in a greater then optimal level of reliance. Because the reduction of regret costs becomes an external benefit of the promisee's actions, the promisee may ignore these costs in determining the extent of his reliance. In order to discourage the promisee from overrelying, the promisor must not be held liable for damages when the promisee knew or should have known that the marginal cost of self-protection was lower than the corresponding marginal reduction in prospective regret costs. This rule gives meaning to the concept of "reasonable reliance" and avoids not only an underinvestment in self-protection by the promisee, but also an overinvestment in precautionary adjustments by the promisor. It fills essentially the same function as does the rule of contributory negligence in tort.

In addition to these risk minimization effects, legally induced qualitative precautionary moves reallocate the risk of regret to the promisee. What can be said of the risk allocation implications of these qualitative adjustments? The allocation of risk to a least-cost risk bearer by the manipulation of legal liability may have efficiency consequences that justify the costs of such adjustments. However, in the case of most nonreciprocal promises, the risk of a regret contingency ultimately will be borne by the promisee in spite of the promisor's risk-bearing advantages. Initially, the imposition of a legal sanction allocates some or all of the risk of a regret contingency to the promisor. But so long as the promisor is free to make qualitative adjustments, by conditioning his promise, he can shift that risk back to the promisee. In some cases, of course, the promisee may be the least-cost risk bearer. However, because it is the enforcement of the promise that removed the risk from the promisee initially, legally induced precautionary moves to shift it back again cannot be regarded as efficiency gains attributable to the liability rule. Thus, in terms of risk allocation, qualitative adjustments have only distributional consequences; their implementation costs may be regarded as net social losses.

This analysis suggest that qualitative precautionary adjustments by the gratuitous promisor have mixed effects. Increasing these adjustments by legally enforcing nonreciprocal promises is optimal, therefore, only when gains in promisee reliance from improved information exceed the net implementation costs of reallocating the risk of regret to the promisee. This implies, as an empirical generalization, that enforcing nonreciprocal promises will improve outcomes when there exists a substantial prospect of beneficial information exchanges through qualitative adjustments. Conversely, in contexts in which self-sanctions are already effective and the prospects of improved information are poor, the social gains from enforcement are negligible and may be exceeded by implementation costs. Nonenforcement of such nonreciprocal promises is thus the optimal choice.

c. An Optimal Damage Formula

The effect of a decision to enforce legally any particular class of nonreciprocal promises depends upon the nature of the sanction imposed for breach. Promisors will respond to higher levels of sanction by increasing their qualitative and quantitative precautions, reducing both the reliability of a given volume of promises and the number of promises actually made.

A necessary starting point in determining an optimal damage rule is to specify the external effects of a nonreciprocal promise as the supply of such promises is increased by one marginal unit. The external effects are the prospective detrimental reliance incurred if the promise is broken and the prospective beneficial reliance enjoyed if the promise is performed. Proper reflection of external effects therefore requires not only that the promisor be charged for the harm expected from broken promises, but also that he be rewarded for the prospective benefits of performance. It is helpful to state this condition symbolically. Let p be the promisor's reasonable, subjective assessment of the probability that he will perform a promise under an existing legal rule calling for damages of D in the event of breach. For the damage rule to deter all promises with net social costs and encourage those with net benefits, the amount of damages awarded must satisfy the following equation:

$$(1 - p)\text{D} = (1 - p)\text{R} - p\text{B}$$

where R and B are the values of detrimental and beneficial reliances, respectively. Assuming that all broken promises are litigated, the left-hand side of the equation represents the expected value of the prospective legal sanction. Because only broken promises are affected by the law, the probability $(1 - p)$ of the promise being broken is used to "discount" the damages D. The values for R and B on the right-hand side of the equation should be understood as those resulting from optimal self-protection by the promisee. Thus, promisees will appropriately minimize the value of the right-hand term, which is the net social cost of the promise. In calculating this prospective net reliance, the magnitudes of the potential detrimental and beneficial reliances are each discounted by their probabilities. When the equation is satisfied through the imposition of optimal damages D, the promisor's internal cost-benefit calculus will reflect the external effects of his promise-making. If the external effects are thus accounted for, the promisor's maximization of his internal net benefits is consistent with supply of the socially optimal quantity and quality of promises. We call this damage rule the "prospective net reliance" formulation.

In some cases, the prospective beneficial reliance from a promise will exceed its prospective detrimental reliance. Because the net external effect of such a promise is beneficial, it would be optimal to reward the making of such promises. However, in the nonreciprocal setting no practical legal mechanism exists for rewarding promises. This limitation renders true optimization impossible; the situation is necessarily second-best. At minimum, promises with prospects of net beneficial reliance should not be the subject of damages if breached. Only promises with prospective net detrimental external effects should be enforce-

able. The prospective net reliance formulation developed above can be used to analyze the optimal level of enforcement. By dividing both sides of the original equation by the probability of breach $(1 - p)$, the following damage rule emerges:

$$\text{D} = \text{R} - \left[\frac{P}{(1 - p)} \right] \text{B}$$

The optimal damage rule thus subtracts from the promisee's reliance cost a fraction of his potential beneficial reliance. This fraction is the ratio of the ex ante subjective probability of performance to that of nonperformance. It determines the extent to which the prospect of beneficial reliance when the promise was made is credited against the promisee's prospective detrimental reliance. Because this ratio may be thought of as an index of the promisor's good faith, we call it the "good-faith ratio." A damage offset based on the good-faith ratio and on the amount of potential beneficial reliance will encourage the optimal quantity and quality of promises by reflecting in the promisor's decision calculus both the harmful and beneficial effects of his promise-making. This optimal legal sanction is likely to be unattainable in an environment of costly legal process and imperfect information. But specifying an optimal sanction permits more rigorous evaluation of the error produced by any practical adjustment attributable to process costs. In addition, the good-faith ratio and the damage offset suggest a possible explanation for the language of the *Restatement of Contracts*, which conditions both the enforceability and the magnitude of reliance-based sanctions upon the "requirements of justice." This language may reflect the view that the prospective beneficial effects of a promise should be considered in effecting a remedy for nonperformance.

The rule suggested by the formula above will admittedly result in a large quantity of uncompensated damages from broken nonreciprocal promises. Although greater damages would deter many injurious transactions, a stricter standard also would deter beneficial transactions in even greater magnitudes. Viewing an already-broken promise, the affected promisee would always prefer the highest possible damage award. But from the ex ante standpoint, a promisee would not wish to discourage a promise that creates a prospect of gain outweighing the risk of uncompensated loss. Such promises are "good bets" for the promisee over the long run, even though some of the promises will result in uncompensated harm. The penalty formulation developed above awards damages both to protect promisees from "bad bet" promises and to avoid deterrence of promises that are "good bets."

...

[In an omitted section the authors conclude that the same principle applies to reciprocal promises and that the different legal treatment of them "may be due to a close empirical identity of reliance and expectation in reciprocal promises." Also "modification of the return promise is a powerful additional adjustment mechanism," which obviously exists only for reciprocal promises. —ed.]

D. *Summary and Implications*

The preceding analysis suggests that the function of promises can be observed more precisely by conceptually distinguishing the effects of the advance information from the actual transfer. Information from promises induces reliance whenever the promisee attaches a positive probability to performance. Reliance responses are beneficial when a promise is kept and detrimental when it is broken. The principal normative justification for permitting promises to be made freely is the belief that, on balance, promissory benefits exceed harms. Legally enforcing promises can sometimes increase this net social gain by encouraging cost-reducing behavior by both promisors and promisees.

The treatment of promises when performance or nonperformance is certain is simple: such promises can be fully enforced so as to maximize benefits or minimize costs respectively. In the sure performance case, enforcement, without deterring the promisor, increases the reliability of the promise to the promisee. In the certain nonperformance case, maximum deterrence of promises serves to prevent a bad-faith promisor from enriching himself at certain cost to the promisee.

The more important case of promises for which performance is potentially uncertain is more complex, because each promise carries both potential benefits and harms that must be balanced. Future contingencies may materialize rendering performance of such promises unattractive to the promisor. The risk of this regret contingency can be allocated several ways. On the one hand, nonenforcement of promises induces self-protective reductions in reliance by the promisee. These, in turn, may trigger reassurance reactions from the promisor. On the other hand, enforcement of promises increases promisee reliance, but also induces precautionary adjustments by the promisor. The social cost of the regret contingency is minimized when the optimal interactive adaptations are encouraged.

An examination of the function of legal rules in optimizing the interactions between the promisor and promisee explains the traditional distinction between nonreciprocal and reciprocal promises. In the case of reciprocal promises, the bargain mechanism provides a feedback of costs and benefits to the promisor and promisee. Thus, the liability rules for reciprocal promises do not directly influence promise-making; instead, they affect the costs of contracting between bargainers. For nonreciprocal promises, however, enforcement substantially shapes the adaptive responses of both parties. For example, enforcement of nonreciprocal promises will optimize social benefits when extra-legal sanctions are minimal and the promisor can be encouraged to adapt the form of the promise to the risk of regret. Calibration of the optimal damages for such enforceable promises requires a consideration of both the beneficial and the detrimental reliance prospectively induced by the promise. Such a prospective net reliance formulation encourages promisors accurately to internalize social effects and thereby induces appropriate qualitative and quantitative adjustments.

But the practical implications of this ideal enforcement scheme must be considered. When nonenforcement is optimal, no measurement difficulties impede its implementation. When enforcement is indicated, implementation of the optimal rule is more difficult. A standard expectation-interest sanction may impose supra-optimal damages and deter socially valuable promise-making by inducing excessive precautionary behavior in promisors. The traditional reliance damage formulation—return of the promisee to the status quo ante—most clearly approximates the optimal level of enforcement. However, despite the language usually invoked, the status quo ante goal is rarely achieved by courts awarding so-called reliance damages. This systematic disparity between principle and practice isolates a central dilemma of promissory liability. True reliance damages, which include the value of opportunities forgone as well as the costs of actions taken, are extraordinarily difficult to measure accurately. Courts have generally responded to this largely unarticulated measurement conundrum by simply reimbursing the promisee for the gross value of any actions taken or actual expenditures incurred in reliance on the promise. The recovery of such expenditures, which we have termed "reimbursement damages," should be distinguished from the theoretical objective of reliance damages.

We have developed the preceding model under an assumption of perfect measurement in order to evaluate the effects of legal rules on promissory behavior. Existing patterns of promissory liability often appear to produce substantial error costs in failing to regulate this conduct efficiently. Can this systematic error be explained? The complexity of the preceding analysis suggests that measurement of the true social cost of promising is likely to be itself a very costly activity. Enforcement costs increase the risk that the promisee's true reliance losses will not be fully recouped. Moreover, process costs necessary to ascertain and implement the optimal level of enforcement may be so high that they exceed the error costs attributable to simpler rules of thumb such as no enforcement, full enforcement, or reimbursement. In Part II we relax the assumptions of perfect measurement and zero process costs to evaluate the efficiency of the rules of promissory obligation from a more practical standpoint.

II. Efficient Rules of Promissory Obligation

The second aspect of the promissory enforcement question asks whether the optimal enforcement model when adjusted for enforcement costs explains current patterns of promissory liability. We address this question first by describing the legal costs necessary to enforce promises and examining the relationship of these costs to different substantive rules. We then evaluate the rules of promissory liability by examining three basic categories of promises: fully bargained-for reciprocal promises within the common law "consideration" model; nonreciprocal promises distinguishable by the parties' inability to adjust interactively the nature and amount of promising; and, finally, the intermediate category of unilateral promises in a reciprocal context, which, under the narrow common law standard, may be unenforceable despite the possibility of bargaining.

. . .

B. *Reciprocal–Bargain Promises: The Consideration Model*

First, we examine reciprocal promises reached by bargaining, for which the common law developed the consideration doctrine.

1. The Functions of Bargain

Evaluating contract rules as cost-reducing surrogates for the theoretically optimal enforcement rule reemphasizes the importance of the distinction between reciprocal and nonreciprocal promises. Promises that satisfy the reciprocal exchange requirement

of consideration are presumptively enforceable. Breach entitles the promisee to full performance compensation. The enforceability of reciprocal promises is supported by a rich normative literature emphasizing the social utility of bargains. But more importantly, as suggested above, the bargain mechanism can reduce discrepancies between optimal and actual enforcement rules.

We have pointed out the identity between detrimental reliance and full-performance expectation whenever markets for promises are competitive. Furthermore, bargaining tends to produce the optimal amount of promissory reliance even when the legal rule deviates from the optimal reliance principle. By modifying contractual terms, the parties can vary the standard liability rule in order to maximize net reliance benefits.

What effects can be predicted from full enforcement of reciprocal bargain promises? As the model developed in Part I suggests, application of sanctions for breach imposes the risk of the regret contingency on the promisor. As the promisor's potential liability is increased, he is encouraged to take precautionary action to minimize the expected liability, by conditioning promises more carefully in negotiations. The promisee, in turn, may bargain for a less restricted promise by paying explicitly for the additional reassurance provided by a compensation award.

Alternatively, a rule denying enforcement of a bargained-for promise reduces precautionary costs incurred by promisors seeking to minimize the risks of regret, because it shifts that risk to the promisee. The promisee may adapt to this increased uncertainty by discounting the price he is willing to pay for the promise. If the promise is actually worth more than the promisee estimates, the promisor will incur costs up to the expected value of the promise in order to assure the promisee of the true worth of the promise. These additional reassurance costs induced by the promisee's adaptive behavior could include the voluntary assumption of legal liability through collateral guarantees or performance bonds.

Thus, because bargainers will attempt to allocate the risk of regret optimally themselves, the effects of enforcement rules depend on the transaction costs of risk allocation. Evaluation of these costs requires an analysis of how bargainers adapt to the risks of regret contingencies. If in certain transactions precautionary efforts by promisors would be more expensive than reassurance, nonenforcement enables the parties to shift the risk of regret more cheaply. Alternatively, when reassurance is more costly, fully enforcing promises induces cheaper precautionary conduct. If each type of transaction can be identified ex ante, specifying the cost-effective rule in advance produces the outcome that the parties would reach if they bargained over legal liability for breach.

. . .

3. *Remedies for Nonperformance of Bargained-for Promises*

The impact of any enforcement rule ultimately depends on the character of the remedy for nonperformance. Full enforcement compensation is the standard recovery for breach of reciprocal-bargain promises, whenever such an award can be determined accurately. The stated objective of this compensation rule is to place the promisee in the same economic position he would have occupied had the promise been performed. As we have argued above, this rule, by imposing a sanction in excess of the social costs of breach, overdeters socially useful promising, except in competitive markets in which expectation is equivalent to reliance. The bargain context, however, enables the parties to vary, with low transactions costs, the legal rule by agreement and thereby mitigate the effects of any remedial distortion. Morever, the disparity between compensatory recovery and optimal reliance damages is usually more than offset by gains in the clarity of the rule. Suppose A promises B $5,000 in exchange for B's agreement to paint A's portrait. After the painting is completed, A reneges. Because the market for similar promises is likely to be thin, the immediate reliance or opportunity costs of A's promise may vary unpredictably from the $5,000 contract price. Furthermore, A's promise and breach will have produced a detrimental adjustment in B's pattern of consumption. The amount of such consequential reliance is even more difficult to measure. Full performance compensation in this example is precisely and objectively measured by the $5,000 face value of A's promise. The administrative advantages of this clear rule outweigh the potential costs of distortion.

When the promisee's expectation includes the consequences of performance, the damage rule becomes more complicated. Suppose A promises to sell B the raw materials for manufacturing 1,000 widgets at the current market price of $5,000. A's breach causes B to lose two weeks of production of widgets. The $5,000 contract price no longer approximates B's expectations from performance. In this situation, B will not be entitled to recover his lost profits from A unless they were foreseeable when the contract was

made and can be proved with reasonable certainty. If B's expectation is unforeseeable or difficult to establish, reimbursement damages may be awarded rather than full performance compensation.

It is tempting to conclude that reimbursement recoveries are always preferable to full-performance damages as a more accurate approximation of the optimal reliance-based sanction. However, as suggested above, reimbursement recoveries are limited on practical grounds to the amount of the expenditures induced by the promise. Courts have not even attempted to ascertain the value of forgone opportunities; expenditures have been reduced to their net value only when a salvage market exists. Thus, a reimbursement remedy is not necessarily a more accurate proxy for the optimal reliance-based sanction than full-performance compensation.

Following a total breach by the promisee, the value of a partial performance by the promisor can also be recouped through a reimbursement recovery. The intricate patterns of recovery in partial performance cases can be explained by variations in magnitude of the costs of proof and valuation. Courts usually award whichever recovery of reimbursement and compensation is readily measurable in monetary terms. In the more common cases in which neither compensation nor reimbursement is easily measured, the promisee may elect either compensation or reimbursement damages for partial performance so long as he is not made better off than his original expectation.

Although objectively measurable recovery has the advantage of reducing process costs, ease of measurement does not fully explain the selection of damage rules. In addition to the uncertainty of the loss, findings of remoteness and unforeseability are used to limit consequential recoveries. Courts appear unwilling to inflict socially harmful overdeterrence when the gains from awarding compensation are attenuated. Furthermore, the damage limitations of uncertainty and unforeseability are not uniformly applied. The doctrines have been rigorously applied in cases in which liability appeared disproportionate to the gains the promisor anticipated from the contract, but have been rarely invoked when recoveries were of more limited magnitude.

These limitations on consequential losses are consistent with the assumption of risk aversion discussed above. If a risk-averse promisor faces potential consequences of breach that are disproportionately large as well as unpredictable, he will increase his precautionary efforts. Limitation of the legal sanction divides the risk of regret between promisors and promisees. Promisors continue to bear the risk of the known and ascertainable consequences of concluded bargains, while promisees bear the risk of uncertain and unforeseeable consequences. A partial reallocation of the risk will reduce promisors' precautionary costs and increase their investment in reassurance. However, the expenditures on reassurance should be less than the investment in precaution under a fully compensatory scheme. First, risk-averse bargainers will choose to forgo gains rather than risk losses of equal magnitude. The cost to the promisee of forgoing profitable but unforeseeable actions in reliance on a promise will be lower than the cost to the promisor of bearing the risks that the promisee will engage in such action and that a regret contingency will arise. Thus, bargainers will prefer to bear the risk of uncertain and potentially severe consequences as promisees rather than as promisors. Second, because the consequences of breach are better known to the promisee, he is better able to select the optimal mix of promisor reassurance and self-protection through limited reliance. In addition, the limitation on the award of damages for unascertainable consequences of breach induces the promisee to disclose to the promisor information that the promisor may not have concerning the consequences of breach. This information would not be disclosed to the promisor under a full-performance compensation rule and benefits from promise-making would not be maximized. Thus, the limitation on damages for unforeseeable consequences of breach increases the efficiency of promissory activity by stimulating the provision of information between bargainers.

. . .

[The authors discuss at some length a hypothetical case of an elderly aunt who promises a valuable Persian rug to a nephew, but dies before transferring it. Although the nephew probably would have relied on the promise by "modify[ing] his consumption habits in adjustment to his suddenly increased expected wealth," this general reliance is difficult to measure and would not be sufficiently definite to satisfy section 90 of either the First or Second Restatement of Contracts.]

[The authors argue that intra-family promises of gifts are very far from the bargain model, that extra-legal sanctions are generally effective in most non-reciprocal settings, and that "the prospect of increasing the exchange of information through qualitative adjustments is small in most donative contexts." They

further find that courts rarely find sufficient foreseeable reliance to enforce familial promises of gifts, and enforce unilateral promises only in contexts approaching the bargaining context of reciprocal promises.]

D. *Unilateral-Bargain Promises: The Expansion of Bargain Theory*

Reciprocal-bargain promises and nonreciprocal promises represent the polar extremes of promissory settings. The recent expansion in promissory liability has been concentrated in the intermediate contexts, in which bargaining and exchange remain a realistic, if not realized, prospect. Indeed, the main source of tension between traditional bargain theory and the optimal enforcement of promises lies in the incongruence between the narrowly drawn consideration model and this broader exchange context. Courts have responded to this tension by using alternative theories of liability to enforce a much wider range of bargain promises, such as subsequent promises to renew an antecedent legal obligation barred by bankruptcy or the statute of limitations. In addition, reliance-based theories have often been employed when rules of consideration deny enforcement. We designate representations lacking any legally enforceable consideration as "unilateral-bargain" promises. Much of the uncertainty concerning the enforcement of such promises arises because the doctrinal support for enforcement has emerged from the gratuitous context. However, although the boundaries have been redefined, the distinction between the enforcement of nonreciprocal and reciprocal promises remains largely undisturbed.

Enforcement rules for unilateral-bargain promises may never be as precisely defined as the provisions regulating other promissory categories. Nevertheless, under recurring circumstances, patterns of enforcement emerge from which individual variables can be isolated. The examination of cases in which courts have recently expanded liability is necessary to isolate the key elements in the enforcement decision.

1. Reduced Transactions Costs

We have suggested that the classic consideration model can be explained by analysis of the transactions costs of exchange. When outcomes are uncertain, the risk of legal liability may be perceived as a greater threat than the risk of uncompensated reliance from a broken promise, because each actor can exercise greater control over his own detrimental reliance than over the potential losses of his promisee.

Thus, all other things equal, forgoing an uncertain gain by reducing reliance will be preferred over suffering an equally uncertain loss of similar magnitude. This assumption helps explain both the offer and acceptance and discharge rules of consideration and the remedial limitations on liability.

Examining the disposition of promissory estoppel claims in bargain settings reveals patterns of enforcement that parallel the design of the consideration model. Promises made in either preliminary or termination negotiations are generally unenforceable under section 90. Alternatively, reliance theories have been used successfully to enforce promises made in the context of an ongoing exchange transaction. Indeed, promises that modify an existing agreement have long been enforced, despite the common law preexisting duty rule, if there is evidence of reasonable reliance. Although the decisions in such "waiver by estoppel" cases often focus doctrinally on equitable estoppel, the impact reliance has on the imposition of liability is clear.

Similarly, courts have enforced a variety of collateral promises reinforcing completed but defective exchanges. For example, in *Wheeler v. White*,[140] after an agreement had been signed, the promisor represented that funds for a projected shopping center would soon be available and convinced the promisee to demolish existing buildings. Although the original agreement was judged indefinite, the subsequent promises of performance were found enforceable under section 90.

By enforcing such promises, the courts have not ventured far beyond the assumptions underlying the consideration model. The requirements for recovery under section 90 have been strictly construed whenever the outcome of bargaining is uncertain, but have been liberally interpreted when the essence of the bargain has been established. When agreements are unclear, risk-averse bargainers prefer to bear the risks of regret contingencies as promisees, and the nonenforcement rule is optimally retained. When the bargain is clear but fails technically, however, parties may prefer pursuing gains to avoiding losses. Enforcement under section 90 allocates the risk of regret to promisors and thereby shifts resources to more efficient precautionary conduct.

These reflections of the assumptions underlying the consideration model also appear in the remedies provided under the doctrine of promissory estoppel. Generally, full-enforcement compensation has been awarded whenever such damages would have been available under the certainty and foreseeability limitations of bargain theory. Reimbursement has been awarded when the harmful consequences of nonperformance were not reasonably foreseeable and the claim for greater damages was too speculative. Although the rhetoric of some of these decisions suggests that reimbursement damages are the preferred recovery under promissory estoppel, the outcomes imply that courts are animated by the same concerns that have produced the design of the consideration model.

· · ·

4. Certainty and Distributional Effects

When considerations of accuracy, transactional efficiency, and bad faith are eliminated, a significant difference remains between the enforcement theories of bargain and reliance. Bargain rules are more certain; reliance rules invite greater flexibility and discretion. Because reliance-based enforcement requires evidence of future facts unknown at the time of bargaining, the availability of such enforcement doctrines increases bargainers' uncertainty as to the risks of legal liability. Uncertainty imposes a social loss that reduces the value of exchange. The inefficiency of a discretionary rule of promissory estoppel may be worth incurring if it results in the achievement of socially desirable distributional goals.[175] However, examination of reliance cases does not yield discernible distributional policies.

Evidence of relative ability to sustain losses or of the reasons for breach is required before the losses, or gains, from the breach can be distributed according to any fairness norms. None of the litigated cases reveals careful exploration of the distributional consequences of alternative decisions. Futhermore, in most cases the redistributional effects of varying rules are difficult to predict. Absent a clear commitment to promissory redistribution, the uncertainty induced by broadly conceived discretionary rules is unjustified. Systematization of the expansion of the bargain model calls for developing clearly articulated liability rules paralleling those that have emerged from the rules of consideration. Such rules can be generally sketched from current patterns of enforcement.

---

[140] 398 S.W.2d 93 (Tex. 1965).

[175] For a discussion of the legitimacy of using contract law to achieve distributional ends, see Kronman, Contract Law and Distributive Justice, 89 Yale L.J. 472 (1980).

Conclusion

Examination of the economic implications of promising reveals a tension between ideal and practical objectives. Because uncertainty cannot be eliminated, it may be tempting to resist systematization of expanding areas of liability. The suggestion that the results in individual cases can safely be predicted by employing a handful of simple economic tools is misguided. Economic concepts are useful, however, in specifying the effects of legal objectives and in observing and isolating systemic patterns of enforcement. The indeterminacy of empirical parameters necessitates the use of assumptions that only crudely approximate the true theoretical objectives. Often the effects of using estimates are unclear, as undetermined factors affect the behavior under examination.[177] Nonetheless, systematic collection and observation of data increases understanding of the regulation of behavior by legal rules.

We have assumed that the economic objective of regulating promises is to maximize the net beneficial reliance derived from promise-making activity. In general, this objective is best achieved by a scheme of promissory enforcement that induces adaptive behavior by the party better able to minimize the risk that future contingencies may materialize and cause the promisor to regret the announcement. Optimal adaptation requires a reduction in the prospective reliance on promising whenever this investment produces a greater decrease in expected harms from nonperformance. Both legal and extra-legal sanctions impose these social costs on the promising parties. Optimal legal sanctions are, therefore, a function of both the magnitude of these extra-legal factors and the parties' relative advantage in risk avoidance. The ideal liability choice ranges from zero enforcement to liability equal to the reasonable detrimental reliance caused by breach. However, because promissory reliance is peculiarly impervious to measurement, alternative rules are often applied as proxies for true reliance.

Promissory liability rules can be examined by classifying promises in three categories along principles of reciprocity and bargain. First, reciprocal promises are distinguishable from nonreciprocal promises on the basis of the ability of bargainers to adjust the volume and form of promising by varying the price of the promise. When such adjustments are not possible, promises are not enforced. Nonenforcement of gratuitous promises is justified because in the nonreciprocal setting, self-sanctions against breach are frequently effective, and promisees are often better able than promisors to adapt to the risks of regret. Second, the narrow consideration model defined by common law delineates a subdivision within the category of reciprocating promises. Enforcement is narrowly limited by assumptions that costs of promise-making are best reduced by precautions at the core of bargaining, and by reassurances on the periphery.

However, courts have used alternate theories of liability to expand enforcement appropriately beyond the confines of the consideration model. Promises have been enforced when increased accuracy, transactional efficiency, or bad faith justified the imposition of liability. These alternative bases of liability have been recently generalized into broad grants of judicial discretion. Although discretion permits the pursuit of distributional goals, it increases the uncertainty facing future bargainers. Absent careful articulation of distributional objectives, the social cost of uncertainty requires the development of clear rules for recoveries grounded on reliance.

---

[177] See Leff, Law and, 87 Yale L.J. 989, 1005-11 (1978).

Relationships As the Basis of Contract

Consent and promise play an indirect role of counterpoint in the writings of Ian Macneil, John Henry Wigmore Professor of Law at Northwestern University. Macneil is best known for his "relational" theory of contract. While his theory has roots both in the Legal Realism of the nineteen thirties and in the empirical research of Stewart Macaulay discussed in Part IA, Macneil can be thought of as an original. Macneil's first major discussions were in two 1974 articles, *The Many Futures of Contracts*, 47 S. Cal. L. Rev. 691 (1974), and *Restatement (Second) of Contracts and Presentiation*, 60 Va. L. Rev. 589 (1974). Between them, these articles total about 150 pages and set the foundation of the theory. Since then

Macneil has published many articles and a book-length group of lectures entitled *The New Social Contract* (1980).

Macneil defined contract as "the projection of exchange into the future," and argued that people project exchange by both promissory and non-promissory means. He distinguished "discrete" or "transactional" exchanges (essentially one-shot deals between relative strangers; his example is a tourist paying cash for gasoline on the Jersey Turnpike) from "relational" or "intertwined" dealings (long-term, and involving people who get to know one another and whose futures are bound together by their dealings; examples include employment, long-term supply contracts and marriage). In long-term relational dealings the parties cannot possibly anticipate every problem; they expect to have to work things out as the months or years go by.

However, "classical" contract law requires that all the terms be expressed (and consented to) at the moment of contracting. To describe this requirement, Macneil resurrected an old, largely forgotten theological term, "presentiation." (Innumerable proofreaders have well-meaningly "corrected" this to "presentation.") According to Macneil, presentiation may be possible to accomplish and may work fairly well in discrete, one-shot deals, but it clashes with the real needs of the parties in long-term relationships.

In an important corollary to his theory, Macneil argues that in a long-term relationship parties act out of more complex and less individualistic motives than the bloodless and faceless rational maximizers of classical economics and classical contract law. Other discussions relevant to this question include Macaulay's material in Part IA, the excerpt quoted from Sir James Fitzjames Stephen in the Atiyah article in this Part, the writing of Roberto Unger, immediately following Macneil, and the material in Part ID ("Other Voices").

Macneil, like many others, uses the term "classical" to refer to the highly formal approach to contract law associated with Christopher Columbus Langdell, Dean of Harvard Law School in the 1870's and inventor of the case method, Samuel Williston, whose great treatise on Contracts first appeared in 1920, and the First Restatement of Contracts, published in 1932. This formalistic approach was severely criticized by the Legal Realists, among them Karl Llewellyn, later the Chief Reporter of the Uniform Commercial Code, and especially by Arthur Corbin, whose own treatise, published in 1950, was the great rival of Williston's. (Corbin was close personally to Williston and worked with him on the First Restatement, but he always argued that formal rules had to give way to working rules based on how people acted in real life.) Macneil refers to the Corbin/Llewellyn approach as "neo-classical." It is reflected in Article Two of the Uniform Commercial Code, now the law in all states but Louisiana, and in the Second Restatement of Contracts, published in 1981. While it arguably has removed some of the excesses of classical contract law, Macneil argues that neo-classical contract law still is based on a model of a discrete transaction with terms presentiated at the magical moment of contracting. In the following article Macneil agrees that the UCC and the Second Restatement have ameliorated some of the problems of classical contract law, for example by permitting courts to supply omitted terms, by easing restrictions on modification by the parties after part performance, and by going past the moment of contracting in deciding when one party's failure to perform discharges the other. Nonetheless, Macneil argued that the "neoclassical system" is too wedded to traditional concepts. His comparison of neo-classical and relational ideas follows. Macneil's relational ideas are both part of and a sharp break with the continuum of contract theory. His refusal to treat consent to presentiated terms as indispensable is heresy to classical contract, but builds on neoclassicism; the same could be said for his attacks on self-interest as the controlling norm. Yet, his relational theory, dependent though it is on neoclassical theory, departs from it in its lack of fervor over freedom of contract and consent. (Contrast Professor Kessler's various contributions to Part IA; Kessler is very much the neoclassicist.) Nonetheless, Macneil fears the intrusion of big government ("Leviathan") into personal dealings. Much of

Macneil's more recent writing has been an attempt to resolve his skepticism about individual ordering through traditional contract law with his distaste for Leviathan.

In his more recent writings Macneil has pointed to solidarity among members of a community as an important source for the norms that ought to govern relational contracts. The concepts of community and solidarity are discussed in the note following this excerpt from Macneil.

Ian R. Macneil, *Contracts: Adjustment of Long-Term Economic Relations Under Classical, Neoclassical, and Relational Contract Law*, 72 Nw. U. L. Rev. 854 (1978)

. . .

Overview of the Limits of a Neoclassical Contract Law System As noted earlier, the two special norms of a classical contract law system are enhancement of discreteness, and expansion and intensification of presentation. Both of these norms aim toward ideals no social or legal system could ever come close to achieving; pure discreteness is an impossibility, as is pure presentation. Thus even the purest classical contract law system is itself a compromise; its spirit and its conceptual structures may be those of pure discreteness and presentation, but its details and its application never can be.

Even apart from these theoretical limitations of a classical contract law system, the limited extent to which it is possible for people to consent to all the terms of a transaction, even a relatively simple and very discrete one, soon forces the development of legal fictions expanding the scope of "consent" far beyond anything remotely close to what the parties ever had in mind. The greatest of these in American law is the objective theory of contract. The classical American contract is founded not upon actual consent but upon objective manifestations of intent. Moreover, in classical law manifestations of intent include whole masses of contract content one, or even both, parties did not know in fact. For example, ordinary run-of-the-mill purchasers of insurance are, in classical law, deemed to have consented not only to all the terms in the policy, which they did not read and could not have understood if they had, but also to all the interpreta-

tions the law would make of those terms. While in theory this enhances presentation (the law presumably being perfectly clear or at least struggling to be so), and may indeed have done so for the insurer, for the insured it commonly has precisely the opposite effect. Nevertheless, it is necessary to cram such absurdities into "objective consent" in order to avoid recognizing the relational characteristics of the system.

Neoclassical contract law partially, but only partially, frees itself of the foregoing difficulties. The freeing comes in the details, not in the overall structure. As suggested above, for example, the neoclassical system displays a good bit of flexibility in adjusting to change, and by no means always does so in terms of fictions about the original intent of the parties. Perhaps one of the most vivid examples of this is Restatement (Second) of Contracts, sections 241 and 242. These define when a failure to perform is material and when unperformed duties under a contract are discharged by the other party's uncured material failure to perform (or offer to perform). Section 242 lists seven circumstances significant in determining the time when the injured party is discharged:

1. the extent to which the injured party will be deprived of the benefit which he reasonably expected;

2. the extent to which the injured party can be adequately compensated for the part of that benefit of which he will be deprived;

Reprinted by special permission of Northwestern University, School of Law, 72, Northwestern University Law Review, 854, (1978).

3. the extent to which the party failing to perform or to offer to perform will suffer forfeiture;

4. the likelihood that the party failing to perform or to offer to perform will cure his failure, taking account of all the circumstances including any reasonable assurances;

5. the extent to which the behavior of the party failing to perform or to offer to perform comports with standards of good faith and fair dealing;

6. the extent to which it reasonably appears to the injured party that delay may prevent or hinder him in making reasonable substitute arrangements;

7. the extent to which the agreement provides for performance without delay, but a material failure to perform or to offer to perform on a stated day does not of itself discharge the other party's remaining duties unless the circumstances, including the language of the agreement, indicate that performance or tender by that day is important.

Of the seven factors, four (3,4,5, and 6) clearly focus on circumstances at the time of the difficulties, rather than following the presentation approach and trying to key back to the original agreement. An element of that is also present in the others. In 1 and 2 "the benefit he reasonably expected" appears to permit more consideration of post-agreement circumstances than would, for example, the phrase "what he was promised." And 7 puts a burden on the injured party to show that timely performance was important beyond simply providing initially in the contract that performance be without delay. (That is only one of the circumstances to be considered.) This too is anti-presentation.

The burgeoning concept of good faith, in large measure within the neoclassical framework, is another largely anti-presentiating, and very much anti-discrete, concept.

But neoclassical contract law can free itself only partially from the limitations posed by obeisance to the twin classical goals of discreteness and presentation. This obeisance is imposed by adherence to an overall structure founded on full consent at the time of initial contracting. As long as such adherence continues, *i.e.*, as long as it remains a neoclassical system, there are limits to the ignoring of discreteness and presentation in favor, for example, of such factors as those listed above respecting Restatement (Second) of Contracts § 242. Nevertheless, the constantly increasing role of ongoing contractual relations in the American economy continues to put immense pressure on the legal system to respond in relational ways.

In the past such pressures have led to the spin-off of many subject areas from the classical, and later the neoclassical, contract law system, *e.g.*, much of corporate law and collective bargaining (to say nothing of marriage, which was never really in). They have thus led to a vast shrinkage of the areas of socioeconomic activity to which the neoclassical system applies.[101] As the earlier discussion in this paper indicates, they have also led to very significant changes leading to the transformation of the Willistonian classical system to what might be called the Realist neoclassical system. The spin-offs can and will continue.

Equally likely, the neoclassical system will continue to evolve in relational directions, while courts and scholars still strive to keep it within the overall classical structure. (This is especially likely in first-year contracts courses in many American law schools and in the casebooks and texts aimed at first-year contracts students and their teachers.) The spin-offs will, however, render the system, as a total system, of less and less practical interest. At the same time, trying to squeeze increasing relational content into the neoclassical system will encounter the same kinds of strains some of my generation are finding in trying to put on the older parts of their wardrobes. Thus, rewards of expanding the neoclassical system will decrease at the same time that intellectual and perhaps other costs of doing so increase.

Elsewhere, I have suggested the possibility that a more encompassing conceptual structure of contract jurisprudence may emerge from the situation just described. Part of such a structure must focus on the issues raised by this paper, adjustment of long-term contractual relations. The concluding section of this paper will deal with some of the consequences of slipping the bounds of the classical contract system alto-

---

[101] See L. Friedman, Contract Law in America (1965); Macneil, Whither Contracts?, 21 J. Legal Educ. 403 (1969). The mistake is sometimes made of concluding that because a subject area has spun off and is widely considered to be a special area, that all elements underlying the classical or neoclassical system disappear from the area. There are hints, or more, of this in G. Gilmore, the Death of Contract (1974), and Friedman & Macaulay, Contract Law and Contract Teaching: Past, Present, and Future, 1967 Wis. L. Rev. 805. . . . Nothing could be farther from the truth. Discreteness and presentation are ever with us in the modern world and will continue to be so; the fact that we now recognize them as integrated into ongoing relations does not eliminate them. . . .

gether, of reducing discreteness and presentation from dominant roles to roles equal or often subordinate to relational norms such as preserving the relation and harmonization of all aspects of the relation, whether discrete or relational.

Contractual Relations: Relational Contract Law

The introduction to the preceding section carefully limits that section to situations where "it is clear that" the long-term economic relations in question are "*between* firms rather than *within* a firm." The situations treated there were, "even in traditional terms, contracts." Such a limitation is unnecessary in introducing the present section. Interfirm contractual relations follow the kinds of patterns discussed here—*e.g.*, in a long-term consortium—but more typical relations of this nature would include such structures as the internal workings of corporations, including relations among management, employees, and stockholders. Corporate relations with long-and short-term creditors, law firms, accounting firms, and managerial and financial consultants may also acquire many of the characteristics discussed and increasingly seem to do so. Collective bargaining, franchising, condominiums, universities, trade unions themselves, large shopping centers, and retirement villages with common facilities of many kinds are other examples now existent. If present trends continue, undoubtedly we shall see new examples, now perhaps entirely unforeseen.

As noted earlier, discreteness and presentation do not disappear from life or law simply because ongoing contractual relations become the organizational mode dominating economic activity. Because they remain with us and because they drastically affect contractual relations, this section will start with an analysis of their role in ongoing relations.

Presentiation and Discreteness in Contractual Relations

However important flexibility for change becomes in economic relations, great need will nevertheless always remain for fixed and reliable planning. Or in the terms emphasized here, presentiation will always occur in economic relations, since it tends to follow planning as a matter of course. Nor does a modern technological economy permit the demise of discreteness. Very specialized products and services, the hallmark of such an economy, produce a high degree of discreteness of behavior, even though their production and use are closely integrated into ongoing relations. When, for example, an automobile manufacturer orders from another manufacturer with which it regularly deals, thousands of piston rings of a specified size, no amount of relational softening of discreteness and presentation will obscure the disaster occurring if the wrong size shows up on the auto assembly line. Nor would the disaster be any less if the failure had occurred in an even more relational pattern, *e.g.*, if the rings had been ordered from another division of the auto manufacturer. Both discreteness and presentation must be served in such an economic process, whether it is carried out between firms by discrete separate orders, between firms under long-established blanket contracts, or within the firm.

Even apart from high demands for reliable planning in a technological society, discreteness is a characteristic inherent in human perception. Moreover, as I have suggested elsewhere, any given "present situation," no matter what its origin, tends to be perceived as highly discrete compared to what lies in the past and what is to come in the future. Thus, the status quo, whatever it is, inevitably has about it a fairly high level of discreteness. This fact, coupled with the human propensity to presentiate on the basis of what is currently in the forefront of the mind, creates strong expectations of the future consistent with status quo. Such expectations tend to be very strong. It is impossible to overstress this phenomenon—it describes not only the conservatism of the nineteenth century Russian peasant but also the intense commitment to change and growth where patterns of change and growth constitute the status quo, *e.g.*, the tenacity in America to patterns of constantly increasing energy consumption.

Expectations created by the above processes can be, and often are, of a magnitude and tenacity as great or greater than those created by good, old-fashioned discrete transactional contracts. Thus, when the phenomenon occurs in contractual relations, any tolerable contract law system must necessarily pay attention to at least some implementation of this kind of discreteness and presentation.

In view of the foregoing, the need for a contract law system enhancing discreteness and presentiation will never disappear. Moreover, it is possible, even likely, that a neoclassical contract law system will continue in existence to deal with those genuine needs. Such a system will, however, continue to rub in an unnecessarily abrasive manner against the realities of coexistence with relational needs for flexibility and change. Only when the parts of the contract law system implementing discreteness and presentation are perceived, intellectually and otherwise, not as an independent system, but only as integral parts of much larger systems, will unnecessary abrasion disappear. By no means will all abrasion disappear, of course, because real conflict exists between the need for reliability of planning and the need for flexibility in economic relations. What will disappear is the abrasion resulting from application of contract law founded on the assumption that all of a contractual relation is encompassed in some original assent to it, where that assumption is manifestly false. The elimination of that assumption not only would eliminate the unnecessary abrasion but also would remove the penultimate classical characteristic justifying calling a contract law system neoclassical.[109]

What replaces the neoclassical system when, and if, all that remains of classical contract law are discreteness and presentation-enhancing segments of far larger systems, segments perhaps often playing roles subordinate to countless other goals, including those of achieving flexibility and change? The remainder of this paper is an introduction to possible answers to that question.

Processes for Flexibility and Change in Contractual Relations

Change, whether caused by forces beyond social control or actively sought, appears to be a permanent characteristic of modern technological societies. Willy-nilly, flexibility comes along with the phenomenon, since the only alternative is a breakdown of the society. But there are processes of flexibility beyond simply bending with each wind of change on an ad hoc basis. Indeed, we have already seen many such processes respecting contracts and have explored the response to them of a neoclassical legal system. We shall look at them again here to see the response of a legal system which is more frankly relational and which has cast off conceptual obeisance to discreteness and presentation by some all-encompassing original assent. Although no such system as yet exists in American law, I shall speak in the present tense; this is justified, perhaps, by the existence of specific terms of contract law, such as collective bargaining, coming close to the patterns described.

The most important processes used for maintaining flexibility are those of exchange itself, whether the sharply focused bargaining characteristic of labor contract renewals or the subtle interplays of day-to-day activities, or a host of other forms taken by exchange. These patterns of exchange take place against the power and normative positions in which the parties find themselves.[110] This means that exchange patterns occur, *inter alia*, against the background of the discrete and presentiated aspects of the relations, whether those aspects were created by explicit prior planning, other existential circumstances, or combinations thereof. This requires harmonization of changes with such a status quo but does not require doctrines such as the doctrine of consideration . . . . There is, however, a substantial difference. In the neoclassical system, the reference point for those questions about the change tends to be the original agreement. In a truly relational approach the reference point is the entire relation as it had developed to the time of the change in question (and in many instances as it has developed since the change). This may or may not include an "original agreement"; and if it does, may or may not result in great deference being given it.

Since contractual relations, such as the employment relation, commonly involve vertical or command-and-subordinate positions of an ongoing nature, *e.g.*, the vice-president in charge of plant operations and his subordinates, much change is brought about by command. As the commands inevitably relate to exchange, as in an order to an employee to report for overtime work, they are techniques for achieving change through nonhorizontal processes, in contrast to those of agreed-upon, horizontal exchange. Again, a relational contract system implements, modifies, or refuses to implement such commands only in the overall context of the whole relation.

When the conflict levels in exchange processes, wherever they may lie on the command-horizontal spectrum, exceed the resolution capacity of bargaining and other exchange processes, other techniques

[109] Penultimate, not ultimate. If we think of the classical contract law system as the antithesis of the status contractual relations of primitive societies—as I believe Maine did in his famous statement about the move from status to contract—one vital characteristic of the classical contract system will remain: the great effect given to planning. Rightly or wrongly we do not think of primitive societies as engaging in a great deal of planning beyond that arising from habit, custom, mores, and customary law of the society. However accurate or inaccurate this view of primitive societies may be, it is a completely inaccurate view of modern technological society with its immense, indeed insatiable, demands for planning and performance of planning. Thus, as already noted, a relational, post-neoclassical contract law system will necessarily retain in context a large measure of the respect for presentiation and discreteness shown by the classical system.

[110] See generally Eisenberg, Private Ordering Through Negotiation: Dispute-Settlement and Rulemaking, 89 Harv. L. Rev. 637 (1976).

of dispute resolution must be utilized. Here we find the most dramatic change from the classical or even neoclassical litigation (or rights arbitration) models. Their function is to put an end to the dispute; and, since resolution of the dispute is all that remains of the discrete transaction, the process is a relatively simple and clean one. This process is rather like the discrete transaction itself: sharp in (by commencing suit) and sharp out (by judgment for defendant or collection of a money judgment by plaintiff).[116] Professor Chayes has recently described this model:

(1) The lawsuit is *bipolar*. Litigation is organized as a contest between two individuals or at least two unitary interests, diametrically opposed, to be decided on a winner-takes-all basis.

(2) Litigation is *retrospective*. The controversy is about an identified set of completed events: whether they occurred, and if so, with what consequences for the legal relations of the parties.

(3) *Right and remedy are interdependent*. The scope of the relief is derived more or less logically from the substantive violation under the general theory that the plaintiff will get compensation measured by the harm caused by the defendant's breach of duty—in contract by giving plaintiff the money he would have had absent the breach; in tort by paying the value of the damage caused.

(4) The lawsuit is a *self-contained* episode. The impact of the judgment is confined to the parties. If plaintiff prevails there is a simple compensatory transfer, usually of money, but occasionally the return of a thing or the performance of a definite act. If defendant prevails, a loss lies where it has fallen. In either case, entry of judgment ends the court's involvement.

(5) The process is *party-initiated* and *party-controlled*. The case is organized and the issues defined by exchanges between the parties. Responsibility for fact development is theirs. The trial judge is a neutral arbiter of their interactions who decides questions of law only if they are put in issue by an appropriate move of a party.[117]

Naturally, no such model will do when the relation is supposed to continue in spite of the dispute, and where a main goal must always be its successful carrying on after the dispute is resolved or otherwise eliminated or avoided.

Professor Chayes went on to develop a morphology of what he terms "public law litigation." Although he does not direct this morphology at contract disputes, I have found it helpful in organizing my thoughts about the processes of dispute resolution in contractual relations. (So modified it focuses on the processes of change in such relations when bargaining and other exchange processes fail.) The following is his morphology, modified where appropriate for use in contractual relations.

1. The scope of the dispute is not exogenously given by contract terms but is shaped by both the parties and the resolver of the dispute—*e.g.*, the arbitrator—and by the entire relation as it has developed and is developing.

2. The party structure is not rigidly bilateral but sprawling and amorphous.

3. The fact inquiry is not only historical and adjudicative but also predictive and legislative.

4. Relief is not conceived primarily (or sometimes at all) as compensation for past wrong in a form logically derived from the substantive liability and confined in its impact to the immediate parties; instead, it is in great (or even entire) measure forward looking, fashioned ad hoc on flexible and broadly remedial lines, often having important consequences for many persons, including absentees.

5. The remedy is not imposed but negotiated and mediated.

6. The award does not terminate the dispute-resolver's role in the relation; instead, the award will require continuing administration by this or other similarly situated dispute-resolvers.

7. The dispute-resolver is not passive, that is, his function is not limited to analysis and statement of governing rules; he is active, with responsibility not only for credible fact evaluation but also for organizing and shaping the dispute processes to ensure a just and viable outcome.

8. The subject matter of the dispute is not between private individuals about private rights but is a grievance about the operation of policies of the overall contractual relation.

In almost every respect the foregoing approaches contrast sharply with a classical contract law system and with the conceptual assumptions of a neoclassical system. For example, two ways by which a classical

---

[116] This is, of course, a parody, especially the very last point. Contrary to the fantasies of the law school classroom, the real beginning of many contract dispute cases won by plaintiffs comes after rendering of a judgment. Then the

deficiencies of execution, and with it the legal remedial system itself, become apparent.

[117] Chayes, The Role of the Judge in Public Law Litigation, 89 Harv. L. Rev. 1281, 1282-83 (1976) (footnotes omitted) (emphasis in original).

contract law system implements its goals of enhancing discreteness and presentation are by limiting strictly the sources considered in establishing the substantive content of the transaction in resolving disputes and by utilizing strictly defined (and narrow) remedies. Both of these methods sharply conflict with the relational approaches outlined above. Similarly, although the neoclassical system can accomplish some of the flexibility of these relational patterns, and utilizes some of them, in toto the patterns go far beyond it. In the neoclassical system the parol evidence rule is hardly dead; the fact inquiry is nowhere nearly as wide-ranging; development of flexible and broad remedies is modest indeed; at the end of the day, remedies are imposed, rather than simply negotiated and mediated until some kind of uneasy (and probably temporary) consensus is reached; more often than not a dispute-resolver does expect to wipe his hands of the matter after the appropriate remedy has been determined; the dispute-resolver, at least when he is a judge, tends to remain passive; and the subject matter of dispute often tends to remain, at least formally and often more substantially, between clear poles of interest and polar rights, rather than overall policies of the contractual relation.

The sharp contrast between the classical (and even neoclassical) limitation of sources of substantive content mentioned above and the broad ranging inquiries of a relational system brings us to a key question concerning the interplay of presentiated and discrete aspects of relations with their nondiscrete, nonpresentiated aspects. The premise of the classical system is that no interplay could occur, because all aspects of the contract are presentiated and discrete. This premise continues to underlie the structure of the neoclassical system, but in actual operation that system shifts to a presumption in favor of limitation, although one subject to considerable erosion. In implementing their premises both classical and neoclassical contract law establish hierarchies for determining content (as noted earlier). Formal communications such as writings control informal communications; linguistic communications control nonlinguistic communications; communicated circumstances control noncommunicated circumstances; and finally utilization of noncommunicated circumstances is always suspect.

Do such hierarchies continue in a relational system? The answer is both yes and no. To the extent that presentiated and discrete aspects of contractual relations are created by written documents, they may reflect very sharp focus of party attention and strong

intentions to be governed by them in the future. Certainly the wage and seniority structures in most collective bargaining agreements exemplify this. Thus, such documents may occupy very dominant positions in the priorities of values of the relation. When this is the case, something analogous to the classical notions previously set out may very properly be applied by the dispute-resolver. There is, however, one big difference. In a system of relational contract law the simple existence of formal communications does not automatically trigger application of the neoclassical hierarchy of presumptions. Rather, a preliminary question must always be asked: do the formal communications indeed reflect the sharp past focus and strong intentions necessary to put these communications high in the priorities of values created by the contractual relation? This question can be answered only by looking at the whole relation, not in the grudging manner of the neoclassical system, but as the very foundation for proceeding further with the hierarchical assumptions, or without them, or with other hierarchies. (An example of the latter occurs in marital disputes: nonlinguistic conduct and informal communications typically far outweigh in importance for resolving such disputes any formal agreements—except sometimes as to property—the parties may have made.)

I feel some temptation to think of the written parts of contractual relations, especially very formal parts, such as collective bargaining agreements and corporate charters and bylaws, as constitutions establishing legislative and administrative processes for the relation. Indeed, that is what many of them are. Nevertheless, danger lurks in this formulation. The danger lies in reintroducing into the law of contractual relations such things as the hierarchies discussed above—not on an ad hoc basis but as a matter of general principle emanating from the concept of "constitution." If that concept or terminology is used to resurrect "constitutions" long decayed and made obsolete by less formally established patterns of communications and behavior, we are, as a matter of principle, back to a relationally dysfunctional neoclassicism. Moreover, only one party or class of parties may know the content of these "constitutions," and they may suffer from other adhesion characteristics. In such circumstances giving them constitutional weight may be very dubious indeed.

This brief treatment of processes of flexibility and change in contractual relations can now serve as a background for consideration of characteristics of substantive change in contractual relations.

The Substance of Change in Contractual Relations

All aspects of contractual relations are subject to the norms characterizing contracts generally, whether they are discrete or relational. As noted earlier these are: (1) permitting and encouraging participation in exchange, (2) promoting reciprocity, (3) reinforcing role patterns appropriate to the various particular kinds of contracts, (4) providing limited freedom for exercise of choice, (5) effectuating planning, and (6) harmonizing the internal and external matrixes of particular contracts. These norms affect change in contractual relations just as they affect all their other aspects.

In addition, I have identified two norms particularly applicable to contractual relations: (1) harmonizing conflict within the internal matrix of the relation, including especially, discrete and presentiated behavior with nondiscrete and nonpresentiated behavior; and (2) preservation of the relation. These norms affect change in contractual relations, just as they affect all their aspects.

A great deal of change in ongoing contractual relations comes about glacially, through small-scale, day-to-day adjustments resulting from an interplay of horizontally arranged exchange—*e.g.*, workers creating new ways of cooperatively defining their work or minor changes in the way in which deliveries are made—and from the flow of day-to-day commands through the vertical patterns of the relation. In addition, within a broad range, change will come about through commands of a more sweeping nature, *e.g.*, to sell the appliance division of the firm or develop a major new line of products. This is, of course, focused change and raises all kinds of problems, not the least of which involve the two relational norms. Moreover, command changes of this magnitude in a modern society almost invariably overlap areas that must be dealt with by horizontal arrangements, *e.g.*, the terms of the collective bargaining agreement governing severance or transfer of old employees and the hiring of new employees. Finally, there are horizontal changes in contractual relations themselves partially or wholly horizontal in origin. If, for example, we consider a collective bargaining agreement as an arrangement separate from the firm itself (by my lights, a somewhat artificial thing to do), the shifting of a major part of a wage increase from cash into layoff compensation would constitute a focused horizontal change.[128]

Similarly, a consortium of businesses determining whether to go into a new line of activity would be engaged in horizontally focused change. We have thus far considered change coming about either through gradual accretion, through command operating within acceptable limits of the relation, or through successful negotiation and agreement. While these offer many problems for a relational contract system and its related legal structure, the big *legal* difficulties come when change is pushed that has failed to come about in those ways. What happens when this occurs?

In answering that question it is well to remember that we are dealing with situations where the desire is to continue the relation, not to terminate it. Moreover, my sense is that normally the most important factor is the status quo; that is to say, that the dispute-resolver will be conservative and will not move far from the status quo. This is borne out by the sense of arbitrators experienced in "interest arbitration" that the base point of such arbitration is the presentiated status quo. Anyone interested in change through the dispute-resolution process has a heavy burden of persuasion. Dispute-resolution processes governed by the norm of continuing the relation are, if this view is correct, essentially conservative.

The foregoing conclusion does not lead to the conclusion that change will not result from this kind of interest-dispute-resolution process. Anyone the least familiar with arbitration of public employee interest disputes knows this. The very fact that a party is willing to press this far suggests in most cases a basis for some change, although bargaining being what it is, probably not as much as the aggressive party tries to get. Moreover, status quo in a dynamic society does not mean a static status quo; as noted earlier in another connection, the status quo itself may very well be one in which changes in a certain direction are expected. If they do not come or come less than expected, then the interest-dispute-resolver is faced with a situation where the status quo calls for change, not for simply sticking to patterns now viewed as obsolete.[131]

---

[128] In the growth society of the past 40 years, such patterns have largely dealt with increments to the wage package, and hence their nature as a fundamental change has been somewhat disguised. In a no-growth or slow-growth society, trade-offs may have to be made between existing cash wages and fringe benefits. Such trade-offs will indeed be perceived as changes. [Macneil's 1978 prediction was borne out in the 1980's —ed.]

[131] "In some cases, such as wages, change over time actually becomes the norm, so that a party who resists an accustomed change may be perceived as himself the proponent of change." Eisenberg, supra note 110, at 676 n. 122.

Exploration of the other relational norm—harmonizing conflicts within the internal social matrix of the relation—reinforces the foregoing conclusions. Such harmonization is unlikely to come through revolutionary changes that conflicting interests have been unable to accede to through negotiation or mediation. Changes typically can be harmonized with the remainder of the relation only by making them consistent with the status quo, again a conservative notion. But it must be noted that if the status quo is a dynamic one moving over time in certain directions-e.g., increasing levels of real wages—change in accord with those patterns is essential to preserve the status quo itself. This is the kind of harmonization we should expect from a dispute-resolver implementing this norm.

My work on developing general contractual norms and relational norms has progressed slowly since *The Many Futures of Contracts*. Certainly other norms besides the two mentioned will have a bearing on change in a system of relational contract law. Two categories should be mentioned, the first of which will have a ring of familiarity to all students of contracts: the restitution, reliance and expectation interests. In a system of discrete transactions, it is now generally accepted that protection of these three interests constitutes a basic norm of contract law. This does not change as we move from classical to neoclassical contract law and on to relational contract law; such interests remain fundamental.

One important change, however, does occur. In classical contract law it is expectations created solely by defined promises and reliance on defined promises that are protected. Only the restitution interest had a broader foundation, and restitution fitted uneasily in the structure of classical contract law, often being conceptualized as not part of that law at all. In neoclassical contract law the expectation and reliance interests remain based primarily on promise, although exceptions do exist. For example, *Drennan v. Star Paving Co.*[134] can be read as holding that reliance on something (industry patterns or common decency?) created the promise rather than the other way around. Restitution, increasingly recognized in neoclassical contract law as an integral part of the system (again perhaps slightly uneasily), stands out as perhaps the least promise-oriented part of the system. In this sense restitution paves the way for treatment of the three contract interests in relational contract law. No longer are those interests bottomed primarily on defined promises, nor are efforts necessary to squeeze them within promissory contexts. In such a system recognition is easily accorded to the creation of such interests arising naturally from *any* behavior patterns within the relation. Substantive changes in relations must therefore take into account the three basic contract interests of restitution, reliance, and expectations, irrespective of their sources.

As illustrative of the foregoing, consider an employee of a small business who has been treated very decently by his employer for thirty years. He quite naturally comes to expect decent treatment throughout the relation including through retirement. Moreover, he relies on that expectation; and if the expectation is not realized, the employer may very well have derived benefits from the reliance by the employee that, in terms of the relation as it existed, are unjustified. We can, and do, infer promises in such situations, but they are far from the defined promises of discrete transactions. Moreover, something besides promise lies behind the social desiderata of seeing that these interests of the employee do not go unprotected. Expectations, as noted earlier, are a form of presentiation however they may be created. When they are reasonable under the circumstances, irrespective of how the circumstances were created, societies tend to be very loath to see them thwarted. An already mentioned example is the reluctance of virtually all of American society to accept even the temporary thwarting of post-World War II expectations of continued economic growth.

The final category of relational norm to be considered here is very open-ended. As contractual relations expand, those relations take on more and more the characteristics of minisocieties and ministates. Indeed, even that is an understatement. In the case of huge bundles of contractual relations, such as a major national or multinational corporation, they take on the characteristics of large societies and large states. But whether small or large, the whole range of social and political norms become pertinent *within* the contractual relations. In ongoing contractual relations we find such broad norms as distributive justice, liberty, human dignity, social equality and inequality, and procedural justice, to mention some of the more vital. Changes in such contractual relations must accord with norms established respecting these matters, just as much as they do the more traditional

---

[134] 51 Cal. 2d 409, 333 P.2d 757 (1958).

contract norms. Changes made ignoring this fact may be very disruptive indeed.[137]

Termination of Contractual Relations

Termination of contractual relations is an extremely complex subject, far too complex to do more than touch here. Nevertheless a number of points should be made. One is that, unlike discrete transactions, many contractual relations are, for all practical purposes, expected never to end. IBM, the relation between the United Auto Workers and General Motors, and Harvard University are expected to go on forever. Even in the face of great trouble, relations of this kind often do not end, but continue on in new forms; *e.g.*, Northeast Airlines is merged into Delta, or rail passenger service is transferred to Amtrak, along with physical facilities, the labor force, and much of the management. The realities of such transformations often evoke processes very similar to relational patterns of change already discussed, rather than clean-cut application of clear rights and obligations in the discrete transactional tradition.

Of course, many long-term contractual relations are recognized (by outsiders, if not always by the participants) as vulnerable to traumatic termination. Small businesses, branch plant operations of large businesses, and in part, marriages, clubs, and many franchises, serve as illustrations. Depending in part on the relations themselves and in part on such external factors as their importance to the community and the political heft of various of their participants, their termination may or may not be treated by the legal system in relational ways, procedurally or substantively.[139] To the extent that they are treated relationally, their terminations will be similar to those massive contractual relations that had not been expected to end at all.

On the other hand, many long-term contractual relations are, from the start, expected to terminate. A small partnership expecting not to take in new members, or marriage without progeny are examples. Many business consortiums are of this nature. When such relations terminate traumatically early, their treatment will follow patterns already discussed. When they follow the expected course, the legal system will treat their termination as it does other aspects of the relation. Some discrete aspects may be given effect; *e.g.*, legacies to the widow will be enforced explicitly. Some aspects may instead invoke relational norms; *e.g.*, the widow, even by will or maybe even by mutual agreement, cannot be cut out of the estate entirely or lose her rights in community property.

A final point to be made is the distinction between termination of a contractual relation and termination of an individual's participation in a contractual relation. Sometimes the two coincide, *e.g.*, the death of a spouse in a childless marriage. But contractual relations outside the nuclear family tend in modern society to be multiperson and to survive the departure or death of individual participants. Further, typically it is the ongoing relation rather than the individual that is the more powerful of the two. Where, as in employment, this fact is coupled with a high degree of dependency of the individual on the particular relation, we are likely to find considerable protection of that dependency. Such protection may grow up internally (*e.g.*, through collective bargaining), may perhaps be coerced in considerable measure from outside (*e.g.*, labor laws and tax provisions favoring pensions), or may simply be imposed (*e.g.*, mandatory contributions by both employer and employee to Social Security). In sum, terminations of long-term contractual relations tend to be like other aspects of relations, messily relational rather than cleanly transactional.

Summary

A system of discrete transactions and its corresponding classical contract law provides for flexibility and change through the market outside the transac-

---

[137] At this point, just as contractual relations exceed the capacities of the neoclassical contract law system, so too the issues exceed the capacities of neoclassical contract law scholars. They must become something else—anthropologists, sociologists, economists, political theorists, and philosophers—to do reasonable justice to the issues raised by contractual relations. Exchange and planning, the basic areas of expertise of the contracts scholar, have now become just two of the many factors in a complete social organism.

[139] E.g., McGrath v. Hilding, 41 N.Y. 2d 625, 363 N. E. 2d 328, 394 N.Y.S. 2d 603 (1977). Plaintiff divorced defendant after three months of marriage and remarried her former husband. During the brief marriage plaintiff contrib-

uted money to building an addition to defendant's house relying on an oral premarital promise to give her a tenancy by the entirety. The promise was not performed, and plaintiff sought equitable relief based on a constructive trust. The lower courts rejected as collateral defendant's offer to prove marital misconduct by plaintiff. The New York Court of Appeals remanded for a new trial, stating that whether defendant's enrichment was unjust could not be determined by inquiring only about an "isolated transaction." Rather it must be a "realistic determination based on a broad view of the human setting involved." Id. at 629, 363 N.E.2d at 331, 394 N.Y.S.2d at 606.

tions, rather than within them. This enables the system to work while the transactions themselves remain highly discrete and presentiated, characteristics preserved and enhanced by classical contract law.

A system of more relational contract and its corresponding neoclassical contract law remains theoretically structured on the discrete and classical models, but involves significant changes. Such contracts, being more complex and of greater duration than discrete transactions, become dysfunctional if too rigid, thereby preventing the high level of presentiation of the discrete transaction. Thus, flexibility, often a great deal of it, needs to be planned into such contracts, or gaps need to be left in the planning to be added as needed. The neoclassical system responds to this by a range of techniques. These run from some open evasion of its primary theoretical commitment to complete presentiation through initial consent on to the more common techniques of stretching consent far beyond its actual bounds and by fictions to squeeze later changes within an initial consent framework.

Somewhere along the line of increasing duration and complexity, trying to force changes into a pattern of original consent becomes both too difficult and too unrewarding to justify the effort, and the contractual relation escapes the bounds of the neoclassical system. That system is replaced by very different adjustment processes of an ongoing-administrative kind in which discreteness and presentiation become merely two of the factors of decision, not the theoretical touchstones. Moreover, the substantive relation of change to the status quo has now altered from what happens in some kind of a market external to the contract to what can be achieved through the political and social processes of the relation, internal and external. This includes internal and external dispute-resolution structures. At this point, the relation has become a minisociety with a vast array of norms beyond the norms centered on exchange and its immediate processes.

Community and Solidarity—Thoughts From Roberto Unger and Patricia Williams

While Ian Macneil is temperamentally distant from the Critical Legal Studies movement, some of his ideas about community and solidarity are not far removed from those of Roberto Mangabeira Unger, the leading theoretician of CLS. Professor Unger was born in South America of European parents. He has published two important books of legal/political/moral/social philosophy, *Knowledge and Politics* and *Law in Modern Society*. He is allied with the Critical Legal Studies movement, and uses some of the methods of "deconstruction" that are popular with CLS. Deconstruction (or "trashing")— is a process of reasoning that is derived from modern French literary theory, particularly that of Jacques Derrida. For an extended discussion of the process, see Jack M. Balkin, *Deconstructive Practice and Legal Theory*, 96 Yale L.J. 743 (1987). However, even under the broad umbrella of CLS, Roberto Unger must be viewed as an original thinker who should not be labeled. Opinions about Unger vary. For a very hostile review, see Ewell, *Unger's Philosophy: A Critical Legal Study*, 97 Yale L.J. 665 (1988). For a defense, see West, *Critical Legal Studies and a Liberal Critic*, 97 Yale L.J. 757 (1988) and other authorities cited in the Ewell article. An even more recent exchange involves Stanley Fish's *Unger and Milton,* 1988 Duke L.J. 975 and H. Jefferson Powell's *The Gospel According to Roberto: A Theological Polemic,* 1988 Duke L.J. 1013.

In 1982 Professor Unger gave a talk to the annual meeting of the Conference on Critical Legal Studies; an expanded version of that talk was published by the Harvard Law Review the following year under the title *The Critical Legal Studies Movement*, 96 Harv. L. Rev. 561 (1983). It has also appeared in book form. The full 115-page article is concerned with the function of the critical approach in all aspects of society, political as well as legal. Within the article Unger has a long discussion of contracts that fairly well explains his "countervision" that community and fairness are more important than freedom of contract and freedom to contract. Some idea of what he is saying and how he says it may be gathered from the following paragraphs, which appear at 96 Harv. L. Rev. 644-45 and 646:

One of [the two especially prominent controlling themes internal to doctrinal analysis] has been the criticism of the stark contrast between contract and community. The starting points of this contrast are a conception of community, as an idyllic haven of harmony, and contract, as a realm of unadulterated self-interest and pure calculation. The actual effect of the contrast, however, is often to accept and to foster the confusion of mutual loyalty with acquiescence in a regime of personalistic power while depriving the elements of trust and interdependence in business life of appropriate legal help. The arrangements and ideas capable of correcting these effects begin by effacing the sharpness of the opposition between contract and community. They end by suggesting a view of contract that can more readily accommodate both a broad range of different sorts of rights or obligations and a conception of community, as a zone of heightened mutual vulnerability, that gives a more satisfactory account of what attracts us to the communal ideal in the first place.

The other major theme of moral vision in my discussion of contract theory has been the search for the conditions under which a regime of contract can avoid becoming the disguise of a power order without being constantly overridden by correction. . . . [His solution] invites a transformation of the institutional basis of economic life and a variety of subversive though ultimately inadequate surrogates for this transformation.

. . .

Revolutions in social life will not be produced by doctrinal breakthroughs even when these breakthroughs influence, as they rightly do, our insight into existing institutions and regnant ideas, the course of ideological debate, and the exercise of judicial authority. When my argument later turns to the critical legal studies movement as a form of political action, it will show that expanded doctrine has a practical task to accomplish both in society at large and in the narrow, subsidiary arena of adjudication.

For another extended critical analysis of contract, see Clare Dalton's *An Essay on the Deconstruction of Contract Doctrine,* 94 Yale L.J. 997 (1985).

Professor Patricia J. Williams is an Associate Professor of Law at the University of Wisconsin. In 1987, while teaching at the CUNY Law School at Queens College, she contributed the following article to a symposium of minority critiques of CLS in the Harvard Civil Right-Civil Liberties Law Review. The article is not primarily about contracts; instead it is an imaginative, thoughtful and particularly well-written consideration of the CLS hostility to rights-based legal analysis, in which Professor Williams considers the many roots that nourish her as a graduate of Wellesley and Harvard Law School who is also the descendent of humans who were bought and sold as slaves. The following short excerpt contrasts her attitudes toward contract-making with those of Peter Gabel, whose essay with Jay Feinman was reprinted in Part IA. It also includes her conclusion.

Patricia J. Williams, *Alchemical Notes: Reconstructing Ideals From Deconstructed Rights*, 22 Harv. CR-CL L. Rev. 401 (1987)

. . .

II. A Tale With Two Stories

A. *Mini-Story* (In Which Peter Gabel and I Set Out to Teach Contracts in the Same Boat While Rowing in Phenomenological Opposition)

Some time ago, Peter Gabel[11] and I taught a contracts class together. Both recent transplants from California to New York, each of us hunted for apartments in between preparing for class and ultimately found places within one week of each other. Inevitably, I suppose, we got into a discussion of trust and distrust as factors in bargain relations. It turned out that Peter had handed over a $900 deposit, in cash, with no lease, no exchange of keys and no receipt, to strangers with whom he had no ties other than a few moments of pleasant conversation.[12] Peter said that he didn't need to sign a lease because it imposed too much formality. The handshake and the good vibes were for him indicators of trust more binding than a distancing form contract. At the time, I told Peter I thought he was stark raving mad, but his faith paid off. His sublessors showed up at the appointed time, keys in hand, to welcome him in. Needless to say, there was absolutely nothing in my experience to prepare me for such a happy ending.

I, meanwhile, had friends who found me an apartment in a building they owned. In *my* rush to show good faith and trustworthiness, I signed a detailed, lengthily-negotiated, finely-printed lease firmly establishing me as the ideal arm's length transactor.

As Peter and I discussed our experiences, I was struck by the similarity of what each of us was seeking, yet in such different terms, and with such polar approaches. We both wanted to establish enduring relationships with the people in whose houses we would be living; we both wanted to enhance trust of ourselves and to allow whatever closeness, whatever friendship, was possible. This similarity of desire, however, could not reconcile our very different rela-

tions to the word of law. Peter, for example, appeared to be extremely self-conscious of his power potential (either real or imagistic) as a white or male or lawyer authority figure. He therefore seemed to go to some lengths to over come the wall which that image might impose. The logical ways of establishing some measure of trust between strangers were for him an avoidance of conventional expressions of power and a preference for informal processes generally.

I, on the other hand, was raised to be acutely conscious of the likelihood that, no matter what degree of professional or professor I became, people would greet and dismiss my black femaleness as unreliable, untrustworthy, hostile, angry, powerless, irrational and probably destitute. Futility and despair are very real parts of my response. Therefore it is helpful for me, even essential for me, to clarify boundary; to show that I can speak the language of lease is my way of enhancing trust of me in my business affairs. As a black, I have been given by this society a strong sense of myself as already too familiar, too personal, too subordinate to white people. I have only recently evolved from being treated as three-fifths of a human,[16] a subpart of the white estate.[17] I grew up in a neighborhood where landlords would not sign leases with their poor, black tenants, and *demanded* that rent be paid in cash; although superficially resembling Peter's transaction, such "informality" in most white-on-black situations signals distrust, not trust. Unlike Peter, I am still engaged in a struggle to set up transactions at arms' length, as legitimately commercial, and to portray myself as a bargainer of separate worth, distinct power, sufficient *rights* to manipulate commerce, rather than to be manipulated as the object of commerce.

Peter, I speculate, would say that a lease or any other formal mechanism would introduce distrust into his relationships and that he would suffer alienation, leading to the commodification of his being and

[11] Peter Gabel was one of the first to bring critical theory to legal analysis; as such he is considered one of the "founders" of Critical Legal Studies.

[12] The people from whom Peter sublet did not want their landlord to know what they were doing—a not uncommon

feature of New York life; they told him they wanted to minimize the "proof."

[16] See U.S. Const. art. I, § 2.

[17] As opposed to being a real part of the white estate. The lease of which I speak was for an apartment in Brooklyn; my search had started in Long Island, where two realtors had refused even to show me apartments in Port Washington and Roslyn.

the degradation of his person to property. In contrast, the lack of a formal relation to the other would leave me estranged. It would risk a figurative isolation from that creative commerce by which I may be recognized as whole, with which I may feed and clothe and shelter myself, by which I may be seen as equal—even if I am stranger. For me, stranger-stranger relations are better than stranger-chattel.

B. *Meta-Mini-Story* (In Which I Reflect Upon My Experiences With Peter, Climb to Celestial Heights While Juggling the Vocabulary of Rights Discourse, and Simultaneously Undo Not a Few Word-Combination Locks)

The unifying theme of Peter's and my experiences (assuming that my hypothesizing about Peter's end of things has any validity at all) is that one's sense of empowerment defines one's relation to the law, in terms of trust-distrust, formality-informality, or rights-no rights (or "needs"). In saying this I am acknowledging and affirming points central to CLS literature: that rights may be unstable and indeterminate. Despite this recognition, however, and despite a mutual struggle to reconcile freedom with alienation, and solidarity with oppression, Peter and I found the expression of our social disillusionment lodged on opposite sides of the rights/needs dichotomy.

On a semantic level, Peter's language of circumstantially-defined need—of informality, of solidarity, of overcoming distance—sounded dangerously like the language of oppression to someone like me who was looking for freedom through the establishment of identity, the *form*-ation of an autonomous social self. To Peter, I am sure, my insistence on the protective distance which rights provide seemed abstract and alienated.

Similarly, while the goals of CLS and of the direct victims of racism may be very much the same, what is too often missing from CLS works is the acknowledgment that our experiences of the same circumstances may be very, very different; the same symbol may mean different things to each of us. At this level, for example, the insistence of Mark Tushnet, Alan Freeman and others that the "needs" of the oppressed should be emphasized rather than their "rights" amounts to no more than a word game. It merely says that the choice has been made to put "needs" in the mouth of a rights discourse—thus transforming "need" into a new form of right. "Need" then joins

"right" in the pantheon of reified representations of what it is that you, I and we want from ourselves and from society.

. . .

[Professor Williams considers the problem of different perceptions, of rights, particularly in light of slavery and the black slaves' status as chattels. —ed.]

Such an expanded frame of rights-reference is the premise of a philosophy of more generously extending rights to all creatures, whether human or beast. It is the basis of those theories of constantly returning cycles which are at the root of environmental reform, and which give "utility" to maintaining the earth in an unexploited form.[88]

III. Conclusion (In Which I Attempt to Rescue From Silence Feelings for Which There Are No Words)

One lesson I never learned in law school, the one lesson I had to learn all by myself, was the degree to which black history in this nation is that of fiercely interwoven patterns of family, as conceived by white men. . . .

. . .

The task for CLS, therefore, is not to discard rights, but to see through or past them so that they reflect a larger definition of privacy, and of property: so that privacy is turned from exclusion based on *self*-regard, into regard for another's fragile, mysterious autonomy; and so that property regains its ancient connotation of being a reflection of that part of the self which by virtue of its very externalization is universal. The task is to expand private property rights into a conception of civil rights, into the right to expect civility from others.

In discarding rights altogether, one discards a symbol too deeply enmeshed in the psyche of the oppressed to lose without trauma and much resistance. Instead, society must *give* them away. Unlock them from reification by giving them to slaves. Give them to trees. Give them to cows. Give them to history. Give them to rivers and rocks. Give to all of society's objects and untouchables the rights of privacy, integrity and self-assertion; give them distance and respect. Flood them with the animating spirit which rights mythology fires in this country's most oppressed psyches, and wash away the shrouds of inanimate object status, so that we may say not that we own gold, but that a luminous golden spirit owns us.

[88] As ought to have been done in Peevyhouse v. Garland Coal & Mining Co., 382 P.2d 109 (1962). There, the Oklahoma Supreme Court refused to enforce a contract provision requiring Garland Coal Company to rehabilitate leased farm and grazing land destroyed by the process of strip-mining.

. . . The restoration of the land, the land's "voice," was viewed as extrinsic, unimportant; since it was not part of the "main purpose" for which the parties had been "righted" (i.e., money-making), that "voice" was permanently silenced.

Where Do We Go From Here?

A conference held at the New York University School of Law in May of 1988 discussed the relation between several theories of contract and the practice of contract law. One of the papers delivered was the following. In it I trace the origins of several of the approaches that can vaguely be gathered under the "relational contracts" umbrella. After discussing such writers as Macaulay, Gilmore and Macneil, I refer to several younger writers' recent extensions of the approach and then look at whether there is any parallel thinking in the courts. My conclusion, much disputed by others, is that consent no longer is as central to contract law as it is made out to be, even though the courts have rarely cited the theorists.

The paper was followed by severe criticism by Professor Steven J. Burton of the University of Iowa Law School and by Jonathan Eddy, a former law professor who is now a distinguished practitioner in the Pacific Northwest. These criticisms are printed following the article in the Annual Survey of American Law. For my response, see Linzer, *Is Consent the Essence of Contract?—Replying to Four Critics*, 1988 Annual Survey of Am. Law 213.

Peter Linzer, *Uncontracts: Context, Contorts and the Relational Approach*, 1988 Ann. Survey of American Law 139

A conventional definition of "contract" is a promise or a set of promises for the breach of which the law will give a remedy. But in the past twenty-five years a number of writers have questioned how accurate the approach implicit in that sort of definition can be. The conventional definition emphasizes promises and judicial remedies, but one line of analysis, the relational approach championed by Ian Macneil, has lead many of us to doubt the magic of the word "promise," while another, the empirical approach of the University of Wisconsin Law School, especially in the writings of Stewart Macaulay, has shown that most business people avoid litigation and work things out rather than seek judicial remedies for explicit paper promises. Still a third approach, associated with Grant Gilmore, has questioned whether the "jurisdictional" lines among contract, tort and property have much intrinsic merit, and has suggested that contract is being "reabsorbed" into the mainstream of tort.

Thus, "Uncontracts." The key question seems to be whether consent and agreement are still the primary elements of contract. In my view, the law has for some time been looking instead to the relationship between the parties, to their dealings both before and after the moment of contracting (if there even is such a moment), and to the entire context in which the parties and their dealings exist. The lines among not only tort and contract, but property as well have increasingly become blurred, and the courts and legislatures (including Congress) are beginning to recognize that rights and duties within a relationship change with time and with the needs not only of the parties but of other people and places affected, and that rights and duties come into existence in ways other than conscious assent to terms at the moment a contract is formed.

In short, there can be forms of contractual liability even though there is no agreement in the usual sense of the word. The thesis questions whether contract law really has much to do with the mutual assent, focused terms and narrow remedies that make up our collective reaction to the word "contracts." I will trace some of the theoretical sources of this "uncontracts" approach, and will try to show that courts have been following the approach more than we (or the courts themselves) realize.

. . .

I

The Persistence Of The Consent Ideal

I assume that most practicing lawyers and most sitting judges believe that the idea of contracts without consent is at best an anomaly and at worst an oxymoron. Although the bulk of academic writers recognize that there are many legitimate occasions for the non-consensual imposition of contractual duties, the main stream continues to believe strongly in the centrality of consent, though with common-sense modifications. This is what has become known as the "neo-classical" approach, exemplified by the Uniform Commercial Code and the Second Restatement of Contracts. . . . Nonetheless, I think that consent has always been subjected to an undertow pulling the sand from underneath it, that it is far from indispensable today, and that it is increasingly being seen as only one of a number of factors affecting contract-like liability.

This is not to say that consent is irrelevant. When parties of roughly equal bargaining power and negotiating sophistication have actually negotiated an express contract, what they had in mind and agreed to should control, especially if both were represented by experienced lawyers. Even in this situation, however, consent, as reflected by the express terms of the contract, has lost considerable force because of factors like the erosion of the parol evidence rule, the expanded use of custom, trade usage, good faith and other implied terms to modify express language, increased use of mistake and impracticability as excuses and a general sense that changed circumstances should trigger renegotiation.

When rights and obligations cannot be traced to an express contract, but instead relate back to an informal and often long-term relationship, or when an express contract is adhesive, it is even harder to find real consent to the duties imposed by courts or by legislatures. To the extent that there is any consent, it is usually attenuated, often little more than being willing to be part of a society that recognizes obligations towards others. In my mind this makes the legal obligations no more consent-based than the tort obligations that are imposed on manufacturers, motorists and even pedestrians walking their dogs. If implied, inferred and imposed "contract" duties are consent-based, then so are tort duties, and consent, promise and agreement cannot be what distinguish contract from tort.

There is nothing wrong with using traditional names as areas of law change. Perhaps something like that is going on, for it seems to me that tort law in practice is personal injury law, property law is almost exclusively concerned with tangible things and contract deals with almost everything else, including most business torts and many tort-like duties im-

posed in the name of implied terms to a largely imaginary contract. This is more than a renaming of topics: it reflects a move away from the Victorian idealization of bargained contract (and with it consent and agreement) as the centerpiece of private legal relations, expressed most famously in Sir Henry Maine's axiom that: "the movement of the progressive societies has hitherto been a movement *from Status to Contract*."

II

The Origin Of The Idea That Consent Is Not Essential To Contract Law

A. *The Brief Reign of the Will Theory*

The purest theoretical belief in consent was the "will theory," which in its most rigid form held that even an uncommunicated change of mind after an acceptance was sent but not yet received would prevent a contract from coming into being. The will theory was in vogue from about 1790 to the mid-nineteenth century, and is largely forgotten today except for its vestige, the phrase "meeting of the minds."

In any event, will theory was bitterly attacked by the generation that came of age between the Civil and First World Wars. The theory of that generation, which became enshrined in the first edition of *Williston On Contracts* in 1920 and in the original *Restatement of Contracts* in 1932, is what we have come to call classical contract law.

. . .

[The article then discusses the downfall of the will theory and argues that even at the height of the objective theory of contracts during the so-called classical period, roughly from the end of the Civil War to the eve of the Second World War, several courts and writers indicated the importance of the relationship between the parties to a contract in construing legal rights and duties. —ed.]

[There follows a discussion of the writings of Stewart Macaulay, Grant Gilmore and Ian Macneil. Some of this discussion has been used in the introductions to the excerpts from these writers in this anthology. The omitted portion ends with Macneil's example of a discrete transaction: a cash sale of gasoline on the Jersey Turnpike. —ed.]

This leads into one of Macneil's most brilliant contributions to contract analysis, albeit one that produced the questionable resurrection of a justly forgotten word: presentation. To "presentiate" means to move the future into the present. In classical contract theory the parties are required to spell out at the time of contracting what should be done when things happen in the future. As Macneil described the system, "the aim was to establish, insofar as the law could, the *entire* relation at the time of the expressions of mutual assent. Total presentation through 100% predictability was sought as of the time of something called the acceptance of an offer."

This works fairly well in the discrete exchange transaction, but intertwined relations involve many factors that cannot be presentiated: the parties cannot plan for every contingency and must continue to plan and adjust their duties throughout the relationship; trouble is expected as a normal part of the relationship; unlike the situation during the discrete bargaining process, in an intertwined relationship the parties have an incentive to share both benefits and burdens, and future cooperation is anticipated. "Finally," wrote Macneil, "the participants never intend or expect to see the whole future of the relation as presentiated at any single time, but view the relation as an ongoing integration of behavior which will grow and vary with events in a largely unforeseeable future . . . ."

D. *The Real Importance of Relational Theory*

In a 1985 article Bill Whitford of the University of Wisconsin argued that Macneil's attacks on discreteness and presentiation have been widely accepted, at least in the academic community.[89] . . .

But Whitford made a penetrating observation: Macneil had a "second great message," that "parties in relational contracts frequently temper wealth maximization goals with other objectives," and this message has had much less impact on the scholars, probably because it is politically unpopular and academically unfashionable in this era of Me Generation wealth maximization. It is this second message that has dominated Macneil's more recent writings such as his 1980 Rosenthal Lectures, published in book form as *The New Social Contract*, and articles with titles like *Exchange Revisited: Individual Utility and Social Solidarity*,[94] *Values in Contract: Internal and External*,[95] and *Efficient Breach of Contract: Circles in the Sky*.[96] It is not, therefore, surprising that Robert Gordon entitled a recent article, *Macaulay, Macneil, and the Discovery of Solidarity and Power in Contract Law*.[97]

E. *Reciprocity, Solidarity and Cooperation*

We can glean what Macneil means by reciprocity, solidarity and cooperation from a number of his works. We might start with his attack on the concept of efficient breach of contract—the notion that under some circumstances a breach can make everyone at least as well off as performance would have and can make some people better off: the breacher breaks his word, seizes another opportunity and pays damages to the promisee of his breached contract. Macneil speaks of the bias of the theory:

That bias is in favor of individual, uncooperative behavior as opposed to behavior requiring the cooperation of the parties. The whole thrust of the Posner analysis is breach first, talk afterwards. . . . And this is so despite the fact that "talking after a breach" may be one of the more expensive forms of conversation to be found, involving as it so often does, engaging high-priced lawyers, and gambits like starting litigation, engaging in discovery, and even trying and appealing cases.

The bias against cooperation demonstrated by the simple-efficient-breach theory should surprise no one familiar with the neo-classical model. . . . That model postulates individuals acting as if the relations in which those individuals exist have no effect on their behavior. Cooperative behavior postulates relations. A model assuming away relationships with the greatest of ease at any stage into favoring uncooperative and—ironically enough—highly inefficient human behavior.[99]

In another article Macneil wrote:

Man is both an entirely selfish creature and an entirely social creature, in that man puts the interests of his fellows ahead of his own interests *at the same time* that he puts his own interests first. . . . Two principles of behavior are essential to the survival of such a creature: solidarity and reciprocity. . . . The two principles of solidarity and reciprocity, neither of which can operate through time without the other, solve this problem. Getting something back for something given neatly releases, or at least reduces, the tension in a creature desiring to be both selfish and social at the same time; and solidarity—a belief in being able to

[89] Whitford, Ian Macneil's Contribution to Contracts Scholarship, 1985 Wis. L. Rev. 545.

[94] Ethics 567 (1986) (hereinafter "Exchange Revisited").

[95] 78 Nw. U. L. Rev. 340 (1983) (hereinafter "Values in Contract").

[96] 68 Va. L. Rev. 947 (1982) (hereinafter "Circles in the Sky").

[97] 1985 Wis. L. Rev. 565. Both the Gordon article, and Whitford's, supra note 89, appeared in a symposium on Macaulay that turned in part into a discussion of Macneil.

[99] Circles in the Sky, supra note 96, at 969.

depend on another—permits the projection of reciprocity through time.[100]

Recently, Macneil listed the relational norms that he derived from relational behavior:

> reciprocity and solidarity, again first among equals, role integrity (requiring consistency, involving internal conflict, and being inherently complex), implementation of planning, effectuation of consent, flexibility, the restitution, reliance, and expectation norms, the power norm justifying both creation and restraint of power, propriety of means, and harmonizing the relation with the internal and external social matrix.[101]

Thus, we have from Ian Macneil an immensely complex theory of contract, increasingly intertwined with a theory of society that includes a strong distaste for bureaucracy and "Leviathan" and a favoring of community and smallness.[102]

F. *New Directions*

Others have built on the ideas underlying Macneil's theories, sometimes going in directions that are very different from his. In 1984, Wallace K. Lightsey, a young practicing lawyer then just out of law school, published an article as noteworthy for its lucidity as for its penetrating thought.[103] Lightsey was generous in acknowledging his intellectual debt to Macneil, but he also built on such disparate writers as the sociologists Emile Durkheim and Alvin Ward Gouldner, the Oxford contracts scholar, Patrick Atiyah, and Roberto Unger, the leading theoretician of Critical Legal Studies. Lightsey's article, entitled *A Critique of the Promise Model of Contract*, was aimed at the "contract as promise" approach of Charles Fried, Harvard contracts and jurisprudence professor and Solicitor General of the United States in the Reagan Administration. Lightsey's conclusion shows the influence of Macneil, but also of many other forebears:

> [T]he discreteness of the promise model hides the fact that trust, expectations, and accompanying

obligations may arise from a variety of sources other than the parties' promises, such as the general interdependence between members of a developed society, the customs and norms of the particular business or social community, similar or previous transactions, or the developing relationship between the parties.

Lightsey offered what he described as "a more accurate conception of contract—contract as the relationship that exists and develops among parties who have made a commitment to a future exchange." Lightsey's model frankly "treats contract as a socio-legal relationship" that "easily accounts for the controlling manner in which society and law shape contractual relationships."

. . .

Lightsey's version of reciprocity is clearly more compatible with the primacy of community than it is with the more individualistic system that bases rights and duties primarily on consent. We have recently learned a lot about some of these communitarian concepts from the writings on feminist (or feminine) jurisprudence.[114] Though the feminist writers have not focused much on contracts,[115] their thesis is most relevant. As Suzanna Sherry described it:

> [T]he feminine perspective views individuals primarily as interconnected members of a community. Nancy Chodorow and Carol Gilligan, in groundbreaking studies on the development of self and morality, have concluded that women tend to have a more intersubjective sense of self than men and that the feminine perspective is therefore more other-directed . . . . The essential difference between the male and female perspectives [is that] . . . "the basic feminine sense of self is connected to the world, the basic masculine sense of self is separate."[116]

Feminist jurisprudence has recently been subjected to a close and critical analysis by Robin West,[117] and it should be apparent that men can think this way as well; after all, the communitarian and relational ap-

---

[100] Values in Contract, supra note 95, at 348 (footnote omitted) (emphasis in original).

[101] Relational Contract Theory as Sociology, 143 J. Institutional and Theoretical Econ. 272, 274 (1987).

[102] See, e.g., Macneil, Bureaucracy, Liberalism, and Community—American Style, 79 Nw. U. L. Rev. 900 (1984-85); Macneil, Exchange Revisited, supra note 94.

[10c] Lightsey, A Critique of the Promise Model of Contract, 26 Wm. & M. L.Rev. 45 (1984).

[114] See, e.g., C. MacKinnon, Feminism Unmodified (1987); West, Jurisprudence and Gender, 55 U. Chi. L. Rev. 1 (1988); Sherry, Civic Virtue and the Feminine Voice in Constitutional Adjudication, 72 Va. L. Rev. 543 (1986); Scales,

The Emergence of Feminist Jurisprudence: An Essay, 95 Yale L.J. 1373 (1986). These works and others are by no means in full agreement. On this, see Robin West's critical study, supra. The writers were powerfully influenced by Carol Gilligan's In a Different Voice (1982) and Nancy Chodorow's The Reproduction of Mothering (1978).

[115] But see Frug, Re-reading Contracts: A Feminist Analysis of a Contracts Casebook, 34 American U. L. Rev. 1065 (1985).

[116] Sherry, supra note 114, at 584-85 (citations omitted), quoting from N. Chodorow, supra note 114.

[117] See West, supra note 114.

proaches to contract were all put forth by men. But the feminist writers show us that rugged individualism, a confrontational rather than compromising approach and an insistence on predetermined rules may be less universal norms than examples of a male outlook that was treated as the norm when women had no voice in the law. As the proportion of women lawyers and women judges increases, the contract approaches that call for continuing rethinking of and compromise in an evolving relationship may come to be seen as considerably more mainstream than in the past.

There remain many questions, especially what reciprocity entails, what a community is and how you get into one. I looked at some of these issues in a study I did a couple of years ago of the erosion of the at-will employment doctrine. I entitled my piece *The Decline of Assent*[118] because an important aspect of it was my contention that not only was there little presentation in informal employment, there also was little focused consent. What consent there was came when someone (often a low-level supervisory employee who worked for a predecessor in interest of the present employer) hired a then-young person to do a job with vague responsibilities, under terms that changed by accretion over many years. I found that courts frequently found rights and duties, but that they had a hard time explaining where these rights and duties came from, and that their rationales, though usually starting from a theory of contract, frequently involved ideas of tort and property more than those of traditional—that is discrete—contract law.

While employment rights are intrinsically important, I was even more interested in what I saw as a breakdown of the boundaries among tort, contract and property, a breakdown that happened because the courts were intuitively moving away from discrete notions of consent and property ownership. In analyzing the courts' responses to the specific issue at hand, one could invoke the economists' concept of the firm—which is, of course, a specialized form of rela-

tionship—to justify finding that the employees had rights in their jobs because of their contribution to and reliance on the existence of the relationship itself. Even more, however, if one focused on relationships rather than on formal concepts of tort, contract and property, many factors came into prominence that traditionally had been thought of as externalities in both economic and legal thinking. It was not that clear results always followed, but that the issues had previously been wrongly framed, whether we were discussing the unilateral termination of a franchise or distributorship, the destruction of a work of art by its putative owner, the uprooting of a professional football team without regard to its fans, or the closing of a plant after one hundred years in a community.

These changes in the jurisprudential boundary lines showed that ideas of property rights were as much a factor as those of tort and contract. There has been some very fine work done in this field, one of the best articles being Margaret Jane Radin's *Property and Personhood*,[124] in which, building on Hegel, Professor Radin argued that some forms of property deserved more protection than others, the key factor being whether a person was dependent on "personal embodiment or self-constitution in terms of 'things.'"[125] This approach does not provide glib answers, but it does suggest not only that most property rights are far from absolute,[126] but that the inquiry should focus on the relationship between the thing said to be protected from interference and the people involved with the thing.

[There follows a discussion of Anthony Jon Waters' article *The Property in the Promise*,[127] excerpted at some length in Part IID of this anthology. —ed.]

Finally, I would point to Joseph William Singer's interesting and recent article entitled *The Reliance Interest in Property*.[136] Singer, who is a member of the Conference on Critical Legal Studies, uses many CLS ideas as well as many of the ideas mentioned here in dealing with the problem of plant closings,

---

[118] Linzer, The Decline of Assent: At-Will Employment as a Case Study of the Breakdown of Private Law Theory, 20 Ga. L. Rev. 323 (1986).

[124] 34 Stan. L. Rev. 957 (1982).

[125] Id. at 958. See also Baker, Property and Its Relation to Constitutionally Protected Liberty, 134 U. Pa. L. Rev. 741 (1986).

[126] A position long accepted by the United States Supreme Court in constitutional law, see Nebbia v. New York, 291 U.S. 502, 523 (1934):

[N]either property rights nor contract rights are absolute; for government cannot exist if the citizen may at will use his property to the detriment of his fellows, or

exercise his freedom of contract to work them harm. Equally fundamental with the private right is that of the public to regulate it in the common interest.

The Court, in an opinion written by Justice Rehnquist, quoted from this passage with approval in PruneYard Shopping Center v. Robins, 447 U.S. 74, 84-85 (1980). On the common law's rejection of absolute property rights, see Powell, The Relationship Between Property Rights and Civil Rights, 15 Hastings L.J. 135 (1963).

[127] Waters, The Property in the Promise: A Study of the Third Party Beneficiary Rule, 98 Harv. L. Rev. 1109 (1985). [This article is excerpted in Part IID. —ed.]

[136] 40 Stan. L. Rev. 611 (1988).

specifically the closing of two steel mills in Youngs-town, Ohio, by United States Steel Corporation (now hiding out as U.S.X. Corp.). Singer's article is exhaustive and thoroughly researched and documented. The interplay among concepts is apparent from his title, which uses a contract notion, the reliance interest, in dealing with what is ostensibly a property issue. In addition, Singer uses the term "reliance" in a broad, societal sense, closer to the Macneilian adjective "relational" than to the narrow sense of Section 90 of either Restatement of Contracts. Singer considers both judicial and legislative ways to protect the interests of workers and cities in the plant that is to be closed. His conclusion shows the influence of the theories that we have discussed:

> Property rights allocate power, and we are suspicious of power. Those without power are vulnerable. Thus the relation between power and vulnerability should be at the heart of our analysis of property rights. Rather than asking "who owns the factory?" we should ask "what relationships should we nurture?" We should encourage people to rely on relationships of mutual dependence by making it possible for everyone to form such relationships and by protecting those who are most vulnerable when those relationships end. Property rights can be justified morally within a common enterprise to the extent they allow people to develop relationships that promote conditions of trust. If T. H. White is right about King Arthur's vision of civilization, then we have an obligation to learn what it would take for us to create the kind of society in which we could trust each other enough to place our lives in each other's hands.[138]

I strongly doubt that Macneil would agree with everything in that paragraph, and I'm not sure that I do, but I do think that much of it is correct, and that it applies as much to contract and tort as to property.

IV

What The Courts Have Done

So much for the theorists. Now let us look at the courts in action. While some courts have cited the theorists, many more, I think, have acted intuitively, without reliance on the signposts in the law reviews. Many decisions that carry out the neo-classical doctrines of the UCC and the Legal Realists have had the effect of moving law-in-operation in relational directions that are more compatible with the "uncontracts" approach than either the neo-classicists or the

courts might have intended. Nonetheless, I think that the courts were right in what they were doing, and right in helping to push the contractual inquiry towards relationship and context and away from consent and bargain.

We can hardly attempt a systematic survey of everything all courts have done, but I would like to discuss three broad areas of substance: the increasing use of tort concepts in contract litigation; the diminishing of presentiation and the increase in demands for cooperation in long-term supply contracts; and the questioning of traditional concepts of contract, property and owners' prerogatives in plant closings, employment and franchise terminations and the movement of sports franchises. But first we should briefly discuss a matter that involves both procedure and substance, and which has had a major effect on contract litigation: the erosion of the parol evidence rule.

. . .

[The article argues that the increasing breakdown of the parol evidence rule has had the effect of getting much more evidence of the relationship between the parties before the jury. It then considers "contorts in action," particularly in cases applying notions of duties of good faith and fair dealing. The discussion of one such case follows. —ed.]

A recent Seventh Circuit case, *Jordan v. Duff and Phelps, Inc.*,[203] applied the anti-fraud provisions of the federal security laws to a corporate employer that allowed an investor who was also an at-will employee to resign and sell back his stock without disclosing that a merger was imminent that would have increased the value of his stock twenty-fold. *Duff and Phelps* is interesting for two reasons. One is that existing caselaw had held that a corporation need not disclose to investors trading in the stock market that merger negotiations were taking place. The majority distinguished the situation before it because the corporation was closely held and because although the investor was an at-will employee:

> The stock component in Jordan's package induced him to stick around and work well. Such an inducement is effective only if the employee reaps the rewards of success as well as the penalties for failure. We do not suppose for a second that if Jordan had not resigned on November 16, the firm could have fired him on January 9 with a little note saying: "Dear Mr. Jordan: There will be a

---

[138] 40 Stan. L. Rev. at 751.

[203] 815 F.2d 429 (7th Cir. 1987).

lucrative merger tomorrow. You have been a wonderful employee, but in order to keep the proceeds of the merger for ourselves, we are letting you go, effective this instant. Here is the $23,000 for your shares." *Had the firm fired Jordan for this stated reason, it would have broken an implied pledge to avoid opportunistic conduct.*

The other interesting point about *Duff and Phelps* is that the majority opinion is by Frank Easterbrook over a dissent by Richard Posner. Judge Easterbrook, like Judge Posner, is a former University of Chicago law professor appointed to the Seventh Circuit by President Reagan. Like Posner he is allied with the law-and-economics approach, and like Posner and Richard Epstein, whose writings he cites in the majority opinion, Easterbrook is quite concerned with contracting parties' assent, actual or inferred. As an example, he wrote that "[t]he silence of the parties may make it necessary to imply other terms—those we are confident the parties would have bargained for if they had signed a written agreement." Immediately after this, though, he wrote that "[o]ne term implied in every written contract and therefore, we suppose, every unwritten one, is that neither party will try to take opportunistic advantage of the other." He backed this statement up with a quotation from Posner's *Economic Analysis of Law*, much to Posner's annoyance. In his dissent, Judge Posner noted that the parties had in fact signed a written shareholder agreement that required the employee to tender back the stock upon termination and which expressly provided that it did not give him any right to be continued in employment by the corporation. He wrote at some length to show that the majority's imposition of a disclosure duty violated what he termed "freedom of contract." I think that the Posner dissent shows that the Easterbrook majority opinion, for all its references to the parties' inferred intent, was really based on their relationship with each other, a relationship that was inconsistent with opportunism and which thus made the employer potentially liable for heavy damages for stock fraud.

[The use of tort concepts has a strong substantive impact on contract litigation. Damages are not limited by the narrow contract rules, it is easier to avoid

the rugged individualism and wealth maximization implicit in much contract thinking, particularly about affirmative duties, and the time focus covers all the dealings, thus minimizing presentation. —ed.]

No one knows where these cases will go, but many ideas come to mind: BNA now has a *Lender Liability Report,* and in its promotional literature tells many horror stories involving massive tort liability when loans fall through; a bonding company lawyer told me about arguments that the surety has a duty to police the contractors that it has bonded, thus opening it up to damages in addition to its bond; an argument could be constructed that a manufacturer should be liable to a distributor if the product involved proves defective and injures the distributor's business reputation—even if the manufacturer has compensated all the consumers. The contorts cases are consistent with "uncontract" theory and are having a major impact on contract litigation. If Macneil and Macaulay are correct in their analysis of how business people deal with each other—and how they should deal with each other, the practice of contract law is beginning to catch up with the real world.

C. *Long-term Supply Contracts*

Article 2 of the Uniform Commercial Code is openly relational in its emphasis on the parties' conduct,[214] its desire that the law follow enlightened business practices,[215] and its attempts to allow business people to solve problems with a minimum of interference from the law.[216] Indeed, in Article One it is expressly stated that one of the three "underlying purposes and policies" of the entire Code is "to permit the continued expansion of commercial practices through custom, usage and agreement of the parties."[217] In a number of cases the courts, either by directly applying the Code or by analogizing from it, have applied a norm of cooperation to a long-term business relationship much in the manner addressed by Macneil, Macaulay and Lightsey, among others.

An example of what I'm getting at is the language used by Judge Clarke of the Eastern District of Virginia in a Miller Act case involving a claim that the contractor agreed to a price increase only because of economic duress.[219] The court said that UCC 2-209

---

[214] E.g., UCC 2-202 (parol evidence rule does not bar evidence of course of dealing, usage of trade or course of performance); 2-204 (conduct recognizing existence of a contract is sufficient to form it); 2-208 (course of performance is relevant to determine meaning of agreement).

[215] See Danzig, A Comment of the Jurisprudence of the Uniform Commercial Code, 27 Stan. L. Rev. 621 (1975).

[216] E.g., UCC 2-311 ("Options and Cooperation Respecting Performance"); 2-508 (cure by seller); 2-609 (right to adequate assurances); 2-615 (b) (allocation by seller among regular customers in cases of partial impracticability).

[217] UCC 1-102 (2) (b).

[219] United States ex rel. Crane Co. v. Progressive Enterprises, 418 F. Supp. 662 (E.D. Va. 1976).

(1), which dispenses with consideration for modifications of existing contracts "would be hollow indeed" if good faith modifications could not be enforced. "In the context of a lengthy, on-going business relationship, seeking modification of a sales price is not uncommon and, given increased costs, is a fair method of doing business in order to preserve the desirability of the relationship for both parties."[220]

A more elaborate example is *Nanakuli Paving and Rock Co. v. Shell Oil Co.,*[221] in which the Ninth Circuit upheld a jury's $220,800 verdict against Shell for breach of contract, holding that despite a contract provision setting a price as "Shell's Posted Price at the time of delivery," Shell was obliged to give an asphalt buyer a period of price protection when the 1973 oil crisis drove up the posted prices. *Nanakuli Paving* can be read as nothing more than an expansive reading of the UCC or it can be read as more overtly relational, but regardless of the label, the effect of a broad reading of several different Code sections was relational both in inquiry and in result.

. . .

D. *Who Owns What?*

Finally, I would like to look briefly at an approach that is only beginning to be taken seriously, that traditional notions of property ownership are not incontrovertible, and that many people and entities other than the traditional owner have rights in an enterprise even if they have no traditional contract, property or tort claim. This argument is not new.

[The article discusses Leon Green's 1937 article, *The Case for the Sit-Down Strike,* reprinted in Part IID of this book. —ed.]

Just as the good faith and fair dealing cases have a cast of tort but have a major impact on dealings that we would view as essentially contractual, here, new ideas of property ownership undercut the long-existing idea that most rights vis-a-vis other individuals come from contract.[255] Thus, if you work for me in an

at-will arrangement, or if you are a fan of my baseball team or if you are a resident of a factory town where my factory has stood for a hundred years, traditionally, you have no rights against me unless you have a contract with me or I have committed a tort against you. I have an owner's prerogative to fire you, to move the team, or to close the plant. They are mine. True, without employees, fans or the town, "my" possessions would be worthless, but that doesn't matter. They still are mine.

The traditional view of property is parallel to the classical view of contract in its respect for individualism. The view that an owner could do what he wanted with his property was the fraternal twin of the view that parties to contracts had no duties other than those that they consciously assented to when they entered into the contract. But, there have always been restrictions on the owner's use of property,[256] and ever since Charles Reich's *The New Property*[257] and Calabresi and Malamed's *One View of the Cathedral,*[258] we have been aware that the real questions are what do we mean by "property" and what do we mean by "property rights"?

Many writers have used the term "property rights in the job," but I see it less metaphorically and more literally than most. I see that phrase as a way of saying that the enterprise in which people work must be viewed as a firm with many members. Particularly with a publicly held corporation, the traditional "owners," the shareholders, have no power, no control, and a bond with the company that can be broken by a call to their broker. They are not even providers of capital, except by buying stock that a thousand trades ago was issued to an actual investor whose money made its way to the company treasury. Their only recourse if they are dissatisfied with management is to vote with their feet—either sell in the market or sell to a corporate raider.[260] The people who do have a bond to the company and who have made a real investment *with* it rather than *in* it are management

[220] 418 F.Supp. at 664.

[221] 664 F.2d 772 (9th Cir. 1981).

[255] See Kessler, Contract as a Principle of Order, in F. Kessler, G. Gilmore and A. T. Kronman, Contracts 1 (3d ed.1986). Kessler's essay is significant not only for its intrinsic worth, but because it is by a great critic of "freedom of contract."

[256] See Powell, The Relationship Between Property Rights and Civil Rights, 15 Hastings L.J. 135 (1963).

[257] 73 Yale L.J. 733 (1964).

[258] Calabresi & Melamed, Property Rules, Liability Rules and Inalienability: One View of the Cathedral, 85 Harv. L. Rev. 1089 (1972).

[260] Even the conservative economists Armen Alchian and Harold Demsetz wrote in their important article, Production, Information Costs, and Economic Organization, 62 Am. Econ. Rev. 777, 789 n.14 (1972) that "[i]nstead of thinking of shareholders as joint owners we can think of them as investors, like bondholders, except that the stockholders are more optimistic than the bondholders about the enterprise prospects." See also L. Lowenstein, What's Wrong With Wall Street 5 (1988): "Investors who thought of themselves as part-owners of a business would never 'tax' themselves, as they in fact do, by turning over their portfolios—taking in each other's washing, as Ben Graham put it—at 160 million shares and more a day."

and workers, as well as the localities that have grown so dependent upon it through years of symbiosis.[261]

Those who are currently claiming what we think of as the prerogatives of ownership are the management. I have no disagreement with their claiming some prerogatives, but I believe these prerogatives come not from ownership (or delegation by the nominal owners), but from the functional needs of the firm and management's contributions to it. Employees and others who have invested their lives or their environment also should have rights *in* the firm, deriving not from traditional contract, tort or property, but from their contribution to it and their close relationship with it.

The employment aspects of this issue have been done to death, but recently there has been interest in what is an equally serious problem—plant closings and runaway shops. I have already mentioned Joseph William Singer's *The Reliance Interest in Property*.[262] In it he discusses *Local 1330, United Steel Workers v. United States Steel Corp.*,[263] in which the Sixth Circuit reluctantly held that U.S. Steel had no obligation to sell its obsolete steel plants to the union and could do what it liked with the plants, thus affirming District Judge Thomas Lambros, who had also wanted to give relief, but had deemed himself without authority to do so. Among Judge Lambros' remarks, quoted both by the Sixth Circuit and by Singer, were the following:

> [I]t seems to me that a property right has arisen from this lengthy, long-established relationship between United States Steel, the steel industry as an institution, the community in Youngstown, the people of Mahoning County and the Mahoning Valley in having given and devoted their lives to this industry. Perhaps not a property right to the extent that can be remedied by compelling U.S. Steel to remain in Youngstown. But I think the law can recognize the property right to the extent that U.S. Steel cannot leave that Mahoning

Valley and the Youngstown area in a state of waste, that it cannot completely abandon its obligation to that community, because certain vested rights have arisen out of this long relationship and institution.[264]

In the end, neither Judge Lambros nor the Court of Appeals believed that it was the place of the courts to create so radical a remedy. . . .

Singer makes out a case for judicial activism in this area. I am on record as believing that the courts are competent to continue the common law tradition by making law—after all, they made most of tort, contract and property law to begin with, and the legislatures always can undo the courts' work if they choose. Nonetheless, I don't expect a rush of courts to embrace Singer's proposal.

But Congress is acting. Both houses passed the Plant Closing Bill by such large margins that President Reagan did not even try to veto it. The provision is modest enough—it requires sixty days' notice of plant closings or major layoffs by big companies, but it still was bitterly attacked by the Chamber of Commerce as "an unprecedented government intrusion into the most fundamental decision-making process of employers." Of course, it isn't at all unprecedented, but it certainly is an intrusion, just as the 1964 Civil Rights Act intruded into the employer's "right" to discriminate in hiring, and the restaurant owner's "right" to refuse to serve blacks; just as the Fair Housing Act intruded into sellers' and landlords' "rights" to perpetuate residential segregation. Whether it will do any good is another matter; the Civil Rights Act has had more success than the Fair Housing Act. But they both reflect Congress's recognition that the old rules of contract, tort and property must give way when there are needs that outweigh them.

. . .

The Plant Closing Law could be just a start. Congress could, if it chose to, require plant closers to give

---

[261] No one could say it better than Leon Green did fifty years ago:

> Both participating groups have contributed heavily to the joint enterprise of industry. The contributions of those who make up the corporate organization on the one hand are visualized in plant, machinery, raw materials and the like. They can be seen, recorded and valued in dollars. We call them property. On the other side are hundreds of personalities who have spent years training their hands and senses to specialized skills; who have set up habitations conveniently located to their work; who have become obligated to families and for the facilities necessary for maintaining them; who have ordered their

> lives and developed disciplines; all to the end that the properties essential to industry may be operated for the profit of the owner group and for their own livelihoods. Their outlays are not so visible, nor so easily measured in dollars, but in gross they may equal or even exceed the contributions of the other group. Both groups are joint adventurers, as it were, in industrial enterprise. . . .

Green, The Case For the Sit-Down Strike, 90 The New Republic 199, 199 (1937).

[262] Supra note 136.

[263] 631 F.2d 1264 (6th Cir. 1980).

[264] 631 F.2d at 1280, quoted in Singer, supra note 136, at 619 (italics omitted).

their employees or the locality rights to buy the plant. Often, this right will be worthless because the plant is outmoded, but Congress could also provide that the plant closer share its claimed savings with those who are contributing to the savings by being impoverished. Alternatively, it could achieve the same effect by requiring significant severance pay, perhaps using the executives' golden parachutes as a model.

Congress could even expand beyond plant closings into industrial relations as a whole. I have little doubt that it would be constitutional for Congress to require profit sharing or productivity bonuses or the use of workers' circles, substituting for the present policy of favoring negotiated contracts one that recognizes the existence of these "relational" policies that are so common in industrialized countries that are beating the pants off our "individualistic" American corporate scheme. I am not saying that this kind of legislation would be politically popular or even very wise. In fact, I would not support a lot of it, because I think the better approach would be for the government to encourage both through exhortation and through financial incentives voluntary solutions that recognize workers as members of the firm. A relational approach would obviously require rethinking by management, but it would require rethinking by unions as well. The old shibboleths about recognizing management as the enemy, and things like distrust of piece work would have to go, just as the management would have to get off its high horse of owners' prerogatives and discrete views of contract rights.[276]

But just as the courts have changed the way contractual relations are carried out by using good faith and cooperational concepts, and just as Congress and the legislatures are chipping away at notions of absolute ownership, parties themselves should be able to do formally what Macaulay and others have shown they do when the lawyers aren't looking. Frank recognition of the relational "uncontracts" approach could help move the Twenty-first Century United States away from a mentality of "we" and "they" to one of "us."

. . .

---

[276] For an expansion of these ideas, see Linzer, Employee Rights and Management Prerogatives: Who Owns the Company?, 3 Law & Policy Rev. ___ (forthcoming).

A Brief Note About Allan Farnsworth's Doubts About Grand Theories

Professor E. Allan Farnsworth of Columbia Law School was the co-reporter of the Restatement (Second) of Contracts, and his recent text has quickly become a leader in the field. In 1986 Professor Farnsworth gave a tongue-in-cheek luncheon speech at a conference of contracts teachers who had gathered to spend two days discussing contract theory. Beginning with a written "quiz" designed to show that a lot of the new ideas weren't so new, Professor Farnsworth expressed his skepticism about the penchant of current writers to spend so much time on elaborate theories of contract. He concluded with this understated bit of advice: "My point is not that these fine articles should not have been written but rather that in the future scholars looking for potential topics might look elsewhere." Farnsworth, *A Fable and A Quiz on Contracts*, 37 J. Legal Educ. 208 (1987).

See also Hillman, *The Crisis in Modern Contract Theory*, 67 Texas L. Rev. 103 (1988).

C.   Where Did Contract Law Come From?

Introduction

The history of anything is interesting and relevant: it exists, and like climbing Mount Everest the reason for doing it can be simply "because it's there." But the common law has always put emphasis on precedent, and the essential conservatism of law suggests that the long existence of a rule puts the burden on those who call for change. Thus, history becomes a political weapon.

Anglo-American contract law has a particularly complex history. The notion of contract is universal and ancient; consider the Covenant between God and the Hebrews or the Orpheus legend. But if we put aside the now-obsolete formal contract under a seal, contract *law* in England has a very shadowy existence, affected more by procedural changes in the forms of action than by anything to do with contract doctrine or theory. It is often difficult to make categorical statements about what contract law was, and this vagueness affects the debate today. Consider, for example, the topic of "contorts," discussed in Part IA by Professors Gilmore and Kessler. If there were rigid rules of contract for hundreds of years, the infusion into contract law of flexible (or open-ended) concepts like unconscionability, good faith and reasonableness might be challenged as an innovation needing considerable justification in light of hundreds of years of hard and fast rules that provided certainty and predictability. But what if the rule-based system itself was a nineteenth-century innovation, imposed on a previously fluid system in response to the industrial revolution, and heavily biased in favor of the emerging new industries? While neither verision of history would compel a given result, each would provide rhetorical support for an appeal to return to the good old way, whichever that might be deemed. In addition, learning what actually went on gives us raw material to use in our current attempt to shape the law to deal with the needs of a "post-industrial" society adjusting to the economic and social changes of the late twentieth century.

The Horwitz-Simpson Debate

There has been interest in the history of contract law for generations. In 1881 Oliver Wendell Holmes, Jr. devoted Lectures VII through IX of *The Common Law* to contract, and James Barr Ames published his history of assumpsit in the second volume of the Harvard Law Review. Ames, *The History of Assumpsit*, 2 Harv. L. Rev. 1, 53 (1888). In more recent times Theodore F. T. Plucknett devoted about fifty pages of his highly regarded history of the common law to a history of contract, see Plucknett, *A Concise History of the Common Law* 628-70 (5th ed. 1956), and Professor A.W.B. Simpson (of whom more below) devoted an entire book to the subject. See A.W.B. Simpson, *A History of the Common Law of Contract* (1975). In addition, Professor E. Allan Farnsworth explored anthropology and other disciplines to inquire, when societies first have enforced bargains, exchange and promises. See Farnsworth, *The Past of Promise: An Historical Introduction to Contract*, 69 Colum. L. Rev. 576 (1969).

In recent years, however, the inquiry has become overtly political, particularly because of the writings of Morton J. Horwitz, whose book, *The Transformation of American Law, 1780-1860* (1977), won the Bancroft Prize in American History for 1978. Professor Horwitz, who teaches at Harvard, had previously published an article, excerpted below, that formed the basis for an important chapter entitled "The Triumph of Contract." His thesis may be briefly stated: prior to the late eighteenth century English law treated contract as simply a means for the conveyance of title to property and did not view contract as a device for apportioning risk or for projecting exchange into the future. The courts did not enforce purely executory contracts and limited the damages to injuries caused by reliance on a breached promise. (Recall Atiyah's similar argument.) The touchstone was not promise or will or consent, but community-based notions of fairness, including notions of a just price and of implied warranties, based not on the parties' supposed state of mind, but on the maxim "a sound price warrants a sound product." In addition, the jury had almost complete control over damages and could adjust them downward when an unfair bargain was the basis of a lawsuit. In the years following the American Revolution the courts here followed a similar approach.

According to Horwitz, as commerce expanded rapidly and as the industrial revolution gained speed, these approaches were at odds with the needs of the increasingly market-based economy. Courts began to speak in terms that rejected objective or community-based standards of value and fairness and to insist that only the parties could judge value. Contract began to be spoken of in terms of the will theory—that rights and duties come into existence only because of the concurrence of the wills of the contracting parties: "the meeting of the minds." The result of this change was the development of the highly crafted system of contract law that eventually became what we call classical contract law. In appearance, this system was value-neutral, but in fact its rule-based system favored the strong and sophisticated bargainer and the entrepreneur.

Despite its influence and favorable reception, Horwitz's view has been much criticized. (It should be noted that Horwitz was an early member of the Critical Legal Studies movement, and that his work has been used as a base by many CLS writers. For an example, see the Gabel and Feinman piece, "Contract Law as Ideology," excerpted in Part IA.) The most notable and rigorous criticism of Horwitz is by Prof. A.W.B. Simpson, an English legal historian who has specialized in contract law, and who now teaches at the University of Michigan Law School. Simpson's 1979 article, *The Horwitz Thesis and the History of Contracts* is excerpted immediately after the Horwitz article. (Horwitz expanded his article when he put it into his book, but since Simpson did not discuss the additions, they will be summarized in the note following the two articles rather than printed out.)

Morton J. Horwitz, *The Historical Foundations of Modern Contract Law*, 87 Harv. L. Rev. 917 (1974)

Modern contract law is fundamentally a creature of the nineteenth century. It arose in both England and America as a reaction to and criticism of the medieval tradition of substantive justice that, surprisingly, had remained a vital part of eighteenth century legal thought, especially in America. Only in the nineteenth century did judges and jurists finally reject the longstanding belief that the justification of contractual obligation is derived from the inherent justice or fairness of an exchange. In its place, they asserted for the first time that the source of the obligation of contract is the convergence of the wills of the contracting parties.

Beginning with the first English treatise on contract, Powell's *Essay Upon the Law of Contracts and Agreements* (1790), a major feature of contract writing has been its denunciation of equitable conceptions of substantive justice as undermining the "rule of law." "[I]t is absolutely necessary for the advantage of the public at large," Powell wrote, "that the rights of the subject should . . . depend upon certain and fixed principles of law, and not upon rules and constructions of equity, which when applied . . . , must be arbitrary and uncertain, depending, in the extent of their application, upon the will and caprice of the judge." The reason why equity "must be arbitrary and uncertain," Powell maintained, was that there could be no principles of substantive justice. A court of equity, for example, should not be permitted to refuse to enforce an agreement for simple "exorbitancy of price" because "it is the consent of parties alone, that fixes the just price of any thing, without reference to the nature of things themselves, or to their intrinsic value . . . . [T]herefore," he concluded, "a man is obliged in conscience to perform a contract which he has entered into, although it be a hard one . . . ." The entire conceptual apparatus of modern contract doctrine—rules dealing with offer and acceptance, the evidentiary function of consideration, and especially canons of interpretation—arose to express this will theory of contract.

Powell's argument against conceptions of intrinsic value and just price reflects major changes in thought associated with the emergence of a market economy. It appears that it was only during the second half of the eighteenth century that national commodities markets began to develop in England. From that time on, "the price of grain was no longer local, but regional; this presupposed [for the first time] the almost general use of money and a wide marketability of goods." In America, widespread markets in government securities arose shortly after the Revolutionary War, and an extensive internal commodities market developed around 1815. The impact of these developments on both English and American contract law was profound. In a market, goods came to be thought of as fungible; the function of contracts correspondingly shifted from that of simply transferring title to a specific item to that of ensuring an expected return. Executory contracts, rare during the eighteenth century, became important as instruments for "futures" agreements; formerly, the economic system had rested on immediate sale and delivery of specific property. And, most importantly, in a society in which value came to be regarded as entirely subjective and in which the only basis for assigning value was the concurrence of arbitrary individual desire, principles of substantive justice were inevitably seen as entailing an "arbitrary and uncertain" standard of value. Substantive justice, according to the earlier view, existed in order to prevent men from using the legal system in order to exploit each other. But where things have no "intrinsic value," there can be no substantive measure of exploitation and the parties are, by definition, equal. Modern contract law was thus

born staunchly proclaiming that all men are equal because all measures of inequality are illusory.

This Article will elaborate the view of the development of modern contract law outlined above. The first Section will describe the distinguishing features of the equitable conception of contract which dominated eighteenth century courts. The second Section will detail the late eighteenth and early nineteenth century disintegration of the equitable conception and the coalesence of new doctrine into the modern will theory of contract.

I. The Equitable Conception of Contract in the Eighteenth Century

The development of contract, it often has been observed, can be divided into three states, which correspond to the history of economic and legal institutions of exchange. In the first stage, all exchange is instantaneous and therefore "involves nothing corresponding to 'contract' in the Anglo-American sense of the term. Each party becomes the owner of a new thing, and his rights rest, not on a promise, but on property." In a second stage "[e]xchange first assumes a contractual aspect when it is left half-completed, so that [only] an obligation on one side remains." The "third and final stage in the development occurs when the executory exchange becomes enforceable." According to orthodox legal history, when English judges declare at the end of the sixteenth century that "every contract executory is an assumpsit in itself," and that "a promise against a promise will maintain an action upon the case," the conception of contract as mutual promises has triumphed and, according to Plucknett, "the process is complete and the result clear. . ."[12] "Damages were soon assessed," Ames added, "not upon the theory of reimbursement for the loss of the thing given for the promise, but upon the principle of compensation for the failure to obtain the thing promised."[13]

It is the purpose of this Section to demonstrate that, contrary to the orthodox view, the process was not complete at the end of the sixteenth century. Instead, one finds that as late as the eighteenth century contract law was still dominated by a title theory of exchange and damages were set under equitable doctrines that ultimately were to be rejected by modern contract law.

To modern eyes, the most distinctive feature of eighteenth century contract law is the subordination

[12] T. Plucknett, A Concise History of the Common Law at 644 (5th ed. 1956).

[13] J. Ames, Lectures on Legal History 144-45 (1913). See also 3 W. Holdsworth, A History of English Law 452 (3d ed. 1923).

of contract to the law of property. In Blackstone's *Commentaries* contract appears for the first time in Book II, which is devoted entirely to the law of property. Contract is classified among such subjects as descent, purchase, and occupancy as one of the many modes of transferring title to a specific thing. Contract appears for the second and last time in a chapter entitled, "Of Injuries to Personal Property." In all, Blackstone's extraordinarily confused treatment of contract ideas occupies only forty pages of his four volume work.

As a result of the subordination of contract to property, eighteenth century jurists endorsed a title theory of contractual exchange according to which a contract functioned to transfer title to the specific thing contracted for. Thus, Blackstone wrote that where a seller fails to deliver goods on an executory contract, "the vendee may seize the goods, or have an action against the vendor for detaining them." Similarly, in the first English treatise on contract, Powell wrote of the remedy for failure to deliver stock on an executory contract as being one for specific performance.

The title theory of exchange was suited to an eighteenth century society in which no extensive markets existed, and goods, therefore, were usually not thought of as being fungible. Exchange was not conceived of in terms of future monetary return, and as a result one finds that expectation damages [i.e., the benefit of the bargain rather than only the out-of-pocket loss (reliance damages) —ed.], were not recognized by eighteenth century courts. Only two reported eighteenth century English cases touch on the question of expectation damages for breach of contract. *Flureau v. Thornhill*[19] (1776) seems to have confronted the question of damages for the loss of a bargain. A purchaser of a lease, who sued for failure to deliver because of a defect in title, sought to recover not only his deposit, but also damages sustained as a result of the lost bargain. The report of the case does not disclose whether the plaintiff attempted to recover the increased value of the lease, or, rather, the loss he had suffered from selling stock to finance the payment. In any event, the court refused to allow him more than restitution of his payment, one judge contemptuously noting that he could not "be entitled to any damages for the fancied goodness of the bargain, which he supposes he has lost."

A second English case involving the damage issue is *Dutch v. Warren*[21] (1720). The case would be irrelevant were it not for the fact that it was regularly cited by later jurists ransacking the English reports for early instances of the recognition of expectation damages. The case represented a buyer's action for restitution of money paid on a stock purchase contract, the price of the stock having fallen by the time delivery was due. Although the court said the case was "well brought; not for the whole money paid, but the damages in not transferring the stock at that time," the case obviously does not establish the modern rule that one may recover expectation damages in excess of the purchase price for failure to deliver stock in a rising market. Indeed, Lord Mansfield referred to it not as establishing a rule for damages, but as illustrating the equitable nature of the action for money had and received.

One of the handful of executory contracts in America before the Revolution appeared in *Boehm v. Engle* (1767), in which two sellers sued a buyer who, alleging bad title, had refused to accept a deed for land. Since Pennsylvania had no equity court in which a seller could have sued for specific performance, Boehm brought "a special action on the case for the consideration money" or contract price, not, it should be emphasized, for the value of the lost bargain. He was thereby suing, in effect, for specific performance and not for the change in value of the land. The suit was therefore consistent with Blackstone's title theory: the contract had transferred title from seller to buyer and all that remained was an action for the price.

To appreciate the radical difference between eighteenth century and modern contract law, consider a case decided during a period in which the demise of the title theory was becoming plain. *Sands v. Taylor* was an 1810 New York suit against a buyer who had received a part shipment of wheat but had refused to receive the remainder contracted for. Under the old title theory, sellers were apparently required to hold the goods until they received the contract price from the buyer. But in *Sands v. Taylor* the sellers immediately "covered" by selling the wheat in the market and thereafter suing the buyer for the difference between market and contract price. While acknowledging that there were "no adjudications in the books, which either establish or deny the rule adopted in this

[19] 2 W. Black 1078, 96 Eng. Rep. 635 (C.P. 1776).
[21] 1 Strange 406, 93 Eng. Rep. 598 (K.B. 1760). For a more complete discussion of the case, see Moses v. Macferlan, 2 Burr. 1005, 1010-11, 97 Eng. Rep. 676 (K.B. 1760) (Mansfield, J.).

case," the court ratified the seller's decision to "cover" and allowed him to sue for the difference. "It is a much fitter rule," it declared, "than to require . . . [the seller] to suffer the property to perish, as a condition on which his right to damages is to depend." In reaching this result the court was forced to fundamentally transform the title theory. The sellers, it said, "were, by necessity . . . thus constituted trustees or agents, for the defendants . . . ." The trust theory was thus created in order to overcome a result which, though inherent in eighteenth century contract conceptions, was becoming increasingly anomalous in a nineteenth century market economy. Under an economic system in which contract was becoming regularly employed for the purpose of speculating on the price of fungible goods, the old title theory of contract, conceived of as creating a property interest in specific goods, had outlived its usefulness. As we shall see in the succeeding Section, the demise of the title theory roughly corresponded to the beginnings of organized markets and the transformation of an economic system that had used contract as simply one means of transferring specific property.

The most important aspect of the eighteenth century conception of exchange is an equitable limitation on contractual obligation. Under the modern will theory, the extent of contractual obligation depends upon the convergence of individual desires. The equitable theory, by contrast, limited and sometimes denied contractual obligation by reference to the fairness of the underlying exchange. The most direct expression of the eighteenth century theory was the well-established doctrine that equity courts would refuse specific enforcement of any contract in which they determined that the consideration was inadequate. The rule was stated by South Carolina's Chancellor Desaussure as late as 1817:

> [I]t would be a great mischief to the community, and a reproach to the justice of the country, if contracts of very great inequality, obtained by fraud, or surprise, or the skillful management of intelligent men, from weakness, or inexperience, or necessity could not be examined into, and set aside.

Four years later, the Chief Justice of New York noted the still widespread opinion of American judges that equity courts would refuse to enforce a contract where the consideration was inadequate.

Supervision of the fairness of contracts was not confined to courts of equity. The same function was performed at law by a substantive doctrine of consideration which allowed the jury to take into account not only whether there was consideration, but also whether it was adequate, before awarding damages. The prevailing legal theory of consideration was expressed by Chancellor Kent as late as 1822, on the very eve of the demise of the doctrine that equity would not enforce unfair bargains.[35] In contract actions at law, he wrote, where a jury determined damages for breach of contract, "relief can be afforded in damages, with a moderation agreeable to equity and good conscience, and . . . the claims and pretensions of each party can be duly attended to, and be admitted to govern the assessment."

Eighteenth century American reports amply support Kent's statement. . . .

. . .

Another indication of the equitable nature of damage judgments in the eighteenth century was the almost universal failure of American courts either to instruct juries in strict damage rules or else to reverse damage judgments with which they disagreed. As a result, the community's sense of fairness was often the dominant standard in contracts cases. A commentator, referring to a 1789 Connecticut commercial case, noted that "[t]he jury were the proper judges, not only of the fact but of the law that was necessarily involved in the issue . . . ." Whatever they believed about the proper allocation between judge and jury on matters of law, most judges were prepared to leave the damage question to the jury. For example, in a 1786 lawsuit in which the jury's award was lower than the agreed contract price, the South Carolina Supreme Court refused to grant a new trial since "this is a case sounding in damages, and . . . the jury have thought proper to give a kind of equitable verdict between the parties . . . ."

Further support for the existence of a substantive doctrine of consideration in the eighteenth century is found in American courts' enforcement of the rule that "a sound price warrants a sound commodity." While there is no direct evidence of a substantive doctrine of consideration in eighteenth century England, several unreported trial decisions supported the "sound price" rule, and as late as 1792 Blackstone's successor in the Vinerian Chair at Oxford, Richard Wooddeson, proclaimed the sound price doctrine to

---

[35] Kent refused to specifically enforce a contract on the grounds of the unfairness of the bargain, but he was to be overruled on appeal. Seymour v. Delancey, 3 Cow. 445 (N.Y. 1824), rev'g 6 Johns. Ch. 222 (N.Y. Ch. 1822).

be good law.[54] Thus, one may conclude that in both England and America, when the selling price was greater than the supposed objective value of the thing bought, juries were permitted to reduce the damages in an action by the seller, and courts would enforce an implied warranty in actions by the buyer.

What we have seen of eighteenth century doctrines suggests that contract law was essentially antagonistic to the interests of commercial classes. The law did not assure a businessman the express value of his bargain, but at most its specific performance. Courts and juries did not honor business agreements on their face, but scrutinized them for the substantive equality of the exchange.

For our purposes, the most important consequence of this hostility was that contract law was insulated from the purposes of commercial transactions. Businessmen settled disputes informally among themselves when they could, referred them to a more formal process of arbitration when they could not, and relied on merchant juries to ameliorate common law rules. And, finally, they endeavored to find legal forms of agreement with which to conduct business transactions free from the equalizing tendencies of courts and juries. Of these forms, the most important was the penal bond.

. . .

. . . If juries were simply instructed to ignore stipulated damages in a bond and to return verdicts for actual damages, bonds could not have represented an important device for avoiding the jury's equitable inquiry into the nature of a transaction. However, it appears that even as late as the last decade of the eighteenth century the number of bonds used to effect business transactions still vastly exceeded the number of ordinary contracts containing mutual promises; this suggests that courts did not have unlimited discretion in cases involving bonds.

The late use of bonds, the absence of widespread markets, and the equitable conception of contract law conspired to retard the development of a law of executory contracts. Indeed, the primitive state of eighteenth century American contract law is underscored by the surprising fact that some American courts did

not enforce executory contracts where there had been no part performance. For example, in *Muir v. Key*, a Virginia case decided in 1787, a buyer of tobacco brought an action for nondelivery on a bond containing mutual promises. In the same action, the seller sued for the price. The jury returned a verdict for the buyer, which the court reversed on the ground that unless the plaintiff had paid in advance he could not sue on the contract. Thus, as late as 1787 in Virginia, there could be no buyer's action on a contract without prepayment. Nor, according to one of the judges could the seller sue without delivery of the tobacco.[65]

The view that part performance was required for contractual obligation seems to have been held elsewhere in eighteenth century America as well. In his study of Massachusetts law, William Nelson states that "[a]s a general rule . . . executory contracts were not enforced . . . in pre-Revolutionary Massachusetts unless the plaintiff pleaded his own performance of his part of the bargain." Thus, in his "Commonplace Book" (1759) John Adams insisted that in "executory Agreements . . . the Performance of the Act is a Condition preecedent [sic] to the Payment." For example, if two men agree on a sale of a horse, Adams wrote, "yet there is no reason that [the seller] should have an Action for the Money before the Horse is delivered."

. . .

. . .

The use of bonds seems to have substantially declined in both England and America during the early decades of the nineteenth century. If, in fact, bonds were still an important vehicle for avoiding inquiry into the fairness of an exchange during the eighteenth century, they became increasingly unnecessary as judges took control of the rules for measuring damages. Furthermore, liquidated damage provisions were not well suited to predicting market fluctuations in an increasingly speculative economy. The result was that the executory contract came gradually to supersede the bond for most nineteenth century business transactions.

Before turning to outright reversals of eighteenth century law, however, it is important to note that

[54] R. Wooddeson, A Systematical View of the Laws of England 415 (1792). On the basis of a doubtfully reported seventeenth century case, Chandelor v. Lopus, Cro. Jac. 4, 79 Eng. Rep. 3 (Ex. 1603), noted in 8 Harv. L. Rev. 282 (1894), it was supposed by later courts that English law had never allowed an action on an implied warranty. See, e.g., Seixas v. Woods, 2 Cai. R. 48 (N.Y. Sup. Ct. 1804). Yet, like

so many other early decisions in English legal history, the court's ruling seems to have been more the product of narrow considerations of pleading than of any direct confrontation with issues of substantive policy. . . .

[65] Some of the language of the judges in the case may allow for other interpretations. . . .

there was a period of uneasy compromise between the old learning and the new. The transitional nature of the late eighteenth and early nineteenth centuries is revealed most explicitly in the confused relationship between the common counts, which by the end of the eighteenth century had emancipated the law of contract from the tyranny of the older forms of action, and Blackstone's 1768 division of the field of contract law into express and implied contracts.[76]

By highlighting the express agreement, Blackstone's division was an early indication of a tendency away from an equitable and toward a will theory of contract law. It also represented an effort to create a theoretical framework as a substitute for the older forms of action. However, Blackstone himself placed the common counts [standard forms of action, particularly those for the restitution of benefits conferred on the defendant —ed.] in the category of implied contracts,[77] which had the significant effect of identifying them with the still dominant equitable conception of contract. Implied contracts, Blackstone wrote, "are such as reason and justice dictate, and which therefore the law presumes that every man has contracted to perform . . . ." For one of the common counts—indebitatus assumpsit for money had and received—Blackstone cited Lord Mansfield's then recent path-breaking decision in *Moses v. Macferlan*,[79] in which the Chief Justice declared: "In one word, the gist of this kind of action is, that the defendant, upon the circumstances of the case, is obliged by the ties of natural justice and equity to refund the money."

As a result of this unrestrained identification of contract with "natural justice and equity," the triumph of the common counts threatened to reinforce the equitable conceptions which Blackstone's distinction between express and implied contracts had appeared to displace as the unifying principle of contract. This persistence of an equitable tradition in English contract law also influenced American courts. . . .

. . .

The transitional nature of the late eighteenth century is thus revealed in the failure of eighteenth century lawyers to perceive any latent theoretical contradictions involved in joining counts on express and implied contract. Their failure to do so undoubtedly resulted from the theoretical confusions underlying the common counts themselves. Two very different conceptions of contract were submerged within actions on the common counts. One was based on an express bargain between the parties; the other derived contractual obligation from "natural justice and equity." But in the eighteenth century there was little occasion to see the two doctrinal strands as contradictory. Contract had not yet become a major subject of common law adjudication. The existence of mercantile arbitration, on one hand, and the predominance of bills of exchange, bonds, and sealed instruments in business dealings, on the other, meant that few of the legal problems that a modern lawyer would identify as contractual entered the common law courts.

In eighteenth century America, the equitable tradition in the common counts was tied not only to a general theory of natural justice but also to an economic system often based on customary prices. The striking existence of this remnant of the medieval just price theory of value can be seen in two Massachusetts colonial cases. In *Tyler v. Richards* (1765), the plaintiff brought indebitatus assumpsit [a form of action based, at least in theory, on actual agreement —ed.] for boarding and schooling the defendant's son. The defendant argued that indebitatus "will not lye; they ought to have brought a *Quantum Meruit* [one of the common counts based on unjust enrichment of the defendant, rather than actual agreement —ed.]." For the plaintiffs, John Adams and Samuel Quincy argued that "[i]t ha[d] always been the Custom of this Court, to allow" the action "if the Services alleged were proved to have been done. As every Man is supposed to assume to pay the customary Price. Assumpsit is always brought for Work done by

---

[76] 3 W. Blackstone, Commentaries *154-64. Blackstone's discussion of express contracts was brief and essentially uninformative. Its most important break with the past lies in his assertion that, except for the seal, ordinary promises were "absolutely the same" as sealed instruments. 3 W. Blackstone, Commentaries *157. Thus, we see the beginnings of a generic conception of contracts united by common principles that transcended the particular form of action under which suits on contracts were brought. But we have yet to see any detailed elaboration of the major categories of nineteenth century contract law: offer and acceptance, con-

sideration, and, most important, rules of contract interpretation.

[77] 3 W. Blackstone, Commentaries *161. He divided implied contracts into two main headings. The first group consisted of obligations imposed by courts or statutes, which arose, Blackstone thought, from an original social contract. Id. at *158-59. A second class, including all of the common counts, arose, he explained "from natural reason, and the just construction of law." Id. at *161. In the latter class, the law assumed "that every man hath engaged to perform what his duty or justice requires." Id.

[79] 2 Burr. 1005, 97 Eng. Rep. 676 (K.B. 1760).

Tradesmen, and is always allowed. The Price for Boarding and Schooling is as much settled in the Country, as it is in the Town for a Yard of Cloth, or a Day's Work by a Carpenter." Adams and Quincy were thus attempting to convince the court that if the value of goods or services was "settled" and bore a "customary Price," there was no difference between this action and indebitatus for a "sum certain." The defendant, however, argued that "[i]f this Proof is admitted, there will be an End of any Distinction between *Indebitatus Assumpsit* and *Quantum meruit.*" The court accepted the defendant's argument and dismissed the action.

In *Pynchon v. Brewster* (1766), the plaintiff brought indebitatus "upon a long Doctor's Bill for Medicines, Travel into the Country and Attendance." This time, Adams, for the defendant, argued on the authority of *Tyler v. Richards* that indebitatus would not lie. The Chief Justice, however, distinguished *Tyler* on the ground that "Travel for Physicians, their Drugs and Attendance, had as fixed a Price as Goods sold by a Shopkeeper, and that it would be a great Hardship upon Physicians to oblige them to lay a *Quantum Meruit.*"

What emerges from these cases is that in America suits in indebitatus were sometimes based on a system of fixed and customary prices. Though the *Richards* court denied the analogy between the price of schooling and the "settled" price for a yard of cloth, it never challenged Adams' premise that the prices of most goods and services were conceived of as "settled." Similarly, while acknowledging the "uncertain" price of schooling, Chief Justice Hutchinson had no doubt that the price of a doctor's medicine and services "had as fixed a Price as Goods sold by a Shopkeeper."

Of course, there could not have been a customary rate for every exchange that might be entered into and sued upon; the jury's power to set a reasonable price in quantum meruit was necessary to fill in the gaps. Indeed, it appears that the jury had discretion to mitigate or enlarge the damages even in indebitatus actions. But the concept of customary prices formed the necessary foundation for a legal system which awarded contract damages according to measures of fairness independent of the terms agreed to by the contracting parties. By the end of the eighteenth century, however, the development of extensive markets undermined this system of customary prices and radically transformed the role of contract in an increasingly commercial society.

II. The Rise of a Market Economy and the Development of the Will Theory of Contract

A. *Early Attacks on Eighteenth Century Contract Doctrine*

For a variety of reasons, it is appropriate to correlate the emergence of the modern law of contract with the first recognition of expectation damages. Executory sales contracts assume a central place in the economic system only when they begin to be used as instruments for "futures" agreements; to accommodate the market function of such agreements the law must grant the contracting parties their expected return. Thus, the recognition of expectation damages marks the rise of the executory contract as an important part of English and American law. Furthermore, the moment at which courts focus on expectation damages, rather than restitution or specific performance to give a remedy for non-delivery, is precisely the time at which contract law begins to separate itself from property. It is at this point that contract begins to be understood not as transferring the title of particular property, but as creating an expected return. Contract then becomes an instrument for protecting against changes in supply and price in a market economy.

The first recognition of expectation damages appeared after 1790 in both England and America in cases involving speculation in stock. Jurists initially attempted to encompass these cases within traditional legal categories. Thus, Lord Mansfield in 1770 referred to a speculative interest in stock as "a new species of property, arisen within the compass of a few years." In 1789 the Connecticut Supreme Court of Errors held that recovery of expectation damages on a contract of stock speculation would be usurious. And as late as 1790, John Powell concluded that specific performance, and not an action for damages, was the proper remedy for failure to deliver stock on a rising market.

These efforts to encompass contracts of stock speculation within the old title theory were soon to be abandoned, however. Between 1799 and 1810 a number of English cases applied the rule of expectation damages for failure to deliver stock on a rising market. In America the transformation occurred a decade earlier, in response to an active "futures" market for speculation in state securities which rapidly developed after the Revolutionary War in anticipation of the assumption of state debts by the new national government. The earliest cases allowing expectation damages on contracts of stock speculation appeared in South Carolina, Virginia, and Pennsylvania.

. . .

In America the application of expectation damages to commodities contracts correlates with the development of extensive internal commodities markets around 1815. The leading case is *Shepherd v. Hampton* (1818), in which the Supreme Court held that the measure of damages for failure to deliver cotton was the difference between the contract price and the market price at the time of delivery. Within the next decade a number of courts worked out the problems of computing expectation damages for commodities contracts, one of them noting that "[m]ost of the [prior] cases in which this principle has been adopted, have grown out of contracts for the delivery and replacing of stock . . . ."

The absorption of commodities transactions into contract law is a major step in the development of a modern law of contracts. As a result of the growth of extensive markets, "futures" contracts became a normal device either to insure against fluctuations in supply and price or simply to speculate. And as a consequence, judges and jurists began to reject eighteenth century legal rules which reflected an underlying conception of contract as fair exchange.

. . .

[Horwitz discusses the efforts of the great British commercial judge, Lord Mansfield in *Pillans v. Van Mierop* in 1765 to eliminate the requirement of consideration in the enforcement of promises, at least between merchants using negotiable instruments. According to Horwitz, by this approach "Mansfield cut the heart out of the traditional equalizing function of consideration." Horwitz further argues that Blackstone argued similarly in his *Commentaries.* Although the Mansfield approach was rejected by the House of Lords in 1778, that decision was not known in America until the early 1800's. "[A] more important factor than the accident of reporting . . . was the congeniality of Mansfield's and Blackstone's views to American judges, whose own opinions were gradually inclining towards a conception of contract as a sacred bargain between private parties." An important New York judge, Brockholst Livingston, made an argument similar to Mansfield's in a dissent in 1805. — ed.]

Like Mansfield's earlier effort, this attack on consideration initially failed, but in its most important respect it ultimately succeeded. It was part of a movement, which had begun in England during Mansfield's tenure and continued throughout the nineteenth century, toward overthrowing the traditional role of courts in regulating the equity of agreements. The underlying logic of the attack on a substantive doctrine of consideration came to fruition in America with the great New York case of *Seymour v. Delancey*[142] (1824), in which a sharply divided High Court of Errors reversed a decision of Chancellor Kent, who had refused to specifically enforce a land contract on the ground of gross inadequacy of consideration between the parties. "Every member of this Court," the majority opinion noted, "must be well aware how much property is held by contract; that purchases are constantly made upon speculation; that the value of real estate is fluctuating . . . ." The result was that there "exists an honest difference of opinion in regard to any bargain, as to its being a beneficial one, or not." The court held that only where the inadequacy of price was itself evidence of fraud would it interfere with the execution of private contracts.

The nineteenth century departure from the equitable conception of contract is particularly obvious in the rapid adoption of the doctrine of caveat emptor. It has already been noted that, despite the supposed ancient lineage of caveat emptor, eighteenth century English and American courts embraced the doctrine that "a sound price warrants a sound commodity." It was only after Lord Mansfield declared in 1778, in one of those casual asides that seem to have been so influential in forging the history of the common law, that the only basis for an action for breach of warranty was an express contract, that the foundation was laid for reconsidering whether an action for breach of an implied warranty would lie. In 1802 the English courts finally considered the policies behind such an action, deciding that no suit on an implied warranty would be allowed. Two years later, in the leading American case of *Seixas v. Woods*,[149] the New York Supreme Court, relying on a doubtfully reported seventeenth century English case, also held that there could be no recovery against a merchant who could not be proved knowingly to have sold defective goods. Other American jurisdictions quickly fell into line.

While the rule of caveat emptor established in *Seixas v. Woods* seems to be the result of one of those frequent accidents of historical misunderstanding,

---

[142] 3 Cow. 445 (N.Y. 1824), rev'g 6 Johns. Ch. 222 (N.Y. Ch. 1822).

[149] 2 Cai. R. 48 (N.Y. Sup. Ct. 1804).

this is hardly sufficient to account for the widespread acceptance of the doctrine of caveat emptor elsewhere in America. Nor are the demands of a market economy a sufficient cause. Although the sound price doctrine was attacked on the ground that there "is no standard to determine whether the vendee has paid a *sound* price," the most consistent legal theorist of the market economy, Gulian Verplanck, devoted his impressive analytical talents to an elaborate critique of the doctrine of caveat emptor.[153] The sudden and complete substitution of caveat emptor in place of the sound price doctrine must therefore be understood as a dramatic overthrow of an important element of the eighteenth century's equitable conception of contract.

B. *The Synthesis of the Will Theory of Contract*

The development of extensive markets at the turn of the century contributed to a substantial erosion of belief in theories of objective value and just price. Markets for future delivery of goods were difficult to explain within a theory of exchange based on giving and receiving equivalents in value. Futures contracts for fungible commodities could only be understood in terms of a fluctuating conception of expected value radically different from the static notion that lay behind contracts for specific goods; a regime of markets and speculation was simply incompatible with a socially imposed standard of value. The rise of a modern law of contract, then, was an outgrowth of an essentially procommercial attack on the theory of objective value which lay at the foundation of the eighteenth century's equitable idea of contract.

We have seen however, that there was a period during which vestiges of the eighteenth century conception of contract coexisted with the emerging will theory. It was not until after 1820 that attacks on the equitable conception began to be generalized to include all aspects of contract law. If value is subjective, nineteenth century contracts theorists reasoned, the function of exchange is to maximize the conflicting and otherwise incommensurable desires of individuals. The role of contract law was not to assure the equity of agreements but simply to enforce only those willed transactions that parties to a contract believed to be to their mutual advantage. The result was a major tendency toward submerging the dominant equitable theory of contract in a conception of

contractual obligation based exclusively on express bargains. In his *Essay on the Law of Contracts* (1822), for example, Daniel Chipman criticized the Vermont system of assigning customary values to goods that were used to pay contract debts. Only the market could establish a fair basis for exchange, Chipman urged. "[L]et money be the sole standard in making all contracts," for "[i]f, therefore, it were possible for courts in the administration of justice, to take this ideal high price as a standard of valuation, every consideration of policy, and a regard for the good of the people would forbid it."

We will see that Nathan Dane's *Abridgment* (1823) and Joseph Story's *Equity Jurisprudence* (1836) also contributed to the demise of the old equitable conceptions. But nowhere were the underlying bases of contract law more brilliantly and systematically rethought than in Gulian C. Verplanck's *An Essay on the Doctrine of Contracts* (1825).

. . .

In refusing to separate law and morals, Verplanck was boldly independent of other theorists of the market economy. But at its deepest level, Verplanck's *Essay* marks the triumph of a subjective theory of value in a market economy. Wishing to base legal doctrine on "the plainer truths of political economy," he insisted that although just price doctrines bore "the impression of a high and pure morality," they were "mixed with error" and arose "from the introduction of a false metaphysic in relation to equality . . . ." Thus, he disputed the view of "[l]awyers and divines . . . that all bargains are made under the ideal of giving and receiving equivalents in value." There could be no "such thing in the literal sense of the words, as adequacy of price [or] equality or inequality of compensation," since "from the very nature of the thing, price depends solely upon the agreement of the parties, being created by it alone. Mere inequality of price, or rather what appears so in the judgment of a third person, cannot, without reference to something else, be any objection to the validity of a sale, or of an agreement to sell."

Verplanck's *Essay* represents an important stage in the process of adapting contract law to the realities of a market economy. Verplanck saw that if value is solely determined by the clash of subjective desire, there can be no objective measure of the fairness of a

---

[153] . . . I have not meant to assert that caveat emptor is more conducive to a market economy than the contrary doctrine of caveat venditor, though this might be independently demonstrated. Rather, I have argued that the importance of caveat emptor lies in its overthrow of both the sound price doctrine and the latter's underlying conception of objective value.

bargain. Since only "facts" are objective, fairness can never be measured in terms of substantive equality. . . .

Though Verplanck's reconsideration of the philosophical foundations of contract law was by far the most penetrating among the American treatise writers, Nathan Dane and Joseph Story were more influential in contributing to the overthrow of an equitable conception of contract. . . .

. . .

Dane was still reflecting an eighteenth century world view in which unequal bargaining power was conceived of as an illegitimate form of duress and in which lack of understanding was not yet identified only with mental disability. And yet in the world of speculation and futures markets, in which all value must simply turn on "an honest difference of opinion," legal doctrine eventually renounced all claims to make judgments about oppression. With the publication of Joseph Story's *Equity Jurisprudence* (1836), American law finally yielded up the ancient notion that the substantive value of an exchange could provide an appropriate measure of the justice of a transaction. "Inadequacy of consideration," Story wrote, "is not then, of itself, a distinct principle of relief in Equity. The Common Law knows no such principle . . . . The value of a thing . . . . must be in its nature fluctuating, and will depend upon ten thousand different circumstances . . . . If Courts of Equity were to unravel all these transactions, they would throw every thing into confusion, and set afloat the contracts of mankind."

The replacement of the equitable conception of contract with the will theory can be seen in Dane's assault on the eighteenth century practice of suing on a theory of implied contract where there had been an express agreement. In a long and unusually polemical technical discussion, Dane argued that once there is an express contract there could be no quantum meruit recovery off the contract on a theory of natural justice and equity. Dane's attack on quantum meruit becomes comprehensible only as an effort to destroy an equitable conception of exchange in light of a newly emerging theory of value based on the subjective desires of contracting parties. Without a socially imposed standard of value, implied contracts make no sense. Where "there is no fixed or unchangeable comparative value between one price of property and another" and all value "depends on the wants and opinions of men," it becomes impossible to measure

damages by reference to customary value. The only basis for measuring contractual obligation, then, derives from the "will" of parties, and the crucial legal issue shifts to whether there has been a "meeting of minds."

The victory of the emerging will theory of contractual obligation was not at first complete. When Theron Metcalf delivered his lectures on contracts in 1828 he still reflected the tension between the old learning and the new. Implied contracts, he wrote, were "inferred from the conduct, situation, or mutual relations of the parties, and enforced by the law on the ground of justice; to compel the performance of a legal and moral duty . . . ." In support of this, he cited Chief Justice Marshall's statement that implied contracts "grow out of the acts of the parties. In such cases, the parties are supposed to have made those stipulations which, as honest, fair, and just men, they ought to have made."[186] Though both Metcalf and Marshall were beginning to pretend that contractual obligation derives only from the will of the parties, their predominant form of expression continued to recognize standards of justice external to the parties. Indeed, Metcalf still maintained that "[i]n sound sense, divested of fiction and technicality, the only true ground, on which an action upon what is called an implied contract can be maintained, is that of justice, duty, and legal obligation."

By the time William W. Story's *Treatise on the Law of Contracts* appeared in 1844, however, the tension between the two theories had dissolved. "Every contract," he wrote, "is founded upon the mutual agreement of the parties . . . ." Both express and implied contracts were "equally founded upon the actual agreement of the parties, and the only distinction between them is in regard to the mode of proof, and belongs to the law of evidence." For implied contracts, he concluded, "the law only supplies that which, although not stated, must be presumed to have been the agreement intended by the parties." Since the only basis for the contractual obligation was the will of the parties, Story now maintained, implied promises "only supply omissions, and do not alter express stipulations"; he was thus prepared to announce the "general rule" that there could be no implied contract where an express agreement already existed.

With Story's announcement of the "general rule," the victory of the will theory of contractual obligation was complete. The entire conceptual apparatus of

---

[186] Ogden v. Saunders, 25 U.S. (12 Wheat.) 341 (1827) . . . .

modern contract doctrine—rules dealing with offer and acceptance, the evidentiary function of consideration, and canons of construction and interpretation—arose to articulate the will theory with which American doctrinal writers expressed the ideology of a market economy in the early nineteenth century.

. . .

Although nineteenth century courts and doctrinal writers did not succeed in entirely destroying the ancient connection between contracts and natural jus-

tice, they were able to elaborate a system that allowed judges to pick and choose among those groups in the population that would be its beneficiaries. And, above all, they succeeded in creating a great intellectual divide between a system of formal rules—which they managed to identify exclusively with the "rule of law"—and those ancient precepts of morality and equity, which they were able to render suspect as subversive of "the rule of law" itself.

A.W.B. Simpson, *The Horwitz Thesis and the History of Contracts*, 46 U. Chi. L. Rev. 533 (1979)

In his article, *The Historical Foundations of Modern Contract Law*, subsequently republished and enlarged as a chapter in *The Transformation of American Law 1780-1860*,[2] Professor Morton J. Horwitz advanced a striking new interpretation of the evolution of American and English contract law in the late eighteenth and nineteenth centuries. This interpretation is related to his general thesis about the "transformation" of American private law in the period covered by the book. Horwitz claims that the private law of the eighteenth century was benign, reflecting the assumptions of a "pre-market economy," and thus its function was to impose a natural and objectively just order upon society. By a variety of mechanisms the law was then adapted to legitimate and facilitate the inequalities of the nineteenth-century market economy in which entrepreneurs flourished and the weak suffered.

I do not propose in this article to consider Horwitz's general thesis, but rather its particular application to certain aspects of contract law. Horwitz argues that there occurred a radical shift in contractual theory in the late eighteenth and early nineteenth centuries. Before the change, the justification of contractual obligation was sought in "the inherent justice or fairness of an exchange." Eighteenth-century courts, concerned with justice, "limited and sometimes denied contractual obligation" when the

underlying exchange was unfair. They assumed that things had their proper price: price, or value, did not depend solely on the operation of market forces. This general philosophy found expression in what Horwitz calls the "equitable conception of contract." The eighteenth century also held to what Horwitz calls the "title theory of exchange"—it understood contract primarily as a mechanism for transferring property and not as a mechanism for securing expectations.

Then, beginning in the last quarter of the eighteenth century, the equitable approach to contract was replaced by the notion that the source of contractual obligation was not the justice of the bargain but the convergence of the wills of the contracting parties. Horwitz elaborately develops a pessimistic interpretation of the cases, presenting what might be regarded as minor changes in the somewhat technical doctrines of contract law as fitting neatly into a process that converted a more humane body of law into a weapon of oppression. Once devised, the new scheme of contract law was reinforced by that most ill-defined of legal ailments, formalism, which supposedly arose after 1825 or 1830, gathered momentum in the 1840's and developed strongly after 1850.

Underlying Horwitz's argument is a romanticized view of English law before the "transformation" and, indeed, before the eighteenth century. But the heart

[2] The article appears as Chapter VI, "The Triumph of

Contract," in M. Horwitz, The Transformation Of American Law 161-210 (1977), with a paragraph, id. at 166 (lines 3-18), and a long passage on "Custom and Contract," id. at 188-210, added. This article will not discuss these additions.

of his argument lies in his view that eighteenth-century contract law reflected an equitable conception or theory of contract, which was "essentially antagonistic to the interests of commercial classes," and that this conception was replaced by an approach more congenial to the needs of a commercial, market economy. As Horwitz presents it, this argument is hard to test against the evidence—partly because it is so general and partly because Horwitz, with true rhetorical mastery, interweaves evidence from England and America, from different periods of time, and from different types of cases. His argument does, however, rest upon a number of specific propositions that can be related to evidence. In his view, eighteenth-century courts (1) did not fully recognize the executory contract; (2) did not award expectation damages; (3) accepted inadequacy of consideration as a well established ground for refusing a decree of specific performance; (4) accepted a "substantive doctrine of consideration" whereby juries in contract cases were to reduce damages where consideration was inadequate; (5) implied a warranty of quality where the price was least the normal price charged for the goods; and (6) allowed the joining of counts in express and implied contract. Horwitz argues that each of these positions was abandoned in the late eighteenth and early nineteenth centuries.

I will address the general issue of Horwitz's view of pre-"transformation" English law in the first part of this article. In the second and major section of the article, I will try to demonstrate, by a detailed investigation of Horwitz's sources, that the evidence he adduces for the specific propositions underlying his thesis is very weak. Horwitz also supports his argument by analyzing treatises on contracts published in the later eighteenth and early nineteenth centuries. The third part of the article will consider that body of evidence. I will conclude with some suggestions regarding the general interpretation of the evolution of contract law in this period.

I. The Good Old Law

Horwitz supports his thesis that, starting in the late eighteenth century, the law of contract was transformed into an instrument of class oppression, with a romanticized view of earlier English law and society. This support is not logically necessary to his thesis. A Marxist might have argued that the English commercial bourgeoisie, linked with elements in the landed classes, forged an equitable theory of contract in the eighteenth century as a weapon in their struggle with a law reflecting earlier, less commercial

times; and that once it triumphed, the new order cut back on the dangerous legal doctrines it had used against the old. But this is emphatically not Horwitz's position. His view of the history of English and American law appears to be linear, not dialectical. He presents the benign and equitable elements in eighteenth-century contractual theory not as innovations associated with the growth of commercial (pre-industrial) capitalism, but as the approach to contract that is appropriate to a precommercial society.

Horwitz suggests in various ways that eighteenth-century English law and society were closer to a simple and morally pure earlier state than to the rapacious world of the nineteenth century. One problem with these suggestions is that the image projected of that earlier state is often skewed. For example, by using expressions like "the medieval tradition of substantive justice," "theories of objective value and just price," "this remnant of the medieval just price theory of value," Horwitz relates his eighteenth-century equitable theory of contract to medieval and presumably postmedieval doctrines associated with notions of just price. Unfortunately, Horwitz tends here to perpetuate a myth that scholars have long attempted to put to rest. His rather vague references should be received with some caution if they are intended to suggest that there was a single doctrine that was generally accepted by medieval or postmedieval secular tribunals dealing with contract law, and that this doctrine was hostile to competitive markets.

The idea of just price goes back in Christian thought at least to St. Augustine of Hippo. From Aquinas onward, the Christian moralists, responding to a rapid growth of commerce in the high Middle Ages, argued in favor of high ethical standards of bargaining. They rejected as sinful all forms of fraud, trickery, and evasion, and all exploitation of the particular weakness of individuals. With this approach, they developed and elaborated notions of the just price of commodities at which commerce could take place without sin. The prevailing view came to be that the just price is fixed by common estimation (*communis aestimatio*) in a fairly conducted market—in the absence of fraud, monopoly, or coercion; value as set by the community was contrasted with special value to the individual. The monopolist, not the market, was seen as the great enemy of the just price. Consequently, in the absence of a fairly conducted market, or when unusually poor conditions of supply or unusually heavy demand threatened to imbalance the market, the just price was to be imposed by legal regulation. It was common enough for prices to be determined that way in medieval and early modern times, but given normal conditions, the fair or just price was the market price, or the price set by ordinary supply and demand.

. . .

The extent to which secular courts in medieval or postmedieval Europe acted upon the views of either the theologians or the civilians raises complex questions on which I am not competent to pronounce. In English common law there is, so far as I am aware, no evidence for the general reception of either. The point I wish to stress here is that neither civilians nor Christian moralists, both trying to adapt received notions to the needs of a society with growing commercial activity, were hostile in principle to a functioning market as a price-setter.

Throughout his analysis, Horwitz implies that eighteenth-century contract law reflected the values of a society whose economy was not only preindustrial in the sense that it has not yet been transformed by the "industrial revolution," but one that was simple, agrarian, and in some sense "pre-market," and which therefore bred values that were "pre-commercial," or at least "antagonistic to the interests of commercial classes." While Horwitz applies these terms to America more than to England, and his sparse evidence comes from America as much as from England, it is in England that the Chancellor and courts supposedly developed the equitable conception of contract. Thus, if the image of economic backwardness he presents is relevant to eighteenth-century Anglo-American contract law, it must be applicable to eighteenth-century English society.

Although there is room for judgment here, the suggestion that English law reflected a relatively simple and primitive economy is odd in a work dealing with the law as it was pronounced by the King's Chancellor and the King's courts in London, not as it was spoken in small borough courts and village tribunals. England, even in the first half of the eighteenth century, was the greatest trading nation in the world, and its trade was supported by a sophisticated mercantile community well versed in techniques of shipping, financing, and insuring cargoes around the world. Equally important, England was second to none in the skill and depth of its commercial and industrial infrastructure. Horwitz emphasizes that a national commodities market grew up in England only in the second half of the eighteenth century. This

is debatable, and not very relevant. Important regional markets affected a large part of the population no later than the beginning of the century; just feeding and supplying London oriented much of the country towards producing for a market. This is not to deny that there were regions, and sections of the population, relatively distant from the world of finance, commerce, and industry. But Horwitz's apparent premise that there must be a national market embracing almost everyone in society before the groups that shape the law can be influenced profoundly by commercial interests and needs is unsupportable. Again, I would not deny that the English aristocracy and gentry sometimes affected to despise commercial values in the eighteenth century (though perhaps no more than in the nineteenth). But to suggest that the law pronounced in Chancery and the common-law courts could ignore the needs of the commercial classes and their powerful allies in Parliament and the court reveals a profound misunderstanding of English politics and society in the eighteenth century and, for that matter, in the seventeenth as well.

These examples can be multiplied. In the second section of this article I will point out that Horwitz sometimes appears to misstate earlier English law in his attempt to show that it was only in the late eighteenth century that the courts and the treatise writers began to transform this law to meet what he conceives to be the needs of a commercial society. I want to close the present section, however, with a more general point. If the eighteenth-century law, in sharp contrast to what was to succeed it, was anticommercial and reflected, as Horwitz puts it, "the medieval tradition of substantive justice," we might expect that the pre-eighteenth-century common law of contract, and particularly the medieval law, would be even more benign and protective. Yet it is quite clear that this was not the case.

The typical medieval contract was the formal contract, the penal bond under seal; the harsh medieval law of the penal bond was notoriously based on the philosophy that those who made beds should lie in them.[42] The law emphatically favored creditors over debtors, and despite the received objections to usury, the law rigorously enforced the recovery of penalties. So far as informal contracts are concerned (the point is palpable for contracts under seal), there is not to be found a single hint in the case law of the fifteenth, sixteenth, or seventeenth centuries of the acceptance

---

[42] On the earlier law of contract, see generally A. Simpson, A History of the Common Law of Contract 88-126

(1975) (substantially incorporating Simpson, The Penal Bond with Conditional Defeasance, 82 L.Q. Rev. 392 (1966)).

of a doctrine of just price. Scholars may attempt to explain away *Chandelor v. Lopus* (1603), but it is more important to notice the complete absence of any suggestions in the case law of implied warranties of quality between 1603 and the late eighteenth century, with the possible exception of contracts for victuals and the very scanty evidence of a different attitude in late medieval common law.

Throughout this period, and long after, imprisonment without term was the fate of the debtor who failed to deliver. As Edmund Plowden put it in 1551, with a certain lack of charm:

> For if one be in Execution he ought to live of his own, and neither the Plaintiff nor the Sheriff is bound to give him Meat or Drink, no more than if one distrains Cattle, and puts them in a Pound . . . . [A]nd if he has no Goods, he shall live of the Charity of others, and if others will give him nothing, let him die in the Name of God, if he will, and impute the Cause of it to his own Fault, for his Presumption and ill Behavior brought him to that Imprisonment.[49]

So spoke the greatest common lawyer of the time, a devout adherent of the old religion and a man who was offered the office of Chancellor by Elizabeth I. It is true that Chancery did, to a considerable extent, soften the extreme rigors of the common law's enthusiasm for creditors' rights—for example, by relieving against penalties, though this jurisdiction was established only in the seventeenth century. If, instead of selecting a short period of the eighteenth century for comparison with the nineteenth, one takes in the medieval common law as a basis for comparison, the picture of a loss of primeval innocence appears most implausible.

Horwitz's thesis does not stand or fall on this issue, of course. Whether he is right in his views about earlier English law, the character of English society before and during the eighteenth century, or the incompatibility of equitable doctrines of contract with the needs of entrepreneurs in an industrial society is ultimately of secondary importance. I will now turn, therefore, to a consideration of the evidence for his view that contract law was fundamentally different in the eighteenth century from what it became in the nineteenth because the eighteenth century accepted an equitable conception of contract that conceived of contract in terms of a "title theory of exchange" and

looked to the fairness of an exchange before it would enforce its terms.

II. The Equitable Conception of Contract

Horwitz's thesis about the transformation of English and American contract law in the period 1780-1860 rests essentially on his interpretation of eighteenth-century English contract law before the transformation. It is my view that the differences Horwitz claims to have discovered between eighteenth-century and early nineteenth-century law are, for the most part, illusory. I am not saying that the law did not change in this period, but that the changes he describes were not the changes that occurred. In particular, many of the doctrines that he identifies as characteristic of the transformation were common in the eighteenth century.

I realize that any major change in the law does not happen overnight. It would not be very significant to find occasional cases in the eighteenth century stating what allegedly became law only in the nineteenth. I have not, therefore, focused on cases that Horwitz ignores, though they are noted where necessary. Rather, the focus of the following analysis is the evidence that Horwitz himself adduces in support of his thesis. Again, to show that his interpretation of the evidence is occasionally at fault would not be very significant, since this would not affect his general thesis. My contention is that Horwitz allowed himself to be misled by his striking and seductive thesis into a general and systematic misinterpretation of the evidence, and that his thesis, once tested in detail, is quite misconceived. In order to make the case for this view it is essential, if at times tedious, to subject his arguments to very close inspection. I can see no other way of testing the validity of a thesis that, if correct, is of great historical importance.

A. The Recognition of Executory Contracts

Horwitz writes that "contrary to the orthodox view, the process [whereby the executory exchange became enforceable] was not complete at the end of the sixteenth century . . . . [A]s late as the eighteenth century contract law was still dominated by a title theory of exchange." It is difficult to come to grips with this position. What does it means to say that the process "was not complete"? No one has claimed that the executory contract played precisely the same role in the sixteenth century as in the eighteenth, or as in

---

[49] Dive v. Maningham, 1 Plowd. 60, 68 (C.P. 1550), reprinted with slight variations in 75 Eng. Rep. 96, 108-09.

the twentieth. In that sense, no process of institutional development is complete until that institution is dead. Similarly, nobody has claimed that the conception of contract as a set of mutual promises drove all other conceptions of contract out of the field in the sixteenth century—it has not done so even today. The issue is, or should be, whether the exchange of promises was a recognized, standard way for parties to conclude a mutually enforceable agreement in the eighteenth century. That the place of executory contracts in early modern English law was different from what it is today does not mean that the law did not fully recognize such contracts. I have set out elsewhere a detailed explanation of the processes whereby so-called executory contracts came to be recognized and, perhaps more important, an analysis of what this expression means,[52] but a short summary here may clarify what Horwitz has misunderstood.

It was settled in the sixteenth century that mutual promises could be consideration for each other. In such a case, a plaintiff could sue for breach without averring performance, the other party being put to his counter-action. The doctrine originated with wagers, where it is logically necessary. Not all exchanges of promises, however, were analyzed as bilateral, executory contracts in the modern sense—as promise-for-promise cases. It might be the intention of the parties that the consideration should be the performance, not the promise. In such a case, the plaintiff had to show performance before he could sue: the promise itself was not actionable because if performance had not yet occurred, there was not yet consideration. An alternative conceptual scheme for achieving the same practical result employed the concept of a condition: the defendant's promised performance might be conditional upon prior or simultaneous performance by the plaintiff, so that the plaintiff would lose unless he could show performance or tender.

Very elaborate rules evolved for these situations.

They offered a guide to whether the parties intended to treat a counter-promise or only its performance as consideration and, using the concept of conditional obligation, dealt with the mutual dependence or independence of promises.[57] Their application caused endless difficulty.[58] The existence of these rules does not mean, however, that contemporaries were "confused" about the nature of contract, and it does not contradict the proposition that the law recognized pure promise-for-promise contracts. Rather, these rules were an integral part of the promise-for-promise doctrine. One can understand what was meant by an executory contract in this period only by keeping in mind the existence of these rules, for they defined the limits of the pure promise-for-promise contract and set forth other ways in which a promise might become the source of a future binding obligation.

Finally, it must be noted that the voluminous case law on the subject, from the mid-sixteenth century until the nineteenth, is primarily concerned with establishing when a plaintiff can sue, rather than when a person may unilaterally withdraw from a promise before breach. In the earliest cases in which the latter issue was aired, it was regarded—however surprising we may find this—as a distinct issue. Eventually, by a process still not understood, it was settled that the giving of a consideration for a promise, whether that consideration was an act or a counter-promise, made the promise binding. When the doctrine of offer and acceptance entered in the nineteenth century, it expressed this view.[60]

. . .

Horwitz also supports his thesis with the argument, limited to America, that American courts did not enforce executory contracts unless there had been at least part performance. His somewhat sparse evidence for this statement is not convincing. The doctrine he reports from John Adams's *Commonplace Book* concerns promise-for-act agreements, in which performance was in standard doctrine a prerequisite

[52] A. Simpson, supra note 42, at 452-70. See generally id. at 406-88.

[57] These rules are associated with the leading cases of Pordage v. Cole, 1 Wms. Saund. 319, 85 Eng. Rep. 449 (K.B. 1669), and Cutter v. Powell, 6 T.R. 320, 101 Eng. Rep. 573 (K.B. 1795).

[58] . . . The rules tended to be regarded as pleading rules, rather than substantive principles of contract law. As Selwyn points out, "[t]he principal difficulty in the construction of agreements consists in discovering, whether the consideration be a condition precedent, a concurrent act, or a mutual promise." W. Selwyn, An Abridgment of the Law of Nisi Prius 109 (3d ed. London 1812). The effect of these rules was that it was most unusual for a plaintiff to be able to sue for breach without showing performance or tender. But this is the situation today as well; it does not mean that the law of contract was [sic "has"? —ed.] abandoned the executory contract. The evidence is discussed in W. Nelson, Americanization of the Common Law 56-59 (1975).

[60] See generally Simpson, Innovation in Nineteenth Century Contract Law, 91 L. Q. Rev. 247 (1975).

of obligation.[73] Orthodox law is also set out in Zephaniah Swift's *A System of the Laws of the State of Connecticut*. Swift, whom Horwitz portrays as wavering between recognition and nonrecognition of executory contracts, merely states what had long been the law and long would be. So far as promise-for-promise cases are concerned, Swift explains that mutual promises can be consideration for each other, but only if the parties so intended. Whether the parties contracted on the basis of mutual promises or on the basis that part performance was required for any obligation to arise is a question of inference from the facts. Swift also explains the mutual dependence rules and gives a particularly clear account of how such rules worked in the law of sale.

. . . Horwitz fails to appreciate the complexity and the function of the rules governing bilateral contracts, which had been settled in all essentials in the sixteenth and seventeenth centuries.

[Professor Simpson continues his detailed analysis of Horwitz's descriptions of contract doctrine for 40 pages. In this deleted portion he discusses expectation damages, specific performance and the inadequacy of consideration, damages at law and the substantive doctrine of consideration, and the sound-price doctrine. Throughout, Simpson gives a close reading to many of the authorities cited by Horwitz and finds that they do not support Horwitz's broad readings. (Whether Simpson discredits Horwitz's conclusions about doctrinal changes is briefly discussed in the note following this article.)

[Simpson concludes this section with a short discussion of the joinder of express and implied contract claims. In reading this portion, it is necessary to understand that until the mid-nineteenth century the English pleading rules were excessively technical and complex, especially in that a case had to fit into one or more existing "forms of action," which were often named by their first words when pleading had been in Law Latin. One of these was "indebitatus assumpsit" ("being indebted he assumed"), which was based on an express promise, not under seal. But there were others like the action for "money had and received" and those for "quantum meruit" ("as much as he deserved") and "quantum valebant" ("as much as they were worth"), which were based on restitutionary notions of unjust enrichment without contract. According to Horwitz, a major change in thinking came when the courts changed the theoretical basis of these latter forms from communal notions of fairness to fictitious "contracts implied in law," and no longer allowed them to be pleaded in the alternative with claims based on express contract. —ed.]

F. Joinder of Express and Implied Contracts

Horwitz associates his older, equitable conception of contract with the rule of pleading that permitted the joinder of counts on express and implied contracts, and the victory of the will theory of contract in the nineteenth century with the disappearance of this rule. In the eighteenth century, for example, in an action of indebitatus assumpsit for the price of goods sold and delivered, the liability was based on an express contract between the parties, whereas in the action for money had and received, the liability might be imposed by law in the absence of any agreement by the defendant. For Horwitz, these two actions reflected "very different conceptions of contract . . . . One was based on an express bargain between the parties; the other derived contractual obligation from 'natural justice and equity.'" Eighteenth-century lawyers, however, did not "perceive any latent theoretical contradictions involved in joining counts on express and implied contract." As a result, "the equitable tradition in the common counts" remained alive. It is not quite clear what Horwitz means by this phrase, but presumably he is implying that the joinder of counts allowed juries to decide in terms of equitable notions inherent in enforcing implied contracts even when there was an express agreement between the parties.

This practice supposedly changed with the collapse of the old conception of contract. "In the nineteenth century the practice of joining counts on express and implied contracts began to be viewed as contradictory, and the rule was ultimately laid down that the existence of an express agreement precludes recovery in quantum meruit." Horwitz supports this by a reference to Story's treatise on contracts in which Story maintains that "[t]he general rule is, that a contact will be implied only where there is no express contract, *'expressum facit cessare tacitum.'*"*

---

[73] The full text makes this quite clear: "In executory Agreements, if the Contract be, that one shall do an Act, and for the doing thereof, the other shall pay &c. the Performance of the Act is a Condition preceedent [sic] to the Payment. Except 1, a Day appointed for Payment of the Money happen before the Thing can be performed. For in this case it is plain the Party relied upon his Remedy." . . .

Adams states the rule with respect to mutually independent promises quite clearly in a passage Horwitz does not quote: "In Case of mutual Promises, one Promise is the Consideration of the other. And in these Cases the Plaintiff is not obliged to aver Performance of his Part.". . .

* ["What is express governs (or "causes to cease") what is implied" —ed.]

Horwitz's account is confused in a number of ways. It is true, of course, that forms of assumpsit were used to enforce different kinds of agreements: express agreements, agreements that were implied only in the sense that they were inferred from conduct, and agreements that were implied in the more radical sense of being imposed by law, irrespective of actual agreement between the parties. It is also true that as a consequence there was a considerable degree of analytical confusion of categories from the seventeenth century onward. But it is mistaken to say that it ever became the rule that counts on express and implied contracts could not be joined. Chitty states the rule in his day to be that "[i]n actions in *form ex contractu*, the plaintiff may join as many different counts as he has causes of action in *assumpsit*." Chitty notes that while it remained usual to add a quantum meruit or valebant count to an indebitatus count, that practice had become unnecessary. The plaintiff could recover "under an *indebitatus* count . . . what may be due to him, although no specific price or sum was agreed upon." Since the indebitatus count could now be used where only a quantum meruit or quantum valebant count could work before, the latter counts had become "in no case necessary." Eventually, these counts passed out of use, and quantum meruit survived as a substantive doctrine, not as a form of pleading.

That it was long a common practice to join counts does not mean that contract would be implied when there was an express contract. The available evidence indicates that a plaintiff used to set forth different counts in the same declaration not to inflate the agreed price by declaring on quantum meruit, but to have something to fall back on "lest he should fail in the proof" of his assumpsit. What Story was expounding in the passage quoted by Horwitz was not a pleading rule, but a substantive doctrine that was not new. It had never been suggested that claims to a quantum meruit—and it is with these that Horwitz is especially concerned—could be used to bypass the agreed price if there was one; insofar as Story's principle involves no more than that, it involves nothing novel.

. . .

[Simpson concludes the section by discussing *Cutter v. Powell*, a famous English case from 1795:] the court there also treated as quite settled that express contracts exclude implied ones: "That where the parties have come to an express contract none can be implied has prevailed so long as to be reduced to an axiom in the law." So it was put by Lord Kenyon in

1795, and Horwitz has provided no evidence to refute it.

. . .

[Professor Simpson similarly criticizes Professor Horwitz's reading of text writers. He then puts forth his conclusion.]

Conclusion

When Horwitz's general account of the dramatic transformation of contract law is broken down into specific propositions, and these are then examined in detail and referred to the evidence, his thesis is found to be oversimplified. Through an unsatisfactory and loose use of evidence, he has made a complex, confused story fall into a preordained pattern. What is still more fundamental, Horwitz appears to me to have made two very dubious assumptions.

The first concerns the interpretation of the growth in scale and elaboration of contract law in the nineteenth century. Essentially, Horwitz views this as a change from one body of substantive law to another, the earlier law favoring the commercial class less than the new. Horwitz is aware, however, that the development of contract law considerably reduced the sovereignty of the jury, whose earlier discretionary power came to be restricted by the newly elaborated law and by the extension of control over the remaining area of discretion. To sustain his pessimistic interpretation, Horwitz is forced into a romanticized view of the eighteenth-century jury, and into attributing to it a consistent and morally appealing doctrinal position. This interpretation is not supported by evidence. Because he believes that a change in substantive doctrine must have taken place, Horwitz fails to grasp the nature of the historical problem: what needs to be explained is this progressive dethronement of the jury, which is accompanied by the generation or reception of law in order not so much to replace or transform older doctrine as to provide law where before there was little or none.

Horwitz's second assumption concerns the relationship between the doctrines he discusses and the exploitation of the poor and weak. Nobody, of course, would doubt the existence of such exploitation in this period, and there is nothing in any way implausible in the claim that certain legal doctrines may facilitate such exploitation. Great care is required, however, in establishing natural links between particular doctrines and human oppression. The sound-price doctrine, for instance, admirable though it may be in some contexts, is not so admirable in others. In the Carolinas, where the doctrine flourished, it turns up in the context of sales of slaves. In the case of *Timrod v. Shoolbred* (1793), assumpsit was brought "for the value of a family of negroes sold at public auction, viz. a fellow called *Stepney*, a ploughman, his wife, a young wench, their daughter and her child, bid off at 170Ł." The day after he was purchased, Stepney broke out with smallpox, from which he died. The purchaser refused to pay unless the price was reduced *pro rata*, and the court agreed, applying the equitable doctrine and reducing the sale price. The court said: "In every contract every imaginable fairness ought to be observed, especially in the sale of negroes, which are a valuable species of property in this country."[418]

In England the implied warranty arose in the context of the sale of horses. The poor did not buy horses; they walked. The doctrine of *laesio enormis* in the civil law protected landowners; in England the case law in chancery on sales at low value and on "catching bargains" with expectant heirs appears to have largely performed the same function. No doubt certain aspects of contract law pressed on the poor—imprisonment for debt is surely the principal villain here. But in the main, I doubt if their lot was much improved by the existence of an implied warranty of quality on the sale of victuals, or made worse by some detail of the rules for the assessment of damages. It was their misfortune to be outside the world in which such luxuries as legal actions at common law or bills in equity much mattered.

---

[418] . . . Hence, the court continued, the implied warranty "of soundness of the thing [sic] sold.". . .

Horwitz's History and Horwitz's Interpretation— His Critics and the Critics of His Critics

Simpson's detailed critique of Horwitz's reading of the cases is about five times as long as the excerpt provided here. Even a strong supporter of Horwitz has admitted that Simpson is daunting. Wythe Holt, in his essay, *Morton Horwitz and the Transformation of American Legal History*, 23 Wm. & M. L. Rev. 663, 700-01 (1982), calls Simpson's work "formidable" and "urbane," but ultimately concludes that Simpson did not manage "substantially to refute Horwitz's reading of the nineteenth-century American cases." Like most commentators, Holt freely admits that he is not competent to get into a deep historical investigation; in the end, he relies on others who are sympathetic to the Horwitz approach. One of the writers that Holt relies on to attack Simpson, Betty Mensch, herself relies on Patrick Atiyah, whose reading of contract history Charles Fried attacked in a book review, relying on Simpson!

In trying to sort out the history, we might look at the debate over the "executory promises" question: did the pre-industrial common law courts view a promise given for a promise as a sufficient basis for a contract claim if a promise was broken before either party relied on the other's word? Horwitz (and Atiyah) say no, while Simpson says yes. But Simpson goes on to add that implied conditions, inferences of intent and the rules of pleading might have made it difficult in practice to recover on a purely executory exchange of promises with no reliance. One might conclude that Horwitz could be faulted for not reading the cases as precisely and rigorously as Simpson, but that Horwitz's (and Atiyah's) position is essentially supported if in fact the courts rarely enforced a pure exchange of promises. From that point it would be possible to go on to the more important point, whether this lack of enforcement supports Horwitz and Atiyah's arguments that contract as an abstract thing, based on free will and a basic liberty to bind oneself, did not exist until the turn of the nineteenth century. This, in turn, would be relevant, though surely not devastating, to the Fried promise approach and the Barnett consent theory of contract.

Most critics of Horwitz have not argued with his reading of the cases, but have vigorously attacked his conspiratorial view of the courts and the legal profession in bringing classical contract theory to prominence. Even more in his book than in the article excerpt, Horwitz makes clear that he does not accept the view that the pro-development legal system evolved naturally and unself-consciously in response to the needs of the industrial revolution and the expansion of commerce in the new nation of the United States. This has led to reviews such as John Phillip Reid's *A Plot Too Doctrinaire,* 55 Tex. L. Rev. 1307 (1977), and Peter Teachout's *Light in Ashes: The Problem of "Respect for the Rule of Law" in American Legal History*, 53 N.Y.U. L. Rev. 241 (1978), which severely criticize Horwitz for his historiography rather than for his history. These and many other critics are in turn criticized in the essay by Wythe Holt cited at the beginning of this article. Professor Holt goes on to offer his own criticisms of Horwitz. The debate is likely to go on.

A Look at a Classroom Classic in Light of the Changing American Economy (herein of Wood v. Lucy, Lady Duff-Gordon)

The following article, by Professor Walter Pratt of Notre Dame, is less overtly political, but still is very much in the modern tradition of trying to integrate changes in legal doctrine with social, economic, political and literary influences of the time and place, in this case, the United States at the turn of the twentieth century. In the process Professor Pratt gives some very entertaining background on the famous case of *Wood v. Lucy, Lady Duff-Gordon*, which appears in or is discussed in virtually every contracts casebook. Professor Pratt does not limit himself to *Wood v. Lucy,* but seeks to show how the courts adapted the rules of contract and public policy to deal with the radical changes in the American economy caused by railroads, futures contracts of commodities and changes in retailing. Our excerpt, however, will concentrate on his discussion of *Wood v. Lucy.* Professor Pratt's article is relevant to the discussion of implied terms, particularly that of good faith and fair dealing, that takes place in Part IIIB, within. The reader may want to return to the Pratt article when reading the later discussion.

I should say that while I am sympathetic to the imposition of substantial duties of good faith in contracts, I am a bit skeptical of the dramatic shift that Professor Pratt sees at the beginning of the twentieth century. To put it differently, I would like to accept all of his conclusions, but I don't think the change in attitude took place as sharply as he does. In fact, the debate over self-interest versus cooperation is still going on; witness Macneil's material in Part IA and the discussion of good faith in Part IIIB, already mentioned. None of this should be taken to denigrate the Pratt article, which I think is very good, but the reader should not suspend his or her own critical facilities, despite Pratt's remarkable breadth of authorities.

Walter F. Pratt, Jr., *American Contract Law At The Turn Of The Century,* 39 S.C. L. Rev. 415 (1988)

I. Introduction

During the past century, contract law, along with most of American society, has undergone a "major transformation." While courts of a hundred or more years ago would have declared an agreement not be enforceable, courts today would routinely consider the same agreement to be a contract. Underlying the transformation in contract law is a fundamental displacement of one image of contract by another. The consequence of that displacement is a greater involvement by courts in policing the performance of contracts.

The result of this transformation in contract law is documented and much discussed. Little, however, has been written to account for the origins of the change. Those accounts that do exist tend toward a generalized explanation that the change was merely one part of a reaction against a style of reasoning known as "formalism." That conventional explanation has taken on an almost legendary character according to which late-nineteenth-century judges had settled into a style of reasoning deductively from a priori rules. Not long thereafter, lore has it, judges of the early twentieth century developed a preference for "scientific" evidence that conclusions worked in practice. As with most legends, there is some truth to this account. But the truth is limited to a description of styles of reasoning. It does little to identify the sources of the reaction against formal rules; and it does even less to explain why courts reached particular results. Specifically, the legend does not account for the courts' transformation of contract law.

Beyond the incomplete portrayal of the development of doctrine is a mischaracterization of the judges who participated in the development. A stock figure in the legend is a late-nineteenth-century judge who is little more than a pertinacious atavist, out of touch with the times, who sought only to obstruct progress. However accurate that caricature might be in public law, in private law it comes perilously close to exceeding the proper bounds of literary license. The actual judges, atavistic though they may have been, proved to be quite pliant in responding to the changes at the turn of the century. Moreover, in their own way, the judges were remarkably in touch with the spirit of the final years of the nineteenth century.

The thesis of this article is that the critical origins of the transformation of contract doctrine lie in the period between 1870 and 1920. In that half century, roughly between the end of Reconstruction and the end of the First World War, the United States came to recognize itself as having changed from a traditional society, characterized by localism and face-to-face communications, to a modern, urban society, characterized by its cosmopolitan nature and by an economy which reached well beyond the village. Intangibly the society had changed from one in which "[p]resent, past, and future [were] essentially the same" to one in which change and uncertainty were dominant and in which links to the past were weakening.

The alterations in contract law matched those in society. The judges of the Reconstruction period viewed contracts as part of a market dominated by small, discrete transactions, as the market had been in the past. But markets were changing, reflecting the acceleration and fruition of many of the developments that had begun in the decades before the Civil War. Instead of being discrete and localized, transactions were now regularly more complex and regional as well as national. In an effort to cope with the newer transactions in an unsettled economy, manufacturers developed new marketing techniques, most often described in terms of vertical and horizontal integration. But the same factors that fueled the movement toward bigger enterprises also produced new contracting practices, characterized by reduced specificity in the terms of agreements. The public debate about the ever larger corporate forms overshadowed all other discussion of economic change. Thus eclipsed, the new contract practices were usually discussed only within judicial opinions. Nevertheless, those opinions reveal concerns about the future of the country akin to the sentiments that dominated the more public debate about large corporations.

Judges at first rejected these new practices by declaring the agreements not to be enforceable as contracts. The new forms failed to fit the existing image of contract; but they had become too popular in the market for the courts long to resist. Recognizing that the doctrines of the past were no longer adequate for the needs of a changing commercial world, the judges modified the doctrines to embrace the greater uncertainty that characterized the new agreements. The judicial adaptations allowed the enforcement of agreements that previously would not have been enforced. But the change produced new difficulties for the judges, who until then had faced only the binary decision of whether or not to enforce an agreement. They now had to attend to the performance of the contract and to the much more complex questions arising from the uncertainties in the agreements themselves. The judicial response to those new difficulties was couched in terms familiar to the emerging communitarian theories of the era. In the language of the courts, the central concept for both enforcement and performance came to be that of "good faith." Through the use of that concept courts strove to preserve some of the moral decency of the rural past while allowing the development of commercial practices for the urban future, with as yet undefined morals. The result was an altered image of contract, one in which the relationship between the parties was closer to a fiducial one than to that of unrelated individuals in a free market.

This article, then, looks to the emergence of the

doctrine of "good faith" as the key to understanding the major transformation in contract law during the past century. As is true with most areas of private law, the path of this doctrinal development is neither straight nor smooth. Rather, because it depends upon the separate courts of many jurisdictions, the path is tortuous and uneven. In an effort to smooth the path and to focus the historical account, this article returns regularly to discussion of a single case, *Wood v. Lucy, Lady Duff-Gordon*,[13] which epitomized the law's developing response to the uncertainty of the late nineteenth century. What may seem, in the 1980's, to be an easy decision was far from easy early in the century, as is apparent from the divisions within the New York courts. Those divisions, along with the facts of the case, make *Wood* an especially useful lens through which to examine the changes in contract law at the turn of the century.[14]

II. *Wood v. Lucy, Lady Duff-Gordon*—Background

A. *The Facts*

The case began as a suit by Otis F. Wood against Lucy, Lady Duff-Gordon for breach of an agreement signed in 1915. According to Wood, the agreement gave him the exclusive right to place Lucy's endorsements on products. Thus, when Lucy herself placed endorsements, Wood contended that he should have a share of the profits from those endorsements. Lucy demurred, arguing that for an agreement to be enforceable it must impose obligations on both parties. This agreement was unenforceable, she contended, because it imposed no duties on Wood. The trial judge overruled the demurrer; he interpreted the agreement as requiring Wood to exercise his "bona fide judgment"—a requirement which the judge thought sufficient to give content to Wood's obligation and thus to make the agreement enforceable. The appellate division unanimously reversed, concluding that the contract was "void for lack of mutuality." The court found nothing in the agreement that required Wood to place any endorsements. Viewed in

that light, there was no obligation in the agreement that could be enforced against Wood. There was therefore no contract that Wood could enforce against Lucy. The court of appeals, by a 4-3 vote, agreed with the trial judge. Judge Cardozo's opinion for the majority used the phrase "reasonable efforts" to describe Wood's obligation.

B. *The Social Milieu*

Although obviously important to the case, Wood and Cardozo were actually little more than supporting characters to the role played by the defendant, Lucy, Lady Duff-Gordon, who was one of the most vibrant symbols of the changing standards of her era. Lucy herself described the change in fashion as one away from individualism. In the years before the death of Queen Victoria in 1901, according to Lucy, "every woman wanted to look individual and unlike everyone else." But as the early years of the twentieth century passed, women's fashion became "almost communal in its tendencies."[18]

Lucy's description of changes in women's fashion was but a cameo portrait of the changes in American society in the years around the turn of the century. There was no overnight transformation into an industrial, urban economy; the changes had begun decades before. In the years after the Civil War, however, the rate and the nature of change so accelerated that it is accurate to describe the economy of the late nineteenth century as significantly different from the economy of mid-century. Perhaps more importantly, many in the United States began to *perceive* the changes as moving significantly and finally away from a nation which was primarily a collection of discrete, small communities or neighborhoods. As the novelist Sherwood Anderson wrote, before the change each town had

a character of its own, and the people who lived in the towns were to each other like members of a great family. . . . [E]very one knew his neighbor and was known to him. Strangers did not come

---

[13] 222 N.Y. 88, 118 N.E. 214 (1917).

[14] I am not the first to see in *Wood* a significant change in the law. Karl Llewellyn, for example, used it to illustrate "a whole new way of reading commercial documents." K. Llewellyn, The Common Law Tradition: Deciding Appeals 34 n.25 (1960). I must also admit that the case makes the historical account much more fun. No other case has links to so much that was symbolic of the modern America—ranging from the Ziegfeld Follies (for which Lucy designed costumes) to the Titantic, that tragically sinkable manifestation of confidence in technology (Lucy and her husband survived the sinking). Other links include the Kewpie doll (Wood was

an advertising agent for the creator of the doll), the modern Olympic movement (Lucy's husband, Cosmo Duff-Gordon was a fencer on the British Olympic team), Queen Victoria (Lucy designed dresses for women attending her funeral, see infra note 57), and Sears, Roebuck's catalogue sales (Lucy agreed to design dresses to be sold by Sears, see infra notes 87-88). For a biography of Lucy and her sister, the novelist Elinor Glyn, see M. Etherington-Smith & J. Pilcher, The "It" Girls (1986).

[18] L. Duff-Gordon, Discretions and Indiscretions 80 (1932).

and go swiftly and mysteriously and there was no constant and confusing roar of machinery and of new projects afoot.

The economy rested on those communities. The essence of production remained the craft; most workers shared the opportunity to put their hands on a product and to identify with it. Likewise, the basis for sales was personal knowledge and trust of those with whom one dealt, even when the transaction extended into a regional market. This personal involvement with production and sales meant that buyers and sellers alike could share the same values. . . .

The United States of 1870 was not yet ready to acknowledge being an urban, industrial nation. According to the census, rural places outnumbered urban places by a ratio of almost five to one. The rural population was almost three times that of the urban population. Not until the census of 1920 would the urban population exceed the rural. Statistics for production and income reflect similar characteristics for the nation. . . .

Thus, by the first decades of the twentieth century, much had changed. "[M]any people living in 1900 could remember when neither railroads nor telegraphs nor telephones existed. In a sense, such people were older than the American economy, a phrase that had seldom been used at the time they were born because it lacked content when economies were local and regional in nature." Two symbols of this new American economy were the city, with its discordant diversity, and the railroad, which provided an impersonal link, often over great distances, between buyers and sellers.

Although not all towns grew to be large cities, the rail lines insured that few would remain isolated. The same lines that brought new products also brought new ideas. The intellectual challenge to existing values matched the economic challenge to existing markets. . . .

The cities and the railroads could offer no consolation; they only reinforced impressions of rapid change and of an increasingly large number of value choices. In the words of one student of the period, "a moral unity corresponding to [the] economic web had not yet emerged." . . . To replace the values of the community, the best that the city and the railroad could offer were the values of commerce. . . . Possibly the most abrupt statement of those values came from the Wizard of Oz, who rejected Dorothy's plea that he must help her because he was strong and she was weak. Responding to Dorothy's plea for justice, Oz said, "In this country everyone must pay for everything he gets. . . . Help me and I will help you."

The new values, unlike the old, could not readily be shared; indeed, because they would exact payment for every exchange, they were the antithesis of sharing. More often than not, they contravened the values of the community, or they were so disparate as to be incoherent. One could therefore sympathize with the reaction of a character in a novel portraying rural life in New England who complained about recent intrusions by strangers coming into her village: "I see so many of these new folks nowadays, that seem to have neither past nor future. Conversation's got to have some root in the past, or else you've got to explain every remark you make, an' it wears a person out."[46] One could just as readily have said "trade" or "bargaining" instead of "conversation."

The reaction to and against the new commercial values was but part of the increasingly prominent belief that the end of the nineteenth century marked a turning point in human history, much like Lucy's designs marked the end of the Victorian era in fashion . . . . In art and literature, for example, that belief found voice through arguments for new "forms" of expression; the old forms were considered inadequate for the new conditions of the twentieth century.

This turmoil, both physical and intellectual, had a profound impact upon the law, possibly the aspect of culture that most prides itself in being influenced by the past, by precedent. Despite that pride, as Cardozo would later write, "[t]he great tides and currents which engulf the rest of men, do not turn aside in their course, and pass the judges by."[50] The value choices inherent in the spreading tracks of economic transactions and the multifarious bustle of the city threatened to overwhelm citizens and judges alike. But lawyers and judges lacked the freedom of artists to declare openly their break with precedent or their disassociation with the forms of the past. Nevertheless, the law underwent a change similar to that in the arts and the rest of American society.

In no area of law was this turbulence of more significance than in contract law, the area of law that arose to establish settled rules to facilitate planning for the future. The turmoil of the late nineteenth cen-

---

[46] S. Jewett, The Country of the Pointed Firs 97 (1896). . . .

[50] B. Cardozo, The Nature of the Judicial Process 168 (1921), *reprinted in* Selected Writings of Benjamin Nathan Cardozo 178 (M. Hall ed. 1967).

tury threatened to put an end to any hope for stability. Contracting, like conversation, had in earlier times been rooted in the past. People who knew one another and who knew the local market, insulated as it was from dramatic shifts in the economy, faced little likelihood of changes in circumstances that would require elaborate agreements or provoke complex disputes. Railroads and cities, however, seemed to disrupt that past by bringing economic uncertainty into the local markets. Parties thus faced the tiring prospect of writing detail upon detail into each agreement if they were to account for every potential event.

As was true of other areas of society, contract law adapted to the changing circumstances. The contours of the developing new consensus were apparent in the 1917 opinion of the New York Court of Appeals in *Wood v. Lucy, Lady Duff-Gordon*. Although the forms often remained the same, the content underwent substantial change. Much like poets who would argue whether free verse retained the form of poetry, so legal scholars would later argue whether the changes which emerged in contract law at the turn of the century retained the form of contract.[54]

III. *Wood v. Lucy, Lady Duff-Gordon*—The Economy

A. *The Contract Between Lucy and Wood*

As she did with the general development of the period, Lucy personified the particular changes in the economy and in contract practice. Very much independent, Lucy renounced the traditions of her generation when she began her own business, designing women's clothing. Like many of the entrepreneurs of the period, Lucy started with little capital. Nevertheless, after overcoming early difficulties, she established herself by 1900 as one of the pre-eminent designers of fashion for women. In a manner typical of the personal style of the American economy during the Reconstruction era, Lucy at first designed only for individual women for specific grand occasions such as coronations and state funerals.[57] Because her designs were created for one woman to wear on a particular occasion, they became known as "personality" dresses.

As the times changed, so did Lucy. First, she became a company, with the name "Lucile." Later, in 1910, she opened a branch office in New York City where she continued to embody the economic

changes by depersonalizing her services. In common with much of the production in the United States, Lucy no longer personally designed each dress for each customer. Instead, she hired others to design and sew; she even began to produce more than one dress of each design. With the change in style and the concentration of population in urban areas, Lucy could now profit from marketing multiple copies of the same design. In addition, Lucy hired a manager for her branch office, further increasing the distance between herself and her customers; she would no longer be able to devote personal attention to each client for each occasion.

Lucy also came to appreciate that something as ephemeral as her name could be of value in the emerging consumer society of the United States. As seller after seller saw production overtake demand in the last years of the nineteenth century, advertising became increasingly important both to inform buyers of products and to persuade customers to buy. To take advantage of that new demand, Lucy turned to an advertising agent, yet another intermediary between herself and her clients.

The agreement with the agent provided that because Wood "possesse[d] a business organization adapted to the placing of such endorsements as the said Lucy, Lady Duff-Gordon, has approved," Lucy agreed to grant Wood "the exclusive right to place such endorsements on such terms and conditions as may in his judgment, and also in the judgment of said Lucy, Lady Duff-Gordon, or A. Merritt, her personal business adviser, be most advantageous" to Lucy and Wood. The agreement was to last for a year and to renew itself automatically unless either party gave ninety days notice of termination.

One aspect of the agreement with Wood is especially important because it represents the most significant change in contract practice and, consequently, the critical challenge to contract doctrine at the turn of the century: The agreement did not fully define Wood's obligation; he was to do whatever his judgment directed, with the consent of Lucy's manager. In the field of advertising it was known as an "open contract." The agreement also contained a second type of contract provision developed in response to the economic uncertainty of the late nineteenth century—Wood's right was *exclusive*. Both aspects of

---

[54] This is in essence the dispute sparked by Professor Gilmore's lectures published under the title The Death of Contract.

[57] Possibly the most spectacular of Lucy's accomplishments was designing different mourning dresses for one

hundred women in Queen Victoria's funeral and then promptly producing different designs for two hundred women for the coronation of King Edward VII. See Sat. Evening Post, Jan. 29, 1927, at 12, 13, 91; The Times (London), Apr. 23, 1935, at 12, col. 3.

the agreement were consequences of Lucy's and Wood's inability to know in advance what opportunities might exist for placing her endorsements. Like other producers who sought to develop new markets, Lucy benefited from the agreement by being freed from having to make decisions about advertising. She could concentrate on her special skill, designing, while Wood concentrated on his presumptive specialty, advertising. From Wood's perspective the agreement was beneficial because it assured him that he would have no competition in his efforts to place Lucy's endorsements. Thus, there would be one less uncertainty in the undeveloped market for her designs.

B. *The Economic Milieu*

Prior to the Civil War, there had been little need to resort to contract to deal with uncertainty. The localized transactions in standardized goods for a primarily agrarian market had insulated commerce from most swings of the economy. . . .

After the war, however, a relatively stable system of money aided the emerging national market for an ever greater variety of products. The development of new markets for new products and increased output required additional planning because uncertainties increased as transactions extended over both longer times and greater distances. New markets also meant more contact with strangers. To complicate matters further, a steady decline of prices and almost periodic panics, or depressions, unsettled the country in the last decades of the nineteenth century. To compensate for the new problems and to reduce uncertainty, parties turned to new forms of contractual arrangements with increasing frequency.

The agreement between Wood and Lucy typified the responses to uncertainty about markets. Like Lucy and Wood, many parties were unable to define the future with precision. They therefore preferred to leave parts of any agreement "open" to await future developments. The techniques of production that emerged during the years of rapid economic expansion after the Civil War left the new industries with uncertainties about their productive capacity. Those industries, therefore, preferred buyers who were willing to leave the quantity term open, agreeing to buy whatever the industry could produce. The resulting agreement came to be known as an "output" contract. Similarly, a buyer who was uncertain about the supply of goods or of the market for the finished product might want a seller to agree to sell only what the buyer would order—a "requirements" contract.

Requirements contracts were especially useful when new markets were opened through advertising or traveling salesmen. The requirements contract permitted an agent or retail outlet to order only the quantity it could actually sell. A common addition to both the output contract and the requirements contract was a provision allowing one party to have an exclusive right to deal with the other, just as Wood and Lucy ostensibly had done. Buyers would agree to sell only the products of particular sellers; or sellers would agree to sell only to particular buyers, usually in a defined geographical area. That type of contract was especially attractive for sellers like Lucy who sought to introduce products into new markets.

One other version of the output contract, and another significant response to uncertainty in the late nineteenth century, arose in the context of developing a specialized market which traded in uncertainty itself and through which risks could be shared among a larger number of individuals. The most significant market of that kind was the farm commodities exchange—the futures market. This market had no direct bearing on the terms of the agreement between Wood and Lucy; but the market did result from factors similar to those which produced the output and requirements contracts. Furthermore, the futures market spawned frequent litigation, much of which served to move courts away from the doctrines of the past, toward a greater acceptance of uncertainty and, therefore, toward acceptance of requirements and output contracts.

. . .

IV. *Wood v. Lucy, Lady Duff-Gordon*—The Law

A. *The Litigation Between Lucy and Wood*

No doubt most of the parties who adopted the new contracting practices never had occasion to test them in court. The first of those who did find themselves involved in litigation, however, had little reason to be confident of the outcome. The very fact of litigation usually meant that the contract had not protected the parties from fluctuation of the market, as they had hoped. Furthermore, once the contract failed, the nature of the transaction meant that the open term would be the very one seized upon by the party seeking to benefit from the change in the economy. With the dispute thereby focused on the open term, the parties presented a direct challenge to the fundamental doctrine that there had to be sufficient certainty for an agreement to be enforced as a contract.

At this juncture, Lucy departed from her role as model. There was no disruption in the market for her endorsements. Instead, she brought Wood's lawsuit upon herself when, in one of the more innovative decisions of her career, she arranged with Sears, Roebuck and Company to sell her dresses through its catalogues.[87] Sears published the first catalogue (which it called a "portfolio") of Lucy's designs for the fall and winter of 1916-1917.[88] That Lucy was once again at the forefront of commercial practice was evident from a comment in the trade journal *Printer's Ink*, which reported that the announcement of the agreement threw "a bomb into the camp of rival mail-order houses." The announcement, the journal further explained, was "by far the most spectacular bid for prestige which this daring advertiser [Sears] has made since it first announced the new handy edition of the Encyclopedia Britannica."[89]

The primary consequence of the arrangement with Sears, however, was to provoke Wood to sue for breach of his agreement with Lucy. As noted previously, Lucy relied upon the traditional response that the agreement lacked mutuality. She lost the first round of the suit when the trial judge denied her motion for judgment on the pleadings. He interpreted the agreement as requiring Wood to exercise his "bona fide judgment"—a requirement which the judge thought sufficient to prevent the agreement from being unenforceable. The appellate division unanimously reversed, concluding that the contract was "void for lack of mutuality." The court held that the agreement did not require Wood to place any endorsements. Viewed in that light, nothing in the agreement could be enforced against Wood.

The disagreement between the two lower New York courts precisely reflected the fluid state of contract doctrine at the turn of the century. Poised between the traditional rule of the appellate division and the modern rule of the trial court, judges throughout the country strove to articulate values in response to the new contractual devices. The "open" nature of the contract between Lucy and Wood challenged the venerated rule of contract law that there could be no contract unless the obligations of the parties were mutual. A late-nineteenth-century American editor of a respected English treatise on contracts phrased the rule this way: "When the only

consideration to sustain the contract is that arising out of mutual promises, the mutuality must be absolute so that each party may have an action in case of breach or neither is bound." The rule could be satisfied only if there were obligations to be imposed on both sides; if an obligation was not fully described, it was not enforceable.

The traditional doctrine formally barred enforcement of the new contracts which left portions of obligations to be defined after the moment of agreement. For example, under an output contract the buyer promised to purchase whatever the seller produced; but, some reasoned, there was no obligation on the part of the seller to produce anything. Similarly, under a requirements contract the seller agreed to sell whatever quantity the buyer ordered; but the buyer had no obligation to order anything. . . . As a result, the very reasons that made the new types of agreements attractive proved to be the basis for denying enforcement.

The evidence of widespread use of the contracts created a dilemma for the courts, a dilemma that emphasized to the judges the weakening power of the past. If they adhered to precedent they would impede what appeared to be a needed contractual practice; if they were to enforce the new agreements, they had to develop a new rationale. They chose to enforce the agreements, but to explain the conclusion in terms of the adage *id certum est quod certum reddi potest* (that is certain which can be made certain). By doing so, the courts were able to change outcomes while appearing to adhere to the old form which required mutuality of obligation. In reality the courts put a markedly different content into that old form. The new content was the result of questions about the nature of obligations that arose once courts decided to enforce the agreements. Could, for example, a buyer seek to profit from a change in the economy and substantially increase its orders from a seller who had agreed to furnish the buyer's requirements? The courts might well have declared the agreements enforceable to the full extent of whatever requirements (or output) a party had. It would not have been implausible to expect that the market and contracting practice would adapt to those circumstances.

[87] Lucy's decision to work with Sears recalled but another example of the intrusion of urban life into rural communities, in this instance through mail-order catalogues. . . .

[88] Portfolio of Lady Duff-Gordon's Original Designs 4 (Sears, Roebuck and Co., Fall & Winter 1916-1917). For advertisements of the portfolio, see Harper's Bazaar, Oct. 1916, at 100-01; McCall's Mag., Nov. 1916, at 92-93.

[89] Sears-Roebuck's Latest Advertising Coup, Printer's Ink, Sept. 21, 1916, at 28; see also G. Weil, Sears, Roebuck, U.S.A. 68 (1977); The Advertising News, Sept. 29, 1916, at 10-11. Despite the excitement created by the announcement, the scheme was a failure. Sears lost more than a quarter of a million dollars on the two portfolios that it published. B. Emmet & J. Jeuck, Catalogues And Counters 225 (1950).

But the courts chose not to take that course. Instead of bowing fully to the values of the market,[99] the judges sought to preserve some of the values of the past by requiring that the contracts be performed in good faith, the "bona fide judgment" required by the trial judge in *Wood*. The key characteristic of the new content for the old form was that the courts, not the parties or the market, would have the primary role in determining what was good faith. Consequently, the courts had both a new focus for their deliberations—performance rather than obligation—and a new standard for judgment—good faith. Together the new focus and the new standard would make the courts much more involved in supervising the performance of contracts.

. . .

[A fourteen-page discussion of judicial responses to output, requirements, and futures contracts is deleted —ed.]

V. *Wood v. Lucy, Lady Duff-Gordon*—The Aftermath

In the process of dealing with uncertainty, many judges came to realize the inadequacy of particular precedents, the old forms of the law. Those judges, like many of their contemporaries, sensed the accuracy of what Cardozo had so brashly said as a student in 1889. The time had come, he observed, "when the old forms seem[ed] ready to decay, and the old rules of action [had] lost their binding force." The judiciary responded through efforts to reconcile the old forms of the law with the new forms of commercial agreement. Once the judges accepted the existence of a new market, however, they confronted a conflict between traditional and modern values. In the disputes about performance of the new agreements, the judges saw not the traditional, accommodating values of the small community, but the new, harsh values of commerce. They saw a market to which, in the words of a character in Henry Fuller's novel *With the Procession*, everyone had "come for the one common, avowed object of making money." The result of that object was that "every man cultivates his own little bed and his neighbor his; but who looks after the paths between? They have become a kind of No Man's Land, and the weeds of a rank iniquity are fast chok-

ing them up." Many judges held similar views about the consequences of a single-minded search for profit, though they expressed them in a different manner; and in a muted way, they set about policing the "paths between."

Almost without exception, courts that enforced output and requirements contracts encountered these agreements after a change in the market presented one party with an opportunity to make substantial profits. To accept the profit-based morality of commerce and enforce the open-term contract without limit did not present the courts with catastrophic choices—it would neither drive anyone out of business nor reward overbearing conduct during negotiations. It would, however, deny one party a share of the bounty newly available to its contractual counterpart. This imbalance was a cause for concern only to those who would not accept the morality of profit as the teleology of the era. Judges expressed that concern with the pejorative observation that to enforce an open-term contract without limit would place one party "at the mercy of the other."

Apprehension that one party was potentially "at the mercy of the other" made it natural for judges to turn to the analogy of the fiduciary and of equity when confronted with disputes about the new contracts. A prime example of that reasoning can be found in *Wigand v. Bachmann-Bechtel Brewing Co.*, the first case in which the highest court of a state held that an obligation of good faith extended to all contracts.[149] This decision of the New York Court of Appeals involved an output contract which obligated the buyer to purchase a waste product from a brewery for five years. The buyer invested a considerable amount of money in preparing to process the waste product. Then, after two years, the brewery sold its facility to another company and attempted to avoid any obligation under the contract by arguing that it no longer had any output. The court of appeals rejected the brewery's position with the observation that to accept the argument would produce an agreement that was too "one-sided." The court further explained its conclusion with the general observation that "[e]very contract implies good faith and fair dealing between the parties to it." The court took its

---

[99] For an argument that the judges sided with mercantile interests, see Feinman, Critical Approaches to Contract Law, 30 UCLA L. Rev. 829 (1983); Gabel & Feinman, Contract Law as Ideology, in The Politics Of Law: A Progressive Critique 172 (D. Kairys ed. 1982).

[149] See 222 N.Y. 272, 277, 118 N.E. 618, 619 (1915). In this conclusion I disagree with Professor Burton's conclu-

sion that "the standard doctrinal formulation of the good faith performance duty was first articulated" in Kirke La Shelle Co. v. Paul Armstrong Co., 263 N.Y. 79, 188 N.E. 163 (1933). Burton, Breach of Contract and the Common Law Duty to Perform in Good Faith, 94 Harv. L. Rev. 369, 370 (1980).

language and principle from cases in which one party had complete control over whether the other party received any benefit at all from the contract. In cases of that sort the courts had routinely concluded that the party with discretion had to act in good faith. For example, in *Simon v. Etgen*, from which the *Wigand* court took its language, the court held that, in the absence of a stated time for performance, a reasonable time would be implied. . . . Thus neither the principle nor even the language of the *Wigand* court was singular. What was portentous was the application of the principle to a contract at the heart of mercantile practice. In a society so dominated by commercial values, it bordered on the heretical for a court even to imply that any part of the relationship between buyer and seller in an output contract resembled that of the fiduciary. Yet that is precisely what the New York courts did at the time of *Wigand* and *Wood*.

. . .

[The author cites two lower court cases from New York State in which courts "castigated" parties for seeking to speculate or to make a windfall at the other party's expense. —ed.]

That castigation represented the final step toward imposing a general duty of good faith on contracting parties. The judicial reaction was comparable to siding with Dorothy in her confrontation with the Wizard of Oz. The judges offered protection solely because the parties were perceived as being weak, without requiring that the parties pay for the protection. The courts had come to realize that the essence of the new contractual practices was sharing. As the nineteenth century struggled to a close, the courts had recognized that mercantile agreements could be no more certain than the uncertain economy itself. The typical relationship between the contracting parties was no longer a discrete transaction based on a particular performance, promised for an assured future. Instead, the parties left open a term in the

agreement, binding themselves to move together into the uncertain future.[161] In recognition of that relationship, the courts had taken a first step toward enforcing the contracts by reasoning that sellers in output contracts could not sell to anyone else, and buyers in requirements contracts could not buy from anyone else.

This new reasoning did more than respond to the formal requirements for mutuality by providing one party with an obligation which could match the obligation of the other party. Binding the fates of the parties so firmly together made it easier for the courts to determine whether there would be limits to the obligation. The close ties between the parties prompted the realization that the relationship between them was akin to one of sharing. Thereafter, courts were able to view parties to the new contracts as being more like partners or co-adventurers than like atomistic elements of a larger economy. The courts were then able to invoke, in the language of both *Woods* and *Wells*, the proscription that no agreement would be allowed to place one party "at the mercy of the other." The phrase referred only to what was perceived as an unseemly rush for profits. Those who sought only profits were branded with the same disparaging label as those who dealt in grain futures. They all were "speculators," immoral because they sought profit without production. One who attempted to speculate was said to have not acted in good faith and therefore could not enforce the contract. The moral opprobrium attached to a pure seeker of profit (who produced nothing) manifested itself in holdings that restricted requirements to actual needs for business. The effect of that limitation was that neither party would be allowed to reap substantial profits without sharing them with the other party.

By so restricting parties to open-term contracts, the courts effected a compromise between traditional and modern values. The courts allowed commercial

---

[161] More recently, Professor Ian Macneil has been a prime proponent of the theory that many contracts are "relational"—they involve more than single, discrete encounters between the parties. See, e.g., . . . Macneil, Contracts: Adjustment of Long-Term Economic Relations Under Classical, Neoclassical, and Relational Contract Law, 72 Nw. U.L. Rev. 854 (1978); Macneil, A Primer of Contract Planning, 48 S. Cal. L. Rev. 627 (1975); Macneil, The Many Futures of Contracts, 47 S. Cal. L.Rev. 691 (1974). In a similar vein, Professor Speidel has written of the obligations arising from long-term contracts:

In short, the long-term supply contract is a bit more complex than the "one-shot" sale of Dobbin or Blackacre. Beyond its obvious economic importance, it complicates,

and perhaps prevents, complete risk planning at the time of contracting. Complete consent is a mirage. Over time, "gaps" in the initial agreement will undoubtedly emerge. At the same time, specialized uses of the contract will increase both the cost of terminating the relationship and the likelihood that the market will be unable to provide an adequate substitute for either party.

Speidel, Court-Imposed Price Adjustments Under Long-Term Supply Contracts, 76 Nw. U.L. Rev. 369, 375 (1981); see also Speidel, Excusable Nonperformance in Sales Contracts: Some Thoughts About Risk Management, 32 S.C.L. Rev. 241 (1980). [The author also cites the works by Stewart Macaulay that are discussed in Part IA of this anthology. —ed.]

practice to develop according to the needs of the market; but they insisted that the development be mediated by values other than those of commerce. In the end, then, both society and its law adapted to uncertainty by turning to embrace it. Sarah Orne Jewett's

well-read sea caption was correct in his observation: "Certainty, not conjecture is what we all desire[d]." But, as he noted, the desire had long been unfulfilled because people had "not looked for truth in the right direction."[168]

[168] S. Jewett, supra note 46, at 23; cf. 3 A. Corbin, Corbin on Contracts § 609, at 689 (1960) ("[C]ertainty in the law is largely an illusion at best, and altogether too high a price

may be paid in the effort to attain it."); Peters, Grant Gilmore and the Illusion of Certainty, 92 Yale L.J. 8 (1982).

D.   Other Voices

Introduction: Generalizing from Carol Gilligan

The title of this section is an allusion to Carol Gilligan's In a Different Voice (1982), in which she proposed that men and women talked about morality and themselves in different voices, "two ways of speaking about moral problems, two modes of describing the relationship between self and others." (p.1) The different voices that Gilligan described are one that speaks about moral problems in terms of abstract and impersonal rules, emphasizing logical progression and universal solutions, and another that speaks in terms of "a world comprised of relationships rather than of people standing alone, a world that coheres through human connection rather than through systems of rules . . . ." (p.29) She concluded that "men and women may speak different languages that they assume are the same, using similar words to encode disparate experiences of self and social relationships," the male approach one of rights, focused on self, and the female approach one of responsibility, within which "lies the truth of an ethic of care, the tie between relationship and responsibility, and the origins of aggression in the failure of connection." (id.)

Gilligan emphasized that the distinctions were not exclusive to one sex or the other, that she sought "to highlight a distinction between two modes of thought and to focus a problem of interpretation rather than to represent a generalization about either sex." (p.2) (In this context it is worth noting that she, like Roberto Unger and many other writers, uses The Merchant of Venice, written after all by a man, to illustrate the different points of view. (p.105)) Gilligan rejects both an "anatomy is destiny" explanation and a claim that women's responses represent immaturity and lack of full intellectual or social development.

> Clearly, these differences arise in a social context where factors of social status and power combine with reproductive biology to shape the experience of males and females and the relations between the sexes. My interest lies in the interaction of experience and thought, in the way we listen to ourselves and to others, in the stories we tell about our lives. (p.2)

While the initial article in this section is a feminist look at a Contracts casebook, the section seeks to generalize on the other voices approach. Included here are a discussion of the role of western religion in contract law and discussions of how two other cultures—the partially westernized but complexly insular one of Japan and the traditional one of an agrarian African tribe—approach contract. Another voice that should be heard in this context is that of Patricia J. Williams, whose Alchemical Notes appear in Part IB. In addition, there is a brief discussion of feminist jurisprudence and its use in general contract theory in the Uncontracts article, also in Part IB. The section concludes with some musings that Patricia A. Tidwell and I have put together on what would happen to our norms of contract law if we listened to its lore, as told in different voices.

Feminist Jurisprudence and Mary Joe Frug's Critique of a Casebook
(herein again of *Wood v. Lucy*, and of *Parker v. Twentieth Century-Fox*)

Inspired in part by Carol Gilligan, there have been a number of writers who have written about feminist (or feminine) jurisprudence, among them Catherine MacKinnon, Susanna Sherry, Robin West, Martha Minow and Ann Swords. These writers have emphasized a communal, relational, problem-solving approach that contrasts sharply with a "masculine" individualism that emphasizes all-or-nothing litigation. This is relevant to the debates that have been excerpted in Parts IA to IC, above, among adherents of a consent-or promise-based view of contracts and those who have emphasized relationship and communal views of fairness. Of this, more in the concluding essay.

Professor Frug, who teaches at the New England School of Law, is not primarily concerned with questions of jurisprudence, although they do appear in her article. She is first concerned with unconscious biases and attitudes *about* women in a casebook written by three men who, far from being bigots, are enlightened and are probably representative of many leaders of the academic community. In the course of her analysis Professor Frug discusses *Wood v. Lucy, Lady Duff-Gordon*, which was discussed at length by Walter Pratt in the concluding article of Part IC, and also discusses *Parker v. Twentieth Century-Fox*, familiarly known to students as "the Shirley MacLaine case." The reader can judge whether Professor Frug's criticisms are well-taken. I will only note that in the next edition of their casebook the editors replaced the picture of Shirley MacLaine complained about by Frug with a more modest one.

Mary Joe Frug, *Re-reading Contracts: A Feminist Analysis of a Contracts Casebook*, 34 American U. L. Rev. 1065 (1985)

Like many other contracts instructors, I presently teach my course from Dawson, Harvey, and Henderson's contracts casebook.[1] This Essay is a feminist examination of that casebook. My objective is critical in character, for I believe a feminist analysis should change one's consciousness. However, I do not intend to deliver a diatribe against the casebook or its editors. Rather, I am writing this for the readers of other casebooks, as well as for readers of *Dawson, Harvey, and Henderson*, in the hope of accomplishing two goals. First, I want to demonstrate that readers' views about gender affect their understanding of a law casebook. Second, I want to demonstrate that gendered aspects of a casebook affect readers' understanding of the law and of themselves. If these endeavors are successful, I hope that casebook readers will be liberated from some of their opinions about gender, opinions that casebooks foster and sustain.

Indeed, this Essay is designed to contribute to the feminist effort to diminish the power that ideas about gender exercise over our lives. I also hope somewhat paradoxically, that exposing and examining gender in a casebook will liberate and vitalize qualities within readers, as well as approaches to contract doctrine, that are currently linked with women.

I. Introductory Explanation

The analysis of *Dawson, Harvey, and Henderson* which follows is primarily concerned with the power of gender in the casebook. It is this focus on gender that makes me claim my analysis is feminist. I use "gender" to mean the reductive, dualistic classification of a wide array of social and psychological characteristics according to biological sex. Gender has power because we use it as a category to explain differences among individuals; it is an idea that orga-

[1] J. Dawson, W. Harvey & S. Henderson, Cases and Comment on Contracts (4th ed. 1982).

nizes and colors many of our responses to others—
what we expect of them, what we hope for them. It
also affects what we desire for ourselves and how others view us. I believe that gender is a significant constraint on the lives of most women and men. It affects how I present myself (my voice, in this Essay),
who my friends are, which students seek me out,
which ones I will care for, and what my work is—
which courses I teach and which scholarly projects I
choose. Indeed, because the explanatory force of gender can be so convincing, gender often functions as a
kind of emotional and rational shortcut. Our reliance
on it, as on any theory, can save us effort. But it can
also induce us to avoid thinking, listening, or responding very carefully. Thus, despite the fact that
we could understand our differences in other ways,
and often do, our ideas about gender have a profound
impact on our lives: they divide us from one another
and from ourselves.

. . .

I have identified my Essay as a feminist analysis
with some reservations. I recognize that the feminist
label may seem uninviting to certain readers, and I
do not want to lose those readers preemptively. Moreover, I believe that the creativity, flexibility, and subordinated opposition that women's life experiences
often demand and cultivate are important to the constitution of feminism. I do not want a "feminist" label
for this project to jeopardize claims that differing
analyses are also feminist. Nevertheless, calling my
analysis "feminist" seems desirable as a way to distinguish my project from the task of eliminating overt
sexism in a book. I fear that "eliminating overt sexism" could seem limited to rooting out instances of
pejorative, demeaning treatment of women in casebooks, and that would not accurately describe my Essay. While I believe eliminating that kind of sexism in
books is an important and challenging enterprise, I
concede at the outset that *Dawson, Harvey, and Henderson* seems cleansed of any gratuitously negative
comments about women. But I believe editors could
conscientiously eliminate all instances of female degradation in their casebooks and still produce books
that would affect readers' views about gender and
that would be subject to multiple interpretations because of readers' gender attitudes. A "feminist" case-

book analysis will be useful, therefore, as long as the
concept of gender has any meaningful content.[12]

. . .

[The author proceeds to "introduce my impressions of a group of typical casebook readers," quoting
a leading modern literary theorist who wrote that
"linguistic and textual facts, rather than being the
objects of interpretation are its products." (See Stanley Fish, *Is There a Text in This Class?* (1980).) Professor Frug describes the following types of readers:
the Feminist, the Woman-Centered Reader, the
Reader With a Chip on the Shoulder, the Innocent
Gentleman, the Reader Who is Undressed for
Success, the Individualist, the Civil Libertarian and
the Undeserving Male or Female Reader. She concedes that these characters may seem stereotyped or
caricatured, but says that "I believe they resemble
students and colleagues I have known in twelve years
of law teaching, and while you may not see yourself
as any one reader, you may see parts of yourself in
more than one." —ed.]

II. An Overview of the Casebook: Dis-covering the Gender of Contract Culture

By segregating social and psychological characteristics into two categories and linking those categories
to one sex or the other, our ideas about gender con-
strain our beliefs about what kinds of work men and
women can do, what their interests are, how they can
act, and how they can feel. In addition, because traits
commonly identified as male are generally more
highly valued than characteristics associated with
women, our ideas about gender have a constituting
effect on the continuing imbalance of power between
men and women. For example, because "men's" work
is considered more important than "women's" work,
and "male" analytical skills are more valued than "female" intuition, women who choose a conventional
woman's job and exhibit common feminine attributes
are likely to have less respect (from women as well as
men), less power, and less money than women who
are more masculine in manner and occupation. I believe that *Dawson, Harvey, and Henderson* strongly
supports this ideology of gender, and my primary objective in this section is to expose how the casebook
functions to sustain and further these gender-related
ideas.

---

[12] I agree with Catharine MacKinnon's eloquent claim
that "the male point of view [is] fundamental to the male
power to create the world in its own image." MacKinnon,
Feminism, Marxism, Method, and the State: Toward Feminist Jurisprudence, 8 Signs: J. of Women in Culture and

Society 635, 640 (1983). As long as our ideas about gender
permit us to divide our views dualistically between male and
female viewpoints, gender will continue to profoundly influence the nature of our lives.

. . .

In providing an overview of the book, I pursue two different kinds of discussion. In the first part, my analysis proceeds from concrete questions regarding women. I look at women as "characters" in the cases, among the "authors" whose decisions or legal commentary the editors have included in the book, and in the language of the book. Most appellate decisions allow one to learn something about the people who are parties in the cases, such as what their jobs are, what activities they undertake that lead to litigation, and occasionally what their characters are like. Judicial descriptions of parties do not, however, stand alone in a casebook. Just as editors are responsible for choosing the cases readers read, they also influence readers' views about the parties in the cases by the comments, elaborations, or questions they include with the decisions. Indeed, as I will show, readers can also interpret the significance of editorial silence about the parties. In addition, readers' views about people in a case will be affected by the people in neighboring cases, so that editorial organization will trigger readers' views regarding gender. Thus, I also observe the effect of the editorial arrangement of women's cases. In this part I shall look at men primarily as a gauge by which to evaluate the treatment of women.

In the second part, my focus shifts to comparisons between abstract characteristics which we commonly attribute to men and characteristics of the casebook. I shall concentrate, in other words, on the analytical, autonomous, abstract, and neutral qualities of the book. Because the book does not exhibit many characteristics commonly characterized as feminine (such as sentimentality, earthiness, and compassion), I use women in this part primarily as a way of understanding what is not womanly. My aim in this second part is to reveal the gendered aspects of the book which do not directly pertain to women. Although I am describing the gender-related aspects of the casebook in both parts of this section, I try to demonstrate the ways in which different casebook readers would interpret the materials the editors have chosen. I want to show not only how the editors' choices affect the readers' views of contract doctrine and their views of themselves, but also the different ways they understand the editors' choices.

[Professor Frug argues that "women's work," often involving service and nuture of others, is deni-

grated in comparison with the jobs men do. Discussing *Fitzpatrick v. Michael,* which denied relief to a practical nurse-housekeeper, and *Dallas Cowboys Football Club v. Harris,* which temporarily enjoined a football player from playing for anyone but the Cowboys, Professor Frug comments: "By combining *Fitzpatrick* with *Dallas Cowboys,* the editors present without apparent embarrassment two opinions involving the "ordinary routine[s] of [American] life" in which judges assert that while nursing, housekeeping, and companionship are not unique services, playing football . . . ah, well, that's another matter." —ed.]

b. *Women's character*

Moving from observations of what women in the casebook do and how their work is valued to what their characters are like, readers who notice gender issues will find women described in stereotypical and unflattering ways in *Dawson, Harvey, and Henderson.* Although the two major case studies included in this Essay are designed to illustrate the effect of such treatment in greater depth, I will briefly offer here the examples of two cases in which the characterization of the women could affect how readers view themselves and, in one instance, how they understand the law.

In *Wood v. Lucy, Lady Duff-Gordon,*[63] Judge Cardozo describes a dispute between a man and a woman who agreed to allow him the exclusive right to promote her fashion designs. The designer broke the agreement with the promoter by selling her products elsewhere, in an apparent attempt to make more money by double-dipping. Lady Duff-Gordon is one of the few women in *Dawson, Harvey, and Henderson* who appears to have had an unconventional, successful career, and she is one of only four parties whose photograph is included in the casebook. Her character, therefore, has more significance than if she were one of many businesswomen, some good, some bad, some in between. Her unique position in the casebook casts her character into prominence, particularly for these readers who are conscious of gender, and from several viewpoints Lady Duff-Gordon's character is disappointing.

Readers who have observed the phenomenal jeans-to-shampoo expansion of designer designated products must wonder how a woman in the early twentieth century could have earned money from dress manufacturers for "a certificate of her approval." The caption under her photograph, reproduced in the

[63] 222 N.Y. 88, 118 N.E. 214 (1917).

casebook from *Good Housekeeping Magazine*, intriguingly states that Lady Duff-Gordon "employ[ed] psychology in designing clothes for women," but Cardozo and the editors do not describe whatever talent, energy, or imagination this woman may have had. Moreover, the decision's treatment of her legal defense does not redeem the greedy fickleness that her breach of contract suggests. Instead, her claim that the contract lacked mutuality of assent seems like a technical attempt to dodge responsibility in Cardozo's skillful exposition of the reasons for his decision against her. Thus, readers who are inclined to look to Lady Duff-Gordon as a role model are likely to observe that as a successful woman she seems undeserving and unethical. This is not a promising message for those readers who seek to abandon conventional women's roles, although it will be reassuring to the Gentleman Reader and the Reader with a Chip on his Shoulder who hope women will be inhibited in their efforts to break away from gender restrictions.

Other readers, who could be among The Feminist Readers or the female Readers with Chips on their Shoulders, might be offended that in one of the rare instances in this casebook in which a woman has a nondependent, untraditional career her work involves commercializing the personal appearance of women. These readers believe the fashion industry exploits and degrades women, and they may feel belittled, angered, or disappointed that a woman with Lady Duff-Gordon's prominence in the casebook is engaged in work they cannot respect.

. . .

[The author then discusses a 1921 Kentucky case involving real property left to a Mrs. Williams by her father. Mrs. Williams' husband is a party rather than she but the editors do not point this out and do not discuss the fact that in those days a married woman frequently could not convey land without her husband's consent. Professor Frug also faults the editors for failing to explore in depth a critical legal factor: Mr. and Mrs. Williams could not convey clear title because, although Mrs. Williams was past the normal age of childbearing, the law presumed that she could still have a child who would have an interest in the property. (This is known in future interests law as the "fertile octogenarian rule," and applies to both sexes.)

[Professor Frug argues that this issue of sexuality and reproduction was at the center of the contracts issue in the particular case, and that the editors' failure to mention it or the women's history issue of married women's incapacity is illustrative of the editorial

silence of which she complains. She continues by discussing other issues of sexuality and reproduction that were ignored, and writes that most contracts casebooks "defer" discussion of such topics to domestic relations and sex discrimination courses. (Cf. The note, *Public Policy From Sunday Contracts to Baby M* in Part IIIB of this anthology.) —ed.]

This deferral is not neutral. By confining issues that particularly concern women to domestic relations or sex discrimination courses, casebooks combine with standard law school curriculums to perpetuate the idea that women's interests are personal, concerning only themselves or their families. Men, in contrast, are concerned with the rest of life. Introducing reproductive technology materials into a contracts casebook would integrate a "woman's" issue into a commercial course, thereby loosening a traditional curricular link between subject matter and the sexes. This change would challenge the gendered message curriculums usually imply regarding the separate interests of men and women.

There may, however, be reasons other than course jurisdiction for excluding women's issues like reproductive technology from *Dawson, Harvey, and Henderson*. In this casebook, the editors use predominantly commercial issues to illustrate the complicated doctrines of mutuality of assent, while more personal issues are used to illustrate the counterprinciples of reliance and promissory estoppel. This commercial and personal dichotomy between the cases invites readers to analogize the stereotypical gender differences between the sexes to the differences between groups of conflicting rules. That is, readers could assume that, because men as a group customarily dominate women, the rules of assent, which are illustrated with cases involving the commercial side of life, where men dominate, must be more significant than the rules of reliance, which are largely illustrated with cases involving the more personal side of life, where women have traditionally been consigned. Excluding "women's" issues from this casebook, therefore, permits the content of the cases to work doctrinally to further gender stereotypes. Because readers interpret gendered clues in cases, the editors' selection and organization of cases subtly communicate a message that estoppel doctrine is subordinate to assent doctrine. Although Dawson, Harvey, and Henderson do not editorially address the relationship between the doctrines, the editors implicitly suggest their views to readers.

Including the reproductive technology materials in this casebook would decrease the power that its gendered messages exercise over readers' views of themselves. . . . Similarly, because these decisions involve obviously personal issues, including them in the casebook would disrupt the commercial/personal dichotomy that presently prevails in the mutual assent and promissory estoppel sections. This would not only break the implicit link the casebook now makes between the sexes and "hard" rules like assent and "soft" rules like "reliance," it would also force Dawson, Harvey, and Henderson to confront their position regarding the relationship of the assent and estoppel rules more straightforwardly. Just as gender provided an analytical shortcut to the courts in [other cases discussed], so gender has permitted Dawson, Harvey, and Henderson to skirt their views about the relationships within legal doctrine in their casebook. Breaking the book's silence on women's issues, therefore, would challenge the power of gender over the casebook editors themselves.

. . .

[Professor Frug objects to the language of the casebook, which uses the masculine pronoun to include the feminine, to the absence of female characters in the casebook's problems and hypothetical questions, and to the failure of the casebook's editors to use opinions and articles by women judges and writers—and to alert the reader to the fact that the pieces are by women. —ed.]

B. *The Maleness of the Casebook*

. . .

. . . My analysis of the maleness of *Dawson, Harvey, and Henderson* proceeds on the assumption that casebook readers generally share my views that analytical intellect, detachment, autonomy, and control seem masculine, whereas emotional intellect, attachment, compassion, and spontaneity seem feminine. I do not claim that these qualities are essential to either sex. In fact, I would argue that they aren't. I only claim to have described my impressions of the way many people understand the content of gender.[138]

1. *The analytical, abstract character of the casebook*

The analytical and abstract character of *Dawson,*

Harvey, and Henderson stems in part from the organizational structure the editors have chosen. The editors have used several organizational techniques that not only are abstract or analytical themselves but that also encourage abstract analysis in casebook readers. . . .

After the opening chapter on remedies, the editors continue to organize the casebook according to doctrinal categories that are divorced from the chronological or relational contexts of contract transactions. This organization also encourages readers to focus on rules in the abstract. Because the structure separates the rules from the more concrete and personalized aspects of the casebook—the case settings, the parties, and even the judges who authored the decisions—the casebook encourages an approach to contracts which can seem exceedingly impersonal.

The extensive use of the case/countercase organizational technique also illustrates the book's analytical and abstract character. This technique could produce concrete rather than abstract readings of conflicting cases if readers could evaluate the factual differences between decisions. The factual distinctions do not speak for themselves, however, and the casebook does not provide any guidance about how to evaluate them. . . .

. . .

My claim that *Dawson, Harvey, and Henderson* seems male because it utilizes organizational techniques and subject matter that are routinely used in legal education may seem fanatical. Using appellate opinions or organizing materials by doctrinal categories shouldn't be considered "male," the Individualist or Civil Libertarian Reader might object: using these things is simply normal. However "normal" the character of this casebook may seem to some readers, its abstract, analytical traits will make it seem male to other readers. One of the problems with the ideology of gender is that men's dominance over women permits the eclipse of traits that are associated with women. Male traits seem standard only because female traits are suppressed from observation and consideration.

In any event, it is disingenuous to claim that this casebook is so "normal" that its analytical and ab-

---

[138] Although the attributions I have made accurately reflect how I think many people would characterize the sexes, I also believe that people attribute qualities to the sexes in a relational way. That is, when women exhibit the traits generally ascribed to men, we tend to think of these traits in comparison to opposing, differently formulated traits linked to men. We make the same comparative adjustments when men exhibit "feminine" characteristics. However, because of

men's traditional dominance over women, the traits which were positive when they were linked with men may seem negative when they are attributed to women. Thus, women may be described as scheming, cold, selfish, and manipulative, when they appear intellectual, detached, autonomous, and in control, while men may be described as uninhibited, loyal, considerate, and easy-going, when they seem emotional, attached, compassionate, and spontaneous.

stract character should not be considered male. Other editors in recent years have departed from the organizational forms and case-conservative content that Dawson, Harvey, and Henderson have chosen. Casebooks that are organized around problems particularly challenge the assertion that this casebook is a standardized, nongendered document, because the problem technique renders casebooks substantially more "feminine" than *Dawson, Harvey, and Henderson*. Problems permit readers to personalize casebooks. Problems require students to undertake tasks that involve their interaction with the materials, that allow them to observe contexts which include settings, characters or issues that often mirror their lives. Casebooks utilizing the problem technique dispute the claim to "normalcy" of a casebook like *Dawson, Harvey, and Henderson*, and the contrasting level of abstraction between the two types of books emphasizes the "maleness" of *Dawson, Harvey, and Henderson*.

. . .

Because the form and content of this casebook together make its analytical and abstract character so predominant, the casebook encourages readers, by example, to cultivate the analytical portions of their intellect, and to separate themselves from their work. Readers do not receive positive reinforcement to nourish their emotional sensibilities or to empathize with clients and their problems as part of legal problem solving. Insofar as the activities that the casebook neglects to nurture are commonly understood as feminine, the casebook subtly warns readers, as future lawyers, to repress the feminine characteristics within themselves.

2. The authoritarian neutrality characteristic

Like many law casebooks, *Dawson, Harvey, and Henderson* seems neutral both in style and content. The editors have not visibly injected themselves or their opinions into the casebook, so that there seems to be no editorial presence in the casebook. Moreover, the editors have selected uncontroversial material to accompany the appellate decisions in the casebook, so that the contents of the casebook are quite unlikely to provoke emotional responses from readers. Although the editors have chosen to evade personal involvement and commitment in their casebook, they never acknowledge that the book's neutrality is deliberately contrived; they do not admit that their casebook has a point of view. Thus, the editors are authoritarian about the casebook's neutrality; they offer readers no

information about what is left unsaid in their casebook. Because most readers associate detachment and control with men, the authoritarian neutrality of this book seems male. . . .

. . .

The primary effect of the authoritarian neutrality I have described thus far is to mislead readers about the kind of questions one can ask about cases and about the kind of legal history that might be relevant to consider in studying contracts. This casebook, like many others, discourages readers from developing ethical, social, and moral opinions on legal issues. Insofar as these questions and opinions seem feminine, because they involve attachment, compassion, and emotion, repressing these questions encourages readers to repress the feminine characteristics within themselves. This promotes a narrow concept of professional conduct, and it also devalues authentic self-development.

. . .

III. Re-Reading Cases: Challenging the Gender of Two Contract Decisions

This section will focus on an extended discussion of two cases in *Dawson, Harvey, and Henderson*. While the previous section concentrated on the impact that the gendered aspects of the casebook have on readers, this section will emphasize the impact that readers' ideas regarding gender have on their understanding of legal doctrine. By analyzing each case from feminist and nonfeminist perspectives, I want to demonstrate that gender-related ideas can be embedded in nonfeminist as well as feminist case readings. My goal in this section is to expose and question the gender constraints that often affect case interpretations, and yet, I also hope this section will arouse interest and respect for gender-related readings that draw on attitudes and concerns commonly linked with women. Specifically, I want the feminist attitudes toward the social history that I describe in conjunction with the first case to change readers' views of that case, and I want the feminist oppositional stance that I adopt in analyzing the second case to lead readers to resist the standard doctrinal synthesis of that material.

A. Shirley MacLaine and the Mitigation of Damages Rule: Re-Uniting Language and Experience in Legal Doctrine

Parker v. Twentieth Century-Fox Film Corp.[168] involves a breach of contract claim against a motion

---

[168] 3 Cal.3d 176, 474 P.2d 689, 89 Cal. Rptr. 737 (1970).

picture studio by a "well-known" actress, whom the editors identify as Shirley MacLaine. Just before production was to begin on a musical entitled "Bloomer Girl," the studio cancelled its contract to pay MacLaine $750,000 to star in the film, offering her instead the role of leading actress in a "western type" movie, "Big Country, Big Man." MacLaine did not accept the offer. The studio opposed her motion for summary judgment on the grounds that her claim for lost wages in "Bloomer Girl" should be reduced by the wages she could have earned in "Big Country, Big Man." This defense is based on the general rule of mitigation of damages, elaborated for casebook readers in the preceding major case: a party injured by breach of contract cannot recover compensation for any damages she could have avoided (or mitigated). The doctrinal issue in *Parker* involves an employee's obligation to avoid damages after her employer has breached their employment agreement: was Shirley MacLaine's claim for compensation foreclosed because of the opportunity, which she refused, to avoid her loss by working in "Big Country, Big Man"? In deciding the case for Shirley MacLaine, the court in *Parker* relied on the fact that, under the mitigation rule, an employee need not avoid damages by accepting "employment of a *different* or *inferior* kind . . . ." The majority concluded that the "'Big Country' lead was . . . both different and inferior:"

The mere circumstance that "Bloomer Girl" was to be a musical review calling upon plaintiff's talents as a dancer as well as actress, and was to be produced in the City of Los Angeles, whereas "Big Country" was a straight dramatic role in a "Western Type" story taking place in an opal mine in Australia, demonstrates the difference in kind between the two employments; the female lead as a dramatic actress in a western style motion picture can by no stretch of imagination be considered the equivalent of or substantially similar to the lead in a song and dance production.

Additionally, the substitute "Big Country" offer proposed to eliminate or impair the director and screenplay approvals accorded to plaintiff under the original "Bloomer Girl" contract . . . and thus constituted an offer of inferior employment. No expertise or judicial notice is required in order to hold that the deprivation or infringement of an employee's rights held under an original employment contract converts the available "other employment" relied upon by the employer to mitigate damages, into inferior employment which the employee need not seek or accept.

The dissenting judge, however, charged that the majority relied on a "superficial listing of differences" between the films, asserting that:

[i]t is not intuitively obvious . . . that the leading female role in a dramatic motion picture is a radically different endeavor from the leading female role in a musical comedy film. Nor is it plain to me that the rather qualified rights of director and screenplay approval contained in the first contract are highly significant matters either in the entertainment industry in general or to this plaintiff in particular. Certainly, none of the declarations introduced by the plaintiff in support of her motion shed any light on these issues. Nor do they attempt to explain why she declined the offer of starring in "Big Country, Big Man."

By calling attention to the majority opinion's conclusory application of the "different or inferior" qualification, the dissenting opinion encourages the casebook reader to feel uncertain about how to use the mitigation rule in the employment context. It will seem unjust, to some readers, that Shirley MacLaine is apparently going to get $750,000, after this decision, for doing nothing. The mitigation rule seems to lose all of its muscle as a result of this "different or inferior" qualification. Would MacLaine have been entitled to damages if she had refused the lead in "Annie Hall," because that extremely successful film is not a musical? Would she have been denied damages if she had turned down "Springtime for Hitler"? How can you tell?

I believe The Feminist Reader and the Reader with a Chip on her Shoulder (as well as other readers who are familiar with feminist social history) might find the majority's application of the "different or inferior" standard much less mysterious than other readers. Their views would be based on their acquaintance either with Amelia Bloomer, a mid-nineteenth century feminist, suffragist, and abolitionist, or with "bloomers," the loose trousers that some women wore under a short skirt, without hoops, multiple petticoats, or restricting underwear, in the early 1850s. (Bloomer, whose magazine, *The Lily*, was the first American magazine published by and for women, publicized and stirred enthusiasm among some women for the trousers, or pantelettes, as they were sometimes known, and they came to be called after her.) These readers might have the intuition, as I did in reading the *Parker* case, that a film entitled "Bloomer Girl" was related in some way to the radical effort feminists in the last century made to achieve more freedom of movement and control over what they wore by reforming their dress. Moreover, simply because Shirley MacLaine is a woman, these readers might assume that the role in "Bloomer Girl" had personal significance for the actress;[177] even if the film treated women's issues in the lighthearted fashion typical of musical comedy, it would still link the actress with events that are historically significant to other women. "Bloomer Girl" would seem different, from this perspective, not only from a western but from other musical comedies, because of its political overtones.

. . .

Although these readers might not know whether "Bloomer Girl" had feminist themes[179] or whether "Big Country, Big Man" portrayed women according to the usual demeaning western stereotype, because of their skepticism about women's roles in westerns and their intuitions regarding "Bloomer Girl's" feminist themes, they might understand MacLaine's rejection of the "Big Country, Big Man" role in terms of their own efforts to reconcile their politics with their careers. These readers would be able to ground the language of the "different or inferior" qualification in their own lives. They might assume that MacLaine not only sought to refuse a role that would be demeaning to her as a woman, but that she also wanted to avoid contributing to the oppressed images of women in popular culture. Rather than thinking that Shirley MacLaine is being paid to do nothing in *Parker*, and that the "different or inferior" qualification to the mitigation rule was unfairly applied, their attitude toward the two films could enable them to infer an ascertainable but complicated standard for determining when the "different or inferior" qualification should be applied in employment cases. That is, they would assume that *Parker* demonstrates that

an employee's serious and recognized personal goals should be respected and protected when they are connected to a concern that is respected and acknowledged by others. Under this interpretation, some degree of mitigation can be required (mitigation does not lose all of its muscle in *Parker*), and yet a wrongly discharged employee would not have to take just any substitute employment. Money would not be the only test for determining whether jobs are comparable, and yet other employment objectives would require social as well as personal significance in order to be protected under the "different or inferior" qualification.

The interpretation of *Parker* generated by feminist attitudes and information about the social history related to the case offers readers useful guidance in applying the "different or inferior" qualification to other situations. This interpretation also allows readers who identify with Shirley MacLaine (because she is a woman) to attribute dignity to her conduct. However, readers of *Dawson, Harvey, and Henderson* will have to struggle to interpret *Parker* in the manner I have described. Inexplicably, the editors omit material that would confirm readers' intuitions that the social context and political significance of the films might explain the application of the "different or inferior" qualification in *Parker*.[182] Dawson, Harvey, and Henderson thus subtly deter readers who are familiar with nineteenth century feminist activists and their work from utilizing their personal connections with the case to understand *Parker*; these readers may even be led to believe that social context and politics are not legitimate interpretive tools. Although readers' intuitions about the *Parker* case may in fact explain the otherwise baffling result of this decision, the casebook does not

---

[177] Although the actress's decision to reject "Big Country, Big Man" may not have been politically motivated, feminists who read the case now may identify MacLaine as a feminist and they are likely to assume that her decision more than twenty years ago was politically motivated. MacLaine has written about her longstanding political activism, as well as her other interests, in several bestselling autobiographical books. . . .

[179] It turns out that "Bloomer Girl" did have feminist themes, as Charles Knapp has pointed out in his contracts casebook. My own intuitions about "Bloomer Girl" were confirmed by reading John Gregory Dunne's review of a book by "Danny Santiago" in the New York Review of Books last year. Dunne, The Secret of Danny Santiago (Book Review), 31 N.Y. Rev. of Books 17 (Aug. 16, 1984) (reviewing D. Santiago, Famous All Over Town (1984)). "Danny Santiago" was revealed in that review to be the nom de plume of Dan James, a Hollywood writer who was blacklisted during the fifties because of his past membership in the Communist

Party. Dunne mentioned that the Broadway musical "Bloomer Girl" was based on a play that James and his wife Lilith co-authored. The inspiration for the James' play stemmed from "a Party-endorsed workshop on women's rights." Id. at 20. Professor Stewart Macaulay, of the University of Wisconsin, who has extensively researched the production and reception of the Broadway "Bloomer Girl," has kindly shared with me some fascinating details he has found about the Broadway play. . . . [Professor Frug finds that the play involved both abolition and the women's movement, and reprints some "bitingly feminist" lyrics by E. Y. Harburg. — ed.]

[182] Well before the fourth edition of Dawson, Harvey, and Henderson was published in 1982, Charles Knapp informed his readers that MacLaine had been connected to feminist causes and that one of the characters in "Bloomer Girl" was "Amelia Jenks ('Dolly') Bloomer . . . a leading advocate of women's rights in the United States during the nineteenth century." . . .

encourage them to draw on those intuitions. It discourages—in the context of these opinions—the sensitivity to what is influential but not said, a sensitivity that women have often found to be a source of strength.

The negative pedagogical effect of omitting information about the feminist themes in "Bloomer Girl" extends to other readers too. Most casebook readers are unlikely to know about Amelia Bloomer or the nineteenth century feminist dress reform effort. Had Dawson, Harvey, and Henderson included the information about "Bloomer Girl," which Charles Knapp provides in his casebook, then feminist attitudes toward the subordination of women in westerns and the importance of dress reform could have been tapped in other readers to develop the complicated, contextualized interpretation of mitigation suggested above. By failing to describe the social context of this case, the editors probably deprive many readers of an interpretation of *Parker* that would advance their understanding of mitigation doctrine.

Although The Feminist Reader or the Reader with a Chip on her Shoulder may pursue her intuitions about *Parker* despite the editors' silence, the editors include a photograph of the actress in the casebook which could distract many of these readers from such an understanding of the majority's result in *Parker*. MacLaine is pictured, pouting, in a fringed, lowcut cocktail dress. Her legs are crossed, a knee is bared, she's wearing open-toe, sling-back high heels, and her cheek is resting on her hand. She might look to some readers like a "sex kitten," an image which is subtly reinforced by the stuffed rabbit tucked under her arm. Her picture, on page forty-seven, is the third illustration in the casebook, following a magisterial full page portrait of Holmes, in judicial robes, on page thirty-one, and then a picture of a bridge, on page forty-three. (The bridge was built by the injured party in the preceding case after he failed to mitigate his damages; it is the object he produced as he piled up his damages.)

Some feminists might relish the contrast between the images of Holmes and MacLaine in that each is wearing a costume that emphasizes the nature of its subject's power—for Holmes, the judicial robes; for MacLaine, the sexy dress and shoes. The conjunction of these illustrations could remind such readers that sexuality has been a considerable source of power for some women. Regarding MacLaine's illustration as a statement that her sex appeal is linked to her exceedingly successful acting career, these readers would believe that their interpretation of the *Parker* case

was sound; MacLaine is exactly the kind of female actress who might have had the courage to stand up to the studio and turn down "Big Country, Big Man."

Many feminist readers, however, might find a different message in these illustrations. Comparing Holmes with MacLaine might remind them of the substantial disparities between the public achievements of men and women. Comparing the picture of the bridge with the picture of MacLaine, these readers might assume they are being shown two "objects" in the mitigation section of the casebook—a bridge and a woman. Because treating women as if they were nothing more than objects for sexual pleasure is a significant feminist concern, these two illustrations could remind feminists that sexuality has often been a form of oppression in women's lives. Thus, MacLaine's photograph could prevent many readers from believing that her refusal to accept the "Big Country, Big Man" role was motivated by her political integrity. Instead, MacLaine's photograph might deter them from considering Amelia Bloomer's significance to the case. How could Shirley MacLaine have stood up to the studio for feminist reasons, they might think; she's not a feminist but a "sex object."

Without any clues in this casebook regarding the feminist themes of "Bloomer Girl," most *Dawson, Harvey, and Henderson* readers will have to find other ways to cope with their uncertainty about the meaning of the "different or inferior" qualification of the mitigation rule. In the remaining pages of this part I shall elaborate interpretations of *Parker* that do not depend on social context or feminist attitudes in order to demonstrate how assumptions regarding gender can also be implicated in interpretations that are not overtly linked with feminism.

The breach of an individual's employment contract sharply presents a basic conflict underlying all mitigation issues. We earnestly want to protect the contract objectives of individual employees against employer breach (they should be compensated for their losses under the contract) and yet we also abhor the idea that such employees should be excused from the communal work ethic by getting paid for doing nothing. The general rule of mitigation of damages favors the communal pole of this conflict (one cannot recover compensation for damages that can be avoided), while the qualification to the general rule, that one need not avoid damages by accepting work of a "different or inferior" kind, favors the individualist pole. Without the qualification, the mitigation rule would swallow an employee's contractual freedom—her employer could fire her with little risk of fiscal responsibility. Thus *Parker*, like all mitigation cases, presents the question of how to resolve in a particular situation a fundamental conflict between the individual and communal claims mediated by the mitigation rule and the "different or inferior" qualification.

To some readers, the conclusory application of the "different or inferior" qualification by the majority in *Parker* will seem like appropriate, if unreasoned deference to individualism. Searching for some rational explanation of the majority's decision, they will conclude that the directorial rights MacLaine would have lost in "Big County, Big Man," in conjunction with the lost opportunity to advance her musical comedy expertise, would justify the application of the "different or inferior" qualification in this case. These readers will agree that MacLaine's autonomy deserved more protection than the general social good that would have come from not letting her off the working hook the rest of us are on.

This interpretation of the case will seem gendered to some readers because the individualism/community duality I have described is generally understood to be gendered. Individualism and autonomy are commonly associated with men while altruism and community are generally linked with women, just as, more concretely, men are usually expected to pursue their individualistic careers single-mindedly while women are expected to subordinate other career objectives to care for their families or to participate in community activities. Readers who justify the majority's decision on the basis of an autonomy rationale are also likely to be influenced in this reading by gender-related ideas about MacLaine and what her objectives were regarding "Bloomer Girl." Thus, some of these readers may approve of MacLaine's efforts to stand up to the studio—to "act like a man"—and the studio be damned, while others may approve of the decision because MacLaine was seeking to protect directorial and approval privileges which these readers understand as participatory and "feminine."

Whatever the particular rationale underlying an interpretation of *Parker* which justifies the majority's decision, it offers readers very little guidance for arguing future employment cases involving a mitigation issue. The majority's conclusory opinion provides readers almost no guidance in how to make an individualist or "masculine" argument. As Judge Sullivan points out in his dissenting opinion, "there will always be differences" between two jobs, and "a su-

perficial listing of differences with no attempt to assess their significance may subvert a valuable legal doctrine."

Because this preceding reading is so unsatisfactory, I believe most readers will be inclined to assume that the majority opinion in the *Parker* decision is an irrational capitulation to individualism. Gender-related ideas may also contribute to this conclusion. As I have stated in an earlier discussion, one way the insignificance of a decision can be suggested to readers is through the organization of the casebook. Because the editors pair *Parker* (the first case in the book in which a woman is a party) with a case setting forth the general obligation of mitigation, readers who link the traditionally inferior status of women to the countercase position of the *Parker* decision will be encouraged to consider the *Parker* rule subordinate to the principal mitigation obligation.

MacLaine's photograph will encourage other readers to treat the *Parker* case skeptically. Because the photograph plays on gender-related ideas about female sexuality, these readers will be reminded that men have historically been able to manage and control the power such a picture suggests in its subject. These readers will be encouraged to believe that the *Parker* rule can be managed and controlled, just as women have been.

Finally, still other readers will be encouraged to dismiss *Parker*'s significance because of the customary disposition in our culture to devalue any kind of women's work. These readers may be dubious at the outset of the opinion about whether acting is *real* work, and MacLaine's sex will foster their belief that *real* employees doing *real* work will not be treated like MacLaine.[192]

Each of these gender-related ideas legitimates a reader's conclusion that *Parker* is incorrectly decided, or insignificant, but the ideas would not help such a reader elaborate altruistic arguments for a different result. Thus, like the earlier interpretation supporting the majority's decision, the dismissive reading of *Parker* disserves readers pedagogically. It fails to offer them guidance for arguing and resolving a mitigation conflict. In addition, because *Parker* is the first major case in the book in which a woman is one of the parties, the dismissive reading is likely to affect the way gender-conscious readers feel about women.

The dismissive reading of the case tempts instruc-

---

[192] A footnote in the dissenting opinion, which informs readers that the mitigation rule "may have had its origin in the bourgeois fear of resubmergence in lower economic classes," may influence readers to adopt the kind of class bias analysis suggested here as an explanation for MacLaine's victory in the case.

tors and students to ridicule MacLaine, to imagine her as an indulged starlet lying around eating chocolates, while the defendants, hard working studio types, struggle to manage their business efficiently despite her arbitrary whims. Some readers may be proud that MacLaine is a woman who manages to "beat the system" by getting paid for doing nothing, but other readers may internalize any disrespect that they think the opinion generates for MacLaine. If these readers believe that women are morally superior to men (and some readers will hold this opinion), they will be shamed if MacLaine, as a woman plaintiff, seems successful because she cleverly manipulated the legal system. In contrast, the misogynist feelings of readers who are undisposed to favor women will be intensified by any derogation of MacLaine; women are just as bad as these readers have always supposed. A distinct advantage of the *Parker* reading based on feminist attitudes toward the social history implicated by the case is that this interpretation will challenge the effect dismissive readings would have on readers; it will encourage feminist as well as nonfeminist readers to rethink their ideas about women.

I am not immune to the diversion *Parker* offers from standard commercial contracts reading. It's fun to talk about the movies. My objective has not been to spoil the fun, but to illuminate some of its darkness. Indeed, *Parker* would be a good case with which to introduce feminist themes into the classroom: as I have argued, feminist attitudes improve its pedagogical usefulness. An interpretation of *Parker* that acknowledges and utilizes feminist attitudes is valuable because it challenges the lessons readers learn from cases such as . . . *Fitzpatrick v. Michael* that gender-related ideas are only helpful to legal interpretations when they draw on negative images of women.

Understanding MacLaine as a powerful actress whose feminist politics are respected by the California Supreme Court could also stimulate readers to draw connections between social contexts and legal decisions, between the experiences of parties in a case and the experiences of readers themselves. Although these interactions are not unique to feminism, they are similar to the skills of "deep reading" many women claim as part of their gendered heritage. Recognizing the value of such skills will affirm, for some readers, an attribute they identify as feminine. Because "women's" attributes are so often less valued than "men's," affirming a "feminine" attribute through an analysis of *Parker* will contribute to the release of gender-related restrictions on our lives.

. . .

IV. Concluding Discussion

. . .

Ideas relating to gender will also affect the way in which instructors determine how a feminist analysis should affect their treatment of *Dawson, Harvey, and Henderson* in class. In my contracts course, for example, I am willing to introduce those parts of this Essay that relate to the relationship between gender and how students understand cases, but I seem reluctant to discuss how the casebook affects students' views of themselves and of gender roles. I thus subordinate the deep pleasure and appreciation many students would derive from having their intuitive responses to the casebook legitimated to my concerns about the negative reactions of other students. I succumb to the position I have disputed in this Essay that doctrinal instruction can be isolated from students' views of themselves.

My reluctance to fully pursue this Essay's ideas in my classroom is a gendered reaction. Like many women law teachers, I am suspicious of the authority and power that students are accustomed to extending to instructors. Because students expect me and I expect myself to be more conciliatory, more deferential, and more understanding than male teachers, I am reluctant to exploit my power in the classroom by introducing some of this controversial material into class.

I am also reluctant to completely incorporate a feminist casebook analysis in class because the analysis is not only radically different from traditional classroom discussion but also closely related to my identity as a woman. Having been educated exclusively by men in the law schools I attended and having taught on predominantly male faculties, I link traditional classroom discussion with men. In order to pursue feminist material in class, I must struggle against the customary deference I have been socialized to extend to men. Challenging the restrictions my own ideas about gender impose on me is an effort I cannot always make.

Because one's own attitudes about gender affect what one believes is acceptable in the classroom and because one's views of what is acceptable in the classroom affect one's attitudes toward gender, any decisions regarding the classroom implications of this Essay must be personal and contextualized, as my own decision has been. Faithfully replicating the analysis set forth in this Essay is unlikely to be a useful way for anyone, even me, to challenge the influence of gender in class discussions of *Dawson, Harvey, and Henderson*. The variety of student—as well as instructor—attitudes needs to be considered. I hope, however, that this Essay has convincingly demonstrated that current classroom conduct is already molding students' views about themselves as men and women and about the relationship between gender and the law. Although the question of how one's treatment of *Dawson, Harvey, and Henderson* should change because of my re-reading cannot be given a uniform answer, there is no way to *avoid* the issue of gender in the classroom. Each of us must address this issue, but for him or herself.

. . .

A feminist analysis of *Dawson, Harvey, and Henderson* can be successful not by being "applied" to other legal writing but by generating other re-readings. Although we need to use gender-related ideas in order to challenge gender constraints, we will only be able to accomplish that objective by constantly re-examining the ideas we are using. Ultimately, in order to challenge gender constraints effectively, our use of gender-related ideas must change with our shifting cultural context and the changes within ourselves. Only by continually re-thinking who we are and why we are making the choices we make can we free ourselves from the belief that our selves are constructed by our sexual identities.

A Japanese Perspective on Contracts

The following article is a collaboration between the late Hiroshi Wagatsuma, a distinguished Japanese anthropologist, and Arthur Rosett, author of one of the leading contracts casebooks and Professor of Law at UCLA. Professor Wagatsuma was trained in social psychology and anthropology at the University of Tokyo, Harvard and Michigan. He taught for many years in the United States and wrote influential publications on Japanese cultural psychology. The son of a preeminent scholar of civil law, Professor Wagatsuma turned late in his life to teaching and research in law at UCLA. He returned to Japan in 1980 and died at 58 in 1985. Professor Rosett, who is well-known in American law, has a strong interest in Asian law as well. The article benefits from the multifaceted lenses through which they view this subject.

As the article points out, formal Japanese commercial law was imported from the German code system in the late nineteenth century, and is thus something of an overlay on the traditional Japanese culture. Courses and articles on Japanese law have become common in recent years, as one might expect with so important a trading partner. In addition, there are now a great many articles on the law of Mainland China. See, e.g., Roderick W. Macneil, *Contract in China: Law, Practice, and Dispute Resolution*, 38 Stan. L. Rev. 303 (1986), on alternatives to traditional Anglo-American dispute resolution. Here, we are more concerned with Japanese attitudes than with the details of Japanese contract doctrines. Japanese corporate and communal approaches to business and labor relations have attracted a lot of attention, but we are often warned that there are great cultural differences that are not to be ignored. The Wagatsuma-Rosett article bears out this warning, but nonetheless gives us material to think about in approaching our own system.

Hiroshi Wagatsuma and Arthur Rosett, *Cultural Attitudes Towards Contract Law: Japan and the United States Compared*, 2 Pacific Basin L.J. 76 (1983)

The Japanese, as well as foreigners who do business with them, commonly have observed that Japanese agreement behavior is strikingly different from that seen in other countries and also diverges from the formal rules of contract law found in Japan's Civil Code. Professor Takeyoshi Kawashima, a leading scholar of the sociology of law, suggests several instances in which these differences are found:

(a) Despite the Civil Code recognition of informal contracts, there is a persistent attitude among Japanese that simple oral agreements concluded without formalities are not binding;

(b) The Code insists that there is either a complete contract comporting a full panoply of rights and obligations, or an unenforceable nullity, whereas in practice the Japanese recognize partial obligations that carry some, but not all, of the binding qualities of contract;

(c) The Code calls for full and detailed statements of the agreement when there is a written contract, while in practice the Japanese rely on incomplete and often cryptic memoranda memorializing the existence of a commitment but not spelling it out completely;

(d) The formal system found in the Code implies that in the event of a dispute there will be an adjudication of rights and wrongs leading to the vindication of the correct position, while Japanese practice seems to prefer compromise and mediation resulting in the accommodation of conflicting claims;

(e) The Code tends to see each contract between two parties as a distinct and isolated transaction, while in practice the Japanese tend to behave as if each contract transaction is merely an integral segment of an ongoing relationship that has duration and significance beyond the life of any particular transaction.

Kawashima understands these differences between norm and behavior in cultural terms. He sees them as specific to Japan and conceives of them developmentally. He expects them to diminish over time as the process of "modernization" produces a convergence between Japanese legal consciousness and the Western values embodied in Japanese law codes.

This paper outlines our attempts to understand these aspects of Japanese behavior and the explanations Kawashima and others have provided. We have struggled together to understand these matters from the different perspectives provided by our separate national cultures and our distinct professional disciplines, in an effort to explain them to our students. As a result, this essay is in part a groping for a hypothesis and in part a working agenda for further research. Perhaps most significantly, it may provide the reader with some sense of the substantial rewards and frustrations of extended interaction between an American law professor and a Japanese psychologist-anthropologist.

We have encountered difficulties in finding reliable observational data on commercial practice in Japan, the U.S., or other Western countries. Professor Kawashima's observation on commercial practices in Japan appears to be at least a generation old. In the United States, the heuristic investigations of Professor Stewart Macaulay of the contracting practices of Wisconsin businessmen date from the 1950s. These crucial deficiencies in the observation of commercial behavior leave us with a number of questions we are unable to answer with certainty and which inspire modesty in our factual assertions. . . .

. . .

Disparity Between Norms and Practices

It seems ironic to us that neither lawyers nor anthropologists are very strong on the facts of commercial contract behavior. The literature of anthropological observation is richer on the practices of so-called "simple cultures" than it is on the practices observable closer to home. Both disciplines insist that social behavior must be compared, tested and reconciled with stated legal norms. Yet lawyers have little concrete information on the extent to which the law's rules and processes actually shape the behavior they are supposed to influence. For over two centuries Anglo-American lawyers have honored, but rarely emulated, the example of Lord Mansfield, who sought guidance from the merchants of London regarding practices to help him decide problems of commercial law.

. . .

[The authors review the history of British commercial law. According to their summary, until the eighteenth century the local and fair courts applied customary practice through the law merchant. At that point, however, the common lawyers imported more formal rules and doctrines that tended to separate law from business practice. —ed.]

This is not the place to describe all the crenellated towers, spacious apartments, winding corridors and dark dungeons of that crystal palace of classical contract law, except to note in passing that a number of its major features were never comfortably accepted by the business community that was subject to its doctrines and rules. More than a century of exposure to the lawyer's concept does not appear to have led businesspersons fully to accept the rules of contract formation, consideration (particularly as it applies to blanket orders and the termination of franchises), the completeness of contract terms, cancellation and modification, and excusing conditions.

Businesspersons have continued to do things in their own way, although they must have recognized that if a dispute ended up in court the lawyers' rules would be applied.

Parenthetically, the Japanese experience is roughly parallel to the Anglo-American in the sense that the codes adopted during the nineteenth-century Meiji Revolution were not derived from subsisting Japanese business practice. Instead they were imposed from outside in an effort to meet the perceived demands of the new economic and political order. Japanese contract law as stated in the Civil Code is an import, borrowed from the German Code and phrased in a synthetic language that had to be invented to convey alien concepts in symbols largely incomprehensible to an ordinary literate Japanese. Introduction of the codes was not aimed primarily at the internal audience of businesspersons who would engage in these transactions, but at an external audience of foreigners who had to be persuaded that the Japanese were "civilized." The twin aims of transplanting this strange legal system to Japanese soil were to support "modernization" and the growth of commercial and industrial interests on the one hand, and to avoid the fate of extraterritoriality and dismembering colonization that befell China with the encroachments of Western imperialism. Both legal cultures therefore found themselves by the early twentieth century in a state of tension between their formal normative statements of contract law and the practices of their business communities. Moderation and resolution of this tension has been a major task for both systems.

A continuing desire to apply business common sense and practice rather than legal rules has been one strong motivation for the growing popularity of commercial arbitration in the past two generations. Similar sentiments have left their mark in the United States on the Uniform Commercial Code, which was drafted about a generation ago and is now the statutory repository of commercial law in virtually every American state. The new Code elevates the importance of course of dealings, trade usage and commercial practice. . . .

. . .

[The authors summarize many provisions of the Uniform Commercial Code, and describe Stewart Macaulay's empirical research. (See Part IA of this anthology.) —ed.]

In many Japanese contracts there are clauses such as, "if in the future a dispute arises between the parties with regard to the rights and duties provided in this contract, the parties will confer in good faith," (sei-i o motte kyōgi suru), or in similar situation, ". . . will settle the dispute harmoniously by consultation" (kyōgi ni yori enman ni kaiketsu suru). These "confer-in-good-faith" and "harmonious-settlement" clauses reveal the basic nature of the Japanese contract. Kawashima's interpretation of the meaning of such clauses is accurate. He says, "in Japanese contract the parties not only do not stipulate in a detailed manner the rights and duties under the contract, but also think that even the rights and duties provided for in the written agreement are tentative rather than definite. Accordingly, when a dispute arises, they think it desirable at that time to fix such rights and duties by means of ad hoc consultation. Therefore, even something such as the due date of a debt is not thought of as something strictly defined but as fixed 'give or take a few days.' The creditor who demands payment of the penalty for delay when payment is only a day or two overdue is thought of as a shylock or an inflexible person. Therefore, it is possible to state that a confer-in-good-faith clause, even if it is not written in a contract document, is, so to speak, tacitly implied in all contracts."

A typical Japanese response to the description of the Officers' and Directors' Errors and Omissions Liability Insurance in the U.S. is the comment, "I could not possibly place myself in the position of a newly employed executive who discusses with the representatives of his new company and of an insurance company as well as with a lawyer the content of the insurance policy that is to protect the company financially in case he is to defalcate with the company's money, or the company is held liable for some damages caused by his fault. How could I feel loyal to the company that needs to protect itself by an insurance from the misdeeds I will never commit? Why couldn't the company *trust* me?" Many Japanese consider liability insurance as deriving from a basic mistrust of humanity (*ningen fushin*).

Health, Illness, Good Faith and Contract

Anglo-American commercial law is primarily the result of common law judicial rulings, not statutory code analysis. These rules arose through a lawyer-dominated process of case decision in relationships that had gone wrong and therefore demanded court intervention. They are not modeled on how things are supposed to work among cooperative businesspersons with healthy ongoing relationships. They emphasize the competitive and antagonistic dimensions of such reality rather than the cooperative and supportive aspects. Looked at the way described above, commercial law can be seen as a kind of medicine for pathological situations, for failed agreements, in which smooth commercial relations have broken down and cooperative transactions have turned sour and ended in conflict. The rules that have emerged over the last century and a half are framed from the perspective of the "doctor" called in to minister to the sick transaction and to resolve the dispute.

Returning to the Japanese situation, it should be clear by now that the so-called traditional Japanese attitude toward contract is not essentially different from that prevalent among American businesspersons. The difference is that in the West contract is used to define rights and duties of the parties by detailed provisions when good-will and trust between the parties have broken down, while the Japanese tend to insist upon the continuing effectiveness of good-will and trust in every situation.

To repeat the medical metaphor, Westerners use contract as a medical device to save a sick relationship in case a relationship loses its original healthy trust, while Japanese social norms demand that the relationship always be healthy. People are forced to behave as if their relationship were continuously healthy even when the bond based upon mutual trust has been damaged. It is as though people are afraid of taking medicine lest they should become really ill because taking a medicine is admitting that one is actually sick. While in the American mind the function of contract is to anticipate possible future strife

and trouble as well as to pre-define disputes and enunciate rights, contract in the Japanese mind is a symbolic expression or reflection of mutual trust that is expected to work favorably for both parties in case of future trouble and never to break down.

Our hypothesis is that Japanese and American perceptions of contract relationships are distinguished by an assumption of healthy trust on the part of the Japanese and a fear of pathology on the part of Americans. To make this hypothesis more convincing let us now discuss three major aspects of Japanese interpersonal relations in general—*tatemae* and *honne*, in-group versus outsider, and the norm of harmony (*wa*).

Stated reasons versus felt reasons for interpersonal behavior—simultaneous conformance to group and personal needs. Two concepts are used by Japanese to describe the tensions between a person's stated reasons or opinion (*tatemae*) and his real intention or motive or feeling (*honne*). These terms describe two sides of a single reality; just as there can be no *omote* (front) without a *ura* (back), there can be no *tatemae* or public character to behavior without its distinct but linked *honne* or private connotation. *Tatemae* is that which one can show or tell others, while *honne* is that which one should not or had better not show or tell others. *Tatemae* is adopted, accepted, stated or asserted as the means of continuing one's social life smoothly, while *honne* is that which one experiences in one's efforts to continue smooth social relationships, and is admitted to one's awareness. At the conversational level, *tatemae* may be an indirection in discourse, while *honne* is a true message underneath. In American society, one may answer one's mother's request to drop by on the next Sunday, "Yes, mother, I'd *love* to come" which is *tatemae*, while one's *honne* may very well be a feeling of reluctance. Japanese frequently use a greater variety of indirections in discourse or polite evasiveness than one may encounter among Americans. Yet, *tatemae* is more than conversational indirection or evasiveness. It can be the expression of one's commitment or compliance to the demands of social norms, while *honne* may be the expression of one's sense of frustration, unwillingness, or feeling that the demands of the norms are unreasonable or impractical.

Traditional Japanese social norms emphasize harmonious interpersonal relations and group solidarity. Self-assertion independent of the group is strongly discouraged and the individual often finds that he must sacrifice personal needs and emotions to avoid confrontation with the group. The harmonious relationship among people (*wa*), as we discuss later, is usually given a top priority and everything else must be subordinated to actualize this value. When they comply with group demands, people may feel unbearably frustrated, or become aware that they are unfairly or unreasonably treated. The Japanese accept such feelings as the natural consequences of social life, although they may not openly announce them. They admit that there is a normative way of doing certain things and they also say they do these things in the normative way. This is the expression of *tatemae*. At the same time they know and may confide to a close friend that it is nearly impossible, highly impractical, unreasonable or unrealistic to do the things in such a way. This admission of impossibility or impracticality is *honne*.

It is not simply that *honne* is truth and *tatemae* is a lie; both *tatemae* and *honne* are the truth for an individual—*tatemae* is true when an individual is expressing his commitment to the norms, and *honne* is true when he is expressing (or admitting to himself) how he feels about them. Whether the things are done actually in the *tatemae* way or *honne* way depends upon the individual and circumstance.

Disparity between operating by rules (*tatemae*) and operating by *ad hoc* judgment (*honne*) may be experienced by Americans also. For example, the criminal statutes state that every person who has committed a crime shall be punished as provided in the law after guilt is proven at a trial (*tatemae*), but the great majority of criminal cases are disposed of without trial at a level of punishment substantially less than that fixed by the statutes. This occurs through application of the discretion of the police, the prosecutor and the judge, and frequently by a process known as plea bargaining (*honne*). Many Americans, however, consider such an implicit and practical system of handling the realities of the criminal courthouse as deviance from norms and judge it "bad."

One factor that makes it difficult for many Americans to understand the Japanese attitude toward *tatemae* and *honne* is the American emphasis upon internal emotional consistency. When they feel positively and negatively toward the same object, they tend to *repress* either their positive or negative feeling so as to establish internal consonance in their minds.[14] Americans find it difficult to live with the cognitive dissonance of ambivalent emotions. They

tend not to admit their ambivalence and to avoid it by repression. One might say that Americans become conscious of either *tatemae* or *honne* only, while Japanese tend to remain consciously ambivalent about many things, so that they remain aware of both *tatemae* and *honne* without suffering from the sense of internal inconsistency. Professor Doi, a psychoanalyst known for his analysis of dependence among Japanese, states that Japanese do not seem to have a very strong urge to overcome ambivalence and to establish the integrity of personality. In this sense the Japanese have a greater tolerance or ambiguity and ambivalence.

This tolerance of ambivalence, which at times may become even a preference for ambiguity, is not limited to feelings and emotions but often extends to cognition as well. To reach a cognitive judgment that x is both A and not-A (for instance, that an oral agreement both is and is not a contract), one may need to repress or reject the possibility that A and not-A are incompatible. That x is both A and not-A appears to be inconsistent. However, Japanese may recognize that x is A (that an agreement is a contract), while leaving some room for the possibility that x is not-A (that the same agreement is not a contract). Especially when they express their own individual opinions or perspective on a certain issue, Japanese often make subtle, indirect, or vague statements, giving an impression that they are stating that x is A (a particular agreement is a contract) while leaving it open, if necessary, that x is not-A (the same agreement is not a contract). Such preference for ambiguity is both a device for avoiding confrontation that may be disturbing to group harmony and a means to leave room for accommodating the group's demands. Japanese often express an opinion that life is full of problems to which no clear-cut solution can be given, and of situations for which there is no logically coherent explanation. Tolerance for ambiguity in social relations is valued as a sign of one's maturity and character of development.

Inner circle versus strangers. Japanese tend to make a sharp distinction between in-group and outgroup, or between those they know very well and those they do not know at all. Within a group, maintenance of harmonious and smooth interpersonal relations, interdependence, and mutual trust is of utmost importance for Japanese. While inner harmony

---

[14] L. A. Festinger, Theory of Cognitive Dissonance (1957).

and solidarity characterize each social group, it follows that there will exist vague animosity, competition, suspicion, or at least indifference between groups. Generally speaking, in-group solidarity and out-group enmity are two sides of the same psychodynamic coin. Aggressive and destructive tendencies that are generated but not allowed to be expressed inside a social group are often directed outward in the form either of hatred focused upon a specific scapegoat or of a diffuse sense of suspicion or indifference toward outsiders. When aggressive self-assertion and confrontation are avoided among the members of a social group they are deprived of opportunities to "air" their pent-up tensions. Consequently, it seems logical to assume that the stronger the emphasis upon in-group harmony and solidarity the more intense the out-group enmity can be.

Japanese like to be among *kigokoro no shireta nakama*, (those whole dispositions are well known to each other). Among the *kigokoro no shireta* friends and colleagues, Japanese can be relaxed, informal,

frank and trusting. Group pressure on each individual member is expected to be very strong but many Japanese often feel that they need no extra efforts to make themselves "fit into" such a congenial group. In such a situation one feels that one is understood by others without verbally expressing and explaining oneself. Very often what is really important for an individual's sense of security and belonging is not so much the actual fact of mutual understanding as the shared assumption of mutual understanding and acceptance.

One may even venture to suggest that while many Americans tend to live with an illusion of complete self-reliance, self-sufficiency and autonomy, many Japanese tend to live with an illusion of total harmony, mutual understanding and consensus among them.[17] A Japan Airlines television advertisement (in Japanese) in Southern California encourages the viewers (supposedly Japanese businessmen and their families stationed in the U.S.) to invite their aged parents and relatives to the U.S. Then it declares,

---

[17] The following anecdotes illustrate the Japanese preference for doing business only with those kigokoro no shireta partners. A young salesman of a sporting goods store began dropping by at the Department of Physical Education at a private college in Tokyo. Once in a while, he would come to the physical education teachers common room, have a conversation with the teachers about the weather or health and leave without mentioning his sales business. About six months passed and the teachers thought the young man was a somewhat unusual, yet very pleasant person. They began ordering from his store some inexpensive commodities such as percussion caps for starting guns. When they needed something quickly, the young man would deliver it within a day, while it would have taken larger stores at least a week. The teachers continued to buy more expensive items from other larger stores but bought less expensive items, like lime, from the young salesman's store, who always delivered the merchandise promptly. The salesman and teachers became closer friends and talked with each other about more intimate matters such as their family life. He began playing chess with some teachers at lunch time. Three years later, his store was selling the department all the sporting goods it needed. Ten years later, the young salesman became independent of the store he had worked for and opened his own store. The physical education department was buying all its sporting goods from his store. When members of other departments needed commodities his store did not deal in, he would buy them elsewhere and deliver them free of charge as his "service to the customers." When a teacher brought something from his store for personal use, he would never ask for payment. The teachers had to ask him to give them bills. He would submit bills reluctantly and would tell the teachers to pay only when they had some "extra money to spend." Twenty years passed since he had first dropped by at the college. One day, he came to one of the elder teachers and said, "Mr. So-and-so, I would like to buy a house. Would you be kind enough to be a guarantor for me when I make a loan from a bank?" The teacher immediately agreed to do so.

. . .

A saleswomen for a life insurance company chose one block of office district in Northern Osaka as her target area. Day after day, she dropped by at every office of every company in the high-rise building in the block and chatted with office workers. As she became acquainted with office workers, she would tell them where bargain sales of food items or clothing were going on. When she found a worker's wife was making handcrafts at home she would volunteer to find customers for her products. In the course of five years, she became a close acquaintance of many workers and even arranged marriages. Now she has a large clientele within her block, has received citations for her successful sales activities from her insurance company and finally bought her own house. R. Iwata, Nihonteki Sensu o Keiei Gaku (Management Science in Japanese Style) (1980).

The Japanese extend their preference for personal acquaintanceship to foreign business partners. According to a Japanese American lawyer familiar with many U.S.-Japan business transactions, the Japanese businessman devotes a great deal of his negotiating energies to acquainting himself with the attitudes, personalities, and thinking of the individuals representing the other party to the contemplated contract. There may even be a tendency on the part of the Japanese businessmen to try to forge a relatively durable and enduring commercial relationship with the other party, tying their companies together with informal understanding and agreements on commercial principles even when the other party is American. The result may be to form a commercial loyalty between the Japanese and American companies, so that "the parties, by virtue of their understanding of and commitment to one another, can be counted upon to work together to achieve a mutually satisfactory solution to the problems." Mori, A Practitioner's Perspective on Negotiations and Communication with Japanese Businessmen, in Current Legal Aspects of Doing Business in Japan and East Asia 47-51 (J. Haley ed. 1978).

"Kigokoro no shireta nikkōki nara anshin desu" (you can be sure of their safe trip on *kigokoro no shireta* JAL planes) as though an intimate relationship could safeguard against highjacking or a mechanical failure!

When a single person whose *kigokoro* is not well known to others—somebody belonging to another company, a person from another village or prefecture, an alumnus of another school—enters the scene, the atmosphere of the circle somehow becomes stiffened or chilled (*za ga shirakeru*), or all present feel strained. Japanese dislike to deal with *doko no uma no hone to mo wakaranu mono* (a horse bone whose origin nobody knows), a stranger with no proper introduction or a reliable sponsor-guarantor who is considered less than fully human!

Those Japanese who are strongly tied to their small groups—family, neighborhood, work, or school groups—do not easily relate to strangers, nor do they find casual acquaintances emotionally rewarding. Individuals A and B, friends of many years, are walking along the street when along comes a third person C, who is an intimate acquaintance of A but who does not know B at all. When this happens in American society, one can expect A to introduce B to C. If A begins to talk with C without introducing B to C, B would feel slighted, ignored and offended. However, when these three individuals are Japanese (or Germans), it often happens that A and C begin talking while B turns around as if socially disappearing from the A-C dyad. When the conversation ends and C walks away, A turns to B and apologizes for impoliteness (*"domo shitsurei itashimashita"*) *not* for not having introduced B to C, but for having kept B waiting.

. . . Compared with the individualistic Americans, Japanese may show a greater degree of conformity to certain group pressures. However, the "group" cannot be just any group. It has to be the group of significant others. The results may be interpreted in the following way: American subjects demonstrated a tendency to relate themselves to a group of "strangers" in the laboratory sufficiently so that the group exerted upon them the pressure to conform, while for the Japanese subjects, people who happen to be sitting together in a psychological laboratory do not constitute a group that is significant enough to elicit conformity.

The same Japanese individuals, compliant, considerate or courteous to insiders, may act in a drastically different, i.e., negative, way toward strangers. Japanese rarely casually relate themselves to strangers. They do not like to do so, nor do they know how to do so. After an appropriate introduction by a third party or through a sustained period of acquaintance, once a Japanese feels at ease with a stranger, that person is no longer an outsider but becomes more or less a member of the inner circle where the norms of harmony, interdependence, and mutual trust dictate.[19] Before dealing with somebody, the Japanese want to become well acquainted with that person so that he or she becomes a *kigokoro no shireta* insider with whom the relationship of unconditional trust is, at least in principle, possible. Such an emphasis on building a business relation upon personal acquaintance may at times override the competitive market motivations based upon price and other terms of trade.[20]

In a relation-based economy, stability of relations, long-term associations, and personal contact are priority values, while in a competitive market economy, stability of relationships must give way to allow for potential shifts in suppliers, customers, and employees to take advantage of changes in competitive conditions.

Wa or Group Harmony. The Japanese are known among Westerners as "group oriented." However, the nature of their group orientation is not always accurately understood. Western social sciences have long looked at the individual and society as two distinct, if not opposing, factors. In order to maintain one's individual identity, highly valued by Western individual-

---

[19] In Japan many gasoline stations give a discount to customers with a charge account but they do not do so to those customers who pay in cash. The reason behind it is that the credit customers are long-time patrons who deserve special service while those who pay in cash are "chance comers." The practice is the opposite in the United States, where cash customers are given a discount over those who buy on credit.

[20] A Japanese individual may feel somewhat unsure of the future of his business transaction with another person and wish to exchange a contract document but will refrain from insisting upon such an exchange, lest his insistence should be interpreted as an expression of lack of trust in the other party. He is likely to be afraid of inviting the criticism, "Why can't you trust my good will? If you do not trust me completely, why do you want to deal with me anyway?" thus the traditional norm of everlasting trust may override the practical necessity of a documented contract. Conversely, however, in many instances the Japanese appear to comply with the transnational norms of commercialism and to accept the need for contract. They exchange contracting documents, with detailed provisions spelled out, but they do so as tatemae, and in actuality they continue their business transactions without paying much attention to the document. Orders may be placed orally and should disputes occur they are settled through an ad hoc consultation.

ism, one must become independent on one's group and assert oneself, if necessary, in defiance of or in rebellion against society. If society becomes oppressive, one must fight for one's freedom, independence and autonomy. In the Western view of group and individual, when priority is given to a group over and above the interest of the individual, the individual is seen as subdued, oppressed, or buried without autonomy. In such a situation, the group may be described as totalitarian. Under normal circumstances, when an individual participates in a group, he does so of his own accord, on a contractual basis, and always retains his ultimate right to withdraw from and become independent of the group. Seen through dualistic Western eyes, Japanese society looks very stifling. In the American mind, a group-oriented individual who gives priority to his group over himself may look like an automaton with no self-identity.

For the Japanese, however, society in essence is not basically opposed to individuals. In contrast to the Western view, an individual is not seen as totally separate and distinct from the group. It is not that an individual, as an entirely distinct entity, asserts himself or herself against, or voluntarily participates in, the group. An individual is, from the beginning, conceived of as a member of the group. In the Japanese conception of individual and group, no group can exist without its individual members and no individual can exist without being a member of his group. Group and individual are conceived of as harmonious with rather than in opposition to each other. What the members of the group share is not limited to work and support; they share goals, so that the goals of the group become those of its members.

Japanese group orientation is based upon the notion that the members of a group cooperate with one another in their collective efforts to define ends, and by so doing each member simultaneously satisfies his individual needs and secures his individual welfare. Such a notion may be called "corporatism." According to this Japanese concept of corporatism, an individual maintains his autonomy through his group efforts. In contrast to the sense of autonomy found in Western individualism, the autonomy of the Japanese may be termed "joint autonomy."

Roughly speaking, Western individualism emphasizes: (1) the establishment of individual ego-identity, its assertion and respect; (2) self-reliance, self-help and self-sufficiency; and (3) a tendency to view inter-personal relations basically as the means for individual, not joint gain.

In contrast with Western individualism, Japanese corporatism emphasizes: (1) interdependence, the notion that social life is based upon mutual help and interdependence among the people; (2) mutual trust, the expectation and conviction that one's trust in others is reciprocated; and (3) a tendency to view inter-personal relationships as an end itself or valuable in its own right, deserving of people's efforts to maintain it.[24]

For the self-concept of a Japanese individual, his or her position in the network of social relations—kinship, marital, age and occupational roles—is much more important than it is for American self-identity. When asked about his occupation an American will mention what he is (an engineer, a sociologist, a secretary), while a Japanese will mention who he works for ("I work for SONY," "I teach at UCLA").[25] Group membership gives the Japanese individual a sense of self-identity and security. It is within this all-important group that the norms demand harmony among the members. Everybody must act according to the conviction that people can trust each other completely. No honest and sincere act may be left unreciprocated, at least as *tatemae*, although this is not realistically possible.

Even in individualistic Western society, trust among people is seen as the healthy state of interpersonal relationship. It should not be difficult, therefore, to appreciate the importance of trust in group oriented Japanese society.

Within a group the recognition of *wa* (group harmony) serves as a limit on the power of any member of the group to act in ways contradictory to the interests of others. A group that recognizes the value of *wa* is led to a system of mutual dependence and decision making by consensus. Power exists and colors relations in Japanese society, but it is moderated by the powerful person's recognition that he must maintain positive relations with those who are weaker.

Illusions of Autonomy and Harmony

Earlier in this essay we suggested that reliance on legal processes in the West often is a therapeutic response to the breakdown of social harmony. In the Western experience, the forces of law are mobilized in response to the breakdown of trust and relation, and are looked to as a corrective of this disharmony.

---

[24] Hsu, Rugged Individualism Reconsidered, 9 The Colorado Quarterly 143 (1960).

[25] C. Nakane, Japanese Society (1970).

The law claims to protect the weak by asserting the overriding legitimacy of legal rights against the imposition of power. This claim rests conceptually on the autonomy and importance of the individual. It is because each individual is important that the weak have legitimate claims on the powerful. It is because each individual is autonomous and can bind himself or herself by choice and will that promises have moral authority. In this framework, it is not only equals who can bind one another by their promises; the promise of the strong to the weak becomes the basis for claims by the less powerful to limit the actions of the more powerful. Through the binding force of promises the ordinary person gains claim to control over those forces in life that are outside ordinary human influence.

To take a rather extreme example from the Hebrew tradition, God and humans are both bound by covenants. People gain claims against the Almighty because God too is bound by law by His promises. Similarly, in English constitutional history the King is understood to be under "God and the Law," and his power is limited in part because he promised in his coronation oath to obey the law. This way of thinking about power, promises and the law had a profoundly revolutionary impact on how the Judaic and later the Christian traditions came to see individuals.

From the time of the Psalmist on, the whole world was understood to be filled and ordered by law. This law is immediately accessible to all and can be discerned in nature, either by studying the grand order of the stars or by looking inward to the order perceived in each human heart. These notions do not play a comparably important role in Oriental traditions. While some echoes and cognates can be found in notions of a universally binding order, there is no comparable idea that the weak can bind and limit the powerful. Confucian political philosophy, for example, does emphasize the importance of the virtue of the Emperor so that when an Emperor abuses his power, thus ceasing to be virtuous and benevolent, the Heaven no longer legitimates his rule. But the idea that this constraint on the Emperor gives an individual a right to demand virtuous rule from the Imperial Authority did not develop in Chinese thought. Confucian ideas adopted in Japan were modified; the notion of the Heaven became more remote and removed from human affairs and the power of the strong knew few external limits. Instead, the expressive aspects of subordinate-superordinate relations were emphasized in terms of mutual dependence of inferiors and superiors on each other, the mutual dependence, *amae*, that binds the two together.

Western insistence on the rights of the weak against the powerful is based on the illusion of individual autonomy and choice, just as the Japanese perspective is based on the *tatemae* of *wa*, the illusion of harmony among disparate parts. When social harmony and mutual trust break down, Western thought is led to resolve the matter in terms of legal rights, while Japanese thought seeks to restore illusory harmony. This is one way to understand the legalization of social and political relations that marks recent periods of American life; the disorder and breakdown of cooperative social structure is seen as the occasion to assert a violation of right, a claim that individual autonomy has been breached. However effective this strategy may be as a means to end a ruptured relationship, assertion of legal rights are not likely to restore harmony to the damaged relationship.

The healthy normal state of social relationships is trust and harmony; these are accepted values of all social systems. Looked at this way, the relative infrequency with which legal rights are asserted is an indication that social coherence continues strong in Japanese society. In Japan the crime rate is the lowest among the highly industrialized nations, family life appears comparatively cohesive and stable, essentially cooperative efforts continue among the workers and management, and the national political structure remains relatively stable.

In contrast, American legalism and litigiousness may simply be a short-term phenomenon, reflecting the social dislocation of a rapidly changing society seeking a new stability. Again, if we have a progressive faith in the underlying health of the social body these distortions should be ameliorated in time by restoration of harmony. There is certainly a widespread recognition that American litigiousness is counter-productive, and that this litigiousness is a reflection of the special interests of the lawyer subculture as opposed to the broader interests of society and the special interests of business clients. This can be seen in increased awareness in the United States of the need to reform litigation practice as well as the Uniform Commercial Code's emphasis on relationship and willingness to let businesspersons set their own rules.

Japanese norms demand that harmony be asserted even when it is not a reality. Japanese are forced to act, even when there is a dispute, as though there is no basic problem between them. This may be *tatemae*, not *honne*, but it shows the social power to create a reality by insisting on an illusion. The Japanese live by the illusion of harmony, while Americans live by the illusion of autonomy and self-sufficiency.

Conclusion

. . .

[W]e have speculatively suggested that the apparent disparity between legal rules and business practice in the United States may in part be the result of the tendency to emphasize the pathological situation, the transaction gone wrong. . . . The coincidence of legal rules and business practices might be greater if both social scientists and lawyers placed greater emphasis on the empirical study of healthy relationships, where relational dealings work effectively among persons who see themselves as sharing common interests and communal membership.

A Religious Approach to Contract

There is no doubt that contract has roots in religion, and that the early role of clerics as the Chancellors in the English equity courts affected its development. This history was traced by a reknown scholar, Professor Harold Berman of Emory University in an engaging article, *The Religious Sources of General Contract Law: An Historical Perspective*, 4 J. Law & Religion 103 (1986). That article appeared in a symposium on Law and Religion, and was followed by a "reply" by Professor Andrew W. McThenia, Jr., who teaches at Washington and Lee University. Professor McThenia's article doesn't really seem to reply to or disagree with Professor Berman's; rather, it goes off on a different tack by considering how today's religious beliefs should affect our contract dealings today. Regardless whether we are Christian, Jewish or not religious at all, McThenia's points bear thinking about.

One might note, however, that McThenia expressly assumes a Judeo-Christian American heritage. This is certainly true, but we should be aware of the increasing presence of Islam and of Asian religions as the combination of new immigration patterns and increased trade with the Middle East, the Indian subcontinent and the Far East begin affecting our ethical consciousness and our commercial practices. Islam is in many ways part of the "Judeo-Christian tradition." (We may soon find that phrase replaced by "people of the Book.") Thanks in part to the oil business, there is much in print about Islamic legal systems, which are intertwined with the Koran much more overtly and directly than our system is with the Bible. See, e.g., Kristin L. Peters Hamlin, *The Impact of Islamic Revivalism on Contract and Usury Law In Iran, Saudi Arabia, and Egypt*, 22 Texas Int'l Law J. 351 (1987). It is harder to find contract material dealing with religions that are not in the Jewish/Christian/Moslem tradition. Remember, however, that there is a short comparison between western and eastern religious attitudes in the preceding article by Wagatsuma and Rosett on Japanese cultural attitudes.

In any event, Professor McThenia's article is not a treatise on religious influences. It is more an application of religious *belief* to contract law. In doing so, Professor McThenia discusses also many of the writers whose works have appeared earlier in this anthology. He offers another voice in the discussion.

Andrew W. McThenia, Jr., *Religion, Story and the Law of Contracts: Reply to Professor Berman,* 4 J. Law and Religion 125 (1986)

Contract law, pronounced dead[1] within the last decade, has undergone a Lazarus-like resurrection. The revival of scholarship runs the gamut from Professor Charles Fried's writing asserting promise as "the moral basis of contract law,"[2] through the *Second Restatement of Contracts* which concedes the legitimacy of more communal based doctrines such as promissory estoppel, to the writings of Professor Ian Macneil who argues that community is "the fundamental root, the base" of contract and the even more collectivist writings of scholars in the Conference on Critical Legal Studies.[6]

This revival of contract scholarship does not yet suggest any unifying theme, but it does, I think, indicate a vigorous search for some means of weaving together seemingly intractable concepts. This symposium on Law and Religion suggests an important area of search. That is, it invites us to examine the shared ethos of our culture. I agree with Professor Berman's observation made elsewhere that law and religion are "two different but interrelated aspects . . . of social experience" and that one cannot flourish without the other. Because both law and religion are aspects of our social experience, one's view of God and the world must certainly affect one's view of the law. Similarly, one's view of the law probably affects how that person views God.[8]

If one's view of the world is that of man as a high stakes gambler, a lonely Robinson Crusoe, or a latter day Horatio Alger living in a minimalist state, then that would suggest a view of contract law not out of sorts with Professor Fried's world of promise. If one thinks that the world is not quite so lonely or individualistic, then she might think of contract in terms of more communal norms of reliance or the prevention of unjust enrichment.

I disagree with Professor Fried's conclusion that the moral basis of contract is promise, for that seems much too limiting to me: I am of the view that Professors Macneil and Unger are more nearly correct in viewing the essence of contract as community. I think the social matrix of the world is more fundamental than promise.

Many Americans, probably a majority, view the world from within the Jewish and Christian traditions. I think it is in our heritage of a covenantal community that we should begin our conversation and search.

As recorded in Mark's gospel:

Jesus said, 'The first commandment is this: Hear, O Israel: The Lord our God is the only Lord. Love the Lord your God with all your heart, with all your soul, with all your mind, and with all your strength. The second is this: Love your neighbor as yourself. There is no other commandment greater than these.' *Mark* 12:29-31.

That "restatement" of the law by Rabbi Jesus contains an important negative principle and the basis for an extremely radical ethic.

The important limitation which we as lawyers need always be mindful of is that the law is not God, the state is not God, Marx is not God nor is capitalism God. To make the law a civil religion is to be idolatrous. One of the two major themes of the biblical tradition is the fear of idolatry, "the fear that man might accept a limited worldly objective as an adequate goal of his striving."[11] We are warned to be especially skeptical of social structures that seek to take the place of God. The political, social, and economic institutions we inherit and are a part of have a profound effect on how we view the world. Yet we often are unaware of how important the effect of institutional forms is upon our moral perceptions. The negative admonition of the Torah and the Gospel warns us to be careful lest we accept the "is" as the "ought."

[1] G. Gilmore, The Death of Contract (1974).
[2] C. Fried, Contract as Promise (1981).
[6] See, e.g., Feinman, Promissory Estoppel and Judicial Method, 97 Harv. L. Rev. 678 (1984); Feinman, Critical Approaches to Contract Law, 30 UCLA L. Rev. 829 (1983) (hereinafter Critical Approaches); M. Horwitz, The Transformation of American Law, 1780-1860 (1977); Kennedy, Form and Substance in Private Law Adjudication, 89 Harv. L. Rev. 1685 (1976); Unger, The Critical Legal Studies Movement, 96 Harv. L. Rev. 563 (1983).
[8] Shaffer, Jurisprudence in Light of the Hebraic Faith, 1 Notre Dame J. of Law, Ethics & Public Policy 77, 108 (1984).
[11] R. Unger, Passion 26 (1984).

The positive theme of this "restatement" of the law by Rabbi Jesus is that love is to be the driving force of humanity. We are called to a personal encounter with one another. It is in our relations with each other that we are transformed. What is fundamental about the Christian tradition is that our identity is constructed around the narrative of the cross. Our identity as individuals and community is reinterpreted by means of the identity of Jesus Christ, a story which culminates in the passion, in the cross. For Christian believers, the point of the passion narratives is not that Jesus died in heroic despair, but that his death was followed by resurrection. . . .

As Harold Berman has said: "Society moves inevitably into the future. But it does so by walking backwards." It is in the shared stories of our tradition that we might find out what is at stake as we search for some way to make sense of modern contract law. The shared stories of our culture are important not to resolve conflicts inherent in modern day contract, but to place the conflicting norms in a matrix which is familiar to most Americans. We do not necessarily learn how to act from the retelling of the stories of our tradition, but we may be able to perceive what is at stake as we think about the seemingly intractable problems of our law of contract. A backward walk in our tradition may show us a way to appreciate the present and to approach the future.

I want to be clear that a return to our origins will not resolve the problems of expectation versus reliance, or, to use Unger's language—conflicting visions of freedom of contract and freedom to contract on the one hand and counter visions of reliance and fairness on the other. In fact, such a journey may well heighten the conflicts. But conflict, too, is valuable.

One of the truths of modern contract law is a recognition that there are conflicting values operating in any serious dispute. But this recognition of disorder and conflict is to a large extent hidden in the way these conflicts are "resolved" in modern contract litigation. The dominant story of contract litigation is of the search for truth by balancing (or mediating) conflicting claims of individual versus communal values before an impartial tribunal. One of the major and important criticisms of contract litigation offered by the Critical Legal Studies writers is to challenge the truth of that story. The erroneous belief that these important conflicts can be reconciled by adjudication tends to disguise the true nature of the conflict between important norms and to knock the sharp edges from the competing values so that they seem fuzzy and relativistic.

An appeal to biblical tradition to understand the moral bases of the competing norms of contract law does not permit the glossing of the neoclassical analysis. Stories from that tradition tell us clearly what is at stake when we make moral claims.

I do not suggest that we look to the Bible to resolve contract disputes, nor do I suggest a reconsecration of law or the return to a theocracy. What I am suggesting is that stories from the Jewish and Christian traditions may shed light on what is at stake when we consider the conflicts between promise and reliance. In my view, this suggestion is legitimate if only because cultures which are influenced by the Bible have a different feeling for history than those shaped by other traditions.

It might be useful to reach back into the biblical stories to see what is involved when we appeal to norms of promise and reliance, two important norms which are often at odds in modern contract disputes.

First, promise. Why should I keep a promise made to you? Professor Fried's analysis of this question is interesting. He analyzes and rejects utilitarian grounds and concludes that the obligation to keep a promise has an independent moral force that cannot be explained by nonpromisory elements such as reliance or benefit. He concludes that the moral force of promise keeping is grounded in the concept of personal autonomy. He does, however, emphasize the importance of trust to the moral obligation of promise keeping. He attempts to associate trust with the concept of personal autonomy, and to avoid linking it to reliance or other communal values. While his argument is powerful, it is ultimately unpersuasive.

I would like to pick up on his argument and suggest another interpretation. As Fried notes, when we use the convention of promising, we invite vulnerability. That gives us power over the other who has made herself vulnerable. What does it mean to be vulnerable? It means that we let down the walls of self-protection which shield us from pain but which also isolate us from love.

There can be nothing more important to the self than to be accepted for what she is; to be shed of the frightening howl of loneliness; to be a person. One can only be fully human when she is accepted, warts and all by her neighbor. That is to be loved. Love can only follow if one acknowledges vulnerability, if one will tear down the walls of self protection which shield us. Yet the paradox of life is that the same walls which shield us from love also protect us from death and destruction. But we cannot have it any other way. To experience love we must risk destruction. We must be vulnerable.

The institution of promise is important in a penultimate sense; it is important because it leads to something else and that something else is the vulnerability that is the necessary soil for love. The Gethsemane story[23] is about many things, but one of its major themes is the necessity for vulnerability in our intimate personal encounters.

. . .

The ultimate value of promise is that it encourages us to trust and to be vulnerable. The law's chief justification and also its chief purpose is, as Harold Berman has noted, "to help create conditions in which love may flourish." That is, I think, the most important reason for enforcing promises.

Another important concept in contract law is reliance. Let me suggest a story which might sharpen our perspective on that notion. The concept of reliance in contract law is often discussed in connection with norms of benevolence, trust, and fairness. Consider for a moment the parable of the Good Samaritan in the Gospel of Luke. On the level of a story of conventional morality it represents an appeal to benevolence or altruism, both aspects of the scriptural virtue of neighborliness. Both of these virtues are appealed to as support for the reliance principle. But the parable is much more radical than that. The question we are asked to consider is: Who is my neighbor? The story was addressed to Jews who would have been expected to identify not with the Samaritan, but with the injured Jew lying by the side of the road. Yet, the parable focuses on the acts of the Samaritan, his goodness, and not on the needs of the injured man. To entertain the possibility that a Samaritan, an outcast who was despised on both racial and religious grounds, would perform good deeds was not just counterintuitive, it was unthinkable. The parable confronts the hearer with a radical challenge to her preconceived notions of reality. It is like asking us to consider that perhaps our neighbors in the times of our need will be Muslim terrorists or Iranians or Russians.

We are challenged beyond benevolence or altruism and asked to reconsider our whole self-constructed universe or order, to "conceive the inconceivable." We are asked to imagine a society in which we recognize our mutual interdependence with brothers and sisters of all kinds and from all stations in life.

It is not that these stories tell us how to act in any given situation. They certainly do not tell us how to resolve contract disputes. Their value, however, is that they tell us how to perceive. Stories tell us how we might view the world. These stories have to do with vision.

One vision these stories offer is that promise is important because it leads us to vulnerability and to love and that we are all vulnerable to pain and death. Who will be our neighbors in that time? Martin Buber captures that vision which I think is important to our consideration of contract norms:

. . . the inmost growth of the self is not accomplished, as people like to suppose today, in man's relation to himself, but in the relation between the one and the other, between men, that is, preeminently in the mutuality of the making present—in the making present of another self and in the knowledge that one is made present in his own self by the other—together with the mutuality of acceptance, of affirmation and confirmation.[28]

He goes on to ask, rhetorically: Is there a way to help which is interpersonal, interhuman, beyond professionalism, and not insular: "I think no human being can give more than this. Making life possible for the other, if only for a moment."

These musings lead me to a vision of community in which promise is important, but primarily because it fosters greater trust and vulnerability and leads to love. Reliance is important because it forces us to see our mutual interdependence.

We are born in community, and I believe that the most important thing we can do in that community is to build and nurture relationships with our neighbors. The biblical call to justice is to create structures in which we can be vulnerable with one another and in which the chance for the transformative personal relationship of love is given primacy. We are called to expand our boundaries and concepts of neighborliness and to accept the stranger into our world.

I do not mean to suggest that communities cannot become tyrannical. The lessons of history are too clear on that to invite argument. We cannot deny those stories of slavery, the oppressive treatment of deviants, and so forth. Our only escape from stories of the tyranny of communities comes from having the courage to confront those stories and to participate in a world that claims our lives in a fundamental fashion, more fundamental than the claims of the state or the law. It comes only if we recognize the ultimate claim that only God is God.

---

[23] See Matthew 26:36-56; Mark 14:32-50; Luke 22:39-53; John 18:1-11.

[28] M. Buber, *Distance and Relation* in The Knowledge of Man 59-71 (Ronald G. Smith trans. 1965).

It is only in such a world that any possibility of acquiring those virtues of hope and patience exists which are capable of countering a tyranny of majoritarian rule or our mutual destruction by rampant individualism. Professor Stanley Hauerwas' comments on this long view of history are apt:

> Without denying that there may be nonreligious accounts of hope and patience, Jews and Christians have been the people that have stressed the particular importance of these virtues. For they are the people formed by the conviction that our existence is bounded by a power that is good and faithful. Moreover they are peoples with a deep stake in history; they believe God has charged them with the task of witnessing to his providential care of our existence. They believe their history is nothing less than the story of God's salvation of them and all people. Such a history does not promise to make the life of virtue easier or our existence safer. Rather such a story, and corresponding society, offers training in the hope and patience necessary to live amid the diversity of the world while trusting that its very plurality reflects the richness of God's creating and redeeming purposes.

My comments offer little advice on what to do. But I think far more important than deciding what to do is to understand who we are. If we talk about that enough, then we might discover what we should do.

Learning From an African Tribe

There is nothing new about looking to anthropology to learn about contract law. In fact, Sir Henry Maine's famous statement "that the movement of progressive societies has hitherto been a movement *from Status to Contract*," was made in the context of mid-Victorian anthropology. In 1969 Professor E. Allan Farnsworth published a highly regarded article entitled *The Past of Promise: An Historical Introduction to Contract*, 69 Colum. L. Rev. 576 (1969), in which he looked at many cultures to ascertain when they first enforced executory promises. (Note, by the way, how many times that question has arisen in the discussions excerpted so far.) Farnsworth's inquiry goes from "primitive" cultures to English and other European uses of promise as a legal concept. Farnsworth's article is accessible and relatively short, and is highly recommended. We should also remember that Ian Macneil, in his first major discussion of relational contracts, *The Many Futures of Contracts*, 47 So. Cal. L. Rev. 691 (1974), made use of anthropology, sociology and even entomology in constructing his theory. That, too, is worth reading.

I prefer, however, to offer the following article because it is concerned with only one group, the Birwa, who live in Botswana, one of the "front-line states" immediately north of South Africa. In the article, Nicholas Mahoney considers the Maine thesis and later expansions of it by modern anthropologists. However, he notes curious conduct by the Birwa. We have read many discussions of communitarianism and the imposition of general social values over negotiated terms. Here we learn that this African tribe uses negotiated formal contracts in some circumstances even when there is a very close relationship between the parties. This sounds anomalous. Surely an agrarian tribe sounds like a paradigm of relationalism. Yet it is contract—not contort, not kinship, not solidarity—that the Birwa use. Let us find out why.

Nicholas Mahoney, *Contract and Neighbourly Exchange Among the Birwa of Botswana*, 21 J. African Law 40 (1977)

Schapera's accounts of the Tswana[2] provide one of the few instances of contract to be found in the "customary" law of African societies in colonial times. Not only were contracts a means used, even between closely related people, for making certain kinds of transactions, but also the Tswana courts were prepared to enforce executory contracts. In this paper I intend to discuss the significance of contracts among the Birwa of independent Botswana, in particular the way in which contracts are used to regulate certain kinds of productive exchanges between co-operating neighbours.

Contracts are not the only means used to regulate neighbourly transactions. A number of different kinds of exchange relationship are established by neighbours in order to secure the various services necessary for their productive activities. The same set of neighbours at different times and for different purposes will render each other friendly assistance, will undertake reciprocal labour exchanges, and will enter into formal contracts. In order to understand why it should be that one set of people should require this range of forms of exchange, and how it is that the different forms can co-exist within single neighbourly relationships, it is necessary to give an outline account of the circumstances of productive activity among the Birwa.

. . .

Exchanges between neighbours at settlements outside of the village can be grouped into three broad categories. They are:

1. *Neighbourly assistance*, which may take a number of forms from the exchange of small gifts between friends to support in emergencies. Such assistance is freely given and sanctioned only by a diffusely defined morality.

2. *Reciprocal labour exchanges*, organized usually between women with neighbouring fields in order to accomplish the tasks of tending or harvesting crops, tasks which could be managed by the women working alone.

3. *Contracts* made between neighbours, acquaintances or strangers for short- or long-term employ-ment and for ploughing. The terms are formally agreed and said to be enforceable in law.

. . .

Contracts

Contract is a term from our own language which has, as well as its everyday usage, a specialized significance in law. Indeed it could be argued that its meaning has become so refined that it is not likely to be an appropriate concept for cross-cultural study. For those, following Maine, who hold an evolutionary view of human society, contract is indeed something peculiar to the modern western world and is seen by them not just as something more developed in the West but as peculiarly characteristic of it, marking it off from earlier, and from contemporary but differently constituted, societies. But evolutionists and anti-evolutionists alike hold in common the view that contract is a specific means by which people can acquire rights and duties and that the incidence of contracts is not unrelated to the kind of social relationship which the contracting parties have. Perhaps the argument which has been put with most force is that contracts are unusual and inappropriate where people's relations with each other are multi-stranded and intense, where most transfers of property and services are made on the basis of people's social positions, and where obligation and generosity are held to be more important than rights. The case of the Birwa neighbourhood set contract is a clear exception to this hypothesis, for among Birwa, as I shall try to demonstrate, many contracts are made precisely because the relations between the parties are multi-stranded and intense.

. . .

Allott, Epstein and Gluckman state that only in modern western law are executory contracts, that is bare promises, protected; in other legal systems protection is only afforded to executed contracts—contracts in which one party has partially or totally fulfilled his obligations. Accordingly it is only under modern western law that damages can be awarded for the mere breach of a verbal or written agreement.

[2] I. Schapera, A handbook of Tswana law and custom, 2nd ed., London, 1955; and "Contract in Tswana Law," in M. Gluckman (ed.), Ideas and procedures in African customary law, 1969, Oxford University Press.

The interest of courts only in disputes arising from partial or total fulfillment of the terms of the agreement by one party *only* in a large number of reported cases gives support to the argument that non-western societies only recognize executed contracts. For example, Epstein observes that in pre-independence Zambia urban courts did not deal with breaches of agreements as such but only wrongs or debts resulting from agreement and fulfillment by one party only. Bohannan notes that "Tiv take these *jir* which, in our classification, might be called contract and they see the debt aspect rather than the contract aspect as the most important point." Because of this focus on debt rather than on breach of an agreement, non-western courts order only the restoration of the original positions of the parties and do not award consequential damages. Furthermore if the indebted party repays what he has received of his own accord he cannot be held liable to fulfil his own obligations under the terms of the agreement. There is, as far as I am aware, only one reported exception to the general pattern in which only executed contracts and the debts to which they are held to give rise are considered to the exclusion of executory contracts and this is the case of the Tswana as reported by Schapera.[4] Schapera stresses that among Tswana the agreement itself was held to be binding on the parties and that courts were prepared to award damages as well as to order repayments in cases where one party had suffered because of the default of the other. Such an attitude among Tswana, it should be stressed, was observed in pre-war Bechuanaland.

The debate over the legal standing of agreements, in concentrating on the point at which a contract is held to be in force, on the issue of debt and on executed contracts, tends to draw attention away from two important issues. The first is that in all the societies considered there were exchange relationships in which the terms of agreements were fixed whether or not a verbal bare promise was held binding in law. That is, contracts as "free agreements of individuals" were made to regulate certain kinds of transactions. It is this specification of rights and obligations by mutual agreement rather than the legal enforceability of the agreements as such that is of primary importance in the following discussion. The second important issue, obscured by the court-centered discussion of enforceability, is that all contracts do not necessarily have to be enforced. As S. F. Moore has noted, "the

most important place where legal rules and ideas operate is outside of the courts." Once this is appreciated the issue of legal enforceability becomes of secondary importance, and it seems that the significance of contracts as mutual agreements has to be found elsewhere.

The distinction between modern, western and other societies in terms of the significance of contract in each has been couched by many in evolutionary terms. Maine's famous passage concerning the movement of progressive societies from relationships governed by status to relationships founded on contract has been echoed in a number of works. Gluckman, for example, states that the Barotse provide an illustration of Maine's thesis, and the changes wrought on pre-contact societies [Sic. It is unclear to me if this is a typographical error for "pre-contract" or if the reference is to societies before their contact with Europeans. —ed.] by colonial incorporation and the development of trade and markets have been seen by many as the replacement of predominantly kinship (or status)-based transactions by exchanges made according to impersonal and contractual market relationships. The evolutionary viewpoint has not, however, gone unchallenged. Lewis has argued that contracts have long held a dominant place in political affairs at all levels in Somalia (then Somaliland) and that there was a complementarity between the principles of clanship and contract and not an opposition nor an evolutionary movement between status/based relationships and those agreed by contract. Pospisil writes that the status-contract dichotomy is founded on various ethnographic misconceptions and illustrates the point with reference to a modern Austrian community. In the

> "North Tirol the rights of individuals in their relations depend *de facto* mostly on the status into which they are born or which they acquire through their occupation, although theoretically and *de jure*, there is available to them a host of contract-types by which they can regulate their roles."

The central issue though does not really rest on the evolutionary or progressive character of certain hypotheses; rather it is more a matter of social relationships and the different means by which rights and duties are conferred and property and services exchanged.

Maine was of the opinion that in pre-industrial so-

---

[4] Cf. Allott, Epstein and Gluckman, "Introduction" to M. Gluckman (ed.), supra note 1, at 77-78, where they note the Tswana case but suggest that its exceptional standing may be due to the effects of colonialism and to "some misunderstanding" on Schapera's part. After 1946 Lozi courts enforced executory contracts.

cieties people's social position—by which he meant their rights, duties, and the rules governing their behaviour—is largely fixed at birth. Indeed their position is fixed to such an extent that the "system leaves the very smallest room for contract." Gluckman, whom I will quote at some length here, develops Maine's thesis. He writes:

> "Lozi hold rights in land and chattels in virtue of their positions as members of political and kinship groupings and most of their work and exchanges are performed with others standing in specific relationships. Free 'contractual' relations between persons not already united by social positions existed, but were proportionately few and unimportant in Lozi life. In this respect a study of Lozi law, as of law in most simple societies, validates Maine's most widely accepted generalization, 'that the movement of progressive societies has hitherto been a movement *from Status to Contract*'."

. . .

The second major point of Gluckman's which I want to emphasize is his view that strictly contractual relations are incompatible with multi-stranded relations:

> "As most important obligations reside in relationships established by birth or marriage, or by political position, the nature of these obligations is defined by the status of the parties involved. All these relationships are marked, in the widest sense, by a stress on generous helpfulness and love and mutual give-and-take. No multiplex relationship can survive if the parties insist on their rights only and try to live by the letter of the law. . . . Lozi law in treating the code of kinship therefore stresses duty and obligation rather than right. Generosity and forebearance are the main obligations; and these are extended to neighbours and fellow-citizens."

In meeting the obligations of their social position people are expected to render more than the minimum required of them and to behave generously with "mutual give-and-take." This is necessary because of the multi-stranded character of social relationships among Lozi. Such relationships, "which are full of strains," are helped to endure only if obligations are stressed rather than rights. Emphasis only on the rights and duties established by contract would be disruptive here because multi-stranded relations "are likely to break if either party tries to live by the letter of rights and duties."

The underlying theme here, as I understand Gluckman's argument, is that of a scale of relations from close kinsman to distant stranger, which is combined with a scale of transactions governed at one end by generosity and at the other by contract, and with a scale of morality from love to self-interest. While his immediate concerns were not the same as were Gluckman's, Sahlins has reached a very similar conclusion and has tried to locate relationships, the regulation of transactions, and their morality along a single continuum.

> "Reciprocity is a whole class of exchanges, a continuum of forms. . . . At one end of the spectrum stands the assistance freely given . . . regarding which an open stipulation of return would be unthinkable and unsociable. At the other pole, self-interested seizure . . . 'negative reciprocity' as Gouldner phrases it. The intervals between them are not merely so many graduations of material balance in exchange, they are intervals of sociability. The distance between the poles of reciprocity is, among other things, social distance."

Sahlins's continuum extends further than does Gluckman's, encompassing as it does relations of negative reciprocity between totally unrelated people; but their conception of a single continuum on which can be placed the social distance between parties to a transaction, the specificity of the terms of the transaction, and the morality governing the exchange is very similar. . . .

My fundamental objection to Gluckman's and Sahlins's hypotheses is an empirical one; among Birwa close kin and neighbours readily make contracts. For these people multi-stranded ties characterized by the generous exchanges of certain services co-exist with the contractual exchanges of others in single relationships. There are indications that such combinations are not unique to the Birwa. Schapera reports that contractual exchanges are made between close kin, even between siblings, among other Tswana groups. Pospisil has reported cases among Kapauku in which contracts were made between co-residents, between a father and son, and between half-brothers. It is my contention that among Birwa contracts are a feature of relations between close kin and neighbours, not because these relations lack a "norm of reciprocity," nor because they are not multi-stranded, but precisely because of their multi-stranded character. My case is that contracts among close kin are made only in regard to specific kinds of transactions and that the purpose of the contracting parties is one of insulating that aspect of their relationship which is characterized by freely given assistance and in which no one counts the cost, from transactions which all hold to be potentially disruptive and which are a regular cause of complaint and dispute. The circumstances of production in neighbourhood sets are such that generous exchanges and potentially disruptive transactions have to be made between the same people. It is here that contracts can be effective.

In referring to contractual agreements, what is usually stressed is the way in which people's obligations to one another are specified: A is to render a specific service to B and B is to pay A a specified amount in return. But the agreement can have another aspect: it can define the limits of the parties' respective responsibilities. A is to render a specific service to B and no more. It is this aspect of contractual agreements which is used to prevent the conflicts arising from certain kinds of transaction from affecting the already existent multi-stranded relationship between the parties.

Contracts are made between neighbours because a multi-stranded relationship characterized by a norm of generosity has to be combined with specific transactions which are regularly disruptive in their effect.

I should make it clear from the outset that not all contracts among Birwa are of this type. Many are made between relative strangers with no other basis for their transaction. While such contracts have very much the same legal form as those made between kin and neighbours, their sociological significance is quite different in that they define minimum obligations rather than maximum responsibilities.

Contracts are made between neighbours for the hiring of labour and of specialized services as well as for other purposes. Here I will deal only with contracts made for ploughing as they are the most common and embody the general features of the many different types.

Ploughing contracts, all of which were formally defined and held to be legally enforceable, were of three main types. The first, "holding the plough" (gotshwara mogoma), was an exchange of labour for the use of ploughing equipment. The second was one in which both households contributed some labour and some equipment; and the third was the purchase of labour and the use of equipment for cash. The first usually involved the understanding that the contributor of labor was entitled to some crop at the end of the season, so that if his first sowing failed the owner of the plough should come a second time to plough

and sow again. The other kinds of contract did not involve this understanding. The three basic types of agreement could be combined in a number of different ways in practice to give a range of actual contracts. In all, the definition of obligations and rights was made clear, and in all the transaction was restricted solely to ploughing and sowing.

It is necessary to distinguish between those more common ploughing contracts which do not involve the use of a tractor and those less common ones which do. Arrangements which make use of animal-drawn ploughs and human labor are constrained by the relative immobility of these factors. To be sure, all can be moved but this is regarded as extremely inconvenient, wasteful, and time-consuming at a stage in the season when timing is of the essence. The tractor on the other hand can move with its trailer loaded up with ploughs, planters, and fuel over large distances, and indeed does so in the course of the ploughing season. For the moment I am concerned only with contracts which *do not* involve tractors.

The relative immobility of people, animals, and light ploughs means that people who wish to hire them have to look to close neighbours in order to do so. Those who want to be employed to carry out ploughing are similarly constrained to find customers close to their settlement. From observation of such ploughing transactions it is apparent that the neighbours involved are regularly fellow members of the same neighbourhood set. In order to understand why formal contracts are made for ploughing exchanges I want to compare the ploughing exchange with ordinary neighbourly exchanges in terms of people's perceptions of the costs incurred in each. Regular exchanges between neighbours, to recapitulate, involve mutual support in emergencies, participation in work groups, and frequent minor gifts and hospitality. What do these transactions cost the people involved and how do they perceive these costs? In short, the answer is that they cost and are held to cost very little. For example, if a person is called to assist another who is sick and thereby fails to weed his field for one day, the loss incurred is hardly measurable; furthermore there is the implicit understanding that one day the favour may well be returned and the balance redressed. When one person assists another in a neighbourly way their relative positions in terms of wealth are likely to remain unaltered. When a person finds a stray animal belonging to his neighbour and calls him over to collect it, the finder of the animal has not contributed to an increase in the wealth of his neighbour but simply prevented a loss: whatever the wealth of each of them was before it is the same afterwards.

How does this compare with relations of ploughing which, after all, could supposedly be organized on the basis of neighbourly goodwill? The timing of ploughing is critical; a delay of only a few days after a period of suitable rainfall can significantly affect crop yields. This fact is clearly perceived by people, and there is the general belief that co-operation in ploughing because of the demands of critical timing cannot only be costly to one of the parties but also significantly affect the relative wealth of those involved. In the arrangement which involves an exchange of labour for the use of equipment it is generally understood that the owner of the equipment has the right to choose the days on which ploughing shall take place, and when he is satisfied with work in his own field will agree to move to the field of the labourer. Thus, whether the whole of the neighbourhood has experienced good rainfall or if the rains have been patchy, as they sometimes are, the owner of the equipment can always choose the optimum moment to plough his own field and therefore is more likely to produce the best crop. Not only is the labourer likely to get a worse crop, but because he has spent time helping the other his activity has directly contributed to the good yields that the equipment owner can expect. In the south of Botswana it has also been noted that ploughing arrangements are perceived to lead to inequalities, though I would not agree with Curtis's suggestion that this is necessarily a recent development. He writes:

"It is widely complained these days that due to the larger acreages people are thought to plough in recent years, and due to the more time-consuming arable practices of today the fields of those who 'put in hands' [contribute labor in exchange for the use of equipment] are often left until it is too late to obtain a reasonable crop."

Even in the arrangements in which labor and services are contributed by both parties one necessarily has his field ploughed first. Arrangements in which there is the hiring of services for cash are also objects of bitter complaint. Among the complaints heard were that the ploughman came too late; he did not come when he had arranged because he was ploughing his own field or that of a more favoured customer; he gave up the job half way through giving some unreasonable excuse and still demanded the normal payment for the job!

Each year the ploughing exchange which is perceived to be costly intrudes into a neighbourly relationship in which few costs are incurred and none counted. I would suggest that the differentiating and conflict-laden ploughing exchanges, exchanges which owe their character to the particular circumstances of ploughing in a particular environment with a particular technology, have somehow to be prevented from damaging the other relations which the parties to the transactions have. The problem is particularly acute, given that both neighbourly goodwill and support and the exchange of ploughing services are equally essential for the maintenance of productive activity. The contract can, in this light, be interpreted as a social (rather than a specifically economic, or legal) device to contain these disruptive exchanges by giving them a short-term specificity: the rights and duties and responsibilities of the parties last only for the duration of ploughing. Only for the duration of the contract, they give the partners clearly measurable rights and responsibilities. By means of this containment a problematic but necessary exchange is prevented from endangering the normal, long-term diffuse understandings which the partners hold. Thus through time the relations between neighbourhood set members can be seen to alternate between long-term diffuseness and short-term specificity, between neighbourly goodwill and complaint, between generalized reciprocity and contract.

Some tractor ploughing contracts resemble those already outlined; others, because of the mobility of the tractor, are something quite different. Contracts made between a tractor-owner and his neighbours, apart from the fact that the tractor-owner can enter into more of them than can an owner of an animal-drawn plough, are sociologically similar to those already discussed. The mobility of the tractor, however, facilitates the negotiation of ploughing contracts with many people outside the owner's neighborhood. The owner generally employs a driver and sends him out to tour many localities looking for ploughing engagements to be performed immediately. The exchange of money for ploughing services takes place in exactly the same way as it does in neighbourhood contracts, but the arrangement is different. Between unrelated parties the contract is a means of establishing a basis of interaction where none other exists; the contract reverts to defining minimum obligations and not maximum responsibilities.

Conclusion

In this paper I have offered an explanation for the apparently unusual practice to be found among Tswana in which formal contracts are negotiated between relatives and neighbours. The explanation developed out of an examination of both the routine and non-routine productive needs of householders, raising their crops and rearing their livestock. Contract was found to be only one of three types of exchange relationship which neighbours used at different times and for different purposes to regulate their many transactions. While ploughing contracts were held by the parties involved to be enforceable in law, in practice litigation over ploughing contracts was not common despite their widespread occurrence. Their purpose, I have argued, was not so much to define minimum obligations and bind the parties to them as to set limits to the responsibilities of the contracting parties and prevent disruptive and intermittent but necessary transactions from damaging a valued neighbourly relationship.

The Flesh-Colored Band Aid:
An essay by Peter Linzer and Patricia A. Tidwell

There is a tension, sometimes overt, sometimes remote between the traditions of the bargain approach and other ideas of contract. We all know the harshness of the old rules, and we are sympathetic with the reforms, but we are troubled by phrases like "as justice requires." The rigid old rules at least gave us answers instead of mushy maybes. Even those of us who are most congenial to relational and communitarian notions sometimes ask ourselves "but how do you structure a relational deal? How do you write a contract of solidarity? How does a jury decide a communitarian contract dispute?" Somehow, in our heart of hearts rules and bargains seem *realer* than general principles and communal notions of loose expectations.[1]

Perhaps the problem lies less with changes in law than it does with our starting place. What we think of as the norms of contract may be more parochial than we realize. Rather than being universal and ineluctable, they may simply be the ways of thinking of those who have dominated our law and legal thinking, particularly upper-middle class white British and American men. We are told by the feminist writers that to many women confrontation, zero-sum results and individualism are not the norms; the norms are compromise, workable results and keeping the enterprise going. We find other norms—some similar, some very different—in the Christian approach of Andrew

McThenia, the complex Japanese attitudes described by Wagatsuma and Rosett, and the interesting use of rigid contract rules to limit and fix duties among closely related members of the Birwa people of Botswana. (On the last, think of how family counselors often recommend parent-child or husband-wife "contracts" for just the same purpose.)

We are less concerned in this essay with the rights and wrongs of particular attitudes than with a couple of lessons from reality: we think of what we know as what is right; and we often are oblivious, or can't even comprehend, that everyone else doesn't think the way we do.[2] For years we "knew" what a flesh-colored band aid was—until black people pointed out that their skin isn't pinkish-beige. We also "knew" that men were better athletes than women, since they were faster and stronger and could beat women at baseball, basketball and tennis. But then someone asked if all that there was to being an athlete was speed and upper-body strength. If precision, endurance and a low center of gravity are alternate qualities of athleticism, women need less patronizing; witness long-distance swimming, equitation, skating and gymnastics. And who knows which sex will hold the marathon record fifty years from now?

We are particularly intrigued by the convergence of a number of current ideas that can be found throughout this book.[3] Both in creating substantive

[1] "Viewed in retrospect, Williston's majestic doctrinal structure may have been silly, but Corbinesque appeals to reasonableness and justice appear sloppy and formless by comparison." Elizabeth Mensch, Freedom of Contract As Ideology, 33 Stan. L. Rev. 753, 769 (1981).

[2] In Edwin A. Abbott's wonderful novel of dimensions and social satire, Flatland (2d & rev'd ed. 1884) (Dover ed. 1952), an inhabitant of the one-dimensional Lineland can see the hero, a square, only as a point. The square's political

troubles in Flatland begin when he has a dream in which he is able to perceive three dimensions.

[3] Examples include relational and communitarian bases of contract (Parts IA and IB); duties of fair bargaining (Part IIA); expanded meanings of reliance (Part IIB) and property rights (Part IID); court-based policing of the contract (Part IIIB); adjustment of long-term contracts in light of mistakes and market changes (Part IIIC); judicial remedies short of all-or-nothing results, and alternative dispute resolution (Part IV).

rights and duties and in providing remedies, these approaches tailor the law to the individual fact situation and to the particular people involved in it. They reject generalized legal rules that, in Richard Epstein's approving words "do not refer to flesh-and-blood individuals, but to those lifeless abstractions, *A* and *B*, about whom nothing else is known or—more to the point—is relevant."[4] To Epstein and other supporters of bargain-based rules, the very abstraction of the common law avoids favoritism and rests on bases of both liberty and equality. Thus, the new ideas are suspect as based on subjectivity and result orientation. But to those coming from another point of view, the abstraction is simply impossible—people are not fungible, and legal rules that ignore this create a false reality. It is said to be "male" to raise arguments of objectivity, reason and rights; as Ann Scales has suggested, many women perceive objectivity as sacrificing context, reason as forbidding emotion, and rights as precluding care.[5] On this line of reasoning the new ideas are fully justified. All we did was change the norm.

Most of these newer approaches were not developed by women,[6] but perhaps they would have been if women had played a larger role sooner in law and politics. It can be argued that the male ideal of justice is that everyone should be treated the same, while the female one is that no one should be hurt. Neither ideal is ever reached, but accepting that there is more than one vision is a major starting point, and it is a point that will become more likely if those in the ever-increasing proportion of women in the law do not become coopted to male norms that they are led to believe are universal and immutable.[7]

Patricia Williams' *Alchemical Notes*, excerpted in Part IB, shows how multi-dimensional points of view can be. Williams is a woman, a black, a law professor and a writer with a sense of her family's history. Her article discusses how her norms differ from those she sympathizes with but diverges from. Like all of us, she draws from her many roots and builds on her many foundations to put forth ideas that do not quite fit into anyone's mold. *Her* flesh-colored band aid looks different. But it is still the color of flesh.

---

[4] Epstein, A Common Law for Labor Relations: A Critique of the New Deal Labor Legislation, 92 Yale L. J. 1357, 1383 (1983).

[5] See Scales, The Emergence of Feminist Jurisprudence: An Essay, 95 Yale L.J. 1373, 1383 (1986).

[6] Women are, however, playing a large role in alternative dispute resolution.

[7] Susan Estrich in her article Rape, 95 Yale L.J. 1087 (1986), and her subsequent book Real Rape, has argued that our criminal law is male-centered in its view of resistance to rape. The male ideal is to struggle and fight, but a woman, physically less strong, frequently with a sleeping child nearby, tries to negotiate, deal, compromise, and talk her way out. This has often been taken for acquiescence or worse, and for a long time women accepted the judgment. But the attitude is changing, in part because of more women lawyers and judges, in part because all women are putting forth their viewpoint with greater vigor. And in part because all of us, men and women, are listening to a voice that wasn't heard before.

Part II
The Formation and Creation
of Contract Rights

A. Contract Formation and Consideration Within the Bargain System

Now that we have looked in some depth at the "why" of contract, it is time to look at how contracts work. We begin by examining how they come into being according to the bargain system. Bargain held sway as the crux of contract formation during the "classical" period (roughly 1870 to World War II), and it still plays a basic role, particularly in carefully negotiated business dealings. We will later look at alternatives to bargain as a source of rights and duties. These include restitution and reliance, the Uniform Commercial Code and property notions evolving from the combination of third party benefi- ciary contracts and federal and state welfare legislation. Some of these concepts will appear within the bargain system, as will references to good faith and other ideas that will reappear in Parts IIIB and C. In this section, however, we are specifically concerned with offer and acceptance, bargained-for consider- ation, promises of gifts and a pressing current problem: "agreements to agree."

Wesley Hohfeld, Arthur Corbin and Precise Legal Terminology

Wesley N. Hohfeld was a brilliant legal scholar who died young in 1918. His best-known contribution to legal thinking was to define a small number of words by giving them tightly fixed meanings and using them to describe legal relations among people. While Hohfeld's own writings are difficult to read, we are fortunate that his approach was championed and restated in accessible form by the great contracts scholar, Arthur L. Corbin. In 1913, when Hohfeld put forth his ideas, Corbin was in his late thirties and already a major figure at Yale Law School. For the rest of his long and productive life Corbin helped to introduce the legal community to Hohfeld's work and to apply it in legal thinking. Corbin's short 1919 Yale Law Journal article, *Legal Analysis and Terminology*, 29 Yale L.J. 163 (1919), briefly and lucidly explains the system itself. I would have reprinted it but for the space limitations of this book.

Hohfeldian analysis, which is far less daunting than its name sounds, is simply a useful tool in keeping ideas straight, particularly the many ideas that we lump together under the term "rights." The Hohfeldian system gives focused and precise meaning to eight terms: right and duty; privilege and no right; power and liability; and immunity and disability. In brief, if you have a "right" that X do something that means, exactly and only, *that you may call upon the government to use its force to make X do that something.* (Normally, this means that you can get damages or specific relief against X, but if your right is protected by the criminal law, right means that the police will arrest him for violating it.) X, under Hohfeld's system of terminology has a "duty" towards you. Right and duty are thus "correlatives": your "right" is X's "duty," neither more nor less. If you have no such right against X, X is said to be "privileged" with respect to you. The correlative of "privilege" is thus "no-right," though, as Corbin said in a 1963 introduction to an edition of Hohfeld, the hyphen in Hohfeld's new word has "made no progress."

The four terms right, duty, privilege and no right are interrelated. The four other terms are also interrelated, and the two sets of four can co-exist. "Power" means the ability to change legal relations with another person. A clear example is the "power" to create a contract where none existed before—by acceptance of an offer. The person subject to the power—in our illustration the offeror—is said to have a "liability." One who is not subject to a power—against whom the other person can not change legal relations—is said to have an "immunity." That other person is said to have a "disability." Powers aren't always beneficial to the person exercising them, and sometimes the very act that is the exercise of the power may not be "privileged." For example, I have a "right" that you refrain from punching me in the nose. You have a "duty" to refrain. You are therefore not "privileged" with respect to my nose. If you violate that duty and punch me, you create a tort action for me against you for battery. That is the exercise of a power, even though (especially because) you were not privileged to do the act that exercised the power. Many exercises of powers, especially those in contract, are privileges; sometimes a person even has a *right* to exercise the power, for example, the offeree's power of acceptance under an irrevocable option contract. (This is because the offeror there has a duty not to revoke his offer.)

Hohfeld's terminology was used in both the Restatement of Property and the Restatement of Contracts. I find it valuable in analyzing the contract formation process, as is shown by the first article in Part II of this anthology, Corbin's seminal *Offer and Acceptance, and Some of the Resulting Legal Relations.*

Not everyone finds Hohfeld useful, and there are modern arguments that Corbin is too narrow when he claims in *Legal Analysis and Terminology*, that "[t]he term 'legal relation' should always be used with reference to two persons, neither more nor less." (Consider the communal claims made in the articles by Macneil, Williams, and Linzer, among others, in Part I, above.) None of this, however, undercuts Hohfeld's analytical value or, for that matter, the entertainment value of Corbin's description of the reaction of Hohfeld's students at Yale to his efforts to teach them his system. See Arthur L. Corbin, *Foreword* to Wesley N. Hohfeld, *Fundamental Legal Conceptions* (1963).

Corbin's Analysis of the Formation Process

In the following article, Arthur Corbin applied Wesley Hohfeld's analytical system to offer and acceptance.

This article, published in 1917, predated Corbin's great treatise on Contracts by more than thirty years. In *The Death of Contract* Grant Gilmore called *Corbin on Contracts* "the greatest law book ever written," but went on to point out that much of it was derived from Corbin's truly revolutionary articles in the early part of the century. This article is surely one of Corbin's most important. It is still brilliant, but we can hardly appreciate how brilliant—and revolutionary—it was seventy years ago, when contract law had not yet been "Corbinized." (In fact, many of the specific doctrinal examples criticized by Corbin are no longer good law, often because of Corbin's criticism of them.)

There are several fine texts that can give a student or a practicing lawyer the up-to-date case law on offer and acceptance. The 1917 Corbin article obviously cannot do that. It is offered for several reasons. First, it describes both the why and the how of contract formation in an analysis that is still appropriate today; indeed, as Gilmore went on to point out in *The Death*, Corbin's ideas are now the mainstream. Second, implicit throughout the article is the central point of all of Corbin's writing on contract—contract is based not on abstract and immutable rules put into play by free-willed actors, but on the society's common sense reactions to what men and women do to achieve solutions to workaday problems. Usually, this will require the courts to figure out what best achieves the reasonably apparent intentions of the parties, but as Corbin says in the last sentence of the article, "[t]he fact, is . . . that the decision will depend upon the notions of the court as to policy, welfare, justice, right and wrong, such notions often being inarticulate and subconscious."

In addition, the article shows the genesis of the changes that led from the rigidly classical notion that the offeror is the master of the bargaining process. to the "neo-classical" idea that he or she may be bound even though the exact terms of the offer are not met. For example, the article's discussion entitled "*Limitations Due to Part Performance*," anticipates the changes made ten to fifteen years later by sections 31, 45 and 90 of the original Restatement of Contracts (now Restatement (Second) secs. 32, 45 and 90). These changes directly and indirectly led to a major displacement of the bargain process by the increasing use of reliance notions, but the displacement did not become dominant until forty or more years after Corbin wrote this article. Similarly, his brief discussions of good faith (in footnote 46) and mutual assent (at the end of the article) anticipate matters that are still controversial today.

Arthur L. Corbin, *Offer and Acceptance, and Some of the Resulting Legal Relations*, 26 Yale L.J. 169 (1917)

In the study and the practice of the law, our constant problem is: what legal relations are the result of facts that occur; or, starting from the other direction with a given set of legal relations (such as a contract, or a debt, or the ownership of land) our problem is: what facts will operate to cause such a result? One may take either starting point; and indeed for the best results, it is necessary to take both, alternately working forward and back, correcting and amplifying our necessarily tentative conclusions. In the present article, the starting point will be the contractual relations themselves, leading back to a consideration of some of the facts and intermediate relations that precede the contract. First, what is a contract and what are its various forms?

The term contract has been used without much discrimination to refer to three different things: (1) the series of operative acts of the parties expressing their assent and resulting in new legal relations; (2) the physical document executed by the parties as an operative fact in itself and as the lasting evidence of their having performed the necessary operative acts; (3) the relations resulting from the operative acts, consisting of a right or rights *in personam* and the corresponding duties, accompanied by certain powers, privileges and immunities.[1] Clearness of thought requires that whenever the term is used, one particular meaning should be consciously adopted and clearly expressed. Very likely it would be most convenient generally to define contract in sense (3), as the legal relations between persons arising from a voluntary expression of intention, and including at least one primary right *in personam*, actual or potential, with its corresponding duty. Unless otherwise indicated, the term contract will be used herein with this meaning.

In determining whether or not a contract exists in any given case, one of our problems is historical in character. What were the facts? What were the acts of the parties and the circumstances that surrounded them? When these have been ascertained the next step is analytical. Immaterial facts must be eliminated, and the rest must be classified as either evidential or operative. The operative facts are those that cause the existence of those legal relations called a contract.

This analysis can only be made, and must be made, with reference to the law of contract. This law is a part of the general legal system under which we live, enforced by the societal organization of which we are part. What the rules of this society are, can be determined only by induction from the judgments and decrees and pronouncements of the past. Under the existing legal system no legal relation is deemed contractual in the absence of certain voluntary acts on the part of two contracting parties. What acts are those which will cause society to come forward with its strong arm? They may well be described as *operative* or *causative*, for they are necessary antecedents to the creation of those legal relations and societal guaranty of compulsion called contract. The analysis of these acts into offer and acceptance, customarily made by writers on contract law, is a convenient one.

An *offer* is an act on the part of one person

Reprinted by permission of the Yale Law Journal Company and Fred B. Rothman and Company from The Yale Law Journal Company, Vol. 26, pp. 169.

[1] For a masterly analysis and classification of jural relations, see an article on Some Fundamental Legal Conceptions as Applied in Judicial Reasoning, in 23 Yale Law Journal 16, by Professor W. N. Hohfeld of the Yale School of Law.

whereby he gives to another the legal power of creating the obligation called contract. An *acceptance* is the exercise of the power conferred by the offer, by the performance of some other act or acts. Both offer and acceptance must be acts expressing assent.

The act constituting an offer and the act constituting an acceptance may each consist in a promise. A promise is an expression of intention that the promisor will conduct himself in a specified way in the future, with an invitation to the promisee to rely thereon. If only one of the acts has this character, the contract is unilateral. If both acts have this character, the contract is bilateral. If neither of the acts has this character, the new set of legal relations, if any exist, is not called obligation. In such case there is no contract in sense (3) adopted above, although there may be one in either of the other senses. Each of these three cases will be discussed below. In none of these cases will the expected legal relations be created unless the acts of the parties comply with the rules relating to mutual assent, consideration, form, capacity of parties, and legality of object. Only certain rules relating to mutual assent will be considered here.

Barter

A mutual, present exchange of lands or chattels creates no contractual duty. If A has apples to sell and B has money, A may offer the apples to B for the money. B may accept by delivering to A the possession of the money. Such a transaction is a barter. The character of the commodities exchanged is not material. Such a transaction creates new physical relations, and in an organized society it creates new legal relations. These new relations arise by the voluntary action and consent of the two parties, but there is no special right *in personam*. There is a contract in sense (1) described above, and a documentary bill of sale would be a contract in sense (2), but there is no contract in sense (3). After such a transaction the apples "belong" to B and the money to A; this means that organized society has created numerous legal relations between each party and every other member of society. . . .

Gift

If A has lands or chattels and executes a gift to B, which B accepts, there are acts of offer and acceptance and there is mutual assent, yet no contractual obligation is created. As in the case of a barter, the only rights involved are property rights or rights *in rem*. The only duties created are those general duties, binding upon non-participating persons as well as upon A. No special right *in personam* is created.

A's rights *in rem* and B's former duties are extinguished, and in lieu thereof similar rights are created in B and similar duties devolve upon A. The same may be said of their respective privileges, powers, immunities, and their correlatives. Thus, there are new legal relations, arising from voluntary acts of offer and acceptance, and such acts would fulfill the first definition of a contract given above. A paper "deed of gift" would satisfy the second definition. The resulting legal relations, however, should not be described as contractual, according to definition (3). All other persons, and not merely A and B, are parties to these new relations.

Contract

If A has apples (or land) to sell, and B has no money, a barter of apples for money is not possible; but A may be willing to deliver his apples to B in return for B's promise to pay money in the future. If B agrees to this, receives the apples and promises to pay the money, a new physical relation exists as to the apples but not as to the money. As in the case of barter, or gift, society creates numerous relations between B and all other persons; as to the apples, he has rights *in rem* against such other persons. B's rights are property rights and not contract rights. But the position of A is very different from that of barter. A has no money, and no rights *in rem*, good as against third persons who are not consenting; but a promise has been made to A by B, the fulfillment of which is commanded by organized society. If B fails to keep his promise, society will at A's request exercise compulsion against B, but will exercise compulsion against no other person. Special legal relations exist between A and B, A having a claim against B that he has against no other person, and B having a duty that rests upon no other person. These relations, with certain others that will not here be discussed, constitute the obligation; and since they arise from expressions of mutual consent, they are *contract*. A's special right against B is called a right *in personam*.

Unilateral And Bilateral Contracts

If the acts of A and B are such as to create a right or rights *in personam*, actual or potential, in favor of A and against B, but no such right in favor of B against A, the contract is called unilateral. If they create mutual rights *in personam* with their corresponding duties, the contract is bilateral. It has sometimes been said that a contract must be binding on both parties or that it is binding on neither, that mutuality of obligation is required; but this is a loose and inaccurate statement. It has no application whatever in the case of unilateral contracts. . . .

. . .

(5) A offers a promise of a reward of $100 to anyone who will arrest X. B, with knowledge of this offer and with intent to accept it, arrests X. A unilateral obligation at once arises.

(6) A writes to B, "Ship me 2 cars XX flour via B. & O., at once, price $10 per bbl. C.O.D." B ships at once as requested.

(7) A sends his brother to B with the following letter of credit, "Let Harry have $100 and I will guarantee repayment in 30 days." B advances $100 as requested.

(8) A promises B to pay him a salary at the rate of $10,000 a year for B's services as superintendent. B may recover at the specified rate for such service as he thereafter renders, but the hiring is a hiring at will.

. . .

Examples (5), (6) and (7) are all cases where a promise is offered for an act. That is, A by promissory words gives to B the power of creating in himself a right *in personam* as against A by doing an act or acts which A desires to be done. In (5) this act is one affecting the physical and legal relations of X, a third party. In (6) B's act effects a substitution of property, A becoming owner of the flour. It also effects a physical change in the location of the goods. In (7) B's act confers property upon Harry, and extinguishes such property in B. It gives B in return a right *in personam* against A, enforceable after 30 days.

A bilateral contract is made in exactly the same way as is a unilateral contract or a barter. The offeror does an act conferring a power upon the offeree, and the offeree does the act that constitutes the exercise of the power. The legal result, however, is a relation consisting of *mutual* rights and duties, special and personal in character. The following are examples of bilateral contracts.

(9) A says to B, "I promise to serve you as bookkeeper for one month in return for your promise to pay me $100." B replies, "I accept."

(10) A writes to B, "I promise to convey Blackacre to you on June 1st in return for your promise to pay me $1,000 at that time. You may accept by cable, using the one word 'Blackacre'." B sends the cable despatch "Blackacre," as requested.

In case (9) the acts of offer and acceptance are oral promissory words. In case (10) the offer is the act of writing and the further acts whereby this writing is brought to the offeree. The acceptance consists of acts by B, whereby he directs the cable company to transmit the word "Blackacre." These acts by B would not customarily amount to a promise to pay $1,000, but in this case they do become such a promise because A will so interpret them and B knows it. In the same way any other act, in itself meaningless, may be specified and may thereby become a return promise.

It is not always an easy matter to determine whether a contract is in fact unilateral or bilateral. Frequently, this determination will have very important results, especially where the offeror has attempted to revoke his offer as explained elsewhere. The form of words used by the parties is not at all conclusive, when examined out of their setting and with the aid of nothing but a dictionary. The meaning of words, as used by the parties to a contract, cannot be determined with mathematical certainty; and the judge who is most certain to do injustice is the pedant who holds contractors to meticulous accuracy in the usage of words and in the construction of sentences.

It can hardly be said that courts are often pedantic in this matter, though it is possible that professors of law may be. The distinction between unilateral and bilateral is not even yet very thoroughly grasped by the multitude of lawyers, a fact which leads them to repeat again and again the erroneous statement that one cannot be bound unless the other is bound. The judges, therefore, are not in general too likely to hold that a proposed contract is unilateral when the parties meant it to be bilateral.

Suppose A writes to B, "I will pay you $5,000 for Blackacre," and B replies, "I accept your offer." This seems to be bilateral, and it is too late for A to revoke. A clearly makes a promise to pay money; and, according to the ordinary understanding of mankind, he requests B to make a return promise to convey the land. But if A has asked an actual conveyance of Blackacre as the equivalent of his promise, there is no contract at all and A may revoke.

In example (8) above, some courts have found in the words of the parties a promise by A to pay to B a year's salary and a return promise by B to serve for a year. In such case the hiring is not at will, but for a year; and this despite the fact that there are no express promissory words of that sort.

In example (6) above, it has often been held that the offeree may accept by mailing a letter containing a promise to supply the goods—an "acceptance of the order," and that a revocation after such acceptance is too late, even though the goods are not yet shipped. It must not be assumed too readily that an order for goods is an offer of a promise in return for title to the goods to be effected by the act of shipment or otherwise. The offeror frequently wishes a return promise, as the offeree understands. The language used may be elliptical, and understood to be so.

Express, Implied, and Tacit Contracts

A brief definition of these terms will suffice here. An express contract is said to exist when the acts of the parties declaring their will and intention are spoken or written words. A tacit contract is any other kind, the acts of the parties being sufficient to express their intention but not consisting of words, either spoken or written. It can easily be seen that a tacit contract is also, in a broader sense, an express one. Words are often lame and halting things in performing their function of expressing thought. It is often true in fact that actions speak louder than words. The term implied contract is generally used to mean exactly the same as tacit contract. The intention of the parties is "implied" or inferred from their actions other than words. For some centuries, however, it has been customary to describe as a "contract implied in law" certain other legal relations, in cases where neither the words of the parties nor their other acts justify an inference that they intended to create such relations. This usage seems to have been due to two reasons: in the earlier cases the courts desired to make the form of action called assumpsit available for the enforcement of certain duties not intentionally assumed; and in some of the later cases the courts desired to avoid the appearance of creating legal rights and duties where the parties had not so agreed. Thus the term implied contract became a slippery one upon which judicial reasoning has not infrequently slipped into error. The legal relations commonly described as contracts implied in law are now coming to be called quasi contracts. It is not necessary here to describe what these are; it is enough to observe that they are not contracts in fact, either express or tacit.

Void, Voidable, And Unenforcible Contracts

. . .

There are next to be considered the acts of offer and acceptance by means of which the foregoing legal relations are finally established, and also some of the intermediate relations that arise prior to the closing of the contract.

The Offer

Definition. An offer is defined above as an act whereby one person confers upon another the power to create contractual relations between them. It has not been customary to describe as a "power" the new legal relation consequent upon an offer;[17] but this term seems to be the most accurate description of that relation. It is similar to the relation existing in the case of agency. The principal, by an act called "appointment," creates in the agent the power of creating (in conjunction with a third person) new legal relations between the principal and a third person. After the one voluntary act of the principal called "appointment," nothing further remains to be done by him; thereafter it is the voluntary act of the agent that is operative to create new relations. So in the case of an offer: the act of the offeror operates to create in the offeree a power, and having so operated it is exhausted; thereafter the voluntary act of the offeree alone will operate to create the new relations called a contract.

The Operative Act. What kind of act creates a power of acceptance and is therefore an offer? It must be an expression of will or intention. It must be an act that leads the offeree reasonably to believe that a power to create a contract is conferred upon him. This applies to the content of the power as well as to the fact of its existence. It is on this ground that we must exclude invitations to deal or acts of mere preliminary negotiation, and acts evidently done in jest or without intent to create legal relations. All these are acts that do not lead others reasonably to believe that they are empowered "to close the contract." So long as it is reasonably apparent that some further act of the offeror is necessary, the offeree has no power to create contractual relations by an act of his own and there is as yet no offer.

Communication. No act can induce another to believe that he is empowered to accept unless he is aware that the act has been performed. So it would seem to be essential that an offer shall be communicated to the offeree, and it has generally been held that acceptance is impossible prior to such communication. Thus, where a reward was offered by publication, for service desired, it has been held that the rendition of the service in ignorance of the offer creates no contract. The contrary has been held in some

---

[17] The first, and the best, presentation of this concept that has been seen by the writer is in the article on Some Fundamental Legal Conceptions as Applied in Judicial Reasoning, in 23 Yale Law Journal 16, 49, by Professor W. N. Hohfeld, to whom the writer acknowledges great indebtedness. In Jordan v. Dobbins (1877) 122 Mass. 168, the court speaks of a continuing guaranty as "a power or authority which he might at any time revoke."

cases. Some judges have thought that where two offers, identical in terms, cross each other in the mail, there is no contract. In these two instances there is no contract if the only way to create a contract is by the machinery of offer and acceptance, regarded as acts expressing consent. In the reward cases, the offeror has acted and has consented; the offeree has acted but his act was not an expression of consent. In the case of crossed offers, each party has acted and has expressed consent; but in so doing, neither has knowingly exercised a power conferred by the other and neither has been induced to believe that he has such a power to exercise. Each has done an act conferring a power upon the other, and either one may now exercise that power by a subsequent act and thus create a contract. There is, however, no inevitable necessity in our adoption of the machinery of offer and acceptance. The rules of contract, like all other rules of law, are based upon mere matters of policy, or belief as to policy. In the process of our evolution we find that some or all of us are following a customary rule. When we become conscious of this fact, we try to express the rule in words and to compel others to obey it by legislative command. We may fail in our attempt, either because the custom supposed is not the custom of the powerful, or because we have failed to express it with accuracy, or because new life conditions require new customs. So, therefore, we may decree that two acts expressing consent, as in the case of crossed offers, shall create contractual relations; or that where an offer has been published, that act empowers others to create contractual relations by doing the acts requested, even though without knowledge of the request. It seems not improbable to the writer that this latter rule will prevail in the future. In the vast majority of cases, however, contracts will be made by offer and acceptance as analyzed above.

Time Limit. An offer having been made and a power having been thereby created, how long will this power continue to exist? The offeror is the creator of the power, and before it leaves his hands he may fashion it to his will. Such is the present decree of society. If he names a specific period for its existence, the offeree can accept only during this period. If the offeror names no period whatever, the power will be held to exist for a reasonable time, to be determined as a fact by the court and dependent upon the circumstances. If the parties are negotiating in each other's presence, the reasonable time will usually be a very short one; but if the offeror indicates that the power of acceptance is to be exercised *in absentia*, the reasonable time will be considerably longer. If the time

taken by the offeree would appear to be reasonable to a reasonably prudent man in his position, the acceptance is operative even though the offeror did not intend the power to exist for so long a period. A reasonable time may be longer than the offeror in fact intended. On the other hand, there seems to be no good reason for holding that the power of acceptance has expired if it can be shown as a fact that the offeror intended that it should still exist. A reasonable time may be longer than the offeror intended, but it can never be less.

Revocation. In most cases the offeror may terminate the power of acceptance prior to the end of the specified period, if any, or of the reasonable time. In the first place he may have expressly provided that the power should be subject to revocation, either by notice to the offeree or without such notice. If he provides for a revocation without notice and by a mere change of his mental state, he can scarcely be said to have conferred any power at all. The power conferred by such an offer is a very flimsy one indeed, for the validity of the acceptance will depend upon the offeror's own will when he is notified of the acceptance. Such an offer is little more, in effect, than an invitation for bids. If the reserved power of revocation is to be exercised by an overt act, then there is a substantial power of acceptance, the validity of the act of acceptance being then not dependent upon the will of the offeror.

Even though the power to revoke has not been expressly reserved by the offeror, it can be said that as a general rule he retains such a power. In such a case, however, the power to revoke can be exercised only in a particular manner. If the offer was made by publication, it has been held that it can be revoked either by actual notice to a claimant or by a notice published in the same manner as was the offer. If the offer was made by personal communication to one or more particular persons, it can be revoked only by giving notice to them, such notice being effective only when received.

. . .

Physical Limitation. Irrevocability may have any one of several meanings: first, that the offeror has no legal power to revoke by any means, lawful or unlawful; second, that he is not legally privileged to revoke, although he may have the legal power; third, that although he has both the legal power and the privilege of revoking by certain means, these means are not within his present physical capacity. Under our law nearly all offers are for a time irrevocable in the third sense. Revocation can take place only after a certain fashion, commonly by giving actual notice to the offeree. So long as it is impossible to reach the offeree with such a notice or to do such other act as may amount to a revocation, the power of acceptance will continue to exist. This means that although the offeror is privileged to revoke and has the legal power to revoke by doing certain acts, the performance of these acts is beyond his limited human capacity.

Contractual Limitation. An offeree's power is irrevocable in the second sense, either by the giving of notice or otherwise, if the offer is put in the form of a conditional covenant or simple contract, or if the offer is accompanied by a promise not to revoke given for a consideration or under seal. In such case the offeror is never privileged to revoke, and he may not even have the legal power. It may be said that these are contracts and are not mere offers; but the fact remains that in all such cases the act of the offeror has conferred upon the offeree a power to create future relations, a power that is in all respects similar to the power conferred by any offer, a power to be exercised by the voluntary act of the offeree alone. The offeree is not bound to do the act that constitutes the condition or acceptance; but if he does do that act, new contractual relations are created. When the courts enforce the duties included among these relations, they do so expressly on the theory that there was an offer that could not be revoked.

If there is in fact a promise to keep the offer open for a specified time, the question of revocation should turn upon the matter of consideration and upon the question of damages. If there is an agreed equivalent given for the promise, a repudiation will beyond doubt create a right to damages. The same result would be reached where the offeree has done detrimental acts in reasonable reliance upon the promsie in those courts adopting the (so-called) estoppel theory of consideration. Further, in this case the offer should be held to be irrevocable and the repudiation of the promise to be wholly without the effect intended, if a subsequent acceptance does not unreasonably increase the damages to be suffered by reason of the breach. In this case, the offer would be irrevocable, in the first (and the best) sense. After a contract has been made, a repudiation by one of the parties creates in the other only a right to such damages as he will suffer after taking all reasonable steps for the prevention of damage. If further performance by him will increase his loss, the other party is under no duty to pay the damages caused by such further

performance. But if such action will not increase his loss, he may proceed with his performance without affecting his claim to damages. In the cases now being considered, whether they be regarded as contracts to hold an offer open or as conditional covenants, the power conferred should be regarded as irrevocable if the execution of the power does not increase the damage to be suffered in case of breach. Such damages are not increased in any respect if the act of acceptance or the fulfillment of the condition consists merely in the giving of a notice or the making of a promise. In spite of an attempted revocation, the offeree still has the power of acceptance; while the offeror lacks not only the privilege of revoking, but also the power to revoke. Thus, suppose that A should offer to convey Blackacre in return for B's promise to pay a price named, and should promise for a consideration or under seal not to withdraw the offer for 30 days. In such a case, acceptance (the act of exercising the power) would be merely the making of a promise to pay the price. This would not in any respect increase the damage suffered by reason of a breach. B's damages, whether for breach of the preliminary option contract, or for breach of the subsequently created contract to convey, would be the value of Blackacre, less the contract price. In cases where B's damage is regarded as irreparable, he should be given a decree for specific performance in equity. The same conclusion follows if the transaction be regarded as a covenant to convey Blackacre on condition that a promise by B to pay the price shall be made within 30 days.

. . .

Specific Performance. An obstacle to specific performance in equity may be supposed to exist in case the option (let us suppose an option to buy) is a contract to hold an offer open instead of a conditional covenant or simple contract. In the latter case there is a completed obligation to convey, and this may be enforced. In the former case there is no such obligation, and none can be made because the option contract has been broken and the offer has been revoked. This obstacle can be avoided by the simple expedient of not seeing it. The asserted impossibility of doing an act has many a time been disproved by doing it. If by definition the thing is impossible, change the definition. The objection can be met verbally in two ways: first, by the easy method of declaring the offer irrevocable and the option contract unbreakable. That this can be done has already been shown above. There is nothing foreign to our law in the idea of an irrevocable power, and the legal relation resulting from an offer is a legal power. The power to accept being still alive, the offeree may exercise it and thus create the obligation to convey, all fit and ready for specific enforcement. The second form of meeting the objection may be preferred by some, but it is the same in essence. Everybody agrees that the option contract creates an obligation that is enforceable. It may be described as a contract to make a contract. Even if the second contract—the obligation to convey—is never formed, equity still has jurisdiction on the ground that money damages are inadequate. Nor is it without the power to enforce a decree. Even if we suppose that equity cannot specifically enforce the contract to make a contract, it can do exactly what it does in all of its decrees for specific performance: it can decree specific *reparation*. In this case a conveyance of the property would be such reparation, for it was the ultimate object of the option contract. Nobody doubts the power of equity to force a conveyance of the *res* and to compel the creation of new rights *in rem*, even though many have supposed that this can be done only by acting *in personam*. Indeed, it seems strange that these same individuals should doubt the power of equity to compel the creation of a new obligation *in personam*, through the medium of an irrevocable power.

Limitations Due to Part Performance. There are still other cases where it has sometimes been held that an offer is irrevocable, even though there is no express promise to hold the offer open. These are offers made in such terms that they can be accepted only by performing a series of acts requiring an appreciable length of time and effort or expense. Upon complete performance of these acts, the power of acceptance becomes irrevocable because it has been fully executed and a contract has resulted; but in a few cases it has been held, contrary to what is generally supposed to be the rule, that the offer becomes irrevocable after the offeree has begun to perform the requested acts of acceptance or has performed a substantial part of such acts. It must be observed that after such a part performance there is as yet no contract, for by hypothesis acceptance was to consist of complete performance. If the offer has become irrevocable, however, the offeree still has the power to create a contract by completing the requested acts, in spite of a notice to the contrary from the offeror. The principle applied in these cases is applicable not merely to offers of unilateral contracts, but also to offers where the offeree is requested to make a return promise and to express it by one or more acts requiring a considerable expenditure of time or money. The cases in point, however, are mostly cases of offers to make a unilateral contract.

In one case, the defendant offered a reward for the arrest and conviction of some criminals. The plaintiff arrested them and induced their confession, but they were not convicted because the defendant wished to use their testimony in other cases and so had the indictments dismissed. It was held that the plaintiff was entitled to the reward.

Again, a defendant delivered a negotiable note in escrow for the plaintiff, to be paid when the plaintiff had completed a line of railway. After part performance by the plaintiff the defendant gave notice of revocation. The court held this notice to be ineffective, saying: "it would be manifestly unjust thereafter to permit the offer that had been made to be withdrawn. The promised consideration had been partly performed, and the contract had taken on a bilateral character."

In another case, a corporation passed a by-law providing that employees should be entitled to a share in the profits after serving for a named period. The plaintiff was discharged one day before he would have been entitled to share under this by-law. His action for such share was sustained, the court saying: "It is true as a general proposition that a party making an offer of a reward may withdraw it before it is accepted. But persons offering rewards must be held to the exercise of good faith and cannot arbitrarily withdraw their offers for the purpose of defeating payment."

A defendant offered to buy all railroad ties "you put on at Gap within the next twelve months." The plaintiff had supplied 1,000 ties and had secured material for 5,000 more, when the defendant gave notice of revocation. The court held the plaintiff to be entitled to damages for failure to take the remaining 5,000 ties.

If an owner has offered a commission to a real estate broker, to be earned by effecting a sale, can the offer be revoked after the broker has spent time and money and may have a sale nearly consummated? In such a case the courts are very ready to make the assumption that there was a bilateral contract, for breach of which the broker is entitled to damages, or that the services of the broker were completed, the acceptance valid, and the reward earned.[46]

Suppose a prize is offered to the winner of a race or to the winner of a voting or guessing contest, under specified rules; can the rules be changed or the offer be withdrawn by the offeror, after substantial acts in reliance thereon by contestants? There are cases tending to justify an inference, though not deciding, that the offer has become irrevocable.

Where a reward has been offered for the return of a lost article, it has been held that the finder has a lien on the article to compel payment of the reward, without stopping to consider whether or not the reward has been earned before delivery. It is apparent that the offer has become irrevocable before delivery.

The rule that offers like the foregoing are revocable at any time prior to complete performance of the acts requested has encountered some criticism. Sometimes a court is astute to find that in fact there was no revocation. In many instances the existence of a bilateral contract has been assumed without close analysis of the facts, in order to render a revocation ineffective. It is often maintained that the offer is irrevocable after the offeree has done an act that binds him to complete the requested performance.

It has been suggested that in cases of the above sort, even in the absence of an express promise not to revoke an offer, a promise not to revoke is implied, the consideration therefor being any substantial act whereby the requested performance is begun. If such an option contract is justly inferable in fact, it is governed by the same rules as an express contract to keep an offer open. This has been discussed above. In many instances, however, the inference of such a promise would be contrary to fact. In those cases the promise would be a fiction and the agreement that the beginning of performance should be the consideration for this promise would likewise be a fiction. The purpose of such a fiction is to make the offer irrevocable and it is based upon a belief as to policy and general advantage. If this is true and if in our process of evolution we have become conscious of the fact, we are ready to discard the fiction and to express in appropriate words the rule and its reason. It might be expressed somewhat like this: Where an offer has been made so that it can be accepted only by per-

forming a series of acts requiring an appreciable length of time and effort or expense, such offer shall be irrevocable after the offeree has begun the performance of the requested acts, unless the offeror expressly reserved the power of revocation.

To this rule there should probably be added some such rule as the following: If the continuation of performance will increase the amount of the offeree's claim, the revocation shall be effective; in such case if the offeree can show with reasonable certainty that he would have performed in full, he shall be entitled to the same damages as if the contract had been a bilateral contract in the beginning.

Possible Unfairness. In this class of cases the question is of some complexity, and it cannot be said that the above rules represent the settled law of any jurisdiction. There is enough reason and authority in their favor, however, to warrant their careful consideration in new legislation, parliamentary or judicial. A possible argument against such rules is that they would operate unfairly and unequally as between offeror and offeree. The offeree will remain free to discontinue performance without any claim for damages arising against him, while the offeror will bear an irrevocable liability. The offeree remains legally privileged and empowered to prevent a contract; the offeror's privilege is wholly gone and in some cases his power of revocation is gone also. It has been our custom to say that both parties must be bound or neither is bound, but this properly applies only to transactions by which it is intended to create bilateral duties. A closer consideration will show that there is no real unfairness on this score. The offeror is the one who invites action by the offeree, and he invites it in such a way that the offeree bears all the risk of loss. The offeror will have to pay nothing if the acceptance is not fully completed, and if it is so completed he has received the requested equivalent for his promise. The offeror has asked for no rights against the offeree and has invested nothing in the hope of such rights and has been induced to do expensive acts in reliance upon such expectation. The offeree may find eventually, after much labor and expense, the complete acceptance by him is impossible or so expensive as to exceed the offered compensation. Complete acceptance may become impossible by reason of a third

---

[46] See Blumenthal v. Goodall (1891) 89 Cal. 251. Where a definite time was fixed for the making of the sale, the broker cannot earn his reward by completing the service after the time. Zeimer v. Antisell (1888) 75 Cal. 509. If the offer has been held open for a reasonable time, and the broker has failed to render the service after a definite attempt, the of-

fer has been said to be revocable if the defendant is acting "in good faith." See Sibbald v. Bethlehem Iron Co. (1881) 83 N. Y. 378; Cadigan v. Crabtree (1904) 186 Mass. 7; Livery v. Miller (1883) 61 Md. 337. The inference may be drawn from these cases that a revocation made unreasonably or "in bad faith" would be ineffective.

party's previous acceptance of the offer. From this it appears that it is fair enough for the one who bears the risk to possess the privilege, while the other, bearing no risk, is deprived of both privilege and power.

Termination of Power by Offeree. The power created by an offer may be terminated not only by the offeror but also by the offeree, the possessor of the power. His mere failure to exercise the power will not in itself cause such a termination, except as such a failure fulfils a condition prescribed by the offeror or by the law. If the offeror has expressly limited the life of the power, he has thereby caused a failure to accept within the prescribed period to be an operative fact. If the power to accept is limited by the law to a "reasonable time," the law has caused failure to accept to be an operative fact. However, in such cases it would be more in accord with the instinct of the average man to designate the act of the offeror as the cause both of the birth of the power to accept and of its death.

It is usually said that the power of acceptance is terminated by the act of the offeree in definitely rejecting the offer or in making a conditional acceptance or counter offer. This is not necessarily true. The offeror is the creator of the power and he may cause it to live in spite of rejections and counter offers. If the offeror should make an offer and at the same time notify the offeree that the power to accept shall exist for two weeks and that a rejection or counter offer shall not terminate it, it can hardly be expected that a court would disregard the offeror's expressed intention. The offeree may still reasonably believe the offer to be open. The same result should follow, even in the absence of an express notice, if the offeror has done any other overt acts expressing such an intention. The real reason why a rejection or a counter offer should terminate the power to accept seems to be the effect that they will probably have upon the thought and actions of the offeror. If in the particular case they have had no effects whatever—and the party asserting rights under a contract must be able to show this—it should be held that the power continues to exist. If, after a rejection or counter offer, the offeror has done no overt act prior to the subsequent act of acceptance, indicating with reasonable certainty that he intends the power still to exist, no doubt it would be held that such an acceptance has only the effect of a new offer; otherwise the acceptor would be wholly at the offeror's mercy, for the latter could prove the overt acts of acceptance, but the acceptor could not prove that the offeror had continued to hold the offer open. If the offeror has in fact done an overt act indicating his intention to continue the existence of the power, there seems to be no practical necessity for a notice of such act to be given to the offeree, except that without such a notice he may never accept. If without such a notice he does accept, he is still being induced to act by the original notice. He is acting in accordance with a power that he thinks he has, and that he has in fact. If he can prove the facts as against the offeror, the latter should be bound. The offeror will have no difficulty in proving the facts as against the offeree, for he has evidence of the acceptance and also of his own overt act continuing the power.

Revocation by Death or Insanity. The general rule is that the power of acceptance is terminated by the death or by the supervening insanity of either the offeror or the offeree. This rule also may be in harmony with the public interest; but there is not, as is often supposed, any compelling necessity for its existence. It may be said that you cannot contract with a dead man; but neither can you force a dead man to pay his debts contracted before his death. Yet the law has no difficulty, in the latter case, in creating legal relations with the dead man's personal representative, and there would be no greater difficulty in declaring the power of acceptance to survive as against the offeror's representative or in favor of the offeree's representative. It may again be suggested that an offer is not a physical sensation or a state of mind. Powers "coupled with an interest" survive the death of the grantor of the power. This rule might well apply to offers where the acceptance is to consist of a series of acts requiring time and labor or expense, and part performance has taken place before notice of the death. It is on similar grounds that option contracts have been enforced, although the acceptance was subsequent to the death of one of the parties. It is generally held that the power created by a continuing guaranty is not destroyed by the death of the guarantor without knowledge thereof by the creditor.

Acceptance

An acceptance is a voluntary act of the offeree whereby he exercises the power conferred upon him by the offer, and thereby creates the set of legal relations called a contract. What acts are sufficient to serve this purpose? We must look first to the terms in which the offer was expressed, either by words or by other conduct. The offeror is the creator of the power and at the time of its creation he has full control over both the fact of its existence and its terms. The offeror has, in the beginning, full power to determine the acts that are to constitute acceptance. After he has once created the power, he may lose his control over it, and may become disabled to change or to revoke it; but the fact that, in the beginning, the offeror has full control of the immediately succeeding relation called a power, is the characteristic that distinguishes contractual relations from non-contractual ones. After the offeror has created the power, the legal consequences thereof are out of his hands, and he may be brought into numerous consequential relations of which he did not dream, and to which he might not have consented. These later relations are nevertheless called contractual.

Silence. There is one limitation upon this power of the offeror. It has been held that he cannot confer a power of accepting by mere silence. In one aspect, this seems to be a not unreasonable limitation. The opposite rule, in such cases, would enable the offeree to await the event, and to deny the fact of acceptance if the contract, now appears to be to his disadvantage, or to assert the fact of acceptance if appearances are to the contrary. This argument, however, proves too much; for it applies with equal force to any positive act that might reasonably be performed even though no offer has been made, and that has no more probative force to establish assent than to establish some other fact. Whether or not it would be so applied may be regarded as doubtful. A strong argument in favor of holding the acceptance good is that the offeror has only himself to blame if the terms of his offer put him at the mercy of the offeree, and that he should not be permitted to escape liability when he has induced the offeree to believe that there is a contract and to act in reliance thereon. The weight of these opposing arguments cannot be determined with certainty; but it will be a rare case where the offeree has not done some overt act which indicates his intention to accept, and in such case the courts would undoubtedly hold that the acceptance was good. This rule must not be confused with the one to the effect that the offeror cannot arbitrarily cause the silence or other ordinarily non-expressive act of the offeree to operate as an acceptance against the will of the offeree. The offeror may, perhaps, confer the power on the offeree to make such an act operate as an acceptance; but he cannot unreasonably deprive the offeree of his pre-existing immunity in doing those acts

or of his power to make them operate otherwise. Thus, if the offeror declares that the offeree shall accept by remaining silent or by eating his breakfast, the offeree cannot be held against his will even though he seems to comply with the terms of the offer. In such a case, the conduct of the offeree may with equal reason be regarded as an expression of quite different intentions and desires. In such case, it might be left to the jury to determine whether or not the act was done with the intention to accept[63] but it would be better to instruct the jury that there is a contract only if the conduct of the offeree has reasonably led the offeror to believe there has been an acceptance.

Impossible Acts. Since the offeror is privileged to make no offer at all, or a power limited as he desires, he may prescribe acts that are wholly impossible or are very difficult. If the prescribed acts are totally impossible, there is in fact no power at all. So, if A apparently offers to contract with B, but prescribes that B must accept yesterday or must accept by going to the moon, no contract can be made. It seems rather fanciful to say that B has a legal power to accept but has not the physical capacity to exercise it. If the prescribed mode of acceptance was that B should lift a 1,000lb. weight, it would not seem so fanciful. B may not at present have the physical capacity to lift the weight, but others have such capacity and B himself may acquire it. The act of going to the moon is also not wholly inconceivable, but the only individual capable of such a Cyclopean undertaking is Noman. The act of accepting yesterday requires the turning back of time and the living of history over again. This seems wholly inconceivable, although Mark Twain's Connecticut Yankee apparently accomplished the feat.

If a particular mode of acceptance has been prescribed by the offeror, the offeree can bring about contractual relations only by acting exactly in the mode prescribed. Nothing else will be "equally as good." It makes no difference how difficult or expensive the prescribed acts may be, except so far as the difficulty or expense may be evidence to indicate that the acts were not in fact prescribed.

Of course society is quite capable of creating powers in B whereby he can create other legal relations with A, even though B wholly disregards the expressed will of A; but in such case we do not call

---

[63] Brian, C.J., once said: "It is trite law that the thought of man is not triable, for even the devil does not know what the thought of man is." Very likely he was mistaken in each of the two statements. See Ashley, Contracts, pp. 51, 52.

those new legal relations contractual. It is here that we reach the boundary line between contract and noncontract.

No Prescribed Acts. Instead of being expressly limited, the offer may prescribe no mode of acceptance whatever. There must be enough to indicate that the offeror intends to create a power of acceptance, but this is quite possible in the absence of any suggestion whatever as to the mode of acceptance. In this case the offeree may accept in any manner that the law deems to be reasonable under the circumstances.

An even larger power of acceptance may be created by the offeror. He may suggest and authorize an acceptance in one or more particular modes, without making them exclusive. In such case, compliance with the suggested mode will close the contract, however unreasonable or unusual the mode may be; but so also will compliance with any other mode that the law deems to be reasonable. In this case, the offeree has all the power that he would have if the mode of acceptance had been exactly prescribed; and in addition thereto, all the power that he would have if no mode of acceptance had been mentioned at all.

The foregoing rules of acceptance are applicable to all kinds of contracts alike, unilateral and bilateral; but in their application certain distinctions are to be observed and some difficulties must be overcome. It is not always easy to determine what mode of acceptance the offeror has required or suggested; a reasonable construction must be put upon his words or other conduct. If the offeror has prescribed no mode of acceptance and if the offeree has not adopted some mode suggested by the offeror, it must be determined whether or not the mode actually adopted is to be deemed reasonable.

Notice. There is some conflict on the question of notice of acceptance. Is the starting of such a notice by the offeree,[66] or the receipt of such a notice by the offeror, one of the necessary operative facts? This question is to be answered by an application of the foregoing principles. The offeror may prescribe either or both as a part of the mode of acceptance. If he does so, the prescribed fact is a sine qua non, whether the proposed contract is unilateral or bilateral. If, however, the offeror prescribes some particular mode of acceptance, not including a notice, none should be required. This is very generally the case

where the offeror requests a return performance but no return promise; and it is generally not the case where he requests a return promise. If A offers his promise of a reward in return for the capture of a felon, or for the destruction of a noxious animal, or for the act of procuring someone to buy certain land, or for the winning of a race, or for the buying and using of a smoke ball and catching the influenza, the acts requested are clearly indicated, and the contract is complete without any act like mailing a notice, and without actual knowledge by the offeror. If A offers his promise of guaranty in return for B's act of advancing money to C, the contract is complete when B has advanced the money. Where, however, A offers either a promise or a performance in return for a promise to be made by B, A does not usually specify any mode of acceptance. In such case, what is the reasonable mode required by the laws? It is a matter of course that B must do some overt act that expresses his intention to accept, but this, in itself, is not enough. The act must be one that B is justified in believing will bring notice to A. In this case, such is the reasonable mode required by the law, because A has asked for a promise—for an assurance upon which he can rely. He cannot rely upon it without knowledge, and it is therefore the custom of reasonable men to do acts that may be expected to give notice to the offeror. It has been vigorously asserted that the contract is not completed until receipt of this notice by the offeror, but the authority against such a doctrine is now overwhelming, both in England and America. This fact shows that the criticisms of the prevailing rule are based upon some *a priori* theory of contract that is not in harmony with human desires and the other facts of life.

What acts are those that may reasonably be regarded as sufficient in the effort to bring knowledge of the acceptance to the offeror? If the parties are negotiating in each others' presence, the act must be one that will bring immediate knowledge. The offeree could not accept by mailing a letter, because in the absence of an extended time for acceptance, such a mode would be unreasonable and unusual. In choosing his mode of acceptance, the offeree must consider the time of delivery, the place of delivery, the certainty of arrival, and the intelligiblity of the expression. If, considering these things, the offeree chooses the customary mode, it is sufficient. It may be suffic-

---

[66] This means the doing of an act that will in the ordinary course of events make the offeror aware of the acceptance.

ient to mail a letter, even though the offer was made orally, if several days were allowed for acceptance. The starting of a telegram by the usual telegraph companies would be equally effective, and in some instances would be effective where the mailing of a letter would not be. If the offer itself was made by mail, it has been supposed that this made the post office an agent of the offeror to receive the letter of acceptance. This theory has been disapproved and seems to have little to support it. It is better to base the rule upon the "usage of trade," or "the ordinary usages of mankind."

So much has been said about the necessity and propriety of mailing a letter of acceptance that it is often taken to be universally required, even where the offeror has himself prescribed another mode of acceptance.

Mutual Assent

The rule generally laid down is that the acts of offer and acceptance must be expressions of assent. This has long been the theory upon which contractual obligations have been enforced, the test question usually put is, what was the intention of the parties? It must not be supposed from this, however, that no contractual relation can exist unless the parties both foresaw and intended it. If two parties have gone through the form of offering and accepting, the law determines the legal relations that follow. Frequently these come with surprise and shock to the parties themselves. It may be said here, as in the law of torts, that the parties are presumed to intend the consequences of their acts, but this is often a violent presumption contrary to fact. To indulge such a presumption is merely to hold that the actual intention of the parties is not the determinative fact, or even that it is wholly immaterial.

Parties are bound by the reasonable meaning of what they said and not by what they thought. If A makes an offer to B which B reasonably understands to have a particular meaning, and so accepts, A is bound in accordance with B's understanding. So also, if A's offer has only one reasonable meaning, B is bound in accordance therewith, even though he accepted supposing the meaning to be otherwise. The operative act creating an obligation is the expression of intention and not the thought process. It may be said that the purpose of the rule is to carry out the intentions of the parties in the great majority of cases; but it seems better to say that its purpose is to secure the fulfillment of the promisee's reasonable expectations as induced by the promisor's act. In the law of contract as in the law of tort, men are expected to live up to the standard of the reasonably prudent man. If there is a misunderstanding and neither party was negligent, there is no contract.[83] The same is true if both are equally negligent.

The legal relations consequent upon offer and acceptance are not wholly dependent, even upon the reasonable meaning of the words and acts of the parties. The law determines these relations in the light of subsequent circumstances, these often being totally unforeseen by the parties. In such cases it is sometimes said that the law will create that relation which the parties would have intended had they foreseen. The fact is, however, that the decision will depend upon the notions of the court as to policy, welfare, justice, right and wrong, such notions often being inarticulate and subconscious.[86]

---

[83] Raffles v. Wichelhaus (1864) 2 H. & C. 906.

[86] "You can always imply a condition in a contract. But why do you imply it? It is because of some belief as to the practice of the community or of a class, or because of some opinion as to policy, or, in short, because of some attitude of yours upon a matter not capable of exact quantitative measurement, and therefore not capable of founding exact logical conclusions." Justice Holmes, The Path of the Law, 10 Harv. L. Rev. 466.

Lon Fuller on Consideration

Lon L. Fuller, one of the great American legal philosophers, taught at Duke and Harvard, among other schools. He is really one of the giants of contract law as well as of jurisprudence, but somehow he doesn't get mentioned quite as often as Corbin, Williston and Karl Llewellyn. Among Fuller's contributions to contract law are his article, *The Reliance Interest in Contract Damages*, written with his student assistant William Perdue in 1936, and his casebook, written in the late 1940's, which revolutionized the teaching of contracts by putting remedies first. The Fuller and Perdue article is probably the best-known article in the contracts literature and is referred to several times in this book. The remedies-first approach in teaching is still controversial, especially among first-year law students.

Here we are concerned with another of Fuller's great contributions, his 1941 Columbia Law Review article, *Consideration and Form*. Snippets of the article, particularly its discussions of the "evidentiary", "cautionary" and "channeling" functions of consideration, appear in many contracts casebooks. However, the entire article appears valuable to me, and it is presented here with very few cuts. I find it particularly interesting when compared with Corbin. Note how essential to Fuller's approach is his view of the centrality of private autonomy, spelled out in Part II. Fuller is no neanderthal; he is well aware that excessive power can undermine freedom of contract, but he makes clear the reasons why he believes that it often is better to allow people "to withdraw assurances they have once given," particularly when there is neither bargain nor reliance and formalities are lacking.

In Part III of the article Fuller considers some of the familiar situations where promises are not backed by bargained-for consideration, including gratuitous promises and unbargained-for reliance. This discussion, as well as his brief discussion of bases of liability other than bargained-for exchange, will lead us into a contemporary discussion by Judge Richard Posner.

Lon L. Fuller, *Consideration and Form*, 41 Colum. L. Rev. 799 (1941)

§1. *Introduction.* What is attempted in this article is an inquiry into the rationale of legal formalities, and an examination of the common-law doctrine of consideration in terms of its underlying policies. That such an investigation will reveal a significant relationship between consideration and form is a proposition not here suggested for the first time; indeed the question has been raised (and sometimes answered affirmatively) whether consideration cannot in the end be reduced entirely to terms of form.

That consideration may have both a "formal" and a "substantive" aspect is apparent when we reflect on the reasons which have been advanced why promises without consideration are not enforced. It has been said that consideration is "for the sake of evidence" and is intended to remove the hazards of mistaken or perjured testimony which would attend the enforcement of promises for which nothing is given in exchange. Again, it is said that enforcement is denied gratuitous promises because such promises are often made impulsively and without proper deliberation. In both these cases the objection relates, not to the content and effect of the promise, but to the manner in which it is made. Objections of this sort, which touch the form rather than the content of the agreement,

will be removed if the making of the promise is attended by some formality or ceremony, as by being under seal. On the other hand, it has been said that the enforcement of gratuitous promises is not an object of sufficient importance to our social and economic order to justify the expenditure of the time and energy necessary to accomplish it. Here the objection is one of "substance" since it touches the significance of the promise made and not merely the circumstances surrounding the making of it.

The task proposed in this article is that of disentangling the "formal" and "substantive" elements in the doctrine of consideration. Since the policies underlying the doctrine are generally left unexamined in the decisions and doctrinal discussions, it will be necessary to postpone taking up the common-law requirement itself until we have examined in general terms the formal and substantive bases of contract liability.

I. The Functions Performed By Legal Formalities

§2. *The Evidentiary Function.* The most obvious function of a legal formality is, to use Austin's words, that of providing "evidence of the existence and purport of the contract, in case of controversy." The need for evidentiary security may be satisfied in a variety of ways: by requiring a writing, or attestation, or the certification of a notary. It may even be satisfied, to some extent, by such a device as the Roman *stipulatio*, which compelled an oral spelling out of the promise in a manner sufficiently ceremonious to impress its terms on participants and possible bystanders.

§3. *The Cautionary Function.* A formality may also perform a cautionary or deterrent function by acting as a check against inconsiderate action. The seal in its original form fulfilled this purpose remarkably well. The affixing and impressing of a wax wafer—symbol in the popular mind of legalism and weightiness—was an excellent device for inducing the circumspective frame of mind appropriate in one pledging his future. To a less extent any requirement of a writing, of course, serves the same purpose, as do requirements of attestation, notarization, etc.

§4. *The Channeling Function.* Though most discussions of the purposes served by formalities go no further than the analysis just presented, this analysis stops short of recognizing one of the most important functions of form. That a legal formality may perform a function not yet described can be shown by the seal. The seal not only insures a satisfactory memorial of the promise and induces deliberation in the making of it. It serves also to mark or signalize the enforceable promise; it furnishes a simple and external test of enforceability. This function of form Ihering described as "the facilitation of judicial diagnosis," and he employed the analogy of coinage in explaining it.

> Form is for a legal transaction what the stamp is for a coin. Just as the stamp of the coin relieves us from the necessity of testing the metallic content and weight—in short, the value of the coin (a test which we could not avoid if uncoined metal were offered to us in payment), in the same way legal formalities relieve the judge of an inquiry whether a legal transaction was intended, and—in case different forms are fixed for different legal transactions—which was intended.

In this passage it is apparent that Ihering has placed an undue emphasis on the utility of form for the judge, to the neglect of its significance for those transacting business out of court. . . . The thing which characterizes the law of contracts and conveyances is that in this field forms are deliberately used, and are intended to be so used, by the parties whose acts are to be judged by the law. To the business man who wishes to make his own or another's promise binding, the seal was at common law available as a device for the accomplishment of his objective. In this aspect form offers a legal framework into which the party may fit his actions, or, to change the figure, it offers channels for the legally effective expression of intention. It is with this aspect of form in mind that I have described the third function of legal formalities as "the channeling function."

In seeking to understand this channeling function of form, perhaps the most useful analogy is that of language, which illustrates both the advantages and dangers of form in the aspect we are now considering. One who wishes to communicate his thoughts to others must force the raw material of meaning into defined and recognizable channels; he must reduce the fleeting entities of wordless thought to the patterns of conventional speech. One planning to enter a legal transaction faces a similar problem. His mind first conceives an economic or sentimental objective, or, more usually, a set of overlapping objectives. He must then, with or without the aid of a lawyer, cast about for the legal transaction (written memorandum, sealed contract, lease, conveyance of the fee, etc.) which will most nearly accomplish these objectives. Just as the use of language contains dangers for the uninitiated, so legal forms are safe only in the hands of those who are familiar with their effects. Ihering explains that the extreme formalism of Roman law was supportable in practice only because of the constant availability of legal advice, *gratis*.

The ideal of language would be the word whose significance remained constant and unaffected by the context in which it was used. Actually there are few words, even in scientific language, which are not capable of taking on a nuance of meaning because of the context in which they occur. So in the law, the ideal type of formal transaction would be the transaction described on the Continent as "abstract," that is, the transaction which is abstracted from the causes which gave rise to it and which has the same legal effect no matter what the context of motives and lay practices in which it occurs. The seal in its original form represented an approach to this ideal, for it will be recalled that extra-formal factors, including even fraud and mistake, were originally without effect on the sealed promise. Most of the formal transactions familiar to modern law, however, fall short of the "abstract" transaction; the channels they cut are not sharply and simply defined. The Statute of Frauds, for example, has only a kind of negative canalizing effect in the sense that it indicates a way by which one may be sure of *not* being bound. On the positive side, the outlines of the channel are blurred because too many factors, including consideration, remain unassimilated into the form.

As a final and very obvious point of comparison between the forms of law and those of language, we may observe that in both fields the actual course of history is determined by a continuous process of compromise between those who wish to preserve the existing patterns and those who wish to rearrange them. Those who are responsible for what Ihering called "the legal alphabet—our judges, legislators, and textwriters—exercise a certain control over the usages of business, but there are times when they, like the lexicographer, must acquiesce in the innovations of the layman. The mere fact that the forms of law and language are set by a balance of opposing tensions does not, of course, insure the soundness of the developments which actually occur. If language sometimes loses valuable distinctions by being too tolerant, the law has lost valuable institutions, like the seal, by being too liberal in interpreting them. On the other hand, in law, as in language, forms have at times been allowed to crystallize to the point where needed innovation has been impeded.

§5. *Interrelations of the Three Functions.* Though I have stated the three functions of legal form separately, it is obvious that there is an intimate connection between them. Generally speaking, whatever tends to accomplish one of these purposes will also tend to accomplish the other two. He who is compelled to do something which will furnish a satisfactory memorial of his intention will be induced to deliberate. Conversely, devices which induce deliberation will usually have an evidentiary value. Devices which insure evidence or prevent inconsiderateness will normally advance the desideratum of channeling, in two different ways. In the first place, he who is compelled to formulate his intention carefully will tend to fit it into legal and business categories. In this way the party is induced to canalize his own intention. In the second place, wherever the requirement of a formality is backed by the sanction of the invalidity of the informal transaction (and this is the means by which requirements of form are normally made effective), a degree of channeling results automatically. Whatever may be its legislative motive, the formality in such a case tends to effect a categorization of transactions into legal and nonlegal.

Just as channeling may result unintentionally from formalities directed toward other ends, so these other ends tend to be satisfied by any device which accomplishes a channeling of expression. There is an evidentiary value in the clarity and definiteness of contour which such a device accomplishes. Anything which effects a neat division between the legal and the non-legal, or between different kinds of legal transactions, will tend also to make apparent to the party the consequences of his action and will suggest deliberation where deliberation is needed. Indeed, we may go further and say that some minimum satisfaction of the desideratum of channeling is necessary before measures designed to prevent inconsiderateness can be effective. This may be illustrated in the holographic will. The necessity of reducing the testator's intention to his own handwriting would seem superficially to offer, not only evidentiary safeguards, but excellent protection against inconsiderateness as well. Where the holographic will fails, however, is as a device for separating the legal wheat from the legally irrelevant chaff. The courts are frequently faced with the difficulty of determining whether a particular document—it may be an informal family letter which happens to be entirely in the handwriting of the sender—reveals the requisite "testamentary intention." This difficulty can only be eliminated by a formality which performs adequately the channeling function, by some external mark which will signalize the testament and distinguish it from non-testamentary expressions of intention. It is obvious that by a kind of reflex action the deficiency of the holographic will from the standpoint of channeling operates to impair its efficacy as a device for inducing deliberation.

§6. *When are Formalities Needed? The Effect of an Informal Satisfaction of the Desiderata Underlying the Use of Formalities.* The analysis of the functions of legal form which has just been presented is useful in answering a question which will assume importance in the later portion of this discussion when a detailed treatment of consideration is undertaken. That question is: In what situations does good legislative policy demand the use of a legal formality? One part of the answer to the question is clear at the outset. Forms must be reserved for relatively important transactions. We must preserve a proportion between means and end; it will scarcely do to require a sealed and witnessed document for the effective sale of a loaf of bread.

But assuming that the transaction in question is of sufficient importance to support the use of a form if a form is needed, how is the existence of this need to be determined? A general answer would run somewhat as follows: *The need for investing a particular transaction with some legal formality will depend upon the extent to which the guaranties that the formality would afford are rendered superfluous by forces native to the situation out of which the transaction arises*—including in these "forces" the habits and conceptions of the transacting parties.

Whether there is any need, for example, to set up a formality designed to induce deliberation will depend upon the degree to which the factual situation, innocent of any legal remolding, tends to bring about the desired circumspective frame of mind. An example from the law of gifts will make this point clear. To accomplish an effective gift of a chattel without resort to the use of documents, delivery of the chattel is ordinarily required and mere donative words are ineffective. It is thought, among other things, that mere words do not sufficiently impress on the donor the significance and seriousness of his act. In an Oregon case however, the donor declared his intention to give a sum of money to the donee and at the same time disclosed to the donee the secret hiding place where he had placed the money. Though the whole donative act consisted merely of words, the court held the gift to be effective. The words which gave access to the money which the donor had so carefully concealed would presumably be accompanied by the same sense of present deprivation which the act of handing over the money would have produced. The situation contained its own guaranty against inconsiderateness.

So far as the channeling function of a formality is concerned it has no place where men's activities are already divided into definite, clear-cut business categories. Where life has already organized itself effectively, there is no need for the law to intervene. It is for this reason that important transactions on the stock and produce markets can safely be carried on in the most "informal" manner. At the other extreme we may cite the negotiations between a house-to-house book salesman and the housewife. Here the situation may be such that the housewife is not certain whether she is being presented with a set of books as a gift, whether she is being asked to trade her letter of recommendation for the books, whether the books are being offered to her on approval, or whether—what is, alas, the fact—a simple sale of the books is being proposed. The ambiguity of the situation is, of course, carefully cultivated and exploited by the canvasser. Some "channeling" here would be highly desirable, though whether a legal form is the most practicable means of bringing it about is, of course, another question.

What has been said in this section demonstrates, I believe, that the problem of "form," when reduced to its underlying policies, extends not merely to "formal" transactions in the usual sense, but to the whole law of contracts and conveyances. Demogue has suggested that even the requirement, imposed in certain cases, that the intention of the parties be express, rather than implied or tacit, is in essence a requirement of form. If our object is to avoid giving sanction to inconsiderate engagements, surely the case for legal redress is stronger against the man who has spelled out his promise than it is against the man who has merely drifted into a situation where he appears to hold out an assurance for the future.

II. The Substantive Bases of Contract Liability

§7. *Private Autonomy.* Among the basic conceptions of contract law the most pervasive and indispensable is the principle of private autonomy. This principle simply means that the law views private individuals as possessing a power to effect, within certain limits, changes in their legal relations. The man who conveys property to another is exercising this power; so is the man who enters a contract. When a court enforces a promise it is merely arming with legal sanction a rule or *lex* previously established by the party himself.[9] This power of the individual to effect changes in his legal relations with others is comparable to the power of a legislature. It is, in fact, only a kind of political prejudice which causes us to use the word "law" in one case and not in the other, a prejudice which did not deter the Ro-

---

[9] What I have called "the principle of private autonomy" is more commonly assumed than discussed in the Anglo-American literature. See, however, Salmond, Jurisprudence (9th ed. 1937) § 23, heading Conventional law; and Vinogradoff, Common-sense In Law (1914) 101-115. The problem generally discussed in this country under the heading "freedom of contract" is the problem of the limits on private autonomy. Cf., Heck, Grundriss des Schuldrechts (1929) § 41.

Cohen's discussion of Contract and Sovereignty and Gardner's discussion of the Specialty Principle and Bargain Principle appear in effect to deal with the principle of private autonomy without using that term. See Cohen, The Basis of Contract (1933) 46 Harv. L. Rev. 553, 585-592; Gardner, An Inquiry into the Principles of the Law of Contracts (1932) 46 Harv. L. Rev. 1, 23, 25.

The principle of private autonomy has nothing to do with the ancient controversy whether the binding effect of a contract derives from "the law" or "the contract." Acceptance of it as a basis of contract liability in no way involves adherence to Marshall's view that "obligation is not conferred on contracts by positive law, but is intrinsic, and is conferred by the act of the parties." Ogden v. Saunders, 12 Wheat. 213, 345 (dissenting opinion) (U. S. 1827). As even Windscheid recognized, the problem is not where the obligation comes from, but why it it is imposed.

mans from applying the word *lex* to the norms established by private agreement.

What has just been stated is not presented as an original insight; the conception described is at least as old as the Twelve Tables. But there is need to reaffirm it, because the issue involved has been obfuscated through the introduction into the discussion of what is called "the will theory of contract." The obfuscation has come partly from the proponents of that theory, but mostly from those who have undertaken to refute it and who, in the process of refutation, have succeeded in throwing the baby out with the bath.

The principle of private autonomy may be translated into terms of the will theory by saying that this principle merely means that the will of the parties sets their legal relations. When the principle is stated in this way certain consequences may seem to follow from it: (1) that the law must concern itself solely with the actual inner intention of the promisor; (2) that the minds of the parties must "meet" at one instant of time before a contract can result; (3) that the law has no power to fill gaps in an agreement and is helpless to deal with contingencies unforseen by the parties; and even (4) that the promisor must be free to change his mind at any time, since it is his will which sets the rule. Since these consequences of the will theory are regarded as unacceptable, the theory is assumed to be refuted by the fact that it entails them.

If we recognize that the will theory is only a figurative way of expressing the principle of private autonomy, we see to what an extent this "refutation" of the will theory really obscures the issues involved. In our country a law-making power is vested in the legislature. This fact is frequently expressed by saying that the will of the legislature is the law. Yet from this hackneyed metaphor we do not feel compelled to draw a set of conclusions paralleling those listed above as deriving from the will theory of contract. Specifically, we do not seek the "actual, inner" intention of individual legislators; we do not insist, except in a very formal way, on proof that a majority of the legislators were actually of one mind at one instant of time; we do not hesitate to fill gaps in defective statutes; and, finally, we do not permit a majority of those who voted for a particular law to nullify it by a later informal declaration that they have changed their minds.

The principle of private autonomy, properly understood, is in no way inconsistent with an "objective" interpretation of contracts. Indeed, we may go farther and say that the so-called objective theory of interpretation in its more extreme applications becomes understandable only in terms of the principle of private autonomy. It has been suggested that in some cases the courts might properly give an interpretation to a written contract inconsistent with the actual understanding of either party.[11] What justification can there be for such a view? We answer, it rests upon the need for promoting the security of transactions. Yet security of transactions presupposes "transactions," in other words, acts of private parties which have a law-making and right-altering function. When we get outside the field of acts having this kind of function as their *raison d'etre*, for example, in the field of tort law, any such uncompromisingly "objective" method of interpreting an act would be incomprehensible.

A legitimate criticism of the principle of private autonomy may be that it is phrased too narrowly, and excludes by implication private heteronomy. If we look at the matter realistically, we see that men not only make private laws for themselves, but also for their fellows. I do not refer here simply to the frequent existence of a gross inequality of bargaining power between contracting parties, nor to the phenomenon of the standardized contract established by one party for a series of routine transactions. Even without excursion into the social reality behind juristic conceptions, a principle of private heteronomy is visible in legal theory itself, as, for example, where it is laid down as a rule of law that the servant is bound to obey the reasonable commands of his master. Here the employer, within the framework of the agreement and subject to judicial veto, is making a part of "the law" of the relation between himself and his employee.

§8. *What Matters Shall be Left to Private Autonomy?* From the fact that a principle of private autonomy is recognized it does not follow that this principle should be given an unlimited application. Law-making by individuals must be kept within its proper sphere, just as, under our constitutional system, law-making by legislatures is kept within its field of competence by the courts. What is the proper sphere of the rule of private autonomy?

In modern society the most familiar field of regu-

---

[11] 1 Williston, Contracts (rev. ed, 1936) § 95.

lation by private autonomy is that having to do with the exchange of goods and services. Paradoxically, it is when contract is performing this most important and pervasive of its functions that we are least apt to conceive of it as a kind of private legislation. If A and B sign articles of partnership we have little difficulty in seeing the analogy between their act and that of a legislature. But if A contracts to buy a ton of coal from B for eight dollars, it seems absurd to conceive of this act as species of private law-making. This is only because we have come to view the distribution of goods through private contract as a part of the order of nature, and we forget that it is only one of several possible ways of accomplishing the same general objective. Coal does not have to be bought and sold; it can be distributed by the decrees of a dictator, or of an elected rationing board. When we allow it to be bought and sold by private agreement, we are, within certain limits, allowing individuals to set their own legal relations with regard to coal.[12]

The principle of private autonomy is not, however, confined to contracts of exchange, and historically it perhaps found its first applications outside the relationship of barter or trade. As modern instances of the exercise of private autonomy outside the field of exchange we may cite gratuitous promises under seal, articles of partnership, and collective labor agreements. In all these cases there may be an element of exchange in the background, just as the whole of society is permeated by a principle of reciprocity. But the fact remains that these transactions do not have as their immediate objective the accomplishment of an exchange of values.

When the principle of private autonomy is extended beyond exchange, where does it stop? The answer to this question is by no means simple, even if it be attempted in terms of some particular system of positive law. I shall not attempt to give such an answer here. One question must, however, be faced. When the principle of private autonomy is extended beyond exchange, can it legitimately be referred to as a "substantive basis of contract liability"? When we say that the contracting parties set the law of their relationship are we not giving a juristic construction of their act rather than a substantive reason for judicial intervention to enforce their agreement? It must

be admitted that in one aspect the principle of private autonomy is a theory of enforcement rather than a reason for enforcement. But in another aspect the principle always implies at least one broad substantive reason for enforcement, which is identical with that underlying government generally. Though occasional philosophers may seem to dispute the proposition, most of us are willing to concede that some kind of regulation of men's relations among themselves is necessary. It is this general desideratum which underlies the principle of private autonomy. Whenever we can reinforce this general need for regulation by a showing that in the particular case private agreement is the best or the only available method of regulation, then in such a case "the principle of private autonomy" may properly be referred to as a "substantive" basis of contract liability.

§9. *Reliance.* A second substantive basis of contract liability lies in a recognition that the breach of a promise may work an injury to one who has changed his position in reliance on the expectation that the promise would be fulfilled. Reliance as a basis of contract liability must not be identified with reliance as a measure of the promisee's recovery. Where the object of the court is to reimburse detrimental reliance, it may measure the loss occasioned through reliance either directly (by looking to see what the promisee actually expended in reliance on the promise), or contractually (by looking to the value of the promised performance out of which the promisee presumably expected to recoup his losses through reliance). If the court's sole object is to reimburse the losses resulting from reliance, it may be expected to prefer the direct measure where that measure may be applied conveniently. But there are various reasons, too complicated for discussion here, why a court may find that measure unworkable and hence prefer the contractual measure, even though its sole object remains that of reimbursing reliance.[15]

What is the relation between reliance and the principle of private autonomy? Occasionally reliance may appear as a distinct basis of liability, excluding the necessity for any resort to the notion of private autonomy. An illustration may be found in some of the cases coming under Section 90 of the Restatement of Contracts. In these cases we are not "uphold-

---

[12] "Bargain is then the social and legal machinery appropriate to arranging affairs in any specialized economy which relies on exchange rather than tradition (the manor) or authority (the army, the U. S. S. R.) for apportionment of productive energy and or product." Llewellyn, What Price Contract? (1931) 40 Yale L. J. 704, 717.

[15] See Fuller and Perdue, The Reliance Interest in Contract Damages (1936-1937) 46 Yale L.J. 52, 66-67 and passim.

ing transactions" but healing losses caused through broken faith. In another class of cases the principle of reimbursing reliance comes into conflict with the principle of private autonomy. These are the cases where a promisee has seriously and, according to ordinary standards of conduct, justifiably relied on a promise which the promisor expressly stipulated should impose no legal liability on him.[16] In still other cases, reliance appears not as an independent or competing basis of liability but as a ground supplementing and reinforcing the principle of private autonomy. For example, while it remains executory, a particular agreement may be regarded as too vague to be enforced; until it has been acted on, such an agreement may be treated as a defective exercise of the power of private autonomy. After reliance, however, the court may be willing to incur the hazards involved in enforcing an indefinite agreement where this is necessary to prevent serious loss to the relying party. The same effect of reliance as reinforcing the principle of private autonomy may be seen in much of the law of waiver. Finally, in some branches of contract law reliance and the principle of private autonomy appear not as reinforcing one another so as to justify judicial intervention where neither alone would be sufficient, but as alternative and independently sufficient bases for imposing liability in the same case. This is perhaps the situation in those cases where the likelihood that reliance will occur influences the court to impose liability on the promisor.[18] On the one hand, we may say that the likelihood of reliance demonstrates that the parties themselves viewed their transaction as an exercise of private autonomy, that they considered that it set their rights and were prepared to act accordingly. On this view, the law simply acquiesces in the parties' conception that their transaction determined their legal relations. On the other hand, we may say that the likelihood that reliance will occur is a sufficient reason for dispensing with proof that it occurred in fact, since where reliance takes negative and intangible forms it may be difficult to prove. On this theory enforcement of the promise is viewed either as protecting an actual reliance which has proba-

bly occurred, or as a kind of prophylactic measure against losses through reliance which will be difficult to prove if they occur.

§10. *Unjust Enrichment.* In return for B's promise to give him a bicycle, A pays B five dollars; B breaks his promise. We may regard this as a case where the injustice resulting from breach of a promise relied on by the promisee is aggravated. The injustice is aggravated because not only has A lost five dollars but B has gained five dollars unjustly. If, following Aristotle, we conceive of justice as being concerned with maintaining a proper proportion of goods among members of society, we may reduce the relations involved to mathematical terms. Suppose A and B have each initially ten units of goods. The relation between them is then one of equivalence, 10:10. A loses five of his units in reliance on a promise by B which B breaks. The resulting relation is 5:10. If, however, A paid these five units over to B, the resulting relation would be 5:15.[20] This comparison shows why unjust enrichment resulting from breach of contract presents a more urgent case for judicial intervention than does mere loss through reliance not resulting in unjust enrichment.

Since unjust enrichment is simply an aggravated case of loss through reliance, all of what was said in the last section is applicable here. When the problem is the quantum of recovery, unjust enrichment may be measured either directly, (by the value of what the promisor received), or contractually, (by the value of the promised equivalent). So too, the prevention of unjust enrichment may sometimes appear openly as a distinct ground of liability (as in suits for restitution for breach of an oral promise "unenforceable" under the Statute of Frauds), and at other times may appear as a basis of liability supplementing and reinforcing the principle of private autonomy (as where the notion of waiver is applied "to prevent forfeiture," and in cases where the inference of a tacit promise of compensation is explained by the court's desire to prevent unjust enrichment).

§11. *Substantive Deterrents to Legal Intervention to Enforce Promises.* I have spoken of "the substan-

---

[16] In a number of recent cases of this sort, involving promises of bonuses to employees, recovery has been permitted. In these cases the principle of reimbursing reliance is regarded as overriding the principle of private autonomy....

[18] Though there are few decisions where the likelihood of reliance is explicitly made a ground for decision, there is reason to suppose that this factor is a potent influence in shaping the law of contracts. See Fuller and Perdue, The Reliance Interest in Contract Damages (1936-1937) 46 Yale L. J. 52, 60-61. Cf. Rutgers v. Lucet, 2 Johns. 92, 95 (N. Y.

1800): "The confidence placed in him [the promisor], and his undertaking to execute the trust, raise a sufficient consideration." The factor of likely reliance may explain why the rejection of an offer, without proof of actual reliance thereon by the offeror, terminates the power of acceptance, and perhaps affords a clue to the rules laid down in connection with the problem of election between inconsistent remedies.

[20] Cf., Aristotle, Nicomachean Ethics, 1132a-1132b.

tive bases of contract liability." It should be noted that the enforcement of promises entails certain costs which constitute substantive objections to the imposition of contract liability. The first of these costs is the obvious one involved in the social effort expended in the legal procedure necessary to enforcement. Enforcement involves, however, another less tangible and more important cost. There is a real need for a field of human intercourse freed from legal restraints, for a field where men may without liability withdraw assurances they have once given. Every time a new type of promise is made enforceable, we reduce the area of this field. The need for a domain of "free-remaining" relations is not merely spiritual. Business deals can often emerge only from a converging series of negotiations, in which each step contains enough assurance to make worthwhile a further exchange of views and yet remains flexible enough to permit a radical readjustment to new situations. To surround with rigid legal sanctions even the first exploratory expressions of intention would not only introduce an unpleasant atmosphere into business negotiations, but would actually hamper commerce. The needs of commerce in this respect are suggested by the fact that in Germany, where the code makes offers binding without consideration, it has become routine to stipulate for a power of revocation.

§12. *The Relation of Form to the Substantive Bases of Contract Liability*. Form has an obvious relationship to the principle of private autonomy. Where men make laws for themselves it is desirable that they should do so under conditions guaranteeing the desiderata described in our analysis of the functions of form. Furthermore, the greater the assurance that these desiderata are satisfied, the larger the scope we may be willing to ascribe to private autonomy. A constitution might permit a legislature to pass laws relating to certain specified subjects in an informal manner, but prescribe a more formal procedure for "extraordinary" enactments, by requiring, for example, successive readings of the bill before it was put to a vote. So, in the law of contracts, we may trust men in the situation of exchange to set their rights with relative informality. Where they go outside the field of exchange, we may require a seal, or appearance before a notary, for the validity of their promises.

When we inquire into the relevance of form to liability founded on reliance or unjust enrichment, it becomes necessary to discriminate between the three functions of form. As to the desiderata implied in the evidentiary and cautionary functions it is clear that

they do not lose their significance simply because the basis of liability has shifted. Even in the law of torts we are concerned with the adequacy of the proof of what occurred in fact, and (sometimes, at least) with the degree of deliberation with which the defendant acted. It is true that in the law of torts these considerations are not usually effectuated in the same way that they are in contract law. This is due to the fact that the channeling function of form becomes, in this field, largely irrelevant, for this function is intimately connected with the principle of private autonomy and loses its significance in fields where that principle has no application. To the extent then, that the basis of promissory liability shifts from the principle of private autonomy to the reimbursement of reliance or the prevention of unjust enrichment, to that extent does the relevance of the channeling function of form decrease. This function loses its relevance altogether at that indefinite point at which it ceases to be appropriate to refer to the acts upon which liability is predicated as a "transaction."

III. The Policies, "Formal" and "Substantive," Underlying The Common-Law Requirement of Consideration

§13. *Reasons for Refusing to Enforce the Gratuitous and Unrelied- on Promise*. A promises to give B $100; B has in no way changed his position in reliance on this promise, and he has neither given nor promised anything in return for it. In such a situation enforcement of the promise is denied both in the common law and in the civil law. We give as our reason, "lack of consideration"; the civilians point to a failure to comply with statutory formalities. In neither case, of course, does the reason assigned explain the policies which justify excluding this promise from enforcement. An explanation in terms of underlying policies can, however, be worked out on the basis of the analysis just completed.

Looking at the case from the standpoint of the substantive bases of contractual liability we observe, first of all, that there is here neither reliance nor unjust enrichment. Furthermore, gratuities such as this one do not present an especially pressing case for the application of the principle of private autonomy, particularly if we bear in mind the substantive deterrents to judicial intervention. While an exchange of goods is a transaction which conduces to the production of wealth and the division of labor, a gift is, in Bufnoir's words, a "sterile transmission." If on "substantive" grounds the balance already inclines away from judicial intervention, the case against enforcement becomes stronger when we draw into account the desiderata underlying the use of formalities. That there is in the instant case a lack of evidentiary and cautionary safeguards is obvious. As to the channeling function of form, we may observe that the promise is made in a field where intention is not naturally canalized. There is nothing here to effect a neat division between tentative and exploratory expressions of intention, on the one hand, and legally effective transactions, on the other. In contrast to the situation of the immediate gift of a chattel (where title will pass by the manual tradition), there is here no "natural formality" on which the courts might seize as a test of enforceability.

§14. *The Contractual Archetype—The Half-Completed Exchange.* A delivers a horse to B in return for B's promise to pay him ten dollars; B defaults on his promise, and A sues for the agreed price. In this case are united all of the factors we have previously analyzed as tending in the direction of enforcement of a promise. On the substantive side, there is reliance by A and unjust enrichment of B. The transaction involves an exchange of economic values, and falls therefore in a field appropriately left to private autonomy in an economy where no other provision is made for the circulation of goods and the division of labor, or where (as perhaps in primitive society) an expanding economy makes the existing provision for those ends seem inadequate. On the side of form, the delivery and acceptance of the horse involve a kind of natural formality, which satisfies the evidentiary, cautionary, and channeling purposes of legal formalities.

Describing this situation as "the contractual archetype," we may take it as our point of departure, dealing with other cases in terms of the degree of their deviation from it. Naturally, all kinds of nuances are here possible, and some minor departures from the pattern were the occasion for dispute in the early history of the action of debt. We are concerned here, however, chiefly with two major deviations from the archetype: the situation of the executory exchange, and the situation of reliance without exchange.

§15. *The Wholly Executory Exchange.* B promises to build a house for A, and A, in return, promises to pay B $5,000 on the completion of the house. B defaults on his promise, and A, without having had occasion to pay anything on the contract, sues B for damages. Judicial intervention in this kind of case ap-

parently began in England toward the end of the sixteenth century. This development we describe by saying that after *Strangborough v. Warner*[25] and related cases the bilateral contract as such became for the first time enforceable. It is now generally assumed that so far as consideration is concerned the executory bilateral contract is on a complete parity with the situation where the plaintiff has already paid the price of the defendant's promised performance. Yet if we examine the executory bilateral contract in terms of the policies underlying consideration, it will become apparent that this assumption is unjustified, and that Lord Holt in reality overshot the mark in his assertion that "where the doing a thing will be a good consideration, a promise to do that thing will be so too."[26]

Where a bilateral contract remains wholly executory the arguments for judicial intervention have been considerably diminished in comparison with the situation of the half-completed exchange. There is here no unjust enrichment. Reliance may or may not exist, but in any event will not be so tangible and direct as where it consists in the rendition of the price of the defendant's performance. On the side of form, we have lost the natural formality involved in the turning over of property or the rendition and acceptance of services. There remains simply the fact that the transaction is an exchange and not a gift. This fact alone does offer some guaranty so far as the cautionary and channeling functions of form are concerned, though, except as the Statute of Frauds interposes to supply the deficiency, evidentiary safeguards are largely lacking. This lessening of the factors arguing for enforcement not only helps to explain why liability in this situation was late in developing, but also explains why even today the executory bilateral contract cannot be put on complete parity with the situation of the half-completed exchange.

In the situation of the half-completed exchange, the element of exchange is only one factor tending toward enforcement. Since that element is there reinforced by reliance, unjust enrichment, and the natural formality involved in the surrender and acceptance of a tangible benefit, it is unnecessary to analyze the concept of exchange closely, and it may properly be left vague. In the executory bilateral contract, on the other hand, the element of exchange

[25] 4 Leo. 3, 74 Eng. Rep. 686 (K.B. 1589).
[26] Thorp v. Thorp, 12 Mod. 455, 459, 88 Eng. Rep. 1448, 1450 (K.B. 1702).

stands largely alone[28] as a basis of liability and its definition becomes crucial. Various definitions are possible. We may define exchange vaguely as a transaction from which each participant derives a benefit, or, more restrictively, as a transaction in which the motives of the parties are primarily economic rather than sentimental. Following Adam Smith, we may say that it is a transaction which, directly or indirectly, conduces to the division of labor. Or we may take Demogue's notion that the most important characteristic of exchange is that it is a situation in which the interests of the transacting parties are opposed, so that the social utility of the contract is guaranteed in some degree by the fact that it emerges as a compromise of those conflicting interests. The problem of choosing among these varying conceptions may seem remote and unimportant, yet it underlines some of the most familiar problems of contract law. For example, suppose a nephew promises his uncle that he will not smoke until he is twenty-one, and the uncle promises him $5,000 as a reward if he will keep his promise. Where the nephew sues after having earned the reward by following the prescribed line of conduct recovery has been permitted.[30] But would such an agreement be enforced as an executory bilateral contract? Could the uncle, for example, sue the nephew for smoking a cigarette? In answering this question it is at once apparent that we are faced with the necessity of defining the particular kind of exchange which is essential to the enforcement of a bilateral contract. A similar problem underlies many of the cases involving "illusory promises."

Like consideration, exchange is a complex concept. To the problem of the executory exchange we may, within a narrower compass, apply the same general approach that we have applied to the problem of consideration as a whole. Here our "archetype" is the business trade of economic values in the form of goods, services, or money. To the degree that a particular case deviates from this archetype, the incentives to judicial intervention decrease, until a point is reached where relief will be denied altogether unless the attenuated element of exchange is reinforced, either on the formal side by some formal or informal satisfaction of the desiderata underlying the use of legal formalities, or on the substantive side by a showing of reliance or unjust enrichment, or of some special need for a regulation of the relations involved by private autonomy.

§16. *Transactions Ancillary to Exchanges.* There are various transactions which, though they are not themselves immediately directed toward accomplishing an exchange, are necessary preliminary steps toward exchanges, or are ancillary to exchanges in process of realization. Among these we may mention offers, promises of unpaid sureties, and what Llewellyn has described as "going transaction adjustments" such as are involved in unilateral concessions or promises of extra compensation granted during performance of a bilateral contract.

. . .

How far legal sanction ought to be extended to these transactions bordering on and surrounding exchanges is a legislative question which cannot be discussed here, though it may be observed that it is precisely in this field that the greatest difference between the common law and the civil law exists. Probably our own law is in need of some reform. The written promise of a surety who guarantees the performance of one party to an exchange, for example, probably ought to be made enforceable without consideration. As to offers, the problem is more difficult, and probably some distinction between kinds of offers is in order.

. . .

§18. *Nominal Consideration.* It has been held that a promise to make a gift may be made binding through the payment of a "nominal" consideration, such as a dollar or a cent. The proper ground for upholding these decisions would seem to be that the desiderata underlying the use of formalities are here satisfied by the fact that the parties have taken the trouble to cast their transaction in the form of an exchange. The promise supported by nominal consideration then becomes enforceable for reasons similar to those which justify the enforcement of the promise under seal. . . .

. . .

§20. *Moral Obligation as Consideration.* Courts have frequently enforced promises on the simple ground that the promisor was only promising to do what he ought to have done anyway. These cases have either been condemned as wanton departures from

---

[28] I say "largely alone" because there is always the possibility that the court will be influenced by actual reliance on the bargain or by the probability that reliance has taken place or will occur.

[30] Hamer v. Sidway, 124 N.Y. 538, 27 N.E. 256 (1891); Lindell v. Rokes, 60 Mo. 249 (1875); Talbott v. Stemmons, 89 Ky. 222 (1889).

legal principle, or reluctantly accepted as involving the kind of compromise logic must inevitably make at times with sentiment. I believe that these decisions are capable of rational defense. When we say the defendant was morally obligated to do the thing he promised, we in effect assert the existence of a substantive ground for enforcing the promise. In a broad sense, a similar line of reasoning justifies the special status accorded by the law to contracts of exchange. Men *ought* to exchange goods and services; therefore when they enter contracts to that end, we enforce those contracts. On the side of form, concern for formal guaranties justifiably diminishes where the promise is backed by a moral obligation to do the thing promised. What does it matter that the promisor may have acted without great deliberation, since he is only promising to do what he should have done without a promise? For the same reason, can we not justifiably overlook some degree of evidentiary insecurity?

In refutation of the notion of "moral consideration" it is sometimes said that a moral obligation plus a mere promise to perform that obligation can no more create legal liability than zero plus zero can have any other sum than zero. But a mathematical analogy at least equally appropriate is the proposition that one-half plus one-half equals one. The court's conviction that the promisor ought to do the thing, plus the promisor's own admission of his obligation, may tilt the scales in favor of enforcement where neither standing alone would be sufficient. If it be argued that moral consideration threatens certainty, the solution would seem to lie, not in rejecting the doctrine, but in taming it by continuing the process of judicial exclusion and inclusion already begun in the cases involving infants' contracts, barred debts, and discharged bankrupts.

§21. *Performance of Legal Duty as Consideration.* The analysis presented in this article is not sufficient for a comprehension of the factors underlying all the situations where courts have talked about "consideration." For example, cases where courts have said that illegal agreements are void for lack of consideration (since the law must close its eyes to an illegal consideration) obviously involve policies going beyond those analyzed in this paper. It is for a similar reason that I have not drawn into the discussion cases laying down the rule that the performance of a legal duty cannot be consideration. These cases involve factors extrinsic to the problems under discussion here. Among those factors are the effects of improper co-

ercion, and the need for preserving the morale of professions, like that of policeman, jockey, and sailor, which involve activities impinging directly on the interests of others. These cases touch the present discussion only in the sense that there is some relation between coercion and the desiderata underlying the use of formalities; whatever tends to guarantee deliberateness in the making of a promise tends in some degree to protect against the milder forms of coercion.

§22. *The Future of Form.* Despite an alleged modern tendency toward "informality," there is little reason to believe that the problem of form will disappear in the future. The desiderata underlying the use of formalities will retain their relevance as long as men make promises to one another. Doubt may legitimately be raised, however, whether there will be any place in the future for what may be called the "blanket formality," the formality which, like the seal, suffices to make any kind of promise, not immoral or illegal, enforceable. It is not that there is no need for such a device. The question is whether with our present-day routinized and institutionalized ways of doing business a "blanket formality" can achieve the desiderata which form is intended to achieve. The net effect of a reform like the Uniform Written Obligations Act, for example, will probably be to add a line or two to unread printed forms and increased embarrassment to the task of judges seeking a way to let a man off from an oppressive bargain without seeming to repudiate the prevailing philosophy of free contract. Under modern conditions perhaps the only devices which would be really effective in achieving the formal desiderata would be that of a nominal consideration actually handed over, or a requirement that the promise be entirely in the handwriting of the promisor. As the holographic will shows, even the second of these devices would be inadequate from the standpoint of the "channeling" function.

§23. *The Future of Consideration.* The future of consideration is tied up to a considerable extent with the future of the principle of private autonomy. If the development of our society continues along the lines it is now following, we may expect, I believe, that private contract as an instrument of exchange will decrease in importance. On the other hand, with an increasing interdependence among the members of society we may expect to see reliance (unbargained-for, or half-bargained-for) become increasingly important as a basis of liability. We may also see an expansion of the principle of private (or semi-private) autonomy to fields outside that of exchange. We get some hint of this second development in the expanding importance of the collective labor agreement. It appears also in the increasing use by business of revocable dealer and distributor agencies, and standing offers, devices which have their *raison d'etre* in furnishing a kind of frame-work or private constitution for future dealings. These changes in business practice will inevitably bring with them in time modifications of the doctrine of consideration. For example, the relationship involved in dealer and jobber agencies is one which calls increasingly for some kind of judicial regulation to prevent hardship and oppression. If the assumption that this relationship is "contractual" coupled with existing definitions of consideration operates to exclude judicial intervention, then legal doctrine should be modified so as to permit bringing this relationship within the control of the law.

It has sometimes been proposed that the doctrine of consideration be "abolished." Such a step would, I believe, be unwise, and in a broad sense even impossible. The *problems* which the doctrine of consideration attempts to solve cannot be abolished. There can be little question that some of these problems do not receive a proper solution in the complex of legal doctrine now grouped under the rubric "consideration." It is equally clear that an original attack on these problems would arrive at some conclusions substantially equivalent to those which result from the doctrine of consideration as now formulated. What needs abolition is not the doctrine of consideration but a conception of legal method which assumes that the doctrine can be understood and applied without reference to the ends it serves. When we have come again to define consideration in terms of its underlying policies the problem of adapting it to new conditions will largely solve itself.

Richard Posner on Promises of Gifts

A perennial problem of the first-year Contracts course is the gift (or donative) promise, which Fuller discussed briefly in *Consideration and Form*. Here we read the analysis of Judge Richard Posner of the United States Court of Appeals for the Seventh Circuit. Before being appointed to the Seventh Circuit Judge Posner taught for many years at the University of Chicago Law School, where he was the most famous member of the "Chicago School" of law and economics. (See the note on *Economic Rationales of Contract* in Part IB, above.)

Although Posner has often been criticized for concealing conservative political values under a veneer of allegedly neutral "positive" or descriptive economic reasoning, this article is not always predictable. Even when he agrees with other analyses, Posner gives a very different rationale. Compare, for example, his disagreement with Fuller over the *reason* why promises for benefits conferred in the past should be enforced. Another valuable article on the topic is Melvin A. Eisenberg's *Donative Promises*, 47 U. Chi. L. Rev. 1 (1970).

Richard A. Posner, *Gratuitous Promises in Economics and Law*, 6 J. Leg. Studies 411 (1977)

The economist tends to think of the making and enforcement of contracts as part of the process by which goods or services are shifted from less to more valuable uses—that is, as part of the process of exchange. The counterpart in (Anglo-American) law to the economist's emphasis on exchange is the principle that promises are not enforceable unless supported by "consideration." This means, roughly speaking, that a promise will not create an enforceable contract unless it is made in exchange for something of value—goods, money, another promise, or whatever. There are, however, a number of exceptions to this principle—cases where a "gratuitous" promise, i.e., one not supported by consideration, does create an enforceable contract. This paper examines those exceptions from the standpoint of economics. For reasons that will appear, a major exception—the promise that reasonably but unintentionally induces reliance by the promisee—is not a focus of inquiry.

The so-called gratuitous promise creates two questions from an economic standpoint. These are discussed together in Part I. The first question is why such promises are ever made by rational economic actors. The second is when, from an economic standpoint, they should be legally enforceable. The answer to the second question should reveal whether the law in this respect follows economics, as has been found in other studies of law in general and contract law in particular.

I. The Economics Of "Gratuitous" Promises

Why would "economic man" ever make a promise without receiving in exchange something of value from the promisee, whether it be money, a promise of future performance beneficial to the promisor, or something else of value to him? It is tempting to answer this question simply by invoking "interdependent utilities." Since people may indeed derive utility or welfare from increases in the utility or welfare of family members, or for that matter of strangers, interdependence may explain why (some) gifts or transfers are made. But it cannot explain why a *promise* to make a transfer in the future is made. Promises, as distinct from transfers, seem related to situations of bilateral performance, of exchange. A promises B $25,000 in exchange for B's building a house for A. B will not build without a promise of payment in advance; A will not pay in advance without B's promise to build. But if A wanted merely to transfer $25,000 to B (his favorite charity), why would he promise B to make the transfer in the future? Why not wait until he is ready to make the transfer and just do it? The purpose of a promise seems to be to induce performance of some sort by the promisee; if reciprocal performance is not desired, there seems no reason to make a promise.

The approach taken here is that a gratuitous promise, to the extent it actually commits the promisor to the promised course of action (an essential qualification), creates utility for the promisor over and above the utility to him of the promised performance. At one level this proposition is a tautology: a promise would not be made unless it conferred utility on the promisor. The interesting question is how it does so. I shall argue that it does so by increasing the present value of an uncertain future stream of transfer payments.

To illustrate, suppose A promises to give $1000 a year for the next 20 years to the B symphony orchestra. The value of the gift to B is the discounted present value of $1000 to be paid yearly over a 20-year period in the future. Among the factors that will be used by B in discounting these expected future receipts to present value is the likelihood that at some time during the 20-year period A will discontinue the annual payments. Depending on B's estimation of A's fickleness, income prospects, etc., the present value of the gift of $1000 a year may be quite small; it may not be much more than $1000. But suppose the gift is actually worth more to B because A is certain to continue the payments throughout the entire period, though this fact is not known to B. If A can make a binding promise to continue the payments in accordance with his intention, B will revalue the gift at its true present worth. The size of the gift (in present-value terms) will be increased at no cost to A. Here is a clear case where the enforcement of a gratuitous promise would increase net social welfare.

This can be seen even more clearly by considering A's alternatives if his promise is not enforceable. One possibility would be for A to promise a larger gift, the discounted value of which to B would equal the true value as known to A. The higher cost of the gift to A would be a measure of the social cost of the unenforceability of his promise. Another possibility would be for A to substitute for the promised series of future transfers a one-time transfer the present value of which would be the same as that of the series of enforceable future transfers. However, the fact that A preferred making a future gift to a present one suggests that they are not perfect substitutes; there are many reasons (including tax and liquidity considerations) why they might not be. Consequently, if A cannot bind himself to make a series of future gifts, he may be led to substitute a one-time transfer, the present value of which is less than that of the series of future gifts, although greater than that of a declared but unenforceable intention to make a series of future gifts.[4] Thus, nonenforceability of gratuitous

---

[4] Compare William M. Landes & Richard A. Posner, The Independent Judiciary in an Interest-Group Perspective, 18 J. Law & Econ. 875 (1975), who argue that the inability of Congress legally to bind future Congresses to honor commitments to interest groups reduces the "price" at which Congress can "sell" prospective legislation to such groups.

promises could tend to bias transfers excessively toward immediacy.

The above analysis rests on the assumption of asymmetry of information between promisor and promisee. Such an assumption may seem implausible: why would not the asymmetry be corrected by a simple communication from A to B, which would make both parties better off? However, because the relevant information concerns A's subjective intentions, the asymmetry is both plausible and difficult to eliminate. A can state his true intentions to B, but how is he to convince B that the statement is correct? One way of making his statement credible is for A to make it costly for himself to lie; embodying the statement in a promise that is legally enforceable does this.

Dispelling uncertainty is not the only function served by making a gratuitous promise binding. Suppose that A really is fickle and B assesses his fickleness accurately. There is then no asymmetry in the information possessed by the parties. But A may still want to make a gift having a present value that is larger than it would be if B's future receipts had to be discounted by the probability that A would actually make each payment when the time came to do so. A will balance the utility to him of making a larger (in present-value terms) gift now against the disutility of losing the freedom to change his mind in the future. He may decide that the utility of the larger gift now is greater, in which event it will be in his self-interest to make a promise that commits him irrevocably. Once again, enforcement of a gratuitous promise will lead to a net increase in social welfare.

The economic case for enforcing the gratuitous promise, it should be noted, is similar to that for enforcing bilateral promises. The failure to enforce bilateral promises would bias exchanges toward those that take place instantaneously, as distinct from those that are completed only over a period of time, even though the former may often be less valuable (as in our examples), or more costly, than the deferred exchange. But the symmetry between gratuitous and bilateral promises has been obscured in conventional legal analysis by a tendency to view a promise as a pure cost to the promisor, a limitation on his freedom of action and nothing more. Under this analysis, if the promisor receives nothing from the promisee in return—if, that is; the promise is unsupported by consideration in the conventional sense—the promise confers no benefit on the promisor and there is therefore no social cost in allowing him to break the promise, at least in the absence of any detrimental reliance by the promisee. For example, A might promise to give B $100 in two weeks. At the end of the two weeks, A changes his mind and decides to keep the $100. His change of mind makes B worse off but A better off; thus there is no basis, in the absence of detrimental reliance by B (e.g. B's taking some time off from work in reliance on receiving the $100), for thinking that A's change of mind has reduced the wealth of the society. But this analysis ignores the fact that being legally bound to make an intended transfer may enhance ex ante the value of the transfer to A and thereby increase the social product, just as in the case of bilateral promises.

One may doubt in light of the foregoing analysis whether the term "gratuitous" promise is useful or even meaningful. To make a binding promise may, as we have seen, be rational maximizing behavior even in the absence of consideration flowing from the promisee. The source of the benefit to the promisor would seem a detail from the standpoint of whether particular promises should be enforced by the law.

II. Optimal Rules For Enforcing "Gratuitous" Promises

The analysis in Part I may seem to imply that all promises, whether compensated or "gratuitous," should be enforced; or at least that enforceability should not depend on whether the promise is one or the other. The second implication has, as we shall see, appeal; but the first is questionable because it ignores the costs to the legal system of enforcing promises. The design of optimal rules of substantive law must always take into account the costs of enforcement. Promises should not be enforced where the enforcement cost—to the extent not borne by the promisor—exceeds the gain from enforcement. The qualification is, of course, essential: if the promisor bore the full costs of enforcement, it would be a matter of indifference to society whether he chose to make enforceable a promise that seemed to confer on him but trivial utility relative to enforcement costs. But it is in fact unlikely—quite apart from the public subsidy of the court system—that such a promisor would bear those costs fully: if he reneged on his promise, and the promisee brought suit against him, the promisor would not be required to defray the promisee's costs of suit. Another category of enforcement costs that are not fully internalized consists of the costs of legal error. Here the focus is not on the promisor but on the mistaken or dishonest "promisee" who imposes on his "promisor" the costs of defending a groundless suit, at the same time incurring litigation costs of his own which have no social value either.

The question whether it is economical for society

to recognize a promise as legally enforceable thus requires a comparison of the utility of the promise to the promisor with the social cost of enforcing the promise.[7] The utility of a "gratuitous" promise (a term I shall continue to use for the sake of convenience) would seem to depend primarily on (1) the size of the promised transfer and (2) the optimal length of the period for completing the transfer (the longer the period, the greater will be the loss of utility from having to substitute an immediate transfer if the promise is not enforceable). The social costs of enforcing the promise depend first of all on the administrative costs of enforcement. These in turn are a function in part of the size of the promised transfer, for expenditures on litigation are an investment in its outcome and therefore tend to be larger, the greater the stakes in the litigation. The social costs of enforcement also depend on the likelihood of an error—e.g., of finding a promise where none in fact was made.

Because the size of the promised transfer appears on both sides of the cost-benefit equation, it is difficult to specify with any confidence the effect of size on the net social gain from enforcement. This issue is pursued in the appendix to this article, where I conclude that the effect is probably positive—i.e., that the case for legal enforcement of gratuitous promises will generally be stronger the larger the promised transfer. In any event, that assumption is employed in the balance of the article.

The criteria developed above should probably be applied to *categories* of promises, rather than to individual promises on a case-by-case basis. Great (and costly!) uncertainty would be created if a gratuitous promisor, in order to know whether his promise was enforceable, would have to predict how a court would apply the criteria directly to the circumstances in which the promise was made.

III. The Approach of the Courts in the Light of Economic Analysis

My purpose in developing optimal criteria of when to enforce gratuitous promises is not to tell judges what to do but to set the stage for another test of the theory that the law, especially the judge-made law and specifically contract law, has been shaped by a concern with achieving efficiency. If the courts in gratuitous-promise cases have reached results generally congruent with the prescriptions of economic analysis, that is some evidence in support of the theory.

The most important class of cases in which promises not supported by consideration are nonetheless enforced consists of those where enforcement is based on detrimental reliance by the promisee. But these cases are properly analyzed in terms different from those developed in this paper. Many of the promises in such cases are in no sense "gratuitous." For example, A might promise B $100 if B would stop smoking. The promise here is *in exchange* for something (perhaps mysteriously) of value to A, namely B's forbearance to smoke. This is bargained reliance and so readily assimilable to the bilateral promise. The exchange element is absent, however, where, for example, A promises B an annuity and in reliance on this promise B gives up his job, incurring costs, though A had no desire or intention that B should give up his job. If B's reliance was reasonable, the promise will be enforced—even though A derived no benefit from B's action and there was, indeed, no genuine element of exchange—in order to deter a form of carelessness (inefficiency) which consists of unjustifiably inducing costly reliance. The rationale for enforcement here is essentially a tort rationale. It makes economic sense but is distinct from the rationale developed in this paper for enforcing (some) gratuitous promises.

A. *General Rule of Nonenforceability*

The general rule is that gratuitous promises are not enforceable. A good example of the rule and its economic logic would be a case where a man promised to take a woman to dinner but later reneged. The man presumably derived some utility from making the promise, and his utility might be greater if the promise were legally binding on him. But the increment in utility, if any, is probably small, both compared to that of the dinner itself and absolutely given the small size of the promised transfer. Moreover, the legal-error costs of enforcing such promises would be high because of the difficulty of distinguishing in casual social relations between a mere present intention, subject to change at will, and a promise intended to be binding on the promisor.

An additional factor reinforces the conclusion that it would be uneconomical to enforce such promises. The administrative costs of enforcement in such a case, while not high in absolute terms, are so high relative to the stakes that legal enforcement would be attempted only rarely. The man in our example would derive only a negligible increment in utility from be-

[7] This type of approach is hinted at in Lon L. Fuller, Consideration and Form, 41 Colum. L. Rev. 799, 815 (1941).

ing able to make a legally binding promise because the woman would know that he knew that in the event he reneged she would not sue. The binding character of the promise would be illusory, and the benefits from its formal status as a binding promise therefore few. But the costs of enforcement would not be negligible.

A moment's reflection will suggest, however, that the analysis would not be materially altered if the dinner promise had been bilateral—if, that is, in return for the man's promise to take her out the woman had promised to accompany him. Where the utility of the promises being exchanged is small, the gains from legal enforcement are likely to be swamped by the costs of enforcement. The law recognizes this and refuses to enforce trivial social promises, especially within the family—where an additional factor, pointing in the same direction, is the existence of an inexpensive alternative to legal enforcement: refusal to engage in promissory transactions in the future. If the husband reneges on his promise, the wife will refuse in the future to perform services in exchange for his promises. Perhaps, then, the real reason for the law's generally not enforcing gratuitous promises is not a belief, which would be economically unsound, that there is a difference in kind between the gratuitous and the bargained-for promise, but an empirical hunch that gratuitous promises tend both to involve small stakes and to be made in family settings where there are economically superior alternatives to legal enforcement.

B. *Past Consideration*

Among the exceptions to the general principle that gratuitous promises will not be enforced are several which are grouped under the rubric of "past consideration." A subsequent promise to pay a debt barred by the statute of limitations, or to pay a debt discharged in bankruptcy, or to pay a debt that is uncollectable because the debtor was a minor at the time the debt was contracted, is legally enforceable even though there is no fresh consideration for the promise. These are classes of promise in which the utility of the promise to the promisor is often great and the costs of enforcement low. First, as regards utility, it should be noted not only that the stakes are often substantial (these are formal debts after all) but that the incremental gain in utility from the enforceable character of the promise may be great. The legal promise conveys information (which a mere stated in-

tention to pay would not) about the promisor's attitude toward the payment of debts barred by a technicality. The information conveyed enhances the promisor's reputation for credit-worthiness and may induce people—not necessarily the promisee himself, which is why the promise itself may not be bilateral— to extend credit to him in the future. And enforcement costs are likely to be low or at least no higher than in conventional bilateral-contract cases because the underlying obligation—the original debt—is fully bilateral. The original debt is not directly enforceable only because of a condition which in the case of the statute of limitations slightly, and in the case of discharge in bankruptcy or voidability by reason of minority not at all, increases the likelihood of error compared to what it would have been in a suit on the original bilateral contract that gave rise to the debt.

The foregoing are cases where, although the promise is not bilateral, the promisor's intent is not donative, that is, not motivated by interdependence between the promisor's and the promisee's utility functions. Another class of "past consideration" cases, however, is best understood on the premise of the law's (implicit) recognition of the existence of interdependent utility functions. These are cases involving promises to compensate rescuers or others who have rendered an unbargained but valuable service to the promisor. The existence of a promise in such a case is strongly attested by the presence of circumstances likely to induce an act of altruism by the promisor toward the promisee. A sees B about to be run down by a speeding car and pushes him out of the way. He saves him but sustains a serious injury in the process. In economic terms, A rescued B because at the moment of danger B's expected utility or wealth was very low; the rescue was like a gift to a starving man. But after the rescue the wealth positions of the parties are dramatically reversed: now A's wealth is low relative to B's since B is whole and A is injured. Hence it is to be expected that B would promise to reward A. The presence of altruistic motivation makes the promise a more plausible one—i.e., one less likely to be a figment of the promisee's imagination—than in the standard unilateral promise case. Stated otherwise, the legal-error costs of enforcing the promise are lower in the rescue case.

The facts of a leading rescue past consideration case, *Webb v. McGowin*,[16] illustrate the benefits that may accrue to the promisor in such cases if the promise is legally enforceable, over and above the benefits

---

[16] 27 Ala. App. 82, 168 So. 196 (1935).

of the transfer itself. The rescued person promised to pay his rescuer $15 every two weeks for the rest of the rescuer's life. This was a generous gift to the extent that the promise was enforceable but a much less generous one to the extent it was not. Had the promisor believed that such a promise was unenforceable, he might have decided instead to make a one-time transfer that might have had a much lower present value than that of the annuity which he in fact promised. Both parties would have been made worse off by this alternative. Hence, it is not surprising that the court held the promise to be enforceable.

Lon Fuller in a well-known article suggested a different rationale for the past-consideration doctrine. Proceeding from the premise that the requirement of consideration is designed in part to prevent people from making promises on the spur of the moment—promises they do not really mean to make and therefore should not be forced to honor (the "cautionary" function of consideration)—he argues that where the promise is to do what the promisor is morally obligated to do anyway, we need not worry whether he is acting deliberately or not—he should have made the promise and that is all that is important. This paternalistic approach is both difficult to square with the basic premises of contract law and an unnecessary embellishment to a theory of the enforcement of gratuitous promises. Fuller is aware of the relevance of economic considerations in explaining the pattern of enforcement and only fails to see that economic analysis can also explain the past-consideration cases.

C. Promises Under Seal

Promises under seal are a traditional and, again, an economically appropriate exception to the requirement that an enforceable promise must be supported by consideration. The requirement of the seal eliminates the major administrative costs associated with the enforcement of unilateral promises. The formalities and written character of the promise reduce both the costs of determining the content of the promise and the probability that the promise was not made or was not intended to be binding.

The abolition by statute of the seal in many states is therefore a mysterious development from the standpoint of efficiency. The decline of this simple but reliable method of making a gratuitous promise binding has been deplored, and various proposals for a substitute method suggested. The legislative character of the abolition movement may reflect simply the difference between the courts and legislatures in the emphasis placed on efficiency. Or, less probably, it may reflect the rise of alternative methods of imparting enforceability to gratuitous promises, such as those discussed in this paper. One way of making a unilateral promise enforceable is for the promisor to exact a merely nominal consideration from the promisee, since courts normally inquire only into the existence and not into the adequacy of the consideration. But not only is this a cumbersome alternative to the promise under seal; increasingly, there is the danger that such a "contract" may be deemed unconscionably one-sided and so not enforced.

D. Charitable Pledges

There is considerable authority for relaxing the requirement of consideration (or reliance) in connection with promises of charitable donations, often to the point where the requirement seems to disappear.[23] This may be thought simply to reflect a special judicial partiality for charity (a partiality that might itself be based on an economic concern for the free-rider or public-good problems that may reduce charitable giving below optimal levels). But that is not an adequate explanation since one effect of enforcement is to increase the cost of making promises of charitable donations by reducing the donor's freedom of action; this could result in an actual decline in charitable giving. An alternative explanation, based on the approach of this paper, does not rely on the meritorious character of charity but instead emphasizes the large size of many charitable donations and the (related) desire of the donor to spread payment of the gift over a significant period of time, for tax, liquidity, or other reasons, as in the symphony-orchestra example discussed earlier.

E. Contract Modification

Often it is possible for a party to make a binding promise, unsupported by any fresh consideration, to modify a term of an existing contract. For example, the payor in a construction contract might agree to pay a higher price to a builder who had encountered unexpected soil conditions. The motives for such promises are various: to gain a reputation for "fair dealing" (really risk sharing), to avoid driving the promisee into bankruptcy (which might prevent his completing performance or raise the cost of his doing so), or even to be altruistic (the contingency giving rise to modification may have dramatically altered the relative wealth position of the parties). In any event, the stakes are often substantial in such cases, while the increment in utility to the promisor may also be substantial because of the length of time over which optimal performance may extend.

Consider the example of the house purchaser who promises the builder a higher than contract price because the builder has encountered some unexpected difficulty which may make it impossible[24] to complete the contract at the agreed price. If the purchaser merely declares his intention of paying the builder a higher price, but is free to renege, the builder may decide not to complete performance but instead to take his chances in bankruptcy court. Yet the promisor dare not pay him the extra price in advance in exchange for the builder's promise to continue, for if the contractor is financially shaky for other reasons, the prepayment may end up in the hands of a trustee in bankruptcy, with the purchaser relegated to the status of an unsecured creditor. This is a clear case where the enforcement of a promise not supported by fresh consideration enhances the welfare of the promisor.

The facts of a real case upholding enforceability of such a promise, *Goebel v. Linn*,[25] are rather similar to those of the last example. The defendants were brewers who had a contract with the plaintiff in the case, an ice company, to supply them with ice at a price not to exceed $2 a ton. An unusually mild winter ruined the local ice "crop" and the ice company informed the defendants that it would not continue to supply them with ice at the contract price. The defendants had a large stock of beer on hand that would spoil without refrigeration, and therefore agreed to pay the ice company $3.50 to continue the supply of ice under the contract. The defendants later repudiated the agreement and the ice company sued. In upholding the plaintiff's claim, the court observed that the defendants

> chose for reasons which they must have deemed sufficient at the time to submit to the company's demand and pay the increased price rather than rely upon their strict rights under the existing contract. . . . Suppose, for example, the defendants had satisfied themselves that the ice company under the very extraordinary circumstances of the entire failure of the local crop of ice must be ruined if their existing contracts were to be insisted

upon, and must be utterly unable to respond in damages; it is plain that then, whether they chose to rely upon their contract or not, it could have been of little or no value to them. Unexpected and extraordinary circumstances had rendered the contract worthless; and they must either make a new arrangement, or, in insisting on holding the ice company to the existing contract, they would ruin the ice company and thereby at the same time ruin themselves.

The result in this case has been criticized on the ground that it exposes promisees to extortion. In economic terms, the making of a contract may confer on the seller a monopoly vis-a-vis the buyer which the seller can exploit by threatening to terminate the contract unless the buyer agrees to pay a higher price than originally agreed upon. The court in *Goebel* was aware of this danger but found that the ice company's claim was not extortionate in this sense. This raises the question, however, whether extortion can be given a meaningful definition in the modification setting. To answer this question, it is helpful to distinguish three situations in which modification might be sought:

1. Nothing has changed since the contract was made, but the promisor, realizing that the remedies for breach of contract would not fully compensate the promisee, gives the promisee the unhappy choice of either paying the promisor more to complete the contract or pursuing his legal remedies.

2. Something has changed since the contract signing: the promisee has given up alternative sources of supply or otherwise increased his dependence on the promisor. If modification is permitted the promisor can extract a monopoly rent from the promisee.

3. Something has changed since the contract signing: an unexpected event which, as in *Goebel v. Linn*, prevents the (willing) promisor from completing the promised performance without a modification of the contract.

The third case is the clearest for allowing modification. The inability of a willing promisor to complete performance removes the factor of strategic behavior that is present in cases one and two. No exploitation of a monopoly position or of the inadequacy of contractual remedies is involved in allowing modification in the third case. The first case might also seem one where modification should be allowed, on the basis of

---

[24] Yet not fall within the bounds of the contract doctrine that allows discharge on grounds of "impossibility"—on which see Richard A. Posner & Andrew M. Rosenfield, Im-

possibility and Related Doctrines in Contract Law: An Economic Analysis, 6 J. Leg. Studies 83 (1977).

[25] 47 Mich. 489, 11 N.W. 284 (1882).

Holmes's "bad man" theory of contract law which has close affinities with the economic approach. The legal obligation of a promisor is to perform or pay damages. If the promisee wants more—wants in effect specific performance—he must pay extra for it.

That is all that seems to be involved in the first case but if we pause to ask why the promisee in the first case would ever agree to pay extra, we shall see that the first case is in reality a version of the second, the monopoly case. If the promisee in the first case has equally good alternative sources of supply, or at least no worse than he had when he made the original contract, he will have no incentive to pay a premium above the contract price for the promisor to perform as agreed; he will allow the promisor to breach and turn elsewhere. He will pay the premium only if his dependence on the promisor has increased since the signing of the contract, i.e., only if the contract gave the promisor a monopoly position vis-a-vis the promisee.

Alaska Packers' Ass'n v. Domenico[27] was such a case. The plaintiffs (technically "libelants") hired out as sailors and fishermen to the defendant (appellant), but soon after beginning work stopped and threatened to quit unless their wages were raised above the agreed amount. Defendant's agent agreed to pay the higher wage demanded but defendant later reneged. The court refused to enforce the modified contract, noting that

> the libelants agreed in writing, for a certain stated compensation, to render their services to the appellant in remote waters where the season for conducting fishing operations is extremely short, and in which enterprise the appellant had a large amount of money invested; and, after having entered upon the discharge of their contract, and at a time when it was impossible for the appellant to secure other men in their places, the libelants, without any valid cause, absolutely refused to continue the services they were under contract to perform unless the appellant would consent to pay them more money.

This seems a clear case where the motive for the modification was simply to exploit a monopoly position conferred on the promisors by the circumstances of the contract. It might seem that the promisee would have been in even worse shape if the men had quit as they threatened to do. However, since their

only motive for threatening to quit was to extract a higher wage, there was probably little danger of their actually quitting. The danger would have been truly negligible had they known that they could not extract an enforceable commitment to pay them a higher wage.[29]

The court in *Alaska Packers'* criticized the earlier result in *Goebel v. Linn*, yet the cases are readily distinguishable, with the help of economic analysis. In *Goebel*, without a modification the promisor might well have terminated the contract, so the modification conferred a real benefit on the promisee. But in *Alaska Packers'* the likelihood of termination was much less since the threat to terminate was not a response to external conditions genuinely impairing the promisor's ability to honor the contract but merely a strategic ploy designed to exploit a monopoly position. A firm rule of nonenforceability in such cases solves the monopoly problem and thereby facilitates the making of contractual arrangements in which the promisee will be dependent on the good faith of the promisor.

One can relate this distinction back to the basic theme of this paper by noting that one effect of enforcing the kind of modification attempted in the *Alaska Packers'* case would be to reduce the benefits of contracting to people in the same situation as the plaintiffs in that case. Seamen thereafter could not expect to be promised a high wage in exchange for agreeing to work for a stated period at that wage, since the employer would know that the seamen were not obliged to honor their promise but could at any time "hold him up" for a higher wage. In a different form, this is the same problem as that of the man who derives little value from promising a future gift because the promise is not binding on him.

An intermediate case between the involuntary threat to terminate (*Goebel v. Linn*) and the monopolistic (*Alaska Packers' Ass'n v. Domenico*) is that of a promisor who threatens to terminate only because a third party has offered him a higher price for his goods. Because the higher price is a genuine opportunity cost of continued compliance with the contract, the promisor should be allowed to terminate subject only to his obligation to make good the promisee's loss from the breach, and hence he should be allowed to negotiate with the promisee over a modification that will compensate the promisor for the lost oppor-

---

[27] 117 Fed 99 (9th Cir. 1902).
[29] If modifications were enforceable in these circumstances; the men might actually quit when the employer

called their bluff in order to enhance the credibility of future threats. This incentive would disappear with a well-settled rule against enforceability.

tunity. This was the result in *Schwartzreich v. Bauman-Basch Inc.* [30]

Conclusion

This paper has treated, perhaps too briefly for some tastes, an area of contract doctrine which seems at first glance utterly resistant to economic analysis because it concerns a form of conduct—the so-called gratuitous promise—that seems to lie outside of the exchange economy altogether. I do not argue that economic analysis can explain every rule and outcome, but only that it gives structure to, and suggests a fundamental economic motivation for, the general legal approach in this area.

The paper makes no attempt to explore the full implications of the economic analysis of gratuity for an understanding of law. The problem of apparent gratuitousness arises where contracts are challenged as resting on merely nominal consideration, where the rights or obligations of gratuitous bailees, invitees, or others are differentiated from those of people doing the same things pursuant to an exchange, in the decision to enforce wills and trusts, in the tax treatment of gifts, and in many other areas. All are areas for fruitful application of economics to law.

Appendix

A Formal Analysis of the Legal Enforcement of Gratuitous Promises

This appendix seeks to push the analysis of the social gains from enforcing gratuitous promises in Part II a bit further, using some extremely simple tools of formal analysis. I realize that a complete formal treatment of the problem would be a good deal more complicated that anything attempted here.

[The appendix is omitted. —ed.]

---

[30] 231 N.Y. 196, 131 N.E. 887 (1921). Indeed, from an economic standpoint a foregone benefit is no different from a direct cost; both are opportunity costs.

Section 2-209(1) of the Uniform Commercial Code provides that absence of consideration is not a defense in an action to enforce a modification of a contract. However, the Official Comment to this section states that the modification must be in "good faith" and implies that, under this standard, the modification in the *Alaska Packers'* case would not be enforced.

"Agreements to Agree"

Although many Contracts courses and casebooks spend a lot of time on the bargaining process, few practicing lawyers run into offer and acceptance problems outside of the "Battle of the Forms" (covered by UCC 2-207). An increasing area of conflict, however, is the situation often referred to rather simplistically as the agreement to agree. As the following pair of articles show, the topic is much subtler and richer. The fact situations can range from completed bargains with the paperwork left to be cleaned up by the lawyers to lease renewal clauses with the new rental left to be fixed in light of future business conditions to express agreements to bargain in good faith or to fix a reasonable price. And there are many variations in between.

Friedrich Kessler and Edith Fine published a trail-blazing article in 1964 in which they discussed the German concept of *culpa in contrahendo* or fault in bargaining. Kessler & Fine, *Culpa in Contrahendo, Bargaining in Good Faith, and Freedom of Contract: A Comparative Study*, 77 Harv. L. Rev. 401 (1964). The concept is well-accepted in the civil law systems of continental Europe, and Kessler and Fine showed that it was not inconsistent with freedom of contract as American law knows it. The article has proved influential both with respect to the question of good faith in bargaining and as to the general duty of good faith under an existing contract. It is further considered in the discussion of good faith in Part IIIB.

In 1969 Professor Charles Knapp of New York University wrote an important article discussing what he called "the contract to bargain." In it Knapp distinguished different types of understandings that fall short of a completed and formalized contract, but that in some circumstances already are enforceable, could become enforceable or could lead to alternative liability. In 1987 Professor E. Allan Farnsworth of Columbia, co-reporter of the Restatement (Second) of Contracts and author of a leading text on contract law, published an article entitled *Precontractual Liability and Preliminary Agreements: Fair Dealing and Failed Negotiations.* The two articles complement each other and show how changed contract formation is from the elegant system put forth by the classic approach—but already criticized by Corbin in 1917.

Charles L. Knapp, *Enforcing the Contract to Bargain,* 44 N.Y.U. L. Rev. 673 (1969)

I. Introduction

A. *Purpose and Scope of the Study*

The main theme of the discussion which follows will be that the common law has failed to deal adequately with many cases in which the parties to a negotiation have reached partial agreement on the terms of their eventual exchange. Such a thesis obviously requires some indulgence on the reader's part, and a certain amount of irreverence as well; to put the reader in the proper frame of mind it may be well to begin with two selections from Professor Corbin's treatise, probably the single most authoritative work in the area of contract law today:

> Frequently agreements are arrived at piecemeal, different terms and items being discussed and agreed upon separately. As long as the parties know that there is an essential term not yet agreed on, there is no contract; the preliminary agreements on specific items are mere preliminary negotiation building up the terms of the final offer that may or may not be made. . . . Further illustrations are to be found in the so-called contract to make a contract. . . . If the document or contract that the parties agree to make is to contain any material term that is not already agreed on, no contract has yet been made; and the so-called "contract to make a contract" is not a contract at all.[1]

No one can go to the moon.[2]

The common law of contracts assumes in general that there is a clear theoretical distinction between what the law calls a "contract" and the relation between those who have merely entered negotiations looking to the formation of a contract. The important difference between the initial stage of preliminary negotiation and the state of contract itself is, of course, that in the latter each party has enforceable rights against the other. Even though these rights may be conditional, and may never become rights to immediate performance, they nevertheless exist in the contemplation of the law—and they exist as soon as the contract comes into being.[3]

Correlative to (but not necessarily dictated by) the proposition that creation of a contract relation results in the immediate existence of rights, is the converse: until the stage of contract is reached, no rights exist because none have been created. . . . Thus, for a common law lawyer, characterizing a particular negotiation situation is likely to be a choice between two alternatives—contract or no-contract.

To some extent, the rigidity of the conceptual distinction thus maintained is weakened by garden variety "legal realism," which readily admits that a court's decision on the question of whether a contract has been created will in some immeasurable but important respect depend on the "moral" or "ethical" quality of the conduct of the parties with respect to

---

[1] 1 A. Corbin, Contracts § 29, at 82-85 (rev. ed. 1963).

[2] 6 A. Corbin, Contracts § 1325, at 337 (rev. ed. 1963). The quoted language is found in the course of an explanation of the term "objective impossibility," and—in one sense, at least—was true when written. Professor Corbin was of course all too aware of the obvious point being made here. See Bibliography of the Published Writings of Arthur Linton Corbin, 74 Yale L.J. 311 n.1 (1964).

[3] The Uniform Commercial Code contains the following language: "An agreement sufficient to constitute a contract for sale may be found even though the moment of its making is undetermined." Uniform Commercial Code § 2-204(2) (1962) (hereinafter cited as UCC). This flexible-sounding provision was apparently not intended to contradict the basic assumption that there is a single point in time when the parties cross the line from non-contract to contract; an earlier version of this provision, somewhat more susceptible to different interpretation ("Conduct by both parties which recognizes the existence of a contract is sufficient to establish a contract for sale even though the moment of its making cannot be determined."), was revised after disapproval by the New York State Law Revision Commission. N.Y. Law Revision Comm'n, Report Relating to the Uniform Commercial Code (Legis. Doc. No. 65A) (1956).

the particular transaction in dispute. Nevertheless, when the dispute is resolved, the court's decision will probably be based on one of two fundamental conclusions: that no contractual rights had been created (and thus none could have been violated); or that the agreement between the parties had reached the stage of a complete and binding contract.

The distinction between contract and non-contract could be phrased in another way, based on the presence or absence of legally enforceable duties: The person who becomes a party to a contract assumes a duty to go forward with the contemplated transaction. . . . One who is not yet bound by a contract, however, has no such duty to go forward. He is at liberty to withdraw completely from the proposed transaction at any time, for any reason. He may choose to enter into a substitute transaction of a similar nature with some third party, or, indeed, to refrain from action altogether in either case without being answerable to the abandoned party for any disappointment to the latter's expectations, however severe this may have been.

Such at least would be the view of the common law. It seems likely, however, that there are in fact many situations in which at some stage of negotiations the views of the negotiating parties as to their own "duty to go forward" would be somewhere between the two extremes described. Most of these cases would be among those customarily put in two of the traditional pigeonholes of contract law the "agreement to agree" cases and the "formal contract contemplated" cases. The first of these categories is comprised primarily of transactions which have reached the stage of full agreement on many, perhaps most, terms of the proposed exchange of performances, plus agreement that an agreement should and probably will later be reached on the remaining terms. The second category includes those cases in which agreement has been reached on many terms of the proposed exchange (probably at least enough to suggest that the parties considered the extent of remaining potential disagreement to be negligible), but it is nevertheless evident that the parties to the negotiation expected to sign later a detailed, formal, written document containing all the terms earlier agreed upon.

In each of these situations, the common law court considers the basic question to be whether at the time the dispute arose a contract had been made. In the "agreement to agree" case, the parties often have failed to achieve "contract" status simply because they did not reach a bargain complete and final

enough to be worthy of (and capable of) legal recognition and enforcement. The intention of the parties not to have a binding contract is perhaps clear, but not of crucial importance. In the "formal contract contemplated" situation, however, the parties may have arrived at an agreement complete enough to satisfy even a demanding court, but the court is wary of enforcing the agreement because it doubts that the parties really intended their promises to be initially enforceable. Here the intention of the parties as to enforceability is said to be of paramount importance.

The draftsmen of the Uniform Commercial Code have undertaken to amend basic rules of contract law in a number of areas where courts have unjustifiably imposed on innocent businessmen the judges' own ideas of what does or does not constitute a sufficiently complete contract. In line with this approach they have modified the "agreement to agree" rule to a considerable degree, so that now under the Code a contract may be found despite a substantial degree of "indefiniteness." The "written contract contemplated" rule, on the other hand, survives today in much the same form as when it was first enunciated. This may be due to the fact that it appears by its very nature to give effect to the real intention of the parties, rather than ignoring it.

It is suggested that in a number of cases, the "agreement to agree" rule—even as liberalized by the U.C.C.—and the "written contract contemplated" rule both run counter to the intentions and expectations of the parties at the time of the transaction under scrutiny. This is because the common law's dichotomy of contract/no-contract does not exhaust the catalog of possible intentions.

There is of course no absolute necessity for making the rules of law coextensive with the parties' ideas of what these rules should be. There are many kinds of conduct most people would label as somehow "wrong," which are neither criminal nor tortious. While "promises should be kept" is a moral stricture of rather general acceptance, the law of contract in general singles out only the "bargained-for" promise as worthy of organized protection.

This insistence on a "bargain," however, does suggest a reason for conforming the law to the private moral code of the parties in the cases under discussion. The Uniform Commercial Code, which, if only by the near-universality of its adoption, must be taken as the most authoritative statement of current American commercial law, purports to be a businessman's code, doing away with "outmoded" rules of law to the extent that they diverge from what businessmen regard as appropriate norms of conduct. In general, it makes a greater effort than the common law to provide means for discovering and following business custom. . . .

The Code thus seeks to follow the businessman into the marketplace, and shape decisions to the facts and norms of business life. If a class of transactions exists in which the law as presently conceived and administered fails to accomplish this goal, then certainly the Code, and perhaps the common law as well, should attempt to adjust existing rules to accommodate to the facts of business life.

The hypothesis here will be that such a class of transactions does exist: that in at least a substantial number of the "agreement to agree" and "formal contract contemplated" cases, the parties—at the relevant stage of negotiations—do consider themselves "morally" or "ethically" bound, but only in a limited way.

In the typical "agreement to agree" case, the parties have clearly intended to make some sort of "bargain"—they contemplate an exchange of performances, not simply a one-sided, gratuitous transfer. However, for some reason, they have postponed a present decision on one or more details of that exchange, such as the time for performance, the precise price to be paid, the terms of payment, or the amounts or varieties of particular goods to be furnished within an overall agreed—amount the possible range of such items is as broad as the whole scope of contracting activity.

At this stage of negotiation, there are a number of possible states of mind which the negotiating parties may have on the question of whether each is "bound" to the other (using "bound" here in the sense of bound by what each would regard as good business ethics):

(1) Each may regard himself and his opposite number as perfectly free for any reason whatsoever to refuse to reach agreement on the outstanding points, and to withdraw from the transaction without being bound to proceed farther with the exchange (except to pay some reasonable amount for any performance which may have already been rendered and received). This is also apt to be the answer of traditional contract common law to the question of whether any legally enforceable bond has been created: that no contract has yet come into existence, and thus no rights exist other than those arising from a duty to make restitution for benefits actually received. No expectation damages can be recovered, because no reasonable expectations have yet been created; no reliance damages can be recovered, because no reliance on such an incomplete transaction is deserving of protection.

(2) Each may regard himself and his opposite number as being fully bound to the proposed exchange unless an excuse exists which would have been sufficient to excuse performance of an ordinary executory contract. Under this view even an eventual failure to reach agreement on the "postponed" points would not of itself be sufficient justification for withdrawal; an impartial arbiter could properly decree the standard of performance in the remaining areas of non-agreement. On the question of whether any legally enforceable bond has been created, this second view might also be the answer given by traditional contract law, based on the assumption that the agreement of the parties is complete, though imperfectly expressed. On any matters left open the parties should, if necessary, be bound in accordance with a standard to be set either by some designated impartial third party or by a court. This approach overcomes the objection that the agreement is too incomplete by finding it no more incomplete than many other perfectly unremarkable commercial contracts in which one or more terms of performance have to be supplied by the court in deciding questions of enforcement.[33]

(3) Finally, it is possible that each of the negotiating parties really regards himself and, the other party not as completely bound, but nonetheless as "committed to the deal," and bound to the extent actual agreement is eventually reached. The parties are bound to try in good faith to reach some agreement and not to withdraw from the proposed exchange for any reason other than the eventual failure to reach such agreement. Implicit in this view of the facts are a number of assumptions: (1) that each party to the negotiations considers the proposed exchange beneficial and has indicated to the other that he can properly be regarded as "committed" to it; (2) that there is a mutual recognition by the parties that important points of substance remain to be decided at some later time, possibly in the light of changing or emergent conditions, but that an immediate decision on such matters would be premature and possibly damaging to one party or the other if conditions should

---

[33] See 1 A. Corbin, Contracts § 95, nn.9 & 10 (rev. ed. 1963). As will be discussed below, this also appears to be the approach of UCC § 2-305, regarding agreements in which "the price is not settled."

develop in an unanticipated way; (3) and finally, that both parties regard the points remaining to be decided as being potential "deal-upsetters"—so material that failure to reach agreement must excuse further performance. This third view of the transaction is one which has no common law counterpart. If the parties are legally bound to each other, then they have impliedly agreed to submit to the court's judgment and terms which for some reason they omitted, left unclear, or reserved for future agreement. If the parties have not so bound themselves, however, they are not bound at all—no contract exists, only an "agreement to agree", and each party is free at any time, and for any reason, to say "I choose to go no farther with this deal."

In the typical "formal contract contemplated" case, the parties have clearly intended a bargain; they have also reached the stage of agreement on at least a number of the material terms of the proposed exchange. However, for some reason, they both apparently contemplate the later execution of a full, formal written document. At this stage of the negotiations, there are once again a number of possible views which the parties may entertain as to the extent to which each of them is "bound," by good business ethics, to the proposed exchange of performances:

(1) Each may regard himself as not bound to anything at all unless and until a formal writing is signed by him, and, further, as being free to refuse to sign that writing for any reason whatsoever. This is one possible view which the law may take as to the extent of the obligation created by the negotiations to date— none at all. A legal conclusion of this sort, which will be presented as the reflection of the parties' intention, is made more likely by the presence of factors such as the following: a) the contract is of a type which requires writing for enforceability under the Statute of Frauds; b) the contract contemplated involves large sums of money; c) the contract has many details; d) the contract is an unusual one, for which a standard form is not available or appropriate; e) the parties were apparently unwilling to proceed with any performance until the formal document was prepared and signed. There are many cases in which it is impossible to believe that the parties intended any liability to attach to either side until final execution of the contemplated formal document.

(2) Each party may really feel that the "formal" document is only a "formality"—some sort of ritual, desirable for one or more reasons, but in no sense a prerequisite to a "binding" agreement.

This second view is, again, not an unlikely one for the law to adopt on the issue of whether in a particular case a binding legal obligation has been created. The likelihood of such an outcome is increased where: a) no independent policy of the law requires a writing for enforceability, or, if it does, the parties have exchanged letters, telegrams or other writings in which the agreed-upon terms are sufficiently reflected; b) the proposed contract appears relatively simple, and does not involve long-term obligations; c) the contemplated "formal" contract is a standard-form document, which itself contains the details necessary for a contract of this sort; or d) the parties themselves, without waiting for the formality of execution, have proceeded to perform, in a way that suggests they believed full and binding agreement to have been reached.

In each of the two preceding characterizations of the "formal contract contemplated" situation, the parties may have actually reached agreement on every detail of their proposed exchange. In any such case where at the relevant point in negotiation there remain terms on which agreement has not been expressly reached, there is yet a third possibility.

(3) It is possible that the principals have carried the "deal" as far as they can, and that they are relying on their agents (almost always including lawyers, but possibly also accountants and other experts) to complete the process of agreement. In this view of the facts, the purpose of preparing the formal document is not simply to postpone creation of an obligation, or even to provide evidence of its existence or terms, but rather to afford these experts an opportunity to add to the total agreement such protection against various risks as they think necessary or prudent. On this assumption, the principals are likely to feel ethically bound to the outlines of the deal as they have hammered it out, the withdrawal of either one based simply on dissatisfaction with those outlines being regarded by both as admittedly unjustified. The principals, however, are likely to consider themselves still morally free to withdraw if and when it should appear that the "second team" of bargainers have raised a substantial issue on which they are unable to agree and which the principals, when apprised of the difficulty, are likewise unable to resolve.

As with the "agreement to agree" discussed above, this third, middle view of the intention of the parties has no common law counterpart. It is similar to the first view in that the execution of a formal writing, or, at least, full agreement on each of its terms, is the point at which the completely binding contract is created. In the eyes of the parties, however, a significant narrowing of the "moral right" to withdraw has occurred at a much earlier time (although immediate commencement of performance is still to be viewed as risky, in light of the continuing possibility of eventual disagreement followed by justified withdrawal).

B. *The Contract to Bargain*

The preceding discussion has preserved the distinction between the "agreement to agree" situation and the "formal-contract-contemplated" situation, resting the distinction on the nature of the reason for delaying agreement: where the delay is to await the occurrence of further events which control the future agreement, the relationship is termed an "agreement to agree"; where the delay is to permit negotiations which will settle the details of a transaction already fully agreed upon in its "essential" terms, the case has been referred to as one where a "formal contract" is "contemplated." Of course, the boundary between the two categories is not always clearly ascertainable, and a given case may well be characterized as falling in either or indeed, in both.

For our purposes, therefore, it will be sufficient to further describe and define the two "middle" positions outlined above, in order to stress the essential similarity between them and the difference between these two categories and other, more conventional analyses. Thus, it has been suggested that in each of the two hypothetical cases above, the parties have reached agreement to such a degree that they regard themselves as bound to each other to the extent that neither can withdraw for an "unjustified" reason, and yet still free enough that neither will be compelled to perform if after good faith bargaining actual agreement cannot be reached. This situation, if recognized at law in the manner suggested, might be most accurately denominated a "contract to bargain." This nomenclature seems accurate for the following reasons: (1) Use of the word "contract" stresses the fact that the relationship, to at least some extent, entails binding obligations, the breach of which will give rise to a legal remedy. (2) Use of the term "bargain" emphasizes that such a contract imposes neither an absolute duty to perform the contemplated exchange, not even an absolute duty to *agree* to perform it. Rather it creates a present duty to "bar-

gain"—to engage, in good faith, in the process of attempting to reach agreement on the terms of the proposed exchange, for as long as may reasonably be required under the circumstances.

As used herein, therefore, the term "contract to bargain" will be used to describe any situation where two or more parties have commenced negotiations looking toward a particular exchange, have reached actual agreement on some important terms of the proposed exchange, have delayed agreement on other terms of real importance, but have nevertheless mutually signified their willingness to be regarded as "committed" to the entire proposed exchange. Each regards withdrawal by the other—for a reason other than failure to reach agreement on the remaining points—as unjustified, and worthy of both moral and legal condemnation.

II. Legal Authority For The Contract To Bargain

A. *Case Law*

The preceding discussion has served to demonstrate that the common law has been not so much resistant as oblivious to the notion that there might be an enforceable contract to bargain. Is there any reason to think that the courts might prove receptive to the analysis outlined above? The answer suggested here is that some authority exists for the duty to bargain as a legally enforceable obligation, that, more importantly, the Uniform Commercial Code furnishes ample room for any judge so disposed to grant enforceable status to the contract to bargain, and that important policies would indeed be furthered by such a decision.

. . .

[Professor Knapp distinguishes *Hoffman v. Red Owl Stores, Inc.*[42] in which a franchise applicant was awarded reliance damages for his expenses incurred during negotiations which eventually fell through. — ed.]

Whatever its consequences in terms of legal recognition of rights and granting of remedies, the contract to bargain is basically a bilateral arrangement; its claim for legal recognition is principally based upon the contention that there are cases where a level of agreement has been reached, and manifested, which is sufficient in the eyes of the parties themselves to bind them, absent good faith justification for withdrawal. A fundamental characteristic of

---

[42] 26 Wis. 2d 683, 133 N.W.2d 267 (1965).

promissory estoppel is its one-sidedness—only one party having enforceable rights against the other. In that respect, *Hoffman*, if it is truly a promissory estoppel situation, is closer to the "firm offer" cases than to the contract to bargain situation. In emphasizing *Hoffman* as authority for the contract to bargain, one runs the risk of subordinating and even obscuring the factor of mutual agreement clearly expressed. Reliance may provide a good additional reason for enforcement of the contract to bargain, and in many cases there may be no remedy for the breach of such a contract unless reliance can be proved. However, there appear to be no compelling reasons for limiting the application of the contract to bargain concept to cases where reliance has taken place, nor indeed is there any justification for applying it at all where—as may have been the case in *Hoffman*—the parties have not both committed themselves to the agreement actually reached, reserving the privilege of bargaining in good faith over the remaining terms.

B. *The Uniform Commercial Code*

Whatever its implications, the *Hoffman* case is precedent in only one jurisdiction, and has yet to give birth to any noteworthy offspring. The Uniform Commercial Code, on the other hand, is law in forty-nine states, and is important not only for the transactions which it expressly governs, but also for the myriad of other contractual relationships which it can influence by analogy. Indeed, evidence is already accumulating that the "general part" of the U.C.C. is the American contract law of the immediate future.[58] This can be seen not only in judicial decisions, but also in the frank attempt of the Restatement to incorporate as much of the U.C.C. as can be decently accommodated in what purports to be a compilation of nonstatutory law.

In order to examine the extent to which the contract to bargain might be comprehended within the general scheme of the U.C.C., consider first the possible objections which traditional contract law would have to its enforcement: no mutuality of obligation; lack of consideration; presence of illusory promises; absence of intention to be bound; "formal contract contemplated"; lack of certainty and definiteness; "agreement to agree."

It is submitted, however, that a number of these objections can easily be disposed of if one really wants to find a basis for enforceability. . . .

. . .

The next objection advanced is that the promises are "illusory" and therefore not binding; this objection is also untenable. The parties may not have promised to go through with the eventual proposed exchange of performances "no matter what," but they have promised to negotiate with each other in good faith toward that end. A promise to negotiate in good faith is non-illusory in two respects: it commits the promisor to a course of action with no condition of subsequent "willingness" on his part; it also results in a substantial narrowing of the promisor's options—his freedom to withdraw from the transaction or enter into a substitute is now restricted. Finally, the contract to bargain may contain elements of both the "formal contract contemplated" and the "agreement to agree" cases. To the extent that such elements in the transaction are symptomatic of an intention not to be legally bound by the tentative agreement, the objection to enforcement would properly be raised. If the intention to be legally bound is clear, however, then objection to enforceability based on lack of such intention is obviously invalid. In this event the presence of the "agreement to agree" element would be a valid reason for denying enforceability to a contract to bargain only if it entailed such a lack of definiteness and certainty of terms as to prevent effective enforcement—the last suggested objection.

Each of the other objections raised above can be overcome without necessarily repudiating the rule on which that objection is based. This one probably cannot. Despite the efforts of some courts and commentators to show that a lack of definiteness does not always import lack of intention to be bound, and that in some cases the remedy for breach may be adjusted to reflect the indefiniteness of the agreement, the common law legal world is too imbued with the hoary precept that "an agreement to agree is not a contract" to change its ways.[68]

The U.C.C., however, accepts the proposition that lack of definiteness does not per se preclude enforcement of rights under an agreement. [Professor

---

[58] Mooney, Old Kontract Principles and Karl's New Kode: An Essay on the Jurisprudence of Our New Commercial Law, 11 Vill. L. Rev. 213, 257-58 (1966).

[68] "[W]e are not persuaded that renewal options in leases are of such an exceptional character as to justify emasculation of one of the basic rules of contract law. An agreement to agree simply does not fix an enforceable obligation." Walker v. Keith, 382 S.W.2d 198, 201 (Ky. 1964).

Knapp discusses U.C.C. 2-204(3)[69] in some detail. He concludes:]

Having met these requirements [i.e., showing that the parties "intended to create a reasonably binding legal relationship" and that there is a reasonably certain basis for giving an appropriate remedy], it appears that the contract to bargain can fit quite comfortably under the umbrella of 2-204(3). Furthermore, it should be noted that legal recognition of the contract to bargain would further a number of policies generally favored by the Code:

. . .

3) Although other points could be raised to demonstrate that the contract to bargain promotes Code policy, there is one in particular that merits consideration because it is of a slightly different nature: it can be contended that decisions like those here argued for are desirable—even necessary—if the Code is to survive as a viable body of law. When the Code was first proposed, one of the chief arguments against its adoption was that the flexibility and potential for change inherent in a common law system would be sacrificed for a rigid system of rules which—however "advanced" or "modern" in their inception—would inevitably become outmoded, stifling further growth. The drafters of the Code tried to overcome this fear in a number of ways, one of which was to build into the Code a number of "expandable" concepts, such as "commercial reasonableness," "good faith," and "unconscionability."[81] Although the courts are not free to contravene the express language of the Code, they must be free within the confines of that language to reach particular decisions not expressly contemplated—perhaps even feared—by the very men who drafted the Code and voted its adoption.

. . .

III. Illustrative Cases

A number of questions remain unanswered. What sort of manifestation of intention will create a contract to bargain? What types of conduct would constitute a breach of such a contract—in other words, what do the very broad terms "good faith" and "bad faith" mean in this context? What sort of remedy would be available for such a breach, even if the law should in theory regard the agreement as a "contract," creating legally-recognized rights? And, finally is the above discussion merely an academic exercise—is there ever going to be an actual contract to bargain?

By examining the facts of a number of relatively recent cases in the "formal contract contemplated" or "agreement to agree" category, one can gain some idea of whether the agreement in question could have been characterized as a contract to bargain; the facts in these cases may also suggest answers to the other questions posed. In addition, a review of such decisions indicates what effect, if any, the adoption of the "contract to bargain" approach would have on either the future state of the law, or the results of the cases themselves.

A. *Contracts to Lease*

. . .

[Knapp discusses *Joseph v. Doraty*,[87] in which parties signed a written agreement providing for a five-year lease at $12,000 annual rent, an option to renew for five more years and a $1000 deposit by the lessees "to show their good faith in consummating the lease to be drawn and subject to the approval" of both parties' attorneys. The parties' attorneys exchanged drafts of a lease, but it was never signed.]

The Ohio Court of Appeals, affirming the trial court's ruling, held that no legally enforceable contract had been made—only "an agreement to enter into an agreement." The court rested its conclusion on two points: the language in the agreement . . . provided that the lease to be executed first had to be approved by counsel for both parties; and the writing made no provision for a number of other matters, "taxes, insurance, utilities (including water), rights of the parties in case of default, destruction by fire, or extent of repairs required by both parties for the portion of the building they agreed to repair."

. . .

. . . The court is right in pointing out that each party did not intend to be fully bound to the agreement as it stood, if his attorney disapproved of it. It appears, however, that the parties had expressed satisfaction with the basic terms of the lease as they had worked them out, and were waiting for their attorneys only to insert the kind of details that attorneys are paid to provide (and which the judge himself volunteered in his opinion). If the parties had been asked

---

[69] "Even though one or more terms are left open a contract for sale does not fail for indefiniteness if the parties have intended to make a contract and there is a reasonably certain basis for giving an appropriate remedy."

[81] See Farnsworth, Good Faith Performance and Commercial Reasonableness Under the Uniform Commercial Code, 30 U. Chi. L. Rev. 666 (1963).

[87] 77 Ohio L. Abs. 381, 144 N.E.2d 111 (Ohio Ct. App. 1957).

at the time they signed their agreement whether each regarded himself as free to withdraw for any reason including simply a better deal somewhere else they both would have probably disclaimed any such privilege of withdrawal. At least each would probably have disclaimed it in the presence of the other party, which may be a good rule of thumb for questions of this sort. If this assumption is correct, then the court could have properly concluded that the privilege of withdrawal was available only where the attorneys were unable to reach agreement in good faith, and was not intended to extend to a withdrawal for unrelated reasons. Unless facts material to this question are omitted from the opinion, the court should then have enforced this agreement as intended by the parties, the defendant being guilty of a breach of contract.

. . .

[Knapp discusses *Walker v. Keith*,[100] in which a small commercial tenant was unable to enforce a renewal option stating

> rental will be fixed in such amount as shall actually be agreed upon by the lessors and the lessee with the monthly rental fixed on the comparative basis of rental values as of the date of the renewal with rental values at this time reflected by the comparative business conditions of the two periods.

The Chancellor, using an advisory jury, fixed a rent for renewal. The Kentucky Court of Appeals reversed.]

It can easily be argued that the court should have held the agreement enforceable and upheld the Chancellor's findings as to the rent for the renewal term. Many courts would take this view; as we have seen, the Uniform Commercial Code in section 2-305 provides for such relief in an analogous situation. Under this approach, it then would not matter whether the provision in question was to be regarded as an agreement to agree, or an agreement to fix price by reference to specific external factors. In either case, the court would determine a "reasonable price" at the time (and place, presumably) for delivery.

This analysis of the contract, however, would not make it a "contract to bargain." As discussed above, the essence of a contract to bargain is that it binds each party only to negotiate in good faith and to refrain from withdrawing for an unrelated reason; it does not bind the parties to a "reasonable agree-

ment" in the event that actual agreement cannot be reached by good faith negotiation. If the renewal option in *Walker* were really to be regarded as a "contract to bargain," however, it appears that the result might well have been the same, since the parties were apparently unable to agree on a figure for the renewal. The court would have had to consider the intention of the parties on these points, of course, in order to determine the proper characterization of the contract. Assuming the court would have been receptive to any of the approaches outlined above, the "reasonable price" approach of section 2-305 might well have been the most appropriate, since the plaintiff had already been in possession for five years and had probably relied on renewal. That the parties had referred to external factors, at least suggests that they had contemplated a "reasonable" rental, in light of prevailing economic conditions at the time of renewal.

. . .

[Knapp discusses] *Borge-Warner Corp. v. Anchor Coupling Co.*,[147] in which plaintiff was seeking specific performance of an alleged contract for sale of the assets of a manufacturing business. Defendants were the manufacturing company, Anchor Coupling Co., and its chief officers and major stockholders, Charles Conroy and Walter Fritsch. The contract was said to be contained in letters of offer and acceptance, written on behalf of Anchor and Borg-Warner, respectively. Conroy later refused to perform under the contract, and this action followed. Defendants Anchor and Conroy moved to dismiss plaintiff's complaint, arguing that Anchor's original letter to plaintiff could not form the basis of a contract, despite the later acceptance. The letter, referring to earlier correspondence from Borg-Warner, affirmed Anchor's intention to enter a contract in accordance with the general terms set out by Borg-Warner, but added certain prerequisites. "[S]uitable assurances" would have to be given "for the retention of the lower level executive personnel" of Anchor, and "mutually satisfactory arrangements" would have to be made "for the continued employ of Charles L. Conroy." The trial court granted defendant Anchor's motion to dismiss, on the ground that no contract existed. The Supreme Court of Illinois, two justices dissenting, reversed and remanded, holding that the parties were not confined to the terms of the writings by the Parol Evidence Rule because of their ambiguity. The court noted that

---

[100] 382 S.W.2d 198 (Ky. 1964).
[147] 16 Ill. 2d 234, 156 N.E.2d 513 (1958).

both the plaintiff and defendant Fritsch had indicated an intention and a belief that a binding contract had been made by the exchange of correspondence. Interpreting the facts in the light most favorable to plaintiff, the court held that a binding contract could be found to exist—one which was not too indefinite for specific performance, because the "mutually satisfactory arrangements" required to be made for Conroy could be taken to mean "reasonably satisfactory."

. . .

A better case could hardly be imagined to demonstrate the dilemma created by the common law for the judge concerned both with justice to the parties and with well-structured legal reasoning. While a majority of the court was persuaded by the parties' intention to make a binding agreement at the time they exchanged the letters, they were forced to take the position either that the contract was complete and binding in the absence of provisions for continued employment of personnel,—*including the second-largest stock-holder*, or that the whole agreement was binding and enforceable—even specifically enforceable—despite the failure of buyer and seller to reach final agreement on the terms of continued employment. As dissenting Justice Schaefer points out, the selling company must have been concerned with the welfare of those personnel, and indeed Conroy himself must have been vitally concerned over the prospects for his continued employment. Justice Schaefer, arguing against the imposition of liability, was forced to take the position that the plaintiff should not even get to the jury, despite the allegation that the parties believed they were concluding a binding contract, acted as though they believed it, and—with only one apparent exception—still believed it.

By contrast, applying the contract to bargain framework to such a situation would permit the court to take notice of, and give effect to, the parties' intention to create a relation which was, at least to some extent, legally binding. Second, it would save the court from inserting "reasonable" terms in the agreement where the terms are of such importance that they should only be decided by the parties. Third, it would direct the attention of the court to another important fact in the case: *Why has the defendant refused to go through with the sale?* If he has simply changed his mind, or now thinks a better price can be found elsewhere, then he should be liable to the plaintiff for breach of contract. If, however, he has withdrawn because negotiations have broken down on the terms of his employment contract, and he has bargained in good faith, then he should be subject to no liability.

Of course, the court may have properly characterized the agreement as a complete and fully binding contract. The common law, however, forces the court to choose one extreme or the other, and, by directing the court's attention to the completeness of the agreement, the law diverts attention from the good faith of the non-performing party, which should be the most important question of all.

E. *Contract for the Sale of Corporate Stock*

Several cases involving contracts for the sale of corporate stock have raised problems of the sort under discussion. *Pennsylvania Co. v. Wilmington Trust Co.*[154] is of particular interest because the court's decision is based on U.C.C. Section 2-204.

. . .

[In *Pennsylvania*, potential buyers; of stock in the Toledo, Peoria and Western Railroad ("T.,P.&W.") held by testamentary trustees had signed letter agreements with the trustees, subject to board and government approvals, and with express understandings that "necessary details" would be worked out by counsel. Under pressure from the beneficiaries, the trustees accepted a rival more attractive offer, arguing that the letter agreement was not binding. In denying the trustees' motion for summary judgment, the court applied U.C.C. 2-204(3) to find a triable issue of fact whether the letter agreement was itself an enforceable contract, despite the unresolved details. —ed.]

There is no need to quarrel with the outcome of the decision. Notice, however, the extent to which the court—even with the aid of the Uniform Commercial Code—was trapped by the all-or-nothing dichotomy of the law of contract. The language is clearly wrong. The result is clearly right. In order to hold defendants liable for breaking a binding contract with plaintiff, the court had to cite the letter agreement between the parties as evidence of a fully-binding contract. The inescapable conclusion is that if the parties should—in the course of agreeing on "all necessary details"—fail to agree on some term, either party could seek legal enforcement of the letter agreement, and the court would decide how the "nec-

[154] 39 Del. Ch. 453, 166 A.2d 726 (Ch. Ct. 1960), aff'd, 40 Del. Ch. 140, 172 A.2d 63 (Sup. Ct. 1961).

essary detail" should be resolved. Note, however, that the letter agreement contained just four terms: the price; the subject matter of the sale; the identities of the parties; and the "understanding" that the T., P. & W. would continue to operate "as an independent organization." Given the multitude of points which attorneys for either side undoubtedly would raise in the course of working out a detailed agreement, and the seriousness with which failure to agree on some of those points would be regarded by one side or the other, it is inconceivable that the letter agreements should be sufficient to make the sale of stock "unstoppable."

What is conceivable, however, is that the defendants should have been held accountable if they withdrew from the transaction *for the sole purpose of getting a better price elsewhere,* as they apparently did. If the agreement of April 15 were regarded as a contract to bargain, the court would no longer be forced to choose between doing justice and talking sense. Regardless of whether the sale would have been completed, the evidence was sufficient to show each party so committed to the basic terms of the proposed exchange that each was bound to attempt in good faith to agree on the remaining terms. Defendants clearly breached that obligation by their bad faith insistence on a higher price.

IV. Some Aspects Of The Contract To Bargain

A. *Intention*

. . .

No court, however, should lightly engage in speculation about the possible intention of the parties; the burden of proof should be on the proponent of a contract to bargain, just as it is on the proponent of any contract. On the other hand, the burden of proof should be no greater than for any other contract—and leaving aside such requirements as the Statute of Frauds—the proponent should not be precluded from relying on oral manifestations of intention.

B. *Good Faith Bargaining*

. . .

Consideration of the "good faith" standard for performance of the contract to bargain suggests two related objections which may be raised to judicial recognition of such contracts. The device may be used to penalize a party merely for "insufficient bargaining." There is, of course, some danger that a party's withdrawal from a contemplated transaction after what he regards as a complete breakdown of negotiations might later be viewed as a failure to bargain long enough, or "reasonably" enough, thus constituting a breach of contract. Plaintiff, however, bears the burden of proof both as to the existence of a contract and as to its breach. In the absence of any additional factors to indicate bad faith (such as acceptance of a better offer from a third party), a court might well find that plaintiff had failed to demonstrate defendant's lack of good faith.

This leads to the second objection that whenever an extraneous factor, such as a better offer from a third party, makes withdrawal from the contract materially advantageous to one party, that party runs the risk of being held liable even if he withdraws from the transaction only after extensive bargaining has failed to produce a complete agreement. Two factors, however, seem to minimize the likelihood of such occurrences. One is the possibility of creating a record of bargaining sufficient to demonstrate that agreement clearly could have been reached had the plaintiff really desired it; second, even those courts willing to recognize the contract to bargain will do so with extreme caution, and only where the justice of plaintiff's claim is virtually beyond question. These two factors suggest that a contract to bargain is likely to be enforced only where there has been either a unilateral withdrawal from negotiations or at least an insistence on terms so clearly unreasonable that they could not have been advanced with any expectation of acceptance, coupled with some demonstrable advantage to be gained by defendant in avoiding the contemplated transaction.

C. *Remedy for Breach*

What sort of remedy should be available for the breach of a contract to bargain? No definitive answer will be attempted here; indeed, there is respectable authority for avoiding such an attempt.[170] The suggestion has already been made that the damage remedy in such a case should extend at least to reimbursement of the plaintiff's reliance expenditures . . . . The harder question is whether the plaintiff's remedy should always be confined to reliance, or should in some cases extend to full compensation for lost expectation.[171] The cases suggest certain factors which bear on this question:

---

[170] Restatement (Second) of Contracts § 90 (remedy in promissory estoppel case may be limited "as justice requires"). Comment e to this section makes some suggestions as to the application of this very vague standard.

[171] See generally Fuller & Perdue, The Reliance Interest in Contract Damages (pts. 1 & 2), 46 Yale L.J. 52, 373 (1936-1937).

[Knapp concludes that many contracts to bargain will have too many essential terms missing to permit expectation remedies to be awarded, but if enough terms are present, disappointed sellers may be able to show a loss through a substitute sale and some buyers may justify recapturing the seller's windfall profits on a sort of unjust enrichment theory.]

The preceding discussion has been concerned with the various measures of damages that might be employed for breach of a contract to bargain. Should such an agreement ever be specifically enforced?

Because of the peculiar nature of the contract to bargain, it is apparent that two types of specific performance are theoretically possible: specific performance of the bargaining process to which defendant had committed himself in the contract, and specific performance of the end-transaction which was to be shaped by the parties pursuant to their initial contract. It seems highly unlikely that a court would grant specific performance of the former type, given the inevitable lapse of time and the likely estrangement of the parties.[175] In many cases an adequate remedy will be available without resorting to enforced bargaining; a court which recognizes the contract to bargain under Section 2-204 of the Commercial Code would probably not regard specific enforcement of this type as being "appropriate," even if no other remedy appeared "adequate."

What then of the second possibility? Should a court ever order specific performance of the exchange on terms which in its opinion would have been agreed on by the parties if good faith bargaining had actually taken place? The discussion above suggests that it should not, since the parties are not consenting to a third party's determination of what constitutes reasonable agreement as to the open terms. It has already been suggested that in some cases the essential terms of the contemplated exchange will have been so far agreed upon that a court could properly frame an expectation remedy in damages. In some cases the terms of that exchange will—by the time of defendant's breach—have been agreed upon in such detail that a court would be justified in rendering a decree of specific performance. If specific performance of the exchange is to be an available remedy for breach of the contract to bargain—even if only in exceptionally clear cases—does the contract to bargain amount to a "reasonable terms" contract, under another name?

Reference to Section 2-305 of the Uniform Commercial Code demonstrates that there is indeed an important distinction between the two types of contract. In the kind of "reasonable price" contract envisioned by 2-305(1), the parties are bound even if they are unable, after good faith negotiation, to agree on such a price. Once the contract has been made, therefore, a legal remedy becomes available to any party who is later disappointed by failure to consummate the exchange. In the contract to bargain case, a remedy would not be available unless the defendant was somehow at fault for the failure to agree. A genuine breakdown in negotiations will not discharge the "reasonable price" contract of 2-305 (1); it would, however, discharge the contract to bargain.

V. Conclusion

It may well be argued that, whatever its disadvantages, the present clear demarcation between contract and non-contract at least has the virtue of certainty, and that to introduce the concept of a contract to bargain as a half-way house between the two will only create uncertainty, and thus breed litigation. The "floodgates" argument is heard whenever it is suggested that a remedy should be made available where it has previously been denied; this does not mean, however, that it always lacks validity.

Here there are at least two countervailing considerations. The amount of uncertainty already prevalent in this area is, as a result of the existing law, not inconsiderable. To mitigate the harshness of the "agreement to agree" cases by introducing the contract to bargain concept may indeed create some additional uncertainty and thus increase litigation; however, the "uncertainty" would largely concern the proper remedy for deserving persons who are currently assured of no remedy at all. The change is not a development to be dreaded.

A franker response, however, is that in the area of commercial bargains between merchants, the floodgates argument is essentially a phony one. The vast preponderance of disputes arising out of the non-performance of commercial agreements do not end up in court. Either some settlement is worked out by the parties, or one side simply abandons its position, and accedes to the claim of the other. No change in any particular axiom of contract law will alter this. Judicial adjustment of contract disputes is the exception rather than the rule, and agreements are kept to the

---

[175] This, despite a discernible trend of courts to grant specific performance in unique situations. See Van Hecke, Changing Emphasis in Specific Performance, 40 N.C.L. Rev. 1 (1961).

extent that they are largely because of extra-legal pressures and sanctions.[178]

What can change, however, is the frame of reference within which settlement negotiations are conducted. The threat of litigation is seldom invoked, but the probable outcome of the unwanted lawsuit is one of the factors—perhaps not decisive, but influential—that determines whether or not to settle, and for how much. If the law should frankly tip the scales against bad faith in the context of a contract to bargain, then such conduct might be deterred. Even if the end result of such a development were merely an increase in the settlements made by those desiring to escape from their agreements, to raise the price of bad faith in this manner seems quite in harmony with the spirit of the Code.

Having attempted to answer the principal arguments against judicial recognition of the contract to bargain, there is one more affirmative argument—perhaps implicit from what has been said before, but worthy of restatement here. Recognition of the contract to bargain would have a beneficial effect on "the law" itself—upon the quality of legal decision-making and the decisions it creates. It would represent a movement away from fiction and toward reality in two related but distinct respects.

There is some evidence in the cases discussed above that courts will respond to the element of bad faith when it is clearly present. If the law persists in declaring bad faith irrelevant in the negotiation process, the court which is faced with clear bad faith conduct will be forced either to find a complete contract where in the absence of bad faith no such contract would be found, or else to write an opinion in which bad faith conduct is either condoned or ignored. Neither of these alternatives makes for "good law," a judicial opinion which, by the moral and logical force of its reasoning, compels acquiescence.

It is also perfectly clear that contracts do not really spring, full-blown, from the collective brows of the parties or their attorneys. It is often difficult to say at what point each party regards himself or the other party as bound. The possible variations are so numerous that the law cannot—and should not—attempt to fashion a different rule for every variety of subjective intention which each party might entertain, if only because such rules would be complex beyond any hope of comprehension, or administration.

Nevertheless, the evidence from cases and our own experience is that parties do often wish to register in an effective way their common commitment to an agreement, while reserving the privilege of differing over points not yet settled. If they have made such an agreement, the law has no business telling them their act of agreement was devoid of legal significance. Nor is the court, in characterizing that agreement, obliged to choose between only two labels, "complete contract" or "mere negotiation," neither of which accurately describes the case. If these were once the only alternatives, they are no longer. Under U.C.C. Section 2-204(3), if the parties intended a contract to bargain, and one of them is found to have breached his duty thereunder, nothing remains for the court but to determine whether an appropriate remedy is available. If there is such a remedy, it should be awarded.

For years, the "contract to make a contract" has been as firmly fixed in the affairs of men as the moon in its track, and yet, because of a seemingly unavoidable logical contradiction, has been as remote from our legal system as the moon seemed to Professor Corbin. The draftsmen of the Code have now bridged this abyss of contradiction; any judge persuaded to cross it will find the step a short one, and the terrain on the far side not as unfamiliar as might have been expected.

---

[178] See Macaulay, Non-Contractual Relations In Business A Preliminary Study, 28 Amer. Soc. Rev. 55, 60-62, 64-65 (1963).

E. Allan Farnsworth, *Precontractual Liability and Preliminary Agreements: Fair Dealing and Failed Negotiations,* 87 Colum. L. Rev. 217 (1987)

Introduction

Ours is an era of "deals"—for the long-term supply of energy, for the development of a shopping center, for the friendly takeover of a corporation, for the signing of a first-round draft choice. Much has been written on how to negotiate such deals. Little has been written on the law governing their negotiation.[2] This Article discusses that law and the recent outpouring of cases that apply it.

The law governing the formation of contracts is usually analyzed in terms of the classic rules of offer and acceptance. They are seductive rules that proceed on a simple premise: two parties exchange proposals until an "offer" by one party is "accepted" by the other forming a contract. Their precise vocabulary of "offer" and "acceptance," of "revocation" and "lapse," of "rejection" and "counter-offer" dissects such tantalizing puzzles as those posed by the "battle of the forms" and contracts by correspondence. But however suited these rules may have been to the measured cadence of contracting in the nineteenth century, they have little to say about the complex processes that lead to major deals today.

Major contractual commitments are typically set out in a lengthy document, or in a set of documents, signed by the parties in multiple copies and exchanged more or less simultaneously at a closing. The terms are reached by negotiations, usually face-to-face over a considerable period of time and often involving corporate officers, bankers, engineers, accountants, lawyers, and others. The negotiations are a far cry from the simple bargaining envisioned by the classic rules of offer and acceptance, which evoke an image of single-issue, adversarial, zero-sum bargaining as opposed to multi-issue, problem-solving, gain-maximizing negotiation.

During the negotiation of such deals there is often no offer or counter-offer for either party to accept, but rather a gradual process in which agreements are reached piecemeal in several "rounds" with a succession of drafts. There may first be an exchange of information and an identification of the parties' interests and differences, then a series of compromises with tentative agreement on major points, and finally a refining of contract terms. The negotiations may begin with managers, who refrain from making offers because they want the terms of any binding commitment to be worked out by their lawyers. Once these original negotiators decide that they have settled those matters that they regard as important, they turn things over to their lawyers. The drafts prepared by the lawyers are not offers because the lawyers lack authority to make offers. When the ultimate agreement is reached, it is often expected that it will be embodied in a document or documents that will be exchanged by the parties at a closing.

If the parties sign and exchange documents at the closing, there is no question that they have given their assent to a contract. There is little occasion to apply the classic rules of offer and acceptance. But if the negotiations fail and no documents are signed and exchanged, a number of questions may arise that the classic rules of offer and acceptance do not address: May a disappointed party have a claim against the other party for having failed to conform to a standard of fair dealing? If so, what is the meaning of fair dealing in this context? And may the disappointed party get restitution? Be reimbursed for out-

---

---

[2] On precontractual negotiations, see J. Schmidt, Negociation et conclusion de contrats (1982); Kessler & Fine, Culpa in Contrahendo, Bargaining in Good Faith, and Freedom of Contract: A Comparative Study, 77 Harv. L. Rev. 401 (1964); Summers, "Good Faith" in General Contract Law and the Sales Provisions of the Uniform Commercial Code, 54 Va. L. Rev. 195, 220-27 (1968). On preliminary agreements, see M. Lutter, Der Letter of Intent (1983) (in German); Dugdale & Lowe, Contracts to Contract and Contracts to Negotiate. 1976 J. Bus. L. 28; Fontaine, Les Lettres d'intention dans la negociation des contrats internationaux, 3 Droit et Pratique du Commerce International 73 (1977); Holmes, The Freedom Not to Contract, 60 Tul. L. Rev. 751, 776-86 (1986); Knapp, Enforcing the Contract to Bargain, 44 N.Y.U. L. Rev. 673 (1969); Schmidt, Preliminary Agreements in International Contract Negotiation, 6 Hous. J. Int'l L. 37 (1983); Trower, Enforceability of Letters of Intent and Other Preliminary Agreements, 24 Rocky Mtn. Min. L. Inst. 347 (1978).

of-pocket expenses? Recover for lost opportunities? As the paradigmatic deal has become larger and more complex, and the typical negotiation has become more complicated and prolonged, these questions have been reaching the courts in increasing numbers. Some observers have concluded that existing contract doctrines are not adequate to the task of protecting the parties. I argue that, on the contrary, those doctrines, imaginatively applied, are both all that are needed and all that are desirable.

The resolution of disputes occasioned by the failure of negotiations depends in any particular case on the legal "regime" under which the parties find themselves as they proceed through the negotiation process to ultimate agreement. In this Article, I identify and sketch the contours of four regimes and consider the requirement of fair dealing in each: the two polar regimes, negotiation and ultimate agreement, and the two intermediate regimes that may result from preliminary agreements, agreement with open terms and agreement to negotiate.

The two polar regimes, negotiation and ultimate agreement, are dealt with in Part I. Under the regime of negotiation, established bases of liability, if creatively used by litigants and liberally applied by courts, afford the parties sufficient protection. The stunted development of these bases in connection with negotiations is not due to any shortcomings in the bases themselves, but rather to the failure of litigants to exploit them fully, including a failure to seek damages for lost opportunities in appropriate cases. And if negotiating parties choose to move quickly to the regime of ultimate agreement in order to avoid the risks to which they are exposed under the regime of negotiation, existing contract law, with its tolerance of conditions, goes far in honoring their choice.

Parties who do not wish to rush to ultimate agreement are free instead to make a preliminary agreement to allocate the risks of their continuing negotiations. Such agreements, in particular agreements with open terms and agreements to negotiate, are the subject of Part II. I contend that existing contract law is fully capable of recognizing and enforcing such preliminary agreements, and that the refusal by some courts to enforce preliminary agreements to negotiate is not a justifiable restriction of party autonomy under existing contract law. Part III discusses

the content of the duty of fair dealing when it is imposed under an agreement to negotiate.[8]

. . .

[Professor Farnsworth devotes the next 43 pages to a discussion of the "polar regimes" of negotiation and ultimate agreement. Our traditional view has been that parties should be left free to negotiate without fear of liability if the negotiations do not lead to a contract. He refers to the risk that a party takes in investing in negotiations that may prove fruitless as the common law's "aleatory view" of negotiations. Nonetheless, though the law of pre-contractual liability is relatively undeveloped, there may be liability under the traditional grounds of unjust enrichment or misrepresentation, because of a specific promise (as in the famous case of *Hoffman v. Red Owl Stores*, 26 Wis. 2d 683, 133 N.W.2d 267 (1965)), or because of general obligation under a theory of good faith in bargaining as put forth in the Kessler and Fine *Culpa in Contrahendo* article mentioned in the introductory note to the Knapp and Farnsworth articles.

[Ultimate agreements, especially long-term ones, may be understood to involve negotiations over modifications. If so, a party may be in breach for refusal to negotiate, and would be bound by a duty of fair dealing during the negotiations. An ultimate agreement may leave one party with discretion over items triggered by outside events. But the discretion is subject to a requirement of fair dealing, and for this reason has been held not to make the party's duties illusory. There also may be preliminary agreements and agreements with open terms. The discussion is magisterial, but space requirements do not permit it to be reprinted.

[Within the discussion is an important one about the measure of damages for breaches under regimes other than ultimate agreement. In most of the fact situations expectation damages would not be likely, either because policy reasons would limit recovery to reliance damages to avoid a windfall to the plaintiff or because expectation damages are too speculative to be awarded. Farnsworth suggests that in the latter situation there is no policy reason why reliance damages should not include lost opportunities for alternative dealings.

[At this point Professor Farnsworth discusses the concept of an "agreement to negotiate." -ed.]

---

[8] "Fair dealing" is used in this Article in preference to "good faith," which is commonly used to refer to such a standard. "Good faith" also denotes the sort of honesty that makes one a good faith purchaser, a reference quite different from that intended here. Both the Uniform Commercial Code and the Restatement (Second) of Contracts couple "fair dealing" with "good faith." U.C.C. § 2-103 (1978); Restatement (Second) of Contracts § 205 (1981).

Sometimes parties are unwilling to make a binding agreement with open terms but wish to undertake a general obligation of fair dealing in their negotiations. The resulting agreements to negotiate have come before the courts with increasing frequency in recent years.

C. Agreement to Negotiate

1. *Nature of the Regime.*—The regime under an agreement to negotiate is similar to that under an agreement with open terms in that it imposes on the parties a duty to negotiate. But it differs in that should negotiations fail, there will be no agreement. Under an agreement with open terms, the parties negotiate with the knowledge that if they fail to reach agreement on the open terms, they will be bound by an ultimate agreement containing the terms on which they have agreed together with those terms that a court will supply. Under an agreement to negotiate, the parties negotiate with the knowledge that if they fail to reach ultimate agreement they will not be bound. The parties to an agreement to negotiate do, however, undertake a general obligation of fair dealings in their negotiations. This often happens when there is a division of responsibility between managers and lawyers.

What is the remedy for breach of such an obligation? The situation here differs from that under the regimes of ultimate agreement and agreement with open terms. There, the obligation of fair dealing is but one obligation that is part of a larger agreement, so that a breach of that obligation might, in an extreme case, be treated as a total breach of that agreement with a resulting claim to damages based on lost expectation. Here, there is no larger agreement and so no possibility of a claim for lost expectations under such an agreement. Furthermore, here there is no way of knowing what the terms of the ultimate agreement would have been, or even whether the parties would have arrived at an ultimate agreement, so

there is no possibility of a claim for lost expectation under such an agreement.[192]

Because of the uncertain scope of an undertaking to negotiate, a court cannot be expected to order its specific performance,[193] though a court might enjoin a party that had undertaken to negotiate exclusively from negotiating with others.[194] Usually the injured party's recourse is to refuse to negotiate and to seek monetary relief. In some situations recovery measured by the restitution interest will be appropriate, as under the regime of negotiation. Generally, however, recovery will be measured by the reliance interest. Reliance damages are particularly appropriate here since a party generally perceives an agreement to negotiate as protecting just that interest, should the other pull out of the negotiations. And the case for counting lost opportunities is strengthened because, in contrast to the regime of negotiation, here the parties explicitly subject themselves to the regime by undertaking to negotiate.[195]

2. *Enforceability of the Agreement.*—Courts have often balked at enforcing agreements to negotiate even if the parties have made it clear that they want to subject themselves to this regime. English courts have been adamant. In 1857, a member of the House of Lords impatiently explained: "An agreement to enter into an agreement upon terms to be afterwards settled between the parties is a contradiction in terms. It is absurd to say that a man enters into an agreement till the terms of that agreement are settled."[196] In 1974, Lord Denning reaffirmed this in a case involving an agreement "to negotiate fair and reasonable contract sums" with the nonsequitur: "If the law does not recognise a contract to enter into a contract (when there is a fundamental term yet to be agreed) it seems to me it cannot recognise a contract to negotiate."

In the United States, where many of the leading cases involve mergers and acquisitions, courts have been of two minds. Some have, like English courts,

---

[192] But see Knapp, supra note 2, at 723 ("In some cases, however, the main terms of performance . . . may have been so agreed upon . . . than an expectation remedy can be computed with as much certainty as is usually required."); see also Air Technology Corp. v. General Elec. Co., 347 Mass. 613, 624-27, 199 N.E.2d 538, 546-48 (1964), in which the court, finding "a contractual association in some form of joint undertaking" between a general contractor and a subcontractor, concluded that the general contractor had not met its obligation "to negotiate a subcontract," and while that obligation was "too uncertain to be enforceable," the subcontractor could recover for the value of the "business opportunity" that it had been promised.

[193] See, e.g., American Broadcasting Cos. v. Wolf, 52 N.Y.2d 394, 420 N.E.2d 363, 438 N.Y.S.2d 482 (1981) (court refused to grant injunctive relief against sportscaster who was in "breach of good faith negotiation provision of a now expired broadcasting contract").

[194] But cf. id. at 394, 420 N.E. 2d at 363 (refusing to enjoin employee from working for another employer in position obtained in violation of promise to negotiate for stated period with former employer).

[195] Knapp appears to take this position. Knapp, supra note 2, at 723-24.

[196] Ridgway v. Wharton, 10 Eng. Rep. 1287, 1313 (H.L. 1857) (Lord Wensleydale).

refused to accord parties the freedom to impose this regime on themselves. Federal courts applying New York law have been the most prominent in refusing on the ground of indefiniteness to enforce explicit agreements to negotiate, whether expressed in terms of "good faith" or "best efforts."

Other courts have been willing to give effect to the parties' expressed intention. *Itek Corp. v. Chicago Aerial Industries*[201] is the leading example. During negotiations for the purchase of Itek's assests by California Aerial Industries (CAI), the parties executed a "letter of intent" confirming the terms of the sale and providing that they "shall make every reasonable effort to agree upon and have prepared . . . a contract providing for the foregoing purchase . . . embodying the above terms and such other terms and conditions as the parties shall agree upon."[202] Itek later consented to a modification of the agreed terms, but CAI, evidently having received a more favorable offer, telegraphed that it would not go ahead with the transaction. Itek sued CAI, which had summary judgment. The Supreme Court of Delaware reversed, reasoning that the letter in which "the parties obligated themselves to 'make every reasonable effort' to agree upon a formal contract . . . obligated each side to attempt in good faith to reach final and formal agreement." It was error to grant summary judgment because there was evidence that in order to accept a more favorable offer, "CAI willfully failed to negotiate in good faith and to make 'every reasonable effort' to agree upon a formal contract, as it was required to do."

This view has gained a substantial following. A few courts have gone to considerable lengths in spelling out an obligation to negotiate from unclear language and suggestive circumstances. There have even been intimations that such an obligation might be implied in law in the absence of any actual assent by the parties. One may doubt the wisdom of those courts that have strained to find an agreement to negotiate in the absence of a clear indication of assent, for if carried to an extreme this would enable courts to impose a general obligation of fair dealing. But there is no compelling justification for those decisions that, in line with the English precedents, have refused to give effect to the intention of the parties when they have made an explicit agreement to negotiate.

Courts have generally been willing to enforce private agreements that do not contravene public policy. The burden lies on the party that would have the court refuse enforcement to show why enforcement should be denied. Courts have advanced two reasons for refusing to enforce explicit agreements to negotiate.

One is that a court cannot fashion an appropriate remedy for the breach of such a duty because there is no way to know what ultimate agreement, if any, would have resulted. This specious argument is sometimes enhanced by characterizing the agreement pejoratively as an "agreement to agree."[209] But the appropriate remedy is not damages for the injured party's lost expectation under the prospective ultimate agreement but damages caused by the injured party's reliance on the agreement to negotiate.[210] If one party breaks off the negotiations before the other has relied on the agreement to negotiate, there is no need to fashion a remedy because no relief is called for.[211] Once the other party has relied, it must prove the loss caused by its reliance, including any lost opportunities.

A more substantial reason for refusing to enforce explicit agreements to negotiate is that a court cannot determine the scope of the obligation of fair dealing under such an agreement. The indefiniteness of the concept of fair dealing is, however, a weak ground for denying relief that involves only the award of reliance damages, for courts generally demand less definiteness when damaged are measured by reliance than when they are measured by expectation.[213] Futhermore, even when expectation damages are claimed under a contract, courts have not balked at applying a standard of fair dealing. Either "good faith" or "best efforts" is sufficient to define a duty or a condition under a contract. Judicial antipathy

---

[201] 248 A.2d 625 (Del. 1968).

[202] Id. at 627. The letter continued: "If the parties fail to agree upon and execute such a contract they shall be under no further obligation to one another." The court read this as absolving the parties from "further obligation" only if such effort failed.

[209] To avoid this, Knapp suggests the term "contract to bargain." Knapp, supra note 2, at 685. This Article suggests "agreement to negotiate."

[210] It might be argued that no loss was caused by the breach of the agreement to negotiate, since the party who broke off the negotiations might have done so without any breach, simply by negotiating fairly but refusing to agree. While this argument has some force where the reliance is not on a misrepresentation or special promise, it seems unlikely to prevail where both breach and loss are clear.

[211] In the case of an agreement to negotiate exclusively, however, a negative injunction may be appropriate.

[213] See E. Farnsworth, Contracts § 3.30, at 209-10.

toward attempts by the parties to a negotiation to impose a duty of fair dealing on themselves by means of an agreement to negotiate seems particularly inconsistent with increasing judicial tolerance toward attempts by the parties to a contract to impose just such a standard on one party by means of a condition of satisfaction.

It is not easy to justify the refusal of courts to recognize a duty of fair dealing under an agreement to negotiate when they have been willing to recognize such a duty under either an ultimate agreement or an agreement with open terms. It can, to be sure, be argued that negotiations are likely to be less complex and far ranging under the last two regimes than under an agreement to negotiate, but this argument is not compelling.

Under an ultimate agreement, the duty of fair dealing extends only to modifications that both parties have chosen to negotiate. But, since potential modifications are ordinarily relatively limited in scope when compared to the agreement as a whole, the negotiations will in practice be similarly limited. Under an agreement with open terms, the duty of fair dealing extends to all terms left open. But since the requirement of definiteness limits the extent to which terms can be left open, the negotiations will again be limited. Under an agreement to negotiate, however, the scope of the negotiations is not so confined.

In practice, however, parties do not usually make agreements to negotiate until the negotiations are well advanced, so that what remains to be negotiated may be no more extensive than if the parties had made an agreement with open terms. Indeed, the negotiations are often so far advanced that the parties will have a choice between making an agreement with open terms and an agreement to negotiate, depending on whether they want to be bound or not, should their negotiations fail through no fault of either. A court that is willing to apply a standard of fair dealing when a number of matters remain to be negotiated under an agreement with open terms should not refuse to apply such a standard when the very same matters remain to be negotiated under an agreement to negotiate.

There will, of course, be occasional cases in which an agreement to negotiate will have been made at such an early stage of negotiations that a court could properly refuse to enforce it. Refusal to enforce the agreement is likely to foreclose at most a claim for expenditures in reliance, since any claim for lost opportunities would probably be foreclosed on the ground that the failure to pursue other opportunities was not justifiable where the negotiations were not advanced.

Concern over the enforceability of agreements to negotiate cannot but discourage their use. It is therefore to be expected that there is relatively little law on the content of the duty of fair dealing under such agreements. If courts are to enforce such agreements, it becomes important to determine that content. We turn to this in Part III.

III. The Meaning Of Fair Dealing

A. *In General*

1. *Sources of Meaning.*—Fair dealing has one meaning where negotiations have resulted in an agreement and an aggrieved party seeks to avoid that agreement for unfairness. Here the claim of unfairness goes to the means used to induce agreement. Judicial experience in dealing with unfairness in this context goes back to the earliest claims of fraud and duress. Fair dealing has a quite different meaning where negotiations have failed to result in an agreement and an aggrieved party seeks to recover reliance damages. Here the claim of unfairness goes to the means used to obstruct agreement. Courts have paid little attention to the meaning of fair dealing in this context. Those that have held that the parties can impose a duty to negotiate on themselves have often, as in the *Itek* case,[216] left the meaning of fair dealing for a lower court to determine at a subsequent trial. Scholars, too, have been more concerned with the imposition of the duty than with its content.

Most scholarly discussions of the meaning of fair dealing in the context of ordinary contract negotiations are modest in their contributions. More is required of a party than the mere absence of malice and fraud, but how much more? The commentary to the Restatement (Second) of Contracts notes only that while its section on "good faith," like the comparable section of the Uniform Commercial Code, "does not deal with good faith in the formation of a contract," bad faith negotiation may be subject to sanctions under more specific rules such as those on fraud and duress. Fisher and Ury observe that it is "often

---

[216] Itek Corp. v. Chicago Aerial Indus., 248 A.2d 625 (Del. 1968).

hard to decide what it means to negotiate in 'good faith'" and that "people draw the line in difference places." They suggest simple analogies such as that of dealing with a good friend or a family member. Summers gives specific instances of bad faith, a few of which involve negotiations, but does not go beyond a discussion of the established category of "negotiating without serious intent to contract" and a discussion of the category of "abusing the privilege to break off negotiations" that is largely confined to an analysis of *Red Owl*. Burton, in discussing good faith performance, urges a general test under which good faith is limited to the exercise of discretion for any purpose within the reasonable contemplation of the parties and bad faith involves the use of discretion to recapture opportunities forgone at formation of the contract, but he does not attempt to apply his analysis to contract negotiations. [For further discussion of good faith, see Part IIIB of this anthology.—ed.]

Knapp offers a more fully developed standard of fair dealing in negotiation, one under which "neither can withdraw for an 'unjustified' reason, and yet . . . neither will be compelled to perform if—after good faith bargaining—actual agreement cannot be reached." Bad faith bargaining may consist of "an insistence on terms so clearly unreasonable that they could not have been advanced with any expectation of acceptance, coupled with some demonstrable advantage to be gained by . . . avoiding the contemplated transaction."

Given the paucity of discussions of the meaning of fair dealing in ordinary contract negotiations, it is of interest to look at cases that interpret the provisions of the National Labor Relations Act (NLRA) that require parties engaged in collective bargaining to bargain in "good faith." The analogy from ordinary contract negotiations to collective bargaining is, to be sure, less than perfect. In ordinary contract negotiations there is no public interest in a successful outcome that is comparable to the interest in preventing labor strife. The relationship between the parties is not necessarily a continuing one, and neither party is bound to deal exclusively with the other. Only occasionally will a party represent the interests of others as a labor union represents the interests of employees. The remedy sought is an award of damages rather than a cease and desist order. And in the absence of an administrative structure to make findings on alleged improprieties in negotiations, such find-

ings must be left to a judge or perhaps a jury. Nevertheless, helpful comparisons can be made, as has been recognized by courts that, in applying the NLRA, have drawn analogies to ordinary contract negotiations.

Although the Act makes the bargainer's state of mind decisive, that state must be inferred from observable conduct. Not only must the employer have "an open mind and a sincere desire to reach an agreement," but a "sincere effort must be made to reach a common ground." Because a party will rarely announce an intention to bargain in bad faith, courts have had to look for subtler manifestations such as refusing to disclose information relevant to the negotiations, rejecting routine provisions, shifting bargaining positions when agreement is near, engaging in dilatory tactics, or withholding agreement on trivial matters. Courts would have to show the same attention to all the circumstances in determining whether parties to ordinary contract negotiations have met a standard of fair dealing.

The Act's requirement of good faith bargaining has not escaped criticism. One court has observed that "[p]robably in few other instances is the task of judging so difficult." An independent study group has concluded that the efficacy of the process employed by the Board and the courts implementing the requirement "is at best doubtful." These criticisms do not, however, diminish the worth of the experience under the Act as a source of analogy.

2. *Language and Other Circumstances.*—Determining the content of the duty of fair dealing under a particular agreement involves, as does determining the content of any contract duty, an inquiry into the expectations of the parties. In making this inquiry a court must look to the language of the agreement and to the surrounding circumstances.

The term most commonly used to describe the duty of fair dealing is "good faith," but parties sometimes use the term "best efforts" instead of or in addition to "good faith." "Best efforts" is generally understood to describe a heavier burden than "good faith,"[233] but it is doubtful that the parties use the terms in different senses in this context. Although many agreements to negotiate say no more than this about the content of the duty, by thoughtful drafting the parties can easily prescribe whether the negotiations are to be exclusive, how long they must continue, what must be disclosed, and what must be held

---

[233] See E. Farnsworth, Contracts § 7.17, at 529.

in confidence. Given the uncertain state of the law on such matters, no drafter should leave them to a court.

Among the most important of the surrounding circumstances are the behavior of the parties up to the time of the agreement and the state of the negotiations at that time. From these, reliable inferences can often be drawn to supplement the language of the agreement. If, as I have suggested, parties do not usually make agreements to negotiate until the negotiations are well along, there will often be a substantial basis for such inferences. Expectations generally build over time, so that the more advanced the negotiations, the more difficult it will be to justify withdrawal. The previous relationship between the parties may also be important. If the parties have dealt with each other on other occasions, the pattern of those earlier negotiations may help to show their expectations in the negotiations in controversy. Evidence of trade practices may do the same.

While the language and other circumstances bear on the content of the duty of fair dealing in any particular case, most claims that a party engaged in unfair dealing to obstruct agreement can be grouped under seven headings: refusal to negotiate, improper tactics, unreasonable proposals, nondisclosure, negotiation with others, reneging, and breaking off negotiations. We turn to them in that order.

B. *Instances of Unfair Dealing*

1. *Refusal to Negotiate.* . . .

2. *Improper Tactics.*—What bargaining tactics are so improper as to be unfair in the context of obstructing agreement? Some tactics, such as fraud and duress, are plainly unfair, but ordinarily induce rather than obstruct agreement. The most troublesome cases in the present context involve inflexibility. For though hard bargaining may prevent agreement, it is often admired. When, if ever, is hard bargaining unfair?

In the context of collective bargaining, stubborn and unyielding bargaining alone is not enough to constitute bad faith, but it is often taken as some evidence of bad faith. An employer that consistently rejects out of hand all of the union's proposals or rigidly adheres to a set of proposals that are patently unacceptable is likely to be found to have bargained in bad faith.

It is unclear whether bad faith can be made out from no more than the assumption of a "take-it-or-

leave-it" position—as where an employer opens with a final "fair" offer and refuses to budge from it. . . .

Although inflexibility in ordinary contract negotiations poses similar difficulties, it is difficult to see why it should not be considered as evidence of unfairness if it is part of a pattern of behavior designed to obstruct agreement. When a party seeks to avoid an agreement, courts are willing to distinguish impermissible economic duress from allowable hard bargaining. They need not shrink from distinguishing unfair stubbornness from justifiable tenacity when negotiations have failed.

3. *Unreasonable Proposals.*—When, if ever, is it unfair to make unreasonable proposals during a negotiation? This has proved a controversial question in collective bargaining cases. . . .

There are obvious reasons why a court dealing with ordinary contract negotiations—lacking the benefit of the expertise of an administrative agency and a body of precedent arising out of similar transactions—should be hesitant to pass on the reasonableness of a party's proposals. Yet it is not impossible to imagine cases in which it would be appropriate to do so. If the parties have provided, as occasionally happens, that the terms to be negotiated are to be "no less favorable" than those of a specified agreement, it is surely not fair dealing to make a proposal that plainly falls below this standard. And even without such a provision, a proposal by a franchisor, for example, to renew the franchise on terms significantly less favorable to the franchisee, though there has been no change in circumstances to justify less favorable treatment, might be evidence of unfair dealing.

4. *Non-disclosure.*—When does fairness require that a party disclose facts on which its bargaining position is based? In some situations, a party's failure to disclose a fact amounts to a misrepresentation. This is so, for example, if disclosure is necessary to correct a previous statement that is no longer true.[257] If the negotiations do not result in agreement, there is no reason why such a failure to speak up should not be the basis for recovery of reliance damages. This would be so, for example, if a party who had begun negotiations with a serious intent to come to terms changed its mind and failed to tell the other party. In general, however, a negotiating party is not expected to go beyond this and disclose information relevant to its bargaining position. A seller need not justify the

---

[257] See Restatement (Second) of Contracts § 161 (1981) for this and other examples.

prices it proposes nor a landlord justify the rents it demands.

A heavier burden of disclosure rests on a fiduciary that negotiates with a beneficiary with respect to matters within the fiduciary relation. . . . It seems not to have been seriously contended, however, that the same requirement of disclosure in negotiations between fiduciary and beneficiary would be appropriate in ordinary contract negotiations.

Under the NLRA, however, courts have imposed on an employer engaged in collective bargaining a broad duty of disclosure—a duty to disclose to the union information relevant to the union's discharge of its function as bargaining representative. In reaching this result, the Supreme Court reasoned:

> Good-faith bargaining necessarily requires that claims made . . . should be honest claims. This is true about an asserted inability to pay an increase in wages. If such an argument is important enough to present in the give and take of bargaining, it is important enough to require some sort of proof of its accuracy.

In defining the content of this duty to disclose, courts have generally rejected employers' attempts to justify nondisclosure on the ground of confidentiality. The imposition of this duty can be justified as a means of forcing employers to abandon unjustified positions, thereby reducing labor strife.

Whatever the merits of this argument, it makes little sense to impose such a duty on parties to ordinary contract negotiations unless they explicitly assume it. Parties to such negotiations may, unlike parties to collective bargaining, be competitors. Even if they are not, they are often concerned that information disclosed during the negotiations not fall into the hands of competitors. Imposing a duty of disclosure on one party would raise the question of the scope of the concomitant duty of confidentiality of the other party. Among the most common types of stop-gap agreements are those providing for disclosure and confidentiality. Given the ease with which the parties themselves can and do deal with the matter of disclosure and related questions of confidentiality, there is scant reason for a court to impose such a requirement of disclosure, beyond that already imposed by the law of misrepresentation. We now turn to the problem of disclosure where a party is engaged in parallel negotiations.

5. *Negotiation with Others.*—Is a party to an agreement to negotiate restricted in conducting parallel negotiations with others? To begin with does fairness ever require a party to negotiate with one other party to the exclusion of all others? Knapp suggests that it does in arguing that "[w]ithdrawal merely because a better offer has been received from a third party . . . seems the most obvious case of bad faith."[264] Yet parallel negotiations are so common in practice and so important to competition that it is hard to see how there can be such a requirement in the absence of an undertaking that negotiations will be exclusive. Collective bargaining does not offer a useful analogy here; since exclusive bargaining is required by statute, there is no occasion for such an undertaking. "Exclusive negotiation" provisions are not, however, unusual in preliminary agreements arising out of ordinary contract negotiations, where they may be assented to by a party who will not grant a right of first refusal.

A typical exclusive-negotiation clause obligates one party to refrain from negotiating with others for a stated period of time. Although not all courts have held such clauses to be unenforceable, three federal district court cases, applying New York law, have taken this position on the ground that they are not sufficiently definite. But in two of the cases the undertaking was not limited in time, so that the court would have had to decide when the obligation of negotiation had been discharged, and an injunction was sought, so that definiteness took on special importance. It seems unlikely that these decisions will be followed by courts that have already shown receptivity to explicit undertakings to negotiate fairly. No drafter of such an undertaking should overlook, however, the importance of specifying a time limit for exclusivity.

6. *Reneging.*—An agreement to negotiate usually sets out, at least in summary form, those terms on which the parties have reached agreement, even though these terms are not binding. Is it unfair dealing to renege on such a commitment? It might seem so, since a common reason for making the agreement to negotiate is to prevent reopening of matters on which agreement has been reached. Indeed, parties who do not want to be precluded from reopening such matters sometimes recite that their agreement is not binding as to them. Nevertheless, even without such a

---

[264] Knapp, supra note 2, at 721. If it is bad faith to withdraw on the receipt of a better offer, it is presumably bad faith to seek to get a better offer by negotiating with a third party.

provision, a party should be free, especially in non-zero sum negotiations, to make creative proposals that may be advantageous to both parties. It should therefore be permissible to offer a concession in return for modification of a term already settled in the agreement. It is, after all, permissible for a party to any contract to do the same in return for a modification of a term of the contract.

The difficult question regards the effect of a party's outright refusal to abide by a term on which agreement has been reached unless the other party makes a concession on a matter still to be negotiated. If the preliminary agreement were one with open terms, rather than one to negotiate, such a refusal would be a repudiation of the agreement and therefore a breach. Even though the agreement is only one to negotiate, the imposition of such a condition would seem, especially if the negotiations are advanced, to amount to a refusal to negotiate and therefore also to be a repudiation and a breach.

This conclusion finds support in labor law, where reneging on a commitment made during collective bargaining may amount to a breach of the duty to bargain in good faith. To take an extreme case, the Act explicitly includes within the duty "the execution of a written contract incorporating any agreement reached if requested by either party." Furthermore, reneging on a commitment made before all of the terms have been agreed upon may also show bad faith. Thus an employer's abrupt refusal to honor a tentative agreement covering some but not all points has been held to support a finding of bad faith. A party can, however, escape such a finding by showing that there was good reason to renege.

7. Breaking Off Negotiations.—The discussion so far has dealt with claims of unfairness that one party would use to justify its breaking off negotiations and seeking reliance damages. This would be an appropriate response for a party who, for example, asserts that the other party's dilatory tactics amount to a refusal to negotiate. But what if the other party breaks off the negotiations? In what circumstances will this give the disappointed party a claim to reliance damages?

There will, of course, be situations in which the other party was justified in breaking off negotiations, and in these the disappointed party is not entitled to

any relief. The other party may have been justified on the ground of unfair dealing by the disappointed party. Or the other party may have been justified on the ground of mistake or changed circumstances. A party to a preliminary agreement should be, if anything, freer than a party to an ultimate agreement to invoke such arguments as mistake, impracticability, and frustration. It may not, for example, be a breach of an agreement to negotiate for the prospective purchaser of a business to back out on the ground of an unexpected drop in its earnings.

But sometimes a party has none of these justifications for breaking off negotiations. The party has simply exhausted its patience and concluded that the negotiations have no chance of success. When is a party justified in breaking off negotiations on this ground? If the undertaking has been carefully drafted, it may contain an outer time limit. But in most cases the answer must be derived from the circumstances.

Under the NLRA, the concept of "impasse" has been developed to deal with a comparable problem when it arises during collective bargaining. If good faith bargaining has resulted in impasse, the employer is no longer forbidden to make unilateral changes in terms of employment. According to a substantial body of case law, an impasse is a "state of facts in which the parties, despite the best of faith, are simply deadlocked." Whether the parties have reached this state has been described as "a matter of judgment" that turns on such factors as the "bargaining history, the good faith of the parties in negotiations, the length of the negotiations, the importance of the . . . issues as to which there is disagreement, [and] the contemporaneous understanding of the parties as to the state of [the] negotiations."

A concept of impasse is essential to the obligation of fair dealing in ordinary contract negotiations. If a party has undertaken to negotiate fairly, it should not be free to change its mind arbitrarily without reasonably exhausting the negotiation process.[279] The Seventh Circuit, for example, has held that a jury could find that a corporation negotiating to sell one of its divisions had violated a commitment under a letter of intent to negotiate in good faith by deciding to keep the division and breaking off negotiations some two

[279] "Each regards withdrawal by the other—for a reason other than the failure to reach agreement on the remaining points—as unjustified . . . ." Knapp, supra note 2, at 685-86.

Knapp, however, regards dealing with another, as well as changing one's mind, as a breach. See supra note 264 and accompanying text.

months later.[280] Implicit in such a conclusion is the assumption that the negotiations had not reached an impasse before they were broken off. The Supreme Court of Colorado has explicitly invoked the concept of impasse, saying that it "presupposes a reasonable effort of good faith bargaining to reach agreement."[281] The court found that there was a question of fact as to whether an impasse had been reached or whether the party who broke off negotiations had refused to negotiate.

But what if a party breaks off negotiations in order to conclude a deal with a third party?[283] The experience under the NLRA is not enlightening on this question because negotiations under the Act are exclusive. A party to an agreement to negotiate who has undertaken to negotiate exclusively with the other is plainly not entitled to conclude a deal with a third party until the period for exclusive negotiation has expired or, absent such a period, until impasse has been reached.

If a party has not agreed to negotiate exclusively, however, it seems unlikely that party can reasonably be expected to forgo the opportunity to conclude a deal with a third party before impasse has been reached. The fact that the party is permitted to engage in parallel negotiations supports this conclusion.[284] The uncertainty as to when impasse is reached and the control that the other party may have over when it is reached make this a practical conclusion. In the absence of a contrary indication, as by the fixing of a time limit for the negotiations, a party should not be expected to forgo other opportunities that might result from parallel negotiations. To take a simple example, if the deal is for the sale of goods for which there is a market, a party should not be expected to give up the advantages that come from changes in the market.

But even if exclusivity is not required, a party may not be as free in dealing with third persons as if there were no agreement to negotiate. It seems reasonable to expect a party who has agreed to negotiate with another party to keep that party informed of relevant proposals from third persons so as to enable it to take account of them in the negotiations. For a party who has made such an agreement to abruptly terminate the negotiations, especially if they are advanced, by accepting a third person's offer without giving the other negotiating party an opportunity to respond to the offer would ordinarily amount to a breach of the duty of fair dealing. Even one who has no right of first refusal may nevertheless be entitled to the opportunity to make a competing proposal.[285] To use the same example of goods for which there is a market, it would not be fair dealing for one party to take advantage of a market shift without first giving the other an opportunity to react to the shift and to respond.

8. *Summary.*—Each party to an agreement to negotiate reasonably expects to be compensated for its justifiable reliance, including lost opportunities, on the other's undertaking to negotiate in accordance with a standard of fair dealing. That standard ordinarily requires at least three things of a party. First, it requires the party actually to negotiate and to refrain from imposing improper conditions. Second, it requires the party to disclose enough about any parallel negotiations as is necessary to allow its counterpart a reasonable opportunity to make competing proposals. Third, it requires the party to continue negotiations until impasse has been reached, or until it is justified on some other ground in breaking off the negotiations.

The standard does not, however, require the party to bargain exclusively, to bargain for any specific length of time, or to disclose the basis of its proposals. Nor does the standard prevent the party from breaking off negotiations for such justifiable reasons as the material failure of its counterpart to perform in accordance with the standard of fair dealing and mistaken or changed conditions, including an opportunity to conclude the deal with a third party. Restrictions on this freedom may, however, be explicitly imposed by the agreement.

---

[280] Chase v. Consolidated Foods Corp., 744 F.2d 566, 571 (7th Cir. 1984).

[281] Vigoda v. Denver Urban Renewal Auth., 646 P.2d 900, 904 (Colo. 1982) (en banc).

[283] If this were regarded as a breach, the third party might be liable for tortious interference with the agreement to negotiate.

[284] There seems no reason why a party should not make separate agreements to negotiate with two other parties. If so, making an ultimate agreement with either party could hardly be a breach of the agreement to negotiate with the other party.

[285] Just as a party who would prefer an option may have to settle for a right of first refusal, a party who would prefer a right of first refusal may have to settle for an agreement to negotiate. Even if a party to such an agreement has no right to the deal on matching a competing offer, such a party may value the right to attempt to make a more attractive offer. This is especially likely if the two offers involve very different terms.

It might be objected that the duty of fair dealing suggested here inevitably involves a court in difficult questions of motive. This is true. If, for example, a party makes a public disclosure of the state of the negotiations, this might be regarded as unfair dealing if motivated by a desire to abort the negotiations but not if motivated by a desire to gain leverage in the negotiations. But this is not a fatal objection. Courts regularly make such determinations of motive in applying the standard of good faith in labor law. And they make analogous decisions as to motive in contract cases when applying the test of honest satisfaction.

A more troubling objection is that imposing a duty of fair dealing on a party that later changes its mind and wants to abort the negotiations may lead to subterfuge, encouraging that party to string the other along in order to avoid a charge of unfair dealing. While that party talked and stalled to impasse, the other party's reliance losses would mount. While this objection might be fatal if it were proposed that courts themselves impose a general duty of fair dealing, it is less convincing as a reason for refusing to enforce an agreement by the parties to impose such a duty on themselves. If the parties conclude that the advantages in an agreement to negotiate outweigh its obvious risks, it is surely not for a court to refuse to honor that conclusion on the basis of a contrary one. Furthermore, if the parties regard the risks as significant, they can limit them by fixing a time when the duty of fair dealing lapses.

Conclusion

Existing contract law has been criticized for failing to deal adequately with the negotiation of deals and, in particular, for failing to protect the rights of parties if their negotiations fail. An application of basic contract law principles to the negotiation process reveals that the criticism is unwarranted. The four regimes that I have identified, to which the parties to negotiations may be subject, provide a satisfactory framework for determining whether liability will attach to a particular type of behavior. Two of these regimes are the familiar polar regimes of negotiation and ultimate agreement. Two are intermediate regimes that the parties may impose on themselves by preliminary agreement—agreement with open terms and agreement to negotiate. Existing contract law is adequate to protect the parties under all four regimes.

Courts have not imposed a general obligation of fair dealing under the regime of negotiation. The dis-

appointed party may, however, have a claim based on restitution, on misrepresentation, or on a specific promise. Recovery for lost opportunities should be allowed in appropriate cases. But courts should not impose a general obligation of fair dealing and abandon the aleatory view of negotiations under which each party bears the risk that its efforts will go uncompensated if the negotiations fail.

Parties can lessen this risk by accelerating the negotiation process so as to reach the other polar regime of ultimate agreement more quickly. Courts have facilitated this through their tolerance for conditions of satisfaction that reserve to a party some of the discretion that it would have had under the regime of negotiation. Parties to an ultimate agreement are under no duty to negotiate a modification, but if they choose to do so they are subject to a general obligation of fair dealing. If their negotiations fail to result in a modification because of one party's breach of that obligation, the disappointed party should have not only a claim for damages for partial breach of the ultimate agreement but, in an extreme situation, the power to terminate that agreement and claim damages for its total breach.

Parties to a preliminary agreement with open terms expect further negotiations over the open terms. If the negotiations fail to result in agreement on the open terms, however, a court will supply the missing terms and enforce the agreement. As under the regime of ultimate agreement, the parties are subject to a general obligation of fair dealing in these negotiations. Again, if their negotiations fail to result in agreement on the open terms because of one party's breach of that obligation, the disappointed party should have not only a claim for damages for partial breach of the agreement with open terms but, in an extreme situation, the power to terminate that agreement and claim damages for total breach.

Parties to a preliminary agreement to negotiate also expect further negotiations. But in contrast to an agreement with open terms, if the negotiations fail to result in ultimate agreement, there will be no enforceable agreement. Some courts have refused to enforce such agreements to negotiate, even where the parties have explicitly undertaken an obligation of fair dealing. These decisions are wrong. Courts generally enforce private agreements that do not offend public policy. They have not balked at enforcing obligations of fair dealing in connection with negotiation under the regimes of ultimate agreement and agreement with open terms. There is no adequate reason to refuse to give effect to the explicit intention of the parties to an agreement to negotiate.

The specific content of the duty of fair dealing has received little attention in appellate opinions or commentary. Attention to basic contract law principles, supplemented by lessons from the resolution of analogous problems under the duty to bargain in good faith in labor law, suggest seven possible types of unfairness: refusal to negotiate, unreasonable proposals, improper tactics, nondisclosure, negotiation with others, reneging, and breaking off negotiations. Under an agreement to negotiate, the standard of fair dealing ordinarily requires: (1) actual negotiations with no imposition of improper conditions; (2) disclosure of enough about parallel negotiations to give a reasonable opportunity to make competing proposals; and (3) continued negotiation until impasse has been reached unless there is another justification for breaking off the negotiations. Absent a contrary understanding and as long as disclosure has been made to the other party, it is not a breach of the duty of fair dealing to conclude a deal with a third person.

The negotiation of deals does not fit into the mold of offer and acceptance, but that does not mean that basic principles of contract law are inadequate to protect the rights of parties if their negotiations fail. By applying those principles to the four regimes that I have identified, courts can reach fair resolutions of disputes that arise out of failed negotiations.

[An appendix with "vignettes" describing "six commonly litigated preliminary agreements" is omitted. —ed.]

B. Restitution and Reliance as Alternatives to Bargain

Restitution's Role in Contract

Restitution or quasi-contract (or implied-in-law contract or quantum meruit or quantum valebant) is, at least in origin, a procedural device designed to return to a plaintiff the value of some act or thing that has unjustly enriched another. Typically, there was no contract between the parties, and there is usually a question why the defendant is under any duty to the plaintiff. This is particularly true when the plaintiff has conferred a benefit on the defendant without being asked to do so. One can see overtones of tort in the restitution concept, especially in the phrase "unjust" enrichment. (As Anthony Jon Waters shows in his article *The Property in the Promise*, reprinted in Part IID, below, restitution also has property origins.)

John W. Wade, long-time Dean of Vanderbilt Law School, co-author of the most widely used torts casebook and co-reporter of the Restatement (Second) of Torts, is one of the most universally admired law teachers. He has for many years been one of the leading authorities on restitution. The following article, written in 1966, discusses many of the fact situations in which restitution is sought because a classic bargain cannot be found. Many of the other leading books and articles on restitution are cited in the notes. Part II of the article details when recovery has been denied, while Parts III and IV look toward a more rational rule permitting recovery when justified. In its more than twenty years of existence, Dean Wade's article has proven influential, primarily, I think, because he offers a rational way of dealing with the tension between our wanting to compensate the person who benefited another and our reluctance to force the other person to pay for something that he never asked for.

John W. Wade, *Restitution for Benefits Conferred Without Request,* 19 Vand. L. Rev. 1183 (1966)

I. Introduction

The principle is now fully recognized in this country that a "person who has been unjustly enriched at the expense of another is required to make restitution to the other." This is the language of the first section of the *Restatement of Restitution.* When one person confers a benefit upon another without the latter's solicitation, the benefit received constitutes an enrichment—a windfall, so to speak. This benefit may take one of several forms. It may involve (1) transferring property to the defendant, (2) saving, preserving or improving his property, (3) rendering personal services for him, or (4) performing for him a duty imposed directly by law or by his own contractual arrangements. In any of these situations there is an enrichment, and the principle quoted above comes into play if the enrichment is "unjust." When is it unjust? Obviously, it would not be so characterized if it were intended as a gift; just as obviously, the opposite is true if the plaintiff acted under legal compulsion and against his will. In making the determination, considerable weight is given to the circumstance that the benefit was not requested by the defendant.

The common law has long had a pronounced policy that benefits may not be forced upon a party against his will, so as to require him to pay for them. This idea has been forcefully expressed on a number of occasions. Said the court in the leading English case, "Liabilities are not to be forced upon people behind their backs any more than you can confer a benefit upon a man against his will." Most of the time this idea has been indicated by applying an epithet to the plaintiff. The term most frequently used is that of "volunteer." Applied to the plaintiff, particularly if it carries the adjective "mere," it has played the "kiss of death" and the sure indication that he will not be allowed to recover. Other derogatory terms used include meddler, intermeddler, interloper, mere stranger, mere impertinence. The Restatement uses the adjective "officious," which carries a somewhat more restricted connotation.[6] All of these terms embody the policy that one should not be required to pay for benefits which he did not solicit and does not desire.

It would not be inappropriate to regard this policy as conflicting with the unjust-enrichment principle, so that the two vie for dominance in general and for application in each fact situation in particular. Most statements of a rule have indicated that the volunteer-policy has prevailed over the unjust-enrichment principle, but a study of the cases indicates that there is a fairly delicate, and somewhat precarious balance between them and that the line of demarcation is a difficult one to draw. Instead of posing the problem in this fashion, however, it may be more accurate, and certainly more illuminating, to explain that the enrichment-principle provides for restitution only when the enrichment is unjust and that the volunteer-policy is a factor of consequence in determining whether or not the enrichment is unjust.

On this basis, the principle that restitution is granted the plaintiff whenever the defendant is unjustly enriched at plaintiff's expense may be regarded as fully applicable to the cases of benefits conferred without request. The task is to determine whether the enrichment is unjust. Perhaps the best way to treat this problem is to examine the cases to see what restrictions they indicate on recovery.[8] These restrictions are somewhat numerous and they may properly be given detailed consideration.

Preliminary reference should be made, however, to another factor which has sometimes played a part. This is the assumption that the granting of restitutionary relief may prove an inducement to a party to act. For this reason, when there is a recognized public interest in having one party intervene to perform another's neglected duty—supplying of necessaries to children, for example, or burial of the dead—restitution is normally granted. This is the purported rea-

---

---

[6] "A person who officiously confers a benefit upon another is not entitled to restitution therefor." Restatement, Restitution § 2 (1937). "Officiousness means interference in the affairs of others not justified by the circumstances under which the interference takes place." Id., comment a.

[8] The leading article on the general subject is Hope, Officiousness, 15 Cornell L.Q. 25 & 205 (1929); see also Dawson, Negotiorum Gestio: The Altruistic Intermeddler, 74 Harv. L. Rev. 817 & 1073 (1961); Heilman, The Rights of the Voluntary Agent Against His Principal in Roman Law and in Anglo-American Law, 4 Tenn. L. Rev. 34 & 76 (1925). . . .

son, also, for the maritime law of salvage—to encourage the rescue of an endangered ship and cargo. This element may therefore tip the balance whenever the court or the legislature feels that intervention should be encouraged.

At an earlier time another factor also influenced results. This was the circumstance that there was no actual contractual relationship between the parties. Today, however, we recognize that there is an obligation imposed by law, not by consent of the parties, and that privity of contract is entirely unnecessary. Other factors may also be of importance in individual cases.

II. Restrictions On Recovery

A. *No Recovery Unless Defendant Has Received a Measurable Enrichment*

This may appear to be a self-evident proposition, and indeed it is implicit in any statement of the enrichment principle. A benefit to the defendant is obviously necessary before he can be held liable. There are, however, certain embellishments on the requirement and explanations of its meaning.

The enrichment may be negative as well as positive. One is enriched not only when he receives an asset but also when someone else performs for him a duty which would be a burden to him. The clearest case is that of one person paying another's debt. The elimination of this obligation is clearly a benefit, and meets this requirement. Of course, other restrictions may still prevent recovery.

But a recovery, when granted, is normally restricted to the net enrichment. This is unlike the case of a benefit which was requested by the defendant, where the cost of purchasing or conferring it is often the measure of recovery, whether the defendant actually realized that amount of net gain or not. The cases most aptly illustrating this point are those involving improvements made on defendant's land under a mistake as to ownership. Here the measure of recovery is generally regarded as the net increase in the value of the land, rather than the cost of making the improvements, if it was more.

If the plaintiff's services did not produce any net value for the defendant, then recovery is usually not justified.[15] A possible exception to this involves personal services to an incapable defendant. Thus, when an unconscious patient was given emergency treatment by a doctor who failed to save him, recovery was allowed.[16] So also when an attorney failed in an action of habeas corpus to release the defendant from an asylum, and she died while he was working on other relief.

There may be other factors which affect the determination of whether there was a true benefit. Thus, when the defendant was contesting the validity of a debt and might have been relieved from paying it, the court held that it was not clear that payment by the plaintiff was beneficial. In another case, the court explained that payment of another's debt is beneficial, "provided no option or privilege of the person primarily or actually liable is thereby intercepted, or abridged or substantially altered." Other situations may easily be conceived where a detriment connected with the benefit causes its value to be outweighed.

A reasonably certain measurement of the enrichment is also needed. Thus, where the plaintiff saves the defendant's life, it certainly would not be thought that the total value of the defendant's life expectancy is the measure of the enrichment. There is, indeed, no accurate basis for measuring the benefit, and this may well be an important reason why courts have been slow to grant recovery in this situation. On the other hand, if the plaintiff is a doctor who has regular fees for treating a patient, this difficulty does not exist and recovery is more freely granted. Similarly, in the case of action to save property from destruction, recovery should not be granted for the full value of the property, and if there is no other way of determining the value of the services, recovery is unlikely.

In this type of situation courts sometimes resort to a device used in actions for breach of contract when the normal measure of damages (what the plaintiff would have received if the contract had been carried out) is so vague as to be almost useless; they take the test of the expense to which the plaintiff has been put—his out-of-pocket loss. Thus, in *Chase v. Corcoran*,[22] where the plaintiff found a damaged boat adrift on the river and recovered and repaired it, he was allowed a reimbursement of his "reasonable expenses of keeping and repairing it." Several other cases are in accord. There are some indications that

---

[15] See, e.g., Mulligan v. Kenny, 34 La. Ann. 50 (1882), where plaintiff replaced some rotted beams and other timbers in a church tower, without consent or approval of defendant. On the basis that the work to repair the tower adequately would still need to be done and would cost as much as if the plaintiff had done no work, the court held that

there could be no recovery. There were other bases, in addition, for a holding for the defendant.

[16] Cotnam v. Wisdom, 83 Ark. 601, 104 S.W. 164 (1907); Matheson v. Smiley, 40 Man. 247, [1932] 1 West Weekly R. 758, [1932] 2 D.L.R. 787.

[22] 106 Mass. 286 (1871).

this approach may also apply to damages incurred by the plaintiff in rendering his service. Thus in *Sheldon v. Sherman*,[25] defendants' logs broke loose from a boom and came to rest down the river on plaintiff's land, where they remained for several months before being reclaimed. The court held that although the defendants were not originally at fault so as to be liable in tort, when they removed the logs, they became responsible for payment of damages on the basis of a promise raised by law. Application of this measure of recovery is less likely to be generally adopted, however, than that of out-of-pocket expenses in rendering the service to the defendant.

An interesting question arises when the plaintiff prevents what would normally be a loss to the defendant, but a third party would have been under a duty to replace that loss. Suppose, for example, that the plaintiff saved the defendant's property from fire, but the property was insured or the defendant would have been able to recover the value of the property from the person who negligently started the fire. What is the enrichment under these circumstances? There seem to be no authorities directly in point, but several cases involving maritime salvage are analogous. The holding in *The Meandros* would suggest that defendant is liable for the value of the services in saving the ship. On the other hand, there are several cases which indicate that the insurance company should be liable since it received a substantial benefit in the prevention of the loss. . . . Several cases indicate that when the salvor's action prevented or reduced a third party's liability to the owner in negligence, he is entitled to salvage from that party. There are helpful analyses, also, in some decisions outside the maritime area. In *Leebov v. United States Fidelity & Guaranty Co.*,[33] where a construction contractor with insurance against his liability for damage to land went to considerable expense to avert an impending landslide, he was allowed to recover expenses against the insurance company.[34] Pertinent also are the numerous cases holding that one who is injured in seeking to rescue another's person or property from danger created by a tortfeasor can recover

from the tortfeasor for his negligence.[36] Although there are gaps in the combined coverage of these cases, the net effect of the combination is the suggestion that if the defendant is held liable for the value of the plaintiff's services, he may recover from the third party whose liability in contract or tort was averted, and that the plaintiff might perhaps have a direct action against that third party. It seems likely that if all three parties are joined in a single suit, plaintiff's chance of recovery would be good. At least, he would be able to show a net benefit in the two defendants.

B. *No Recovery if Plaintiff Intended to Act Gratuitously*

Quite obviously an enrichment is not unjust if it was bestowed upon the defendant as a gift. Nor should one be allowed to recover for services which he rendered without any intent to charge for them. A change of circumstances so that the plaintiff does not now wish to render a gift is normally held not to alter the result. Once having made the gift or rendered the gratuitous service he cannot now change his mind and seek to recover because of new conditions. On the other hand, if a gift is made under a mistake as to existing circumstances, although earlier cases denied restitutionary relief, the more recent cases usually permit recovery when the actual circumstances make it equitable. If the mistake is to a material fact inducing the making of the gift, the donative intent should no longer be controlling and restitution may be granted.

Perhaps a majority of the cases in which the presence or absence of intent to charge is involved are concerned with services rendered to relatives living in the home. Courts have declared that while it is normally presumed that one who renders services intends to charge for them, the presumption is that they are gratuitous when they are rendered to a relative; other factors, such as the reciprocal rendering of services, the nature of the services, the closeness of the relationship of the parties, may affect the determination.[43] Actually, most of these cases turn upon

---

[25] 42 N.Y. 484 (1870), affirming 42 Barb. 368 (N.Y. Sup. Ct. 1864).

[33] 401 Pa. 477, 165 A.2d 82 (1960).

[34] Said the court: "It would be a strange kind of argument and an equivocal type of justice which would hold that the defendant would be compelled to pay out, let us say, the sum of $100,000 if the plaintiff had not prevented what would have been inevitable, and yet not be called upon to pay the smaller sum which the plaintiff actually expended to avoid a foreseeable disaster." Id. at 481, 165 A.2d at 84. But

cf. Fair v. Traders & Gen. Ins. Co., 235 Ark. 185, 357 S.W.2d 544 (1962), when an oil driller acted to minimize damage to adjoining property and was not allowed to recover for his expense from the insurance company on the ground that the possible damage was too speculative.

[36] The leading case is Wagner v. International Ry., 232 N.Y. 176, 133 N.E. 437 (1921).

[43] See generally Havinghurst, Services in the Home—A Study in Contract Concepts in Domestic Relations, 41 Yale L.J. 386 (1932).

the question of whether there is a true contract between the parties to pay for the services—a contract implied-in-fact from the circumstances. But these same circumstances also affect the determination as to whether quasi-contractual or restitutionary relief should be granted. For, even though there is no contract implied in fact, a restitutionary remedy may be available. If the recipient of the services is incapable of contracting, for example, the same question is present as to whether or not a gift was intended. Gratuitous services may also be the basis for a quasi-contractual recovery, if mistake vitiates the reason for the gratuity.

When the courts speak of presumptions in family-services cases, they are speaking of presumptions of fact, which are subject to being rebutted by a showing that the facts are actually otherwise. In a different group of cases, however, the presumption is treated as a rule of law. The first case of significance is *Bartholomew v. Jackson*, where plaintiff, having saved defendant's wheat stack from a fire, received a jury verdict of fifty cents as the value of his services. The court reversed, saying: "If a man humanely bestows his labor, and even risks his life, in voluntarily aiding to preserve his neighbor's house from destruction by fire, the law considers the service rendered as gratuitous, and it, therefore, forms no ground of action." The Louisiana court applied the same approach to a flood, and the Oregon court in a flight of eloquence seemed to apply it more broadly.[50]

These are all early cases and their authority is now somewhat doubtful. More recent cases permitting recovery when a doctor renders emergency services to an unconscious person may perhaps be distinguished on the ground that the doctor is normally acting as a professional person and expecting to charge. Even so, this indicates that there is not an inflexible rule of law, but that the facts should control. The presumption should appropriately be treated as it is in the family-service cases, as an indication of the normal assumption to be drawn from the facts as to the plaintiff's intention—that he acted in the emergency without any thought of charging

the defendant for his services—but subject to rebuttal by other available facts. And if the plaintiff incurs expenses in rendering the emergency aid, he would not normally be expecting to make a gift of this to the defendant. If there is any presumption as to this, it should be that the plaintiff is expecting reimbursement.

. . .

C. *No Recovery if Defendant Refuses to Accept the Benefit, Unless It Is an Appropriate Performance of a Legal Duty*

Benefits cannot be forced upon a party who declines to receive them. This is tacitly assumed in many cases and expressly stated in a few. Thus, in the early case of *Stokes v. Lewis*[58] where one parish paid the quota of another, Lord Mansfield held that there could be no recovery when the payment was made "in spite of their teeth." And in *Stern v. Haas*, where plaintiff lighted and cleaned a common passageway against defendant's will, contribution was not allowed. Several cases have held that a plaintiff may not charge the defendant with money expended in keeping the defendant's chattel, when the latter has indicated he no longer wants the chattel and will not be responsible for it. In others, a plaintiff who obtained a temporary injunction preventing interference with his activities, was not permitted to recover for the enrichment thus created in the defendant. In all of these cases the plaintiff's conduct can be characterized as officious.

There is one recognized exception to this rule, although its precise scope has not been clearly delineated. If the defendant fails to perform a duty imposed upon him by the law, under suitable circumstances a plaintiff may perform it for him and be granted restitutionary relief. The most clearly established illustration involves the obligation of a man to provide necessaries for his family. Numerous cases hold that when he refuses to meet his obligation a third person may perform it and hold him liable. Thus in the striking case of *Carr v. Anderson*,[64] where the defendant's wife had been committed to a mental in-

---

[50] Glenn v. Savage, 14 Ore. 567, 13 Pac. 442 (1887). The plaintiff had saved some building materials of the defendant which had fallen into the Columbia River. Said the court: "The law will never permit a friendly act or such as was intended to be an act of kindness or benevolence, to be afterwards converted into a pecuniary demand; it would be doing violence to some of the kindest and best effusions of the heart, to suffer them afterwards to be perverted by sordid avarice. Whatever differences may arise afterwards among men, let those meritorious and generous acts remain lasting monuments of the good offices intended in the days of good

neighborhood and friendship; and let no after circumstances ever tarnish or obliterate them from the recollection of the parties." Id. at 577-78, 13 Pac. at 448. In Mathie v. Hancock, 78 Vt. 414, 63 Atl. 143 (1906), where plaintiff supplied feed to the horses of a decedent, the court gave, among other reasons for holding for the defendant, that it did not "appear that he expected compensation, and that cannot be inferred." This is not a conclusive presumption but seems to deny the effect of circumstantial evidence.

[58] 1 T.R. 20, 99 Eng. Rep. 949 (K.B. 1785).

[64] 154 Minn. 162, 191 N.W. 407 (1923).

stitution and he apparently wanted to keep her there, he was held liable to an attorney for services rendered in having her declared competent and released.[65]

Another group of cases has involved the failure of a local government, or its agency, to perform a duty imposed upon it by statute. Thus, recovery has been allowed to one who performed the defendant's duty of providing necessaries for a pauper (especially in case of an emergency), supplying transportation to school children, preparing a public road and arranging for publication in a county newspaper.

A study of these cases indicates several limitations on the scope of the exception. . . .

. . .

D. *No Recovery for Benefits Conferred Without Suitable Opportunity to Decline, In Absence of Reasonable Excuse for Failure to Afford Opportunity*

A person is ordinarily not required to pay for benefits which were thrust upon him with no opportunity to refuse them. The fact that he is enriched is not enough, if he cannot avoid the enrichment.[81]

On the other hand, if the plaintiff, before bestowing the benefit on the defendant, notifies him and thus gives an opportunity to decline, the defendant, if he accepts the benefit, will be held liable. This may be on the basis of an actual contract—one implied-in-fact from the conduct of the parties, to pay the reasonable value; or it may be in restitution on the basis of an obligation imposed by law to pay for the enrichment. A similar problem arises when the defendant did not have an opportunity to decline the benefit before the plaintiff acted, but on a later occasion had the opportunity to elect whether or not to take it. Here, too, it would appear that if he takes the benefit, he should be liable. The real question is whether he has a suitable opportunity to accept or decline. Two boat cases illustrate. In *Chase v. Corcoran*, plaintiff rescued a drifting boat and repaired it when he could not locate the owner. Later, defendant claimed it and brought replevin when plaintiff insisted on payment. The court held that plaintiff might recover the cost of storage and repairs, since defendant could have cho-

sen to let the finder keep the boat. In *J. L. Carpenter Co. v. Richardson*, a motorboat was left with plaintiff to be tuned, but plaintiff did additional work on it. Defendant was held not liable for the unordered work, since he "was entitled to the use of his motorboat, and in order to use it was obliged to avail himself of such work as the plaintiff had performed on it."[87] The distinction is hard to express, yet it clearly exists. One who had apparently abandoned property is not put to an unreasonable election when required either to pay for the expense of saving and preserving it or to leave it with the finder. It is unreasonable, however, to expect the owner of valuable property to give up that property if he is unable to reject additional and unrequested benefit. In the case of improvements made upon defendant's land, he has an election if they are removable, but not if they are incorporated into the land.

On this basis it would appear that when defendant's debt is paid by plaintiff, defendant always has an option to accept or reject it, since he could insist that he had not accepted the payment and intended to pay the debt himself, all of this without injuring himself in any way or giving up anything. Although some courts have taken this viewpoint, the majority position disregards it. The position is less applicable to the performance of other contractual obligations.

1. Excuse

Even in a case where defendant was afforded no opportunity to accept or decline the benefit, restitution may still be granted against him if there was a reasonable excuse for failure to make the opportunity available. When is it not necessary to provide the option to the defendant? There are several types of situations.

(a). *Defendant Under Legal Obligation.*—If the defendant is under obligation to perform a legal duty, such that if he refused to perform the plaintiff might perform for him and be entitled to restitution, then it may be that plaintiff can proceed to perform for him without notifying him and giving him the opportunity. But ordinarily this can be done safely only in the situation where it is obvious that giving the opportu-

---

[65] Said the court: "It is unimportant that the husband, who does not furnish the necessary, does not want it furnished, or forbids its furnishing, or declares in advance that he will not pay. The law imposes the obligation, and enforces it by a contract remedy." Id. at 165, 191 N.W. at 407.

[81] Though the law does not impose a liability on him to pay, he should be able to bind himself a promise to compensate for the enrichment. Thus, in Drake v. Bell, 26 Misc. 237, 55 N.Y. Supp. 945 (Sup. Ct. 1899), where defendant's house was replastered and painted by mistake, a promise to pay

the reasonable value was enforced. See generally Note, Promissory Obligations Based on Past Benefits or Other Moral Consideration, 7 U. Chi. L. Rev. 124 (1939).

[87] Compare the remarks of Pollock, C.J., in the argument in Taylor v. Laird, 25 L.J. Ex. 329, 332 (1856): "Suppose I clean your property without your knowledge, have I then a claim on you for payment? How can you help it? . . . The benefit of the service could not be rejected without refusing the property itself."

nity would be useless. Defendant should be afforded the chance of performing the legal duty himself unless his conduct or other circumstances manifestly indicate that he would have refused to exercise that chance. Of course, if he has already refused to perform or is clearly in default, there is no need to give him an additional opportunity.

(b). *Plaintiff Under Legal Compulsion.*—If the plaintiff is under a legal duty so that in performing his own obligation he discharges a duty of the defendant, he is normally excused from the requirement that he give the defendant an opportunity to perform. Of course, if the plaintiff's liability does not arise until after the defendant is in default, plaintiff is not under legal compulsion until his liability arises. The cases usually involve sureties, and joint tortfeasors. They need not be treated in detail here.[92]

(c). *Plaintiff Acts to Protect His Own Property or Interests.*—The leading case is the early one of *Exall v. Partridge.* Plaintiff's coach, left with defendants to be repaired, was seized by defendants' landlord as distress for rent in arrears, and he was forced to pay the rent to repossess it. It was held that he was entitled to restitution. Similar cases involve the payment of a senior mortgage by a junior mortgagee to protect his interest; or payment of taxes by a mortgagee.

In other situations, the plaintiff acts to protect an interest rather than property. Thus, in *Zurich General Accident & Liability Insurance Co. v. Klein,*[96] defendant sold property which had an unknown tax lien on it, and plaintiff, insurance company for the attorney who had searched the titles and failed to locate the lien, paid the lien. Plaintiff was held entitled to restitution. An interesting case in this connection is *Rivers v. Roe,* where a bank clerk, accepting payment on a note from defendant, later showed up twenty-five pounds short and was required by the bank to pay it. He was permitted to recover from the defendant on proof that the total amount had not been paid. Courts differ as to whether plaintiff must have been acting to prevent a legal liability on his part. Thus two early cases disagree as to whether a sheriff who failed to execute on property, paying the amount himself, can obtain reimbursement, and two recent cases similarly disagree as to whether a party who claims he was not negligent but nevertheless pays the amount of the injured party's loss can recover against the person who he claims to have been negligent.

(d). *Plaintiff Confers Benefit Under Mistake.*—If plaintiff pays defendant's debt under the mistaken apprehension that he was himself under a duty to do it or that he was protecting his own property, there is less reason to treat him as being officious, and the courts will usually grant restitution. The mistake excuses plaintiff from the requirement of giving defendant an opportunity to decline, when he is not placed in a worse position by the creation of an obligation to reimburse the plaintiff. His duty to pay is merely transferred to another party. A similar result is usually reached when the plaintiff mistakenly performs defendant's legal obligation. Somewhat analogous are the cases where plaintiff gratuitously provides necessaries for the defendant under the mistaken apprehension that the latter is financially unable to provide them himself. Again, recent cases allow recovery.

A somewhat different situation exists when plaintiff has by mistake added improvements to defendant's property. Plaintiff's situation is not materially different, since his mistake is still the reason for his failure to give defendant an opportunity to decline. But defendant's situation is quite different; now, unwanted and unneeded benefits may be forced upon him. For this reason, a majority of the courts have stated that restitution is not granted. Even here, however, a good number of cases have granted restitution, and if the "betterment statutes" are added to this group, restitution is granted in a substantial number of states. There is a clear enrichment, and the balancing process of weighing the equities of the mistaken plaintiff and the unconsenting defendant is a delicate one, whether done by court or legislature. It is easy to see why the states are divided.

On principle there would be more reason to grant restitution when the plaintiff has made necessary repairs rather than unneeded improvements. Several cases, however, have refused recovery, and it is not possible to say that this is the law.

(e). *Plaintiff Acts Under an Emergency.*—If an emergency exists so that plaintiff cannot give defendant an opportunity to decline the benefit before acting, this may excuse him from that requirement. If other requirements are met, restitution is normally granted, provided the plaintiff has acted reasonably.

Thus, in the saving of life, a physician, who is regarded as not intending to render his services gratuitously, and whose services can be properly reduced to

---

[92] See generally Restatement, Restitution §§ 76-102 (1937).

[96] 181 Pa. Super. 48, 121 A.2d 893 (1956).

terms of a measurable benefit, is granted restitution. A similar result is reached where a person saves or preserves another's property, so long as his services are not treated as gratuitous and a properly measurable benefit is bestowed. Cases involving funeral expenses also come within this principle. Obviously, there is no opportunity to present the matter to the decedent's estate, or its representative, for decision. And finally, restitutionary relief is also awarded in those cases where the plaintiff looks after animals of a decedent, pending the qualifying of a representative of the estate who can take over.

(f). *Plaintiff Acts Under a Moral Responsibility.*— In a number of cases a plaintiff has been granted restitution when he was not under a legal obligation to perform a duty for the defendant but where he had a moral obligation to act. In most of these cases the discussion is posed in terms of the plaintiff's classification as a volunteer or not, relief depending upon the classification.

Thus, in *Ford v. United States*,[112] plaintiff, an American soldier in England, had stolen money from an Englishman. The United States Government reimbursed the victim in accordance with an American statute, and later caught plaintiff and confiscated some of his money. In his action for the money, the Government was able to counterclaim for the amount it had paid, on the ground that it had "a moral obligation to respond for depredations committed by a member of our armed forces." In several cases, where the defendant had breached a contract to provide support to a third party, a close relative of that party who supplied the support was allowed to recover on the ground that lie was acting under "moral compulsion." In a case where a wife paid her husband's obligation, the court spoke of a "moral duty or at least a moral privilege." In an interesting pair of cases, an agent negotiated a contract for a principal, and, though not legally bound, paid the third party when the principal reneged on the contract. An early English case denied recovery against the principal, but the North Carolina case granted it. Mere courtesy or accommodation for a friend does not meet the requirement here.

. . .

E. *No Recovery for Benefits Incidentally Conferred*

Where a plaintiff in the performance of his own duty incidentally confers a benefit on the defendant,

it is usually held that restitution is not available. Thus, where one in possession of land hires the plaintiff to put an improvement on it, the fact that this inures to the benefit of the owner does not create liability to make restitution. Similarly, where one benefits another's property in improving his own property or promoting his own interest in some manner, restitution is not granted.

A more difficult question has arisen when an attorney has rendered services which benefit not only the persons who employed him but also other claimants similarly placed. Thus, in *Felton v. Finley*,[123] the attorney was employed by two nephews to break the will of an uncle; three others, who had refused to join in the employment of plaintiff or the suit, then decided to benefit from the results. The Idaho court first held that the plaintiff might recover since the defendants had voluntarily accepted the benefits of the services, but then changed its mind and held for the defendants. On the other hand, in *Winton v. Amos*,[124] the United States Supreme Court held that attorneys who had, under employment with certain members of an Indian group, rendered lobbying services which allegedly made Federal funds available to all members of the group, would be entitled to an "equitable charge upon the funds and lands for a reasonable and proportionate contribution toward value of services rendered and expenses incurred." The Court found applicable the principle that one with a common interest in a trust fund who saves it from destruction is entitled to reimbursement from the fund or the other beneficiaries, and also spoke of the "curious analogy to the salvage services of the maritime law."

The distinction between the incidental-benefit cases and the cases where the plaintiff confers a benefit on defendant in protection of his own property or interests is one only of degree, and the attorney cases are close to the uncertain borderline. The courts may be especially inclined to hold liability when the defendants consciously and voluntarily elect to accept the benefits.

III. Special Problems

A. *Law and Equity*

Because of the historical development of some areas of the law of restitution, relief has been more freely given in equity than at law, and there have been differences in the form of the remedy. There is less of

---

[112] 88 F. Supp. 263 (Ct. Cl. 1950).
[123] 69 Idaho 381, 209 P.2d 899 (1959).

[124] 255 U.S. 373 (1921).

this in the area involving benefits conferred without request than in several other fields.

The equitable remedy of subrogation may of course, be available when relief is granted for paying the debt of another. But because of the traditional maxim that equity will not aid a volunteer, though it involves a misapplication in connection with the type of volunteer involved here, equity has not developed a more liberal set of rules regarding the person who pays the debt of another. A series of lower court decisions during the early part of this century suggested that the English courts of equity were about to develop a position permitting recovery as a general rule. The Court of Appeal in 1938 apparently repudiated them, however, and indicated that the common law rule of no-recovery would apply in equity too.

One place where the rules of equity have been more liberal is in regard to the putting of improvements on land under mistake as to ownership. It is quite generally held that when the owner seeks equitable relief, the court of equity will require him to do equity and to compensate for the value of the improvements, as a condition of receiving assistance. In some jurisdictions a stronger position has been taken and it is held that a court of equity will grant affirmative restitutionary relief.

B. *Paying Another's Debt*

It is not clear why the courts have continued to hold with such rigidity that one who pays another's debt is not entitled to restitution from him. At early common law, a chose in action was not assignable for reasons of champerty and maintenance. For a long time, however, it has been held that a debt is freely assignable, without regard to the consent of the debtor. Even officious motives on the part of the payor-purchaser make no difference so long as he obtains a valid assignment. Where there is no express assignment, the position of the debtor is not made worse than it was prior to the payment, if the payment is treated as the equivalent of an assignment. Indeed, some courts have spoken of an equitable assignment which puts the payor in the position to enforce the original obligation as his own.

One objection which has sometimes been raised to this suggestion is that the payment amounts to a discharge of the debt, which therefore no longer exists to be enforced. This argument is merely technical, and any validity in it is met by adopting the approach of equity in utilizing the remedy of subrogation. There, equity retains or revives the lien for the benefit of the payor, who steps into the shoes of the origi-

nal obligee. This is also what happens when one pays an unsecured debt of another, and the only reason why subrogation has not been applied is the old maxim that equity will not aid a volunteer. With the free assignability of choses in action there is no longer any reason to look on the payor with more disfavor than an assignee. Since the payor merely steps into the shoes of the original creditor, he cannot change the original obligation, and the debtor's burden is in no way increased.

Look at the situation now from the standpoint of the debtor. If he has his debt paid and has no further obligation, he has clearly been enriched. And he just as clearly has a full opportunity to accept or decline the benefit. If he wishes, he may elect to disregard the payment and to insist that he be permitted to pay his own debt to the creditor. On the other hand, if he accepts the payment of his debt, he accepts the enrichment and should be required to make restitution. A procedural device which would make this clear but which apparently has not been utilized, would be for the plaintiff to join the debtor and the creditor in a single action, suing in the alternative. If the debtor elects to regard the plaintiff's action as a payment of his debt, he should be liable on the ground of his unjust enrichment; if he elects to regard it as not being a payment, he is still under obligation to the creditor, and the creditor should be liable to the plaintiff on the ground of his unjust enrichment. This method of bringing suit, if used, might constitute a means of bringing the substantive law into accord with modern conditions.

Whatever validity the no-relief-for-the-volunteer rule has, it does not apply to the payment of another's debt. For the opposite rule could not increase the debtor's burden; and the true volunteer, the officious person who is consciously trying to interfere in the debtor's affairs, can do that anyway by taking an express assignment. The no-recovery rule damages only the altruistic individual who was trying to help, or the person who was acting under a mistake. Is any social policy promoted by this anomaly? No, not even logical consistency is promoted by it.

C. *Relationship to the Law of Salvage and the Civil Law*

The law of salvage, as applied by both British and American courts, affords a marked contrast to the restrictive attitude of the common law. One who saves property from impending danger at sea is held entitled to compensation. His compensation includes reimbursement of his expenses, the value of his services, a consideration of the benefit to the owner, involving the value of the property, and a reasonable reward in addition. To enforce it he is given a lien on the property. To be entitled to relief he must prove that he is a volunteer; a preexisting duty disqualifies him.

No adequate explanation has been given for this remarkable contrast with the common law, other than the historical development. It was referred to by Chief Justice Marshall in *Mason v. Ship Blaireau*,[144] but without explanation. In *Falcke v. Scottish Imperial Insurance Co.*,[145] the English Court of Appeal expressly rejected an analogy to salvage and refused to allow recovery by one who paid the obligation of another in order to have an insurance policy.[146] The only discovered case where the salvage analogy was used to allow recovery is the United States Supreme Court case of *Winton v. Amos*, where an attorney who obtained a fund for some claimants was given equitable charge on it to permit compensation against others; no reference was made there to the restrictive common law cases.

The practical explanation of the difference between the common law and the maritime law may be that they are two different systems of law, with entirely different backgrounds. Yet it may be pertinent to see the reasons given by the courts for the salvage rule. On several occasions, the assertion has been made that it is founded upon principles of equity. Frequently, it is said that the rule is based on the policy of encouraging mariners to undertake the task of rescue by offering a reward. And it is sometimes added that there is the countervailing policy of withdrawing the "temptation to embezzlement and dishonesty" by allowing him "a liberal compensation." The extent to which these reasons may apply to activities on land should be apparent after reflection. Do they not have a reasonable application to emergency rescues of property or land? The only real difference is that custom has now developed so that the salvor at sea al-

ways expects compensation and there is no presumption of gratuity.

The Roman law had a doctrine of *negotiorum gestio*, under which one might take charge of the affairs of his absent neighbor and manage them in the latter's interest; he was then allowed to recover for the value of his services if they were beneficial. The doctrine passed into the civil law of the continent and, while its career has been somewhat varied in several European countries, it is still found and used in their law.[151]

The attitude here is that of encouraging a man to act in an altruistic fashion in aiding another. No deprecating remarks are made about the volunteer or the intermeddler, and there is no refusal to grant him relief. The common law has steadfastly refused to adopt this attitude. Some have explained it on the basis of the difference in temperament of the Anglo-Saxon and the Latin, suggesting that the characteristic independence of the former is not to be found in the latter.[153] The difference in the law may perhaps have started on this basis, but it now seems more historic than anything else.

The prime significance of the law of salvage and that of the civil law is that they indicate that a fully developed system of law may operate effectively under a principle which seeks to encourage rather than discourage and deprecate the rendering of aid to another without his prior request. The law of salvage is administered by our own courts without difficulty.

D. *Liens*

When restitution is granted to the person who voluntarily confers a benefit on another, it is only rarely that he is given a lien. . . .

IV. Conclusion

The restrictions on recovery which have been spelled out at considerable length have all been presented from a negative standpoint.

---

[144] 6 U.S. (2 Cranch) 240 (1804). "If the property of an individual on land be exposed to the greatest peril, and be saved by the voluntary exertions of any person whatever; if valuable goods be rescued from a house in flames, at the imminent hazard of life by the salvor, no remuneration in the shape of salvage is allowed. The act is highly meritorious, and the service is as great as if rendered at sea. Yet the claim for salvage could not, perhaps, be supported. It is certainly not made. Let precisely the same service, at precisely the same hazard be rendered at sea, and a very ample reward will be bestowed in the courts of justice." Id. at 266.

[145] 34 Ch. D. 234 (C.A. 1886).

[146] Said Bowen, L.J.: "The maritime law, for the purposes of public policy and for the advantage of trade, imposes in

these cases a liability upon the thing saved, a liability which is a special consequence arising out of the character of mercantile enterprises, the nature of sea perils, and the fact that the thing saved was saved under great stress and exceptional circumstances." Id. at 248-49.

[151] A thorough and penetrating treatment of the doctrine in modern European law is to be found in Dawson, Negotiorum Gestio: The Altruistic Intermeddler, 74 Harv. L. Rev. 817 & 1073 (1961); see also Dawson, Unjust Enrichment 55-61, 136-40 (1951).

[153] See Allen, Legal Duties, 40 Yale L.J. 331, 375 (1931); Hope, Officiousness, 15 Cornell L.Q. 25, 29 (1929). This is characterized as "nonsense" in Stoljar, Quasi-Contract 161 n.4 (1964).

It may now be possible to summarize them and present a general principle stated in a positive fashion.

Perhaps the following two sentences will prove helpful in this regard:

One who, without intent to act gratuitously, confers a measurable benefit upon another, is entitled to restitution, if he affords the other an opportunity to decline the benefit or else has a reasonable excuse for failing to do so. If the other refuses to receive the benefit, he is not required to make restitution unless the actor justifiably performs for the other a duty imposed upon him by law.

Note that this is a statement of a general principle. It does not purport to be a rule providing for results with precision. Such a rule, or even a set of such rules, does not appear to be possible, or even desirable. This statement contains numerous terms which obviously require considerable discretion in their application, and allow the court considerable leeway.[159] On the other hand, it does purport to give direction to the line of thought of the court, and it aids in putting meaning in the adjective "unjust," in the phrase, unjust enrichment.

Note also that the statement eschews any use of expressions like "volunteer" or "officious." Any study of the cases indicates that these words have been question-begging epithets which have had the effect of creating a personal disability in the plaintiff. The policy that benefits cannot be forced upon a person against his will is incorporated into the statement, but hopefully in a more meaningful and less emotional fashion.

No attempt will be made to show the application of this statement of general principle to the various types of fact situations involving the saving, preserving or improving of life or property, or the performance of another's duties. A careful tracing of the application to these situations indicates that the statement may be interpreted to explain the existing holdings and to aid in reaching decisions.

In two types of situations it may have a liberalizing effect. One involves the payment of the debt of another. Here the language on which the decision would turn is that of the "opportunity to decline the benefit." Courts holding for the defendant may explain by saying that the opportunity must exist before the payment is made (unless there is a reasonable excuse). It is quite appropriate to say, however, that the opportunity may exist later; and that the defendant has a true opportunity to decline by insisting that he pay the debt himself. This would produce a different result, but one which should be encouraged.

The other situation involves the placing of improvement on land under mistake as to ownership. Here the language on which the decision will turn is "reasonable excuse for failure" to afford an opportunity to decline. The majority rule has been stated that restitution is not granted. But a number of courts have consistently allowed it, and a number of states have changed the rule by statute. The existence of a statutory change and the procedural device of permitting recovery when the owner brings an action have undoubtedly taken care of many cases where the courts would more forthrightly have permitted recovery by judicial decision if it had been necessary. The phrase "reasonable excuse" does not compel either result, but would seem to be more persuasive toward allowing recovery.

The existence of the "betterment statutes," the "finder statutes," the "Good Samaritan statutes" and others is an indication of dissatisfaction with the traditional rule of no-recovery. It may well be argued that our law as a whole has become much more cognizant of social needs and less insistent upon the attitude of rugged individualism. Courts today would probably be less likely to take a doctrinaire approach, but ready instead to attempt carefully to balance the interests and claims of the parties. They would be less likely to do this, that is, if they were not frequently led astray from the real problems by the question-begging epithet, volunteer.

The effort here has been to pose a statement of

---

[159] There is little value here to paraphrase or annotate the whole statement. Some of the expressions which require discretionary interpretation are the following:

"intent to act gratuitously." This permits consideration of custom and use of presumptions—of fact, not law. It could have been phrased in terms of "intent to charge" as the Restatement does, the difference, of course, being one of burden of proof. In Blackwood v. Southern Ry., 178 N.C. 343, 100 S.E. 610 (1910) it is put, "not intended to be gratuitous."

"measurable benefit."

"opportunity to decline the benefit." There can be difference of viewpoint as to whether there is an opportunity or not. Like "refuses to receive the benefit," this does not apply to refusal to pay for it.

"reasonable excuse." This is one of the broadest terms in the statement, covering several factors and affording considerable discretion. But it makes the exercise of discretion manifest rather than disguised.

"justifiably performs . . . a duty." This is the most indefinite expression in the statement. Yet it offers an approach which avoids an emotional epithet and promotes frank consideration of the factors involved.

the general principle which utilizes the valid idea behind the term but does not permit it automatically to

impose a disability upon the plaintiff, barring him at
the threshold of the court.

Section 90 and the First Restatement—
The Gilmore Version and the Evidence From the Time

I don't think there is much dissent from the claim that the inclusion of section 90 in the original Restatement of Contracts was the most important event in twentieth century American contract law. Ironically, the First Restatement is often said to be the ultimate flowering of the rigidly classical bargain theory, and its centerpiece was its section 75, which strictly limited consideration for a promise to something that was "bargained for and given in exchange for the promise." Section 90 appeared in a separate part of the Restatement without cross-reference to section 75. It provided that:

A promise which the promisor should reasonably expect to induce action or forebearance of a definite and substantial character on the part of the promisee and which does induce such action or forbearance is binding if injustice can be avoided only by enforcement of the promise.

On pages 58 to 65 of *The Death of Contract* Grant Gilmore gives a version of how the First Restatement came to have both Sections 75 and 90. Professor Samuel Williston of Harvard was the Reporter of the Restatement, with Arthur Corbin as his chief advisor. Gilmore attributes the high quality of the Restatement to the collaboration, but continues: "No doubt it was also their joint participation—bearing in mind that Williston and Corbin held antithetical points of view on almost every conceivable point of law—that accounts for the schizophrenic quality which makes the *Restatement*, viewed historically, the fascinating document which it is."

According to Gilmore, when Williston proposed the description of consideration eventually adopted as section 75, Corbin submitted a very different proposal that would have avoided the strict bargained-for exchange approach and that instead used a very loose definition allowing anything that showed that a party took its promise seriously to qualify as consideration. After this approach was rejected, Corbin brought in a list of many cases enforcing contracts where no bargain could be found in the sense used in section 75. Often, the cases used the term "estoppel," although traditionally, estoppel had been limited to statements of existing facts, not promises of future action. According to Gilmore:

The Restaters, honorable men, evidently found Corbin's argument unanswerable. However, instead of reopening the debate on the consideration definition, they elected to stand by § 75 but to add a new section—§ 90—incorporating the estoppel idea although without using the word "estoppel." The extent to which the new section § 90 was to be allowed to undercut the underlying principle of § 75 was left entirely unresolved.

G. Gilmore, The Death of Contract at 64. Gilmore goes on to conclude that as to section 90, "no one had any idea what the damn thing meant."

Gilmore was careful to describe the story as Professor Corbin's version and to warn in an endnote that he was reproducing, in the 1970's, the substance of a series of conversations that had taken place twenty years earlier concerning events that had happened twenty or thirty years before that. As he put it, "obviously there is bound to be a certain amount of slippage between what really happened and this second-hand reconstruction of what happened." Id. at 128 n. 135. Gilmore's cautions are usually ignored, which does neither him nor history a favor.

There is no reason to reject Gilmore's anecdote, but it is worth noting the comment of Anthony Jon Waters, who wrote the following (in an article dedicated to Gilmore):

Corbin's own account is very different from the "Williston versus Corbin" struggle depicted by Gilmore: "[Williston] often said that § 90 was my Section, but the fact is that it is now in exactly the form in which he *first* submitted it." Letter from Arthur Corbin to Robert Braucher (Jan. 27, 1961) (Braucher Papers, Manuscript Div., Harvard Law School Library).

Waters, *The Property In the Promise: A Study of the Third Party Beneficiary Rule*, 98 Harv. L. Rev. 1109, 1198 n. 418, at 1199. The Waters article is excerpted in Part IID of this anthology.

It was Williston who had to defend section 90 (then numbered section 88) when it came before the members of the American Law Institute—self-proclaimed leaders of the bench and bar—in 1926. A small exchange from the proceedings—Williston's discussion with Frederic Coudert, a distinguished New York lawyer, of Johnny and the car—is often reproduced as evidence of Williston's narrow view of the section and of his extreme formalism. The full debate, however, shows Williston to have defended section 88 energetically, and with a sense of the importance of doing justice that belies the received wisdom of Williston the old fuddy-duddy. The debate, which is not very long, is reproduced below almost in full, with only a few cross-references removed. Williston comes through as a much more human figure, and as one who understood the importance of the new concept. None of this is to suggest that Williston would have accepted the applications of the reliance concept made in the second half of the century, but it fills in gaps left by those who treat Gilmore's version as the whole story.

Debate on Section 88 (Later Section 90) of the Restatement of Contracts, 4 American Law Institute Proceedings Appendix 85-114 (1926)

Mr. Wickersham: With the Reporter thus strengthened against his Advisers, perhaps the Institute would be willing to pass on to the next section. Are there any observations on Section 86? (After a pause) We will turn to 87; Section 88.

"Section 88. A promise which the promisor should reasonably expect to induce action or forbearance of a definite and substantial character on the part of the promisee and which does induce such action or forbearance is binding if injustice can be avoided only by enforcement of the promise."

Edwin G. Norman (Massachusetts): I was requested to ask a question with reference to this section and I do it as a member of the Subcommittee from Massachusetts appointed by the Massachusetts members of this association, and that is as to the meaning of the word "injustice" and as to its application, whether it is to be applied to the promisee or the injustice suffered by someone else, and whether it means a pecuniary loss or any injustice?

Mr. Williston: I suppose the fair inference is that it does mean injustice to the promisee; but whether it

means pecuniary loss or loss of some other kind is not defined.

Of course, this section has excited a good deal of discussion. It excited discussion among the Advisers.

It excited discussion in the Council. It is the section that is most elaborately considered in the commentaries on the Restatement of Contracts.

Pages 14 to 20 deal exclusively with reasons for this section. There are a number of cases here grouped together that are law everywhere which support the section, though often dealt with as a half dozen different subjects. There are other cases which are law in some states but not everywhere, commonly grouped under such words as promises supported by "moral consideration." In some courts these words mean that there is a legal obligation. In other courts they rather abruptly induce the decision, "judgment for the defendant."

Now, if the law is to be simplified or clarified, one must try to reduce to broader or more general principles, so far as possible, large groups of cases where the courts reach a decision in favor of enforcing promises because of such reasons as are stated in

Section 88, although the courts may not formulate the reasons in just those words.

Unquestionably, the word "injustice," to which Mr. Norman specifically refers and inquires about, leaves a certain leeway one way or the other to the judge. As someone expressed it, in regard to this section if you bind up too closely, with definite mathematical rules the law of consideration, the boiler will burst. You have got to leave the court a certain leeway outside of those mathematical and exact rules. This section is, so to speak, the safety valve for the subject of consideration.

That is the reasoning on which the section is based. I hope the section will appeal to you, but I have at least given the reason for it. As to the specific inquiry what injustice means, it means something indefinite and the meaning is purposely left somewhat indefinite.

. . .

Mr. Norman: May I also ask one more question, and that is as to the example given in (c) on page 34? It says that A promises B that if B will go to college and complete his course, he will give him $5000. On those facts, I inquire whether it is possible to construe them to mean that there would be a pecuniary loss to B, who paid his college expenses, or a pecuniary loss to the parent to pay them; or perhaps there might be no injustice; it might be of benefit to him to go to college for a short time.

Mr. Williston: I think that is arguable. It would be open to discussion, whether there is a benefit to him to go to college for a short time, if he has his expenses paid for that short time. But in the illustration as given, it is apparent that the promisor does not pay his expenses while he is there. I should be of the opinion that it was unjust under the circumstances as stated in the illustration for the promisor not to do what he said he would.

Morrison R. Waite (Ohio): Why is not that a contract under Section 73? [This became Section 75 of the First Restatement and Section 71 of the Second. It deals with bargained-for exchange. -ed.] Is it not an act done by a promisee which is a consideration?

Mr. Williston: That is possible, but I think it is a case of a gift on condition or promise of gift on condition rather than a bargain. The case is typical of a class that gives a good deal of opportunity for discussion in law schools and elsewhere. A says to his nephew "If you go to Europe I will pay your expenses." Now, that may be a contract, or it may be merely a promised gift on condition. If the act is purely beneficial to the promisee, and the promisor gets nothing out of it, the usual implication and the natural implication, is that it is a promise to give something on a contingency that happens rather than a bargain to secure some performance in return for the promise.

Victor Morawetz (New York): This section says that a promise of the kind described, that is one which would reasonably be expected to induce definite action and which does induce such action, is binding. I take it that this means that the promise although not binding when made, becomes binding by reason of the subsequent action. Am I right as to that, Mr. Williston?

Mr. Williston: You are.

Mr. Morawetz: In order that this section may apply the promisor must reasonably expect to induce certain definite action to be taken. Now, it seems to me that instead of dealing with this matter under the head of consideration, it would go more appropriately under the head of offers. What happens in these cases is that the law holds that if a man makes a promise to induce another to do a certain act, he will be held to have made an offer of a unilateral promise to take effect upon the performance of the act.

Mr. Williston: Let me put a case to you, Mr. Morawetz. Johnny says, "I want to buy a Buick car." Uncle says, "Well, I will give you $1000." Do you call that an offer of a contract?

Mr. Morawetz: It depends on the circumstances.

Mr. Williston: I will give you any circumstances that you want that are not yet disclosed.

Mr. Morawetz: If the surrounding facts make it reasonable to construe that as a statement that I will give you $1000 if you will buy a Buick car—

Mr. Williston: He does not say that; he simply knows that-that $1,000 is going to be relied on by the nephew for the purchase of a car. I want to cover more in Section 88 than offers. I understand perfectly well what you have in mind, as offers for unilateral contracts, and they are covered under offers; but this section covers a case where there is a promise to give and the promisor knows that the promisee will rely upon the proposed gift in certain definite ways. I promise to give you Blackacre, and you go on Blackacre and build a house on Blackacre. That is not an offer on the part of the promisor but aside from Section 88, it is a promise on which specific performance will lie today anywhere.

Merritt Lane (New Jersey): May I ask the Reporter whether it was not the intent to cover under

Section 88 what is now usually treated under the head of equitable estoppel?

Mr. Williston: I should say that was a very bad name for it.

Mr. Lane: What would you call it?

Mr. Williston: I dont know; and nearly anything can be called estoppel. When a lawyer or a judge does not know what other name to give for his decision to decide a case in a certain way, he says there is an estoppel; but I should like to confine the meaning of the word to a misrepresentation of some fact that was relied upon. There is no misrepresentation of fact here; there is simply a gratuitous promise which the promisor knows is gratuitous and which the promisee knows is gratuitous. I have in my treatise used the term "promissory estoppel" for this sort of case; but there is the danger that the inference will be drawn that wherever a promise is reasonably relied upon it becomes binding. That would go farther than Section 88.

. . .

Mr. Morawetz: It is correct that we should understand that under this section a man may always rely upon the promise which is made to induce a certain action?

Mr. Williston: Yes, of a substantial and definite character.

Mr. Morawetz: Of a definite character.

Mr. Williston: And substantial.

Mr. Morawetz: And substantial. That is, in other words, any promise which is made to induce definite action of a substantial and definite character, a man may depend upon, and he can render it binding by that action.

Mr. Williston: The qualification is necessary, if injustice can be avoided only by enforcement of the promise. The reason of that insertion I should perhaps explain. In some cases, in many cases perhaps, it will be possible for the promisee, if he is induced to do some act or pay some money, to recover back what he has given or the value of what he has done. If the court can get out of the difficulty by restoring the *status quo*, there is no necessity of enforcing the promise, but if detriment has been incurred by the promisee of a definite and substantial character and the *status quo* cannot be restored, then the proposition is that the court should enforce the promise.

William Prickett (Delaware): May I ask the Reporter if in the example he gave of Johnny and the car, his uncle's promise would be enforceable when Johnny buys the car?

Mr. Williston: I should say so, because the promise was made as a direct reply to Johnny's expression of a desire for a car. The uncle should certainly expect that the next thing that would happen would be that Johnny would run around the corner to the Buick agency and get a car and perhaps sign some promissory notes for it.

Mr. Prickett: Suppose Johnny pays no money down.

Mr. Williston: If he has got the car and is liable for the price he gets the $1000 under this Section. So long as he has not got the car, however, he has incurred no substantial injury by the withdrawal of the promise.

Mr. Prickett: My idea is this: If he gets the car and pays no money down, if the car is taken away from him, has he suffered any substantial injury?

Mr. Williston: Oh, I think he has, as long as he is liable for the price. Whether the dealer, instead of suing for the price, or in addition to suing for the price, could replevy the car, does not seem to me material.

Mr. Prickett: His liability for the price of the car would be sufficient substantial injury?

Mr. Williston: I think so, and it is injury not only in a pecuniary sense but in reputation. Johnny would not like to be put in the position of having contracted, and thus becoming bound to pay for a car, and also put in the position of a defaulter. I am willing to interpret injustice more widely than as suggested by Mr. Norman, as merely pecuniary loss.

Mr.   : I have difficulty with the words, "of a definite and substantial character," and it strikes me that they are not necessary in view of the classifications in lines 17 and 18. I should like to hear the reasons for their insertion.

Mr. Williston: So far as possible simply to obviate the sort of point that Mr. Norman makes. Injustice is a word that is more or less indefinite anyway, and I wished as far as possible to characterize it. Certainly, I should dislike very much to leave out the word "substantial," and I think the word, "definite" ought to be left in. Those words narrow the Section undoubtedly. If you leave them out, you make the Section broader and I think add to its vagueness. Perhaps, I may illustrate. The uncle says to Johnny, simply out of a clear sky, "I am going to give you $1000." The money is to be a present, and perhaps Johnny is expected to invest it—there is no telling. Then Johnny launches forth into high life. Under the section as it stands, there could be no recovery on the promise even though it might be somewhat hard on the boy that he had so ventured forth and then found he could not get the money to support his venture. We have not gone so far as to say that any reliance on a gratuitous promise will render the promise enforceable provided injustice cannot be otherwise avoided.

We have confined the Section to the case where a reasonable person would say that the promisor expected the man to do just what he did or that he ought to have expected it.

George E. Crothers (California): May I not suggest that this falls within Section 709 of the California Civil Code, as one of those acts or statements intended to mislead another, coming under the head of deceit, and would it not be better to leave it under deceit rather than under Contracts and the remedy in damages?

Mr. Williston: I do not regard a promise to do something in the future as deceitful merely because the promise is broken. If a man promises something intending at the time he makes the promise not to perform it, that is deceit, and if the promise is made fraudulently, he may in most jurisdictions be the subject of damages for a tort; but to call a promise deceit merely because the promisor, although intending to keep it when he makes it, afterwards decides not to, is to my mind a misuse of language.

Frederic R. Coudert (New York): May I ask the learned Reporter, as I am unfamiliar with the literature on that particular subject, whether it could not be properly and logically supported on the ground of a quasi-contractual relation, because it would be necessary for the judge to decide first, whether substantial justice required that it be enforced rather than merely whether it falls within the technical rules of contracts. Would not that partake somewhat of the language of a quasi-contractual obligation rather than of a true contractual obligation?

Mr. Williston: I should say not. I should say anything was truly contractual where a promisor makes a promise and that promise is enforced. A contract to my mind is a binding promise, and in the case we are referring to, under the stated circumstances, the promise itself is binding. In such a case as I suggested a few moments ago where the status quo can be restored, the promise would not be binding; and what the plaintiff will obtain is not the enforcement of the promise but the recovery of what he has given, or payment for what he has done. Such an obligation is quasi-contractual; but if what the court is asked to do and what it does, is to enforce the actual promise

that is made, whatever reason the court has for doing it, you are enforcing a contract.

Mr. Coudert: But is it not true that it only enforces it because justice requires it and not because it is a rule of contract law? I do not quarrel at all with it; it may be the necessary statement; but I am a little confused by the predicate that substantial justice can be done only in that way. Is that the only way to get at the existence of a true contract?

Mr. Williston: I do not care in what way you may make your true contracts. The definition of contract in the first part of the section is a binding promise. If any law in any state says that a promise is binding under certain circumstances, then that promise is a contract.

Robert B. Tunstall (Virginia): Going back to the example of Johnny and his car. Suppose the car had been a Ford instead of a Buick, costing $600. I take it in view of the obligation to pay $1000, it would be equally binding if Johnny should acquire a Ford?

Mr. Williston: I don't know. Why should you say that?

Mr. Tunstall: There is no limitation in the statement as I read it, that the performance of the promisor is limited to the detriment suffered by the promisee.

Mr. Williston: Consider these words: "which the promisor should reasonably expect to induce action of a definite and substantial character and which does induce such action." Now, are you supposing that the promisor would reasonably expect that Johnny should buy any kind of car he liked? If so, I stand for your conclusion.

Mr. Tunstall: I am taking simply the illustration that is given, that Johnny says "I want to buy a Ford" and uncle says "I will give you a thousand dollars."

Mr. Williston: Oh, Johnny says he wants to buy a Ford this time?

Mr. Tunstall: Possibly, not being familiar with the market price of a Ford, the uncle says, "I will give you $1000." Now, is the uncle obligated for the $1000 or for the price of the Ford?

Mr. Williston: I think he might be bound for the $1000.

Mr. Tunstall: That is how I should interpret it, because otherwise the point made by Mr. Coudert would limit recovery to the price of the Ford and so also an action of deceit would limit it to the price of a Ford; but if it is a promise and the promise is binding, the uncle would be bound for $1000 irrespective of the detriment suffered by the promisee.

Frederick W. Mansfield (Massachusetts): It seems to me, Mr. Chairman, and gentlemen, that the trouble with this Section if there is any trouble with it, is that it appears to merge into the realm of equity. I am sorry that the learned Reporter disposed of the suggestion that this came into the field of equitable estoppel so quickly, because I think there is something in that objection. Really, what this section really means is that if any person, depending upon a promise, which probably could not be enforced, does something to change his position in reliance upon that promise, that then equity comes in and estops the other man from denying the validity of the promise. For instance, if a promise is made which does not satisfy the Statute of Frauds but relying on the promise, the other party changes his position to his detriment, then the first man is not allowed to set up the Statute of Frauds in defense—does not that verge into the field of equity, and is not that the cause of this present discussion?

Mr. Williston: I think not. In the case you put of the Statute of Frauds, the court of equity may do something if the promise relates to lands, and otherwise not. Equity does not relieve merely on the ground of what you call equitable estoppel; you have to have a case where the subject matter of the bargain is what the court will deal with. In the cases I have cited in the commentary in support of this sort of thing, some of the cases are equity and some are not. I will confess, I have used the word estoppel in connection with this sort of case in my treatises; but I have used the word promissory in front of it. I rather insist on the use of the word promissory in front of it, if you are going to talk about estoppel, because there is a difference, and the difference should be kept in mind, between misrepresenting an existing fact, and thereby becoming estopped to deny its truth and simply making a promise on which the promisee relies. He relies on the fact that it will be performed. You are not making any misrepresentation there. The promisor presumably means exactly what he says when he makes the promise. He does not intend to deceive. Only when the time comes around to perform the promise, circumstances have changed, or he has changed his mind, and he concludes not to perform it.

Now, there is no broad doctrine that wherever a man makes a promise, a gratuitous promise, and the other relies upon it, the promisee can recover on the promise, and we do not dare in Section 88 make any such broad statement that wherever a gratuitous promise is made and the promisee relies on it to his injury, he may enforce it; that is going far beyond the law and far beyond what we should dare to say.

Mr. Mansfield: But, Mr. Reporter, the only time that the promise is enforced under Section 88 is when injustice cannot be avoided otherwise. That looks like equity to me.

Mr. Williston: Courts of law sometimes have a little interest as to whether injustice can be avoided.

Mr. Mansfield: In other words, if injustice can be avoided, the promise is not enforced.

Mr. Williston: Yes.

Mr. Mansfield: That looks to me more like the elastic application of equity rather than like the hard and fast rules of law.

Mr. Williston: I should say to that, that this restatement of Contracts has nothing to do with the procedure of law or equity. Different remedies may be appropriate in the two forums, but a contract should be recognized as such in any court. I should regret to have a rule which said in effect, this is a contract in equity but is no contract in law; that is a kind of a hybrid I should dislike to manufacture. (Laughter.)

Mr. Mansfield: May I say one more word about it? Would your rule be acceptable if it stopped at the word, "binding" . . .? [See the text of Section 88 at the beginning of this material. -ed.]

Mr. Williston: It would be a broader rule than it is now. It would cut out the cases where the *status quo* can be restored, and therefore where there is perhaps a simpler way of dealing with the question than by enforcing the promise. I suppose that such objection as is likely to be made to Section 88 as it stands is it goes beyond existing law and goes too far. You are now suggesting making it go further, because you would let in more cases, you would enforce more cases if you left out the final words.

Mr. Coudert: Allow me to trespass once more, Mr. Reporter, by asking this question. Please let me see if I understand it rightly. Would you say, Mr. Reporter, in your case of Johnny and the uncle, the uncle promising the $1000 and Johnny buying the car—say, he goes out and buys the car for $500—that uncle would be liable for $1000 or would he be liable for $500?

Mr. Williston: If Johnny had done what he was expected to do, or is acting within the limits of his uncle's expectation, I think the uncle would be liable for $1000; but not otherwise.

Mr. Coudert: In other words, substantial justice would require that uncle should be penalized in the sum of $500.

Mr. Williston: Why do you say "penalized?"

Mr. Coudert: By saving $500.

Mr. Williston: Why do you say "penalized?"

Mr. Coudert: Because substantial justice there would require, it seems to me, that Johnny get his money for his car, but should he get his car and $500 more? I don't see.

Mr. Williston: Of course, it would be possible to say that for Section 88 should be substituted a section in the restatement of quasi contract that under these circumstances the promisee should be allowed to cover such a sum as would represent the injury he had suffered. Consider this case. A promisor promises Blackacre to Johnny and Johnny goes and builds a house on it. Does he get the price of the house, or does he get the land with the house on it, too? The law is, he gets the land with the house on it. That is only one of a number of illustrations given in the commentaries, where the promise is enforced under these circumstances. They are all special classes of cases, it is true; but so far as they go they support the contractual and not the quasi-contractual theory.

Mr. Coudert: Then I think you should stand by and strike out the words "substantial justice,"; justice does not enter into it.

Mr. Wickersham: Are there any further remarks?

Mr. Morawetz: I am not quarrelling with the idea of this Section, but I do think the section is not clear. The purpose of these Restatements is to clarify the law, to make it more certain. It seems to me that this Section would have the contrary effect. If I were a judge on reading this section I should not know where to draw the line. It seems to me that the Reporter and his Advisers would help the situation very much if they would revise this section by making it more definite, by stating more clearly what they mean.

Mr. Williston: It cannot be made more definite. The variety of circumstances that may arise is such that it is impossible to enumerate them all. The section can, of course, be stricken out and you can leave in the law of Contracts only the cases where there are the exact requirements for an ordinary bargain. You are then within the realm of perfect certainty; but if you try to go beyond that———

Alexander R. Lawton (Georgia) (interposing): May I ask the Reporter if this is not the answer? All your rules are based on an assumed state of facts. An assumed state of facts leaves open the question of fact, for example, what is a definite character, what is a substantial character, and in this particular case, what is injustice? Is it possible to state it except by stating a conclusion of facts, and that conclusion of

fact depends in every case upon the particular circumstances of what the remedy should be?

Mr. Williston: I think you have stated it with perfect truth. You are going to have the same question a little further on. When the question arises, when will a breach of one party to a bilateral contract excuse the other. It will excuse the other if there is a material and substantial breach, and if it is more just to let the promisor off from performing because of the injury by the party making the return promise, or whether it is more just to compel the injured party to perform his promise and seek remedy in a cross action for what he has suffered. There is no way in the law to get rid of some of those questions where mathematics will not help.

Maurice H. Donahue (Ohio): It does not seem to me that Section 88 is indefinite or uncertain or that the application of the principle therein announced would require the adjustment of equities between the parties.

On the contrary, the right of the promisee to recover upon such a promise, would, under the provisions of this section, depend upon whether, in reliance upon the promise, the promisee had suffered a substantial loss, expended money or incurred liability, that he would not have suffered, expended or incurred except for the promise. If these or either of these facts, appear from the evidence, and the amounts or amount substantial, the promisee would be entitled to recover upon the promise according to its terms and condition regardless of the extent of the loss, the money expended, or the liability incurred. If this is the law, then it would seem to be clearly stated in Section 88.

Homer Albers (Massachusetts): I am still not satisfied that Johnny could have the car and $500 both, if he bought a second-hand Buick for $500; but could not that be made clear, that it depended on the question of what the offer really was? Is it not a fair construction of uncle's offer to say I will give you $500 towards the purchase of a Buick car, which would reconcile the theoretical proposition and then apply it practically to that answer?

Mr. Williston: Uncle might say that and he might say the other thing; I cannot construe what all uncles will say.

Mr. Albers: But could you say what the court would say under that definite statement of uncle's?

Mr. Williston: My statement is that the court has no business to make the uncle say anything except what he did say, and that it is the function of the court to give the natural meaning to the uncle's words whatever they were under the particular circumstances of the case.

Mr. Lane: It seems to me that if there is anything in this discussion that this question has developed, it is that it is impossible to draft a section which will substantially cover or even pretend to cover all cases, and it seems to me that that necessarily throws it over into the domain of equity, and there is where I think it belongs.

George T. Page (Illinois): I was going to ask if you would stop with the word "binding," whether it would be a contract?

Mr. Williston: Oh, yes; my definition in the first part of the Restatement is that wherever a promise is binding, it is a contract.

Judge Page: Then would it not better explain, perhaps, the purpose of the section if between the word "binding" and the word "is," you would put the words, "and will be enforced," if injustice can be avoided only be enforcement.

Mr. Williston: No; I do not like that, because then you say it is binding whether injustice can be avoided or not.

Judge Page: Everybody else seems to like the other. I wanted to know what those words add to the section.

Mr. Williston: Why, they qualify the word "binding." It is not binding necessarily because the action or forbearance of a definite character is induced.

Judge Page: To get back to Johnny, how is injustice going to be done Johnny if he is not going to get the other $500; how is he going to be done an injustice, if he only paid $500 for the car?

Mr. Williston: How is he going to get the $500 he has paid for the car?

Judge Page: The probabilities are that the uncle would be willing to give him the $500.

Mr. Williston: Well, we do not legislate for that kind of uncle; it is the other kind we are speaking about.

Judge Page: Then your section means this: that simply because uncle cannot be made to pay $500, which Johnny has promised, uncle has to put in $500 more to make the thing even?

Mr. Williston: Either the promise is binding or it is not. If the promise is binding it has to be enforced as it is made. As I said to Mr. Coudert, I could leave this whole thing to the subject of quasi contracts so that the promisee under those circumstances shall never recover on the promise but he shall recover such an amount as will fairly compensate him for any injury incurred; but it seems to me you have to take one leg

or the other. You have either to say the promise is binding or you have to go on the theory of restoring the *status quo*. Now, there are a lot of things which I have cited in my Commentaries where the court enforces a promise and does not go on the theory of restoring the *status quo*. In the case I put of Johnny building a house on Blackacre, he gets Blackacre, he does not get what he has spent on the house; he gets Blackacre, whether it is worth four or five times as much as the house.

Ira P. Hildebrand (Texas): Mr. Chairman, I dislike very much to disagree with Professor Williston. I have taught the subject of Contracts for many years and if Section 88 is approved, fifteen of my neat illustrations given to the classes will evaporate. (Laughter). I give to my classes all the illustrations set forth by Professor Williston in the Restatement and some others. One illustration that I give is, suppose I say to a newsboy, "If you will come to my house Christmas I will give you $5.00." Everybody understands that the walking to my house by the newsboy is not the requested consideration for my promise. Therefore, the promise is but a promised gift upon condition; and even though the newsboy walks six miles to my house he cannot recover. This is what I was taught by Professor Williston twenty-five years ago. Professor Williston seems to have changed his mind. I merely wish to say that I still agree with Kirksey v. Kirksey and Cooper v. the Presbyterian Church. The cases that are opposed to the Cooper case are set forth in Professor Williston's case book on Contracts. I do not believe we should reject what Judge Cardozo says is law in De Cicco v. Schweizer, *viz.*: "Nothing is consideration that is not regarded as such by both parties." I think that Professor Williston has almost limited his proposition to that statement by the phrase "expect to induce action or forbearance of a definite and substantial character." I do not believe that we should go even that far.

In other words I do not believe that we should substitute "promissory estoppel" for consideration. If Section 88 is approved the law of Contracts becomes too indefinite. The phrase "if injustice can be avoided only by enforcement of the promise" is objectionable and makes it very difficult to determine whether there is a contract. In other words, when is the offer accepted? Is it when the detriment is suffered or only after the court or jury determines whether injustice can be avoided only by enforcement of the promise?

If I say to my nephew, "If you will buy a Ford car I will give you $1000"; or if I say, "If you will promise to buy a Ford car I will promise to give you $10,000,"

either contract is binding, since the detriment suffered by the nephew was the requested consideration
for my promise. But if out of the blue sky I say to my
class that I am going to give each one of you $50 next
Christmas and one of the students in view of this
promised gift buys a Ford car on credit he should not
recover even though he smashes the car before
Christmas Day. Under Section 88 I will be forced to
comply with my promised gift, provided the student
told me the day before I made the promise that he
was thinking of buying a Ford car. The same would be
true of my promise to give my neighbor's boy $5000
next year if I had heard him beg his father for a
Buick car where he bought the car in view of my
promised gift. I do not think we should go that far.

Mr. Williston: Neither do I.

Mr. Hildebrand: I think we should hold to the old
landmarks on this proposition and say only where I
call for that action as a consideration for my offer
should the contract be binding.

Mr. Williston: I should like to cite one or two of
the cases that I have cited in the Commentaries in
regard to this question because I suppose they may
not all have been read.

In the first place, there are the charitable sub-
scription cases. A man promises to give $5000 to-
wards a new church. The very name charitable implies what is the truth and it is a promised gift to the
church, and the promisee understands it is a gift. The
church or the trustees of the church go ahead and
incur obligations on the strength of it and they enforce that promise almost everywhere in this country.

Now, it is simply misuse of words to say that there
is any bargain there. The emphasis laid both by the
last speaker and by Mr. Morawetz on whether you say
if you will do this, I will do thus and so, is enforced
emphasis. Parties do not use in real life language of
any such nicety; but the question does arise whether
a reasonable person would understand that certain
action was requested as a bargain as an exchange for
the promise or whether the promisor was promising
the benefit to the promisee, and that whatever was to
be done by the promisee was to be done for the promisee's own advantage and not for the promisor's.
There is no bargain, but there is recovery. Those
cases are not in equity, they are at law.

Then there are other classes of cases. Here is a
case that arose in the New York Court of Appeals
recently. A promise was made by a gratuitous bailee
to take out insurance on the bailed property. He did
not do it. Of course, the promisee, the owner of the
property, had expected him to and had relied on him.

But there was no consideration for the promise. The
court said the bailee, apart from the promise, would
be liable for the destruction of the goods, if due to his
gross negligence; but being a gratuitous bailee, gross
negligence would be necessary, and the court said
that there was no gross negligence. But the court enforced the promise and held the promisor was liable
because the owner of the goods naturally assumed
that the insurance would be taken out and that the
owner would be affected, and that case was not in
equity.

A lot of cases that go under the name of waiver,
are really cases of promises falling within this description. They are promises to perform in spite of
some non-performance of a condition or requirement
of the contract. Relying on a promise, the condition is
not complied with, and yet the promisee recovers.

Promises to make marriage settlements form another class. A promises to make a marriage settlement. He does not ask for the marriage of his daughter as consideration. He is not making a bargain, he
just makes a promise. The marriage takes place and
both in England and in the United States the settlement has to be made.

Now, these cases all depend really on the principles which I have tried to state in Section 88. If you
strike out Section 88 and leave things as they stand,
then all those promises which I have just stated, and
others which I will not repeat, become unenforceable.
It seems to me impossible merely to strike out Section 88. You can enumerate all the classes of cases
which I have enumerated and have a number of special instances, and then another instance will come
up and it will not be covered by the Restatement. If
the law is to be simplified, it seems to me it must be
done by coordinating the classes of cases rather than
by enumerating a lot of special instances. That is the
reason why I defend Section 88.

May I say a word as to the suggestion of the Reporter and his Advisers further considering this and
improving it? It was long considered by the Reporter
and his Advisers. It came before the Council and the
Council was not inclined to accept it, and a committee of the Council was appointed to consult with the
Reporter and his Advisers with this clause in mind as
the chief one which was to be dealt with, and of that
committee of three, I should say at least two and one-
half were opposed to it. And after consideration and
examination of the authorities every suggestion that
they had made or had in mind seemed to them inadequate. The first thing that seemed possible was to
take these different sets of cases and say, simply

grouping them together, that there were exceptions to the rule and that a contract required consideration at the time. But I think the complete answer to that and the one that satisfied the committee is this statement of the Reporter on page 19 of the Commentaries:

"If the law is to be simplified and clarified, it can be done only by coordinating the decisions under general rules, not by stating empirically a succession of specific cases without any binding thread of principle."

And it was because of the multitude of these cases, cases which were law cases, that treating it as a matter of equity was very soon given up. We had to adopt some general principle which would be stated as a section of this Restatement which would cover the mass of authorities and it is perfectly useless to shut one's eyes to those authorities because every now and then there is a case found where the promise is enforced though it is gratuitous.

The question whether words really amount to a promise, applies to Section 88 as well as elsewhere. Whether words are intended as a contract, or to be a binding promise, or are merely as an expression of good will indicating the present intention to give money to somebody when he does something, that has been dealt with elsewhere in this Restatement. I thought it was in this part of the Restatement, but I do not see it; but that question has been considered.

When you say to a young man, "I will give you $1000 the day you enter college," you having heard that he wants to go to college, is that a promise? Of course, it may be a contract. A man hears that a boy wants to go to college, and he says to him "the day you enter, that day you get $1000," or, "the day you pass your examinations, you will have $1000."

There has been an immense amount of time spent by different sets of people in trying to get some language that might be more limited, which it was felt would be the spirit of the Institute, and the spirit of the Council. It is recognized that this is a broad statement, which would make it difficult to say, when anything was done following a promise, whether the promise was a binding contract.

Arthur J. Tuttle (Michigan): I know that the three illustrations given are all of the kind that are binding promises and so many suggestions have been made that possibly this Section 88 might stop with the word "forbearance" in line 17, that it occurred to me that possibly it might help us if an illustration could be suggested by someone where it would not be bind-

ing. I have tried to think of one and I cannot think of a case that would come within the definition of not doing an injustice if the promise were definite and substantial and the promisee had done that definite and substantial thing. I presume there are illustrations, but I cannot think of any and it occurred to me that if we could have one of these illustrations, it might help us.

George T. McDermott (Kansas): It occurred to me that perhaps this disagreement between the uncle and the nephew is probably taken care of by the phrase "if injustice can be avoided only by the enforcement of the promise." In answer to the last gentlemen, I take it if this boy had bought this Buick car and had paid $1000 (the uncle intending he should have it for his pleasure and comfort) and the next hour turned around and sold it for $1000, the nephew would suffer no injustice if the uncle were not held for $1000 for the simple reason he only had the car an hour and had his $1000 back.

With reference to the uncle offering the boy $1000 if he would buy a comparatively new Buick, and he goes out and buys a $500 Buick, it is an injustice if he makes him pay $1000, and it is an injustice to the boy if he does not get anything. Suppose the uncle goes to the boy and says: "I understood you only paid $500 for that car." The boy admits that is true. The uncle says: "Well, here is your $500," he makes him a legal tender of that amount, and the boy refuses to take it and sues him for the $1000. Is it the judgment of the Reporter that when the court determines the question of what is an injustice, he will take it in the light of the facts that exist at the time of the trial and say to the boy the injustice can be avoided by denying your claim for relief because your uncle made a valid tender of $500, which you refused to take?

Mr. Williston: I think that is a very good case. Also we might suppose the uncle went to the dealer and the dealer said "I am perfectly willing to take the car back." That might be a case, and I think that case you put is very good.

Judge Tuttle: My illustration of the interpretation would be this: that if the uncle said to the boy "I will give you $1000 if you will buy a Buick car and keep it ten minutes and then resell it," then that would be the definite thing. But on the other hand if he said "You buy a Buick and keep it and enjoy it," then that would be the definite thing. The suggestion that has been made is not intended as a trick, but in the end it is a trick illustration and does not put straight the proposition.

Mr. Williston: It seems to me it did. It was put to illustrate the point that you were raising, whether injustice could be avoided. Grant that what the uncle meant was purchasing the car just as the boy did, still injustice can be avoided if the boy gets his money back and the uncle is willing to pay.

. . .

O. H. Burns (Louisiana): Does it follow because a man says, "I will give you $1000" that the promisee can recover the $1000?

Mr. Williston: No.

Mr. Burns: Is it a question of damages there?

Mr. Williston: I suppose it is a question of damages, but the question of damages for breach of a promise is ordinarily such a sum that will put the promisee in as good a position as he would have been in if the promise had been kept, not as good a position as he would have been in if the promise had not been made, not a restoration of the *status quo*; but if we say that there is recovery at all, the damages for breach of a contract are such as would exist if the contract had been carried out in full.

Mr. Coudert: Could not an injustice be done by placing these in the category of quasi contracts rather than trying to twist the facts into a contract in order to do justice where it won't always work out justice?

Mr. Williston: What has that to do with the cases I have cited? They are not based on quasi contract, they are based on the idea of enforcing the promises that are made.

Henry S. Drinker, Jr. (Pennsylvania): The thing that particularly commends itself to me in this section is that by the use of the words, "if injustice can be avoided," the Reporter and the Institute acknowledge that here is a case that does not exactly tally with the strict conception. They frankly acknowledge that there is an exception and carefully circumscribe it with these admirably chosen words, "of a definite and substantial character," so it cannot be abused.

In practically every branch of the law, I believe there is a case like that, that is based on hardship and injustice, but instead of being acknowledged it is covered up with a phrase like estoppel or *res gestae* or something of that kind, and that is supposed to mean something.

Professor Williston says that it is a safety valve, that it is worded this way as a safety valve, whereas, as it is in the law now, cases of this sort were apt to get into legal garbage barrels where our slop is thrown in, and there taken up by somebody that does

not read them with understanding, so that they are diverted from their original and proper purpose. I think the Institute will do a great service to the law if it picks out these exceptions and circumscribes them as Professor Williston has done. This labels them all so we will know exactly what they are.

Mr. Burns: I have noted that much of the opposition to Section 88, now under consideration, has taken the form that the doctrine therein set out is essentially an equitable one and that for that reason it has no place in this connection.

Now, personally, I cannot see the force of that argument.

Suppose we agree with those gentlemen who object on the ground that it is in nature essentially an equitable doctrine. It is not an unheard of thing for a court of law to adopt what is by its nature and in its origin an equitable doctrine, and I should judge from certain of the cases which the Reporter cited a moment ago in support of his position that that very thing has happened as regards this particular doctrine.

Another objection which I notice has been raised to this Section is that it ought to be placed under the head of quasi-contractual obligations. It strikes me that as a matter of theory or logic, it might be difficult to put the case on the one side or the other of the line of demarcation between a duty imposed by the party and a duty imposed by the law; but it would seem that if it be classified under the head of quasi-contractual liability, the question of damages would be a material consideration, and that it might be objected that in certain cases damages, if it were regarded as quasi-contractual liability, would be insufficient.

For those two reasons I, personally, am heartily in accord with Section 88. I believe it would be a most unfortunate thing if this meeting should choose to reject Mr. Williston's suggestion. I think, as said by the speaker who preceded me, that it represents an enlightened view in regard to the doctrine of consideration, that it affords a safety valve, that it furnishes an element of elasticity and that it reveals an endeavor to save the doctrine of consideration from an unreasonable rigidity. It would be most unfortunate in my opinion to reject it.

Mr. Wickersham: Have we finished with the discussion of this Section?

Mr.   : One further suggestion in reference to this, it seems to me that the language that injustice can be avoided only by enforcement of the promise, is understood by some of our members as meaning that the court of law is going to deal with that proposition as a court of equity. Perhaps, if it read: "induce such action or forbearance is binding if refusal to enforce it would work injustice."

I think that is the idea I got from it at the start. I do not know whether that is the real meaning of it. If it is, I think that would end the discussion.

Mr. Williston: Yes, that is the intended meaning: "if refusal to enforce it would work an injustice."

Mr. Wickersham: The Reporter will take that in consideration:

We will now pass to Section 89. Are there any comments? . . .

The Expansion of the Reliance/Promissory Estoppel Concept

Section 90 uses neither the term "promissory estoppel" nor "reliance," though it requires both a promise and foreseeable action or forbearance induced by it. For the most part the terms have come to be used interchangeably, though some recent writers have used one term or the other to emphasize the importance of either the promise or the reliance. Here, they will be used interchangeably. For a generation after the First Restatement was published in 1932 there was debate in the courts and the literature over the legitimacy of the concept as a basis of contract liability and, assuming its legitimacy, over whether it could be justifiably used in situations other than family gifts and pledges of charitable donations. A famous early example is Learned Hand's opinion in *James Baird Co. v. Gimbel Bros.*, 64 F.2d 344 (2d Cir. 1933). The acceptance of the reliance concept and its expansion into business dealings is traceable to Justice Roger Traynor's opinion in *Drennan v. Star Paving Co.*, 51 Cal. 2d 409, 333 P.2d 757 (1958), involving a mistaken bid on a construction contract, although there were earlier cases going the same way.

In 1969, Professor Stanley Henderson, now the F.D.G. Ribble Professor at the University of Virginia Law School, published *Promissory Estoppel and Traditional Contract Doctrine*, which showed that the old debate was concluded and that a new one had begun. As Henderson says near the beginning, although the draftsmen of Section 90 had had gratutitous promises in mind, "[t]he usual setting out of which a Section 90 promise currently emerges, however, is commercial, not benevolent." The new question was how far ought the reliance concept be applied when the bargaining process had begun but had either broken down or was incomplete when reliance occurred. Professor Henderson's article follows. Besides its forward look, it includes a useful background discussion of Section 90 and its relation to the bargain concept.

Stanley D. Henderson, *Promissory Estoppel and Traditional Contract Doctrine*, 78 Yale L.J. 343 (1969)

I. Introduction

Recent decisions[1] invoking Section 90 of the Restatement of Contracts demonstrate that the doctrine of promissory estoppel embodied in that section[2] is playing an important role in the fixing of

Reprinted by permission of The Yale Law Journal Company and Fred B. Rothman and Company from The Yale Law Journal Company, Vol. 78, pp. 343.

[1] This article is concerned primarily with decisions rendered during the course of the past ten years. For discussions of earlier collections of promissory estoppel cases, see Shattuck, Gratuitous Promissor—A New Writ?, 35 Mich. L. Rev. 908 (1937); Boyer, Promissory Estoppel.: Principle from Precedents, 50 Mich. L. Rev. 639, 873 (1952); Annot., 48 A.L.R.2d 1069 (1956); 22 Minn. L. Rev. 843 (1939); Note, The Measure of Damages for Breach of a Contract Created by Action in Reliance, 48 Yale L.J. 1036 (1939).

[2] Restatement of Contracts § 90 (1932) provides:
    A promise which the promisor should reasonably expect to induce action or forbearance of a definite and

limits of contractual responsibility. Promissory estoppel is, however, today serving functions quite different from those contemplated by the draftsmen of Section 90. The principal application of the doctrine is no longer in the limited area of gratuitous promises, but in the much broader field of bargain transactions. A number of earlier cases, to be sure, did apply promissory estoppel to gratuitous promises made in a business setting. But both courts and commentators understood that the basis of enforcement was that the promisor had failed to prescribe a return for his promise. Indeed, the basic elements of promissory estoppel doctrine have been fashioned in the context of the explicit assumption that the doctrine properly operates outside the bargain relationship.

The usual setting out of which a Section 90 promise currently emerges, however, is commercial, not benevolent. More important, the promise which calls for application of Section 90 is typically one which contemplates an exchange. Section 90 has thus grown from a device for enforcing certain gratuitous promises into a useful, though little understood, contract tool for recognizing the reliance element in bargain transactions as well.

Expanded application of any legal doctrine naturally raises questions about practical consequences and effective limits. With respect to Section 90, the implications of expansion are to be found in the manner in which theories of reliance upon promises are shaping the evolution and application of other principles to which our system of contract has traditionally been committed, particularly the "bargain principle" of consideration and the "assent principle" of offer-acceptance. The purpose of this discussion is to examine the extent to which familiar rules of contract formation, validation and adjustment have been affected by, and have themselves shaped the course of, expanded use of the promissory estoppel concept of Section 90.

II. Tensions Between the Reliance Principle and the Bargain Principle

Injury to the person or property of one who justifiably relied on the undertaking of another was apparently the earliest basis upon which informal contracts were enforced in the action of assumpsit.[8] And reliance, whether actual or probable, was an essential ingredient in the evolutionary process through which consideration doctrine developed as the keystone of traditional contract law. But despite the early prominence of the element of reasonable reliance in contract, the requirement of "bargain" or "exchange," apparently an extension of the idea of *quid pro quo* in the action of debt, has emerged as the core of consideration doctrine. The classifications of responsibility which we have come to regard as conventional, and which have been accorded blackletter status in the *Restatement of Contracts*, evidence a preoccupation with the belief that only promises for which some agreed price has been paid are deserving of enforcement. Thus, according to the catechism of consideration, action in reliance upon a promise is sufficient reason for enforcement only when the action is bargained for by the promisor and given in return by the promisee.

. . .

Thus the importance of bargain in practical affairs, reinforced by the priority accorded it in law, has made it difficult for courts to isolate the reliance problem and to handle it with consistency. The notion that bargain represents a calculated effort by the promisor to satisfy some desire, usually economic, operates to make the conduct of the promisee of secondary importance. Because of the prevailing policy that the element of bargain, standing alone, justifies enforcement, action in reliance is commonly seen as a tool for sorting out motives which bear on the issue of exchange. The fact that the promisee may have incurred expense, or otherwise have relied to his det-

---

substantial character on the part of the promisee and which does induce such action or forbearance is binding if injustice can be avoided only by enforcement of the promise.

The tentative draft of the Restatement (Second) of Contracts proposes that Section 90 be altered to read as follows:

A promise which the promisor should reasonably expect to induce action or forbearance on the part of the promisee or a third person and which does induce such action or forbearance is binding if injustice can be avoided only by enforcement of the promise. The remedy granted for breach may be limited as justice requires.

Restatement (Second) of Contracts § 90 (Tent. Draft No. 2, 1965).

Because the doctrine of promissory estoppel and the rules of Section 90 are customarily understood to refer to the same general theory of reliance, they will be used interchangeably in this discussion. The objections to using the phrase "promissory estoppel" to describe the doctrine of enforceability because of action in reliance are noted in 1A A. Corbin, Contracts § 204 (rev. ed.1963) [hereinafter cited as Corbin].

[8] See generally Ames, The History of Assumpsit, 2 Harv. L. Rev. 1, 53 (1888); Holdsworth, The Modern History of the Doctrine of Consideration, 2 Boston U.L. Rev. 87, 174 (1922).

riment, is subsumed in considerations about whether the promisor, in accordance with the rules of offer and acceptance, has received the particular advantage which prompted his promise. Reliance, under this approach, functions not as a substantive ground for enforcement, but as a vehicle for identification of some other ground for enforcement.

Moreover, the disposition to treat action in reliance as proof of bargain rather than as an independent basis of enforcement most seriously impairs the reliance principle in the very cases in which reliance is likely to be the only available ground for relief. Because the cases which most clearly warrant the application of Section 90 seldom involve reliance which is beneficial to the promisor, a causal relation between putative bargain and factual reliance is likely to be difficult to find. The risk that action in reliance will be found to be not sufficiently serious to justify application of Section 90, or to be merely a condition of a gratuitous promise, is thereby increased. In addition, in the absence of benefit conferred, the enrichment factor is not available to give color to reliance or to support relief along restitutionary lines.

Not even the preference of the courts for the detriment branch of consideration has diminished the appeal of bargain as the prevailing context of analysis and decision. Rather than freeing the reliance factor of its subordinate status, the effect of broadening the meaning of detriment to include practically any conduct of the promisee has been to encourage a corresponding expansion of the bargain concept. This development was predictable so long as the expansion of the concept of detriment took place within a frame of reference which concentrated attention upon events surrounding the making of the promise, rather than upon the consequences of non-performance. It is now true that conventional theory can be manipulated so as to protect even gratuitous promises. But while the holdings in such cases may be approved, their circuitous reasoning tends to confuse the law of reliance by converting change of position in any form or degree into consideration. The disposition of judges, adverted to above, to talk the language of familiar doctrine adds to the pressure to fit the reliance principle of promissory estoppel into the mold of consideration rules: Thus despite the *Restatement* directive that Section 90 promises are enforceable without consideration, the theme of consideration is in fact the point of departure for nearly every judicial discussion

of promissory estoppel. Consequently, it is fashionable to portray the doctrine of promissory estoppel as some kind of stand-in for consideration. If promissory estoppel cannot be extricated from the language and label of consideration, the elements of Section 90 are likely to function as little more than an extension of the criteria of the latter.

III. The Functions of Section 90 in the Bargaining Process

While the pressures discussed above have tended to assimilate Section 90 into the consideration-centered framework of traditional contract law, blurring the outlines of reliance theory in the process, the domestication of the section has at the same time had the effect of expanding the sphere of application accorded the theory of promissory estoppel by the courts. Before discussing the details of this expansion, however, it is worth considering briefly some of its general background and implications.

A. *General Background*

It must first be remembered that the tradition which produced Section 90 necessitated the extraction of a broad generalization from an assortment of cases which are not reducible to a systematic pattern. The oral promise of land, followed by entry and improvements, brings into play a wide range of considerations, including the enrichment factor, the history of equity, the Statute of Frauds, and property concepts relating to the status of title. Policy considerations of a different kind are responsible for the varied theories which have been used to protect charitable subscriptions, and help explain why the ablest of judges might strain conventional theory in order to enforce gift promises to charities. Tort analogies focusing upon consequential losses have apparently influenced the treatment of the gratuitous bailee. At the same time, the degree to which the estoppel idea is reinforced by voluntary dealings or relationships of blood or family undoubtedly accounts for the historical protection of a host of promises reliance upon which gives rise to varying degrees of injustice.

. . .

It has been noted above that on practically every occasion on which the courts have dealt explicitly with Section 90 in recent years, the promise in question has been made either in contemplation of a commercial return or in the course of commercial negotiations.[37] . . .

---

[37] The author has uncovered more than 100 decisions during the period in question in which promissory estoppel was considered as the ground of decision in a clear bargain transaction. In more than one-third of those cases, the theory of Section 90 was used as the sole or alternative basis for enforcement.

And if the gratuitous promise is no longer relevant to the theory of Section 90, policy considerations developed in relation to the conventional idea of promissory estoppel will have to be carefully examined before Section 90 is made a vehicle for relieving injustices occasioned by business bargains.

The most obvious consequence of the application of Section 90 in areas other than that of the gratuitous promise is that the distinguishing characteristics of conventional theories are obscured. It is standard practice in a good many jurisdictions to plead the theory of consideration simultaneously with that of promissory estoppel, urging the same allegations and evidence in support of both theories. Occasionally, it is true, the facts of a given case lend themselves to analysis under either approach. But although the use of alternative theories by a litigant is entirely consistent with good practice, a large number of courts are invoking both promissory estoppel and consideration doctrine in their opinions without any recognition of differences in theory. It can be argued that obscuring the distinct criteria of the bargain and reliance principles provides the courts with increased flexibility and ensures wider enforcement of deserving promises. But judicial intertwining of the two theories can cut the other way as well, preventing plaintiffs from circumventing certain obstacles peculiar to one or the other theory. . . .

The breadth of statement of Section 90 has facilitated movement of reliance theory into the realm of bargain. Because of the flexibility which results from the generalized phrasing of the doctrine, many courts have apparently concluded that cases can be decided more easily by the use of promissory estoppel than by consideration rules. . . .

The broad language of Section 90 also enables courts to avoid struggling with the more unintelligible aspects of consideration doctrine, such as the so-called requirement of "mutuality of obligation."

More important, the use of Section 90 avoids the necessity of unduly stretching the concept of bargain in certain cases. Because of the reluctance of the common law to inquire into the adequacy of consideration, it has been possible to manipulate the test of bargain so as to extend protection to transactions in which the element of exchange is not easily observed. The opinions in such cases, however, disclose some discomfort in the handling of conventional theory. The line between bargain and gift is often vague, and an examination of the motives of the parties may be less than conclusive.[51] Then, too, a court may feel some reluctance to lend support to a contrived exchange which is designed only to effect a gift. Further, the inclination to reduce bargain to a "request"[53] has confused the law in that it tends to make the conditional gift look like an exchange. In light of these conceptual and definitional problems, the appeal of Section 90 and its neat criteria of promissory estoppel is understandable.

Perhaps the most interesting aspect of the recent Section 90 decisions, however, is that significant expansion into the bargain area has occurred in spite of well-established precedent to the contrary. In the years immediately following the drafting of Section 90 it was customary for the courts to exhibit reluctance to extend promissory estoppel to commercial transactions. A major source of this reluctance was the classic case of *James Baird Co. v. Gimbel Bros., Inc.*,[54] in which Learned Hand held that promissory estoppel was inapplicable to a bargain promise which occasioned reliance not constituting performance of the consideration sought by the promisor. An offer which bargains for a promise, he reasoned, is not binding until the specific return asked for is made. If a promise contains conditions about acceptance or performance, they are entitled to full effect. Hence reliance not in the form of the specified equivalent cannot affect the freedom which offer-acceptance doctrine guarantees to the promisor. It follows that the conditional character of an offer which proposes an exchange precludes the application of Section 90 because, of necessity, reliance which fails to satisfy the conditions is unreasonable. Thus, as Judge Hand felt compelled to conclude, promissory estoppel is restricted to "donative" promises. The element of exchange which marks off the bargain promise also serves to identify the boundaries beyond which promissory estoppel is not permitted.

The effect of *Baird* was to bar the application of Section 90 to an offer for a bilateral contract. The

---

[51] As a practical matter, the requirement of "mutual inducement" between promise and consideration has always tended to lead to an exploration of subjective factors clustered around the idea of "motive." The notion that motive is an essential test of consideration, though rejected by the Restatement Of Contracts § 84(a) (1932), still has life left in it today.

[53] The real problem with interpreting a request by the promisor in terms of consideration is that it simply cannot be said that every request imports a promise.

[54] 64 F.2d 344 (2d Cir. 1933). Defendant subcontractor, claiming a mistake in computation, revoked his offer to supply materials after the general contractor had relied by incorporating the offer in the bid for the prime contract.

restriction, in actual practice, has never been completely accepted.[58] But it was not until the 1958 decision in *Drennan v. Star Paving Co.*[59] that a theoretical bridge to the bilateral contract was constructed. On facts almost identical to those in *Baird*, the *Drennan* court, primarily on the basis of an analogy to the unilateral contract provisions of Section 45 of the *Restatement*, held that a general contractor's reliance on a paving subcontractor's bid had the effect of making the bid irrevocable. The technique was first to find in the offer an implied subsidiary promise not to revoke, based upon the promisee's reasonable and foreseeable change of position in reliance upon the offer. Once the subsidiary promise, which was unsupported by consideration and therefore gratuitous, had been implied, the reference to Section 90 in the comment to Section 45[62] was the vehicle for invoking promissory estoppel as the ground for enforcement.

Justice Traynor's opinion for the court in *Drennan* is a landmark because it opens up for exploration ground not previously considered available to Section 90. In challenging the rationale of the *Baird* decision, it also represents one of the few serious efforts to provide a theoretical basis for the application of promissory estoppel in the context of business transactions. It should be noted, however, that the theory articulated in *Drennan* is far from a license to enlarge the scope of Section 90 without limit. The effect of the case is only to make certain offers irrevocable until the offeree has had a reasonable opportunity to accept, which may explain why *Drennan* has not been widely invoked outside its factual setting.

Aside from the interest created by *Drennan*, there appears to be no widespread concern with the disparity between the orthodox theory of promissory estoppel and current applications of Section 90. Nor is there agreement as to the continuing vitality of the Baird rationale. Many of the courts that face the issue squarely still assert that Section 90 is applicable only to unconditional, or non-bargain, promises. Yet the number of instances in which a court explores and applies both bargain consideration and promissory estoppel theories in the same case casts doubt on such assertions. It may well be that our notions of

what qualifies as reasonable reliance on even a highly conditional offer are circumscribing freedoms which orthodox rules have previously assured to the promisor. If reliance upon a bargain promise seems to justify some form of relief, the tendency in the cases is to concentrate upon the particular elements of Section 90 rather than upon the proper function of that section in the context of general contract theory.[66] The practical result is that promisors are required to assume greater responsibility for expensive action occasioned by their promises, regardless of the conditions under which the promises were made.

With these general problems in mind, we turn to a closer examination of the various ways in which promissory estoppel is being used today.

B. *Preliminary Negotiations and Defective Promises*

The offer-acceptance rules which dominate contract formation reflect the importance we attach to bargains arrived at through the interplay of private interests. The general objective of these assorted rules is to guarantee parties seeking an exchange extensive freedom to express, or to refuse to express, a willingness to be bound. Thus, a proposal does not ordinarily subject the proposer to liability unless a variety of safeguards are satisfied. Numerous rules permit a change of mind in the course of bargaining. Doubtful responses operate to keep negotiations alive. The occurrence of such fortuitous events as death, supervening impossibility or frustration, insanity, and delay wipe clean the slate. The difficulties resulting from communication across great distances are taken into account in determining whether a party shall be held to have agreed to a contract. In short, the rules which regulate the bargaining process seek to insure that, in most instances, obligation attaches only when it has been deliberately undertaken.

Because the doctrine of promissory estoppel imposes liability without regard to expressed intention, its use in pre-agreement negotiations is bound to alter the traditional scheme of offer and acceptance. This is particularly so where, after lengthy and expensive negotiations, no agreement is in fact reached. In just such a case the Supreme Court of Wisconsin,

---

[58] E.g., Robert Gordon, Inc. v. Ingersoll-Rand Co., 117 F.2d 654 (7th Cir. 1941); Northwestern Eng'r Co. v. Ellerman, 69 S.D. 397, 10 N.W.2d 879 (1943).

[59] 51 Cal. 2d 409, 333 P.2d 757 (1958).

[62] In discussing the theory of an implied promise not to revoke, Restatement § 45 says that "merely acting in justifiable reliance on an offer may in some cases serve as sufficient reason for making a promise binding (see § 90)." Restatement of Contracts § 45, comment b at 54 (1932).

[66] What this means essentially is that the traditional distinction between bargained-for and unbargained-for reliance is being abandoned.

solely on the ground of promissory estoppel, approved an assessment of damages against a party whose unfulfilled "promises and assurances," made in the course of bargaining, had left the other party with extensive reliance losses. *Hoffman v. Red Owl Stores, Inc.*[72] evolved from a proposal by defendant to establish plaintiff in one of its stores as a franchise operator, provided plaintiff would invest a specified amount of capital and perform certain other conditions. The parties discussed the matter in various stages for more than two years, with defendant at each stage assuring plaintiff that he would get his franchise upon performance of the stated conditions, some of which were added as matters progressed.[73] The termination of negotiations apparently resulted from defendant's insistence that plaintiff supply an amount of capital nearly twice the sum originally requested. By that time, as a result of defendant's urging, plaintiff had sold his bakery business and building, sold a small grocery operation which had been purchased in order to gain experience, made a payment on the site for the proposed franchise, incurred moving expenses and arranged for a house rental. The Wisconsin court, reasoning that promissory estoppel contemplates an award of such damages "as are necessary to prevent injustice," awarded plaintiff the amount of the actual expenses and losses he had incurred.

The *Hoffman* decision is highly significant in several respects. First, it must be recognized that the responsibilities imposed by the decision upon a contract negotiator who induces prejudicial reliance, and then withdraws, are somewhat unusual. If the case is thought of as involving a promise to consummate a deal, it sounds a retreat from the common law view that breach of an agreement to agree is not actionable. In addition, Hoffman may be viewed as establishing the beginnings of an "important new legal duty of good faith in the conduct of contract negotiations." But for our purposes, the significance of the case lies in the manner in which it rationalizes its application of Section 90. The parties in *Hoffman* dealt with each other with the intent of effecting a business exchange without reaching agreement on a contract. In fact, the failure to reach agreement upon essential terms prevented defendant's promises from

achieving even the level of an operative offer. Nevertheless, the absence of the elements of a traditional contract was deemed immaterial in an action grounded on promissory estoppel.[79] In the judgment of the court, enforcement of a promise under Section 90 is not based on breach of contract, nor is it "the equivalent of a breach of contract action."

By freeing the promise which triggers application of the section from the context of offer-acceptance rules, *Hoffman* does away with the bridge commonly used to link promissory estoppel with orthodox consideration doctrine. The key to the court's opinion is its apparent belief that the conventional use of promissory estoppel as a "substitute for consideration" in connection with gratuitous promises is now obsolete and that Section 90 should serve as a distinct basis of liability without regard to theories of bargain, contract, or consideration. The criteria which justify and limit the application of promissory estoppel are to be determined exclusively by what Section 90 says about the effects of nonperformance of promises. The factual context out of which a given case evolves, whether bargain or gratuity, is presumably beside the point. If the tests of Section 90 are satisfied, *Hoffman* arguably makes promissory estoppel applicable throughout the negotiating process.

. . .

It may be expected, however, that the courts will not allow Section 90 free rein in bargain negotiation contexts. If promissory estoppel is to provide a standard of fairness by which the conduct of negotiations may be judged, it is likely that the courts will examine the reasonableness of alleged reliance with some care. Deliberate risk-taking prior to agreement will clearly be treated differently from a change of position in response to a promise. The taking of steps designed primarily to enhance the chances of reaching agreement, moreover, even if requested by the other party, involves the risk that benefits derived will render loss difficult to demonstrate in court. Promisees seeking to invoke Section 90 on the basis of pre-agreement action in reliance are particularly vulnerable to the claim that ordinary care was not exercised. Where protracted business negotiations involve a number of parties, as was the case in *Corbit v.*

---

[72] 26 Wis. 2d 683, 133 N.W.2d 267 (1965).

[73] The court expressly found that the evidence would not support a finding that defendant's promises were made in "bad faith with any present intent that they would not be fulfilled . . . ." Id. at 695, 133 N.W.2d at 273.

[79] The Hoffman court emphasized that Section 90 imposes no requirement that a promise giving rise to the doctrine of promissory estoppel be "so comprehensive in scope as to meet the requirements of an offer . . . ." Id. at 698, 133 N.W.2d at 275.

J.I. Case Co.,[91] or a complex transaction, as in *Doven-muehle, Inc. v. K-Way Associates*,[92] the problems of proof of the elements of promissory estoppel are similar to those commonly associated with conspiracy litigation—the significance of action in reliance may simply be lost in a host of evidentiary disputes. Considerations like these, together with the broad scope of judicial review made available by the generalized tests of Section 90, may well minimize the hazards of hasty applications of the reliance doctrine in bargain contexts.

Section 90 is also being used as a basis for enforcement of promises which under traditional theory would be held indefinite and hence unenforceable. It has long been customary for the courts and commentators to recite that only a *genuine* promise will support an action grounded on promissory estoppel. The idea behind the requirement is simply that promissory estoppel protects reasonable reliance, and that, in the nature of things, reliance is reasonable only if it is induced by an actual promise. With the movement of Section 90 into the area of bargains, the promise foundation of the reliance doctrine is subject to additional stress in connection with promises that are "indefinite" because vague or incomplete, or ones that are "illusory" because, in reality, they promise nothing.

. . .

Generally, however, the trend is toward wider use of Section 90 to enforce bargains which are otherwise unenforceable for indefiniteness under conventional rules. In the Texas case of *Wheeler v. White*,[98] a written agreement purported to obligate defendant to obtain or furnish plaintiff with construction financing for a shopping center. In reliance upon defendant's assurances that the financing would be provided, plaintiff proceeded to demolish existing buildings and generally prepare the site for the new venture. Upon learning that the loan would not be made, plaintiff sued to recover damages for breach of the written contract. Because the writing failed to

particularize the terms upon, which the loan was to be repaid, the intermediate appellate court affirmed the trial court's finding that the contract was too indefinite to enforce. The Texas Supreme Court agreed that indefiniteness precluded recovery on a conventional breach of contract theory, but reversed and remanded on the ground that the complaint stated a cause of action on the theory of promissory estoppel.[101] The decision was explicitly premised on the proposition that detrimental reliance occasioned by "an otherwise unenforceable promise" may present a "substantial and compelling claim for relief" under Section 90.

A group of cases involving franchised dealer contracts provide further evidence of the impact of Section 90 upon traditionally unenforceable bargains. The broad powers typically reserved to one or both parties to the franchise arrangement generally do not meet the criteria of established consideration doctrine. If the agreement imposes no real obligation on a party, or is expressly terminable at will, a court may well find the agreement illusory and therefore void for lack of mutuality of obligation. A decision adopting this rationale could be expected to deny recovery of a dealer's reliance losses as well. Nevertheless, over the years some limited protection of reliance losses has been recognized on the basis of the tort notion that a dealer ought to be entitled to enjoy the fruits of a franchise or distributorship at least for a period of time which permits him to recoup his investment.[106] And there is little doubt that Section 90 significantly reinforces the various reasons for reimbursement of a dealer's reliance losses.

So long as a dealer restricts his lawsuit to expenses actually incurred, Section 90 will apparently allow recovery without opening the Pandora's box of problems relating to the general unenforceability of dealership agreements. And even if lost profits are sought as well, Section 90 may still be of assistance, by way of the doctrine that an exclusive dealership agreement supported by consideration "additional"

---

[91] 70 Wash. 2d 522, 424 P.2d 290 (1967).

[92] 388 F.2d 940 (7th Cir. 1968).

[98] 398 S.W.2d 93 (Tex. Sup. Ct. 1965).

[101] The court stated that lost profits are not recoverable under the theory of promissory estoppel; rather, "the promisee is to be allowed to recover no more than reliance damages measured by the detriment sustained." 398 S.W.2d at 97.

[106] For discussion and cases see Gellhorn, Limitations on Contract Termination Rights—Franchise Cancellations, 1967 Duke L.J. 465, 479-83 (1967). As to the period of time for recoupment of a dealer's investment, see Clausen &

Sons, Inc. v. Theo. Hamm Brewing Co., 395 F.2d 388 (8th Cir. 1968), which leaves open the possibility that 13 years might not be unreasonable.

A well known case usually associated with promissory estoppel, Goodman v. Dicker, 169 F.2d 684 (D.C. Cir. 1948), may represent nothing more than a sophisticated application of this earlier line of cases. Though the court does not mention Section 90, perhaps because of some fairly obvious difficulties with the specific requirements of that section, the case is significant because reliance is the ground for recovery of expenses incurred in preparation to operate under a franchise which was never granted.

to the personal services of the dealer, even though expressly terminable at will, is enforceable for a reasonable time and may be terminated without cause only upon notice. The practical effect of this doctrine is that cancellation without notice gives rise to a damage claim which may include the profit margin on sales the dealer might have made during the time the agreement would have been effective after receipt of notice. The significance of promissory estoppel in this connection is that it may be treated as satisfying the requirement of "additional consideration," thereby extending limited protection to the expectation interest.

When a court finds that a bargain promise is indefinite or illusory, or that it lacks mutuality, it is really saying that the theory of consideration, as applied to the particular facts, has not been satisfied. If the court then proceeds on the theory of promissory estoppel, the necessary implication is that the bargain requirement is not as essential in exchange transactions as orthodox doctrine would have us believe. Rather, detrimental reliance emerges as the decisive factor; the promise itself is no longer as significant as the harm it precipitates. The cases of unenforceable bargains—whether for lack of agreement, indefiniteness of language or lack of mutuality of obligation—clearly demonstrate that when reliance is justifiable and serious, the promise requirement of Section 90 is not difficult to satisfy. Indeed, there is considerable evidence that strict requirements of promissory language are not being applied in Section 90 cases today. Section 90 promises are more frequently implied from conduct than was previously true, and patterns of conduct which resembles factual representations rather than promises often suffice.

These uses of Section 90 in the bargain context have the obvious effect of limiting powers traditionally exercised by offerors. The danger in this development is that the insistence of traditional theory upon clear promises, upon close attention to the reasonableness of conduct in reliance, and upon external indicia of intent to be bound, fulfill a valid purpose and should not be hastily discarded in the effort to protect every relying promisee. That consideration rules perform a vital function in providing evidence that "something happened" should not be overlooked. Whether or not the limitations inherent in Section 90

will keep the reliance principle within bounds in the bargain context will ultimately depend upon the degree to which courts recognize the dangers of imposing liability too readily in the formative stages of the bargaining process.

C. *The Reinforcement of Offers Through Reliance*

While the general problems relating to the revocability of offers, particularly those presented in the construction bidding cases, have been the subject of much study and discussion, the application of Section 90 to offers raises a number of questions which have not yet been answered.

It should be recalled that contract doctrine generally classifies offers under the same consideration rules as promises. Thus, unless an offer is supported by consideration, the offeror retains the power to revoke until the moment of acceptance. If the offer is expressly or impliedly "firm," the potential injustice of the operation of the revocation rule is obvious. One avenue of escape is made available by consideration doctrine in the part performance rule of Section 45 of the *Restatement.*[117] The principle of that section, however, does not provide a foundation sufficiently broad to include many cases of justifiable reliance arising today. It is expressly limited to offers for unilateral contracts and precludes revocation prior to acceptance only where the action in reliance constitutes a part of the actual performance made the price of the offer. If justifiable reliance in the form of *preparations* to perform is to have the effect of preventing revocation, the most readily available theory is that of promissory estoppel. Yet, aside from the construction bidding cases, there is little evidence that non-performance reliance upon unaccepted offers prompts explicit use of Section 90 as a ground of irrevocability. And even in those cases in which the section is applied, the mode of application is vulnerable to objections of inconsistency, invalid analogy, and circuitous reasoning.

The outcome of current construction bidding litigation usually depends upon the extent to which a particular court accepts the *Drennan* route around the obstacles of *Baird*. In view of the frequent applications of Section 90 to bargains, it is surprising that *Baird* has retained as much vitality as it has. Aside from the technicalities of theory, the blunt thrust of the case is that Section 90 has no relevance to a

---

[117] E.g. Brackenbury v. Hodgkin, 116 Me. 399, 102 A. 106 (1917).

promise which offers a bargain. A number of courts have, in effect, adopted this philosophy, depriving themselves of a flexible tool for conforming law to common commercial expectations and practices. The liberalizing effect of Justice Traynor's opinion in *Drennan* is therefore a valuable contribution to legal doctrine. However, because the opinion may well be relied upon to justify continued expansion of Section 90, the difficulties with the *Drennan* application of promissory estoppel to offers ought to be kept in mind.

. . .

There are obvious advantages in frank recognition that foreseeable and substantial reliance upon unaccepted offers, standing alone, is a sufficient reason for binding offerors. The tentative draft of the second *Restatement of Contracts* takes this position in a new section dealing with reliance prior to acceptance. Its approach makes clear that the reliance principle is applicable to bargains, whether unilateral or bilateral in form. . . .

. . .

E. *Readjustment in On-going Transactions*

Perhaps the most conventional application of promissory estoppel occurs when a relationship, usually contractual, has already been established and the rendering of performance has begun. One of the parties then promises to vary or forfeit a non-essential term or condition of the contract, or to surrender a defense which may arise in the future. The promise is typically unsupported by consideration, and the reliance which it induces is not actionable under strict contract theory because of the rule that performance of legal duties already owed the promisor is not consideration. But if the promise relates to the future and induces a material change of position, the intention of "waiver" or "abandonment" expressed in the promise combines with the general estoppel idea to give rise to promissory estoppel.

. . .

IV. The Impact of the Estoppel Principle

In addition to resisting pressures exerted by bar-

gain concepts, Section 90 must also be extricated from the influence of traditional estoppel doctrine if it is to establish an identity of its own. The limiting effects of the estoppel principle stem from an historical distinction which has little real meaning today. The common definition of estoppel in pais, or equitable estoppel,[182] is based upon the assumption that a promise as to the future is normally distinguishable from a factual representation about the past or present. But because many of the estoppel cases can be interpreted to involve an express or implied promise rather than a representation of fact, the narrow definition of equitable estoppel has never adequately covered all the cases to which the estoppel principle might fairly be applied. It was therefore inevitable that a rule of promissory estoppel would develop in recognition of the applicability of the estoppel principle to promises. The basic difficulty with this innovation is that the underlying theory of estoppel is not mechanically suited for application to promises. To "estop" the maker of a statement of fact by sealing his mouth in court has the effect of establishing a factual basis for an action, which, standing alone, will support recovery. The consequences of misleading conduct supply the injury, and the estoppel theory renders the representor powerless to dispute the facts upon which liability is based.

The situation becomes more complex when estoppel is applied to a promise. In the first place, enforcement goes beyond a represented status quo. As to theory, the mechanics of promissory estoppel produce liability by the technique of "estoppel to deny consideration." In effect a promise which is unenforceable under consideration rules is enforced by creating the impression that a form of consideration exists.[187]

The significant point is that while the reliance principle of Section 90 is widely understood as independent of the common definition of estoppel, the technicalities which derive from the common definition continue to influence the application of promissory estoppel.[188] Decision after decision disposes of Section 90 in the language of equitable estoppel, as if there were no real difference between the theories.

---

[182] The species of estoppel which equity puts upon a person who has made a false representation or a concealment of material facts, with knowledge of the facts, to a party ignorant of the truth of the matter, with the intention that the other party should act upon it, and with the result that such party is actually induced to act upon it to his damage. Black's Law Dictionary 632 (4th ed. 1951). A good discussion of the rules of equitable estoppel appears in Barnett v. Wolfolk, 149 W. Va. 246, 140 S.E.2d 466 (1965).

[187] In conventional language, estoppel to deny consider-

ation provides a "substitute" for consideration. As a practical matter, it is estoppel theory which supplies the legal framework for the imposition of liability. Cf. Bray v. Gardner, 268 F. Supp. 328, 332 E.D., Tenn. 1967): ". . . in the absence of statute, the doctrine of estoppel is available to protect a right; never to create one."

[188] The wide use of the popular phrase "promissory estoppel" undoubtedly contributes to the belief that Section 90 is properly classified under an estoppel heading. As a result, attention is diverted from the reliance principle which underlies Section 90.

Estoppel precedents are used to give content to the specific elements of Section 90, as well as to dispose of broad issues of promissory estoppel. The old fact-promise distinction may be employed to preclude liability under either equitable or promissory estoppel. . . . The essentially defensive tradition of equitable estoppel not only dominates the fashioning of remedial relief under Section 90, but, by necessary implication, brings in question the expansion of promissory estoppel as an affirmative basis of responsibility. The most striking consequence of preoccupation with estoppel concepts is that the courts fail to recognize that application of Section 90 does in fact involve a contract. It should be recalled that the expanded use of promissory estoppel in the forward-looking case of *Hoffman v. Red Owl Stores, Inc.*, was expressly premised upon a finding that Section 90 did not rest upon, nor was equivalent to, a contract. Other courts have similarly dissociated promissory estoppel from contract. If such decisions are merely saying that Section 90 does not depend upon bargain consideration, the distinction is of course accurate. But there is a general failure to recognize that Section 90 is catalogued under the heading of informal contracts without consideration. As a result, attention is diverted from the specific language of the section, which says that a "promise" is "binding" when detrimental reliance creates "injustice" which can be avoided only by "enforcement of the promise."

The consequences of failure to recognize promissory estoppel as a contract doctrine are felt principally in the area of remedies. After scholarly and exhaustive analysis, the issue of whether damages awarded under Section 90 should be limited to protection of the reliance interest, or measured by the full expectation interest, is still unsettled.[197] In practice, even the most progressive expansions of Section 90 often cling to a damage measure derived from the defensive theory of estoppel.[198] There are occasions, to be sure, where the limitations of estoppel theory are circumvented by employing Section 90 to effect a recovery in excess of reliance losses. It is interesting to note, however, that the cases which use Section 90 as the ground for awarding the promised performance typically involve bargain transactions in which consideration might arguably have been found. This suggests that identification with contract doctrine is

indeed essential if promissory estoppel is to be broadly accepted as a vehicle for protecting the expectation interest. To the extent that estoppel intervenes to obscure the contract theory, the reimbursement of reliance losses alone will likely develop as the standard damage measure under Section 90.

A further influence upon Section 90 is to be observed in the tradition of equity which underlies estoppel. The specific concern of Section 90 with "injustice," standing alone, contemplates broad judicial discretion to make use of equitable principles. The risk inherent in such discretion is that equities arising from sources other than Section 90 may operate to modify the requirements of that Section. For example, the historical tests of a remedy in equity do not necessarily determine the availability of promissory estoppel. Nor does Section 90 authorize a conventional "balancing of the equities," especially in the light of the principal concern of the section for the effects of non-performance upon the promisee. If the particular remedy sought sounds in equity, the elements of promissory estoppel have on occasion drawn meaning from doctrines indigenous to the ethics of equity.

Since promissory estoppel is a peculiarly equitable doctrine designed to deal with situations which, in total impact, necessarily call into play discretionary powers, it is desirable that the elements of Section 90 remain sufficiently pliable. They should not, however, be subject to unlimited modification in the name of estoppel or equity. If it is remembered that the rules of promissory estoppel create a contract grounded on the effects of reliance, indiscriminate use of estoppel notions will be minimized. The complicating factor is that the element of detrimental reliance is essential to both estoppel and Section 90. If Section 90 is to be unraveled from the estoppel tradition, controlling importance must be given the specific tests of that section in weighing the factors which bear on relief.

V. The Collision of Promissory Estoppel and Legislative Policies

. . .

VI. Inherent Limitations of the Reliance Theory

The granting of relief under Section 90 depends ultimately upon a judgment that enforcement is necessary to avoid injustice. Such a requirement serves

---

[197] The definitive work is Fuller & Perdue, The Reliance Interest in Contract Damages, 46 Yale L.J. 52, 373 (1936, 1937).

[198] See, e.g., Dovenmuehle, Inc. v. K-Way Associates, 388 F.2d 940 (7th Cir. 1968) (dissent); Hoffman v. Red Owl

Stores, Inc., 26 Wis. 2d 683, 133 N.W.2d 267 (1965); Wheeler v. White, 398 S.W.2d 93 (Tex. 1965). Recoveries in the franchise dealer cases are consistent with measuring protection by the reliance interest.

as a reminder that not all promisees who suffer reliance injuries are entitled to the protections of the section. More important, the notion that justice determines the limits of responsibility means that promissory estoppel is informed by a basic test of fairness. The doctrine thus allows courts wide latitude in redistributing losses resulting from unfilled promises. At the same time, it must be recognized that the very flexibility of Section 90 prevents its reduction to a precise formula or series of tests. In consequence, as the foregoing discussion should have demonstrated, it is difficult if not impossible to abstract and describe any single theory of the operation of the reliance principle of Section 90. Now that the role being played by that section has been examined in some detail at each stage of the contracting process, however, certain general observations and suggestions are in order. Because the language of Section 90 appears to call for the enforcement of the promised performance, rather than an award of reliance losses, it is customary for the courts to dwell upon the requirement that reliance be "of a definite and substantial character." The trouble with this statement is that it seems to get translated into rigid tests which suggest that some specific degree of reliance must be shown in order to recover. If, on the other hand, limited or partial enforcement comes to be recognized as the norm in Section 90 cases,[223] the test of substantial reliance is likely to merge with the test of "injustice." The result will be that the extent of relief will reflect and be tailored to the extent of reliance, encouraging development of a more effective working concept concentrating inquiry upon the foreseeability and seriousness of reliance.

A party who seeks to rest liability on reliance grounds must be prepared to carry a substantial burden of argument and proof. Problems of proof of actual loss, particularly where reliance takes the form of forbearance, have been crucially significant in a number of instances where recovery has been denied under the promissory estoppel label. The handling of the mistake factor in the construction bidding cases is representative of more general attitudes about the

responsibilities a promisee is expected to assume concerning the reasonableness of his conduct. If damages are difficult to assess or the consequences of reliance hard to unravel, the chances of success on a theory of promissory estoppel may be impaired. And even if recovery is won in the trial court, the broad scope of judicial review permitted by promissory estoppel increases the possibility of reversal, especially where a large damage recovery is involved.

In addition, the subject matter of the action may significantly influence the outcome of litigation. For example, attempts to expand insurance coverage by resort to Section 90 are likely to founder upon familiar rules pertaining to the limited operation of estoppel doctrine. Courts are also reluctant to use Section 90 to make a promisor an insurer or guarantor. And it will be remembered that promissory estoppel has had little success in cases involving the employment relation and franchised dealers—areas marked by longstanding confusion in the theory of consideration. If, on the other hand, action in reliance is taken by a third person who is a beneficiary of the promise, there appears to be support developing for application of the theory of Section 90.[230] . . .

Possibly the greatest risk in electing to proceed on a theory of promissory estoppel is that the concept of reliance, and hence injustice, will be tested by the criteria of common law consideration. In view of the frequency with which Section 90 is raised today in the context of commercial exchange, it should not be surprising that principles of bargain reliance became confused with the requirements of promissory estoppel. The chief difficulty with this tendency is that if the reliance element of Section 90 is reduced to common law notions of "legal detriment," any real assessment of the merits of the alleged action in reliance is unlikely to occur.[233] One court has even gone so far as to suggest that, for purposes of Section 90, forbearance is not prejudicial unless it consists of "an abandonment or deferment of an enforceable right."[234] This insistence upon the classic terminology of consideration is symptomatic of a general desire to give familiar meaning to the elements of Section 90. But

---

[223] See cases cited at note 198 supra. Because the Tentative Draft of Section 90 in the Restatement (Second, adds a new sentence recognizing the possibility of partial enforcement, the requirement that action in reliance have "a definite and substantial character" is abandoned. See Restatement (Second) of Contracts § 90, Reporter's Note.

[230] Hoffman v. Red Owl Stores, Inc., 26 Wis. 2d 683, 133 N.W.2d 267 (1965), extends the protections of Section 90 to claims of third party beneficiaries. Restatement (Second) of

Contracts § 90 expressly includes "a third person" within the operation of the reliance principle.

[233] As suggested earlier, the confusion of price or bargain with the principle of injustice underlying Section 90 tends to distort the reliance concept. . . .

[234] Overlock v. Central Vt. Pub. Serv. Corp., 126 Vt. 549, 237 A.2d 356. 359 (1967). See also 440 Pitts v. McGraw-Edison Co., 329 F.2d 412, 416 (6th Cir. 1964) (". . . plaintiff gave up nothing to which he was legally entitled . . .").

it woodenly directs attention away from considerations of justice and the extent of reliance, and focuses instead upon relatively inflexible and narrow bargain-oriented rules. As has been pointed out above, since the typical commercial case in which Section 90 is invoked will satisfy some of the elements of both theories, it is not surprising that bargain principles permeate judicial treatment of the reliance factor. Nevertheless, if the principles of fairness and avoidance of injustice underlying Section 90 are to serve their intended function, some effort must be made to distinguish reliance from bargain elements and to allow the former some autonomy of application.

Given the vast factual differences among the Section 90 cases, any attempt to dispose of the problems of promissory reliance by a single formula is hazardous because no formula can be comprehensive enough to resolve every case satisfactorily. But the major impact of promissory estoppel in recent years may be that it has made the whole matter of classification or definition less important in the decision of contract cases. Change is in fact being effected by quiet manipulation of the familiar labels. To this extent, protection of the reliance interest ultimately depends upon the total impact of a given case rather than upon the technicalities of classification.

At this stage the principal difficulty is that the purposes to be served by Section 90 in the setting of bargains have not been sufficiently identified or examined. If the reason for enforcing a bargain promise on a non-bargain theory is to protect reasonable reliance in conduct, the criteria of consideration are not of central importance. However, the policies which underlie orthodox contract rules are quite relevant to the expansion of Section 90 in commercial cases. No persuasive public policy may preclude a recovery where injury is occasioned by a gratuitous promise. But if a reliance claim arises in the bargain context, policy considerations relating to the security of expectations come into play. It is probable that the next stage of development of Section 90 will evidence concern with these broader aspects of the reliance theory.

Reliance in the Years to Come

In an interesting and perceptive (and exhaustive) article, Michael B. Metzger and Michael J. Phillips, both then Associate Professors of Business Law in the Graduate School of Business at Indiana University, traced what they saw as a role for promissory estoppel independent of contract doctrines such as the Statute of Frauds and damage limitations. Metzger and Phillips, *The Emergence of Promissory Estoppel As An Independent Theory of Recovery*, 35 Rutgers L. Rev. 472 (1983). Others have argued that reliance can be analyzed within a consent-based contract system. For examples, see Randy Barnett and Mary E. Becker's *Beyond Reliance: Promissory Estoppel, Contract Formalities, and Misrepresentations*, 15 Hofstra L. Rev. 443 (1987), and Juliet P. Kostristky's *A New Theory of Assent-Based Liability Emerging Under the Guise of Promissory Estoppel: An Explanation and Defense*, 33 Wayne L. Rev. 895 (1987).

The two following articles consider the concept in a more generalized social context. Daniel A. Farber and John A. Matheson, both of the University of Minnesota Law School, discuss what they call, building on the economist Arthur Okun, "the invisible handshake," and argue that some promises deserve enforcement on a promissory estoppel theory that does not require reliance. On top of this, Farber and Matheson argue that promises may be inferred from conduct, a position supported by both the Restatement (Second) and Professor Henderson. Jay Feinman, of Rutgers-Camden, focuses on reliance, but gives reliance a meaning that is broader and more societal than has been traditional, and that is something like Ian Macneil's relational approach. (Farber and Matheson also acknowledge Macneil's approach.) Both articles spend a fair amount of attention on employment, in which dealings are often made in a context that fits neither traditional bargain nor traditional reliance.

If contract is based on either consent or promise while tort is based on societal compulsion, it can be argued that the looser the definitions of promise and reliance become, the closer contract comes to tort, or, at least, the more the concepts coalesce. (This point, which is derived from Gilmore's "contorts," is addressed in the Uncontracts article, excerpted in Part IB.) Farber and Matheson dispute this near the end of their introduction (at notes 11 and 12). They argue that "stripped of its heightened individualism," contract law deals with the creation of economically productive relationships, while tort is concerned with "the independent individual's right to be free of interference that is unreasonable according to community standards." On this basis, they put promissory estoppel "within the domain of contract—while trying at the same time to imbue contract law with some of the concern with community standards that has been the attraction of tort-based theories of promissory estoppel."

The dispute may be more definitional than real. On the other hand, it can be argued that emphasis on promise and individual will understates the diffuse nature of relationships like employment, for instance, those among factory, worker and town, which Farber and Matheson discuss in some detail. Feinman considers something of this when he discusses "artificial notions of discrete promise and discrete reliance" in the brief excerpt that is included below. Both of the articles are well worth reading in full.

Daniel A. Farber and John H. Matheson, *Beyond Promissory Estoppel: Contract Law and the "Invisible Handshake*," 52 U. Chi. L. Rev. 903 (1985)

Employers do, in fact, rely heavily on the "invisible handshake" as a substitute for the invisible hand that cannot operate effectively in the career labor market. While nonunion firms do make commitments that are morally, and even legally, binding for a year ahead upon wage rates (and, for some salaried employees, on total earnings), they generally opt for implicit rather than explicit contracts beyond that period. Apparently employers believe they can influence the long-term expectations of workers favorably with nonbinding statements that preserve much of their own flexibility.

Arthur Okun[1]

As every law student knows, promissory estoppel is based on detrimental reliance. Law students share this idea with the American Law Institute and with treatise writers. Indeed, promissory estoppel is one of the few points of agreement between the critical legal scholars on the left and the law and economics writers on the right. Both agree that reliance has been the foundation of promissory estoppel,[4] and both accuse the courts of incoherence in applying the doctrine.

We have recently surveyed over two hundred promissory estoppel cases decided in the last ten years. Our conclusion is that reliance is no longer the key to promissory estoppel.[7] Although courts still feel constrained to speak the language of reliance, their holdings can best be understood and harmonized on other grounds.

Part I of this article reports the results of our survey. It documents the declining role of reliance in establishing liability and determining remedies. It also suggests that most cases denying recovery, purport-

---

[1] Arthur Okun, Prices and Quantities: A Macroeconomic Analysis 89 (1981).

[4] For critical legal studies approaches, see Feinman, Critical Approaches to Contract Law, 30 UCLA L. Rev. 829, 854-56 (1983) (discussing Hoffman v. Red Owl Stores, Inc., 26 Wis. 2d 683, 133 N.W.2d 267 (1967), as recognizing reliance theory of contract); Mensch, Book Review, 33 Stan. L. Rev. 753, 769-70 (1981) (reviewing Patrick Atiyah, The Rise and Fall of Freedom of Contract (1979) (critiquing use of a reliance vocabulary). On the law and economics side, see Goetz

& Scott, Enforcing Promises: An Examination of the Basis of Contract, 89 Yale L. J. 1261, 1266-70, 1314-21 (1980) (discussing reliance, defined as consumption changes made by plaintiffs in anticipation of fulfillment of promises, as basis of promissory enforcement).

[7] That the reliance interest is central to contract law in general has been recognized since the publication of Fuller & Perdue, The Reliance Interest in Contract Damages (pts. 1 & 2), 46 Yale L. J. 52, 373 (1936-37). . . .

When we state that our proposed rule is not reliance-based, we mean that it does not base recovery upon proof of reliance in the indivdual case. The policy we seek to promote, however, is one of encouraging reliance.

edly for lack of reasonable reliance, can be readily explained on other grounds. Part II explores the implications of these findings. We believe that a new rule of promissory liability is emerging from the courts' encounters with an economy in which Okun's "invisible handshake" is increasingly important. The rule is quite simple: any promise made in furtherance of an economic activity is enforceable.[8]

Our proposed rule unifies promissory estoppel and other exceptions to the consideration requirement with consideration doctrine itself. In each instance, the underlying legal policy is to protect the ability of individuals to trust promises in circumstances in which that trust is socially beneficial. Traditional consideration doctrine allows trust to function in contexts such as sales, leases, insurance, and loans—key economic arrangements that could not function effectively without legal enforceability. Promises involving firm offers, sureties, and options are enforceable without consideration because some economically useful transactions would otherwise be difficult to structure. Promissory estoppel fills a similar function by enforcing promises in other settings not amenable to traditional bargaining transactions, in which reliance is beneficial both to the promisor and to society as a whole.

In our view, the expansion of promissory estoppel is not, as some have argued, proof that contract is in the process of being swallowed up by tort.[11] Rather, promissory estoppel is being transformed into a new theory of distinctly contractual obligation.[12] We also think, for reasons that will appear more fully in Part II, that our proposed rule not only harmonizes many otherwise inconsistent cases, but also furthers the often divergent values proclaimed by the law and economics writers and the critical legal scholars. Besides

serving the interest of economic efficiency, our proposed rule also furthers the important moral value of mutual trust.

I. Promissory Estoppel Today: The Changing Framework of Enforcement

To investigate the current evolution of promissory estoppel, we undertook a systematic review of the recent cases. We collected every case in the past ten years citing Section 90 of either Restatement, and categorized the outcomes. The results were somewhat unexpected.

A. *The Expansion of Promissory Estoppel*

Our first finding concerned the range of cases in which promissory estoppel was applied. Despite its tentative origins and its initial restriction to donative promises, promissory estoppel is regularly applied to the gamut of commercial contexts. Classic construction bid cases appear often, as do employee compensation and pension cases. But promissory estoppel has also been invoked in cases involving lease agreements, stock purchases, and promissory notes.

Second, promissory estoppel is no longer merely a fall-back theory of recovery. Rather, courts are now comfortable enough with the doctrine to use it as a primary basis of enforcement. Courts often "decline to address the issue of whether a contract was ever formed between the parties,[19]" relying instead on promissory estoppel even when no apparent barrier exists to recovery on a traditional contract theory.

Third, reliance plays little role in the determination of remedies. This should not be cause for surprise—the first *Restatement of Contracts* contemplated full enforcement of promises even when reliance was the basis for enforcement. But some important early cases limited recovery to reliance dam-

---

[8] This rule is set out in detail in a proposed section for the third Restatement, infra.

[11] See Grant Gilmore, The Death of Contract 87 (1974) ("'contract' is being reabsorbed into the mainstream of 'tort'"). . . .

[12] An analysis of the difference between contract and tort would occupy a treatise, particularly if the discussion were to be historically sensitive. . . .

Nonetheless, there does still seem to be some sense in distinguishing between contract-based and tort-based theories of obligation, if only to be able to document the closing of the gaps between them. The classical starting point of contract law is the autonomous domain of voluntary private ordering. . . . But stripped of its heightened individualism, contract law, with its stress on the creation and internal dynamics of economically productive relationships, remains a vital source of support for long-term planning and coordination in social relationships. See generally Ian Macneil, The New Social Contract (1980) [hereinafter cited as I. Macneil,

Social Contract]. Tort law, in contrast, originates in protection of the independent individual's rights to be free of interference that is unreasonable according to community standards. . . . But the core concepts of tort law continue to stress compensation for injury to individual activity. It is in the sense of concern with the affirmative creation of economic relationships, as opposed to the avoidance of interference with autonomous action, that our theory places its expansion of promissory estoppel firmly within the domain of contract—while trying at the same time to imbue contract law with some of the concern with community standards that has been the attraction of tort-based theories of promissory obligation.

[19] . . .

This finding bears out Henderson's early observation that promissory estoppel often forms the basis of decision in cases involving bargain transactions. See Henderson, Promissory Estoppel and Traditional Contract Doctrine, 78 Yale L.J. 343 (1969). . . .

ages, and the drafters of the second *Restatement* found it necessary to accommodate such limitations: they stated that "recognition of the possibility of partial enforcement" was their major innovation. Despite this possibility, however, recent cases are heavily weighted towards the award of full expectation damages. The amount of awards for lost profits may be substantial. Courts are also willing to grant equitable remedies, such as specific performance or injunctive relief, in cases decided on a promissory estoppel theory.

Our fourth and most important finding is the diminished role of reliance in determining liability. The essential requirement for liability on a promissory estoppel theory has traditionally been some specific action in justifiable reliance on the promise. This requirement of an identifiable detriment no longer defines the boundary of enforceability.

Perhaps the best example of a court applying promissory estoppel where the presence of clear and substantial detrimental reliance is doubtful at best is *Vastoler v. American Can Co.*[28] Solomon Vastoler worked for American Can for several periods between 1937 and 1978, when he retired with a pension. He had worked as an hourly employee from 1937 to 1946, from 1947 to 1952, and from 1958 to 1963. He was promoted to a salaried supervisory position in 1963. Vastoler was reluctant to accept the promotion because "from a financial standpoint of view, initially, he [Vastoler] was not benefitting by this promotion." Vastoler testified that he told the plant manager that the promotion would leave him worse off financially, and that he would only accept the promotion if the company agreed to alter the terms of its pension plan in his favor. According to the express terms of the pension plan, Vastoler's resignation in 1952 meant that his time of service was to be measured from 1958 rather than from 1937; Vastoler claimed that the company promised him credit for his pre-1958 years of service in order to convince him to accept the promotion. When the company refused to calculate Vastoler's pension benefits on the basis of the longer term of service, he sued to recover on a promissory estoppel theory.[31] Vastoler

claimed that he altered his position to his detriment by accepting the promotion and that justice required enforcement of the promise.

The trial court granted summary judgment against Vastoler on the promissory estoppel claim, stating that "'nothing at all has been shown to indicate such a disadvantage to him . . . by accepting the transfer as to make it imperative that the promise be adhered to in order to avoid obvious and manifest injustice.'" The appellate court reversed. The court admitted that, despite Vastoler's fears to the contrary, the financial package and job security he received as a salaried supervisor were better than what he would have received as an hourly employee. But the district court was faulted for viewing these financial outcomes as determinative of lack of detrimental reliance.

The appellate court first suggested that the comparison between the financial situation of a salaried supervisor and that of an hourly employee of the same company was an erroneous basis for determining lack of detrimental reliance. "The American job market is broader than American Can Company, and this was especially true during the great economic expansion of the 1960's." The court appeared further to suggest that Vastoler's ultimate economic position was not relevant to the inquiry because it was "merely a matter of coincidence that over the years Vastoler's financial benefits may have equalled or bettered those he would have earned had he not accepted the promotion to supervisor. Reliance is measured by the terms of the agreement, not by benefits extraneous, albeit incidental, to the agreement."

Second, the appellate court criticized the district court for failing "to consider the human dynamics and anxieties inherent in supervisory positions." Even apart from any financial detriment, the court found sufficient detrimental reliance to support a promissory estoppel claim in "the stress and emotional trauma"[37] that may accompany supervisory responsibilities.

Vastoler is an instance of a court straining to find detrimental reliance in order to enforce a promise. So far as the record indicates, Vastoler's sole objection

---

[28] 700 F.2d 916 (3d Cir. 1983).

[31] Vastoler also claimed that the terms of the pension plan mandated past service credit from 1937 rather than from 1958. This claim was rejected by both the district and the appellate courts. Id. at 918. It is noteworthy, however, that Vastoler could have argued that a bargain was made through his negotiations with the plant manager. The appellate court stated that "[t]he record shows . . . that Vastoler accepted the promotion, a transfer that was apparently de-

sired more by the Company than by Vastoler, *in exchange for* the full recognition of his past service." Id. at 920 (emphasis added). Vastoler, then, may be an example of the use of promissory estoppel instead of traditional contract doctrine in the context of a bargaining transaction. See supra note 19 and accompanying text.

[37] Id. No evidence of such emotional detriment appears to have been on the record.

to promotion was financial, and his financial position was in fact improved as a result of the promotion. The court's suggestion that failure to gain the benefit of the promise might constitute the detriment required for recovery on a promissory estoppel theory, even if the plaintiff's change in position is to his financial benefit, indicates that detrimental reliance has veered far from its traditional meaning. Enforcement of a promise appears to be desired for its own sake, rather than because "justice" so requires in light of the peculiar situation of a particular plaintiff. And if psychological factors are sufficient to support a claim of promissory estoppel, relatively few promises will fail to qualify for enforcement.

A similar result was reached in *Oates v. Teamsters Affiliates Pension Plan*.[38] . . .

. . .

In *Oates*, as in *Vastoler*, the court adopted a definition of detrimental reliance that permits enforcement of promises on a promissory estoppel theory even when the plaintiff's action does not substantially worsen his position. More significantly, both courts suggested that the comparison between the promisee's position before and after taking action in reliance on the promise is irrelevant to the inquiry. It is the mere taking of action that is defined in *Oates* as detrimental reliance. Thus, the theory of promissory estoppel put forth in *Oates* has as much in common with traditional contract doctrine as it does with detrimental reliance as a basis for recovery.[43] In these cases, promissory estoppel has expanded beyond its traditional function of protecting a promisee who has changed his or her position for the worse as a result of the promise.

B. *The Scope of the Expansion*

Admittedly, the expansion of promissory estoppel beyond detrimental reliance has not been smooth. Some uncertainty and apparent contradiction still appear in the cases. We do not claim that all the cases can be reconciled with the conclusion that detrimental reliance is no longer the key to promissory estoppel. But we believe that much of the dissonance is the result of courts using the language of reliance to take account of three factors which quite correctly tip the balance in favor of recovery: (1) the presence of a credible promise; (2) the promisor's authority to make the promise; and (3) the existence of a benefit to the promisor from economic activity. These factors do more than account for inconsistencies in the reported cases. They also define the limits of an emerging theory of contractual obligation.

1. *The Presence of a Credible Promise.* Promise-making is the linchpin of liability under both traditional contract doctrine and promissory estoppel. The requirement of a promise makes liability turn on the voluntary assumption of duty, and thus underlies the function of contract law as a promoter of voluntary agreements. But courts have long had trouble distinguishing binding commitments from other communications such as opinions, predictions, or negotiations.[45]

This issue has not disappeared in the modern cases. If anything, it is even more likely to arise with the relatively informal statements that often form the basis of promissory estoppel claims. The less formal the parties' actions, the greater must be the court's attention to their context. Focusing on the issue of whether a promise has been made explains the differing results in some otherwise superficially similar cases.

[The authors discuss cases involving physicians' assurances, guidelines in franchise application booklets, waivers, and promises inferred from conduct. — ed.]

2. *The Promisor's Authority to Make the Promise.* The person making an otherwise actionable promise sometimes lacks the authority to bind the organization involved and cannot reasonably be understood to have such authority. The expansive scope and hierarchy of modern enterprise makes such limitations on authority unavoidable. Because agency law has all but disappeared as a separate legal discipline, attorneys, judges, and law clerks are ill-equipped to perceive agency issues. Often opinions refer to a lack of rea-

---

[38] 482 F. Supp. 481 (D.D.C. 1979).

[43] For the observation that promissory estoppel is often applied in the context of bargain transactions, see Henderson, supra note 19, at 345-50.

[45] Courts often resort to conclusory language in finding that a manifestation rises to the level of a promise. This is not surprising. Judges called upon to determine whether a promise has been made must look beyond the words and acts which constitute the transaction to the nature of the relationship between the parties and the circumstances sur-

rounding their actions. But relationships and surrounding circumstances do not speak for themselves. They must be interpreted by judges on the basis of the expectations likely to arise between similarly situated parties. The conclusory tone follows because we are being told what we ought already to understand as members of the community. It is inherent in the use of an objective standard—under both traditional contract and promissory estoppel theories of obligation—to determine whether a commitment was voluntarily made.

sonable reliance in cases in which the reliance is unreasonable largely because of the promisor's evident lack of authority.

. . .

3. *The Importance of Benefit to the Promisor from Economic Activity.* As we have seen, courts have manipulated the reliance concept to find liability in a number of promissory estoppel cases. A fuller understanding of this expansion of promissory liability can be gained through an examination of the way in which courts have strained traditional bargain concepts in similar factual settings.

Pine River State Bank v. Mettille[71] exemplifies this expansion of the bargain concept. In *Pine River*, an at-will employee was discharged without benefit of the procedural safeguards laid out in an employee handbook distributed while he was an employee. The trial court found for the employee on grounds of breach of contract. On appeal, the employer argued that the handbook could not be considered a modification of the terms of the at-will employment contract because no consideration existed for the handbook's increased job security protections. Under traditional contract theory this argument carries much force. The job security provisions were not bargained for; no identifiable exchange from the employee was specified.[72] The Minnesota Supreme Court affirmed, however, finding that the handbook was an offer of a unilateral contract and that the employee's "continued performance despite his freedom to leave" constituted both acceptance and consideration.

Use of the unilateral contract device to enforce one-sided modifications of ongoing relationships has found increasing favor. Technically, however, plaintiffs in such cases receive a windfall, for the change in terms is not bargained for and does not require any additional commitment from or detriment to them. In *Pine River*, the employer clearly anticipated some benefits from improved procedural safeguards, but specified no clearly defined conduct by the worker as the price of the new benefits. Workers clearly were not buying the benefits by promising to work for any

specified period. Nor was there any understanding that the promised rights would vest only after some period of additional work. A court might hold that simply showing up for work the next day was the bargained-for exchange. But is this really true to the intent of the parties? Nothing in the handbook suggested that the new benefits were a bonus simply for showing up for work the day after the handbook came out, nor would the employer want the employee to think that so little was expected in return.

The employer typically does expect benefits from such arrangements, such as obtaining lower turnover or keeping out a union. But while "inferences of reciprocity can be drawn" when these understandings are reached, it distorts the facts to say that anything specific has been exchanged. Judges do construct conventional contracts in such cases, but only a Cardozo could make them seem plausible. Nonetheless, such judicial creativity represents a recognition that the promises in such cases are not gratuitous in the ordinary sense of the word.[77]

The expansion of the notion of consideration in cases like *Pine River* to enforce promises that are neither bargained for nor gratuitous closely parallels the expansion of detrimental reliance in cases like *Vastoler*. It is not surprising to find courts imposing liability when the defendant has made a promise in the expectation of receiving an economic benefit from the plaintiff. Quite apart from any unjust enrichment which might have resulted from the promise, breach of a promise seems especially unjust when the promisor was willing to reap economic benefits from the promise but not to pay the price. The simple idea that one must "accept the bitter with the sweet" is a core intuition underlying these cases. Similarly, the absence of a prospect of benefit to the promisor from economic activity argues against enforceability. Our survey of the promissory estoppel cases suggests that courts have been responsive to the presence or absence of such a benefit from economic activity.

[The authors contrast the "economic activity" in two insurance cases. In *Prudential Ins. Co. v. Clark,*[80] the company was held to its agent's promise

---

[71] 333 N.W.2d 622 (Minn. 1983).

[72] See generally Pettit, Modern Unilateral Contracts, 63 B.U.L. Rev. 551, 559-67 (1983).

[77] The reality that some promises have non-quantifiable yet tangible economic benefits is not lost on judges. See Toussaint v. Blue Cross & Blue Shield, 408 Mich. 579, 613, 292 N.W.2d 880, 892 (1980) ("The employer secures an orderly, cooperative and loyal work force . . . . It is enough that the employer chooses, presumably in its own interest, to cre-

ate [such] an environment . . . . The employer has then created a situation 'instinct with an obligation.'") (quoting Cardozo's opinion in Wood v. Lucy, Lady Duff-Gordon, 222 N.Y. 88, 91, 118 N.E. 214, 214 (1917); Thompson v. St. Regis Paper Co., 102 Wash. 2d 219, 229-30, 685 P.2d 1081, 1087 (1984) (employers make promises in manuals "to create an atmosphere of fair treatment and job security").

[80] 456 F.2d 932 (5th Cir. 1972).

that it would issue a policy without war risk or aviation exclusions. The insured had given up such a policy and replaced it with Prudential's, but the Prudential policy contained the exclusion clauses despite the agent's promise. In *Marker v. Preferred Life Ins. Co.,*[83] an insurance agent who had written a policy on some land promised the buyers, also agents for the same company, that he would notify them before the policy expired. He failed to do so, and the property was damaged, but the company was not held liable for his promise. —ed.]

The essence of the *Marker* decision, obfuscated by the reliance analysis, is that the promise was not made in furtherance of any economic relationship or activity. The defendant in *Marker* was not making a promise to a prospective client (or even to someone likely to steer business his way in the future) since the plaintiff's father was also an agent with the same company. The defendant neither sought nor saw a prospective benefit or ongoing relationship, and none was offered by the plaintiff. Under these circumstances, where the promise is not related to current or prospective activity between the parties, nonenforcement appears reasonable. In *Clark,* on the other hand, the promise was made to obtain a new insurance customer. Traditional promissory estoppel analysis obscures the decisive distinction between these two cases, namely, benefit to the promisor.

II. Redefining The Basis Of Promissory Obligation

Two factors appear to coalesce in cases in which promissory obligation has been expanded beyond its traditional boundaries. First, as suggested above, the promisor's primary motive for making the promise is typically to obtain an economic benefit. Second, the enforced promises generally occur in the context of a relationship that is or is expected to be ongoing rather than in the context of a discrete transaction.

These relationships are characterized by a need for a high level of mutual confidence and trust.

A. *Economic Benefit in Ongoing Relationships: Closing the Relational Gap in Contract Law*

Economic motives underlie many of the kinds of employer promises which have been enforced through the expansion of promissory estoppel and unilateral contract doctrines. The employer attempts to produce employment conditions in which employees are comfortable and relatively secure in order to gain increased loyalty and productivity from them. But as cases like *Pine River* demonstrate, the anticipated benefits cannot readily be reduced to the terms of a traditional bargain. We believe that recent expansions of promissory obligation are based upon the insight that an economic exchange need not be seen as taking place in an isolated transaction or at a specific time, nor need it be manifested by an identifiable increase in the promisor's economic assets. In the context of ongoing relationships, exchange is a continuing rather than a discrete event.[90] Where such relationships are highly interdependent, economic benefit is likely to be sought through informal understandings that reinforce the relationship, rather than through discrete bargains.

Consider again the typical employee's position. An employee has a substantial investment in a job and is expected to make increased future investments. He or she has acquired job-specific skills, which are less valuable on the market than to the present employer. At least some of the benefits to be obtained from employment, like pensions or promotions, are not immediate. The employee faces high search costs, including the risk of a prolonged period of unemployment, if he or she decides to obtain another job. Finally, the employee's mobility may be restricted by consumption choices based on his or her employment situation, such as home ownership. Hence, the employee

---

[83] 211 Kan. 427, 506 P.2d 1163 (1973).

[90] Ian Macneil has led the attack on notions of promissory obligation that are modelled on the "paradigm [of] the transaction of neoclassical microeconomics," in which "no relation exists between the parties apart from the simple exchange of goods." I. Macneil, Social Contract, supra note 12, at 10. For elaboration of Macneil's theory of relational contract, which he defines as "involving relations other than a discrete exchange," id., see Macneil, Values in Contract: Internal and External, 78 Nw. U.L. Rev. 340 (1983); Macneil, Efficient Breach of Contract: Circles in the Sky, 68 Va. L. Rev. 947 (1982); Macneil, Economic Analysis of Contractual Relations: Its Shortfalls and the Need for a "Rich Classificatory Apparatus," 75 Nw. U.L. Rev. 1018 (1981); Macneil, The Many Futures of Contracts, 47 S. Cal. L. Rev. 691 (1974);

Macneil, Restatement (Second) of Contracts and Presentiation, 60 Va. L. Rev. 589 (1974).

. . .

Macneil's "relational foundations" are based, as are those of our approach, on trust. But our approach to relational contracts differs from Macneil's in some respects. First, Macneil applies his theory to some kinds of agreements which do not fit within our "economic activity" test. See, e.g., I. Macneil, Social Contract, supra note 12, at 20 (including marriage as a "contractual relation"). Second, Macneil does not stress the existence of a promise in his definition of contract. Instead, he sees promise-making as but one of several ways in which legitimate expectations arise. . . .

normally has a strong stake in the continuation and development of an ongoing relationship with the employer.

The employer has different but not wholly dissimilar needs. The employer has invested in the selection and on-the-job training of the employee, an investment that can be lost through employee turnover. Moreover, the employer cannot supervise employees closely enough to ensure that they invest their best efforts. The employer would therefore like to use an incentive system and other inducements to encourage effort. Thus, like the employee, the employer has a stake in the quality of the employment relationship.

This mutual interest in a long-term and amicable relationship is part of the explanation Okun[91] and Thurow[92] give for the behavior of the labor market. For example, classical economics suggests that if someone were to come along and offer to perform an employee's job at a reduced rate, the employer would fire the existing employee and replace him by the lower cost employee. Yet in reality this never happens. The reason is that the employer cannot afford to take action that will discourage employees from making long-term investments in their jobs. For example, much on-the-job training is actually given by older employees, who will have little incentive to provide such training if they fear their own jobs may be at stake. To maximize the benefits of their relationship, both sides need a certain amount of trust.

Up until this point, relationships characterized by interdependence and thus by a need for trust have been described as though they were exceptional. This description could not be further from the truth. The network of interdependence in modern economic relations extends far beyond the ongoing relationship between specific parties to the very structure of the modern economy. Modern economic relations are dependent upon institutions which themselves are based on trust. The firm, an essential economic unit, can function only if employees and employer have at least limited trust in each other. Markets for goods can exist only if sellers normally can be trusted to make future deliveries of nondefective products. Insurance, credit, and investment can exist only when the other party generally can be trusted to pay.

These institutional arrangements are not only valuable to the individuals involved in specific transactions. They are also valuable to society as a whole. . . .

Because trust is essential to our basic economic institutions, it is a public good. One individual breaking trust in a dramatic way, or many individuals breaking trust less dramatically, can lead to short-run benefits for those individuals but create negative externalities. The willingness of others to trust is impaired, requiring them to invest in precautions or insure themselves against the increased risk of betrayal.[96] Such externalities exist because of asymmetrical information: the promisor necessarily has better information about his own trustworthiness than does the promisee. For example, in the short run employers can profit by making commitments to employees, obtaining the resulting benefits, and then reneging. But in the long run, enforcement benefits promisors as a group by fostering the reliance from which they seek to benefit. Conversely, trustworthy individuals confer a social benefit by increasing the general perception of trust, thereby allowing others to decrease such costs.

Seen in this light, the cases in which courts have pushed the doctrine of promissory estoppel beyond its stated justification and technical limitations are characterized by a strong need both by the parties and society for a high level of trust. They involve relationships in which one party must depend on the word of the other to engage in socially beneficial reliance. In the employee cases, the socially beneficial reliance takes the form of higher job performance and lower turnover. In subcontracting cases, that reliance takes the form of a more efficient bidding process in which general contractors are able to give bids directly reflecting the information they receive from subcontractors. The point in these cases is not that reliance has taken place in a particular instance, but rather that reliance should be encouraged among participants in a class of activities. To restate our initial

---

[91] A. Okun, supra note 1, at 81-133 (describing choice of "career" labor strategy over "casual" labor strategy, with resulting need for arrangements to counter distrust in longer-term employment relationships).

[92] Lester Thurow, Dangerous Currents: The State of Economics 184-215 (1983) (discussing employee motivation and critiquing the "price-auction" model's disavowal of its importance).

[96] The Tylenol incident was a dramatic example of the value of confidence. As long as people could be trusted not to tamper with medicines, medicines could be sold without elaborate safeguards. Once that trust was violated, it became necessary to spend millions of dollars for improved product security.

observation, the role of reliance in establishing liability and determining damages *in individual cases* is on the decline—but reliance, in the form of trust, is on the rise as the *policy* behind legal rules of promissory obligation.

B. *The Proposed Rule*

A revised rule of promissory obligation should accept the fundamental fact that commitments are often made to promote economic activity and obtain economic benefits without any specific bargained-for exchange. Promisors expect various benefits to flow from their promise-making. A rule that gives force to this expectation simply reinforces the traditional free-will basis of promissory liability, albeit in an expanded context of relational and institutional interdependence.

Our proposed rule is simply that commitments made in furtherance of economic activity should be enforced. Partial steps toward this rule can be found in Section 90 of the *Restatement (Second) of Contracts*, as well as in various exceptions to the consideration doctrine intended to further useful commercial arrangements.[98] The proposed rule is a major departure from traditional contract law in that it requires neither satisfaction of traditional notions of consideration nor the specific showing of detriment associated with promissory estoppel. But the rule sounds within contract law, and operates within its traditional area of concern: promissory economic exchange.

Just as the proposed rule emerges from recent judicial expansions of promissory estoppel, its boundaries are suggested by the limits of that expansion. Our survey demonstrated that courts have been influenced to refrain from imposing liability by absence of a credible promise, absence of authority to make the promise, and absence of projected benefit to the promisor from economic activity. These factors also constitute the limits of promissory liability under the proposed rule.

. . .

As included in the *Restatement (Third) of Contracts*, with accompanying comments and illustrations, our proposed rule would appear as follows:

Section 71. Enforceability of Promises

A Promise is enforceable when made in furtherance of an economic activity.

Comment:

a. Rationale and Relation to Other Rules. This section deals with what has traditionally been called consideration—namely, the legal conclusion that a promise is enforceable. Prior rules tested every promise or modification to determine whether the promise was conditioned on some tangible bargained-for exchange. The present section eliminates the need for finding a specific bargained-for promise or performance for each promise or modification. Rather, the key determination is whether the promise is designed to induce the creation of or to aid in the continuation of economic activity. The rule posits the social and economic utility of promises made in furtherance of economic activity.

The term "economic activity" includes sales of goods and services, leases, loans, insurance and employment arrangements, and similar transactions, whether involving businesses or individuals. The operations of organized charities are considered economic activities for purposes of this section. The requirement that the promise be "in furtherance" of the economic activity carries the implication that the promisor must expect a benefit to result from the promise. This expectation of benefit is to be demonstrated on the basis of an objective standard, and may often be presumed from the circumstances.

If the requirement of promise in furtherance of economic activity is met, there is no additional requirement of (1) a gain, advantage, or benefit to the promisor or a loss, disadvantage, reliance, or detriment to the promisee; (2) equivalence in the values exchanged; or (3) mutuality of obligation. Further, many of the promises denominated under the Restatement, Second, of Contracts as without consideration would be enforceable under this section if they occur in furtherance of economic activity. See, e.g., Restatement, Second, of Contracts § 87 (options contracts), § 88 (guarantees), § 89 (modifications), § 90 (promises enforced on the basis of reliance). Modern courts have made significant strides toward accomplishing the effect of this section by expanding the notion of the performance required for creation of a unilateral contract or by diluting the concept of reliance in promissory estoppel situations.

. . .

[The authors' Illustrations 1-5 are omitted. —ed.]

b. Promises, Acts and Resulting Relations.[104] This

---

[98] U.C.C. § 2-205 (1978) (firm offers); Restatement (Second) § 87 (option contract); id. § 88 (guaranty).

[104] The next two subsections draw heavily on the discussion of promises in Restatement (Second) § 2.

section requires that a promise have been made. A promise is a manifestation of intention to act or refrain from acting in a specified way, so made as to justify a promisee in understanding that a commitment has been made. A promise may be stated in words, either orally or in writing, or may be inferred wholly or partly from conduct. Compare Restatement, Second, of Contracts sections 18-19 (manifestation of assent). Both language and conduct are to be understood in the light of the circumstances, including course of performance, course of dealing, or usage of trade.

. . .

c. *Opinions and Predictions.* A promise must be distinguished from a statement of opinion or a mere prediction of future events. Whether manifestations rise to the level of a promise depends on various factors, including the clarity of the manifestations, the nature of the relationship between the parties, and the circumstances surrounding the manifestations.

Illustrations:

6. A, a long-term employee with B corporation, sues for severance pay after being separated from the company. The basis of A's claim is a portion of the employee handbook entitled "Separation Allowance." The Separation Allowance section states that "[t]he inclusion of a schedule of separation allowances in the handbook, together with the conditions governing their payment, . . . is not intended nor is it to be interpreted to establish a contractual relationship with the employee." The last page of the handbook also contains an express, conspicuous disclaimer. Absent other circumstances indicating that B corporation had an express policy of not observing the stated limitations or that a reasonable employee would not have seen or understood the disclaimers, A's claim under this section fails.[106]

7. Physician B performed a tubal ligation on his patient, A. Several months after the operation B told A that A had nothing to worry about and that it was impossible for her to have any more children. Within a year A becomes pregnant. B's statement, in the context of the ordinary doctor/patient relationship, should have been seen as a mere therapeutic reassurance, not a promise.

d. Agency Limitations. . . .

. . .

C. *Possible Objections to the Proposed Rule*

Several objections are likely to be made to a proposal that dispenses with reliance as a requirement for enforcing promises. First, it might be argued that reliance-based liability adequately protects the value of trust, which we have identified as the core concern of contract law. The main response to this objection is that reliance on promises in furtherance of economic activity often takes forms that are exceedingly difficult to prove. In the employment setting, for example, proving that an employee has worked harder or done a better job of training new workers may be close to impossible. The argument for enforcing such promises even in the absence of proof of reliance closely parallels the traditional argument for enforcing executory contracts without requiring proof of reliance:

Unless agreements can be relied upon, they are of little use. A rule of law that only protected a promisee who had actually relied upon a promise would, in practice, tend to discourage reliance. The difficulties in proving and valuing reliance are such that a person in business would hesitate to rely on a promise if the legal sanction were important to him. These difficulties are especially acute when a party has relied by forgoing other opportunities, as in the case of the buyer who contracts with a seller for the future delivery of apples and who would have made arrangements to get them from another source had the seller not promised to deliver them. "To encourage reliance we must . . . dispense with its proof."[111]

A second possible objection is that imposing liability on potential promisors will deter them from revealing information about their future intentions to those in the position to benefit from that information. The simple answer is that economic actors are free to make any statements they desire without fear of liability, so long as the other party understands that they are not committing themselves, are stating only their current intentions, and may change their mind at any time. In other words, where potential promisors are less than confident of their future con-

---

[106] See Kari v. General Motors Corp., 79 Mich. App. 93, 261 N.W.2d 222, rev'd, 402 Mich. 926, 282 N.W.2d 925 (1977).

[111] E. Farnsworth, Contracts, § 1.6, at 18-19 (quoting Fuller & Purdue, supra note 7, at 62) (citations and footnotes omitted). The traditional justifications for dispensing with consideration for options are similar. See Restatement (Second) § 87 comment a.

duct, the proposed rule fosters better information transmission by encouraging them to reveal their uncertainties. This information will help to insure that promisors will be trusted only insofar as they are worthy of trust.

A third objection is that legal liability will.deprive economic actors of needed flexibility. But flexibility is not hampered by requiring accurate disclosure of uncertainty. If a promisee is not made aware that the promise made to him is meant to be flexible, the promisee's conduct will be premised on a false understanding of the seriousness of the promisor's commitment. . . . In short, flexibility is best created by the combination of accurate disclosure and predictable enforcement.

Another objection is more general. Why should someone who has neither relied on a promise nor given anything in exchange for the promise be able to sue the promisor? Does a promisee who has neither incurred a detriment nor conferred a benefit receive a morally undeserved windfall from enforcement of a promise? Three moral arguments can be made in favor of plaintiffs suing under these "naked" promises. First, these plaintiffs are suing under a legal rule that itself has a moral claim to acceptance. If our underlying theory is correct, the rule benefits all economic actors in the long run. Thus, the rule would gain universal acceptance behind only the thinnest Rawlsian "veil of ignorance" and therefore creates not only legal but moral claims.[114] Second, if these plaintiffs are not allowed recovery, the defendant may be said to enjoy a windfall. Having made a promise in order to capture a benefit for himself, the defendant cannot fairly be allowed to enrich himself by breaching the promise. In other words, a strong element of potential unjust enrichment is present. Third, promises may be thought to create moral obligations over and above the obligations enforced by the legal system on the basis of the technical requirements of considerations or reliance. Hence, any plaintiff suing on a promise has at least a prima facie moral claim to enforcement.

The most telling objection to our rule builds on this last argument and suggests that our rule does not go far enough. Why not provide for enforcement of all promises, rather than limit enforcement to those promises made in an economic setting? Although we have defined "economic activity" broadly,[116] some promises clearly are not included, such as intrafamiliar donative promises. Unlike promises made in an economic setting, these promises are not generally made to coordinate activities or generate reliance beneficial to the promisor. The presumption of utility that underlies our proposed enforcement of promises in furtherance of economic activity thus does not apply to such donative promises. This response, however, merely underscores the fact that our approach reinforces the moral value of trust only insofar as trust serves to support the functioning of the modern economic system.

We accept this characterization of our approach, but do not take it as a criticism. While the proposed rule addresses the often divergent concerns of the law and economics and critical legal studies approaches, it would be foolhardy to claim to synthesize them into a unified alternative perspective. We have aimed to broaden the scope of contract law to acknowledge and reinforce the value of trust for the broad range of economic relations that shape our daily lives—economic relations that have been hidden from the scrutiny of traditional contract law. There are certainly other kinds of relationships that help to constitute the life of the community. The areas of law that govern these relationships—family law is an example—may well need to be reformed in order to protect values similar to those that we have identified in the field of contract law. But we do not expect that a single legal rule can begin to capture the full spectrum of social relations.

D. Application of the Proposed Rule

The effect of the proposed Section 71 can be explored by applying it to a controversial recent case, *United Steel Workers, Local 1330 v. United States Steel Corp.*,[119] which involved the closing of two steel plants near Youngstown, Ohio. Plaintiffs alleged that defendants had promised to keep the plants open if the workers made them profitable. Plaintiffs acknowledged that "the minimum features of a formal legal contract," such as a fixed contract period and "specified mutual consideration," were missing.

---

[114] See generally John Rawls, A Theory of Justice 3-192 (1971) (discussing the principle of "justice as fairness").

[116] See proposed § 71 comment (a), supra text following note 99. For an argument for even broader enforcement of promises, see Knapp, Book Review, 82 Mich. L. Rev. 932,

938-47 (1984) (reviewing E. Allen Farnsworth, Contracts (1982)).

[119] 492 F. Supp. 1 (N.D. Ohio), aff'd in part and vacated in part on other grounds, 631 F.2d 1264 (6th Cir. 1980).

Plaintiffs' primary claim was based on promissory estoppel. The district court rejected the promissory estoppel claim on three grounds: (1) no definite promise was made; (2) the individuals making the statements were not defendant's officers, but employees and public relations agents; and (3) even if a promise had been made, the achievement of profitability was a condition precedent of defendant's obligations under that promise, and the Youngstown facilities did not become profitable. The Sixth Circuit affirmed.

According to the approach set forth by our proposed rule, *Local 1330* was wrongly decided. The employees and the company had, over the years, developed the kind of interdependent relationship that promotes action on the basis of an "invisible handshake." U.S. Steel must be understood to have sought economic benefits by leading employees to increase their efforts. A traumatic time such as that surrounding a possible plant closing creates both a need to cooperate to salvage the operations and an atmosphere of distrust. In such a setting, the need to reinforce trust with legal sanctions is especially strong.

Seen in the context of surrounding circumstances, the promises made and the authority of those making the promises were sufficiently clear to support recovery under the proposed Section 71 of the third *Restatement*. As the appellate court noted, "It is beyond argument that the local management of U.S. Steel's Youngstown plants engaged in a major campaign to enlist employee participation in an all-out effort to make these two plants profitable in order to prevent their being closed." But local management was not the only source of this effort. Many statements were made by agents of U.S. Steel at all levels, from the chairman of the board on down, to the effect that operations would be maintained if the plant became profitable.[123]

The appellate court's discussion then focused on the question of whether the Youngstown plants did in fact become profitable—with profitability identified as a condition precedent of the obligation that U.S. Steel was alleged to have incurred. The parties presented conflicting accounting methods to measure profitability. The district court adopted the methods proposed by U.S. Steel, those of "normal corporate profit accounting;" the appellate court stated that it could not hold that "the District Judge erred legally or was "clearly erroneous" in so doing.

The appellate court faulted the plaintiffs for defining profit as the difference between the direct costs of a plant's operations and the total selling price of its products. While stating that "any multiplant corporation could quickly go bankrupt if such a definition of profit was employed generally and over any period of time," the court acknowledged that "this version of Youngstown profitability was employed by the Youngstown management in setting a goal for its employees and in statements that described achieving that goal." And, beginning in April, 1978, and continuing through November, 1979, the company commented to both employees and the public that the plant had become profitable according to those standards.

The representations of profitability were unequivocal and were calculated to invoke the workers' trust. Nonetheless, both the district and appellate courts found that the employees should not have relied on these representations.

The standard of Restatement (Second) of Contracts § 90, upon which plaintiff-appellants rely, however, is one of reasonable expectability of the "promise" detrimentally relied upon. The District Judge did not find, nor can we, that reliance upon a promise to keep these plants open on the basis of coverage of plant fixed costs was within reasonable expectability.

In short, the employees relied on the promise as the employer intended, but their reliance was not "within reasonable expectability."

We find this result unconscionable. Whatever the prevailing definition of "profit" in corporate accounting, a continuous and consistent pattern of declaring the plants profitable, commending the employees for their achievements, and urging them forward should have tipped the scales against defendant U.S. Steel on this issue. There can be little doubt from the steady stream of communications about the achievement of profitability that employees did as they were expected to do when they relied on the representations of profitability.

The fact that the *Local 1330* courts placed such emphasis on the meaning of one term, "profitability," may well underscore the need for a rule which, like the proposed Section 71, examines the full context in which promises are made with a view to their social

---

[123] See, e.g. id. at 1273 (item p: a televised statement by the chairman of the board). The statement also mentioned the possible relevance of costs of compliance with environ- mental regulations, but U.S. Steel did not allege such costs to have arisen.

effects. The district court best described the nature of the relationship between U.S. Steel, its employees, and the surrounding community: "Everything that has happened in the Mahoning Valley has been happening for many years because of steel. . . . [T]o accommodate that industry, lives and destinies of the inhabitants of that community were based and planned on the basis of that institution: Steel." U.S. Steel had drawn "the lifeblood of the community" for its many years in the Youngstown area. The company had a strong community base and a stable work force that was willing to engage in the kind of long-term planning and commitment which is economically beneficial and perhaps even essential to a major industry.

However U.S. Steel might have understood its long-term economic interests, there can be little doubt that it received economic benefits from the extraordinary efforts of its workers in the period between the initial rumors of shut-down and its final decision to close the Youngstown plants. As the Virginia Supreme Court observed in a similar case, a company needs "the continued services of loyal and efficient employees" to perform the task of winding down operations.[132] Although that case involved the use of promises of severance pay to achieve orderly sale of the company as a going concern, the court's basic observation that major readjustments require industrial peace applies to plant closings as well. In either case, continued productivity and avoidance of damage to property enhance the value of the firm's resources.

In the long run, allowing breach of the employer's promise in this situation injures society as a whole. Employees will be less likely to put forth the extra effort to save a plant if employers can violate their promises by semantic quibbles. In breaching its understanding with its employees, U.S. Steel polluted the pool of trust from which it had drawn. The pool is large and individual breaches of trust may be small, but the effect of pollution is cumulative. Not only justice to the employees, but also society's interest in preserving the integrity of a vital social resource, require enforcement of the employer's promise in this situation. The proposed Section 71 would do just that.

E. Critical Legal Studies and the Proposed Rule

Although we have focused on the economic rationale for our proposed rule of promissory obligation, the rule is also bolstered by moral considerations. Like the critical legal scholars, we view human social life as a positive good, and we believe that contract law implicates communitarian values. The value of trust, which forms the basis of the *entitlement* to rely, is the starting point of our theory of promissory obligation. Reliance is not protected in order to compensate individuals who have suffered a wrong, as some writers have argued.[133] Rather, promises are enforced in order to foster a society in which people can confidently rely on each other. Such a society is morally superior to the state of constrained avarice depicted by "bad man" theories of legal obligation.[134]

As the above discussion of *Local 1330* demonstrates, however, our approach differs from what might be expected from the critical legal scholars. Duncan Kennedy, working from a critical legal studies perspective, agrees that the plaintiffs in *Local 1330* should have prevailed, but for different reasons:

> The case was wrongly decided because the court should have implied into every contract of employment between the company and an individual worker the following term: As part payment for the worker's labor, the company promised that in the event it wished to terminate the manufacture of steel in the plant, it would convey the plant to the union in trust for the present workers (along with recently laid-off and retired workers). The company further impliedly promised to condition the conveyance so that if the union as trustee attempted to sell the plant or convert it to a use that would substantially reduce the economic benefit it generated for the town, the town would become the owner in fee simple. I would make this implied promise on the part of the company nonwaivable . . . [135]

Kennedy would imply such a term in order to achieve the three objectives that, according to his theory, form the basis for contract enforcement: paternalism, the redistribution of wealth, and efficiency.

To Kennedy, a properly paternalistic court would recognize that:

[132] Dulany Foods, Inc. v. Ayers, 220 Va. 502, 508, 260 S.E.2d 196, 200 (1979).
[133] See, e.g., Patrick Atiyah, Promises, Morals, and Law 40-42 (1981).
[134] See Oliver Wendell Holmes, Jr., The Path of the Law, in Collected Legal Papers 170 (1920).
[135] Kennedy, Distributive and Paternalistic Motives in Contract and Tort Law, With Special Reference to Compulsory Terms and Unequal Bargaining Power, 41 Md. L. Rev. 563, 630 (1982).

[a] basic reason why workers have not in the past bargained for and won the kind of property interest in manufacturing enterprises that this term would represent seems to have been that they have miscalculated their true interests. They have underestimated the long-term value of worker control. . . . They have overestimated the stability of basic arrangements between labor and management, and also overestimated the benefits of a relatively quiet life, with plenty of material goods and no responsibility.

In short, "[p]eople are idiots,"[137] and courts must engage in paternalistic intervention to save them from the effects of false consciousness.

Professor Kennedy is not explicit as to the redistributive effects of his proposed solution. Because of his focus on the company's relationship with its employees and the town, he is likely to lose track of the benefits that might result from relocation. If a new plant were opened in another town, the residents of that community would gain the kind of benefits the *Local 1330* plaintiffs were about to lose. From the perspective of wealth redistribution, the gainers might well be people who are presently worse off than the union members who are suing—particularly if the plant relocates in the Third World. Stated more generally, communitarian values must operate within a community, and the solutions to social problems are deceptively simple if the affected community is defined too narrowly.[138]

As to efficiency, Professor Kennedy generally overlooks one of the basic lessons of economics: firms are not passive in the face of legal rules. Their future conduct will be affected as they take the rules into account. For instance, faced by Kennedy's rule of law, companies will be reluctant to open new plants or to expand existing plants because by doing so they will

be freezing their capital. Instead, they will move to jurisdictions with more favorable legal rules, or work a plant until it becomes unproductive for lack of capital improvement, leaving a worthless legacy to the workers and the town. To the extent they cannot do so, the return on capital will diminish—a result with possible effects on savings and economic growth that may be damaging to the economy as a whole.

Our own approach fosters many of Kennedy's goals, but within the constraints of economic reality. We do not categorically reject the possibility that employers should have non-negotiable duties of fairness toward employees, but we do see serious difficulties in such proposals. We take the more modest step of holding employers to their express representations. This approach does not protect against the distortions created by false consciousness. But it is likely to protect against the exploitation of employees by employers who falsely appeal to employee self-interest by making promises they do not keep. We believe this is an approach that courts are beginning to take, and one that is worth taking.

Conclusion

The traditional view of contract law divides promissory liability into two categories. By far the larger category involves the bargained-for exchange of promises for other consideration. These bargains are enforced, even in the absence of reliance, in order to protect the parties' expectation that future conduct will be governed by present commitments. The other, much smaller category, is that of promissory estoppel. Here, liability is imposed to remedy the injury to promisees who have relied on promises in vain.

Based on our survey of recent promissory estoppel cases, we believe that promissory estoppel is losing its link with reliance. In key cases promises have been

[137] Id. at 633. Real uncertainity, rather than false consciousness, may account for why even rational actors would be hesitant to bargain for such a contract term. Even Kennedy admits to some uncertainty about the effects of his proposed rule. Id. at 631 ("if I had been the district court judge in the case, I would have imposed it, with some trepidation and a great deal of curiosity about what would happen next").

[138] Feinman, supra note 4, at 858-59, suggests an approach to Local 1330 similar to Kennedy's. According to Feinman, "the case has potential for creative revolutionary thinking in addition to legal advocacy or mass organizing." Id. at 859.

Reconstructing the contract case [Local 1330] can help us visualize what a more just system would look like and what is necessary to achieve it. "Freedom of con-

tract" in the utopian vision requires a social order in which people possess the practical ability to connect with each other to find meaning in their lives through common endeavor, a freedom that denies the life and death power of distant corporate managers over workers and their town.

Id. at 859-60. Again, however, while we find the goal laudable, a more realistic approach is necessary. Steel is not a local industry. A steel plant uses raw materials brought from distant markets, and sells products to firms that themselves have far-flung markets. Maintaining an inefficient plant in Ohio might require eliminating foreign imports, which would harm not only American consumers but also workers in Japan and Korea. It is not just "distant corporate managers" who exercise life and death power over steel towns; it is also the world economy.

enforced with only the weakest showing of any detriment to the promisee. Reliance-based damages are the exception, not the rule. With the decline of reliance, promissory estoppel is moving away from tort law. It has become a means of enforcing promises differing in doctrinal detail from traditional contract law but sharing a common goal. That goal, we have argued, is to foster trust between economic actors. Trust is a moral good, but it is also an economic asset. It allows coordination and planning between economic actors and fosters the formation of valuable economic institutions.

Perhaps in an earlier age traditional contract law was adequate to foster the degree of trust society needed in economic activities. Today, an increasingly interdependent society needs to foster trust in a variety of relationships not readily organized through the device of the formal contract. Promissory estoppel is one of several mechanisms courts have used to try to close what we have called the "relational gap" in contract law.

In our view, recent cases expansively applying promissory estoppel are steps on the road to a broader rule of promissory obligation. We have proposed as a new standard for enforcement that all promises made in furtherance of economic activities be enforced without regard to the presence of consideration or reliance. Although we recognize that courts have not yet articulated this standard, we believe they are moving in this direction.

We do not wish to overstate our claims for our approach. Like Corbin, we are skeptical of claims that the common law can be reduced to a simple set of rules, as well as claims that the proper resolution of contracts issues can be deduced from some set of abstract principles. And although we think our description of the cases we surveyed is a fair one, we certainly do not claim that every case can be neatly fit within our framework.[140] Law is much too untidy for that. Perhaps most importantly, our rule does not pretend to be an eternal verity. It is tailored to provide for enforcement of promises in the kinds of relationships that are central to the contemporary economy.

On the other hand, we do believe that our approach is a distinct improvement over that of the current *Restatement*. As a description of the cases, the current Section 90 offers very little guidance because it fails to identify the factors that are actually decisive in determining the outcomes of the cases. Our proposed Section 71 admittedly does not account for every case, but it does provide much surer guidance in understanding the case law. As a normative statement, the promissory estoppel doctrine expressed in Section 90 has raised more questions than it has answered. In every case, it has required that courts return to first principles to ask whether "injustice can be avoided only by enforcement of the promise."[141] Busy judges, we think, deserve better guidance.

We do not claim to have finally resolved the problem of promissory obligation. We do contend, however, that our approach is both a distinct improvement over the current view and a modest step toward a fairer social order.

---

[140] For example, our proposed rule does not attempt to address the issue of past consideration. See, e.g., Webb v. McGowin, 27 Ala. App. 82, 168 So. 196 (1935) (enforcing a promise to pay an annuity to a man who was severely injured while saving the promisor's life). The second Restatement's explanation of this result is keyed to the benefit received by the promisor. See Restatement (Second) § 86 comment d, illustration 7. We suspect, however, that the harm suffered by the promisee is at least as important in understanding the result. In any event, although we do not question the result in Webb, we have made no attempt to incorporate it within our proposed rule.

[141] Restatement (Second) § 90. It may well be that all legal rules are ultimately based on the moral values of the judges, and that hard cases may require a judge to resort to consulting these values directly. As the quoted language shows, however, the current Section 90 makes every case a hard case. Indeed, since the remedy "may be limited as justice requires," the remedy becomes a separate issue again requiring a resort to ultimate moral values. If we are going to include rules this indeterminate in the Restatement, we might as well do a little editing of Section 90 and reduce all of contract law to a single rule: "a promise is binding. . . if injustice can be avoided only by enforcement of the promise."

Jay M. Feinman, *The Meaning of Reliance: A Historical Perspective,*
1984 Wis. L. Rev. 1373

. . .

IV.

The expansion of reliance doctrine, like all law-making, is an attempt to order a disorderly world. In developing and applying legal doctrine, lawyers, judges and legal scholars seek both to reflect their perception of relations in society and to present an ideal picture of those relations. An interpretation of reliance, then, should seek to elucidate the values inherent in the doctrine, as well as examine the ways in which the doctrine has been developed to idealize social relations. Such an interpretation, drawing on the interpretive map sketched in the previous section, leads to the conclusion that reliance doctrine makes existing social relations appear to be good and necessary when they actually are neither.

Classical legal and social thought had drawn a comforting if forbidding picture of a world in which rugged individuals were both free to and forced to compete with each other, ostensibly as equals in the arenas of free contract, private property, and laissez-faire. But people came to see that the picture was distorted, as a portrayal of the world they knew and as an ideal of the world to which they aspired. The world they and we know contains some institutions of great social and economic power and many individuals of limited resources; for both large and small, cooperation and interdependence are as important as competition in producing the good life. The world to which we aspire balances personal initiative and freedom with social responsibility and communal sharing. The expansion of reliance represents a three-fold effort to represent the real world, to present the ideal world, and to deny the gap between the two.

Reliance's representation of the actual is part of a rejection of the abstraction and unreality of classical thought. The world does not conform to the discrete transactional ideal of classical contract law, and the law cannot force it to do so. The image presented in the reliance case law accommodates the uncertainties and irregularities of commercial behavior and the frequency of transactions between unequals.

Recognizing the fact of non-contractual reliance leads to the statement of a new ideal image of behav-ior, different from but no less abstract than the classical image of unregulated competition. The modern image of contract conceives people to be "partners in a moral community [defined by] equity and the balancing of interests according to standards of fair dealing" where the law is the "active enforcer of the newly conceived notion of the general welfare." Reliance doctrine is a means of affirming the existence of trust and cooperation among the members of that community.

Thus reliance doctrine is an accommodation of the real and the ideal. But instead of being held out as a goal to be achieved, the ideal is posited as the actual. The picture of a society governed by a moral consensus is presented as an accurate portrayal of the world. Each reliance case involves a choice among conflicting interests against a background of inequity, but the choice and the inequity are concealed by the claims that the proper resolution of the dispute is immanent in the situation being adjudicated or is derived by an objective normative calculus. The meaning of reliance, then, is the affirmation of truth but also the concealment of falsehood in the world.

My description of the meaning of reliance for its advocates—in a sense, its meaning for us as members of the legal community—is essentially its role as a corrective to the abstraction and unreality of classical contract law in light of a changed perception of the social universe. The doctrine's power lies in its statement of a more concrete, attractive reality and ideal, in contrast to the apparent wrongness of classical doctrine. However, it falters in representing the real world as if it was the ideal, presenting a false image of a just economic sphere regulated by moral principles while failing to effect a change to such a world.

Reliance has been powerfully appealing because it dereifies. "Reify" and "dereify" are sometimes derided as critical jargon, but they are evocative and accurate. As its etymology suggests,[22] to reify is to endow an abstraction, such as a concept, a relationship, or a doctrine, with the quality of being concrete, fixed, or thing-like. Classical contract law posited an individualistic, competitive concept of bargain as the

---

[22] From the Latin res, meaning "thing." See generally Gabel, Reification in Legal Reasoning, 3 Research L. & Soc. 25 (1980).

core of contract in law and society, but regarded the concept as a naturally existing and immutable reality, rather than as a historically particular policy choice. Reliance doctrine demonstrated that the bargain concept inaccurately reflected social circumstances and incompletely defined the available contract principles; that is, reliance "dereified" contract by concretizing it and showing its inconsistencies.

There is, I believe, a widely held view that the dereification of contract that began with Corbin and Cardozo and has continued to the present has been a success: contract doctrine has been substantially purged of its prior impurities so that it now closely approximates commercial behavior and social norms and is therefore theoretically "correct." That view is wrong, and the error demonstrates the difference between liberal and critical analysis. To descend further into critical jargon, the dereification process that contract has undergone has not been critical because it has not been "counterhegemonic dereification." "Hegemony" is the dominance in a society of a set of beliefs, relations, and institutions, a dominance accomplished more through cultural conditioning than through the threat or use of force. "Counterhegemonic dereification," then, breaks down concepts such as legal doctrines in a way that demonstrates how they support the status quo.

Reliance's liberal dereification modified one doctrine perceived to be inconsistent with commercial reality and with predominant social norms through another doctrine perceived to better represent that reality and those norms. But this dereification is incomplete and hegemonic because it legitimates the status quo rather than significantly altering legal relations. Though flexible in principle, in practice reliance has been used in a restricted form. The counterprinciple of reliance was accommodated with the bargain principle in a reformed version of traditional contract thinking and the doctrine has been applied in limited contexts, addressing only particular trades or usages. Reliance, then, has led to limited changes in lawyers' perception of social reality and in that reality itself.

What we need, then, is counterhegemonic dereification as a source of critical doctrine. Let me conclude with some comments concerning employment relations, an area in which reliance issues frequently arise.

Traditional bargain formation and consideration doctrine required a high degree of presentiation[24] at the commencement of an employment relation. All elements of the relationship were encapsulated in a single artificial contract formed at the moment of contracting. Subsequent promises or representations by the employer concerning benefits or compensation were unenforceable, except through tortuous and transparently result-oriented manipulations of doctrine. In some reliance cases courts have enforced such promises, typically where the promise or representation is fairly specific, even if it conflicts with other statements of the employer, and where the employee can demonstrate a particular act in reliance on the promise. These results grow out of a sense of the employment relation as one in which changes can be made over time, even in the absence of specific bargains concerning the changes.

Suppose we were to extend that analysis. We might point out that the current analysis is still constrained by artificial notions of discrete promise and discrete reliance. These restricted concepts legitimate a situation in which control over most aspects of the employment relation typically rests with the employer. Only in the exceptional situation in which the employee can demonstrate an explicit promise and a particular act of reliance is the employer bound. In fact, future-regarding actions by employer (promises) and employee (reliance) are more common and less discrete than that. There may be little reason to distinguish pre-contractual, discrete contractual, and post-contractual elements in a long-term relation.

Moving in this direction requires us to immerse ourselves ever more in the life situations from which the legal issues arise. That, too, is interpretive activity, and it can best be achieved when we draw closer to those whose situations we seek to interpret. One thing we must do, then, is seek to involve in the process of lawmaking more of those subject to the law, an involvement that must be fuller than that permitted by the reified roles of "litigant" or "citizen."

This analysis also requires intensive and extensive consideration of the range of norms involved in the contracting process. Only in the narrowest sense is reliance doctrine about actions induced by promises. Reliance seen more broadly is about mutuality, solidarity, and power in particular relations and in soci-

---

[24] To presentiate is to cause aspects of the future to be perceived as if they were in the present. See Macneil, Restatement (Second) of Contracts and Presentiation, 60 Va. L. Rev. 589 (1974).

ety. A critical use of reliance requires us to consider all of those qualities in formulating doctrine.

These directions suggest new possibilities for reliance doctrine. Perhaps reliance doctrine should be extended to grant employees the right to a safe workplace, reasonable benefits, fair treatment, and the tenure of employment during good behavior. Perhaps reliance doctrine ought to provide protection against plant closings. Perhaps it even should provide a cause of action against the state requiring adequate training for employment and a fulfilling job.

Needless to say, this list of new reliance theories and the process that might produce them is intended to be provocative rather than precise or comprehensive. But none of these things is unthinkable. My view of the history of reliance, as of legal history in general, is one of alternatives chosen and foregone. Why we choose some and forgo others is complex. Examining our past choices and forcing into the open our present choices seem to me to be worthy endeavors.

C.   The Role of the Uniform Commercial Code

The UCC, Karl Llewellyn, and Common Law Contracts

The Uniform Commercial Code has been a major influence, perhaps the major influence, on American contract law in the second half of the twentieth century. Its origins go back at least to 1936 when Karl N. Llewellyn began work on a revision of the Uniform Sales Act, then some forty years old. The project expanded globally when the decision was made in the nineteen-forties to write a comprehensive code that would cover many (though not all) aspects of commercial transactions rather than focusing only on sales.

Throughout the late forties and fifties, the "proposed" Code was the subject of great controversy. Some of that controversy is mentioned in the article by Eugene F. Mooney, which follows, and other aspects are discussed in Arthur Leff's "Emperor's New Clause" article, which appears in Part IIIB. Samuel Williston had been the draftsman of the Uniform Sales Act, and his article opposing the new Code, Williston, *The Law of Sales in the Proposed Uniform Commercial Code*, 63 Harv. L. Rev. 561 (1950), written when he was nearly ninety, is his last major work. Almost simultaneously, Arthur Corbin, a youth of 75, wrote in support of the Code. Corbin, *The Uniform Commercial Code—Sales; Should It Be Enacted?*, 59 Yale L.J. 821 (1950). Corbin, who was protective of Williston as Williston aged, wrote a remarkable first footnote that tells us a lot about the two men, and that made prescient comments as well about the Code:

> The writer has carefully read the critical article in the Harvard Law Review by his dearly beloved friend and revered teacher (outside the schoolroom), Samuel Williston. While differing in its conclusions the present article is not written as an "answer" to that criticism; our relations for many years have been such that a "controversy" between us is inconceivable. This is being written, without the knowledge or advice of any person, as an affirmative support of the Code by an enthusiastic advocate of its enactment by Congress and the States. The Code and its accompanying comment have been made use of at every relevant spot in the writer's forthcoming general treatise on the law of Contracts. Just as in the case of the Restatements, they will serve a useful purpose there even if the Code should never be enacted as a statute.

Since those early days, much has been written about the Code and common law contracts. Two of the many possible examples are Richard Danzig's *A Comment on the Jurisprudence of the Uniform Commercial Code*, 27 Stan. L. Rev. 621 (1975), and Robert A. Hillman's *A Study of Uniform Commercial Code Methodology: Contract Modification Under Article Two*, 59 N.C. L. Rev. 335 (1981). Article Two has not been limited by the courts to sales of goods in a literal sense, but has often been applied to contracts structuring distributorships and franchises that in turn deal in goods. It has been used by analogy when it was not applicable even on a broad reading of its scope. And the Restatement (Second) of Contracts openly borrowed concepts like good faith and unconscionability from the Code and declared that they applied to all contracts regardless of subject matter.

Eugene F. Mooney's article, *Old Kontract Principles and Karl's New Kode: An Essay on the Jurisprudence of Our New Commercial Law*, shows the influences both of the mid-sixties, when it was written, and of Karl Llewellyn, who was the Chief Reporter of the Code, and whose legal philosophy was a strong influence on it. Its discussion simultaneously relates back to Part IIA on contract formation and forward to the discussions of good faith and unconscionability in Part IIIB. More than twenty years after Mooney pubished the article, there can easily be found critics who see Mooney as starry-eyed. To this non-specialist in the Code, however, Mooney appears to see in the Code what Llewellyn intended to be found there. Despite the Code's many technical rules, it has overarching principles of fairness, commercial reasonableness and a preference for business practice over rigid legal rules.

Eugene F. Mooney, *Old Kontract Principles and Karl's New Kode: An Essay on the Jurisprudence of Our New Commercial Law*, 11 Villanova L. Rev. 213 (1966)

The Contract Parable*

When the World was very young and long before society reached its present state of perfection people began making contracts. Freud's Oedipus Legend recites that the Primeval Father and the Primeval Mother had an exclusive dealing arrangement. The Brother Clan by mutual agreement killed the Father and appropriated the Mother for their own use. Thereafter to keep peace among themselves they entered into the Social Contract. This was the first Bilateral Contract. Despite good intentions, however, the parties constantly bickered over this unwritten contract and it became apparent the entire venture needed to be reconstituted.

When God opened negotiations with the Children of Israel they promptly demanded a firm written offer which would satisfy the Statute of Frauds, so Moses was sent back up Mount Sinai to draft the stone tablets. The essence of the offer was that if the Children of Israel would act a certain way then God would do thus and so. This was the first Unilateral Contract. Early construction of the contract was in strict compliance with the Parol Evidence Rule, but subsequent liberal interpretation discovered it was open-ended so Gentiles could be included and Subcontracting was permitted. This should have been a sufficient arrangement for everyone. The Farmers were reasonably satisfied with it but the Merchants were not. Moreover, despite a considerable interpretive gloss a number of loopholes were uncovered and the terms were too harsh because the Contract required that all Subcontracts be fully performed.

So the next attempt took up the problem of what agreements should be enforced. Both the Romans and Early Church Fathers were inclined to enforce all agreements if there was causa. But foreign merchants were notoriously Godless men who would take one's money and give him nothing so we let them make up their own law. Thus two or three different approaches developed over the centuries: 1) The Romans simply required fair dealing in Good Faith and enforced every agreement except a nudum pactum, *2) Other Europeans were more realistic and required the posting of hostages as security for performance of the under-*

---

* Inspiration for this parable summing up all the author has been able to learn about the law of contract, and, indeed for this entire article is traceable directly to D. J. Swift

Teufelsdrockh, Jurisprudence, The Crown of Civilization— Being Also The Principles of Writing Jurisprudence Made Clear To Neophytes, 5 U. Chi. Rev. 171 (1938). Most of the principles set forth in that article have been here employed: it was impossible to capture the style but hopefully some of the overtones of that article also appear here.

taking, 3) The English were the most realistic and required the assumpsit to be sworn out twice, put in writing, a hostage be posted and a quid pro quo be given. This was the beginning of the Common Law of Contract. The Foreign Merchant Problem was solved when Lord Mansfield began to let them sue on their contracts in his Common Law Court in order to keep them out of Equity.

Things moved swiftly after that and within a few centuries we dropped the purely ceremonial requirements of the English system. When Slade's case broke in 1606 no one was outraged that only a single sworn assumpsit was required and if supported by a peppercorn it was binding. We discovered that good faith actually had nothing to do with contract, which was an omnipotent expression of human will binding on the courts, society and God in that order. The English Sale of Goods Act was the final expression of a matchless state of contract perfection, embodying the true meaning of contract as a legal obligation arising out of a promise supported by consideration.

So you see when we all came over to America the whole matter had settled into black-letter rules: 1) Contracts must be covered by a writing and supported by consideration, for it would be immoral to allow them out in public nude and without visible means of support, 2) Foreign merchants have their own law which is too devious for common lawyers, 3) Mutual assent to a contract embodies Omnipotent Human Will and is the only obligation binding anyone to do anything for anyone else so it should be strictly construed, and 4) God can revoke His offer at any time before it is accepted by the requested act; but if He defaults no decree for specific performance will issue although He may have to answer to a writ of indebitatus assumpsit.

I. Introduction

Is There A Contract? What The Hell![1]

The subject is almost as insane as the parable. One recalls with horror his first semester in law school and the course in Contracts I. The whole matter of offer, acceptance and consideration is deliciously painful, like "possession" in Personal Property, "seizin" in Real Property, and "duty" in Torts. Struggling through cases deliberately chosen by the case book editor to bewilder, one sought guidance from Williston, Corbin, and the Restatement of Contracts.

Yet they all seemed to say the same thing in much the same words with only nitpicking differences, and in desperation one committed to memory the miniscule distinctions in dogma drawn by Williston and Corbin and struck the balance where he thought the Restatement dictated. All this frantic mental juggling took place without for a moment understanding what it was all about, if anything. One thing was clear, however: The traditional contract construct was the key to Paradise and one learned it or flunked.

Actually, the construct was quite simple and easy to understand once it had been mentally assimilated. This was accomplished through hours of unbelievable monotony in the library relieved by brief moments of stark terror socratically superinduced in the classroom. We learned that there are certain expressions of mutual assent to which the law appends an obligation arising from the express or plainly implied "promises" of the parties. The legal obligation is strictly limited to the promises. These promises are discovered in the unvarying method by which human beings contract with each other, namely, by means of "offers" embodying "promises" directed by "offerors" to particular "offerees" who "accept" by manifesting assent either by tendering a promise or an act. The agreement thus made is enforcible at law or in equity if and only if the promises involved "detriment to the promisor." Otherwise the agreement was not supported by "consideration" and was a bare nudum pactum. Case variations were hung on the construct like ornaments on a Christmas tree, glittering but essentially useless.

One visualized the whole thing as if it were a door hasp into which the lock of consideration was snapped, or a hinge with the linchpin of consideration fitting smoothly into the aligned holes. It was all so professionally neat that one commentator was prompted to remark:

> The Langdell School's amazing theory of consideration and unilateral contract is not only the most familiar American example [of "the vigorous, almost rigid German theories of construction and dogmatics"], but the most clean of line, most bald of eye-deflecting cover: the consideration needed to support a promise must be bargained for; it must be the precise something bargained for; the something bargained for must be precise. Acceptance and the provision of consideration

---

[1] The subtitle is taken from the delightful "Ballade Of The Class in Contracts" by Professor Karl N. Llewyllyn which appears in Llewellyn, Put In His Thumb 39-40 (1931), and which begins: "Is there a contract? What the hell!"

coincide like equal triangles, superimposed, and, superposed, exclude all variant dimensions of "conditions." If "an act" is called for by an offer, that very "act" complete, and nothing else or less, though by a hair, is what is needed; only the other party to the bargain can accept; only "he" can give consideration; only "he" acquire rights. Nothing could be more simply stated, more rigorously thought, more tightly integrated, more fascinatingly absurd to teach, more easy to "apply."[2]

Such mental pictures were irresistible, and more than one lawyer upon first discovering that the contract law of many other nations requires neither "consideration" nor any functional equivalent has been heard to remark querulously, "But what holds the contract together?"

From this simplistic construct of obligation-based-on-promise derived all those conceptualistic torments of Contracts I. The concept of "offer" brought forth problems involving "illusory" offers, agreements to contract and bilateral-or-unilateralness, all of which stem inexorably from the conceptual necessity for discovering in the particular fact-transaction the precise "power" created in the offeree. The notion of "acceptance" spawned terrible classroom conundrums involving communication of the acceptance and the absolute absurdity of the "ribbon-matching" cases, culminating in the ever-fruitful offer-to-make-a-unilateral-contract if the offeree will climb a flagpole (mow the lawn, chop the wood, walk across a bridge, and so forth ad nauseum) which is revoked at the last instant. Revocability also generated those hairy problems concerning withdrawal of options and the burning question whether revocation of the reward offered for Lincoln's assassin should have been in a local, regional or national newspaper. Such technicalities are absolute requisites when one believes that the promisor is in complete control of his "offer" in every conceivable respect and is entitled to receive from the promisee exactly what his offer demands in precisely the manner it prescribes. The doctrine of consideration gave us intellectual peppercorns. One grappled with such awe-inspiring problems as benefit-to-the-promisee versus detriment-to-the-promisor, whether a promise could be consideration for a promise, and whether void, voidable, barred, redundant, economically valueless or silly promises could be consideration for anything. The comfortable artificiali-

ties of the traditional contract construct led Professor Llewellyn to note with delicious irony that:

The rules of Offer and Acceptance have been worked over; they have been written over; they have been shaped and rubbed smooth with pumice, they wear the rich deep polish of a thousand classrooms; they have a grip on the vision and indeed on the affections held by no other rules "of law," real or pseudo. For it was Offer and Acceptance which first led each of us out of laydom into The Law. Puzzled, befogged, adrift in the strange words and technique of cases, with only our sane feeling of what was decent for a compass, we felt the warm sun suddenly, we knew that we were arriving, we knew we too could "think like a lawyer": That was when we learned to down seasickness as A revoked when B was almost up the flag-pole. Within the first October, we had achieved a technical glee in justifying judgment then for A; and succulent memory lingers, of the way our dumber brethren were pilloried as Laymen still.[3]

This is a serious charge but the indictment is well-grounded. A formidable bill of particulars was drawn up long ago by a distinguished group of legal realists which is devastating and persuasive even today. Particular aspects of the construct have been successfully challenged from time to time virtually since its inception by such luminaries as Whittier, Ballantine, Oliphant, Ferson, Corbin and other giants of contract law. Their assaults on the Langdell-Williston construct were based mainly on specific manifestations of its illogic or inconsistency. But for forty years the most careful, persistent and effective critic of the Langdell-Williston-Restatement construct was Professor Karl N. Llewellyn whose complaints pointed out the damagingly unrealistic nature of the whole orthodox offer-acceptance-consideration trichotomy and its progeny of meaningless technicalities. . . . Time after time and through cumulating instances he emphasized that despite the doctrinal handcuffs the courts amazingly did justice, reached results reasonable under the circumstances, and were perceptive to the demands of a changing commercial society. Over and over he emphasized that business arrangements, not family transactions, are a more reasonable foundation upon which theories of contract should be based, because

[2] Llewellyn, Jurisprudence 172 (1962).
[3] Llewellyn, On Our Case-Law of Contract: Offer And Acceptance, I, 48 Yale L.J. 1, 32 (1938).

[I]t is not safe to reason about business cases from cases in which an uncle became interested in having his nephew see Europe, go to Yale, abstain from nicotine, or christen his infant heir "Alvardus Torrington, III." And it may even be urged that safe conclusions as to business cases of the more ordinary variety cannot be derived from what courts or scholars rule about the idiosyncratic desires of one *A* to see one *B* climb a fifty-foot greased flag-pole or push a peanut across the Brooklyn Bridge.

This is not only delightful criticism, it is trenchant good sense. The overwhelming majority of contracts are made in the course of business transactions, and of these the largest percentage are sale or sale-oriented contracts. Yet virtually the entire American Bar is composed of lawyers, judges and professors who were nurtured on the artificialities of peppercornism. We are all comfortably at home there:

> This is therefore no area of "rules" to be disturbed. It is an area where we want no disturbance, and will brook none. It is the Rabbit-Hole down which we fell into the Law, and to him who has gone down it, no queer phenomenon is strange; he has been magicked; the logic of Wonderland we then entered makes mere discrepant decision negligible. And it is not only hard, it is obnoxious, for any of us who have gone through that experience to even conceive of Offer and Acceptance as perhaps in need of re-examination.[8]

But re-examination was necessary and it could have been foreseen that Llewellyn would be the one to do it.

Many good and valuable compilations of the particular Restatement of Contracts rules changed by the Uniform Commercial Code have appeared in print over the past fifteen years. These new rules have almost uniformly been viewed by commentators as no more than sensible exceptions to particular unfortunate rules of contract law which had been negligently permitted to grow up unrelated to given business practices. . . .

There is a completely different, iconoclastic view of the matter, one which ignores the slight modifications of particular rules and focuses on the major jurisprudential shift in the structure of the contract construct made by the Code. Commercial law in this country is or soon will be the Uniform Commercial Code and thus is firmly rooted in the rich soil of the "life-situation" of business agreements made in the context of the contemporary processes of the primary commercial activity in this country. This was done, insofar as statutory language can do so, by framing the entire Code so as to ground the contract obligation on good faith mercantile agreements embodying the parties' bargain within the functional economic structures relating to goods distribution in this country. No mere language change was contemplated. No mere piecemeal modification of Restatement rules was involved. Not only was the amelioration of particular legalistic hardships on business intended, nothing less than the substitution of a dynamic and transactionally-oriented agreement construct for the old and static offer-acceptance-consideration model was attempted.

Viewed thus, Code rule changes cannot meaningfully be examined as mere isolated tailoring alterations. The old suit has been totally remodelled, the high peaked lapels were blunted, the coat cut down to be single-breasted, the padding excised from the shoulders and the pleats removed from the pants. An old suit cut from the cloth of the common law was turned into a modern set of threads. The new suit could be described by noting the precise details of alteration in terms such as freedom of contract, offer, acceptance, consideration, assignability, statute of frauds, anticipatory repudiation and remedies, but the true significance of the change in contract principles would be missed. The suit is now designed not for the portly buyer and seller of title to goods, but for the wiry, slender dealer in goods. One could similarly list the many changes in the law of negotiable instruments and in the law of secured transactions. But the former list would not clearly reflect the real change made by the Code, and the latter list would be so long and redundant that it would be buried under detail. Only by viewing the whole Code and its constituent parts ideographically can the full impact of the change be understood. Examination of these hundreds of changes by means of verbalinear analysis could easily take longer than the sixteen years already spent drafting and revising the Code. Even if it *could* be done, the point of primary significance would escape notice again: the Uniform Commercial Code was conceived, drafted, and enacted into statutory law as a *code* and not a mere collection of statutory rules. As such it has unifying features, threads running across the cloth, repeating patterns of rules embodying concepts common to the whole, and legal

---

[8] Llewellyn supra note 3, at 32.

"base lines" along which the Code articles are laid out. Three of the most important of these base lines are:

1) The legal obligation of contract arises from the agreement-in-fact of the parties and not their "promises";

2) The Code as a whole and each of its parts is predicated on a functional economic construct of goods distribution in this country and not on abstractions of the law of contracts;

3) The ultimate affirmative touchstone for judicial decision on commercial contract matters under the Code is mercantile good faith and fair dealing.

Copious quotations from Karl Llewellyn's writings are of greater significance than mere criticisms from the past of the traditional contract construct. They can be seen in retrospect as something more than professorial bombast or persnickety complaints destined never to be remembered. Because of the smashing legislative success of the Uniform Commercial Code the attitudes and opinions of Karl Llewellyn can be neither forgotten nor ignored. Those attitudes are built into the Code forever.

Llewellyn had formed most of his ideas about contract law before he began drafting the Code. While in the midst of publishing a series of brilliant articles undertaking a fundamental re-examination of the law of commercial contracts, Llewellyn became the chairman of the Code committee of the Commission on Uniform State Laws. During the ensuing decade he worked unceasingly toward comprehensive codification of commercial law.

Although much of the actual drafting of the various articles was done by committees, Llewellyn was the coordinator and, as such, exercised both tremendous influence and practical control over the whole project. He and Professor Corbin served on the committee drafting the sales article and in great measure Llewellyn wrote that section of the Code to suit himself.[16] The first version was published in 1949 and although there have been numerous and extensive revisions since then, the sales article and the all-important introductory article (Article 1) retain most of the characteristics built into them by Llewellyn.

. . .

The burden of this monograph is that Professor Karl Llewellyn implemented his ideas on the law of contract by imbedding them into the Uniform Commercial Code in such manner that they are now virtually inextricable. More importantly, he built the Code so as to embody a commercial contract construct substantially different from the orthodox contract construct by statutorily substituting obligation-based-on-transaction for obligation-based-on-promise. This theory is fascinatingly persuasive for those like myself, who had long wondered what fine madness underlay the plethora of contract rule changes wrought by the Code.

II. From Promise to Agreement and a Bit Beyond

The concept of "promise" was and is of critical importance to traditional contract law, but the word seldom appears in the Code. This alone marks a significant departure from the nomenclature of the law of contract. Relying completely on the mental picture of face-to-face dealing by means of personal "promises," the Restatement of Contracts repeatedly uses the term as virtually synonymous with "contract" or "undertaking," a combination of acts *and* "intangible duties" or "the moral duty" to perform. Since it is the ultimate fact in traditional contract law it cannot be defined in concrete terms because it signifies a mixture of fact and law.

The validity of the entire Langdell-Williston-Restatement construct was briskly challenged by Llewellyn in 1937. Announcing his deliberate intention to recanvass the field of contract law in a series of studies, Llewellyn gave as his explanation for this monumental task he was undertaking that Orthodoxy's formulations were suspect. . . .

One can only suppose the virtual omission of "promise" from the Code was a deliberate and calculated effort to free contract from an indefensible image and an undefinable foundation word. The third episode of his projected recanvassing of the law of contract took up this precise point in a passage where he noted that "the traditional base-line of a century back" is that "the essential basis of contracting is *Agreement*." . . . [According to Llewellyn, "promise"

---

[16] Llewellyn and Professor Soia Mentschikoff were the reporter and assistant reporter on the Uniform Revised Sales Act which was the first major subdivision of the proposed Code. Later they became chief reporter and associate chief reporter for the whole Code. Braucher, The Legislative History of the Uniform Commercial Code, 58 Colum. L. Rev.

798 (1958). Llewellyn's influence was particularly strong during the early drafting stages, and even after industry and government groups became pointedly interested in the project around 1952, and participated heavily in the actual drafting thereafter, Llewellyn was able to hold much of the alteration to language changes. . . .

is too focused to capture the functional meaning of "agreement." —ed.]

Nor does the phrase "mutual assent" quite fill the bill. Crippled permanently by the legal theological battles over "subjective" versus "objective" tests, encrusted with the barnacles of "meeting of the minds" problems and rife with the promissory connotations of the word "assent," use of the mutual assent litany would augur confusion further compounded. The phrase has always carried the distressing implication that there was a *single* proposition to which the contracting parties humbly acquiesced, a proposition existing completely extraneous to the parties and their transactions . . . . Something much more realistic, comprehensive and cleanly factual than either "promise" or "mutual assent" was required. . . . Resort by the Code to the older word "agreement" was thus both a return to the original understanding of the essence of contract obligation and a more concrete reference to contemporary commercial transactions.

. . . Grounding contract on agreement-in-fact, however manifested, the Code wipes out with one sweep the whole figment of promise-for-a-promise-or-promise-for-an-act. Llewellyn proposed at that point in his thinking not so much a massive conceptual shift *away* from something called "promise" to something called "agreement," but more nearly a broader conceptual base for contract, unified by removal of the false dichotomy between promises and acts of acceptance dictated by Orthodoxy's emphasis on "promise," and a more commonsense "single approach to acceptance for business deals" in meeting the functional problems arising from the initiation of business transactions. In other words, the making of business contracts should be viewed by the law as involving not only the exchange of factual promises or the tendering of unverbalized acquiescence, but, more realistically, as the commencement of a continuing process of agreement in the broader, more familiar sense.

That he still had this in mind when he fashioned the Code cannot be doubted when the introductory article itself is consulted. . . . The 1962 definition provides:

> (3) "Agreement" means the bargain of the parties in fact as found in their language or by implication from other circumstances including course of dealing or usage of trade or course of performance. . . . (section 1–201 (3))

There is the implication that under the original [1949] definition of agreement a contract obligation could be founded upon: 1) language of the parties, or 2) course

of dealing, or 3) usage of trade, or 4) course of performance, or 5) other circumstances; but that the 1962 definition eliminates the fifth basis and through phraseological rearrangement creates a series of possibilities for contract obligations arising from:

1) language of the parties, or
2) other circumstances provided in the act, including [but not limited to?]
  a) course of dealing, or
  b) usage of trade, or
  c) course of performance.

This does not seem to modify the basic meaning of the original 1949 language. Even more importantly, this key definition substantially reflects Llewellyn's meaning of obligation-based-on-transaction and manifests his deliberate intention to effect the precise alterations in the contract construct he urged in 1939.

This point can be traced still further in the Code. Both the 1949 and the current versions of the Code irrevocably structure the agreement-in-fact idea into the law of sales contracts by providing in section 2-204 that "a contract for sale of goods may be made in any manner sufficient to show agreement," including conduct by the parties recognizing the existence of a contract. The secured transactions article provides that "a security interest cannot attach until there is agreement," citing specifically to the agreement definition of Article 1. This same "agreement" definition also is imported into the letters of credit article where the issuer's obligation to its customer is set forth in section 5-109. . . . [T]he more illuminating aspect of this section appears in comment 1, which states:

> The extent of the issuer's obligation to its customer is based upon the agreement between the two. Like all agreements within the Code that agreement is the bargain of the parties in fact as defined in Section 1-201 (3) . . . and includes the obligation of good faith imposed by Section 1-203 and the observance of any course of dealing or usage of trade made applicable by Section 1-205.

A forward reference to Part IV of this essay serves to emphasize the essential unity of Llewellyn's thought as manifested in the Code, for in the Code section quoted above the two baselines of Agreement and Commercial Good Faith are explicitly linked.

These examples not only echo the theme of section 1-201(3) that a broader jurisprudential base than promise has been laid for the law of sales, letters of credit, and secured transactions; but a more noticeable and more important fact is that the seeming multitude of changes in particular traditional rules of contract law gain new significance by reference to the Code emphasis on obligation-based-on-agreement-in fact. Viewed in the polarized light of Llewellyn's attitudes concerning orthodox contract law, this return by the Code to older and more realistic ideas lends significance to the rule changes which loom forth from the dry-as-dust statutory language of our new commercial law.

III. A Transactional Construct

. . .

The Code takes a fresh start and is framed around our present goods distribution system. This shows up clearly when the two are considered together. . . . That Karl Llewellyn *was* concerned because the orthodox offer-acceptance-consideration construct was predicated on a static, unrealistic conception of 18th century face-to-face commercial exchanges, is manifested in many of his published expressions. The closing stanza of his monumental two-part study of the law of sales warranty in 1937 alludes to the increasing prevalence of the commercial phenomenon of the "continuing transaction" which our law of contract regards in helpless amazement. He noted:

> Consider, for instance, the queer rules which courts indulge, severing *each* contract between two parties from each other contract—*e.g.*, in regard to whether buyer's default on one excuses seller's performance on "*another*." No businessman or credit department could think that way: what they see is "an account" in arrears, on certain "items." The law has, thus far, failed to come close to perception of these standing relations, and has failed to develop tools to pick them up or deal with them.[24]

Attempting to summarize some of the legal aspects of this settled commercial practice, he noted the need for open terms in contracts, a commercial (substantial) performance doctrine in place of the legal (strict) performance standard in sales, a "less-than-full-contract-damage" sanction for binding going-relation arrangements, and frank recognition that what may be "good policy" in goods-distributing relations might be intolerable in labor-relations. Thirty years ago he noted, "that sales law is already being affected by going-relations, of one sort or another, in ways which flout old contract and sales theory."

. . .

But the best evidence of the extent to which the Code is geared to dynamic, flowing, on-going commercial process is the fact that the very warp and woof of the Code itself testifies to the fact. For a point of beginning visualize the general goods distribution process in this country today by means of an ideograph symbolizing the essential economic functions together with the various articles of the Code. . . .

. . .

A similar analysis of the key articles themselves reveals a repetition of functional arrangement based closely upon the settled fact-patterns of commercial practice in the particular field of activity. These key articles cover sales, negotiable instruments, bank collections and secured transactions—articles 2, 3, 4 and 9. Only a sketchy discussion of the respective processes will be reproduced here in an attempt to minimize reader boredom. Yet it should be apparent immediately that upon the whited bones of these frames grow the living sinews of the Code rules. The basic parameter for each Code article is the typical chronological sequence of the particular commercial process involved.

A. *Sales Law*

The *Sales Construct* is a two-party model which embodies the basic sales processes of "contracting," "delivery," "acceptance," "breach" and "remedies." This feature has been elliptically noted by many commentators. Professor Mentschikoff, in her recent discussion of the Code, sketches through the arrangement of the parts in the sales article.[29] We are all familiar with the functional disorganization of the old Uniform Sales Act which was vaguely arranged along contract concept lines. The Code remedies that particular blemish in our commercial law and takes a functionally-oriented approach to do so by proceeding through the typical sales transaction systematically from contracting to performance to lawsuit. This is life.

Wedded to the functional sales construct are major changes relating to legal concepts of "contracting." More than mere rules changes, these alterations signify a clear rejection of the traditional construct and reinforce the shift from promise to agreement.

. . .

[24] Llewellyn, On Warranty of Quality, And Society: II, 37 Colum. L. Rev. 341, 376-77 (1937).

[29] Mentschikoff, Highlights of the Uniform Commercial Code, 27 Mod. L. Rev. 167, 172 (1964).

. . . The comments to [section 2-206] make clear that "any reasonable manner of acceptance is intended to be regarded as available unless the offeror has made quite clear" that it will not, that *either* shipment *or* a promise by the offeree initiates the deal in law, and the *beginning* of performance plus *notice* thereof to the offeror makes the contract. The "Ribbon Matching" law of contract stems directly from the rigorous conceptualism of offer-acceptance, and Orthodoxy has always demanded that both the content and mode of the acceptance correlate one-to-one with the content and mode of the offer. This absurdity has now disappeared from commercial law. Moreover, comment 4 states that under subsection 1 (b) a shipment of nonconforming goods may amount to an acceptance "intended to close the bargain, even though it proves to have been at the same time a breach." One schooled in Orthodoxy cannot imagine how such a thing could happen;[30] but to the functionally-oriented visionary it is all quite simple.

Inexorably eradicating old doctrine root and branch, the Code settles the "battle of the forms" by providing in section 2-207 that express acceptance varying the terms of the offer amounts not to a conceptual counteroffer but instead "operates as an acceptance," unless designated to be conditional upon assent by the offeror, whereupon any such additional terms will normally become a part of merchants' contracts unless the offer specifies otherwise, the additional terms materially alter the contract or express objection to them is promptly given. Comment 2 specifies that "a proposed deal which in commercial understanding has in fact been closed is recognized as a contract."

[Section 2-207 has not been as successful as Professor Mooney evidently expected it to be. Could its failure be due to its not being radical enough? Doesn't the section continue the attempt to find mutual assent in a "battle of the forms" in which neither side ever reads the other's boiler-plate? See the Macaulay articles in Part IA. —ed.]

These two provisions substantially implement the "single approach to business contracting" advocated by Llewellyn in 1939 and wipe out Orthodoxy's great dichotomy in the field of sales contracts.

The hoary old consideration doctrine is treated almost as harshly. Mercantile offers in writing may be irrevocable for ninety days without being "supported" by consideration because the business practice of contracting for goods both needs and utilizes the firm offer in writing identified as such.[32] Llewellyn noted this many years ago. But a more graphic affront to the consideration doctrine is contained in the blunt statement of section 2-209(1) that "an agreement modifying a contract within this article needs no consideration to be binding," and subsection (4) will permit many abortive modification agreements to "operate as a waiver." The comments clearly indicate that a requirement of consideration for such modification agreements would be mere "technicality." Alas, once-mighty legal doctrine is humbled by mere business expediency!

Numerous other specific changes in the Restatement and sales rules are made throughout the body of article 2, some large and some small, but all significant. . . . There are many other contract rule changes in the sales article. Significant ones concern warranty, remedies, and quasi-remedies. Arguably, the "quasi-remedies" represent the substantial performance and less-than-full-contract damage principles Llewellyn cried out for many years ago.

Particular modifications in contract law are apparently miniscule but have enormous significance when viewed in the light of the suggested jurisprudential shift from contract back to (economic) status. Thus the "open terms" provisions of the Code strike at the heart of the orthodox indefiniteness doctrine of ancient vintage by expressly validating contracts which specify neither price, place of delivery, time of delivery nor time of performance. Only the total quantity must be definite although the assortment need not. Section 2-204(3) sets forth basic Code doctrine that such an open-term contract "does not fail for indefiniteness if the parties have intended to make a contract" and some appropriate remedy can be framed, and the comment to that provision notes that it "states the principle as to "open terms" underlying later sections of the article." More to the point, the open price term provision rejects both the orthodox contract rule that "an agreement to agree is unenforcible" and the whole "indefiniteness" doctrine on grounds that ". . . where the dominant intention of the parties [is] to have the deal continue to be binding on both. . ." the contract is valid.[39]

---

[30] "How a nonconforming shipment can be both an acceptance and a breach I cannot imagine." Williston, The Proposed Commercial Code, 63 Harv. L. Rev. 561, 577 (1950).

[32] Uniform Commercial Code § 2-205.
[39] Uniform Commercial Code § 2-305, comment 1.

Functional approach to goods distribution, coupled with both major doctrinal modifications and minor rules changes all compel the conclusion that the sales article alterations are consistent with this conspiracy theory of the Code.

. . .

IV. Courts in League with Commercial Decency

Karl Llewellyn's first thoughts on the problem of implementing a general obligation of good faith in commercial transactions was to restore Lord Mansfield's merchant jury. The virtues of this device were that the triers of fact would themselves be imbued with and have the best understanding of what types of commercial conduct met the prevailing standards of commercial good faith and fair dealing. By means of this device, plus the fortuitous ascendance of strong common law commercial judges, the law merchant first became incorporated into the common law. Such a decision-making mechanism has the added feature of a built-in pipeline straight to the vital source of commercial law, namely, the customs, practices and institutions of the business society. Commercial law could thereby remain current, alive and in contact with the world of commerce. This idea never bore fruit, however, and does not appear in any of the published versions of the Code.

His next approach was to impose the general obligation of good faith performance on every contracting party and define good faith as both "honesty in fact" and "observance of the reasonable commercial standards of any business or trade in which he is engaged." The latter element was excised by the American Bar Association's Section on Corporation, Banking and Business Law by 1952, thereby destroying the unitary concept of good faith performance applicable throughout the Code.[53]

Perhaps in desperation, the present elaborate and fragmented scheme embodying the good faith obligation was re-introduced into the Code piecemeal. That pattern appears as a phrase in the text here, an expanded comment there, and surreptitious cross-referencing back and forth between definitions, substantive provisions and sections addressed primarily to courts. Sadly enough it is problematical whether Llewellyn was able to restore to health the fatally crip-

pled general obligation of good faith and commercial fair dealing.[54] The courts may be able to find one. Spelling out precisely how such an assertion may be established by reference to the Code provisions themselves is a most difficult exercise in Code-dialing. Yet it can be demonstrated to a fair degree of persuasiveness that one more factor evidencing the massive jurisprudential shift by the Code away from traditional contract principles is its emphasis on a commercial good faith ground for judicial decision.

The general theory of contract grew up at Law and not in Equity. Orthodox contract doctrine makes no meaningful differentiation among contracting parties in terms of the roles they play in the economy. Merchants are treated like everyone else. Generally speaking, our law requires courts to enforce contracts as drawn by the parties absent mental incompetence, fraud, deceit, mistake or when something called "public policy" intervenes. In some circumstances the law will decline to enforce a contract for a party who has disqualified himself from receiving the aid of a court of Equity. Little leeway for "interpretation" is provided a court by the offer-acceptance-consideration construct because it places maximum emphasis upon the express or fairly implied-in-fact promises of the parties. Although frequently cited in judicial opinions as makeweight, the notion of good faith and fair dealing is almost never an explicit ground for decision in commercial contracts cases. . . .

. . .

[According to Mooney, the Code revives the Roman Law notion of a general obligation of good faith in performance. —ed.] Thus another one of Karl Llewellyn's legal "base lines" came to be expressly incorporated in the Code. There may be no effective general obligation of good faith in the law of contract, but in the law of commercial contracts there is an obligation of commercial good faith.

The Code concept of commercial good faith is complex, has substance and judicial weight. The "good faith" of family relations can provide little or no guidance in judicial decision-making because the notion is rooted in "good morals" and thus has the legal characteristics of the chancellor's foot. Nor is the Code concept merely the rather cynical "good

[53] Farnsworth, Good Faith Performance and Commercial Reasonableness Under the Uniform, Commercial Code, 30 U. Chi. L. Rev. 666, 673 (1963).

[54] This seems to be generally accepted as the unfortunate truth by both Mentschikoff, supra note 29, and

Farnsworth, supra note 53, and is probably true as far as it goes. The assertion being made herein, however, is not quite the same. Technically speaking no general duty exists—jurisprudentially, good faith is a baseline. [On this question, see the "Summers-Burton Debate" in Part IIIB. —ed.]

faith" of the "layman" which is roughly equated to any-conduct-this-side-of-crime. The Code concept of good faith commercial dealing is inextricably linked with commercial customs and usages and consigned for implementation to the judiciary.

A. Commercial Good Faith Concept

Any fair appraisal of the "good faith" requirements imposed by the Uniform Commercial Code will reveal a significant jurisprudential shift toward obligation-based-on-transactional fair dealing. The Code imposes on every contracting party the general "obligation of good faith in its performance or enforcement," and throughout the Code specific provisions in every article impose an explicit good faith requirement, in several contexts. Professor Farnsworth has stated that "good faith" is mentioned at least fifty times in the 400 sections of the Code. . . . But the sheer number of references does not alone establish that the good faith obligation is "a basic principle running throughout this Act." Nor would mere proof of that assertion thereby establish its juridical significance without further reference to the substantive *content* of the good faith principle including the legal mechanism with which the Code proposes to implement any such vague principle.

The Code definition of "good faith" is "honesty in fact in the conduct or transaction concerned."[57] This is a subjective quality in "good faith purchase" and normally an objective one in "good faith performance."[58] But a more meaningful statement of the commercial good faith *principle* appears in the comment to the section which imposes the general obligation of good faith:

> The principle involved is that in commercial transactions good faith is required in the performance and enforcement of all agreements or duties . . . [and] is further implemented by section 1–205 on course of dealing and usage of trade . . . [and concerning sales,] contracts made by a merchant have incorporated in them the explicit standard not only of honesty in fact (section 1–201), but also of observance by the merchant of reasonable

commercial standards of fair dealing in the trade.[59]

This "principle" is called "central to the entire Code," and together with express reliance on "current course" aspects of commercial activity and "custom, usage and agreement of the parties," hopefully will "give freedom to individual action while preventing surprise and traps for the unwary." The jurisprudential essence of the commercial good faith concept promulgated in the Code is "the linking of the good faith obligation of performance with reasonable commercial standards" which runs throughout the entire Code, although "its formulation . . . [in particular articles] reflects a functional difference in situation."

Five particular types of commercial good faith have been identified in the Code: 1) the general obligation of good faith performance of contracts, 2) mercantile good faith performance, 3) good faith purchase (of goods or paper), 4) good faith enforcement of legal remedies, most often explicitly accompanied by the recurring phrase "commercially reasonable," and, 5) good faith diligence. The most persuasive categorization of these many faces of good faith is that the particular substantive content of a given good faith provision depends upon its functional context. . . .

Technically speaking, it may be impossible for even the most diligent dialer of Code provisions to spell out the precise legalistic path through the trackless forest of text, comments and cross-references whereby one starts with the general obligation of good faith performance, converts into honesty-in-fact plus observance-of-reasonable-commercial-standards-of-fair-dealing-in-the-trade and arrives at automatic construction of the statutory phrase "good faith" to include both criteria. Llewellyn may have failed to restore in effect the original general obligation of good faith excised in 1952, as Professor Farnsworth speculates,[71] but there would seem to be little doubt that he succeeded in several respects. The Code clearly imposes on all Code contracting parties the duty of subjective honesty in fact and obligates sales merchant parties also to observe commercial standards

---

[57] Uniform Commercial Code § 1-201(19).

[58] Farnsworth notes that an objective "good faith" must be intended in the good faith performance aspects of the Code because:

> Would a test based on the individual's actual state of mind with no appeal to common practices make any sense in these cases? Surely the test is not whether one party actually believed that he was acting decently, fairly

or reasonably. Surely he must do more than form an honest judgment. Otherwise no more than knowing and deliberate unfairness, maliciousness, trickery and deceit would be forbidden.

Farnsworth, supra note 53, at 672.

[59] Uniform Commercial Code § 1-203, comment 19.

[71] Farnsworth, supra note 53, at 676-77.

of fair dealing in their trade. In addition, depending upon the particular context, a professional will be explicitly bound by his trade standards of fair dealing or, at the bare minimum, will be subject to trade customs including those relating to fair dealing. This scheme touches most Code parties. Moreover, perhaps the tortuous manual and mental dexterity suggested above is unnecessary because of the Code provisions specifically directed to courts and which set up rules for interpreting all agreements under the Code.

B. *Mechanism for Implementation*

I suppose everyone would agree that whatever else one may pump into the magic phrase "commercial standards of fair dealing," at rock-bottom its content rests on the particular commercial context to which the provision embodying it or its synonym applies. This suggests that courts are to find the precise content of the mercantile good faith standard in the facts of the case and not in the words of the Code.

Specific rules for the guidance of courts interpreting contracts under the Code comes from several points. . . . But the Code does more than admonish in general terms; it provides generally for the superimposition of commercial fair dealing in good faith by means of express statutory language in innumerable sections and comments, and, more importantly, the introductory article which is applicable to the entire Code, provides a mechanism for courts to open the contract and pour into its language the Roman wine of good faith.

. . . Specific citation to section 1-203 [in the comment to section 1-205 (course of dealing and usage of trade)] links up the general obligation of good faith, commercial customs and usages, unconscionable contracts and judicial interpretation of *all* agreements under the Code in what Llewellyn was wont to call an "iron section" because the duty cannot be avoided by contract. (Section 1-102(3)—"the obligations of good faith . . . may not be disclaimed by agreement," and comment 2 cites specifically to section 1−205.)

These all link up and section 1−205 (4) prescribes the rules for judicial interpretation of Code agreements in light of applicable trade custom and usage.
. . .

Combination of these provisions into a meaningful judicial interpretation system culminates in the following grounds for interpretation of commercial agreements under the Code in the order of preference:

1) The express terms; and

2) Course of dealing or usage of trade; or,

3) Course of performance under section 2-208.

Essential to any such determination of meaning is trade custom concerning commercial standards of fair dealing in the parties' vocation or fairly implied by their prior course of dealing. In addition, the court is to take such factors into account where the good faith and commercial fair dealing criteria are explicitly imposed by the particular Code provision applicable to the precise point in controversy.

The syllogism cast at the beginning of this monograph closes smoothly by calling attention to the uncanny parallelism displayed by the judicial interpretation mechanism in section 1-205 and the definition of agreement which marks the substantive beginning of the Code. Agreement is the bargain of the parties in fact manifested by their language or other circumstances "including course of dealing or usage of trade or course of performance" under sections 1-205 and 2-208 (section 1-201(3)). Courts are to give meaning to commercial agreements by reference to the parties' language "and by their action, read and interpreted in light of commercial practices and other surrounding circumstances" (section 1-205, comment 3). This entire operation should be judicially conducted by means of a liberal construction and application of the Code so as to promote the expansion of commercial practices (section 1-101).

One may call this jurisprudential theme whatever he chooses but it seems clear that it is a baseline. It is here called "commercial good faith" to distinguish it from the many different technical kinds of specific and general duties of good faith. Grounding judicial interpretation of commercial agreements on trade custom and usage, including general and special duties of good faith, is a far cry from the emphasis by traditional contract law on "contract" concepts and it permits courts to continue doing what they have been doing all along, namely, seeking meaning from trade custom, without having to manipulate contract concepts in order to reach a reasonable result.

V. The Pedagogigal Values of Bookburning

Our general theory of contract has been mortally wounded by the Uniform Commercial Code. Not killed outright by the blow, its grip on the law is greatly weakened. It will surely suffer most pitiably under the combined effects of the Code and our increasing awareness of the unbridgeable gap between contract theology and the realities of the socio-economic workings of our industrial democracy. Thirty-five years ago Karl Llewellyn gave warning of what was to come when he looked down the years and sounded the trumpet-call for reform in his characteristic legal-romantic prose:

> Marginal cases, Hospital cases, most of our cases well may be. Much doctrine, however sweetly spun, serves chiefly to grow grey with dust against the rafters. Overwhelming is the certainty that any synthesis which is to match with the meaning of the law in Life must expand beyond the futile limits set by present legal theory to include great blocks of what we know as property, and equity, and remedies, to cover as well the most significant parts of business associations, and who knows what besides. Overwhelming is the realization of how far a law still built in the ideology of Adam Smith has been meshed into the new order of mass-production, mass-relationships. Overwhelming in no less measure is the conviction that broad forms of words are chaos, that only in close study of the facts salvation lies.[74]

The Code may not accomplish that in one fell swoop. But it rests at a threshold between old doctrine and new jurisprudence and represents the flower of the legal realist movement in American law. The Code is a "fresh start" in more ways than one.

There is increasing evidence that rotting old contract doctrine has been supporting a law of contract which, at least since the Civil War, has been utterly irrelevant to commercial life in this country. Durkheim's intuitive study of the non-legal elements in business[75] is even now in the process of being validated by empirically based studies of current business contracting practices. Tentative returns from a comprehensive study being conducted by Professor Stewart Macaulay indicate that the business world seldom uses our contract law, fears and distrusts both contract law and lawyers and is unlikely to change in the future.[76] [See Part IA. —ed.]

. . .

. . . How useful is a law of contract to a society whose members refuse to pay any attention to it in making their contracts, who avoid it whenever possible in settling contract disputes and whose conduct is not affected by it in any demonstrable way?

But the greatest disservice of all is re-inculcation by the law schools of each succeeding generation of lawyers and judges. Contracts may well be the jurisprudential Typhoid Mary of the law. Once the law student is exposed to this high art of obfuscation there may be no hope for the patient. . . .

The perspicacious have begun to sense the jurisprudential earthquake, however, and Professor Edward J. Murphy, himself a budding contracts casebook producer, has recently noted the profound impact of Code concepts on such hardy perennials as Williston on Contracts, and has pointed the direction the Dutch Elm Blight of the Code will take through the forest of old contract doctrine.[88] Even more significant is the fact that the Second Restatement of Contracts has capitulated many strategic positions to Karl Llewellyn under the doctrinal pressures generated by the Code. Professor Robert Braucher notes candidly that in the Second Restatement "particular effort has been made to reconcile both black letter and comment . . . with such statutory formulations as the Uniform Commercial Code."[89] He first tacitly acknowledges the impact of the legal realists of the 1930's, especially Karl Llewellyn, upon the Restatement theory of contract, and then notes that the great dichotomy between unilateral and bilateral contract, which Llewellyn castigated so adroitly, has been dropped; and, finally, he lists some areas of doctrinal change attributable to Llewellyn's Code: mutual assent, option contracts, revocability, indefiniteness, and acceptance. All in all, Llewellyn nearly swept the board clean. Yet at a recent workshop on the Uniform Commercial Code an overwhelming number of the contracts and commercial law professors present indicated that commercial law is still be-

---

[74] Llewellyn, What Price Contract?, 40 Yale L.J. 704, 751 (1931).

[75] Durkheim, The Division Of Labor In Society 227 (1964).

[76] Macaulay, Non-Contractual Relations in Business: A Preliminary Study, 1963 Amer. Soc. Rev. 55.

[88] Murphy, reviewing Williston, Contracts (3d ed. 1960), 37 Notre Dame Law. 465 (1962), suggests that the Code may provide a basis for counsel to argue in analogous cases, viz., leases now held invalid because they are an "agreement to agree" and unenforcible under traditional contracts rules, or

employment contracts now too "indefinite" to be enforced. Of these types of situations he notes:

> Will not the Code help force at least a reappraisal of similar decisions? It takes no crystal ball, in my opinion. to foresee a trend toward greater judicial enforcement of many heretofore "vague and indefinite" promises. Similarly, may we not expect the number of so-called "illusory promises" to decline sharply, since the Code imposes a fundamental obligation upon all parties to act in good faith?

[89] Braucher, Offer and Acceptance in the Second Restatement, 74 Yale L.J. 302 (1964).

ing taught from the same old cases in the same old way. Offer-acceptance-consideration and *Slade's* case still rule in the classroom.

A thousand old professorial notes may have to burn and ten thousand pounds of dusty hornbooks may be lost in the conflagration, but a more realistic theory of contract will have to be formulated in order to accommodate this Code. It will not fit into the general theory of contract taught today. Reformation will have to be undertaken if the law schools expect to educate young men who are not technologically unemployable the day they graduate. The Code offers the first and best baseline for that better theory.

So goes *this* contract parable.

D. Third Party Rights, Public Law, and Property Interests Within Contracts

Tony Waters' Use of the Past and Present to Find the Future

Anthony Jon Waters, known to everyone in the legal education world as Tony, is an Englishman who teaches at the University of Maryland School of Law. After undergraduate work in England, Waters was a Bigelow Fellow at the University of Chicago Law School and then took a Master of Laws degree at Yale. In the following article Waters shows a typically English interest in the forms of action at common law, which, though long dead, are said to rule us from the grave. He applies his understanding to provide insights into the 1859 New York case of *Lawrence v. Fox*, which created the third party beneficiary doctrine, and to apply these insights into contemporary problems of who can sue under public welfare contracts between government and entrepreneurs designed to benefit a large class of individuals.

Waters' careful gleaning of the records of the old Buffalo, New York Superior Court led to a colorful explanation of why Lawrence, who appeared to have a perfectly good claim against "one Holly," who admitedly owed him money, instead sued Fox, who had promised "Holly" that he, Fox, would pay Lawrence. The exigencies of the three parties' dealings led the New York Court of Appeals to make a major change in the law of standing to sue on a contractual promise. According to Waters, the court saw Fox's promise to "Holly" as a restitutionary property interest of Lawrence, reachable under the common count for "money had and received."

While early courts, Samuel Williston and the First Restatement limited recovery to "donee" and "creditor" beneficiaries, Arthur Corbin argued for general enforcement of promises made for a third party's benefit, and the Second Restatement, with Corbin's blessing, adopted the term "intended beneficiary," which is arguably a broader scope than the two older categories taken together. Waters, in a section that is summarized in the excerpt, described Corbin's fifty year battle for general enforceability of third party promises, a battle in which Corbin proves to have been rather disingenuous in his arguments.

This is of serious historical interest, but Waters also puts it to use to analyze the most controversial current use of the third party beneficiary doctrine. Governments, both federal and local, often enter into contracts that subsidize a party who promises in return to give some particular benefit to underprivileged members of the public. Sometimes the recipient of the subsidy breaks his promise, but the goverment fails to follow up. May the members of the public sue the recipient as third party beneficiaries? Waters sees the answer in a property analysis of their claim under the contract between the government and the defendant.

Ever since Charles Reich's famous article, *The New Property*, 73 Yale L.J. 733 (1964), it has been common to recognize government entitlements as a form of property. Since the members of the benefited class are intended by the government to be benefited by the promise made in exchange for the government largess, Waters argues that they should be deemed to have a restitutionary or quasi-contractual property interest in the entitlements created by the contract, and should be able to enforce the promise made for their benefit to the government. This article has drawn a great deal of attention because it is interesting on so many different levels. At one level it involves a clear promise made in exchange for clear consideration; the only issue is one of standing to sue, and takes us back to the "privity of contract" involved in *Lawrence v. Fox* in 1859. On a different level, though, Waters' fusion of property, restitution and contract is another example of the breakdown of jurisprudential boundary lines discussed in the excerpts from Gilmore and Linzer in Part I. Waters goes still further by conflating public and private law: these contracts differ from ordinary third party beneficiary contracts by being directly traceable to some form of public welfare legislation, normally a statute that seeks to achieve a socially desired end not by direct government action, but by a subsidy to a private party in return for his promise to benefit those now seeking to enforce his promise to the government.

Not only is the article intellectually exciting, both in its analysis of the currently controversial issue of the government entitlements and in its implications for future problems, it is enormously entertaining, particularly in its reconstruction of what went on that day in 1854 in Mr. Purdy Meritt's, on Washington Street, near the Erie Canal in Buffalo, New York.

Anthony Jon Waters, *The Property In the Promise: A Study of the Third Party Beneficiary Rule*,* 98 Harv. L. Rev. 1109 (1985)

This is a study of one common law rule. From its inception a century and a quarter ago to the present day, the third party beneficiary rule has remained unique to this country. In all other common law countries, no non-party to a contract may enforce it, save by statutory exception to the general rule. In the United States, since the New York Court of Appeals decided *Lawrence v. Fox*[2] in 1859, it has become generally accepted that a third party (one not party to the contract) may enforce a contractual obligation made for his or her benefit.

The detail of *Lawrence v. Fox*, from trial to ultimate disposition, provides an instructive lesson about the way in which abrupt change can occur in the course of reasoning from precedent. The relationship between this abstract process of doctrinal development and its real-life impact becomes the more interesting when one considers that the rule enabling a non-party to enforce an undertaking made for his or her benefit is essentially altruistic: it is concerned with the welfare of someone outside of the act of contracting. By contrast, the mainstream of American

contract law at the time of *Lawrence v. Fox*, and for at least half a century thereafter, was more nearly atomistic, jealously guarding the autonomy of contracting parties by insisting upon "privity of contract" between plaintiff and defendant. The rights of so-called third parties had long been beyond the scope of contractual obligation, the "stranger" to the contract having no obligation under it (no mutuality of obligation), not being a party to it (no privity), and having given nothing in exchange for the right claimed (no consideration moving from him). The rule that enables a "beneficiary" of a contract to enforce its beneficial terms defies the basic structure of traditional, bargain-based contract doctrine.

But the fact of this minor theoretical revolution is less important than its present-day consequence. Third party beneficiary doctrine is the vehicle by which a novel species of common law right has developed as a consequence of the widespread use of funding contracts in the distribution of the benefits of public programs. The heresy inherent in allowing an outsider into the contractual relationship—always as

---

* I dedicate this essay, as befits its subject, to three people: to the late Grant Gilmore, who inspired, advised, and encouraged me in this undertaking; to my father, Montague Waters, Q. C., who taught me most of what I know about the law; and to my mother, Jessica, who endured many of those lessons and oft intervened as the reasonable person.

[2] 20 N.Y. 268 (1859).

a beneficiary laying claim, never as a party bound to perform—has been turned to advantage by many individual plaintiffs in what we might call welfare law. More specifically, the third party beneficiary rule has enabled a number of beneficiaries of public programs to secure their intended benefits by private suit.

A growing recognition of rights to intangibles protected as property under the due process clauses led Charles Reich to write "The New Property," published in 1964.[8] Reich's insight, which was soon absorbed into the mainstream of American legal thought, was that a new and significant species of property right had developed within federal constitutional law. This "property" is created by government for the benefit of certain classes of individuals. It invariably involves governmental "largess" (as Reich termed it), which is manifested in what have come to be called entitlements. Although courts and commentators have generally recognized the existence of such rights, they have raised questions about the propriety of private enforcement. The cases have focused mainly on the notion of an implied private right of action, the idea that a court may "find" a legislative intent to permit an individual to enforce a federal statute in the absence of express language to that effect. Tests have been developed and applied by the federal courts to determine whether or not a private right of action is appropriate and, hence, to be inferred.[9]

The link between the third party beneficiary rule and public law questions about private rights of action is their common concern with an individual's access to some beneficial interest in the thing, be it a statute or a contract. Indeed, for many years the first test applied in determining whether a court should infer a private right of action from a statute was whether the plaintiff was a member of the class that the legislature intended to benefit—essentially the same test that courts apply in determining whether a

plaintiff is an "intended beneficiary" under the Second Restatement of Contracts.[10] In both instances, the status of a particular person or group of people in relation to the intended benefit of the statute, or contract, is central. Where a sizeable group of people is involved, as is now commonly the case, the consequences of recognizing third party rights to enforce a federal funding contract can be far-reaching, particularly if the same court holds that those people have no "private right" to enforce the statute that precipitated, authorized, and informed the funding contract.

An analysis of cases involving both types of claim—on the statute and on the contract—occupies the third and final Part of this essay. It demonstrates that the third party beneficiary's right is more accurately described and better understood as a restitutionary right to intangible property than as a contract right, at least in this group of cases, and arguably in all cases. Moreover, in these terms, the third party rule is true to its own heritage (which is the subject of the earlier parts of this essay) in emerging as a means of vindicating essentially proprietary claims; this heritage suggests principles of decision significantly different from those now applied in cases of this kind.

This study begins with an examination of *Lawrence v. Fox*, the case that gave us the initial formulation of the third party beneficiary rule. Part I spans the years from 1854, the date of the transaction upon which Lawrence based his claim, to 1859, the year the New York Court of Appeals, in a plurality opinion, upheld Lawrence's right to enforce Fox's promise which, though not made to Lawrence, nor to his agent, nor in his presence, was made for his benefit. This detailed history of the case shows how the third party rule came into being, the product of a merger of two distinct theories of recovery. An action on the promise (contract) was merged with a proprietary action that depended on the fiction of "a promise im-

---

[8] Reich, The New Property, 73 Yale L.J. 733 (1964) [hereinafter cited as Reich, New Property]; see also Reich, Individual Rights and Social Welfare. The Emerging Legal Issues, 74 Yale L.J. 1245 (1965) [hereinafter cited as Reich, Individual Rights] (arguing that it was time for lawyers to get involved in the protection and clarification of the legal rights of beneficiaries of social welfare programs).

[9] In J.I. Case Co. v. Borak, 377 U.S. 426 (1964), and Cort v. Ash, 422 U.S. 66 (1975), the Supreme Court encouraged lower federal courts to infer private rights of action within relatively broad limits. But in more recent years, the Supreme Court has increasingly restricted the availability of private rights of action where none is expressly provided by

the statute. See sources cited infra note 286. The restriction seems to have induced plaintiffs' attorneys to resort to the alternative third party beneficiary action with much greater frequency in the past two or three years than ever before.

[10] In third party beneficiary actions, the intent of the promisee "to give the beneficiary the benefit of the promised performance," Restatement (Second) Of Contracts § 302 (1979), is the counterpart of the intent of a legislature, as used in determining whether a plaintiff who claims a private right of action is "one of the class for whose *especial* benefit the statute was enacted," see Cort v. Ash, 422 U.S. 66, 78 (1975) (quoting Texas & P.R.R. v. Rigsby, 241 U.S. 33, 39 (1916)) (emphasis added).

plied by law" (quasi-contract). Whether it was advocate's ingenuity, judicial inventiveness, or pure chance that contributed most to the rule's creation is a question incapable of tidy resolution, but this study of the seminal case does resolve the long-standing mystery of how third party contract rights came into being.

The second Part of this Article deals impressionistically with the question of how this new rule, quite at odds with received wisdom, became all but universally accepted in American jurisdictions, state and federal. This inquiry centers on some remarkable clues found in the work of Arthur Corbin, Professor of Law at Yale Law School, author of six articles on the subject of third party contract rights, and highly influential in the formulation of both Restatements of Contracts. Between the years 1918 and 1930, Corbin managed nothing less than a campaign on behalf of the third party beneficiary rule, singling out for a special brand of jurisprudential hounding those jurisdictions that denied or tightly limited third party recovery and basing much of his work on flagrant misrepresentation of the law of those states. It is an extraordinary story of how one well-placed academic influenced the development of the common law, and it provides a chronological link between the case study in Part I and the discussion in Part III of how and why the doctrine has become so important today.

I. The Great Case of *Lawrence v. Fox*, 1854—1859

A. *Background*

As one might have guessed about an idea so plainly at odds with the received wisdom of its time, the rule of *Lawrence v. Fox* is the product of a freakish combination of events. The facts of the case, the rules of pleading, and the substantive law were each in doubt or in flux, and each was resolved in such a way as to make possible the birth of the third party beneficiary rule. In order to appreciate how and why these elements combined as they did, it is necessary to delve in some depth into the history of the action "for money had and received for and to the use of the plaintiff," for it was in that form that Lawrence's action against Fox was brought.[11]

1. *The Common Counts.* —[The action for money had and received was one of the "common counts,"

forms of action that had become standardized over the centuries. It was a form of "indebitatus assumpsit" ("being indebted, he promised"), which had in turn evolved to avoid the procedural difficulties of the old action for debt. Originally, it had been necessary in indebitatus assumpsit to prove both an underlying debt and a subsequent promise to repay it, but at the turn of the seventeenth century, *Slade's Case* turned the promise into a fiction, and left the plaintiff to prove only that he had a proprietary right to something being withheld by the defendant. This is said to be the beginning of quasi-contract and promises implied by law.

[By the time of *Lawrence v. Fox*, the action for money had and received had become a residual category for situations that didn't fit into other forms of action, but the New York courts strictly observed its proprietary limitations, giving relief only if they could describe the defendant as a trustee for the true owner-plaintiff. —ed.]

Thus, in a case in which the plaintiff could establish ownership of money being held by the defendant, a promise "implied by law"—a pure fiction—was employed to permit recovery of plaintiff's property. But where the plaintiff's claim was instead founded on a promise by the defendant, then the action, being an action "on the promise," could be maintained only if the plaintiff had complied with the requisites of contractual liability; if the plaintiff was not a party to the promise (no privity), his action would fail.

The two theories of recovery were conceptually distinct and did not overlap. Indeed, a "no-man's land" lay between them. For example, if it could be shown that in the plaintiff's absence someone had lent money to the defendant, who promised to discharge that (promissory) obligation by making payment to the plaintiff, then the plaintiff's cause fell squarely within the unclaimed legal territory that lay between an action on the promise and an action for money had and received. An action on the promise would fail, most obviously for want of privity, and an action for money had and received would not lie because the defendant had no property belonging to the plaintiff: he was not a trustee, but a borrower. *Lawrence v. Fox* involved just such a situation. The case thus presented two appellate courts with the task of

---

[11] See Record at 1, Lawrence v. Fox, 20 N.Y. 268 (1859) (copy available at Harvard Law School Library) [hereinafter cited as Record] (reprinting complaint).

The original Record, which includes the bill of exceptions, and the briefs submitted to the Court of Appeals were in the Law Library of the State University of New York at

Buffalo in 1978, when I copied them there. The documents were apparently misplaced or discarded during a subsequent reorganization and clearing out of the library's collections; the Library of the Eighth Judicial District of New York, in Buffalo, N.Y., to which the documents were reputedly sent, disclaims any knowledge of them.

explaining Lawrence's right to recover so as to prevent his cause from failing—which, given the facts of the case, would have been manifestly unfair.

2. *The Field Code.*—To understand the solution that emerged, we must take account of one other circumstance. *Lawrence v. Fox* was litigated in the immediate aftermath of the Field codification. In 1856, New York pleading rules were in a state of flux, creating particular uncertainty, where the Code changed rather than consolidated prior law.

Codification wrought two changes in the law of pleading that bear directly on *Lawrence v. Fox*, one specific, the other general. Specifically, the Field Code abolished the common counts, of which the action for money had and received was one. More generally, the Code shifted the emphasis from form to substance, from the law to the facts. No longer was it fatal for the plaintiff to select the wrong legal form; he had only to persuade the court that he had a cause.

The potential for creating new theories of liability was inherent in this development, and in *Lawrence v. Fox* that potential was realized. The courts were no longer bound to a single theory of recovery, and this flexibility permitted them to meld a proprietary interest—resembling a beneficiary's interest in a trust—with a promissory interest—resembling the right of a party to a contract. Lawrence was neither the beneficiary of a trust of which Fox was trustee, nor a party to the contract being sued upon. But thanks to the Field Code, a smart lawyer, and several sympathetic judges, he became the first third party beneficiary.

B. *The Trial*

The facts of *Lawrence v. Fox*, as recounted by the New York Court of Appeals, are these: One Holly, declaring that he owed Lawrence three hundred dollars, lent that amount to Fox, who promised Holly that he would repay it to Lawrence the next day. Fox did not pay, and Lawrence sued him. Lawrence prevailed at trial, on appeal, and, finally, in the New York Court of Appeals. What the Court of Appeals called the "principle of law" of the case is "that [when] a promise [is] made to one for the benefit of another, he for whose benefit it is made may bring an action for its breach." The mystery of *Lawrence v. Fox* is why

Lawrence chose the tortuous route of suing Fox, with whom he had not dealt, rather than sue Holly, who was, it appears, his debtor.

1. *Suing the Debtor's Debtor.*—From the records of the case, we learn that "Holly" was in fact one Hawley, referred to in the complaint as Samuel Hawley. The Buffalo census of 1855 lists no Samuel Hawley, but of the eighteen Hawleys who are listed, only one appears to have had sufficient means to have been involved in a three hundred dollar cash transaction. He was Merwin Spencer Hawley, a prominent merchant.

In 1854, when the transaction took place, three hundred dollars was a very large amount of money.[45] Even among successful entrepreneurs, a loan the size of Hawley's to Fox, to be repaid a day later, must have been out of the ordinary. At trial in the Superior Court in Buffalo, Fox's attorney, Jared Torrance, shed some light on the nature of that transaction. The only witness in the case was William Riley, by whom Lawrence's attorney, Edward Chapin, had proved that Hawley paid three hundred dollars to Fox; that Hawley told Fox that he, Hawley, owed that amount to Lawrence; and that Fox promised Hawley that he would repay that amount to Lawrence. On cross-examination, Torrance elicited four facts: that Lawrence was not present when Hawley made the loan to Fox; that the deal took place at Mr. Purdy Merritt's on Washington Street; that there were "two or three persons present . . . doing nothing but standing near them"; and that Hawley counted out the money as he handed it to Fox.

The first fact, that Lawrence was not present, formed the basis of Fox's privity defense. This defense makes sense only in an action based on contract, a point to which we shall return. For now, it is the other three facts—the location, the bystanders, and the cash being counted out—that are noteworthy, for they suggest the milieu in which the transaction took place, and help to explain its character.

William Riley, the witness, was a horse dealer. He did his business near the canal, the life line of Buffalo's then-thriving commerce. Not many steps away was Mr. Purdy Merritt's establishment, where the transaction took place; Merritt was also a horse dealer. Torrance's cross-examination presented a more complete picture: two well-to-do merchants in a

---

[45] Grover Cleveland wrote to his sister that he was to be paid a salary of $500 in 1858, his third year with a Buffalo law firm. See A. Nevins, Grover Cleveland 40, 43 (1932). The average annual income per worker in New York State in 1840 has been estimated at between $238 and $288, the higher figure including wages of workers engaged in commerce.

horse dealer's establishment down by the canal; a large amount of cash changing hands; and several other people present, loitering. Of these facts, not the least significant was the location:

> Canal Street was more than a street. It was the name of a district, a small and sinful neighborhood . . . . As late as the 1800's, there were ninety-three saloons there, among which were sprinkled fifteen other dives known as concert halls plus sundry establishments designed to separate the sucker from his money as swiftly as possible, painlessly by preference, but painfully if necessary . . . . It must have been an eternal mystery to the clergy and the good people of the town why the Lord never wiped out this nineteenth century example of Sodom and Gamorrah with a storm or a great wave from Lake Erie.[53]

In his cross-examination of Riley, Attorney Torrance had gone as far as he could go to set the scene for what he then sought to prove directly, also by William Riley: that Hawley lent the money to Fox for Fox to gamble with it, and that this unlawful purpose was known to Hawley.

Trial Judge Joseph Masten did not, however, permit Riley to testify to the alleged link with gambling. Attorney Chapin, for Lawrence, successfully objected on two grounds, neither of which bears upon the probable truth or untruth of the evidence that Riley was prepared to give. As to that question, the facts that Torrance had already elicited do suggest a setting in which gambling could have been taking place. But there is one more fact, this one uncontroverted, that is entirely consistent with the allegation of a connection with gambling and is difficult to explain otherwise. That fact—the central mystery of this case—is that Lawrence chose to sue not his debtor, Hawley, but his debtor's debtor, Fox. If, as seems to be the fact, Hawley was a person of considerable wealth in Buffalo, and if, as alleged, he owed three hundred dollars to Lawrence, then Lawrence must have had compelling reason to neglect the obvious action—suing Hawley—in favor of the much more difficult task of seeking recovery from Fox. A gambling debt would have presented just such a reason. If Hawley's debt to Lawrence from the day before, in the round sum of three hundred dollars, was itself the outcome of gambling and thus unenforceable at law,

Lawrence was well advised to look for someone other than Hawley to sue. Furthermore, if we look to the law of gamblers rather than the law of commerce, it is clear that Fox, and not Hawley, was both the villain and the obvious person to pursue.

Commercial transactions were not then and are not now structured in such a way as to leave a creditor with no better means of recovery than to sue his debtor's debtor.[59] The series of events described in *Lawrence v. Fox* makes no commercial sense. Had Hawley's dealings with Fox conformed to the norms of commercial behavior, Hawley would have requested a negotiable instrument either made out to Lawrence, or to be endorsed in his favor, in return for his loan to Fox. And had Lawrence's dealings with Hawley been of a kind condoned and upheld by the law of the land, then Lawrence would surely have sued Hawley, and not Fox. It is not surprising, therefore, that there was no theory of recovery in the law of contract by which Lawrence could collect from Fox.

Had William Riley's further evidence been admitted, and not controverted, Torrance, for Fox, would presumably have argued that the indirect link with gambling tainted Hawley's loan to Fox so as to make it unrecoverable, there being New York case law to support that position. Chapin, for Lawrence, would have argued the opposite—that the loan itself was distinct from, and not tainted by, the borrower's purpose in borrowing, even if known to the lender.

But Judge Masten did not admit the evidence. Chapin successfully raised two objections, each sustained, so the question was avoided altogether. Although the allegation of taint played no direct role at trial, this reconstruction of the case strongly suggests that some taint affecting Hawley's debt to Lawrence played a decisive part in the formulation of the "rule of *Lawrence v. Fox*" on appeal. To understand how that is so, we must consider the task that initially confronted Chapin.

[Chapin needed a cause of action that minimized the facts of the dealings among Lawrence, Fox and Hawley. Prior to the trial Chapin avoided characterizing the transfer of funds from Hawley to Fox as a loan, because traditionally a loan could not be recovered by the common count of money had and received. After winning the trial he abandoned this

---

[53] L. Graham, Niagara Country 205-06 (1949).

[59] Cf King of Spain v. Oliver, 14 F. Cas. 572, 577 (C.C.D. Pa. 1816) (No. 7813) ("[T]here is no principle in law, which will sanction an action by the creditor, against the debtor of his debtor, upon the ground of contract; for this plain reason, that there is no privity between them.").

strategy, perhaps because the Field Code made the issue less critical. The effect was to present the appellate courts with the opportunity to treat the matter as an amalgam between a property claim by Lawrence for the money in Fox's possession and one based on Fox's promise to Hawley that he would pay it to Lawrence —ed.].

C. On Appeal to the General Term, in Buffalo

[Though it seems anomalous to our modern eyes, the trial judge, Judge Masten, also sat in the General Term, the intermediate appellate court, and wrote the opinion upholding his ruling for Lawrence in the trial court. —ed.]

It would have been easy to afford Lawrence recovery of the money if Fox had been, in effect, a trustee; and it would then have made sense to conclude that what Hawley said about owing that amount to Lawrence, when he delivered the money to Fox, was a part of Lawrence's action because it established, or helped to establish, that the money belonged to Lawrence. But once it was established that Fox borrowed the money, no claim based on that idea—a constructive trust—could lie. Judge Masten retained the analytic framework of an action for money had and received, while acknowledging that Hawley's delivery was a loan.

The consequence was the creation of a kind of "property in the promise," a right that resembles a right to fungible property (money), but which is in fact a right to a sum certain arising out of the defendant's promissory obligation. Judge Masten's retaining a had-and-received approach—forced on him, perhaps, by the posture of Torrance's appeal—to what we now call an action on the promise resulted in an obviously hybrid formulation, as is suggested by the concluding paragraph of his opinion:

> The consideration of the defendant's promise was the loan of money by [Hawley] to him, and having made the promise to pay the money to the plaintiff upon a good consideration, there was enough in the case to throw the burthen upon him of showing that the plaintiff had no interest in the promise.

This language is, in the main, the language of an action on the promise. But in concluding that the defendant had the burden of showing that the plaintiff "had no interest in the promise" (proprietary lan-

guage), Judge Masten departed markedly from the law of contract and articulated the idea of a property interest arising from a promise. It would be for the New York Court of Appeals, through Judge Gray, to refine this new hybrid, while declaring in ringing terms that there was nothing new about it.

D. In the Court of Appeals, Albany

In the New York Court of Appeals, Lawrence v. Fox generated three judicial opinions. Two of them, however awkwardly, upheld Lawrence's recovery, and the third, a vigorous dissent, deplored the court's great departure from prior law.

Judge Gray, for a plurality of the court, wrote the opinion that was to become a blueprint for the law of creditor beneficiaries. He overcame the central legal obstacle—that Lawrence was neither a party to the contract, nor the owner of funds being held by Fox—by holding that because of the debtor-creditor relationship between Hawley and Lawrence, Lawrence had the right to enforce Fox's promise. Authority for that proposition was, to say the least, meager, compelling Judge Gray (much assisted by Chapin's brief) to work assiduously with bits and pieces of disparate cases to uphold Lawrence's recovery below. He concluded: "[I]f . . . it could be shown that a more strict and technically accurate application of the rules applied, would lead to a different result (which I by no means concede), the effort should not be made in the face of manifest justice."

Torrance, for Fox, argued three grounds of appeal, one of which was the hearsay objection dealt with by Judge Masten below. The hearsay question in Lawrence v. Fox was strategically positioned between two rather different notions of Lawrence's cause of action. Had the Court of Appeals held that Lawrence actually had to prove Hawley's debt, then we could say that Lawrence's right to enforce Fox's promise was derived in part from Hawley's debt to him. In contrast, if the court had held that no proof of that debt was called for, then Lawrence's right would seem to arise entirely out of Fox's transaction with Hawley and, thus, would not in any sense be derived from Hawley's debt to Lawrence.[104] The vehicle for deciding in legal terms whether Lawrence's claim against Fox did or did not derive from Hawley's debt, was the hearsay question. Judge Gray fashioned a middle road, and so left a central uncertainty that

---

[104] This distinction corresponds in part to the distinction between an action for money had and received and an action on the promise. . . .

remained with the creditor beneficiary rule until the American Law Institute abandoned that classification in 1967.

The hearsay objection raised two questions: did Lawrence need to prove the debt and, if so, was Riley's testimony sufficient proof? Judge Gray responded to those two questions thus: "All the defendant had the right to demand in this case was evidence which, as between [Hawley] and the plaintiff, was competent to establish the relation between them of debtor and creditor. For that purpose the evidence was clearly competent . . . ."

The implicit distinction between proving the debt and proving "the relation between them of debtor and creditor" was later to cause a good deal of confusion in the case law. . . .

If our earlier reconstruction of events is essentially accurate—specifically, if Hawley's debt to Lawrence was unenforceable because it was a gambling debt—then the Delphic distinction between proving the debt and proving the debtor-creditor relationship may represent the ultimate expression of Chapin's triumph, for it enabled Judge Gray to walk the very tightrope that Chapin walked when he drafted the complaint and when he proved his case. The complaint alleged that Hawley was indebted to Lawrence; the evidence adduced in support tended to show only that Hawley said he owed three hundred dollars to Lawrence when he made arrangements with Fox for Fox to pay Lawrence. This stopped short of proving the debt itself; but it did tend to prove "the relation between them of debtor and creditor." The relationship explained why Hawley procured Fox's promise to pay Lawrence, and it established the equity of the claim.

In summary, we can see that Judge Gray's hitherto mysterious statement of what the plaintiff had to prove is intelligible as the product of a chain of events. First—we assume—Lawrence's claim against Hawley was unenforceable; second, in drafting Lawrence's claim against Fox, Chapin alleged that Hawley was indebted to Lawrence; third, in proving his case, Chapin stopped short of proving the debt, but did prove that the alleged debtor, Hawley, admitted the debt and made arrangements with Fox to have it paid off; fourth, Torrance, for Fox, challenged Riley's testimony as hearsay; and fifth, Judge Gray ruled that Riley's evidence was not inadmissible hearsay to prove "the relation between [Hawley and Lawrence] of debtor and creditor." Making the most of the evidence available, Judge Gray held that the combina-

tion of Lawrence's allegation, Hawley's conduct, and Fox's promise sufficed for Lawrence to enforce that promise, at least "in the face of manifest justice." And this is the origin of the very curious fact that the creditor beneficiary did not actually have to be a creditor.

Torrance, for Fox, preserved two further grounds of appeal: that Fox's agreement with Hawley was void for want of consideration moving between the parties, and that Lawrence could not enforce Fox's promise because he was not a party to the contract Lurking behind both arguments was the fact that Fox had borrowed the money, which, in Torrance's view, rendered inapplicable the cases that had employed proprietary concepts to permit a "third party" to recover. In other words, the fact that Fox was a borrower rather than a trustee rendered his obligation promissory. Want of consideration moving from the plaintiff, and lack of privity, Torrance argued, were each sufficient to prevent Lawrence from enforcing Fox's promise.

Judge Gray took a different view of things. In response to Torrance's consideration argument, he relied on *Farley v. Cleveland* and two later cases that reaffirmed it. In *Farley*, one Moon owed a certain quantity of hay to Farley, a debt evidenced by Moon's note. Moon sold that amount of hay to Cleveland in Farley's presence, the buyer agreeing to pay Farley the value of the hay, and Farley assenting to the arrangement. Cleveland did not pay, and Farley sued him. . . .

. . .

Farley v. Cleveland was, among other things, an instance of consideration (the hay) apparently moving from someone other than the plaintiff, and for this reason it enabled Judge Gray to refute Torrance's "want of consideration" argument. But the damage done to Fox's case by the introduction of *Farley* extended beyond the single issue of consideration, for the case appeared to sanction third party enforcement of a promise. On closer inspection, we see that it involved enforcement by one of two promisees, and not enforcement by a non-party. The case did not support the kind of action that Lawrence brought against Fox, but it did serve Judge Gray's purpose by giving the general impression of sanctioning third party enforcement of a promise.

Judge Gray's discussion of consideration does not address the question of privity, Fox's remaining ground of appeal. Torrance's argument was that Lawrence, unlike Farley, was not a party to the contract and therefore could not enforce Fox's promise. In disposing of this argument, while conceding that Lawrence was not in privity, Judge Gray relied on cases dependent on some kind of trust, real or constructive. Torrance had pointed out that these were proprietary claims that depended on a principle peculiar to the law of trusts, and that Fox was no trustee. But Judge Gray had the last word:

> [C]oncede them all to have been cases of trusts, and it proves nothing against the application of the rule to this case. . . . The principle illustrated . . . has been applied to trust cases, not because it was exclusively applicable to those cases, but because it was a principle of law, and as such applicable to those cases.

In that sweeping statement, Judge Gray threw open a door that had been ever closed, the door that now admitted a stranger into the hallowed chamber of contract enforcement.

This bold response was thought necessary to upholding Lawrence's recovery only because Hawley's delivery of money to Fox was a loan, the critical fact that had been added by hand to the bill of exceptions. In support of his decision, Judge Gray reached for cases that were decided unambiguously in terms of a trust, a fact that he seemed to concede. That is, he used a proprietary explanation for upholding Lawrence's action on the promise, and so consolidated the merger of property with promise that began when someone took a pen to the bill of exceptions back in 1857, and was furthered by Judge Masten's awkward, hybrid explanation at General Term. In so doing, Judge Gray introduced a brand new rule into the legal world in order to explain Lawrence's recovery from Fox.

E. Consequences

The hybrid origins of the action that emerged from *Lawrence v. Fox* have long been masked by its formulation as an action on the promise.[126] Yet in its modern application, the third party beneficiary rule bears as much resemblance to a proprietary claim as to a conventional contract action. In both respects—its formulation and its application—the present-day doctrine is faithful to the case from which it is derived, and it is as imprecisely classified as was Lawrence's claim against Fox.

So long as the object of the suit remained a bag of coins or a bundle of bills, it did not much matter whether the plaintiff's right was thought about as a right to the property, being money, or as a right to enforce the defendant's promise to pay. But when the object of such suits is broadened to include the benefit of all promises of which the plaintiff is "an intended beneficiary,"[128] the transformation from an essentially proprietary claim (had and received), to an action on the promise, matters very much. If the courts had persisted in looking for trust property, had-and-received style, before upholding the third party's claim, the third party beneficiary rule would never have attained its present importance, specifically in relation to the benefits of public programs.[129]

It is one of the ironies of this story that the broadly equitable third party beneficiary rule, which today enables the beneficiaries of government programs, among others, to secure their intended benefits, grew out of what were apparently gambling-related transactions that took place in Purdy Merritt's establishment down by the canal, in Buffalo, in 1854. Twenty years later a eulogist wrote of Arthur W. Fox:

> There are not many men in Buffalo whose death would be more deeply regretted . . . . Possessing remarkable business enterprise and ability, he was also a man of strict and rigid integrity, always fulfilling in letter and spirit any engagement or undertaking into which he entered. Of him it might with literal truth be said, "his word is as good as his bond."

[Waters provides a necrology of the main players in the case. Chapin, Lawrence's attorney, died a hero's death in the Civil War; Fox was killed in 1874 when his buggy was hit by a train; Hawley died peacefully in his eightieth year in 1887; Judge Masten died of an apoplectic seizure in 1871; and defense

---

[126] Street observes:

[F]rom Slade's Case until this good day there has been more or less confusion in the minds of legal thinkers between the conceptions of contractual duty imposed by law [quasi-contract] and the conception of the obligation of promise . . . . Men have talked about the implied promise, which is nominally the foundation of the action of indebitatus assumpsit, until they have actually come to think that the same concep-

tion of liability is here presented to view as in the ordinary engagement by actual promise.

This very confusion made Lawrence v. Fox possible. And by permitting Lawrence to sue upon Fox's promise to Hawley, the court advanced the confusion to the stage of conflation.

[128] See Restatement (Second) of Contracts § 302(1) (1979).

[129] This application of the modern third party beneficiary rule is discussed in Part III.

counsel Torrance of consumption in 1872. Lawrence, who started the whole thing, "was never found." Those who enjoy a good obituary will want to consult the full article.

[In the twenty-five page Part II, entitled "The Corbin Connection, 1918-1967," Waters explores the role of Arthur Corbin in proselytizing for acceptance of a general right of recovery for third party beneficiaries. According to Waters, Williston saw third party recovery as an anomaly that was sometimes justified by the equities of the case, while Corbin, by contrast, "pushed for the recognition of third party enforcement as the general rule rather than the exception." Corbin wrote six law review articles between 1918 and 1930 in which he explored different aspects of the case law on third party beneficiaries, and attempted to show that cases denying recovery were not only wrong, but out of the main stream of their jurisdiction's legal thought. Waters finds Corbin less than ingenious in his scholarship. He examines in detail Corbin's article on Pennsylvania's case law, and concludes:

> Thus, Corbin "clarified" Pennsylvania law by pummeling it into submission. He simply ignored the grounds of decision articulated by the courts, rejected the notion that these cases were exceptional, and concluded that the cases supported a general rule that favored third party suits. But the importance of his Pennsylvania article lies not so much in his method as in his achievement. What Corbin did by lumping all third party recoveries together was to merge property and promise, just as the New York Court of Appeals, in 1859, had merged the action for money had and received with an action on the promise. The cases from which he drew his general rule were not as clearly founded on property notions as was the action for money had and received, but they were property-based in a broad sense, and his merger-by-generalization was essentially the same as the seminal merger in *Lawrence v. Fox*.

[While Corbin supported the First Restatement's general acceptance of the third party beneficiary doctrine, he did not favor its limitation of the concept to "donee" and "creditor" beneficiaries. In fact, he had indicated as early as 1918 that the test should be whether the contracting parties intended to create a right in a third party. He repeated this in his treatise in 1951. In 1959, at Corbin's own suggestion, he was invited by the American Law Institute to comment systematically on the First Restatement of Contracts with an eye towards its revision and updating. Corbin corresponded with Judge Robert Braucher, the original Reporter of the Second Restatement, and it appears that he was a great influence on Braucher's decision to scrap the old system of donee and creditor beneficiaries for one category of "intended" beneficiaries. We may now return to Professor Waters. — ed.]

The substitution of the "intended beneficiary" formulation for the "donee" and "creditor" categories, whatever the reasons and influences behind that change, had far-reaching, unforeseen consequences for the development of the third party beneficiary rule. Since the passage of the 1964 Civil Rights Act, federal funding of public programs has frequently been conditioned on the recipient's complying with one or another federal statute. Invariably, the statute defines the class intended to be benefited by the program, so that where a funding contract calls for compliance with the statute, the class of intended beneficiaries of the contract is clearly defined. Those who are intended beneficiaries of the statute would seem to be intended beneficiaries of the contract as well, irrespective of whether they have a right to enforce the statute directly. A moment's thought suggests that plaintiffs of this kind, who are typically beneficiaries of public programs (such as Medicaid) or members of minority groups intended to be protected by anti-discrimination statutes, are neither donees nor creditors of the promisee, the federal government. We cannot say that one or the other of those categories would not have been made to accommodate beneficiaries of federal funding contracts, but we can say that the substitution of the "intended beneficiary" for the "donee" and "creditor" classifications rendered the third party beneficiary rule obviously suitable for this application, which it was not before.

Arthur Linton Corbin had more influence on the sustained development of this rule than anyone else before him or since. It was at least an abiding interest, perhaps an obsession, throughout the latter half of his life. As we have seen, his scholarship in this area was meticulous, if not always accurate. Evidently, for him, the end justified the means, and that end was formally accomplished when the American Law Institute gave its blessing to the "intended beneficiary" formulation. When Corbin died in 1967, that ultimate victory was within sight, his extraordinary campaign at an end.

III. The Property In The Promise, 1964 To The Present

This final part of the essay chronicles the evolution of the third party beneficiary rule into a vehicle for securing the benefits of statutes in general, and of public programs in particular, by private suit. This development, which has taken place over the past twenty years or so, is closely related to the development of judicial tests for determining whether, in the absence of statutory language expressly creating a private right of action, such a right should be "implied" in order to permit a private suit based on breach of the statute.

The so-called implied private right of action has fallen into disfavor in recent years as the Supreme Court has increasingly restricted its use.[286] During these same years, the number of cases in which plaintiffs have raised third party beneficiary claims instead of, or in addition to seeking an implied private right of action, has increased dramatically. This Part focuses on these cases for two reasons: to demonstrate the growing significance of the third party beneficiary rule, and to show that in its application to contracts involving statutory entitlements, the rule that derives from *Lawrence v. Fox* remains remarkably true to its origins in lending itself to the vindication of essentially proprietary rights. The quasi-contractual, restitutionary origins of the rule suggest principles of decision in cases involving public program beneficiaries that differ significantly from the principles applicable to third party beneficiary claims arising out of commercial contracts with the government.

I shall take the year 1964 as the beginning of the modern era of third party beneficiary law. In that year, the American Law Institute produced its first draft of the Second Restatement of Contracts; Congress enacted the Civil Rights Act of 1964;[289] Charles Reich published "The New Property";[290] and the Supreme Court decided *J.I. Case Co. v. Borak*.[291] Each of these events played a part in shaping modern third party beneficiary law, but because the law of implied private rights of action provides the backdrop, I shall

begin with *Borak* and refer to the other events in due course.

A. *Implied Private Rights of Action*

[Although *Borak* permitted a private right of enforcement under the federal securities laws, in 1975, in *Cort v. Ash* the Supreme Court cut back on this right by establishing a "four pronged test" in Professor Waters' words: "(1) whether the plaintiff is a member of the class for whose special benefit Congress enacted the federal statute; (2) whether there is any indication of legislative intent concerning private actions; (3) whether the implication of such a right is consistent with the purposes underlying the legislative scheme; and (4) whether the cause of action is one traditionally relegated to state law." By 1979 the Court was treating the *Cort* factors as merely "relevant" rather than determinative, and held that the Court's task was "solely" to determine whether Congress had intended to create a private right of action—even if it was clear that the plaintiffs were the intended beneficiaries of the statute in question, they might not be allowed to bring a private action on their own behalf. Thus, the second and third prongs of the *Cort* test became dominant if an individual tried to sue directly under a federal entitlement statute. However, the first and fourth prongs of *Cort* fit very nicely into the intended beneficiary approach of the Second Restatement. —ed.]

B. *The Third Party Beneficiary Alternative*

In the years since 1964, more than two hundred federal cases have either involved or discussed both a third party beneficiary claim and a claim to an implied private right of action to enforce a statute. More than half of these cases were decided in the 1980s, and almost one-third of them were decided during the period 1976 to 1979. Thus, of the roughly two hundred cases decided since 1964, about ninety percent post-date 1975, when the Supreme Court decided Cort v. Ash.

Although I claim no precise relationship between the rate at which claimants have been denied implied rights of action and the frequency of third party ben-

[286] See Universities Research Ass'n, Inc. v. Coutu, 450 U.S. 754, 770-84 (1981); Kissinger v. Reporters Comm. for Freedom of the Press, 445 U.S. 136, 148-50 (1980); Transamerica Mortgage Advisors, Inc. v. Lewis, 444 U.S. 11, 19-24 (1979); Touche Ross & Co. v. Redington, 442 U.S. 560, 568-78 (1979); Chrysler Corp. v. Brown, 441 U.S. 281, 290-94 (1979). For a concise discussion of this trend, see Comment,

Implied Private Rights of Action: The Courts Search for Limitations in a Confused Area of the Law, 13 Cum. L. Rev. 569, 577-92 (1983).
[289] Pub. L. No. 88-352, 78 Stat. 241 (codified as amended at 42 U.S.C. §§ 1971, 1975a-1975d, 2000a-2000h (1982)).
[290] Reich, New Property, supra note 8.
[291] 377 U.S. 426 (1964).

eficiary claims, claimants are increasingly using the third party beneficiary rule as an alternative to an implied private right of action claim. Typically, pursuant to a statute, a funding contract binds the recipient of federal funds to play some role in furthering the purpose behind that statute. The requirement may involve affirmative action in hiring handicapped individuals pursuant to the Rehabilitation Act of 1973,[310] or compliance with Medicare regulations intended to protect residents of nursing homes, or admission of black children to desegregated public school systems pursuant to title VI of the Civil Rights Act of 1964. In each of these situations, and many others like them, an individual or a class has used the third party beneficiary rule to claim the benefits of the statutory scheme. In this respect, the action "on the contract" is very similar to the private action "on the statute." Formally, however, the two kinds of action are worlds apart, and claimants have been able to employ the third party beneficiary rule where an action on the statute would have failed.

The two forms of action can have different results because they invoke different tests. A plaintiff who satisfies the first prong of *Cort's* four-part test is, of course, very likely to be an intended beneficiary of any contract in which the promisor agrees to abide by the statute. Because a contract beneficiary need not be concerned with the separate question of a right of action—as are *Cort's* second and third prongs—a third party beneficiary claim is more likely to prevail than an action on the statute. And the fourth *Cort* factor—whether the claim is one traditionally relegated to state law—has led a number of courts to hold that no private right of action should be implied precisely because the plaintiff had a state law claim as a third party beneficiary.

Yet these doctrinal distinctions have not persuaded all courts that the third party beneficiary claim deserves consideration independent of the statutory claim. Indeed, we are now in a period of judicial resistance to this use of the rule; courts are resorting to a variety of devices to turn away the contract claim, without consideration of its merits. . . .

. . .

[Professor Waters devotes nearly 15 pages to close analysis of cases in which state courts and federal

district courts and courts of appeals have used third party beneficiary reasoning in cases in which a contract was required in some way by a federal statute. (He does note, however, that some courts have refused to follow this approach, seeing it as nothing but a formalistic end-run around the Supreme Court's restrictions on private rights of action under federal statutes.) Some of the cases using third party beneficiary contract reasoning involved shareholders' rights under contracts between stock exchanges and the Securities and Exchange Commission in which the exchange agreed to comply with federal securities laws. A different fact situation was involved in *Bossier Parish School Board v. Lemon*, 370 F.2d 847 (5th Cir.), *cert. denied*, 388 U.S. 911 (1967), where children of Air Force personnel were held entitled to go to desegregated schools as beneficiaries of a contract under which the United States gave funding to the local school board, and the Board agreed to admit Air Force children on the same terms as other children in the district. Another case found beneficiary rights in Medicaid patients under a contract by which a nursing home owner agreed with a state to abide by the state's federally-approved plan. Other cases involved rights of tenants in federally subsidized housing. The landlord had failed in some way to comply with federal regulations, to the tenants' detriment. Because the landlord had received a subsidy under a contract with the government, the courts found third party beneficiary rights in the tenants, and standing to recover their loss from the landlord.

[One of the housing cases that Waters discusses is *Zigas v. Superior Court*, 120 Cal. App. 3d 827, 174 Cal. Rptr. 806 (1981), in which the California Court of Appeal held for the tenant-plaintiffs who had been overcharged rent in violation of an agreement between their landlord and the federal government. The court distinguished a 1974 California Supreme Court case, *Martinez v. Socoma Companies*, which had refused to apply a third party beneficiary theory to a similar though not identical case, relying on Section 145 of the First Restatement of Contracts (followed in Section 313 of the Second Restatement), which limited recovery by the general public under government contracts. —ed.]

The rule of section 145, or something like it, is

---

[310] "Any contract in excess of $2,500 entered into by any Federal department or agency . . . shall contain a provision requiring that . . . the party contracting with the United States shall take affirmative action to employ and advance in employment qualified handicapped individuals . . . ." Reha-

bilitation Act of 1973, § 503, 29 U.S.C. § 793 (1982). This section has generated considerable litigation over the twin claims of an implied private right of action to enforce the statute and of intended beneficiary status in relation to the contracts subject to § 503.

needed when a contractor contracts with a governmental entity, because the work to be done—be it repairing a street or building a bridge—is for the benefit of the public. Application of the untrammeled third party beneficiary rule here would permit all members of the public intended to be benefited by the performance of the contract to recover consequential damages from the contractor in the event of breach. Section 145 protects the contractor from that possibility by laying down a rule that no member of the public may sue on contracts with the government unless the contract manifests an intention that the contractor be so liable. In *Zigas*, the remedy sought was a refund of money that had been paid by the plaintiffs to the defendants; the claim did not involve consequential damages, and the plaintiffs were not "members of the public" in the sense in which that phrase is used in section 145. As Judge Feinberg put it [in *Zigas*]: "[T]he money sought is not a consequence of the breach, it is the breach."

Judge Feinberg's awkward sentence harks back to the origin of the third party beneficiary rule, to the distinction between a promissory obligation to pay money and a restitutionary obligation to hand over money being wrongfully held. In these terms, the plaintiffs' claim in Zigas was a restitutionary claim and therefore ought not to have been governed by the rule of section 145, which was designed to deal with claims based on promissory obligations. This analysis suggests that two distinct strands remain in the modern third party beneficiary rule, strands derived from the two bodies of law that were merged in *Lawrence v. Fox*. It is more than sheer coincidence that the claim in *Zigas* would have fit comfortably into the old common count for "money had and received for and to the use of the plaintiff"; that count was routinely used to recover money paid in error, or in excess of the amount owed, by the plaintiff to the defendant. The restitutionary "branch" of the third party rule presents itself in pure form in *Zigas*. Just like the had-and-received action from which it is descended, the third party beneficiary rule is used here to vindicate a kind of proprietary right. As we have come to accept a much broader notion of intangible property

in recent years, so the rule has been brought to bear upon kinds of property that are significantly different from the bag of coins that was usually the focus of the had-and-received actions of old. In *Zigas*, however, the common count would have done the job, and done it more simply. The case illustrates rather well how the old, narrow action inhibits the broad, modern rule.

C. *The Property in the Promise*

Thus far in Part III, we have considered implied private rights of action, the third party beneficiary alternative, and the relationship between them. But we ought not lose sight of the quasi-contractual origins of the "contract law" rule that offers intended beneficiaries this alternative approach. In particular, the equitable property idea on which the action for money had and received was based has much in common with a species of constitutionally protected property that has evolved in recent years.

1. *Public Law and the "New Property."*—During the past twenty years or so, the federal courts have recognized and developed a theory of constitutionally protected property that was first fully articulated by Charles Reich in his influential 1964 article, "The New Property." This "new property" consists of governmentally created rights, typically the right to the tangible and intangible benefits of social welfare programs.[392] Reich argued that such new property rights should be afforded procedural safeguards. Soon thereafter, the Supreme Court embraced the new property concept, according procedural due process protection to certain statutory entitlements.

. . .

Constitutionally protected rights to intangible property, many of which are not "property rights" within the common law meaning of that term, are by now well established. Those that concern us here are the "new property" rights created by the government for the benefit of particular groups—specifically, what have come to be called statutory entitlements. Where such rights are protected as "property," it is the statute that creates the property and the due process clause that protects it.[399] Examples of statu-

---

[392] "Examples are Social Security benefits, unemployment compensation, aid to dependent children, veterans benefits, and the whole scheme of state and local welfare." Reich, New Property, supra note 8, at 734. "[T]oday more and more of our wealth takes the form of rights or status rather than of tangible goods." Id. at 738. "To the individual, these new forms . . . are the basis of his various statuses in society, and may therefore be the most meaningful and dis-

tinctive wealth he possesses." Id. at 739; see also Reich, Individual Rights, supra note 8, at 1255-56 (describing the concept of "entitlement").

[399] Justice Blackmun has referred to the "familiar two-part inquiry: we must determine whether [the plaintiff] was deprived of a protected interest, and, if so, what process was his due." Logan v. Zimmerman Brush Co., 455 U.S. 422, 428 (1982).

tory entitlements that have passed muster in the Supreme Court are welfare benefits, old-age benefits, federal civil service employment, and social security benefits.

2. *Private Law and "Equitable Property."* The origin of the rule that enables third party beneficiaries to secure compliance with federal statutes lies in quasi-contract, specifically, in the old common count for "money had and received for and to the use of the plaintiff." Yet this action was not precisely a property claim. A plaintiff stating a claim for money had and received did not, for example, have to identify specific funds, but the defendant's right to act other than as trustee of the money would defeat the claim. . . . On this analysis, what is involved is a kind of "equitable property," as distinct from the common law notion of property.

The doctrinal innovation involved in *Lawrence v. Fox* was the substitution of the promise to pay money for the equitable property in the money itself. The rule of *Lawrence v. Fox* made the defendant a "constructive trustee" of the benefit of the promise, extending the potential of the action considerably. So long as the promise remained a promise to pay money, this legal sleight of hand did not matter very much. But once courts developed a generalized right of "intended beneficiaries" to enforce promises of all kinds, this type of "equitable property" was enlarged enormously.

This analysis of the role now being played by the third party beneficiary rule is supported not only by the history of the rule, but also by the nature of the rights it secures. Rights acquired by third party beneficiaries under contracts that are a part of statutory schemes of distribution and protection have a great deal in common with the kinds of rights the Supreme Court has held to be protected property under the due process clauses. This similarity is especially obvious with respect to intangible, "new property" rights, which are not encompassed by traditional legal concepts of property.

Setting aside for a moment the notion that the third party's right, thus created, is a "contract right," the right may be thought of in terms of its restitutionary, quasi-contractual origins. Quasi-contractual rights were dependent on the fiction of a promise "implied by law" from the facts of the case—facts such as the receipt of money by the defendant for and to the use of the plaintiff. If a federal agency pays a subsidy to a provider of low-income housing to be credited toward the rent of an identified tenant, the tenant could maintain an action for money had and

received, were it available, against the recipient of the funds if they were not so applied and could certainly recover as an intended beneficiary of the contract under which funds were paid. Thus, where money earmarked for the plaintiff's use or credit is the object of the claim, the grievance is virtually identical to that involved in *Lawrence v. Fox*.

The same analysis applies where an apartment house owner charges rents in excess of the maximum permitted under its mortgage agreement with the federal government, and the tenants sue for a refund. The plaintiffs' claim is rather straightforward: "We want our money back!" But the response of the law can be rather sophisticated, offering several formally distinct avenues to the same remedy. That which most accurately describes the grievance is the action for money had and received, which is as straightforward and as primitive as the claim itself. But this simple tool from yesteryear has been mislaid in the process of doctrinal development; an action "on the promise" or another "on the statute" must be made to do the job.

Turning from the particular case of money paid to the credit of an identified beneficiary to cases of federal funding contracts generally, we move away from something very much like the "old property" idea toward something that more closely resembles the "new property." Indeed, that so many modern third party beneficiary cases are class actions—status-based actions that straddle the divide between public and private law by making a nominally private law claim on behalf of a class created by statute—emphasizes the similarity between these cases and those involving statutory entitlements considered property for due process purposes.

These cases are the culmination of a series of evolutionary events. The first event was the development of the kind of equitable property involved in the action for money had and received and arguably in all restitutionary actions. Then, in *Lawrence v. Fox*, the "property in the promise" displaced the "property in the money" as the basis of the claim. Later, this idea of a beneficial interest in a contractual obligation was generalized, culminating in the Second Restatement's exorcising the vestiges of the tie to money by abolishing the "creditor" and "donee" beneficiaries and approving a formulation of the third party beneficiary rule that applies to any promise of which there is an intended beneficiary.

. . .

The third party beneficiary's right, then, is better understood, and more precisely classified, as a restitutionary right to intangible property—the benefit of a promise—than as a contract action. This characterization is not limited to those cases in which the benefits being sought happen to resemble intangible benefits that have been constitutionally protected as property, but those cases do illustrate one point particularly well: there is sometimes a marked similarity between the kinds of rights constitutionally protected as property and those secured by the third party beneficiary rule that derives historically from a private law notion of equitable property. Given that both notions of property developed teleologically, one to protect due process values as they affect groups of citizens, the other for the more limited purpose of achieving "justice as between man and man" in the form of restitution, it is not surprising that each should now address the same contemporary social concern over intangible property rights.

D. *Form and Substance*

In this Section, I shall attempt to make use of the preceding analysis of the public program beneficiary's "contract right" as a restitutionary right to intangible property by demonstrating that the principles applicable to restitutionary claims in general are the appropriate principles for dealing with this kind of claim in particular. First I shall distinguish these principles from those appropriate to dealing with third party beneficiary claims arising out of commercial contracts with the government. Then I shall argue that because the Second Restatement's guidelines for dealing with third party beneficiary claims based on government contracts are applicable only to commercial contracts with the government, we must look to the history of the third party beneficiary rule—specifically to its restitutionary. antecedents—for guidance.

. . .

The third party beneficiary rule raises the same general problem in [cases treating it as an end-run around the restrictions on private rights of action under federal statutes] that it has raised from the beginning: by affording an enforceable right where there was none before, it tends to unsettle neighboring doctrines. *Slade's Case* and its progeny had that effect on the action of debt; *Lawrence v. Fox* and its immediate progeny had that effect on pockets of law that were based on exceptions to the general rule that no stranger to a contract could enforce it. And now the broad "intended beneficiary" rule has come to threaten the stability of the law of implied private rights of action, a stability that the Supreme Court

has worked hard to achieve over the past twenty years. This latest struggle between two forms of claim is directly descended from the celebrated struggle that gave birth to the promise implied by law for the sake of the remedy in *Slade's Case* and from the less celebrated battle of wits that produced the original third party beneficiary rule in *Lawrence v. Fox*. Today's struggle is between those who favor the enforcement of public programs through widespread recognition of private rights of action and those who do not.

1. *Distinguishing the Contractual and Quasi-Contractual Branches of the Modern Third Party Beneficiary Rule*.—What now purports to be a general rule about contract liability to third parties is the product of the merger of a restitutionary, trust-like concept with an action on the promise. The cases arising under the third party beneficiary rule today can usefully be broken down into two groups that correspond to its history: those that are descended from the quasi-contractual side of the family and those that are extensions of "straight" contract law. Different principles are appropriate to each. In particular, third party beneficiary claims that arise out of public programs, as distinct from commercial transactions, should be treated in accord with broad restitutionary principles, rather than be subjected to rules that were formulated to limit consequential damages for breach of contract.

Although courts that have upheld third party beneficiary claims to the benefits of public programs have very often ignored it, there has always been a Restatement rule dealing specifically with the application of the third party beneficiary rule "to contracts with a government or governmental agency." That rule is now found in section 313 of the Second Restatement, the successor to the First Restatement's section 145. The main principle enshrined in section 313 makes much more sense when applied to general commercial obligations than to public programs that have intended beneficiaries; it derives from the contract side of the family and does not fit well with claims that more nearly resemble restitutionary actions. I propose to use the rule stated in section 313 as a device for unraveling the two strands of liability that have been merged and as a reference point for formulating a different set of principles that should be applied to claims not satisfactorily addressed by the existing rule.

. . .

[Section 313(2) denies recovery to members of the general public for consequential damages when a contract with the government is breached by someone providing a service used by the general public. Section 313 is concerned with the problem exemplified by the Cardozo opinion in *H.R. Moch Co. v. Rensselaer Water Co.*, 247 N.Y. 160, 159 N.E. 896 (1928), where a water company contracted to provide a city with water for fire hydrants and was sued by a member of the public whose warehouse was destroyed when the water pressure proved inadequate. The court held the plaintiff an incidental beneficiary, unable to recover for the breach, pointing to the "crushing burden" that consequential liability would have if the breaching party were held liable to the general public. —ed.]

In the particular context of contracts with government, section 313(2) attempts no more than to place a clear limit on consequential damages in circumstances in which the third party beneficiary rule, combined with the usual measure of contract damages, would otherwise wreak havoc on the first generation of mail carriers and water companies to come before the courts. Without such a limit, the second generation would have to insure against such risks, and we would all be paying more to receive water and to send mail. Instead, in cases like *Moch*, the rule articulated in section 313(2) intervenes to limit the liability of those contracting with the government, and in so doing puts the burden on the property owner and on the user of the mails to insure against loss.

Cases that involve beneficiaries of public programs typically do not involve consequential damages or insurable risks. The remedy sought is almost always some kind of injunctive relief, often resembling specific performance, intended to achieve such objectives as admittance to nonsegregated public schools, the right to remain in a particular nursing home, employment under a federally funded jobs program, or special instruction in the English language for non-English-speaking school children. The grievances involved in these cases are different from those involved in commercial transactions. The plaintiffs are not so much "members of the public" as identifiable classes, usually described and created by statute, for whose particular benefit some arm of the federal government has imposed an obligation on the defendant. Not only are the section 313 terms "consequential damages" and "members of the public" inappropriate

here, but policy considerations such as "the likelihood of impairment of service or of excessive financial burden, and the availability of alternatives such as insurance" are simply inapplicable to cases that represent the restitutionary rather than the contractual branch of third party beneficiary doctrine. Such cases ought to be dealt with by reference to other principles.

The drafters of section 313 did not entirely disregard beneficiaries of public programs. The rider to section 313(1) identifies contravention of "the policy of the law authorizing the contract" as a reason for not applying the general law of contract beneficiaries, and the accompanying comment includes "governmental control over the litigation and settlement of claims" as a factor that renders a direct action against the promisor "inappropriate." The reporter's note to section 313 acknowledges: "[T]he category of government contracts is not monolithic. In addition to the traditional disputes over contracts to provide services to the general public . . . recent cases have involved rights of poor people in federal-state social services agreements . . . ."

Having acknowledged the existence of this group of cases, and that they are not represented in the illustrations of section 313, the reporter's note offers only this guidance: "In deciding whether the agreement was intended to create contractual rights in third parties, the nature of the agreement, the identity of the alleged intended beneficiaries and the specific duty said to have been created toward them are all factors to be considered." Lord Mansfield said something similar, but more direct, in 1760, in a celebrated and expansive statement about the equitable nature of the action for money had and received:

> This kind of equitable action . . . is very beneficial, and therefore much encouraged . . . . [I]t lies [for example] for money . . . got through . . . an undue advantage taken of the plaintiff's situation, contrary to laws made for the protection of persons under those circumstances. . . . [T]he gist of this kind of action is, that the defendant, upon the circumstances of the case, is obliged by the ties of natural justice and equity to refund the money.[453]

The modern third party beneficiary rule is an expansion and generalization of the old action for money had and received. In cases in which it is used to secure benefits that are classified for some related

[453] Moses v. Macferlan, 2 Burr. 1005, 1012, 97 Eng. Rep. 676, 680-81 (K.B. 1760) "We have only to substitute "make restitution' for the last three words of [Lord Mansfield's] statement to make it appropriate for the whole law of restitution." R. Goff & G. Jones, The Law of Restitution 12 (2d ed. 1978).

purpose as intangible property, we may observe that our property rights have changed more significantly than the mechanism by which we vindicate them. The notion of property that was the basis of the action for money had and received—a restitutionary claim to money—has been displaced by a much broader idea that closely resembles the new property. But the restitutionary principle on which the old action depended has not been displaced. That principle, or something very much like it, remains at the heart of third party beneficiary claims to what Charles Reich called "government largess."

2. *Restitutionary Principles and Public Programs.*—The characterization just offered suggests principles of decision that go beyond the vague guidelines of the reporter's note and "the weighing of considerations peculiar to particular situations." They are principles deeply rooted in the history of the third party beneficiary rule, and they afford a substantial legal basis for treating third party beneficiary claims that arise from public programs in broadly restitutionary terms.

The most authoritative modern statement of the general principles of restitution is found in Tentative Draft No. 1 of the Second Restatement of Restitution, under the heading "The General Principle: Unjust Enrichment": "A person who receives a benefit by reason of an infringement of another person's interest, or of loss suffered by the other, owes restitution to him in the manner and amount necessary to prevent unjust enrichment." A comment adds that "[a] breach of contract often results in unjust enrichment of the party in breach and gives rise to a right to restitution in the other party." When a link in the chain of distribution of new property rights—a school board, a nursing home operator, or a landlord—has received federal funds to be spent for the benefit of an identifiable group, there is a benefit conferred. When the promisor fails to distribute the promised benefits, he is unjustly enriched "by reason of an infringement of another person's interest."

These broadly equitable restitutionary principles are perfectly suited to dealing with third party claims to the intended benefits of public programs, as several factors that appear repeatedly in this group of cases suggest. Often, some element of unjust enrichment is present, as when the defendant receives federal funds intended to be used for the benefit of the

plaintiff, but does not provide the intended benefits. Frequently, an equitable remedy, rather than damages, is sought, and that remedy reflects a right quite different from the expectation interest that is typically created by contract. For example, plaintiffs may be students seeking admission to public schools free from racial segregation, or tenants seeking injunctive relief to upgrade living conditions in a housing project, or handicapped or racial minority plaintiffs seeking the benefits of an affirmative action program in job distribution. Often, the right that is the subject of the suit is some kind of entitlement created specifically for the benefit of the plaintiff (or plaintiff class). If the very same kind of right has already been held to be constitutionally protected property, then it is that much easier to regard it as a property right.

In these cases, "a relational duty" is often at least as good a description of the defendant's obligation to the plaintiff as "a willed undertaking." In 1924 Dean Pound warned:

Nothing could be more unhappy than to put trusts under contract, as if the legal transaction of becoming trustee were analogous to a contract and all liability flowed therefrom. Nothing is gained and much confusion is invited when we attempt to treat common-law relational duties in terms of willed undertakings.[459]

These forebodings did not deter Professor Williston from relying on a deed analogy in defense of the Restatement rule that gave donee beneficiaries an immediate vested interest, and Arthur Corbin, in his efforts to extend the scope of the third party beneficiary rule, paid no heed to the distinction between proprietary and promissory explanations of the third party beneficiary's right. Indeed, the merger of certain common law relational duties with contractual willed undertakings is intrinsic to the third party beneficiary rule: Judge Gray's use of trust principles was central to the original formulation of the rule of *Lawrence v. Fox.*

The designation "relational duty" is especially appropriate when the obligation is to a class of people of a certain status (typically, a status created by statute), and there is a proprietary nexus, such as the school buildings that were built with federal monies in *Lemon*, or the rent overcharges that were the subject of suit in *Zigas*. The subject-matter of these cases is not, as a rule, commercial endeavor, and

---

[459] Pound, Preliminary Report on Classification of the Law, 2 A.L.I. Proc. 381, 422 (1924).

what I earlier described as the "contract law questions" that are the basis of cases like *Moch*, and of the rule of section 313, are not the right questions to ask about cases that involve new property rights. The issue is not the extent of liability for consequential damages for breach, which is the concern of the rule of section 313. The issue is access to the intended benefits of public programs.

Where some or all of the factors that distinguish the "restitutionary" cases from the "bargain-based" cases are present, courts should consider factors beyond those set out in section 313, and decide such claims according to the broadly equitable considerations that gave rise to the third party beneficiary rule in the first place. After all, had Fox been permitted to keep the money, he would have been unjustly enriched. The equitable considerations that drove the New York Court of Appeals in 1859 to devise a rule that would uphold Lawrence's recovery are equally valid today, in the context of private rights and public programs.

IV. Conclusion

In the history of ideas, 1859 was a notable year. In January, Karl Marx completed *The Critique of Political Economy*. In early August, Richard Wagner finished *Tristan and Isolde*. On November 24, Charles Darwin's *The Origin of Species* first appeared. And on December 23, the New York Court of Appeals handed down its decision in *Lawrence v. Fox*. Each of these events marks a turning point in the evolution of its own field.

This essay has been about evolution—and not just about the evolution of a legal rule, but about one aspect of our social evolution. As the subject for a study in doctrinal development, the third party beneficiary rule has proved to be extraordinarily revealing of the three main activities that contribute to case law change: litigation, with all its vicissitudes; academic commentary and reformulation, with its demonstrated potential for influencing the courts; and the changing patterns of life itself—in this instance, a greatly increased social concern for disadvantaged people. The third party beneficiary rule has come to reflect and to be allied with that increased social concern. As Friedrich Kessler and Grant Gilmore observed fifteen years ago:

> The eventual triumph of the third party beneficiary idea may be looked on as still another instance of the progressive liberalization or erosion of the rigid rules of the late nineteenth century theory of contractual obligation. . . . To the nineteenth century legal mind the propositions that no man was his brother's keeper, that the race was to the swift and that the devil should take the hindmost seemed not only obvious but morally right. The most striking feature of nineteenth century contract theory is the narrow scope of social duty which it implicitly assumed. In our own century we have witnessed what it does not seem too fanciful to describe as a socialization of our theory of contract. The progressive expansion of the range of non-parties allowed to sue as contract beneficiaries as well as of the situations in which they have been allowed to sue is one of the entries to be made in this ledger.

The "socialization of our theory of contract" presents itself at each of the three stages that are the subject of this essay. From the first, the third party beneficiary rule clashed with both the structure and the import of traditional contract law, and "the eventual triumph of the third party beneficiary idea" is surely a significant contribution to the death of Contract. At the second stage—the marketing stage—we find Arthur Corbin waging a campaign on behalf of the third party beneficiary rule, apparently driven by the intrinsic equity of the rule he was promoting. While that episode has an undeniable appeal to the jurisprurient interest, we should not overlook its teaching. Corbin's campaign illustrates that the general acceptance of the third party beneficiary doctrine has been a triumph of equity over doctrine. In a paradox characteristic of our legal system, it has been a formalistic triumph of substance over form. And at the third stage—the present day—we find the phenomenon of socialization manifested much more obviously. We find intended beneficiaries of public programs attempting to use the broad, modern rule as an alternative to the increasingly unavailable route of an implied right of action.

The broad, modern "intended beneficiary" rule is now poised on the fringes of public law and is perfectly suited to reversing the trend whereby intended beneficiaries of public programs have increasingly been denied access to the courts. If it does that—if it goes some or all of the way toward reversing that trend—the third party beneficiary rule will be doing in a new context and on a larger scale what it has been doing all along. It will be doing what it was bred to do.

What Leon Green Saw

Leon Green was a dominant figure in tort law for most of the first two-thirds of this century. He was part of the brilliant faculty, led by Thomas Swan and Arthur Corbin, who created the modern Yale Law School around and soon after the First World War. In the twenties he was called to succeed John Henry Wigmore as dean at Northwestern, a position he held for some twenty years. In the later part of his life he returned to his native Texas to teach at the University of Texas until he was nearly ninety. One of Green's contributions to tort law was to argue that in addition to injuries to person and property, the law should recognize injuries to relations. (For a discussion from the tort point of view, see Wex S. Malone's *Torts in a Nutshell—Injuries to Family, Social and Trade Relations* (1979), especially chapter 1.) His several articles on injuries to relations were a major influence on the development of the relational approach to contracts, discussed in Part IB.

The following article by Green appeared in The New Republic for March 24, 1937, during the bloody sit-down strikes through which the United Auto Workers were able to organize the automobile factories in Detroit and Flint, Michigan. The organizing effort was aided when Governor Frank Murphy, later Attorney General of the United States and still later a Justice of the United States Supreme Court, refused to call out the National Guard to evict the workers from the plants. While the article was a very much a part of its time (it was followed by Kenneth Rexroth's *Requiem for the Dead in Spain*), it remains relevant today. We have just seen Congress overwhelmingly pass the Plant Closing Bill, requiring sixty days' notice before a corporation can close down a major operation. The ideas discussed in the Barnett, Macneil and Linzer articles in Part IB, in the Hohfeld note and the Knapp and Farnsworth articles in Part IIA, in the Farber & Matheson and Feinman articles in Part IIB, in the Waters article here in Part IID, and in the note on *Public Policy From Sunday Contracts to Baby M*, among others in Part IIIB, all can be rethought when we ask the questions what do we mean by property ownership and what do we mean by rights. Though Leon Green wrote more than fifty years ago, and changed some of his views in later years, his article is still futuristic. But the future may be coming.

Leon Green, *The Case for the Sit-Down Strike,* 90 The New Republic 199 (1937)

The sit-down strike presents a new problem for government and industrialists. The first reaction was that the sit-down strikers were mere trespassers against whom the equitable remedy of injunction was available. But this quick analysis seems to have been far too simple. As is frequently the case, what seems at first to be a simple situation upon further examination turns out to be one so compactly complex that its difficulties become apparent only after the closest study. Some conservative lawyers have, therefore, been slow, and doubtless will continue to be slow, in concluding the argument against the employees on the surface analysis which was at first brought forward.

The respective interests of employer and employee in their relations with each other have full recognition under the common law, statutes and constitutions of Anglo-American jurisdictions. Within the past century everything affecting their relations has changed completely. The personal master has become an industrial corporation, a conglomerate of thousands of stockholders, bondholders, directors, corporate officials, managers, superintendents and assistants of all sorts. The personal servant has become a labor union, itself a conglomerate of persons and organization almost as far-flung and equally as difficult to visualize as the corporation. The simple handcraft has become the highly coordinated mechanized mass-production processes of industry.

The industrial relation resulting from these changes differs as greatly from the simple relation of master and hired hand as does the modern industrial corporation from the personal master, the labor union from the personal servant, or industrial mechanization from simple handcraft. It is the result of a long, tedious, costly, evolutionary process. And the sit-down strike is but the latest step in the struggle between a large mass of employers operating under an institution know as an industrial corporation and an equally large or larger mass of employees operating or attempting to operate under a somewhat similar institution known as a labor union, to work out their respective rights, duties and privileges in industrial enterprise—enterprise resulting from the joint efforts of what we oversimplify as capital and labor.

The industrial enterprise is not made up merely of land, brick, mortar and machinery on the one hand, and personal services of many individuals on the other. These two great interests of property and personality are both essential to the enterprise, but each alone is meaningless to the industrial world. *It is their joinder that creates the third great interest, the industrial relation upon which industry is based*. It is their joinder that brings into existence this something distinct from its parental forbears as a child is distinct from its parents, or a corporation from its stockholders, a partnership from its members; about which cluster rights, duties, liabilities and immunities not yet clearly articulated in terms of legal theory except as they are recognized as relations equal in dignity and value to those of property or personality.

That this something which has been in the process of development for a century or more has an existence all its own, as much so as the family or the corporation, both of which in like manner are made up of an indefinite number of similar relational interests, is all too clear. And that it—as the family and corporation have come to be by a process of evolution in human affairs—is a usable, workable, recognizable concept, requires no demonstration further than common observation and experience.

The industrial relation in its initial or formative state is the result of a contractual nexus between the two parental organisms of industry—those who supply its property-capital on the one hand and those who supply its service-capital on the other. But as in the case of family, corporate, partnership, carrier, and all other important relations, the slender tie of the initial contract is overgrown by a network of tissue, nerves and tendons, as it were, which gives the relation its significance. The respective rights, duties, privileges and immunities of the parties to the industrial relation are too numerous to recite here, but they are well known.

Both participating groups have contributed heavily to the joint enterprise of industry. The contributions of those who make up the corporate organization on the one hand are visualized in plant, machinery, raw materials and the like. They can be seen, recorded and valued in dollars. We call them property. On the other side are hundreds of personalities who have spent years training their hands and senses to specialized skills; who have set up habitations conveniently located to their work; who have become obligated to families and for facilities necessary for maintaining them; who have ordered their lives and developed disciplines; all to the end that the properties essential to industry may be operated for the profit of the owner group and for their own livelihoods. Their outlays are not so visible, nor so easily measured in dollars, but in gross they may equal or even exceed the contributions of the other group. Both groups are joint adventurers, as it were, in industrial enterprise. Both have and necessarily must have a voice in the matters of common concern. Both must have protection adequate to their interests as against the world at large as well as against the undue demands of each other.

Disputes have frequently arisen between employers and employees. Normally they have arisen on complaint of employees. In order to give weight to their demands, concert of effort was the first step. This resulted ultimately in the recognition of the union organization. Then came the strike, the closed shop, the union card, the sympathetic strike, followed by picketing, bombing, boycotts and collective bargaining. These in turn were met in various ways, the lockout, strike-breakers, criminal prosecutions, injunctions, yellow-dog contracts, company unions, espionage and the like. An effective measure on one side has always called for a counter measure on the other. Like the less complex carrier-passenger relations, the relation between insurer and insured, the oil and gas lessor and lessee and every other such relation, the industrial relation has been built slowly but certainly upon the reactions of the parties, the public generally and government to practices which have been employed by the one party and the other.

From such a background has come the sit-down strike. It is a refinement that could only result from years of struggle and bitter experience. Having found the walk-out ineffective and picketing, boycotts, sympathetic strikes and other measures severely restricted by law, unions have used the sit-down strike to avoid the difficulties of them all, to be more effective. Instead of employees severing their relations and thereby automatically placing themselves outside as dissatisfied former employees, they now insist on maintaining their relations while they negotiate about their complaints. Once they sever the relations they become strangers to the enterprise and trespassers if they remain upon the employer's premises, but as employees they stay at their posts ready to work upon condition that the employer shall negotiate with them. Thus they retain their interest in and relation to the common enterprise.

Moreover, they deny the employer the power to discharge them and thereby sever the relations they have with the industry. They insist that by negotiation some basis be reached upon which work of the enterprise may be continued. The right to fire is an incident of the simplest form of contract, that of employment at the will of both parties; it has no place in a relation which is based upon infinitely more than mere contract. A wife cannot fire her husband, a parent his child, a corporate stockholder other stockholders, one partner another member of the firm, an insurer the insured, a carrier its passengers, with impunity. Neither can an employer fire his employees*en masse*. These other relations are at best only analogous, but they give point. All institutions built upon relational interests of the groups concerned must submit to the obligations which have grown up around the particular relation, and if it is to be destroyed it must be done subject to such obligations.

The right to fire is a right to end the relation. Clear enough in the simplest form of relations, it does not obtain between a group employer on the one hand as against group employees on the other. An industrial corporation cannot fire an industrial union. Industry has grown beyond that stage. To protect himself against incompetence, dishonesty or malicious damage, it is the employer's right to fire the individual employee who refuses to respect his obligations. But used as a means of weakening an organization of employees, or as a means of refusing to negotiate with them about their common enterprise, the right to fire has no place. In the one instance it is used in defense of his interests; in the other it becomes a means to destroy the strength of the em-

ployee group and to escape the obligation to negotiate the industrial difference. It is thus that employees may peacefully sit and wait until their complaints are ironed out through negotiations between their representatives and the representatives of the corporate group of owners. They do not operate or do injury to the owner's property. They make no adverse claim of possession to the premises they occupy. They merely occupy them because they are an incident to the industry in which they have an interest. If more were needed they could well claim a license coupled with an interest in the premises devoted to the enterprise. But they sit to negotiate some affair pertinent to their relation to industry.

And this is their right. If so, it is equally their right to protect themselves against attack.

Whither does this right lead? What are its implications? What are its limitations?

Strangely enough, though government has provided means for protecting every other important relation, it has not provided any means to settle the disputes of industrial employer and employee. They are not justiciable matters; the courts afford no remedy to either party. Political and economic, broad and irreducible to legal theory, the courts have left such disputes alone.

Is this then to be an empty right? Does government offer no protection to these interests when assailed by the parties themselves? Is this right a dead end?

Not by a long shot! True it is that government offers nothing affirmatively for the protection of employees' relational interests against the refusal of an employer to negotiate their differences, *but neither does government offer an employer affirmative relief or protection*, in absence of violence or fraud on the part of employees directed against his interests. Employer and employee hold their fates as to their common relations in their own hands. In that fact is found the significance of the sit-down strike. It gives employees a means of forcing negotiation, and such a means without the severance of the relations, without violence or other unlawful conduct.

But suppose negotiation results in failure, what then? Here is the gap that government has not filled and the one it must fill before we go very much farther. No one else can fill the gap. But until it has done so, there is nothing a court can do to adjudicate the issues between industrial employers and industrial employees and it will therefore not intervene in behalf of either party. It will not rob employees of the advantage which falls to them as an incident of their relation. Their presence in the industrial plant so long as they refrain from fraud or violence does not violate their obligations as employees; they are not trespassers; they are still employees with all their relations intact. Nor should a court seek an excuse to take jurisdiction of such a situation on some incidental point and thereby prejudice the main dispute when it has no power to settle it directly. The courts have no part to play in such matters in absence of violence or fraud; they should leave the parties where they are; they have no means of their own to work fair settlements and they should await the action of government through some agency better equipped to deal with such problems.

A court of equity will not act in absence of the invasion of a clear legal right. Even then injunction is a matter of sound discretion. It only became available in labor disputes where violence or its threat or some form of fraud against person or property was said to be involved. When neither is present injunction has no part to play in labor disputes. In the peaceful sit-down strike the only claim as the basis for injunctive relief is the occupation of the industrial plant. But that is only an incident to the industrial relation which the industrial employee enjoys in the employer's property devoted to the enterprise. As long as it is occupied in good faith awaiting the adjustment of differences growing out of the industrial relation, occupation of the plant is not merely a privilege but the employee's right.

And thus it is that the sit-down strike may be the last step in the long, costly, brutal and in many respects unintelligent struggle through which the industrial enterprise with its congeries of relations has evolved. Such is the history of most human institutions. But this struggle should now be over. Having won their recognition as joint adventurers in industry, the industrial relation having assumed so large a place in our social organism, employees should now be willing to submit their complaints, when negotiations have failed, to a duly organized, safeguarded and intelligent government agency so constituted as to have the confidence of employers, employees and the public at large. The implications of such a method of settling disputes cannot be developed here. Both groups would doubtless be equally fearful of such a suggestion, and they will not accept it until they are certain that they are meeting on an equal basis before a public that is wholeheartedly devoted to fair play between them. It is enough to say that such an arrangement would necessitate responsible leadership of the highest type on the part of both groups, and that each group, along with the public, would have everything to gain and nothing to lose. The attitude of English capital, English labor, English public and English government at home and in the commonwealths has definitely pointed the way here.

This in brief is the case for the sit-down strike. It rests upon four fundamental propositions:

1. Employees have an interest in the industrial relation distinct from any property interest or interest of personality. Such interest is a valuable one of the same dignity as that of property and is given the recognition and protection of the courts as property.

2. Disputes between employers and employees with respect to industrial relations involve economic and political questions outside the jurisdictions of the courts; the problems involved are of such great difficulty administratively that courts will not undertake to adjudicate them but will leave them to other agencies of government and to the parties themselves in absence of such agencies.

3. Courts will not prejudice the issues between industrial employers and employees by assuming jurisdiction of issues incidental to the main dispute in absence of physical violence or fraud directed against the persons or property of the parties.

4. Occupation in good faith and peacefully of a plant devoted to industry by employees awaiting the adjustment of differences growing out of the industrial relation is but an incident of the industrial relation and in no sense unlawful.

Part III
Contracts in Action

A. The Interpretation of Contracts

Words and Meaning

Once it is decided that some sort of contractual obligation has come into existence, there remains the problem of figuring out what the parties meant by what they said. We can easily understand interpretation problems arising when a contract is oral, but problems often arise when there is a written contract. The more precisely written the contract, the more likely a court is to read it literally. This seems like common sense, but as we have become more sophisticated about word usage, semantics and linguistics, we have become less certain that words ever have fixed and "plain" meanings.

We begin with an article that Arthur Corbin wrote very near the end of his long and prolific life. At 90 Corbin updated the pocket parts to his treatise and included four new sections dealing with interpretation and related matters. With his consent, the Cornell Law Quarterly adapted and published the new matter as *The Interpretation of Words and the Parol Evidence Rule*. Corbin had written about language over his whole career, and had been very influential in the erosion of the rigid view of the parol evidence rule, which permitted no outside evidence if an "integrated" contract was not "ambiguous on its face." Not long after Corbin's article was published, E. Allan Farnsworth, relatively near the beginning of his career, published an influential article entitled *"Meaning" in the Law of Contracts*. Both Corbin and Farnsworth discuss the well-known "what is chicken?" case, *Frigaliment v. B.N.S. Int'l Sales Corp.*, and Farnsworth also discusses another staple, the *Peerless* case, *Raffles v. Wichelhaus*.

Arthur L. Corbin, *The Interpretation of Words and the Parol Evidence Rule,* 50 Cornell L.Q. 161 (1965)

Growth of the Law, in Spite of Long Repetition of Formalistic Rules

At an earlier date, this author warned that "in advising clients and in predicting court decisions, it must always be borne in mind that the assumption of uniformity and certainty in the meaning of language, however erroneous, has been made so often and so long that it will be repeated many times in the future."[1] This prediction has been fully borne out in the court opinions that have been published in the fourteen years since it was made. It is still being said,

sometimes as the ratio decidendi but more often as a dictum representing established law, that extrinsic evidence is not admissible to aid the court in the interpretation of a written contract (an integration) if the written words are themselves plain and clear and unambiguous. This is said even by a court that declares the rule to be a rule of substantive law and not a rule of evidence.

Is not this continuous repetition in itself sufficient to make the statement a well settled rule of substantive law, even though it results at times in the court's

---

[1] Corbin, Contracts § 542, at 112 (2d ed. 1960).

making a contract for the parties in disregard of their actual intention? Hard cases, they say, must not be allowed to make bad law. Contracting parties must be made to know that it is their written words that constitute their contract, not their intentions that they try to express in the words. They, not the court, have chosen the words; and they, not the court, have made the contract. Its legal operation must be in accordance with the meaning that the words convey to the court, not the meaning that they intend to convey. Is not an author, or even a dissenting judge, guilty of the utmost temerity (and even of folly) to deny the accuracy, the justice, and the necessity of the repeated rule?

There are times when an author is incompetent, and even intellectually and morally dishonest, if he fails to attack an often repeated statement of law. This is such a case; one that has had many precedents throughout our legal history. There are many court decisions, made by highly respected courts, that are inconsistent with the repeated rule. If extrinsic evidence is admitted without objection, the trial court is never reversed for considering it in the process of interpretation. There are many cases, practically never subjected to criticism, in which the court has considered extrinsic evidence as a basis for finding that the written words are ambiguous; instead of ambiguity admitting the evidence, the evidence establishes the ambiguity. Learned judges have often differed as to whether the written words are ambiguous, each one sometimes asserting that *his* meaning is plain and clear. All that any court has to do in order to admit relevant extrinsic evidence is to assert that the written words are ambiguous; this has been done in many cases in which the ordinary reader can perceive no ambiguity until he sees the extrinsic evidence.

There are general rules that are universally accepted that are inconsistent with the stated rule here criticized. The cardinal rule with which all interpretation begins is that its purpose is to ascertain the intention of the parties. The criticized rule, if actually applied, excludes proof of their actual intention. It is universally agreed that it is the first duty of the court to put itself in the position of the parties at the time the contract was made; it is wholly impossible to do this without being informed by extrinsic evidence of the circumstances surrounding the making of the contract. These include the character of the subject matter, the nature of the business, the antecedent offers and counter offers and the communications of the parties with each other in the process of negotiation, the purposes of the parties which they expect to realize in the performance of the contract.[2] The court must put itself "in the shoes" of the parties; is it justified in drawing on the "shoes" of one party and not of the other, or only one "shoe" of each, or no "shoe" at all? Shall an author, or a court, disregard the cardinal general rules and accept without criticism a commonly asserted subsidiary rule that is inconsistent with them? If we wish to profit by the mistakes as well as by the wisdom of the past, it is necessary to look back over our legal history. Such a look informs us that law never begins with a system of rules and doctrines and principles, each (presumably) eternal, unchangeable, perfect (and perfectly worded with one true meaning). Such a look informs us that law is in a constant process of development and change; that laws are put into words by men—men who are not all-wise and capable of foresight into the distant future—and that these words are repeated by other men for shorter or longer periods of time, packing new meanings into the words as the exigencies of life require, finally (after a century of confusion) abandoning them altogether. A few examples of such a historical development may be profitable.

Consider the law of third party beneficiaries. No informed lawyer or judge doubts that by the common, judge-made law such beneficiaries have enforceable

[2] [After referring to several labor cases in which federal courts of appeals admitted "evidence of the background and negotiations of the bargaining" to ascertain the parties' intentions as to meaning, Corbin continued:] Unless the court wishes to make the contract for the parties in the sole light of its own linguistic education and experience, it must always know the situation and relations of the parties and its dominant purpose. Without thus putting itself in the position of the parties, a court cannot know whether the language of the contract is susceptible of more than one interpretation, cannot determine thedominant purpose of the parties, and cannot arrive at the reasonable and sensible meaning.

In Pocius v. Halvorsen, 30 Ill. 2d 73, 76, 195 N.E.2d 137, 140 (1964), the court emphasized:

The intention of the parties, it is true, must govern; but the experience of human affairs teaches courts that this intention is not to be sought merely in the apparent meaning of the language used, but this language may be enlarged or limited by reference to the circumstances surrounding the parties and the object they evidently had in view.

Here, the parties were in the relation of attorney and client. The court considered the interpretation that had been placed upon the contract by the parties, although the payments made by the client prior to termination of the litigation did not tend wholly in her favor.

legal rights. And yet it is only a short lifetime since teachers ceased teaching and writers ceased writing and judges ceased holding that privity of contract is necessary, that two parties cannot by contract create a legal right in a third, and that a stranger to the consideration cannot enforce a promise. For at least two centuries, the "law" on this subject had been in confusion, a fact that did not prevent thousands of dogmatic statements of the law.

. . .

. . . Must the consideration for a promise still be a detriment to the promisee? Is it still true that action in reliance on a promise cannot impart validity to what before was void?

For centuries a bilateral contract was unknown to the courts (although ignorant individuals probably performed them). And after they were recognized as enforceable, it took two centuries more to get rid of the doctrine that such exchanged promises were mutually independent, so that each one could be enforced even though the other had been repudiated. To many courts, this was just and right. Should not a man who has made a binding promise keep to his word and be compelled to do so? He had exactly the same remedy against the other party, who was likewise bound. Perfect equality, was it not?

I shall continue to do my best to clarify the process and the law of interpretation, of both words and acts as symbols of expression; to demonstrate that no man can determine the meaning of written words by merely glueing his eyes within the four corners of a square paper; to convince that it is men who give meanings to words and that words in themselves have no meaning; and to demonstrate that, when a judge refuses to consider relevant extrinsic evidence on the ground that the meaning of written words is to him plain and clear, his decision is formed by and wholly based upon the completely extrinsic evidence of his own personal education and experience.

At no place and at no time have I asserted that there is no difference between language that is plain and clear and language that is ambiguous, or that a judge should give no weight to the extrinsic evidence of his own education and experience. In view of the common efforts of attorneys at law to base interpretation on irrelevant and incredible extrinsic evidence and upon mere forensic assertion in place of any evidence, the extrinsic evidence of the judge's own education and experience (of which he necessarily takes judicial notice) may well be decisive. But in every case he should realize that this evidence, known only to himself, may not be the best evidence; that he must hold it at every point subject to correction; and that the purpose of all the evidence is the ascertainment of the intention of the parties (their meaning), and not the meaning that the written words convey to himself or to any third persons, few or many, reasonably intelligent or otherwise.

Process of Interpretation—Objective Meanings

The case of *Frigaliment Importing Co. v. B.N.S. Int'l Sales Corp.*,[3] is well suited for use in illustrating the process of interpretation. A contract for the sale of goods by the defendant, a New York corporation, to the plaintiff, a Swiss corporation, was confirmed in the following form:

US Fresh Frozen Chicken, Grade A, Government Inspected, Eviscerated 2 1/2-3 lbs. and 1 1/2-2 lbs., each, all chickens individually wrapped in cryovac packed in secured fiber cartons or wooden boxes, suitable for export

75,000 lbs. 2 1/2-3 lbs . . . . .at $33.00
25,000 lbs. 1 1/2-2 lbs . . . . .at $36.50
per 100 lbs. FAS New York.

Scheduled May 10, 1957, pursuant to instructions from Penson & Co., New York.

When the initial shipment arrived in Switzerland, on May 28, the plaintiff found that the 2 1/2-3 lbs. birds were not young chicken suitable for broiling or frying, but stewing chicken, or fowl. The plaintiff sued for damages, asserting that the delivery of stewing chicken or fowl was a breach. New York law was applicable. Was this an ambiguous contract, or a valid contract at all? How is the court to determine?

The court said, "The issue is, what is chicken?" Also, "Since the word 'chicken' standing alone is ambiguous, I turn first to see whether the contract itself offers any aid to its interpretation." The word chicken did not stand alone; and whatever meanings (if any) it might have standing alone, do not determine the issue. The word as used by the parties is in a context of other words, a context of negotiations by cable and by word of mouth in New York, a context of variable usages by other people (in their own variable contexts).

The court said:

Assuming that both parties were acting in gocd faith, the case nicely illustrates Holmes' remark

[3] 190 F. Supp. 116 (S.D.N.Y. 1960).

that the making of a contract depends not on the agreement of two minds in one intention, but on the agreement of two sets of external signs—not on the parties having *meant* the same thing but on their having said the same thing. [The Path of the Law, in Collected Legal Papers p. 178.] I have concluded that plaintiff has not sustained its burden of persuasion that the contract used "chicken" in the narrower sense.

Observe, first, that in this case, regarding the writing as an integration, there were not two sets of external signs. The plaintiff made no objection to the defendant's written confirmation; and the court does not suggest that the contract comprised any different set of words. It is this one set of words that constitutes the contract that the court is interpreting. The court must, indeed, interpret this set of words in the light of surrounding circumstances, the oral and cabled communications; the usages of other persons; but these collateral factors do not constitute any part of the contract that is being interpreted.

Secondly, since the contract, the subject matter of interpretation, consisted of only one set of written words, they were the words of both parties alike. These parties *said* the same thing. Holmes' statement, if it is interpreted in accordance with his own theory (i.e., interpreting it objectively, by what he *said* and not by what he *meant*), lends no support to the court's decision. It should not be sacrilege to suggest that there is an ambiguity in Holmes' use of the word said; in using it, Holmes may have put into it the meaning *the thought that the words convey to others*, but not *the words themselves* and not *the thought that the user intended to convey*. In this case, the parties expressed their thoughts by the same identical set of words; but the thoughts that they intended to convey were not identical. Nor were the thoughts (the meanings) that this set of words would convey to various third persons identical.

Thirdly, it was not the contract that used the word chicken, in any sense, narrower or broader. It is only men who use words as a means of conveying thoughts. The two parties adopted the words that they put into the present written instrument (the "integration"), including the word chicken. Each of them used these words to convey a meaning—*his* meaning. Assuming good faith (as the court does), the meanings that they gave to these words were not identical; there was no meeting of the minds. The words that they said (in writing) were identical; but these words did not say (Holmes' word) the same thoughts to each other. (Note the double usage of the verb say.)

Fourthly, if the identical words did not convey the same thoughts, were the parties legally bound by a valid contract? We have all been made aware, largely by the work of Holmes himself, that a party may be bound by a valid contract in accordance with an interpretation that was not his own. This is true of transactions conducted orally, in which the parties do not use identical words, or by a series of letters not identically worded. It is true also of cases like the present one, in which the parties have adopted a single set of words, now commonly described as an integration. If the parties, in good faith, understood the words of this integration differently, under what circumstances and for what reasons will the court penalize the defendant for not performing in accordance with the plaintiff's different interpretation? It is only when the facts are such that the court believes that the defendant is in some way at fault in not giving the words the same interpretation as the plaintiff did. This is expressed in various ways: the defendant was negligent, he had reason to know, he should have known. Then there is always the possibility that *he did know* and that his present assertions are not in good faith. Instead of expressing the reason in terms of fault, it may be explained on the ground that the general welfare requires the security of expectations reasonably induced by the defendant's assent to the words used; but this merely states the matter in another form. It passes the buck to a determination of what is reasonable. It must be borne in mind that both parties may have been negligent or that neither may have been, that both may have been equally reasonable or unreasonable, that the plaintiff may have had as much "reason to know" as the defendant had. In making the determination, the court is judging the parties and their use of words by the understandings and usages of other men, at the same time making some indeterminate allowance for the special mentality, experience, and education of the contracting parties themselves.

In determining whether the defendant was legally bound to deliver only young and tender birds, sometimes described as broilers and fryers, and not more mature and relatively tough hens and roosters that have to be stewed, the court was not interpreting the word chicken, standing alone; but rather in a context of other words in the integration, in the broader context of relevant communications, and the still broader context of the linguistic usages of other men. Dictionary usage could not be decisive, for "Dictionaries give both meanings, as well as some others not relevant here." Moreover, no dictionary interprets the word chicken in its present context. The court very properly said: "I turn first to see whether the contract itself [the "integration" as a whole] offers any aid to its interpretation."

The fifty or more words of the integration itself did not make the interpretation plain and unambiguous to the judge. It might have seemed otherwise to the present writer if he had been the judge. In his own linguistic experience and education, he had heard of broilers and fryers, and also of fowl; but to him the word chickens included them all. For ten years on a Kansas farm it had been a regular job to feed the chickens, with no suggestion that the old hens and roosters were to be excluded. In the campaign of 1928, the country was informed that one of the issues was "a chicken in every pot," obviously a bird for stewing. But in spite of his limited knowledge of other people's usages, he would have admitted extrinsic evidence, as the court did in this case. The integration itself contained certain descriptive elements: The birds sold must be US, Grade A, not over 3 lbs. each, and Government Inspected; but no one asserted that these terms segregated the young from the old or the tender from the tough. Evidence was admitted to show that the Department of Agriculture inspected chickens, including thereunder six classes beginning with broiler and ending with cock or old rooster, expressly including hen or stewing chicken or fowl. But the integration made no distinct reference to the Department's classification. Other extrinsic evidence included trade usages in New York, which the plaintiff testified used chicken to include only broilers and fryers. But the defendant testified that it had only that year entered the poultry trade; and the court says it is quite plain that defendant's belief [as to trade usage] was to the contrary. A New York buyer for the Swiss trade testified that on chicken I would definitely understand a broiler, but also that he was careful to say broiler when he intended to exclude fowl. A dealer who had supplied the defendant with some of the birds sold to the plaintiff testified that chicken in the poultry industry meant "the male species . . . that could be a broiler, a fryer or a roaster" but not a "stewing chicken," and that he had induced the defendant to use the term "stewing chicken" in its confirmation with him. The price paid to this dealer by the defendant was 30¢ per lb. Cablegrams, both antecedent and subsequent to the closing of the deal, were admitted. These were mostly in German; but they used the English word chicken. Plaintiff testified that the word was used be-

cause it understood it to mean broilers; also, that in German (well understood by defendant) chicken would be translated as "Brathuhn" and not by the more general term "Huhn." There was other extrinsic testimony.

Other terms used in the opinion, besides the word "chicken," might well be regarded as "ambiguous." What is the "poultry trade" and what witnesses were competent to speak for the usages of the persons engaged therein? The word "broiler" has its uncertain aspects. Was the manager of an "eviscerating" company, who testified that to him "chicken" meant "anything except a goose, a turkey, or a duck," engaged in the "poultry trade"? Does the term include both domestic and foreign transactions, both wholesale and retail? The plaintiff could have got much support from housewives and cooks, American as well as Swiss, who expect and actually receive a "broiler" when they order a "chicken" at a "supermarket." Would their testimony be admissible? And yet if they ordered a "5 lb. chicken," they would expect and receive a "fowl." What line in weight or age distinguishes a "broiler" from a "fowl"?

Finally the court said:

When all the evidence is reviewed it is clear that defendant believed it could comply with the contract by delivering stewing chicken in the 2 1/2-3 lbs. size. Defendant's subjective intent would not be significant if this did not coincide with *an objective* meaning of "chicken." Here it did coincide with *one of the dictionary meanings*, with the definition in the Department of Agriculture Regulations to which the contract made at least *oblique* reference, with at least *some usage* in the trade, with the *realities* of the market, and with what plaintiff's spokesman had *said*. Plaintiff asserts it to be equally plain that plaintiff's own subjective intent was to obtain broilers and fryers; the only evidence against this is the material as to market prices and this may not have been sufficiently brought home. In any event it is unnecessary to determine that issue. For plaintiff has the burden of showing that "chicken" was used in the narrower rather than the broader sense, and this it has not sustained.[10]

From this it appears that chicken has *more than one* objective meaning; that all the meanings in any dictionary are objective meanings; that the meaning of the "Department" of Agriculture (if it has one) is

---

[10] Id. at 121. [Emphasis added.]

an objective meaning; that meanings given by various persons in the poultry trade are objective meanings; that the subjective meaning of the defendant is significant if it coincides with an objective meaning; and that the plaintiff's subjective meaning does not have to be determined (even though it too did coincide with an objective meaning) only because it had the burden of proving that the word was used to mean broilers only. The court does not say by *whom* the word was used; but the words of the integration were the words of both parties. The issue before the court was as to how it was used *by these two parties*, in this particular context, in this specific case. No exception is here taken to the court's decision; but if the parties had been reversed and the seller had been suing for damages or for the purchase price, the burden of proof that the word was used in the broader sense would have been on the seller. The plaintiff (purchaser) lost this case, not because the word has *one objective meaning* by which the parties were bound, but because it failed to show that the defendant either "knew" or had reason to know that the plaintiff intended to buy broilers only and assented to the words of the integration with the understanding that chicken excluded birds that would have to be stewed.

The opinion of the court and a careful analysis of the facts and the evidence both lead to the conclusion that chicken has no single objective meaning, and that any meaning is an objective meaning if it is given to the word in any context by any person other than the two contracting parties.

. . .

Semantic Stone Walls—What Are They Made Of?

A Warehouseman's Licensing Act provided that any person applying for such a license must file a bond for the security of depositors of goods, and also that any person making such a deposit should have a right of action on the bond in case of the warehouseman's default. This statute contained a preliminary "glossary" of definitions of terms, including this: "'person' shall mean an individual, corporation, partnership . . . but shall not mean the United States or Iowa State Government or any subdivision or agency of either." Later, the defendant and a surety company executed such a bond; and the United States deposited grain in his warehouse. The United States brought suit on his bond for his failure to return the grain so deposited. The court held that the United States could not maintain the suit for the reason that it was expressly excluded as a beneficiary. The court said that "when the plaintiff comes along the statutory path to the second statutory provision [authorizing suit] it is met with a semantic stone wall."[45]

In view of the experience of the United States in purchasing agricultural crops at high prices and the extent to which it has deposited grain in storage warehouses, the author of this article had a distinct shock on reading the court's opinion, resulting in some thought as to the nature and the resistant quality of the wall that barred its way in an attempt to get damages for the loss of its stolen grain. It is certain that, although figures of speech have a literary charm they may have unfortunate results in law suits if taken literally. He observed, first, that in this case the wall was not in fact a wall of stone, against which it is futile to "butt one's head." The stone of which this wall was composed was "semantic stone." The stones of which this wall was composed were mere words. And a long experience in the use of words, by himself as well as by other men, had demonstrated that the thoughts that they express or convey are variables, depending on verbal context and surrounding circumstances and purposes in view of the linguistic education and experience of their users and their hearers or readers (not excluding judges). This is true whether the words are in a statute, a contract, a novel by Henry James, or a poem by Robert Browning. A word has no meaning apart from these factors; much less does it have an objective meaning, one true meaning. Consider the variable meanings that have been given to such words as chicken, democracy, income, value, dollar, or, and meaning itself.

In seeing the "semantic stone wall" blocking the remedy of the United States, the court was merely applying the doctrine so often repeated in judicial opinions, that when the words of a statute or of a contract are plain and clear and unambiguous, no interpretation is required and no extrinsic evidence is admissible—evidence of antecedent history and surrounding circumstances and purposes and usages of the parties.[46] The judge looks at the words of the

---

[45] United States v. West View Grain Co., 189 F. Supp. 482, 487 (N.D. Iowa 1960).

[46] William Graham Sumner once said, "if you want war, nourish a doctrine." In law, if you wish to destroy the judicial system, nourish and apply the doctrines—the formalistic rules—of the past. There are, indeed, those who love and nourish them and who become angry at those who attack them. Certainty is an illusion; but we love our illusions. Repose is not the destiny of man; but we yearn for repose.

written document alone and *knows* their true meaning by virtue of judicial notice.

Were the words of the Warehouseman's Act ambiguous? Looking at the words of the statute alone, this author sees no ambiguity. All persons seeking a license must give bond; and all persons injured by default may sue on the bond. But the word persons as used in this statute means all individuals and corporations except the United States and the State of Iowa. What is ambiguous about that? To discover ambiguity, we must resort to extrinsic evidence of history and purposes and surrounding circumstances; and when all this extrinsic evidence is before us, we discover not ambiguity but mistake, error in the definition, bad lexicography.

Fortunately we have had to wait only three years for the judicial correction of the mistake. In less than one year, the legislature corrected the mistake of its lexicographer; but its correction had no retroactive operation as to antecedent bonds. The United States not only forced a settlement in *West View*; it brought two other suits against the sureties of two other defaulting warehousemen, brought on identical bonds affected by the same Warehouseman's Act (unamended). In these two suits, a new district judge, sitting in the same State of Iowa, heard a new and better argument, and respectfully disapproved the *West View* decision.[47] He saw the same "semantic stone wall"; but he saw too that it was made of words and not of stone. He could not reform the statute or correct the lexicographic mistake; but he could and did correct the error of his judicial brother. He heard the extrinsic evidence of history and purpose and circumstances; and he found that the intention of the legislature was not in accord with the glossary definition. Its intention was to exclude the United States and the State of Iowa from the requirement of giving bond if they chose to operate a warehouse, and not to exclude them from rights as grain depositors in a private warehouse. He also held that the glossary definition in the statute was applicable to the statute alone, whether corrected or uncorrected, and not to bonds (or other documents) executed by surety companies. The process of interpretation of the bond is to determine the meaning and intention of the parties to the bond. There was no "semantic stone wall" included in the words of the bond.

Extrinsic Evidence a Necessary Aid in the Interpretation of Written Words

The preceding paragraphs were written as supplements to chapters 25 and 26 of the author's treatise on the Law of Contracts. Chapter 25 develops in detail the author's theory and practice in the interpretation of written language. Chapter 26 deals with the so-called Parol Evidence Rule. The present article, therefore, must be understood as bringing support, on the basis of the most recent judicial decisions and opinions, to the theories and reasoning presented in those chapters. In the remainder of the present article, the author will merely present, in abbreviated form, some of the important conclusions more fully stated and supported there.

First and foremost, extrinsic evidence is always necessary in the interpretation of a written instrument: in determining the meaning and intention of the parties who executed or relied upon it, in applying it to the objects and persons involved in the litigated or otherwise disputed issues, in determining the specific legal operation that justice requires to be given to the written instrument. In this process of interpretation, no relevant credible evidence is inadmissible merely because it is extrinsic; all such evidence is necessarily extrinsic. When a court makes the often repeated statement that the written words are so plain and clear and unambiguous that they need no interpretation and that evidence is not admissible, it is making an interpretation on the sole basis of the extrinsic evidence of its own linguistic experience and education, of which it merely takes judicial notice.

The so-called parol evidence rule is not a rule of evidence and has no application in the process of interpretation of a written instrument. It is now most commonly described as a rule of substantive law, even by a court that erroneously applies it to exclude relevant credible evidence. The supposed rule is so variable in its formulation, and its application as an exclusionary rule is so generally avoided in so many ways, that it is erroneous and unjust to apply it for the purpose of excluding evidence that is offered in aid of interpretation. When it is established by relevant credible evidence that the parties have mutually assented to a specific written instrument as a complete and accurate statement of the terms of their contract

[47] United States v. Tyler, 220 F. Supp. 386 (N.D. Iowa, 1963); United States v. Merchants Mut. Bonding Co., 220 F. Supp. 163 (N.D. Iowa 1963).

(an integration) and the words of that instrument have been properly interpreted with the aid of all relevant extrinsic evidence, that instrument operates as a discharge of all antecedent agreements and negotiations (oral or written) that are inconsistent therewith. This is a rule of substantive contract law, not a rule of evidence. Such antecedent agreements (oral or written) are not rendered inadmissible in evidence; they are merely rendered inoperative by having been discharged by a subsequent agreement that has been duly proved and interpreted.

Whenever a person has made to another person a written promise for which that other has given a consideration or in reliance on which he has reasonably changed his position, the court in its interpretation of the words of that promise must take into account the intention and understanding of each of the two parties—the "meaning" attributed to the words by each of them. If they have inconsistent intentions and understandings, having given materially different interpretations to the words, no valid contract has been made unless the conduct of the promisor has been

such that he is equitably estopped from asserting his own interpretation as against that given to his words by the promisee. A promisor may be legally bound in accordance with the promisee's intention and understanding if he actually knew or had reason to know such intention and understanding. The promisor is thus bound, not because the promisee's interpretation is the one and only true or objective interpretation of the written words, but because he knew or had reason to know the understanding of the promisee and permitted him to act in reliance thereon. In determining whether a promisor is bound by reason of his having had reason to know (without actual knowledge), his conduct must be considered in relation to all the circumstances of the case, including the customs and usages of other men in similar circumstances. Among these usages are the usages of words, as reported in respectable dictionaries and testified to by competent witnesses. Not one of the usages, however, constitutes the one true and objective meaning by which the promisor or anybody else is bound.

E. Allan Farnsworth, *"Meaning" in the Law of Contracts,* 76 Yale L.J. 939 (1967)

Introduction

Although contract disputes often turn on the interpretation of contract language, this subject has received relatively little attention, especially when compared to that lavished on the interpretation of statutory language. This article will examine some of the conflicting assumptions American courts make in interpreting contract language, and will offer some suggestions for change.

A number of writers have taken pains to distinguish the process of interpretation from that of construction, a distinction that goes back to Lieber. He defined interpretation as "the art of finding out . . . the sense which their author intended [words] to convey." Construction, on the other hand, "is the drawing of conclusions respecting subjects, that lie beyond the direct expression of the text, from elements known from and given in the text—conclusions which are in

the spirit, though not within the letter of the text."[2] To Lieber, then, the boundary between interpretation and construction was the boundary between "letter," or "direct expression," and "spirit."

Corbin has stated the modern version of the distinction. He limited the process of interpretation to the language of the contract and argued that interpretation is "the process whereby one person gives a meaning to the symbols of expression used by the other person." In contrast, construction of the contract is the determination of the contract's "legal operation—its effect upon the action of courts and administrative officials." On this view, while the "meaning" given by the parties to "the symbols of expression" may be clear, the process of construction could lead a court to depart from that "meaning." Williston drew a slightly different distinction. He defined interpretation as the task of determining the

Reprinted by permission of The Yale Law Journal Company and Fred B. Rothman and Company from The Yale Law Journal Company, Vol. 76, pp. 939.

[2] F. Lieber, Legal and Political Hermeneutics 11, 44 (3d ed. 1880).

"meaning" of expressions used in an agreement, but this task is accomplished by the application of something he called "the legal standard" to these expressions. This idea of using a legal standard will turn out to have important consequences on Williston's view of the parol evidence rule—a view that differs significantly from Corbin's. As for construction, Williston defined it as the determination of "the legal meaning of the entire contract."

"Interpretation" will be used here in this modern sense to refer to the process by which courts determine the "meaning" of the language. We are not concerned with overriding legal rules which may render contract language ineffective after it has been interpreted. Nor are we concerned with "gap filling" by which the absence of contract language is remedied. Our concern is exclusively with contract language and its meaning.

The Search for "Meaning"

In Semantics

Writers on semantics have characterized "meaning" as "the arch-ambiguity,"[5] as "a harlot among words . . . a temptress who can seduce the writer and the speaker from the path of intellectual chastity." They tend to shun the term. However, the semanticists Ogden and Richards, who produced a representative list of sixteen main definitions of the word "meaning" as used by philosophers, could have found more grist for their mill in writings on contract law.

Some philosophers, following the distinction suggested by John Stuart Mill, have defined "meaning" as the connotation or intension of a word (the characteristics which determine the objects to which it can correctly be applied and which mark them out from other objects) as opposed to its denotation or extension (the objects to which the word correctly applies). Thus according to the contemporary philosopher Quine, the terms "creature with a heart" and "creature with a kidney" are perhaps alike in denotation, as denoting the same objects, but are unlike in connotation, and therefore unlike in "meaning."[10]

Ogden and Richards rejected this definition of "meaning" as "highly artificial" and as relying on a concept of "correct usage". . . .

. . .

The temptation to look to semantics for help in coping with contract language is aggravated by the fact that in form it is deceptively similar to the language of science, with which semantics has been mainly concerned. The terms of a contract ("Seller will deliver the goods to Buyer at Seller's warehouse") may be similar in form to the laws of science ("Ice will melt at 32 degrees F"), but they are totally different in significance. Since the language of scientific discourse is used descriptively, our concern is mainly with its truth. Since contract language is used to control behavior, our concern is mainly with the expectations that it incites in the contracting parties. This is not to say that contract law has no concern for truth, for if the seller sells wood as "braziletto," a court may be called upon to decide whether it is in fact braziletto or peachum. But such questions of fact, which concern truth, arise only after questions of law, which concern the expectations of the parties, have been answered: Was the seller bound to deliver braziletto rather than peachum? The answers to these questions turn not on truth but on the expectations of the parties, and it is there that we must look in our search for the "meaning" of contract language.

In Contract Interpretation

One of the doctrines that is said to have retarded the development of contract law is the "subjective theory," under which it was supposed that the creation of a contractual obligation required a coincidence of the actual mental process of both parties, "a meeting of the minds." Generations of crusaders have so succeeded in extirpating this view that Judge Learned Hand could record, in his oft-quoted dictum, that

A contract has, strictly speaking, nothing to do with the personal, or individual, intent of the parties . . . . If . . . it were proved by twenty bishops that either party, when he used the words, intended something else than the usual meaning which the law imposes upon them, he would still be held, unless there were some mutual mistake or something else of the sort.

Note that Hand, with typical crusader's zeal, denied not only the *necessity* of a "meeting of the minds," but even its *relevance.*

. . .

[Professor Farnsworth gives an entertaining history of the term "meeting of the minds" and notes that while the concept of subjective intention to contract had only brief impact, courts still pay lip service

---

[5] C. Ogden & I. Richards, The Meaning of Meaning 104 (8th ed. 1947) [hereinafter cited as Ogden & Richards].

[10] W. Quine, From A Logical Point Of View 21 (1952).

to the phrase in contract formation cases. The phrase, however, has ceased to have practical consequences in this area of contract law. —ed.]

The grip of the metaphor in matters of contract interpretation must have appeared even more tenuous. Here, too, courts reiterated the requirement that there be a meeting of the minds, but here there was never a recognized body of case law . . . that gave it practical consequences. No responsible authority seems ever to have suggested that the process of interpretation dealt only with those terms on which there was a meeting of the minds at the time of the agreement. Unhappily, many commentators, as exemplified by Hand's dictum, have jumped from the premise that a meeting of the minds is unnecessary to the conclusion that the actual intentions of the parties are irrelevant to the process of interpretation.

We can explore the merit of this conclusion by formulating three competing definitions of "meaning" which differ in the extent to which they take account of the actual intentions of the parties. These three definitions are:

(1) That to which either party believes the other to be referring.

(2) That to which either party refers.

(3) That to which either party ought to be referring.

The first definition was proposed by the eighteenth-century moral philosopher, William Paley, who maintained that a promise is to be performed in "the sense . . . in which the promisor believed that the promisee accepted the promise." In support of his principle, Paley put his case of Temures who, after promising the garrison of Sebasta that no blood should be shed if they surrendered, buried them alive when they accepted his terms. It was the sense in which he should have apprehended that the garrison received his promise that should have controlled. John Austin criticized this rule of pure expectation on the ground that it would be particularly unfair in the case where the promisor underrates the promisee's expectation. Archbishop Whately amended the rule so that "the right meaning of any expression is that which may be *fairly presumed to be understood* by it." So transformed, this rule derived from Paley is essentially that later adopted for unintegrated contracts by both Williston and the *Restatement*. The *Restatement* sets up a standard of "reasonable expecta-

tion" under which "words or other manifestations of intention forming an agreement . . . are given the meaning which the party making the manifestations should reasonably expect that the other party would give to them . . . ." The first definition has now become one of *reasonable* belief: that to which one party has reason to believe the other party is referring. Note that at no point in its evolution has this definition of "meaning" taken any account of either party's actual expectation, as opposed to what the other party believed, or had reason to believe, it to be.

The second definition is purely subjective. Although no modern writer favors it as an exclusive test, Corbin argued for a modified version of it:

[A] party should be permitted to determine the operative meaning of the words of agreement by proving that both parties so understood them or that he so understood them and the other party knew that he did, or that he so understood them and the other party had reason to know that he did.[41]

Thus recast, the second definition defines meaning as that to which either party refers *if* it is the same as that to which the other party refers or believes or has reason to believe the first party to be referring. This definition does take account of the parties' actual expectations.

The third definition, that to which either party ought to be referring, involves the consideration of "common usage," criticized by Ogden and Richards in their discussion of the definition of meaning as connotation. It relies upon the way in which language is used in the community, and it is commonly associated with definitions found in dictionaries. This is the standard that the *Restatement* and Williston bid us apply to integrated agreements, and it will be discussed later in connection with the search for "plain meaning." Note that this definition, like the first, takes no account of either party's actual expectation. For the present, however, our attention will be confined to the first two definitions.

These two definitions, in their modified forms, can be compared through a series of hypotheticals based on the celebrated case of *Raffles v. Wichelhaus*.[43] In that case, it will be recalled, the parties ageed upon the sale of cotton to arrive "ex Peerless" from Bombay without realizing that there were two ships named "Peerless" leaving Bombay at different times.

---

[41] 3 Corbin § 538, at 59-61. See also Corbin, Conditions in the Law of Contract, 28 Yale L. J. 739, 740 (1919).

[43] 159 Eng. Rep. 375 (Ex. 1864).

The buyer had in mind the ship that sailed in October, and the seller had in mind the ship that sailed in December. The court held that there was no contract. At the outset it may be well to dispose of the exceptional group of cases of which the "Peerless" case itself is typical.

Illustration 1. A offered to sell B goods shipped from Bombay "ex Peerless." B accepted. There were two steamers of the name "Peerless" sailing from Bombay at materially different times. A referred to Peerless No. 1, and he neither believed nor had reason to believe that B referred to Peerless No. 2. B referred to Peerless No. 2, and he neither believed nor had reason to believe that A referred to Peerless No. 1.

Under the first definition, no meaning of "Peerless" can be determined because neither party had reason to believe that the other referred to a different ship. Under the second definition, no meaning of "Peerless" can be determined because each party referred to a different ship and in neither case did the other believe or have reason to believe this. Such cases rarely arise, and when they do, they are often dealt with under the rubric of "mistake." Neither definition fares better than the other and courts have reluctantly followed the original "Peerless" case in holding that no contract has been formed.

More significant are the cases in which the parties make different references, but one and only one party has reason to know that made by the other.

Illustration 2. The facts being otherwise as stated in Illustration 1, A referred to Peerless No. 1 but had reason to believe that B referred to Peerless No. 2. B referred to Peerless No. 2, and he neither believed nor had reason to believe that A referred to Peerless No. 1.

Under the first definition, the meaning of "Peerless" is Peerless No. 2 because A believed that B referred to Peerless No. 2. Under the second definition, the meaning of "Peerless" is also Peerless No. 2 because B referred to Peerless No. 2 and A had reason to believe it. The great majority of the cases relied upon by the proponents of both definitions turn out on inspection to be instances of this sort in which the result would have been the same regardless of which definition had been used. The frequency of this kind of situation bears out the fact that it is human nature for a contracting party to tend to give the language an interpretation favorable to himself, even when he suspects that it differs from that of the other party.

Another large group of cases comprehends those in which it cannot be established what reference was made either by one party, or by both parties.

Illustration 3. The facts being otherwise as stated in Illustration 1, it cannot be established to what A referred, but he had reason to believe that B referred to Peerless No. 2. It cannot be established to what B referred, but he neither believed nor had reason to believe that A referred to Peerless No. 1.

Under the first definition, the meaning of "Peerless" is Peerless No. 2, for the same reason given under Illustration 2. Under the second definition, however, no meaning of Peerless can be determined since it is not known what either actually referred to. In such situations, which are of frequent occurrence, the first definition must be applied if a contract is to result.

In many contemporary business transactions, no thought is given by the parties to many matters that are likely later to become important in the event of controversy. Perhaps the contract is embodied in a printed form which has not been prepared by either party; perhaps its clauses have been lifted from a form book; perhaps the deal is a routine one struck by minor functionaries for two contracting business giants. For these and many other reasons the court may have no choice but to look to a standard of reasonableness.

But this is not to say that the references actually made by the parties should not be controlling if it should be possible to establish what they were and that they were the same.

Illustration 4. The facts being otherwise as stated in Illustration 1, A referred to Peerless No. 1 but had reason to believe that B referred to Peerless No. 2. B, however, referred to Peerless No. 1 and had reason to believe that A referred to Peerless No. 2.

Under the first definition, the meaning of "Peerless" is Peerless No. 2, because each party had reason to believe that the other referred to that ship. Under the second definition the meaning of "Peerless" is Peerless No. 1 because both parties referred to that ship (even though it may not have been reasonable for them to have done so).

Illustration 5. The facts being otherwise as stated in Illustration 1, A referred to Peerless No. 1 and had reason to believe that B did too. B referred to Peerless No. 1 but had reason to believe that A referred to Peerless No. 2.

Under the first definition there are two conflicting "meanings" of "Peerless" because each party had reason to believe that the other referred to a different ship. Under the second definition the meaning of "Peerless" is Peerless No. 1 because each party referred to this ship.

It is difficult to believe, however, that any court would reach the results required by the first definition in these last two illustrations. It is hardly surprising that opinions in which that definition has been applied and where the issue has been presented in these stark terms are not to be found. On the other hand, *Berke Moore Co. v. Phoenix Bridge Co.*[46] well illustrates the proper application of the second definition to this kind of situation. There a general contractor undertook to construct the superstructure of a bridge for New Hampshire upon terms which allowed it $12.60 per square yard of concrete on the bridge deck. It then engaged a subcontractor to do the concrete work for $12.00 per square yard of "concrete surface included in the bridge deck." The subcontractor claimed that it was entitled to payment for the number of square yards included in the outer surfaces of the deck, including top, bottom and sides, a total of 8,100. The general contractor refused to pay for more than the number of square yards contained in the upper surface of the deck, a total of 4,184, for which it had been paid by the state. The trial court concluded that at the time of contracting both parties intended that payment be made according to the latter formula. It relied upon their negotiations in concluding that this had been the intention of the subcontractor at the time of contracting. Although there was no direct evidence of the general contractor's intention at that time, the trial court concluded that it must have been the same since the parties, both experienced contractors, had reached very similar figures of $12.60 and $12.00, while the area claimed by the subcontractor was nearly twice that insisted upon by the general contractor. The Supreme Court of New Hampshire upheld the trial court's conclusion, adding:

> The rule which precludes the use of the understanding of one party alone is designed to prevent imposition of his private understanding upon the other party to a bilateral transaction . . . . But when it appears that the understanding of one is the understanding of both, no violation of the rule

results from determination of the mutual understanding according to that of one alone.

> Where the understanding is mutual, it ceases to be the "private," understanding of one party.

Since the court could determine that to which each party referred by the words "concrete surface included in the bridge deck," and since each party made the same reference, it was able to determine the meaning of the language without ever having to determine that to which neither party had reason to believe the other referred. Other opinions are in accord with the point that if the two parties made the same reference, it is unnecessary to decide whether the reference was a reasonable one or what either party had reason to believe.

The point is not that there must be a "meeting of the minds" in order for there to be a contract, but only that if there should be a "meeting of the minds," it ought to be controlling in matters of interpretation regardless of what either party had reason to believe. Corbin maintained that "it is certain that the purpose of the court is in all cases the ascertainment of the 'intention of the parties' if they had one in common." Folke Schmidt assumed that "all agree upon one very essential point: that what both parties have intended should decide the content of the agreement." And happily, the draftsmen of the *Restatement Second of Contracts* appear to have tacitly adopted the same principle.

The object of contract law is to protect the justifiable expectations of the contracting parties themselves, not those of third parties, even reasonable third parties. A formula, such as the first definition, which takes no account of the actual expectation of either party is unlikely to render good service. "Meaning" for the purpose of contract interpretation should therefore be defined as: (1) that to which either party refers, where it can be determined and where it can be established that it is the same as that to which the other party refers, or believes or has reason to believe the first party to be referring; and, only failing this, (2) that to which either party has reason to believe the other to be referring. Interpretation then becomes the process applied to the language of the parties by which this meaning is determined. It is sometimes supposed, however, that

---

[46] 98 N.H. 261, 98 A.2d 150 (1953). But cf. Eustis Mining Co. v. Beer, Sondheimer & Co., 239 Fed. 976 (S.D.N.Y. 1917).

language can be so clear that no recourse need be had to external circumstances to determine its meaning. Are there circumstances under which the meaning of language is so "plain" that some other definition of that term is appropriate?

The Search for Plain Meaning

In Semantics

The very concept of plain meaning finds scant support in semantics, where one of the cardinal teachings is the fallibility of language as a means of communication. Waismann lamented that,

> Ordinary language simply has not got the "hardness," the logical hardness, to cut axioms in it. It needs something like a metallic substance to carve a deductive system out of it such as Euclid's. But common speech? If you begin to draw inferences it soon begins to go "soft" and fluffs up somewhere. You may just as well carve cameos on a cheese soufflé. [52]

Much of this softness of language comes from the differing ways in which we learn to use words, for the use of a symbol for communication is ordinarily preceded by an elaborate process of conditioning which may vary greatly with the individual. According to Skinner, a leading figure among psychologists and philosophers who study language learning, this process takes place in roughly the following manner. In late infancy children begin to emit sounds in a random way, to babble. The parents show pleasure when they hear patterns that sound like words among the random noises. Their display of pleasure serves as a reward for the child, which reinforces both his ability and desire to repeat these sound-patterns. In this way a vocabulary is acquired. The child learns to use this vocabulary correctly and to respond to words themselves as stimuli by associating words with the stimuli presented at the time of a rewarded bit of babbling. A rudimentary form of trial and error serves to weed out irrelevant stimuli.

This account of language learning shows two reasons why vagueness pervades language. First, each person learns words on the basis of different sets of stimuli. To borrow Quine's example of the word "red," some will have learned this word in situations where red was sharply contrasted with other colors that differ greatly; others will have learned it by being rewarded for distinguishing red from other reddish colors. It seems clear that the former group will use "red" more freely than the latter group. Second, the abilities of people to group stimulations into sets differ somewhat. Thus, some children will simply respond "red" when either a red object or a crimson object comes into view and will remain incapable of distinguishing them.

Quine has built upon Skinner's theory of language learning to explain the concept of vagueness. According to Quine, "stimulations eliciting a verbal response, say 'red,' are best depicted as forming not a neatly bounded class but a distribution about a central norm." [54] The idea of a central norm is useful in explaining the concept of vagueness, for a word is vague to the extent that it can apply to stimuli that depart from its central norm.

Contract language abounds in perturbing examples of vagueness. The parties provide for the removal of "all the dirt" on a tract; may sand from a stratum of subsoil be taken? [55] An American seller and a Swiss buyer agree upon the sale of "chicken"; is stewing chicken "chicken"? [56] Vagueness may even infect a term that has an apparently precise connotation. The parties contract for the sale of horsemeat scraps "Minimum 50% protein"; may evidence be admitted to show that by trade usage scraps containing 49.5% or more conform? [57]

Ambiguity, properly defined, is an entirely distinct concept from that of vagueness. A word that may or may not be applicable to marginal objects is vague. But a word may also have two entirely different connotations so that it may be applied to an object and be at the same time both clearly appropriate and inappropriate, as the word "light" may be when applied to dark feathers. [58] Such a word is ambiguous.

. . .

Ambiguities may be classified into those of term and those of syntax. As Young has pointed out, true

[52] Waismann, How I See Philosophty, in Logical Positivism 345 (A. Ayer ed. 1959).

[54] W. Quine, Word and Object 85 (1960). See also Id. at 126.

[55] See Highley v. Phillips, 176 Md. 463, 5 A.2d 824 (1939) (held: yes).

[56] See Frigaliment Importing Co. v. B.N.S. Int'l Sales Corp., 190 F. Supp. 116 (S.D.N.Y. 1960) (held: for seller).

[57] See Hurst v. Lake & Co., 141 Ore. 306, 16 P.2d 627 (1932) (held: yes).

[58] The example is from W. Quine, Word and Object 129 (1960).

examples of ambiguity of term are rare in contract cases. A contract specifies "tons"; are they to be long or short tons? A charter party provides that a vessel must be "double-rigged," which by usage can refer to either two winches and two booms per hatch, or four of each per hatch; how many must the vessel have? An important variety of ambiguity of term, for our purposes, is proper name ambiguity, the kind of ambiguity that plagued Shakespeare's Cinna,[66] the kind of ambiguity that we deliberately create when we name a child after someone. It was this kind of ambiguity that was involved in the celebrated case of the ships "Peerless."

An ambiguity of syntax is, in the strictest sense, an ambiguity of grammatical structure, of what is syntactically connected with what. A classic example is, "And Satan trembles when he sees/ The weakest saint upon his knees," in which the ambiguity is that of pronominal reference.

Ambiguity of syntax is probably a more common cause of contract disputes than is ambiguity of term. An insurance policy covers any "disease of organs of the body not common to both sexes"; does it include a fibroid tumor (which can occur on any organ) of the womb?

A contract provides that, "Before the livestock is removed from the possession of the carrier or mingled with other livestock, the shipper . . . shall inform in writing the delivery carrier of any visible injuries to the livestock"; is it enough that he notify before mingling although after removal?

Ambiguity in contracts may also result from inconsistent or conflicting language. A buyer agrees to pay "at the rate of $1.25 per M" for all the timber on a designated tract, and that "the entire sale and purchase price of said lumber is $1400.00"; how much must he pay for 4,000 M feet? In many of these cases the conflict is between language in a form contract and that added by the parties for the particular transaction. A printed warranty in the sale of a house requires the owner to give notice of breach "within one year from . . . the date of initial occupancy" and also provides that "notice of nonconformity must be delivered no later than January 6, 1957," the date having been inserted by hand; when must the buyer give notice if he moves in on May 16, 1955?

It would be wrong to assume that the failure of contract language to dispose of a dispute that later arises is invariably due to some inherent fallibility of language as a means of communication. The parties may simply not have foreseen the problem at the time of contracting. An insurance contract on a motor vessel covers "collision with any other ship or vessel"; is a collision with an anchored flying boat included? Or one or both may have foreseen the problem but deliberately refrained from raising it during the negotiations for fear that they might fail—the lawyer who "wakes these sleeping dogs" by insisting that they be resolved may cost his client the bargain. An elderly lady enters a home for the aged, paying a lump sum, to be returned to her "if it should be found advisable to discontinue her stay" during a two-month probationary period; must the home refund her money if she dies within that time?" Or both may have foreseen the problem but chosen to deal with it only in general terms, delegating the ultimate resolution of particular controversies to the appropriate forum. A contract for the sale of wool requires "prompt" shipment from New Zealand to Philadelphia; does shipment in 52 days conform? It is interesting to note that while either ambiguity or vagueness may result from the other causes just suggested, only vagueness is suitable for use in such a conscious attempt at delegation.

Having seen, then, that vagueness and ambiguity represent different concepts and that for various reasons they pervade contract language, we now pursue the search for "plain meaning" into the field of contract interpretation itself.

In Contract Interpretation

The concept of a plain meaning of language has found a more hospitable climate in the field of contract law than it has in semantics. The problem is not, however, that courts engaged in interpreting contracts have assumed that there is always a fixed connection between a word and its referent. While they may have made that assumption for the interpretation of such formal instruments as wills and deeds, they seem not to have done so for the interpretation of informal contracts, since from earliest times courts have been willing to vary the meaning of words according to custom or usage. An early example is *Wing v. Earle*, decided in Queen's Bench in 1592. The defendant had contracted to sell wooded land near the town of Rye to the plaintiff. A statute

---

[66] "Cinna: I am Cinna the poet . . . . I am not Cinna the conspirator! Second Plebian: It is no matter, his name's Cinna; pluck but his name out of his heart and turn him going."

Julius Caesar, III, iii.

designed to prevent the depletion of woodlands by iron mills forbade the use for the making of iron of any wood within four miles of Rye, and it was made a condition of the contract that the land in question be four miles from Rye. The land was over four miles from Rye by the nearest route, but less than four miles as the crow flies. Generally, distances were measured by the "English form," that is, by the nearest route, and they were so measured under the statute. Nevertheless the plaintiff had judgment because the case was on the condition and not the statute, and it was the local usage to measure it "as a bird shall fly."

While courts engaged in contract interpretation, then, have not adopted the idea that there is *always* a fixed and inevitable connection between word and object, they have found it difficult to rid themselves of the influence of this view. They have tended to attribute a definitive quality to written words. This tendency is exemplified by the parol evidence rule, which deserves close examination in light of the points we have just discussed.

Of the parol evidence rule, Thayer wrote: "Few things are darker than this, or fuller of subtle difficulties." Typically, the rule is called into play where the parties have reduced their contract to writing after oral or written negotiations in which they have given assurances, made promises, or reached understandings. When, in the event of litigation, one of them seeks to introduce evidence of these negotiations to support his version of the contract, he will be met with this rule which, if it applies, will preclude his reliance on such "parol evidence," that is to say, on prior oral or written or contemporaneous oral negotiations.

The principle behind the parol evidence rule has been the subject of speculation. McCormick saw it through the eyes of an authority on evidence. He argued that where parties of unequal economic status advance conflicting claims based upon the written word and the oral word, respectively, the party relying on the written word is more likely to be the richer, the one relying on the oral word the poorer. Since, under these circumstances, the jury is not likely to take sufficient account of the unreliability of the narrative of an interested witness, there is a "grave danger that honest expectations, based upon carefully considered written transactions, may be defeated." McCormick's explanation is faulty, however, since it goes only to prior *oral* negotiations and fails to account for the exclusion of prior *written* negotia-

tions, as to which his arguments have little force. A more satisfactory rationale is that of Corbin, who viewed it as a specialist in contracts:

> Any contract, however made or evidenced, can be discharged or modified by subsequent agreement of the parties. . . . This, it is believed, is the substance of what has been unfortunately called the "parol evidence rule." . . . If the foregoing is true of antecedent contracts that were once legally operative and enforceable, it is equally true of preliminary negotiations that were not themselves mutually agreed upon or enforceable at law. . . . [T]he legal relations of the parties are now governed by the terms of the new agreement. This is so because it is the agreement of today, whether that which had happened yesterday was itself a contract or was nothing more than inoperative negotiation.

For the rule to apply at all, a court must first conclude that the parties regarded the documents as a sort of exclusive memorial of their transaction, an "integration." This happens if the parties adopt a writing as the final, complete, and exclusive expression of their agreement. Once it is judicially determined that the agreement is "integrated," then the parol evidence rule applies, and prior oral or written and contemporaneous oral agreements are "inoperative to add to or to vary the agreement." It is generally recognized, however, that this prohibition against addition and variation does not necessarily preclude resort to parol evidence when it is offered for the purpose of interpretation of language. Here there are two conflicting views.

Under the older and more restrictive, parol evidence may only be used for the purpose of interpretation where the language in the writing is "ambiguous." The decision to admit parol evidence, that is, consists of two steps: first, one decides whether the language is ambiguous; second, if it is ambiguous, then one admits parol evidence only for the purpose of clearing up that ambiguity. This is the view adopted both by Williston and by the *Restatement of Contracts*. The standard for integrated agreements is a variant of the last of the three definitions of meaning set out earlier, "That to which either party ought to be referring." Accordingly, the *Restatement* provides that in the absence of ambiguity, the standard of interpretation to be applied to an integration is "the meaning that would be attached . . . by a reasonably intelligent person" familiar with all operative usages and knowing all the circumstances other than oral statements by the parties about what they intended the words to mean.

Under the newer and more liberal view championed by Corbin, the parol evidence rule is not applicable at all to matters of interpretation. On this view there is only one standard, applicable alike to integrated and unintegrated agreements, and parol evidence is always admissible in either of these two cases so long as it is used for the purpose of interpretation. The court need not first determine that the language is "ambiguous." This latter version of the rule seems more meaningful.[90]

The principal instance in which the two views give conflicting results occurs when the parties reach an oral understanding whose meaning differs from what would be inferred by the *Restatement*'s "reasonably intelligent person." This can be illustrated by another example based on the Peerless case.

Illustration 6. A, by an agreement evidenced by an integration, contracted to sell B goods shipped from Bombay "ex Peerless." There were two steamers of the name "Peerless" sailing from Bombay at materially different times. A and B orally agreed that they were referring to Peerless No. 1, but a reasonably intelligent person acquainted with all operative usages and knowing all the circumstances, other than the oral agreement, would have referred to Peerless No. 2.[91]

Under the more restrictive view, it will be remembered, the court must determine whether "Peerless" as used in the writing is ambiguous. Assuming that it would conclude that it is not, parol evidence would be excluded. And since the reasonably intelligent person would have referred to Peerless No. 2, the court will find that to be the meaning of "Peerless." Under the more liberal view, however, since the purpose for which the evidence is offered is clearly that of "interpretation" of "Peerless," the court will admit evidence of the oral agreement and find the "meaning" of "Peerless" to be Peerless No. 1.

Under the more restrictive view, therefore, the parties do not have absolute freedom to attach special meanings to ordinary words. This view is kin to the much discredited "plain meaning" rule in the field of

statutory interpretation, which excludes from consideration the statute's legislative history where the meaning of the statutory language is "plain." For if parol evidence may only be used to interpret the language of an integrated agreement where that language is ambiguous, the effect is to exclude the "transactional history" of the contract where the meaning of the integration is "plain."

The problem then becomes one of determining what constitutes ambiguity for this purpose. A hoary distinction between a patent ambiguity, one apparent from the face of the writing (*e.g.*, that inherent in "and" or "or"), and a latent ambiguity, one apparent only from extrinsic circumstances (*e.g.*, that inherent in "Peerless") has come down to us from Bacon's maxims. The distinction has long been used to explain the result in the "Peerless" case, which is then regarded as being limited to latent ambiguities. Thayer, however, rejected the distinction as an "unprofitable subtlety" and it appears to have lost currency. Once it is recognized, as Quine has shown, that the referent of a word is heavily dependent upon its context, the distinction becomes blurred and many supposedly latent ambiguities can be seen instead as patent ones. Thus once the ambiguity *inherent* in proper names is granted, even the supposedly latent ambiguity in the "Peerless" case takes on the character of a patent one, apparent on its face to an observer versed in Quine.

Generally, the term "ambiguity" is used loosely under the more restrictive view of the parol evidence rule, so that it includes not only patent and latent ambiguities, but vagueness as well. In one recent case, for example, the issue was whether the word "liabilities" included liabilities that were unknown and unforeseen and not stated on the balance sheet." Strictly, the problem was one of the vagueness of "liabilities" and not of its ambiguity. The court, nevertheless, held that parol evidence was admissible because the word "liability" was ambiguous, explaining: "An ambiguous contract is one capable of being understood in more senses than one; an agreement obscure in meaning through indefiniteness of expression, or having a double meaning." In other words, the court

---

[90] Corbin, The Interpretation of Words and the Parol Evidence Rule, 50 Cornell L.Q. 161 (1965). This view seems to be supported by Uniform Commercial Code § 2-202, which states the parol evidence rule so as to forbid contradiction but not interpretation, without regard to "ambiguity."

[91] The comparable Restatement example is Illustration 1 to § 230, which involves an integrated agreement for the sale of certain patents, which A, the seller, understands to

be only the English, but B, the buyer, understands to be the English, French and American. If a reasonable person under the standard of limited usage would understand this as a sale of the English and American, but not French, patents, then A and B are bound by the meaning. As Corbin points out, this example seems to be a distortion of Preston v. Luck, 27 Ch. D. 497 (1884). See 3 Corbin § 539 n.60.

defined "ambiguity" to include vagueness as well as ambiguity, and then admitted parol evidence where only vagueness existed. Indeed, some formulations of the traditional view specifically use the term "uncertainty" in addition to "ambiguity." Furthermore, courts have become increasingly willing to recognize the presence of both ambiguity and vagueness.

In spite of this liberalization of the more restrictive view, is there any excuse for the continued insistence upon ambiguity or vagueness in the integration in an era when the concept of a "plain" meaning of words has become justifiably suspect? Williston defended the more restrictive view on the ground that in unintegrated contracts the parties are not primarily paying attention to the symbols which they are using but have in mind the things for which the symbols stand. He claimed that just the opposite is true in the case of an integration. The basis for this assumption does not appear, and the image of the parties considering the things for which the symbols stand rather than the symbols themselves seems as appropriate to a contract made on a standard printed form containing an integration clause among its boilerplate as to a more informal sort of transaction. On a more practical level, Williston suggested that exclusion of parol evidence, even for the purpose of interpretation, may be dictated by two factors: first by fairness to the other party, who may have been justified in assuming an intention different from that which actually existed; and second, by the desirability of a reasonable certainty of proof of the terms of the contract. The first argument is scarcely compelling if it has been determined that *both* parties used words in a way different from that dictated by general or limited usage. As to the second, the curious fact that the *Restatement* formulation of the more restrictive view speaks only to "oral statements," while the parol evidence rule generally applies to prior written statements as well, suggests that this branch of the rule places more reliance on the desirability of certainty of proof for its justification. Since, however interpretation is ordinarily regarded as a matter of law rather than one of fact, so that it falls within the province of judge rather than of jury, there is an adequate safeguard, if one is needed, against the risk of insubstantial evidence.

The more liberal view is more persuasive. This view makes it unnecessary to determine whether the language of an integrated writing is "plain" as op-posed to "ambiguous" or "vague." Instead the task is to characterize the process involved as that of "interpreting" the writing on the one hand, or as that of "adding to" or "varying" it on the other. The distinction can be justified on the ground that although the writing is an integration and the parties have assented to it as a complete and exclusive statement of terms, the imprecise nature of language still leaves room for interpretation.

The question is then, when does "interpretation" end and "addition" or "variation" begin? The answer under the definition of "interpretation," arrived at earlier must be, interpretation ends with the resolution of problems which derive from the failure of language, that is to say with the resolution of ambiguity and vagueness. Accordingly, even under the liberal view, parol evidence is admissible only where vagueness or ambiguity is claimed. In many cases this will produce the same result as the restrictive view—that parol evidence is admissible only where the meaning of the writing is not "plain." The principal departure is that while the restrictive view confines the court to the language of the integration itself and requires it to decide whether there is ambiguity or vagueness, the liberal view simply requires the court to look to the purpose for which the parol evidence is sought to be introduced, without the necessity of deciding beforehand whether the language is, in fact, ambiguous or vague. The significance of this difference will be more apparent after a discussiom of some of the cases in which courts have wrestled with these problems.

Many of the cases in which courts claim to have rejected the more liberal view and excluded parol evidence which was offered for the purpose of interpretation turn out on careful analysis to be cases in which the evidence was not actually offered for this purpose at all. In *Imbach v. Schultz*,[102] for example, an integrated deposit receipt for a real estate deal contained an agreement to pay "as commission on closing the sum of Eighteen Thousand Five Hundred 18,500 Dollars, or one-half the deposit in case same is forfeited by purchaser." The sum was written and the words "on closing" were interlined in ink on a printed form. When the purchaser defaulted, the broker claimed one half of the $15,000 deposit, or $7,500. The seller maintained that he had an understanding with the broker that nothing was to be paid unless the sale was closed. The Supreme Court of California

---

[102] 58 Cal. 2d 585, 377 P.2d 272, 27 Cal. Rptr. 160 (1962).

held it error to admit this. Parol evidence is "not admissible when it is offered, as here, to give the terms of the agreement a meaning to which they are not reasonably susceptible. . . ." But here the evidence was noted for the purpose of *interpretation* of the language of the contract. No term was claimed to be vague or ambiguous. Rather, the evidence was offered to establish an additional term that plainly contradicted the terms of the integrated writing.

Where, in contrast to the case just discussed, parol evidence is offered purely for the purpose of interpretation, courts have generally been ready to admit it, at least after a finding of "vagueness" or "ambiguity." *Asheville Mica Co. v. Commodity Credit Corp.*[105] is typical. The CCC and the General Service Administration both had contracts to buy mica from the plaintiff. The CCC agreed to match any increase in "the unit prices under GSA's purchase contracts." The plaintiff negotiated new contracts with the GSA, but the CCC refused to match these prices, claiming that the term "GSA's purchase contracts" referred only to contracts in existence at the time the contracts with the CCC were made. The federal court of appeals reversed the district court, which had held that the contract sued upon was "so clear on its face as to preclude resort to oral testimony . . . ." The court of appeals relied on parol evidence and approved Corbin's view that parol evidence is always admissible for the purpose of interpretation. Since the purpose for which the evidence was offered was to clear up the claimed vagueness of the word "contracts" and to show that the new contracts were "contracts," the court was correct in its conclusion that only interpretation was involved. Although on this view it was unnecessary for the court to find vagueness or ambiguity, it gratuitously added that "the provision in question is not wholly unambiguous" since it was not limited to existing contracts with GSA.

Upon elimination of the first group of cases in which the rejection of the more liberal view has concerned controversies not actually involving interpretation, and of the second group where courts admitted parol evidence offered for the purposes of interpretation, there remains, of course, a hard core of cases in which the more liberal view has been rejected. *American Sumatra Tobacco Corp. v. Willis*[108] is an example. A tobacco grower was sued on his contract to sell his "entire crop . . . to be grown by me on

about 30 acres." He offered parol evidence to show that he had two farms, that only one of them was referred to by the contract, and that his crop had failed on that farm. The court held that this evidence should have been excluded under the parol evidence rule. Parol evidence was "not admissible to vary, alter, or contradict the terms of a complete and unambiguous written contract." Under the more liberal view this unsatisfactory result would have been avoided. The evidence would have been admitted since it was offered for the purpose of interpretation; that is, to resolve a claimed ambiguity in the term "30 acres." Applicability of the parol evidence rule would have turned simply upon a determination of the purpose for which the evidence was offered, not upon a decision as to whether or not the term was ambiguous.

A similar problem arises in connection with what are sometimes referred to as "private conventions" as to interpretation. Holmes argued against accepting parol evidence of such conventions where the language was "plain," and rejected the notion that the parties to a contract, making sense as it was written, could show that they had orally agreed "that when they wrote five hundred feet it should mean one hundred inches, or that Bunker Hill Monument should signify Old South Church."[110] But as applied to cases of private conventions as well as generally, the unhappy effect of this more restrictive view is to impose upon contracting parties interpretations that were expected by neither of them. It has been suggested that reformation is the proper remedy in these cases. These are not, however, situations where the parties have mistakenly used words which they did not intend, and so where reformation is appropriate to insert the correct words. These are situations where the parties have used the very words intended by them, but have used them in a way not sanctioned by the usage of others. Reformation is neither a necessary nor even an appropriate remedy; judicial interpretation is sufficient.

It is increasingly difficult to justify the restrictive view of the parol evidence rule. Once it is recognized that all language is infected with ambiguity and vagueness, it is senseless to ask a court to determine whether particular language is "ambiguous" or "vague" as opposed to "plain." But it is possible to give content to the terms "ambiguity" and "vague-

[105] 335 F.2d 768 (2d Cir. 1964).
[108] 170 F.2d 215 (5th Cir. 1948).

[110] Holmes, The Theory of Legal Interpretation, 12 Harv. L. Rev. 417, 420 (1899). . . .

ness," and it does make sense to ask a court to determine whether evidence is offered for the purpose of resolving ambiguity or vagueness. By limiting "interpretation" to the resolution of ambiguity or vagueness, we can give meaningful content to the more liberal rule.

Contract Interpretation and "High Weirdness"

In 1968, shortly after the Corbin and Farnsworth articles appeared, the Supreme Court of California virtually emasculated the parol evidence rule in three cases, *Masterson v. Sine*, 68 Cal.2d 222, 486 P.2d 561, 65 Cal. Rptr. 545 (1968); *Pacific Gas & Electric Co. v. G. W. Thomas Drayage & Rigging Co.*, 69 Cal. 2d 33, 442 P.2d 641, 69 Cal. Rptr. 561 (1968); and *Delta Dynamics v. Arioto*, 69 Cal. 2d 525, 446 P.2d 785, 72 Cal. Rptr. 785 (1968). Each opinion was written by Chief Justice Roger Traynor. In *Masterson* Traynor cited many contracts authorities, but in *G. W. Thomas Drayage* Traynor added to the legal writers references to writers on anthropology and semantics, and rejected the notion of a plain meaning as "a remnant of a primitive faith in the inherent potency and inherent meaning of words." To this statement he appended a footnote citing primitive associations of words and magic.

L. Gordon Crovitz, an editorial writer for the Wall Street Journal, recently took on Traynor's *G. W. Thomas Drayage* opinion in a short article with the excellent title of "Saving Contracts From High Wierdness." That article follows. (While Mr. Crovitz's opinions on contract interpretation are worth reading, he doesn't seem to understand that under the rule of *Erie R.R. v. Tompkins*, decided by the Supreme Court more than fifty years ago, a federal judge in a diversity case *must* apply state substantive law whether he agrees with it or not.)

On the merits of the parol evidence rule issue, it should be noted in support of Mr. Crovitz that by the third of the 1968 cases, Justice Stanley Mosk, a wise and progressive judge who had joined in the first two of Traynor's opinions, dissented, saying that "[g]iven two experienced businessmen dealing at arm's length, both represented by competent counsel, it has become virtually impossible under recently evolving rules of evidence to draft a written contract that will produce predictable results in court." However, it can also be argued that the supporters of the parol evidence rule really are distrustful of the jury system. It would be possible to let in whatever evidence was deemed relevant, but to instruct the jury to be skeptical of after-the-fact stories when contract language was drafted by skillful lawyers for both sides. This might be the solution in the particular case discussed by Mr. Crovitz.

The idea that there is no such thing as a core meaning of words and certainly no fixed meaning was one of the matters debated by two great legal philosophers, H. L. A. Hart and Lon Fuller, in 1958. Hart, *Positivism and the Separation of Law and Morals*, 71 Harv. L. Rev. 593 (1958); Fuller, *Positivism and Fidelity to Law—A Reply to Professor Hart*, 72 Harv. L. Rev. 630 (1958). Thus, in the "what is chicken?" case, *Frigaliment*, there are those who contend that the court was wrong to pose the question as if it had a definite answer. In addition, a number of writers have applied modern literary criticism and linguistic theory to law. See, e.g., the symposia on Law and Literature at 39 Mercer L. Rev. 739-935 (1988), and 60 Tex. L. Rev. 373-586 (1982); and Donald H. J. Hermann's *Phenomenology, Structuralism, Hermeneutics, and Legal Study: Applications of Contemporary Continental Thought to Legal Phenomena*, 36 U. Miami L. Rev. 379 (1982). Some of these writers argue that no text has meaning without the active participation of the reader as creator, and without recognizing the role of the "interpretive community" of which the reader is or is not a part. This idea, associated with Stanley Fish who teaches in both the Law School and the English Department at Duke, is in turn derived from Thomas Kuhn's classic of modern philosophy of science, *The Structure of Scientific Revolutions*. On the other hand, it can be traced back at least to Nietzche, who wrote in the nineteenth century that the author is not superior to his text, but rather "is, after all, only a condition of the work, the soil from which it grows, perhaps only the manure on that soil." Mr. Crovitz is alluding to some of these approaches when he scornfully refers to "the deconstructionist theory of the Critical Legal Studies movement."

L. Gordon Crovitz, *Saving Contracts From High Weirdness*, Wall Street Journal, August 3, 1988, p. 16.

The counterrevolution is gaining a beachhead where judicial activism began—in California. The voters replaced the Rose Bird court, and now a member of the federal appeals court in Pasadena is on a one-judge campaign to restore both common law and judicial restraint.

A ruling in a contract dispute issued in May by conservative Judge Alex Kozinski, appointed by President Reagan in 1985 at the record young age of 34, at first seems mystifying in that it reverses a lower-court decision that seemed like an eminently sensible reaction to the litigation explosion. Last year, District Court Judge James Ideman tossed out as baseless a suit by some sophisticated plaintiffs trying to wiggle out of contract obligations. Judge Ideman even assessed a penalty against them for bringing a frivolous case. Judge Kozinski reversed the decision on the ground that after 20 years of judicial activism no contract claim is so ridiculous that it can't win in California.

Law-and-Morality Tale

This riddle is a law-and-morality tale with something for everyone: Litigation-happy lawyers; 1960s judges citing moonbeam legal evidence including "the Swedish peasant custom of curing sick cattle"; and a judge, Mr. Kozinski, who escaped the arbitrary laws of Bucharest when he emigrated in 1962, now hoping to restore the ancient Anglo-American concept of sanctity of contract.

The roots of *Trident Center v. Connecticut General Life Insurance* are in the decision by two of Los Angeles's big law firms, along with two other investing partners, to build their own office towers. The law firms Manatt, Phelps, Rothenberg & Phillips and Mitchell, Silberberg & Knupp decided on a pioneering area for office buildings in West Los Angeles, just off the San Diego Freeway. They borrowed $56.5 million in 1983 to build Trident Center. An office glut soon developed, and carrying the mortgage took a big bite out of the law partners' draw.

At the same time, interest rates fell below the loan's fixed rate. The lawyers went to court, arguing that despite what the contract said about 12-1/4% interest over 15 years, they could prepay the loan subject to a 10% prepayment penalty. They would then refinance at a lower rate.

But the contract was clear that there could be no prepayment for the first 12 years. The promissory note said that Trident "shall not have the right to prepay the principal amount hereof in whole or in part before January 1996." The plaintiffs wanted to offer evidence from the contract negotiations that despite the language, the parties intended that a prepayment was possible at their option. Judge Ideman refused, citing the "parol evidence rule" that extrinsic evidence can't be used to interpret, vary or add to the terms of an unambiguous written agreement.

Judge Ideman went further, and invoked the federal rule against frivolous cases to assess $56,000 in penalties on the plaintiffs for bringing the case. "Plaintiff's contention that it misunderstood the terms in the note and deed of trust is not credible especially since the plaintiff has two reputable law firms as its general partners," he wrote. "No reasonable person, much less firms of able attorneys, could possibly misunderstand this crystal-clear language. . . .Therefore, this action was brought in bad faith."

In his reversal, Judge Kozinski agrees that the language is "devoid of ambiguity." He also agrees that "Trident is attempting to obtain judicial sterilization of its intended default." And he agrees it would be wrong to "truncate the lender's remedies and deprive Connecticut General of its bargained-for protection." Yet he nevertheless ruled the plaintiffs can introduce evidence outside the contract to contradict the written agreement.

There is method in Judge Kozinski's apparent madness. He insists that judicial restraint means that federal judges must be bound by the precedents of state courts when interpreting state law, no matter how awful, until the precedents are changed.

And the precedent here is a real doozy: the 1968 California Supreme Court decision, *Pacific Gas & Electric v. G.W. Thomas Drayage & Rigging*. In that case, there was a clear indemnification provision in a contract, but the court said the words didn't settle the matter. The plaintiffs could present other evidence, which the judges could use to allocate the parties' risks regardless of the contract.

The opinion by then-Chief Justice Roger Traynor rejected the common-law notion that parties must be free to negotiate among themselves. This old view that individuals can use words—that is, contracts—to allocate risks and rewards, he wrote, "is a remnant of a primitive faith in the inherent potency and inherent meaning of words." He concluded that "Words, however, do not have absolute and constant referents."

Judge Traynor went on to cite semantic and anthropologic evidence for his proposition that only primitives ascribe binding meaning to words. This supporting reference appears in what may be the single weirdest footnote in the history of U.S. courts:

"E.g., 'The elaborate system of taboo and verbal prohibitions in primitive groups; the ancient Egyptian myth of Khern, the apotheosis of the words, and of Thoth, the Scribe of Truth, the Giver of Words and Script, the Master of Incantations; the avoidance of the name of God in Brahmanism, Judaism and Islam; totemistic and protective names in medieval Turkish and Finno-Ugrian languages; the misplaced verbal scruples of Precieuses; the Swedish peasant custom of curing sick cattle smitten by witchcraft, by making them swallow a page torn out of the psalter and put in dough. . . .' from Ullman, the Principles of Semantics."

Whatever the Finno-Ugrians had to say, Judge Kozinski emphasizes in his opinion that freewheeling judicial reinterpretations of contracts have made California a dangerous place to do business. Judge Kozinski says "*Pacific Gas* casts a long shadow of uncertainty over all transactions negotiated and executed under the law of California. As *Trident Center* illustrates, even when the transaction is very sizable, even if it involves only sophisticated parties, even if it was negotiated with the aid of counsel, even if it results in contract language that is devoid of ambigu-

ity, costly and protracted litigation cannot be avoided if one party has a strong enough motive for challenging the contract."

In dismissing the frivolous-case fine, Judge Kozinski concludes that "at fault, it seems to us, are not the parties and their lawyers, but the legal system that encourages this kind of lawsuit." He also notes that the activist judges' view of contracts creates problems for other areas of law. "If we are unwilling to say that the parties, dealing face to face, can come up with language that binds them, how can we send anyone to jail for violating statutes consisting of mere words. . . ?"

For that matter, how can Judge Kozinski be sure he knows what the mere words of *Pacific Gas* mean? Such *reductio ad absurdum* reasoning, undermining the rule of law, is what the deconstructionist theory of the Critical Legal Studies movement is all about.

It didn't take long before litigants caught on. After reading the Kozinski opinion, lawyers for Metromedia Inc., which relies on an equally clear contract in a case concerning the ownership of videotapes, urged the California Supreme Court to heed this warning. Metromedia's attorney, Theodore Olson, recently urged the justices, "If anything is to remain of the integrity of written contracts in California, it is necessary for this court to intervene."

This is not the first time a legal system has ignored contract law. The *Pennzoil v. Texaco* case put investors world-wide on notice that anything could happen in a Texas courtroom. Nor is this the first time Judge Kozinski has spoken out for a return to traditional contract law.

'An Important Civilizing Concept'

In February, he decided a case from Guam where the plaintiff wanted to get out of a release he had signed with an automobile insurance company in exchange for a settlement. "Despite recent cynicism, sanctity of contract remains an important civilizing concept," he wrote. "It embodies some very important ideas about the nature of human existence and about personal rights and responsibilities: that people have the right, within the scope of what is lawful, to fix their legal relationship by private agreement; that the future is inherently unknowable and that individuals have different visions of what it may bring . . . and that enforcement of these agreements will not be held hostage to delay, uncertainty, the cost of litigation or the generosity of juries."

The freedom to write contracts and the duty to

abide by their terms are features of American life so basic that it's hard to believe they could be litigated

Yet this is where the law has now led. Judge Kozinski did his best to embarrass the judicial activists into retreat. We will now see if they have any shame.

B. Public Policy, Good Faith, Economic Duress and Unconscionability: Collective Values And Individual Choices (Or Is It All Just Paternalism?)

While not everyone would agree, it can be argued that the four concepts discussed in this section are unified by a concept of collective values that override freedom of contract. To use public policy as an example, if A promises to commit murder in exchange for B's promise of ten thousand dollars, no court will enforce the agreement even if both consented freely and with full understanding. Such a contract used to be called an "illegal contract," but today it is more common to refer to it as "against public policy." While the murder contract might constitute a criminal conspiracy, it often is not a crime to make an "illegal" contract (though it might be a crime to execute it). In addition, courts may refuse to enforce a contract that does not actually violate a criminal law, but may enforce others that do technically violate a law, criminal or civil. In all these "public policy" cases, the question is whether the courts should lend their enforcement powers to some voluntarily agreed upon arrangement that is said to be contrary to some overriding social policy. Similar collisions between what is said to be free contracting and supposed social norms can be found in the other areas covered in this section. They all are subject to the charge that they patronize the apparently favored party and can only be justified as paternalism. Of these charges, more throughout the section and in the concluding note.

1. Public Policy

Walter Gellhorn and Public Policy

Walter M. Gellhorn is University Professor Emeritus at Columbia, where he has taught since 1933. Gellhorn was part of a generation of whiz kids who joined the Columbia law faculty in the early thirties and affected legal education throughout the middle third of the century and beyond. Gellhorn is best known as a great expert on administrative law, but his interests have always been catholic. He was one of the first American writers to introduce the concept of the ombudsman from Scandinavian society; when Gellhorn first wrote about it in the mid-sixties no one could pronounce the word, which now is a commonplace. Although not primarily a torts teacher, Gellhorn—at 82—recently published a comparison of American and New Zealand approaches to medical accidents, *Medical Malpractice Litigation (U.S.)—Medical Mishap Compensation (N.Z.)*, 75 Cornell L. Rev. 170 (1988). Gellhorn was also not primarily a contracts teacher, but he wrote, more than fifty years ago, the classic discussion of public policy as a ground for invalidating contracts. The article follows, almost in its entirety. (A short discussion of contracts made on Sundays is cut since the topic is superannuated.) The article has been influential in pointing the inquiry on public policy away from rules about violations of particular statutes, etc., and towards the key word "policy."

A major area of public policy that remains today is that of the enforcement of employees' agreements not to compete after leaving their current employment. Two important articles on this topic are Milton Handler and Daniel E. Lazaroff, *Restraint of Trade and the Restatement (Second) of Contracts*, 57 N.Y.U. L. Rev. 669 (1982); and Harlan Blake, *Employee Agreements Not to Compete*, 73 Harv. L. Rev. 625 (1960). After the Gellhorn article, we will consider the implications of public policy analysis in an even more contemporary context: surrogate parenting and the *Baby M* case.

Walter Gellhorn, *Contracts and Public Policy*, 35 Colum. L. Rev. 679 (1935)

The "well-settled rule" to the effect that contracts will not be enforced if in violation of a penal statute is applied in many instances with an unthinking rigidity, quite without regard to its rationale. Thus applied, it leads the courts into a morass of obscurities, supposed distinctions, and questionable techniques of decision. A different path, enabling the courts to skirt that morass, is open. Neither precedent nor legislative insistence compels unintelligence.

From early times Anglo-American courts have refused to enforce illegal contracts, that is, those that are "opposed to public policy." As a rule, no substantial distinctions were made by the courts among situations where the contract bore an element of criminality, where the contract might prove to be a step in the commission of the crime (either by way of making its commission possible or by way of enjoying its fruits), and where the contract was merely shocking to the sense of justice and of the fitness of things. In each instance the judges, as representing the community conscience, declared that such contracts should not be executed with the court's assistance, because to assist in their enforcement would be to encourage conduct which was inimical to the public welfare. Until a relatively recent day, be it noted, too, criminal conduct was by definition largely limited to the common law crimes; the full bloom of penal statutes describing new offenses had not yet been attained, and the courts were themselves largely the moulders of thought concerning what was criminal.

When the simplicity of the law-making structure passed, however, and when judges were at least nominally relegated to the role of interstitialists, a web of complexity was cast over what had before seemed to be the easy application of a corollary rule. Now the legislature was the authoritative denouncer of conduct. Now the statutes, rather than judges' opinions, determined what acts were to be regarded as antisocial, that is, against public policy. And now the lawmakers, with a wide range of choice before them, could select the penalties they thought best suited to the proscribed conduct, and, by a generalization, lay down the rule to guide the judiciary in making appropriate disposition of the particular case that might later arise. Acts thought to be undesirable could be discouraged or desired results could be achieved (among other ways) by altering procedural rules, by creating a tort liability or by removing or establishing defenses against such a liability, by imposing taxes, by conditioning the enjoyment of a privilege upon the surrender of some other privilege or upon the performance of an affirmative act, by withdrawing the protection of legal process in the enforcement of claims, by various money impositions, by penalties in the form of fine and imprisonment or both, or by a combination of two or more of these methods.

But when the legislature selected only one sanction to enforce compliance with what it regarded as the public interest, the courts at once came face to face with the problem whether the selection of one negatived the desirability of also utilizing another.

The difficulty, though similar to, was distinct from that with which the courts wrestled when they were perplexed by lacunae or inconsistencies in the law. Whether murderers should be permitted to inherit from their victims;[12] whether unprincipled police methods, as, for instance, flagrant examples of entrapment, should relieve a defendant from punishment for the commission of acts which a statute in terms forbade; whether a sheriff should be prosecuted for interfering with the United States mails when he had arrested a carrier charged with murder—these questions and questions like them were solved by a dubious "interpretation" of the underlying statutes to enable the courts to reach what they considered the "equitable" result. In other instances, faced with the necessity of enforcing the statutes according to their words or of reading into them exceptions or addenda to cover cases which had clearly not been contemplated by the enacting legislatures, the courts, with a modest shrug, have disclaimed the power to make law and have indulged a rigorous application of the statutes.

When, however, the circumstances of a case

---

[12] Riggs v. Palmer, 115 N.Y. 506, 22 N.E. 188 (1889); Estate of Wilkins, 192 Wis. 111, 211 N.W. 652 (1927); and see Effect Upon a Murderer's Estate of Statutes Precluding Murderer's Inheritance from Victim (1934) 44 Yale L. J. 164.

brought it within the very terms of a controlling statute or, at least, so nearly within the reach of its words as to make the relationship plain, the judiciary encountered an even more perplexing problem. No longer could they attach a penal sanction to what had not been otherwise denominated a crime. But could they add to a legislatively declared sanction, civil or penal, the threat of further civil consequences? Thus, one who, contrary to a statute making such conduct tortious, persisted in invading another's right of privacy by publishing his photograph without consent, would not be punished therefor as though he had committed a misdemeanor, no matter how strongly the court might feel that such acts merited punishment. Suppose, however, the existence of a statute which did make such conduct criminal but not tortious. Should the courts then refuse to lend their process to actions upon contracts which, if executed, would violate the statute, or should they hold that the penal sanction had been deemed sufficient by the legislature as a punishment for one who acted contrary to the law? Should they even entertain an action sounding in tort, brought by the person whose privacy had been invaded against the person who had committed the crime of publishing the photograph? [18]

In the field of contracts, in particular, the courts have failed to develop a useful approach to the type of questions just put. The difficulty has lain in their general unwillingness to accept realistically the proposition that the legislature, when adopting a penal statute, has rarely had in mind the problems of contract law that may later arise. Legislators are prone to regard the criminal law as the definitive disposition of undesirable activities. Make something a crime and that thing will promptly disappear, except in so far as a few depraved individuals may continue in their wayward course. If, contrary to expectation, the antisocial manifestations do not vanish forthwith, the cure is a more stringent punishment, to intimidate recalcitrants into a law-abiding frame of mind. Time after time has this progression of ideas appeared; it is almost a pattern of habit with legislators and, even more generally, with the public at large. Despite this general poverty of imagination upon the part of the statute-makers, the courts have persisted in speculating (and in reaching divergent conclusions) as to

whether the legislature "intended" contracts to be treated as void when they ran afoul of laws which penalized some act of the contractors but which said nothing concerning enforcement of the bargains.

Some judges have felt that the imposition of a penalty upon one who disobeyed a statutory command was tantamount to a legislative prohibition of all contracts bearing a relation to the act of disobedience. Others have taken the stand that where no civil sanction was expressly provided, the courts should refuse to supply one; the legislature, evidently enough, had selected what it deemed to be an adequate penalty for lawlessness and the courts should regard that penalty as a "sufficient punishment." Still other courts have undertaken to differentiate their decisions according to whether the contracts in question related to *mala prohibita* or *mala in se*—"that acute distinction between *mala in se*, and *mala prohibita,* which being so shrewd and sounding so pretty, and being in Latin has no sort of an occasion to have any meaning to it; accordingly it has none." Further distinctions have been made between contracts which contravened statutes designed solely for revenue purposes and, on the other hand, statutes which were intended to be prohibitory or which stated conditions "for the benefit of the public"; but the difficulty of drawing the line between the one type and the other vitiates the effectiveness of the distinction, and in any event it is unrealistic to say that the legislature intended or that it did not intend that contracts should be held invalid if in violation of such statutes.

By way of ameliorating the harsh results that would sometimes follow the strict application of the common law maxims which underlie the "void for illegality" rule, courts have also spun fine theories concerning "collateral illegality" and "new and independent considerations." "If a plaintiff can establish his case without directly relying on the illegality, then he can recover"; so runs the dogma. Its application requires nice judgment concerning the remoteness of the connection between the contract in suit and the illegality of the consideration or of the conduct of the parties to the contract. Not only does it seem little calculated to assist in a sharp analysis of the issues involved,[22] but, quite apart from any criticism that may be made on that score, this doctrine has evoked

---

[18] It is not intended to treat herein the various problems of tort law that are created by violations of penal statutes. They are well discussed by Prof. Clarence Morris in The Relation of Criminal Statutes to Tort Liability (1933) 46 Harv. L. Rev. 453. 20.Bentham, Comment on the Commentaries (Everett ed. 1928) 80. See The Distinction Between

Mala Prohibita and Mala in Se in Criminal Law (1930) 30 Columbia Law Rev. 74.

[22] That is to say, inquiries into collaterality, remoteness, newness of consideration and the like may or may not help to determine the answer to the question. Should this particular contract be enforced as being consonant with public

the ireful comment of the quasi-contractualists, who see in it a subjugation of substance to form, that is, order of proof. "In many cases the rule would prevent the relief of persons who are the victims of actual fraud or oppression, or who are intended to be protected by the law which makes the contract illegal. For in order to establish the right to restitution, a plaintiff must prove the circumstances under which he conferred the benefit. This means that he must put the contract in evidence, and if the contract were unlawful on its face he would thereby establish the fact that he was *in pari delicto*, regardless of the circumstances of the formation of the contract and of the purpose of the law in prohibiting it."

The judicial plowing of the soil in this field has led to the growth of patent inanities. Because a contract is part of an illegal transaction is no reason for disregarding its existence or for declining to weigh the consequences of holding it to be void.[26] Nor should a court's disposition of a contract be dependent solely upon whether it purports to find the presence or absence of a purely imaginary legislative intent that a given result be reached.

To inject a rational basis of decision it is necessary to sweep aside the cliches and pseudo-scientific measures which now customarily accompany examination of the question whether courts should enforce contracts in this category. Some courts have already frankly reverted to the old position. They have refused to lend their aid to contracts which they deemed to be contrary to public policy. They have exercised their inherent power to avoid permitting their process to be used for antisocial ends—exercised this power not because legislatively directed to do so in a particular case, but because, in their own discretion, they deemed such an exercise necessary as a protection of the public welfare against noxious consequences.[27]

But the discarding of the present juggling with a non-existent statutory intent must not carry with it the discarding of judicial dependence on the legislative judgment. Statutes denouncing conduct as criminal must continue to be, as they now are, the starting point of the judges' excursions into territory uncharted.

What does or does not represent the general interest is for the legislature to determine. Equipped to make factual investigations, constituted so that in greater or lesser degree it is responsive to the judgments and desires of that balance of interests known as the general public, the legislature must today be regarded as the court of last resort in resolving the clamorous claims for one policy or another. Less and less, even in the disposition of constitutional questions, do the courts seek to substitute for the legislative judgment their own convictions concerning what is wisdom. With diminishing frequency does the student find contemporary counterparts of the frank declaration that "the paternalistic theory of government is to me odious. The utmost liberty to the individual . . . is both the limitation and duty of government," with which comment Justice Brewer once sought to justify his conclusion that a regulatory statute was unconstitutional. Indulgence in subjectivism does still on occasion convert the United States Supreme Court into a super-legislature. But the occasions are happily becoming less numerous. In the complexities of modern life, prejudice and presupposition may no longer be permitted to guide constitutional judgments. The former embarrassing confusions of functions is abating. In the usually less controversial matters which are the subjects of penal statutes there is still smaller reason, or tendency, for the courts to question the definitiveness of the legislative conclusion that what has been proscribed is in fact something which, if not impeded, would operate to the public detriment. In short, every definition of a crime contains an implicit declaration that the results of the prohibited conduct are "against public policy," and there is no justification for the courts' hesitating

---

policy? The stated inquiries are perhaps properly made to acquire information with which to answer the question, but they do not hold in themselves the conclusion. Compare Graves v. Johnson, 179 Mass. 53, 60 N.E. 383 (1901).

[26] It would of course be unfair to say that courts always fail to balance the considerations involved in treating an "illegal" contract. . . . On the other hand, the countenancing of shocking immorality is seen in some of the decisions. In Levy v. Kansas City, Kan., 168 Fed. 524 (C.C.A. 8th 1909), the plaintiff sued to recover $5000 he had paid pursuant to an ordinance authorizing the licensing, upon payment of that sum, of the business of book making and pool selling. A state statute prohibited that business. Two days after plaintiff commenced business, he alleged, the city was instigated

and induced by those who were conducting a rival business to revoke his license and thus to prevent him from carrying on his illegal business. Recovery of the $5000 was denied, the court being of opinion that the controlling issue was the righteousness of the plaintiff's acts; "those of the defendant have little materiality," though they were characterized as "despicable" and "abhorrent to the sense of fairness."

[27] Cf. Fidelity & Deposit Co. of Maryland v. Grand Nat. Bank, 2 F. Supp. 666, 668 (E.D. Mo. 1933): "The question of how close illegality must be woven into a transaction in order to taint it is often difficult to determine. The principle to be applied is one of general public policy, and the inquiry is not alone as to the effect of a particular transaction, but whether its tendency is in the direction of public detriment."

(and slight disposition on their part to hesitate) in accepting that declaration as an appraisal conclusive for the moment, of what is in fact "against public policy."

Having accepted these determinations as embodying the value judgments they were themselves wont to make in an earlier day, the courts must now be prepared to utilize them in weighing the question whether they will aid in enforcing contracts which, while not expressly banned by the legislature, have some tendency to bring about the results which have been officially stigmatized as undesirable. The penal statutes thus become significant not as controlling the disposition of a civil case, but as enlightening the judiciary concerning specific "public policies." In approaching the cases, the judges are not bound to regard as void every contract which seems in some way to fall within the general aura of the criminal law, but only those whose enforcement, they are persuaded, after respectfully studying the "public policy" involved, will disserve the general interest as it has been indicated by the legislature.

The significance of this approach to contract questions is made clearer upon examination of particular cases in which, as is often true, more than one "public policy" is to be affected by the decision.

1. "Whatever is done in contravention of a prohibitory law is void, although the nullity be not formally directed." Thus reads a Louisiana statute which, though part of a civil code, is roughly declaratory of the common law.

In 1924, one Hill, a telegraph operator for the Missouri Pacific Railway, was injured by a robber while he was protecting his employer's property at the town of Tioga, Louisiana. Shortly after this incident, Hill agreed with the railroad to continue in its employ and to relinquish any claim he might be able to assert against it on account of the injuries he had suffered. On its part, the railroad agreed to employ Hill until he was eligible for a pension, in 1933. Nineteen months before the date on which Hill might have retired, and some seven years after the making of the agreement, Hill was discharged on a "trumped-up charge" of drunkenness while on duty. He thereupon brought suit against the railroad to recover for the earnings he had lost in consequence of the breach of the contract.

Judge Dawkins, sitting in the United States District Court for the Western District of Louisiana, interpreted the contract as calling for a bilateral undertaking: a promise by Hill to work for the railroad until he was seventy, or a period of nine years, in return for the railroad's promise of continued employment during that period. This questionable reading of the agreement brought it within the terms of a statute prohibiting adults to bind themselves to labor for terms longer than five years, hence it followed, according to the court, that Hill was without redress, since contracts made in violation of a prohibitory statute are void.[35]

Thus this labor statute, which was no doubt adopted in the first instance as a protection of workers against peonage, was utilized as a shield behind which the employer might with impunity contract with its servants. The claim relinquished by Hill in return for an assurance of security of tenure in his employment seems to have been of slight merit; but many a worker has surrendered a cause of action not because proffered compensation, but because promised future employment.

When, as in that case, the court feels bound without more ado to ignore a contract because it seems violative of a criminal law, it fails to accord proper consideration to other social desiderata, possibly expressed in other statutes, which are also worthy of the court's attention. Refusal to give Hill a remedy may, conceivably have added some compulsive force to the penalties of the Louisiana Labor Law; but it did so perhaps at the cost of encouraging sharp dealing by claim agents. The result of that case, though said to be controlled by a declaratory statute, resembles that reached in the absence of any direction where the courts have failed to apprehend that their task was, first, to discover the reasons for and the policy to be served by the related penal statute; and second, to consider, *as an independent matter*, whether the particular contracts before them should or should not be nullified in the light of all the circumstances, of which the penal statute is only one.

2. In *Short v. Bullion-Beck & Champion Mining Company*[37] the plaintiff sued to recover a sum alleged to be due him for overtime work. He asserted that during a period of five months he had worked twelve hours per day at his employer's request. A state statute provided that the maximum "period of employment" should be eight hours per day and punished "any person, body corporate, agent, manager or employer" who violated the act. The court construed

[35] Hill v. Missouri Pacific Ry. Co., 8 F. Supp. 80 (W.D. La. 1933), discussed in (1935) 35 Columbia Law Rev. 297.

[37] 20 Utah 20, 57 Pac. 720 (1899).

this statute as meaning not only that the employer was subject to a penalty, but also that the employee who worked for more than eight hours, was guilty of a crime. It held, accordingly, that the plaintiff, in working twelve hours, had engaged in a criminal enterprise jointly with his employer, and hence that he was not entitled to recover for the value of his services.

The interpretation of the relevant penal statute seems strained. But even if that interpretation should be fully accepted, the result of the case was still not inevitable. The legislature had not prescribed it; the legislature had said no more than that inducing to work—or, even, working—in certain occupations for more than eight hours per day was "against public policy" because of deleterious effects upon public health. Was that public policy effectuated by enforcing the rule (also founded upon a public policy) that persons who engaged in illegal occupations should not be assisted in securing compensation for their excess, though illegal, services? On the face of the case a negative answer seems clearly, required. To suppose that the decision would deter employees from undertaking over-time work would mean the rejection of the observation made by the United States Supreme Court in considering the validity of the very same statute involved here:[38]

> "The legislature has also recognized the fact, which the experience of legislatures in many states has corroborated, that the proprietors of these establishments and their operatives do not stand upon an equality, and that their interests are, to a certain extent, conflicting. The former naturally desire to obtain as much labor as possible from their employees, while the latter are often induced by the fear of discharge to conform to regulations which their judgment, fairly exercised, would pronounce to be detrimental to their health or strength. In other words, the proprietors lay down the rules and the laborers are practically constrained to obey them."

If the decision affected the policy of limiting work-hours, it could affect it only adversely, since the employer was assured immunity against the necessity of paying wages for any over-time services.

3. Some courts have held that negotiable instruments are unenforcible even in the hands of bona fide purchasers, where they originated out of an illegal transaction. It may well be questioned whether such

holdings serve to assist in suppressing the evils that attended the creation of the instruments so much as they disserve the public interest in the free circulation of negotiable paper.

. . .

5. Another problem that frequently results in litigation arises when equipment is furnished for use in an illegal activity. According to Section 602 (1) of the Contracts Restatement, the improper use vitiates a contract only if the intended purpose of the equipment involves serious moral turpitude (or unless a statute prohibits recovery). As illustration, it is stated that if A sells B a shotgun on credit, knowing that the gun will be used by B in hunting without a license, A can recover the contract price. But if B, to A's knowledge, bought the gun to use in committing a robbery, A could not recover. It often happens that furnishings are supplied by persons who know they are to be used in houses of prostitution. Under the rule stated, may the furnisher successfully maintain an action on the contract? The results of the cases are not consistent. But none of the opinions, so far as the writer is aware, discusses the question from the standpoint of the effectiveness of one result or another upon the policy considerations involved. Does failure to permit recovery on such contracts in fact deter the establishment of houses of prostitution? Or does it encourage prostitutes to purchase freely, knowing that their promises are unenforcible? Is a useful distinction to be drawn between ordinary dealers and persons who regularly engage in business with the underworld? Questions like these are not asked or answered by the courts. Here, as in this whole field, there is tacit assumption that refusal to enforce a contract is an effective sanction to compel observance of penal statutes. In many cases the assumption is well founded. Men of affairs, in undertaking a business relationship, do pause to consider what redress they may have in the event that contractual obligations are not observed. But is this so in every instance? May it not be true that in some circumstances knowledge of unenforcibility of contracts is not so widely disseminated among potential creditors (*e.g.*, small furniture dealers) as among a group of prospective debtors (*e.g.*, prostitutes)? And in any event, if refusal to enforce the contracts between supplier-of-equipment and criminal is deemed to be of some service in deterring the commission of crimes in which the equipment might be used, why must the crime involve "serious moral turpitude" to invalidate

---

[38] Holden v. Hardy, 169 U.S. 366, 397 (1898).

the contract? If on the other hand there is a policy argument to be urged in favor of keeping untrammeled the ordinary processes of bargain and sale, that policy should be evaluated. At present it usually either remains wholly unrecognized or is arbitrarily accorded complete supremacy.

These illustrations indicate not that the courts should reappraise the facts to discover whether given conduct is antisocial, but that they must often balance competing "public policies," must weigh one result against another, must search the whole of statute law for aid in making a wise decision. The process of determination should not be markedly different from that which characterizes the courts' use of judicial opinions in solving common law cases. It is axiomatic that the rules of law in the hornbooks are of limited utility in litigated cases, because the cases customarily do not fall into the neat factual patterns to which the rules have been attached. Combinations of facts bring with them combinations of rules, each with its claim to be recognized as "the governing principle"; here, the courts are forced to make not an automatic decision based on *the* rule, but a decision based on conflicting rules. The reasons for the rules are to be studied, the *consequences* of applying one rather than the other are to be evaluated. The effects of the decision on subsequent cases are to be considered. The clear cases (that is, the cases which unquestionably fall within *the* rule) are used as analogies, with which are compared the complex cases (which unquestionably do not fall within *the* rule as it has theretofore been stated and applied). Now, where statutes supplant the rules as developed by the courts, the judicial process need undergo no essential change; the only alteration should be in the materials that are to be employed as the basis of deliberation. Instead of precedent and case-law analogies, the statutes are available.[45] Let it be realized, however, that they are only points of departure, only analogies, though exceptionally informative and persuasive and illuminating analogies; to regard the statutory suggestions as controlling every case which bears some resemblance or relation to the stuff of the statute, would be to fetter this branch of judicial work with the same rusty chains of conceptualism that have so long impeded the growth of decisional law.

This approach, if utilized by the courts, lends added significance to non-penal statutes which contain indications of what are "public policies." It also makes available in the decision of cases the statutes of states other than the state of jurisdiction. Where they employ this method of attack, the courts will refuse to enforce a contract not "because it is illegal" or because the legislature "intended that a person making such a contract should be punished," but because they have satisfied themselves that, in the light of what has been indicated to them by legislative bodies, at home or abroad, the contract is against public policy. Criminality is not a requisite element; punishment (in the sense of retribution for undesirable conduct) is not a primary purpose. No novelty is involved in a refusal to enforce a contract which relieves against liability for negligence or which involves the commission of a tort, even though no statute requires that result. Similarly, the courts should frown upon contracts which, though not touching a penal statute, involve other conduct which has been inveighed against by the legislature. What is suggested is not an extension of the scope of judicial disapprobation of contracts, for at all times the courts have freely declared that noncriminal agreements might be against public policy and consequently, unenforcible.[46] What is urged is, again, merely that legislative judgments should be used as indicators of the occasion for employment of the common law rule governing the validity of contracts.

For example, the New York statute which gives redress to an individual whose privacy has been invaded should be considered by the courts as they should consider a similar penal statute, in the event that they are called upon to enforce an agreement having some relation to the doing of the act declared to be tortious. If the legislative judgment was that the publication of unauthorized photographs was

---

[45] See the extremely useful essay of J. M. Landis, Statutes and the Sources of Law, in Harvard Legal Essays (1934) 213. The suggestive discussion in that paper is valuable as a basis for any thinking concerning the significance of the legislative judgments.

[46] See, e.g., discussion in Diamond Match Co. v. Roeber, 106 N.Y. 473, 479 et seq., 13 N.E. 419, 420 (1887). And see Holland v. Sheehan, 108 Minn. 362, 367, 122 N.W. 1, 3 (1909); "We are not required to look exclusively to statutory enactments in determining questions of public policy. Con-

stitutions and statutes are evidence of the general policy of a state; but when confronted with questions of general public policy, as defined in the books, the courts go beyond express legislation and look to the whole body of the law—statutory, common, and judicial decisions. Public policy requires of courts of equity protection from unjust and unconscionable bargains, though no statutory authority is granted by legislation." See also Reiner v. North American Newspaper Alliance, 259 N.Y. 250, 181 N.E. 561 (1932).

against public policy because of possible disturbances of the peace or because of possible blackmailing threats to embarrass the person photographed, the courts should deem it immaterial that the statute carries a civil instead of a penal sanction. The nature of the sanction in some instances will indicate that the legislature found no public interest to be involved; but the single circumstance that, instead of a new crime, a new cause of action was created, should not be determinative. On the other hand, mere legislative definition of a tort should not foreclose judicial recognition of contracts.

Similarly, where legislative materials are used as sources of information and as analogies, there need be no direct connection in terms between statutes and the contract under judicial consideration. James M. Landis, in addressing the Association of American Law Schools in 1934, suggested that the courts should with hesitancy enforce "yellow-dog contracts." [In these contracts employees agreed, as a condition of employment, not to join a labor union. Until the Norris-LaGuardia Act was passed, the employer could use these contracts to obtain an injunction against labor organizers for inducing the workers to breach the contract. —ed.] In 1917, in the *Hitchman* case,[47] the Supreme Court thought that, as a matter of public policy, such contracts warranted judicial protection. But in 1930, the Senate, after thorough consideration, rejected the nomination of Judge John J. Parker to sit on the Supreme Court, largely because he had followed and applied the *Hitchman* case. Later, when Congress adopted the Norris-LaGuardia Act, not a single voice was raised in defense of yellow-dog contracts as such; even the opponents of the measure did not argue that such agreements deserved protection. In the event of a suit to enforce such a contract or to recover damages from one who induced its violation, these matters should be worthy of a court's consideration as important legal facts. They are more significant than prior inexpert judicial pronouncements that such contracts are not against public policy, and hence must be honored.

Again, the statutes of other jurisdictions may be useful as informing the court of considerations which it might otherwise ignore. In other fields the judges have shown more and more liberality in employing the laws of other states as aids in reaching sound results in cases not controlled by any statute operative in the forum. So long as its own legislature has not clearly directed a court to enforce or to ignore contracts of a given nature, the court is free to decide for itself whether or not such contracts are against public policy. It is clear that of most weight would be local statutes having some bearing upon the subject matter of the contract. But where such statutes are lacking, there is no reason why the scope of the search for information should not be widened to include examination of pertinent conclusions in other jurisdictions. Utilizations of judicial opinions are not uncommon and are accepted as an appropriate aid in making similar determinations; legislative opinions upon the same matters should be employed with, if anything, more confidence in their helpfulness.

The method here urged warrants employment by the courts of administrative pronouncements, which are suggestive indications of what is "public policy." When a legislature has delegated to a body of experts the task of formulating rules for public guidance, those rules merit the dignity of being deemed authoritative and informed judgments upon the issues at stake. To be sure, unlike statutes, they are infrequently generally known or widely available for study by the public. But this circumstance, while it may clearly be significant in particular cases, should not operate to induce disregard by the courts of this rich mine of information. Again, the question is not whether a party to a contract deserves to be punished because he entered into the contract, but it is whether the public deserves to be protected against harm that might result from execution of the contract.

In a recent New York case it was held that a contract violating a city ordinance is illegal to the same extent as a contract violating an enactment of the legislature. If a particular transaction is in fact inimical to the public welfare, the nature of the source of knowledge concerning that fact is immaterial; the circumstance that municipal assemblies are inferior in governmental status to state legislatures should not obscure recognition that the former are in a better position than the latter to gauge many local needs. True, numerous ordinances deal with petty antisocialisms; but this should mean only that in some instances the courts will adjudge them to be overborne by other considerations which make desirable the enforcement of contractual liabilities. . . .

---

[47] Hitchman Coal & Coke Co. v. Mitchell, 245 U.S. 229 (1917).

Conclusion

The obvious criticism of any suggestion that the validity of contracts should depend upon an independent judicial answer to the question whether they comport with public policy, is that too much uncertainty would thus be injected into contractual relationships. If "public policy" should be defined as something having no relationship to the judgments formulated by Constitutions, statutes, and prior judicial and non-judicial investigations, but as being ascertainable only by an unassisted judicial discovery of "what is naturally and inherently just and right between man and man," there would be much to be said in favor of the criticism. But if a determination of the relevant public policy rests upon authoritative legislative pronouncement and upon intelligent effort to procure informative data, the criticism loses force. Of course it is true that in many situations neither courts nor the lawyers who argue before them have knowledge necessary to determine whether desirable public ends are to be attained by enforcement or refusal to enforce particular contracts. Just so, today, they have not the knowledge (nor do they very assiduously seek to acquire the knowledge) necessary to determine whether one decision or another will better serve the particular legislative purpose they discern in a penal statute. To make either determination, the good lawyer or the good judge must become adept in making essentially non-"legal" judgments based upon essentially non-"legal" materials.

Certainty of prediction, moreover, diminishes in importance when it means only that an undesirable result may be predicted with certainty in many cases. Indeed, it is questionable that a greater degree of unpredictability will be introduced into the law of contracts than is now to be found there. The plethora of cases in the appellate courts dealing with illegal bargains itself indicates uncertainty concerning the applicability of the outwardly simple rules. In fact, the existing judicial techniques in large measure are directed toward the ascertainment of public policy; the only suggestion here made relates to the nature and limitations of one type of source material—legislative and administrative texts. Surely an intelligent attack upon a complex problem is not to be disregarded solely because the result of deliberation may be no better known in advance than it is now.

Unquestionably there will be poor judgments if courts discard the existing set of rules that are supposed to govern the illegality of contracts, just as poor judgments and unhappy results may be found among current adjudications.[57] But the lines will be more sharply drawn, the attention of the judges focussed more directly upon the essential nature of their task. Doubt concerning the eventual determination of the issue of public policy may serve to prevent the formation of contracts which are close to the border line, though not certainly across it. But perhaps this in itself is a consequence to be desired, for public policies may well be served by the existence of a twilight zone in which steps are taken but cautiously.

[57] An instance of what appears to the writer to be bad judgment concerning policy is Coules v. Pharris, 212 Wis. 558, 250 N.W. 404 (1933) . . . . There the court decided that it was of public importance, as a sanction for the immigration laws, to deny recovery in a suit for wages earned by an alien who had entered the country illegally. The court said that it should not assist one who was, while unlawfully in the country, in competition with American laborers. The doctrine of "collateral illegality" was brushed aside.

Public Policy From Sunday Contracts to Baby M.

As mentioned in the introduction to the Gellhorn article, I cut from it a short discussion of "Sunday contracts," since today there is typically no problem with the enforcement of contracts made on Sundays. That we go from an outdated topic to one as contemporary as surrogate parenting shows the fluidity of the public policy concept. Surrogate parenting has become commercially viable because of a combination of technological change and demographics. Although artificial insemination has been around for at least a generation, we now have an aging baby boom population that frequently put off having children until the wife's having a first child became problematic. At the same time, abortion and other factors have made adoptive children, particularly white children, difficult to find.

In the Matter of Baby M, 109 N.J. 396, 537 A.2d 1227 (1988), made surrogate motherhood contracts a national topic. The literature on the New Jersey Supreme Court's decision has only begun to appear. See, *e.g.,* June R. Carbone's *The Role of Contract Principles in Determining the Validity of Surrogacy Contracts,* 28 Santa Clara L. Rev. 581 (1988). Earlier articles are cited in the Carbone article.

Baby M put the collision of public policy and freedom of contract in high relief. A childless couple, the Sterns, he a bio-chemist, she a pediatrician, desired a child. Mr. Stern's family had been largely exterminated by the Nazis, and he wished to perpetuate the line. Dr. Stern suffered from multiple sclerosis, which made a pregnancy worrisome, if not dangerous or impossible. Through a private company that made surrogate parenting arrangements for a substantial fee ($7500), Mr. Stern was put in touch with a married woman named Mary Beth Whitehead who had two children of her own. Mr. Stern and Mr. and Mrs. Whitehead agreed in a written contract, prepared by a lawyer, that Mrs. Whitehead would be artificially impregnated with Mr. Stern's semen, that her expenses during pregnancy would be paid by Mr. Stern, that if she had a live birth she would be paid $10,000, and that she agreed in advance to the adoption of the child by Mr. Stern and to the termination of her parental rights.

After giving birth to a daughter, Mrs. Whitehead turned the baby over to the Sterns, but soon felt that she could not go ahead with the arrangement that she had agreed to. A lurid series of events followed: the Sterns allowed Mrs. Whitehead to take the baby for a few days, she refused to return the baby, the Sterns obtained an ex parte custody change, Mrs. Whitehead fled with the baby and hid in a series of some twenty motels in Florida, the Sterns "recaptured" the baby with help from Florida police, and Mrs. Whitehead asked the New Jersey courts to void the agreement and award her custody.

The trial court awarded custody to Mr. Stern, finding that Mrs. Whitehead was bound by her agreement. Despite its enforcement of the contract, the trial court heard extensive testimony about the best interests of the child before exercising its discretionary power to grant specific performance. On appeal, the Supreme Court of New Jersey affirmed the award of custody to Mr. Stern, but completely rejected any contract reasoning, and remanded the case for a determination of Mrs. Whitehead's visitation rights, strongly suggesting that visitation should be allowed. (On remand Mrs. Whitehead was given substantial rights of visitation.)

The New Jersey Supreme Court's opinion is some one hundred pages long and contains a sensitive (but still controversial) assessment of the custody and visitation questions. From the point of view of this section, however, it is its approach to the contract of surrogacy that is most apt. The court made clear that it was not surrogacy that was the evil. It was the combination of payment of money to the natural mother and the attempt to make irrevocable her pre-birth (or even pre-conception) consent to giving up the child that the court found against public policy. Unlike the trial court, the New Jersey Supreme Court treated the case as either an adoption or custody case, and found that the surrogacy contract violated several statutes that forbade payments in adoption cases and that made mothers' surrenders of custody and consent to adoption revocable in private placements. The court said that "the determinative aspect is the vulnerability of the natural mother who decides to surrender her child in the absence of institutional safeguards."

Passing to non-statutory considerations, the Supreme Court considered the nature of consent under a contract of surrogacy:

> Under the contract, the natural mother is irrevocably committed before she knows the strength of her bond with her child. She never makes a totally voluntary, informed decision, for quite clearly any decision prior to the baby's birth is, in the most important sense, uninformed, and any decision after that, compelled by a pre-existing contractual commitment, the threat of a lawsuit, and the inducement of a $10,000 payment, is less than totally voluntary.

In addition, the payment of money for bearing a child had economic and class overtones. True, not every surrogate mother was impoverished. Nonetheless, as the court put it, "we doubt that infertile couples in the low-income bracket will find upper income surrogates." The court also noted that the contract could be a "potential degredation of some women."

But even more than the statutory, consent or exploitation issues, it was a general sense of public policy that led the court to hold surrogacy *contracts* unenforceable:

> Putting aside the issue of how compelling her need for money may have been, and how significant her understanding of the consequences, we suggest that her consent is irrelevant. There are, in a civilized society, some things that money cannot buy.

The New Jersey Supreme Court's public policy approach is consistent with that of Professor Margaret Jane Radin of the University of Southern California in her article, *Market-Inalienability*, 100 Harv. L. Rev. 1849 (1987), which is cited in the opinion. Professor Radin, who previously wrote the seminal *Property and Personhood*, 34 Stan. L. Rev. 957 (1982), argues in *Market-Inalienability*, that some things should not be turned into commodities, that the law should not allow them to be bought and sold. In the Thirteenth Amendment we, as a nation, took this attitude towards slavery and serfdom, but many law and economics writers have "commodified" such concepts as the family, see Gary Becker, *A Treatise on the Family* (1981), and the buying and selling of babies for adoption, see Richard Posner and Elizabeth Landes, *The Economics of the Baby Shortage*, 7 J. Leg. Stud. 323 (1978). (The Posner and Landes article was serious, as opposed to Jonathan Swift's *A Modest Proposal*, to which it has been derisively compared, but Judge Posner has more recently said that he does not advocate a free market in babies. Posner, *Mischaracterized Views*, 69 Judicature 321 (1986).) Professor Radin, who discussed surrogate parenting among other examples, concluded that there was no ideal solution, and suggested "a form of market-alienability similar to our regime for ordinary adoption" as "the better non-ideal solution." This allows surrogate parenting, but prevents the mother from making an irrevocable consent before birth.

It should be apparent that if we decide that some thing or some right is not "market-alienable," it cannot be transferred by an enforceable contract. (Compare the consent theory of Randy Barnett, reprinted in Part IB.) We can only decide what we are willing or unwilling to "commodify" by searching our system of values, whether in enacting legislation or in resolving whether a contract should be enforced by a court. In either case, what we are talking about is that same public policy that Walter Gellhorn wrote about more than fifty years ago.

2. Good Faith and Fair Dealing

The Good Faith Concept and the Summers-Burton Debate

The notion that one has a duty to carry out a contract in good faith is not new. It goes back at least to cases from the New York Court of Appeals around the First World War. Some of these are discussed in the Pratt article in Part IC. The concept got a tremendous boost when the Uniform Commercial Code provided in its section 1-203 that "Every contract or duty within this Act imposes an obligation of good faith in its performance or enforcement." The Code defined good faith generally as merely "honesty in fact," but further provided in section 2-103 that within the sale of goods article in the case of a merchant good faith also included "the observance of reasonable commercial standards of fair dealing in the trade." The Second Restatement extended the duty of "good faith and fair dealing" to all contracts, but gave the term no definition.

The first major article on the topic was Friedrich Kessler and Edith Fine's *Culpa In Contrahendo, Bargaining in Good Faith, and Freedom of Contract: A Comparative Study*, 77 Harv. L. Rev. 401 (1964), in which the authors explored the German concept of culpa in contrahendo or bad faith in bargaining, and suggested that similar ideas had a place in American law. While much of their article was concerned with pre-contractual applications of good faith (compare the Knapp and Farnsworth articles in Part IIA), Kessler and Fine did not draw a sharp line between conduct before and during a contract. They also showed that good faith was not inconsistent with a notion of freedom of contract.

Soon after Kessler and Fine, Professor Robert S. Summers, then of Oregon, now of Cornell, published *"Good Faith" in General Contract Law and the Sales Provisions of the Uniform Commercial Code*, 54 Va. L. Rev. 195 (1968), which put forth the important notion that good faith is an "excluder" that is best left undefined and best understood as excluding activities that are deemed bad faith.

It is a phrase without general meaning (or meanings) of its own and serves to exclude a wide range of heterogenous forms of bad faith. In a particular context the phrase takes on specific meaning, but usually this is only by way of contrast with the specific form of bad faith actually or hypothetically ruled out.

Summers traced the history of the U.C.C. 1-203 (19) definition of good faith generally as "honesty in fact in the conduct or transaction concerned," and proposed that the definition be scrapped. While this proposal has gone nowhere, Summers' article has been influential, and many of his suggestions that seemed visionary in 1968 have come to pass or been exceeded. Though he gave many examples of conduct that courts had found to have been done in bad faith, Summers argued forcefully against a definition other than an excluder. To his own rhetorical charge that he was "just a moralist trying to foist your ideas of good faith off on others," he answered that "legal good faith, in the case law, is not identical with moral good faith, though it must be admitted that the two overlap." Perhaps more important, "insofar as legal good faith incorporates morals, which require a party to act in ways he ought to act anyway, I see nothing to object to. . . . At the least, a judge should always be willing to intervene to enforce minimal standards of just dealing as well as the spirit of any consummated deal."

In 1980 Professor Steven J. Burton of Iowa published *Breach of Contract and the Common Law Duty to Perform in Good Faith*, 94 Harv. L. Rev. 369 (1980). While not radically different from Summers', Burton's approach stressed the parties' prior bargaining over opportunities. Using what he called a cost perspective, Burton argued that good faith meant that a party could not exercise his discretion under a contract to recapture previously forgone opportunities. In 1982, in a Cornell Law Review symposium on the Restatement (Second) of Contracts, Summers returned to the fray, discussing the Restatement's approach to good faith, which was greatly influenced by his 1968 article. Summers also criticized Burton's approach at some length, which prompted a 1984 reply by Burton in the Iowa Law Review. Excerpts from the more recent Summers and Burton articles follow. The differences between the relatively narrow Burton approach and the more broad-ranging Summers approach are important as bad faith breach of contract becomes an increasingly popular cause of action, particularly in insurance, employment and lender liability cases. (On this, see the *Uncontracts* article in Part IB.)

Robert S. Summers, *The General Duty of Good Faith—Its Recognition and Conceptualization*, 67 Cornell L. Rev. 810 (1982)

Introduction

The text of section 205 of the Restatement (Second) of Contracts, adopted by the American Law Institute in 1979 and published in final form in 1981, provides:

§ 205. *Duty of Good Faith and Fair Dealing*
Every contract imposes upon each party a duty of good faith and fair dealing in its performance and its enforcement.

This section, together with its accompanying Comment and Reporter's Note, recognizes and conceptualizes a general duty of good faith and fair dealing in the performance and enforcement of contracts in American law. In addition, a number of other sections and Comments particularize the bearing of this general duty in various ways.

The first Restatement of Contracts, which appeared in 1932, did not include a section comparable to section 205. This new section reflects one of the truly major advances in American contract law during the past fifty years.

The late Robert Braucher, then Professor of Law at Harvard Law School, was the Reporter for the *Restatement Second* during the years when section 205 was in embryo, and he drafted it. Professor Braucher acknowledged that an article I wrote on the subject published in 1968 substantially influenced the recognition and conceptualization of good faith in section 205.[5] It is therefore probably not inappropriate for me to offer some remarks on the occasion of its final official publication. I hasten to say, however, that I now have relatively little to add to my earlier, somewhat extended study, with perhaps two exceptions.

The questions I will consider briefly here are these: What was the basis upon which the general duty in section 205 was recognized? How did the draftsman conceptualize good faith in section 205, and how might one respond to the various criticisms that have been made of this type of conceptualization? And is there anything of general value that draftsmen, judges, and others might learn about conceptualization for the law's purposes from our legal experience thus far with efforts to conceptualize good faith? In addressing these questions, I will not set forth and discuss the now vast body of judge-made and statutory law in the background. A large number of articles, including my own earlier one, treat this law at length.[7]

Section 205 represents a major advance for several reasons. First, the sheer volume of case law and statutory development it reflects is vast. Second, the section symbolizes a commitment to the most fundamental objectives a legal system can have—justice, and justice according to law. Thus, it is of a piece with explicit requirements of "contractual morality" such as the unconscionability doctrine and various general equitable principles. The increasing recognition of such requirements is one of the hallmarks of the law of our time. Third, although the general duty of good faith and fair dealing is no more than a minimal requirement (rather than a high ideal), its relevance in contractual matters is peculiarly wide-ranging, and it rules out many varieties of bad faith in a diverse array of contexts. Fourth, section 205 embodies a general requirement that has a distinctively significant role to play in the law. It is a kind of "safety valve" to which judges may turn to fill gaps and qualify or limit rights and duties otherwise arising under rules of law and specific contract language.[11] Finally, as an explicit general requirement, it has all the advantages of a direct and overt tool rather than an indirect and covert one. In the long history of contract, judges who have not had such a tool ready to hand have either had to leave bad faith unredressed or resort to indirect and covert means, thereby fictionalizing the law or otherwise begetting unclarity, unpredictability, or inequity.[13]

. . .

I. Recognition

The general requirement of good faith recognized in section 205 is based on numerous judicial opinions imposing a duty of good faith, several major statutory developments, and the published writings of professors of law. By the late 1960s, when section 205 (then numbered section 231) was being drafted, the accumulation of case law imposing a duty of contractual good faith outside contexts of "good-faith purchase" was considerable. In particular, the courts of two leading states, New York and California, had by then rendered many decisions affording relief for various forms of bad faith in contractual relations; the corpus of decisions from other jurisdictions was sizeable too. Moreover, no American case had been found in which the court said that "good faith is not required in the performance of a contract or in enforcement of a contract." In my 1968 article, I sought to

---

[5] The article is Summers, "Good Faith" in General Contract Law and the Sales Provisions of the Uniform Commercial Code, 54 Va. L. Rev. 195 (1968).

[7] See Burton, Good Faith Performance of a Contract Within Article 2 of the Uniform Commercial Code, 67 Iowa L. Rev. 1 (1981) [hereinafter cited as Article 2 Good Faith]; Burton, Breach of Contract and the Common Law Duty to Perform in Good Faith, 94 Harv. L. Rev. 369 (1980) [herein-

after cited as Breach of Contract]; Summers, Good Faith, supra note 5, at 203, 216-52 (citing cases).

[11] See Ellinghaus, In Defense of Unconscionability, 78 Yale L.J. 757, 779-80 (1969).

[13] For numerous examples of such resort, see Holmes, A Contextual Study of Commercial Good Faith: Good Faith Disclosure in Contract Formation, 39 U. Pitt. L. Rev. 381, 388-89 (1978); Summers, Good Faith, supra note 5, at 231.

provide a survey and catalogue of many of the relevant cases. Thus there were many decisions in which judges had recognized and ruled out a number of general types of bad faith in performance, including: evasion of the spirit of the deal; lack of diligence and slacking off; wilful rendering of only substantial performance; abuse of a power to determine compliance; and interference with, or failure to cooperate in, the other party's performance. In such cases, the courts went beyond the more familiar standards of performance—for example, the specific terms of agreements, general gap-filler law, course of dealing, and custom and usage—and invoked a general requirement of good faith. Many courts proceeded similarly in coping with various forms of bad faith in the assertion, settlement, and litigation of contract claims and defenses. Among other things, they ruled out bad faith in the form of: conjuring up a pretended dispute in order, for example, to lay a basis for a settlement; asserting an overreaching or "weaseling" interpretation or construction of contract language; taking advantage of another's necessitous circumstances to secure a favorable modification; making harassing demands for assurances of performance; wrongfully refusing to accept performance; wilfully failing to mitigate damages; and abusing a power to determine compliance or to terminate a contract. In section 205 of the *Restatement Second*, and in the accompanying Comment and Reporter's Note, Professor Braucher adopted nearly all of the foregoing categories, and most of the Illustrations in the Comment are based on cases decided before 1970 that fall into these categories.

The *Restatement Second* "authority" for section 205 was not, however, confined to general contract case law. The authority for the section 205 requirement—as distinguished from the conceptualization of good faith that it incorporates—also included statutory law, particularly provisions of the Uniform Commercial Code. By the late 1960s, this new uniform act had been adopted in a majority of states. Many of its sections and Comments imposed specific duties of good faith. Moreover, one of its most famous provisions is section 1-203, which states that "[e]very contract or duty within this Act imposes an obligation of good faith in its performance or enforcement." This general obligation was, in the 1950s, a major innovation in American statutory law, and is the closest ancestral authority for the *Restatement Second*'s section 205. It is hardly surprising, then, that the first Comment to section 205 opens with references to Uniform Commercial Code provisions on good faith. The

next section of this Article, dealing with the conceptualization of good faith in the *Restatement Second* suggests, however, that the Uniform Commercial Code and the *Restatement Second* diverge significantly.

. . .

II. Conceptualization

I will begin with some preliminary remarks on the general problem of conceptualization as it arises for draftsmen and others in the law. I will then describe the "excluder" conceptualization of good faith in section 205 and the Comment, explain its origins, and contrast it with the conceptualization of good faith in the Uniform Commercial Code. I will also consider the extent to which section 205 is consistent with the "rule of law" and values associated with that ideal.

A. *The General Problem of Conceptualization*

As the term is used here, a "conceptualization" is an intellectual construct that represents or embodies an idea formulated in words for some general or special purpose or purposes. When a draftsman is formulating a legal requirement, he may be called upon to conceptualize some idea, or ideas, to appear in the explicit language of the requirement itself or in an accompanying official Comment or other authoritative legislative history. . . .

. . .

[Professor Summers lists six types of conceptualizations, and suggests that some ideas may be conceptualized in more than one way, but that for others only one of the methods may work. —ed.]

B. *"Excluder" Conceptualizations*

Some ideas yield to this mode of conceptualization, and it has been my view since the mid-1960's that this is true of the idea of good faith. I will not here repeat the extended excluder analysis of good faith that I set forth in my 1968 article. I will merely summarize its essence. In my view, some words and phrases do not have a general positive meaning of their own within the contexts or realms of discourse in which they are at home. Instead, these words or phrases function to rule out various things according to context. The notion that some ideas are of this character was not my invention and is hardly novel. The excluder conceptualization may have appeared first in Aristotle's writings. The late Professor J.L. Austin of Oxford University made much of it. His discussion of the term "real" is illuminating:

That is, a definite sense attaches to the assertion that something is real, a real such-and-such, only in the light of a specific way in which it might be, or might have been, *not* real. "A real duck" differs from the simple "a duck" only in that it is used to exclude various ways of being not a real duck—but a dummy, a toy, a picture, a decoy, &c.; and moreover I don't know *just* how to take the assertion that it's a real duck unless I know *just* what, on that particular occasion, the speaker has it in mind to exclude. This, of course, is why the attempt to find a characteristic common to all things that are or could be called "real" is doomed to failure; the function of "real" is not to contribute positively to the characterization of anything, but to exclude possible ways of being *not* real—and these ways are both numerous for particular kinds of things, and liable to be quite different for things of different kinds. It is this identity of general function combined with immense diversity in specific applications which gives to the word "real" the, at first sight, baffling feature of having neither one single "meaning," nor yet ambiguity, a number of different meanings.[36]

In addition to the word "real," itself not really a word much used in the law, one might cite many other notions at work in the law that do yield best to an excluder analysis. . . . Requirements of equality in many branches of the law probably yield best to an excluder analysis, according to which these requirements rule out a heterogeneous variety of forms of unjustified discrimination. Presumably the same goes for certain legal requirements of fairness. One scholar has even claimed that the notion of justice itself is best analyzed in these terms.

In my view, good faith in the general requirement of good faith in ordinary moral dealings, and in the general case law of contract up to the late 1960's, was most felicitously conceptualized as an "excluder." That is, it was not appropriately formulable in terms of some general positive meaning—through the specification of a set of necessary and sufficient conditions, for example; rather, it functioned as an excluder to rule out a wide range of heterogeneous forms of bad faith. This is not to say that paraphrase, example, and other methods of conceptualization cannot also cast still further light on this corner of the law. Nor is it to deny the distinctively illuminating power of the purposes behind such a requirement in determining its scope and limits, a topic to which I

will return. Nor, finally, is it to deny that judges should try to articulate criteria to be used to decide whether particular conduct claimed to be in bad faith really is so—criteria that must inevitably vary somewhat from context to context. I will return later to this topic as well.

C. *The Restatement's Conceptualization of Good Faith as an "Excluder"*

Professor Braucher did not attempt to provide a conceptualization of any assumed general positive content of the expression "good faith" as it appears in section 205, nor did he seek to so conceptualize it in the Comments or Reporter's Note to section 205. Thus, for example, he did not undertake to define good faith in terms of some assumed general, invariant, and synonymous meaning such as "honesty in fact in the . . . transaction," as did the draftsman of the Uniform Commercial Code. Indeed, he provided no general definition of good faith at all. All this, of course, is consistent with the excluder analysis.

He did assume, as did I in my 1968 article, that it is possible to formulate specific positive meanings for particular uses of "good faith," by way of contrast with the specific forms of bad faith being ruled out in the context. These meanings would vary "somewhat with the context."[43] But he did not then go on to try to generalize from these and set forth a single, positive, and unified general meaning of good faith as used in section 205. Rather, he stressed that the section 205 requirement of good faith "excludes a variety of types of conduct characterized as involving 'bad faith,'" including evasion of the spirit of the bargain, lack of diligence and slacking off, abuse of a power to specify terms, conjuring up a dispute to force a settlement or modification, wilfully failing to mitigate damages, and so on. Many theorists have been tempted to try to conceptualize all these forms of bad faith, partly in terms of some necessary or singular "mental element," such as a "bad motive." But Professor Braucher saw that this would not do either, and stated: "Subterfuges and evasions violate the obligation of good faith in performance even though the actor believes his conduct to be justified. But the obligation goes further: bad faith may be overt or may consist of inaction, and fair dealing may require more than honesty."

Professor Braucher did go on to try to articulate the general purposes of the section: that of securing

---

[36] J. Austin, Sense and Sensibilia 70-71 (G. Warnock ed 1962) (emphasis in original).

[43] Restatement (Second) of Contracts § 205, Comment a (1979).

"faithfulness to an agreed common purpose and consistency with the justified expectations of the other party," and compliance with "community standards of decency, fairness or reasonableness." But this is not the same as specifying a general positive meaning for the expression as it appears in section 205. This remains true even if one concedes, as I certainly would, that the section must be interpreted and applied in light of its purposes. Furthermore, as a corollary of the excluder conceptualization, Professor Braucher stressed that a "complete catalogue of types of bad faith is impossible."

In my view, the conceptualization of good faith as an excluder in section 205, the Comment, and the Reporter's Note satisfies the relevant criteria of adequacy. It is sufficiently faithful to the nature of the basic idea involved, and it is aptly designed to serve the general substantive purposes of the legal requirement involved, including the fulfillment of just expectations. Also, it is not defined restrictively and therefore can be deployed in unforeseen circumstances as a kind of safety valve; it also can sufficiently serve the more general purposes connoted by the phrase "the rule of law." For now I will only undertake specific discussion of this last point.

D. Consistency of the Restatement Conceptualization with the "Rule of Law"

The rule of law does not require that all forms of law consist of rules.[49] Section 205 itself, with its excluder conceptualization, is not a rule; it is more in the nature of a principle or maxim, and if I am right, this is as it should be. Section 205 is an unusually "circumstance-bound" requirement, and excludes highly varied forms of bad faith, many of which become identifiable only in the context of circumstantial detail of a kind that defies comprehensive formulation in a single rule. Those who would insist in the name of the rule of law that all forms of law must consist of specific detailed rules addressed to narrow patterns of fact have very likely not thought through the implications of their position.[51] In the field of commercial law alone, this would require substantial

revision, including an overhaul of the Uniform Commercial Code. Not only would section 1-203 on good faith have to go, but so would section 1-103 on general equitable principles and section 2-302 on unconscionability. Many other provisions would at least have to be revised and narrowed.

Although section 205 of the *Restatement Second* is as it should be, it does not follow that the numerous and varied contexts to which it is addressed cannot, *in addition*, be governed by still other forms of "good-faith" law. As we have seen, the *Restatement Second* itself includes several further provisions that, among other things, purport to particularize the requirement of section 205 in given contexts. Beyond these provisions, one can identify three further (to some extent overlapping) forms of good-faith law addressed to many of these contexts which are now either more or less fully formed or in process of development. First, we now have a vast accumulation of *holdings with stated reasons*. The generality implicit (and sometimes explicit) in this form of law is often considerable. Second, courts and scholars are now, for some of these contexts, beginning to formulate *lists of criteria* for identifying specific forms of bad faith.[54] The generality of such criteria represents a form of law of long-standing respectability in our legal experience. It was law of this type that I had in mind when, in my earlier piece, I wrote that: "No effort has been made here to identify the criteria which judges ought to use in deciding particular conduct is in bad faith, although enough has been said to show that these criteria must vary from context to context." Third, the accumulation of experience with respect to some contexts might be sufficiently extensive, and the circumstantial attributes of these contexts sufficiently amenable, to permit the formulation of *detailed rules* that rule out specific forms of bad faith. I have not tried my hand at constructing such rules, but I would not be surprised if some could now be so formulated to go beyond those already recognized in the Restatement Second sections that are corollaries of section 205.

. . .

---

[49] See generally R. Dworkin, Taking Rights Seriously ch. 2 (1978); L. Fuller, The Morality of Law (2d ed. 1969).

[51] Nor have they thought through their motives. I have met lawyers from time to time who seem to believe that those responsible for the law always owe lawyers an obligation to create and package that law in the form of tiny bits, the scope of which is always totally certain and easily ascertainable in advance. Why? Because, it is said, lawyers must earn a livelihood and law of this sort is the kind most saleable to clients!

[54] The most detailed example to date is probably Professor Hillman's treatment of bad faith modifications of contracts. See Hillman, Contract Modification Under the Restatement (Second) of Contracts, 67 Cornell L. Rev. 680 (1982); Hillman, Policing Contract Modifications Under the U.C.C.: Good Faith and the Doctrine of Economic Duress, 64 Iowa L. Rev. 849 (1979). For another example of an effort to articulate specific criteria in still another context, see Holmes, supra note 13, at 451.

In my view, a judge in a novel case posing an issue of good faith under section 205 with its excluder conceptualization is far from lacking meaningful guidance of the kind legitimately to be demanded in the name of the rule of law. He should start with the language of the section. Second, he should turn to the purposes of section 205 as set forth mainly in Comment a. These purposive rationales will infuse the excluder analysis with meaning in all the ways that purposive interpretation is known generally to provide guidance to judges (as in the case of statutes). Third, after completing this, he should seek guidance by the time-honored common-law method of reasoning by analogy, not only from past cases, but from the various illustrations set forth in the Comments to section 205. Such reasoning, particularly that which is done with an eye to the *reasons* given by prior judges, can provide substantial insight into how novel cases should be decided. Fourth, also in light of the purposes of section 205 and any general analogies, he can analyze the relevant facts—alleged or proven—to see what specific reasons these facts, and the values they implicate, generate for and against characterizing the action or inaction in question as bad-faith behavior. Fifth, because of the very nature of the problem, the excluder analysis is not only faithful to the reality involved, but it is itself a distinctive source of illumination. It does not focus on some presumed positive and unitary element or cluster of elements called "good faith"; instead, it focuses on whether the alleged form of bad-faith behavior really is, in the context, ruled out by section 205, when considered in light of its purposes and in relation to the facts of the case. The foregoing factors do not exhaust all the forms of guidance that section 205 provides, but they are more than sufficient to rebut the charge that a section in which good faith is conceptualized as an excluder leaves the judges at sea and the "law" merely whatever the judges say it is.

It may be added that the lengthy German experience with a comparably general requirement of good faith in its contract law has not been a legally unhappy one. The requirement has not proliferated into the kind of mere ad hoc judicial caprice that some critics of a section such as *Restatement Second* section 205 presumably would have predicted.[59]

E. *Relative Inferiority of the Uniform Commercial Code Conceptualization*

As we have seen, the Uniform Commercial Code includes a general section like *Restatement Second* section 205. Section 1-203 of the Code provides that "[e]very contract or duty within this Act imposes an obligation of good faith in its performance or enforcement." In addition, many sections of the Uniform Commercial Code, and numerous Official Comments, impose particular duties of good faith.

This body of Code law served as one of the authoritative underpinnings of the *Restatement Second*'s section 205. But there ends the Code influence.[61] Section 205 conceptualizes good faith as an excluder; the Code's section 1-203 does not do so. The Code section and accompanying definitions generally conceptualize good faith as "honesty in fact." Professor E. Allan Farnsworth observed in 1963 that this restrictive conceptualization of good faith "enfeebled" the Code's section 1-203, because many forms of contractual bad faith do not involve dishonesty as such.[63] In my 1968 article I sought to demonstrate the truth of this at some length. The narrowness of the foregoing conceptualization was only partially mitigated by the fact that the honesty definition was prefaced with the words "unless the context otherwise requires," and that certain other sections of the Code incorporated a less restrictive definition. Here, then, is a striking example of the failure of a draftsman (Professor Karl N. Llewellyn) to conceptualize an idea in a manner sufficiently faithful to its own basic character. This underscores the importance of recognizing problems of conceptualization in the law for what they are—they are not merely formal matters of selecting linguistic expressions.

Professor Braucher understood as much. He recognized that the Code's general conceptualization of good faith as "honesty in fact" was too narrow. He stated, in particular, that a "focus on honesty is appropriate to cases of good-faith purchase; it is less so in cases of good-faith performance." In drafting sec-

---

[59] See generally J. Dawson, The Oracles of Law 461-502 (1968). I have not, incidentally, sought to apply the excluder analysis to the German case law, but it seems more than a little likely that it would apply.

[61] It should also be noted that both formulations are restricted to "performance" and "enforcement"; they do not explicitly extend to the negotiation stage. Some differences in wording might be noted, too: (1) the Restatement Second

includes the words "and fair dealing," but the Code provision does not, and (2) the Code provision applies the requirement of good faith to every "contract or duty within this Act," whereas the Restatement Second applies only to "every contract."

[63] Farnsworth, Good Faith Performance and Commercial Reasonableness Under the Uniform Commerical Code, 30 U. Chi. L. Rev. 666, 673-74 (1963).

tion 205, he was mindful of the impossibility of devising a definition of a general positive meaning for good faith that would avoid the twin hazards of colliding with the Scylla of restrictive specificity and spiraling into the Charybdis of vacuous generality. He eschewed general definitions altogether and instead conceptualized the requirement of good faith in section 205, the Comment, and the Reporter's Note in terms of excluder analysis. Thus, section 205 of the *Restatement Second* is superior in conceptualization to its Uniform Commercial Code counterpart.

III. Some Replies To Criticisms

The type of general requirement of good faith embodied in section 205, including its excluder conceptualization, has already generated considerable commentary. Most of the commentators agree that some such requirement is desirable, but many offer criticisms and suggestions for improvement. Because I believe that section 205 is on the whole an admirable piece of work, I will here address and respond to a number of criticisms directed, implicitly or explicitly, to that section. I will devote a number of my remarks to the writings of Professor Steven Burton, who has recently published two articles[70] that should, if any can, arouse me from my dogmatic slumbers.

A. *The Rationales for a Good-Faith Requirement*

The rationales for a general requirement of good faith, such as those appearing in section 205, are of fundamental significance. They provide judges with indispensable guidance and may even serve as a kind of unifying "theory" that, if anything can, ties various decisions together. In my view, there are two primary rationales for such a section: it is a means to "justice and to justice according to law." Professor Braucher did not adopt this specific formulation, but the overlap between the language he used and my own formulation is great. In his view, the good-faith requirement serves: (1) "faithfulness to an agreed common purpose and consistency with the justified expectations of the other party," and (2) "community standards of decency, fairness or reasonableness." In the general case law, judges have frequently recognized that these rationales are significantly moral.

Some commentators seem to deny that the foregoing justice-oriented rationales really are the true rationales of general good-faith requirements, and/or that they are significantly moral. Yet rationales such as the foregoing are the ones most commonly stated in the case law. Moreover, Professor Braucher's language, quoted above, is the exact language of Comment a of section 205.

It is not uncommon today to find a theorist claiming that the most "appropriate" rationale for a provision such as section 205 is economic, at least in its application to good faith performance.[75] The requirement is said to enhance economic efficiency by reducing the costs of contracting, including "the costs of gathering information with which to choose one's contract partners, negotiating and drafting contracts, and risk taking with respect to the future."[76] The general requirement of good faith accomplishes all this by "allowing parties to rely on the law in place of incurring some of these costs." The "economically rational person" will thus "substitut[e] good faith at the margin." This claimed economic rationale requires several responses. First, it is ahistoric. As already indicated, the historical evidence favors other rationales. Second, these other rationales, at least so far as good-faith performance is concerned, are largely moral and include the principle *pacta sunt servanda* ("the obligation to keep agreements"). To say that this principle is part of the rationale for a section such as 205 is hardly to render that section "superfluous." It is one function of the good-faith performance doctrine to enforce the spirit of deals, including their unspecified inner logic. Indeed, it has even been said that "it is the potential for a lack of clarity and completeness that necessitates the implication of the good faith covenant in every contract." Third, it is in any case rather speculative that the rationale is economic—even in regard to a duty of good-faith performance. We really do not *know* whether general recognition of this duty is economically efficient. Many more types of costs would first have to be counted, including the allocable costs of running a legal system that administers such a doctrine. It might turn out only that the doctrine is not economically inefficient—or not obviously so—and this would be a slender reed, indeed, on which to rest section 205. Fourth, it is one function of rationales to generate, in light of the facts and law, specific reasons for the decisions of particular cases. The extent to which an economic rationale such as the one proferred can do this efficiently and otherwise satisfactorily is, as yet, undemonstrated and problematic, a

---

[70] Burton, Breach of Contract, supra note 7; Burton, Article 2 Good Faith, supra note 7.

[75] See, e.g., Burton, Breach of Contracts, supra note 7, at 392-94.

[76] Id. at 393.

matter that Mr. Kelley and I have sought to treat at length elsewhere.[82]

. . .

C. The General Indefinability of Good Faith

Many commentators suggest that they are willing to accept that good faith cannot, as such, be usefully defined in terms of a single, general, positive meaning, but most of them still find this state of affairs rather difficult to live with. At one point or another, in text or in footnote, they try their hand at what seems to be tendered as a general definition. Here are some of the results:

—Good faith is an "absence of intention to harm a legally protected pecuniary interest." [quoting Steven Burton]

—Good faith performance "occurs when a party's discretion is exercised for any purpose within the reasonable contemplation of the parties at the time of formation—to capture opportunities that were preserved upon entering the contract, interpreted objectively." [quoting Burton again]

—Good faith and fair conduct consists of action "according to reasonable standards set by customary practices and by known individual expectations." [quoting Holmes, *supra* note 13]

My view is that all such efforts to define good faith, *for purposes of a section like 205*, are misguided. Such formulations provide very little, if any, genuine *definitional* guidance. Moreover, some of them may restrictively distort the scope of the general requirement of good faith. For example, the factors relevant in the context may not be confined to what "custom" and communicted "expectations" dictate. In addition, such formulations may lead judges and lawyers to ponder and argue over *the* meaning of good faith and in this or other ways divert focus away from the issue of whether a claimed form of bad faith really is, in light of all relevant circumstantial detail, to be so characterized. Finally, the very idea of good faith, if I am right, is simply not the kind of idea that is susceptible of such a definitional approach.

All this is not to say that some of the phrases appearing in the foregoing proferred definitions have no relevant utility. As fragments of statements of *rationales* for the requirement of good faith, they plainly do. But to provide a rationale for a requirement is one thing; to define the ideas that figure in the requirement itself is another.

D. The Determination of Bad Faith in Novel Cases— The Burton Model

Professor Burton, in a most interesting essay in the *Harvard Law Review*, recently proposed a model decision procedure for the resolution of novel cases posing issues of good-faith *performance*. The essence of his model is as follows. One of the two parties will always have what Professor Burton calls "discretion to perform." At the time of contracting, that party will have given up some of his freedom of action, which Professor Burton calls "forgone opportunities" (to that party, a "cost" of contracting). Bad-faith contractual activity is then defined as "exercising discretion" to recapture one or more of the opportunities forgone upon entering a contract. To determine whether an opportunity was in fact forgone, it is necessary to inquire into the reasonable expectations of the "dependent party" (the other party). The party with discretion to perform acts in good faith if he does not attempt to recapture a forgone opportunity. Professor Burton also argues that "whether a particular discretion-exercising party acted to recapture forgone opportunities is a question of subjective intent"—a "subjective inquiry." Moreover, the "objective inquiry" into the dependent party's reasonable expectations is not alone "dispositive." Indeed, Professor Burton stresses that instead the inquiry into state of mind is "of central importance."

We may adopt one of Professor Burton's illustrations to try to demonstrate his model at work. Assume that L and T entered into a lease providing that T was to pay rentals as a percentage of the gross receipts of T's business on the premises. T also had another store in the same town. From time to time, he diverted customers to that other store (where he owned the premises), thereby reducing the rentals otherwise payable to L. For this, L sued T, claiming that T's diversionary tactics were in bad faith. Here, according to Professor Burton, a court should presumably find (1) that a reasonable person in L's position expected to receive rentals not depleted by T's diversionary acts, and (2) that T acted with the subjective intention of recapturing a forgone opportunity.

---

[82] Summers & Kelley, Economists' Reasons for Common Law Decisions—A Preliminary Inquiry, 1 Oxford J. Legal Stud. 213 (1981).

Professor Burton, unlike many who have criticized general requirements of good faith, does believe in them and has sought to direct his efforts largely to making them more effective. Moreover, he does not ultimately seek to resolve issues of good faith under a general requirement like section 205 through a general definition of some presumed positive content of that phrase. He also concedes that what a general good-faith requirement rules out varies to some extent depending on the context. And he generally seeks to focus on the reasons for ruling out claimed forms of bad faith. In all these respects, despite some misleading protestations to the contrary, his approach is itself generally consistent with the spirit of section 205, including its excluder conceptualization.

Professor Burton makes a number of claims on behalf of his approach, as opposed to what he calls the "traditional" approach (born not so long ago in the history of the common law and including, presumably, that of section 205). First, he says that his approach provides more analytical focus. It isolates "with greater particularity the factors that must be considered in determining good or bad-faith performance." Instead of an "amorphous totality of factual circumstances," we have an inquiry into reasonable expectations of the "dependent party" and the subjective intent of the "discretion-exercising" party—all to determine precisely whether the discretion-exercising party has acted to recapture forgone opportunities so as to constitute bad faith. Is this analysis necessarily any more focused than that of section 205 in a novel good-faith performance case? Does it focus on the right things? Does it go far enough? These are large questions, and I cannot now do full justice to them. I have already tried to show in this Article that section 205 provides judges with considerable guidance, not merely in novel performance cases but in performance and enforcement cases generally. It is true that Professor Burton's model introduces new terminology and appears to reduce to two questions; but I do not see that anything turns on this. Why, for example, should it "advance the analysis" to inquire whether the discretion-exercising party is seeking to "recapture forgone opportunities," rather than whether his actions fall outside the reasonable expectations of the dependent party in light of the various

factors in the circumstances that legitimately shape those expectations? Or why does it help (if it does) in our foregoing lease illustration to inquire whether the tenant, in diverting customers, was trying to recapture costs incurred in entering the contract, rather than whether what the tenant did was, all things considered, contrary to the spirit of the deal?

One may also question whether the Burton model really focuses on the right things. For example, does the subjective inquiry into the discretion-exercising party's state of mind really have the central importance that is claimed? Part of the claim, as I understand it, is that this inquiry is *typically* relevant, not just contingently so. This does not accord with section 205. Moreover, in a great many well-decided performance cases, courts give little or no consideration to this factor.[106] Indeed, its independent significance in the Burton model is at least in some areas problematic. Consider, again, the lease illustration. If the court decides that the reasonable expectations of the landlord rule out the tenant's acts of diverting customers to his other store, what if anything would it add to inquire into the tenant's state of mind? It is said (a) that the "traditional analysis" focuses mainly on benefits due the promisee under the agreement and (b) that this is inadequate because the promisor may be "entitled" to withhold something in good faith. Whether or not (a) is true, (b) does not follow. If what is due the promisee really does exclude what the promisor wants to withhold, then that will be dispositive. What one is "entitled" to withhold depends on what is due the promisee. (This is not to say that an inquiry into the promisor's state of mind can never have independent significance in good-faith performance cases.)

Further, in my view the Burton model does not go far enough. That is, it does not provide as much focus as section 205 of the *Restatement Second* and the general case law now permit. I suspect that it is now possible to develop useful lists of factors generally relevant to the determination of good-faith performance in a number of different performance contexts. Professor Burton seems content, for example, to leave the general test of reasonableness of expectations relatively unanalyzed. Yet Professors Hillman[108] and Holmes[109] have shown, in comparable good-faith

---

[106] See generally Summers, Good Faith, supra note 5, 232-43 (citing cases). The main case that Professor Burton cites on the subjective inquiry is a case in which the contract embodied a clause requiring that the promisee be satisfied with performance. Burton, Breach of Contract, supra note

7, at 390 (citing Isbell v. Anderson Carriage Co., 170 Mich. 304, 136 N.W. 457 (1912).

[108] See the articles by Professor Hillman in note 54 supra.

[109] See Holmes, supra note 13.

contexts, that a closer analysis and differentiation of relevant factors is possible. Nothing in the excluder conceptualization embodied in section 205 is inconsistent with the articulation of such criteria. A general requirement of good faith can rule out forms of bad faith identifiable by reference to these criteria. Indeed, as I have already suggested, some such criteria in some contexts may now be ripe for formulation in rules.

Professor Burton claims that, in addition to more focus, his model provides more generality than other approaches and thus is more "law-like." In particular, he thinks it is less a "license" for the exercise of ad hoc judicial intuition. Again, I fail to see why there is any less generality in the *Restatement Second* approach. . . .

Finally, Professor Burton claims that his model provides a useful new "perspective and policy framework" within which good-faith performance issues are more manageable. Close analysis suggests, however, that it is less general than Professor Burton makes it seem, and that it introduces economic ideas and terminology that may breed uncertainty or confusion. I will say something further only about the first of these observations. The model is less general because it is in truth drawn mainly from those cases in which contracting parties have in fact conferred on one of the parties some genuine discretionary power in matters of performance. Many good-faith performance cases are not of this kind; they do not confer *discretion* to perform in some way. It is not difficult to discern the likely motive here behind the Burton model. The maneuver of adopting a conceptual framework in which one party is always considered to have discretion felicitously generates the *possibility* that the "discretion-exercising" party might have failed to perform in good faith, and thus seems to give pervasive point to the "subjective inquiry" of such central importance in the model. After all, "a party with discretion may withhold all benefits for good reasons." In many cases posing issues of good-faith performance, however, there will be no such discretion and therefore no such possibility. And even when this is not so, the subjective inquiry may lack independent significance.

E. *Good Faith and Moralism*

One commentator recently expressed strong concern that courts may very likely overextend a general requirement of good faith of the kind embodied in section 205, the Comments, and the Reporter's Note, all in the name of altruism, Good Samaritanism, general benevolence, moral idealism, or the like.[118] The shortest answer to this concern is that the extensive case law to date does not reveal any significant tendency of this kind.[119] But a bit more should be said on this point.

The risk of overextension is inherent in any doctrine. Experience to date indicates that the risk is not great with regard to section 205. This is hardly surprising. Our contract law has been relatively free of moralism, especially any forms legitimately describable as "Good Samaritanism" or the like. Moreover, legal good faith is not identical with moral good faith. In any event, a requirement of good faith is a minimal standard rather than a high ideal. In addition, section 205, the Comment, and the Reporter's Note incorporate safeguards. And the determinations of trial judges and jurors are subject to various forms of review.

The ultimate question is whether the gain is worth the risk. I cannot say that all the cases so far soundly decided in major part on the basis of a general obligation of good faith would certainly have been decided the other way in the absence of such an obligation; yet certainly some of them would have. And it is also certain that some private parties acting out of court would have acted differently in interpreting contracts and settling contract disputes in the absence of such an obligation. Finally, it must be conceded that in the days before such an obligation was generally recognized, some judges sometimes used indirect and covert tools to remedy bad faith; yet this involved costs, too.

Conclusion

The final adoption and publication of section 205 is fairly certain to accelerate the growth of general contract law on good faith. At least two major tasks remain here for contract scholars. They will have a continuing responsibility to try to evaluate, systema-

---

[118] Gillette, Limitations on the Obligation of Good Faith, 1981 Duke L.J. 619.

[119] Indeed, Professor Gillette is hard pressed to find any cases that look at all like the beginnings of a parade of horribles.

tize, and when the time comes, refine, this case law into more discrete categories and forms of law. They will also have the interesting task, as the case law grows, of identifying its implications for numerous other general doctrines of contract law. The discovery and recognition of these implications is almost certain to be a rich source of insight into the deeper mysteries of the social institution of contract.

Steven J. Burton, *More on Good Faith Performance of a Contract: A Reply to Professor Summers,* 69 Iowa L. Rev. 497 (1984)

In a recent article in the *Cornell Law Review*,[1] Professor Robert S. Summers devotes almost nine pages to a strong criticism of my two articles on the obligation to perform a contract in good faith.[2] The occasion for Professor Summers' effort was a symposium on the *Restatement (Second) of Contracts.*[3] Section 205 of the *Restatement (Second)* recognizes the good faith performance obligation and largely adopts the approach to good faith suggested by Professor Summers in an earlier article.[5] The recent article defends the *Restatement*-Summers conceptualization of the good faith performance obligation against a sometimes presumed rejection of it in my work.[6]

Professor Summers protests too much. One need not consider his thesis to have been wrong-headed in order to find value in mine. There are, however, significant differences between Professor Summers' approach and mine. I will endeavor in this short reply to clarify those differences and to show in what ways my approach may be preferable.

I.

The case and statutory law on the general obligation of good faith in contract law, including the obligation to perform a contract in good faith, developed largely in this century. Professor Summers' 1968 article was the first extensive effort to collect and analyze the cases. It was an impressive research effort because none of the available research tools then recognized the existence of the obligation as such. It also was an admirable early effort to understand and conceptualize the apparently new doctrine, which the courts had left largely unexplained in their opinions. The drafters of the *Restatement (Second)* surely exercised good judgment in 1970 by recognizing the good faith performance obligation and by explaining it largely on the basis of Professor Summers' work.

Professor Summers' main thesis was that the good faith obligation is best conceptualized as an "excluder." That is to say, paraphrasing the philosopher J.L. Austin, that any attempt to find a characteristic common to all instances of good faith performance is doomed to failure; the function of "good faith" is not to contribute positively to the characterization of anything, but to exclude possible ways of being in bad faith, which are both numerous and varied. Excluder analysis thus considers it impossible to state the necessary and sufficient factual conditions for a finding of good faith or bad faith. More important, excluder analysis shifts attention to instances of bad faith, of-

[1] Summers, The General Duty of Good Faith—Its Recognition and Conceptualization, 67 Cornell L. Rev. 810 (1982) [hereinafter cited as Summers 1982].

[2] Burton, Breach of Contract and the Common Law Duty to Perform in Good Faith, 94 Harv. L. Rev. 369 (1980) [hereinafter cited as Burton 1980]; Burton, Good Faith Performance of a Contract Within Article 2 of the Uniform Commercial Code, 67 Iowa L. Rev. 1 (1981) [hereinafter cited as Burton 1981].

[3] Symposium: The Restatement (Second) of Contacts, 67 Cornell L. Rev. 631 (1982).

[5] Summers, "Good Faith" in General Contract Law and the Sales Provisions of the Uniform Commercial Code, 54 Va. L. Rev. 195 (1968) [hereinafter cited as Summers 1968].

[6] Professor Summers interprets my criticism of what I have referred to as the "traditional approach" as a criticism of the Restatement-Summers approach. See Summers 1982, supra note 1 at 831. However, the "traditional approach" that I find incomplete is the emphasis on determining breach by asking only whether the promisee received the fruits or benefits of the contract. Burton 1980, supra note 2, at 372, 374-76; Burton 1981, supra note 2, at 3, 5-6. Professor Summers' excluder analysis, as I understand it, is not committed to this "benefit perspective," which contrasts with a "cost perspective" developed in Burton 1980, supra note 2, at 373-78.

338 A CONTRACTS ANTHOLOGY

fering a list of such instances from which one may reason analogically in light of the rationale of the doctrine. Professor Summers offered the following rationale: "[I]t is a means to 'justice and to justice according to law.'"

Having adopted the excluder approach, Professor Summers classified some bad faith performance cases in one of six general categories, not regarded as exhaustive: evasion of the spirit of the deal; lack of diligence and slacking off; willful rendering of only substantial performance; abuse of a power to specify terms; abuse of a power to determine compliance; and interference with, or failure to cooperate in, the other party's performance. The *Restatement (Second)* commentary generally follows this approach, adding that "[g]ood faith performance . . . of a contract emphasizes faithfulness to an agreed common purpose and consistency with the justified expectations of the other party; it excludes a variety of types of conduct characterized as involving 'bad faith' because they violate community standards of decency, fairness or reasonableness."[14] Together with the *Restatement (Second)* illustrations and a fair number of case citations, the foregoing summarizes what the *Restatement*-Summers approach offers to a lawyer or judge.

The *Restatement*-Summers formulation is inspired by the view that the good faith performance doctrine "is of a piece with explicit requirements of 'contractual morality' such as the unconscionability doctrine and various general equitable principles." "Contractual morality" implies a ground for judicial decision that lies outside of and may take precedence over the agreement of the parties. Explaining the good faith performance doctrine in such terms implies that courts typically use the doctrine to render agreed terms unenforceable or to impose obligations that are incompatible with the agreement reached at formation. Moreover, such an explanation implies that the vagueness of doing "justice and justice according to law," or ruling out "abuses" of powers to specify terms or to determine compliance, is a virtue. Such vagueness enables courts to decide each case accord-

ing to the felt requirements of morality under the particular circumstances.

II.

In my view, courts generally do not use the good faith performance doctrine to override the agreement of the parties. Rather, the good faith performance doctrine is used to effectuate the intentions of the parties, or to protect their reasonable expectations, through interpretation and implication. Courts might override agreed contract terms on grounds of "contractual morality" when the contract is unconscionable or otherwise unenforceable at formation, when estoppel or waiver are properly invoked, or when performance is impossible or commercially impracticable. They might resort to considerations of fairness or justice to interpret or supply terms when the intentions of the parties or their reasonable expectations cannot be reasonably ascertained. But it is hard to see what justifies a court in disregarding the agreement of the parties on grounds of "contractual morality" when the intentions of the parties or their reasonable expectations can be reasonably ascertained, and none of the above-mentioned doctrines properly are invoked.

More important, the decided cases on the whole do not support the view that the good faith performance doctrine incorporates vague requirements of contractual morality into the law of contract performance and breach.[18] Both the U.C.C. and the common-law cases make clear that the parties are free to determine by agreement what good faith will permit or require of them. The remedies awarded in cases of bad faith performance are the same as those awarded for any normal breach of contract, suggesting that the implied covenant of good faith protects the same interests that are protected when enforcing express promises. The New York Court of Appeals—the leading exponent of the good faith performance doctrine—recently confirmed that the doctrine serves to further the agreement of the parties, not to override any part of it:

---

[14] Restatement (Second) of Contracts § 205 comment a (1981). Professor Summers approves of the addition. Summers 1982, supra note 1, at 826. The addition probably reflects the influence of Professor Farnsworth. See Farnsworth, Good Faith Performance and Commercial Reasonableness Under the Uniform Commercial Code, 30 U. Chi. L. Rev. 666, 669 (1963).

[18] Professor Summers probably thinks that the good faith performance cases typically are cases in which the reasonable expectations of the parties cannot be reasonably as-

certained, based on his sample of cases decided before 1968. I think that the good faith performance cases typically are cases in which the reasonable expectations of the parties can be reasonably ascertained, using an objective theory of contract interpretation and a cost perspective on the contractual expectation interest, based on a sample of over 400 cases decided before 1983. Without the cost perspective, many cases might well appear to be much as Professor Summers characterizes them.

New York does recognize that in appropriate circumstances an obligation of good faith and fair dealing on the part of a party to a contract may be implied and, if implied will be enforced . . . . In such instances the implied obligation is in aid and furtherance of the other terms of the agreement of the parties. No obligation can be implied, however, which would be inconsistent with other terms of the contractual relationship.[21]

The explanatory task presumptively is to show how the good faith performance doctrine helps to further the agreement of the parties, if we can. My study of the cases led me to the conclusion that good faith performance of a contract occurs when a party with discretion in performance exercises its discretion for any purpose within the reasonable contemplation of the parties at the time of contract formation—to capture alternative opportunities that were preserved on entering the contract, interpreted objectively. As a corollary, bad faith performance occurs when such a party uses its discretion to recapture opportunities forgone (costs incurred) on entering the contract. This explanation draws on a "cost perspective" from which I analyze the contractual expectation interest and the concept of a breach of contract. It employs the language of modern microeconomics, though not necessarily normative economic theory. I will explain these relatively abstract formulations below.

The concept of "discretion in performance" refers to one party's power after contract formation to set or control the terms of performance. The parties by express agreement commonly confer discretion on one of them, as in output and requirements contracts, floating-price contracts, conditions of satisfaction and other conditions within the control of one party, or contracts that require one party to set or control the time for performance. In each of these situations, the parties at formation defer a decision regarding what the contract will permit or require of them in performance. The parties provide in the contract that one of them will determine what performance is required (for example, a condition of personal satisfaction or particulars of performance to be set by one party), or that circumstances within the control of one of them will determine what is required (for example, an output contract or price based on a per-

centage of gross receipts of the buyer). In either case, the contract confers discretion on one party to determine later the precise content of its own or the other party's legal duty at performance.

Discretion in performance may arise with similar effect due to omission or a lack of clarity in the express terms of the contract. Unlike cases in which the parties agree to defer a decision and to confer discretion on one of them, the discretion in these cases does not arise by the agreement of the parties. When the express contract does not clearly establish the performance duties of the parties, the effect is that each party has discretion to determine its own performance duty, subject to the implied covenant of good faith and other implied terms. I did not say that "one party is always considered to have discretion," as Professor Summers reported. Good faith performance is required in every contract because the problems of omission and lack of clarity can arise in every contract.

The concept of discretion in performance is essential to understanding the good faith performance doctrine as it has been employed by the courts. Consider Professor Summers' use of one of my "illustrations" to demonstrate my model at work:

Assume that L and T entered into a lease providing that T was to pay rentals as a percentage of the gross receipts of T's business on the premises. T also had another store in the same town. From time to time, he diverted customers to that other store (where he owned the premises), thereby reducing the rentals otherwise payable to L. For this, L sued T, claiming that T's diversionary tactics were in bad faith. Here, according to Professor Burton, a court should presumably find (1) that a reasonable person in L's position expected to receive rentals not depleted by T's diversionary acts, and (2) that T acted with the subjective intention of recapturing a forgone opportunity.

I could not possibly say whether T acted in bad faith on the facts stated by Professor Summers. I would say that T enjoys discretion in performance unless the express terms of the contract clearly govern how he deals with customers in relation to his two stores. The point is that the act of diverting customers to the other store *itself is legally neutral for purposes of determining whether T breached the contract.* If T

[21] Murphy v. American Home Prods. Corp., 58 N.Y.2d 293, 304-05, 448 N.E.2d 86, 91, 461 N.Y.S.2d 232, 237 (1983) (citations omitted) (holding that discharged "whistle-blower" failed to state a claim of breach of contract terminable at will); see also Broad v. Rockwell Int'l Corp., 642 F.2d 929, 957 (5th Cir. 1981).

used his discretion to send customers to the other store because the inventories differ and the customers thus would be better served, there is good authority for doubting that T has breached the contract. If T used his discretion to send customers to the other store for the "sole purpose" of bringing gross receipts down at the leased premises, there is good authority for concluding that T breached the contract. Consequently, it is necessary to focus attention on whether the discretion-exercising party used its discretion for an improper purpose, despite the well-known difficulties of an inquiry into subjective intent.

Additionally, it would be useful to say something in general terms about which purposes are proper or improper, if we can. It is a step forward to say, as have a few courts, that the discretion-exercising party must act for a purpose within the reasonable contemplation of the parties at formation. That draws our attention to the intention of the parties or their reasonable expectations at formation, and away from duties imposed on the parties irrespective of their "assent." This is consistent with the decided cases on the whole. However, the totality of the factual circumstances at formation is amorphous. The contemplation standard fails in any way to distinguish relevant from irrelevant facts within that realm.

The language of microeconomics, with its emphasis on opportunity costs, makes it possible to take a further step forward. Traditionally, the contractual expectation interest is viewed as comprising the property, services, or money to be received by the promisee. I call this the "benefit perspective" because it directs our attention to the benefits of the contract to the promisee. From this perspective, to determine whether a contract was breached we ask whether the promisee in fact received the benefits to be transferred under the contract terms. The benefit perspective is wholly adequate for a large number of contract cases, such as those in which the terms of the contract identify the benefits due to be transferred under the contract to the promisee. An inquiry into the promisor's subjective intent is not necessary in such cases.

The benefit perspective alone is inadequate when a promisee claims that a discretion-exercising promisor breached a contract by failing to perform in good faith. The soundness of this claim cannot be determined by focusing on the express terms and what benefits, if any, the promisee in fact received from the discretion-exercising promisor. The express terms of the contract identify or reveal the discretion, not the benefits due to be transferred under the contract to the promisee. The soundness of this claim depends on whether the discretion-exercising promisor exercised its discretion in good faith. But this implied term also does not identify the benefits due to be transferred in any case; indeed, the cases make clear that a discretion-exercising promisor is entitled to withhold all benefits if it does so for good reason.[36] The benefit perspective is inadequate in such cases because the express and implied terms of the contract do not identify the benefits due the promisee.

I argue that the contractual expectation interest also encompasses the reasonably expected cost of performance to the promisor. I call this the "cost perspective" because it directs our attention to the other side of the coin—alternative opportunities forgone by a promisor on entering a particular contract. From the cost perspective, a person who takes the opportunity to enter a particular binding contract forgoes opportunities to employ elsewhere the resources required for the performance of that contract. A person who (intentionally) breaches a contract normally does so to redirect resources to other opportunities that turn out to be more attractive than the contract. A breach of contract thus may be described in general as a "recapture" of opportunities forgone on entering the contract. More important, a breach of contract by failing to perform in good faith can be described as a use of discretion in performance to recapture opportunities forgone on entering the contract. To determine whether a contract was breached, from the cost perspective, we ask whether the promisor in fact paid the reasonably expected cost of performance.

Whether the promisee is entitled to receive benefits claimed to be due under a contract with discretion in performance can be determined if we ask whether the promisor paid the reasonably expected cost of performance. A discretion-exercising promisor who uses its discretion to recapture forgone opportunities necessarily redirects to other opportunities the resources that were committed at formation to performance of the contract. It follows that the resources earmarked at formation for the promised

---

[36] See, e.g., U.C.C. § 2-306 comment 2 (1978) ("[a] shutdown by a requirements buyer for lack of orders might be permissible . . . .").

performance will not be received in fact by the promisee. Harm to the promisee's expectation interest can be inferred from the promisor's recapture of forgone opportunities. Consequently, a promisor who uses discretion in performance to recapture forgone opportunities acts for an improper purpose, fails to keep its promise, and is in breach of contract.

Assume, for example, that a potato chip company contracts with a grower for a set quantity of potatoes at a set price, provided that each shipment is satisfactory for making potato chips. The satisfaction clause confers discretion in performance on the company because the contract empowers the company to judge the quality of tendered potatoes at the time of tender, and to accept or reject them in accordance with its judgment. But its discretion is not unlimited. Surely the grower reasonably expects that by contracting the company gives up the opportunity to later substitute potatoes from the spot market for the contract potatoes because the market price falls below the contract price. The very purpose of contracting at a set price is to make that commitment. It is not strained to say that the grower reasonably expects (and the company impliedly promises) that the company will not substitute spot-market potatoes for contract potatoes in a falling market only to save money. In other words, the company impliedly promises not to recapture the opportunity that was forgone by contracting at a set price.

Assume further that the company rejects deliveries in a falling market, claiming that the contract potatoes would not "chip" satisfactorily, as a pretext to take advantage of the lower market prices. From the benefit perspective, we would ask only whether the company received satisfactory potatoes and, if so, whether the grower received the price. *Evidence of the falling market would seem to be irrelevant*. From the cost perspective, we would ask whether the company rejected the potatoes because they were unsatisfactory (in which case substituting spot-market potatoes is an alternative opportunity preserved on contracting) or because the company could buy more cheaply elsewhere (in which case substituting spot-market potatoes is recapturing an alternative opportunity forgone on contracting). Thus, *evidence of a falling market clearly would be relevant*. The cost perspective explains why evidence of rising or falling markets so often is considered in good faith performance cases, as in the case from which this example is drawn. Accordingly, the cost perspective calls attention to important facts in a good faith performance case better than the benefit perspective does, without

displacing the benefit perspective for those cases in which it is useful.

The discretion-exercising promisor that uses its discretion to recapture a forgone opportunity does not withhold the anticipated benefits of the contract for a legitimate reason. A principal function of the law of contracts is to protect the reasonable expectations of the parties. Just as a promisee may have a reasonable expectation that it will receive the promised benefits when they are identifiable, the promisee may have a reasonable expectation that a discretion-exercising promisor will pay the (impliedly) promised cost of performance. That is to say that the promisee may have a reasonable expectation that a discretion-exercising promisor will keep its promise—that it will not use its discretion to recapture opportunities forgone on contracting.

To summarize, one may pose two questions to determine whether a discretion-exercising promisor breached a contract by using its discretion in bad faith: (1) At formation, what were the reasonably expected costs of performance (forgone opportunities) to the discretion-exercising promisor? (2) At performance, did the discretion-exercising promisor use its discretion to recapture an opportunity forgone on contracting? The first focuses attention on the time of formation and is an objective inquiry into the reasonable expectations of the promisee as to opportunities forgone by the discretion-exercising promisor by contracting. The second is an inquiry into subjective intent at the time for performance. Having made these determinations, one then can conclude with reason whether the dependent party's claim that it did not receive what it was entitled to receive is or is not sound.

III.

Professor Summers questions the value of this analysis:

> It is true that Professor Burton's model introduces new terminology and appears to reduce to two questions; but I do not see that anything turns on this. Why, for example, would it "advance the analysis" to inquire whether the discretion-exercising party is seeking to "recapture forgone opportunities," rather than whether his actions fall outside the reasonable expectations of the dependent party in light of the various factors in the circumstances that legitimately shape those expectations? Or why does it help (if it does) in our foregoing lease illustration to inquire whether the tenant, in diverting customers, was trying to re-

capture costs incurred in entering the contract, rather than whether what the tenant did was, all things considered, contrary to the spirit of the deal?

These are important questions that challenge the theoretical underpinnings of my work, which were not emphasized explicitly in the previous articles. I will discuss more completely why explaining the good faith performance doctrine in terms of 'discretion in performance' and 'recapturing forgone opportunities' improves upon formulations like protecting 'the reasonable expectations of the parties' or not acting 'contrary to the spirit of the deal, all things considered.' As Professor Summers says, my goal was to make the good faith performance obligation more effective. Does such a change in terminology "advance the analysis"?

Preliminarily, let it be clear that both of us fully agree that one cannot state a 'positive definition' of good faith or bad faith performance. That is to say that there is no one fact or set of facts that is present in all cases of one class or the other as a sign of its membership in the class. One cannot state the necessary and sufficient factual conditions for a finding of good faith or bad faith. Decisions in good faith performance cases therefore cannot be made by a wholly deductive method of reasoning. Excluder analysis takes this view, but adopting this view does not commit one to excluder analysis.

The *Restatement*-Summers formulation says, in paraphrase: 'Do not ask what good faith is; ask what courts have found to be instances of bad faith and reason by analogy from them to do justice and to protect the reasonable expectations of the parties.' My principal difficulty with excluder analysis is its singular focus on cases of bad faith. Most of the relevant performance cases hold that a party acted in good faith. These precedents also are useful in the treatment of new cases. One need not adopt a 'positive definition' to consider analogically whether a particular case is more like those precedents finding good faith performance or more like those finding bad faith performance. Moreover, a linguistic formulation should help us to understand the distinction between both groups of cases.

The original Summers article left us with excluder analysis and a categorization and description of a number of cases finding bad faith. Significantly, the new Summers article adds that the excluder conceptualization is consistent with articulating "criteria" to "rule out forms of bad faith identifiable by refer-

ence to these criteria." By this, Professor Summers means that we can "develop useful lists of factors generally relevant to the determination of good-faith performance in a number of different performance contexts."

It thus appears that Professor Summers and I both regard the *Restatement*-Summers formulations as way stations on the road to something better. He would like to retain the way station formulations and elaborate on them. He might want to say, for example, 'one must not act contrary to the spirit of the deal; in determining whether one has done so, do justice and protect the reasonable expectations of the parties, taking into account the following factors, *inter alia* . . . .' *But Professor Summers has given us no such list of factors for good faith performance cases,* nor has anyone else. We are left, for now, with 'one must not act contrary to the spirit of the deal, all things considered' (and other like formulations), 'do justice,' 'protect the reasonable expectations of the parties,' and 'reason by analogy from past cases of bad faith.' Whether these way station formulations should be retained, of course, should be an open question pending an improved understanding of the doctrine.

. . .

. . . Professor Summers' preference for "lists of factors generally relevant to the determination" favors one form that could be employed, in theory. If we had such a list and it were authoritative we could claim that the facts in two cases each include a factor on the list—that is, plausibly can be described in the abstract language of the factor—and thus are alike in a relevant respect. A second form that could be employed, however, is the general description or model—a simplified representation of a complex reality. With this form, our ability plausibly to describe two cases each in the abstract language of the model suggests similarity in an important respect, if the model is an authoritative one. Unlike most lists of factors, the general description technique encourages us to focus on complex webs of relationships among the facts.

The cost perspective employs this second method. It describes a breach of contract by failing to perform in good faith in abstract terms as a 'use of discretion in performance to recapture forgone opportunities,' as a way of summarizing a more elaborate general description. In the two previous articles, I showed how a multitude of performance cases plausibly can be described in, this language. Further, I showed that the cases finding good faith and bad faith performance can be distinguished in this language. Because so many of the cases thus can be explained in the language of the cost perspective, I claim that it is a useful formulation that calls our attention to the important facts in these cases. Whether it will become an authoritative formulation depends on its acceptance by the courts. I am happy to report that the discretion-in-performance concept, which Professor Summers finds so unacceptable, seems well on its way to general judicial acceptance in this context.

By contrast, I do not find that saying 'one must not act contrary to the spirit of the deal, all things considered,' tells me as much about which similarities and differences are important and which are not. Saying that we should 'do justice and justice under the law' is an obvious truism that tells me even less that is of practical utility in reasoning analogically with the cases. Saying that we should 'protect the reasonable expectations of the parties' seems to me useful. But is our understanding not a step further advanced if we elaborate by dividing reasonable expectations into two subcategories: expectations as to benefits to be received by the promisee and expectations as to costs (forgone opportunities) to be born by the promisor? Do we not search more intelligently for the important factual similarities and differences if we augment the language of the traditional benefit perspective with the language of the cost perspective?

Thus, a basic reason why the *Restatement*-Summers formulations are less helpful is their relative lack of focus. Surely we could say, for example, that a multitude of contract doctrines require us to reason analogically from the cases to do justice and to protect the reasonable expectations of the parties. But each doctrine should make its own contribution or be discarded as redundant or superfluous. Explaining a particular doctrine, like the good faith performance doctrine, requires us to say something that distinguishes it functionally from the other contract doctrines. For the foregoing reasons, I submit that the language of 'discretion in performance' and 'recapturing forgone opportunities' both does that better than the *Restatement*-Summers formulations and is faithful to the precedents.

IV.

In the end, the question is whether one's formulation helps lawyers and judges to distinguish the cases that find good faith performance from those that find bad faith performance. I cannot imagine how 'not acting contrary to the spirit of the deal, all things considered' (and other like formulations) can found a distinction, save by the most patent bootstrap argument. Given the impossibility of 'positive definition' and our imperfect understanding of language, I hope that I have offered a distinction and an analysis of the cases that will be helpful to lawyers and judges as a practical matter.

3. Economic Duress

The Concept of Economic Duress

The defense of duress goes far back in the history of contract law, at least in the sense of someone holding a knife to the signatory's throat or moving his hand against his will. Even the idea that economic need undermines free will is old, going back at least to the eighteenth century. For some reason, the leading modern articles on economic duress came out largely simultaneously. In 1937, John P. Dawson, then of Michigan and later of Harvard, published *Economic Duress and Fair Exchange in French and German Law*, 11 Tul. L. Rev. 345 (1937), 12 Tul. L. Rev. 42 (1937), discussing continental notions, which were affected by the Roman Law concept of *laesio enormis*, which allowed rescission in land sales when the price received was less than half the "value" of the property sold. In 1942, John Dalzell of the University of North Carolina published *Duress by Economic Pressure*, 20 N.C. L. Rev. 237, 341 (1942), and the following year Robert L. Hale of Columbia contributed *Bargaining, Duress, and Economic Liberty*, 43 Colum. L. Rev. 603 (1943), to a still-challenging symposium on *Compulsory Contract*, 43 Colum. L. Rev. 564-752 (1943). Dawson had been working on an article at the same time, but though he completed in it 1942, the Second World War intervened and he did not publish it until 1947, paying tribute to Dalzell and Hale, but discussing their contributions only peripherally. Dawson, *Economic Duress—An Essay in Perspective*, 47 Mich. L. Rev. 254 (1947).

Remarkably, each of these writers agreed that economic duress should have less to do with supposed loss of free will through hard choice (a given in a market economy) than with the fairness or unfairness of the resulting contract. In the nearly fifty years since they wrote, this view seems to have been accepted with respect to contract modifications. The old pre-existing duty cases prevented renegotiation because of lack of consideration on one side, but really had a policing function (for good or evil—see *Alaska Packers' Assn. v. Domenico*, 117 F. 99 (9th Cir. 1902)). Today, it is easy to modify a contract, but the problem remains of coercion by one party seeking to recapture what he previously bargained away. This can be handled as a matter of good faith under either the Burton or Summers approaches or as a matter of unconscionability (see the Epstein and Eisenberg articles in this section). Or it can be handled as economic duress. The name given seems less important than the idea that the court can evaluate both the fairness of the bargain and the fairness of the methods used to get to it. (On this point, contrast the Leff and Eisenberg articles below.)

While the use of economic duress as a policing device seems to be less in fashion today than good faith and unconscionability, the duress articles have had a major influence on the later doctrines. All of them are good, but the Hale article is intriguing because it is less concerned with duress as an excuse than it is with the whole question of economic imbalance and bargaining in a free enterprise system.

Robert L. Hale, *Bargaining, Duress, and Economic Liberty*, 43 Colum. L. Rev. 603 (1943)

We live in what is known as a free economy. We did, at least, before it was subjected to the controls necessitated by the war, or, as some would say, before the advent of the New Deal. Government and law did not tell us what part each of us must play in the process of production, or assign to each of us our respective rations of coffee, gasoline or other materials. What work we should do and how much we might consume were determined by a process known as freedom of contract. Yet in that process there was more coercion, and government and law played a more significant part, than is generally realized.

That men may live, they must either be in a position each to produce the material necessities of life for his own use, or there must be some adequate incentive for production of the goods and services which people other than the producers may enjoy, and some means by which individual consumers can acquire some portion of them. . . . Almost every article or service that is produced is the fruit of the combined efforts of countless people, each working on a fractional part of the product. But the product is consumed only in small part, if at all, by its producers. Other people consume it, and the producers of this product consume the products of other people's labor. Goods are turned out collectively and consumed individually. Individuals could conceivably be conscripted to contribute their respective efforts to the collective process of production, and the products could be rationed out to each for his individual consumption. These are not the methods of our free economy. We rely instead, for the most part, on bargaining. There are few, if any, who own enough of the collective output of goods ready for consumption to satisfy their needs for more than a brief period in the future. Some persons own more than enough of certain types of goods, but they must perforce acquire the use of other types as well. The owner of a shoe factory is in no danger of going ill-shod—he may wear his own shoes. But he cannot live on shoes alone. Like everyone else, he must *buy* food or starve. . . .

The owner of the shoes or the food or any other product can insist on other people keeping their hands off his products. Should he so insist, the government will back him up with force. The owner of the money can likewise insist on other people keeping their hands off his money, and the government will likewise back *him* up with force. By *threatening* to maintain the legal barrier against the use of his shoes, their owner may be able to obtain a certain amount of money as the price of not carrying out his threat. And by threatening to maintain the legal barrier against the use of his money, the purchaser may be able to obtain a certain amount of shoes as the price of not withholding the money. A bargain is finally struck, each party consenting to its terms in order to avert the consequences with which the other threatens him.

This does not mean, of course, that in each purchase of a commodity, there is unfriendliness, or deliberation and haggling over terms. Market conditions may have standardized prices, so that each party knows that any haggling would be futile. Nevertheless the transaction is based on the bargaining power of the two parties. The seller would not part with the shoes, or produce them in the first place, if the law enabled him to get the buyer's money without doing so, nor would the buyer part with his money if the law enabled him to obtain the shoes without payment.

. . .

How, then, does any purchaser obtain the money that will enable him to consume? We have already seem that the owner of products obtains it, by selling his products to buyers. But how did he come to be the owner of the products? The answer which first suggests itself is that he produced them. . . . But the answer is not wholly true. The owner did not produce the shoes by his own efforts alone. Other people have taken part in the production too—not only his employees, but those who have advanced the necessary capital, or taken any part in the production of the raw materials and fuel which he uses, or in transporting them to his factory.

Yet of all these innumerable producers of the shoes, only the owner of the factory acquires title to them. The others have all, at some time or another, waived their claims to any share in the ownership of the shoes. They have done so in a series of bargaining transactions, in which they received money, or promises to pay money. Through this series of bargains, the owner of the plant has acquired the full right of ownership in the shoes. This right enables him, if he is successful, to obtain from his customers more than enough to repay all the outlays he has made to the other participants—enough more to compensate him

for his risk and labor in organizing and managing the plant, and perhaps even more than this.

As a result of these innumerable bargains, the owner and the other participants in the production obtain their respective money incomes, and these money incomes determine the share that each may obtain of the total goods and services turned out by the collective efforts of all the other members of society. And it is as a result of these bargains, or in anticipation of them, that each participant in these collective productive efforts makes his contribution. We rely on the bargaining process to serve the conflicting interests of individuals in securing a share of the collective output of society, and also to serve their common interest in the creation of that collective output.

Though these bargains lead to vast differences in the economic positions of different persons, whether as producers or as consumers, these differences have all resulted from transactions into which each has entered without any explicit requirement of law that he do so. But while there is no explicit legal requirement that one enter into any particular transaction, one's freedom to decline to do so is nevertheless circumscribed. One chooses to enter into any given transaction in order to avoid the threat of something worse—threats which impinge with unequal weight on different members of society. The fact that he exercised a choice does not indicate lack of compulsion. Even a slave makes a choice. The compulsion which drives him to work operates through his own will power. He makes the "voluntary" muscular movements which the work calls for, in order to escape some threat; and though he exercises will power and makes a choice, still, since he is making it under threat, his servitude is called "involuntary." And one who obeys some compulsory requirement of the law in order to avoid a penalty is likewise making a choice. If he has the physical power to disobey, his obedience is not a matter of physical necessity, but of choice. Yet no one would deny that the requirement of the law is a compulsory one. It restricts his liberty to act out of conformity to it.

Government has power to compel one to choose obedience, since it can threaten disobedience with death, imprisonment, or seizure of property. Private individuals are not permitted to make such threats to other individuals, save in exceptional circumstances such as self-defense. But there are other threats which may lawfully be made to induce a party to enter into a transaction. In the complex bargains made in the course of production, some parties who deal with the manufacturer surrender a portion of their property, others their liberty not to work for him, in order to avert his threat to withhold his money, while he, in turn, surrenders some part of the money he now owns, or some part of his right to keep from them money he may obtain in the future, to avert their threats of withholding from him their raw materials or their labor. And he may have surrendered property in the past, and the freedom to abstain from labor, in order to attain his position as owner of the plant and its products, and so to obtain the money with which to avert the threats of owners of the things he wishes to consume, to withhold those things from him. In consenting to enter into any bargain, each party yields to the threats of the other. In the absence of corrective legislation, each party, in order to induce the other to enter into a transaction, may generally threaten to exercise any of his legal rights and privileges, no matter how disadvantageous that exercise may be to the other party. As Justice Holmes said in 1896 in a well known dissenting opinion in *Vegelahn v. Guntner,*[1]

> ... The word "threats" often is used as if, when it appeared that threats had been made, it appeared that unlawful conduct had begun. But it depends on what you threaten. As a general rule, even if subject to some exceptions, what you may do in a certain event you may threaten to do, that is, give warning of your intention to do in that event, and thus allow the other person the chance of avoiding the consequences.

As Holmes indicated in this passage, however, the law makes some exceptions to this general rule, even apart from legislation aimed at economic reforms. Many courts, for instance, follow what is known as the *prima facie* tort doctrine. As formulated in the classic statement of Lord Bowen in *Mogul Steamship Co. v. McGregor, Gow & Co.,*[2] "intentionally to do that which is calculated in the ordinary course of events to damage, and which does, in fact, damage another in that person's property or trade, is actionable if done without just cause or excuse." When the damaging act is done for the purpose of bringing the other party to terms, courts which follow this doctrine will hold the act unlawful, even though in ordinary circumstances it would not be, if they think the terms insisted on do not justify the infliction of the damage.

As Holmes said long ago,[3] the ground of decision "really comes down to a proposition of policy.". . .

. . .

Not only will courts sometimes forbid the commission of harmful acts which are otherwise lawful when motivated by a purpose which fails to justify the harm; they will sometimes refuse to aid a party to enforce a duty which someone else owes him when he desires enforcement for an unjustified end; or, for the same reason, they may refuse to permit him to employ those private means of enforcement which are normally open to him—as when the owner of land removes another's property from it, which is there without permission. Ordinarily the law not only permits the holder of a check to present it for collection to the bank on which it is drawn at any time the holder may choose, but also stands ready to enforce the bank's legal duty to pay it when presented. But in *American Bank & Trust Co. v. Federal Reserve Bank of Atlanta*[10] it was held unlawful for the Federal Reserve Bank to accumulate checks on country banks, as they alleged it was doing, and present them in a body for the purpose of forcing the country banks to keep so much cash in their vaults as to be driven out of business, as the alternative to submitting to the Reserve Bank's alleged insistence that they join the reserve system. If the allegations could be proved, it was held, the Reserve Bank should be enjoined from collecting checks except in the usual way. To determine whether the Reserve Bank was authorized to follow the course alleged, said Justice Holmes, "it is not enough to refer to the general right of a holder of checks to present them but it is necessary to consider whether the collection of checks and presenting them in a body for the purpose of breaking down the plaintiffs' business as now conducted is justified by the ulterior purpose in view."

. . .

In some of the cases in which courts refuse to grant specific enforcement of a duty, or to permit the injured party to put an end to its breach they nevertheless award him damages. But these are frequently measured by some other criterion than what the plaintiff might have obtained in a bargain from the defendant, under threat of stopping the breach of the duty outright. In *Vincent v. Lake Erie Transportation Co.,*[13] the Minnesota Supreme Court sustained

---

[1] 167 Mass. 92, 107 (1896).
[2] L. R. 23 Q.B.D. 598, 613 (1889).
[3] Privilege, Malice and Intent (1894) 8 Harv. L. Rev. 1, 8.

Reprinted in Holmes, Collected Legal Papers (1921), 117, 128.
[10] 256 U.S. 350 (1921).
[13] 109 Minn. 456 (1910).

an award of $500 for damage to a dock caused by a vessel whose owners kept it moored to the dock during a sudden and unusual storm which would otherwise probably have destroyed the vessel. In sustaining the award, the court evidently regarded the act of keeping the vessel moored a technical invasion of the dock owner's property rights; yet it went out of its way to justify the invasion, and remarked that "the situation was one in which the ordinary rules regulating property rights were suspended by forces beyond human control." It intimated that the dockowner could not lawfully have done what under ordinary circumstances, would have been permissible—that is, unmoor the vessel and cast her adrift; for its citation of the Vermont case of *Ploof v. Putnam*,[14] in which a dockowner's unmooring under similar circumstances was held unlawful, was apparently with approval. In short, the dockowner seems to have had a "right" not to have the vessel moored to the dock, even during the storm, but would not have been permitted to exercise that right, but only to be paid for not exercising it. And what he was paid was for the physical damage to the dock, not for the loss of the bargaining power which he might have exerted against the owners of the vessel, had he been able to threaten to exercise his property right.

In *Smith v. Staso Milling Co.*,[15] the Circuit Court of Appeals modified an injunction granted by the District Court against a slate crushing mill, which restrained it from continuing an admitted invasion of the property rights of the owner of a nearby summer residence, by polluting the air with dust. Damages were awarded, but they were measured by the loss which the plaintiff suffered by being prevented from leasing his house as a residence. As in the *Vincent* case, they were not measured by what he might have exacted from the mill by threatening to cause it to cease operations by enforcing his right to have the pollution stopped. In fact the court intimated that one reason for refusing to put an end to the admitted invasion of the plaintiff's property right was that such action might put the plaintiff in a position to enact too much money from the defendant, as the price of letting him continue to operate the mill.

"The very right on which the injured party stands," said Learned Hand, Cir. J., "is a quantitative compromise between two conflicting interests. What may be an entirely tolerable adjustment, when the result is only to award damages for the injury done, may become no better than a means of extortion if the result is absolutely to curtail the defendant's enjoyment of his land. Even though the defendant has no power to condemn, at times it may be proper to require of him no more than to make good the whole injury once and for all."

There are statutes making extortion of money a crime. And there are doctrines that in a civil action, one may recover money paid under duress or avoid a contract made under duress. But all money is paid, and all contracts are made, to avert some kinds of threats. What are the peculiar earmarks which characterize some types of threat as "extortion" or "duress," in contradistinction to other types which the law regards as innocent?

. . .

[Professor Hale discusses commercial boycotts, extortion, and other ways of obtaining property or money by threat. He rejects the idea that a party must be deprived of all free will to be able to claim duress, quoting Holmes: "It is always for the interest of a party under duress to choose the lesser of two evils." Duress may be found when based on a threat to do something that in itself is lawful. Sometimes, as with threats of criminal prosecution, the decision to treat a threat as duress may be based on a notion of perverting a public measure for private gain. —ed.]

Even privileges and rights, however, which are accorded for the private benefit of their possessor may sometimes be denied when a threat is made to exercise them in order to obtain some abnormal private advantage. We have already referred to such cases, where parties were not allowed to institute a boycott by means otherwise innocent, or to accumulate checks on a bank for the purpose of forcing it to change its business methods, or to enforce their patent rights for the purpose of securing a monopoly in an unpatented article, or to enforce their property rights in such a way as to serve as a means of "extortion." Courts will not always permit a person to realize on the full nuisance value of his rights and privileges, even those rights and privileges which it accords to him for his private benefit. On the other hand, they do not always thwart the realization of a nuisance value.

In *Mayor of Bradford v. Pickles*,[34] Lord Macnaghten, rendering one of the opinions in the House

[14] 81 Vt. 471 (1908).
[15] 18 F.(2d) 736 (C.C.A. 2d, 1927).

[34] [1895] A. C. 587.

of Lords, suggested that the doing of an otherwise lawful act for the sole purpose of being bought off was quite lawful. The Town sought damages from Pickles for having sunk a shaft in his own land for the malicious purpose of intercepting the flow of underground water to the Town's reservoir. It was held that he had an "absolute right" to do so, whatever his motive. But Lord Macnaghten went further, and, while regarding the existence of malice as irrelevant, denied its existence, saying, in what he termed "palliation" of Pickles's conduct, that

> it may be taken that his real object was to show that he was master of the situation, and to force the corporation [the Town] to buy him out at a price satisfactory to himself. Well, he has something to sell, or, at any rate, he has something which he can prevent other people enjoying unless he is paid for it. . . . His conduct may seem shocking to a moral philosopher. But where is the malice?

It is diffcult to see why an act should be permitted when done for the sole purpose of exacting money from another in return for no service rendered, and no sacrifice incurred. And courts have, on occasion, ordered the restoration of what they regard as "exorbitant" payments, even though they were only exacted by threats to exercise rights and privileges which are accorded for private advantages. The test seems to be a quantitative one, the decision turning not so much on the nature of the threat, as on the amount exacted. Where the sum is "reasonable," the transaction is not characterized as "duress," even though it is exacted by precisely the same pressure as that used to exact an "exorbitant" sum. In *United States v. Bethlehem Steel Corp.*,[36] Justice Black, speaking of the government's abandonment of one of its demands in the course of preliminary negotiations during the first World War, in deference to what he regarded as a reasonable insistence by Bethlehem, said: "And if the government's abandonment of its position is to be regarded as evidence of compulsion, we should have to find compulsion in every contract in which one of the parties makes a concession to a demand, however reasonable, of the other side." We should indeed, for every concession is made to avert a threat. The reasonableness or unreasonableness of a demand has nothing to do with its compulsory or non-compulsory character. Obedience to law is compulsory, however reasonable the law. But the fact that

a contract is made under compulsion is not sufficient ground to invalidate for duress. The test of validity is not compulsion (which is always present), but the quantitative reasonableness of the terms.

Courts will sometimes annul or modify contracts, because the person who enters into them is thought to be too inexperienced or ignorant to bargain effectively with such rights as he has. Thus an infant can avoid a contract, and the courts will give jealous scrutiny to contracts made by seamen, who are regarded as "wards in admiralty." Even when the party is not inexperienced or ignorant, courts will sometimes annul what they regard as unconscionable contracts when advantage has been taken of a party's necessities. As Justice Frankfurter said, in his dissenting opinion in the *Bethlehem* case:

> . . . Fraud and physical duress are not the only grounds upon which courts refuse to enforce contracts. The law is not so primitive that it sanctions every injustice except brute force and downright fraud. More specifically, the courts generally refuse to lend themselves to the enforcement of a "bargain" in which one party has unjustly taken advantage of the economic necessities of the other. "And there is great reason and justice in this rule, for necessitous men are not, truly speaking, free men, but, to answer a present exigency, will submit to any terms that the crafty may impose upon them." Vernon v. Bethell, 2 Eden 110, 113. So wrote Lord Chancellor Northington in 1761.

> . . .

Assuming with Frankfurter, however, that the government was in the position of a "necessitous person," it would not, of course, follow that every bargain that it made out of necessity was oppressive to it. All would agree that Bethlehem should receive *some* compensation for building the ships, just as a salvor should receive some reward for going to the rescue of a ship in distress. Black insisted that, "if there was a 'traffic of profit' here, it was not the unanticipated result of an accident as in the salvage cases.". . .

These remarks suggest that, in determining whether a contract is so oppressive that it should be annulled or modified on the ground of duress, when the party accused of duress has only threatened to exercise some right or privilege whose use for bargaining purposes is not wholly banned, a court will only inquire whether there is a discrepancy between

---

[36] 315 U. S. 289, 302 (1942).

the amount exacted and the *anticpated* result of the other party's needs, or the *standard* established by common practice. That a payment was agreed to under the pressure of necessities does not suffice to make it exorbitant. The services of a wrecking truck or of a salvaging vessel or for that matter, of a physician, are required only because of necessities; but not every contract to pay for such service will be annulled. No court would be likely to annul a contract to pay for the services of a wrecking truck, unless the proprietor of the service station had taken advantage of some "unanticipated" necessity of the driver in distress, beyond the ordinary necessities of such drivers, and forced him to agree to pay appreciably more than the "standard" rate established by common practice. Where there is a market for the services, the standard rate, based on anticipated necessities, would correspond to the market rate. In several of the cases cited by Frankfurter where a contract was annulled, one party, under the stress of necessity, had either sold property for less than its market value, or bought property for more.

"Market value" is a somewhat ambiguous term. In one sense, the price at which any sale takes place is its market value—the value for which the property or service is exchanged on the actual market in which the buyer and seller participate. But when a sale is said to take place at a price above or below the market value, reference is made to what the property *would* sell for in a hypothetical "normal" market, in which other parties might have made bids, had not the buyer or seller been prevented by ignorance or pressing necessity from seeking them out. A driver in distress may be forced to pay his rescuer far more than he would have to if aware of the charges made by other service stations, or if circumstances permitted him to resort to them. If courts refuse to enforce the contract to pay more than the "normal" market value, they do not allow the rescuer to profit from the driver's distress, *except* to the extent that the "anticipated" distress of drivers in general affects the normal market value of the service. They will not inquire, apparently, into whether the normal market value itself, resulting from the mutual coercion of buyers and sellers of the service, is so high or so low as to give an undue advantage to one side or the other. Nor are they the appropriate organs to make such an inquiry.

. . .

But because courts can do nothing to revise the underlying pattern of market relationships, it does not follow that other organs of government should make no attempt to accord greater freedom to the economically weak from the restrictions which stronger individuals place upon them by means of the coercive bargaining power which the law now permits or enables them to exert. Nor does it follow that courts should, in the name of liberty and equality, thwart such attempts to increase and to equalize the economic liberty of the weak. The fact that transactions do not deviate from normal market values does not necessarily indicate that there is a fair relation between the respective bargaining powers of the parties. The market value of a property or a service is merely a measure of the strength of the bargaining power of the person who owns the one or renders the other, under the particular legal rights with which the law endows him, and the legal restrictions which it places on others. To hold unequal bargaining power economically justified, merely because each party obtains the market value of what he sells, no more and no less, is to beg the question.

As a result of governmental and private coercion under what is mistakenly called *laissez faire*, the economic liberty of some is curtailed to the advantage of others, while the economic liberty of all is curtailed to some degree. Absolute freedom in economic matters is of course out of the question. The most we can attain is a relative degree of freedom, with the restrictions on each person's liberty as tolerable as we can make them. It would be impossible for everyone to have unrestricted freedom to make use of any material goods of which there are not enough to go round. If some exercised a freedom to take all the goods they desired, the freedom of others to consume those goods would be gone. There can be no freedom to consume what does not exist, or what other consumers have already appropriated. To protect a consumer's liberty from annihilation at the hands of other consumers, the law curtails it in a more methodical and less drastic way, by forbidding the use of goods without the consent of the owner. In practice this means that the liberty to consume is conditioned on the payment of the market price. When, as in time of war, a price high enough to keep the demand down to the amount available is deemed to place too great a limitation on the freedom of the less well-to-do consumer, the price is kept down by law. We then add a supplementary restriction on the freedom to consume, in order to protect it from being destroyed by the activities of hoarders. Freedom to consume is then conditioned, not only on the possession of money, but also on the possession of rationing coupons.

Liberty to consume would be restricted far more drastically than it is were there no restrictions on that other aspect of economic liberty, freedom to abstain from producing. We do not have slave labor, but there are nevertheless compulsions which force people to work. These compulsions affect different people in varying degree, and are usually far more tolerable than slavery, or than the famine which would doubtless ensue were there no compulsions to work at all. In our industrial society, an employee works in order to make a bargain with his employer and thus obtain the money with which to free himself from some of the restrictions which other people's property rights place on his freedom to consume. He induces the employer to pay him his wage by *threatening* not to work for him, and then not carrying out his threat. Not carrying it out involves temporary surrender of his liberty to be idle. He *must* surrender that liberty, under penalty of not having freedom to consume more than his present means would enable him to.

But the degree to which men surrender liberty in the sphere of production, in order to increase their freedom to consume, varies. One who is endowed by nature or by superior educational opportunities with the ability to render services which are relatively scarce and for which there is great demand, may be able to insist on a high salary as the price of not withholding that ability from the employer, and thus may attain a large measure of freedom to consume. Or he may organize a business of his own and with the profits buy his freedom to consume. At the same time the surrender of his liberty to be idle may involve little if any sacrifice, for the work is apt to be agreeable, or at least more so than idleness. And he may have a large measure of discretion (or liberty) in deciding just *how* he is to perform his work, whereas those who have to take inferior jobs may have to do just what they are told by superiors throughout the working day. The liberty of these people as producers is more closely restricted than is that of those who can bargain for supervisory positions, or who can become entrepreneurs, and for this greater sacrifice of liberty in the process of production, they generally gain less freedom as consumers, being able to bargain only for low wages. The market value of their labor may be low, reflecting the low degree of compulsion they can bring to the bargaining process, as compared to the compulsion brought to bear by the employer.

The employer's power to induce people to work for him depends largely on the fact that the law previously restricts the liberty of these people to consume, while he has the power, through the payment of wages to release them to some extent from these restrictions. He has little power over those whose freedom to consume is relatively unrestricted, because they have large independent means, or who can secure freedom to consume from other employers, because of their ability to render services of a sort that is scarce and in great demand. Those who own enough property have sufficient liberty to consume, without yielding any of their liberty to be idle. Their property rights enable them to exert pressure of great effectiveness to induce people to enter into bargains to pay them money. The law endows them with the power to call on the governmental authorities to keep others from using what they own. For merely not exercising this power, they can obtain large money rewards, by leasing or selling it to someone who will utilize it. These rewards may in many instances amount only to postponed payments for services which the owners have rendered in the past in the process of production, but frequently they greatly exceed any such amount. In fact the owner may have rendered no services whatever himself, but may have acquired his property by government grant or by virtue of the fact that the law assigns property rights to those named in the will of the previous owner, or, if he makes no will, according to the intestacy laws. Bargaining power would be different were it not that the law endows some with rights that are more advantageous than those with which it endows others.

It is with these unequal rights that men bargain and exert pressure on one another. These rights give birth to the unequal fruits of bargaining. There may be sound reasons of economic policy to justify all the economic inequalities that flow from unequal rights. If so, these reasons must be more specific than a broad policy of private property and freedom of contract. With different rules as to the assignment of property rights, particularly by way of inheritance or government grant, we could have just as strict a protection of each person's property rights, and just as little governmental interference with freedom of contract, but a very different pattern of economic relationships. Moreover, by judicious legal limitation on the bargaining power of the economically and legally stronger, it is conceivable that the economically weak would acquire greater freedom of contract than they now have—freedom to resist more effectively the bargaining power of the strong, and to obtain better terms.

If more ambitious governmental activities, in the way of public works, government enterprises and deficit financing at appropriate times, would result in full employment in periods when there would otherwise be business stagnation, then these government activities, far from reducing the economic liberty of individuals, might greatly enlarge it. People who cannot find jobs have no freedom to bargain for wages, and without wages they have very little freedom to consume. In so far as a certain amount of government enterprise would eliminate unemployment, it would increase the demand for the products of private industry. The freedom of private enterprise is at present restricted during periods of business stagnation by its inability to bargain with non-existent customers among the unemployed. Full employment would strike down these restrictions. Whether government activities of the type indicated would in fact increase the total output of society, and with it not only the security and well-being, but the economic liberty as well, of most people, is a question that can be answered only in economic terms. There is no *a priori* reason for regarding planned governmental intervention in the economic sphere as inimical to economic liberty, or even to that special form of it known as free enterprise. We shall have governmental intervention anyway, even if unplanned, in the form of the enforcement of property rights assigned to different individuals according to legal rules laid down by the government. It is this unplanned governmental intervention which restricts economic liberty so drastically and so unequally at present.

4. Unconscionability

Two Attacks on Unconscionability

Under section 2-302 of the Uniform Commercial Code a court may limit or refuse to enforce a contract clause or even the entire contract if it "finds the contract or any clause of the contract to have been unconscionable at the time it was made." This has proven to be one of the most controversial sections in Article Two, and spawned a number of famous cases, several involving welfare consumers. Unlike good faith, which the Code defined in two different ways, unconscionability is left undefined. As will be recalled from the introductory note to the Summers-Burton debate, Professor Summers criticized the idea of defining good faith, and called for elimination of the definition.

In the following article, the late Professor Arthur Leff of Yale traced the path by which the unconscionability notion was left undefined and strongly criticized the lack of definition. One may contrast Leff's attitude towards the Code's approach with that of Eugene Mooney in his *Old Kontract Principles and Karl's New Kode*, reprinted in Part IIC. (The Leff and Mooney articles appeared almost simultaneously, in law reviews published in the same city. Their differences are striking.)

Leff, who died young from lung cancer, was greatly liked and of unquestioned brilliance. This is probably his most famous article. Its tone can be sensed from its title: *Unconscionability and the Code—The Emperor's New Clause*. (Notice how his rhetoric intertwines with his analysis. Who can get terribly concerned with something labeled "bargaining naughtiness"?) Leff's brilliance and cleverness can be irritating, but his conclusion about the use of unconscionability to patronize the poor and to deprive them of the capacity to decide their own style of living is profound and disturbing.

Leff's division of unconscionability into the procedural and the substantive has gained many adherents, among them Professor Richard Epstein of the University of Chicago, who is one of the academic leaders of economic libertarianism. Epstein is a prolific writer, author of a leading torts casebook, and a great polemicist for right-libertarianism. He has many admirers and many adversaries. Indeed, some of his most vigorous adversaries are also his admirers. For what has been called "trenchant" criticism of Epstein, see Linzer, *The Decline of Assent: At-Will Employment as a Case Study of the Breakdown of Private Law Theory*, 20 Ga. L. Rev. 393, 409-15 (1986).

Arthur A. Leff, *Unconscionability and the Code—The Emperor's New Clause*, 115 U. Pa. L. Rev. 485 (1967)

Introduction

This paper is devoted wholly to section 2-302 of the Uniform Commercial Code, the so-called unconscionability clause. It is, however, not primarily an essay on commercial law. Rather it is intended to be a study in statutory pathology, an examination in some depth of the misdrafting of one section of a massive, codifying statute and the misinterpretations which came to surround it. The paper therefore is not intended as a commentary upon the content or drafting technique of the Code as a whole or even of the Sales article. The focus of this study is section 2-302, and excursions into other provisions of the Code are made only to help illuminate that primary target. . . .

Let us begin the story the way so many good stories begin, with ritual incantation: to make a contract one needs (i) parties with capacity, (ii) manifested assent, and (iii) consideration. This is all very simple.[7] If these criteria are met, a party to the resulting nexus who has made promises is obligated to carry them out, unless he can maintain successfully one of the standard contract-law defenses, such as fraud, duress, mistake, impossibility or illegality. These "defenses" might be classified in diverse ways to serve various analytical purposes. For our particular needs, however, there is a simple way of grouping them which is signally illuminating: some of these defenses have to do with the *process of contracting* and others have to do with the resulting *contract*. When fraud and duress are involved, for instance, the focus of attention is on what took place between the parties at the making of the contract. With illegality, on the other hand, the material question is instead the content of the contract once "made." The law may legitimately be interested both in the way agreements come about and in what they provide. A "contract" gotten at gunpoint may be avoided; a classic dicker over Dobbin may come to naught if horse owning is illegal. Hereafter, to distinguish the two interests, I shall often refer to bargaining naughtiness as "procedural unconscionability," and to evils in the resulting contract as "substantive unconscionability."

Getting down to cases, section 2-302 of the Uniform Commercial Code provides in its entirety as follows:

Section 2-302. Unconscionable Contract or Clause.

(1) If the court as a matter of law finds the contract or any clause of the contract to have been unconscionable at the time it was made the court may refuse to enforce the contract, or it may enforce the remainder of the contract without the unconscionable clause, or it may so limit the application of any unconscionable clause as to avoid any unconscionable result.

(2) When it is claimed or appears to the court that the contract or any clause thereof may be unconscionable the parties shall be afforded a reasonable opportunity to present evidence as to its commercial setting, purpose, and effect to aid the court in making the determination.

If reading this section makes anything clear it is that reading this section alone makes nothing clear about the meaning of "unconscionable" except perhaps that it is pejorative. More particularly, one cannot tell from the statute whether the key concept is something to be predicated on the bargaining process or on the bargain or on some combination of the two, that is, to use our terminology, whether it is procedural or substantive. Nonetheless, determining whether the section's target is a species of quasi-fraud or quasi-duress, or whether it is a species of quasi-illegality, is obviously the key to the bite and scope of the provision.

---

[7] This simplicity is, of course, of a rather special kind. Robert Frost once remarked (at a "saying" of his poetry): "e equals mc2; what's so hard about that? Of course, what e, m and c is harder."

One central thesis of this essay is that the drafts-men[11] failed fully to appreciate the significance of the unconscionability concept's necessary procedure-substance dichotomy and that such failure is one of the primary reasons for section 2-302's final amorphous unintelligibility and its accompanying commentary's final irrelevance. This I think can most clearly be shown by an examination in detail of the drafting history of the provision and its accompanying comments, from the beginning (prior to 1941) to the present version. The examination will proceed first from the point of view of what that history discloses about the transformations of procedural unconscionability, and then the focus will shift to substantive unconscionability. Thereafter, I shall examine the equity-specific performance "unconscionability" doctrine to show its total inapplicability to the problems dealt with in the Code, hence pointing out the irrelevance of substantially all of the standard commentary on the section. I shall close by examining the reported cases thus far affected by section 2-302, and their dangerous (though understandable) tendency. The central purpose of the paper will be to illustrate the progressive abstraction, attentuation and eventual destruction of meaning in an important single statutory provision, in response to pressures the nature of which can only be guessed.

. . .

[Professor Leff traces in considerable detail the drafting of the predecessors to section 2-302, beginning in 1941. He argues that the earlier versions permitted invalidation only when a party did not make use of freedom of contract (i.e., did not consciously understand, read, intend to be bound by a provision), but that a notion of substantive unconscionability crept in.]

[By 1949 the] draft cut the developing Gordian knot by saying, in effect, that an unconscionable clause is an unconscionable clause, no matter how it got into the contract. The policy determination was made, in effect, that one could use his superior bargaining power only so far. A legislature being presented with the 1949 draft would have had a fighting chance of knowing what it was being called upon to import into the law of Sales.

Alas, the draftsmen's impulse toward transparency of intention was but ephemeral. It lasted only

until the next printed draft of the Code came out in May 1950. The statute itself remained almost unchanged from its 1949 incarnation. But the comments, oh my, the comments. As a starter, comments 3 and 4 from the prior version, the two comments which explicitly discussed and distinguished substantive and procedural unconscionability, were totally deleted. There was substituted, however, a newly minted first comment, which read in its entirety as follows:

This section is intended to make it possible for the courts to police explicitly against the contracts or clauses which they find to be unconscionable. In the past such policing has been accomplished by adverse construction of language, by manipulation of the rules of offer and acceptance or by determination that the clause is contrary to public policy or to the dominant purpose of the contract. This section is intended to allow the court to pass on the unconscionability of the contract or particular clause therein and to make a conclusion of law as to its unconscionability. The basic test is whether in the light of the general commercial background and the commercial needs of the particular trade or case the clauses involved are so one-sided as not to be expected to be included in the agreement. The principal [sic] is one of prevention of unfair surprises and not of disturbance of allocation of risks because of superior bargaining power. The underlying basis of this section is illustrated by the results in cases such as the following . . . . [40]

As I shall discuss anon, this new comment raised substantial problems through its obfuscation of what "unconscionability" as a substantive thing applicable to a single contractual provision might be. But equally significant was the diffusion of the section's attitude toward contracting conduct. Briefly put, is the manner in which a provision gets into a contract relevant or not? If the contracting process is relevant, what standards does one use to judge the adequacy of that process? Is "reading" enough (can you or can't you be surprised by what you have read?) or "understanding" or "bargaining"? If some form of bargaining over a specific clause goes on, but the seller can and does adopt a take-it-or-leave-it position, is the buyer bound if he takes it? The important thing is not so much that the comment to the 1950

---

[11] I shall use "draftsmen" throughout to refer to that imaginary construct which corporately produced the final Code and the final version of § 2-302. From time to time I shall use the singular form "draftsman," to refer to the late Karl Llewellyn who, at least at the earliest drafting stages,

did the major share of the actual drafting, especially of the Sales article. . . .
. . .
[40] 1950 Draft § 2-302, comment 1. Following the colon were the ten cases cited in the current version of the Code.

version does not clearly answer those particular questions, but that it clearly replaced a draft which did.

The 1949 version's confrontation of the difficulty was to be the last; succeeding drafts of 2-302 were to back further and further away from any stand on the relevance of contracting procedure to a finding of "unconscionability." While the section itself did not change in any manner material to that problem after the 1950 changes, the comments did—subtly perhaps, but importantly.[41] For instance, the 1950 comment had described an unconscionable clause as one "so one sided as not to be expected." The comment to the 1952 draft, however, condemned instead clauses "so one sided as to be unconscionable." This particular transformation I find most instructive on the development of 2-302's language in general. The 1950 comment had pointed to a recognizable human situation; it had, if you will, a dramatic situation somewhere behind it. It may have been impossible to tell in advance what clause might turn out to be so unexpectable as to be *unfairly* surprising, but at least it was clear that one was looking for one of the indicia of surprise—a dropped jaw, perhaps. Some variation from what a contracting party might reasonably have been lulled into expecting (or, more likely, not expecting) was the focus. That would be a scene describing the interaction of real people. Obviously relevant to unconscionability posed as a question of "surprise" would be whether the clause ought to have been pointed out especially, or explained, or at the very least not hidden in fine print and verbal complexity. The test might have been stated, "if he had read this clause, and if he had understood it, what is it likely that he would have done?" If the answer were "exclaimed" or "questioned" or even perhaps "looked quizzical" (the expected reaction need not have been at the level of a silent-movie seduction) then there might arguably have been enough wrong with such a clause's method of importation into the contract to justify its lancing. The 1950 comment at least made the question one of a person's state of mind, and its factual justification. But when it was decided in the 1952 draft to describe unconscionability as "so one sided as to be unconscionable," all dramatic focus was destroyed. The movement of the drafting was from definition in terms of drama to definition in terms of

abstraction. By 1952 unconscionability was defined in terms of itself.

Still another major change was made in the 1952 comment. To the draft as it appeared in 1950 the material indicated by italics below was added:

The principle is one of the prevention of *oppression and* unfair surprise (*Cf. Campbell Soup Co. v. Wentz, 172 F. 2d 80, 3d Cir. 1948*) and not of disturbance of allocation of risks because of superior bargaining power.

The relevance, if any, of the *Campbell Soup* decision and the doctrine of equity unconscionability will be discussed shortly. At this point, however, while the historical progression of the treatment of procedural unconscionability is being surveyed, it is especially illuminating to discuss what "oppression" might possibly have meant. Given the emerging diffusing trend of the statute brought to its peak in this 1952 draft,[44] it should come as no surprise to anyone to discover that the word "oppression," apparently chosen to clarify the meaning of unconscionability, should be almost perfectly ambiguous. Oppression, strictly as a linguistic and syntactical matter, might refer to what took place between the parties at the time they entered into the contract in question (a sort of quasi-duress), or it might just as well refer to the effect of that contract upon the complaining party. As it happens, it is not easy to think of a word better designed to leave in a state of perfect uncertainty whether the focus of the section was to be upon the contracting process or the contract.

If one takes the position that "oppression" refers to the nature of the contract rather than to the contracting process, then the word may add to one's feeling for what "unconscionability" might be: it is something that is not only unexpected but hard on the complaining party. That harshness should be a component of unconscionability will hardly come as startling illumination to anyone, but it does add some explicit coloration to an implicit expectation. If, however, "oppression" describes something in the bargaining process, one is merely more puzzled. Prior to its appearance one would have, under the guidance of the reference to "unfair surprises," focused his attention upon various modes of deception which might have been practiced on the complaining party. One

---

[41] This propensity of the draftsmen to make material changes in the Code by modifying the comment rather than the statute has not gone unnoticed. . . .

[44] Note, for instance, this subtle linguistic modification: the 1950 draft's "surprises" became in the 1952 draft "sur-

prise." This is a nice example of the progressive regression of § 2-302's language from recognizable commercial "plot" to abstraction. Substituting "surprise" for "surprises" has much the same effect as substituting the abstract plural "man" for the pictorial plural "men."

would have looked to factors such as absence of opportunity to read or ability to read, the size of the type used, the unnecessary verbal complexity of the provision in question and so forth. What factors would suffice to do the trick might not be clear, but the relevant inquiry would have been intelligibly circumscribed. With the suggestion that "oppression" was to be henceforth relevant, however, there appeared a new dimension. It was as if the comment had said that if for some reason the aggrieved party could not effectively have objected to the provision in question, even if he knew about it and understood it, that is, *even if he were not surprised*, then the provision would still be destructible as unconscionable. What could be clearer?

Well, what could be clearer, and what in fact was clearer, was the statement in the 1949 draft comment that it was the intention of the draftsmen to cover those clauses which in fact were totally bargained but just too harsh to permit. That particularly explicit comment, however, was eliminated very shortly after it appeared. Is one to take that the gist of that comment was deemed to have returned with all of its vigor in this new compressed form? I am easily churlish enough to suggest that drafting compression has its limits, and that if one were trying to convey such a signally radical position it would have been well to do so in a somewhat less Delphic manner than by the unexplained insertion of the single word "oppression." Moreover, even this circuitous implication that the full meaning of "oppression" encompassed "forced by strong bargaining" is somewhat lessened by the presence in the 1952 draft of an element which did not appear in the 1949 version, the express disclaimer of any intention to meddle with "superior bargaining power." Since "true" duress expectedly remained an available defense in commercial contracts even after the adoption of the Code, "oppression" must lie somewhere between duress and superior bargaining power, a rather narrow niche indeed. Why all this ambiguity?

The answer, I think, is reasonably clear. The draftsmen were faced with several possibilities. They could have said that if a certain level of bargaining elaborateness were reached, any resulting contract (short of illegality) would be invulnerable to later judicial meddling. That, however, would most likely have necessitated some fuller description of what type of bargaining procedure was envisioned as sufficiently immunizing. That is, they would have had to return to what seems to have been the basic conception (though not necessarily to the exact language or to the discursive style) of the original 1941 version. This, as the earliest draft itself showed, presented exceedingly difficult drafting problems. Alternatively, the draftsmen could finally have espoused the position taken in the 1949 draft, that there were some contractual provisions, presently unspecifiable, which could not be permitted under the Code no matter how fully bargained between the parties. This position, however, might well have been unacceptable to important backers of the Code (not to mention to legislatures) if it had been set forth in the high relief in which it was graven in the 1949 comment. Thus faced with a dilemma, the difficulty of the first alternative and the unpopularity of the second, the draftsmen opted for a third solution. They fudged.

. . .

[The cases cited in the Official Comments to section 2-302 involve form contracts, not oppressive bargains or even oppressive bargaining.] The frank adoption of the position that any form contract was open to clause-by-clause policing, however, as Professor Llewellyn pointed out very early in the game, leaves this problem: the use of form contracts is a social good; it is the contracting-process component of the mass transaction, and the mass sales transaction has exceeding economic utility.[64] The form contract is designed *not* to be read or pondered; if it is or has to be it loses much of its utility. But not reading it leads to attempts at aggrandizement by form. The law's problem, therefore, is to discourage dickering and overreaching simultaneously. For this it needs some new device, since in theory at least, until the time of the mass form, it was the dickering which discouraged the overreaching. If this new device, however, is making all printed forms open to after-the-fact *ad hoc* judicial second guessing, there is the danger that the efficiency of mass transactions will be seriously impaired. Moreover, once one faces the fact that the "vice" in the contracting process is nothing more than the use of a form contract, the internal justification for interfering with the parties' transaction becomes attenuated. It becomes exceedingly harder to justify suspension of the ordinary rule that a *sui juris* person who signs his name is bound to what is over his signature. After all, preprinting one's contracts is hardly *malum in se*.

---

64 Llewellyn, Book Review, 52 Harv. L. Rev. 700, 701 (1939).

This tension seems to have led some commentators on 2-302 to suggest that the contracting-procedure element which will permit scrutiny for unconscionability is not the mere use of a form but the use of a form *plus* something else. That is, they have felt impelled to find some "vice" to justify the judicial meddling. And they have identified this form-plus situation with the "contract of adhesion," contract to which one of the parties must either "adhere" entirely or refuse altogether. In such a contract, a party may not bargain minutely over form or content, but must take it as is, if at all. . . . The essence of the adhesion contract is not its "formishness" (that is just a symptom), but the fact that one of the parties has, at least for the purposes of the transaction in question, some of the powers of a monopolist. . . . How it comes about is less important than the fact that it exists; the hallmark of the adhesion contract, and its alleged evil, is that the purveyor of such a contract is in the position for one reason or another to refuse to bargain, to put the other party to a take-it-or-leave-it option.

The dramatic situation which typically frames the contract of adhesion, therefore, is the merchant-consumer retail sale. But while it is very hard to imagine many adhesion contracts which are not at the same time form contracts, it is very simple to imagine form contracts which are not contracts of adhesion. In fact, there is one species of contract, one which most likely accounts for the bulk of commercial contracting in the nation, which is ordinarily a form contract but not an adhesion contract—the merchant-to-merchant form-pad contract, the subject matter of the "battle of the forms." These form-pad deals may on occasion be adhesion deals too, but they certainly need not be. Indeed, there is often a sharp gulf between the typical contract of adhesion and the typical businessmen's battle of the forms. In a very large number of cases businessmen dealing with each other are not forced to take or leave each other's forms. They do not have so limited a market (or knowledge) that they cannot deal elsewhere, and they can, if they wish, argue about even the minutiae of the transaction. As a general rule, however, they do not so wish. They prefer instead to maneuver like Renaissance condottieri for the cheap and bloodless positional victory that comes with the "making" of the contract on their own form. . . .

. . .

Let us assume, however, that despite the references to the businessman's form-pad deal, the proce-dural unconscionability component of section 2-302 is at the adhesion-contract level rather than at the mere form-contract level; that is, that something more than mere preprinting must be shown before the resultant contract becomes subject to meddling under 2-302. It is exceedingly important to note that the only thing such a determination does is to set the level of contract-*insulating* conduct. One may now argue that a contract which has a sufficient number of indicia of compulsion to be fairly described as a contract of adhesion is not something upon which a party can rely to protect the provisions therein from the Code's unconscionability section. In other words, the adhesion contract becomes an exception to the usual rule that one is bound to that which he signs. But that cannot mean that all contracts of adhesion are void, or that all clauses contained in contracts of adhesion are going to be stricken under 2-302. The presentation of an adhesion contract to a person is not, like the presentation of a pistol to his head, sufficient, if proven, to prevent the enforcement of the contract no matter how "fair" its terms. The provisions of the telephone company tariffs and of the common carrier's tickets are ordinarily binding; one cannot get out from under a provision of that sort by showing only that one could not have bargained about it. Thus, once it is decided that a certain contract is vulnerable to scrutiny under 2-302 because its bargaining was not sufficiently angelic to insulate it from the section, the problem of the unconscionability provision of the Code still remains unsolved: granted that the contract is now open to 2-302, when is it, or a portion of it, "unconscionable"?

Substantive Unconscionability

Drafting History

. . .

This idea, that "unconscionability" meant something like overall contractual imbalance, was maintained all the way up to the 1948 version of section 2-302. At that point came a change of immense significance. The 1948 version read in its entirety as follows:

Section 23. Unconscionable Contract or Clause.

(1) If the court finds the contract to be unconscionable, it may refuse to enforce the contract or strike any unconscionable clauses and enforce the rest of the contract or substitute for the stricken clause such provision as would be implied under this Act if the stricken clause had never existed.

(2) A contract not unconscionable in its entirety

but containing an unconscionable clause, whether a form clause or not, may be enforced with any such clause stricken.

This draft says bluntly that a court may excise from a not unconscionable contract any single "unconscionable" clause, and the comment accompanying the 1949 version (in which version the text of the section itself is not changed from the 1948 draft) says it just as bluntly:

> Under this section the court, in its discretion, may refuse to enforce the contract as a whole if it is permeated by the unconscionability or it may strike any single clause or group of clauses which are so tainted or which are contrary to the essential purpose of the agreement.

From this point on in the drafting history of section 2-302 the concept of single-clause unconscionability was fixed; no substantial changes were made in this regard in the text of the statute or its accompanying comments. The current comment 2[109] was present in essentially its final form as early as the 1950 draft.

This progression through the drafts of the idea of substantive unconscionability, from overall imbalance to one-clause naughtiness, is the most important single transformation disclosed by a study of the drafting history. Determining which contracts are substantively unconscionable is a difficult enough job even if one's conception of substantive unconscionability is something like "gross imbalance," or "lopsidedness." After all, even a lopsided contract might in some cases be hard to identify; what if X got seven risks and Y got five—or four to three—or two to one? The spuriousness of the quantification lurking in the idea of a contract suffering from "overall imbalance," is a potential plague for close cases. Compared, however, with the difficulties of dealing with a concept of one-clause unconscionability, it is pure vanilla. . . .

. . .

. . . [I]f one decides to police contracts on a clause-by-clause basis, he finds that he has merely substituted the highly abstract word "unconscionable" for the possibility of more concrete and particularized thinking about particular problems of social policy. Should warranty disclaimers be permitted? If so, should they be with respect to consumer goods?

Should parties be allowed to agree about what law will govern their contract? To what extent, if any, should a party be permitted to limit his liability under a contract? All of these questions need decision. *But not one of them is helped toward solution by being subsumed in a section as a species of "unconscionability."* The word "unconscionable," as finally used in the Code, describes neither the dramatic situation of two persons bargaining nor the "imbalance" or "lopsidedness" or other quality of the resulting contract, but rather describes the emotional state of the trier which will justify his use of the section. In other words, the attitudes relevant under section 2-302 are not those of the parties but those of the judges. The pictures to be sought in the facts are not of the varieties of oppressive or surprising negotiations, nor of oppressive or surprising contracts, but rather of oppressed or surprised judges. But what may permissibly make the judges' pulses race or their cheeks redden, so as to justify the destruction of a particular provision, is, one would suppose, what the judge ought to have been told by the statute. In short, once the movement was made to a conception of one-clause unconscionability, and the "overall-imbalance" rubric was abandoned as insufficient, the statute and its commentary had been stripped of any power to guide the decision of what the "bad" single provisions might be like. And the enormous significance of this failure may be illustrated by a careful consideration of the ten cases described as disclosing the "underlying basis" of the section, and the interesting way they failed to fill the gap.

The Official-Comment Cases

The ten cases do illustrate the one-clause-unconscionability theory, each really involving only one offensive "unconscionable" clause. But there are only two types of naughty clauses represented: warranty disclaimers and remedy limitations. Given this arresting fact alone, one might be tempted to conclude that the purpose of section 2-302 was to render warranty disclaimers and remedy limitations per se unconscionable. Nor indeed would the world, even the commercial world, come to an end if parties were forbidden either to disclaim warranties or to withhold from each other any of the total panoply of remedies for breach of contract which the Code provides. In other

---

[109] Under this section the court, in its discretion, may refuse to enforce the contract as a whole if it is permeated by the unconscionability, or it may strike any single clause or group of clauses which are so tainted or which are contrary

to the essential purpose of the agreement, or it may simply limit unconscionable clauses so as to avoid unconscionable results. U.C.C. § 2-302, comment 2.

places in the Code the draftsmen have felt free flatly to forbid particular contractual provisions, agreement between the parties or not.

Unfortunately for the solution of the problem now before us, that road was not the one taken. It is perfectly clear that under the Code warranties may be disclaimed, and remedies for breach may be modified and limited; neither are per se unconscionable. . . .

. . .

. . . It appears to be a matter of common assumption that section 2-302 is applicable to warranty disclaimers. I find this, frankly, incredible. Here is 2-316 which sets forth clear, specific and anything but easy-to-meet standards for disclaiming warranties. It is a highly detailed section, the comments to which disclose full awareness of the problem at hand. It contains no reference of any kind to section 2-302, although nine other sections of article 2 contain such references. In such circumstances the usually bland assumptions that a disclaimer which meets the requirements of 2-316 might still be strikable as "unconscionable" under 2-302 seems explainable, if at all, as oversight, wishful thinking or (in a rare case) attempted sneakiness.

Of course, the emotional pressure to reach a no-disclaimer result via the unconscionability route if it cannot be done otherwise is understandable. One need only point out that if in the *Henningsen* case [142] the auto manufacturers had gotten together to agree upon a form of disclaimer clause which accorded with the requirements of section 2-316, under my view, Mrs. Henningsen's serious personal injuries would have to go uncompensated. This would be so even though the auto manufacturers had the oligopolistic power to make the terms of their contracts unbargainable. Any court might find it intolerable to allow a rich auto manufacturer to avoid making restitution for injuries suffered through the breakdown of a dangerous instrument it manufactured merely because it had made verbal compliance with a talismanic form of words which may not have been read or understood by the purchaser, and about which he could have done nothing even if he had read, understood and objected. Such a decision would be an exceedingly painful one to announce. But that *is* what the statute says. There is nothing to prevent a legislature from regulating certain particular contractual provisions out of existence, as they have done on innumerable occasions in the past. Certainly there is not much force remaining

in simplistic freedom-of-contract arguments that legislatures may not determine, as a matter of policy, that some things in contracts just won't go. The Code itself goes that route in other places and there would have been nothing offensive in doing so with respect to warranty disclaimers, especially with respect to consumer goods. What is offensive is the seeming attempt on the part of some commentators to nullify the legislative determination that warranty disclaimers, for the time being at least, may continue. Even legislatures, one would think, are entitled to some protection from oppression and unfair surprise.

If one concludes, however, as I do, that if there is one sales-contract provision to which 2-302 does not apply it is the warranty disclaimer, then both kinds of clauses dealt with in the official-comment cases are totally regulated by sections of the Code other than 2-302. But may one not reason by analogy from the warranty-disclaimer and remedy-limitation clauses at issue in the official comment cases to clauses which are "like" them but do not have any specific applicable section of the Code? The answer, I think, is no. First let us recall that we are not talking here of procedural unconscionability. Assuming that a certain level of bargaining nastiness is reached, any harsh clause may be strikable; but we are talking, remember, of form contracts, or at most of contracts of adhesion, contracts whose provisions cannot be handled in any per se simplified manner. Thus we are speaking of what is "like" a warranty disclaimer as a substantive provision. What is that? Basically, it is a provision which shifts a risk from party A to party B when party A is, arguably, better able to appreciate, avoid and stand that risk. Put briefly, can we assume that a provision is unconscionable and voidable if (a) it is in a form contract or a contract of adhesion and (b) it makes the poorer party stand a substantial loss which the richer party could stand better? Moreover, it must be recalled that the Code most specifically did not declare warranty disclaimers and remedy limitations void. Instead it regulated them in detail. Is one to assume that while the paradigms are to be regulated the clauses "like" them are to be voided instead? What analogy suggests here is not similarity of treatment, but unspecified variation instead.

. . .

[Professor Leff discusses equity cases in some detail. He concludes:] Briefly put, when one examines any number of these equity cases at all it becomes

[142] Henningsen v. Bloomfield Motors, Inc., 32 N.J. 358, 161 A.2d 69 (1960).

abundantly clear that over and above fraud, misrepresentation, mistake and duress there is a whole universe of *kinds of bargaining* which, while not sufficient to justify the voiding of a contract, will support a refusal specifically to enforce it, and that beyond the illegality and "against public policy" rubrics of law, are *kinds of contracts* which equity will not affirmatively aid.

Within the ambit of those factors of contract-procuring behavior which would result in a denial of specific performance, a bewildering number of permutations work to inform the chancellor's discretion. In these cases one runs continually into the old, the young, the ignorant, the necessitous, the illiterate, the improvident, the drunken, the naive and the sick, all on one side of the transaction, with the sharp and hard on the other. Language of quasi-fraud and quasi-duress abounds. Certain whole classes of presumptive sillies like sailors and heirs and farmers and women continually wander on and off stage. Those not certifiably crazy, but nonetheless pretty peculiar, are often to be found. And in most of the cases, of course, several of these factors appear in combination.[202] It might be assumed, therefore, that one setting out to find a body of decisions which might give contour and limits to a word like "unconscionability," at least insofar as that word might have something to do with the insufficiency of the bargaining process, would find in these cases riches beyond the dreams of judicial avarice. There is, however, one weakness in using these cases as a guide to the meaning of unconscionability in section 2-302: they are all irrelevant—for two reasons. First, the equity cases are of interest, if at all, only for giving outline to the limits of procedural unconscionability; they cannot define what kind of clause might be substantively unconscionable because they all involve only one form of substantive unconscionability—overall imbalance. Second, on procedural unconscionability, the dramatic situations which have produced the contracts which have produced the equity cases are exceedingly unlikely to be reproduced in a Sales context except on the very rarest of occasions, and thus their details do not inform the sales-contract decision a bit.

. . .

Merely that there is no a priori reason why doctrines developed in equity might not fit equally well in law actions, does not justify the jumped conclusion

that all equitable doctrines fit equally well at law. Put more concretely for present purposes, the practice of denying specific performance in equity to contracts because of their "unconscionability," does not *necessarily* make any sense when applied to the law of Sales. It might be sensible. In fact, it isn't.

Almost without exception, actions for specific performance were (and are) brought with respect to transactions involving real property. Article 2 of the Code governs "goods" only, and real property is not a species of "goods". . . .

. . .

Most important, real property is likely to be the only thing that relatively unsophisticated people have which is worth tricking them out of. Farmers have farms and old ladies have old homesteads. The equity cases are replete with factual patterns involving the old being bilked, and farmers sweet-talked into ruinous trades. Courts would be most solicitous to impede land transfers by the poor sillies of the world.

It is out of these special attributes of land, making up the *Gestalt* of real property (as opposed to the "goods" of the Code), that there arise those repeated dramatic vignettes with which the Chancellors were continually faced—the abused old and unsophisticated young, the slicker and the farmer, the money lender and the expectant heir. This cast of characters, to a large extent determined by the nature of the commodity, led to the various forms of overreaching which, while not quite adding up to fraud or duress, formed the pictures of bargaining processes which the chancellors declared "unconscionable." But mark: *all of these are pictures of individual overreachings.* In other words, more important than the uniqueness of each piece of land (but connected with it) is *the uniqueness of each land transaction.* The dramatic situations which were presented and decided under the equity unconscionability doctrine were most particularly those kinds of overreaching which take place, and can only take place, when there is individualized bargaining. The equity criteria are fitted only to nonmass transactions.

And that is precisely what the Code in general and section 2-302 in particular is not designed to cover. The unconscionability section of the Code is primarily focused on the merchant-to-merchant form-pad deal, the merchant-to-consumer adhesion transaction, the modern mass-sale transaction. To decide whether one

[202] See, e.g., Banaghan v. Malaney, 200 Mass. 46, 85 N.E. 839 (1908), involving an "aged, inexperienced and ignorant woman."

of these mass transactions is to be allowed to stand, the discriminations and discussions by the equity courts of various gradations of quasi-fraud and quasi-duress are about as useful as a goiter. Section 2-302 is a child of the mass transaction, and the state of health of little old ladies and the shade of rapaciousness of their favorite nephews is not going to inform one's decision. Thus, all of the jolly references to the good old equity doctrine, if they are supposed to indicate a source for determining procedural unconscionability under the Code, are woefully misguided and misguiding. Equity dealt with the pathology of bargaining. The Code deals with the pathology of nonbargaining.

Substantive Unconscionability in Equity

If, then, the references to the equity doctrine are to be other than delusive, the mass of equity cases must help to define the kinds of contracts and contract clauses (as distinguished from the kinds of contracting behavior) which are unconscionable. Alas, that hope is also bootless. There is only one thing which equity recognized as substantive unconscionability: inadequate consideration (or, to put it another way, "gross overall imbalance"). . . .

This important fact, that all of the equity unconscionability decisions really depend upon a finding of inadequate overall consideration has been obscured by the fact that the really live issue in this area, the subject of a controversy lasting centuries, was not whether inadequate consideration was a *necessary* cause of the denial of specific performance, but whether it was a *sufficient* cause. . . . Thus the only factor of substantive unconscionability which could be presented in an action for specific performance was that of disproportion of price, *i.e.*, overall imbalance. The Code draftsmen, however, quite specifically determined, after an early impulse to the contrary, that section 2-302 would be applicable not only to contracts which were unbalanced in an overall sense, but also to those containing single "unconscionable" clauses. Since under this approach a separate substantive determination must be made on a clause-by-clause basis, the equity doctrine's weighing technique is generally irrelevant.

To summarize, there are two separate social policies which are embodied in the equity unconscionability doctrine. The first is that bargaining naughtiness, once it reaches a certain level, ought to avail the practitioner naught. The second is directed not against

bargaining conduct (except insofar as certain results often are strong evidence of certain conduct otherwise unproved) but against results, and embodies the doctrine (also present in *laesio enormis* statutes) that the infliction of serious hardship demands special justification. The first of these social policies cannot be reflected in section 2-302 in any helpful way unless one takes the position that everything in a form contract or an adhesion contract is to be stricken upon the nondrafting party's request, for that is the type of transaction with which the section is designed to deal. The second policy, that harsh results not be permitted irrespective of the fairness of the bargaining process or the unfairness of the provision at the time of the drafting, is an attractive one because of the ease of its administration; it is not at all hard to identify a harsh result when it has come about. The difficulty with adapting that doctrine to the Code provision is that substantially all of the important provisions in a normal sales contract are *potentially* exceedingly harsh. Generally they are inserted to determine who will stand a loss, perhaps a total loss, if a particular happening happens, or at least to give a huge litigation advantage to one of the parties should the question come up. . . . Thus "unconscionability" cannot be equated with "harshness" as an abstract matter. Certain particular clauses may indeed be declared impermissible as a matter of policy; that is how a usury statute operates, and consumer protection statutes embody numerous interdictions of specific contractual provisions. But the hallmark of unconscionability cannot be the harshness of the result without more, because sales clauses are designed to be harsh. Unless one says that *all* losses should be split or spread (as has been suggested in special contexts), a harsh result without more, even if the result of an adhesion or form-contract provision, cannot identify the impermissible.

If the unconscionability of a clause at the time it was made cannot be determined by looking at its eventual harsh effect then the test of unconscionability to be applied to any individual clause of a commercial contract is no further clarified. When is a warranty disclaimer "unconscionable"? Not, obviously, when it succeeds in disclaiming a warranty, but when it is as a matter of social policy "bad" that the warranty be disclaimable. When is that? One can argue about the answer, but at least when the question is asked in that way, one is arguably arguing about the right sub-questions, not about the content of an *n*th level abstraction like "unconscionability." Alas, 2-302 steers the latter course.[237]

. . .

The Cases "Using" 2-302

As the history of 2-302, and the suggested guides to its operation have now been discussed, it is time to analyze those cases in which 2-302 has so far been actually involved. Strictly speaking, only one reported case relies upon section 2-302 of the Code even as an alternative ground of holding. In *American Home Improvement, Inc. v. MacIver*,[255] the plaintiff was in the business of selling and installing home improvements. It agreed with the defendant to "furnish and install 14 combination windows and one door" and "flintcoat the side walls" on defendant's home, all for $1,759.00. Since the defendant was apparently unwilling or unable to pay cash, the plaintiff undertook to arrange long-term financing, and furnished defendant with an application to a finance company (apparently in some way allied or affiliated with the plaintiff). This application was shortly "accepted," and defendant was notified in writing that his payments for the improvements would be $42.81 per month for sixty months (a grand total of $2,568.60) which included "principal, interest and life and disability insurance." Plaintiff commenced work, but after it had completed only a negligible portion of the job it was asked by defendant to stop and it complied, thereafter suing defendant for damages for breach of contract.

On these facts, the New Hampshire court need never have reached any unconscionability question. There was in effect in the jurisdiction a "truth-in-lending" statute which applied to the transaction. The court could have relied upon that statute to strike the contract, and indeed did so as an alternative ground of decision. But the court most specifically made it a point not to rest its decision solely upon the disclosure statute. It said:

There is another and independent reason why the recovery should be barred in the present case because the transaction was unconscionable. "The courts have often avoided the enforcement of unconscionable provisions in long printed standardized contracts, in part by the process of '*interpretation*' against the parties using them, and in part by the method used by Lord Nelson at Copenhagen." 1 Corbin, Contracts, s. 128 (1963). Without using either of these methods reliance can be placed upon the Uniform Commercial Code (U.C.C. 2-302(1)) [quotation of section omitted].

. . .

Inasmuch as the defendants have received little or nothing of value and under the transaction they entered into they were paying $1,609 for goods and services valued at far less, the contract should not be enforced because of its unconscionable features. This is not a new thought or a new rule in this jurisdiction. See Morrill v. Bank, 90 N.H. 358, 365, 9 A.2d 519, 525; "It has long been the law in this state that contracts may be declared void because unconscionable and oppressive . . . ."

All right, then. As of the time of writing, the only case which has relied upon section 2-302 as a basis of decision has decided that "unconscionable" means "too expensive." And certainly there is no immutable principle displayed in fixed stars that would make that particular meaning of unconscionable inconceivable. I have earlier suggested that in fact that was the primary meaning of unconscionability in some of the early drafts of the Code, and that it was its *only* meaning as used by courts of equity. Certainly the idea that a strikingly disproportionate exchange should be voidable has not destroyed the commerce of the many jurisdictions which utilize a *laesio enormis* doctrine in one form or another.[260] On the other hand one may certainly speculate on whether the legislatures which have flocked to embrace the Code would

[237] One other difference between the equity doctrine and § 2-302 should be mentioned here. Under the equity doctrine, the result of a refusal to enforce was, at least theoretically, not total failure of the plaintiff's cause, but only to a remission to his rights "at law." Such "right" at law in fact might not exist. One empirical study (dealing, however, with only fifty-six cases) has suggested that as a general rule one who loses in equity loses for good. Frank & Endicott, Defenses in Equity and "Legal Rights," 14 La. L. Rev. 380 (1954). One suspects, however, that the Chancellors thought there was a real remedy at law, and that the litigants did too; else the actions for cancellation and the judges' agoniz-

ing over them make little sense. See, e.g., Day v. Newman, 2 Cox 77, 83, 30 Eng. Rep. 36, 38 (Ch. 1788).

[255] 105 N.H. 435, 201 A.2d 886 (1964).

[260] E.g., Code Civil art. 1134 (Fr. 58th ed. 1959) (5/12 of value); Civil Code § 138 (Ger. 10th ed. Palandt 1952) ("strikingly disproportionate"), La. Civ. Code Ann. art. 1861(2) (West 1952) (1/2 of value). Moreover, according to an exceedingly interesting recent book, the Barotse of Northern Rhodesia also know fair-price and aesio enormis doctrines. See Gluckman, The Ideas in Barotse Jurisprudence 192-93 (1965). So much for you, Tom Hobbes.

have been willing to adopt a provision which frankly and openly declared that overcharges of some large but unspecified degree could be invalidated by courts on an *ad hoc* basis, at least as part of a *commercial* code.

Let us assume, however, that a system of jurisprudence ought to have some way to deal with transactions in which one party is giving up vastly more than he is getting, and that this purpose is at least one of those that section 2-302 is designed to serve. Even given that assumption, one has still to ask whether the best way to inject that supervisory power into the law is to subsume it under a high-level abstraction like "unconscionability." After all, a *laesio enormis* type of statute is not very hard to draft, as either a flat-percentage or a "grossly-too-much" provision. The decision in the *MacIver* case exposes the weaknesses of abstraction so deliciously that it justifies esurient consideration.

[Professor Leff's "esurient consideration" of the *MacIver* case is omitted. He argues that the court ignored such legitimate seller's costs as salesmen's commissions and costs of distribution, and incorrectly computed the interest rate to arrive at an inflated number. The real evil, in his mind, is that section 2-302 encourages the court to go by guesswork, just as it did. —ed.]

. . .

As noted earlier, the *MacIver* case is the only one reported which has relied upon 2-302 as a basis of decision. One very recent case, however, which has attracted substantial attention from the commentators, clearly would have been decided on the basis of 2-302 had the statute been in effect at the time of the relevant transaction, and in fact was decided as if the section were the law of the jurisdiction. In that case, *Williams v. Walker-Thomas Furniture Co.*, [268] the appellant, a Mrs. Williams, "a person of limited education separated from her husband," had, during the period 1957-1962, purchased "a number of household items" from appellee furniture company on printed-form installment sale contracts (in the transparent guise of leases). One sentence in this printed contract, part of "a long paragraph in extremely fine print" had the net effect of keeping

a balance due on every item purchased until the balance due on all items, whenever purchased, was

liquidated. As a result, the debt incurred at the time of purchase of each item was secured by the right to repossess all the items previously purchased by the same purchaser. . . .

When Mrs. Williams' outstanding balance was only $164, she bought a $515 stereo phonograph set. At the time of this purchase, the furniture company was perfectly aware (since the information was endorsed on the back of the installment contract) that Mrs. Williams' sole income was a government payment (apparently some species of relief) of $218 per month. The Circuit Court opinion also indicated that the store knew that Mrs. Williams was supposed to support herself and her seven children on that amount (though that seems not to have been endorsed on the back of the contract). At any rate, the stereo set was apparently just too great a burden for the $218 per month to bear. Mrs. Williams defaulted, the store replevied every item it could lay its hands on and won in the trial court and the intermediate appeals court. On appeal to the United States Court of Appeals for the District of Columbia Circuit, the case was remanded to make findings on the issue of unconscionability.

For those of us who have an instinctive and infallible sense of justice (and which of us does not), any other result in this case is unimaginable. But there are grounds for quibbling about the court's (and the Code's) methodology. Judge Wright found unconscionability easy to describe:

Unconscionability has generally been recognized to include an absence of meaningful choice on the part of one of the parties together with contract terms which are unreasonably favorable to the other party . . . . [In the footnote which supports this statement, citation is to *Henningsen v. Bloomfield Motors, Inc.*, 32 N.J. 358, 161 A.2d 69 (1960), and *Campbell Soup Co. v. Wentz*, 172 F.2d 80 (3d Cir. 1948) only.] In many cases the meaningfulness of the choice is negated by a gross inequality of bargaining power.[277]

That is, there is immediate recognition that unconscionability has to have two foci, the negotiation which led to the contract and that contract's terms. As for the procedural aspect, while there is no finding that this was the only credit furniture store open to Mrs. Williams, or that even if it were not, they all had substantially the same contract (which was the

[268] 350 F.2d 445 (D.C. Cir. 1965), remanding 198 A.2d 914 (D.C. Mun. Ct. App. 1964).

[277] Compare § 2-302, comment 1: "The principle [of the section] is . . . not [one] of disturbance of allocation of risks because of superior bargaining power."

situation in the *Henningsen* case so heavily relied upon by the court), one may assume that the form Mrs. Williams signed was essentially the only kind of form open to her. A person's "relevant market" may fairly be the one he can reasonably be expected to know about or dare to use. In other words, the local stores may be a local person's relevant market because of his ignorance, and if they are all as one on something, as to him they are a monopoly. And besides, in this case the court made an almost-finding of contracting procedures which went beyond the mere use of a form or even of a contract of adhesion, which reached, in fact, at least some level of quasi-fraud. Judge Wright asks:

> Did each party to the contract, considering his obvious education or lack of it, have a reasonable opportunity to understand the terms of the contract, or were the important terms hidden in a maze of fine print and minimized by deceptive sales practices?

There was apparently no problem with the answer, for after giving lip service to the "usual rule" that one who signs an agreement is bound to all of its terms, he said:

> But when a party of little bargaining power, and hence little real choice, signs a commercially unreasonable contract with little or no knowledge of its terms . . . the usual rule . . . should be abandoned . . . .[281]

It is hard to fault the court's argument on the procedural unconscionability aspects of this case. While it might sometimes be difficult to decide whether a species or level of bargaining ought to protect a contract from section 2-302, it is not difficult here. If the unconscionability section is to be applicable to any contract, it must be to one "bargained" as this one was.

But there is no need to labor this point. Finding that the bargaining procedure involved will not insulate the contract from judicial scrutiny under section 2-302 is only the first and less difficult step in the process of using that section. Once one decides that the contract is vulnerable to judicial meddling, there still remains to be decided whether the provision or contract is "unconscionable." For that determination Judge Wright also articulated a test:

> In determining reasonableness or fairness, the primary concern must be with the terms of the

contract considered in light of the circumstances existing when the contract was made. The test is not simple, nor can it be mechanically applied. The terms are to be considered "in the light of the general commercial background and the commercial needs of the particular trade or case" [citing "Comment, Uniform Commercial Code sec. 2-307," but obviously meaning 2-302]. Corbin suggests the test as being whether the terms are "so extreme as to appear unconscionable according to the mores and business practices of the time and place." . . . We think this formulation correctly states the test to be applied in those cases where no meaningful choice was exercised upon entering the contract.

How does that test apply to the *Williams* facts? What is it about Mrs. Williams' contract which is "unconscionable"? Surprisingly, the answer is not clear, even about *what* in the contract is bad. It seems, however, that there are two possibilities. First, it may be that the provision by which each item purchased became security for all items purchased was the objectionable feature of the contract. Or it might be that the furniture company sold this expensive stereo set to this particular party which forms the unconscionability of the contract. If the vice is the add-on clause, then one encounters the now-familiar problem: such a clause is hardly such a moral outrage as by itself meets Judge Wright's standard of being "so extreme as to appear unconscionable according to the mores and business practices of the time and place." The lower court in the *Williams* case called attention, for instance, to a Maryland statute regulating retail installment sales under which Mrs. Williams might have been relieved, noting with regret that the statute was not in effect in the District. What was not pointed out by the lower court (and *certainly* not by the upper court) was that the State of Maryland had found nothing illegal per se about add-on provisions, in fact specifically permitting them and setting out to regulate them in some detail. Of the thirty-seven jurisdictions which have statutes regulating retail installment sales, only one has a provision making add-on clauses impermissible. In such circumstances it does seem a bit much to find "so extreme as to appear unconscionable according to the mores and business practices of the time and place" an add-on clause in the District of Columbia which is used and statutorily permitted almost everyplace else, including contiguous Maryland. One's gorge can hardly be expected to rise with such nice geographic selectivity.

If one is not convinced that the unconscionability inheres in the add-on provision, it may be argued that it inheres in the contract as a whole, in the act of having sold this expensive item to a poor person knowing of her poverty. This is quite clearly the primary significance of the case to some of the commentators. That is the kind of action which the Maryland statute does not deal with, nor do any of the statutes like it: the unconscionability of aiding or encouraging a person to live beyond his means (without much hope of eventual success). Well, why not make that "unconscionable" for purposes of section 2-302? After all, in this case Walker-Thomas did know for a fact that Mrs. Williams was on relief; they knew her income and needs with great particularity: $218 per month and seven children. This case does not present any of the sticky close questions of how much of what a seller would have to know (or inquire about) before being deemed to know that the buyer shouldn't buy. Moreover, what Mrs. Williams bought this time was a stereo record player. No one could argue that such an article is a "necessity" to a relief client, and thus the dissenting judge's suggestion that "what is a luxury to some may seem an outright necessity to others" hardly applies in this case. Who can doubt but that this purchase was a frill? So in this case all we would have is a holding that one cannot enforce a contract pursuant to which one has sold luxuries to a poor person (or at least one on relief) with knowledge or reason to know that he will not be able to pay for them. This is just another class distinction, and distinctions among persons on the bases of the "class" to which they belong, that is, on the basis of some common supra-personal characteristics, is exceedingly common in the law (not to mention life). Such a process immensely simplifies decision by limiting the required inquiry to the person's membership in the class. Once that determination is made, a certain legal result will flow. The classic instance is the majority-minority dichotomy. Persons under twenty-one cannot, as a general rule, make self-binding contracts. This may be considered a shorthand form of a syllogism which would go something like (a) persons lacking sufficient probity ought not to be allowed to bind themselves; (b) all persons under twenty-one

lack sufficient probity; (c) persons under twenty-one cannot bind themselves. This illustrates some of the strengths and weakneses of the class system. The rule is easy to administer because a party's age is much easier to determine than his probity. The difficulty is that the easier the classification the less likely it is to be accurate, because classes are, in fact, hardly ever wholly homogeneous. In our case, for instance, the "minor premise," is false; not all persons under twenty-one lack sufficient probity to bind themselves. [The age of majority is now commonly eighteen. —ed.]

When faced with the difficulties inherent in deciding the bargaining fairness of any given transaction, the equity courts, in working out *their* unconscionability doctrine, similarly leaned heavily on relatively gross classifications. In effect, they seem continually to have taken a kind of *sub rosa* judicial notice of the amount of power of certain classes of people to take care of themselves, often without too much inquiry into the actual individual bargaining situation. And it is arguable that sometimes they were wrong; not all old ladies or farmers are without defenses. Put briefly, the typical has a tendency to become stereotypical, with what may be unpleasant results even for the beneficiaries of the judicial benevolence. One can see it enshrined in the old English equity courts' jolly treatment of English seamen as members of a happy, fun-loving race (with, one supposes, a fine sense of rhythm), but certainly not to be trusted to take care of themselves. What effect, if any, this had upon the sailors is hidden behind the judicial chuckles as they protected their loyal sailor boys, but one cannot help wondering how many sailors managed to get credit at any reasonable price. In other words, the benevolent have a tendency to colonize, whether geographically or legally.[296]

Far more economically significant and widespread as an example of the Chancellors' temptation toward stereotypical jurisprudence is found in the expectant-heir cases. The most important thing about expectant-heir cases is that there are expectant-heir cases, classifiable separately as such in treatises. The Chancellors did not find unfairness in the price and refuse to enforce because they had no conception of how an expectancy had to be discounted for risk; that kind of sophistication came early.[298] They just set out to protect heirs from the full effect of their tendency to live

[296] See F. Cohen, Indian Wardship: The Twilight of a Myth, in The Legal Conscience 328 (L. Cohen ed. 1960); cf. Williams v. Walker-Thomas Furniture Co., 350 F.2d 445 (D.C. Cir. 1965).

[298] The leading case of Earl of Chesterfield v. Janssen, 2 Ves. Sr. 125, 28 Eng. Rep. 82 (Ch. 1750), for instance, contains a sophisticated judicial discussion of the economic problems involved.

beyond their governors' life expectancies. This was easy to do; it was rare that a judge had to enter into too long a discussion of the actual facts, or to face the real basis of his easy decision in the battle between his (there but for the grace of God) grandson and the most-likely-Jewish moneylender. After all, he had the rubric "unconscionable" with which to explain (to himself and to the public) that decision.

Thus, when one asks why a court (like the District of Columbia Court in the *Williams* case) ought not be allowed to subsume its social decisions under a high-level abstraction like "unconscionability," one may point to the equity cases so many other commentators have pointed to, but for a different reason. One may suggest that first (and less important) it tends to make the true bases of decisions more hidden to those trying to use them as the basis of future planning. But more important, it tends to permit a court to be nondisclosive about the basis of its decision even to itself; the class determination is so easy and so tempting (and often so heart-warming). More particularly with respect to the *Williams* case concept that the poor should be discouraged from frill-buying, no legislature in America could be persuaded openly to pass such a statute, nor should any be permitted to do so sneakily. If the selling of frills to the poor is to be discouraged, if the traditional middle-class virtues of thrift and child care are to be fostered in the deserving poor by a commercial statute, if one wants to protect a class, improvident by definition, from the depredations of another class, it is at least arguable that one should just up and do so—but clearly. This is not to suggest, for a moment, anything as stupid as that some "freedom-of-contract" concept ought to prevent, for instance, the statutory interdiction of an eleven-hour day. It is only to say that when you forbid a contractual practice, you ought to have the political nerve to do so with some understanding (and some disclosure) of what you are doing.[300]

Conclusion

I have attempted to describe in some detail the pathology, developmental, morphological and functional, of section 2-302 of the Code and its official and unofficial commentaries. The gist of the tale is simple: it is hard to give up an emotionally satisfying incantation, and the way to keep the glow without the trouble of the meaning is continually to increase the abstraction level of the drafting and explaining language. If for one reason or another (in this case the desire to forward the passage of the whole Code) the academic community is generally friendly to the drafting effort, a single provision in a massive Code may get by even if it has, really, no reality referent, and all of its explanatory material ranges between the irrelevant and the misleading. That this happened with respect to 2-302 the few cases using it are beginning to show more and more clearly. The world is not going to come to an end. The courts will most likely adjust, encrusting the irritating aspects of the section with a smoothing nacre of more or less reasonable applications, or the legislatures may act if things get out of hand. Commerce in any event is not going to grind to a halt because of the weaknesses in 2-302. But the lesson of its drafting ought nevertheless to be learned: it is easy to say nothing with words. Even if those words make one feel all warm inside, the result of sedulously preventing thought about them is likely to lead to more trouble than the draftsmen's cozy glow is worth, as a matter not only of statutory elegance but of effect in the world being regulated. Subsuming problems is not as good as solving them, and may in fact retard solutions instead. Or, once more to quote Karl Llewellyn (to whom, after all, the last word justly belongs), "Covert tools are never reliable tools."[301]

---

[300] In Henningsen v. Bloomfield Motors, Inc., 32 N.J. 358, 161 A.2d 69 (1960), continually cited in the Williams case (see 350 F.2d at 448 n.2, 449 nn.6 & 7, 450 n.12), it is most significant that the court did not have § 2-302 to work with. It was forced, therefore, to face the relevant policy questions, which it did in a many-paged opinion. In other words, in Henningsen the New Jersey court was forced to talk about the basis for its decision; in Williams and MacIver the courts were most particularly enabled not to.

[301] Llewellyn, The Common Law Tradition 365 (1960), quoting Llewellyn, Book Review, 52 Harv. L. Rev. 700, 703 (1939).

Richard A. Epstein, *Unconscionability: A Critical Reappraisal,* 18 J. L. & Econ. 293 (1973)

I. Introduction

The classical conception of contract at common law had as its first premise the belief that private agreements should be enforced in accordance with their terms. That premise of course was subject to important qualifications. Promises procured by fraud, duress, or undue influence were not generally enforced by the courts; and the same was true with certain exceptions of promises made by infants and incompetents. Again, agreements that had as their object illegal ends were usually not enforced, as, for example in cases of bribes of public officials or contracts to kill third persons. Yet even after these exceptions are taken into account, there was still one ground on which the initial premise could not be challenged: the terms of private agreements could not be set aside because the court found them to be harsh, unconscionable, or unjust. The reasonableness of the terms of a private agreement was the business of the parties to that agreement. True, there were numerous cases in which the language of the contract stood in need of judicial interpretation, but once that task was done there was no place for a court to impose upon the parties its own views about their rights and duties. "Public policy" was an "unruly horse," to be mounted only in exceptional cases and then only with care.

This general regime of freedom of contract can be defended from two points of view. One defense is utilitarian. So long as the tort law protects the interests of strangers to the agreement, its enforcement will tend to maximize the welfare of the parties to it, and therefore the good of the society as a whole.[2] The alternative defense is on libertarian grounds. One of the first functions of the law is to guarantee to individuals a sphere of influence in which they will be able to operate, without having to justify themselves to the state or to third parties: if one individual is entitled to do within the confines of the tort law what he pleases with what he owns, then two individuals who operate with those same constraints should have the same right with respect to their mutual affairs against the rest of the world.

Whatever its merits, however, it is fair to say that this traditional view of the law of contract has been in general retreat in recent years. That decline is reflected in part in the cool reception given to doctrines of laissez-faire, its economic counterpart, since the late nineteenth century, or at least since the New Deal. The total "hands off" policy with respect to economic matters is regarded as incorrect in most political discussions almost as a matter of course, and the same view is taken, moreover, toward a more subtle form of laissez-faire that views all government interference in economic matters as an evil until shown to be good. Instead, the opposite point of view is increasingly urged: market solutions—those which presuppose a regime of freedom of contract—are sure to be inadequate, and the only question worth debating concerns the appropriate form of public intervention. That attitude has, moreover, worked its way (as these things usually happen) into the fabric of the legal system, for today, more than ever, courts are willing to set aside the provisions of private agreements.

One of the major conceptual tools used by courts in their assault upon private agreements has been the doctrine of unconscionability. That doctrine has a place in contract law, but it is not the one usually assigned it by its advocates. The doctrine should not, in my view, allow courts to act as roving commissions to set aside those agreements whose substantive terms they find objectionable. Instead, it should be used only to allow courts to police the process whereby private agreements are formed, and in that connection, only to facilitate the setting aside of agreements that are as a matter of probabilities likely to be vitiated by the classical defenses of duress, fraud, or incompetence.[7] In order to show how

---

[2] The crucial question for the tort law concerns the scope and identification of the "interests" to be protected. On the one hand, they could be defined as to include the expectation of profit from trade, in which case all economic harm would fall within the scope of the tort law. On the other hand, they could cover the exclusive use and possession of one's person and property, in which case most forms of economic harm would fall outside the protection of the tort law. For a defense and elaboration of the second point of view, see Richard A. Epstein, Intentional Harms, 4 J. Leg. Studies 391 (1975).

[7] The concern is, in other words, with what has been aptly called "procedural unconscionability." Leff, Unconscionability and the Code—The Emperor's New Clause, 115 U. Pa.L.Rev. 337, 487 (1969).

the doctrine of unconscionability can function usefully in this manner, we shall examine first the traditional limitations upon the freedom of contract. That done, we shall show how a doctrine of unconscionability, when properly used, enables us to further at an acceptable cost the ends served by these classical limitations.

With a place for unconscionability thus established, we shall explore the results achieved when the doctrine of unconscionability is used to oust on substantive grounds the terms of private agreements that have been formed by unexceptionable means. While this examination cannot demonstrate conclusively that the substantive doctrine necessarily will have harmful effects, it can, I think, show that use of the doctrine tends on balance to work more harm than good, and should therefore be abandoned.

II. Traditional Common Law Defenses

[In Part II Professor Epstein considers the traditional defenses of duress, fraudulent misrepresentation and incapacity based on "infancy, insanity, and drunkenness." He approves of these within limits: duress should be limited to physical threats and threats to breach an existing obligaton, but should not be used to redress uneven bargaining power; fraudulent misrepresentation should cover lies, half-truths and deliberate cover-ups of defects but should not encompass a duty to disclose facts unknown to another bargaining party; incapacity ("incompetence") is justified, but merchants who rely on minors' lies about their age should be allowed recovery in restitution or fraud. —ed.]

III. Unconscionability Applied

[In Part III Epstein approves of the use of "procedural" unconscionability to encompass the traditional defenses so as to make it easier to raise the defenses. He approves of protecting heirs against improvident alienation of their expectations, and continues. —ed.]

One of the strengths of the unconscionability doctrine is its flexibility, an attribute much needed because it is difficult to identify in advance all of the kinds of situations to which it might in principle apply. One recent case, for example, that appears to warrant the application of unconscionability rules, involves recently returned prisoners of the Vietnam war. After receipt of accumulated back pay, these men were approached by experienced salesmen who proceeded to sell them unattractive municipal bonds. These transactions should as a class be set aside at the option of the buyers. We have here a narrow class of purchasers, vulnerable by reason of their long cap-

tivity, given sudden control over substantial funds. Opposite them are salesmen who know how to exploit them. Proof of fraud is apt to be difficult in this case, even if the fraud itself is likely. Setting aside the transaction gives the shrewd buyer a chance to repudiate an arm's length deal he does not like, but it is highly unlikely that many buyers took conscious advantage of this legal benefit. It is also possible that some proper transactions will be set aside, but again those costs are apt to be small, measured against the gains derived. But the limits of the principle must be noted. The case should go the other way if, for example, these men on their own initiative went to a brokerage house to purchase these same bonds.

The limitations on the use of consciability doctrines are as important as their application. Should, for example, the doctrine be used to protect those who are poor, unemployed, on welfare, or members of disadvantaged racial or ethnic groups? The perils of this course are great. First, it is difficult, if not impossible, to assert that the persons who fall into any or all of these classes are not in general competent to fend for themselves in most market situations. They are not infants, impressionable heirs, or gullible prisoners of war. Second, the subject matter of the transactions is for the most part standard consumer goods that are sold in generally competitive markets, and not interests in trust funds or real estate difficult to value even under the best of circumstances. The costs of setting these transactions aside, moreover, are apt to be quite great, for it will be more expensive for members of the "protected" class to contract on their own behalf within a complex web of legal rules. In addition, there will no doubt be both opportunity and incentive for many to take advantage of the rights conferred upon them by law to manipulate the system to their own advantage. The absence of protective rules will have costs, measured by the tainted transactions given full legal effect, but these costs, all things considered, are apt to be lower than those incurred by demanding proof of fraud to set the transactions aside.

In consumer transactions, therefore, it will be necessary to take great care in specifying the circumstances where protective rules should be adopted in order to prevent fraud or duress. One possible case that might warrant the use of such protective rules involves door-to-door salesmen, who often rely on both high pressure tactics and outright fraud to complete a sale. Yet I suspect that the unconscionability doctrine functions at best as a very blunt instrument in cases of this sort, and that it is better to adopt some legislative solution to control the problem. Here for example it is possible to specify a short "cooling off" period in which the buyer is allowed as a matter of positive law to disaffirm the contract of sale at his own option without a showing of fraud or duress. In this context, moreover, it might even be desirable, given the costs of such a rule upon honest merchants, for the legislature to adopt one rule for encyclopedias and quite another for beauty products, particularly if different levels of abuse are involved in the two cases. We are not faced with an elegant question of legal theory or with a moral question of great urgency. The only issue is what combination of common law doctrine and legislative enactment will work to miminize the abuses in consumer transactions.

IV. Substantive Unconscionability

In this last section we shall deal with the doctrine of unconscionability in a way that first puts to one side all the considerations about fraud, duress, and incompetence. Instead, our attention shifts to the cases in which courts will strike down either whole contracts or, more frequently, particular clauses on the ground that they are, as a *substantive* matter only, unfair and unconscionable. It is difficult in the abstract to insist that no contract language invites invalidation for these reasons. But the crucial point is that most clauses that do *in fact* appear in agreements cannot be fairly challenged on those grounds. It is difficult to know what principles identify the "just term," and for the same reasons that make it so difficult to determine the "just price." And the problem with substantive unconscionability is further increased because the clauses so attacked are, at the time of formation, arguably in the interests of both parties to the agreement. I cannot within the compass of this paper examine most, let alone all, of the clauses that have been attacked on substantive grounds over the years. But the examination of a few typical clauses, drawn from both consumer and commercial transactions, can illustrate the pattern of argument appropriate to cases of this sort.

a. *"Add-On" Clauses*

One sort of clause that has come under both judicial and statutory scrutiny is the so-called "add-on" clause used in consumer credit sales. These clauses govern the security interest taken back by the seller, and, in one common form, provide that all previous

goods purchased by the buyer from the seller will secure the debts incurred with the current purchase. The security agreement also provides that each payment made with respect to any of the items purchased would be applied against all outstanding balances, allowing the seller in effect to retain his security interest in all the goods sold until the debts with respect to all items are discharged. A single default on a single payment could trigger the plaintiff's right to repossess all the goods subject to the comprehensive security arrangement.[36]

Although agreements of this kind can, and have, been attacked on unconscionability grounds, they make good sense in the cases to which they apply. One of the major risks to the seller of personal property is that the goods sold will lose value, be it through use or abuse, more rapidly than the purchase price is paid off. The buyer can, and quite often does, have a "negative" equity in the goods. The seller, therefore, who takes back a security interest only in the goods sold, runs the real risk that repossession of the single item sold will still leave him with a loss on the transaction as a whole, taking into account the costs of interest and collection. One way to handle this problem is to require the purchaser of the goods to make a larger cash down payment, but that, of course, is something which many buyers, particularly those of limited means, do not want to do. Another alternative is for the buyer to provide the seller with additional collateral; yet here the best collateral is doubtless in goods sold by the seller to the buyer. Other goods already in the possession of the buyer may be of uncertain value, and they may well be subject to prior liens. Again, they may be of a sort that the seller cannot conveniently resell in the ordinary course of his business. Even if the goods are suitable collateral for the loan, it could take a good deal of time and effort for the seller to determine that fact. The "add-on" clause allows both parties to benefit from the reduction in costs in the setting up of a security arrangement.

The case for the add-on clauses is strengthened, moreover, when we note its legal effects. As between the buyer and seller the clause allows the seller to collect on his unpaid debt without having to avail himself of the awkward procedures established for unsecured creditors. The clause assures the seller that the value he has furnished the buyer will, if need be, first

[36] One such clause [was] central to the important case of Williams v. Walker-Thomas Furniture Co., 350 F.2d 445 (D.C. Cir. 1965).

be used to satisfy his own claims and not those of third parties. The only disadvantage to the buyer therefore is that he will not be able to use the goods purchased to obtain some economic benefit in a subsequent transaction. But it is difficult in a commercial context to see why a seller should not be paid before his buyer or third parties are able to use the goods he furnished for their own satisfaction.

The sense of these clauses, regardless of the particular form which they take, is demonstrated anew, moreover, once we realize that they operate within one very strong constraint, often imposed by statute, which restricts the creditor in a secured transaction to the recovery of principal, interest and costs in cases of default by the buyer. Within the framework of these limitations, the add-on clause can do no harm at all, for it only makes it more certain that the seller will be able to collect that to which on any view he is entitled.

b. "Waiver-of Defense" Clauses

Unconscionability arguments have been used to attack other clauses that govern the financing of consumer sales. Thus in many cases where the goods are purchased on an installment contract, the seller's rights under the contract are then sold, usually at a discount, to a finance company, which is then entitled to collect the payments as they come due from the buyer. In order to insulate itself from the disputes between the buyer and the seller of the goods, the company often insists that the original contract of sale include a term for its benefit which requires the buyer to continue to pay his installments to it even if the seller has not made good, for example, his warranty obligations.

In spite of the enthusiasm for consumer protection, it is unwise to strike these clauses down as unconscionable. Suppose the seller sold goods under warranty for cash. The buyer then could only get the seller to honor the warranty by request or, that failing, by legal action; the withholding of payment is no longer a possible alternative. I take it, however, that no one would argue that this arrangement is unconscionable, even though it leaves the buyer at risk on the warranty. Why then should the position be different if he is at risk because he has waived his defenses against the finance company?

The same point can be made if we consider another alternative method of financing the purchase of consumer goods. Suppose the seller says to the buyer of his goods, "If you wish to buy them on time, you must take out a bank loan for credit." Under that arrangement, the buyer remains unconditionally liable on his note to the bank even if his seller is in breach of his warranty obligation. If that arrangement is not unconscionable, why should it be unconscionable for the buyer to have no remedy against the lender because he happens to be chosen by the seller instead of the buyer?

There are also strong economic reasons that indicate that it is no one's interest, ex ante, to prohibit finance companies from disassociating themselves from the disputes between buyer and seller. The main advantage of seller financing over buyer financing is that it allows the parties to reduce the transaction costs of putting the credit arrangement together when security interests are necessary. Yet if that arrangement is incumbered by involving the finance company in disputes in which it wants no part, then there will be a shift to less desirable modes of financing. If it is argued that the finance companies should be held liable because they are better able to supervise the general activities of sellers, the quick answer is that if that is the case, then they will agree to do so as a matter of course for a fee. The fact that they do not is a strong suggestion that they have neither time nor skill to get involved in the narrow disputes which are apt to arise in consumer cases. What knowledge does the finance company have on the question of whether the buyer tampered with goods or used them in accordance with instructions? If buyers want protection against having to pay the price where there is a defect in the goods in question, then they should deal with sellers who carry their own contracts.[39] Whether that arrangement is preferable as an economic matter to one that contemplates third party financing is not the question that should be asked by the legal system. So long as both have their uses, as is likely the case, there is no principled justification for the judicial or legislative prohibition of either of them.

c. Exclusion of Liability for Consequential Damage

A close examination of still other clauses that have been incorporated into standard form contracts reveals that they too should be able to escape from the

[39] Here one can even take the argument one step farther. If all parties who carry their own contracts refuse to allow breach of warranty to be a complete defense against the payment of installment obligations, there will be a good reason for them so doing: to wit, that most of the claims are manufactured as excuses for non-payment.

taint of unconscionability. In *Collins v. Uniroyal Inc.*,[40] a case of quite recent vintage, the defendant tire company sold a tire under a contract of sale which contained the following guarantee.

> Road Hazard—In addition, every such U.S. Royal Master tire, when used in normal passenger car service, is guaranteed during the life of the original tread against blowouts, cuts, bruises, and similar injury rendering the tire unserviceable. Tires which are punctured or abused, by being run flat, improperly aligned, balanced, or inflated, cut by chains or obstructions on vehicle, damaged by fire, collision or vandalism, or by other means, and "seconds" are not subject to the road hazard provision of this Guarantee.

> This Guarantee does not cover consequential damage, and the liability of the manufacturer is limited to repairing or replacing the tire in accordance with the stipulation contained in this Guarantee. No other guarantee or warranty, express or implied, is made.

The purchaser of the tire was killed when the car he was driving went out of control after the tire blew out. The weight of the evidence established that no defect whatsoever in the tire caused the accident, ruling out recovery on any tort theory of products liability. The New Jersey Supreme Court held, however, that the limitation in the warranty against the recovery of consequential damages was unconscionable under the Uniform Commercial Code, and that the defendant accordingly was liable on a contract theory for the death of the decedent.[43]

The Court's argument in support of that conclusion is, I believe, erroneous. Under the New Jersey law, the defendant was required by statute to sell the tire with only a warranty of merchantability, under which its liability is triggered only if the tire is defective. The defendant here gave the buyer an extra measure of protection under its supplemental warranty, without which the plaintiff concededly could have recovered nothing. What is achieved by holding the defendant liable because it gave the plaintiff protection not required by statute when the effect of the decision may well be to reduce the protection that

sellers will give their purchasers? Is it in the general interest of consumers that Uniroyal not include warranties of the sort provided in this case?

Thus far we have assumed that there is justification for a rule that treats all limitations against recovery for consequential damages for personal injury as prima facie unconscionable. Yet even that restriction itself is not beyond criticism. In typical actions for breach of the warranty of merchantability, the plaintiff must show something beyond his own injury in the use of the goods in order to recover consequential damages. Indeed the very restrictions about proper use and maintenance incorporated into the warranty in *Collins* apply with equal force to the straightforward warranty of merchantability. It might well be wise for a seller to tell his buyers that it is too difficult for him to determine whether a particular injury is attributable to his own manufacture, to the plaintiff's conduct, or to some external cause. The best solution might be to offer the tire at a lower price, leaving the buyer, if he chooses, to purchase insurance elsewhere against this particular risk. In this manner, market mechanisms could work to bring about the best distribution of risks between the parties, superior to that ordained by statute.

. . .

e. *"Termination-at-will" Clauses*

Unconscionability arguments are not restricted to consumer contexts. To take but one instance of its application in commercial cases, consider a provision common to many franchise agreements that allows the franchisor to terminate the franchise at will, without, in other words, having to give any justification for his actions. The attack against such clauses is based upon the belief that they allow the franchisor to act as a tyrant, who can cut off his franchisee at whim, even before he has recouped his start-up costs in the venture.

While these clauses are indeed open to this kind of abuse, there are reasons that make their adoption work in general in the interests of both parties to the agreement. The franchisor is concerned with, first, the profitability of the particular outlet and, second, with the impact that its operation will have upon his entire enterprise. If the franchise could be termi-

---

[40] 64 N.J. 260, 315 A.2d 16 (1974).

[43] "Consequential damages may be limited or excluded unless the limitation or exclusion is unconscionable. Limitation of consequential damages for injury to the person in the case of consumer goods is prima facie unconscionable but limitation of damages where the loss is commercial is not."

U.C.C. § 2-719(3). Note that there is no explanation given of the force of the words "prima facie" or what facts might be sufficient to override them. Note too the language of § 2-719 leaves the court that applies it with ample discretion in the particular case.

nated only "with cause," his settlement costs on termination are apt to be high no matter what the circumstances, for the franchisee always could litigate the matter. If those costs deter the franchisor from termination, he loses the benefits of a substitute franchisee, while being forced to suffer from the continued erosion of his good will. All these costs are reduced, if not eliminated, if termination can be at will.

From the point of view of the franchisee, the clause need not work harm, and may do good. If the franchisee makes a good profit, it will not, in general, be in the economic interest of the franchisor to invoke the clause, as termination of the franchise will make him worse off. Indeed, the good franchisee may well want a termination-at-will clause to be included in all franchise agreements, because he may rightly perceive that the franchisor acts in his interest when he terminates a weak franchisee whose conduct erodes the goodwill of the entire enterprise, including his own. The real conflict, in other words, is not between franchisor and franchisee, but between franchisee and franchisee, as the franchisor acts in effect as the *de facto* agent of the superior franchisees. Where termination appears warranted, moreover, a franchisor has incentives to act in a manner which, no matter how informal, appears to be fair if he wishes to retain his other franchisees and attract new franchisees. When we look, therefore, at both the economic pressures and the contract terms, the termination-at-will clause may well be the best solution for both parties. The issue is not whether the clause will be required, but only whether it should be allowed. On that question, there is no need for judicial or legislative intervention so long as there are common circumstances in which the use of this clause is appropriate. Those who might wish to ban the use of the clause labor under a much greater burden than those who only want to permit its use, and that burden is not met by the invocation of unconscionability arguments.

Conclusion

In this paper I have sought to defend against modern attacks the principle of freedom of contract which was central to the classical common law. Properly understood, that position does not require a court to enforce every contract brought before it. It does, however, demand that the reasons invoked for not enforcing the contract be of one of two sorts. Either there must be proof of some defect in the process of contract formation (be it duress, fraud or undue influence); or there must be, but only within narrow limits, some incompetence of the party against whom the agreement is to be enforced. The doctrine of unconscionability is important in both these respects because it can, if wisely applied, allow the courts to police these two types of problems, and thereby improve the general administration of the contract law. Yet when the doctrine of unconscionability is used in its substantive dimension, be it in a commercial or consumer context, it serves only to undercut the private right of contract in a manner that is apt to do more social harm than good. The result of the analysis is the same even if we view the question of unconscionability from the lofty perspective of public policy. "[I]f there is one thing which more than another public policy requires, it is that men of full age and competent understanding shall have the utmost liberty of contracting, and that their contracts when entered into freely and voluntarily shall be held sacred and shall be enforced by Courts of justice."[52]

---

[52] Printing and Numerical Registering Co. v. Sampson L. R. 19 Eq. 462, 465 (1875).

Defenses of the Unconscionability Concept

Not long after Leff's *Emperor's New Clause* article appeared, M. P. Ellinghaus of the University of Melbourne published *In Defense of Unconscionability*, 78 Yale L.J. 757 (1969), challenging Leff's basic thesis. Ellinghaus began his conclusion by saying:

I have tried to show that Section 2-302 is more than mere incantation; that it has a number of "reality referents," and that it is not too difficult, given an appropriate initial disposition and a little concentration, to flush those referents out of their thickets. To go to great lengths to prove the opposite amounts in the end merely to a demonstration of the self-evident: that "unconscionability" is a residual category of shifting content and expansible nature. The thesis of this essay has been, of course, that we cannot do without such regrettably vague standards.

78 Yale L.J. at 814-15. In this respect, Ellinghaus takes a position similar to that taken by Robert Summers in the "good faith" debate excerpted earlier in this section, although Ellinghaus relies primarily on the writing of his fellow Australian, Julius Stone. The Ellinghaus article discussed Leff in great detail, both on the history and interpretation of section 2-302 and on the reading of the cases on unconscionability, and predicted that the unconscionability principle would be expanded beyond the compass of Article Two and transactions in goods. That prediction seems to have been borne out. The Ellinghaus article is worth reading.

We have here, however, a short excerpt from a more recent article, *The Bargain Principle and Its Limits*, 95 Harv. L. Rev. 741 (1982), by Melvin Aron Eisenberg, Professor of Law at Berkeley, and a very important authority on both contracts and corporation law. This article was one of series that Eisenberg wrote on contract theory and practice, and only part of the article is actually devoted to unconscionability. Professor Eisenberg, a hard-headed, untrendy "neo-classicist" who fully understands economic reasoning, rejects the Leff dichotomy of procedural and substantive unconsconability as too rigid. Instead, Professor Eisenberg uses the approach of Thomas Kuhn, author of *The Structure of Scientific Revolutions*, to suggest that unconscionability is less an anomaly of the bargain principle than a new "paradigm" that, standing alongside the bargain principle, must govern our general thinking about contracts. His movement from the reconciliation of "anomalies" to the claim of a new "paradigm" follows Kuhn's description of the way scientific discovery works. Kuhn argues that scientists often see anomalies in the existing paradigms such as Newtonian physics, but that it often takes a younger generation or someone not raised on the existing paradigm to rethink the anomalies into a new paradigm such as Einstein's theory of relativity. Often the pathfinders themselves refuse to accept the new paradigms that still later scientists trace to the earlier work.

The anomalies of bargain and freedom of contract were seen by many of the legal realists, but the seminal (an overused word, but justified here) discussion was in Friedrich Kessler's *Contracts of Adhesion—Some Thoughts About Freedom of Contract*, 43 Colum. L. Rev. 629 (1943). Kessler, raised and educated in Europe, tried to cleanse the freedom of contract paradigm of the anomalies caused by adhesion contracts, and has remained faithful to what he sees as true freedom of contract throughout his long career. See the Kessler-Gilmore "dialogue" that begins Part IA. Nonetheless, Kessler may really have been the pathfinder who alerted us to a new paradigm that he, himself has rejected.

On the specifics of adhesion contracts, Todd Rakoff has argued that contract law must be entirely rethought—"reconstructed"—to take into account the problems—and benefits—of form contracts. Rakoff, *Contracts of Adhesion: An Essay in Reconstruction*, 96 Harv. L. Rev. 1174 (1983). Eric Mills Holmes and Dagmar Thurmann have built on both Rakoff and German law in proposing a complex theory to replace current American law, which they describe as "a tortuous and tortured legal jujitsu of sundry attempts to find a doctrine and a structure." Holmes and Thurmann, *A New and Old Theory For Adjudicating Standardized Contracts*, 17 Ga. J. Int'l & Comp. L. 323 (1987). Others have argued that Eisenberg, Kessler and other neo-classicists do not go far enough. See the contort, relational and communitarian discussions in Parts IA and IB. The broader issues of paternalism are discussed in the note following the Eisenberg article.

Melvin Aron Eisenberg, *The Bargain Principle and Its Limits,* 95 Harv. L. Rev. 741 (1982)

The institution of contract is central to our social and legal systems, both as reality and as metaphor. At the present time, however, the institution is in conceptual disarray. In the late nineteenth and early twentieth centuries, scholars and courts constructed a philosophical system of contract law characterized in substantial part by logical deduction from received axioms. This system fell into inevitable decline because it failed to recognize that deduction is a means, not an end, and that the purpose of contract law is not simply to create conditions of liability, but also to respond to the social process of promising. As part of this decline, in the last thirty to forty years there has been a wholesome reaction against logical deduction as a dominant mode of contract reasoning. Unfortunately, that reaction has often been accompanied by a wholesale retreat from any conceptualization of contract law—a retreat represented in its extreme forms by suggestions that contract is being absorbed into tort[2] or that there is no institution of contract as such, but only particular transaction-types.[3] These approaches neglect the possibility of reconceptualizing contract law through the development of principles that are intellectually coherent, yet sufficiently open-textured to account for human reality and to unfold over time. This Article is the second of a series attempting such a reconceptualization.[4]

The subject of this Article is the bargain principle and its limits. By bargain, I mean an exchange in which each party views the performance that he undertakes as the price of the performance undertaken by the other. Although parties may barter bargained-for performances without making any promises, contract law is concerned with those bargains that involve a present promise to render a future performance—that is, that involve an exchange over time. By the bargain principle, I mean the common law rule that, in the absence of a traditional defense relating to the quality of consent (such as duress, incapacity, misrepresentation, or mutual mistake), the

courts will enforce a bargain according to its terms, with the object of putting a bargain-promisee in as good a position as if the bargain had been performed.

. . .

. . .

II. The Principle Of Unconscionability

Each of the arguments supporting the bargain principle has considerable force, even outside the context of the exemplary case. Each, however, overstates its claim when it is extended beyond that case. The argument that objective value is neither a meaningful nor an appropriate concept can be countered by observing that the law often measures objective value in bargains that are not made in a perfectly competitive market. For example, off-market contracts between a beneficiary and his trustee or between a fiduciary and his corporation are customarily subject to review for objective fairness. . . . The argument that revising a bargained-for price may unfairly convert a party who has rendered a bargained-for performance into an involuntary actor can be countered by a similar objection. If the price was not set by a mechanism that is regarded as fair, such as a competitive market, it may not be unfair or undesirable to revise it judicially. Many rules of law induce some form of involuntary behavior.

The argument based on the need to facilitate credit transactions and private planning depends for its weight on the strength of the policy behind facilitation, which in turn depends in part on the quality of the market in which the contract is made. In any event, not all types of credit transactions are necessarily to be encouraged, not all bargains involve planning, and in some transactions occurring off competitive markets a party might not be deterred from contracting by the prospect of a reduction in price.

The argument based on the efficiency of contract price is fully effective only to the extent that the relevant market does not materially differ from a per-

---

[2] See G. Gilmore, The Death Of Contract 87-94 (1974).

[3] See Mueller, Contract Remedies: Business Fact and Legal Fantasy, 1967 Wis. L. Rev. 833, 833-34; cf. G. Gilmore, supra note 2 (arguing general collapse of traditional con-

tract doctrine); Friedman & Macaulay, Contract Law and Contract Teaching: Past, Present and Future, 1967 Wis. L. Rev. 805, 812 (fundamental concepts of contract law "too general and abstract to regulate current, socially significant business problems").

[4] See Eisenberg, Donative Promises, 47 U. Chi. L. Rev. I (1979).

fectly competitive market. In fact, however, many contracts are made in markets that are highly imperfect.

In short, while the arguments supporting the bargain principle are weighty and suggest that limits on the principle should be imposed cautiously, they are not conclusive. Always, therefore, there has been a strong countercurrent against the bargain principle. Equity courts have long reviewed contracts for fairness when equitable relief has been sought. Within recent years the principle has emerged—first in section 2-302 of the Uniform Commercial Code, then in the cases, and later in section 208 of the *Restatement (Second) of Contracts*, other uniform acts, and the *Restatement (Second) of Property*—that law courts too may limit or deny enforcement of a bargain promise when the bargain is "unconscionable."

To understand the significance of this principle, it is useful to invoke the concept of a paradigm, in the sense developed by Thomas Kuhn in *The Structure of Scientific Revolutions*. As used by Kuhn, a paradigm is a model, principle, or theory that explains most or all phenomena within its scope, but is sufficiently open-ended to leave room for the resolution of further problems and ambiguities.[28] At the time of its formation, a paradigm looks both backward and forward. Looking backward, the paradigm permits and indeed requires the reconstruction of prior explanations. Looking forward, the paradigm will be applied and extended, by further articulation and specification, to resolve additional problems and ambiguities and to uncover new or previously disregarded phenomena. But as the paradigm is applied and extended in this manner, it typically happens that anomalies— phenomena the paradigm does not account for—are uncovered. These anomalies may eventually lead to the formation of an entirely new paradigm.

The history of contract law, read retrospectively, suggests that the bargain principle, while long implicit, at some point emerged as a controlling paradigm in the area of consideration. Since that time, the law of consideration has been concerned to a great extent with the articulation and specification of that paradigm. For example, courts and scholars have analyzed over the years such problems as why executory bargains should be enforceable and how to treat bargains involving a performance that was already legally required, transactions that are bargains in

form but not in substance, bargains in which one of the promises is illusory, and unbargained-for reliance.

When the concept of unconscionability was first made explicit by the Uniform Commercial Code, the initial effort was to reconcile it with the bargain principle. A major step in this direction was a distinction, drawn in 1967 by Arthur Leff, between "procedural" and "substantive" unconscionability. Leff defined procedural unconscionability as fault or unfairness in the bargaining *process*; substantive unconscionability as fault or unfairness in the bargaining *outcome*— that is, unfairness of terms. The effect (if not the purpose) of this distinction, which influenced much of the later analysis,[38] was to domesticate unconscionability by accepting the concept insofar as it could be made harmonious with the bargain principle (that is, insofar as it was "procedural"), while rejecting its wider implication that in appropriate cases the courts might review bargains for fairness of terms. Correspondingly, much of the scholarly literature and case law concerning unconscionability has emphasized the element of unfair surprise, in which a major underpinning of the bargain principle—knowing assent—is absent by hypothesis.

Over the last fifteen years, however, there have been strong indications that the principle of unconscionability authorizes a review of elements well beyond unfair surprise, including, in appropriate cases, fairness of terms. For example, comment c to section 208 of the *Restatement (Second) of Contracts* states that "[t]heoretically it is possible for a contract to be oppressive taken as a whole, even though there is no weakness in the bargaining process." Similarly, section 5.108(4)(c) of the Uniform Consumer Credit Code lists as a factor to be considered in determining whether a transaction is unconscionable "gross disparity between the price of the property or services . . . [and their value] measured by the price at which similar property or services are readily obtainable in credit transactions by like consumers." And a number of cases have held or indicated that the principle of unconscionability permits enforcement of a promise to be limited on the basis of unfair price alone.

As these phenomena have accumulated, it has become clear that they constitute anomalies under the bargain principle, and can be explained only on the basis of an expanded, paradigmatic concept of unconscionability that is not limited to procedural elements

---

[28] T. Kuhn, The Structure Of Scientific Revolutions 10, 23, 181-87 (2d ed. 1970).

[38] See e.g. Epstein, Unconscionability: A Critical Reappraisal, 18 J.L. & Econ. 293 (1975).

such as unfair surprise. This new paradigm does not replace the bargain principle, which is based on sound sense and continues to govern the normal case. Rather, the new paradigm creates a theoretical framework that explains most of the limits that have been or should be placed upon that principle, based on the quality of the bargain. What lies ahead is to articulate and extend the unconscionability paradigm through the development of specific norms, other than unfair surprise, that can guide the resolution of specific cases. The balance of Part II is devoted to the development of four such norms, relating to exploitation of distress, transactional incapacity, susceptibility to unfair persuasion, and price-ignorance.

It is not the purpose of Part II to exhaust the concept of unconscionability. Quite the contrary: a basic thesis of this Article is that unconscionability is a paradigmatic concept that can never be exhaustively described. It is, however, a major purpose of Part II to suggest a methodology by which specific unconscionability norms should be developed. Accordingly, the norms described in this Part are important not only in themselves, but also as demonstrations of that methodology. Three general propositions underlie the methodology, and should be stated at the outset: (1) Since the bargain principle rests on arguments of fairness and efficiency, it is appropriate to develop and apply a specific unconscionability norm whenever a class of cases can be identified in which neither fairness nor efficiency support the bargain principle's application. (2) The development and application of specific unconscionability norms is closely related to the manner in which the relevant market deviates from a perfectly competitive market. (3) The distinction between procedural and substantive unconscionability is too rigid to provide significant help in either the development or the application of such norms.

. . .

[A discussion of parties who contract while in distress, such as an injured and stranded traveler, is omitted. We pick up with the conclusion of a discussion of "transactional capacity." —ed.] The doctrine of transactional capacity is not limited to cases where a promisor lacks capacity to understand the value of the performances to be exchanged; it also applies to cases in which the promisor can understand the value of the performance called for but lacks capacity to understand the meaning of contractual provisions

governing the parties' rights in the event of nonperformance. This application is most likely to occur in transactions involving form contracts prepared by relatively sophisticated sellers who deal regularly with relatively unsophisticated buyers. Such transactions raise a special problem. A wide range of buyers are likely to use any given form. Some will be capable of understanding virtually any provision, while others will not. Of those who do not, some might have refused to enter into the contract if they had understood the provision, while others would have gone ahead. Because the agent of the seller who deals with a given buyer may not know the category into which the buyer falls, how should the doctrine of transactional incapacity be applied in form contract cases?

The answer is, if a provision changes the rights that a buyer would otherwise have on nonperformance in a manner the seller knows or should know many buyers would probably not knowingly agree to, it is unconscionable to word the provision in language the seller knows or should know many buyers will lack capacity to understand. For example, in the well-known case of *Williams v. Walker-Thomas Furniture Co.*,[80] the buyer regularly purchased furniture and home appliances from the seller on installment credit. The purchase agreements were printed contracts in the form of chattel leases, which contained the following provision:

> [T]he amount of each periodical installment payment to be made by [purchaser] to the Company under this present lease shall be inclusive of and not in addition to the amount of each installment payment to be made by [purchaser] under such prior leases, bills, or accounts; and all payments now and hereafter made by [purchaser] shall be credited pro rata on all outstanding leases, bills and accounts due the Company by [purchaser] at the time each such payment is made.

The effect of this provision was that until the buyer was completely out of debt to the seller, no item she had ever purchased from it would be completely paid off, even though the balances due on some of the items might be worked down (as they were in *Williams*) to a few cents. As a result, no such item would be immune from procedures for summary recovery under replevin statutes, or would fall within the protection of statutes exempting defined classes of property from attachment to satisfy judgments.

---

[80] 350 F.2d 445 (D.C. Cir. 1965).

The seller certainly knew or should have known that many (indeed almost all) buyers would lack capacity to understand the effect of this provision, and probably knew or should have known that if buyers had understood that effect, many would have refused to sign. Under traditional legal rules, the provision would probably have nevertheless bound the buyer on the theory that she had a duty to read the contract and be aware of its contents. Indeed, this was just what happened in *Williams* in the lower court. If such a provision was inconspicuous, most modern courts would probably not enforce it, under the unconscionability norm of unfair surprise. Thus, in its opinion remanding the case, the United States Court of Appeals for the District of Columbia Circuit emphasized the importance of determining whether the term was "hidden in a maze of fine print." But such a provision should be deemed unconscionable, under the doctrine of transactional incapacity, even if it is conspicuous to the eye. Thus, in *Gerhardt v. Continental Insurance Cos.*[86] the court struck down an obscurely worded exception to a comprehensive insurance policy on the ground that it was "neither conspicuous *nor* plain and clear." In *Weaver v. American Oil Co.*,[88] involving a complex and legalistically phrased provision under which the operator of an Amoco gas station indemnified Amoco against Amoco's own negligence, the court said: "The party seeking to enforce such a contract has the burden of showing that the provisions were explained to the other party and *came to his knowledge and there was in fact a real and voluntary meeting of the minds and not merely an objective meeting.*"

What should be the remedy in such cases? Ordinarily, the balance of the contract should stand, but the rights of the parties should be those that would have prevailed in the absence of the relevant term— unless the seller shows either that he explained the term, that it was conspicuous and the buyer had the capacity to understand its effect, or, perhaps, that if the buyer had understood it he would nevertheless have signed. The remedy hardly seems severe, since its only effect is that the parties are governed by a presumably fair rule of law, and the seller can avoid even this effect by writing the term in plain English and presenting it in a manner that avoids unfair surprise.

C. *Unfair Persuasion*

In a perfectly competitive market, persuasion ordinarily plays little or no role in contract formation: buyers and sellers either take the uniform market price of a homogeneous commodity, or they do not. Away from such a market, however, persuasion may play an important role. This opens the possibility that a party who is normally capable of acting in a deliberative manner may be rendered temporarily unable to do so by unfair persuasion.

. . .

Although the principle of unconscionability allows the courts to adopt the doctrine of unfair persuasion on analytical grounds alone, some support for the doctrine can be found even in existing case law. A good example is *Odorizzi v. Bloomfield School District*,[94] decided by the California District Court of Appeal in 1966. According to the complaint, Odorizzi, an elementary school teacher, had been arrested on criminal charges of homosexual activity. After he had been questioned by the police, booked, released on bail, and gone forty hours without sleep, two school district officials came to his apartment. The officials advised Odorizzi that if he did not resign immediately he would be dismissed and his arrest would be publicized, jeopardizing his chances of securing employment elsewhere, but that if he resigned at once the incident would not be publicized. Odorizzi then resigned, and the criminal charges were later dismissed. The court held that on these facts Odorizzi was entitled to reinstatement. Undue influence, the court said, involves two aspects—undue susceptibility and undue pressure:

> Undue influence in its second aspect involves an application of excessive strength by a dominant subject against a servient object. Judicial consideration of this second element in undue influence has been relatively rare, for there are few cases denying persons who persuade but do not misrepresent the benefit of their bargain. Yet logically, the same legal consequences should apply to the results of excessive strength as to the results of undue weakness. Whether from weakness on one side, or strength on the other, or a combination of the two, undue influence occurs whenever there results "that kind of influence or supremacy of one mind over another by which that other is pre-

---

[86] 48 N.J. 291, 225 A.2d 328 (1966).
[88] 257 Ind. 458, 276 N.E.2d 144(1971).

[94] 246 Cal. App. 2d 123, 54 Cal. Rptr. 533 (1966).

vented from acting according to his own wish or judgment, and whereby the will of the person is overborne and he is induced to do or forbear to do an act which he would not do, or would do, if left to act freely."

Support for a doctrine of unfair persuasion can also be found in rules that permit a buyer who has made a contract in his own home to rescind during a specified "cooling-off" period, typically three days. Such rules have been adopted by a number of state legislatures, by the Commissioners on Uniform State Laws in the Uniform Consumer Credit Code, by the Federal Trade Commission, and by Congress with regard to home improvement contracts. The diverse agencies adopting these rules gave recognition to the problem of a transitory state of acquiescence produced by unfair means, and fixed a reasonable boundary line for determining the time within which such a state may be expected to lapse. The principle underlying these rules supports a comparable rule applicable to transactions outside the home.

. . .

Assume, however, that in some cases it will be difficult to distinguish between normal sales talk and unfair persuasion, so that the doctrine of unfair persuasion would enable some consumers to back out of a transaction in which the persuasion was not actually unfair. Even under this assumption, the problem is not particularly worrisome. Observation suggests that reputable merchants commonly permit consumers to return unused merchandise for refund or credit. Accordingly, erroneous application of the doctrine of unfair persuasion in the consumer context would do no more than produce a result that is often obtainable from reputable merchants even without judicial intervention.

D. Price-Ignorance

One condition of a perfectly competitive market is a homogeneous marketplace in which cost-free information concerning price is readily available. When this condition is not satisfied and marketplaces are differentiated, the price of a homogeneous commodity in a given marketplace may be strikingly higher than the price at which the commodity is normally sold. For example, the *New York Times* recently reported as follows on a group of Manhattan stores,

most of them clustered on Fifth Avenue, which apparently specialize in one-shot sales, often to tourists:

[S]uch shops . . . [offer] $40 radios for $80, $30 calculators for $95 and ivory and jade collectibles, so-called, at similarly inflated prices, according to cases cited by the New York City Department of Consumer Affairs. . . .

Similarly, a number of cases have concerned door-to-door sales at a price more than twice as high as that charged for comparable commodities in conventional retail marketplaces. For example, in *Toker v. Westerman*,[102] People's Foods sold a stripped-down refrigerator-freezer for $899.98 plus a credit charge, when the evidence showed that the normal retail price of this model was $350-400 and that the most expensive model of comparable size, equipped with extra features, retailed for only $500. In *Kugler v. Romain*,[103] Romain was engaged in selling door-to-door a set of books bearing a cash price of $249.50, when the usual retail price for comparable books was approximately $108-110.

In analyzing whether the seller has acted wrongfully in such cases, we must first determine what accounts for the disparity between the contract price and the normal retail price. Let us begin with the Fifth Avenue stores described in the *Times* article. These sellers appear to offer little or no advantage over nearby stores that sell the same commodities at list price. Since no consumer would knowingly pay twice that price in the absence of such advantage, it seems clear that the price disparity in this case is based on the ignorance of some consumers concerning normal retail prices and on their assumption that further search is unnecessary because a merchant-seller's price for a homogeneous commodity is almost certainly representative of the prevailing price.

Accordingly, one method for dealing with such transactions would be to adopt a rule that a merchant who offers homogeneous commodities at fixed prices impliedly represents that the offered price is not strikingly disproportionate to its prevailing price at other readily accessible marketplaces—giving due weight to the merchant's tangible and intangible advantages over other merchants, its reputation, and the normal range of pricing variations. On every aspect of a sale transaction except price, the old doctrine of caveat emptor has given way to the doctrines

---

[102] 113 N.J. Super. 452, 274 A.2d 78 (Union County D. Ct. 1970).

[103] 58 N.J. 522, 279 A.2d 640 (1971).

that a seller will be held to his express representations and that the very act of sale gives rise to implied warranties. The theory of caveat emptor was that the obligation to ensure quality was on the buyer; to put it differently, that it was the buyer's task to search for defects in the product. The buyer therefore absorbed the loss if he did not search or searched inadequately. The theory of implied warranty, on the other hand, is that holding out a product for sale creates certain expectations in a buyer—for example, that the goods are fit for the ordinary purposes for which such goods are used—and that these expectations should be protected unless the seller has explicitly negated them.

Caveat emptor might be viewed as justified in its day if we assume that when this doctrine prevailed, buyers had little or no confidence in sellers and therefore had no expectation of quality beyond such expectations as arose from their own search. In a modern economy, however, buyers place confidence in merchant-sellers regarding a great variety of product attributes, and most merchants work hard to engender and maintain that confidence. So too with price . . . . In particular, it would conform to modern understanding to adopt a rule that a merchant who offers a homogeneous commodity at a fixed price impliedly represents that the price is not strikingly disproportionate to that at which the commodity is normally sold in readily accessible marketplaces, giving due weight to the merchant's relevant advantages, reputation, and normal price variations.

Under such a rule, however, whether the seller knew or had reason to know that the price quotation was strikingly disproportionate would be irrelevant. The rule would therefore not be based on a concept of fault, and accordingly would go beyond the concept of unconscionability. For now, it is not necessary to go that far. Instead, it suffices to adopt the fault-based doctrine that it is unconscionable for a merchant to exploit a consumer's price-ignorance by offering a homogeneous commodity at a price he knows or has reason to know is strikingly disproportionate in the stated manner. Application of the bargain principle to such cases is unsupported by either of that principle's two major props. Fairness does not support application of the principle, since the promisee has violated conventional morality by making a kind of misrepresentation and by exploiting the promisor's ignorance of a body of cheaply acquired and readily available knowledge (as opposed to knowledge that is generated by the promisee's own skill and diligence).

Efficiency considerations are at worst neutral: since the commodity is by hypothesis selling at a much lower price in comparable marketplaces, it hardly seems likely that the higher price is required to move the commodity to its highest-valued uses or to allocate properly the factors necessary for its production. Indeed, it is arguable that by reducing wasteful search, a prohibition on exploitation of price-ignorance would lead to greater efficiency than would enforcing the bargain to its full extent. A consumer who knows that the law prohibits a merchant from charging a price for a homogeneous commodity that the merchant knows or should know strikingly exceeds the prevailing price in comparable marketplaces can make a more or less informed decision on whether the likelihood of finding a moderately lower price justifies the cost of searching for such a price. In contrast, a consumer who knows that the law does not prohibit such behavior may feel constrained to search several marketplaces for every purchase, lest he be exploited in the first marketplace.

Thus far, no assumption has been made concerning the seller's profits. Is the argument affected if the seller's profits are not above normal? To explore this issue, let us return to door-to-door sales at prices very much higher than those charged for comparable goods at conventional retail outlets, which I shall refer to hereinafter as high-price door-to-door selling. Assume, for purposes of argument, that high-price door-to-door sellers do not earn above-normal profits. In that case, they are recovering their costs but not much more, and their high prices must therefore reflect high costs. This in turn raises two issues. First, can prices be deemed unconscionable if the seller is only covering its costs, including a fair return? Second, if a high-cost seller is making only normal profits, can it not be inferred that the costs are translated into consumer benefits? The two issues are intimately connected, since if the seller's costs are completely translated into consumer benefits, its price can hardly be deemed unconscionable.

To address these issues, consider two possible models of high-price door-to-door selling. Under one model, prices are high because these sellers offer nonprice benefits that consumers value to the extent of the difference between the contract price and the normal retail price. In particular, these sellers may bring to a buyer's attention information the buyer did not previously have—for example, that a certain type of product exists. Under this model the sellers' high prices are justified, since the consumer is paying for both a commodity and a special service. Indeed, it might be argued that any lower price would be economically inefficient. If sellers were forced to charge a lower price, some or all would have to withdraw from the business. To the extent such sellers are engaged in the provision of information, their withdrawal would result in the provision of less information. Potential buyers who would have valued the commodity at an amount as high as or higher than the price actually charged would therefore be deprived of the utility derived from making the purchase.

The second model is much less flattering. Under this model, high-price door-to-door firms are not selling information, but searching out and exploiting price-ignorant buyers.[111] Each completed sale has a very high cost because each salesperson must spend considerable time and effort searching for uninformed buyers. The cost of that time and effort is subsidized by completed sales.

It seems likely that the second model describes high-price door-to-door selling better than the first. It is hard to believe that a consumer operating from behind the veil would value the benefits of high-price door-to-door selling to the extent the first model presupposes. (That is, if consumers were given a choice between: (1) no visits by high-price door-to-door sellers, at the cost of occasionally missing out on information concerning new commodities; or (2) periodic visits, at the cost of unknowingly paying twice or more the normal retail price of a commodity on occasion, it is hard to believe that many would choose the second alternative.) If this is true, refusing to enforce contracts with high-price door-to-door sellers to their full extent would not necessarily reduce the satisfaction of buyers as a class, even if some sellers were forced out of business. Call a high-price door-to-door seller who is forced out of the market by a rule against exploitation of price ignorance SI. By hypothesis, products comparable to the commodity sold by SI are available in other marketplaces, and the buyer would purchase in those marketplaces if he had the relevant information. It seems likely that many of the persons who would buy the commodity from SI would sooner or later visit one of these marketplaces and discover the commodity and its normal retail price. In

effect, SI is engaged in intercepting such persons before they have undertaken a price search themselves. For those buyers, at least, the withdrawal of SI from the door-to-door market would result in *increased* utility whenever the difference between the price charged by SI and the normal retail price exceeded the utility lost by not having the use of the commodity between the date on which the buyer would have purchased it from SI and the date on which the buyer actually purchased it. To this differential must be added the amount of wasteful search, by those buyers who would like to deal with door-to-door sellers, that can be forgone under a doctrine prohibiting exploitation of price-ignorance by such sellers.

In short, if, as seems likely, the second model describes high-price door-to-door sales better than the first, the fact that such sellers earn only normal returns becomes irrelevant. In terms of fairness, conduct may be exploitive even if it does not produce above-normal returns. In terms of efficiency, profits are normal only because the seller incurs the socially wasteful cost of searching out and intercepting the price-ignorant. Even if the seller's prices do provide only a fair return on investment, the investment is not one that the law should promote by enforcing a recovery that reimburses those unproductive costs.

A doctrine prohibiting the exploitation of price-ignorance is sufficiently justified by the principle of unconscionability. In addition, it is but a modest extension of section 5.108(4)(c) of the Uniform Consumer Credit Code, which provides that in determining whether a consumer credit sale is unconscionable, consideration shall be given to "gross disparity between the price of the property or services sold . . . and the value of the property or services measured by the price at which similar property or services are readily obtainable in credit transactions by like consumers." The doctrine also finds support in the results of cases involving door-to-door selling. For example, in *Toker v. Westerman*,[115] the buyer had purchased a freezer for $899.98 plus a credit charge. The retail price of comparable units was $350-400. Buyer made payments of $655.85 and then stopped, and seller's assignee sued for the remaining balance. The court held that the seller and his assignee had already received a reasonable sum, and gave judgment

---

[111] The activity of shoppers in conventional retail marketplaces will usually (although not always) keep prices in such marketplaces competitive. See Schwartz & Wilde, Intervening in Markets on the Basis of Imperfect Information: A Legal and Economic Analysis, 127 U. Pa. L. Rev. 630 (1979).

Sellers therefore have an incentive to try to seek out buyers who do not frequent normal retail marketplaces, and going door-to-door is one way to do this.

[115] 113 N.J. Super. 452, 274 A.2d 78 (Union County D. Ct. 1970).

to the buyer. Similarly, in *Jones v. Star Credit Corp.*,[116] the buyer had purchased a food-freezer for $900 plus a credit charge of over $400. The retail price of a comparable unit was $300. Buyer paid $619.88 and then brought suit to reform the contract. The court ordered that the contract be reformed by changing the price to the amount the buyer had paid.

Finally, the doctrine is supported by—and helps rationalize—the language of door-to-door cases in which the courts stressed that the contract price far exceeded the retail price in conventional market-places, and concluded that "exorbitant price . . . makes this contract unconscionable and therefore unenforceable"; that it is "unconscionable . . . [to sell] goods for approximately 2 1/2 times their reasonable retail value"; or that "the value disparity itself leads inevitably to the felt conclusion that knowing advantage was taken of the plaintiffs."

. . .

IV. Conclusion

The first great problem of contract law—usually subsumed under the heading of consideration—is what *kinds* of promises the law should enforce. This problem, however, is tightly linked with another: the *extent* to which a certain kind of promise should be enforced. Indeed, on a deep level the two problems are virtually inseparable. The proposition that promises made as part of a bargain ought to be enforced is relatively straightforward; the real question is to what extent.

The traditional answer to this question is embodied in the paradigmatic bargain principle, namely, that damages for the unexcused breach of a bargain promise should invariably be measured by the value that the promised performance would have had to the plaintiff, regardless of the value for which the defendant's promise was exchanged.

. . .

Until recently, courts have tended either to apply the bargain principle to cases raising such problems, despite the difficulties this application presents, or to deal with these difficulties in covert and unsystematic ways. Over the past thirty years, however, a new paradigmatic principle—unconscionability—has emerged. This principle explains and justifies the limits that should be placed upon the bargain principle on the basis of the quality of a bargain.

Looking backward, the new paradigm enables us to reconstruct prior theory and phenomena by pro-

viding a general explanation for a wide variety of contract concepts that heretofore seemed distinct. So, for example, duress may now be seen as simply a special case of the exploitation of distress; undue influence may now be seen as simply a special case of unfair persuasion; and the prohibition against exploiting palpable unilateral mistake may now be seen as a specific norm of unconscionability. Similarly, the apparent anomaly of review for fairness in courts of equity and admiralty can be explained by the new paradigm, while guidelines can now be set for that review; and the doctrine of general incapacity might be reformulated to apply only when exploitation is present.

Looking forward, the paradigm must be articulated and extended through the development of more specific norms to guide the resolution of specific cases, provide affirmative relief to exploited parties, and channel the discretion of administrators and legislators. In accomplishing this task, it now appears that the distinction between procedural and substantive unconscionability, which may have served a useful purpose at an earlier stage, does not provide much help once the relatively obvious norms of unconscionability, such as unfair surprise, have been articulated. For example, it is both difficult and unproductive to classify as exclusively either "substantive" or "procedural" the problems posed by the extraction of an unduly high price from a person who is in distress, lacks transactional capacity, or is price-ignorant. Development of more specific norms must instead proceed by the identification of classes of cases in which neither fairness nor efficiency supports the application of the bargain principle—an effort that can be guided in part by the reconstruction and extension of existing contract doctrines.

. . .

Placing limits on the bargain principle is not cost-free. A major advantage of that principle, at least in theory is its conceptual simplicity and the ease with which it can be administered. To apply the principle, it need only be determined whether a bargain was made, and if so, what remedy is required to put the innocent party in the position he would have been in had the bargain been performed. Development of specific unconscionability norms and limitations on the full reach of the bargain principle in certain types of executory contracts make doctrine more complex by singling out certain transaction-types for special

[116] 59 Misc. 2d 189, 298 N.Y.S.2d 264 (Sup. Ct. 1969).

treatment. Administration is also made more complex and problematical by requiring decisions on such issues as whether a given course of conduct was exploitive or whether a given price was unfairly high.

The simplicity of the bargain principle, however, is partly a mirage. Concepts of fairness were smuggled into contract law even when the principle seemed most secure, through doctrines such as the legal-duty rule and the principle of mutuality. Partly because these doctrines are allowed to achieve their ends only

in a covert fashion, they operate in an extremely technical manner and are riddled with legalistic exceptions. Furthermore, an increase in the complexity of some areas of law may be desirable, if it accurately mirrors the increased complexity of social and economic life. Placing limits on the bargain principle involves costs of administration. Failure to place such limits, however, involves still greater costs to the system of justice.

5. Paternalism

The Problem of Paternalism

Arthur Leff argues in his *Emperor's New Clause* article that interference with bargains, at least bargains made without overt overreaching, is paternalistic, and that paternalism is the patronizing of those we think are entitled to less freedom to make mistakes than we are. Two important thinkers have written extensively on the issue. In *Paternalism and the Law of Contracts*, 92 Yale L.J. 763 (1983), Leff's colleague at Yale, Anthony T. Kronman, co-author of a leading casebook on contracts and a writer on legal philosophy, argued that there are many restrictions on freedom of contract, some of which are paternalistic in the sense that their purpose is to prevent people from harming themselves, but that paternalistic rules do not "derive . . . from a single principle, nor is there any one idea that best explains them all." He argues that while nondisclaimable warranties can be justified in economic terms, other "paternalistic" interferences can not, but that all those he identifies can be justified on moral grounds. "[I]n each case, however, the justification turns upon a different principle or ideal: distributive fairness, self-respect, and the value of judgment or moral imagination. The concept of paternalism conceals too much philosophical variety to be useful in itself; it wrongly suggests that all paternalistic restrictions address a single problem and must be justified by a single principle, or not at all."

Duncan Kennedy of Harvard is one of the most visible members of the Critical Legal Studies movement. He has produced some fine writing, including his *Form and Substance in Private Law Adjudication*, 89 Harv. L. Rev. 1685 (1976), which should be read. In a long but readable article with the awful title *Distributive and Paternalist Motives In Contract and Tort Law, With Special Reference to Compulsory Terms and Unequal Bargaining Power*, 41 Md. L. Rev. 563 (1982), Kennedy stated his "most important points" as:

First, distributive and paternalistic motives play a central role in explaining the rules of the contract and tort systems with respect to agreements. Second, these motives explain far better than any notion of rectifying unequal bargaining power the widespread legal institution of compulsory terms in areas such as the allocation of risk. Third, the notion that paternalist intervention can be justified only by the "incapacity" of the person the decision maker is trying to protect is wrong—the basis of paternalism is empathy or love, and its legitimate operation cannot be constricted to situations in which its object lacks "free will."

However, Kennedy concedes that there is a great danger that the decision-maker will misread the values and motivations of those who are poorer (and darker-skinned) than he, and that he will impose his own value system. (Note again the parallel to Leff.) Nonetheless, Kennedy concludes that a principle of anti-paternalism cannot be justified. He ends up with the sort of utopian (or perhaps merely hopeful) non-conclusion that is often said to be typical of Critical Legal Studies writing:

> In short, the decision maker should be damned if he doesn't [intervene paternalistically] as well as damned if he does. Let's face it: he's almost certainly a middle or upper middle class person, or a person who identifies with those classes in his heart. If he is concerned about failures of intuition, about the limits of empathy, he has two alternatives he should try before declaring himself a public life anti-paternalist and passing by on the other side. The first is to investigate the consciousness of those he isn't supposed to mess with. This means breaking down the barriers of segregation by knowing others, rather than just making rules for them.
>
> The second is to go beyond exploration to the task of helping mobilize the groups on whose part one may have to act paternalistically. . . . And if they're mobilized, there's more chance they will be able to dispense with your services. That is the true paternal goal: that the other should surpass you both in knowledge and in power, and share both.

Kennedy's article is briefly referred to in the Farber and Matheson *Invisible Handshake* piece in Part IIB.

C.   Changing (Saving?) the Parties' Deal: Mistake and Impracticability

Mistakes

Every contracts book has some reference to the old standbys of the literature of mistake: Rose 2d of Aberlone, the supposedly barren cow who turned out to be pregnant; the two Ships Peerless; the stone whose value (we are asked to believe) neither the jeweler nor the little girl knew. Today, however, the issue is likely to be tied into a question of a duty on one party to disclose information not known to the other. For example, A buys B's farm land for a fair price, but neglects to mention that he knows that it is likely to have valuable mineral deposits. B later seeks rescission or reformation. While B may claim fraud or misrepresentation, if the topic of mineral rights never came up, and if the land is in a part of the country where mining and drilling is uncommon, B may claim mistake: A knew a fact about the land that B didn't. The duty to disclose (or, conversely, the privilege not to disclose) is relevant to claims of both misrepresentation and mistake. Professor Anthony T. Kronman, formerly of the University of Chicago and now of Yale, has provided a very well-received analysis of the problems of disclosure and mistake, *Mistake, Disclosure, Information, and the Law of Contracts*, 7 J. Legal Stud. 1 (1978). Professor Kronman uses economic reasoning (without any mathematics) in arguing that information that is the result of deliberate search should be treated as a property right not subject to disclosure while information picked up casually should be disclosed.

There is a lot to be said for the Kronman position. However, a party with the wherewithal to engage in costly information searches is likely to be the wealthier party. Thus, the arguments of efficiency may be complicated by issues of wealth distribution. When Farmer B complains, should it be enough for A to answer that he paid B the going rate (or better) for the land, and that he invested millions in geological surveys that lead him to believe that B's land was worth one hundred million dollars? It is possible that if A had to share his information with sellers he would be discouraged from investing in the search. Thus, the land might go underutilized, a loss in efficiency to the society. On the other hand, there is no way that B could have invested in the search, since he doesn't have millions to invest. (It should be borne in mind, though, that if B had asked "Do you know anything about minerals on this land?", A could not say no today without committing fraud.) Is B's lack of wealth or sophistication relevant? Clearly relevant to the answer to that question are the notions of economic duress, unconscionability, good faith in bargaining, and generally, the overlaps among property, tort and contract concepts.

Anthony T. Kronman, *Mistake, Disclosure, Information, and the Law of Contracts,* 7 J. Legal Stud. 1 (1978)

Introduction

This paper attempts to explain an apparent inconsistency in the law of contracts. On the one hand, there are many contract cases—generally classified under the rubric of unilateral mistake—which hold that a promisor is excused from his obligation to either perform or pay damages when he is mistaken about some important fact and his error is known (or should be known) to the other party. On the other hand, cases may also be found which state that in some circumstances one party to a contract is entitled to withhold information he knows the other party lacks. These latter cases typically rest upon the proposition that the party with knowledge does not owe the other party a "duty of disclosure."

Although these two lines of cases employ different doctrinal techniques, they both address essentially the same question: if one party to a contract knows or has reason to know that the other party is mistaken about a particular fact, does the knowledgeable party have a duty to speak up or may he remain silent and capitalize on the other party's error? The aim of this paper is to provide a theory which will explain why some contract cases impose such a duty and others do not.

The paper is divided into three parts. In the first part, I discuss the problem of unilateral mistake and offer an economic justification for the rule that a unilaterally mistaken promisor is excused when his error is known or should be known to the other party. In the second part of the paper, I propose a distinction between two kinds or information—information which is the result of a deliberate search and information which has been casually acquired. I argue that a legal privilege of nondisclosure is in effect a property right and attempt to show that where special knowledge or information is the fruit of a deliberate search the assignment of a property right of this sort is required in order to insure production of the

information at a socially desirable level. I then attempt to show that a distinction between deliberately and casually acquired information is useful in explaining why disclosure is required in some contract cases but not in others.

In the third, and concluding, part of the paper, I return briefly to the problem of unilateral mistake, in order to reconcile the apparent conflict between the two lines of cases described above. I argue that this apparent conflict disappears when the unilateral mistake cases are viewed from the perspective developed in the second part of the paper.

I. Mistake and the Allocation of Risk.

Every contractual agreement is predicated upon a number of factual assumptions about the world. Some of these assumptions are shared by the parties to the contract and some are not. It is always possible that a particular factual assumption is mistaken. From an economic point of view, the risk of such a mistake (whether it be the mistake of only one party, or both) represents a cost. It is a cost to the contracting parties themselves and to society as a whole since the actual occurrence of a mistake always (potentially) increases the resources which must be devoted to the process of allocating goods to their highest-valuing users.

There are basically two ways in which this particular cost can be reduced to an optimal level. First, one or both of the parties can take steps to prevent the mistake from occurring. Second, to the extent a mistake cannot be prevented, either party (or both) can insure against the risk of its occurrence by purchasing insurance from a professional insurer or by self-insuring.

In what follows, I shall be concerned exclusively with the prevention of mistakes. Although this limitation might appear arbitrary, it is warranted by the fact that most mistake cases involve errors which can be prevented at a reasonable cost. Where a risk cannot be prevented at a reasonable cost—which is true of many of the risks associated with what the law calls "supervening impossibilities"—insurance is the only effective means of risk reduction. (This is why the concept of insurance unavoidably plays a more prominent role in the treatment of impossibility than it does in the analysis of mistake.) Information is the antidote to mistake. Although information is costly to produce, one individual may be able to obtain relevant information more cheaply than another. If the parties to a contract are acting rationally, they will minimize the joint costs of a potential mistake by assigning the risk of its occurrence to the party who is the better (cheaper) information-gatherer. Where the parties have actually assigned the risk—whether explicitly, or implicitly through their adherence to trade custom and past patterns of dealing—their own allocation must be respected. Where they have not—and there is a resulting gap in the contract—a court concerned with economic efficiency should impose the risk on the better information-gatherer. This is so for familiar reasons: by allocating the risk in this way, an efficiency-minded court reduces the transaction costs of the contracting process itself.

The most important doctrinal distinction in the law of mistake is the one drawn between "mutual" and "unilateral" mistakes. Traditionally courts have been more reluctant to excuse a mistaken promisor where he alone is mistaken than where the other party is mistaken as to the same fact. Although relief for unilateral mistake has been liberalized during the last half-century (to the point where some commentators have questioned the utility of the distinction between unilateral and mutual mistake and a few have even urged its abolition), it is still "black-letter" law that a promisor whose mistake is not shared by the other party is less likely to be relieved of his duty to perform than a promisor whose mistake happens to be mutual.

Viewed broadly, the distinction between mutual and unilateral mistake makes sense from an economic point of view. Where both parties to a contract are mistaken about the same fact or state of affairs, deciding which of them would have been better able to prevent the mistake may well require a detailed inquiry regarding the nature of the mistake and the (economic) role or position of each of the parties involved. But where only one party is mistaken, it is reasonable to assume that he is in a better position than the other party to prevent his own error. As we

shall see, this is not true in every case, but it provides a useful beginning point for analysis and helps to explain the generic difference between mutual and unilateral mistakes.

. . .

In the past, it was often asserted that, absent fraud or misrepresentation, a unilateral mistake never justifies excusing the mistaken party from his duty to perform or pay damages. This is certainly no longer the law, and Corbin has demonstrated that in all probability it never was. One well-established exception protects the unilaterally mistaken promisor whose error is known or reasonably should be known to the other party. Relief has long been available in this case despite the fact that the promisor's mistake is not shared by the other party to the contract.

For example, if a bidder submits a bid containing a clerical error or miscalculation, and the mistake is either evident on the face of the bid or may reasonably be inferred from a discrepancy between it and other bids, the bidder will typically be permitted to withdraw the bid without having to pay damages (even after the bid has been accepted and in some cases relied upon by the other party). Or, to take another example, suppose that, A submits a proposed contract in writing to B and knows that B has misread the document. If B accepts the proposed contract, upon discovering his error, he may avoid his obligations under the contract and has no duty to compensate A for A's lost expectation. A closely related situation involves the offer which is "too good to be true." One receiving such an offer cannot "snap it up"; if he does so, the offeror may withdraw the offer despite the fact that it has been accepted.

In each of the cases just described, one party is mistaken and the other has actual knowledge or reason to know of his mistake. The mistaken party in each case is excused from meeting any contractual obligations owed to the party with knowledge.

A rule of this sort is a sensible one. While it is true that in each of the cases just described the mistaken party is likely to be the one best able to prevent the mistake from occurring in the first place (by exercising care in preparing his bid or in reading the proposed contract which has been submitted to him), the other party may be able to rectify the mistake more cheaply in the interim between its occurrence and the formation of the contract. At one moment in time the mistaken party is the better mistake-preventer (information-gatherer). At some subsequent moment, however, the other party may be the better preventer because of his superior access to relevant information that will disclose the mistake and thus allow its correction. This may be so, for example, if he has other bids to compare with the mistaken one since this will provide him with information which the bidder himself lacks. . . .

The cases in which relief is granted to a unilaterally mistaken promisor on the grounds that his mistake was known or reasonably knowable by the other party appear, however, to conflict sharply with another line of cases.

These cases deal with the related problems of fraud and disclosure: if one party to a contract knows that the other is mistaken as to some material fact, is it fraud for the party with knowledge to fail to disclose the error and may the mistaken party avoid the contract on the theory that he was owed a duty of disclosure? This question is not always answered in the same way. In some cases, courts typically find a duty to disclose and in others they do not. It is the latter group of cases—those not requiring disclosure—which appear to conflict with the rule that a unilateral mistake will excuse if the other party knows or has reason to know of its existence. In the cases not requiring disclosure, one party is mistaken and the other party knows or has reason to know it. Can these cases be reconciled with those which stand for the proposition that a unilateral mistake plus knowledge or reason to know will excuse the mistaken party? More particularly, can the apparent divergence between these two lines of cases be explained on economic grounds?

The rest of this paper is devoted to answering these two questions. In brief, the answer I propose is as follows. Where nondisclosure is permitted (or put differently, where the knowledgeable party's contract rights are enforced despite his failure to disclose a known mistake), the knowledge involved is typically the product of a costly search. A rule permitting nondisclosure is the only effective way of providing an incentive to invest in the production of such knowledge. By contrast, in the cases requiring disclosure,[25] and in those excusing a unilaterally mistaken promi-

sor because the other party knew or had reason to know of his error, the knowledgeable party's special information is typically not the fruit of a deliberate search. Although information of this sort is socially useful as well, a disclosure requirement will not cause a sharp reduction in the amount of such information which is actually produced. If one takes into account the investment costs incurred in the deliberate production of information, the two apparently divergent lines of cases described above may both be seen as conforming (roughly) to the principle of efficiency, which requires that the risk of a unilateral mistake be placed on the most effective risk-preventer.

II. The Production of Information and the Duty to Disclose

A. *General Considerations*

It is appropriate to begin a discussion of fraud and nondisclosure in contract law with the celebrated case of *Laidlaw v. Organ.*[26] Organ was a New Orleans commission merchant engaged in the purchase and sale of tobacco. Early on the morning of February 19, 1815, he was informed by a Mr. Shepherd that a peace treaty had been signed at Ghent by American and British officers, formally ending the War of 1812. Mr. Shepherd (who was himself interested in the profits of the transaction involved in *Laidlaw v. Organ*) had obtained information regarding the treaty from his brother who, along with two other gentlemen, brought the news from the British Fleet. (What Shepherd's brother and his companions were doing with the British Fleet is not disclosed.)

Knowledge of the treaty was made public in a handbill circulated around eight o'clock on the morning of the nineteenth. However, before the treaty's existence had been publicized ("soon after sunrise" according to the reported version of the case), Organ, knowing of the treaty, called on a representative of the Laidlaw firm and entered into a contract for the purchase of 111 hogsheads of tobacco. Before agreeing to sell the tobacco, the Laidlaw representative "asked if there was any news which was calculated to enhance the price or value of the article about to be

[25] Although throughout the paper I use the expression "duty to disclose," the duty involved is typically not a true legal obligation. If the party with knowledge fails to disclose the other party's error, his failure to do so will give the mistaken party grounds for avoiding any contract which has been concluded between them. In the absence of such a contract, however, the knowing party has no positive duty to disclose—that is, nondisclosure will not by itself give the

mistaken party the right to sue him for damages. Of course, in some cases—for example, where there is a fiduciary relation between the parties—a positive duty of this latter sort may exist. Where it does, a failure to disclose is not simply a defense to the knowing party's suit to enforce the other party's contractual obligations; it also provides the mistaken party with an independent cause of action for damages.

[26] Laidlaw v. Organ, 15 U.S. (2 Wheat.) 178.

purchased." It is unclear what response, if any, Organ made to this inquiry.[27]

As a result of the news of the treaty—which signalled an end to the naval blockade of New Orleans—the market price of tobacco quickly rose by 30 to 50 percent. Laidlaw refused to deliver the tobacco as he had originally promised. Organ subsequently brought suit to recover damages and to block Laidlaw from otherwise disposing of the goods in controversy. Although the report of the case is unclear, it appears that the trial judge directed a verdict in Organ's favor. The case was appealed to the United States Supreme Court which in an opinion by Chief Justice Marshall remanded with directions for a new trial. The Court concluded that the question "whether any imposition was practiced by the vendee upon the vendor ought to have been submitted to the jury" and that as a result "the absolute instruction of the judge was erroneous." Marshall's opinion is more famous, however, for its dictum than for its holding:

> The question in this case is, whether the intelligence of extrinsic circumstances, which might influence the price of the commodity, and which was exclusively within the knowledge of the vendee, ought to have been communicated by him to the vendor? The court is of opinion that he was not bound to communicate it. It would be difficult to circumscribe the contrary doctrine within proper limits, where the means of intelligence are equally accessible to both parties. But at the same time, each party must take care not to say or do anything tending to impose upon the other.

Although Marshall's dictum in *Laidlaw v. Organ* has been sharply criticized, it is still generally regarded as an accurate statement of the law (when properly interpreted). The broad rule which Marshall endorses has usually been justified on three related grounds: that it conforms to the legitimate expectations of commercial parties and thus accurately reflects the (harsh) morality of the marketplace; that in a contract for the sale of goods each party takes the risk that his own evaluation of the worth of the goods may be erroneous; or finally, that it justly rewards the intelligence and industry of the party with special knowledge (in this case, the buyer). This last idea may be elaborated in the following way.

News of the treaty of Ghent affected the price of tobacco in New Orleans. Price measures the relative value of commodities: information regarding the treaty revealed a new state of affairs in which the value of tobacco—relative to other goods and to tobacco-substitutes in particular—had altered. An alteration of this sort is almost certain to affect the allocation of social resources. If the price of tobacco to suppliers rises, for example, farmers will be encouraged to plant more tobacco and tobacco merchants may be prepared to pay more to get their goods to and from market. In this way, the proportion of society's (limited) resources devoted to the production and transportation of tobacco will be increased. Information revealing a change in circumstances which alters the relative value of a particular commodity will always have some (perhaps unmeasurable) allocative impact. (In addition, of course, information of this sort will have distributive consequences: the owners of tobacco or of rights to tobacco will be relatively wealthier after the price rise, assuming that other prices have not risen or have not risen as fast.)

From a social point of view, it is desirable that information which reveals a change in circumstances affecting the relative value of commodities reach the market as quickly as possible (or put differently, that the time between the change itself and its comprehension and assessment be minimized). If a farmer who would have planted tobacco had he known of the change plants peanuts instead, he will have to choose between either uprooting one crop and substituting another (which may be prohibitively expensive and will in any case be costly), or devoting his land to a nonoptimal use. In either case, both the individual farmer and society as a whole will be worse off than if he had planted tobacco to begin with. The sooner information of the change reaches the farmer, the less likely it is that social resources will be wasted.

. . .

In some cases, the individuals who supply information have obtained it by a deliberate search; in other cases, their information has been acquired casually. A securities analyst, for example, acquires information about a particular corporation in a deliberate fashion—by carefully studying evidence of its economic performance. By contrast, a businessman who ac-

---

[27] If Organ denied that he had heard any news of this sort, he would have committed a fraud. It may even be, in light of Laidlaw's direct question, that silence on Organ's part was fraudulent. William W. Story, A Treatise on the Law of Contracts 444 n.2 (2d ed. 1847). In my discussion of the case, and of the general rule which Marshall lays down in his famous dictum, I have put aside any question of fraud on Organ's part.

quires a valuable piece of information when he accidentally overhears a conversation on a bus acquires the information casually.

As it is used here, the term "deliberately acquired information" means information whose acquisition entails costs which would not have been incurred but for the likelihood, however great, that the information in question would actually be produced. These costs may include, of course, not only direct search costs (the cost of examining the corporation's annual statement) but the costs of developing an initial expertise as well (for example, the cost of attending business school). If the costs incurred in acquiring the information (the cost of the bus ticket in the second example) would have been incurred in any case—that is, whether or not the information was forthcoming—the information may be said to have been casually acquired. The distinction between deliberately and casually acquired information is a short-hand way of expressing this economic difference. Although in reality it may be difficult to determine whether any particular item of information has been acquired in one way or the other, the distinction between these two types of information has—as I hope to show—considerable analytical usefulness.

If information has been deliberately acquired (in the sense defined above), and its possessor is denied the benefits of having and using it, he will have an incentive to reduce (or curtail entirely) his production of such information in the future. This is in fact merely a consequence of defining deliberately acquired information in the way that I have, since one who acquires information of this sort will by definition have incurred costs which he would have avoided had it not been for the prospect of the benefits he has now been denied. By being denied the same benefits, one who has casually acquired information will not be discouraged from doing what—for independent reasons—he would have done in any case.

. . .

One effective way of insuring that an individual will benefit from the possession of information (or anything else for that matter) is to assign him a property right in the information itself—a right or entitlement to invoke the coercive machinery of the state in order to exclude others from its use and enjoyment. The benefits of possession become secure only when the state transforms the possesor of information into an owner by investing him with a legally enforceable property right of some sort or other. The assignment of property rights in information is a familiar feature of our legal system. The legal protection accorded patented inventions and certain trade secrets are two obvious examples.

One (seldom noticed) way in which the legal system can establish property rights in information is by permitting an informed party to enter—and enforce—contracts which his information suggests are profitable without disclosing the information to the other party. Imposing a duty to disclose upon the knowledgeable party deprives him of a private advantage which the information would otherwise afford. A duty to disclose is tantamount to a requirement that the benefit on the information be publicly shared and is thus antithetical to the notion of a property right which—whatever else it may entail—always requires the legal protection of private appropriation.

. . .

It is unclear, from the report of the case, whether the buyer in *Laidlaw* casually acquired his information or made a deliberate investment in seeking it out (for example, by cultivating a network of valuable commercial "friendships"). If we assume the buyer casually acquired his knowledge of the treaty, requiring him to disclose the information to his seller (that is, denying him a property right in the information) will have no significant effect on his future behavior. Since one who casually acquires information makes no investment in its acquisition, subjecting him to a duty to disclose is not likely to reduce the amount of socially useful information which he actually generates. Of course, if the buyer in *Laidlaw* acquired his knowledge of the treaty as the result of a deliberate and costly search, a disclosure requirement will deprive him of any private benefit which he might otherwise realize from possession of the information and should discourage him from making similar investments in the future.

In addition, since it would enable the seller to appropriate the buyer's information without cost and would eliminate the danger of his being lured unwittingly into a losing contract by one possessing superior knowledge, a disclosure requirement will also reduce the seller's incentive to search. Denying the buyer a property right in deliberately acquired information will therefore discourage both buyers and sellers from investing in the development of expertise and in the actual search for information. The assignment of such a right will not only protect the investment of the party possessing the special knowledge, it will also impose an opportunity cost on the other party and thus give him an incentive to undertake a (cost-justified) search of his own.

If we assume that courts can easily discriminate between those who have acquired information casually and those who have acquired it deliberately, plausible economic considerations might well justify imposing a duty to disclose on a case-by-case basis (imposing it where the information has been casually acquired, refusing to impose it where the information is the fruit of a deliberate search). A party who has casually acquired information is, at the time of the transaction, likely to be a better (cheaper) mistake-preventer than the mistaken party with whom he deals—regardless of the fact that both parties initially had equal access to the information in question. One who has deliberately acquired information is also in a position to prevent the other party's error. But in determining the cost to the knowledgeable party or preventing the mistake (by disclosure), we must include whatever investment he has made in acquiring the information in the first place. This investment will represent a loss to him if the other party can avoid the contract on the grounds that the party with the information owes him a duty of disclosure.

If we take this cost into account, it is no longer clear that the party with knowledge is the cheaper mistake-preventer when his knowledge has been deliberately acquired. Indeed, the opposite conclusion seems more plausible. In this case, therefore, a rule permitting nondisclosure (which has the effect of imposing the risk of a mistake on the mistaken party) corresponds to the arrangement the parties themselves would have been likely to adopt if they had negotiated an explicit allocation or the risk at the time they entered the contract. The parties to a contract are always free to allocate this particular risk by including an appropriate disclaimer in the terms of their agreement. Where they have failed to do so, however, the object or the law of contracts should be (as it is elsewhere) to reduce transaction costs by providing a legal rule which approximates the arrangement the parties would have chosen for themselves if they had deliberately addressed the problem. This consideration, coupled with the reduction in the production of socially useful information which is likely to follow from subjecting him to a disclosure requirement, suggests that allocative efficiency is best served by permitting one who possesses deliberately acquired information to enter and enforce favorable bargains without disclosing what he knows. A rule which calls for case-by-case application of a disclosure requirement is likely, however, to involve factual issues that will be difficult (and expensive) to resolve.

Laidlaw itself illustrates this point nicely. On the facts of the case, as we have them, it is impossible to determine whether the buyer actualy made a deliberate investment in acquiring information regarding the treaty. The cost of administering a disclosure requirement on a case-by-case basis is likely to be substantial.

As an alternative, one might uniformly apply a blanket rule (of disclosure or nondisclosure) across each class of cases involving the same sort of information (for example, information about market conditions or about defects in property held for sale). In determining the appropriate blanket rule for a particular class of cases, it would first be necessary to decide whether the kind of information involved is (on the whole) more likely to be generated by chance or by deliberate searching. The greater the likelihood that such information will be deliberately produced rather than casually discovered, the more plausible the assumption becomes that a blanket rule permitting nondisclosure will have benefits that outweigh its costs.

In *Laidlaw*, for example, the information involved concerned changing market conditions. The results in that case may be justified (from the more general perspective just described) on the grounds that information regarding the state of the market is typically (although not in every case) the product of a deliberate search. The large number of individuals who are actually engaged in the production of such information lends some empirical support to this proposition.

B. *The Case Law*

The distinction between deliberately and casually acquired information helps us to understand the pattern exhibited by the cases in which a duty to disclose is asserted by one party or the other. By and large, the cases requiring disclosure involve information which is likely to have been casually acquired (in the sense defined above). The cases permitting nondisclosure, on the other hand, involve information which, on the whole, is likely to have been deliberately produced. Taken as a group, the disclosure cases give at least the appearance of promoting allocative efficiency by limiting the assignment of property rights to those types of information which are likely to be the fruit of a deliberate investment (either in the development of expertise or in actual searching).

The economic rationale for permitting nondisclosure is nicely illustrated by several cases involving the purchase of real estate where the buyer had reason to believe in the existence of a subsurface oil or mineral deposit unkown to the seller. . . .

. . .

[Professor Kronman discusses oil and uranium cases where the buyer was not held to a duty to disclose information about hidden value, information that was the product of a costly search. The search would have been discouraged by a disclosure requirement. He also notes cases giving sellers of homes a similar privilege of non-disclosure of termite infestation, but contrasts a more recent termite case. —ed.]

Eighteen years later [(in 1960)], in *Obde v. Schlemeyer*,[68] a Washington seller was held to have a duty to disclose under identical circumstances. The Washington court concluded that the seller had a duty to speak up, "regardless of the [buyer's] failure to ask any questions relative to the possibility of termites," since the condition was "clearly latent—not readily observable upon reasonable inspection." The court bolstered its argument with a long quotation from an article by Professor Keeton:

It is of course apparent that the content of the maxim "caveat emptor," used in its broader meaning of imposing risks on both parties to a transaction, has been greatly limited since its origin. When Lord Cairns stated in Peek v. Gurney that there was no duty to disclose facts, however morally censurable their non-disclosure may be, he was stating the law as shaped by an individualistic philosophy based upon freedom of contract. It was not concerned with morals. In the present state of the law, the decisions show a drawing away from this idea, and there can be seen an attempt by many courts to reach a just result in so far as possible, but yet maintaining the degree of certainty which the law must have. The statement may often be found that if either party to a contract of sale conceals or suppresses a material fact which he is in good faith bound to disclose then his silence is fraudulent.

The attitude of the courts toward non-disclosure is undergoing a change and contrary to Lord Cairns' famous remark it would seem that the object of the law in these cases should be to impose on parties to the transaction a duty to speak whenever justice, equity, and fair dealing demand it.

However one feels about Professor Keeton's moral claim, requiring the disclosure of latent defects makes good sense from the more limited perspective offered here. In the first place, it is likely to be expensive for the buyer to discover such defects; the discovery of a latent defect will almost always require something more than an ordinary search. Even where neither party has knowledge of the defect, it may be efficient to allocate to the seller the risk of a mistaken belief that no defect exists, on the grounds that of the two parties he is likely to be the cheapest mistake-preventer.

Where the seller actually knows of the defect, and the buyer does not, the seller is clearly the party best able to avoid the buyer's mistake at least cost—unless the seller has made a deliberate investment in acquiring his knowledge which he would not have made had he known he would be required to disclose to purchasers of the property any defects he discovered.

. . . A disclosure requirement is unlikely to have a substantial effect on the level of investment by homeowners in the detection of termites: the point is not that information regarding termites is costless (it isn't), but that a disclosure requirement would not be likely to reduce the production of such information. This represents an important distinction between cases like *Obde*, on the one hand, and those like *Laidlaw* . . . on the other.

A seller of goods might argue that a rule requiring him to disclose latent defects will discourage him from developing (socially useful) expertise regarding the qualities or attributes of the goods he is selling: if he cannot enjoy its fruits by selling without disclosure, what incentive will he have to acquire such expertise in the first place? This argument is rather unconvincing. A seller benefits in many different ways from his knowledge of the various attributes which his goods possess. For example, expertise of this sort enables him to be more efficient in purchasing materials, and reduces the likelihood that he will fail to identify any special advantage his goods enjoy (and therefore undersell them). Because the benefits which he derives from such knowledge are many and varied, it is unlikely that a duty to disclose latent defects will by itself seriously impair a seller's incentive to invest in acquiring knowledge regarding the attributes of what he sells.

By contrast, the usefulness of market information (as distinct from information regarding the attributes of goods held for sale) is substantially reduced by imposing a duty to disclose on its possessor. It is doubtful whether the benefits of market information which are not eliminated by a disclosure requirement are

---

[68] Obde v. Schlemeyer, 56 Wash. 2d 449, 353 P.2d 672 (1960).

sufficient by themselves to justify a deliberate investment in its production. Consequently, even if we regard these two kinds of information—market information and product information—as equally useful from a social point of view, a legal rule requiring disclosure is likely to have a different impact upon the production of each. It follows from what I have just said that a rule permitting nondisclosure of market information is sensible whether the party possessing the information is a buyer or a seller. Thus, if the seller in *Laidlaw* had known the treaty would have a depressing effect on the price of cotton and had sold to the buyer without disclosing this fact, the economic considerations favoring enforcement would be the same as where the buyer had acquired special information. Although economic considerations would appear to support similar treatment for buyers and sellers possessing market information, these same considerations may justify different treatment where product information is involved. It should be clear, from what I have already said, that there is no inconsistency in requiring sellers to disclose latent defects, while not requiring buyers to disclose latent advantages.

The latent defect cases have an interesting analogue in the insurance field. An applicant for a life insurance policy is usually held to have a duty to disclose known "defects" in his own constitution . . . [E]ven in the absence of fraud, an applicant is usually held to have a positive duty to speak up even where he has not been asked a specific question. In this respect, the same disclosure is required of one who purchases an insurance policy as is required of a seller who sells a house with a latent defect (such as a termite infestation). From an economic point of view, these two cases are quite similar and it is therefore understandable that the same disclosure requirement should be applied to each. Because of his intimate familiarity with his own medical history and symptoms, an applicant for an insurance policy will typically be in a better position than the insurance company itself to prevent a mistake by the company regarding some latent defect in the applicant's constitution. More importantly, an applicant will have a strong incentive to acquire information concerning his own health whether or not we impose a disclosure requirement on him. In this sense, he resembles the homeowner who will have an incentive to protect his home from destruction by termites whether we require him to disclose the existence of a termite infestation or not. Both the homeowner and the insurance applicant have an independent reason for producing information of this sort, and the value to them of the information will in most cases be unimpaired by a disclosure requirement.

. . .

Conclusion

In this paper, I have emphasized the way in which one branch of the law of contracts promotes efficiency by encouraging the deliberate search for socially useful information. It does so, I have argued, by giving the possessor of such information the right to deal with others without disclosing what he knows. This right is in essence a property right, and I have tried to show that the law tends to recognize a right of this sort where the information is the result of a deliberate and costly search and not to recognize it where the information has been casually acquired. This basic distinction between two kinds of information (and the theory of property rights which is based upon it) introduces order into the disclosure cases and eliminates the apparent conflict between those cases which permit nondisclosure and the well-established rule that a unilaterally mistaken promisor will be excused if his error is or reasonably should be known by the other party.

. . .

Adjusting Long-Term Contracts: Impracticability and Freedom of Contract

While mistakes can happen in any context, impracticability usually comes up in long-term contracts of supply or services. In the 1950's the closing of the Suez Canal caused many shipping dislocations. The 1970's produced many even more dramatic economic cataclysms coming out of the oil boycotts. Both of these events produced a lot of litigation and perhaps even more law review articles. Several of the articles use economic analysis, the best-known being Posner and Rosenfield, *Impossibility and Related Doctrines in Contract Law: An Economic Analysis*, 6 J. Legal Stud. 83 (1977). Another interesting economic analysis is that of Paul L. Joskow in *Commercial Impossibility, The Uranium Market and the Westinghouse Case*, 6 J. Legal Stud. 119 (1977). These and other articles on impracticability are excerpted in Anthony T. Kronman and Richard A. Posner, *The Economics of Contract Law* (1979). Several writers have considered the role of cooperation during a long-term contract. Not surprisingly, Ian Macneil is one of these. In fact, that is the principal burden of his article, *Contracts: Adjustment of Long-Term Economic Relations*, etc., excerpted in Part IB. A more recent example, using game theory and risk-sharing to reconcile bargain with relational notions, is Professor Robert E. Scott's *Conflict and Cooperation in Long-Term Contracts*, 75 Calif. L. Rev. 2005 (1987).

Common law courts frequently rewrote ("reformed") contracts to correct parties' mistakes, but if an unforeseen event made a contract impossible to perform (or more likely, "economically impracticable"), the only remedy that the common law courts offered was discharge of the parties from all their duties under the contract. That all-or-nothing result discouraged judicial intervention. The Uniform Commercial Code's comment to section 2-615 suggested that duties could be judicially modified in light of shortages, and in one famous case (settled while on appeal), the trial judge used the law of mistake to rewrite a contract to share the spoils of what would have been a windfall to one party when a pricing index did not work in the hyperinflation of the mid-seventies. That case, *Aluminum Company of America v. Essex Group*, 499 F. Supp. 53 (W.D. Pa. 1980), is discussed in each of the following articles. (It is also discussed in Stewart Macaulay's *An Empirical View of Contract*, excerpted in Part IA, where he suggests that only law professors have been impressed with the *ALCOA* case.)

Richard E. Speidel of Northwestern is co-author of leading casebooks in both Contracts and Commercial Law. Speidel is on record as believing that "contorts" should not be allowed to swamp the central position of consent in contract; nonetheless, he has written several important articles on the role of courts in filling gaps and even imposing adjustments when unexpected things happen in long-term contracts. His article *Court-Imposed Price Adjustments Under Long-Term Supply Contracts*, 76 Nw. L. Rev. 369 (1981), discusses the *ALCOA* case in detail, and argues that modification rather than all-or-nothing liability can be justified under traditional contract doctrines and practices. Below are excerpts from a shorter discussion, Speidel's Caplan Lecture at the University of Pittsburgh, *The New Spirit of Contract*. Speidel takes an overview of the evolution of contract law, and then applies it to justify a flexible judicial approach to long-term contract. Central to Speidel's thesis are the good faith concept and an argument that we need more flexible remedies than the traditional ones used in breach of contract cases. On this second point, see also William F. Young's *Half Measures*, 81 Colum. L. Rev. 19 (1981), and the note on *Judicially Imposed Compromise—The Wisdom of Solomon?* in Part IV. Robert A. Hillman of Cornell recently added his analysis to the discussion. Hillman also speaks for court modification, but he differs somewhat from Speidel and shows his sensitivity to the parties' autonomy by trying to limit the court involvement to cases in which it seems consistent with what the parties really intended (in a broad sense). His approach can be compared profitably with the Knapp and Farnsworth articles on agreements to negotiate in Part IIA, as well as with Macneil's in Part IB. Professor Hillman's article, *Court Adjustments of Long-Term Contracts: An Analysis Under Modern Contract Law*, 1987 Duke L.J. 1, follows Speidel.

John P. Dawson's name came up prominently in the discussion of economic duress. During a very long academic career Professor Dawson, of Michigan and Harvard, brought many new ideas into contract and restitution law. He often educated his fellow Americans about ideas from Europe that could be applied in this country. One of the areas in which he brought in European ideas was the judicial revision of frustrated contracts. Despite his role in this area and his openness to new ideas, Professor Dawson found himself dissatisfied. In what may have been his last work, written in 1984, Professor Dawson wrote critically of *ALCOA*, and of Speidel. Professor Hillman replied to Dawson in his 1987 article, but it seems only right to give Professor Dawson the last word on the subject. The Dawson article is pungent and funny, as well as being a most effective argument against judicial intervention in contract performance, no matter how relational the contracts are.

Richard E. Speidel, *The New Spirit of Contract*, 2 J. Law & Comm. 193 (1982)

My text is taken from the opinion of Judge Hubert Teitelbaum in *Aluminum Co. of America v. Essex Group, Inc.*,[1] decided in 1980 in the Western District of Pennsylvania. In that case, the parties had entered into a seventeen-year contract for the processing of aluminum ore into ingots. After seven years of performance, ALCOA claimed that the price term, a production cost index, had failed its essential purpose due to changed circumstances and that the appropriate remedy was an equitable price adjustment. The court found that the changed circumstances, which caused a dramatic increase in energy costs, were (1) not foreseeable at the time of contracting as likely to occur and that (2) ALCOA's projected loss of $60 million over the balance of the contract made performance "commercially senseless." Expressed in the language of contemporary contract law, the changes were "contingenc[ies] the nonoccurrence of which was a basic assumption" of the contract and their occurrence made performance "as agreed" impracticable.

The court held that although ALCOA was entitled to *some* relief, it was not a discharge from the contract. Rather, the court deleted the production cost index and imposed in the "gap" a new price term, derived partly from expressed intention and partly from the court's sense of fairness. This unprecedented equitable reformation was done without Essex' consent in the name of a "new" spirit of contract.

What is this "new" spirit that supported the imposition of a price adjustment without mutual consent? According to the court, this spirit directed the court to give close attention to: (1) the legitimate business aims of the parties as supplemented by the "customs and expectations of the particular business community;" (2) their purpose of "avoiding the risks of great losses;" and (3) the need to frame a remedy to preserve the essence of the agreement. Stated another way, within the general purposes of the parties, the "new" spirit contained three pegs: contextualization, loss avoidance and flexible remedies. Coming as it does in the wake of Grant Gilmore's assertion that contract is dead—that is, that the classical theory of contract with its emphasis upon "manifested mutual assent to a bargain" has come unglued[4]—this "new" spirit is both provocative and vaguely disturbing. Is it for good or for evil? Before we can answer that question, perhaps we should know something about the "old" spirit of contract.

I. The Classical Theory: The "Old" Spirit Of Contract

The word spirit usually depicts an elusive force which is central to life. A spirit can be uneven and wild. But one normally celebrates a vital spirit that prompts the pursuit of aspiration or sparks defiance against tyranny. One does not celebrate the spirit of martial law. Shakespeare, as usual, caught the essence:

> I see you stand like greyhounds in the slips, straining upon the start. The game's afoot: Follow your spirit; and upon this charge cry "God for Harry, England and St. George."[5]

One celebrates the "Spirit of Liberty," as did Learned Hand,[6] or the two concepts of liberty, "freedom to" and "freedom from," as did Sir Isaiah Berlin.[7] In fact, the spirit of a people at any given time may be measured by the opportunity and incentive to exercise "freedom to" and the felt necessity to assert "freedom from." Similarly, the nature of a society and its legal order may be determined by the force and permissible scope of these two concepts of liberty and how the inevitable tension between them is resolved.

If I may now suggest the obvious, the law of contracts as administered by courts constantly reflects the tension between "freedom to" and "freedom from." . . .

Under the classical system—a system that, among

---

[1] Aluminum Co. of America v. Essex Group, Inc., 499 F. Supp. 53 (W.D. Pa. 1980). For a full discussion of the ALCOA case and related problems, see Speidel, Court-Imposed Price Adjustments Under Long-Term Supply Contracts, 76 Nw. U.L. Rev. 369 (1981).

[4] G. Gilmore, The Death Of Contract (1974).

[5] W. Shakespeare, Henry V, IIIi, 31.

[6] L. Hand, The Spirit Of Liberty 189-191 (I. Dillard 3d ed. 1960). For Hand, the "spirit" of liberty was restrained. It is the spirit "which is not too sure that it is right; . . . which seeks to understand the minds of other[s]; . . . which weighs their interests along side its own without bias . . . ."

[7] I. Berlin, Two Concepts of Liberty, in Four Essays on Liberty 118 (1969).

other things, required promises, mutual assent and consideration for liability, and measured obligation under an objective test—one had an immediate sense that "freedom to," that is enforcement, caught the "old" spirit of contract. Contracts are devices by which private parties implement personal or business plans. Bargains, when performed, increase the satisfaction of both parties, and, when combined with other exchange transactions in the market, contribute to increased wealth for all. Thus, as a nineteenth century judge put it, "if there is one thing which . . . public policy requires, it is that men of full age and competent understanding shall have the utmost liberty of contracting, and that their contracts when entered into freely and voluntarily shall be held sacred and shall be enforced by Courts of Justice."[9]

. . .

The other side of the enforcement coin is "freedom from" contract. Contract liability, of course, will not be imposed upon a person without consent. However, suppose that person seeks to exit from a bargain to which he has assented for reasons other than a breach by the other party. Harry Jones has reminded us that contract law provides an important function by protecting one party from the exercise by the other party of excessive market power in fact:[14] the court can avoid the contract and return the parties to the pre-assent position. Harold Havighurst concluded that in this guise, contract law performed the role of a leveller—it gave the weak a chance to enforce promises against the strong and, to the extent that the "will" of the strong was excessive, also lent protection to the weak. With this "blend of equalities," therefore, the contract institution leaned toward liberty.

Despite this optimism, "classical" contract law was not particularly sensitive to claims of hardship, disproportion or disadvantage. It was (1) difficult to establish fraud and duress, (2) everyone had a duty to read and understand what they signed, (3) excuse for mistake or changed circumstances was limited and (4) unless an infant or incompetent, everyone was held to the standard of that rational, efficient, "reasonable"

person. In short, it was an uphill battle to escape from the bargain because the other party exercised allegedly "excessive" market power and, to this extent, this result reinforced the sense that the "old" spirit of contract was enforcement.

Even so, the classical model permitted more "freedom from" contract than the emphasis upon enforcement would suggest.[17] . . .

. . .

[Professor Speidel points to the requirement of mutuality of obligation, the parol evidence and plain meaning rules, harsh enforcement of express conditions and the preference for money damages over specific performance (discussed in Part IV of this anthology) as ways in which the classical system often allowed in practice the privilege of unilateral exit that it denied in theory. —ed.]

On balance, then, let me suggest a working hypothesis: the "classical" theory of contract, despite its apparent emphasis on enforcement, provided considerable room for exit. In short, the key feature of the "old spirit of contract" may have been the scope of "freedom from" liability rather than the notion of enforcement underlying "freedom to." Unlike Judge Teitelbaum's "new" spirit, the classical theory also preferred rules over standards, eschewed contextualization, was relatively insensitive to claims of hardship and limited remedial flexibility by its preference for damages. In the time since the highwater mark of the classical theory, the completion of the first Restatement of Contracts in 1933, what has happened to uncork this "new" spirit? More importantly, does the "new" spirit as identified by the court in ALCOA catch the essence of the changes under way?

II. A Shift in Method—The Role of Hardship, Fairness and Good Faith in the Enforcement of Bargains

Let us turn first to the "what has happened" question, a complete answer to which would take several days. There has been a shift from the classical system to what Ian Macneil has called a "neoclassical" system of contract.[29] This system finds its intellectual roots in the work of Karl Llewellyn and the great

---

[9] Printing and Numerical Registering Co. v. Sampson, 19 L.R. Eq. 462 465 (1875) See also Inman v. Clyde Hall Drilling Co., 369 P.2d 498 (Alaska 1962) ("As a matter of judicial policy the court should maintain and enforce contracts, rather than enable parties to escape from the obligations they have chosen to incur.") Enforcement of contracts is also a legitimate function of government in what Robert Nozick has called the "night-watchman" or "minimal" state of classical liberal theory. R. Nozick, Anarchy State And Utopia 26 (1974).

[14] Jones, The Jurisprudence of Contracts, 44 U. Cin. L. Rev. 43, 50 (1975). See also Jones, The Rule of Law and the Welfare State, 58 Colum. L. Rev. 143 (1958).
[17] By "freedom from" I mean the exercise of unilateral power to avoid or exit from a contractual relationship with little or no cost.
[29] Unlike classical contract law which is modeled on discrete transactions and presumes presentation neoclassical contract law (1) recognizes that full presentation is neither possible nor desirable in less discrete transactions, (2) pro-

treatise of Corbin and is embodied in Article 2 of the Uniform Commercial Code (UCC) and the Restatement (Second) of Contracts. The shift reveals important changes in both method and substance and, on balance, constitutes a victory for enforcement over exit.

The shift in method supports one peg of Judge Teitelbaum's "new" spirit: that in the search for agreement the court should ascertain the legitimate business aims of the contract as supplemented by the "customs and expectations of the particular business community." The preference is for standards rather than reasoning downward from abstract rules in the sky, and agreement in fact rather than some limited concept of promise.

. . .

[Among Speidel's examples are the Restatment (Second)'s encouragement of judicial "gap-filling," its willingness to find liability from the entire context of the parties' dealings, its desire to avoid hardship through forfeiture and unreimbursed reliance and its excuse of non-material conditions. —ed.]

Again, if a promisor induces but does not bargain for reasonable reliance that does not benefit that promisor, there are compelling reasons for imposing liability on that promisor. Reliance in the Restatement (Second) has emerged as the basis for an expanded theory of contract liability. Existing in addition to the bargain contract, it reflects the most significant single expansion of promissory liability in the last fifty years. The scope of protection may be limited, however, by the power of the court to restrict recovery to the reliance interest when justice requires. Nevertheless, here is expanded protection against the hardship of induced but unreimbursed reliance.

Whether these developments tend toward enforcement or exit is less important than what they symbolize: the recognition that hardship in various garbs provides a justification for the court to police the transaction in the interest of fairness. To this extent, they are generally consistent with the second peg of ALCOA's "new" spirit of contract: "loss avoidance." But these important developments arguably pale before another: the triumph of the duty of good faith in the performance and enforcement of bargains. This duty, expressed as a standard, is imposed regardless

of consent. Its presence alone increases the scope of contract liability by limiting the exercise by one party of what might be called unilateral power. In short, it further reduces the range of "freedom from" contract. If, then, the "old" spirit of contract heralded the virtues, economic or otherwise, of "freedom from," the triumph of increased enforcement implicit in the duty of good faith signals an important new mix in the two concepts of liberty.

III. The Duty To Modify

It is now time to return to ALCOA. The basic problem was not new. ALCOA claimed that the occurrence of events not anticipated at the time of contracting as likely to occur had made performance of the long-term contract impracticable. The court agreed and held that ALCOA was entitled to "some relief." In moves quite consistent with the neo-classical model, the court employed standards to assist in determining risk allocation and "gap" filling and was responsive to the hardship that ALCOA would suffer if compelled by specific performance to perform the contract under the original price term.

To this extent, the first two pegs of the "new" spirit of contract find firm support in Article 2 of the UCC and in the Restatement (Second). The unprecedented advance was in the remedy selected by the court. The remedy framed to preserve the "essence of the agreement" and to provide "some relief" was equitable reformation rather than discharge. This adjustment approach finds little or no support in the basic sources of neo-classical contract law, including equity jurisprudence.[41] Yet it marks a substantial limitation upon "freedom from," here, the power of one party to refuse without liability to accept a proposed modification whether or not that modification is fair and reasonable.

Viewed from this perspective, the third peg of ALCOA's "new" spirit of contract, "flexible remedies," finds less support in the UCC and Restatement than exists for the first two pegs and, in fact, has been greeted with some hostility by other courts.

It seems to me that ALCOA got the remedial cart before the good faith horse. In the balance of this Article, I will argue that the court should have first considered whether Essex had a good faith duty to accept any modification proposed by ALCOA. If not,

---

vides flexibility for adjustment and planning and, (3) when disputes arise, focuses as much upon events at the time of the dispute as upon the agreement at the time of contracting.

[41] But see Young, Half Measures, 81 Colum. L. Rev. 19 (1981).

the court's "flexible" remedy is not appropriate. If there was a duty, a court imposed price adjustment, whether through reformation or a conditional specific performance decree,[43] could be appropriate. Phrased another way, the crucial question is whether Essex had any duty to be a "commercial good Samaritan," and this turns on the quality of the *ex post* bargaining.

There are three basic questions in the good faith game: (1) What is the scope of the duty? (2) What is bad faith? and (3) What is the appropriate remedy for bad faith? The present triumph of good faith is found in the pervasive scope of the duty: Section 205 of the Restatement (Second) states that "every contract imposes upon each party a duty of good faith and fair dealing in its performance and its enforcement." This broadly gauged standard focuses attention on particular conduct and circumstances at the time of performance or enforcement rather than at the time of contracting. The unanswered and hotly debated questions are when is the duty violated and what are the remedies? More to the point, did Essex have a good faith duty to accept a modification when and if proposed by ALCOA and, if so, would a bad faith refusal justify the remedy of reformation and a court imposed price adjustment?

A useful start is to search for examples of opportunistic behavior by one party to the exchange which, arguably, amount to bad faith. Of the many possibilities, three examples of bad faith advantage-taking, or the exercise of "self interest with guile,"[44] should suffice.

Example one: *A* agrees to purchase goods or services from *B* for a fixed price. The market price drops, *B* commits a minor breach, and *A*, intending to take advantage of the market shift, rejects the performance and cancels the contract. *A*, by using a minor breach to recapture an opportunity foregone at the time of contracting, has enforced the contract in bad faith. *A*'s cancellation, therefore, is a breach of contract.

Example two: *B* agrees to purchase 60% of *S*'s output for five years at a fixed price. After two years, the market price drops sharply. In response, *S* increases his output by 30% and demands that *B* take and pay for 60% of the increased output at the contract price. The exercise by *S* of its control over output is in bad faith, and *B*, at a minimum, is not required to take more than 60% of some reasonable prior output.

Example three: *A* grants to *B* a distributorship for a stated term, subject to a clause reserving to *A* the power to terminate "at any time without notice." Under the UCC, the Restatement, and most case law, *A* must exercise the termination power in good faith. The termination is in bad faith, and thus a breach of contract, when *B* has not had a reasonable opportunity to capitalize on his investment or *A* is motivated primarily by a desire to recapture *B*'s opportunity rather than honest dissatisfaction with *B*'s performance.[47]

However analyzed, ALCOA is not precisely one of these cases. ALCOA did not seek to take advantage of an opportunity foregone at contracting, because ALCOA did not assume the risk. Further, neither party attempted to exercise discretion, whether in performance or enforcement, expressly reserved to it in the contract. However, the changed circumstances caused extreme economic hardship to ALCOA and produced windfall or unbargained for gains to Essex. Given this combination of hardship to ALCOA and gain to Essex, was it bad faith for Essex to seek specific performance of the contract as originally agreed without accepting a proposed modification which was fair and reasonable under the circumstances? If the answer is yes, then Essex, indeed, has a duty to become a "commercial good Samaritan."[48]

This complex question has parallels in the "duty to rescue" problem in the law of torts. To date, no court has held that there is such a contractual duty, especially where the advantaged party has not caused the peril and the disadvantaged party has, for one reason

[43] On the conditional decree, see Speidel, supra note 1, at 415-419.

[44] Williamson, Transaction Cost Economics: The Governance of Contractual Relations, 22 J. L. & Econ. 233, 234 n.3 (1979). As Professor Goldberg has put it:

[N]ot all people are saints all of the time; as the relationship unfolds there will be opportunities for one party to take advantage of the other's vulnerability, to engage in strategic behavior, or to follow his own interests at the expense of the other party. The actors will, on occasion, behave opportunistically.

Goldberg, Relational Exchange: Economics and Complex Contracts 23 Am. Behavioral Scientist 337 (1980). See generally Muris, Opportunistic Behavior and the Law of Contracts, 65 Minn. L. Rev. 521 (1981).

[47] There is some disagreement over whether the good faith duty regulates the exercise of unconditional termination power. . . .

[48] In ALCOA, the court did not evaluate the parties' efforts to reach an agreed adjustment. After concluding that the parties had failed to agree, the court stated: "Essex was under no duty or pressure to agree to revise the contract." 499 F. Supp. at 81.

or another, assumed the risk. Beyond a narrow band of affirmative responsibilities associated with breach of contract by failure to cooperate,[51] "freedom from" in this area is well preserved.

One justification for this result is a philosophical and moral aversion to the imposition of non-consensual duties in support of a generalized principle of altruism, the effect of which is to restrict liberty and accomplish a redistribution of resources.[52] If altruism is the "new" spirit of contract, then contract, indeed, has become a tort devoted to an egalitarian, collectivist spirit. A more focused justification has recently been advanced by Professor Clayton Gillette.[53] He argues that good faith does not include a duty to be a "commercial good Samaritan" where the economic peril was not created by the obligor and the contract does not create a duty to be concerned by an allocation of risks. His reasons, derived from commercial policy, are that the imposition of a duty here "subjects bargains to inconsistent and uncertain enforcement, and does not produce offsetting benefits in commercial conduct."

Further, he argues that the vagueness of the good faith standard mitigates its independent force and that the lack of certainty in appropriate remedies impairs the predictability which ought to exist in commercial transactions. Although cooperation, generosity and altruism should be encouraged, they should not be required. Presumably, Gillette would conclude in the ALCOA case that Essex had no duty to aid ALCOA by adjustment or otherwise and, similarly, that the court had no power to impose a price adjustment without Essex' consent.

This position, bolstered by philosophical and policy grounds, is the underpinning of the spirit of "freedom from" in classical contract law and libertarian philosophy. But can a case be made for imposing a duty on the advantaged party to accept a "fair and equitable" adjustment proposal made by the disadvantaged party? If so, what remedies are appropri-

ate? Keeping the ALCOA facts in mind, a tentative case can be made that does not convert the law of contracts into a pervasive duty to be altruistic.

First, the disadvantaged party must propose a modification that would be enforceable if accepted by the advantaged party. Under the Restatement (Second), this occurs if the disrupted contract is not "fully performed on either side" and if the modification is "fair and equitable in view of circumstances not anticipated by the parties when the contract was made."[57] The changed circumstances are similar to but less than those required to discharge a contract for impracticability. This first requirement both neutralizes any opportunism by the disadvantaged party, e.g., duress, and affirms that agreed adjustments are preferred—that contract is available to resolve the dilemma and has been employed by the disadvantaged party.

Second, it must be clear that the disadvantaged party did not assume the risk of the unanticipated event by agreement, or under the test stated in the UCC in section 2-615(a), or otherwise. If the disadvantaged party did assume the risk, then the advantaged party has no duty to accept any proposed modification. The risk assumption question is complicated, and the answer will probably not be clear at the time that the adjustment is proposed. Why should the advantaged party be held to reject at his peril? Because it is in this precise situation—where there are substantial unbargained-for gains and losses caused by unanticipated events—that a case for the duty to rescue can be made. In this setting where the risk of changed circumstances has not been allocated to either party, a refusal to adjust by the advantaged party leaves all of the loss on the disadvantaged party and permits the advantaged party to salt away all of the gains. Short of discharging the contract and leaving the parties to restitution, a duty to adjust is necessary to avoid opportunism.

Thus, imposing the duty here is consistent with

---

[51] See U.C.C. § 2-311; Restatement (Second) of Contracts § 205 (1979), comment (d) (bad faith performance includes "interferences with or failure to cooperate in the other party's performance"); Patterson, Constructive Conditions in Contracts 903, 928-42 (1942) (arguing that a duty to cooperate exists when failure to act produces unjust enrichment).

[52] See C. Fried, Contract As Promise: A Theory Of Contractual Obligation 85-91 (1981) (arguing that good faith as honesty is compatible with the "promise principle" but good faith as "loyalty" is not); Kronman, Contract Law and Distributive Justice, 89 Yale L. J. 472 (1980). See also Gordley, Equality in Exchange, 69 Cal. L. Rev. 1587 (1981).

[53] Gillette, Limitations on the Obligation of Good Faith, 1981 Duke L. J. 619.

[57] Restatement (Second) Of Contracts § 89 (1979). See U.C.C. § 2-209 (1) and comment 2, where it states that a modification "needs no consideration to be binding" but that the "extortion of a 'modification' without legitimate commercial reason is ineffective as a violation of the duty of good faith." The extensive literature on this problem focuses exclusively upon the enforceability of an agreed modification rather than the duty, if any, of the advantaged party to negotiate or to agree. See, e.g., Muris, supra note 44, at 532-552; Hillman, A Study of Uniform Commercial Code Methodology: Contract Modification Under Article Two, 59 N.C.L. Rev. 335 (1981). But see Speidel, supra note 1, at 404-419.

emerging notions of good faith performance and AL-COA's second peg in the "new" spirit, loss avoidance. More importantly, it is an imposition with little damage to the requirement of consent in contract law. Since there is a "gap" in the agreement on risk allocation, even that staunch defender of the "promise principle," Professor Charles Fried, argues that the parties have "some obligation to share unexpected benefits and losses in the case of an accident" in the course of a joint enterprise where they are not strangers to each other.[59] This "sharing principle" is derived from a more general principle of altruism and is similar to what has been called the duty of "easy rescue" in the law of torts.

Last, this conclusion is bolstered by what might be the imperatives of an emerging theory of relational contract law. In ALCOA, the parties, at the time of contracting, were unable adequately to deal with certain changed circumstances over the duration of a seventeen-year contract. Yet preserving the contract was important to the parties and to third parties dependent upon its performance but not represented in the litigation. Ian Macneil has argued that in situations such as this there are relational norms that the contract should be preserved and conflict harmonized by adjustment. These norms put a high premium upon developing mechanisms for adjustment over time and good faith efforts to adjust in the light of change.[61] Thus, if in an ALCOA-type case, the court concludes that the disadvantaged party is entitled to "some relief" but not discharge, and the advantaged party has refused to accept a reasonable adjustment in light of risks that the disadvantaged party did not assume, relational theory also supports a court imposed adjustment to preserve the contract, to adjust the price and to avoid the twin devils of unbargained-for hardship and unjust enrichment.[62]

IV. Conclusion

A grudging conclusion in this brief study is that the "new" spirit of contract is a form of tort—a duty of good faith in performance and enforcement of a contract imposed without the parties' consent. This duty, however defined and enforced, is one more limitation upon "freedom from" contract and cannot be

viewed with joy by those who celebrate the virtues of classical contract law. The danger is that any duty imposed upon an advantaged party for the protection of the disadvantaged, whether to avoid opportunism or to promote altruism, will be used to rewrite agreements and to redistribute resources in the name of fairness or equality. Perhaps, then, the doctrine of "commercial good Samaritan" should be rejected for the law of contracts.

On the other hand, I have suggested that (1) sensitivity to hardship, the risk of which has not been allocated, (2) concerns about opportunism or unfair advantage taking, and (3) the emerging imperatives of relational contract theory support a limited imposition without imperiling the delicate balance between "freedom from" and "freedom to." I have argued that when changed circumstances, the risk of which the disadvantaged party did not assume, cause extreme hardship and imperil the relationship, the advantaged party acts in bad faith if he fails to accept a proposed modification that would be enforceable if accepted. This refusal ignores the economic hardship to the disadvantaged party, further imperils a relationship that should be preserved and permits the advantaged party to reap unbargained-for gains. Within these constraints, a bad faith refusal justifies a court imposed price adjustment, whether by reformation or as a conditional decree, on terms that are reasonable in light of the unanticipated events. Finally, I have argued the ALCOA went too far, too fast with the remedy of a court imposed price adjustment. The court should have asked and answered the good faith question discussed above before imposing a price adjustment without the consent of both parties.

Nevertheless, ALCOA is a forefront case in contemporary contract law. Two of the three pegs of its "new" spirit of contract are firmly rooted in the post-realist, neo-classical system of contract. The third peg, flexible remedies, may be a bit ahead of its time, especially when invoked before the potential of good faith is exhausted in the adjustment process. But as a harbinger of a day when the emphasis in commercial litigation is less on issues of liability and more upon appropriate remedies, particularly equitable remedies, ALCOA cannot be ignored.

---

[59] C. Fried, supra note 52, at 72-73. See Coons, Compromise as Precise Justice, 68 Calif. L. Rev. 250 (1980).

[61] For a fuller discussion of Macneil's ideas, see Speidel, supra note 1, at 400-404.

[62] Compare the "risk allocation" clause drafted and defended by Professor John Murray in Murray, Long-Term Supply Contracts: Foreseeing the Unforseeable, Proceedings, Eastern Mineral Law Foundation, Second Annual Institute, 2-28 & 29 (1981).

Robert A. Hillman, *Court Adjustment of Long-Term Contracts: An Analysis Under Modern Contract Law*, (1987) Duke L.J. 1

A manufacturer or utility, contemplating long-term energy needs, enters a twenty-year fuel supply agreement. The buyer and supplier agree on a base price, subject to periodic adjustment based on increased costs of production. The agreement initially is satisfactory to both parties. Then, due to an unanticipated event such as an oil embargo or high inflation, costs dramatically rise and outpace the price-adjustment provision. Because continued performance will result in substantial losses, the supplier proposes an adjustment of the price formula. The buyer refuses to adjust and the supplier, preferring the uncertain results of litigation to certain continuing losses, repudiates the agreement. The buyer then seeks specific performance.[1]

A court may respond in a variety of ways to the problem posed by these facts. It can hold the supplier to the contract by granting the buyer specific performance or damages. Conversely, under the impracticability doctrine, the court can excuse the supplier from performing. Or, it can grant relief based on a party's restitution or reliance interest. In the alternative, the court can try to induce a settlement, for example, by deferring any holding and ordering the parties to bargain further. Finally, the court can adjust the contract, such as by modifying the terms of the agreement and conditioning specific performance on acceptance of the changes. Courts typically have followed the first approach, barring any relief to the supplier.[4] The last approach, court adjustment, has enjoyed little judicial acceptance.[5]

Opposition to court adjustment is typically founded on one or more of the following concerns. First, the supplier promised to perform a carefully planned agreement, and, therefore, assumed the risk of the onerous circumstances. By adjusting the parties' well-planned agreement, courts would threaten freedom of contract, produce uncertainty, and deter planning. Second, even if the supplier were entitled to some relief, courts lack sufficient information and expertise to determine precisely when adjustment is appropriate.[7] Again, the present approach—either the supplier is excused or it must perform or pay damages—has the virtue of certainty. Additional categories would only confuse. Third, in long-term contract settings, courts have insufficient guidance on the appropriate terms of an adjustment, and, in any event, judges are personally ill-equipped to adjust complex commercial contracts. The results would be haphazard, and, again, would deter planning. Fourth, court adjustment would be bad policy, for example, because it would increase the costs of contracting by causing parties to draft around the rule of adjustment, thus deterring some parties from entering long-term arrangements.

In this article, I analyze when, if ever, court adjustment is appropriate. I argue that the supplier is entitled to some form of relief in at least some situations, that these situations can be identified with sufficient precision, that courts have adequate tools to shape appropriate relief, and that court adjustment is good policy in limited, but distinct, circumstances.[12]

---

[1] Or, before the buyer brings an action, the supplier might bring an action seeking reformation of the contract or a finding of impracticability. The hypothetical is based loosely on Missouri Pub. Serv. Co. v. Peabody Coal Co., 583 S.W.2d 721 (Mo. Ct. App.), cert. denied, 444 U.S. 865 (1979).

[4] See Speidel, Court-Imposed Price Adjustments Under Long-Term Supply Contracts, 76 NW U. L. Rev. 369, 376 (1981); see also Bernina Distribs., Inc. v. Bernina Sewing Mach. Co., 646 F.2d 434, 439-40 (10th Cir. 1981) (cost increases alone do not render contract impracticable; court will order specific performance).

[5] Only one court has adjusted a long-term contract in a situation similar to the one described in the opening problem. See Aluminum Co. of Am. (Alcoa) v. Essex Group, Inc., 499 F. Supp. 53 (W.D. Pa. 1980). . . .

Although court adjustment is relatively novel in our legal system, it is common in others. See, e.g., Dawson, Judicial Revision of Frustrated Contracts: Germany, 63 B.U.L. Rev. 1039 (1983).

[7] See Dawson, Judicial Revision of Frustrated Contracts: The United States, 64 B.U.L. Rev. 1, 31 (1984).

[12] Others have written about the problem of court adjustment. The leading article in support of court adjustment is Speidel, supra note 4. This article differs from Professor Speidel's excellent work in three ways. First, I develop an agreement model which justifies court adjustment (hence I refer to court adjustment rather than court-imposed adjustment), whereas Professor Speidel relied on a gap model almost exclusively. Second, I respond to criticism of court adjustment generated by Professor Speidel's thoughtful piece. For articles critical of adjustment, see Dawson, supra note 7, and Gillette, Commercial Rationality and the Duty to Adjust Long-Term Contracts, 69 Minn. L. Rev. 521 (1985). Third, I analyze more fully the kinds of relief appropriate in court adjustment.

In Part I, I identify two situations in which court adjustment is appropriate. The first situation calling for adjustment, the "agreement model," occurs when the supplier reasonably expects the buyer to adjust in case of a serious disruption. The buyer's failure to adjust is a breach of contract. The agreement model accounts for the "relational" realities of many contract settings through a theory of the parties' implicit risk allocation. The second situation calling for adjustment, the "gap model," occurs when the supplier has no reasonable expectation of adjustment, but the parties simply fail to allocate the risk of some calamitous event. The supplier will suffer substantial harm from continued performance, but the buyer has materially relied on that performance. The gap model is based primarily on the fairness principle that the parties should agree to share unallocated losses.

In Part II, I argue that when a court identifies a situation ripe for court adjustment, that remedy should not be abandoned on impracticality or policy grounds. I therefore discuss possible approaches to court adjustment and respond to the criticisms outlined above. Because a remedy should be as certain and simple as possible, I conclude that in many situations court adjustment should be limited to adjustment of the duration of the agreement. Using the contract-law response to the problem of terminable-at-will franchise agreements as a model, I suggest that supply contracts should continue only for a period sufficient to enable the buyer to recoup its reliance expenses.

I. Recognition Of A Duty To Adjust

A. *The Agreement Model.*

Because most contracting parties are aware that conditions may change during the course of their agreement and that allocating all risks is impossible, too costly, or unnecessary,[17] many long-term contracts expressly require adjustment of terms in light of changed circumstances. For example, some coal contracts include a "gross inequities adjustment provision," which requires the parties to negotiate in good faith to resolve "inequities" resulting from eco-

nomic conditions that the parties did not contemplate at the time they made their agreement.[18] Alternatively, the parties may expressly agree that the price or other provision is merely a projection and is subject to further negotiation. In either case, when the supplier seeks negotiation under the flexibility-preserving term, the supplier is attempting to perform the contract, not avoid it. The buyer's refusal to bargain would be a breach.

Even if the supply contract contains no express agreement to adjust, the circumstances existing at the time of contracting may demonstrate that the parties intended such a duty. Consider the following typical backdrop to long-term contracting. The parties enjoy relatively equal bargaining strength, are familiar with each other, and have previously dealt with each other. The subject matter of the contract, although not involving a standardized commodity, is also not unusual (for example, the sale of coal). The parties are therefore comfortable with little formality. In addition, the parties want to continue to deal with each other because they are aware of the costs of finding a market substitute after investing in a relationship and after forming understandings that lower the cost of doing business. In short, the parties want to continue a profitable relationship and maintain their goodwill and reputation in their industry.

Such parties to long-term contracts also are interested in ensuring a supply or a market at a reasonable price, not in making wagers about market shifts. Although they expect disruptions during the course of the agreement, the parties do not attempt to plan for nebulous risks, and they may even fail to allocate some foreseeable but remote risks because allocation costs too much; or may rock the boat. Put another way, both parties can increase mutual gains from the contract by remaining flexible after signing the contract, thereby saving costs related to planning for risks and bickering after contract breakdown.

With these relational realities explicit, the issue is whether the agreement, although silent on the duty to adjust in exigent circumstances, includes such a duty. In some situations, the answer is "yes."[30] First,

---

[17] On the limits of planning, see Macaulay, The Use and Non-Use of Contract in the Manufacturing Industry, Prac. Law., Nov. 1963, at 13, 17-18.

[18] These provisions are common in long-term contracts. See Goldberg, Price Adjustment in Long-Term Contracts, 1985 Wis. L. Rev. 527, 529 n.5; Joskow, Vertical Integration and Long-Term Contracts: The Case of Coal-Burning Electric Generating Plants, 1 J. L. Econ. & Organization 33, 73 (1985). In coal contracts a "market reopener" provision is also common. Such a provision typically allows either party

to notify the other that the contract price is inconsistent with the market price. After notice, the parties must negotiate in good faith for an adjustment or, failing to agree, go to arbitration. Scott, Coal Supply Agreements, 23 Rocky Mtn. Min. L. Inst. 107, 131-32 (1977).

[30] See Goetz & Scott, The Limits of Expanded Choice: An Analysis of the Interactions Between Express and Implied Contract Terms, 73 Calif. L. Rev. 261, 277 n.47 (1985) ("[U]nofficial or other context-generated understandings might be legally enforceable, implied terms").

the circumstances may support a finding of a trade custom of adjustment, or previous adjustments between the buyer and the supplier may constitute a course of dealing or a course of performance. The Uniform Commercial Code encourages resort to such evidence in interpreting the parties' agreement on the theory that, unless excluded, the parties intended to incorporate the trade custom, course of dealing, or course of performance.[34] Thus, although silent on adjustment, an agreement may require it. Again, a refusal to adjust would be a breach.

Apart from any duty based on trade custom, course of dealing or course of performance, a party may have a good-faith duty to adjust. In problems of performance, good faith requires "cooperation on the part of one party to the contract so that another party will not be deprived of his reasonable expectations."[37] In our example, then, performance by the buyer contrary to the supplier's reasonable expectations is in bad faith. The supplier's argument is that, as a result of the circumstances at or after the time of contracting, each party reasonably expected the other to act consistently with its interests by being flexible and cooperating to preserve the relationship when serious trouble arose.

Adjustment often may be precisely what the parties expect. The best way to maintain an informal, harmonious relationship, preserve goodwill and reputation, and protect one's investment is to remain flexible and avoid disputes and litigation. Indeed, disagreements in longterm settings are most often settled without pursuing legal remedies. Contracting parties view their obligations as growing not only out of the contract, but also out of the norms of their relationship such as cooperation and compromise. As Karl Llewellyn long ago pointed out, the written contract is only a "rough indication around which [real working] relations vary." For example, when confronted with large cost increases, one coal supplier recently requested relief from more than forty utilities. Only two utilities balked, and the contract of one of those that refused had less than a year to run.

Obviously, not every contract raises a duty to adjust if something goes awry. If the scenario is not what I have described—for example, if the agreement is a large one-time deal involving a standardized commodity—a reasonable party might not expect the other to adjust. . . .

. . .

A duty to adjust, therefore, can override express contract terms such as fixed-price terms or even price-adjustment formulas, provided that the parties reasonably expect those terms to yield to the implied duty. The amount of bargaining over a particular express provision and the parties' purpose in including the provision are obviously critical in determining whether adjustment trumps an express provision. . . .

. . .

Although it fails to discuss the adjustment duty, *Aluminum Co. of America (Alcoa) v. Essex Group, Inc.*[55] is an example of a case in which a price formula apparently failed to achieve the parties' goal of limiting their risks. The parties agreed to refer to the Wholesale Price Index-Industrial Commodities (WPI) to adjust the nonlabor production costs borne by Alcoa in converting alumina to aluminum for Essex. The price formula included a ceiling on how much Essex would be required to pay, but no floor. The WPI failed to reflect unanticipated cost increases due to oil price inflation and pollution control, causing Alcoa a projected loss of over sixty million dollars for the remainder of the contract. Alcoa argued that the WPI did not work as the parties intended and that relief was appropriate.

The district court agreed. In its view, the issue was whether the parties intended the WPI to apply regardless of the circumstances, or whether they intended the index to apply only within a range of potential cost fluctuations, with additional adjustments to be made through further bargaining when the range was exceeded. Weighing all the circumstances, the court found that the parties intended the latter. . . .

A foreseeability test may help in determining

---

[34] The UCC focuses on the parties' bargain in fact, as found in the written agreement and in course of dealing, usage of trade, or course of performance. Id. § 1-201(3). See also Nanakuli Paving & Rock Co. v. Shell Oil Co., 664 F.2d 772, 796-805 (9th Cir. 1981) (collecting cases); American Mach. & Tool Co. v. Strite-Anderson Mfg. Co., 353 N.W.2d 592, 598 (Minn. Ct. App. 1984); Campbell v. Hostetter Farms, Inc., 251 Pa. Super. 232, 237-39, 380 A.2d 463, 466 (1977). See generally Kirst, Usage of Trade and Course of Dealing: Subversion of the UCC Theory, 1977 U. Ill. L.F. 811.

Reliance on trade custom and the like to determine the parties' intentions is by no means novel—it is part of a "new spirit of contract." See Speidel, The New Spirit of Contract, 2 J. L. & Com. 193, 199-200 (1982).

[37] Farnsworth, Good Faith Performance and Commercial Reasonableness Under the Uniform Commercial Code, 30 U. Chi. L. Rev. 666, 669 (1963).

[55] 499 F. Supp. 53 (W.D. Pa. 1980).

whether a duty to adjust arises, For example, we can assume that parties to a long-term contract intend that any detailed price-adjustment formula apply to readily foreseeable circumstances—after all, why else draft such a provision? Suppose, however, that the supply contract contains a fixed-price term. Some courts assume that absent an express allocation of risk, the parties must have intended to assign all foreseeable risks to the supplier.[64] As we have seen, however, the parties may have failed to allocate even foreseeable risks; the parties may have decided that a carefully negotiated allocation of risks would not suit their interests. They may, for example, have thought that such a contract would be insufficiently flexible or would sour a prosperous relationship. The parties also may have determined that further negotiation about risk allocation would not be cost-effective. Supporting these determinations may be the expectation that if the risk comes to pass, the parties will cooperate to deal with it. In a fixed-price contract, then, there is no persuasive reason why even foreseeable risks must fall automatically on a party rather than trigger an adjustment duty.[68] In fact, these arguments concerning the fallibility of the foreseeability test suggest that even a price-adjustment formula may not be designed to allocate some foreseeable but remote and harmful risks.

Assuming that an implied agreement to adjust exists in some circumstances, we still must determine what magnitude of disruption would trigger the duty. As in most areas of the law (including the current approach to the impracticability doctrine), no precise line can be drawn. Still, some guidance is possible. Generally, the greater the disruption, the greater the likelihood that a duty to adjust will arise. For example, express provisions calling for an adjustment often require "gross inequities." In such situations, the parties would view performance of the contract without an adjustment as ultimately detrimental to both sides. Obviously, in many cases it will not serve the buyer's interests if the supplier is driven out of business or to bankruptcy and therefore cannot continue

to supply the buyer. The implied adjustment duty should be no less stringent. In fact, the potential harm to a party must approximate that of a party who historically has been excused from performance under the impracticability doctrine.[70] . . .

The argument under the agreement model in favor of a good-faith duty to adjust in certain circumstances is thus based on the realities of business expectations. As such, the argument is vulnerable to the criticism that contract law should not necessarily reflect the "morals of the marketplace." Certainly, patently unfair practices, such as a merchant's unconscionable behavior toward a consumer in adhesion contract situations, should be regulated. When, however, the parties' practices consist not of advantage-taking, but of sharing and cooperation, and both parties intended to incorporate such practices, enforcing the accepted mores should be encouraged.

. . .

B. *The "Gap" Model.*

The principal justification for an adjustment duty under the agreement model derives from the principle of freedom of contract. There is often a fine line, however, between enforcing the parties' intentions and judicial gap filling, especially when those intentions are gleaned from the circumstances rather than an express agreement. An independent justification exists, however, for an adjustment duty in some cases in which the evidence is insufficient to find an express or implied agreement to adjust. The duty is based on the desirability of requiring the parties to share unallocated losses.

The realities of planning suggest that a particular risk, such as an oil embargo or runaway inflation, may be unallocated. If parties explicitly or implicitly agree not to deal with such a problem because it is too remote, too costly to provide for, or too likely to upset the deal, there is little reason based on the agreement for placing the risk solely on either party. Although contracts are entered for the purpose of ensuring performance in an unpredictable future, rea-

[64] See, e.g., Raner v. Goldberg, 244 N.Y. 438, 441, 155 N.E. 733, 734 (1927); see also Hillman, An Analysis of the Cessation of Contractual Relations, 68 Cornell L. Rev. 617, 625 (1983).

[68] See Hillman, supra note 64, at 625. Courts applying the foreseeability test must also determine whether a contingency was foreseeable. All commercial contingencies may be foreseeable to some extent; a more realistic question is how foreseeable was the occurrence. See Aluminum Co. of Am. (Alcoa) v. Essex Group, Inc., 499 F. Supp. 53, 70 (W.D. Pa. 1980) (the "proper question" is whether the parties be-

lieved an outcome was "highly unlikely".) The greater the foreseeability, the more likely the parties' price provision was intended to take care of the contingency. Because determining the extent of foreseeability requires difficult line drawing, one suspects that other factors often control the foreseeability determination. For example, a court may find that calamitous cost increases due to an oil boycott were unforeseeable, while less drastic increases were foreseeable. See Hillman, supra note 64, at 625.

[70] Typically courts require close to a 100% increase in costs. See Hillman, supra note 64, at 652 nn.219-20.

sonable parties often do not expect a promisor to act as an insurer by performing regardless of calamitous circumstances. This is true even in contracts containing price-adjustment features, if these features are designed to deal only with a certain magnitude and species of risk.

. . .

[Professor Hillman discusses a hypothetical contract between a utility and a supplier whose costs increase by more than 100%. —ed.] The traditional approach to this problem is all or nothing: either the supplier is excused or the utility is entitled to performance under the contract. Courts rarely favor the supplier in such cases. Instead, they retreat to a "finding" that the supplier promised to perform and therefore assumed the risk of even an oil embargo.[85] In reality, confronted with the adage that courts should not make contracts for the parties and with remedial inflexibility in the face of strong interests on both sides, the court may simply opt for a facile solution.[86]

Does the all-or-nothing approach make sense? In a gap situation, where the parties' agreement does not justify a refusal to adjust and where both parties have strong contradictory interests, it would be better to recognize a duty to adjust and enforce the duty through appropriate remedies. First, an adjustment duty is even-handed. Both parties have significant interests worthy of protection in a situation in which there is little reason to favor either one completely.[87] An adjustment duty also avoids unexpected gain by one party at the cost of catastrophe for the other, when neither is earned. Moreover, an adjustment duty helps both parties ultimately to benefit from their contract. Finally, in an atmosphere of flexibility and cooperation, an adjustment duty may reflect what the parties would have agreed to at the time of contracting had they addressed the problem of changed circumstances.

II. Court Adjustment

Assuming the court finds a duty to adjust and the parties have failed to adjust, the question of fashioning an appropriate remedy confronts the court. When the buyer's bad faith is the cause of the failure to adjust, one approach would be to find that adjustment is an implied condition precedent to the supplier's performance and to excuse the supplier. Modeled after the general contract law approach to breaches of contract, this response would be appropriate whenever the buyer's particularly unreasonable response to the exigent circumstances casts doubt on the buyer's future satisfactory performance. Because determining whether the buyer is acting in bad faith will often be very difficult—requiring the court to weigh adjustment offers and other potentially ambiguous conduct of the parties—and because cessation is typically onerous and wasteful, the court should rarely excuse the supplier.

A less severe approach would be to order the parties to engage in good faith bargaining, mediation, or other dispute resolution techniques. Such an order may prompt the parties to reach some reasonable agreement. If the parties still do not reach agreement, or if the court believes such an approach would be fruitless, a third approach would be for the court itself to adjust the contract.

I do not dispute the proposition that a court is far from ideally suited to adjust long-term contracts. Litigation costs time and money and a judge can rarely make a better contract for the parties than they could make for themselves.[96] This does not mean, however, that courts should not be allowed to adjust long-term contracts of parties who cannot privately resolve their dispute. Rather, the shortcomings of court adjustment only serve to emphasize that courts should be creative in encouraging the parties to settle. The discussion in this section, however, assumes the court has failed to induce private settlement. In short, we now confront the hard question: Is court adjustment ever appropriate when the parties cannot reach agreement themselves?

A. *Judicial Standards for Adjusting Long-Term Contracts.*

Professor Dawson opposed court adjustment of

---

[85] But see Trakman, Winner Take Some: Loss Sharing and Commerical Impracticability, 69 Minn. L. Rev. 471, 486-87 (1985) (courts have recognized that risk of change in conditions should not always be allocated to the promisor).

[86] One critic aptly observed: "Dominated by our all-or-nothing notions of recovery, we have almost totally ignored what would appear in many situations to be the eminently sensible split-the-loss solution." Mueller, Contract Remedies: Business Fact and Legal Fantasy, 1967 Wis. L. Rev. 833, 837.

[87] See Hillman, supra note 64, at 629-34, 650-55; Speidel, supra note 4, at 406. See generally Coons, Approaches to Court Imposed Compromise—The Uses of Doubt and Reason, 58 Nw. U.L. Rev. 750 (1964) (discussing the prospect and appropriate limitations on the imposition of settlement on parties).

[96] Dawson, supra note 7, at 36. But Professor Dawson conceded that parties are unlikely to adjust voluntarily after initial breakdown. Id. at 29-30 (German experience indicated that many parties lacked incentive to renegotiate in inflationary period).

long-term contracts because he believed that courts lack sufficient standards to reshape the contract to reflect what the parties should have agreed to ex post or what they would have agreed to ex ante. In the absence of standards, the argument goes, a court enjoys unbounded discretion to create a new contract for the parties.

Even Professor Dawson conceded that court adjustment may be appropriate when the court does no more than extend party-agreed standards found in their contract. . . .

Although party-agreed standards in long-term contracts often offer only an imperfect guide to expectations—after all, the parties typically expect flexibility and cooperation and may have had no expectations at all with respect to the current circumstances—the situation is far from hopeless. The goal of court adjustment is to preserve the parties' purposes and to avoid unbargained-for gains by one party or losses by the other. In situations ripe for adjustment, the supplier sought an assured market and cost coverage and the buyer sought an assured supply at a reasonable price. The parties did not intend to permit the supplier to raise prices without a corresponding increase in its costs. Similarly, the parties did not intend to permit the buyer to take advantage of an exigent market situation by raising its own prices to third parties (such as a utility increasing its rates or spot selling on the market), while at the same time insisting on the supplier's performance at preinflation prices.

Within these broad parameters, more concrete guidance may be available to help a court adjust the contract. For example, a court could refer to other similar supply contracts formulated or adjusted under current conditions by the supplier or other contracting parties to determine an appropriate pricing formula. Such models should not be difficult to find. For example, all but two utilities agreed to adjust when a coal supplier recently requested relief from over forty utilities. A court also has the benefit of any party documents or statements concerning the purpose of cost-adjustment features in the contract. For example, if the adjustment provision was intended to ensure coverage of the supplier's costs plus a certain profit, a court could adjust the contract to ensure such a result. A court could also apportion allocated

and unallocated risks. If an oil embargo and safety regulations both cause a cost increase but the parties allocated the latter risk to the supplier, the adjustment should reflect only the former cause of the increase. Finally, a court could refer to any settlement offers made by the parties.[110]

Instead of focusing on the parties' expectations, a court could employ a restitutionary theory and base adjustment on the buyer's windfall. Of course, the court must consider the parties' contract expectations when deciding which gains are a windfall to the buyer. In some situations this may not be too difficult. For example, in *Alcoa*, the parties did not contemplate that Essex would spot-sell aluminum on the market. When Alcoa's costs increased, however, and the market price of aluminum dramatically rose, Essex began to do just that. Arguably, all of Essex's gain from such conduct was unjust enrichment. The problem with a restitutionary approach, however, is that it would be difficult to adjust the contract to account not only for the realized unjust gain, but also for the future market fluctuations and other uncertainties that may favor the supplier.

A less ambitious approach would be to base adjustment on a reliance theory modeled after the judicial response to the problem of terminable-at-will franchise agreements. Some courts have held that terminating a franchise agreement of indefinite duration is wrongful if the franchisee has not had reasonable time to recoup its investment. Although the franchisee's remedy is often limited to damages, some courts enjoin such wrongful terminations. Similarly, a court could enjoin a supplier from ceasing a long-term supply contract until the buyer had reasonable time to recoup its reasonable reliance expenses. Court adjustment would be limited to the contract's duration term.

. . .

Like the expectation and restitutionary approaches to the problem of adjustment, recoupment challenges the courts. Still, recoupment simplifies the problem. It requires no new pricing formula that may fail to reflect unanticipated future changes of conditions over a potentially long period of time. Instead, recoupment alleviates the harshness to the buyer of immediate termination, while it simultaneously acknowledges the supplier's legitimate interests in ces-

[110] For example, in Missouri Pub. Serv. Co. v. Peabody Coal Co., 583 S.W.2d 721 (Mo. Ct. App.), cert. denied, 444 U.S. 865 (1979), the coal supplier proposed a coal price of $10.60 per ton and new price adjustment features including a gross inequity clause at a time that coal was selling for $17.00 on the market and the buyer was paying $7.83 per ton under the contract. The buyer countered with an offer of an increase of $1.00 per ton. Brief for Peabody Coal Co.

sation of the contract.

Alternatively, a court could base adjustment on re-coupment, but instead of ordering specific perform-ance of the contract for a limited duration, the court could calculate a payment by the supplier necessary to "buy-out" the contract. . . . This approach would require the court to calculate a precise money figure. For this reason, it is less attractive than limiting the contract duration; the latter approach allows the court to "hedge" with respect to the ultimate matter of dollars and cents.

B. *Judicial Competence to Adjust Long-Term Contracts.*

Some commentators argue that adjusting long-term contracts, which requires determining whether risks were allocated, understanding and applying complex accounting data, and foreseeing the future, is simply too complex for judges. These commenta-tors believe that judges lack both the parties' exper-tise concerning the subject matter and prior training or experience in creating contract terms.[123] The ar-gument is not overly persuasive. The problem of com-plex cases is not unique to the performance of long-term contracts. Consider, for example, the substantive and remedial complexities of securities, patent, and antitrust cases. The judicial incompe-tence argument casts doubt on our entire judicial sys-tem. Furthermore, the argument erroneously im-pugns all judicial adjustment, and overlooks the practicality of a modest adjustment such as specific performance for a limited duration or a cash buy-out designed to recoup the buyer's reliance expense.

Doubtful also is whether alternative dispute reso-lution forums (or, in extreme cases, the legislature) would be superior to judicial adjustment. Alternative dispute resolvers such as arbitrators or neutral third parties are not inherently better qualified to resolve adjustment problems. Nor is the problem suited for a legislative solution. In precisely such a problem as this, flexible approaches are needed, approaches that are geared to the particular facts and to the parties' idiosyncratic interests.

. . .

C. *Judicial Adjustment as a Restriction of the Par-ties' Autonomy.*

Critics also argue that court adjustment restricts the parties' autonomy and, in effect, remakes the contract for the parties.[131] But assume that a court can approximate the adjustment the parties should have made. Under the agreement model, the parties reasonably expect adjustment; court adjustment is therefore a form of specific performance that sup-ports, rather than defeats, the parties' expectations.

Similarly, court adjustment under the gap model does not impinge on the parties' freedom because the parties have created no law to govern their rights and duties. A buyer could, of course, enter a contract in which the supplier expressly insures performance re-gardless of the circumstances. Or the supplier could expressly provide for release from the contract under onerous circumstances (for example, when costs are equal to or greater than the contract price). In such cases, ignoring the contract allocation of risk would impinge on freedom of contract. But if such an agree-ment was not made, neither party is contractually en-titled to any particular resolution of the problem when an unallocated risk arises. Nevertheless, be-cause the parties are joined in an enterprise that en-courages reliance and creates expectations, neither party should have the unilateral right to insist on per-formance or to walk away from the deal. Of course, the parties are free after contract breakdown to agree on a new approach to govern their affairs. The parties' failure to set their own agenda at that time or at the time of initial contracting constitutes im-plicit consent to the court's intervention to adjust the agreement for them.[135]

Although classical contract law typically decides cases involving assertions of impracticability in an all-or-nothing fashion, it does not follow that a sup-plier or buyer in a true gap situation has the right to such a determination. Because of informal planning or loose drafting and because of the lack of clarity of contract rules on the subject (When is a risk foresee-able? When is performance impractical?), most true gap cases do not fit neatly on one side of the imprac-ticability line. In fact, one suspects that in gap cases

---

[123] See, e.g., Dawson, supra note 7, at 17-18.

[131] See Dawson, supra note 7, at 18 ("If the contract that was previously in force has through frustration ceased to exist, how can the parties to it be compelled to accept a 'contract' that is manufactured by a court to replace it?")

[135] In Goetz & Scott, supra note 30, at 317, the authors refer to "indeterminate formulations" in relational con-tracts, which "implicitly instruct the dispute-resolver to con-strue the contract equitably."

the issue of whether a supplier has a "right" to cease performing or the buyer a "right" to specific performance turns on the court's determination of whether the supplier would be hurt badly enough by performance. To argue that the supplier or buyer has a "right" to a release or to performance, then, hinges upon a largely unsupportable belief in the clarity of contract rules in the true gap setting.

A related argument against court adjustment is that it forces parties to perform in an unhappy marriage that would be better terminated. Parties in litigation have demonstrated their inability to perform without a costly breakdown, the argument goes, and it is therefore unlikely that they would do better in the future even under a more equitable arrangement. Limiting adjustment to the duration term reflects this concern and minimizes this problem. But if a court does opt to adjust the price, thus removing an inequity in the agreement, perhaps the parties will do better. In addition, the buyer need not be forced to perform under the adjusted regime. The court could grant the buyer specific performance, conditioned on the buyer's acceptance of the adjustment.[138] Thus the buyer would have the choice to either end the deal or accept performance of the adjusted contract. The supplier should not be heard to complain if the buyer chooses specific performance because the adjustment would largely obviate the supplier's reasons for seeking a release in the first place.

Ultimately, the criticism that court adjustment is an impermissible interference into the parties' freedom of contract fails to recognize that courts under current doctrine often "make" contracts for the parties. The UCC, for example, sets forth statutory gap-fillers, instructs the courts to carve up unconscionable contracts, and authorizes orders of specific performance under terms the court views as "just." In fact, a UCC comment authorizes precisely the approach suggested in this article.[142] In addition, courts, using their equity powers, have a tradition of

adjusting contracts. For example, courts have long whittled away at covenants not to compete, adjusting the duration, area, and substance of such promises.

D. Is Court Adjustment Bad Policy?

Is court adjustment an unsound approach on policy grounds? For example, will it increase the cost of contracting (i.e., will it be inefficient)? Will it promote disputes? Will it decrease the number of settlements of disputes prior to or during litigation? Will it promote unfairness?

It is unlikely that the world is going to change very much from the limited recognition of an adjustment duty and from some remedial flexibility in the face of a party's unwillingness to adjust when the duty arises. First, the change of approach is modest. The duty to adjust would arise in few cases, and the remedy need not be dramatic. In addition, in circumstances in which such a duty may arise, the parties could easily avoid it by clear contract drafting.

Second, parties to long-term contracts frequently pay little attention to contract rules. Instead, extralegal factors such as the need to preserve the relationship or avoid the costs and delays of litigation control the parties' conduct. It is therefore unlikely that any adjustment rule will have much effect on future behavior of the parties. They simply will continue doing what they have been doing.

Third, to the extent that a modest adjustment regime has any effect on the cost of contracting, that effect arguably will be salutary. The now familiar efficiency argument maintains that the "superior risk bearer" should suffer an unallocated loss, because the parties would have placed the loss on that party had they allocated it. Because it reflects what the parties would have done, such an approach saves transaction costs—future parties will not have to negotiate and draft around a different rule—and therefore promotes allocative efficiency.[151]. . .

This efficiency theory does not apply to the agreement model because there is no gap to fill. Based on

[138] See Dawson, supra note 7, at 32-33 (conditional decree is an "expedient with old and respectable credentials"); Speidel, supra note 4, at 417 (conditional grant of specific performance is the "most direct and least offensive" approach); see also Wooster Republican Printing Co. v. Channel 17, Inc., 533 F. Supp. 601, 621-22 (W.D. Mo. 1981) (ordering specific performance where performance was not impossible and buyer was willing to accept less than full performance), aff'd, 682 F.2d 165 (8th Cir. 1982); Humble Oil & Ref. Co. v. DeLoache, 297 F. Supp. 647, 656 (D.S.C. 1969) (granting specific performance where plaintiff agreed to re-

form of lease option); U.C.C. § 2-716(2) (1977) ("The decree for specific performance may include such terms and conditions . . . as the court may deem "just.")

[142] Id. § 2-615 comment 6 ("In situations in which neither sense nor justice is served by either answer when the issue is posed in flat terms of 'excuse' or 'no excuse,' adjustment under the various provisions of this Article is necessary . . . .")

[151] See, e.g., Posner & Rosenfield, Impossibility and Related Doctrines in Contract Law: An Economic Analysis, 6 J. Legal Stud. 83, 97-108 (1977).

the parties' intentions, the agreement includes an implied adjustment duty. Under the gap model, the contract does not allocate the risk of the unforeseen event and does not contain an adjustment duty. The circumstances suggest, however, that the parties would have included an adjustment duty if they had dealt with the problem at the formation stage. They would not have placed all the risk on one party. Parties will therefore incur costs contracting around the harsh "superior risk bearer" rule, which may deter some parties from entering contracts. Moreover, in light of the high termination costs involved, we can assume that the parties would select a remedy that would preserve the deal—not ensure its demise. Thus a rule recognizing a potential adjustment duty and, ultimately, even the possibility of court adjustment, may be more efficient and supportive of long-term contracting.[155]

Determining the precise effect that court adjustment will have on the parties' performance would require substantial empirical investigation; such investigation might tell us what approach to adjustment, if any, helps to avoid disputes and leads to more and fairer party settlements of disputes when they do occur. For now, I offer some preliminary observations.

When contract rules clearly define the parties' obligations, the parties may be less likely to "test" the rules in adverse circumstances. Clear rules may thus facilitate performance and help avoid disputes. Similarly, when a dispute does arise, clear rules that enable the parties to determine their settling prices inexpensively may promote settlement. . . .

. . .

Despite the long odds against winning a complete release from any duty to perform, the existing all-or-nothing approach of impracticability may actually encourage suppliers to cease performance and refuse settlement. The hope for a complete release may explain, for example, why the dispute between Westinghouse Electric and operators of forty-nine nuclear power plants concerning Westinghouse's agreement to supply uranium to the plants was not settled prior to a court decision. Westinghouse had agreed to supply uranium to the plants at up to twelve dollars a pound, but the market price then rose sharply to over forty dollars a pound. Westinghouse projected its losses at over two billion dol-

lars. After a decision that Westinghouse was liable for expectation damages, the utility owners of the plants agreed to settle under "extremely lenient terms." Presumably the utilities would have been willing to settle under terms at least as favorable to Westinghouse prior to incurring all of the costs of litigation. This suggests that Westinghouse must have held out, hoping to win a complete release from its duties under the contract.

Although the effect of a limited court adjustment approach on the frequency of party disputes and settlements may be unclear,[164] the quality of settlement is likely to improve. In cases ripe for adjustment, neither party will be able to assert bargaining leverage because each will know that the court is unlikely to decide totally in its favor. This is especially important in the long-term contract setting where the parties typically make significant investments in the contract, where there are few market alternatives and, thus, where the party favored by the existing approach may take advantage of its bargaining leverage to extract significant concessions.

In conclusion, even if a court adjustment regime marginally increased disputes and marginally decreased settlements, it would not necessarily be undesirable. Avoiding disputes or maximizing the settlement rate ultimately may be less important than implementing a just method of resolving disputes. In short, the benefits of court adjustment in terms of fairness to particular parties may outweigh any costs such as diminished settlement of disputes. In fact, at the margin perhaps a fair resolution of disputes maximizes the benefits to society of long-term contracts by encouraging people to enter into them.

III. Conclusion

I neither argue that court adjustment is always proper, nor that parties cannot contract out of it. Court adjustment, however, is appropriate in some circumstances that are sufficiently identifiable. The "relational" realities of modern-day, long-term contracting suggest that when an unanticipated disruption causes calamitous losses to a party, a duty to adjust may arise. Further, if the court finds a duty to adjust, the court can, in some circumstances and often in modest ways, adjust the contract for the parties. Although these "relational" facts support the

---

[155] See Speidel, supra note 4, at 390-400 (discussing the pros and cons of the efficiency arguments).

[164] At least one judge believes court adjustment can "best maintain the integrity of the long-term contractual relation-

ship" when interparty negotiation fails to lead to a fair outcome. McGinnis v. Cayton, 312 S.E.2d 765, 779 (W. Va. 1984) (Harshbarger, J., concurring).

recognition of an adjustment duty, this does not mean that we must find a radical, new way of looking at contract.[167] We must only pay closer attention to the more accurate factual premises of the relational view as seen in business practice, and we must be willing to show greater courage in fashioning appropriate remedies.

---

[167] "[O]ne can be a soldier in the relational contract army without urging a repudiation of existing doctrine." Kidwell, A Caveat, 1985 Wis. L. Rev. 615, 621-22.

John P. Dawson, *Judicial Revision of Frustrated Contracts: The United States*, 64 B.U.L. Rev. 1 (1984)

One of the significant changes in the law of contract in recent decades has been the expansion of unforeseen change of conditions as a ground for discharge of contract obligations. More recently several authors have proposed to go one step further by ordering, instead of discharge, a revision to be accomplished by court order after the court had found that its intervention in some form was needed. The argument usually advanced to explain this result is that discharge, if it were granted, would be on the ground that an event had occurred for which the parties themselves could not have provided, for by hypothesis they had not foreseen it. From this premise the conclusion is drawn that a court should intervene to fill what is thus found to be an unintended gap and do for the parties what they, with good reason, could not do for themselves. If this argument comes to be more widely accepted our judges have the prospect of acquiring some new tasks of considerable difficulty and magnitude, though first they will need to find somewhere a higher source that had conferred these powers on them.

An earlier article in this Review described the experience of Germany with court-ordered revision of contracts where the intended balance or purpose had been destroyed by unexpected events.[1] My aim was to show how extensive powers to rewrite such contracts were assumed by German courts, using doctrines that were not to be found in the German Civil Code but were created by the courts themselves. They were formulated in terms that closely resembled the doctrines now used by our own courts. The German judiciary, highly conservative by training and conviction, ventured onto this unmapped terrain with hesitation and reluctance, only when the pressures to do so became severe. The pressures were generated by a nation-wide economic disaster, an inflation of the national currency, the mark, that escaped all control and ended in effect with its repudiation. After a new and stable currency had been established the legislature set about the task of restoring to creditors some part of the wealth that their government had destroyed through meeting its own imperative needs by resort to the printing press. The claims of these creditors lay heavily on the nation's conscience, as Germany's high court had itself declared. For standard types of money debt expressed in familiar, stereotyped forms, formulas usable in legislation were quite readily devised. But legislative draftsmen were unable to invent any criteria at all for the vast range of other transactions, many of them framed as exchange transactions, that inflation had distorted beyond recognition. So the statute left all the rest for the courts to handle, with no guidance more explicit than the abstruse comment that their "revalorization" was to proceed "in accordance with general principles of law." The courts were not directed, but inferred they were expected, to salvage the transactions left in their charge and to enforce them if they could. So for years thereafter—well into the 1930's—German courts were heavily engaged in "free" revalorization, rewriting clauses in contracts that called for

---

[1] Dawson, Judicial Revision of Frustrated Contracts: Germany, 63 B.U.L. Rev. 1039 (1983).

money payments and doing their best to recreate all the varied transactions in which such clauses had been used.

So it is not surprising that German courts responded as vigorously as they did to the thinly veiled appeal of the legislature to join in what was evidently conceived as a program of reconstruction—salvaging private transactions by restoring to provisions for money payment some of the content that inflation had drained away. But no such motive can explain the readiness in more recent times with which West German courts have rewritten all kinds of contracts for all kinds of reasons. In the 1920's and 30's German courts had been almost solely preoccupied with only one form of unforeseen change—drastic change in the purchasing power of money. Since the Second World War this ground for judicial intervention has not reappeared, though the law reports reveal a full catalogue of all the private misfortunes that can bring the performance of private contracts to a halt. In all such cases if the disruptive effect is drastic enough to excuse further performance, the preferred solution, instead of discharge, will be for a court to revise the transaction, substituting new terms that the court invents and that are made binding by its order. This solution will be preferred in the sense that it will be employed unless it is clear that court-ordered revision could not produce an imitation "contract" that the parties could perform and that would bear a recognizable resemblance to the transaction that it replaced.

It will be evident as the discussion proceeds that on this issue—whether the frustration of contracts through unforeseen events confers on judges a power to revise them—a wide divergence has developed between German and American law. This divergence may be due merely to our good fortune, that our society has not yet encountered disasters of the same magnitude as that experienced by Germany in the 1920's; for if we do, no one can predict what the response of our courts will be. But there are some among us who now seriously urge that we should not wait until catastrophe overtakes us but should adopt this now as the preferred solution. Whether we should is the question to be discussed.

It will be necessary first to describe briefly the sources in our present-day contract law that have some bearing on this question. The next step will be to consider certain forms of disruption through unforeseen events for which court-ordered adjustment

is beneficial, needed and fully authorized under law that is now in force. A survey will follow of a variety of situations in which courts might have been tempted to impose substantive changes by mandatory court order.

I. The Current Tests For Frustration

Much comment has been provoked by the section of the Uniform Commercial Code that provides a test for the intervening obstacles that will excuse a seller from performance of a contract of sale. It states that a seller's delay in delivering or his failure to deliver the subject of the sale will not constitute a breach if performance as agreed "has been made impracticable by the occurrence of a contingency the non-occurrence of which was a basic assumption on which the contract was made."[2] This section deals only with one narrow topic—default by a seller of goods—but its language seemed to the draftsmen of the *Second Restatement of Contracts* to express better than earlier formulations the trends apparent in modern court decisions. The main innovation of the Commercial Code was its redefinition of impossibility, so that it is enough for performance to become "impracticable." The *Restatement* adopted this and made it applicable to contracts of all kinds. The formula that required a finding that it had been a "basic assumption" of the contract that no such contingency would occur was adopted not only for all forms of "impracticability of performance" but also for the closely related case of frustration of "a party's principal purpose." These formulas have already come into widespread use. The method of analysis that they imply is extended further by the *Restatement* to include both "impracticability" and frustration of purpose that already existed at the time the contract was made, though not then known to the party prejudiced by it. Such situations form part of a larger group that have usually been classified under the heading of mistake, but the Restaters concluded quite rightly that the date of origin of the inability to perform or of the circumstance that defeats a main purpose should not produce any important difference.

There is no word or phrase in English that will adequately characterize all the kinds of disruption that can result from events that had not been foreseen or the discovery of facts that had been unknown. In Germany there is one inclusive phrase that is used wherever the disruption seems to justify the intervention of some court. Whatever form the intervention

---

[2] U.C.C. § 2-615 (1978).

may take, the reason for it will almost certainly be said to be that "the foundations of the transaction" have been destroyed or undermined. The only word in English that carries with it in this context a similar meaning is the word "frustration." I shall use it to describe all those situations in which the agreed performance has been prevented (has become "impracticable") or can no longer accomplish its principal purpose, whether the cause arose only after the date of the contract or existed at the time, undiscovered.

The remedy contemplated by the U.C.C. and the Restatement clearly is the traditional remedy of Anglo-American law for impossibility of performance—discharge of both parties from any duty of further performance with restitution, if needed, of any performance already rendered. The principal source of confusion, however, has recently been a brief comment by the draftsmen of the Code section on this topic:

> In situations in which neither sense nor justice is served by either answer when the issue is posed in flat terms of "excuse" or "no excuse," adjustment under the various provisions of this Article is necessary, especially the sections on good faith, on insecurity and assurance and on the reading of all provisions in the light of their purposes, and the general policy of this Act to use equitable principles in furtherance of commercial standards and good faith.

The possibilities for confusion were certainly not reduced by the enigmatic section that the draftsmen inserted in the *Second Restatement*, at the conclusion of the chapter on Impracticability and Frustration:

> In any case governed by the rules stated in this chapter, if those rules together with the rules stated in Chapter 16 [on remedies] will not avoid injustice, the court may grant relief on such terms as justice requires including protection of the parties' reliance interests.

Both passages suggest that something new will be added both by the court-ordered "adjustment" that is proposed in the comment on the Code and by the "terms" to be supplied "as justice requires." Are there limits on what can be added?

II. Adjustments Authorized Under Existing Law

[At this point, Professor Dawson reviews cases in which courts traditionally adjusted contract duties under American law. He finds that the adjustments normally took place only in situations where the court could easily discern the parties' intentions as to apportionment of reciprocal rights and duties, even if

the apportionment was not specified in the agreement. He gives examples of installment contracts where performance of part but not all was made impossible, contracts where compensation was specified for each of several duties and some were performable but others were not, and land sales where the acreage was mistaken and where the total price could easily be figured on a per-acre basis and adjusted arithmetically. He also notes that in most of the cases arising out of the closing of the Suez Canal in 1956, the courts refused to give ships additional compensation for the longer voyage around the Cape of Good Hope. Professor Dawson recognizes, however, that these cases typically found that the closing of the Canal had been foreseeable when the contracts were made, and suggests that had the frustration been found, additional compensation could have been awarded in restitution, the computation usually being figured at the contract rate.

[Dawson then remarks: "Perhaps it is because our courts in these cases have been for the most part so circumspect that when their conduct wanders off limits it can be truly bizarre." He discusses *National Presto Industries v. United States*, 338 F.2d 99 (Ct. Cl. 1964), *cert. denied*, 380 U.S. 962 (1965), in which the Court of Claims was faced with a claim by a supplier of artillery shells. The Army wanted Presto to use a manufacturing method avoiding the use of lathes, a method that Presto kept insisting would not work. The contract was silent on lathes. Presto tried, unsuccessfully, to use the non-lathe method, and later sought additional compensation for its losses from the unsuccessful experiment. Dawson sees the case as involving an assumption of risk by Presto, which did not have a provision protecting it put in the contract, and as posing the question "how far should one go in reimbursing reliance loss through a liability in damages when it is assumed that there has been no fault in anyone?" —ed.]

But the court had no need to pause and display whatever distress it felt over this painful question. For it thought—or at any rate said—that the remedy needed was reformation. This is of course the old-time remedy of equity courts for mistakes in written expression, aiming to correct a document in order to make it say what the parties to it had agreed it should say. In the instant case no one seemed disposed to go through a ceremony so idle as amending the writing that the parties had signed but that had already been fully performed. It would be enough merely to imagine the change, but its object this time would be different—to make the document say not what the parties had agreed it should say (for it had done precisely that) but what the court decides it should have said in view of all the later trouble. This was that the government, the buyer, guaranteed the seller in making the shells against loss in acting on the government's claim that in making them no turning on lathes was needed. This would permit recovery for (1) expenditures in testing and delay in determining that this was not true and (2) extra costs of using lathes when it was found that turning was needed. But wait, reader, for a last-minute correction: the government had learned something it had wanted to know (a benefit that could not be measured) and suppliers should have incentives not to pile up unnecessary costs (no one knew how much of this had occurred). So a cleaver would produce a cleaner result—divide all the losses, necessary or not, by two, with one-half assigned to each side. Thus the court ended by making one contribution, to the peace of mind of those who for years have been urging without avail that when problems become so hard that a rational solution cannot be found, we should rely on arithmetic and simply divide the losses by the number of parties.[48]

. . .

Whether or not such an extension [of recovery for reliance losses in the wake of discharge through frustration of *non*-governmental contracts] does occur, we can be thankful at least that the *Presto* case has not provided a model for this or any other innovation. Its fate in the court from which it emerged, the United States Court of Claims, has been well described: that court "has since beaten a hasty if not embarrassed retreat . . ., limiting it to a special set of facts that seem never to recur."[52] In recent debates among the authors over the power of courts to revise frustrated contracts this case does not appear as an exhibit to which anyone points with pride. But it is still useful as a reminder that American courts are just as capable as West German courts of uncontrollable aberrations when they conceive their mission in the "reformation" of frustrated contracts as the *Presto* case did: one in which the court authorized to dispose of the case "can mold its relief to achieve any fair result

within the broadest perimeter of the charter the parties have established for themselves."[53]

III. Frustration Through Widely Operative Changes In Price

A. *Change by Direct Court Order*

There remain some situations not yet discussed in which it has been somewhat more common for our courts to be asked to revise contract terms rather than grant full-scale discharge. They constitute a group only in the sense that they have one feature in common—the unexpected change (or the unexpected discovery) has taken the form of a widespread increase in price (i.e., the procurement cost) of some resource that one party must have in order to accomplish his agreed performance. An unexpected increase in the cost of performance is certainly not a unique feature in frustration cases, for that was found in a high percentage of the situations that have just been discussed. But in them the increased cost was usually due to some change that had a direct effect on some identified physical asset or course of conduct—an order from a source empowered to command that certain sewer pipes shall no longer be used to pollute or an international waterway that had shortened voyages shall be closed. But where the change consists of nothing more than a rise in the procurement cost of some asset or service that one party must have and the rise is one of wide incidence in the economy, as it is likely to be, prudence dictates the warning that other promisors are very likely to have claims of equal merit to be relieved of their duties; their number multiplies as the price rise spreads. Even the courts of West Germany, which seem to assume that the rewriting of frustrated contracts is so beneficial that hesitancy on their part is not needed, have shown it strongly here.

It is something more than coincidence that this is the group of recent cases in which courts have been most strongly urged to rewrite price rather than discharge exchanges that, it was urged, had been seriously disrupted by this means. They all concerned sales of goods or a service on which the buyer claimed to be so dependent and with performance

---

[48] This has been urged, though with attempts to be more persuasive than I have been, in D. Dobbs, Remedies 268-69 (1973); . . . A reasoned argument for this Solomonic solution to be used generally in situations where either facts or the choice of the governing rule is "indeterminate" is presented by Coons, Approaches to Court-Imposed Compromise—The Uses of Doubt and Reason, 58 Nw. U. L. Rev. 750 (1964) and

Coons, Compromise as Precise Justice, 68 Calif. L. Rev. 250 (1980) (deriving support for this solution from the requirement of equality in judicial administration).

[52] Speidel, Court-Imposed Price Adjustments Under Long-Term Supply Contracts, 76 Nw. U. L. Rev. 369, 379 n.47 (1981).

[53] Presto, 338 F.2d at 112.

stretched over a long enough time to make damages for breach hard to calculate. So the buyers in several cases sued for specific performance. This meant that the sellers acquired the seeming advantage of being able to appeal to the discretion of a court exercising "equity" powers, urging it to refuse a remedy within the old equity tradition unless the judge's own standards of good conscience and fairness were fully met by the case before him. From this discretion older decisions had derived a power to impose terms which would not be directly binding on the successful party but with which he must comply in order to secure from the court any aid in enforcing a decree.

This was the dilemma with which the Atlas Corporation sought to confront an Iowa power company to which it had agreed to supply for four years uranium concentrate, to be used for producing nuclear power. The sale price was to rise by small increments from $7.10 a pound in 1975 to $8.45 in 1978. But by 1978 the market price had risen to more than $43.00 a pound and the costs for Atlas of producing it were somewhere in that range. In the year 1976, for example, Atlas claimed that it had incurred a net loss on this contract alone of $ 1.8 million; larger losses were expected later. To this disaster various factors had contributed, a large increase in wages and other production costs, some of them due to governmental controls aimed at greater safety and environmental protection, but central was a shortage of uranium, leading to higher prices and a decision by Atlas to employ a lower grade. The court was left with questions it could not answer: some, but how much, of Atlas' losses were due to its own decisions, some, but how much, should have been foreseen? It was impossible to track losses to their causes, and a court "cannot pick a price out of the air." So the court granted the specific performance that the buyer had sued for without the "reformation" (price increase) that the seller sought.[57]

There have been other cases in which specific performance sought by buyers has been granted while price revison, even as a mere condition to the remedy granted, was being denied. All the contracts involved commodities whose market price was very likely to rise in response to the sharp rise in the 1970's in petroleum prices. The most emphasized reason for refusing to undertake any price revision was that ex-

perienced traders had good reason to foresee a rise in the prices of petroleum and its products. The inclusion in a contract of sale of a clause tied to an index that provided for price escalation was taken to reinforce this conclusion and in the court's view to set limits to the allowance for rises in price that the contracting parties had been willing to make. So far as court opinions gave any clues, the fact that these issues arose by way of defense to actions for specific performance did not introduce any different tests than if the supplier were affirmatively suing to secure a discharge. These cases, in other words, in no way suggest the phenomenon so prevalent in West German courts—a readiness to undertake revision of terms in order to "adjust" contracts to unexpected changes—changes that would be entirely insufficient to produce full-scale discharge. If our courts had any such purpose in mind the most plausible way to disguise it would be as a purely defensive maneuver when courts were asked to exercise "equity" powers.

Miscalculation by a supplier reached a new scale of magnitude in the contracts of Westinghouse Electric to supply 49 nuclear power plants with their requirements of uranium. The 27 utilities that owned the sites where these plants were projected wanted assurances before making the necessary huge investment in nuclear plant and equipment, of which Westinghouse was a major supplier. The assurances they received took the form of contracts, mostly made in the early 1970's, for Westinghouse to supply the requirements of uranium for these plants when in operation, at fixed prices—$8.00 or $10.00 (up to $12.00) a pound. They were mostly made in the early 1970's and the market price of uranium began to rise sharply in 1974. In September, 1975, when Westinghouse announced that it could not and would not perform further, the market price approached $40.00 a pound and later went higher. The guesses as to how much Westinghouse would lose if it performed all its contracts for their full terms (on the doubtful assumption they could procure the supplies) started from a base of two billion dollars and went considerably higher. In actions for damages by thirteen power companies, consolidated in a trial that lasted six months, the conclusion reached by the trial judge was that Westinghouse had no sufficient excuse and was liable full scale for expectancy damages.[60] Unfortu-

[57] Iowa Elec. Light & Power Co. v. Atlas Corp., 467 F. Supp. 129 (N.D. Iowa 1978), rev'd on other grounds, 603 F.2d 1301 (8th Cir. 1979), cert. denied, 445 U.S. 911 (1980).
[60] Since this decision has not been reported, the main

events have been described only in newspaper reports. The 13 actions for damages brought in different parts of the country were consolidated for trial in Virginia in In re Westinghouse Elec. Corp. Uranium Contracts Litig., 405 F.

nately for posterity a reasoned opinion was not filed but this may have been just as well for Westinghouse, since its damage-claim creditors, motivated presumably by their own self-interest in preserving it as a fully functioning enterprise, agreed to settlements that were vastly more lenient than any that a court would have been bold enough to propose.

So the question becomes whether, as the interests at stake rise higher on a scale of magnitude and the complexities of the performances multiply, these are reasons for judges to intervene and impose new terms that to them will seem more workable and fair. This strange inversion of ideas occurred in one case that was even more grotesque than the Presto case, for the remedy given in *Aluminum Co. of America v. Essex Group, Inc. (Alcoa)* was not damages for losses through performance already completed, but the manufacture of a new price term that was to govern future performance for a potential eight years. The contract thus revised had been made in 1967 by a colossus, the Aluminum Company of America (Alcoa), with another large conglomerate, the Essex Group (Essex), that among other things manufactures metal products. Alcoa undertook for 16 years (extensible by Essex for 5 years more) to smelt specified quantities that Essex supplied of the primary component of aluminum (alumina) and redeliver it to Essex as aluminum.[62] This service was to be performed at a plant owned by Alcoa in Warwick, Indiana.

The price was set at a base figure of 15 cents a pound but included in this total were three components whose prices were variable. One was tied to an index of construction costs nation-wide, another to the costs of labor at the Warwick plant itself, and a third—applied to 3 of the original 15 cents—to an index of wholesale prices for industrial commodities maintained by the United States Department of Labor. The use of this index had been proposed by Alcoa after close study of its past performance had shown that prior to 1967, when the contract was signed, fluctuations in this index had coincided closely with variations in production costs at Alcoa's Warwick plant. For the first seven years after the contract was

signed all went well and Alcoa turned a handsome profit on the smelting service it supplied. Then the rise in "non-labor" costs at the Warwick plant, especially the cost of electric energy (a leading element of cost in smelting), exceeded the rise in the Labor Department index, so that in the two years 1977 and 1978 Alcoa lost $12 million, not quite half its profit in the first nine years. For the remaining years Alcoa conjectured that its loss on the contract would exceed $60 million and the judge accepted this estimate though it had no basis in ascertainable facts and was sharply challenged by Essex.

For the evident purpose of opening the way to the "reformation" that Alcoa sought the court strenuously tried to demonstrate that the rise in the cost of energy, occurring years after the contract was formed, was a mistake of fact. It was as much a mistake of present fact, I would say, as though at the time two parties agreed on the rental for one day of rooms from which a royal procession could be observed, both parties had believed the king to be a vigorous outdoor type with a strong resistance to colds though later, on the crucial day, a bad cold forced him to stay home in his palace in bed. Describing the parties' miscalculation as a mistake of present fact would change nothing in the case and most certainly would not confer on a court a power to reduce the rent to the sum it found the rented space to be worth for looking out on empty streets. In the *Alcoa* case, I believe, the court was misled by a leading treatise in drawing the inference that for reformation there is no need for an enforceable contract to which the writing was intended and can be made to conform.[65] The court did concede that in the case before it any such purpose could not be accomplished for the contract had said precisely what the parties had intended it to say. But the court flatly rejected "the hoary maxim" that the courts will not make a contract for the parties. So it ordered that the complex scheme for price determination approved by the parties, tied to three price indices, was to be entirely replaced by one invented by the court and shifting completely to a cost-plus basis. Under its scheme the costs of production incurred during each quarter at

Supp. 316 (J.P.M.D.L. 1975). A useful comment on this aspect appears in Note, In re Westinghouse: Commercial Impracticability As A Contractual Defense, 47 UMKC L. Rev. 650 (1979). An excellent account of the economic and legal background and of the astonishing lack of foresight shown by the Westinghouse management is given by Joskow, Commercial Impossibility, The Uranium Market and the Westinghouse Case, 6 J. Legal Stud. 119, 143-50 (1977).

[62] Aluminum Co. of America v. Essex Group, Inc., 499 F. Supp. 53 (W.D. Pa. 1980).

[65] 3 G. Palmer Restitution, § 13.9 contains the comments that misled the court. This may have been because the author, in my view, overstates his own contention that reformation quite often will "produce a contract which contract doctrine does not support." Id. at 54. . . .

the Warwick plant were all to be added up after each quarter had ended and Essex was then to pay prices that would ensure to Alcoa for all the aluminum it delivered a profit of one cent a pound.

The judge claimed that in reaching out for this bizarre solution he was inspired by becoming modesty: "the court willingly concedes that the managements of Alcoa and Essex are better able to conduct their business than is the court." But he claimed also that his information, being derived from hindsight, was "far superior" to that of the parties when they had made their contract and that a rule precluding adjustments by courts would have had "the perverse effect" of discouraging the parties from resolving this dispute or future disputes on their own. Only slightly paraphrased, this suggestion seems to mean that when basic provisions are revised by a judge, who knows only what he can learn from presiding at a trial, the result will probably be so unacceptable to both parties that by their own agreement they will reject the dictated terms and reassert the right that they fortunately still retain, to recover control over their own affairs. If that was his object it was soon realized in the *Alcoa* case. The judge's decree was appealed and after argument had been heard in the Court of Appeals for the Third Circuit but before that court could decide, a settlement was reached, Alcoa's action to "reform" was voluntarily dismissed and Alcoa surrendered any rights it had acquired under the trial court decree.[71]

This is, I believe, the only instance in which an American court has claimed power to recast by its own direct order, without some transparent disguise like "reformation," an essential term in an exchange that was still in progress when some unforeseen external event produced major imbalance. This form of "adjustment" to govern the performances not yet rendered is the one recommended by some authors in American law reviews.[72] In West Germany this is the treatment that is now normally given frustrated contracts, a treatment described with the hope that our own courts can be dissuaded from a course so disastrous for the coherence and rationality of our law of contract.[73]

B. *Conditional Relief as a Means of Eliciting Assent to Change*

If the reclaiming of frustrated contracts through "adjustments" in their terms were an objective to which our courts became committed, would anything be gained by seeking support from consent by the parties, one or both? We can safely start from the premise that the parties, if they agreed, could readily accomplish the announced purpose, unaided. If the parties have incentives strong enough for them to work out and agree on a substitute for the discharged agreement they will be entirely free to do so without encouragement or facilities that any court has supplied. The only impediment that our law of contract might have presented—the pre-existing duty rule—will presumably not apply if the duties on both sides have been discharged; if it did it could in any case be very easily evaded. But the question remains whether there would be some advantage in creating inducements for the parties to renegotiate the terms of contracts that unexpected events have superseded, even visiting a failure to do so with some deprivation—such as the denial of a remedy sought—unless "reasonable" efforts were made to secure the assent of both to a change.

Indirect pressures of this kind had a short history in German decisions rendered during the course of the great inflation. They were introduced by a division of the German high court that believed it had no power to revise contract terms, even in contracts that inflation had so grossly distorted that by the tests then used they should be discharged. Duties both to make and to respond to proposals for revision of terms were derived by the court from the omnipresent "good faith" clause on which depended all the other measures invented by courts to deal with the effects of inflation. Much litigation resulted over issues that can only be described as issues of ceremonial or protocol—the fairness of proposals made, receptivity or obduracy in the responses made, readiness shown by counter-proposals. It soon became apparent that the motivations of the parties usually worked in directly opposite directions, for the effects of the changes that were occurring so rapidly brought

[71] This I have learned through private communication from counsel for Essex who had requested me to comment on the briefs that were being prepared for the appeal by Essex. I had thus considerably earlier an opportunity to form a highly adverse opinion of the trial court's decision.

[72] Zindel, Equitable Reformation of Long-Term Contracts—The New Spirit of Alcoa, 1982 Utah L. Rev. 985;

Note, U.C.C. § 2-615: Excusing the Impracticable, 60 B.U.L. Rev. 575 (1980); Note, Sharp Inflationary Increases in Cost as an Excuse From Performance of Contract, 50 Notre Dame Law. 297 (1974). The views of Professor Richard Speidel will be discussed in the following section.

[73] See Dawson, supra note 1.

gains to one that usually matched closely the losses of the other. A seller, for example, would usually have no impulse to offer new terms attractive to the buyer, for cancellation of the sale was what the seller would most desire; but to hold the seller to the original, unmodified terms of the contract came to be considered too severe a sanction. The buyer, on the other hand, would usually be willing to offer more acceptable terms but this of itself would not ensure their acceptance. Often in order to produce a contract a court would find it necessary to say—you *should* have accepted this reasonable proposal, so we will treat you as though you did. But when one stopped to examine the matter more closely there was not much difference between a "contract" that resulted from a court's adoption of the new terms proposed by one party and one whose terms had been entirely invented by a court. In either case the judgment and the authority of a court must both be interposed as a substitute for the assent that was lacking.

Much more often the interlude for the manufacture of new bargains that was assigned in each case was used for formal exchanges and guarded replies and tended to produce only delay. And the anomaly was that for parties whose incentives were strong no such interludes were needed, for the parties at all times had remained entirely free to displace the old with new agreements without facilities provided by any court. These maneuvers were evidently found to be a wasteful diversion of effort for they disappeared altogether after a short interval, about three years. And since the Second World War, when court-ordered revision of frustrated contracts has become a normal and expected result, one finds no mention at all of these interludes assigned to provide a semblance of party-assent.

In an extended discussion of the *Alcoa* case, some other, quite different reasons have been presented for providing the parties to frustrated contracts with opportunities to renegotiate their terms. After expressing admiration for that "trail-blazer" case,[75] the author criticizes it only for its failure to provide such a planned interlude during which the parties could be judged for their readiness to engage in bargaining in "good faith." In the "long-term supply contract," which he considers the *Alcoa* case to be, the author asserts that there is a duty "to preserve and adjust"

the contract relation, a duty that falls in particular on the party who has gained an advantage through some unforeseen change. This is because the "new spirit" that, as he views it, is coming to pervade our contract law condemns "opportunism" and "improper advantage-taking," and requires that all such gains be shared. So for the one who has acquired the advantage, a refusal to negotiate for an adjustment of the contract would imperil the contract relation itself, produce conflict, and leave him with a gain that is "unfair" and "undeserved." The sanctions? So long as he fails to "bargain in good faith," if the advantaged party seeks specific performance this remedy should be denied and the other party, to whom has accrued a *dis*advantage, can suspend his own performance until an accommodation has been reached. But more than this, if bargaining ensues and the *dis*advantaged party makes an "equitable" proposal which the advantaged party then rejects, the court at that point acquires the power to declare that these rejected terms are binding and have replaced the corresponding terms of the original contract. The author describes this as the appropriate penalty for a failure to bargain in "good faith." From another point of view there is a certain anomaly here—that it is the express refusal by one to assent to a proposal made by the other that transforms that proposal into a "contract" binding on both.

The troublesome question for me at least, is—how far would the *Alcoa* case and the glosses like this that are being written to praise it carry us along the route that German courts have travelled? The main directions of both are clearly the same. There is also one other respect in which they follow parallel lines: an ambiguity that seems to be deliberately maintained as to how disruptive the unforeseen change must be for courts to acquire the power to "readjust" terms. In Germany this question does not seem even to be discussed, though it is plain that some of the corrections made by German courts have been for disruptions that were minor indeed. It is true, of course, that when court-ordered revision has come to be the outcome expected the temptation will be strong to disregard tests that would have had to be met if the end result for the transaction were to be its complete dissolution. The same ambiguity seems to me to pervade the *Alcoa* case, nor do I find more guidance in

completely what the parties had agreed it should say. Instead the court described the case as one in which it was awarding "equitable restitution," this being, of course, the last thing it was.

the comments of its leading admirer. Yet surely it would make a vast difference in the reliability and usefulness of contracts in our society if our courts were to acquire a broad mandate to rewrite contract terms that had, as a result of unforeseen events, produced on one side an unexpected gain. But perhaps the time has not yet come to be concerned. This power to "readjust" is conceived by the author who advocates it most strongly to be merely a means of enforcing a duty to bargain in "good faith" for the surrender of such "underserved" [sic; "undeserved"? —ed.] gains, great or small. If this is all that it is, there is no need to expect any great consequences. For as another recent case has said in discussing this theme: a contention that a party to a contract "was in bad faith for failure to do what it had no obligation to do cannot withstand scrutiny."[79]

One other device that is old and familiar for eliciting consent to substantive change is the conditional decree used where an equitable remedy (such as specific performance) is sought. The conditional decree is of course a familiar feature of many forms of equitable relief. . . .

The freedom exercised in the past by equity courts in fixing conditions to the remedies they awarded was derived from the premise that those remedies were merely a supplement to those established long before by the common law. Since equity courts were endowed with discretion that could be exercised by a total refusal of all equitable relief, it was thought to follow that such relief could be granted on the court's own terms. If the terms were not satisfactory to the one bringing the action he was left free to discontinue and resort to his remedy in damages, which was left intact. . . .

Should this expedient, a condition aiming to induce the adoption of new terms manufactured by a court, be considered now to be part of the standard equipment of American courts if they were to undertake on a much larger scale to refashion contracts thrown awry by unforeseen events? It remains, as I have said, an expedient with old and respectable credentials, little used though it is. Nevertheless I do not predict for it an expanding future, since as a device for alleviating hardship it rests on some built-in dilemmas.

The remedy of specific performance has been commonly used, of course, to enforce contracts for the sale of land. The remedy is granted routinely, no effort is made to require a showing that the land in question is unusually hard to appraise, and in truth it usually is not. So as the discrepancy between contract price and land value widens the provable damages mount, as will the sum that is to be extracted by indirect means from the litigant to whom the remedy is granted. As the damage remedy becomes more productive and the charge for equitable relief goes up, it will be the rare case in which a litigant who was left free to forego his rights under the equity decree will have reason to pursue the equity remedy further.

Where other commodities (other than land) or services, perhaps, have been the subjects of exchange agreements, the problems presented will be somewhat different. Here in almost all cases it will still be essential to show that a remedy in damages would be seriously deficient. There is, of course, no necessary connection between measuring the interests that a promisee may have in securing a promised performance and difficulties in calculating the supplement to the price that a court might wish to induce him to pay. But if it turns out that this desired supplement can be calculated with relative ease, the comments I have just made on the dilemmas arising in sales of land would seem to apply with equal force. One could expect more often that the difficulties in measuring the losses that a breach would cause and difficulties in measuring the costs of a replacement for the promised performance would be fused together in one composite maze. And what needs emphasis most is that damages that are really hard to measure through evidence supplied to a jury will be just as hard to measure, for the same reasons, when the evidence is supplied to a judge.

A recent illustration is a dispute over the debris left behind by one of the sales of uranium by Westinghouse. The sale had been made to a utility, producer of electric power, with a clause in which Westinghouse promised to remove from the plant of the buyer all uranium from which the usable energy had been extracted. For years Westinghouse had failed to comply with this undertaking and the power company asserted that unless the resulting accumulation of ra-

---

[79] Louisiana Power & Light v. Allegheny Ludlum Indus., 517 F. Supp. 1319, 1330 (E.D. La. 1981). . . . The court reviewed the recent course of decision and emphatically rejected the Alcoa decision, especially its delusion that subse-

quent events within the range of risks that were assumed can provide ground for relief by simply being described as mutual mistake.

dioactive waste was removed, its plant would have to close—it could not say precisely when but in four years was its best guess. The power company also asserted that it would be "extremely difficult if not impossible" to find another agency that would undertake to remove the waste. Westinghouse gave the excuse that it planned to reprocess the spent uranium when removed and thereby recoup some $16 million or more, but this had proved difficult to arrange and in 1977 was prohibited by federal legislation. The court held nevertheless that since Westinghouse had undertaken to remove the spent fuel and its difficulties were within the risks that it should have foreseen, specific performance should be awarded.[85]

Would it have been preferable for the court to insert a condition to the order for removal of the radioactive waste, providing that enforcement of the order could begin only when the power company had reimbursed Westinghouse for its unexpectedly higher cost in removing and safely disposing of the waste? This sum under standard procedure would be for the court to fix. Such a half-way measure could be defended (not very convincingly, I confess) by arguing that the reprocessing planned by Westinghouse, now no longer possible, would have aided in disposal of the waste and the great volume of radioactive waste that had in the meantime poured forth nationwide had left it few disposal sites. So the court would then set about establishing (hopefully with credible evidence) what an enterprise qualified to dispose of radioactive waste would charge if one could be found (the power company had not succeeded in finding one), the costs of constructing or digging safe places of storage, the nature and costs of the safeguards that would be needed for the environment over a long and uncertain future time. A damage remedy that was forced to deal with such issues would indeed be inadequate; for the remedy in equity there plainly was a great need. One objection to the introduction of such a condition would be its net effect in requiring the buyer, if it was to continue to use its overencumbered plant, to assume the money cost of all the burdens and risks that the seller had assumed. But another objection, which should be in any case fatal, would be that these costs which in a damage action would be beyond the range of human calculation could not be more readily measured by judges, who do not possess supernatural insight even in their exercise of equity powers.

IV. Conclusion

The court-ordered revisions of frustrated contracts that this survey has reviewed involved at the outset some changes that the courts were entirely willing to make and that seemed to be altogether desirable and needed. They involved no more than the extension of standards on which the parties had already agreed and adopted as terms of their contracts to situations that had been unexpected and for which the parties therefore had not provided. Controversy arose only where the revision to accomplish its purpose must create new substantive standards that some court must invent to define the performances due from the parties, one or both. Our courts when asked had consistently refused to undertake such tasks and were clear in their reasons why this lay well outside the functions assigned to them. They had refused, that is, until four years ago when a federal trial judge gave some peculiar reasons for concluding that he had the power to rewrite a contract in which Alcoa agreed to process metal owned by a conglomerate, the Essex Group. The judge's contribution proved, however, to be not very helpful. The dissatisfied parties agreed to substitute for the "contract" that the judge had contrived, a new version that they themselves had prepared. Appellate review of the judge's order was imminent but was foreclosed when the appeal by Essex was abandoned. So the *Alcoa* opinion is a lonely monument on a bleak landscape, the only instance in which an American judge has tried to dictate entirely different substantive terms (in this instance the price) in a contract that was still being actively performed. This may explain why so much attention has been given to the frustrated venture of a single trial judge whose fancy was unusually free.

The *Alcoa* opinion has an admirer who has presented some reasons why other courts too should be encouraged to rewrite the terms of other contracts—at any rate those that he would characterize, as he does that in the *Alcoa* case, as "long term supply contracts." This is a phrase that he does not try to define—how "long" the duration, what can be "supplied" (are land and personal services, for example, to be wholly excluded?).[86] Nor is it clear whether the supervening event or discovery must have had effects so drastic that total discharge of the contract would have been justified. Of the reasons given for rewrit-

[85] In re Westinghouse Elec. Corp., 517 F. Supp. 440 (E.D. Va. 1981).

[86] Speidel, supra note 52, at 373-75. There is evidently room for debate, for as the author recognizes, id. n.37, the

Alcoa case itself was not a sale of goods but a service supplied—the smelting of alumina that Essex throughout continued to own. As to how long—at one point, id. at 373, the author mentions twenty years and in Alcoa itself the con-ing such contracts the first and most prominent reason where the duration is to be "long" is the great difficulty in foreseeing and providing for all the contingencies that may arise; even when some might be in some degree foreseen they may have consequences whose nature and extent could not be and were not foreseen. Over this proposition there is not likely to be dispute from those whose life-span has fallen, through no choice of their own, within the twentieth century.

The question then must be what consequences follow from it. In this setting does it mean that judges have advantages in forecasting the future that are denied to the stumbling, undiscerning human beings that produce most of our contracts? By the time questions requiring such forecasts can reach a judge he will have acquired the considerable advantage that hindsight gives—he can see what has happened to this particular contract. But by that time, so will the parties. Any effort he makes to rewrite the contract will aim, of course, to project it into the future. All the resources of language, the escalation clauses, conditions and reservations that qualify obligations, are just as available to the parties as they are to any judge. Does anyone seriously contend that a judge, by virtue of the skills and insight needed for him to acquire judicial office and by virtue also of the experience that it provides, becomes better equipped than the parties concerned to reconcile their divergent, often conflicting interests, to devise the terms that can govern a complex enterprise and ensure its future survival? The judges I have known are human too. Perhaps I have not met enough judges.

The argument for empowering courts to manufacture substitute "contracts" seems to rest on the premise that without the compulsion of a court decree the parties after frustration has occurred and their performance is excused will lose all incentives to use productively the assets that they had previously committed. That this would be a misfortune and should be prevented is evidently believed by the leading admirer of the *Alcoa* case, and particularly, he argues, in two situations. One of them is the long-term contract for which large resources are needed but one of the parties acquires still more resources by new expenditures—expenditures made in reliance although not in performance of the contract. Of course this

may happen. But then again, it may not and the argument that a judge should contrive and impose his own version of a "contract" is not made to depend on whether it did or not. And then if it did, I would again ask, what reason would there be for expecting that their owners would permit valuable assets to be destroyed or wasted—though it might be that they could continue in use only through a new contract made—freely made with someone else? The other type of situation the author describes is that in which a buyer needs and uses the commodity or service "supplied" for the purpose of rendering a performance on which third persons come to depend. As described, the connections of these "dependents" are so remote that they would not be taken into account for any other purpose. But again, the first question is whether such measures are needed, whether valuable, potentially profitable resources will not continue in any event to be used for the purposes for which they were planned and are well adapted. And then, if for any cluster out of a thousand reasons the parties decide they will not use them in this way, are we to understand that they must?

The first reason that I have urged (for me it is a sufficient reason) for judges to abstain from rewriting the contracts of other people is that they are not qualified for such tasks. Nothing in their prior training as lawyers or their experience in directing litigation and giving coherence to its results will qualify them to invent viable new designs for disrupted enterprises, now gone awry, that the persons most concerned had tried to construct but without success. As one able author has contended, judges, trained as judges, are "institutionally incapable" of achieving success in such undertakings.[89]

The second reason, however, is important enough to be stated first for it raises an issue that I regard as a major issue of civil liberty. The question that I have repeatedly raised but have not tried to answer is the question—when an unforeseen event has so drastically altered a contract that the parties to it are fully excused from its further performance, from what source does any court derive the power to impose on them a new contract without the free assent of both? Where rescission is awarded on any of the other standard grounds—fraud, mistake,[90] substantial breach, defective capacity, duress—no one has even

tract was for sixteen years, extensible by Essex for another five. What is wrong with 10 or 5 or even less if difficulty in forecasting the future is a primary factor?

[89] Schwartz, Sales Law and Inflation, 50 S. Cal. L. Rev. 1 (1976).

[90] If one could imagine, as I cannot, that an unexpected rise in energy costs occurring nine years after the contract was a mistake of present fact, it would have to be described, as the court itself said, 499 F. Supp. at 64-65, as a mistake in a "basic assumption." For this the standard remedies, if any

suggested that such a power lay hidden somewhere. For myself, I do not propose to spend time looking for the source of the power. I am convinced that it does not exist.

---

were to be granted, would all require rescission of the contract. How far-fetched the notion of court-ordered revision would have seemed in such a case can be illustrated by imagining a variation on a time-worn relic of our contract law, the sale of the fertile cow. Sherwood v. Walker, 66 Mich. 568, 33 N.W. 919 (1887). The cow was Rose of Aberlone, of distinguished Scottish lineage, who was believed by its owner to be sterile and was sold to a local banker for a price that was calculated to be her value as beef. She was in fact pregnant at the time of the sale and therefore worth about ten times the price agreed. Should the seller be told that he could not keep the cow, as the court allowed him to do in the original case, and that he must deliver her to the buyer, but that he would be given judgment for the value of a well-bred pregnant cow (the two attributes, I assume, being compatible in a cow), an amount that the court would fix with perhaps the help of a jury? If the buyer then protested that he did not want the cow if he had to pay for it a sum possibly ten times as much as he had agreed to pay, there would not be much comfort in the only justification that a judge could give—that being a banker he could afford it.

Part IV
Remedies

Introductory Note

Contract remedies deserve more space than they can be given here. There are many aspects to remedies, and the topic has received a great deal of attention both from writers using traditional doctrinal analysis and from those using economic reasoning. Unfortunately, the articles tend to be long, either because they must set up economic assumptions or because they have many examples or both. As a result, this section gives only a sampling of the rich literature. As a partial substitute, the notes attempt to give the reader leads to many other articles, and to indicate some of the major areas of controversy. The leading texts on contracts all have good overviews of remedies. Of particular note is Farnsworth, *Contracts* (1982), in which Professor Farnsworth built on his well-known article, *Legal Remedies for Breach of Contract*, 70 Colum. L. Rev. 1145 (1970).

Traditional Contract Remedies and the Question of Efficient Breach

In Part I of this book there were several discussions of "expectation" and "reliance" damages, one of the debates being over why a party who has not relied at all on a broken promise should nonetheless get all of the "benefit of the bargain" if the other party repudiates before any performance has taken place. While this particular issue suggests that contract damages may sometimes provide windfalls, for the most part, the remedial theory underlying traditional contract law is undercompensatory and totally unconcerned with the morality of promise-breaking. In a famous passage, Holmes wrote:

> The duty to keep a contract at common law means a prediction that you must pay damages if you do not keep it—and nothing else. If you commit a tort, you are liable to pay a compensatory sum. If you commit a contract, you are liable to pay a compensatory sum unless the promised event comes to pass, and that is all the difference. But such a mode of looking at the matter stinks in the nostrils of those who think it advantageous to get as much ethics into the law as they can.

Holmes, *The Path of the Law*, 10 Harv. L. Rev. 457 (1897), Collected Legal Papers 167 (1920). Holmes's view was controversial even in its own day, but it has retained its vitality. It receives qualified approval in the Introductory Note to Chapter 16 (Remedies) of the Restatement (Second) of Contracts:

> The traditional goal of the law of contract remedies has not been compulsion of the promisor to perform his promise but compensation of the promisee for the loss resulting from the breach. "Willful" breaches have not been distinguished from other breaches, punitive damages have not been awarded for breach of contract, and specific performance has not been granted where compensation in damages is an adequate substitute for the injured party. In general, therefore, a party may find it advantageous to refuse to perform a contract if he will still have a net gain after he has fully compensated the injured party for the resulting loss.

This last idea has received the engaging name of "efficient breach of contract." The idea is not that parties should be free to break their contracts, but that they should be allowed to do so *if they can fully compensate the other party and still make a profit from the substitute deal*. Here is an illustration:

Assume that Athos owns a woodworking factory capable of taking on one more major project. He contracts to supply Porthos with 100,000 chairs at $10 per chair, which will bring Athos a net profit of $2 per chair, or $200,000 on the contract. Before any work takes place, Aramis, who sells tables, approaches Athos. Although there are several chair factories in the area, only Athos's factory can make tables. If Athos will supply Aramis with 50,000 tables, Aramis will pay him $40 per table. Athos can produce the tables for $25, so he can make a profit of $750,000 if he uses his factory for Aramis's tables. But to do so, he must breach his contract with Porthos. There are other chair factories, and Porthos will be able to get the chairs from one of them—for example from D'Artagnan's. Let us assume that because of his distress situation Porthos will have to pay D'Artagnan 20% more than Athos's price for comparable chairs, and that Porthos will sustain $100,000 in incidental administrative costs and consequential costs such as damages for delay to his customers. Even with these costs, Porthos will lose only $300,000 because of Athos's breach, and Athos can reimburse him in full and still make $450,000 profit, over twice the profit from his contract with Porthos.

Linzer, *On the Amorality of Contract Remedies—Efficiency, Equity, and the Second Restatement*, 81 Colum. L. Rev. 111, 114 (1981). Similar illustrations can be found throughout the law and economics literature, for instance in Judge Richard Posner's *Economic Analysis of Law*. The idea is that it would be economically wasteful to the society as a whole if Athos were prevented from taking on Aramis's job, since Aramis wouldn't get his tables. If Athos is allowed to breach, Porthos ends up with the chairs and full compensation, Aramis gets his tables, and Athos makes a bigger profit.

To my mind, however, the concept was effectively demolished by Ian Macneil in *Efficient Breach of Contract: Circles In the Sky*, 68 Va. L. Rev. 947 (1982), in which he used the quoted example for disection. (To my relief, he did note that its author "is setting up the Posner model for the purpose of showing its limitations," and "is hardly a stirring proponent of the analysis.")

Macneil pointed out that efficient breach theory was often based on unrealistic price differentials (as in the Four Musketeers illustration where Athos makes a twenty-five percent markup on chairs but a sixty percent markup on tables; if tables are so profitable, why don't his competitors make them?), and that it ignores the true costs of litigation, where many costs, most notably attorneys' fees, are not recoverable. Although the illustration attempts to include transaction costs in the calculus, many transaction costs are not recoverable, especially the real costs of lost confidence in long-range business dealings. The economists usually say that this is a matter of politics—all the costs should be included, and if the legal system doesn't allow some, that's not the fault of economics. However, that point is often lost. In fact, few victims of breach even come close to breaking even. Former California Chief Justice Rose Bird argued that many commercial contracts have an implied understanding that they may be breached in good faith if all compensatory damages are paid. She urged a broader view of compensatory damages for the very purpose of protecting the supposed right to breach deliberately, but in good faith, to take a better deal. See her dissent in *Seaman's Direct Buying Service v. Standard Oil Co.*, 36 Cal. 3d 752, 686 P.2d 1158, 206 Cal. Rptr. 354 (1984).

The efficiency issue has many ramifications for contract remedies. For instance, one of the rationales why specific performance is not generally available is that it would deter "efficient breaches." Alan Schwartz of Yale argued forcefully in *The Case for Specific Performance*, 89 Yale L.J. 271 (1979), that economic efficiency would be well-served by a general availability of specific performance, and the Linzer article cited above argued that there was no dichotomy between economic efficiency and a morality of keeping promises, and that valuation of the promised performance will be more accurate if specific performance is granted and the parties are allowed to bargain out of the decree. A more recent argument for increased availability of specific performance on efficiency grounds appears in Ulen, *The Efficiency of Specific Performance: Toward a Unified Theory of Contract Remedies*, 83 Mich. L. Rev.

341 (1984). The present system of modest availability of specific relief was well defended by Anthony T. Kronman, *Specific Performance,* 45 U. Chi. L. Rev. 351 (1978), and by Edward M. Yorio in *In Defense of Money Damages for Breach of Contract,* 82 Colum. L. Rev. 1365 (1982).

Another area of concern is the extent to which more generous measures of damages would comport with efficiency. The present system of contract damages limits recovery by rules of certainty and foreseeability, by a general refusal to allow damages for emotional injury and by a great reluctance to award punitive damages. With no contract equivalent of pain and suffering, attorneys' fees come out of the dollar and cents loss actually suffered by the plaintiff. All of these factors make it very unlikely that the non-breaching party will come even close to breaking even, and also make it difficult to find lawyers to take contract cases on a contingent fee. This has ominous overtones for the justice system. As Farnsworth said in the famous closing line to his 1970 remedies article, "All in all, our system of legal remedies for breach of contract, heavily influenced by the economic philosophy of free enterprise, has shown a marked solicitude for men who do not keep their promises." 70 Colum. L. Rev. at 1216.

Traditional Contract Damages

The most famous contracts article ever written is Lon L. Fuller and William R. Perdue, Jr., *The Reliance Interest in Contract Damages* (parts 1&2), 46 Yale L.J. 52, 373 (1936-37). Fuller was then teaching at Duke, where Perdue was his student assistant. Fuller soon went to Harvard where he became Carter Professor of General Jurisprudence, while Perdue went on to a distinguished career as a practicing lawyer and business executive. The article popularized the terms expectation, restitution and reliance interests, which are expressly adopted in section 344 of the Restatement (Second) of Contracts. While the article contains a famous justification for the protection of the expectation interest (i.e., the benefit of the bargain), its real contribution was to argue that in many situations it would be proper for a court to limit its award to a party's out-of-pocket "reliance" damages.

A generation after the article appeared, there was, as mentioned in Part IIB, increased recognition of reliance as a substantive basis for liability. The Fuller and Perdue approach allowed courts to give some relief where none had been available before, but to limit the remedy to the reliance interest. Thus, the article simultaneously influenced contract toward greater expansion and greater contraction of recovery. It should be noted that while the reliance measure will normally be less than expectations, it can be fairly generous, and arguably more fully compensatory, if a party's lost opportunities are considered reliance damages. This is discussed by Professor Farnsworth in his *Precontractual Liability* article, excerpted in Part IIA. In addition, Professor Daniel Friedmann of Tel-Aviv University has argued that the restitution measure should be used expansively. Friedmann, *Restitution of Benefits Obtained Through the Appropriation of Property or the Commission of a Wrong,* 80 Colum. L. Rev. 504 (1980).

In the following article, written almost fifty years after Fuller and Perdue, Professors Robert Cooter and Melvin Aron Eisenberg of Boalt Hall, the University of California, Berkeley, consider the expectation and reliance measures of damages from a modern point of view. Both authors are well-versed in efficiency economics and they use the tools of economic analysis along with other methods of legal reasoning. (The economically unwashed (like the editor) have nothing to fear. Professors Cooter and Eisenberg write readable English and several graphs and references to more technical economic analyses have been deleted.) Unlike the work of some users of efficiency reasoning, the Cooter and Eisenberg results are not always predictable politically, showing that there may be a place for economic reasoning regardless of one's normative point of view—or political values.

In their conclusion, the authors discuss the Fuller and Perdue article as well as the attacks on expectation damages made by Patrick Atiyah and Morton Horwitz discussed in Part I of this book. In all, while this article does not give all the answers to contract damages, it is a rewarding and illuminating discussion from an enlightened point of view. Other valuable discussions of traditional contract remedies include Farnsworth, *Legal Remedies for Breach of Contract*, 70 Colum. L. Rev. 1145 (1970); Vernon, *Expectancy Damages for Breach of Contract: A Primer and Critique*, 1976 Wash. U. L.Q. 179; and Kornhauser, *An Introduction to the Economic Analysis of Contract Remedies*, 57 U. Colo. L. Rev. 683 (1986).

Robert Cooter and Melvin Aron Eisenberg, *Damages for Breach of Contract*, 73 Calif. L. Rev. 1434 (1985)

. . .

IV. What Measure Of Damages Should The Law Prefer?

A. *The General Case*

We now consider whether reliance or expectation damages should be preferred on breach of a bargain contract. In examining this question, we turn from problems of definition to problems of fairness and policy.

In many cases, the issue of selecting between reliance and expectation damages is not significant, because the two measures will yield virtually identical damages. In particular, as shown in Part III, Section A, in a competitive market reliance damages normally will equal expectation damages unless the seller's business conduct is described by the statistical-breach model. [This "model" will be briefly discussed below. —ed.] While it is true that few markets satisfy all the conditions of perfect competition, many come close enough so that the difference between expectation and reliance damages would be insignificant.

The question remains what measure of damages should be used in cases where expectation and reliance may materially diverge. We begin our analysis of that question with the concept of efficient contract terms.

Economists often distinguish between efficiency and distribution. For present purposes, efficiency concerns the amount of value created by a contract, and distribution concerns the division of that value between the parties. Economists say that a contract is efficient if its terms maximize the value that can be created by the contemplated exchange. Put differently, if a contract is inefficient, revising the inefficient terms can increase the value it creates.

The distinction between distribution and efficiency parallels a distinction between the price and nonprice terms of a contract. Adjusting *nonprice* terms often makes it possible to control a contract's efficiency. For example, suppose that our hypothetical contract for a boat includes a term that imposes very high liquidated damages if Seller breaches. There are many types of precaution Seller can take to decrease the probability of breach, such as ordering materials well in advance, hiring extra workers to protect against someone's quitting or falling ill, and reserving drydock facilities needed in the final stages of construction. If the very high liquidated-damages term is enforceable, it may cause Seller to take excessive precaution, in the sense that the cost of the precaution to Seller is greater than the value to Buyer of the increased probability that Seller will perform. In that case, the liquidated damages term is inefficient. If, however, the term is modified by reducing the liquidated damages, the saving to Seller from taking less precaution would exceed the cost to Buyer of exposure to additional risk of nonperformance. This would result in a net increase in the value created by the contract.

The *price* term of a contract controls the distribution of the value that the contract creates. Revision of an inefficient nonprice term can produce an increase in value, and this increase can be distributed between the parties by adjusting the price term so that each party is better off. Thus in the boat case, an increase in value from adjusting the liquidated-damages provision, initially enjoyed by Seller, could be split with Buyer by lowering the price of the boat. The revised contract, containing lower liquidated damages and a lower price, would make both parties better off. Put differently, the original contract stipulates damages in the event of Seller's breach, thus creating a right

---

From similar article originally published in the California Law Review, Vol. 73, N0.5, October 1985, pages 1434-1481.

in Buyer. If Seller is willing to pay more for a modification of this right than the price Buyer would demand, efficiency requires that the contract be modified. In this respect, the exchange of legal rights is no different than the exchange of ordinary commodities.

Under ideal conditions—that is, where negotiation and drafting are cost-free—self-interest compels a rational buyer and seller to create an efficient contract, so that the process of bargaining leads to the maximization of the value a contract creates. In practice, however, there are many obstacles to creating efficient contracts. For example, it is costly to write contract terms. Instead of including explicit terms covering all contingencies, therefore, most contracts leave many issues to be resolved by the courts in case an irreconcilable dispute should arise. Specifically, many contracts leave out terms covering damages for breach, and the courts, in effect, must fill in the contract with legal damages rules.

The damage rules that the courts apply to fill in contracts should be both fair and efficient. Contracts negotiated under ideal conditions will be efficient, and enforcing the terms of such contracts will usually be regarded as fair. Thus we take as a theorem that a damage rule is both fair and efficient if it corresponds to the terms that rational parties situated like the contracting parties would have reached when bargaining under ideal conditions.

The question then is, why might rational parties, who address the issue, choose an expectation measure over a reliance measure? One reason is administrative: it is usually easier to establish in court the value of performance than the extent of reliance. The very fact of reliance is often difficult to prove, as in cases where the reliance consists of passive inaction (such as failure to pursue alternatives) rather than a positive change of position. Even if the fact of reliance can be proved, reliance damages may be difficult to measure. In a noncompetitive market, for example, reliance damages would normally be calculated by the opportunity-cost formula, which requires determining the forgone price. Often, however, the forgone price is very hard to determine, as where the commodity is so unusual that there is no way to establish exactly what the next-best alternative buyer would have paid. In contrast, expectation damages are based on the contract price, which is known, rather than the forgone price, which is speculative. This administrative consideration has implications for both fairness and efficiency. In terms of fairness, the difficulty of proving reliance damages might, paradoxically, result in a failure to protect the reliance

interest unless an expectation measure is chosen. In terms of efficiency, a damage measure that was difficult to prove, and therefore unreliable, would undercut the goal of facilitating private planning.

An intimately related set of considerations has to do with the incentive effects of the expectation and reliance measures. Most contracts are made with the expectation of mutual gain. As shown in Part I, this gain can be measured by the profits created for firms or the consumer's surplus created for individuals. The total gain to both parties—the surplus from exchange—is the value created by the contract. The terms of a contract have incentive effects upon behavior that influence how much value the contract will create. Accordingly, one index to whether a damage rule would have been agreed to by rational parties situated like the contracting parties, and bargaining under ideal conditions, is whether the rule provides incentives for efficient behavior.

Contract damage rules influence several types of behavior, such as searching for trading partners, negotiating exchanges, drafting contracts, keeping or breaking promises, relying upon promises, mitigating damages caused by broken promises, and resolving disputes about broken promises. A complete account of the incentive effects of various damage rules would model the effects on all these types of behavior. Instead of aiming for completeness, we will focus on incentives to perform contracts, to take precautions against breach, and to rely on contracts. To illustrate, in our boat example Seller must decide whether to perform, and how much precaution to take to assure that he will be able to perform, and Buyer must decide how much to rely on Seller's promise (e.g., whether to make a contract for dock space to begin when the boat is scheduled to be delivered). These three decisions concern the rate of breach, the amount of precaution, and the extent of reliance.

1. Performance

We begin with the incentive effects of damage measures on the decision whether to perform, that is, on the rate of breach. A contract involves a promise by at least one party, and it is always possible that events will induce a promisor to refuse to perform, either because performance has become unprofitable or because an alternative performance has become more profitable. If a promisor were liable only for the promisee's reliance damages, the value of the promisor's performance to the promisee would not enter into a purely self-interested calculation by the promisor whether to perform. In contrast, expectation damages place on the promisor the promisee's loss of his share of the contract's value in the event of breach, and thereby sweep that loss into the promisor's calculus of self-interest.

The effect of expectation damages on the promisor's calculations can be stated in terms of externalities. Economists say that an externality exists when one person imposes a cost upon another without paying for it. Incentives for performance are efficient if they compel a promisor to balance the cost to him of performing against the losses to himself and to others that will result if he does not perform. If the promisor does not perform, the promisee loses his share of the value of the contract. If the promisor is liable for that loss, he internalizes not only his own loss but the losses to the promisee that result from his failure to perform. In contrast, if the promisor is liable only for reliance damages, he will not internalize the full value of performance to the promisee. Thus expectation damages create efficient incentives for the promisor's performance, while reliance damages do not, unless they are identical to expectation damages.

By directly affecting the probability that the promisor will perform, the expectation measure has an indirect effect upon the promisee's behavior, which can be stated in terms of planning. Knowing that expectation damages give the promisor strong incentives to perform, the promisee will be more confident that his reliance on the promisor will not expose him to undue risk. The promisee can therefore plan more effectively, because once a contract is made he can order his affairs with the confidence that he will realize its value, whether by performance or damages. In contrast, under a regime of reliance damages, a promisee could plan only on the basis that if breach occurs the law will put him back to where he was when he started. Since planning is by nature forward-looking, this backward-looking nature of reliance damages would be a shaky foundation for ordering complex affairs. Furthermore, it is in the promisor's interest that the promisee be able to plan reliably, because the ability to do so will make the promisee willing to pay a higher price for the promise.

These ideas can also be expressed in institutional terms. The purpose of the social institution of bargain is to create joint value through exchange. In recognition of the desirability of creating value in this manner, the legal institution of contract supports the social institution of the bargain with official sanctions. It is rational to design the legal sanctions so that the joint value from exchange is maximized. This goal is achieved by protecting the expectation interest.

2. Precaution

One reason breach may occur is that the contract has become unprofitable to the promisor due to an increase in his cost of performance. Another reason is that circumstances have changed so that performance has become impracticable, although there is no legal excuse for nonperformance. In either case, the promisor might have forestalled the motivation for breach if he had taken appropriate precautions against the change in cost or circumstances. In the boat case, for example, Seller could have ordered materials well in advance to avoid a price rise, hired extra workers to protect against someone quitting or falling ill, and reserved drydock facilities necessary for the final stages of construction to ensure their availability when needed. Precaution is usually costly in terms of money, time, or effort. From an efficiency standpoint, however, this cost must be balanced against the resulting benefits—a reduction in the probability of breach, and a consequent enhancement of the likelihood that the value of the contract will be realized.

The argument that expectation damages provide incentives for the efficient amount of precaution is the same as the argument that expectation damages provide incentives for the efficient rate of performance. Incentives for precaution are efficient if they compel the promisor to balance the cost of his precaution against the cost of failing to take precaution, including the risk to the promisee of losing his share of the contract's value. In the absence of liability for the promisee's expectation damages, the latter cost would not enter into a purely self-interested calculation by the promisor, and the promisor's incentive for precaution would therefore be inadequate. By placing on the promisor the promisee's risk of losing his share of the contract's value in the event of breach, that risk can be swept into the promisor's calculus of self-interest. Expectation damages, which make the promisor liable for the promisee's loss of value caused by the breach, therefore cause the promisor to internalize the cost of his failure to take adequate precaution, facilitate planning by the promisee, and create incentives for efficient precaution against breach. Reliance damages, which are not based on the value of the contract to the promisee, do not create efficient incentives for precaution except where they equal expectation damages.

3. Reliance

Once a contract has been made, a party may take various actions in reliance upon it. Some such actions fall into the category of performance or preparation for performance. For all practical purposes, these actions are not within the contracting party's discretion. The very purpose of the contract is to commit the party to perform and, by implication, to do whatever is necessary to prepare for performance. If one party does not perform, he is in breach and unable to establish rights against his contracting partner.

There is, however, another category of reliance whose nature or extent is discretionary. The most important component of this category consists of reliance that is neither explicitly nor implicitly required under the contract, although it will enable the relying party to benefit more from the contract. In the boat case, for example, Buyer might buy special navigational equipment in advance so that he can take transoceanic trips as soon as the boat is delivered, rather than postponing his enjoyment of such travel by awaiting delivery of the boat before ordering the special equipment. We will use the term "surplus-enhancing reliance" to refer to discretionary reliance by a contracting party that is undertaken to increase the surplus over and above what he would enjoy had he simply done what was explicitly or implicitly required under the contract.

Typically, surplus-enhancing reliance increases not only the surplus from performance of the contract, but also the loss that will result if the promisor breaches. For example, if Seller in the boat case breaches, Buyer might have to sell the special navigational equipment at a loss. Economists say that a gamble gets more risky as the spread in value between winning and losing increases. More risk involves the possibility of a larger gain and the possibility of a larger loss. Reliance that will enhance the surplus from a contract usually increases the risk involved in a contract.

In the preceding Sections we argued that the rate of breach and the extent of precaution by the promisor are efficient under a regime of expectation damages. The effect of a damages regime on surplus-enhancing reliance is more complex. A rule placing all the costs of such reliance on the promisor might be thought desirable on the ground that it would allow the promisee to plan as if the contract will be performed. On the other hand, we know that not all contracts are performed. Indeed, sometimes both parties can be made better off by nonperformance. It can therefore be argued that it is efficient for a promisee to engage in surplus-enhancing reliance only to the extent that such reliance is profitable given the probability of nonperformance.

Assume, for example, that Lessor agrees to lease commercial premises to Lessee for a new retail store, beginning on July 1. To maximize the value of the contract, Lessee may take various steps in reliance prior to July 1, such as advertising the opening of the store. If it is certain that Lessor will deliver the premises on time, Lessee will make advertising expenditures up to the point where one more dollar of expense will produce one more dollar of profit. Assume the level of surplus-enhancing reliance under this state of the word is X dollars. Now suppose that Lessee realizes there is a given probability of nonperformance by Lessor, say p. On the assumption that p is not zero, the efficient level of reliance, which maximizes the expected value of the contract, is less than X dollars. Presumably, therefore, Lessee should factor the probability p into his calculations and spend less than X dollars for advertising. Correspondingly, if a damage measure creates incentives for Lessee to spend X dollars, the measure may be thought to create an incentive for inefficient behavior. We will use the term overreliance to refer to reliance that is inefficient in this sense.

The potential for inefficient overreliance should not be overemphasized, because it is limited to forms of reliance that increase the benefit and risk associated with the contract. Thus the possibility of overreliance often is not salient in the case of sellers. Typically, a seller's reliance consists solely of preparing to perform and performing, and its discretion involves forms of precaution, such as scheduling. Overreliance also is typically not a salient problem for buyers in the case of contracts for homogenous commodities that are readily available on a competitive market. It is usually efficient for a buyer of such commodities to rely as if the seller's performance were certain, because even if the seller does breach, the buyer can normally replace the breached item with an identical commodity on the market, and thereby put his reliance to full use. For present purposes, however, the important point is not the precise extent of the problem, but that a potential for overreliance can exist.

Both the reliance and the expectation measures might be interpreted to require a breaching promisor to compensate the promisee for all of the promisee's actual reliance, whether efficient or not. For example, the Lessee in the hypothetical might be allowed to recover all of his advertising costs under a reliance measure, on the theory that the costs were incurred in reliance and now have gone to waste. He might be allowed to recover all of his advertising costs under an expectation measure, on the theory that if Lessor had performed, Lessee not only would have captured his expected net profit, but also would have recouped his advertising costs. Such interpretations would create incentives for overreliance, because the promisee's expenditures on advertising would, in effect, be insured by the promisor.

The problem can be avoided, however, if the reliance and expectation measures are interpreted to provide for invariant damages with respect to reliance. A measure of damages is invariant with respect to reliance if the promisee cannot increase the promisor's liability by additional reliance over a given baseline. Under those conditions, the promisee internalizes the risk of reliance over the baseline, so that the damage measure will not in itself cause him to overrely. A familiar example is provided by liquidated damages. To illustrate, suppose that in the retail-store hypothetical, the lease validly specified that Lessor would pay $500 per week for late completion, up to a maximum of $8,000. The damages that Lessee could recover on Lessor's breach would then be unaffected by the extent of Lessee's advertising or other surplus-enhancing reliance. Thus the liquidation of damages makes damages invariant with respect to reliance.

Similarly, the reliance and expectation measures can be interpreted as invariant with respect to reliance by limiting recovery on the basis of reliance to costs that are reasonably incurred. Such an interpretation would make the two measures invariant, because reasonability is an objective test. Under this test, therefore, actual reliance in excess of reasonable reliance would not be compensated, and the risk of reliance above the reasonability baseline would be internalized by the promisee. If the reasonability baseline was set at the level of efficient reliance, then overreliance would be uncompensated and the promisee would bear its full cost.

Arguably, such an interpretation already prevails under existing law. Both the expectation and reliance measures undoubtedly contemplate that only reasonable reliance will be compensated. The question for present purposes is what kinds of factors determine reasonability. If economic analysis suggests that it is inefficient to engage in surplus-enhancing reliance without regard to the likelihood of breach, that analysis can be read into the meaning of reasonability. Accordingly, although either the expectation or the reli-

ance measure can be interpreted in a way that might create incentives for overreliance in some cases, there is nothing in the nature of these measures that requires such an interpretation, and there is good reason for interpreting them in a manner that would not give rise to overreliance. Under such an interpretation, both the expectation and the reliance measures would lead to an efficient level of reliance.

In short, where expectation and reliance damages diverge, expectation damages are preferable because they better assure that reliance will be compensated, better facilitate planning, provide better incentives for efficient performance and precaution, and provide no worse incentives for overreliance.

B. *The Limits of the Expectation Principle*

In the preceding Section, we showed why expectation damages are normally fair and efficient. In this Section, we shall discuss a special problem with expectation damages that arises when a seller's business conduct corresponds to our fishing or statistical-breach models.

[The "statistical-breach model" involves sellers whose market includes a high, but statistically predictable number of breaches, for example, airlines who can predict that ten percent of their passengers will be no-shows. The "fishing model" is described in a passage that appears earlier in the article:—ed.]

Example E: Seller supplies branded plumbingware to plumbing subcontractors under an exclusive territorial franchise. Seller's practice is to keep in inventory a full line of three colors and selected models in other colors. If a buyer wants merchandise that Seller does not have in inventory, Seller orders the models and colors the buyer wants. Seller always charges the manufacturer's suggested list price. Buyer places an order for models and colors that Seller does not have in inventory, but later refuses to accept the merchandise because of changed conditions in his business. Seller retains the breached items in inventory and shortly thereafter sells them to someone else at the list price. Seller sues Buyer for breach of contract.

We call the model that describes business conduct of this type (*Example E*) the fishing model, because the seller sets out plumbingware at a fixed price as bait and fishes for customers. If one fish gets away from a fisherman, the rest of the catch is unaffected by the escape; losing one fish does not enable a fisherman to catch another fish. Similarly, the effect of

Buyer's breach in *Example E* is the loss of one sale, and that loss does not make another sale possible.

In analyzing this problem, we shall return to the theorem that a contract term can be deemed both fair and efficient if it corresponds to the term that rational parties would probably have agreed to if they had bargained under ideal conditions (that is, if negotiation and drafting were cost-free). Based on this theorem, we shall distinguish between the expectation principle and what we shall call the expectation theory. The expectation *theory*—which follows from the theorem—is that in case of breach the injured party's recovery should be measured under the damage rule the parties probably would have agreed to at the time of contract-formation if they had bargained under ideal conditions and had addressed the issue. The expectation *principle*—which is a doctrinal principle of contract law—is that in case of breach the injured party should be put in a position as good as he would have enjoyed had the contract been performed. The principle gives fair expression to the theory in most but not all cases.

We begin with the fishing model. Here the seller supplies commodities to all buyers at a fixed price, so that breach causes a reduction in sales volume. At least at first glance, the lost-surplus formula—and more particularly, the "lost-volume" measure of damages—is necessary to compensate for this reduction in volume. However, there has been much controversy in secondary literature concerning the propriety of lost-volume damages in such circumstances. Whether expectation damages are appropriate when the injured party's method of doing business is best described by the fishing model or by the statistical-planning model, and if so, how to correctly measure the seller's expectation, are difficult questions, to which we now turn.

Prior to the adoption of the Uniform Commercial Code, a seller's measure of damages for breach of a contract for the sale of goods was governed by the Uniform Sales Act. That Act provided that if there was an available market for the goods, the seller's damages normally were to be measured by the difference between the market price and the contract price. In contrast, section 2-708(2) of the U.C.C provides that if the difference between contract price and market price is inadequate to put the seller in as good a position as performance would have done, the seller's damages are to be measured by the profit, "including reasonable overhead," that he would have made from the buyer's full performance. The case law

holds that this alternative measure is to be used when the seller conducts his business in such a manner that the breach did not enable him to make a substitute sale (a sale he would not otherwise have made), so that as a result of the breach the seller loses volume. To put the matter in terms of the analysis in this Article, the Uniform Sales Act provided that in a contract for the sale of goods the seller was normally entitled only to substitute-price damages. In contrast, the U.C.C. provides that the seller can recover lost-surplus damages when appropriate. The case law holds that lost-surplus damages are appropriate when the seller's method of doing business is best described by the fishing model.

The routine award of lost-surplus damages for the buyer's breach of a contract for the sale of goods is a relatively recent phenomenon. Such damages have long been routinely awarded, however, for the buyer's breach of a contract for the provision of services. Consider, for example, the following illustration:

> *Example F*: *B*, a manufacturer, wants to have an office building constructed for its headquarters on property it owns. *S*, a contractor, agrees to construct the building for $5 million. *S*'s projected out-of-pocket cost of construction is $4.3 million. The contract is entered into on May 1, 1983; construction is to begin on August 1, 1983, and to be completed on May 1, 1984. Payment is to be made in installments as the building progresses. On July 15, 1983, *B* repudiates the contract.

The fairness and efficiency grounds adduced in Part IV, Section A to justify expectation damages also support the award of expectation damages in general, and lost-surplus damages in particular, in cases like *Example F*. A contractor's capacity to take on jobs normally is constrained by such factors as bonding limits and depth of management. Ordinarily, a contractor will attempt to take on as many jobs as it can within the limit of these constraints. Accordingly, it is likely that by virtue of making the breached contract, the contractor will have forgone the opportunity to make another contract, which would have yielded its own surplus. The contractor is also likely to incur other opportunity costs, such as allocating executive time to planning or performing the contract. Fairness normally requires that a victim of breach at least be compensated for his costs, including his opportunity costs. However, it would often be very difficult for the contractor to quantify his opportunity costs and prove them in court. It may be difficult for the contractor to establish that an opportunity to make another contract was forgone, if only because, having made the breached contract, he stopped searching for other opportunities. The allocation of executives' time to a project, and the related planning costs, are also difficult to establish. Because of these difficulties, a reliance measure would be unpredictable in its application. Unpredictability of application is an obstacle both to protecting the contractor's reliance interest, as required for fairness, and to reliable planning, as required for efficiency. In addition, expectation damages make the buyer internalize the benefits of the contract to the parties, and thereby provide him with efficient incentives in making decisions concerning performance and precaution, and further assure reliability in planning.

The same reasoning supports measuring the contractor's expectation by the lost-surplus formula. In theory, the substitute-price formula might be used in such cases, if the contractor completed construction of the building and sold it to an alternative buyer. In practice, when the buyer breaches, the contractor usually must abandon the project, because normally the construction is to occur on the buyer's land, or it is tailored expressly for the buyer, or completion would violate the principle of mitigation of damages or expose the contractor to undue business risks. Furthermore, lost-surplus damages, and not substitute-price damages, will cause the buyer to internalize the full benefits of the contract to the contractor, and thereby assure reliable planning and provide the buyer with the correct efficiency incentives in making decisions concerning performance and precaution. Thus the lost-surplus formula normally will be the appropriate formula to measure expectation damages in cases like *Example F*.

The analysis applied to *Example F* can be extended to most contracts involving the provision of services to merchant-buyers. It may also be extended in substantial part to contracts for the sale of goods to a merchant-buyer by a seller whose method of doing business is best described by the fishing model (as in *Example E*). The analysis may break down, however, where the buyer is a consumer of nonindividualized or "off-the-shelf" services, as in the following example:

Example G: Seller owns a dancing school. He sets a fee of $300 for each 20-session class, and allows preenrollment when accompanied by a down payment of $30. Seller's teachers are on contract, and the building in which classes are conducted is held under a long-term lease, so Seller's out-of-pocket cost for conducting any given class is virtually nil. Buyer preenrolls on May 1 for a class beginning on July 1. By May 20, Buyer's circumstances have changed, and he cancels. The class was undersubscribed, so Buyer's enrollment did not preclude Seller from contracting with another student, and Buyer's cancellation did not enable Seller to enroll a student who would not otherwise have been enrolled. Seller now sues Buyer to recover $270, the difference (calculated under the lost-surplus formula) between the profits it would have earned if the Buyer performed, and the profits it will actually earn given Buyer's cancellation.

If Seller can recover $270, Buyer will have paid the full $300 contract price to Seller although he has received no lessons. Such a recovery would not be easy to justify on the ground that the expectation measure is required to protect the reliance interest in a bargain context. By hypothesis, Seller has incurred neither out-of-pocket nor opportunity costs. Would such a recovery be justified by considerations of efficiency? In Part IV, Section A, we argued that a damage rule should cause a promisor to internalize the value of the contract, so as to provide incentives for efficient rate of breach and efficient precaution. This argument applies to *Example G*, but there is a broader set of efficiency considerations that must be discussed to reach a satisfactory conclusion.

To begin the broader analysis, recall first the theorem that a contract term can be deemed both fair and efficient if it corresponds to the term that rational parties situated like the contracting parties would probably have agreed to if they were bargaining under ideal conditions. Recall next the expectation theory, which follows from this theorem: expectation damages should be based on the measure that rational parties situated like the contracting parties would probably have agreed to if they had bargained under ideal conditions and addressed the issue. In analyzing whether the parties in *Example G* would probably have agreed that if Buyer breached, Seller's damages would be measured by its lost surplus, the relevant question is why someone in Buyer's position would make a contract on May 1, rather than simply wait until July 1 and enroll on the first day of class. Consumers normally do not make contracts like that in *Example G* for the purpose of allocating the risk of price changes, or speculating in the market for dancing lessons. Rather, the typical purposes of such contracting are to ensure supply (that is, to ensure a place in the class) and, perhaps, to commit oneself to an action.

Given these purposes, it seems unlikely that Buyer would have agreed ex ante to a provision that if he cancelled in advance he would pay the entire tuition. In effect, such a provision would allocate to Buyer all the risks entailed by his change of mind. Buyer would be unlikely to accept such a risk allocation, because it would be greatly disproportionate to both the benefit to be derived (which is not the dancing lesson itself, but the reservation of a place in line and the personal commitment), and the harm inflicted on Seller in terms of how much worse off he is as a result of having made the contract. Seller, for its part, would not be likely to insist on such a risk allocation, because (a) if he did so he would diminish his profitability, since too few consumers would sign contracts; (b) it would be unnecessary to do so, in light of the relatively low degree of harm he will suffer; and (c) as we shall show, Seller could utilize other mechanisms that would address his needs at significantly less cost (and therefore greater acceptability) to Buyer than lost-surplus damages.[47]

Are lost-surplus damages required to provide the correct incentives to Buyer for performance and precaution? Since these efficiency considerations concern incentives, they are premised on the assumption that the parties know how damages will be measured, or that the damage measure used by the courts corresponds to the measure the parties had reason to expect the courts would use or corresponds to a term the parties probably would have agreed to if they had bargained under ideal conditions and addressed the issue. Measuring damages by a given formula cannot affect a party's incentives if he does not know, have reason to expect, or probably would have agreed that damages will be measured by that formula. Given Buyer's purposes for entering into the contract, his consumer status, and the likelihood that he would not have agreed ex ante to a lost-surplus formula, it is hard to imagine that Buyer would have known or reasonably expected that damages would be measured this way by the courts.

Are lost-surplus damages justified on the grounds that they are necessary to enable Seller to plan effectively? Although firm proof is lacking, the available evidence tends to suggest that firms selling services to consumers can and do plan effectively without expecting to collect damages measured under the lost-surplus formula. For example, the problem raised by *Example G* is characteristic of any contract for tuition, and such contracts often involve relatively large amounts. Nevertheless, many and perhaps most schools provide for refunding tuition on a declining basis if the student drops out.

The lack of a planning justification for lost-surplus damages is particularly clear in the case of a seller whose method of doing business is accurately described by the statistical-planning model. By hypothesis, such a seller does not make plans on the basis that any particular contract will be kept. If the seller's statistical forecast is reasonably accurate, his planning is therefore not interrupted by any single breach, or even by a number of breaches. Indeed, if the seller's forecast is correct, he may be said to realize his ex ante expectation in spite of breach. Such a seller therefore can plan reliably even if his damages are not measured by the lost-surplus formula.

Accordingly, in contracts for off-the-shelf services to be provided to a consumer, lost-surplus damages normally are not required by either efficiency or fairness considerations, particularly where the statistical-planning model is applicable. Rather, damages in such cases should be based on the amount necessary to (a) reimburse the seller for incidental costs, (b) provide enough deterrence to facilitate planning, and (c) pay for the buyer's benefit in having had a place reserved. A formula that reflects these three elements would probably be the formula the parties would have agreed to ex ante had they addressed the issue and bargained under ideal conditions.

The measurement required need not be difficult. In most cases, the law could treat a deposit by the buyer as a tacit liquidated-damages provision even if the contract does not so provide. It seems likely that most consumers expect that if they cancel a contract for off-the-shelf services they will lose their deposit

---

[47] If Seller had been operating at full capacity, and reserved a place for a Buyer, he may have turned away an alternative customer. If Buyer's place was not eventually filled, Seller will have incurred an opportunity cost equal to the contract price. One way to handle this problem is to permit Seller to recover his lost surplus in such a case under a reliance theory, with the burden on Seller to prove both that he was operating at full capacity and that he turned away another customer because of his contract with Buyer. However, if Buyer would probably not have agreed to lost-surplus damages ex ante, recovery of lost surplus might be inappropriate even on a reliance theory, unless the parties contracted to that effect.

(whether or not the contract so provides) but nothing more. Setting damages equivalent to either an explicit liquidated damages clause or the amount of any deposit therefore would satisfy the expectation theory, unless the buyer was not aware of the liquidated-damages clause or the amount of the deposit was clearly in excess of what the buyer would probably have expected to forfeit on cancellation.[49] In cases where the seller neither includes a liquidated-damages provision nor requires a deposit, the law might limit damages to reliance or to the substitute-price formula, or might impose a charge based on the customary level of deposits required in the relevant industry, on the ground that this practice shows what similarly situated sellers and buyers would agree to under like circumstances.

Expectation damages measured in this way might be denominated "cancellation-charge damages." The manner in which such damages should operate can be illustrated by the airline business. The airlines' overbooking system is an application of the statistical-planning model of doing business. By use of this system, airlines can make reliable plans even without requiring no-show passengers to pay lost-surplus damages (which would be almost equal to the entire cost of the ticket if a plane has vacant seats, since there is almost no out-of-pocket cost for carrying one additional passenger). On the other hand, if passengers can make multiple bookings without cost, they may have an incentive to do so, thereby increasing the airlines' costs and making it more expensive for the airlines to compile and administer their forecasts. However, a reasonable cancellation charge would normally be sufficient to induce a passenger not to engage in multiple bookings, because if he does so he will end up paying more than the cost of the ticket for his flight. Accordingly, airlines characteristically do not attempt to collect lost-surplus damages, but do sometimes impose cancellation charges.

Let us now apply this analysis to the sale of relatively homogeneous goods by a merchant to a consumer, as in the following hypothetical:

Example H: Buyer, a high school teacher, wants to buy a new Buick. After shopping around, Buyer decides to buy at Seller's dealership, since Seller's price matches the lowest price available from competing dealers and Seller has a good reputation for servicing. On October 1, Buyer signs a contract to buy from Seller a new Buick, with specified accessories, for $10,000, delivery on December 1. Buyer puts down a deposit of $250. On November 1, before the factory has begun to fill Seller's order for Buyer's car, Buyer repudiates the contract. Seller's factory cost for the Buick ordered by Buyer is $8,500, and Seller can buy as many new Buicks from the factory as it sells.

Much the same analysis can be made in this kind of case as in *Example G*. Under the lost-surplus formula, Seller would recover $1500. This result is not as draconian as the application of that formula in cases like *Example G*. Seller's projected out-of-pocket cost is significant, and the recovery therefore would be well below the entire amount of the contract price. Nevertheless, the result is not easy to justify on the theory that lost-surplus damages are required to protect the reliance interest, since Seller will have incurred little or no cost at the time of the breach. Similarly, it is unlikely that Buyer would have agreed ex ante to a provision measuring damages for cancellation in this manner. It is unlikely too that lost-surplus damages are necessary to provide Buyer with the correct incentives for efficient behavior, because Buyer probably believes that at worst he will lose his deposit. Finally, it is unlikely that lost-surplus damages are required to enable Seller to plan effectively, since Seller is likely to use a combination of the statistical-planning model and deposits to deal with the problem of breach. Indeed, casual investigation suggests that few mass retailers—including few new-car dealerships—bring suits for breach of executory contracts. Accordingly, Seller's damages should be limited to the deposit.

Conclusion

Fairness seems to require that a person who breaches a contract should pay compensation to the victim of breach for the injury he suffers as a result. But the meanings of the terms "compensation" and "injury" are fundamentally ambiguous. Under a reliance conception, the uninjured state is the condition the victim would have been in if he had not made the contract with the breaching party. Under an expectation conception, the uninjured state is the condition the victim would have been in if the breaching party had performed the contract. Which conception should govern is far from obvious.

Under certain conditions, it is unnecessary to choose between these two conceptions. In perfectly competitive markets where the rate of breach is low and the seller's business conduct is described by the

---

[49] U.C.C. § 2-718 would be relevant here.

traditional economic model, expectation and reliance damages will be virtually equivalent. This equivalence also will hold in imperfectly competitive markets, if market conditions do not vary materially from those of perfect competition and the seller's business conduct conforms to the traditional model applicable to these markets.

Often, however, the two measures may diverge significantly. This may occur, for example, in imperfectly competitive markets whose conditions differ materially from those of perfectly competitive markets, or in which the seller's business conduct is best characterized by the fishing model. The question of choice between competing conceptions of injury and compensation then becomes material. Traditionally, courts and commentators were united in holding that the expectation conception of injury governed in such cases. In fact, prior to the 1930's the reliance principle operated in only a covert manner. However, with the promulgation in 1932 of section 90 of the Restatement of Contracts, and the publication in 1934 [sic — ed.] of Fuller and Perdue's landmark article *The Reliance Interest in Contract Damages*,[51] the reliance principle began to undergo a process of steady and impressive growth. Until the last ten years or so, this growth served to expand liability in contract. Recently, however, some commentators have taken the position that the reliance principle should be used to reduce liability, by substituting the reliance conception for the expectation conception in the law of damages.[52]

The reasons for this position are complex. Partly it is an attack on the very institution of contract: liability based on reliance may be conceptualized as liability in tort. It also results, however, from the apparent lack of a clear rationale for expectation damages. The reliance conception of injury reflects the basic intuition that if somebody is worse off than he was before, he has been hurt. The expectation conception reflects a much more subtle intuition, and indeed it is plausible to argue that the mere defeat of an expectation is not a very serious injury.

One purpose of this Article has been to explore the meanings of the expectation and reliance conceptions of damages, and to develop the basic formulas through which these conceptions can be expressed. A second purpose has been to show that the expectation conception has a sound basis in both fairness and

policy. As a matter of fairness, one who breaches a contract ought at a minimum to compensate the promisee's reliance, and in many or most cases the expectation measure yields virtually the same damages as the reliance measure, but is much easier to administer. As a matter of policy, expectation damages best facilitate planning. As a matter of both fairness and policy, a damage measure is appropriate if it is the measure the parties probably would have chosen if they had bargained under ideal conditions and addressed the issue, and in most cases the parties to a bargain probably would have chosen the expectation measure, because it protects reliance, facilitates planning, and provides the correct incentives for performance and precaution.

Another purpose of this Article has been to show that the term expectation is itself ambiguous. One meaning of the term, which we call the expectation principle, is that a victim of breach should be put in the position he would have been if the contract had been performed. A second meaning, which we call the expectation theory, is that damages should be based on the measure that parties situated like the contracting parties probably would have agreed to, if they had bargained under ideal conditions and addressed the damages issue. Still a third meaning, which we call statistical expectation, is that if a person makes a number of comparable contracts with a known probable rate of breach, he should enjoy the overall profit level he expected to achieve, rather than the profit level he would have achieved if the rate of breach were zero. We suggest that where the expectation principle and the expectation theory diverge— which is particularly likely where a seller forms a statistical expectation—the theory rather than the principle should govern. Thus in many cases involving consumers, where damages under the expectation priniciple would be measured by the seller's lost volume, the parties would probably have agreed to a much smaller measure of damages (such as forfeit of a deposit) if they had addressed the issue. It is this measure that should govern.

Indeed, it seems likely that the assault by some commentators on expectation damages results in part from the intuition that damages measured under the expectation principle are out of place in just such cases. This intuition is correct, but the way the problem should be dealt with is not by denying expecta-

---

[51] Fuller & Perdue, The Reliance Interest in Contract Damages (pts. 1 & 2), 46 Yale L.J. 52, 373 (1936-1937).

[52] See, e.g., P.S. Atiyah, The Rise and Fall of Freedom of Contract 1-7, 754-64 (1979); see also Horwitz, The Historical Foundations of Modern Contract Law, 87 Harv. L. Rev. 917 (1974).

tion damages, but by reconceptualizing the expectation interest in such cases through use of the
expectation theory.

Judicially Imposed Compromise—The Wisdom of Solomon?

Throughout this book there have been many substantive discussions of relational contracts, and of the need for cooperation among the parties to contracts. One such discussion took place in the Spiedel, Hillman and Dawson articles in Part IIIC on adjustment of long-term contracts. A major hurdle for any attempt at judicially imposed cooperation is the traditional limitation of common-law remedies to an all-or-nothing result. Although Professors Speidel and Hillman refer to the power of courts of equity to shape remedies and condition decrees on some modification by the winning party, Professor Dawson claimed that they had painted the courts of equity as more free-wheeling than they really were. In any event, most contracts cases involve only claims for money damages, and the courts have never had a power to impose compromises if either party insists on a trial. It should be apparent that the traditional process fits better with a bargain-based system of contract than it does with a relational one.

Professor John E. Coons, now of Boalt Hall, Berkeley, has published two provocative articles calling on courts to impose compromises, Coons, *Approaches to Court-Imposed Compromise—The Uses of Doubt and Reason*, 58 Nw. U. L. Rev. 750 (1964), and Coons, *Compromise as Precise Justice*, 68 Calif. L. Rev. 250 (1980). His articles are referred to by Professor Dawson, and served as an important influence on an article by Professor William F. Young of Columbia, *Half Measures*, 81 Colum. L. Rev. 19 (1981), which appeared in a symposium on the Second Restatement of Contracts. Young is a far from effusive supporter of the notion, but he does give it some backing. If Young and Coons are correct in asserting a power in common law courts to take "half-measures," a powerful lever is created to move parties in long-term, relational contracts to compromise disputes. We are told by empiricists like Stewart Macaulay that businesspeople usually compromise, and that the traditional all-or-nothing judicial approach works against this instinct. We also know that in practice, most lawsuits are settled and many judges force or at least encourage settlement through informal pressure. Overt recognition of a power to award only partial damages would mesh nicely with the substantive approaches advocated by Ian Macneil, Richard Speidel and Robert Hillman. On the other hand, the power is subject to the criticisms leveled by Dawson, who was not impressed with the concept. If the courts are not able or willing to give half-measures, is that an argument for alternative methods of dispute resolution?

Changing the Measure of Contract Damages— and Using Remedies Not Based on Contract

In recent years many articles have suggested "supra-compensatory" damages. (The term I believe, is Edward Yorio's in *In Defense of Money Damages for Breach of Contract*, 82 Colum. L. Rev. 1365 (1982).) Among these are John A. Sebert, Jr.'s *Punitive and Nonpecuniary Damages in Actions Based Upon Contract: Toward Achieving the Objective of Full Compensation*, 33 U.C.L.A. L. Rev. 1565 (1986); Patricia H. Marschall's *Willfulness: A Crucial Factor in Choosing Remedies for Breach of Contract*, 24 Ariz. L. Rev. 733 (1982); Daniel Farber's *Reassessing the Economic Efficiency of Compensatory Damages for Breach of Contract*, 66 Va. L. Rev. 1443 (1980), and a work-in-progress by Professor W. David Slawson of the University of Southern California on damages for bad faith breach of contract.

The Sebert article shows in some detail that many courts have expanded the measure of contract recovery in the last few years. One major vehicle has been to find a tort of bad faith breach of contract, a topic discussed substantively at several earlier points in this book, among them the Summers-Burton debate over good faith in Part IIIB(2), the Knapp and Farnsworth articles on agreements to bargain or negotiate in Part IIA, and the Uncontracts article in Part IB. See also Anderson, *Good Faith in the Enforcement of Contracts*, 73 Iowa L. Rev. 299 (1988). The effect of using tort remedies in what are essentially contract cases is to moot the traditional debate over contract remedies by going around them. The result is to make contract litigation much more lucrative, and arguably to put greater pressure on a contract breacher to settle for the victim's full loss, even if part of that loss would not be recoverable under the traditional contract damage rules. Critics of this expansion of recovery argue that it produces windfalls and leads to blackmail and economic inefficiency. For an argument that better results could be reached by expanding traditional contract remedies and widening the scope of liability within contract for bad faith conduct, see Note, *Tort Remedies for Breach of Contract: The Expansion of Tortious Breach of the Implied Covenant of Good Faith and Fair Dealing Into the Commercial Realm*, 86 Colum. L. Rev. 377 (1986).

Still another way in which contract-like cases may have expanded remedies is the use of statutory remedies such as consumer statutes and unfair and deceptive trade practice acts. These statutory remedies often provide attorneys' fees to successful plaintiffs and authorize the award of punitive or multiple damages as a matter of right. Although the statutes were intended to benefit consumers, particularly poor consumers, they have often been applied in ways that benefit business plaintiffs and Yuppies fighting the BMW dealer. (In Texas, it is almost an automatic reaction for a lawyer to put in a Deceptive Trade Practices Act count in a contract complaint. I would consider it close to malpractice for a Texas lawyer not to make a conscious assessment whether a contract claim can be fit into the Texas DTPA.)

In the following article, originally given at the 1988 Association of American Law Schools Annual Meeting, Professor Stewart Macaulay of Wisconsin, that eternal gadfly who has appeared prominently throughout this book, took a wry look at what had been done to consumer protection and deceptive trade practice statutes in the years since consumer protection lost its sexiness. In the process he kept up his attack on the teaching of contract law, and its lack of contact with what students always call "the real world."

Stewart Macaulay, *Bambi Meets Godzilla: Contracts Scholarship and Teaching vs. State Unfair and Deceptive Trade Practices and Consumer Protection Statutes*,* 26 Houston L. Rev. No. 4 (1989)

Wolfgang Friedmann saw traditional contract law as the home of free market values, but he pointed out that statutes and administrative regulations were shifting contract values to those of the welfare state.[1]

Lawrence Friedman argued that classic contract law was the law of left-overs—areas too new or too unimportant to warrant their own statute. While these insights both are over twenty years old and true, they

---

* This paper is based on a talk given at the Association of American Law Schools meeting in Miami, Florida, January 9, 1988. Dr. Jacqueline Macaulay took time from her law practice to edit it. My colleagues John Kidwell and Bill Whitford offered valuable suggestions. They all greatly improved the document. However, I didn't take all their good advice, and, as always, all errors remain mine alone.

[1] I was reminded of Friedmann's comment by Ian Macneil. See Macneil, Book Review, 14 Journal of Law and Society 373 (1987). Friedmann's ideas appear in his Law in a Changing Society 90 (1959).

seldom affect contracts teaching or research. Academic contracts celebrates free market capitalism. The few exceptions serve to show that everything is under control. In this picture, capitalist contract doctrine plays Godzilla, the monster that overwhelms the Bambi of statutes which, at best, create minor and trivial exceptions to the general law of contract. However, when we walk outside the doors of the academy and see contract in society, it is not so clear who is playing what part.

First, I'll look at some of our practice. Then I'll review state unfair and deceptive trade practices statutes which may invade much of contract's turf. Finally, I'll offer some explanations for our inattention to these statutes and draw a few conclusions.

Peripheries Nibble Away at Cores.

Duncan Kennedy describes academic contract study as core and periphery.[3] Our tradition offers a core of doctrine which seems hard and rational. However, there is also a periphery of soft exceptions which make minor corrections so we may achieve justice in unusual situations. Kennedy argues that, in practice, the periphery swallows the core. As exceptions expand, the rule becomes little more than "it depends." For example, take promissory estoppel, waiver and the Uniform Commercial Code's many sections which seriously undercut the traditional consideration doctrine. Then to make matters even more incoherent, traditionalist judges can counterattack. Professor Llewellyn, in the U.C.C., told judges to search for substantive justice using the grand style of reasoning. However, his innovations concerning requirements contracts and the parol evidence rule can be offset by a strict reading of the Code's Statute of Frauds.

Academic contract is not an empirical study. We have no systematic way of discovering which doctrines are being used, abused or forgotten. We miss new doctrines that displace old ones. We may not see that a peripheral rule has almost destroyed one of our core concepts. Or, worse yet, our theory may delegitimate one soft exception and confine it to a small place. Nonetheless, we may overlook other laws, particularly statutes, which eat away the foundations of our conventional wisdom.

Long ago in law school, I learned that courts were not interested in the fairness of contract negotiations. Of course, fraud and duress were defenses, but few people could meet their requirements. Courts also were not interested in the outcome of bargains. Judges told us that they were interested in the existence but not the adequacy of consideration. People had a duty to take care of themselves. A deal is a deal, and there is nothing wrong with driving a hard bargain.

Then came the reformist 1960s. *Williams v. Walker-Thomas*[6] became the contract teachers' morality play. Evil Walker-Thomas preyed on a poor welfare mother. If she missed a payment on one item, then Walker-Thomas had rigged matters so that they could clean out her apartment and take away everything she ever had bought from them. The trial court wanted to help Mrs. Williams, but the judge thought his hands were tied. The Walker-Thomas transaction took place before the U.C.C. went into effect in the District of Columbia. As a result, the court could not find the cross-collateral clause unconscionable under Section 2-302. A legal services office appealed the case. Judge Skelly Wright rode to the rescue. Much to our amazement, he told us that unconscionability always had been part of the common-law in the District. Most of us would have thought that unconscionability was only a limitation on specific performance before this decision.[7] The *denouement*? As usual, the case was remanded for findings on unconscionability and then settled.[8]

The *Williams* decision quickly became a favorite of law review and casebook authors. It still is. For example, my survey of 14 casebooks published since 1980 shows that nearly everyone teaches it. Originally, the *Williams* case showed how a progressive judge could use the U.C.C. to fashion weapons for legal services programs in the War on Poverty. Students eager to battle for the poor might be reassured that contracts was up to date and with it.

Today, if we explore appellate reports dealing with Section 2-302 via a Lexis search, we find that people such as Mrs. Williams have almost disappeared from judicial opinions.[9] Yet *Williams v. Walker-Thomas* remains in the casebooks and law reviews. Why? Notes

[3] Kennedy, Form and Substance in Private Law Adjudication, 89 Harv. L. Rev. 1685, 1737 (1976).

[6] 350 F.2d 445 (D.C. Cir. 1965).

[7] See Campbell Soup Co. v. Wentz, 172 F.2d 80 (3d Cir. 1948).

[8] The Chief Staff Attorney of the District of Columbia Legal Assistance Office said that Walker-Thomas dropped

all claims against Mrs. Williams and paid her the reasonable value of the used items it had taken from her. See Dostert, Appellate Restatement of Unconscionability: Civil Legal Aid at Work, 54 A.B.A.J. 1183, 1186 (1968).

[9] Business people assert unconscionability in incredible numbers. Most lose. Perhaps the farmer faced with what David Stockman called disinvestment is the Mrs. Williams of

and questions as well as a few articles suggest that *Williams* now plays a very different role in the drama of this era. Writers see the case as an expression of knee-jerk liberalism. Students follow the grand tradition of hissing the villain and cheering the hero, and then contracts professors use the case to trap them. We hope that our privileged students have some empathy for Mrs. Williams, but once the class accepts Judge Wright's decision, the professor moves in. On one hand, we may be hurting poor welfare mothers in the name of helping them. Welfare mothers are poor credit risks, and if they cannot make contracts that bind, they will not be able to make contracts at all.[10] Walker-Thomas demanded cross-collateral clauses to minimize its losses from defaulting debtors. These clauses must be necessary. If they weren't, competitors would offer goods to welfare mothers on a different basis to gain sales. Mrs. Williams was able to share in the consumer society which she saw on her television set only because Walker-Thomas found a way to profit by supplying these goods to her. If we regulate too much, we risk taking away her chance to improve her situation if only a little. Efficiency and the rule of law yield a just society, and Yuppie students can relax and seek big salaries because this is the best of all possible worlds.[11]

Once many students begin to nod in agreement, the professor can bound to the opposite side of the ideological street. *Williams* is wrong because it is little more than a gesture when so much more is needed. Judge Wright can be seen as a mad field marshal leading a column of cardboard tanks against an enemy with real weapons. Mrs. Williams wasn't

likely to find buying appliances at reasonable prices on reasonable terms much easier in the future. Judge Wright couldn't order VISA or Sears to issue a credit card to her. After the decision, Mrs. Williams was still a welfare mother living in the inner city.[12] The case did little to open opportunities for her or her children. The opinion is largely liberal symbolism. It blinds us to the structural changes needed to attack poverty. Liberal students usually become uneasy when they recognize that marginal reform is not enough.

Indeed, if the government wanted to provide appliances to the poor, it could do it far more directly than by funding a legal services program to assert U.C.C. § 2-302. Those in the military or in diplomatic service overseas can buy goods at a post exchange. Why not establish PX's for those on welfare, selling goods at fair prices on fair terms? The government could use its buying power to shop for higher quality at lower prices and share this gain with Mrs. Williams and others in her position. By this time the liberal students are squirming and the conservatives are anguished. The professor, of course, continues to pour gasoline on the fire.

What about the problems of paternalism?[13] If Mrs. Williams can learn to cope with Walker-Thomas, she can cope better with the rest of her circumstances. She may be empowered to better her situation. Indeed, the government PX scheme or anything similar is likely to offer what experts or bureaucrats decide she should want rather than what she does want. Paternalism involves treating her as less than a competent person.[14] All we know is that she is poor and

---

the 1980s. See John Deere Leasing Co. v. Blubaugh, 636 F.Supp. 1569 (D. Kans. 1986) ("This court is surprised that a reputable company such as Deere would stoop to this." At 1571.); A & M Produce Co. v. FMC Corp., 135 Cal.App.3d 473, 186 Cal.Rptr 114 (4th Dist. 1982) ("No experienced farmer would spend $32,000 for equipment which could not process his tomatoes before they rot and no fair and honest merchant would sell such equipment with representations negated in its own sales contract.")

[10] Compare Judge Posner's opinion in Selmer Co. v. Blakeslee-Midwest Co., 704 F.2d 924 (7th Cir. 1983).

[11] But compare Greenberg, Easy Terms, Hard Times: Complaint Handling in the Ghetto, in L. Nader (ed.) No Access to Law: Alternatives to the American Judicial System at 379 (1980). It is hard to imagine understanding the Williams case without reading Greenberg's account of the business practices of Walker-Thomas. To a great extent, the case involves the assumptions created by a long-term continuing relationship, what Sally Falk Moore calls a fictive friendship. See Moore, Law and Social Change: The Semi-Autonomous Social Field as an Appropriate Subject of Study, 7 Law & Society Rev. 719, 727-729 (1973).

[12] My colleague Professor Daniel Bernstein and law stu-

dents at Howard University tried to find what had happened to Mrs. Williams. Unfortunately, they could not trace her.

[13] See Kennedy, Distributive and Paternalist Motives in Contract and Tort Law, with Special Reference to Compulsory Terms and Unequal Bargaining Power, 41 Maryland L. Rev. 563 (1982); Kronman, Paternalism and the Law of Contracts, 92 Yale L.J. 763 (1983). Some students have suggested that the term should be maternalism. They argue that mothers take care of children's problems, acting in their best interests while fathers seldom do this. Fathers just decide important questions, refusing to allow their children any voice. I hope such stereotypes are unwarranted. Others prefer parentalism. I continue to use paternalism, but I could be persuaded to change.

[14] Professor Patricia Williams writes of her experiences at the Harvard Law School: "I learned to undo images of power with images of powerlessness; to clothe the victims of excessive power in utter, bereft naivete; to cast them as defenseless supplicants raising—pleading—the defenses of duress, undue influence and fraud. I learned that the best way to give voice to those whose voice had been suppressed was to argue that they had no voice." She then continues in a footnote: "[a] quick review of almost any contracts text will

uneducated; that doesn't mean that she doesn't know her own self interest better than liberal reformers or social workers hampered by bureaucratic constraints.

It all produces lively classes and allows students to learn something of the War on Poverty—what they now see as ancient history. However, we cannot stop with Mrs. Williams' story or this exercise will come at the price of straying far from where the action seems to be in the 1980s. There is still another periphery attacking the core of contract doctrine, but it has been largely unnoticed.

Over the past twenty or thirty years, many states have passed unfair and deceptive trade practices acts (UDTP). Some of these statutes have overturned much of contracts' conventional wisdom, and there are other statutes lurking in the shadows that have the potential to do this. Contracts scholars must watch these developments carefully if they want their articles and courses to have real contact with the worlds in which their students will practice.

Many of these statutes stick to arming state attorneys general with weapons to use against unfair trade practices.[15] Some statutes also create private causes of actions, often with a chance to recover double, treble or punitive damages as well as attorneys fees. Legal services programs have brought many of the reported cases. The substantive standards vary, but almost always they favor plaintiffs far more than the common law or Uniform Commercial Code § 2-302. Professor Sebert divides "comprehensive state deceptive practices laws . . . into three rough categories: [1] Little FTC Acts, [2] Consumer Fraud Acts, and [3] Deceptive Trade Practices Acts."[16] Little FTC Acts prohibit "unfair methods of competition and unfair or deceptive acts or practices." Consumer Fraud Acts, though phrased in varying terms, normally contain broad general prohibitions against deceptive acts

or practices, any deception or fraud, or unconscionable commercial practices. Deceptive Trade Practices Acts contain express prohibitions against many specified deceptive practices and catch-all provisions. For example, the Michigan Consumer Protection Act[17] lists 29 methods, acts and practices as "[u]nfair, unconscionable, or deceptive methods, acts or practices in the conduct of trade or commerce . . ." Some of the more interesting ones include:

Taking advantage of the consumer's inability reasonably to protect his interests by reason of disability, illiteracy, or inability to understand the language of an agreement presented by the other party to the transaction who knows or reasonably should know of the consumer's inability.

(y) Gross discrepancies between the oral representations of the seller and the written agreement covering the same transaction or failure of the other party to the transaction to provide the promised benefits.

(z) Charging the consumer a price which is grossly in excess of the price at which similar property or services are sold. . . .

(bb) Making a representation of fact or statement of fact material to the transaction such that a person reasonably believes the represented or suggested state of affairs to be other than it actually is.

(cc) Failing to reveal facts which are material to the transaction in light of representations of fact made in a positive manner.

Statutes such as Michigan's suggest major changes in the common law, but much will turn on what courts do with them. Decisions in five states indicate that the judiciary has a great deal of discretion when faced by such qualitative standards.[18]

---

show that most successful defenses feature women, particularly if they are old and widowed; illiterates; blacks and other minorities; the abjectly poor; and the old and infirm. A white male student of mine once remarked that he couldn't imagine 'reconfiguring his manhood' to live up to the 'publicly craven defenselessness' of defenses like duress and undue influence." Williams, Alchemical Notes: Reconstructing Ideals From Deconstructed Rights, 22 Harvard Civil Rights-Civil Liberties L. Rev. 401, 419-420 n. 54 (1987).

[15] For a very critical analysis, see Silbey & Bittner, The Availability of Law, 4 Law & Policy Q. 399 (1982); Bernstine, Prosecutorial Discretion of Selected State Attorney General Offices, 20 Howard L.J. 247 (1977). However, some attorneys general have taken action under this legislation. . . .

[16] See Sebert, State Government: Consumer Protection in the States and Local Communities, in State Studies Prepared for the National Institute for Consumer Justice (1973). The statutes are analyzed in great detail in Dunbar,

Consumer Protection: The Practical Effectiveness of State Deceptive Trade Practices Legislation, 59 Tulane L. Rev. 427 (1984).

[17] 24 Michigan Comp. Laws Ann §§ 445.901, 445.903 (1987).

[18] This discussion is based on a selection of appellate cases, or what Karl Llewellyn called taking "test borings." I looked at the cases cited by law review writers and appellate opinions from Georgia, Kansas, Michigan, Texas and Washington. Washington has a "Little FTC Act." Georgia has a consumer protection statute. Kansas, Michigan and Texas all have more elaborate deceptive trade practices and consumer protection acts. Furthermore, Dunbar in the Tulane survey says "[r]oughly half of all reported state court decisions involving private consumer actions have arisen in Texas, under its Deceptive Trade Practice and Consumer Protection Act of 1973." Dunbar, supra note 16, 59 Tulane L. Rev. 427, 449 (1984). Of course, we all must be aware that

Some cases decided under these statutes remind us of Mrs. Williams' problems. For example, in *McRaild v. Shepard Lincoln Mercury*,[19] Legal Assistance of St. Clair County brought an action against an auto dealer under the Michigan Consumer Act. The plaintiff recovered $11,551.31 as damages, costs and attorneys' fees. Plaintiff, a widow, traded her $43,000 house and her 1978 Buick, for $11,000 and a 1980 Lincoln Mark VI automobile worth $17,000. Moreover, she remained obligated on the mortgage on the house. She wanted to sell because she no longer wanted to maintain the house and wanted to travel. The trial court found that the Michigan Act had been violated because defendants' actions confused plaintiff, the consideration that plaintiff exchanged for the car was grossly excessive, and the defendants took advantage of plaintiff. The appellate court affirmed, saying no more than "we are not left with a definite and firm conviction that the trial court made a mistake."

In *Murphy v. McNamara*,[20] Buyer agreed to pay $16 a week for a television set. If she made payments for 78 weeks, she would own it. She entered the deal because she could get a set without establishing credit. She was a welfare mother with four minor children. She was not told that the total she would pay under the contract was $1268 or that the retail sales price for the set was $499. She made payments totaling $436. She stopped paying when she read a newspaper article criticizing the plan. Defendant threatened her with arrest if she did not pay, causing her emotional distress.

New Haven Legal Services sought to prevent the seller from repossessing the set by self-help or from initiating a criminal complaint. Buyer was granted a temporary injunction, pending trial of the case. The Connecticut statute provides "[n]o person shall engage in unfair methods of competition and unfair or deceptive acts or practices in the conduct of any trade or commerce."

The court said, "the plaintiff relies on the unconscionable bargain extracted by the defendant in requiring her to pay over two and one-half times the regular retail sales price of the television set for the extension of credit, the failure to advise her of the true purchase price she would pay over the eighteen month period, and the unscrupulous collection practice of threatening her with arrest. This court has no doubt that these practices offend the CUTPA and come within its proscriptions." It noted: "[T]he act must be applied to protect the unthinking, the unsuspecting and the credulous as well as the sophisticated." The court continued the injunction against the harsh collection practices, pending final resolution of the suit. Appellate cases suggest, however, that middle class and rich consumers are the usual beneficiaries of these statutes. The poor consumer seems protected only marginally.[21] Many of the cases involve new automobiles. Indeed, my students think the Texas statute was designed to see that J.R. Ewing is protected from bad deals. The headnotes written for two Texas cases remind us that we are getting far from Mrs. Williams' situation:

> Finding that manufacturer [Mercedes-Benz] knowingly engaged in unconscionable course of action by failing to provide proper replacement parts for car was sufficiently supported by evidence of manufacturer's repeated, unsuccessful attempt to provide replacement parts for car, which resulted in gross disparity between value buyer gave for car and value he received.

> Automobile purchaser's payment of $55,175 for car which was not in deliverable condition and was in effect repossessed from him, for which he was not reimbursed, supported finding of unconscionability in deceptive trade practices action.

Some of these unfair and deceptive trade practices acts are not limited to consumers buying items for personal use. Eight states allow businesses to sue while in six others the statutory language would appear to allow them to do so. Texas allows businesses to sue as long as the business does not have "assets of $25 million or more." For example, in *Tri-Continental Leasing Corp. v. Law Office of Richard W. Burns*,[25] a vendor of copying machines approached a lawyer and

appellate cases may present a highly distorted view of what is going on in lawyers' offices, settlement negotiations and trial courts. Moreover, consumer disputing is an area where we find many other-than-legal dispute resolution mechanisms. See Macaulay, Lawyers and Consumer Protection Laws, 14 Law & Society Rev. 115 (1979).

[19] 141 Mich.App. 406, 367 N.W.2d 404 (1985).

[20] 36 Conn. Supp. 183, 416 A.2d. 170 (1979).

[21] We can speculate and imagine that these statutes and other consumer protection laws are tools legal services programs and other lawyers use to help the poor. Perhaps the threat to invoke these laws helps gain settlements for the poor. As always, we can observe that legal scholars know little about what lawyers do, and we are only beginning to bring our picture of practice into sharper focus by empirical study.

[25] 710 S.W.2d 604 (Tex. App.-Houston [1st] 1986, writ ref'd n.r.e.).

arranged a lease of a machine on a printed lease form. The machine constantly malfunctioned. The lawyer refused to pay installments, the machine was repossessed and sold, and the equipment lessor sued for a default judgment. The case turned on disclaimers in the form contract. They said that the equipment was leased "as is." The trial court found this provision unconscionable because there was a gross disparity between the value received and the consideration paid. The court pointed out that the lawyer was unfamiliar with copiers. Until he tried the machine in his office, he could not determine whether it was in good condition. "The trial court could reasonably have decided that . . . [the salesman], being in a superior position of knowledge, took advantage of [the lawyer] to a 'grossly unfair degree' by representing that the machine would perform its intended function." As a result, "the trial court's finding of unconscionability precludes conclusive effect being given to the stipulation that the parties' entire agreement is set forth in the lease, subject to modification only by a writing signed by [the lessor's] executive officer."[26]

Finally, in *Honeywell v. Imperial Condominium Assn, Inc.),*[27] a condominium association purchased a contract to service its heating and air conditioning system. During the negotiations a salesman distributed Honeywell's promotional literature. The literature made representations greater than the obligation assumed by Honeywell in a written form contract. Honeywell's representations concerning the quality and benefits of its services did not accurately depict those actually received. Thus, the promotional literature could be introduced to show that Honeywell

had violated the Texas statute. The court noted that the parol evidence rule does not apply in a DTPA suit.

So What? Substantive Concerns for Contracts Scholarship.

What might contracts scholars know if we recognized the existence of these unfair trade practices statutes? At least in those situations where the statutes apply, some questions we often ask have been answered. Other questions may be answered, but we will have to wait for courts to interpret the legislation to be sure. If we fail to tell our students that this legislation exists, they may overlook it when they enter practice. This risk is greater when the case doesn't involve enough to justify exhaustive research. If we fail to consider these statutes when we write about contracts problems, our discussion may be incomplete and misleading.

These statutes may affect our analysis of a number of problems. Of course, these statutes differ in the extent to which they offer relatively precise standards. For example, some statutes, such as Connecticut's, say only "[n]o person shall engage in . . . unfair or deceptive acts or practices in the conduct of any trade or commerce."[28] Others, such as the Kansas Consumer Protection Act,[29] prohibit unconscionable practices and then offer many examples of these practices. My colleague, Professor Whitford, has suggested that we can expect statutes such as the Connecticut act to do little more than U.C.C. § 2-302. He asks why we should expect judges to be willing to attack "unfair or deceptive" acts or practices when they have not been ready to do much to overturn "unconscionable" ones. On the other hand, he argues

---

[26] However, the court did note "[o]ur holding in this case does not constitute a general condemnation of the contract clauses in question."

Weitzel v. Barnes, 691 S.W.2d 598 (Tex. 1985) may go further, but we must reconstruct the facts from both the majority and dissenting opinion. Apparently, a lawyer drafted a contract under which he was the buyer of a used house. The contract gave the lawyer the right to inspect the plumbing and air conditioning systems and demand repairs. The contract provided that it was "the entire agreement of the parties and cannot be changed except by the written consent of all parties hereto." The lawyer discovered a condemned notice on the house. The lawyer moved in without having the house inspected. The city's representative refused to discuss the matter with the lawyer, stating that the city could deal only with the seller. The lawyer called the seller, and he told the lawyer that the house met the Fort Worth code standards. A few weeks later, the lawyer sued the seller for misrepresenting that the house complied with the city's code standards. The trial judge found for the lawyer and awarded treble damages and attorneys' fees.

The Supreme Court of Texas affirmed. It found that the parol evidence rule was not applicable. There was no effort to show a breach of contract. "The oral misrepresentations, which were made both before and after the execution of the agreement, constitute the basis of this cause of action, so traditional contractual notions do not apply." The dissenting judge asserted "[t]his case demonstrates how far we have strayed from the Legislature's intent of protecting the uneducated, the unsophisticated and the poor against the false, misleading and deceptive practices. I cannot believe that the Legislature ever intended for the Deceptive Trade Practices Act to be used to bail out an attorney who does not inspect the used house he purchases even though he had actual notice, prior to closing, that the city had condemned the property."

[27] 716 S.W.2d 75 (Tex.App.-Dallas 1986, no writ).
[28] Conn. Gen. Stat. § 42-110b(a).
[29] Kans. Stat. Ann. § 50-627.

that more detailed provisions offer hesitant judges guidance and might have some substantial impact.[30] While his argument seems plausible, my research for this paper cannot settle the matter. For example, there have been several pro-consumer cases under the very general Connecticut statute. Nonetheless, the great burst of pro-consumer cases was provoked by the very detailed Texas statute. One possibility is that unlike U.C.C. § 2-302, many of the general unfair and deceptive trade practices statute provide for attorneys' fees and punitive or multiple damages.

This may prompt more litigation which, in turn, may bring more cases before the courts. More cases might mean more real atrocity stories which would move judges to respond. Nonetheless, as a lawyer representing a client, I would be happy to discover the more specific provisions of statutes such as those in Texas, Michigan and Kansas.

At least the more detailed statutes might affect the way we think about a number of classic problems. For example, Professors Slawson and Rakoff have written about the gap between the real deal and the paper deal. Parties negotiate at least certain terms of their contract. Then one asks the other to sign a standard form contract or standard terms and conditions are introduced into the transaction in some other way. The other party often will sign without understanding or even reading the standard terms. Moreover, the side that drafted the terms will know the other side won't read and understand. Slawson thinks courts should seek the reasonable expectations of the parties. Rakoff would place the burden of showing that any term changing the underlying law was reasonable on the one drafting it. The DTPA statutes may open the door to these approaches. As we've seen, the Texas courts have not let terms in forms override their Deceptive Trade Practices Act.

Professor Unger notes that our contract law contains both individualistic and altruistic strands. As part of a much larger program to provoke social change, he argues that courts should fashion standards which require bargainers to consider each other's interests. He criticizes liberal doctrines such as economic duress which grant courts "a roving commission to correct the most egregious and overt forms of an omnipresent type of disparity." To what extent are these statutes an expression of the altruis-

tic strand he finds as part of the contradictions in contract doctrine? What do the statutes suggest about the chances his program might be implemented? Do the statutes grant more than a roving commission to correct only the most egregious and overt forms of unfairness? Consider the detail in the Michigan statute, for example. That statute prohibits such things as "charging the consumer a price which is grossly in excess of the price at which similar property or services are sold. . . ." and "failing to reveal facts which are material to the transaction in light of representations of fact made in a positive manner." While both provisions point toward altruism, neither is a bright line rule and much is left to discretion and judgment.

Professor Linzer argues that rights flow from reasonable expectations generated by relationships rather than classic mutual assent. Employees, for example, make transaction-specific investments and have dignitary interests. Many of the unfair and deceptive trade practices statutes would allow courts to protect expectations generated by relationships rather than focusing on the point of mutual assent. For example, the *Williams* case could have been analyzed in relational terms. As Greenberg notes,[37] Walker-Thomas conducted its business through about 30 door-to-door people who were both sales representatives and collection agents. One representative dealt with each customer throughout the relationship and got to know the customer's family, playing the role of a friend who visited regularly. Since most Walker-Thomas' customers' primary source of income was the monthly benefit check, the sales representative scheduled visits to a customer's apartment on the day when the check was likely to arrive. Poor people have difficulty cashing checks, and there is a high risk of being robbed just after they cash them. Walker-Thomas' representatives carried money and would cash welfare checks and deduct the required payment. They knew the customer's income and saw the apartment. They often suggested that the customer needed a new television set or a new couch and showed the customer how he or she could pay for it. If their suggestions failed one week, they would be repeated, perhaps in a different form, on the next visit. When the customer faced financial difficulty, the sales representative could allow extra time for

---

[30] See Whitford, Structuring Consumer Protection Legislation to Maximize Effectiveness, 1981 Wis. L. Rev. 1018, 1042-1043.

[37] Greenberg, Easy Terms, Hard Times: Complaint Handling in the Ghetto, in L. Nader (ed.) No Access to Law: Alternatives to the American Judicial System at 379 (1980).

payment. In the (*Williams*) case, use of the cross-collateral clause may have violated the tacit assumptions of the customer-representative relationship. Here a friend turned into a hostile aggressor, cleaning out Mrs. Williams' apartment as a form of coercion. While Walker-Thomas' representative wasn't a fiduciary, he was hardly a stranger dealing at arms-length either. Again at least some of the UDTP statutes offer a means of breaking with traditional case law and recognizing a relational interest worthy of protection. Walker-Thomas' management of the relationship could be viewed as a "deceptive practice."

Professor Rice has emphasized the costs of a diversity of approaches to substantive justice. Much business in this country is conducted nationally or regionally. A large corporation may be faced with great diversity in the rules governing their business. Some states follow the common law and a restrictive reading of the Uniform Commercial Code while others have enacted something such as the Texas Deceptive Trade Practices Act. Many statutes fall in between these extremes. Brandeis praised the states as social laboratories which could learn from trial and error as they took different approaches. However, business must create procedures to adapt to different rules or comply with the most strict one.[38] Rice suggests that our diversity of laws involves significant costs, and his argument is plausible. At the same time these statutes may offer benefits to the public which outweigh these costs. We need empirical study of the impact of these statutes. We should expect that Texas will provide a good test case for a first effort.[39] My July 1987 Lexis search, for example, asked only for cases mentioning the Texas statute after 1985. I found 169 reported appellate decisions of the Texas and federal courts. Many involved home builders and remodelers; slightly fewer involved automobile dealers. If any UDTP statute can be expected to have an impact on business practices, it should be this one. At present, we know little about the costs and benefits of the Texas DTPA.

These statutes also could serve to bring politics and power into our discussion of contract law. During the 1960s and 1970s, legislators found it hard to oppose these statutes while in the 1980s we have heard about the glories of deregulation. Moreover, the statutes, by creating qualitative standards rather than bright line rules, grant wide discretion to judges. There are many roads to the bench in different states and at different times, and judges carry with them varying strands of both legal and popular culture. Some judges may see these statutes as a progressive reform, while others will view them as a costly and silly interference with business and the market.

For example, Georgia and Kansas judges have limited their statutes. Their actions show the power of what Roscoe Pound called "taught tradition" which supports business interests by limiting unsound reformist statutes. Georgia judges have read their statute so that it applies only to consumer transactions narrowly defined. Alleged misrepresentations, for example, must be to consumers *generally* and not to only a particular consumer.[40] The Georgia courts seem to have reduced their statute to a limited regulation of selling expensive cars.

Heidt v. Potamkin Chrysler-Plymouth, Inc.,[41] shows that the more things seem to change, the more they stay the same. There, a buyer alleged that an automobile dealer had agreed orally to pay off the balance still due on the buyer's trade-in. However, the form contract said the buyer was responsible for paying off any balance due. The trial court directed a verdict for the dealer. The appellate court affirmed. Under the Georgia Fair Business Practices Act one seeking relief must have relied on the misrepresentation. Here the buyer had a duty to read the contract, and so he could not have relied on the oral representation. The court explained why it so confined the statute: "[i]t is not the intent of the FBPA to protect consumers from their own lack of diligence and to render every written and ostensibly final sale of a product a potential source of liability for the seller."

---

[38] See Rice, Product Quality Laws and the Economics of Federalism, 65 Boston U.L. Rev. 1 (1985). Professor Rice is the authority on unfair and deceptive trade practices statutes. See, e.g., Rice, Uniform Consumer Sales Practices Act—Damages Remedies: The NCCUSL Giveth and Taketh Away, 67 Northwestern U.L.Rev. 369 (1972); Rice, New Private Remedies for Consumers: The Amendment of Chapter 93A, 54 Mass. L.Q. 307 (1969); Rice, Remedies, Enforcement Procedures and the Duality of Consumer Transactions Problems, 48 Boston U.L.Rev. 559 (1968).

[39] See the Wall Street Journal, Nov. 27, 1987, at 10, col. 1. (Southern Methodist University's "Center for Enterprising . . . identif[ies] Texas's civil justice system as the biggest barrier to attracting business to the state.") We can wonder what kind of proof was offered to support this statement.

[40] See Burdakin v. Hub Motor Co., 183 Ga.App.90, 357 S.E.2d 839 (1987).

[41] 181 Ga.App. 903, 354 S.E.2d 440, 442 (1987).

Or, in Professor Patricia Williams' words, the rule means that "[t]erms with respect to which the constructed reality (or governing narrative) of a given power structure agree, may not be contradicted. . . ."[42]

The Kansas courts have denied relief to a Mrs. Williams, but then granted relief to the buyer of an expensive sports car when the dealer failed to tell her that it would be unable to get the car. In *Remco Enterprises, Inc. v. Houston*,[43] the Wyandotte Co. Legal Aid Society defended an action under the Kansas Consumer Protection Act. It sought to have plaintiff declared the owner of a television set with no further indebtedness due the plaintiff.

On September 11, 1980, Remco had made a contract with defendant whereby she rented a stereo component set. If she made 69 payments of $12, she would own it. She complied with this contract. On September 13th, she made a similar arrangement for a television. She would own it if she made 104 weekly payments of $17 each. She made 68 payments and then defaulted. Remco sued to recover the set and past due rental payments. The buyer was a 20 year old single mother of three. She had completed only the ninth grade in school and was dependent upon AFDC payments of $320 per month. The appellate court affirmed the trial courts finding that the arrangement was not unconscionable. It said:

> Although defendant would have had to pay 108% more than a cash customer, defendant received the benefit of not being responsible for service or repairs to the TV set, of not having to undergo a credit check or make a downpayment, and of having the option to cancel the agreement at any time after one week. Most importantly, she received the benefit and use of a TV set which she might not have otherwise had. Although in retrospect it may seem to have been a bad bargain, the price disparity does not rise to the level of unconscionability. . . . [D]efendant knew that she could return the set at any time she desired to terminate the agreement, that she knew how to multiply 104 (weeks) times 17 (dollars), that she was of average intelligence and was not taken advantage of by the

seller. . . . The record is devoid of any evidence of deceptive or oppressive practices, overreaching, intentional misstatements, or concealment of facts by plaintiff.[44]

However, in *Willman v. Ewen*,[45] the Supreme Court of Kansas enforced the Consumer Protection Act. A woman made a contract with a dealer to buy a "1978 Chevrolet Corvette Indianapolis 500 Pace Car" for $13,800. For over three months the dealer misled her into believing that General Motors would fill her order. This, the court said in denying a motion for summary judgment, could have deprived her of the opportunity to obtain a pace car from another source. The dealer's actions after it failed to deliver the car were more than just a breach of contract, and they came within the Kansas statute.

How do we put the two Kansas cases together? Perhaps it is unfair to say no more than Kansas judges will protect buyers of Corvettes but not poor welfare mothers who buy television sets. If we could not find a better distinction, I would wonder about the values of the kinds of people who become Kansas appellate judges. Of course, one case involves a misrepresentation while the other involves only charging too much. Yet the Kansas statute lists as a factor to consider in determining unconscionability "that, when the consumer transaction was entered into, the price grossly exceeded the price at which similar property or services were similarly available in similar transactions by similar consumers."[46] Another factor is "that the transaction the supplier induced the consumer to enter into was excessively onesided in favor of the supplier."[47] Moreover, I am troubled by what I see as the insignificant reliance by the consumer in the case where she won. However, I cannot imagine why anyone would spend $13,000 for a 1978 Chevrolet Corvette Indianapolis 500 Pace Car in the first place.

The United States Supreme Court has helped large corporations cope with bothersome state regulation, all in the name of the virtues of alternative dispute resolution. Corporate lawyers often put arbitration clauses in form contracts which otherwise would be subject to state regulation. Of course, firms

[42] Williams, Alchemical Notes: Reconstructing Ideals From Deconstructed Rights, 22 Harvard Civil Rights-Civil Liberties L. Rev. 401, 424 (1987).
[43] 9 Kan.App.2d 296, 677 P.2d 567 (1984).

[44] Contrast the Connecticut decision, Murphy v. McNamara, supra, note 20.
[45] 634 P.2d 1061 (1981).
[46] Kans. Stat. Ann. § 50-627(b)(1) (1987).
[47] Id. at § 50-627(b)(5).

creating the procedures usually retain some control over who will arbitrate. Also arbitrators usually have more pro-business values than jurors, and they seldom award large amounts as damages. In *Southland Corp. v. Keating*,[48] the Supreme Court upheld this method of offsetting, controlling or influencing state regulation of dependent relationships. The federal arbitration act prevails over state regulatory statutes. Following the *Southland* decision, a federal Court of Appeals ruled that an arbitration clause in a franchise agreement makes a claim of unconscionability under the Texas DTPA subject to arbitration.[49]

I think an honest teacher must present the judicial reaction to these unfair and deceptive trade practices statutes as highly disputed politics. We cannot teach modern contract law with a straight face unless we consider such things as the significance of the wild spiral of governors who have appointed the justices of the Supreme Court of California or why and how Judges Posner, Easterbrook, Coffee and Manion got to the United States Court of Appeals for the Seventh Circuit. And, at least until recently, we should have expected the Texas Supreme Court to read a UDTP statute very differently than an intermediate appellate court in Georgia or Kansas. The roads to those courts are different.

Why have contracts scholars paid so little attention to unfair and deceptive trade practices legislation? Perhaps these statutes bring political considerations too close to the surface. Or perhaps these statutes offer little to a scholar trying to build a consistent analytical theory based on values of individual responsibility and market controls. The statutes and the cases interpreting them differ state by state, and so we cannot build a clean general theory about contracts which includes them. Or perhaps most scholars just don't know much about the statutes, and their research techniques aren't likely to turn up cases interpreting them.

A Conclusion.

But if all is periphery or politics, what do we have to teach or write about? We must remember Betty Mensch's argument that Williston continues to live because he provides structure to ward off the chaos of realism.[50] One of my students appeared in class with a slogan on her book bag that sums up so much: "I've given up my search for truth. Now all I want is a good fantasy!"

Even if we look at these statutes, all of our tradition may not be lost. Judges in many states have and will confine the impact of these statutes to less than we might expect by reading their texts in isolation. Even in Texas, the sky is not the limit. We must remember *MacDonald v. Texaco, Inc.*,[51] where the plaintiff sued for damages under the state's Deceptive Trade Practices Act. MacDonald asked at an Esso station if they could install a fuel filter on his van. The Esso employees could not, but they directed him to a local Texaco station. There a mechanic attempted to do the work, but he set the van and its contents on fire. When the van owner sued Texaco under the Texas DTPA, the trial court granted Texaco's motion for summary judgment. The Court of Appeals affirmed. The owner, the court said, had not shown that his reliance on Texaco's misrepresentation was the "producing cause" of his loss.

What misrepresentation, you might ask. Remember when Bob Hope told us, "You can trust you car to the man who wears the star." This was the alleged misrepresentation. The court said, "MacDonald's admissions clearly establish that MacDonald was not drawn to Ray Hajevandi's Texaco station by any fond memories of Texaco advertising jingles. He stated in his interrogatory answers, 'I asked if there was a service station open where there was a mechanic. I was told that the Texaco station did mechanical work.'"

Suppose, however, the plaintiff had gone to the Texaco station because of Texaco's commercial? Think of what this might have done to television if he had won on this ground! Think of what it might have done to contracts teaching and research! Indeed, think what it might mean if we could trust our large corporations. As my student's book bag said, "all I want is a good fantasy!"

---

[48] 465 U.S. 1 (1984). See, e.g., Note, Resolving the Conflict Between Arbitration Clauses and Claims under Unfair and Deceptive Practices Acts, 64 Boston Univ. L.Rev. 377 (1984). Compare Faruki, The Defense of Terminated Dealer Litigation: A Survey of Legal and Strategic Considerations, 46 Ohio St. L.J. 925, 940-44 (1985).

[49] See Ommani v. Doctor's Associations, Inc., 789 F.2d 298 (5th Cir. 1986).

[50] "Viewed in retrospect, Williston's majestic doctrinal structure may have been silly, but Corbinesque appeals to reasonableness and justice appear sloppy and formless by comparison. Williston's structure was, at least, a real structure, however misguided. Perhaps much Willistonian dogma survives simply because it provides a challenging intellectual game to learn and teach in law school—more fun than the close attention to commercial detail required by thoroughgoing realism." Mensch, Freedom of Contract as Ideology, 33 Stan. L.Rev. 753, 769 (1981).

[51] 713 S.W.2d 203 (Tex.App.-Corpus Christi 1986, no writ).

Alternative Dispute Resolution and Its Promise for Contracts

Alternative dispute resolution, commonly called ADR (though others want to call it simply "Dispute Resolution"), has burst into the legal consciousness. It has become part of many law schools' curriculums and there are already several casebooks on the market, among them Goldberg, Green & Sander, *Dispute Resolution* (Little Brown 1985); Riskin & Westbrook, *Materials on Alternative Dispute Processing and Lawyers* (West 1985); Kanowitz, *Cases and Materials on Alternative Dispute Resolution* (West 1985), and, most recently, Leeson & Johnston, *Ending It: Dispute Resolution in America* (Anderson 1988). A foundation book on the topic is J. Auerbach, *Justice Without Law? Resolving Disputes Without Lawyers* (1983).

We begin with an article giving a quick overview of the topic, written by Frank E. A. Sander of Harvard, co-author of one of the casebooks. It is followed by a review of the casebook by Carrie Menkel-Meadow of UCLA. The excerpts from Professor Menkel-Meadow's review are concerned less with the particular casebook than with policy questions surrounding ADR.

Another review of the same casebook, by Professor Sally Engle Merry, an anthropologist at Wellesley, 100 Harv. L. Rev. 2057 (1987), raised some points that Professor Menkel-Meadow alludes to near the end of her essay. According to Professor Merry, who has written on dispute procedures in other cultures, ADR "expresses an anti-law ideology, claiming that nonadversarial ways of resolving conflict can create a better world." But ADR has been taken over by the lawyers and the courts, and is in danger of losing its different point of view and becoming instead a weak form of litigation.

In an earlier note in this section of the book it was suggested that traditional judicial remedies fit better with a bargain-based system of contract than one based on relations and community values. It is just these ideas of relations and values that are supposed to be served by ADR. However, avoiding the judicial system is not found by every writer to be a virtue. (Consider Macaulay's attack on arbitration as an end run around deceptive trade practice acts in *Bambi Meets Godzilla* in this section.)

In *Against Settlement*, 93 Yale L.J. 1073 (1983), Owen Fiss of Yale argued that the judicial system produces justice, and that the ADR movement was primarily motivated by a desire to reduce court loads and to achieve repose by getting people to compromise their rights. Andrew W. McThenia and Thomas L. Shaffer of Washington and Lee University responded to Fiss in *For Reconciliation*, 94 Yale L.J. 1660 (1985), in which they argued that the Judeo-Christian values shared by most Americans can lead to the restoration of the relationship between disputing parties and to their reconciliation through the mediation of the community. (The flavor of the article is like that of McThenia's *Religion, Story and the Law of Contracts*, which appears in the Different Voices section (Part ID) of this book.) Fiss then responded with *Out of Eden*, 94 Yale L.J. 1669 (1985), in which he suggested that McThenia and Shaffer were working from an atypical model of a small insular community. "But once we stop thinking about the Anabaptists and start thinking about Chicago, once we stop thinking about the ancient Hebrews and Christians and turn to modern America," there is no reason to assume that the "community" can answer the needs of those who "turn to the courts because they have to."

As Fiss sees it, the political impetus behind ADR involves distrust of the state, and of active government:

> Adjudication is more likely to do justice than conversation, mediation, arbitration, settlement, rent-a-judge, mini-trials, community moots or any other contrivance of ADR, precisely because it vests the power of the state in officials who act as trustees for the public, who are highly visible, and who are committed to reason. What we need at the moment is not another assault on this form of public power, whether from the periphery or the center, or whether inspired by religion or politics, but a renewed appreciation of all that it promises.

Fiss is more concerned with public law problems than contracts. Closer to our topic, Timothy P. Terrell, of Emory, has argued in *Rights and Wrongs in the Rush to Repose on the Jurisprudential*

Dangers of Alternative Dispute Resolution," 36 Emory L.J. 541 (1987), against the claim that litigation is inherently individualistic while ADR is communitarian. "The existence of law does not . . . reflect a basic deficiency in our community; instead, in a very fundamental sense, law *is* our community. We express that vital and unavoidable connection in the well-known phrase 'the rule of law' . . . ." He continues:

> Individual rights, as a consequence, far from being antithetical to our sense of community, are a reflection of it. Moreover, individual rights need not spring from an extreme version of individualism, for our community is based on interdependence rather than severe and counterfactual independence. We need not ask whether the community came first and the individual second, or the individual first and the community second. Neither is a byproduct of the other, for they arrived and travel together.

Like Fiss, Terrell argues that advocates of ADR "often appear to have a superficial understanding of the normative implications of conflict and its resolution." While he says that he is not contending that conflict is good and peaceful coexistence is bad, Terrell concludes:

> The peaceful resolution of disputes seems to me of less moral importance than the issues at stake in the disputes. Remedies, in other words, are properly the function of rules and rights, and not the other way around. To the extent advocates of ADR argue otherwise, the burden of persuasion remains on them . . . . I, for one, have yet to be persuaded.

In reading the Sander and Menkel-Meadow pieces that follow, consider ADR in light of the substantive arguments that have been made by some (but by no means by all) of the writers in this anthology: is it time to rethink the devil-take-the-hindmost attitude associated with classical contract law, to think in terms of reciprocity and solidarity rather than individual wealth maximization, to work things out by talking and compromise rather than by using hired gun lawyers to fight in a courtroom? Bear in mind the criticisms that have been summarized in this note. Is ADR the remedial vehicle needed to carry out the relational and communal approaches to contract or has it been oversold? Is it too radical a departure from our litigation system or is it not radical enough? Above all, are ideas of community too amorphous to be of value, or are they based on a false sense of homogeneity. Is it wiser after all to leave most things up to individuals, and to rely on their self-interest to protect their rights?

Frank E.A. Sander, *Alternative Methods of Dispute Resolution: An Overview*, 37 U. Fla. L. Rev. 1 (1985)

I. Introduction

Beginning in the late sixties, American society witnessed an extraordinary flowering of interest in alternative forms of dispute settlement. This interest emanated from a wide variety of sources ranging from the Chief Justice of the United States Supreme Court to corporate general counsel, the organized Bar and various lay groups. Following a decade or so of virtually unabashed enthusiasm, serious questions and doubts are now being raised. Additionally, we are slowly accumulating limited data concerning viable models and empirical effects. Hence, this may be an opportune time for evaluating and exploring promising future directions.

Perhaps a good place to begin is with some definitions. What exactly do we mean by "alternative dispute resolution mechanisms" (ADRMs)? Alternative to what? Presumably "alternative" is used as a substitute for the traditional dispute resolution mechanism, the court. Interestingly enough, however, courts do not resolve most disputes. The literature on dispute processing and dispute transformation has delineated ways in which grievances may be turned into ongoing disputes, and the myriad ways in which disputes may be resolved by means other than court adjudication. In fact, disputes that cannot be readily adjusted may be presented initially to a whole host of dispute processors such as arbitrators, mediators, fact-finders or ombudsmen. If the dispute is ultimately filed in court, approximately 90-95 percent of these disputes are settled by negotiation, with little or no court litigation. Hence, the argument for "alternatives" is not based on the need to find a substitute for court adjudication. Rather, it is based on the need to gain a better understanding of the functioning of these alternative mechanisms and processes.

. . .

From this brief and fragmentary history, four goals of the alternatives movement emerge:

1) to relieve court congestion, as well as undue cost and delay;

2) to enhance community involvement in the dispute resolution process;

3) to facilitate access to justice;

4) to provide more "effective" dispute resolution.

These goals might overlap and conflict. Consider, for example, the problem of "excessive" access. If society is too ready to provide access for all kinds of disputes, this will lengthen the queue and aggravate the congestion problem. Similarly, measures aimed at relieving court congestion would take a very different form from measures designed to enhance community control over dispute settlement. Hence, it is essential to think clearly and precisely about the reasons for pursuing ADRMs.

Considering the complex social conditions that have led to court congestion and concomitant delay, it seems specious to assume an appropriate use of alternatives can significantly affect court case loads. This is not to say that a cautious and informed use of ancillary mechanisms to screen court cases is not worth undertaking. On the contrary, such a program holds considerable promise. But the notion that a pervasive use of arbitration and mediation will solve "the court crisis" seems misguided. The principal promise of alternatives stems from the third and fourth goals set forth above. Our primary efforts should be directed toward these two goals. And since the access goal can only be fulfilled by providing access to an ADRM that is appropriate for the particular dispute, the third and fourth goals in effect coalesce.

II. Current Types of Disputes and Programs

This section presents a brief overview of the rich variety of ADRMs presently in use. Of necessity the picture will be somewhat fragmentary and conclusory. Because many mechanisms involve a blend or sequence of different dispute processes, it might be useful first to provide a brief restatement of the basic processes.

The most common and familiar form of dispute settlement between two parties is bargaining or negotiation. Negotiation offers the great advantage of allowing the parties themselves to control the process and the solution. Sometimes, however, disputants are unable to settle the dispute, and a third party must be engaged. If a third party joins the negotiations, the parties must determine whether he or she has power to impose a solution on the parties, or whether the third party is simply to help the disputants arrive at their own solution. The latter role is commonly referred to as conciliation or mediation. The former might entail some form of adjudication, by a court, an administrative agency, or a private adjudicator, also known as an arbitrator.

A. Labor Mediation and Arbitration

The model for many of the current mechanisms is the system developed during World War II for handling grievances arising under collective bargaining agreements. Typically, such agreements provide for a series of steps whereby an employee with a grievance first complains to his foreman. Next a meeting occurs between the Union Committee and the Plant Committee. Finally, if the matter cannot be resolved within the plant by negotiation, the parties select an outside arbitrator, often with the assistance of the American Arbitration Association or the Federal Mediation and Conciliation Service. This procedure is comparatively expeditious and inexpensive, even though recent complaints suggest it is becoming more formal, costly, and time-consuming. In short, it is too much like the court system it was originally designed to circumvent.

. . .

B. Commercial Arbitration

Long before the rise of labor arbitration, commercial contract disputes were submitted to arbitration by a panel of experts in the industry. This mechanism works particularly well in industries where a continuing relationship exists between the parties. Such cases necessitate an expeditious and amicable method by which one or more individuals familiar with the trade practices can resolve the disputes. The American Arbitration Association now handles close to 10,000 of these disputes each year. In addition, an untold number are handled similarly under private industry agreements.

C. *Consumer Disputes*

In a sense, consumer disputes could be subsumed under the category of commercial arbitration. Consumer disputes, however, typically involve smaller claims. Additionally, consumer contract agreements rarely provide for arbitration of disputes.

In recent years several mechanisms have been developed for extra-judicial handling of consumer disputes. Some states have created consumer protection divisions within the attorney general's office, where such claims are sought to be mediated, often by volunteers. Likewise, some industry groups, such as the Better Business Bureaus, have established procedures for arbitrating such claims. Some industries (e.g., automobiles and major appliances) even set up panels providing free arbitration of the consumer's claim. Of course, consumer claims also can be presented in small claims court and, where available, to media action programs such as Call for Action, where the service provided is not really dispute resolution but information and referral. Because of the clout wielded by these latter groups, they sometimes act in effect like mediators or ombudsmen in adjusting consumer grievances. A recent study, however, suggests the effectiveness and accessibility of some of the mechanisms may be suspect.[21]

D. *Interpersonal Disputes*

One of the best examples of the need for new dispute resolution mechanisms can be seen with respect to various types of interpersonal disputes. Here, the tendency of courts to look backwards and produce winners and losers is least responsive to the needs of the parties, who usually are seeking to resolve present controversies and avoid future disputes. Mediation, which helps the parties settle their problems jointly, is far more suited to this task than adjudication.

1. Neighborhood Justice Centers

In the past decade well over two hundred community dispute centers have been created. These are known by various names, ranging from "citizen complaint center" to "neighborhood justice center."

These centers are either free-standing institutions or are affiliated with the court. Center referrals are received from the court, prosecutor, police or other community agencies; some disputants also come on a walk-in basis. The kinds of cases handled vary widely, from landlord-tenant disputes to domestic and neighbor quarrels.

Although dispute centers vary greatly, two differing prototypes deserve exploration. One, commonly attached to a prosecutor's office, features rapid screening of a large number of cases to determine whether quick settlement might be possible and desirable. These programs involve high-volume processing in very short sessions, which law students often conduct. Whether this process should be viewed as true mediation is open to question.

In contrast to this approach is the more typical mediation, conducted by a professionally trained mediator or by a person drawn from the neighborhood who has received mediation training. Two or three mediators often conduct these mediations, which typically last three to four hours. These meetings allow disputants a full opportunity to present their views, and permit the mediators to meet with each of the disputants separately before attempting to reach agreement.

On the whole, the experience with these projects has been encouraging, although further public education is needed to stimulate greater resort to these unfamiliar institutions. Americans appear too prone to presume that anyone engaged in a dispute should take it to a lawyer or court. Ironically, the individuals who do use the new projects find them helpful and satisfying, and the agreements reached appear to endure. New York recently became the first state to recognize the value of these agencies by providing public funding for them.

2. Divorce Mediation

. . .

3. Parent/Child Disputes

. . .

E. *Intra-institutional Disputes*

Some institutions have recently applied the grievance machinery model of the labor sector to their intra-institutional settings. For example, a California prison established a grievance committee comprising prisoners and supervisory personnel to air prisoner

---

[21] No Access to Law: Alternatives to the American Judicial System (L. Nader ed. 1980).

complaints. If the case could not be resolved internally, it would be submitted, at least in an advisory capacity, to an outside arbitrator. This process features initial consideration by a group with representation from both sides, and the possibility of ultimate submission to an outside authority. This process has been replicated in other correctional facilities and other institutional settings, such as schools.

. . .

F. *Claims Against the Government*

The ombudsman institution first arose in Scandinavia in response to citizen's complaints against the government. A number of American states and municipalities now have ombudsmen. An analogue of the ombudsman concept has been the development of media action lines such as Call for Action on television.

G. *Public Disputes*

Most of the controversies considered previously involve two disputants, with relatively concrete, defined concerns. In recent years, however, more large-scale disputes have arisen involving a multiplicity of parties and interests. Examples of such disputes are community conflicts over whether a facility should be built in the area, certain racial controversies, major claims to land holdings by native Americans, and environmental disputes. Such cases have proved to be far more intractable, and have often required a combination of litigation and mediation. A number of organizations, most of them privately sponsored, have sought to develop special expertise in the handling of such cases.

H. *Court-Annexed Mechanisms*

Most of the mechanisms discussed thus far are primarily found in the private dispute resolution sector and are not a part of the formal court structure. In an attempt to make courts more responsive to the emerging alternatives movement, ADRMs have been incorporated in one way or another into the court system. In that respect, these developments represent a partial foreshadowing of the "multi-door courthouse" notion more fully explored in Section III below.

1. Small Claims Adjudication and Mediation

Over fifty years ago courts were recognized as too elaborate and expensive for simple cases involving only small claims. This led to the creation of small claims court, where litigants themselves, without lawyers, can present their disputes. These actions normally involve claims of not more than $1,000 and result in a type of quick, rough justice. Some scholars

have recently raised serious questions about the efficacy of small claims courts. Nevertheless, the institution appears to be an essentially durable one that has carved a place in the catalog of useful dispute settlement mechanisms. An interesting recent variant has been utilization of mediation in small claims court.

2. Compulsory Arbitration

Following a 1950's experiment in Philadelphia a number of jurisdictions have recently passed legislation requiring all monetary claims cases up to a certain limit (generally around $10,000-$15,000) to be initially processed by arbitration. In view of the prevailing right to trial by jury, a right to *de novo* review must then be accorded in the courts. However, such recourse to the courts might be subjected to cost sanctions if the petitioner does not prevail in court. Absent such a sanction, the net result might be to substitute two proceedings for the previous one. A similar program was begun on an experimental basis in three federal district courts. Preliminary data from these experiments are encouraging, and show that even where a sizeable percentage of the cases are appealed to court, very few proceed to trial.

3. Malpractice Screening

Following the malpractice "crisis" in the mid-seventies, a number of states set up special procedures for malpractice actions. Often the parties are initially required to arbitrate their differences. In other jurisdictions, such as Massachusetts, a screening panel is established, consisting of a doctor, lawyer and judge. The panel determines whether a *prima facie* case is established. If not, the plaintiff may proceed only by putting up a bond for the defendant's costs. The success of these experiments has varied. In some states, the special procedures have been abandoned or declared unconstitutional. In others, the mechanisms have worked well to screen out spurious claims.

4. Large Litigation

Many of the devices discussed above are applicable only to what has sometimes been referred to as "minor disputes." Some devices have also been developed to deal specifically with large and complex litigation.

a. Rent-a-Judge

Arbitration often employs experienced individuals such as retired judges to arbitrate difficult cases. Such use of arbitration, by consent of the parties, is quite different from that discussed in Section 2 above, where reference to arbitration is compulsory rather than consensual.

A variant of this practice has developed in some jurisdictions, notably California. It calls for parties to select a retired judge to hear the case, much as an arbitrator would. The procedures applied are the same as those that would apply in court, except as otherwise modified by the parties. Most notably, the judge's decision has the same force and effect as a judgment entered by a regular court.

The Rent-a-Judge procedure raises important policy questions. For example, should parties be able to hire the best available judges under circumstances where their decision has the full force of law, just as if the case had been decided in court? How does this practice square with the notion of equal access to the courts regardless of means? What will be the impact of such a practice on the regular judiciary? These questions and others deserve more discussion than they have received thus far.

b. Mini-Trial

Ten years ago some imaginative litigants in the federal district court in California developed an innovative extrajudicial mechanism to aid in the settlement of complex and protracted litigation. The procedure calls for the parties to select an experienced individual to preside at a two-day information exchange. Each party has one day to present its case in any form it desires, including questions for the opposing side. The highest official of each party, assuming a corporate litigant, must attend this hearing. At the end of the proceeding, the two top officials confer, without their lawyers, to evaluate the case. In the seminal case utilizing this innovative procedure, the parties promptly settled. If an agreement is not reached, then the presiding official will give his view concerning how the case would be resolved in court. The parties then use this additional information to discuss settlement. If settlement is not achieved, the procedure has no evidentiary effect and the case returns to court. In virtually all cases which have utilized this procedure, however, settlement has been achieved. The procedure has the additional virtue that it can be readily adapted to different situations (e.g., the presider can be dispensed with, more or less time can be allowed for the presentations).

. . . .

Carrie Menkel-Meadow, *Dispute Resolution: The Periphery Becomes the Core*, 69 Judicature 300 (1986) [Review of Stephen B. Goldberg, Eric D. Green and Frank E. A. Sander, Dispute Resolution (1985)]

In recent years a subject called "alternative dispute resolution" has garnered much attention in the literature of judicial administration, litigation management, legal scholarship and legal education. Some call this attention a social movement because it calls for greater access to courts and greater flexibility in resolving a myriad of social and legal problems. Others see the developments encompassed by the phrase "alternative dispute resolution" as a problematic effort to streamline litigation and to privatize and separate some disputes from others. For me, one of the more interesting aspects of this development has been the misnomer attached to the "movement." For the processes included—negotiation, arbitration, mediation, summary proceedings—are hardly alternatives: they are the norm for dispute resolution. Litigation in the form of trial held in court is, in fact, the "alternative" when over 90 per cent of all cases, civil and criminal, are settled before trial.

. . . .

Why ADR Now?

In their preface, the authors suggest that although many forms of dispute resolution now popular (such as arbitration and negotiation), are not new, the late 1960s produced a "flowering of interest in alternative forms of dispute settlement." (p. 3) This development arose because of the confluence of the increase in legal rights asserted through lawsuits in a time of legal and social activism with a decrease in the number or quality of social institutions (churches, families, communities, schools and local government units) able to deal with and resolve these new competing demands. Thus, the volume of cases increased and there was a need to "process" them.

At the same time, many of the "movements" of the 1960s also demanded not only more substantive rights, but greater procedural rights, flexibility, and participation in the determination of disputes. "Maximum feasible participation" was a phrase attached to many social programs of the '60s, and this theme is echoed in many of the attempts to return disputes to the communities in which they occurred. Intellectual developments in this period, such as the work of Laura Nader in dispute studies in other cultures[2] and Lon Fuller in legal scholarship,[3] suggested experimenting with other forms of resolving different types of disputes, leading to such concrete developments as the neighborhood justice centers. This period also saw the rise of anti-professionalism, or at least a demystification of professional work and a demand for lay or client participation in legal services as well as other professionally delivered help. It seems clear to us now that the themes of this period were participation, flexibility of both process and result and access to justice of those previously foreclosed, as well as extension of models of procedural justice into such other domains as the workplace, local community and family.

In the mid-1970s another stream of interest in "alternative" dispute resolution came from different sources. The American Bar Association established a Special Committee on Minor Disputes, the Chief Justice began speaking out on the need to deflect some cases out of the judicial machinery into other forms of dispute processing, and large law firms, the insurance industry and companies with large litigation budgets began to study and consider faster and cheaper ways of managing disputes at a time when court dockets "seemed" congested and litigation costs seemed grossly out of line. In addition, complex and technical cases were being decided by those (both judge and jury) who might not have the technical expertise to understand the underlying dispute. To this wing of the alternative dispute resolution movement the important themes are efficiency, speed of proc-

essing, transaction costs in getting disputes resolved and technical competance for "best" results.

In the 1980's we sit listening to a cacophony of voices talking about dispute resolution for a number of different reasons and raising a number of different values, rationales and justifications for a wide variety of different proposals. The social forces which join to bring us this interest in dispute resolution—both practical and theoretical—are themselves sometimes in dispute or conflict. Is ADR outside of courts being suggested at a time when certain groups have recently obtained their rights in civil rights, torts, or warranties? Are the well-endowed better able to buy the dispute resolution device that best meets their needs? Has one wing of ADR, motivated by cost savings and efficiency, coopted the process begun by others seeking humane values in the resolution of disputes?

Thus, the timing of interest in dispute resolution is propitious. Activists, theorists and practitioners alike have come to understand that courts and court-like adjudication is not the only way to resolve a dispute. Given the many different ways disputes can be resolved, we should consider, study and, in the law schools, teach about all of them so that dispute resolvers—lawyers, judges and clients—can make intelligent judgments about which forms to use and why. Most important, we can begin to ask, as Lon Fuller did in 1962, what are the different moralities of each dispute resolution device, and what are the social, political and jurisprudential effects of choosing one form or another. Our consideration of these issues will be greatly enhanced by works like *Dispute Resolution* which brings these themes and issues to the forefront of our attention, rather than at the periphery such as in speeches, instead of cases, in digressions in civil procedure instead of in courses on dispute resolution, and in sidelights in litigation training rather than training of its own.

Emerging Themes

Goldberg, Green and Sander have worked hard and fast to produce this first text in dispute resolution. They have provided an excellent overview of the primary and hybrid processes, and have identified the major themes and policy issues presented by this confluence of interest from many different quarters in dispute resolution. Since they have taken the plunge

---

[2] Nader & Todd, The Disputing Process—Law in Ten Societies (New York, NY: Columbia University Press, 1978).

[3] Fuller, Mediation—Its Form and Functions, 44 So. Cal. L. Rev. 305 (1971); Fuller, The Forms and Limits of Adjudication, 92 Harv. L. Rev. 353 (1979).

and gone first with their choices about how to treat this material, it will be easier for those who follow to see what works and what doesn't. As a friendly critic I will explore their major themes, organizing principles and choices with an eye toward seeing how *Dispute Resolution* best can be used in teaching about the core activities of dispute resolution.

The first organizing principle appears to be the order they chose for exploring dispute resolution processes. The authors begin with the most voluntary, two-party form of negotiation and move to increased roles for third party intervenors and more compulsory processes in dispute resolution—mediation, adjudication and arbitration. These are what the authors identify as the "primary" processes: the pure forms with relatively clear roles for the participants—direct negotiators, facilitators and deciders; with variations on those themes. The authors then move to the hybrid processes: variations and combinations of these primary forms—the negotiation/adjudication/arbitration of the minitrial, summary jury trial, med-arb, special masters and expert fact-finders.

Perhaps if the authors had begun with adjudication they might have provided another focus and a somewhat easier way for novitiates in this field to understand it. Students, for example, will, in the present world, still know more about adjudication than any of the other processes and it would be useful, therefore, to introduce other forms of dispute resolution in juxtaposition to what students have come to see as the "norm" or core concern of dispute resolvers.

. . .

As the different processes are presented in the book, there is a need for more conceptual organization and questioning about the very deep issues that transcend form. One could ask of each form, for example, if it is an expression of the qualitative side of dispute resolution (the hope for better solutions, greater party participation) or quantitative dispute resolution (more disputes can be handled more easily, cheaper, faster this way). As Fuller suggests, what are the moralities of each form? Does mediation place a higher value on agreement and peace as Fuller and Fiss suggest where adjudication and arbitration place a higher value on the rule of law and "justice?"

My own view on this important question is that it is not a simple question of form—both forms express both values, depending on the nature of the dispute, who the parties are and who the third parties are.

But organizing the material to probe this question repeatedly with respect to each of the surveyed topics might deepen students' understanding of the why's, as well as the how's of dispute resolution processes.

. . .

Critical and Policy Issues

The authors present an excellent list of critical and policy issues that can be applied across the board to all forms of dispute resolution (pages 13-14), such as noting that the early euphoric advocacy for these "alternatives" has worn off; why hasn't ADR become the accepted core for dispute processing? Should particular forms of dispute resolution be made compulsory or does that destroy the essence of "alternative" dispute resolution? Can disputes be prospectively assigned to the appropriate form of dispute resolution? Will such dispute "tracking" result in class-based segregations where some forms will be available to those who can pay and others only to those who have few resources? Will the use of private dispute resolution with an emphasis on compromise and accommodation threaten our system of public accountability and rule-making? Will dispute resolution in "alternative" forms become as "bureaucratized" as the present court system? How should dispute resolution be managed? Should there be separately trained dispute resolvers, new professionals with new skills, or lay people assisting other lay people? How should dispute resolution forms other than court-managed litigation be financed? What are the implications of private or public financing?

These are very important questions. Some are implicitly critical of the alternative dispute resolution proposals for new forms. Although many of these issues are touched on in questions at the conclusion of each chapter and in greater depth in Chapter 13, "Overcoming Impediments to the Use of Alternative Dispute Resolution," it seems to me that the critical issues are not sufficiently canvassed in each of the chapters devoted to the particular processes of dispute resolution. The mediation chapter, for example, should present and deal with critiques of mediation from feminist quarters, where it is argued that people of disparate power will abuse each other in informal processes. Both the mediation and arbitration sections should take on the question of hybridization to the point of bastardization of both processes when mixes of role occur, such as when the mediator "suggests" solutions to the point of "deciding" a dispute, and the arbitrator enlists the parties' "participation" in the award to the point of abdicating responsibility for the decision. (An issue which is explored well in the hybrid section on med-arb (p.247-268)).

. . .

Core and Periphery

The appearance of *Dispute Resolution* presents us with an important opportunity to reorient the way we think of legal processes. In virtually all law schools, law is taught from the appellate opinion and procedure is taught from the rules for conducting trials and the litigation which precedes the trial. A broader conception of dispute resolution gives us the opportunity to teach future lawyers that their function may be more complex (and worthwhile) than simply engaging in traditional litigation.

I have argued elsewhere that court models of dispute resolution too narrowly limit our conception of what is possible in resolving disputes. We tend to think of the sort of solutions courts are empowered to award—money damages and injunctions—and to argue for these things with appeals to principles that would be recognized in court, even when we are disputing outside of the court. Others have framed this argument in different terminology with similar effect. Mnookin & Kornhauser argue that the rules provided by courts give the parties the bargaining chips they use in their dealings in bargaining "in the shadow of the law." Galanter has argued that disputing is one large process called "litigotiation," where clear boundaries between litigation (through adjudication) and negotiations are blurred in the similarities of behaviors and arguments.

The emergence of a book like *Dispute Resolution* enables us to see how simplistic such a view of disputing is and its simplicity is deceptive. The different processes described and illustrated in *Dispute Resolution* through case studies, descriptions and sample procedural rules demonstrate how much more varied our studies should be and how much more diverse our teaching should be. In their own review of the impediments to the use of alternative dispute resolution (p. 486-7), the authors suggest the crucial role played by lawyers in thwarting attempts to try different processes. Lawyers work with what they are familiar with. The control they exert over their knowledge of the litigation system to advise clients is an important dimension of limiting what is made available to clients. Thus, the early education of law students to understand the varieties of dispute processing seems crucial. As the teaching of different methods of dispute resolution makes its way through the law schools, new entrants to the profession will educate their clients, their seniors at the bar and bench, and more importantly, their adversaries in disputing. I have already seen the fruits of such labors as students of mine join law firms with a commitment to exploring other ways of disputing.

The crucial issue in the teaching of dispute resolution is to make the "peripheral" concern of ADR a "core" concern. To the extent that ADR is tacked on as just another class in civil procedure or torts, students will continue to see courts and trial and appellate adjudication as the core legal activity. More importantly, while the reading of cases does teach the skill of "thinking like a lawyer" in litigating by teaching how to select the relevant, how to distinguish one situation from another, a complete education in dispute resolution must include other skills—such as conflict resolution, fact investigation and preparation, questioning, judgment, problem solving and empathy training, to name a few. For those who seek to specialize in particular fields, such as environmental or family dispute resolution, skills must be combined with complex substantive knowledge (technical and psychological respectively) and legal information. This means that dispute resolution must be taught pervasively in all courses and must be integated into the process and substantive concerns of all areas of law.

Thus, discussions of changes in products liability policy should include discussion of mini-trials and the Asbestos Claims Facility. Contracts courses should treat the issue of preventive conflict resolution by discussing and engaging in the drafting of dispute resolution clauses, exploring the differences between arbitration, mediation or "good faith" negotiation clauses.[29] Advanced courses will be necessary, too, since skills training in these areas (negotiation, arbitration award drafting, mediation facilitation, mini-trial presentation) requires close supervision and the opportunity for repeated behavioral exercises.

. . .

. . . One interesting sociological question to which attention should be paid in this context is who is doing this teaching? To what extent are the "core" subject teachers working in this area and to what extent

---

[29] See Gray, Dispute Resolution Clauses—Some Thoughts on Ends and Means, 2 Alternatives 12 (1984).

have we created another "marginalized" entry into the legal curriculum? It is no accident that in some schools the ADR teachers are the keepers of the '60s flames, either in their commitments to access issues or clinical education methodologies. It seems to me that with the pervasiveness of disputes in our social and political lives, issues in considering how we should best resolve disputes—public, private, large and small—is central to our concerns in creating and maintaining a legal system, both from a proceduralist and substantive perspective. Thus, we cannot afford to leave these important issues to the periphery of our curriculum.

. . .

Dispute Resolution by Goldberg, Green and Sander heralds the earnest study of dispute resolution in the law schools. This "new" field is still in a state of flux with many important issues to be addressed—public accountability, segregation of dispute resolution structures, quality of justice vs. efficiency of justice concerns, standardization or bureaucratization vs. flexibility and open-ended creativity in new institution building, compulsory vs. voluntary processes, power imbalances and the relation of informal procedures to our formal rule making structures, to name a few. But the formal introduction of these issues) into legal scholarship and legal education is to be welcomed. I applaud this first entry into the field as we begin to watch the further development of the emerging issues in dispute resolution as all forms of dispute resolution penetrate the core of adjudication, now taught and conceived as the "only" worthy form of dispute resolution.

Epilogue: Gilmore on Corbin on Cardozo on Law

In 1964 the Yale Law Journal celebrated Arthur Corbin's ninetieth birthday by dedicating an issue to him. In that issue appeared one of Grant Gilmore's finest articles, *The Assignee of Contract Rights and His Precarious Security*, 74 Yale L.J. 217 (1964). As a sort of preface to the article, Professor Gilmore paid his own tribute to Corbin. I know no better way to close this book.

Grant Gilmore, *The Assignee of Contract Rights and His Precarious Security*, 74 Yale L.J. 217 (1964)

Professor Corbin

For several years after I began teaching the first-year course in Contracts at the Law School, Professor Corbin graciously came, once each year, to teach one class. These were great occasions; in addition to the students officially enrolled, as many more attended as could squeeze their way into the classroom. I told my own students that, in Professor Corbin's classes, a person called on to engage in Socratic dialogue with the instructor stood up in the full glare of publicity instead of remaining seated in comfortable anonymity. In advance of the class I gave Professor Corbin the names of half a dozen students whom I conceived to be among the brightest and hoped for the best. Fortunately there were no scandals, and, year by year, Professor Corbin seemed to be content with the current crop of law students.

Having no use for sentimental reminiscence, Professor Corbin would teach, with undiminished vigor and skill, for fifty minutes. The one indulgence which he permitted himself was that, at the end, he would read a passage from *The Nature of the Judicial Process*. Cardozo's description of his own search for certainty in the law, and his ultimate realization that certainty is not the goal, was evidently deeply meaningful to Professor Corbin. I have thought, listening to him read Cardozo's words, that the quest which the great judge so movingly describes had been the great scholar's quest as well.

The words with which Professor Corbin chose to conclude the last class which he taught at the Yale Law School were these:

I was much troubled in spirit, in my first years upon the bench, to find how trackless was the ocean on which I had embarked. I sought for certainty. I was oppressed and disheartened when I found that the quest for it was futile. I was trying to reach land, the solid land of fixed and settled rules, the paradise of a justice that would declare itself by tokens plainer and more commanding than its pale and glimmering reflections in my own vacillating mind and conscience. I found "with the voyagers in Browning's 'Paracelsus' that the real heaven was always beyond." As the years have gone by, and as I have reflected more and more upon the nature of the judicial process, I have become reconciled to the uncertainty, because I have grown to see it as inevitable. I have grown to see that the process in its highest reaches is not discovery, but creation; and that the doubts and misgivings, the hopes and fears, are part of the travail of mind, the pangs of death and the pangs of birth, in which principles that have served their day expire, and new principles are born.[*]

[*] Cardozo, The Nature of the Judicial Process 166-67 (1921).

Table of Classroom Favorites

This table is designed to help students find discussions of cases that frequently appear in Contracts casebooks. The reference is usually to the first time the case is cited in the article. Occasionally, it is to one or more full discussions that do not take place at the time of the first citation. When the entire article or a whole section discusses a case continually, "passim" is used.

Wood v. Lucy, Lady Duff-Gordon

Zigas v. Superior Court